D1096365

The Lincoln Encyclopedia

THE MACMILLAN COMPANY
NEW YORK · BOSTON · CHICAGO · DALLAS
ATLANTA · SAN FRANCISCO

MACMILLAN AND CO., Limited
LONDON · BOMBAY · CALCUTTA · MADRAS
MELBOURNE

THE MACMILLAN COMPANY
OF CANADA, Limited
TORONTO

THE
LINCOLN
ENCYCLOPEDIA

THE SPOKEN AND WRITTEN WORDS OF

A. Lincoln

ARRANGED FOR READY REFERENCE

COMPILED AND EDITED BY

ARCHER H. SHAW

With an Introduction by David C. Mearns
Assistant Librarian, Library of Congress

THE MACMILLAN COMPANY : NEW YORK

1950

COPYRIGHT, 1950, by

THE MACMILLAN COMPANY

All rights reserved—no part of this book may be reproduced in any form without permission in writing from the publisher, except by a reviewer who wishes to quote brief passages in connection with a review written for inclusion in magazine or newspaper.

PRINTED IN THE UNITED STATES OF AMERICA

TO CLARA

INTRODUCTION

The President was going home to vote. In the afternoon, as his train rolled toward the West, he telegraphed to Washington requesting verification of a Lincoln phrase which he proposed to employ in a final appeal to the electorate. On Capitol Hill a little band, not wholly unaccustomed to such exercise, went to work. The quarry was elusive. Fingers ran up and down the pages of Nicolay and Hay, Tandy, Lapsley, Tracy, Angle, and the rest. For a time it was tedious merely; it became frantic and even frenzied when the White House began a series of peremptory demands for result. At nightfall one or two of the searchers absented themselves for a hurried supper and then rejoined their colleagues who were still hard at it. There was now a sense of discouragement, compulsion, and helplessness. There was weariness as well. Shortly after three o'clock in the morning, an elbow swept a slender volume from the shelf. It fell open, and the one who stretched to pick it up found his thumb resting on the hunted lines! The day could be called a day.

Now dropping books upon the floor, or hurling them at walls, is sometimes an admirable reference procedure. Its successful adoption was witnessed on another occasion when the inquirer was a statesman fond of alternating his Lincoln with his Kipling. Generally speaking, however, it is useful only as relief to feelings, and there are those who condemn it as implicitly destructive. It should, in other words, be practiced only sparingly, and then as a last resort. Far better to rely on a divining rod contrived of intelligence, imagination, and ingenuity. When *it* fails, reliance must be placed on simple doggedness.

Once, a professor at Columbia University, writing for the New York *Times,* chanced to cite Mr. Lincoln's approval of the American Union as "the last best hope of earth." The issue was delivered in due course to an ornament-strewn desk in the Executive Mansion, and its occupant, whose eyes could hear as well as see, came upon that rounded, ringing declaration. He was delighted with it. He determined to endow it with an even greater circulation. He sent word of his intention and insisted on its source. As a consequence, there was a muster of the company which, under not dissimilar circumstances, had been engaged in behalf of his predecessor. Again the quest was, for long hours, earnest and devoted and fruitless. Again the frailties of existing indices were startlingly and painfully revealed. But at last came word that it had been seen recently in the columns of that metropolitan daily, and the case was suddenly broken. It was broken by a long-distance call to Professor Henry Steele Commager. Up to that moment the closing sentences of the Annual Message of December 1, 1862, had not been impressed upon the public consciousness and imprisoned in the concordances. They have now.

But there is no isolation for these instances. Over and over again, for more than eighty years, they have been repeated until they have acquired some of the aspects of a national pastime. Mr. Lincoln is the most quotable notable in history. His writings constitute the American scriptures, the testaments of democracy, the trade-marks of tradition, the prescriptions of the patriots. No state paper, no pious or outraged editorial, no schoolboy's essay, no dizzy flight of oratory, can be accepted as quite authentic unless it glows with some proudly borrowed Lincolnism, and echoes with the sounds of that strange man from Illinois. The discovery, application, and exploitation of a startling Lincoln passage is an engrossing, exciting, and personally elevating enterprise; but for the historian, the librarian, the bibliographer, or the documentarian it is a tantalizing experience, sometimes marred by frustration and blurred with indignant astonishment. For numbered among his prolific disciples are those who adduce his sentiments with charming and innocent irrelevancy, snatch lines from their context, and successfully impose upon the credulity of their fellow citizens. Yet those whose business it is to keep the record straight have been obliged to labor without instruments fashioned to their purpose. It is as though the amateurs conspired against them.

Mr. Jefferson for years has had his Foley, and Theodore Roosevelt his Hart and Ferliger, but until the appearance of Archer Shaw, Mr. Lincoln has been denied the comfort and assurance of a cyclopedist.

His spirit must be as gratified as are the spirits of his students, for out of some five thousand monographs in Lincoln literature, there have been but a meager handful of reference books to help them, and now for the first time (so far as I am aware) have Mr. Lincoln's expressions been extracted, systematically arranged, and presented in a dictionary form. It is high time.

For Mr. Shaw this has been a labor of love, and as such it deserves to be happily regarded. His task was formidable; it is necessary only to examine the titles listed in the Key and Explanation to understand the dispersal of Lincoln sources and the imposing number of Lincoln authorities which have had to be consulted. But he has accomplished more than the survival of an endurance test; he has reduced the acknowledged utterances of the foremost American to a discipline whereby they may be readily recovered. This is not to say that use of his *Encyclopedia* will be either instantly rewarding or effortlessly automatic. The reader must accommodate himself to Mr. Shaw's assignment of subject headings and project his own purpose in terms of the compiler's organization of material. In this he will not infrequently find his ideas and Mr. Shaw's at sharp and distressing variance; but it is evidence of Mr. Shaw's good humor and good sense that he cheerfully accepts the situation and declines to be dissuaded by it. There is not now, nor will there ever be, a universally agreeable schedule of arbitrary entries, but even the most querulous and most unreasonable of men prefers such a schedule to the alternative of anarchy. What is infinitely more important is the fact that Mr. Shaw's arrangement works. Over a period of several months this subscriber has put it to the test, and unfailingly it has responded. Because this is so, he can commend it without reservation, convinced that it will be to others as helpful as it has been to him.

There are three blessings which it confers: (1) the anxious composer seeking illustration, example, or embellishment for his own writing will find Mr. Lincoln's prose assorted for his choosing—to him it will be convenience; (2) the documentarian will find the source of the writer's choice—to him it will be relief and fixation and overtaken time; (3) the scholar will find beginnings—to him it will be neither vehicle nor destination but a mounting block, a point of departure, a setting-out. But beyond these bounties there is a special fascination, for here starkly displayed, dissected, for everyone to see, is the person of Mr. Lincoln himself, the steady progress of his faith, his opinions, his purpose; the compromises which he discarded; the impulses which drove him; the circumstances which changed him; the attributes which separately and in combination distinguished him; and from these elements there emerges a new and enduring concept of the whole man, who was somehow greater than the sum of all his parts.

DAVID C. MEARNS
Assistant librarian
Library of Congress

Washington, D. C.

PREFACE

Many years of employment as an editorial writer for a metropolitan newspaper impressed upon the editor and compiler of this volume the need for some concise book of reference to the words of Abraham Lincoln.

More than eighty years have passed since Lincoln's active pen was laid down for the last time, and his lips were stilled in death, but Lincoln's words still live in the hearts of millions, gaining in power and significance as time goes by.

The effort here has been to prepare a volume of ready reference, suitable to the convenience of a writer or lecturer who may himself lack the time to dig deeply into a Lincoln text for some desired quotation or idea. The importance of simplification has been kept in mind. Long quotations have been avoided whenever possible. Cross references have been supplied to help locate a quotation if it is not found where first sought. They will also facilitate the finding of additional quotations on kindred subjects.

It is inevitable that in such a volume there may lurk many a disappointment. Quotations which Lincoln disciples might insist it should contain may be omitted. To such seekers-in-vain I can only reply by reminding them that scores, perhaps hundreds, of so-called Lincoln quotations, some of them long popular, unhappily lack authenticity. They may, or may not, sound like Lincoln, but a conscientious compiler finds himself regretfully unable to establish their genuineness.

"One of the hardest problems in historical criticism," writes Harry E. Pratt, Lincoln student and scholar, "is that of assessing the reliability of reminiscences." Men too often remember what is convenient or pleasant or at the moment popular to remember. Such recollections obviously have small place in a book of reference which puts authenticity above every other consideration.

Reminiscences have furnished the basis for innumerable and worth-while books on Lincoln. In the main, presumably, they are as accurate as they are entertaining and enlightening. Into that field, however, the present volume chooses not to enter. These quotations are pegged as to exact time, place, and circumstance. References to volume and page give readers the opportunity to pursue the subject further, to study their context, if they are so inclined.

Some may be surprised to find here quotations from the famous "lost speech" delivered at Bloomington on May 29, 1856. Many Lincoln students reject altogether the text which purports to represent that important utterance, since it did not make its appearance until a few years ago and is admittedly based on notes which, although taken at the time, were not expanded into manuscript form until long afterward. However, as capable a scholar as Arthur Brooks Lapsley considers the text authentic enough for inclusion in his *Writings of Abraham Lincoln*. This writer accepts his judgment.

It will be observed that where more than a single quotation is given on one subject, they appear in chronological order. Thus, read consecutively, they may be taken to reflect in some measure the logical development of Lincoln's thinking on particular subjects, as events influenced his reasoning and his policies advanced to maturity.

No one else can be as conscious of the defects of this volume as is the editor and compiler, or as regretful that it is not more nearly perfect. Such as it is, however, with all its faults, and with whatever merits it may possess, it is hopefully launched on a sea already thickly dotted with craft alike sustained by the deathless fame of America's greatest President.

II

The words of Abraham Lincoln will live as long as the conscience and memory of man.

It was Lincoln's lot to live in a period of his country's history when old citadels of political thought were under deadly fire and when men with strange new devices were challenging the very foundations of the Republic. Could a nation founded, like America, upon the principles of the equality of men, maintain itself against a world contrary-minded? In particular, as Lincoln himself suggested the question, must a government be either too weak to withstand attack from abroad or at home, or so strong as necessarily to nullify the guarantees of freedom?

The issue was determined by battle, as the wiser men of the day knew it must be. Thus decisively answered, the question itself does not recur. Government of, by, and for the people, once and for all time established its power to stand.

Lincoln early sensed the deeper meaning of the conflict he saw approaching. With astonishing accuracy he interpreted its significance and prepared the ground on which the defenders of an ancient faith must meet the test. The result, world-wide in its promise to mankind, gloriously vindicated his wisdom, his patience under stress, and the high quality of his statesmanship.

Although Lincoln was a prolific writer of letters and a popular speaker on topics which stirred great masses of people, few men ever wasted fewer words. His self-taught command of English was unexcelled, as witness the Gettysburg Address; but he used this excellence, never for display, but always to further some cause. He spoke to influence men's minds. His letters, for the most part, were letters of appeal, of serious criticism or of direction. He was famed in Illinois as a raconteur, but his stories were habitually inspired by some useful purpose. He weighed words, as on a precision scale, to determine their effect. He had none to squander in verbosity.

The result is that these words of Lincoln, spoken and recorded in the heat of a historic political struggle, stand today not only as a milestone on the road to universal civil and religious liberty, but, more important, as a code of principles on which progress along that course must inevitably be based.

Certainly there can be no lasting triumph for good except it be founded on justice and truth. In the utterances of Lincoln, profound in thought but simple in expression, one sees justice and truth working together toward a common end. The immortal truths of the Declaration of Independence were thus repeated and given new emphasis three-quarters of a century after Jefferson had penned them. While the assassin in the Washington playhouse destroyed the physical man, his act served merely to increase the stature of the statesman. Armed and armored with truth, justice, and respect for law, Lincoln, as spokesman for freedom, remained, and remains, invincible.

As he himself said of another's, Lincoln's declarations are the veritable precepts of a free society. Believers in the fundamental equality of men, those who devoutly believe that society's best hope for peace, progress, and contentment lies in enlightened self-government find now, as they found then, a mine of encouragement in the words of one who sprang from common, humble men, voiced their thoughts, sympathized with their aspirations, and trusted their integrity.

Lincoln's words, the expression of his sublime faith in men, live after him, a stimulation and a challenge. Free men look to them as political gospel; men who still long to be free find in them a guidepost to the attainment of their hopes. Lincoln dreamed their dreams, spoke the language of their hearts, put into everlasting phrases the substance of their hopes. For his creed embraced the world. The cause he labored incessantly to advance contemplates a universe at last forever free.

Thus a perpetual freshness is found in the words of Lincoln. He made effective weapons of truths as old as mankind, and as ever new as tomorrow morning. With them as guide and inspiration, men can win their way to liberty, if they will, or retain a liberty already won, if they think it worth striving for. Just as the character of Lincoln continues to stand foursquare, like the Pyramid of Cheops, amid the shifting sands of a world in turmoil, his words possess an indestructible quality. They will lose nothing in power or significance as long as men are men and the ideal of political freedom remains alive in the human heart. Neither time nor circumstance alters them. Only the enemies of liberty deny their validity.

A. H. S.

KEY AND EXPLANATION

A majority of the quotations appearing here are taken from the speeches, papers, and letters contained in the Gettysburg edition of *Lincoln's Complete Works*, published by Francis D. Tandy Co., New York, in 1905. This twelve-volume edition represents an expansion of the two-volume work, edited by John G. Nicolay and John Hay and published by the Century Co., New York, in 1894. Wherever in this volume, therefore, a quotation is credited merely to a volume and page, the reference is to this Tandy edition.

In the more than forty years since this edition was published, however, a great number of new Lincoln utterances have been brought to light. They appear in successive volumes by various authors, and must be studied by one who would offer a comprehensive book of quotations.

The present compiler has roamed far and wide among the works of these and other students of Lincoln literature. He is sensible of the debt he owes them and takes this opportunity to express his thanks. Without their help, whatever small merit this book may have would be much smaller.

The following table gives the key by which the source of each quotation may be determined. The key name is on the left, followed by the full title of the volume where the quotation may be found:

Angle—*New Letters and Papers of Lincoln,* compiled by Paul M. Angle. Boston, Houghton, 1930.

Arnold—*Life of Abraham Lincoln,* by Isaac N. Arnold. Chicago, McClurg, 1901.

Bartlett—*Life and Public Services of Abraham Lincoln,* by D. W. Bartlett. Cincinnati, Broaders & Co., 1860.

Basler—*Abraham Lincoln: His Speeches and Writings,* edited with critical and analytical notes by Roy P. Basler. Cleveland, World Pub. Co., 1946.

Brooks—*Abraham Lincoln,* by Noah Brooks. Washington, National Tribune, 1888.

Brown—*Lincoln Letters* at Brown University and other Providence libraries. Brown University Library, 1927.

Burt—Article in *Century,* February, 1907, by Col. Silas W. Burt.

Carpenter—*Six Months at the White House with Abraham Lincoln,* by F. B. Carpenter. New York, Hurd & Houghton, 1866.

Coffin—*Abraham Lincoln,* by Charles Carleton Coffin. New York, Harper, 1892.

Diary—*Diary of a Public Man* (author unknown). Chicago, Abraham Lincoln Book Shop, 1945.

Diplomat—*Diplomat in Carpet Slippers,* by Jay Monaghan. Indianapolis, Bobbs-Merrill, 1944.

Du Bose—*General Joseph Wheeler and the Army of the Tennessee,* by John M. Du Bose. New York, Neale Pub. Co., 1912.

Eulogy—*Eulogy of Abraham Lincoln,* by Henry Champion Deming. Hartford, Conn., A. N. Clark & Co., 1865.

Follett—*Lives and Speeches of Abraham Lincoln and Hannibal Hamlin. New York,* W. A. Townsend & Co.; Columbus, Ohio, Follett, Foster & Co., 1860.

Foner—*Business and Slavery,* by Philip S. Foner. University of North Carolina Press, 1941.

Gilmore—*Personal Recollections of Abraham Lincoln and the Civil War,* by James R. Gilmore. Boston, L. C. Page & Co., 1898.

Hay—*Lincoln and the Civil War in the Diaries and Letters of John Hay,* selected and with an introduction by Tyler Dennett. New York, Dodd, 1939.

Herndon—*The True Story of a Great Life,* by William H. Herndon and Jesse William Weik. Chicago, Bedford, Clarke & Co., 1889.

Hertz—*Abraham Lincoln: A New Portrait,* by Emanuel Hertz, 2 vols. New York, Liveright, 1931.

Hill—*Abraham Lincoln, Man of God,* by John Wesley Hill. New York, Putnam, 1920.

F. T. Hill—*Lincoln, the Lawyer,* by Frederick Trevor Hill, New York, Century, 1906.

History and Overthrow—*History of Abraham Lincoln and the Overthrow of Slavery,* by Isaac N. Arnold. Chicago, S. C. Griggs & Co., 1871.

Keckley—*Behind the Scenes,* by Elizabeth Keckley. New York, G. W. Carleton & Co., 1868.

Kelley—*Lincoln and Stanton,* by William D. Kelley. New York, Putnam, 1885.

Lang—*Wit and Wisdom of Abraham Lincoln,* ed. by H. Jack Lang. New York, Greenberg, 1941.

Lapsley—*Writings of Abraham Lincoln,* ed. by Arthur Brooks Lapsley, 8 vols. New York, Lamb Pub. Co., 1905.

Layman's Faith—*The Layman's Faith,* by Isaac N. Arnold. Chicago, Fergus Printing Co., 1882.

Locke—*Reminiscences of Abraham Lincoln,* by David R. Locke, ed. by Allan Thorndike Rice. New York, North American Pub. Co., 1886.

Lore—*Lincoln Lore,* bulletin of the Lincoln National Life Foundation, published weekly at Fort Wayne, Ind.

McClure—*"Abe" Lincoln's Yarns and Stories,* ed. by A. K. McClure. Chicago, Educational Co., 1901.

Messages—*Messages and Papers of the President.* Washington, Bureau of National Literature, 1897.

Morgan—*Our Presidents,* by James Morgan. New York, Macmillan, 1926.

N. & H.—*Complete Works of Abraham Lincoln,* ed. by John G. Nicolay and John Hay, 2 vols. New York, Century, 1894.

Voice and Pen—*Abraham Lincoln's Voice and Pen,* by G. M. Van Buren. Cincinnati, Robert Clarke & Co., 1890.

Quarterly—*Abraham Lincoln Quarterly.* Springfield, Ill., Abraham Lincoln Association.

R. T. L.—The Robert Todd Lincoln Papers, Library of Congress, Washington (opened to public, 1947).

Reveille—*Reveille in Washington,* by Margaret Leech. New York, Harper, 1941.

Richards—*Abraham Lincoln, the Lawyer-Statesman,* by John T. Richards. Boston, Houghton, 1916.

Russell—*My Diary, North and South,* by William Howard Russell. London, Bradbury & Evans, 1863.

Schurz—*Reminiscences of Carl Schurz.* New York, Doubleday, 1907.

Selby—*Stories and Speeches of Abraham Lincoln,* by Paul Selby. Chicago, Thompson & Thomas, 1900.

Starr—*Lincoln and the Railroads,* by John W. Starr, Jr. New York, Dodd, 1927.

Stephenson—*An Autobiography of Abraham Lincoln,* compiled by Nathaniel Wright Stephenson. Indianapolis, Bobbs-Merrill, 1926.

Stern—*Life and Writings of Abraham Lincoln,* ed. by Philip Van Doren Stern. New York, Random House, 1940.

Table Talk—*Table Talk of Abraham Lincoln,* ed. William O. Stoddard. New York, Stokes, 1894.

Tarbell—*Life of Abraham Lincoln,* by Ida M. Tarbell, 4 vols. New York, Lincoln Historical Society, 1903.

Townsend—*Real Life of Abraham Lincoln,* by George Alfred Townsend. New York, Bible House, 1867.

Tracy—*Uncollected Letters of Abraham Lincoln,* brought together by Gilbert A. Tracy. Boston, Houghton, 1917.

Tribune, *Chicago Tribune, Its First Hundred Years,* by Philip Kinsley. New York, Knopf, 1943.

War Years—*Abraham Lincoln: The War Years,* by Carl Sandburg, 4 vols. New York, Harcourt, 1939.

Weed—*Autobiography of Thurlow Weed.* Boston, Houghton, 1884.

Welles—*Diary of Gideon Welles,* 3 vols. Boston, Houghton, 1911.

Whitney—*Life on the Circuit with Lincoln,* by Henry C. Whitney. Boston, Estes & Lauriat, 1892.

Brackets are used in the following text to enclose words not found in a quotation itself, but supplied by the editor to clarify its meaning.

A comma is inserted in the subtitle of a quotation or group of quotations when it has been advisable to avoid the awkward necessity of repeating the title itself.

Ellipsis marks indicate the omission of words deemed by the editor not essential to the sense or significance of a quotation.

The names of states are omitted where thought unnecessary for the sake of clarity. When not otherwise indicated, it may be understood that the state of Illinois is meant; except in cases like Cincinnati or Buffalo, for instance, where but one city of the name is generally recognized and its state is well known.

A. H. S.

The Lincoln Encyclopedia

A.B.C. Schools, attended by Lincoln—Before leaving Kentucky he [Abraham Lincoln] and his sister were sent, for short periods, to A.B.C. schools, the first kept by Zachariah Riney, and the second by Caleb Hazel.—*Autobiography, June 1, 1860.* N. & H.* I, 638.

Abel, blood of, "crying to Heaven against him"—*See* MEXICAN WAR, Polk's attempt to justify, 2.

Abolition, doctrines of, decried—*See* SLAVERY, wrong of, 1.

Abolition, how define?—I know of no word in the language that has been used so much as that one "Abolitionist." Having no definition, it has no meaning unless taken as designating a person who is abolishing something. If that be its signification, the supporters of Frémont are not Abolitionists. . . . They tell us we are in company with men who have long been known as Abolitionists. What care we how many may feel disposed to labor for our cause?—*Speech, Kalamazoo, Mich., Aug. 27, 1856.* Stern, 406.

Abolition, radical advocates of, receive execration—Those who would shiver into fragments the Union of these states, tear to tatters its now venerated Constitution, and even burn the last copy of the Bible, rather than slavery continue a single hour, together with all their more halting sympathizers, have received, and are receiving their just execration; and the name and opinions and influence of Mr. [Henry] Clay are fully, and, as I trust, effectually and enduringly arrayed against them.—*Speech, Springfield, July 16, 1852.* II, 172.

Abolition, strongest argument for—No man can [embrace the Freeport Doctrine] who does not give the Abolitionists an argument to deny the obligation enjoined by the Constitution to enact a fugitive slave law. Try it now. It is the strongest Abolition argument ever made. I say, if that Dred Scott decision is correct, then the right to hold slaves in a territory is equally a constitutional right with the right of a slaveholder to have his runaway returned. No man can

* Nicolay and Hay. See Key.

show the distinction between them.—*Debate, Alton, Oct. 15, 1858.* V, 70.
2.—The man who argues that by unfriendly legislation, in spite of that constitutional right [as claimed by the Supreme Court], slavery can be driven from the territories, cannot avoid furnishing an argument by which Abolitionists may deny the obligation to return fugitives, and claim the power to pass laws unfriendly to the right of the slaveholder to reclaim his fugitive.—*Debate, Alton, Oct. 15, 1858.* N. & H. I, 513.
3.—I defy anybody . . . to show that there is an iota of difference between the constitutional right to reclaim a fugitive [slave] and the constitutional right to hold a slave, in a territory, provided this Dred Scott decision is correct. I defy any man to make an argument that will justify unfriendly legislation to deprive a slaveholder of his right to hold his slave in a territory [as suggested by Douglas], that will not equally in all its length, breadth and thickness, furnish an argument for nullifying the fugitive slave law. Why, there is not such an Abolitionist in the nation as Douglas, after all.—*Debate, Alton, Oct. 15, 1858.* V, 70.

Abolition, "terrible name"—Men who will march up to the mouth of a loaded cannon without shrinking will run from the terrible name of "Abolitionist," even when uttered by a worthless creature whom they, with good reason, despise.—*Speech, Bloomington, May 29, 1856.* Lapsley II, 252.

Abolition, Virginians advocated—Petitions for the abolition of slavery were presented to the very first Congress by Virginia and Massachusetts alike.—*Speech, Bloomington, May 29, 1856.* Lapsley II, 256.
2.—Abolition societies existed as far south as Virginia; and it is a well known fact that Washington, Jefferson, Madison, Lee, Henry, Mason and Pendleton were qualified Abolitionists, and much more radical on that subject than the Whig and Democratic parties claim to be today.—*Speech, Bloomington, May 29, 1856.* Lapsley II, 257.
3.—In the colonial time, Mason, Pendleton, and Jefferson were as hostile to slavery in Virginia as Otis, Ames and the Adamses were in Massachusetts; and

Virginia made as earnest an effort to get rid of it as old Massachusetts did.—*Speech, Bloomington, May 29, 1856.* Lapsley II, 258.

4.—In the constitutional convention, George Mason of Virginia made a more violent abolition speech than my friends Lovejoy or [Ichabod] Codding would desire to make here today—a speech which could not be safely repeated anywhere on southern soil in this enlightened year.—*Speech, Bloomington, May 29, 1856.* Lapsley II, 259.

5.—Within the memory of men now present the leading statesmen of Virginia could make genuine, red-hot Abolitionist speeches in old Virginia.—*Speech, Bloomington, May 29, 1856.* Lapsley II, 274.

Abolition, war not waged to promote—*See* UNION, preservation of, first duty, 15.

Abolition, Whigs and—Your third question is: "And have we as a party ever gained anything by falling in company with Abolitionists?" Yes—we gained our only national victory by falling in company with them in the election of Gen. Harrison—Not that we fell into Abolition doctrines; but we took up a man whose position induced them to join us in his election.—*To Usher F. Linden, March 22, 1848.* Hertz II, 566.

Abolitionize, plot to, parties denied—In regard to this matter about a contract that was made between Judge Trumbull and myself . . . I wish simply to say what I have said to him [Douglas] before, that he cannot know whether it is true or not, and I do know there is not a word of truth in it.—*Debate, Jonesboro, Sept. 15, 1858.* IV, 35.

2.—I contradicted it [the Douglas charge] instantly, and it has been contradicted by Judge Trumbull, while nobody has produced any proof, because there is none.—*Debate, Jonesboro, Sept. 15, 1858.* IV, 36.

3.—In regard to this matter about Trumbull and myself having made a bargain to sell out the entire Whig and Democratic parties in 1854, Judge Douglas brings forward no evidence to sustain his charge, except the speech Matheny is said to have made in 1856, in which he told a cock-and-bull story, upon the same moral principles that Judge Douglas tells it here today. . . . I have twice told Judge Douglas to his face that from beginning to end there is not a word of truth in it. I have called upon him for the proof, and he does not at all meet me . . . by producing the record; because there was no record for him to bring.—*Debate, Charleston, Sept. 18, 1858.* IV, 189.

4.—At Ottawa he [Douglas] led off by charging a bargain, somewhat corrupt in its character, upon Trumbull and myself—that we had entered into a bargain,

one of the terms of which was that Trumbull was to abolitionize the old Democratic party and I, Lincoln, was to abolitionize the old Whig party—I pretending to be as good an old-line Whig as ever. Judge Douglas may not understand that he implicated my truthfulness and honor when he said I was doing one thing and pretending another.—*Debate, Quincy, Oct. 13, 1858.* IV, 325.

Absenteeism—*See* CIVIL WAR, army reduced by "absenteeism."

Absolutism, danger of—*See* EMANCIPATION PROCLAMATION, argument against extension of.

Acquaintance, promotes liking—From the first appearance of man upon the earth down to very recent times, the words "stranger" and "enemy" were quite or almost synonymous. Long after civilized nations had defined robbery and murder as high crimes, and had affixed severe punishments to them, when practiced among and upon their own people respectively, it was deemed no offense, but even meritorious, to rob and murder and enslave strangers, whether as nations or as individuals. Even yet, this has not totally disappeared. The man of the highest moral cultivation, in spite of all which abstract principle can do, likes him whom he does know better than him whom he does not know.—*Speech, Milwaukee, Sept. 30, 1859.* V, 236.

2.—I hope, in a word, that when we become better acquainted—and I say it with great confidence—we shall like each other better.—*Speech, reply to mayor of Washington, Feb. 27, 1861.* VI, 166.

"Act Well Your Part"—"Act well your part, there all the honor lies." He who does something at the head of a regiment will eclipse him who does nothing at the head of a hundred.—*To Gen. Hunter, Dec. 31, 1861.* VII, 70.

Action, pleas for—Temporizing will not do longer; now is the time for decision—for firm, persistent, resolute action.—*Speech, Bloomington, May 29, 1856.* Lapsley II, 250.

2.—Do not delay a single regiment, but hasten everything forward as soon as one regiment is ready.—*To Gov. Morton, Aug. 15, 1861.* VI, 343.

3.—Please do not lose time in this matter.—*To Gen. Halleck, Jan. 1, 1862.* VII, 71.

4.—Delay is ruining us.—*To Gen. Buell, Jan. 7, 1862.* VII, 74.

5.—[This] letter from Gen. Halleck . . . is exceedingly discouraging. As everywhere else, nothing can be done.—*Indorsement on letter of Halleck, Jan. 10, 1862.* VII, 78.

6.—I suppose the whole force which has gone forward to you is with you by this time; and if so, I think it is the precise time for you to strike a blow. By delay the enemy will relatively gain upon you—that is, he will gain faster by fortifications and reinforcements than you can by reinforcements alone.—*To Gen. McClellan, April 9, 1862.* VII, 143.

7.—Once more let me tell you it is indispensable to you that you strike a blow. . . . The country will not fail to note—is now noting—that the present hesitation to move upon an entrenched enemy is but the story of Manassas repeated. . . . You must act.—*To Gen. McClellan, April 9, 1862.* VII, 143.

8.—Your call for Parrott guns from Washington alarms me, chiefly because it argues indefinite procrastination. Is anything to be done?—*To Gen. McClellan, May 1, 1862.* VII, 152.

9.—Everything now depends upon the celerity and vigor of your movement.—*To Gen. McDowell, May 24, 1862.* VII, 181.

10.—Put the utmost speed into it. Do not lose a minute.—*To Gen. Frémont, May 24, 1862.* VII, 179.

11.—I think the time is near when you must either attack Richmond or give up the job and come to the defense of Washington. . . . Let me hear from you instantly.—*To Gen. McClellan, May 25, 1862.* VII, 183.

12.—I hope he [Gen. McDowell] will put all possible energy and speed into the effort.—*To Sec. Chase, May 25, 1862.* VII, 185.

13.—Assuming this, it is for you a question of legs. Put in all the speed you can.—*To Gen. McDowell, May 28, 1862.* VII, 198.

14.—The quicker you send [recruits for army], the fewer you will have to send. Time is everything. Please act in view of this.—*To governors, July 3, 1862.* VII, 256.

15.—Please do what you can, and do it quickly. Time is everything.—*To Gov. Andrew Johnson, July 3, 1862.* Hertz II, 871.

16.—We do not need more [new troops], nor, indeed, so many, if we could have the smaller number very soon.—*To Sec. Stanton, July 22, 1862.* VII, 287.

17.—It is very important for some regiments to arrive here at once. What lack you from us? What can we do to expedite matters?—*To Gov. Curtin, Aug. 12, 1862.* VII, 310.

18.—The forces you speak of will be of no imaginable service if they cannot go forward with a little more expedition.—*To Lorenzo Thomas, July 8, 1863.* IX, 23.

19.—Please do not lose a moment.—*To Gen. Burnside, Sept. 21, 1863.* IX, 132.

Adam, compared with descendant—The most that can be said is that, according to his chance, he [Adam] may have been quite as much a man as his very self-complacent descendant. Little as what he knew, let the youngster discard all he has learned from others, and then show, if he can, any advantage on his side.—*Lecture, Springfield, Feb. 22, 1859.* V, 102.

Adam, First of Old Fogies*—Take . . . the first of all Old Fogies, Father Adam. . . . He must have been very ignorant, and simple in his habits. He had had no sufficient time to learn much by observation, and he had no near neighbors to teach him anything. No part of his breakfast had been brought from the other side of the world; and it is quite probable he had no conception of the world having any other side. In all these things, it is very plain, he was no equal of Young America. . . . In the way of land and livestock [however] Adam was quite in the ascendent. . . . He had dominion over all the earth. . . . The land has been sadly divided out since; but never fret, Young America will re-annex it!—*Lecture, Springfield, Feb. 22, 1859.* V, 101.

Adam, joins Eve in first invention—He [Adam] seems not to have been a very observing man at first; for it appears he went about naked a considerable length of time before he even noticed that obvious fact. But when he did observe it, the observation was not lost upon him; for it immediately led to the first of all inventions of which we have any direct account—the fig leaf apron. . . . [But this] first invention was a joint operation, Eve having shared with Adam the getting up of the Apron. And, indeed, judging from the fact that sewing has come down to our times as "woman's work," it is very possible that she took the leading part—he, perhaps, doing no more than to stand by and thread the needle.—*Lecture, Springfield, Feb. 22, 1859.* V, 104.

Adams, James—*See* CHARACTER, no whining about. *See* LAWYER OR LIAR.

Adams, John, death of—The two men most distinguished in the framing and support of the Declaration of Independence were Thomas Jefferson and John Adams—the one having penned it, and the other sustained it most forcibly in debate—the only two of the 55 who signed it that were elected President of the United States. Precisely 50 years after they had put their hands to the paper, it pleased

* After 1850 thousands of the "emerging generation" of Democratic voters, with eyes on the rising political star of Douglas, began calling themselves "Young America." Men who refused to subscribe to their advanced dogmas were, in their opinion, "Old Fogies."

Almighty God to take both from this stage of action. This was indeed an extraordinary and remarkable event in our history.—*Response to serenade, July 7, 1863.* IX, 20.

Admiral P. Tordenskiold—I deem it my duty to recommend an appropriation in behalf of the owners of the Norwegian bark *Admiral P. Tordenskiold,* which vessel was in May, 1861, prevented by the commander of the blockading force off Charleston from leaving that port with cargo, notwithstanding a similar privilege had shortly before been granted to an English vessel.—*Second annual message, Dec. 1, 1862.* VIII, 96.

Advancement, universal order—Advancement—improvement in condition—is the order of things in a society of equals.—*Fragment, July 1, 1854.* II, 185.

Advertising, Democrats get too much—No member of the cabinet knows so well as yourself the great anxiety I felt for Gen. Taylor's election and consequently none could so well appreciate my anxiety for the success of his administration—Therefore I address you—It seems here that the government advertising, or a great part of it, is given to the Democratic papers—This gives offense to the Whig papers; and, if persisted in, will leave the administration without any newspaper support whatever. It causes or will cause the Whig editors to fall off, while the Democratic ones will not be brought in.—*To W. B. Preston, April 20, 1849.* Hertz II, 595.

Advice to Man Condemned to Die—*See* DEITY, mercy of, 2.

Aesop—*See* UNION, strength in.

African Slave Trade, abolition of, not a compromise—[Douglas says] "the abolition of the African slave-trade is a compromise of the Constitution." I deny it. . . . It is a mere barren assertion, made simply for the purpose of getting up a distinction between the revival of the African slave-trade and his "great principle" [popular sovereignty].—*Speech, Columbus, Ohio, Sept. 16, 1859.* V, 183.
2.—Compromise! What word of compromise was there about it? Why, the public sense was then in favor of the abolition of the slave-trade; but there was at the time a very great commercial interest involved in it, and extensive capital in that branch of trade. There were doubtless the incipient stages of improvement in the South in the way of farming, dependent on the slave-trade, and they made a proposition to Congress to abolish the trade after allowing it 20 years, a sufficient time for the capital and commerce engaged in it to be transferred to other channels. They made no

provision that it should be abolished in 20 years; I do not doubt that they expected it would be; but they made no bargain about it.—*Speech, Columbus, Ohio, Sept. 16, 1859.* V, 184.
3.—I repeat, there is nothing in the history of those times in favor of that matter being a compromise of the Constitution.—*Speech, Columbus, Ohio, Sept. 16, 1859.* V, 185.
4.—He [Douglas] has written a letter . . . declaring his opposition to the repeal of the laws that prohibit the African slave-trade. He bases his opposition to such repeal upon the ground that these laws are themselves one of the compromises of the Constitution of the United States. . . . I think there is abundant contemporaneous history to show that the framers of the Constitution expected it to be abolished. But while they so expected, they gave nothing for that expectation, and they put no provision in the Constitution requiring it should be abolished.—*Speech, Cincinnati, Sept. 17, 1859.* V, 208.

African Slave Trade, Congress once controlled in territories—*See* TERRITORIES, slavery in, once controlled by Congress.

African Slave Trade, Declaration of Independence and—*See* DECLARATION OF INDEPENDENCE, slave-trade denunciation omitted from.

African Slave Trade, fight against, was long in Britain—I have not allowed myself to forget that the abolition of the slave trade by Great Britain was agitated a hundred years before it was a final success; that the measure had its open fire-eating opponents; its inferior race opponents; its negro equality opponents; and its religion and good order opponents; that all these opponents got offices, and their adversaries got none. But I have also remembered that though they blazed, like tallow candles for a century, at last they flickered in the socket, died out, stank in the dark for a brief season, and were remembered no more, even by the smell. School boys know that Wilberforce and Granville Sharp helped that course forward; but who can now name a single man who labored to retard it?—*Notes, autumn, 1858.* Hertz II, 705.

African Slave Trade, no asylum for traders—If Congress should think that proceedings in such cases lack the authority of law, or ought to be further regulated by it, I recommend that provision be made for effectually preventing foreign slave traders from acquiring domicile and facilities for their criminal occupation in our country.—*Fourth annual message, Dec. 6, 1864.* X, 288.

African Slave Trade, not suppressed—The African slave-trade is not yet effectually suppressed.—*Speech, Peoria, Oct. 16, 1854.* II, 223.

African Slave Trade, progress against—It is a subject of gratulation that the efforts which have been made for the suppression of this inhuman traffic have been recently attended with unusual success.—*First annual message, Dec. 3, 1861.* VII, 47.

African Slave Trade, revival of, resisted—We must prevent the revival of the African slave trade, because . . . the general welfare does require the prevention.—*Speeches in Kansas, Dec. 1-5, 1859.* V, 279.

African Slave Trade, slavery extension akin to—The law which forbids the bringing of slaves from Africa, and that which has so long forbidden the taking of them into Nebraska, can hardly be distinguished on any moral principle, and the repeal of the former could find quite as plausible excuses as that of the latter.—*Speech, Peoria, Oct. 16, 1854.* II, 208.
Repeated at Urbana, Oct. 24, 1854. Hertz, II, 635.
Repeated at Ottawa, Aug. 21, 1858. III, 228.
2.—I am aware, you may say, that taking slaves from the states to Nebraska does not make slaves of freemen; but the African slave trader can say just as much. He does not catch free negroes and bring them here. He finds them already in the hands of their black captors, and he honestly buys them at the rate of a red cotton handkerchief a head. This is very cheap, and it is a great abridgment of the sacred right of self-government to hang men for engaging in this profitable trade.—*Speech, Peoria, Oct. 16, 1854.* II, 231.
Repeated at Urbana, Oct. 24, 1854. Hertz II, 646.
3.—If it is a sacred right for the people of Nebraska to take and hold slaves there, it is equally their sacred right to buy them where they can buy them cheapest; and that, undoubtedly, will be on the coast of Africa, provided you will consent not to hang them for going there to buy them. You must remove this restriction, too, from the sacred right of self-government.—*Speech, Peoria, Oct. 16, 1854.* II, 231.
Repeated at Urbana, Oct. 24, 1854. Hertz II, 646.
4.—And if you can do this [introduce slavery] in free Kansas, and it is allowed to stand, the next thing you will see is shiploads of negroes from Africa at the wharf at Charleston; for the one thing is as truly lawful as the other; and these are the bastard notions we have got to stamp out, else they will stamp us out.—*Speech, Bloomington, May 29, 1856.* Lapsley II, 272.
5.—A leading Douglas Democratic newspaper thinks Douglas's superior talent will be needed to resist the revival of the African slave-trade. . . . But . . . how can he resist it? For years he has labored to prove it a sacred right of white men to take negro slaves into the new territories. Can he possibly show that it is less a sacred right to buy them where they can be bought cheapest?—*Speech, Springfield, June 16, 1858.* III, 13.
6.—There is no reason in favor of sending slavery to Kansas that might not be adduced in support of the African slave trade. Each is demanded by the profitableness of the traffic thus made in opening a new slave mart, and not from the rightfulness of it. They are upon a common basis, and should be alike condemned.—*Speech, Carlinville, Aug. 31, 1858.* Angle, 190.
7.—Douglas's popular sovereignty, accepted by the public mind as a just principle, nationalizes slavery, and revives the African slave trade inevitably. Taking slaves into new territories, and buying slaves in Africa, are identical things, identical rights or identical wrongs, and the argument which establishes one will establish the other. Try a thousand years for a sound reason why Congress shall not hinder the people of Kansas from having slaves, and when you have found it, it will be an equally good one why Congress should not hinder the people of Georgia from importing slaves from Africa.—*To Samuel Galloway, July 28, 1859.* V, 137.
8.—I now put this proposition, that Judge Douglas's popular sovereignty applied will reopen the African slave trade; and I will demonstrate it by any variety of ways in which you can turn the subject and look at it.—*Speech, Columbus, Ohio, Sept. 16, 1859.* V, 182.
9.—The people of Georgia are as much entitled to popular sovereignty and to buy slaves in Africa, if they want them, as the people of the territory are to have slaves, if they want them, and I defy any man on earth to show any distinction between the two things —to show that the one is either more wicked or more unlawful; to show, on original principles, that one is better or worse than the other; or to show by the Constitution that one differs a whit from the other.—*Speech, Columbus, Ohio, Sept. 16, 1859.* V, 182.
10.—I ask any man, dealing honestly with himself, to point out a distinction [between slavery extension and slave purchases in Africa].—*Speech, Columbus, Ohio, Sept. 16, 1859.* V, 182.
11.—At the time of the formation of the Constitution, public expectation was that the slave trade would be abolished, but no more so than that the spread of slavery into the territories should be restrained.—*Speech, Columbus, Ohio, Sept. 16, 1859.* V, 184.

12.—[If the Douglas principle is established, we shall] be ready for Jeff Davis and Stephens, and other leaders of that company, to sound the bugle for the revival of the slave-trade, for the second Dred Scott decision, for the flood of slavery to be poured over the free states, while we shall be here tied down and helpless, and run over like sheep.—*Speech, Columbus, Ohio, Sept. 16, 1859.* V, 185.

13.—If this principle of Douglas [of Douglas's popular sovereignty] is established, that there is no wrong in slavery, and whoever wants it has a right to have it; that it is a matter of dollars and cents; a sort of question of how they shall deal with brutes; that between us and the negro there is no sort of question, but that at the South the question is between the negro and the crocodile; that it is a mere question of policy; that there is a perfect right, according to interest, to do just as you please—when this is done, where this doctrine prevails, the miners and sappers will have formed public opinion for the [African] slave-trade—*Speech, Columbus, Ohio, Sept. 16, 1859.* V, 185.

14.—Douglas's popular sovereignty, establishing his sacred right in the people [to have slavery wherever they wish], if you please, if carried to its logical conclusion, gives equally the sacred right to the people of the states or the territories themselves to buy slaves wherever they can buy them cheapest; and if any man can show how the people of Kansas have a better right to slaves because they want them, than the people of Georgia have to buy them in Africa, I want him to do so.—*Speech, Cincinnati, Sept. 17, 1859.* V, 206.

15.—He [Douglas] says that it is the sacred right of the man who goes into the territories to have slavery if he wants it. Grant this for the argument's sake. Is it not the sacred right of the man who don't go there, equally to buy slaves in Africa if he wants them? Can you point out the difference?—*Speech, Cincinnati, Sept. 17, 1859.* V, 206.

16.—If it is "popular sovereignty" for the people to have slaves because they want them, it is popular sovereignty for them to buy them in Africa, because they desire to do so.—*Speech, Cincinnati, Sept. 17, 1859.* V, 207.

17.—It is as easy to prove that the framers of the Constitution of the United States expected that slavery should be prohibited from extending into the new territories, as it is to prove that it was expected that the slave-trade should be abolished. Both these things were expected.—*Speech, Cincinnati, Sept. 17, 1859.* V, 208.

18.—Who can show that one people have a better right to carry slaves to where they have never been, than another people have to buy slaves wherever they please, even in Africa?—*Speech, Leavenworth, Kan., Dec. 3, 1859.* Angle, 233.
See SLAVERY, "sacred right" of.

African Slave Trade, suppression of, by treaty—I transmit to Congress a copy of a treaty for the suppression of the African slave-trade, between the United States and Her Britannic Majesty. . . . It is desirable that such legislation as may be necessary to carry the treaty into effect should be enacted as soon as may comport with the convenience of Congress.—*Message to Congress, June 10, 1862.* VII, 215.

2.—The treaty with Great Britain for the suppression of the slave-trade has been put into operation with a good prospect of complete success. It is an occasion of special pleasure to acknowledge that the execution of it on the part of Her Majesty's government has been marked with a jealous respect for the authority of the United States and the rights of their moral and loyal citizens.—*Second annual message, Dec. 1, 1862.* VIII, 95.

3.—The supplemental treaty between the United States and Great Britain for the suppression of the African slave-trade . . . has been . . . carried into execution. It is believed that so far as American ports and American citizens are concerned, that inhuman and odious traffic has been brought to an end.—*Third annual message, Dec. 8, 1863.* IX, 225.

African Slave Trade, to help Liberia fight—*See* LIBERIA, gunboat suggested for.

Agitator and Deserter—*See* VALLANDIGHAM, C. L., arrest of, explained, 1.

Agreement, more important than terms of—Between public measures regarded as antagonistic, there is often less real difference in their bearing on the public weal, than there is between the dispute being kept up, or being settled either way.—*Speech, Chicago, July 25, 1850.* Angle, 75.

Agricultural Fairs, Utility of—Agricultural fairs . . . render more pleasant, and more strong and durable, the bond of social and political union among us.—*Speech, Milwaukee, Sept. 30, 1859.* V, 236.

2.—The chief use of agricultural fairs is to aid in improving the great calling of agriculture in all its departments and minute divisions; to make mutual exchange of agricultural discoveries, information, and knowledge; so that, at the end, all may know everything which may have been known to but one or to but a few, at the beginning; to bring together especially all which is supposed to be not generally known because of recent discovery or invention.—*Speech, Milwaukee, Sept. 30, 1859.* V, 237.

3.—By exciting emulation for premiums, and for the pride and honor of success—of triumph, in some sort —to stimulate that discovery and invention into extraordinary activity.—*Speech, Milwaukee, Sept. 30, 1859.* V, 238.

Agriculture, agreeable occupation—No other human occupation opens so wide a field for the profitable and agreeable combination of labor with cultivated thought as agriculture.—*Speech, Milwaukee, Sept. 30, 1859.* V, 252.
2.—The mind already trained to thought in the country school, or higher school, cannot fail to find there [in agriculture] an exhaustless source of enjoyment.—*Speech, Milwaukee, Sept. 30, 1859.* Basler, 503.
3.—Soils, seeds, and seasons—hedges, ditches and fences—draining, droughts and irrigation—plowing, hoeing and harrowing—reaping, mowing and threshing—saving crops, pests of crops, diseases of crops, and what will prevent or cure them—implements, utensils, and machines, their relative merits, and how to improve them—hogs, horses and cattle—sheep, goats and poultry—trees, shrubs, fruits, plants, and flowers—the thousand things of which these are specimens—each a world of study within itself.—*Speech, Milwaukee, Sept. 30, 1859.* V, 253.

Agriculture, bureau of, recommended—Agriculture, confessedly the largest interest in the nation, has not a department nor a bureau, but a clerkship only, assigned to it in the government. . . . It is fortunate that this great interest is so independent in its nature as not to have demanded and extorted more from the government. . . . I venture the opinion that an agricultural and statistical bureau might profitably be organized.—*First annual message, Dec. 3, 1861.* VII, 46.

Agriculture, Department of, deserves support—The creation of this [agricultural] department was for the immediate benefit of a large class of our most valuable citizens, and I trust that the liberal basis on which it has been organized will not only meet your approbation, but that it will realize at no distant day all the fondest anticipations of its most sanguine friends and become the fruitful source of advantage to all our people.—*Second annual message, Dec. 1, 1862.* VIII, 110.

Agriculture, Department of, established—To carry out the provisions of the act of Congress of the 15th of May last, I have caused the Department of Agriculture of the United States to be organized. The commissioner informs me that within the period of a few months this department has established an extensive system of correspondence and exchanges, both at home and abroad, which promises to effect highly beneficial results.—*Second annual message, Dec. 1, 1862.* VIII, 109.

Agriculture, Department of, is people's—The agricultural department . . . is peculiarly the people's department in which they feel more directly concerned than any other.—*Fourth annual message, Dec. 6, 1864.* X, 302.

Agriculture, farmers' interest paramount—Farmers, being the most numerous class, it follows that their interest is the largest interest. It also follows that that interest is most worthy of all to be cherished and cultivated—that if there be inevitable conflict between that interest and any other, that other should yield. —*Speech, Milwaukee, Sept. 30, 1859.* Basler, 495.

Agriculture, farmers "neither better nor worse"—My opinion of them [farmers as a class] is that, in proportion to numbers, they are neither better nor worse than other people. In the nature of things they are more numerous than any other class; and I believe there really are more attempts at flattering them than any other, the reason for which I cannot perceive, unless it be that they cast more votes than any other. —*Speech, Milwaukee, Sept. 30, 1859.* V, 238.

Agriculture, fosters independence—Ere long the most valuable of all arts will be the art of deriving a comfortable subsistence from the smallest area of soil. No community whose every member possesses this art, can ever be the victim of oppression in any of its forms. Such community will be alike independent of crowned kings, money kings and land kings.—*Speech, Milwaukee, Sept. 30, 1859.* V, 254.

Agriculture, horsepower in harvesting—In the highest degree of perfection yet reached in applying the horsepower to harvesting, fully nine-tenths of the power is expended by the animal in carrying himself and dragging the machine over the field, leaving certainly not more than one-tenth to be applied directly to the only end of the whole operation—the gathering in of the grain, and clipping the straw. What I have said of harvesting is true in a greater or less degree of mowing, plowing, gathering in of crops generally, and indeed of almost all farm work.— *Speech, Milwaukee, Sept. 30, 1859.* V, 242.
Repeated at Springfield, Nov. 7, 1860. Hertz II, 789.

Agriculture, mammoth farms seldom profitable—The ambition for broad acres leads to poor farming, even with men of energy. I scarcely ever knew a mammoth farm to sustain itself, much less to return a profit upon the outlay. . . . Mammoth farms are like tools

or weapons too heavy to be handled.—*Speech, Milwaukee, Sept. 30, 1859*. V, 244.
Repeated at Springfield, Nov. 7, 1860. Hertz II, 790.

Agriculture, "most valuable of all arts"—Population must increase rapidly, more rapidly than in former times, and ere long the most valuable of all arts will be the art of deriving a comfortable subsistence from the smallest area of soil.—*Speech, Milwaukee, Sept. 30, 1859*. V, 254.

Agriculture, no farmer—I have no farm, nor ever expect to have, and consequently have not studied the subject enough to be much interested in it.—*To Joshua F. Speed, March 27, 1842*. I, 214.

Agriculture, steam power in—The successful application of steam-power to farm work is a desideratum—especially a steam plow. It is not enough that a machine operated by steam will really plow. To be successful it must, all things considered, plow better than can be done with animal power. It must do all the work as well, and cheaper; or more rapidly, so as to get through more perfectly in season; or in some way afford an advantage over plowing with animals, else it is no success. I have never seen a machine intended for a steam plow.—*Speech, Milwaukee, Sept. 30, 1859*. Basler, 498.
2.—That one [steam plow] which shall be so contrived as to apply the larger proportion of its power to the cutting and turning of the soil, and the smallest to the moving itself over the field, will be the best one.—*Speech, Milwaukee, Sept. 30, 1859*. V, 245.
3.—Our thanks, and something more substantial than thanks, are due to every man engaged in the effort to produce a successful steam plow.—*Speech, Milwaukee, Sept. 30, 1859*. V, 247.

Agriculture, thorough cultivation urged—My first suggestion is an inquiry into the effects of greater thoroughness in all the departments of agriculture than now prevails in the Northwest—perhaps I might say in America. To speak entirely within bounds, it is known that 50 bushels of wheat, or 100 bushels of Indian corn, can be produced from an acre. Less than a year ago I saw it stated that a man, by extraordinary care and labor, had produced of wheat what was equal to 200 bushels from an acre. But take 50 of wheat and 100 of corn, to be a probability and compare it with the actual crops of the country. Many years ago I saw it stated in a Patent Office report that 18 bushels was the average crop throughout the United States; and this year an intelligent farmer of Illinois assured me that he did not believe the land harvested in that state this season had yielded more

than an average of eight bushels to the acre. . . . It is true that heretofore we have had better crops with no better cultivation; but I believe it is also true that the soil has never been pushed up to one-half of its capacity.—*Speech, Milwaukee, Sept. 30, 1859*. V, 239.
Repeated at Springfield, Nov. 7, 1860. Hertz II, 788.
2.—What would be the effect upon the farming interest to push the soil up to something near its full capacity? Unquestionably it will take more labor to produce 50 bushels [of wheat] from an acre than it will to produce ten bushels from the same acre; but will it take more labor to produce 50 bushels from one acre than from five?—*Speech, Milwaukee, Sept. 30, 1859*. V, 240.
Repeated at Springfield, Nov. 7, 1860. Hertz II, 789.
3.—There are some probable, and several certain, advantages in favor of the thorough practice [in soil cultivation]. It is probable it would develop those unknown causes which of late years have cut down our crops below their former average. It is almost certain, I think, that by deeper plowing, analysis of soils, experiments with manures and varieties of seeds, observance of seasons, and the like, these causes would be found. It is certain that thorough cultivation would spare half, or more than half, the cost of land, simply because the same product would be got from half, or from less than half, the quantity of land.—*Speech, Milwaukee, Sept. 30, 1859*. Basler, 496.
4.—[Thorough cultivation] would also spare a large proportion of the expense of making and maintaining inclosures—the same whether such inclosures should be hedges, ditches or fences. This, again, is a heavy item—heavy at first, and heavy in its continual demand for repairs.—*Speech, Milwaukee, Sept. 30, 1859*. V, 241.
Repeated at Springfield, Nov. 7, 1860. Hertz II, 788.
5.—Again, a great amount of "locomotion" is spared by thorough cultivation. Take 50 bushels of wheat, ready for the harvest, standing upon a single acre, and it can be harvested in any of the known ways, with less than half the labor which would be required if it were spread over five acres.—*Speech, Milwaukee, Sept. 30, 1859*. V, 242.
Repeated at Springfield, Nov. 7, 1860. Hertz II, 788.
6.—The effect of thorough cultivation upon the farmer's own mind, and in reaction through his mind back upon his business, is perhaps quite equal to any other of its effects. Every man is proud of what he does well, and no man is proud of that he does not well. With the former his heart is in his work, and he will do twice as much of it with less fatigue; the latter he performs a little imperfectly, looks at in disgust, turns from it, and imagines himself exceedingly tired—the little he has done comes to nothing for

want of finishing.—*Speech, Milwaukee, Sept. 30, 1859.*
V, 243.

7.—The man who produces a good full crop will scarcely ever let any part of it go to waste; he will keep up the inclosures about it, and allow neither man nor beast to trespass upon it. He will gather it in due season, and store it in perfect security.—*Speech, Milwaukee, Sept. 30, 1859.* Basler, 497. Repeated at Springfield, Nov. 7, 1860. Hertz II, 790.

Albany Resolutions—*See* CIVIL WAR, Albany resolutions on.

See WAR POWER, use of, defended, 5, 7, 8.

Alexander, challenged—I would like to know who is the great Alexander that talks so oracularly about "if the President keeps his word" and Banks not having "capacity to run an omnibus on Broadway." How has this Alexander's immense light been obscured hitherto?—*To F. P. Blair, July 30, 1863.* IX, 49.

Alienage—*See* ALIENS, status of, in war, 4.

Aliens, if Know-Nothings get control—*See* KNOW-NOTHING PARTY, principles of, challenged, 2.

Aliens, justice to—Injuries unforeseen by the government and unintended, may, in some cases have been inflicted on the subjects or citizens of foreign countries, both at sea and on land, by persons in the service of the United States. As this government expects redress from other powers when similar injuries are inflicted by persons in their service upon citizens of the United States, we must be prepared to do justice to foreigners. If the existing judicial tribunals are inadequate to this purpose, a special court may be authorized, with power to hear and decide such claims of the character referred to as may have arisen under treaties and the public law.—*Third annual message, Dec. 8, 1863.* IX, 231.

Aliens, Massachusetts Republicans criticized for "tilting against"—*See* REPUBLICAN PARTY, threats to unity, 3.

Aliens, status of, in war—It is the duty of all aliens residing in the United States to submit to and obey the laws, and respect authority of the government. . . . They cannot be required to take an oath of allegiance to this government, because it conflicts with the duty they owe to their own sovereigns. All such obligations heretofore taken are therefore remitted and annulled. Military commanders will refrain from imposing similar obligations in the future.—*Military order, July 22, 1862.* Hertz II, 873.

2.—Whereas it is claimed in behalf of persons of foreign birth . . . who have heretofore declared on oath their intentions to become citizens . . . and who have not exercised the right of suffrage or any other political franchise under the laws of the United States or of any of the states thereof, that they are not absolutely concluded by their aforesaid declaration of intention from renouncing their purpose to become citizens and that, on the contrary, such persons, under treaties or the law of nations, retain a right to renounce that purpose and to forego the privileges of citizenship and residence within the United States. . . . Now, therefore . . . I do hereby order and proclaim that no plea of alienage will be received or allowed to exempt from the obligations [of military service] any person of foreign birth who shall have declared his intention to become a citizen. —*Proclamation, May 8, 1863.* VIII, 267.

3.—Incidents occurring in the progress of our civil war have forced upon my attention the uncertain state of international questions touching the rights of foreigners in this country and of United States citizens abroad. In regard to some governments these rights are at least partially defined by treaties. In no instance, however, is it expressly stipulated that in the event of civil war a foreigner residing in the country within the lines of the insurgents is to be exempted from the rule which classes him as a belligerent, in whose behalf the government of his country cannot expect any privileges or immunities distinct from that character. I regret to say, however, that such claims have been put forward, and in some instances in behalf of foreigners who have lived in the United States the greater part of their lives. There is reason to believe that many persons born in foreign countries who have declared their intention to become citizens, or who have been fully naturalized, have evaded the military duty required of them by denying the fact and thereby throwing upon the government the burden of proof. It has been found difficult or impracticable to obtain this proof, from the want of guides to the proper sources of information.—*Third annual message, Dec. 8, 1863.* IX, 227.

4.—The right of suffrage has often been assumed and exercised by aliens under the pretense of naturalization, which they have disavowed when drafted into the military service. I submit the expediency of such an amendment of the law as will make the fact of voting an estopel against any plea of exemption from military service or other civic obligation on the ground of alienage.—*Third annual message, Dec. 8, 1863.* IX, 228.

"All Men Are Created Equal," ancient faith—*See* SLAVERY, wrong of, 4.

"All Men Are Created Equal"—*See* EQUALITY.
See "'APPLE OF GOLD,' pictures of silver."

Allaying Plaster—*See* KANSAS-NEBRASKA ACT, ended period of peace.

Allen, Robert, "favor" of, rejected—*See* "FAVOR," rejected.

Alliance, bipartisan, denied—*See* DOUGLAS-BUCHANAN FEUD, Republicans welcome.

Ambition, confession of—Every man is said to have his peculiar ambition. Whether it be true or not, I can say, for one, that I have no other so great as that of being truly esteemed by my fellow-men, by rendering myself worthy of their esteem. How far I shall succeed in gratifying this ambition, is yet to be developed.—*Address to Sangamon County, March 9, 1832.* I, 8.
2.—I claim no extraordinary exemption from personal ambition. That I like preferment as well as the average of men may be admitted. But I protest I have not entered upon this hard contest [for United States senator] solely, or even chiefly, for a mere personal object.—*Notes, Oct. 1, 1858.* IV, 214.
3.—Ambition has been ascribed to me. God knows how sincerely I prayed from the first that this field of ambition might not be opened. I claim no insensibility to political honors; but today, could the Missouri restrictions be restored, and the whole slavery question be placed on the same old grounds of "toleration" by necessity where it exists, with unyielding hostility to the spread of it, on principle, I would, in consideration, gladly agree that Judge Douglas should never be out, and I never in, an office so long as we both or either, live.—*Speech, Springfield, Oct. 30, 1858.* Angle, 198.
4.—I have never professed an indifference to the honors of official station; and were I to do so now, I should only make myself ridiculous. Yet I have never failed—do not now fail—to recognize that in the Republican cause there is a higher aim than that of mere office.—*Notes, 1858.* Hertz II, 705.

Ambition, driving power of—It is to deny what the history of the world tells us is true, to suppose that men of ambition and talents will not continue to spring up amongst us. And when they do, they will as naturally seek the gratification of their ruling passion as others have done before them. The question then is, Can that gratification be found in supporting and maintaining an edifice that has been erected by others? Most certain, it cannot! Many great and good men, sufficiently qualified for any task they should undertake, may ever be found whose ambition would

aspire to nothing beyond a seat in Congress, a gubernatorial or a presidential chair; but such belong not to the family of the lion or the tribe of the eagle. What! think you these places would satisfy an Alexander, a Caesar, or a Napoleon?—*Speech, Springfield, Jan. 27, 1837.* I, 46.
2.—Towering genius disdains a beaten path. It seeks regions hitherto unexplored. It sees no distinction in adding story to story upon the monuments of fame erected to the memory of others. It denies that it is glory enough to serve under any chief. It scorns to tread in the footsteps of any predecessor, however illustrious. It thirsts and burns for distinction; and, if possible, will have it, whether at the expense of emancipating slaves or enslaving free men.—*Speech, Springfield, Jan. 27, 1837.* I, 46.
3.—Is it unreasonable, then, to expect that some man possessed of the loftiest genius, coupled with ambition sufficient to push it to its utmost stretch, will at some time spring up amongst us? And when such a one does, it will require the people to be united with each other, attached to the government and laws, and generally intelligent, successfully to frustrate his designs. Distinction will be his paramount object, and although he would as willingly, perhaps, more so, acquire it by doing good as harm, yet, that opportunity being past, and nothing left to be done in the way of building up, he would set boldly to the task of pulling down.—*Speech, Springfield, Jan. 27, 1837.* I, 47.

America, anxiety for—*See* CIVIL WAR, aftermath feared.

America, "beneficial toward mankind"—A fair examination of history has served to authorize a belief that the past actions and influences of the United States were generally regarded as having been beneficial toward mankind. I have therefore reckoned upon the forbearance of nations.—*To workers of Manchester, Jan. 19, 1863.* VIII, 195.

America, citizens of, are brothers—Let us at all times remember that all American citizens are brothers of a common country, and should dwell together in the bonds of fraternal feeling.—*Speech, Springfield, Nov. 20, 1860.* VI, 72.

America, comparison in principles—We find a people on the Northeast, who have a different government from ours, being ruled by a queen. Turning to the South, we see a people who, while they boast of being free, keep their fellow-beings in bondage. Compare free states with either; shall we say here we have no interest in keeping that principle [liberty] alive?

—Speech, Kalamazoo, Mich., Aug. 27, 1856. Stern, 404.

America, dangerous tendencies in—We hope that all danger [to the nation] may be overcome; but to conclude that no danger may ever arise would itself be extremely dangerous. There are now, and will hereafter be, many causes dangerous in their tendencies, which have not existed heretofore, and which are not too insignificant to merit attention.—*Speech, Springfield, Jan. 27, 1837.* I, 44.
2.—We live in the midst of alarms; anxiety beclouds the future; we expect some new disaster with each newspaper we read. Are we in a healthful political state? Are not the tendencies plain? Do not the signs of the times point plainly the way in which we are going?—*Speech, Bloomington, May 29, 1856.* Lapsley II, 256.

America, dedication to—Many free countries have lost their liberty, and ours may lose hers; but if she shall, be it my proudest plume, not that I was the last to desert, but that I never deserted her. . . . I cannot deny that all may be swept away. Broken by it, I, too, may be; bow to it I never will.—*Speech, Springfield, Dec. 20, 1839.* I, 137.
2.—If ever I feel the soul within me elevate and expand to those dimensions not wholly unworthy of its Almighty Architect, it is when I contemplate the course of my country, deserted by all the world beside, and I standing up boldly and alone, and hurling defiance at her victorious oppressors. Here, without contemplating consequences, before high heaven and in the face of the world, I swear eternal fidelity to the just cause, as I deem it, of the land of my life, my liberty and my love.—*Speech, Springfield, Dec. 20, 1839.* I, 138.
3.—If, after all, we shall fail, be it so. We still shall have the proud consolation of saying to our consciences, and to a departed shade of our country's freedom, that the cause approved by our judgment, and adored by our hearts, in disaster, in chains, in torture, in death, we never faltered in defending.—*Speech, Springfield, Dec. 20, 1839.* I, 139.
4.—It is for us, the living, rather, to be dedicated here to the unfinished work which they who fought here have thus far so nobly advanced. It is rather for us to be here dedicated to the great task remaining before us—that from these honored dead we take increased devotion to that cause for which they gave the last full measure of devotion.—*Gettysburg Address, Nov. 19, 1863.* IX, 210.

America, equal treatment for, insisted on—The United States, whatever claim or pretense may have existed heretofore, are now, at least entitled to claim and concede an entire and friendly equality of rights and hospitalities with all maritime nations.—*Proclamation, April 11, 1865.* XI, 83.

America, future rulers of—Your friend, Leroy C. Driggs, tells me you are a very earnest friend of mine, for which please allow me to thank you. You and those of your age [twelve] are to take charge of this country when we older ones shall have gone; and I am glad to learn that you already take so lively an interest in what just now so deeply concerns us.—*To Willie Smith, Feb. 23, 1864.* Angle, 343.

America, grown great—We are a great empire. We are 80 years old. We stand at once the wonder and the admiration of the whole world, and we must inquire what it is that has given us so much prosperity, and we shall understand that to give up that one thing [free government] would be to give up all future prosperity. This cause is that every man can make himself. It has been said that such a race of prosperity has been run nowhere else.—*Speech, Kalamazoo, Mich., Aug. 27, 1856.* Stern, 404.
2.—We are now a mighty nation; we are thirty, or about thirty, million people, and we own and inhabit about one-fifteenth part of the dry land of the whole earth. We run our memory back over the pages of history for about eighty-two years, and we discover that we were then a very small people, in point of numbers vastly inferior to what we now are, with a vastly less extent of country, with vastly less of everything we deem desirable among men. We look upon the change as exceedingly advantageous to us and to our posterity, and we fix upon something that happened away back as in some way or other being connected with this rise of prosperity. We find a race of men living in that day whom we claim as our fathers and grandfathers; they were iron men; they fought for the principle that they were contending for; and we understand that by what they did it has followed that the degree of prosperity which we now enjoy has come to us.—*Speech, Chicago, July 10, 1858.* III, 46.

America, inheritance—We, the American people . . . find ourselves in the peaceful possession of the fairest portion of the earth as regards extent of territory, fertility of soil, and salubrity of climate. We find ourselves under the government of a system of political institutions conducing more essentially to the ends of civil and religious liberty than any of which the history of former times tells us. We, when mounting the stage of existence, found ourselves the legal inheritors of those fundamental blessings.—*Speech, Springfield, Jan. 27, 1837.* I, 35.

America, "land of liberty"—*See* LIBERTY, preservation of, a duty, 2.

America, "land of the free"—*See* "LAND OF THE FREE, HOME OF THE BRAVE," is America?

America, leads in improvements—The human family originated somewhere in Asia, and have worked their way principally westward. Just now in civilization and the arts the people of Asia are entirely behind those of Europe; those of the east of Europe are behind those of the west of it; while we, here in America, think we discover, and invent, and improve faster than any of them. They may think it arrogance; but they cannot deny that Russia has called on us to show her how to build steamboats and railroads, while in the older parts of Asia they scarcely know that such things as steamboats and railroads exist. —*Lecture, Springfield, Feb. 22, 1858. V, 112.*

America, people of, called hypocrites—*See* SLAVERY, extension of, opposed, 2.

America, suicide only peril of—If destruction be our lot we must ourselves be its author and finisher. As a nation of freemen, we must live through all time, or die by suicide.—*Speech, Springfield, Jan. 27, 1837. I, 37.*
2.—While ever a state of feeling such as this [reverence for law] shall universally or even very generally prevail throughout the nation, vain will be every effort, and fruitless every attempt, to subvert our national freedom.—*Speech, Springfield, Jan. 27, 1837. I, 43.*

America, thanks for—For the great Republic—for the principle it lives by and keeps alive—for man's vast future—thanks to all.—*To James C. Conkling, Aug. 26, 1863. IX, 101.*

American Baptist Home Mission Society, thanked—In response to the preamble and resolutions of the American Baptist Home Mission Society, which you did me the honor to represent, I can only thank you for thus adding to the effective and almost unanimous support which the Christian communities are so zealously giving to the country and to liberty. Indeed, it is difficult to conceive how it could be otherwise with anyone professing Christianity, or even having ordinary perceptions of right and wrong.— *To Dr. Ide and others, May 30, 1864. X, 109.*

American Colonization Society, praise for—It [American Colonization Society] was one of the most cherished objects of his [Henry Clay's] direct care and consideration, and the association of his name with it has probably been its very greatest collateral sup-

port. . . . This suggestion of the possible ultimate redemption of the African race and African continent was made 25 years ago. Every succeeding year has added strength to the hope of its realization. May it indeed be realized.—*Speech, Springfield, July 16, 1852. II, 175.*

American Flag, each star brings happiness—I am invited and called before you to participate in raising above Independence Hall the flag of our country, with an additional star upon it [that of Kansas]. . . . I wish to call your attention that, under the blessing of God, each additional star added to that flag has given additional prosperity and happiness to this country, until it has advanced to its present condition; and its welfare in the future, as well as in the past, is in your hands. Cultivating the spirit that animated our fathers, who gave renown and celebrity to this hall, cherishing that fraternal feeling which has so long characterized us as a nation, excluding passion, ill temper, and precipitate action on all occasions, I think we may promise ourselves that not only the new star placed upon that flag shall be permitted to remain there to our permanent prosperity for years to come, but additional ones shall from time to time be placed there until we shall number, as was anticipated by the great historian, five hundred millions of happy and prosperous people.— *Speech, Independence Hall, Philadelphia, Feb. 22, 1861. VI, 159.*

American Flag, its raising an omen—When [at Independence Hall] . . . the cord was pulled, and it [American flag] floated gloriously to the wind, without an accident, in the bright, glowing sunshine of the morning, I could not help hoping that there was in the entire success of that beautiful ceremony at least something of an omen of what is to come. Nor could I help feeling then, as I have often felt, that in the whole of that proceeding I was a very humble instrument. I had not provided the flag; I had not made the arrangements for elevating it to its place; I had applied but a very small portion of even my feeble strength in raising it.—*Speech to Pennsylvania legislature, Feb. 22, 1861. VI, 163.*

American Government—*See* GOVERNMENT (AMERICAN).

American Party—*See* KNOW-NOTHING PARTY.

American People, "most intelligent, and happiest"— *See* PEOPLE, relied on to save Union, 10.

"American Solon"—*See* WALKER, ROBERT J., characterized.

American Tract Society—What has jarred and shaken the great American Tract Society—not yet splitting it, but sure to divide it in the end? Is it not this same mighty deep-seated power [the "endeavor to spread" slavery] that somehow operates on the minds of men, exciting and stirring them up in every avenue of society—in politics, in religion, in literature, in morals, in all the manifold relations of life?—*Debate, Alton, Oct. 15, 1858.* V, 55.

"Americanism," trouble from—*See* CAMPAIGN OF 1858, hopeful.

Amnesty, discretion urged—I somewhat dread the effect of your Special Order No. 61, dated March 7, 1864. I have found that men who have not been even suspected of disloyalty are very averse to taking an oath of any sort as a condition to exercising an ordinary right of citizenship. The point will probably be made that while men may, without an oath, assemble in a noisy political meeting, they must take the oath to assemble as a religious meeting.—*To Gen. Rosecrans, April 4, 1864.* X, 63.

Amnesty, door open for a year—A year ago general pardon and amnesty, upon specified terms, were offered to all except certain designated classes. . . . Thus practically the door has been for a full year open to all except such as were not in condition to make free choice; that is, such as were in custody or under constraint. It is still so open to all. But the time may come, probably will come, when public duty shall demand that it be closed and that in lieu more rigorous measures than heretofore shall be adopted.—*Fourth annual message, Dec. 6, 1864.* X, 309.

Amnesty, penitence alone essential—When a man is sincerely penitent for his misdeeds, and gives satisfactory evidence of the same, he can safely be pardoned, and there is no exception to the rule.—*To White House group, April 30, 1864.* Carpenter, 102.

Amnesty, proclamation of, constitutional—On examination of this proclamation it will appear, as is believed, that nothing is attempted beyond what is amply justified by the Constitution. . . . The Constitution authorizes the executive to grant or withhold the pardon at his own absolute discretion; and this includes the power to grant on terms, as is fully established by judicial and other authorities.—*Third annual message, Dec. 8, 1863.* IX, 248.
2.—For these and other reasons it is thought best that support of these measures [Acts of Congress, proclamations] shall be included in the oath; and it is believed the executive may lawfully claim it in return for pardon and restoration of forfeited rights, which he has clear constitutional power to withhold alto-

gether, or grant upon the terms which he shall deem wisest for the public interest.—*Third annual message, Dec. 8, 1863.* IX, 250.

Amnesty, proclamation of, explained—The oath in the proclamation of Dec. 8 is intended for those who may voluntarily take it, and not for those who may be constrained to take it in order to escape actual imprisonment or punishment. It is intended that the latter class shall abide the granting or withholding of the pardoning power in the usual way.—*To Judge Ogden Hoffman, Dec. 15, 1863.* IX, 258.
2.—I . . . proclaim and declare that the said proclamation [of Dec. 8, 1863] does not apply to the class of persons who, at the time they seek to obtain the benefits thereof by taking the oath thereby prescribed, are in military, naval, or civil confinement or custody, or under bonds, or on parole of the civil, military or naval authorities, or agents of the United States, as prisoners of war, or persons detained for offenses of any kind, either before or after conviction; and that, on the contrary, it does apply only to those persons who, being yet at large, and free from arrest, confinement or duress, shall voluntarily come forward and take the said oath, with the purpose of restoring peace, and establishing the national authority. Prisoners excluded from the amnesty offered in the said proclamation may apply to the President for clemency, like all other offenders.—*Proclamation, March 26, 1864.* X, 58.

Amnesty, purpose of proclamation—The objects of that proclamation [of Dec. 8, 1863] were to suppress the rebellion and to restore the authority of the United States.—*Proclamation, March 26, 1864.* X, 58.

Amnesty, terms of, declared—I . . . do proclaim and make known to all persons who, directly or by implication, participated in the existing rebellion, except as hereinafter excepted, that a full pardon is hereby granted to them and each of them, with restoration of all rights of property, except as to slaves and in property cases where rights of third parties shall have intervened, and upon the condition that every such person shall take and subscribe an oath and thenceforward keep and maintain such oath inviolate, and which oath shall be registered for permanent preservation and shall be of the tenor and effect following, to wit:
I— ———, do solemnly swear, in the presence of Almighty God, that I will henceforth faithfully support, protect and defend the Constitution of the United States and the Union of states thereunder; and that I will in like manner abide by and faithfully support all acts of Congress passed during the existing rebellion with ref-

erence to slaves, so long and so far as not repealed, modified or held void by Congress or by decision of the Supreme Court; and that I will in like manner abide by and faithfully support all proclamations by the president made during the existing rebellion having reference to slaves, so long and so far as not modified or declared void by decision of the Supreme Court. So help me, God!

The persons exempted from the benefits of the foregoing provisions are all who are, or shall have been, civil or diplomatic officers or agents of the so-called Confederate government; all who have left judicial stations under the United States to aid the rebellion; all who are or shall have been military or naval officers of said so-called Confederate government above the rank of colonel in the army or of lieutenant in the navy; all who have left seats in the United States Congress to aid the rebellion; all who resigned commissions in the army or navy of the United States and afterward aided the rebellion; and all who have engaged in any way in treating colored persons, or white persons in charge of such, otherwise than lawfully as prisoners of war, and which persons may have been found in the United States service as soldiers, seamen, or in any other capacity.—*Proclamation, Dec. 8, 1863.* IX, 219.

2.—But if it be proper to require, as a test of admission to the political body, an oath of allegiance to the Constitution of the United States, and to the Union under it, why also the laws and proclamations in regard to slavery? These laws and proclamations were enacted and put forth for the purpose of aiding in the suppression of the rebellion. To give them their fullest effect, there had to be a pledge for their maintenance. In my judgment they have aided, and will further aid, the cause for which they were intended. To abandon them would be not only to relinquish a lever of power, but would also be a cruel and astounding breach of faith.—*Third annual message, Dec. 8, 1863.* IX, 247.

3.—Saying that, on certain terms, certain classes will be pardoned, with rights restored, it is not said that other classes, or other terms, will never be included. —*Third annual message, Dec. 8, 1863.* IX, 251.

Amnesty, war prisoners and—I am so pressed in regard to prisoners of war in our custody, whose homes are within our lines, and who wish not to be exchanged, but to take the oath and be discharged, that I hope you will pardon me for again calling up the subject. My impression is that we will not ever force the exchange of any of this class; that, taking the oath and being discharged, none of them will again go to the rebellion; but the rebellion coming to them, a considerable percentage of them, probably not a majority, would join it; that, by a cautious discrimination, the number so discharged would not be large

enough to do any considerable mischief in any event, will relieve distress in at least some meritorious cases, and would give me some relief from an intolerable pressure.—*To Sec. Stanton, March 18, 1864.* X, 44.

2.—I see your dispatch to the secretary of war, objecting to rebel prisoners being allowed to take the oath and go free. Supposing that I am responsible for what is done in this way, I think fit to say there is no general rule of action, allowing prisoners to be discharged merely on taking the oath. What has been done is that members of Congress come to me, from time to time, with lists of names, alleging that from personal knowledge, and the evidence of reliable persons, they are satisfied that it is safe to discharge the particular persons named in the lists, and I have indorsed their discharge. These members are chiefly from the border states, and those they get discharged are their neighbors and neighbors' sons. . . . The number I have discharged has been rather larger than I liked, reaching, I should think, an average of 50 a day since the recent general exchange commenced. On the same grounds, last year, I discharged quite a number at different times, aggregating perhaps 1000 Missourians and Kentuckians; and their members, returning here since the prisoners' return to their homes, report to me only two cases of proving false. Doubtless some more have proved false; but, on the whole, I believe that what I have done in this way has done good rather than harm.—*To Gen. Grant, March 9, 1865.* XI, 50.

Anarchy, essence of secession—*See* SECESSION means disintegration, 2.

Ancient Faith—*See* LIBERTY, danger to, 2.

See SLAVERY, wrong of, 4.

"And This, Too, Shall Pass Away"—It is said an eastern monarch once charged his wise men to invent him a sentence to be ever in view, and which should be true and appropriate in all times and situations. They presented him the words, "And this, too, shall pass away." How much it expresses! How chastening in the hour of pride! How consoling in the depths of affliction! . . . And yet, let us hope, it is not quite true. Let us hope, rather, that by the best cultivation of the physical world beneath and around us, and the best intellectual and moral world within us, we shall secure an individual, social and political prosperity and happiness, whose course shall be onward and upward, and which, while the earth endures, shall not pass away.—*Speech, Milwaukee, Sept. 30, 1859.* V, 255.

Anderson, Robert, appreciation of—A few days ago I caused an official letter to be written to you, through the war department, expressive of the approbation and gratitude I considered due you and your command from this government. I now write this as a purely private and social letter to say that I shall be much gratified to see you here at your earliest convenience, when and where I can personally testify my appreciation of your services and fidelity.—*To Maj. Anderson, May 1, 1861.* VI, 260.

2.— . . . reposing special trust and confidence in the patriotism, valor, fidelity, and ability of Col. Robert Anderson.—*Executive order, May 7, 1861.* VI, 267.

3.—And now, my dear General, allow me to assure you that we here are all your sincere friends.—*To Gen. Anderson, Aug. 15, 1863.* Angle, 332.

"Animal Must Be Very Slim"—*See* HOOKER, JOSEPH, suggestions to, 3.

Annapolis—*See* NAVAL ACADEMY.

Ant, parable of—*See* SLAVERY, wrong of, 2.

Antecedents, in place of party platforms—*See* POLITICAL PLATFORMS, candidates and, 3.

"Apple of Discord"—*See* SLAVERY, disturbing element, 1.

" 'Apple of Gold,' pictures of silver"—The assertion of that principle [equality of men], at that time, was the word "fitly spoken" which has proved an "apple of gold" to us. The Union and the Constitution are the pictures of silver, subsequently framed around it. The picture was made, not to conceal or destroy the apple, but to adorn and preserve it. The picture was made for the apple—not the apple for the picture. So let us act that neither the picture nor apple shall ever be blurred or broken. That we may so act, we must study and understand the points of danger.—*Fragment, date uncertain.* Angle, 240.

Apple-Sized Tears—*See* WHIG PARTY, apple-sized tears from.

Apprenticeship, for freed men—*See* EMANCIPATION, slave states "need not be hurt by."

Argument, how stop false?—*See* GAG, can't fashion, for Douglas.

Argumentation, two methods of—There are two ways of establishing a proposition. One is by trying to demonstrate it upon reason; and the other is, to show that great men in former times have thought so and so, and thus to pass it by the weight of pure authority.—*Speech, Columbus, Ohio, Sept. 16, 1859.* V, 172.

Arkansas, free-state constitution for, urged—*See* RECONSTRUCTION, Arkansas, 4.

"Armed Neutrality," disunion in disguise—In the border states, so-called—in fact, the middle states—there are those who favor a policy which they called "armed neutrality"; that is, an arming of those states to prevent the Union forces passing one way or the disunion forces the other over their soil. This would be disunion completed. . . . At a stroke it would take all the trouble off the hands of secession, except only what proceeds from the external blockade. It would do for the disunionists that which of all things they most desire—feed them well and give them disunion without a struggle of their own. It recognizes no fidelity to the Constitution, no obligation to maintain the Union.—*Message to Congress, July 4, 1861.* VI, 307.

Arms, not enough available—You do not receive arms from us as fast as you need them; but it is because we have not near enough to meet all the pressing demands, and we are obliged to share around what we have, sending the larger share to the points which appear to need them most. We have great hopes that our own supply will be ample before long, so that you and all others can have as many as you need.—*To Gov. O. P. Morton, Sept. 29, 1861.* VII, 1.

2.—Some of your forces are without arms, but the same is true here and at every other place where we have considerable bodies of troops.—*To Gen. McClernand, Oct. 10, 1861.* VII, 19.

Armstrong, Hannah, letter to—*See* GRATITUDE, testimony to.

Army—*See* UNION TROOPS.

Army Corps Organization, favored by all except McClellan—I ordered the army corps organization not merely on the unanimous opinion of the twelve generals whom you had selected and assigned as generals of divisions, but also on the unanimous opinion of every military man I could get an opinion from—and every modern military book—yourself only excepted. . . . Your struggle against it is received in quarters which we cannot entirely disregard . . . as merely an effort to pamper one or two pets and to persecute and degrade their supposed rivals. . . . Are you strong enough—are you strong enough, even with my help —to set your foot upon the necks of Sumner, Heintzelman, and Keyes all at once? This is a practical and very serious question for you.—*To Gen. McClellan, May 9, 1862.* VII, 156.

Army Desertion, equal guilt—He who dissuades one man from volunteering, or induces one soldier to desert, weakens the Union cause as much as he who kills a Union soldier in battle.—*To Erastus Corning and others, June 12, 1863.* VIII, 303.

See VALLANDIGHAM, C. L., arrest of, explained.

Army Desertion, Ohio Democrats encourage—*See* OHIO DEMOCRATS, attitude of, toward war, 2.

Army Desertion, pardons offered—I . . . do issue this my proclamation, as required by said [recent] act [of Congress], ordering and requiring all deserters to return to their proper posts; and I do hereby notify them that all deserters who shall within 60 days from the date of this proclamation—viz., on or before the 10th day of May, 1865—return to service or report themselves to a provost marshal, shall be pardoned, on condition that they return to their regiments or companies, or to such other organizations as they may be assigned, and serve the remainder of their original term of enlistment, and, in addition, thereto a period equal to the time lost by desertion.—*Proclamation, March 11, 1865.* XI, 52.

Army Desertion, report of intended—*See* FORT KEARNY, desertion report a humbug?

Army Desertion, serious case—Can there be a worse case than to desert, and with letters persuading others to desert? I cannot interpose without a better showing than you have made.—*To E. P. Evans, Nov. 23, 1863.* IX, 214.

Army Desertion, serious evil—The desertion of the army is now the most serious evil we have to encounter.—*To Mary A. Livermore and friend, Sept., 1862.* War Years I, 554.

See CIVIL WAR, army reduced by "absenteeism."

Army Desertion, war prolonged by—Whereas evildisposed and disloyal persons at sundry places have enticed and procured soldiers to desert and absent themselves from their regiments, thereby weakening the strength of the armies and prolonging the war, giving aid and comfort to the enemies, and cruelly exposing the gallant and faithful soldiers remaining in the ranks to increased hardships and dangers; I do therefore call upon all patriotic and faithful citizens to oppose and resist the aforementioned dangerous and treasonable crimes; and to aid in restoring to their regiments all soldiers absent without leave.—*Proclamation, March 10, 1863.* VIII, 225.

Army, harmed by speculation—*See* SPECULATION, diverts army from fighting.

Army of the Potomac, generals disappoint—It is the same old story of this Army of the Potomac. Imbecility, inefficiency—don't want to do—is defending the capital. . . . Oh, it is terrible, terrible, this weakness, this indifference, of our Potomac generals, with such

armies of good and brave men. . . . But what can I do, with such generals as we have? Who among them is any better than Meade? To sweep away the whole of them from the chief command and substitute a new man would cause a shock, and be likely to lead to combinations and troubles greater than we now have. I see all the difficulties as you do. They oppress me.—*To Sec. Welles, Sept. 21, 1863.* Welles I, 439.

Army of the Potomac, "last of"—*See* GETTYSBURG, full advantage of victory sacrificed, 4.

Army of the Potomac, "McClellan's body-guard"—It is called the Army of the Potomac, but it is only McClellan's body-guard. . . . If McClellan is not using the army I should like to borrow it for a while.—*Remarks by President.* VII, 141. Footnote.

Army of the Potomac, praised for Fredericksburg—I have just read your commanding general's preliminary report of the battle of Fredericksburg. Although you were not successful, the attempt was not an error nor the failure other than an accident. The courage with which you in an open field maintained the contest against an entrenched foe and the consummate skill and success with which you crossed and recrossed the river in the face of the enemy show that you possess all the qualities of a great army, which will yet give victory to the cause of the country and of popular government.—*To Army of the Potomac, Dec. 22, 1862.* VIII, 149.

Army of the Potomac, praised for Gettysburg—The President announces to the country that news from the Army of the Potomac up to 10 o'clock P.M. of the 3d is such as to cover that army with the highest honor, to promise a great success to the cause of the Union and to claim the condolence of all for the many gallant fallen.—*Executive order, July 4, 1863.* IX, 17.

Army, officers who resigned from—*See* UNION TROOPS, tributes to, 2, 3.

Army Recruits, relative values of—It is a very important consideration, too, that one recruited into an old regiment is nearly or quite equal in value to two in a new one.—*To Sec. Stanton, July 22, 1862.* VII, 287.

Articles of Association—*See* UNION, inviolability of, 5.

Articles of Confederation—*See* UNION, inviolability of, 5, 9.

Artists, aid to—I have some wish that Thomas D. Jones of Cincinnati and John J. Piatt, now in this city, should have some of those moderate sized consulates which facilitate artists a little in their profession. Please watch for chances.—*To Sec. Seward, March 6, 1865.* XI, 47.

Asia, backward continent—*See* AMERICA, leads in improvements.

Assassination, no protection against—I long ago made up my mind that if anybody wants to kill me, he will do it. If I wore a shirt of mail and kept myself surrounded by a body-guard, it would be all the same. There are a thousand ways to getting at a man if it is desired that he should be killed.—*To Noah Brooks, Spring, 1863.* Scribner's, March, 1878.

Assassination, "not American"—Oh, assassination of public officers is not an American crime.—*To Gen. Butler, Sept. 18, 1863.* Table Talk, 115.

Assassination, preferred—*See* SELF-GOVERNMENT, can it survive? 1.

Assassination, seldom successful—*See* BROWN, JOHN, "effort was peculiar."

Assassination, "systematically committed"—It is said, I know not whether truly, that in some parts of Missouri assassinations are systematically committed upon returned rebels who wish to ground arms and behave themselves. This should not be. Of course, I have not heard that you give countenance or wink at such assassinations.—*To Gen. Rosecrans, April 4, 1864.* X, 64.

Atlanta, Sherman thanked for taking—*See* SHERMAN, WILLIAM T., appreciation of, 2.

Atlantic Telegraph, favored—I have favored the project for connecting the United States with Europe by an Atlantic telegraph, and a similar project to extend the telegraph from San Francisco, to connect by a Pacific telegraph with the line which is being extended across the Russian empire.—*Second annual message, Dec. 1, 1862.* VIII, 99.
2.—I recommend to your favorable consideration the subject of an international telegraph across the Atlantic, and also a telegraph between this capital and the national forts along the Atlantic seaboard, and the Gulf of Mexico. Such communications, established with any reasonable outlay, would be economical as well as effective aids to the diplomatic, military and naval service.—*Third annual message, Dec. 8, 1863.* IX, 229.
3.—I learn with much satisfaction that the noble design of a telegraphic communication between the eastern coast of America and Great Britain has been renewed, with full expectation of its early accomplishment.—*Fourth annual message, Dec. 6, 1864.* X, 286.

"Attainder of Treason," Constitution violated—For the causes of treason and the ingredients of treason not amounting to the full crime, it [bill passed by Congress] declares forfeiture extending beyond the lives of the guilty parties; whereas the Constitution of the United States declares that "no attainder of treason shall work corruption of blood, or forfeiture, except during the life of the person attainted." . . . With great respect I am constrained to say I think this feature of the act is unconstitutional.—*Message to House, July 17, 1862.* VII, 285.

Autobiography, Lincoln's—I am young, and unknown to many of you. I was born, and have ever remained, in the most humble walks of life. I have no wealthy or popular relations or friends to recommend me.—*Address to Sangamon County, March 9, 1832.* I, 8.
2.—It would astonish, if not amuse, the older citizens, to learn that I—a stranger, friendless, uneducated, penniless boy, working on a flatboat at ten dollars a month—have been put down here as the candidate of pride, wealth, and aristocratic family distinction.—*To M. M. Morris, March 26, 1843.* I, 262.
3.—The judge [Douglas] is woefully at fault about his early friend Lincoln being a "grocery-keeper." I don't know that it would be a great sin if I had been; but he is mistaken. Lincoln never kept a grocery anywhere in the world. It is true that Lincoln did work the latter part of one winter in a little stillhouse up at the head of a hollow.—*Debaté, Ottawa, Aug. 21, 1858.* III, 230.
4.—In '32 I voted for Henry Clay, in '36 for the Hugh L. White ticket, in '40 for "Tip and Tyler." In '44 I made the last great effort for "Old Harry of the West." . . . But we got gloriously whipped. Taylor was elected in '48, and we fought nobly for Scott in '52.—*Speech, Carlinville, Aug. 31, 1858.* Angle, 190.
5.—I was with the old-line Whigs from the origin to the end of that party.—*Debate, Alton, Oct. 15, 1858.* V, 38.
6.—Herewith is a little sketch, as you requested. There is not much of it, for the reason, I suppose, that there is not much of me.—*To J. W. Fell, Dec. 20, 1859.* V, 286.
7.—My parents were both born in Virginia, of undistinguished families—of second families, perhaps I should say.—*To J. W. Fell, Dec. 20, 1859.* V, 286.
8.—[I was] always a Whig in politics; and generally on the Whig electoral tickets, making active canvasses.—*To J. W. Fell, Dec. 20, 1859.* V, 288.
9.—I am not ashamed to confess that 25 years ago I was a hired laborer, mauling rails, at work on a flatboat—just what might happen to any poor man's son.

I want every man to have a chance.—*Speech, New Haven, Conn., March 6, 1860.* V, 361.

10.—He [Lincoln's father] settled in an unbroken forest [in Indiana], and the clearing away of surplus wood was the great task ahead. Abraham [the future president], though very young, was large of his age, and had an ax put into his hands at once; and from that time till within his twenty-third year he was almost constantly handling that most useful instrument —less, of course, in plowing and harvesting seasons. At this place Abraham took an early start as a hunter, which was never much improved afterward. A few days before the completion of his eighth year, in the absence of his father, a flock of wild turkeys approached the new log cabin, and Abraham with a rifle-gun, standing inside, shot through a crack and killed one of them. He has never since pulled a trigger on any larger game.—*Autobiography, June 1, 1860.* VI, 26.

11.—His [Lincoln's] father and family settled a new place . . . about ten miles westerly from Decatur. Here they built a log cabin . . . and made sufficient of rails to fence ten acres of ground. . . . These are, or are supposed to be, the rails about which so much is being said just now, though these are far from being the first or only rails ever made by Abraham [the future President].—*Autobiography, June 1, 1860.* VI, 29.

12.—Abraham [the future President] joined a volunteer company [for the Black Hawk War], and, to his own surprise, was elected captain of it. He says he has not since had any success in life which gave him so much satisfaction. . . Returning from the campaign, and encouraged by his great popularity among his immediate neighbors, he the same year ran for the legislature, and was beaten. . . . It was the only time Abraham was ever beaten on a direct vote of the people.—*Autobiography, June 1, 1860.* VI, 31.

13.—He [Lincoln] studied what he should do— thought of learning the blacksmith trade—thought of trying to study law—rather thought he could not succeed at that without a better education. Before long, strangely enough, a man offered to sell, and did sell, to Abraham and another as poor as himself, an old stock of goods upon credit. They opened as merchants. . . . Of course, they did nothing but get deeper in debt. . . . The store winked out.—*Autobiography, June 1, 1860.* VI, 32.

14.—He [Lincoln] was appointed postmaster at Salem —the office being too insignificant to make politics an objection.—*Autobiography, June 1, 1860.* VI, 32.

15.—The surveyor of Sangamon offered to depute to Abraham that portion of his work which was within his part of the county. He accepted, procured a com-

pass and chain, studied Flint and Gibson a little, and went at it. This procured bread, and kept body and soul together.—*Autobiography, June 1, 1860.* VI, 38.

16.—It seems as if the question whether my first name is "Abraham" or "Abram" will never be settled. It is "Abraham."—*To George Ashmun, June 4, 1860.* VI, 38.

17.—Like you, I belonged to the Whig party from its origin to its close.—*To Samuel Haycraft, June 4, 1860.* VI, 39.

18.—I was born in Kentucky, raised in Indiana, reside in Illinois, and now, here, it is my duty to care equally for the good people of all the states.—*Speech to Indiana regiment, March 17, 1865.* XI, 55.

"Babel of Confusion"—For us here to control him [Gen. Wright] there on the ground would be a babel of confusion which would be utterly ruinous.—*To Gen. Boyle, Sept. 12, 1862.* Lapsley VI, 134.

Baker, Edward, characterized—A good hand to raise a breeze.—*To E. B. Washburne, April 30, 1848.* II, 16.

Balance of Powers, essential to American plan of government—*See* SLAVERY, no interference with, in slave states, 33.

Ballot better than bullets—Through all this [turmoil in Nebraska] bowie knives and six-shooters are seen plainly enough; but never a glimpse of a ballot-box. —*Speech, Peoria, Oct. 16, 1854.* II, 239.

2.—You can better succeed with the ballot. You can peaceably then redeem the government and preserve the liberties of mankind through your votes and voice and moral influence. . . . Let there be peace. Revolutionize through the ballot-box.—*To Free-Soilers, Springfield, 1855.* Herndon, 380.

3.—Do not mistake that the ballot is stronger than the bullet. Therefore, let the legions of slavery use bullets; but let us wait patiently till November and fire ballots at them in return; and by that peaceful policy I believe we shall ultimately win.—*Speech, Bloomington, May 29, 1856.* Lapsley II, 269.

4.—To give the victory to the right, not bloody bullets, but peaceful ballots only are necessary. Thanks to our good old Constitution, and organization under it, these alone are necessary.—*Notes, Oct. 1, 1858.* IV, 235.

5.—We have the means provided for the expression of our belief in regard to slavery; it is through the ballot box—the peaceful method provided by the Constitution.—*Speech, Elwood, Dec. 1, 1859.* Angle, 229.

6.—It is now for them [the people] to demonstrate to the world that those who can fairly carry an election can also suppress a rebellion; that ballots are the rightful and peaceful successors of bullets and that when ballots have been fairly and constitutionally decided there can be no successful appeal, except to ballots themselves at succeeding elections.—*Message to Congress, July 4, 1861.* VI, 322.

7.—[When peace comes] it will then have been proved that among free men there can be no appeal from the ballot to the bullet, and that they who take such appeal are sure to lose their case and pay the cost.—*To J. C. Conkling, Aug. 26, 1863.* IX, 101.

Ballot, protection of—That so much of the governor's message as relates to fraudulent voting, and other fraudulent practices at elections, be referred to the committee on elections, with instructions to said committee to prepare and report to the House a bill for such act as may in their judgment afford the greatest possible protection of the elective franchise against all frauds of all sorts whatever.—*Resolution, Illinois legislature, Nov. 28, 1840.* I, 152.

Ballot, "protection of the flag"—*See* NEGRO SUFFRAGE, favored, 2.

Ballot, use without fear—It only needs that every right-thinking man shall go to the polls, and without fear or prejudice vote as he thinks.—*Notes, Oct. 1, 1858.* IV, 236.

Ballot, voters who neglect—*See* WEST VIRGINIA, argument for admission of, 1. 2.

Baltimore, calamities of, deplored—I have deplored the calamities which the sympathy of some misguided citizens of Maryland has brought down upon that patriotic and heretofore flourishing state. The prosperity of Baltimore up to the 19th of April last was one of the wonders produced by the American Union. He who strangles himself, for whatever motive, is not more unreasonable than were those citizens of Baltimore, who, in a single night, destroyed the Baltimore & Ohio railroad, the Northern Pennsylvania railroad and the railroad from Baltimore to Philadelphia. From that day when that mad transaction occurred, the government of the United States has been diligently engaged in endeavoring to restore those great avenues to their former usefulness and at the same time, to save Baltimore and Maryland from the danger of complete ruin through an unnecessary and unnatural rebellion.—*Reply to delegation of Baltimore workmen, Nov. 15, 1861.* Hertz II, 845.

Baltimore, change in three years—Calling to mind that we are in Baltimore, we cannot fail to note that the world moves. Looking upon these many people assembled here to serve, as they best may, the soldiers

of the Union, it occurs at once that three years ago the same soldiers could not so much as pass through Baltimore. The change from then till now is both great and gratifying. Blessings on the brave men who have wrought the change, and the fair women who strive to reward them for it.—*Speech to Sanitary Fair, Baltimore, April 18, 1864.* X, 76.

Baltimore, policy toward—Let Baltimore be held as now, with a gentle, but firm and certain hand—*Memorandum, July 26, 1861.* VI, 332.

Baltimore, troops may avoid—For the future troops must be brought here, but I make no point of bringing them through Baltimore. Without any military knowledge myself, of course I must leave details to Gen. Scott. He hastily said this morning in the presence of these gentlemen, "March them around Baltimore and not through it." I sincerely hope the general, on fuller reflection, will consider this practical and proper, and that you will not object to it. By this a collision of the people of Baltimore with the troops will be avoided, unless they go out of their way to seek it.—*To Gov. Hicks and Mayor Brown, April 20, 1861.* VI, 251.

Baltimore American—*See* LINCOLN, ABRAHAM, personal traits and reactions, 6.

See SLAVERY, Gulf states would suffer.

Bancroft, George, recognized—Hold on—I know you; you are—History, History of the United States—Mr. —Mr. Bancroft, Mr. George Bancroft.—*To Mr. Bancroft, Feb. 23, 1864.* Quarterly, Sept. 1945, p. 345.

Banking and Currency, banking associations urged—Fluctuations in the value of currency are always injurious, and to reduce these fluctuations to the lowest possible point will always be a leading purpose in wise legislation. Convertibility, prompt and certain convertibility, into coin is generally acknowledged to be the best and surest safeguard against them; and it is extremely doubtful whether a circulation of United States notes payable in coin and sufficiently large for the wants of the people can be permanently, usefully and safely maintained. Is there, then, any other mode in which the necessary provision for the public wants can be made and the great advantages of a safe and uniform currency secured? I know of none which promises so certain results and is at the same time so unobjectionable as the organization of banking associations, under a general act of Congress, well guarded in its provisions. To such associations the government might furnish circulating notes on the security of United States bonds deposited in the treasury. These notes . . . being uniform in appearance and security and convertible always into coin, would at once protect labor against the wiles of a vicious currency and facilitate commerce by cheap and safe exchanges. . . . The public credit, moreover, would be greatly improved and the negotiation of new loans greatly facilitated by the steady market demand for government bonds which the adoption of the proposed system would create.—*Second annual message, Dec. 1, 1862.* VIII, 101.

Banking and Currency, circulation needs control—It seems very plain that continued issues of United States notes without any check to the issues of suspended banks and without adequate provision for the raising of money by loans and for funding the issues so as to keep them within due limits must soon produce disastrous consequences. . . . That Congress has power to regulate the currency of the country can hardly admit of doubt, and that a judicious measure to prevent the deterioration of this currency, by a reasonable taxation of bank circulation or otherwise, is needed seems equally clear. Independently of this general consideration, it would be unjust to the people at large to exempt banks enjoying the special privilege of circulation from their just proportion of the public burdens.—*Message to Congress, Jan. 17, 1863.* VIII, 191.

2.—It seems clear that the treasury cannot be successfully conducted unless the government can exercise a restraining power over the banknote circulation of the country.—*Fourth annual message, Dec. 6, 1864.* X, 295.

See COST OF LIVING, dangerous steps toward higher.

Banking and Currency, greenbacks' origin—I have long determined to make public the origin of the greenback. . . . When troublous times fell upon us, and my shoulders, though broad and willing, were weak, and myself surrounded by such circumstances and such people that I knew not whom to trust, then I said in my extremity," I will send for Col. Taylor; he will know what to do." I think it was in January, 1862, on or about the 16th, that I did so. You came, and I said to you, "What shall we do?" Said you: "Why, issue treasury notes bearing no interest, printed on the best banking paper. Issue enough to pay off the army expenses, and declare it legal tender." Chase thought it a hazardous thing, but we finally accomplished it, and gave to the people of the Republic the greatest blessing they ever had—their own paper to pay off their debts.—*To Col. E. D. Taylor, Dec., 1864.* Hertz II, 957.

Banking and Currency, "sound and uniform"—No duty is more imperative on that [the national] government than the duty it owes the people of furnishing them a sound and uniform currency.—*Speech, Springfield, Dec. 20, 1839.* I, 110.

2.—During the existing war it is peculiarly the duty of the national government to secure to the people a sound circulating medium.—*Message to Senate, June 23, 1862.* VII, 232.

Banks, Nathaniel P., appreciation of—I need a man of Democratic antecedents from New England. . . . I have had an intimation that Gov. Banks would yet accept a place in the cabinet.—*To Hannibal Hamlin, Nov., 1860.* War Years I, 154.

2.—Being a poor correspondent is the only apology I offer for not having sooner tendered my thanks for your very successful and very valuable military operations this year. The final stroke in opening the Mississippi never should, and I think never will, be forgotten.—*To Gen. Banks, Aug. 5, 1863.* IX, 56.

3.—My thanks for your successful and valuable operations in Texas.—*To Gen. Banks, Dec. 24, 1863.* IX, 274.

4.—Your confidence in the practicability of constructing a free government speedily for Louisiana, and your zeal to accomplish it, are very gratifying.—*To Gen. Banks, Jan. 13, 1864.* IX, 282.

5.—I know you are dissatisfied, which pains me much, but I wish not to be argued with further. I entertain no abatement of confidence or friendship for you.—*To Gen. Banks, Dec. 2, 1864.* X, 279.

Banks, Nathanial P., chided for "impedimenta"—I have just been overwhelmed and confounded with a sight of a requisition made by you which, I am assured, cannot be filled and got off within an hour short of two months. . . . My dear General, this expending and piling up of *impedimenta* has been, so far, almost our ruin, and will be our final ruin if it is not abandoned. If you had the articles of this requisition upon the wharf, with the necessary animals to make them of any use, and forage for the animals, you could not get vessels together in two weeks to carry the whole, to say nothing of your twenty thousand men; and having the vessels, you could not put the cargoes aboard in two weeks more. . . . You would be better off anywhere, and especially where you are going, for not having a thousand wagons doing nothing but hauling forage to feed the animals that draw them, and taking at least two thousand men to care for the wagons and animals, who otherwise might be two thousand good soldiers.—*To Gen. Banks, Nov. 22, 1862.* VIII, 81.

Banks, Nathaniel P., consideration for—Now, dear General, do not think this is an ill-natured letter; it is the very reverse.—*To Gen. Banks, Nov. 22, 1862.* VIII, 83.

2.—In superseding you, by returning Gen. Butler to command the Department of the Gulf, I have trusted that you not understand me as being indifferent to your feelings and your honor. I would be as careful of yours as of my own.—*To Gen. Banks, 1863.* Angle, 313.

3.—I deeply regret to have said or done anything which could give you pain or uneasiness.—*To Gen. Banks, Dec. 24, 1864.* IX, 273.

Banks, Nathaniel P., master in Louisiana—*See* RE-CONSTRUCTION, Louisiana, 11.

Barbarism, relapse into—*See* WAR, no barbarities in civilized.

Bargain, "hug tighter" if bad—My old father used to have a saying that "if you make a bad bargain, hug it all the tighter"; and it occurs to me that if the bargain you have just closed [marriage] can possibly be called a bad one, it is certainly the most pleasant one for applying that maxim which my fancy can by any effort picture.—*To Joshua F. Speed, Feb. 25, 1842.* I, 213.

"Bastard logic"—*See* SLAVERY, Moloch of.

Bates, Edward, appraised as presidential candidate—*See* CAMPAIGN OF 1860, preconvention candidates appraised.

"Bates Egg in the South"—*See* NOMINATION OF 1860, attitude toward, 4.

Bayonets, ineffective against slavery—*See* SLAVERY, bayonets ineffective.

Bear Drops Cub, when hard pressed—*See* DOUGLAS, STEPHEN A., characterized, 26.

Bell, John, Douglas strategy toward—*See* CAMPAIGN OF 1860, Douglas strategy in.

"Best of the Bargain"—I appear before you that I may see you and that you may see me; and I am willing to admit that, so far as the ladies are concerned, I have the best of the bargain, though I wish it to be understood that I do not make the same acknowledgment concerning the men.—*Speech Utica, N.Y., Feb. 18, 1861.* VI, 136.

2.—I come merely to see you, and allow you to see me. And I have to say to you, as I have said frequently on my journey, that, in the sight, I have the best of the bargain.—*Speech, New York, Feb. 20, 1861.* Hertz II, 807.

3.—There appears to be a desire to see more of me, and I can only say that from my position, especially when I look around the gallery [bowing to the ladies] I feel I have decidedly the best of the bargain, and in this matter I am for no compromise here.—*Speech, Jersey City, Feb. 21, 1861.* Hertz II, 807.

4.—I have no speech to make, but merely appear to see you and let you look at me; and as to the latter, I think I have greatly the best of the bargain.—*Speech, Trenton, N.J., Feb. 21, 1861.* Hertz II, 808.

5.—I came only to see you, and to give you the opportunity to see me; and I say to you, as I have before said towards where there were so many handsome ladies there are here, I think I have decidedly the best of the bargain.—*Speech, Hudson, N.Y., Feb. 19, 1861.* VI, 144.

6.—Well, in the matter of looking at one another, I have altogether the advantage.—*To woman caller, Feb. 19, 1864.* Welles I, 528.

Bible, "best gift of God"—In regard to this great book, I have but to say, it is the best gift God has given to men. All the good Savior gave to the world was communicated through this book. But for it we could not know right from wrong. All things most desirable for man's welfare, here and hereafter, are to be found portrayed in it.—*Reply to committee presenting Bible, Sept. 9, 1864.* X, 218.

Bible, "cure for Blues"—Tell your mother that I have not got her present—an "Oxford" Bible—with me, but I intend to read it regularly when I return home. I doubt not that it is really, as she says, the best cure for the blues, could one but take it according to the truth.—*To Mary Speed, Sept. 27, 1841.* I, 180.

Bible, education encourages reading of—*See* EDUCATION, importance of.

Bible, maxims cited—The good old maxims of the Bible are applicable, and truly applicable, to human affairs, and in this [consideration of plans for anti-slavery contest in 1860], as in other things, we may say here that he who is not for us is against us; he who gathereth not with us, scattereth.—*Speech, Cincinnati, Sept. 17, 1859.* V, 234.

See CAMPAIGN OF 1860, silence is candidate's best policy, 6.

See DEITY, purpose of, toward slavery.

See EQUALITY, doctrine of Declaration explained, 4.

See KANSAS, slavery's test case.

See MEXICAN WAR, acts of aggression, 3.

See MORAL PERFECTION, goal to strive for.

See RELIGION, attitude toward, 4.

See SLAVERY, Christian duty and.

See SLAVERY, wrong of, 28.

Bible, parallel cited in Lovejoy martyrdom—*See* LOVEJOY, ELIJAH P., biblical comparison.

Bible, "poor hand to quote"—My friend has said to me that I am a poor hand to quote Scripture. I will try it again, however.—*Speech, Chicago, July 10, 1858.* III, 50.

Bible, quoted against "holy men of the South"—*See* CHURCH, insulted by "professedly holy men of the South."

Bible, slavery and—In many of the slave states . . . you [Kentuckians] are trying to establish the rightfulness of slavery, by reference to the Bible. You are trying to show that slavery existed in Bible times by divine ordinance. Now Douglas is wiser than you for your own benefit, upon that subject. Douglas knows that whenever you establish that slavery was right by the Bible, it will occur that that slavery was the slavery of the white man, of men without reference to color—, and he knows very well that you may entertain that idea in Kentucky as much as you please, but you will never win any northern support for it. He makes the wiser argument for you; he makes the argument that the slavery of the black man, the slavery of the man who has a skin of a different color from your own, is right.—*Speech, Cincinnati, Sept. 17, 1859.* V, 202.

See SLAVERY, Christian duty and.

Bible, truth of, never denied—*See* RELIGION, attitude toward, 1.

Bill of Rights, freedoms not jeopardized by military arrests—*See* WAR POWER, use of, defended, 8.

Biographies, appraisal of—Biographies as generally written are not only misleading, but false. . . . I've wondered why book publishers and merchants don't have blank biographies on their shelves, always ready for an emergency; so that, if a man happens to die, his heirs or his friends, if they wish to perpetuate his memory, can purchase one already written but with blanks. These blanks they can at their pleasure, fill up with rosy sentences full of high-sounding praise. In most instances they commemorate a lie, and cheat posterity out of the truth.—*To W. H. Herndon, 1856.* Herndon, 147.

Biography, not authorized—Messrs. Follett, Foster & Co's Life of me is not by my authority; and I have scarcely been so much astounded by anything, as their public announcement that it is authorized by me. They have fallen into some strange misunderstanding. I certainly knew they were contemplating publishing a biography, and I certainly did not object to their doing so, upon their own responsibility. I even took pains to facilitate them. But at the same time, I made myself tiresome, if not hoarse, with repeating to Mr. Howard, their only agent seen by me, my protest that I authorized nothing—Would be responsible for nothing. . . . As a matter, wholly my own, I would authorize no biography, without time and opportunity to carefully examine and consider every word of it; and, in this case, in the nature of things, I can have no such time and opportunity. But, in my present position, when, by the lessons of the past, and the united voices of all discreet friends, I can neither write nor speak a word for the public, how dare I to send forth, by my authority, a volume of hundreds of pages, for adversaries to make points upon without end? Were I to do so, the convention would have a right to reassemble and substitute another name for mine.—*To Samuel Galloway, June 19, 1860.* VI, 40.

Bird Trap—*See* REPUBLICAN PARTY, warned against Douglas, 4.

Birds, soldiers are not—*See* MARYLAND, troops must cross.

Bitterness, harvest of—We are aware that it is sometimes a temporary gratification, when a friend cannot succeed, to be able to choose between opponents; but we believe that that gratification is the seed-time which never fails to be followed by a most abundant harvest of bitterness.—*Whig circular, March 1, 1843.* I, 251.

Bixby Letter—I have been shown in the files of the War Department a statement of the adjutant general of Massachusetts that you are the mother of five sons who have died gloriously on the field of battle. I feel how weak and fruitless must be any words of mine which should attempt to beguile you from the grief of a loss so overwhelming. But I cannot refrain from tendering you the consolation that may be found in the thanks of the republic they died to save. I pray that our Heavenly Father may assuage the anguish of your bereavement, and leave you only the cherished memory of the loved and lost, and the solemn pride that must be yours to have laid so costly a sacrifice upon the altar of freedom.—*To Mrs. Bixby, Nov. 21, 1864.* X, 274.

Black Hawk War, "hero" of—*See* LINCOLN, ABRAHAM, "military hero."

Black Hawk War, soldiers trade places—The transfer of [David] Rankin from my company occurred as follows: Rankin, having lost his horse at Dixon's Ferry, and having acquaintance in one of the foot companies who were going down the river, was desirous to go with them, and one Galishen, being an acquaintance of mine, wished to leave it and join mine; this being the case, it was agreed that they should exchange places and answer to each other's names, as it was expected that we all would be discharged in a very few days.—*To E. C. Blankenship, Aug. 10, 1833.* I, 10.

"Black Laws"—*See* MISSOURI COMPROMISE, gave Missouri slaves.

"Black Republicans," Douglas expected to join—*See* DOUGLAS, STEPHEN A., expected to turn Republican.

"Black Republicans," if they elect President—*See* BROWN, JOHN, secessionists face same fate as.

"Black Republicans," one of them—I say . . . to the Kentuckians that I am what they call, as I understand it, a "Black Republican."—*Speech, Cincinnati, Sept. 17, 1859.* V, 195.

"Black Republicans," their estimate of Douglas—*See* DOUGLAS, STEPHEN A., expected to turn Republican.

"Black Republicans"—*See* REPUBLICAN PARTY, South's attitude toward.

Blackberries, major generalships not as plentiful as—I fully appreciate Gen. Pope's splendid achievements, with their valuable results, but you must know that major-generalships in the regular army are not as plentiful as blackberries.—*To R. Yates and William Butler, April 10, 1862.* V, 145.

Blackmail and Spoils—Frequent complaints are made to me that persons endeavoring to bring in cotton in strict accordance with the trade regulations of the treasury department are frustrated by seizures by district attorneys, marshals and provost-marshals, and others, on various pretenses, all looking to blackmail and spoils. I wish, if you can find time, you would look into this matter within your department, and, finding these abuses to exist, break them up, in your power, so that fair dealing under the regulations can proceed.—*To Gen. Canby, July 25, 1864.* X, 172.

Blair, Frank P., advice to—My wish . . . is compounded of what I believe will be best for the country and best for him [Maj. Gen. Frank P. Blair], and it is that he will come here, put his military commission in my hands, take his seat [in the House of Representatives], go into caucus with our friends, abide the nominations, help elect the nominees and thus to organize a House of Representatives which will really support the government in the war. If the result shall be the election of himself as speaker, let him serve in that position; if not, let him retake his commission and return to the army. . . . He is young yet. He has abundant talents, quite enough to occupy all his time without devoting any to temper. . . . The foregoing is what I would say if Frank were my brother, instead of yours.—*To Montgomery Blair, Nov. 2, 1863.* IX, 195.

Blair, Frank P., family pride in—The Blairs have to an unusual degree the spirit of clan. Their family is a closed corporation. Frank is their hope and pride. —*To White House group, Dec. 9, 1863.* Hay, 133.

Blair, Frank P., fights for emancipation—*See* SLAVERY, Democratic policy toward, 5, 11.

Blair, Montgomery, resignation of, accepted—You have generously said to me more than once that whenever your resignation [as postmaster general] could be a relief to me it was at my disposal. The time has come. You very well know that this proceeds from no dissatisfaction of mine with you personally or officially. Your uniform kindness has been unsurpassed by that of any friend. . . . In the three years and a half during which you have administered the general post office, I remember no single complaint against you in connection therewith.—*To Mr. Blair, Sept. 23, 1864.* X, 228.

Blair, Montgomery, supported against complaining generals—*See* CABINET, dismissals up to president alone, 1.

Blisters, might have to sit on—*See* ELECTION OF 1864, people's business.

Blockade, cotton and—By the external blockade, the price [of cotton] is made certainly six times as great as it was. And yet the enemy gets through at least one-sixth part as much in a given period, say a year, as if there were no blockade, and receives as much for it as he would for a full crop in time of peace. The effect, in substance, is that we give him six ordinary crops without the trouble of producing any but the first; and at the same time leave his fields and his laborers free to produce provisions. You know how this keeps up his armies at home, and produces supplies from abroad.—*To Gen. Canby, Dec. 12, 1864.* X, 312.
2.—We cannot give up the blockade, and hence it becomes immensely important to us to get the cotton away from him [the enemy]. Better give him guns for

it than let him as now, get both guns and ammunition.—*To Gen. Canby, Dec. 12, 1864.* X, 313.

Blockade, effect of, on currency—*See* GOLD, effected by cotton escaping through blockade.

Blockade, questions incident to—Questions of great intricacy and importance have arisen out of the blockade and other belligerent operations between the government and several maritime powers, but they have been discussed and, as far as was possible, accommodated in a spirit of frankness, justice and mutual good will.—*Third annual message, Dec. 8, 1863.* IX, 224.

Blockade, mistakes of—A blockade of 3,000 miles of sea coast could not be established and vigorously enforced in a season of great commercial activity like the present without committing occasional mistakes and inflicting unintentional injuries upon foreign nations and their subjects.—*Second annual message, Dec. 1, 1862.* VIII, 95.

Blockade, success of—The extensive blockade has been constantly increasing in efficiency as the navy has expanded, yet on so long a line it has so far been impossible to entirely suppress illicit trade. . . . It appears that more than 1,000 vessels have been captured since the blockade was instituted, and that the value of prizes already sent in for adjudication amounts to more than $13,000,000.—*Third annual message, Dec. 8, 1863.* IX, 236.

Blockade, three ports reopened—The ports of Norfolk, Fernandina and Pensacola have been reopened by proclamation. It is hoped that foreign merchants will now consider whether it is not safer and more profitable to themselves, as well as just to the United States, to resort to these and other open ports than it is to pursue, through many hazards, and at vast cost, a contrabrand trade with other ports which are closed, if not by actual military occupation, at least by a lawful and effective blockade.—*Fourth annual message, Dec. 6, 1864.* X, 288.

Blockade—*See* PERTHSHIRE, BRITISH SHIP.

Bloodshed, emancipation avoids—And then the latter [plan for compensated emancipation] will cost no blood, no precious life. It will be a saving of both.—*Second annual message, Dec. 1, 1862.* VIII, 125.
2.—It is much—very much—that it [compensated emancipation] would cost no blood at all.—*Second annual message, Dec. 1, 1862.* VIII, 129.
3.—Is it doubted, then, that the plan [of compensated emancipation] I propose, if adopted, would shorten the war, and thus lessen its expenditure of money and of blood?—*Second annual message, Dec. 1, 1862.* VIII, 130.

Bloodshed, to be avoided if possible—While I have been proud to see today the finest military array, I think, that I have ever seen . . . allow me to express the hope that in the shedding of blood their services may never be needed, especially in the shedding of fraternal blood. It shall be my endeavor to preserve the peace of the country so far as it can possibly be done consistently with the maintenance of the institutions of the country. With my consent, or without my great displeasure, this country shall never witness the shedding of one drop of blood in fraternal strife. —*Speech, reply to Gov. Curtin, Harrisburg, Feb. 22, 1861.* VI, 161.
2.—I desire to repeat, in order to preclude any possible misconstruction, that I do most sincerely hope that we shall have no use for them [Pennsylvania troops]; that it will never become their duty to shed blood, and most especially never to shed fraternal blood. I promise that so far as I may have wisdom to direct, if so painful a result shall in any wise be brought about, it shall be through no fault of mine. —*Speech, Pennsylvania legislature, Feb. 22, 1861.* VI, 164.
3.—Pressed as we are by lapse of time, I am glad to hear you say this [that Grant proposed to hold an important position with fewer men]; and yet I do hope you may find a way that the effort shall not be desperate in the sense of a great loss of life.—*To Gen. Grant, July 17, 1864.* X, 160.

See EMANCIPATION, financial aspects of compensated, 6.

Bloodshed, unnecessary—In my view of the present aspect of affairs, there is no need of bloodshed and war. There is no necessity for it. I am not in favor of such a course; and I may say in advance there will be no bloodshed unless it is forced upon the government. The government will not use force, unless force is used against it.—*Address, Philadelphia, Feb. 22, 1861.* VI, 158.
2.—In doing this [defending the Union] there need be no bloodshed or violence, and there shall be none unless it be forced upon the national authority. The power confided to me will be used to hold, occupy and maintain the property and places belonging to the Government and to collect the duties and imposts; but beyond what may be necessary for these objects, there will be no invasion, no using of force against the people anywhere.—*First inaugural, March 4, 1861.* VI, 175.

"Bloody Hand"—*See* KANSAS-NEBRASKA ACT, opens territories to slavery, 4.

"Blue Light" Burners—*See* POLITICAL PLATFORMS, proposals for 1860 rejected, 3.

Blue Lodges—Then there are "blue lodges"—as they call them—everywhere doing their secret and deadly work.—*Speech, Bloomington, May 29, 1856.* Lapsley II, 271.

Bluebottle Fly, Chase likened to—*See* CHASE, SALMON P., relations with Lincoln, 5.

Blunt, James G., accused of helping Judge Lynch— I regret to find you denouncing so many persons as liars, scoundrels, fools, thieves, and persecutors of yourself. . . . My appointment of you first as a brigadier, and then as a major-general, was evidence of my appreciation of your services and I have since marked but one thing in connection with you with which to be dissatisfied. The sending of a military order 25 miles outside of your lines, and all military lines, to take men charged with no offense against the military, out of the hands of the courts, to be turned over to a mob to be hanged, can find no precedent to justify it. Judge Lynch sometimes takes jurisdiction of cases which prove too strong for the courts; but this is the first case within my knowledge wherein the court being able to maintain jurisdiction against Judge Lynch, the military has come to the assistance of the latter.—*To Gen. Blunt, Aug. 18, 1863.* IX, 87.

"Board at Home"—I understand the main body of the enemy is very near you, so near that you could "board at home," so to speak, and menace or attack him any day.—*To Gen. Rosecrans, Oct. 4, 1863.* IX, 154.

Bond Forfeiture, courts to say when—I understand that provost-marshals in different parts of Missouri are assuming to decide that the conditions of bonds are forfeited, and therefore are seizing and selling property to pay damages. This, if true, is both outrageous and ridiculous. Do not allow it. The courts, and not provost-marshals, are to decide such questions unless when military necessity makes an exception.—*To Gen. Pope, Feb. 12, 1865.* XI, 33.

Boots, parable of new—The idea that we could [depend on tonnage duties for harbor development] involves the same absurdity as the Irish bull about the new boots. "I shall niver git 'em on," says Patrick, "till I wear 'em a day or two, and stretch 'em a little." We shall never make a canal by tonnage duties until it shall already have been made a while, so the

tonnage can get into it.—*Speech in Congress, June 20, 1848.* II, 42.

Border States, attitude of, toward Union—The border states, so called, were not uniform in their action, some of them being almost for the Union, while in others . . . the Union sentiment was nearly repressed and silenced.—*Message to Congress, July 4, 1861.* VI, 305.
2.—There are 50,000 bayonets in the Union armies from the border slave states. It would be a serious matter if, in consequence of a [emancipation] proclamation such as you desire, they should go over to the rebels. I do not think they all would—not so many, indeed, as a year ago, or six months ago—not so many today as yesterday. Every day increases their Union feeling. They are also getting their pride enlisted, and want to beat the rebels.—*Reply to committee from Chicago churches, Sept. 13, 1862.* VIII, 33.

See "ARMED NEUTRALITY," disunion in disguise.

Border States, Congressmen from, urged to support emancipation—*See* CIVIL WAR, will end slavery if continued.

See EMANCIPATION, states appealed to for, compensated, 3.

See SELF-GOVERNMENT, importance of, 1, 2.

Borrowing, folly of continuous—As an individual who undertakes to live by borrowing soon finds his original means devoured by interest, and next, no one left to borrow from, so must it be with a government. —*Whig circular, March 4, 1843.* I, 246.

Boston, honors Jefferson—Bearing in mind that about seventy years ago two great political parties were formed in this country, that Thomas Jefferson was the head of one of them and Boston the headquarters of the other, it is both curious and interesting that those supposed to descend politically from the party opposed to Jefferson should now be celebrating his birthday in their own original seat of empire, while those claiming political descent from him have nearly ceased to breathe his name everywhere.—*To H. L. Pierce and others, April 6, 1859.* V, 124.

Boston Courier—*See* PRESS, some papers unfair.

Boy, letter to—*See* AMERICA, future rulers of.

Boys, disobedient, not needed—The United States don't need boys who disobey their parents.—*To Sec. Welles, no date.* Tracy, 237.

Breath, not enough—*See* EMANCIPATION PROCLAMATION (PRELIMINARY), doubtfully received.

Breckinridge, John C., alarmed by Douglas strategy —*See* CAMPAIGN OF 1860, Douglas's strategy in.

Breckinridge, John C., might have been arrested— *See* CONFEDERATE GENERALS, might have been arrested.

Bridegroom, counsel for—I know what the painful point with you is at all times when you are unhappy; it is an apprehension that you do not love her as you should. What nonsense! How came you to court her? . . . But you say you reasoned yourself into it. What do you mean by that? Was it not that you found yourself unable to reason yourself out of it? Say candidly, were not those heavenly black eyes the whole basis of all your early reasoning on the subject?—*To Joshua F. Speed, Jan. 3, 1852.* I, 184.

British King, blamed for American slavery—*See* SLAVERY, policy of the fathers, 2.

See GREAT BRITAIN, blamed for slavery.

British Ministry, attitude toward Civil War—*See* CIVIL WAR, foreign nations' attitude toward, 9, 12.

British Ministry, Civil War policy to help—*See* CIVIL WAR, foreign nations' attitude toward, 10.

"Broken Eggs"—*See* EMANCIPATION PROCLAMATION, no retraction of, 1.

See RECONSTRUCTION, Louisiana, 3.

Brooks, Preston S., slavery and the fathers—*See* SLAVERY, toward ultimate extinction, 9.

See SLAVERY, perpetuation of, 6, 8, 9.

Brough, John, nothing against—I deeply regret that you were not renominated, not that I have aught against Brough. On the contrary, like yourself, I say hurrah for Brough!—*To David Tod, June 18, 1863.* VIII, 326.

Brown, B. Gratz, fights for emancipation—*See* SLAVERY, Democratic policy on, 5.

Brown, John, "effort was peculiar"—John Brown's effort [at Harper's Ferry] was peculiar. It was not a slave insurrection. It was an attempt by white men to get up a revolt among slaves, in which the slaves refused to participate. In fact, it was so absurd that the slaves, with all their ignorance, saw plainly enough it could not succeed. That affair, in its philosophy, corresponds with the many attempts, related in history, at the assassination of kings and emperors. An enthusiast broods over the oppression of a people till he fancies himself commissioned by Heaven to liber-

ate them. He ventures the attempt, which ends in little else than his own execution.—*Cooper Institute address, New York, Feb. 27, 1860.* V, 318.

Brown, John, no Republican implicated—John Brown was no Republican. You [slave sympathizers] have never implicated a single Republican in that Harper's Ferry enterprise. We tell you if any member of the Republican party is guilty in that matter, you know it or you do not know it. If you do know it, you are inexcusable not to designate the man and prove the fact. If you do not know it, you are inexcusable to assert it; and especially for persisting in the assertion after you have tried and failed to make the proof.—*Cooper Institute address, New York, Feb. 27, 1860.* V, 314.
Repeated at New Haven, Conn., March 6, 1860. V, 358.

Brown, John, qualified praise of—John Brown has shown great courage, rare unselfishness, as even Gov. Wise testifies. But no man, north or south, can approve of violence or crime.—*Speech, Elwood, Kan., Dec. 1, 1859.* Angle, 229.

Brown, John, secessionists face same fate as—Your own statement [as Democrats] is that if the Black Republicans elect a President, you "won't stand it." You will break up the Union. If we shall constitutionally elect a President, it will be our duty to see that you submit. Old John Brown has been executed for treason against a state. We cannot object, even though he agreed with us in thinking slavery wrong. That cannot excuse violence, bloodshed and treason. It could avail him nothing that he might think himself right. So, if we constitutionally elect a President, and therefore you undertake to destroy the Union, it will be our duty to deal with you as old John Brown has been dealt with. We shall try to do our duty. We hope and believe that in no section will a majority so act as to render such extreme measures necessary. —*Speech, Leavenworth, Kan., Dec. 3, 1859.* XI, 115.

Browne, Charles Farrar—*See* WARD, ARTEMUS.

Buchanan, (Commodore) Franklin, might have been arrested—*See* CONFEDERATE GENERALS, might have been arrested.

Buchanan, James, "claws burnt off"—From much dragging of chestnuts from the fire for others to eat, his [Buchanan's] claws are burnt off to the gristle, and he is thrown aside as unfit for further use.— *Speech, Springfield, Dec. 10, 1856.* II, 309.

Buchanan, James, "giving away the case"—Every hour adds to the difficulties I am called upon to meet, and the present administration does nothing to check the tendency toward dissolution. I, who have been called to meet this awful responsibility, am compelled to remain here doing nothing to avert it or lessen its force when it comes to me. Secession is being fostered rather than repressed, and if the doctrine meets with general acceptance in the border states, it will be a great blow to the government. I suppose you will never forget that trial down in Montgomery county, where the lawyer associated with you gave away the whole case in his opening speech. I saw you signaling to him, but you couldn't stop him. Now, that's just the way with me and Buchanan. He is giving away the case, and I have nothing to say, and can't stop him.—*To Joseph Gillespie, Jan., 1861.* Stephenson, 214.

Buchanan, James, minority choice—[President Pierce] considers the result [election of Buchanan] a signal triumph of good principles and good men, and a very pointed rebuke of bad ones. He says the people did it. He forgets that the "people," as he complacently calls only those who voted for Buchanan, are in a minority of the whole people by about 400,000 votes—one full tenth of all the vote. Remembering this, he might perceive that the "rebuke" may not be quite as durable as he seems to think—that the majority may not choose to remain permanently rebuked by that minority.—*Speech, Chicago, Dec. 10, 1856.* II, 308.
2.—All of us who did not vote for Mr. Buchanan, taken together, are a majority of 400,000.—*Speech, Chicago, Dec. 10, 1856.* II, 311.
3.—Since then [his introduction of the Kansas-Nebraska bill] he [Douglas] has seen himself superseded in a presidential nomination by one indorsing the general doctrine of his measure, but at the same time standing clear of the odium of its untimely agitation and its gross breach of public faith; and he has seen that successful rival constitutionally elected, not by the strength of friends, but by the division of adversaries, being in a popular minority of nearly 400,000 votes.—*Speech, Chicago, June 27, 1857.* II, 328.
4.—Mr. Buchanan was elected, and the indorsement [of the proslavery program] such as it was, secured. . . . The indorsement, however, fell short of a clear majority by nearly 400,000 votes, and so, perhaps, was not overwhelmingly reliable and satisfactory.—*Speech, Springfield, June 16, 1858.* III, 5.

Buchanan, James, part in proslavery program—*See* SLAVERY, conspiracy to promote, 4, 5.

Buchanan, James, false prophet—*See* PROPHECY, false, touching slavery, 4.

Buckner, Simon B., might have been arrested—*See* CONFEDERATE GENERALS, might have been arrested.

Budget, government, suggested—*See* INTERNAL IMPROVEMENTS, budget plan suggested for.

Buell, Don Carlos, promotion for, suggested—If Gen. McClellan thinks it proper to make Buell a major general, enabling Sherman to return to Kentucky, it would rather please me.—*Indorsement on letter of James Guthrie, Nov. 27, 1861.* R. T. L.

Buell, Don Carlos, successors of, and McClellan disappoint—*See* MC CLELLAN, GEORGE B., successors of, and Buell disappoint.

Bull-Dog Grip—*See* GRANT, U. S., advice to, 1.

Bullets, ballot and—*See* BALLOT, better than bullets.

"Bullocks to Slaughter"—*See* MILITARY DRAFT, can't wait, 2.

Burbridge, S. G., thanked—Please accept my congratulations and thanks for yourself and command. —*To Gen. Burbridge, June 14, 1864.* X, 125.

Burnside, Ambrose E., advice to—Be cautious, and do not understand that the government or country is driving you.—*To Gen. Burnside, Jan. 8, 1863.* VIII, 181.

Burnside, Ambrose E., appreciation of—A thousand thanks for the late successes you have given us.—*To Gen. Burnside, Sept. 11, 1863.* IX, 118.

See ROSECRANS, WILLIAM S., opportunity of, 2.

Burnside, Ambrose E., criticized—Yours of the 23d . . . makes me doubt whether I am awake or dreaming. I have been struggling for ten days, first through Gen. Halleck, and then directly, to get you to go to assist Gen. Rosecrans in an extremity, and you have repeatedly declared you would do it, and yet you steadily move the contrary way.—*To Gen. Burnside, Sept. 25, 1863.* IX, 13 (not sent).

Burnside, Ambrose E., resignation of, not desired— I do not yet see how I could profit by changing the command of the Army of the Potomac; and if I did, I should not wish to do so by accepting the resignation of your commission.—*To Gen. Burnside, Jan. 8, 1863.* VIII, 181.
2.—When I shall wish to supersede you I will let you know.—*To Gen. Burnside, May 29, 1863.* VIII, 286.
3.—We cannot allow you to resign until things shall be a little more settled in East Tennessee.—*To Gen. Burnside, Sept. 11, 1863.* IX, 118.

Bushwhacking, complaint reported—Complaint is made to me that Gen. Brown does not do his best to suppress bushwhacking. Please ascertain and report to me.—*To Gen. Rosecrans, June 24, 1864.* X, 134.

Bushwhacking, war on Republican antislavery stand characterized—A great deal of this war with us [on the slavery issue] nowadays is mere bushwhacking. At the battle of Waterloo, when Napoleon's cavalry had charged again and again upon the unbroken squares of British infantry, at last they were giving up the attempt, and going off in disorder, when some of the officers, in mere vexation and complete despair, fired their pistols at the solid squares. The Democrats are in that sort of extreme desperation; it is nothing else. —*Speech, New Haven, Conn., March 6, 1860.* V, 357.
2.—Another specimen of this bushwhacking—that "shoe strike" [in New England].—*Speech, New Haven, Conn., March 6, 1860.* V, 360.

"Butchering Business"—*See* LINCOLN, ABRAHAM, personal traits and reactions, 18.

"But," how would Pierce's father spell it?—*See* PIERCE, FRANKLIN, "arguments" for.

Butler, Benjamin F., appreciation of—On behalf of yourself, officers and men, please accept my hearty thanks for what you and they have so far done.—*To Gen. Butler, May 18, 1864.* X, 105.
2.—I surely need not to assure you that I have no doubt of your loyalty and devoted patriotism.—*To Gen. Butler, Aug. 9, 1864.* X, 321.

"Buts," "Ifs" and "Ands"—*See* UNION, do-nothing friends of, 4.

Butterfield, Justin, general land office and—*See* GENERAL LAND OFFICE, Butterfield not entitled to.

"By the Throat"—*See* ROSECRANS, WILLIAM S., opportunity of, 2.

Cabinet, balanced—You seem to forget that I expect to be there [in the cabinet]; and counting me as one, you see how nicely the cabinet would be balanced [between Whigs and Democrats].—*Interview, Thurlow Weed, Dec. 1860.* Weed, 610.

Cabinet, Chase necessary to—*See* CHASE, SALMON P., appointment of, necessary.

Cabinet, dismissals from, up to President alone—Your note . . . inclosing Gen. Halleck's letter . . . relative to offensive remarks supposed to have been made by the postmaster general concerning the military officers on duty about Washington is received. The general's letter in substance demands that if I approve the remarks I shall strike the names of those officers from the rolls; and that if I do not approve them the postmaster general shall be dismissed from the cabinet. Whether the remarks were really made I do not know, nor do I suppose such knowledge is necessary to a correct response. If they were made, I do not approve them; and yet, under the circumstances, I would not dismiss a member of the cabinet therefor. I do not consider what may have been hastily said in a moment of vexation at so severe a loss is sufficient ground for so grave a step. Besides this, truth is generally the best vindication against slander. I propose continuing to be myself the judge as to when a member of the cabinet shall be dismissed.—*To Sec. Stanton, July 14, 1864.* X, 157.
2.—I must myself be the judge how long to retain and when to remove any of you [cabinet members] from his position. It would greatly pain me to discover any of you endeavoring to procure another's removal, or in any way to prejudice him before the public. Such endeavor would be a wrong to me, and, much worse, a wrong to the country.—*Memorandum read to cabinet, July 14, 1864.* X, 158.

Cabinet, how and when formed—The truth is, and I may as well state the facts to you, for others know them, on the day of the presidential election, the operator of the telegraph in Springfield placed his instrument at my disposal. I was there without leaving, after the returns began to come in, until we had enough to satisfy us how the election had gone. This was about 2 in the morning of Wednesday. I went home but not to get much sleep, for I then felt, as I never had before, the responsibility that was upon me. I began at once to feel that I needed support— others to share with me the burden. This was on Wednesday morning, and before the sun went down I had made up my cabinet. It was almost the same that I finally appointed. One or two changes were made, and the particular position of one or two was unsettled.—*To White House group, Aug. 15, 1862.* Welles, I, 81.

Cabinet, policy in relation to—When a general line of policy is adopted, I apprehend there is no danger of its being changed without good reason, or continuing to be a subject of unnecessary debate; still, upon points arising in its progress I wish, and suppose I am entitled to have, the advice of all the cabinet.— *To W. H. Seward, April 1, 1861.* VI, 237.
2.—In cabinet my view is that in questions affecting the whole country there should be full and frequent consultations, and that nothing should be done particularly affecting any department without consultation with the head of that department.—*Memorandum, July 4, 1864.* Hertz II, 935.

Cabinet, southern men for?—We hear such frequent allusions to a supposed purpose on the part of Mr. Lincoln to call into his cabinet two or three southern gentlemen from the parties opposed to him politically, that we are prompted to ask a few questions. First, is it known that any such gentlemen of character would accept a place in the cabinet? Second, if yea, on what terms does he surrender to Mr. Lincoln, or Mr. Lincoln to him, on the political differences between them; or do they enter upon the administration in open opposition to each other?—*Editorial, Illinois* Journal, *Dec. 12, 1860.* VI, 78.
2.—It certainly would be of some advantage if you would know who are to be at the heads of the War and Navy Departments; but until I can ascertain definitely whether I can get any suitable men from the South, and who, and how many, I cannot well decide.—*To W. H. Seward, Jan. 3, 1861.* VI, 91.

Cabinet, states entitled to places in—Pennsylvania, any more than New York or Ohio, cannot be overlooked. Her strong Republican vote entitles her to a representative in the cabinet.—*Interview, Thurlow Weed, Dec., 1860.* Weed, 608.

Cabinet, trouble in forming—As to the matter of the cabinet, mentioned by you, I can only say I shall have a great deal of trouble, do the best I can.—*To William Cullen Bryant, Dec. 29, 1860.* VI, 89.
2.—I shall have trouble with every other northern cabinet appointment [except that of Seward], so much so that I shall have to defer them as long as possible, to avoid being teased to insanity to make changes.—*To W. H. Seward, Jan. 12, 1861.* VI, 95.

Cabinet, West needs seat in—In these days of cabinet making, we out west are awake as well as others. . . . The West is not only entitled to, but is in need of, one member of the [Taylor] cabinet.—*To William Schouler, Feb. 2, 1849.* II, 100.

Caesar's Hair, shade of, unimportant—I personally wish Jacob Freese of New Jersey to be appointed colonel for a colored regiment, and this regardless of whether he can tell the exact shade of Julius Caesar's hair.—*To Sec. Stanton, Nov. 11, 1863.* IX, 206.

Calhoun, John C., first to assail Declaration—*See* DECLARATION OF INDEPENDENCE, hostility toward, 1.

California, "best part"—[California] was by far the best part of our acquisition from Mexico.—*Speech, Peoria, Oct. 16, 1854.* II, 203.
2.—They [antislavery men] . . . got California into the Union as a free state. This was by far the best

part of all they had struggled for by the Wilmot Proviso.—*Speech, Peoria, Oct. 16, 1854.* II, 214. Repeated at Urbana, Oct. 24, 1854. Hertz II, 638.

California, kept out of Union—There California stood, kept out of the Union because she would not let slavery into her borders.—*Speech, Peoria, Oct. 16, 1854.* II, 201.

California, treasure-ships protected—I directed that an armed revenue cutter should proceed to sea, to afford protection to the commercial marine, and especially the California treasure-ships then on their way to this coast.—*Message to Congress, May 26, 1862.* VII, 190.

Cameron, Simon, appointment of, withdrawn—When you were here, about the last of December, I handed you a letter saying I should at the proper time nominate you to the Senate for a place in the cabinet. . . . You have not as yet signified to me whether you would accept the appointment, and with much pain I now say to you that you will relieve me from great embarrassment by allowing me to recall that offer. This springs from an unexpected complication, and not from any change of my view as to the ability or faithfulness with which you would discharge the duties of the place.—*To Simon Cameron, Jan. 3, 1861.* VI, 97.

Cameron, Simon, cabinet possibility—Then comes the danger that the protectionists of Pennsylvania will be dissatisfied [if Cameron is not given the Treasury appointment]; and to clear this difficulty Gen. C[ameron] must be brought to cooperate. He would readily do this for the War Department. But then comes the fierce opposition to his having any department, threatening even to send charges into the Senate to procure his rejection by that body. Now, what I would like most, and what I think he should prefer too, under the circumstances, would be to retain his place in the Senate. . . . I may mention before closing that besides the very fixed opposition to Gen. C. he is more amply recommended for a place in the cabinet than any other man.—*To Lyman Trumbull, Jan. 7, 1861.* Tracy, 174.

Cameron, Simon, confidence and esteem—I . . . tender to your acceptance . . . the post of minister to Russia. Should you accept it, you will bear with you the assurance of my undiminished confidence, of my affectionate esteem, and of my sure expectation that, near the great sovereign whose personal and hereditary friendship for the United States so much endears him to Americans, you will be able to render services to your country not less important than those you could render at home.—*To Simon Cameron, Jan. 11, 1862.*   VII, 80.

2.—His [Cameron's] fidelity, probity, and good conduct.—*To Czar Alexander II of Russia, April 8, 1862.* Hertz II, 855.

Cameron, Simon, defense of—I should be wanting equally in candor and in justice if I should leave the censure expressed in this [House] resolution to rest exclusively or chiefly upon Mr. Cameron. . . . It is due to Mr. Cameron to say that, although he fully approved the proceedings, they were not moved nor suggested by him, and that not only the President but all the other heads of departments were at least equally responsible with him for whatever error, wrong or fault was committed in the premises.—*Message to Congress, May 26, 1862.*   VII, 193.

Cameron, Simon, not much of Democrat—I suppose we could say of Gen. Cameron that he is not Democrat enough to hurt him.—*Interview, Thurlow Weed, Dec., 1860.*   Weed, 610.

Cameron, Simon, Presidency and—If the Republicans of the great state of Pennsylvania shall present Mr. Cameron as their candidate for the Presidency, such an indorsement of his fitness for the place could scarcely be deemed insufficient.—*To W. E. Frazer, Nov. 1, 1859.*   V, 258.

Campaign of 1840, hopeful for Illinois—The nomination of Harrison takes first-rate. You know I am never sanguine; but I believe we will carry this state. —*To John T. Stuart, Jan. 20, 1840.*   I, 147.

Campaign of 1848, victory forecast—One unmistakable sign [of success] is that all the odds and ends are with us—Barnburners, Native Americans, Tyler men, disappointed office-seeking Locofocos, and the Lord knows what. This is important, if for nothing else, in showing which way the wind blows. Taylor's nomination takes the Locos on the blind side. It turns the war thunder against them. The war is now to them the gallows of Haman, which they built for us, and on which they are doomed to be hanged themselves.—*To Archibald Williams, June 12, 1848.*   II, 27.

2.—The news [touching Taylor's chance for election] we are receiving here [in Washington] now, by letters from all quarters, is steadily on the rise; we have none lately of a discouraging character.—*To Thaddeus Stevens, Sept. 3, 1848.*   Angle, 48.

Campaign of 1852, Democrats' do-nothing platform —Take the present Democratic platform, and it does not propose to do a single thing. It is full of declarations as to what ought not to be done, but no one

[thing] to be done. If there is in it even an inference in favor of any positive action by the Democracy, should they again get into power, it only extends to the collecting of a sufficient revenue to pay their own salaries, including perhaps constructive mileage to senators. Propose a course of policy that shall ultimately supplant the monstrous folly of bringing untold millions of iron, thousands of miles across water and land, while our own hills and mountains are groaning with the best quality in the world, and in quantity sufficient for ten such worlds, and the cry instantly is "no." Propose to remove a snag, a rock, or a sand bar from a lake or river, and the cry still is "no."—*Speech, Springfield, Aug. 26, 1852.*   Angle, 104.

See PIERCE, FRANKLIN.

Campaign of 1856, Fillmore endangers Frémont—I very cheerfully give you my opinion as to the prospects of the presidential election in this state & Indiana; premising that I am a Frémont man, so you can make due allowance for my partiality. I have no doubt, then, that the opposition to Buchanan are in the majority in both these states; but, that opposition being divided between Frémont and Fillmore, places both states in some danger. . . . The Fillmore men have no power in either state, beyond dividing strength, and thereby bettering the chances of Buchanan. They know this; and I still think the bulk of them will think better than to throw away their votes for such an object.—*To Artemus Hale, July 28, 1856.*   Angle, 163.

2.—I understand you are a Fillmore man. . . . If you would like to defeat Buchanan and his gang, allow me a word with you: Does anyone pretend that Fillmore can carry the vote of this state? I have not heard a single man pretend so. Every vote taken from Frémont and given to Fillmore is just so much in favor of Buchanan. The Buchanan men see this; and hence their great anxiety in favor of the Fillmore movement. They know where the shoe pinches. They now greatly prefer having a man of your character go for Fillmore than for Buchanan because they expect several to go with you, who would go for Frémont if you were to go directly for Buchanan.—*To John Bennett, Aug. 4, 1856.*   II, 295.

3.—You who hate slavery and love freedom, why not, as Fillmore and Buchanan are on the same ground, vote for Frémont? Why not vote for the man who takes your side of the question?—*Speech, Kalamazoo, Mich., Aug. 27, 1856.*   Stern, 403.

4.—Let me prove to you that every vote withheld from Frémont, and given to Fillmore, in this state, actually lessens Fillmore's chances of being President.

Suppose Buchanan gets all the slave states, and Pennsylvania, and any other one state besides; then he is elected, no matter who gets all the rest. But suppose Fillmore gets the two slave states of Maryland and Kentucky; then Buchanan is not elected; Fillmore goes into the House of Representatives, and may be made President by a compromise. But suppose again Fillmore's friends throw away a few thousand votes on him, in Indiana or Illinois, it will inevitably give those states to Buchanan, which will more than compensate him for the loss of Maryland and Kentucky, will elect him, and leave Fillmore no chance in the H. R., or out of it. . . . As Mr. Fillmore has no possible chance to carry Illinois for himself, it is plainly his interest to let Frémont take it. . . . Be not deceived. Buchanan is the hard horse to beat in this race. Let him have Illinois, and nothing can beat him.—*To Ed. Lawrence, Sept. 8, 1856.* Hertz II, 687. Repeated, in substance, to Luther Hill, same date. Hertz II, 688.
Repeated to Harrison Maltby, same date,   II, 297.

Campaign of 1856, issue defined—What is the question between the parties, respectively represented by Buchanan and Frémont? Simply this: Shall slavery be allowed to extend into U.S. territories, now legally free? Buchanan says it shall; and Frémont says it shall not. That is the naked issue, and the whole of it.—*Fragment, no date.* Hertz II, 681.
2.—This is the question: Shall the government of the United States prohibit slavery in the United States?—*Speech, Kalamazoo, Mich., Aug, 27, 1856.* Stern, 401.

Campaign of 1856, plan to save Illinois—A union of our strength, to be effected in some way, is indispensable to our carrying the state against Buchanan. The inherent obstacle to any plan of union lies in the fact that of the Germans which we now have with us, large numbers will fall away so soon as it is seen that their votes, cast with us, may possibly be used to elevate Mr. Fillmore. If this inherent difficulty were out of the way, one small improvement on your plan occurs to me. It is this. Let Frémont and Fillmore men unite on one entire ticket, with the understanding that that ticket, if elected, shall cast the vote of the state for whichever of the two shall be known to have received the larger number of electoral votes in the other states.—*To James Berdan, July 10, 1856.* Angle, 162.

Campaign of 1858, "as a gentleman"—I set out in this campaign with the intention of conducting it strictly as a gentleman, in substance at least, if not in outside polish. The latter I shall never be, but that which constitutes the inside of a gentleman I hope I understand, and am not less inclined to practice than others. It was my purpose and expectation that this canvass would be conducted upon principle, with fairness on both sides, and it shall not be my fault if this purpose and expectation shall be given up.—*Speech, Springfield, July 17, 1858.* III, 171.

Campaign of 1858, hopeful—I think our prospects gradually and steadily grow better, though we are not yet out of the woods by a great deal. There is still some effort to make trouble out of "Americanism." If that were out of the way, for all the rest, I believe we should be out of the woods.—*To E. B. Washburne, May 15, 1858.* II, 360.

Campaign of 1858, in review—I have borne laborious and, in some respects to myself, a painful part in the contest. Through all, I have neither assailed, nor wrestled with any part of the Constitution. . . . I have said that in some respects the contest has been painful to me. Myself, and those with whom I act, have been constantly accused of a purpose to destroy the Union; and bespattered with every imaginable odious epithet; and some who were friends, as it were but yesterday, have made themselves most active in this. I have cultivated patience, and made no attempt at a retort.—*Speech, Springfield, Oct. 30, 1858.* Angle, 197.
2.—Douglas had the ingenuity to be supported in the late contest both as the best means to break down and to uphold the slave interests. No ingenuity can keep those antagonistic elements in harmony long. Another explosion will come.—*To Henry Ashbury, Nov. 19, 1858.* V, 94.

Campaign of 1858, no treachery suspected—Of all the avowed friends I had in the canvass of last year, I do not suspect any of having acted treacherously to me, or to our cause.—*To George W. Dole, G. S. Hubbard and W. H. Brown, Dec. 14, 1859.* V, 284.

Campaign of 1858, Republican handicaps in—In regard to the legislature [where United States senator is to be elected], we, the Republicans, labor under some disadvantages. In the first place, we have a legislature to elect upon an apportionment of the representation made several years ago, when the proportion of population was far greater in the South—as compared with the North—than it now is; and inasmuch as our opponents have almost the entire sway in the South, and we a correspondingly large majority in the North, the fact that we are now to be represented as we were years ago, when the population was different, is to us a very great disadvantage.—*Speech, Springfield, July 17, 1858.* III, 155.

2.—Another disadvantage under which we labor is that there are one or two Democratic senators who will be members of the next legislature, and will vote for the election of [United States] senator, who are holding over in districts in which we could, on all reasonable calculation, elect men of our own, if we only had the chance of an election.—*Speech, Springfield, July 17, 1858.* III, 156.

3.—We [Republicans] have to fight this battle [against slavery] upon principle alone. . . . So I hope those with whom I am surrounded have principle enough to nerve themselves for the task, and leave nothing undone that can fairly be done to bring about the right result.—*Speech, Springfield, July 17, 1858.* III, 158.

Campaign of 1858, some Republicans favor Douglas —What does the New York *Tribune* mean by its constant eulogizing, and admiring, and magnifying Douglas? Does it, in this, speak the sentiments of the Republicans at Washington? Have they concluded that the Republican cause, generally, can be best promoted by sacrificing us here in Illinois? If so, we would like to know it soon; it will save us a great deal of labor to surrender at once. . . . I am not complaining—I only wish a fair understanding.—*To Lyman Trumbull, Dec. 28, 1857.* Tracy, 83.

2.—Some of our eastern Republican friends [are inclined to] favor Douglas. . . . I have believed—I do believe now—that [Horace] Greeley, for instance, would be rather pleased to see Douglas re-elected over me or any other Republican; and yet I do not believe it is so because of any secret arrangement with Douglas. It is because he thinks Douglas's superior position, reputation, experience, ability, if you please, would more than compensate for his lack of a pure Republican position, and therefore his re-election do the general cause of Republicanism more good than would the election of any one of our better undistinguished pure Republicans. . . . He [Greeley] denies that he directly is taking part in favor of Douglas, and I believe him. Still his feeling constantly manifests itself in his paper so extensively read in Illinois, is, and will continue to be, a drag upon us.—*To Charles L. Wilson, June 1, 1858.* II, 362.

3.—As to the inclination of some Republicans to favor Douglas, that is one of the chances I have to run, and which I intend to run with patience.—*To W. H. Lamon, June 11, 1858.* II, 366.

Campaign of 1858, victory may be delayed—I cannot but regard it as possible that the higher object of this contest may not be completely attained within the term of my natural life. But I cannot doubt either

that it will come in due time. Even in this view, I am proud, in my passing speck of time, to contribute an humble mite to that glorious consummation, which my own poor eyes may not last to see.—*Notes, 1858.* Hertz II, 705.

Campaign of 1860, advice to Missouri friend—There is now a Republican electoral ticket in Missouri, so that you can vote for me if your neighbors will let you. I would advise you not to get into any trouble about it.—*To Nathaniel Grigsby, Sept. 20, 1860.* Tracy, 163.

Campaign of 1860, Douglas strategy in—Douglas is managing the Bell element with great adroitness. He has his men in Kentucky to vote for the Bell candidate, producing a result which has badly alarmed Breckinridge, and at the same time has induced the Bell men to suppose that Bell will certainly be President if they can keep a few northern states away from us by throwing them to Douglas. . . . You have seen that Bell tickets have been put on the track both here and in Indiana. In both cases the object has been, I think, the same as the Hunt movement in New York—to throw states to Douglas.—*To Thurlow Weed, Aug. 17, 1860.* VI, 51.

Campaign of 1860, North-South fusion suggested— There are many men in the slave states for any one of whom I could cheerfully vote for either President or Vice President, provided he would enable me to do so with safety to the Republican cause, without lowering the Republican standard. This is the indispensable condition of union with us; it is idle to talk of any other. Any other would be as fruitless to the South as distasteful to the North, the whole ending in common defeat.—*To M. W. Delahay, May 14, 1859.* V, 128.

2.—Let a union be attempted on the basis of ignoring the slavery question, and magnifying other questions which the people are just now not caring about, and it will result in gaining no single electoral vote in the South, and losing every one in the North.— *To M. W. Delahay, May 14, 1859.* V, 129.

3.—As to the matter of fusion I am for it, if it can be had on Republican grounds; and I am not for it on any other terms. A fusion on any other terms would be as foolish as unprincipled. It would lose the whole North, while the common enemy would still carry the whole South. . . . I am against letting down the Republican standard a hair's breadth.—*To Dr. Theodore Canisius, May 17, 1859.* V, 130.

4.—I know that it is very desirable with me, as with everybody else, that all the elements of the Opposition [to slavery] shall unite in the next presidential election, and in all future time. . . . If the terms can be arranged, I am in favor of the union. But suppose we take up some man and put him upon one end or the other of the ticket, who declares against us in regard to the prevention of the extension of slavery, who turns up his nose and says he is tired of hearing anything more about it, who is more against us than against the enemy—what will be the issue? . . . He won't get a single vote anywhere, except, perhaps, in the state of Maryland.—*Speech, Cincinnati, Sept. 17, 1859.* V, 233.

5.—There are plenty of men in the slave states that are altogether good enough for me to be either President or Vice President, provided they will profess their sympathy with our [antislavery] purpose, and will place themselves on such ground that our men, upon principle, can vote for them. There are scores of them—good men in their character for intelligence, and talent and integrity. If such an one will place himself upon the right ground, I am for his occupying one place upon the next Republican or Opposition ticket. I will heartily go for him.—*Speech, Cincinnati, Sept. 17, 1859.* V, 234.

6.—I should be glad to have some of the many good, able, and noble men of the South to place themselves where we can confer upon them the high honor of an election upon one or the other end of our ticket. It would do my soul good to do that thing. It would enable us to teach them that, inasmuch as we select one of their number to carry out our principles, we are free from the charge that we mean more than we say.—*Speech, Cincinnati, Sept. 17, 1859.* V, 235.

7.—A hope is often expressed that all the elements of opposition to the so-called Democracy may unite in the next presidential election; and to favor this it is suggested that at least one candidate on the opposition national ticket must be resident in the slave states. I strongly sympathize with this hope; and the particular suggestion presents no difficulty to me. . . . But there is a difficulty. . . . Will those good men of the South occupy any ground upon which we of the free states can vote for them? There is the rub.—*Speeches in Kansas, Dec. 1-5, 1859.* V, 273.

8.—The simple problem [touching political fusion for 1860] is: Will any good and capable man of the South allow the Republicans to elect him [President or Vice President] on their own platform? If such a man can be found, I believe the thing can be done. It can be done in no other way.—*Speeches in Kansas, Dec. 1-5, 1859.* V, 275.

9.—What do we gain, say some, by such a union? In yielding a share of the high honors and offices to you [men of the South], you gain the assurance that ours is not a mere struggle to secure those honors and offices for one section. You gain the assurance that we mean no more than we say in our platforms, else we would not entrust you to execute them. You gain the assurance that we intend no invasion of your rights or your honor, else we would not make one of you the executor of the laws and commander of the army and navy.—*Speeches in Kansas, Dec. 1-5, 1859.* V, 275.

10.—As a matter of mere partisan policy, there is no reason for and much against any letting down of the Republican party in order to form a union with the southern opposition. By no possibility can a union ticket secure a single electoral vote in the South, unless the Republican platform be so far let down as to lose every electoral vote in the North.—*Speeches in Kansas, Dec. 1-5, 1859.* V, 275.

11.—There is no successful basis of union but for some good southern man to allow us of the North to elect him square on our platform. Plainly, it is that or nothing.—*Speeches in Kansas, Dec. 1-5, 1859.* V, 276.

See POLITICAL PLATFORMS, proposals for 1860 rejected, 2.

Campaign of 1860, preconvention candidates appraised—I think neither Seward nor Bates can carry Illinois, if Douglas shall be on the track; and that either of them can, if he shall not be. I rather think McLean could carry it with D. on or off; in other words, I think McLean is stronger in Illinois, taking all sections of it, than either S. or B.; and I think S. the weakest of the three. I hear no objection to Mr. McLean except his age, but that objection seems to occur to everyone; and it is possible it might leave him no stronger than the others.—*To Lyman Trumbull, April 29, 1859.* Tracy, 143.

2.—I think Mr. Seward is the very best candidate we could have for the north of Illinois, and the very worst for the south of it. The estimate of Gov. Chase here is neither better nor worse than that of Seward, except that he is a newer man. They are regarded as being almost the same, seniority giving Seward the inside track. Mr. Bates, I think, would be the best man for the south of our state, and the worst for the north of it. If Judge McLean was fifteen, or even ten, years younger, I think he would be stronger than either, in our state, taken as a whole; but his great age, and the recollection of the deaths of Harrison and Taylor have, so far, prevented his being much spoken of here.—*To R. M. Corwine, April 6, 1860.* Tracy, 138.

Campaign of 1860, silence is candidate's best policy—I would cheerfully answer your questions in regard to the fugitive-slave law, were it not that I consider it would be both imprudent and contrary to the reasonable expectations of friends for me to write, or speak, anything on doctrinal points now. Besides this, my published speeches contain nearly all I could willingly say now. Justice and fairness to all is the utmost I have said or will say.—*To T. A. Cheney, Aug. 14, 1860.* VI, 48.

2.—It has been my purpose since I have been placed in my present position to make no speeches.—*Speech, Springfield, Aug. 14, 1860.* VI, 49.

3.—As to our uneasy friends in New York—if there be such—all that can be said is, "Justice and fairness to all." More than this has not been, and cannot be said to any.—*To James E. Harvey, Aug. 14, 1860.* Hertz II, 782.

4.—Your letter asking me, "Are you in favor of a tariff and protection to American industry?" is received. The convention which nominated me, by the twelfth plank of their platform, selected their position on this question; and I have declared my approval of the platform. . . . Now, if I were to publicly shift the position or add or subtract anything, the convention would have the right, and probably would be inclined, to displace me as its candidate. And I feel confident that you, on reflection, would not wish me to give private assurances to be seen by some and kept secret from others.—*To G. Yoke Tams, Sept. 22, 1860.* VI, 58.

5.—Does not my acceptance pledge me to that [Chicago] convention? And am I at liberty to do more, if I were inclined?—*To J. E. Harvey, Oct. 2, 1860.* VI, 62.

6.—I appreciate your motive when you suggest the propriety of my writing something disclaiming all intention to interfere with slaves or slavery in the states; but in my judgment it would do no good. I have already done this many, many times; and it is in print, and open to all to read. Those who will not read or heed what I have already publicly said would not read or heed a repetition of it. "If they hear not Moses nor the prophets, neither will they be persuaded though one rose from the dead."—*To William S. Speer, Oct. 23, 1860.* VI, 63.

7.—Your suggestion that I in a certain event shall write a letter setting forth my conservative views and intentions is certainly a very worthy one. But would it do any good? If I were to labor a month I could not express my conservative views and intentions more clearly and strongly than they were expressed in our platform and in the many speeches already in print and before the public. And yet even you, who do occasionally speak of me in terms of personal kindness, give no prominence to these oft-repeated expressions of conservative views and intentions, but

busy yourself [as editor of the Louisville *Journal*] with appeals to all conservative men to vote for Douglas—to vote any way which can possibly defeat me—thus impressing your readers that you think I am the very worst man living. If what I have already said has failed to convince you, no repetition of it would convince you.—*To George D. Prentice, Oct. 29, 1860.* VI, 66.

8.—For the good men of the South—and I regard the majority of them as such—I have no objection to repeat seventy and seven times. But I have bad men to deal with, both North and South; men who are eager for something new upon which to base new misrepresentations; men who like to frighten me, or at least to fix upon me the character of timidity and cowardice. They would seize upon almost any letter I could write as being an "awful coming down." I intend keeping my eye upon these gentlemen, and to not unnecessarily put any weapons in their hands.—*To George D. Prentice, Oct. 29, 1860.* VI, 67.

9.—Allow me to beg that you will not live in much apprehension of my precipitating a letter upon the public.—*To G. G. Fogg, Oct. 31, 1860.* Tracy, 167.

Campaign of 1860, victory forecast—So far as I can learn, the nominations start well everywhere; and, if they get no setback, it would seem as if they are going through.—*To E. B. Washburne, May 26, 1860.* VI, 20.

2.—The thing starts well everywhere—too well, I almost fear, to last.—*To C. B. Smith, May 26, 1860.* VI, 21.

3.—Gov. Reeder was here last evening direct from Pennsylvania. He is entirely confident of that state, and of the general result. . . . He [Thurlow Weed] asked for nothing; and said New York is safe, without condition.—*To Lyman Trumbull, June 5, 1860.* Stephenson, 202.

4.—We know not what a day may bring forth, but today it looks as if the Chicago ticket will be elected. I think the chances were more than equal that we [Republicans] could have beaten the Democracy united. Divided as it is, its chances appear indeed very slim. But great is Democracy in resources; and it may yet give its fortunes a turn. It is under great temptation to do something.—*To A. G. Henry, July 4, 1860.* VI, 42.

5.—The prospect of Republican success now appears very flattering, so far as I can perceive.—*To Hannibal Hamlin, July 18, 1860.* VI, 44.

6.—I hesitate to say it, but it really appears now as if the success of the Republican ticket is inevitable.—*To Simeon Francis, Aug. 4, 1860.* Quarterly, March, 1940, p. 57.

7.—I have a good deal of private correspondence; and without giving details, I will only say it all looks very favorable to our success.—*To A. G. Henry, Sept. 22, 1860.* VI, 58.

8.—So far as I have private information, the prospect for the election looks quite encouraging.—*To B. F. James, Sept. 26, 1860.* Hertz II, 787.

Campaign of 1864, public letter refused—I beg you to pardon me for having concluded that it is not best for me now to write a general letter to a political meeting. First, I believe it is not customary for one holding the office [of President], and being a candidate for re-election, to do so; and, secondly, a public letter must be written with some care, and at some expense of them, so that having begun with your meeting, I could not well refuse others, and yet could not get through with all having equal claims.—*To Isaac M. Schermerhorn, Sept. 12, 1864.* X, 223.

Campaign of 1864, victory held improbable—This morning, as for some days past, it seems exceedingly probable that this administration will not be re-elected. Then it will be my duty to so cooperate with the President-elect as to save the Union between the election and the inauguration; as he will have secured his election on such ground that he cannot possibly save it afterward.—*Memorandum, Aug. 23, 1864.* X, 203.

Campaign Pledges, won't buy with—*See* NOMINATION OF 1860, attitude toward, 7.

Campbell, Thomas H.—An honest man, of thorough business capacity. . . . No man can be more safely trusted.—*To Sec. Chase, March 10, 1862.* VII, 128.

Canada, "not unfriendly"—*See* GREAT LAKES, fortifications suggested, 2.

Canada, slave refugees in—If Canada now had as many horses as she has slaves belonging to Americans, I should think it just cause for war if she did not surrender them on demand.—*Speech, Leavenworth, Kan., Dec. 3, 1859.* Angle, 234.

Canby, Edward R. S.—*See* FARRAGUT, DAVID G., thanked for victories.

"Cancer,"—*See* LIBERTY, prosperity and, threatened by slavery.

Cane, donor's name illegible—Herewith is the manuscript letter for the gentleman who sent me a cane through your hands. For my life I cannot make out his name; and therefore I cut it from his letter and paste it on, as you see.—*To Gov. A. G. Curtin, July 25, 1864.* X, 171.

Capital, labor and—*See* LABOR, relationship of, and capital.

Capitalists, "fleece the people"—These capitalists generally act harmoniously and in concert, to fleece the people, and now, that they have got into a quarrel with themselves, we are called upon to appropriate the people's money to settle the quarrel.—*Speech to Illinois Legislature, Jan., 1837.* I, 24.

Carlin (Thomas), court decision in case—*See* JUDICIAL DECISIONS, Douglas's attitude toward, 11.

Carney, Thomas, relations with Lane—It is not my recollection that I said to you Senator Lane would probably oppose raising troops in Kansas because it would confer patronage upon you. What I did say was, that he would probably oppose it because he and you were in a mood of each opposing whatever the other should propose.—*Indorsement on letter of Gov. Carney's, May 14, 1864.* X, 100.

See PATRONAGE, "demoralizing." 1.

Carpetbaggers, not wanted in Congress—*See* RECONSTRUCTION, Louisiana, 5.

Cass, Lewis D., eating capacity of—And at eating, too, his [Cass's] capacities are shown to be quite wonderful. From October, 1821, to May, 1822, he ate ten rations a day in Michigan, ten rations a day here in Washington, and near five dollars' worth a day on the road between the two places! And then there is an important discovery in his example—the art of being paid for what one eats, instead of having to pay for it. Hereafter if any nice young man should owe a bill which he cannot pay in any other way, he can just board it out!—*Speech in Congress, July 27, 1848.* II, 83.

2.—We have all heard of the animal standing in doubt between two stacks of hay and starving to death. The like of that would never happen to Gen. Cass. Place the stacks a thousand miles apart, he would stand stock-still midway between them, and eat them both at once, and the green grass along the line would be apt to suffer some, too.—*Speech in Congress, July 27, 1848.* II, 83.

3.—By all means make him President, gentlemen. He will feed you bounteously—if—if there is any left after he shall have helped himself.—*Speech in Congress, July 27, 1848.* II, 83.

Cass, Lewis D., military figure of—All his biographies —and they are legion—have him [Cass] in hand, tying him to a military tail, like so many mischievous boys tying a dog to a bladder of beans. True, the material they have is very limited, but they drive at it with might and main. He *invaded* Canada without resistance, and *outv*aded it without pursuit. . . . [There remains] the mooted question of the broken sword. Some authors say he [Cass] broke it, some say he threw it away, and others, who ought to know, say nothing about it. Perhaps it would be a fair historical compromise to say, if he did not break it, he did not do anything else with it. It is quite certain I did not break my sword, for I had none to break; but I bent a musket pretty badly on one occasion. [*See* LINCOLN, ABRAHAM, "military hero."] If Cass broke his sword, the idea is that he broke it in desperation. If Gen. Cass went in advance of me in picking huckleberries, I guess I surpassed him in charges upon the wild onions. If he saw any live, fighting Indians, it was more than I did; but I had a good many bloody struggles with mosquitoes, and although I never fainted from loss of blood, I can truly say I was often very hungry. Mr. Speaker, if I should ever conclude to doff whatever our Democratic friends may suppose there is of black cockade federalism about me, and therefore they shall take me up as their candidate for the Presidency, I protest they shall not make fun of me, as they have of Gen. Cass, by attempting to write me into a military hero.—*Speech in Congress, July 27, 1848.* II, 74.

2.—He [Cass] was volunteer aid to Gen. Harrison on the day of the battle of the Thames; and as you [Democrats] said in 1840, Harrison was picking huckleberries two miles off while the battle was fought. I suppose it is a just conclusion with you to say Cass was aiding Harrison to pick huckleberries.— *Speech in Congress, July 27, 1848.* II, 75.

3.—Gen Cass is a general of splendidly successful charges—charges, to be sure, not upon the enemy, but upon the public treasury.—*Speech in Congress, July 27, 1848.* II, 80.

See LINCOLN, ABRAHAM, "military hero."

Cass, Lewis D., Nicholson letter and popular sovereignty—*See* POPULAR SOVEREIGNTY, what did Douglas invent?

Cass, Lewis D., physical capacity of—I have introduced Gen. Cass's accounts here chiefly to show the wonderful physical capacities of the man. They show that he not only did the labor of several men at the same time, but that he often did it at several places, many hundreds of miles apart, at the same time.— *Speech in Congress, July 27, 1848.* II, 83.

Cass, Lewis D., Van Buren and—He [Cass] and Van Buren are the same "manner of men," and, like Van Buren, he will never desert you till you desert him.— *Speech in Congress, July 27, 1848.* II, 79.

Catholic Church, archbishop asked to suggest names for chaplain—*See* CHAPLAINS, sought for hospitals.

Catholics, if Know-Nothings get control—*See* KNOW-NOTHING PARTY, principles of, challenged, 2.

Catchwords, indicate demoralization—We note our political demoralization in the catchwords that are coming into such common use; on the one hand, "freedom shriekers," and sometimes "freedom screechers," and, on the other hand, "border ruffians," and that fully deserved. And the significance of catchwords cannot pass unheeded, for they constitute a sign of the times.—*Speech, Bloomington, May 29, 1856.* Lapsley II, 268.

Caucus, support for, asked—*See* CONGRESS, war supporters only.

Cause, dependence on good—Stand by the cause, and the cause will see you through.—*To B. Clarke Lundy and others, July 28, 1856.* Tracy, 68.

Causes and Effects—*See* HISTORY, repeats.

Censorship, Lincoln exercises—*See* GREELEY, HORACE, correspondence censored.

Censorship, ordered—It is ordered that all correspondence and communication, verbally or by writing, printing or telegraphing, respecting operations by the army or military movements on land or water, or respecting the troops, camps, arsenals, intrenchments or military affairs within the several military districts, by which intelligence shall be, directly or indirectly, given to the enemy, without the authority and sanction of the major-gentral in command, be, and the same are, absolutely prohibited.—*Executive order, Aug. 7, 1861.* Messages VIII, 3240.

Centenarian, thanked—I take the liberty of writing to you to express my personal gratitude for the compliment paid me by the suffrage of a citizen so venerable. [Deacon Phillips of Sturbridge, Mass., was 104 years old when he voted for Lincoln, and had voted at every presidential election since the formation of the government.] The example of such devotion for civic duties in one whose days have already been extended an average lifetime beyond the Psalmist's limit, cannot but be valuable and fruitful. It is not for myself only, but for the country which you have in your sphere served so long and so well, that I thank you.—*To John Phillips, Nov. 21, 1864.* X, 276.

Chair, gift of, acknowledged—The chair which you designate as the "chair of state" is duly at hand and gratefully accepted. In view of what it symbolizes, might it not be called the "chair of state and the Union of states"? The conception of the maker is a pretty, a patriotic, and a national one.—*To D. V. Bell, June 5, 1860.* Angle, 246.

"Chair of State"—*See* CHAIR, gift of, acknowledged.

Chaplains, sought for hospitals—I find no law authorizing the appointment of chaplains for our hospitals; and yet the services of chaplains are more needed, perhaps, in the hospitals than with the healthy soldiers in the field. With this view, I have given a sort of *quasi* appointment—a copy of which I inclose—to each of three Protestant ministers, who have accepted and entered upon the duties. If you perceive no objection, I will thank you to give me the names of one or more suitable persons of the Catholic Church, to whom I may with propriety tender the same service.—*To Archbishop Hughes, Oct. 21, 1861.* VII, 8.
2.—By mere omission, I presume, Congress has failed to provide chaplains for hospitals occupied by volunteers. . . . I further suggest that general provision be made for chaplains at hospitals as well as with the regiments.—*First annual message, Dec. 3, 1861.* VII, 36.

Character, no whining about—I have a character to defend as well as Gen. [James] Adams, but I disdain to whine about it as he does.—*To editor Sangamo Journal, Sept. 9, 1837.* I, 75.

Charity, rules of, and of slavery conflict—*See* NEGRO, justice to, 4.

Charles I, lost his head—Upon questions of history I must refer you to Mr. Seward, for he is posted in such things, and I don't pretend to be bright. My only distinct recollection of the matter [Confederate Commissioner Hunter had suggested that Lincoln should follow the example of Charles and treat with men in rebellion] is that Charles lost his head.—*To Confederate peace conference, Feb. 3, 1865.* Carpenter, 213.

Charleston, S.C., debt owed to—I intend at present, always leaving an opportunity for change of mind, to fill Fortress Monroe with men and stores, blockade the ports effectually, provide for the entire safety of the capital, keep them quietly employed in this way, and then go to Charleston and pay her the little debt we are owing her [for capture of Fort Sumter].—*To Sec. Smith, April 25, 1861.* Hay, 11.

Charleston Courier—I have heard of but one Whig who has been to the [Mexican] war attempting to justify the President's conduct. That one was Capt.

Bishop, editor of the Charleston *Courier,* and a very clever fellow.—*To William H. Herndon, Feb. 1, 1848.* I, 351.

Charleston Mercury, "salivated by"—Try . . . to circulate W. L. Garrison's *Liberator* where most men are salivated by the excessive use of the Charleston *Mercury.*—*To John J. Crittenden, Dec. 22, 1859.* Tracy, 121.

Chase, pleasures of—With the catching end the pleasures of the chase.—*Speech, Springfield, Jan., 1837.* I, 46.

Chase, Salmon P., appointment of, necessary—Gen. C[ameron] has not been offered the Treasury and I think will not be. It seems to me not only highly proper but a necessity that Gov. Chase shall take that place. His ability, firmness, and purity of character produce this propriety; and that he alone can reconcile Mr. Byrant and his class to the appointment of Gov. S. to the State Department produces the necessity.—*To Lyman Trumbull, Jan. 7, 1861.* Tracy, 173.

Chase, Salmon P., arouses ire of slavery men—Why did they [proslavery men in Congress] stand there taunting and quibbling at Chase?—*Debate, Freeport, Aug. 27, 1858.* III, 289.

Chase, Salmon P., avoids proslavery trap—*See* SLAVERY, conspiracy to promote, 17.

Chase, Salmon P., relations with Lincoln—Allow me also to thank you as being one of the very few distinguished men, whose sympathies we in Illinois did receive last year, of all those whose sympathy we thought we had reason to expect.—*To Mr. Chase, April 30, 1859.* Hertz II, 751.
2.—As to Gov. Chase, I have a kind side for him. He was one of the few distinguished men of the nation who gave us, in Illinois, their sympathy last year. I never saw him, but suppose him to be able and right-minded; but still he may not be the most suitable as a candidate for the Presidency.—*To Samuel Galloway, July 28, 1859.* V, 137.
3.—I especially wish to do no ungenerous thing toward Gov. Chase, because he gave us his sympathy in 1858 when scarcely any other distinguished man did. —*To Samuel Galloway, March 24, 1860.* VI, 8.
4.—If he [Chase] becomes President, all right. I hope we may never have a worse man. I have all along clearly seen his plan of strengthening himself. Whenever he sees that an important matter is troubling me, if I am compelled to decide it in a way to give offense to a man of some influence he always ranged himself in opposition to me and persuades the victim

that he would have arranged it differently. . . . I am entirely indifferent to his success or failure in these schemes; so long as he does his duty as head of the Treasury Department.—*To John Hay, Oct. 18, 1863.* Hay, 100.

5.—I suppose he [Chase] will, like the bluebottle fly, lay his eggs in every rotten spot he can find.—*To John Hay, Oct. 28, 1863.* Hay, 110.

6.—I fully concur with you that neither of us can be justly held responsible for what our respective friends may do without our instigation or countenance; and I assure you, as you have assured me, that no assault has been made upon you by my instigation or with my countenance. Whether you shall remain at the head of the Treasury Department is a question which I will not allow myself to consider from any standpoint other than my judgment of the public service, and, in that view, I do not perceive occasion for a change.—*To Sec. Chase, Feb. 29, 1864.* X, 26.

7.—I will no longer continue the association [with Chase]. I am ready and willing to resign the office of President, and let you have Mr. Hamlin for your President, but I will not longer endure the state I have been in.—*To group of senators, June 30, 1864.* War Years III, 115.

Chase, Salmon P., resignation of, accepted—Your resignation of the office of Secretary of the Treasury . . . is accepted. Of all I have said in commendation of your ability and fidelity I have nothing to unsay; and yet you and I have reached a point of mutual embarrassment in our official relations which it seems cannot be overcome or longer sustained consistently with the public service.—*To Sec. Chase, June 30, 1864.* X, 140.

Chestnut Horse—*See* HORSECHESTNUT AND CHESTNUT HORSE.

Chicago, Republicans of, thanked—It gives me peculiar pleasure to find an opportunity under such favorable circumstances to return my thanks for the gallant support that the Republicans of the city of Chicago and of the state gave to the cause in which we were all engaged in the late momentous struggle in Illinois. —*Speech, Chicago, March 1, 1859.* V, 114.

Chicago Convention (1864), may swing toward violence—*See* PEOPLE, opposed to violence.

Chicago Platform (1860)—*See* NOMINATION OF 1860, accepted.

See POLITICAL PLATFORMS, proposals for 1860 rejected.

Chicago Times, "blind rage" of—In its blind rage to assail me, it has seized upon a vague recollection of

[Congressman John] Henry's vote, and appropriated it to me. I scarcely think anyone is quite vile enough to make such a charge in such terms, without some slight belief in the truth of it.—*To J. Medill, June 25, 1858.* Angle, 180.

Chicago Times, embarrassed by suspension of—In regard to the order of Gen. Burnside suspending the Chicago *Times,* now nearly a year ago, I can only say I was embarrassed with the question between what was due to the military service on the one hand, and the liberty of the press on the other, and I believe it was the dispatch of Senator Trumbull and yourself, added to the proceedings of the meeting which it brought me, that turned the scale in favor of my revoking the order.—*To I. N. Arnold, May 25, 1864.* X, 108.

See FREEDOM OF OPINION.

Chicago Times, "not a word of truth"—*See* MEXICAN WAR, voting record explained, 6.

Chicago Times, story of—Upon the repeal of the Missouri Compromise, the Democratic newspapers at Chicago went over to the opposition. Thereupon the *Times* was established by friends of the administration, Senator Douglas being the most prominent in establishing it. . . . On the political separation between Mr. Buchanan and Senator Douglas, the *Times* adhered to the senator, and was the ablest paper in his support through his senatorial contest with Mr. Lincoln.—*To editor of Washington* Chronicle, *June 6, 1863.* VIII, 393.

Chicago Times, suspension of, should end—I have received additional dispatches, which, with former ones, induce me to believe we should revoke or suspend the order suspending the Chicago *Times.*—*To Sec. Stanton, June 4, 1863.* VIII, 290.

Chicago Tribune, editor of, rebuked—And you [Joseph] Medill, you are acting like a coward. You and your *Tribune* has had more influence than any other paper in the Northwest in making this war. You can influence great masses, and yet you cry to be spared at a moment when your cause is suffering.—*To Mr. Medill, 1864.* McClure, 188.

Chicago Tribune, grateful to—Herewith is a little draft to pay for your daily another year from today. I suppose I shall take the *Press & Tribune* so long as it and I both live, unless I become unable to pay for it. In its devotion to our cause always, and to me personally last year, I owe it a debt of gratitude, which I fear I shall never be able to pay.—*To* Press & Tribune, *June 15, 1859.* Hertz II, 755.

Children, "good things"—*See* COLONIZATION, appeal for, to colored men.

Children of Israel—*See* SLAVERY, Egypt's experience with.

China, bows to the West—The rebellion which has long been flagrant in China has at last been suppressed, with the cooperating good offices of this government and the other western commercial states. . . . China seems to be accepting with hearty good will the conventional laws which regulate commercial and social intercourse among the western nations.—*Fourth annual message, Dec. 6, 1864.* X, 287.

China, claims against—I repeat the recommendation of my predecessor . . . in regard to the disposition of the surplus which will probably remain after satisfying the claims of American citizens against China pursuant to the awards of the commissioners under the act of the 3d of March, 1859. If, however, it should not be deemed advisable to carry that recommendation into effect, I would suggest that authority be given for investing the principal . . . in good securities, with a view to the satisfaction of such other just claims of our citizens against China as are not unlikely to arise hereafter in the course of our extensive trade with that empire.—*First annual message, Dec. 3, 1861.* VII, 32.

Choate, Rufus, calls Declaration "string of glittering generalities"—*See* DECLARATION OF INDEPENDENCE, hostility toward, 5.

Christian Charity—*See* MISSOURI, way to peace in, 2.

Christian Commission, commended—Your Christian and benevolent undertaking for the benefit of the soldiers is too obviously proper and praiseworthy to admit of any difference of opinion.—*To George H. Stuart, Dec. 12, 1861.* Hertz II, 846.
2.—I cannot withhold my approval of the meeting [sponsored by the Christian Commission] and its worthy objects.—*To Rev. Alexander Reed, Feb. 22, 1863.* VIII, 217.
3.—The Christian Commission, with all its Christian and benevolent labors.—*Speech, Philadelphia, June 16, 1864.* X, 127.

Christian Duty—*See* SLAVERY, Christian duty and.

Christian Faith—*See* INDIAN TRIBES, friendlier relations with, foreseen.

Christianity, attitude toward—*See* RELIGION, attitude toward.

Church, at odds on slavery—*See* SLAVERY, churches wrangle and crack.

Church, Christian charity urged—It seems . . . there is danger of the different religious denominations having some collision in their ministering among the colored people about Port Royal and elsewhere. I should think each church should minister according to its own rules, without interference by others differing from them; and if there still be difficulties about places of worship, a real Christian charity and forbearance on the part of all might obviate it.—*To S. Peck, Sept. 29, 1862.* Hertz II, 884.

Church, government must not run—The United States Government must not . . . undertake to run the churches. When an individual in a church or out of it becomes dangerous to the public interest, he must be checked; but let the churches, as such, take care of themselves. It will not do for the United States to appoint trustees, supervisors or other agents for the churches.—*To Gen. S. R. Curtis, Jan. 2, 1863.* VIII, 169.
2.—I have never interfered, nor thought of interfering, as to who shall or shall not preach in any church; nor have I knowingly or believingly tolerated anyone else to so interfere by my authority.—*To O. D. Filley, Dec. 22, 1863.* IX, 270.
3.—I will not have control of any church on any side. —*To O. D. Filley, Dec. 22, 1863.* IX, 271.
4.—In no event was anyone to interfere, by my authority, as to who should or should not preach in any church.—*Indorsement on petition, Dec. 22, 1863.* IX, 271.
5.—If the military have military need of the church building, let them keep it; otherwise let them get out of it, and leave it and its owners alone except for causes that justify the arrest of anyone.—*Memorandum, March 4, 1864.* X, 30.
6.—My view is that the United States should not appoint trustees for, or in any way take charge of, any church as such.—*Indorsement, March 15, 1864.* X, 42.
7.—I say again, if there is no military need for the building [church at Memphis], leave it alone, neither putting any one in nor out of it, except on finding some one preaching or practicing treason, in which case lay hands upon him just as if he were doing the same thing in any other building or in the streets or highways.—*Indorsement, May 13, 1864.* X, 99.

Church, insulted by "professedly holy men of South"—When, a year or two ago, those professedly holy men of the South met in the semblance of prayer and devotion, and, in the name of Him who said, "As ye would all men should do unto you, do ye even so unto them," appealed to the Christian world to aid them in doing to a whole race of men as they would have no man do unto themselves, to my way of thinking they contemned and insulted God and his church far more than did Satan when he tempted the Saviour with the kingdoms of the earth. The devil was no more false, and far less hypocritical. But let me forbear, remembering it is also written, "Judge not lest ye be judged."—*To Dr. Ide and others, May 30, 1864.* X, 110.

Church, opposed to Lincoln—There was the strangest combination of church influence against me [as a candidate for congressional nomination]. Baker [Lincoln's opponent] is a Campbellite; and therefore, as I suppose, with few exceptions got all that church. My wife has some relations in the Presbyterian churches, and some with the Episcopal churches; and therefore, wherever it would tell, I was set down as either the one or the other, while it was everywhere contended that no Christian ought to go for me, because I belonged to no church, was suspected of being a deist and had talked about fighting a duel.—*To M. Morris, March 26, 1843.* I, 262.

Church, gratitude toward—I have had great cause for gratitude for the support so unanimously given by all Christian denominations of the country.—*Reply to Baptist delegation, May 14, 1864.* X, 101.

Church, service of—*See* METHODIST CHURCH, thanked, 2.

Cincinnati, characterized—Good old Cincinnati.—*Speech, Cincinnati, Feb. 12, 1861.* VI, 116.

Cincinnati Platform (1856), Douglas and Dred Scott decision—*See* JUDICIAL DECISIONS, Douglas's attitude toward, 1, 3, 9.

Circuit Courts, proposes change in—*See* SUPREME COURT, modifications suggested.

Civil and Religious Liberty.—*See* LIBERTY, CIVIL AND RELIGIOUS.

Civil Liberty—*See,* LIBERTY, CIVIL.

Civil War; aftermath feared—We may congratulate ourselves that this cruel war is nearing its end. It has cost a vast amount of treasure and blood. . . . It has indeed been a trying hour for the Republic; but I see in the near future a crisis approaching that unnerves me and causes me to tremble for the safety of my country. As a result of the war, corporations have been enthroned and an era of corruption in high places will follow, and the money power of the country will endeavor to prolong its reign by working upon the prejudices of the people until all wealth is aggregated in a few hands, and the Republic is destroyed. I feel at this moment more anxiety for the

safety of my country than ever before, even in the midst of war.—No date. Hertz II, 954.

Civil War, Albany resolutions on—The resolutions [adopted at Albany, May 16], as I understand them, are resolvable into two propositions—first, the expression of a purpose to sustain the cause of the Union, to secure peace through victory, and to support the administration in every constitutional and lawful measure to suppress the rebellion; and, secondly, a declaration of censure upon the administration for supposed unconstitutional action, such as the making of military arrests. And from the two propositions a third is deduced, which is that the gentlemen composing the meeting are resolved on doing their part to maintain our common government and country, despite the folly or wickedness, as they may conceive, of my administration. The position is eminently patriotic and as such I thank the meeting, and congratulate the nation for it. My own purpose is the same; so that the meeting and myself have a common object, and can have no difference, except in the choice of means or measures for effecting that object. —*To Erastus Corning and others, June 12, 1863.* VIII, 289.

See DEMOCRATIC PARTY, attitude of, toward war effort, 1.

Civil War, army reduced by "absenteeism"—Nothing is operating so ruinously upon us everywhere as "absenteeism." It positively will not do for me to grant leaves of absence in cases not sufficient to procure them under the regular rules. It would astonish you to know the extent of the evil of "absenteeism." We scarcely have more than half the men we are paying on the spot for service anywhere.—*To T. J. Henderson, Dec. 20, 1862.* Lapsley II, 223.

See ARMY DESERTION, serious evil.

Civil War, begun on unequal terms—The rebellion thus begun soon ran into the present Civil War; and, in certain respects, it began on very unequal terms between the parties. The insurgents had been preparing for it more than thirty years, while the government had taken no steps to resist them. The former had carefully considered all the means which could be turned to their account. It undoubtedly was a well-pondered reliance with them that in their own unrestricted effort to destroy the Union, Constitution and law, all together, the government would, in great degree, be restrained by the same Constitution and law from arresting their progress.—*To Erastus Corning and others, June 12, 1863.* VIII, 301.

Civil War, better days ahead—I hope that, far advanced in life as many of you are, you will, gentlemen, yet live to see better days than those which it is now our misfortune to behold.—*To visiting veterans of 1812, July 4, 1863.* Hertz II, 893.

Civil War, both sides surprised—When the war began three years ago neither party, nor any man, expected it would last till now. Each looked for the end, in some way, long ere today. Neither did any anticipate that domestic slavery would be much affected by the war. But here we are; the war has not ended, and slavery has been much affected—how much, needs not now be recounted.—*Speech, Baltimore, April 18, 1864.* X, 76.
2.—Neither party expected for the war the magnitude or the duration it has already attained. Neither anticipated that the cause of the conflict might cease with, or even before, the conflict itself should cease. Each looked for an earlier triumph, and a result less fundamental and astounding.—*Second inaugural, March 4, 1865.* XI, 45.

Civil War, Burdens of, cheerfully borne—It is believed . . . that by no people were the burdens incident to a great war ever more cheerfully borne [than by Americans in this war].—*Third annual message, Dec. 8, 1863.* IX, 233.

Civil War, contrasting aims in—On the side of the Union it [Civil War] is a struggle to maintain in the world that form and substance of government whose leading object is to elevate the condition of men, lift artificial burdens from all shoulders and clear the paths of laudable pursuits for all; to afford all an unfettered start and a fair chance in the race of life. This is the leading object of the government for whose existence we contend.—*Message to Congress, July 4, 1861.* VI, 321.
2.—I look upon it [Civil War] as an attempt on the one hand to overwhelm and destroy the national existence, while on our part we are striving to maintain the government and institutions of our fathers, to enjoy them ourselves, and transmit them to our children and our childrens' children, forever. To do this the constitutional administration of our government must be sustained.—*Speech to 148th Ohio regiment, Aug. 31, 1864.* X, 208.
3.—The preservation of our Union was not the sole avowed object for which the war was commenced. It was commenced for precisely the reverse object—to destroy the Union.—*Unfinished letter to Isaac M. Schermerhorn, Sept. 12, 1864.* X, 221.

See CIVIL WAR, slavery cause of, 4.

Civil War, dark days in—*See* CRITICAL DAYS, confront North.

Civil War, dedication to task of winning—It is for us, the living . . . to be dedicated here to the unfinished work which they who fought here have thus far so nobly advanced. It is . . . for us to be here dedicated to the great task remaining before us—that from these honored dead we take increased devotion to that cause for which they gave the last full measure of devotion; that we here highly resolve that these dead shall not have died in vain; that this nation, under God, shall have a new birth of freedom; and that government of the people, by the people, for the people shall not perish from the earth.—*Gettysburg Address, Nov. 19, 1863.* IX, 210.

Civil War, determination to continue—I hope there will be no trouble, but I will make the South a graveyard rather than see a slavery gospel triumph, or successful secession lose this government to the cause of the people and representative institutions.—*To W. H. Herndon, winter, 1861.* Townsend, 11.
2.—War has been made, and continues to be, an indispensable means to this end [preservation of the Union.] A practical reacknowledgment of the national authority would render the war unnecessary, and it would at once cease. If, however, resistance continues, the war must also continue; and it is impossible to foresee all the incidents which may attend and all the ruin which may follow it. Such as may seem indispensable, or may obviously promise great efficiency toward ending the struggle, must and will come.—*Message to Congress, March 6, 1862.* VII, 114.
3.—I expect to maintain this contest until successful, or till I die, or am conquered, or my term expires, or Congress or the country forsake me; and I would publicly appeal for this new force [100,000 men] were it not that I fear a general panic and stampede would follow, so hard it is to have a thing understood as it really is.—*To Sec. Seward, June 30, 1862.* VII, 241.
4.—What would you do in my position? Would you drop the war where it is? Or would you prosecute it in the future with elder-stalk squirts charged with rose water? Would you deal lighter blows rather than heavier ones? . . . I shall do all I can to save the government, which is my sworn duty as well as my personal inclination.—*To Cuthbert Bullitt, July 28, 1862.* VII, 297.

See CIVIL WAR, when will it end?

Civil War, extra-legal steps at beginning of—*See* WAR POWER, use of, defended, 2.

Civil War, fall of 1862 in review—The kindest words coming from Europe [in the fall of 1862] were uttered in accents of pity that we were too blind to surrender a hopeless cause. Our commerce was suffering greatly by a few armed vessels built upon and furnished from foreign shores, and we were threatened with such additions from the same quarter as would sweep our trade from the sea and raise our blockade. We had failed to elicit from European governments anything hopeful upon this subject.—*Third annual message, Dec. 8, 1863. IX, 245.*

Civil War, foreign intervention averted—It has pleased Almighty God to vouchsafe signal victories to the land and naval forces engaged in suppressing an internal rebellion, and at the same time to avert from our country the dangers of foreign intervention and invasion.—*Thanksgiving proclamation, April 10, 1862. VII, 144.*

Civil War, foreign nations' attitude toward—The forbearance of this government has been so extraordinary and so long continued as to lead some foreign nations to shape their action as if they supposed the early destruction of our national Union was probable. While this on discovery gave the executive some concern, he is now happy to say that the sovereignty and rights of the United States are now everywhere practically respected by foreign powers, and a general sympathy with the country is manifest throughout the world.—*Message to Congress, July 4, 1861. VI, 311.*

2.—You will not be surprised to learn that, in the peculiar exigencies of the times, our intercourse with foreign nations has been attended with profound solicitude, chiefly turning upon our own domestic affairs. A disloyal portion of the American people have, during the whole year, been engaged in an attempt to divide and destroy the Union. A nation which endures factious domestic division is exposed to disrespect abroad; and one party, if not both, is sure, sooner or later, to invoke foreign intervention. Nations thus tempted are not always able to resist the counsels of seeming expediency and ungenerous ambition, although measures adopted under such influences seldom fail to be unfortunate and injurious to those adopting them—*First annual message, Dec. 3, 1861. VII, 28.*

3.—The disloyal citizens of the United States who have offered the ruin of our country in return for the aid and comfort which they have invoked abroad have received less patronage and encouragement than they probably expected. If it were just to suppose, as the insurgents have seemed to assume, that foreign nations in this case, discarding all moral, social and treaty obligations, would act solely and selfishly for the most speedy restoration of commerce, including especially the acquisition of cotton, those nations appear as yet not to have seen their way to their object more directly or clearly through the destruction than through the preservation of the Union. If we could dare to believe that foreign nations are actuated by no higher principle than this, I am quite sure a sound argument could be made to show them that they can reach their aim more readily and easily by aiding to crush this rebellion than by giving encouragement to it.—*First annual message, Dec. 3, 1861. VII, 29.*

4.—The principal lever relied on by the insurgents for exciting foreign nations to hostility against us . . . is the embarrassment of commerce. Those nations, however, not improbably saw from the first that it was the Union which made as well our foreign as our domestic commerce. They can scarcely have failed to perceive that the effort for disunion produces the existing difficulty, and that one strong nation promises more durable peace and a more extensive, valuable and reliable commerce than can the same nation broken into hostile fragments.—*First annual message, Dec. 3, 1861. VII, 29.*

5.—I venture to hope it will appear that we have practiced prudence and liberality toward foreign powers, averting causes of irritation, and with firmness maintaining our own rights and honor.—*First annual message, Dec. 3, 1861. VII, 30.*

6.—I cannot imagine any European power would dare to recognize and aid the Southern Confederacy if it becomes clear that the Confederacy stands for slavery and the Union for freedom.—*Interview, Carl Schurz, Jan. 1862. Schurz II, 309.*

7.—If the condition of our relations with other nations is less gratifying than it has usually been at former periods, it is certainly more satisfactory than a nation so unhappily distracted as we might reasonably have apprehended. In the month of June last there were some grounds to expect that the maritime powers which at the beginning of our domestic difficulties so unwisely and unnecessarily, as we think, recognized the insurgents, would soon recede from that position, which has proved only less injurious to themselves than to our own country. But the temporary reverses which afterwards befell the national arms and which were exaggerated by our own disloyal citizens aboard, have hitherto delayed that act of simple justice.—*Second annual message, Dec. 1, 1862. VIII, 93.*

8.—The civil war, which has radically changed for the moment the occupations and habits of the American people, has necessarily disturbed the social condition and affected very deeply the prosperity of the nations with which we have carried on a commerce that has been steadily increasing throughout a period of half a century. It has at the same time excited political ambitions and apprehensions which have produced a profound agitation throughout the civilized world. In this unusual agitation we have forborne from taking part in any controversy between foreign states and between parties or factions in such states. We have attempted no propagandism and acknowledged no revolution. . . . Our struggle has been, of course, contemplated by foreign nations with reference less to its own merits than to its supposed and often exaggerated effects and consequences resulting to those nations themselves.—*Second annual message, Dec. 1, 1862.* VIII, 94.

9.—I have, therefore, reckoned upon the forbearance of nations. Circumstances—to some of which you kindly allude—induce me especially to expect that if justice and good faith should be practiced by the United States, they would encounter no hostile influence on the part of Great Britain.—*To workers of Manchester, Jan. 19, 1863.* VIII, 195.

10.—What I propose is in strict accord with international law, and is therefore unobjectionable; whilst, if it does no other good, it will contribute to sustain a considerable portion of the present British ministry in their places who, if displaced, are sure to be replaced by others more unfavorable to us—*Instructions to Secretary of Navy, July 25, 1863.* XI, 128.

11.—In the midst of a civil war of unequalled magnitude and severity, which has sometimes seemed to foreign states to invite and provoke their aggression, peace has been preserved with all nations.—*Thanksgiving Proclamation, Oct. 3, 1863.* IX, 151.

12.—We remain in peace and friendship with foreign powers. The efforts of disloyal citizens of the United States to involve us in foreign wars to aid an inexcusable insurrection have been unavailing. Her Britannic Majesty's government, as was justly expected, have exercised their authority to prevent the departure of new hostile expeditions from British ports. The emperor of France has by a like proceeding promptly vindicated the neutrality which he proclaimed at the beginning of the contest.—*Third annual message, Dec. 8, 1863.* IX, 224.

13.—It is possible that if it were a new and open question, the maritime powers, with the lights they now enjoy, would not concede the privileges of a naval belligerent to the insurgents of the United States, destitute, as they are, and always have been, equally of ships of war and of ports and harbors. Disloyal emissaries have been neither less assiduous

nor more successful during the last year than they were before that time in their efforts, under favor of that privilege, to embroil our country in foreign wars. The desire and determination of the government of the maritime states to defeat that design are believed to be as sincere as, and cannot be more correct than, our own.—*Fourth annual message, Dec. 6, 1864.* X, 288.

Civil War, Honor to home front—See HOME FRONT, honor to those who serve.

Civil War, hundred-day volunteers thanked—The term of one hundred days for which volunteers from the states of Indiana, Illinois, Iowa and Wisconsin volunteered . . . to aid in the campaign of Gen. Sherman having expired, the President directs an official acknowledgment to be made of their patriotic service. It was their good fortune to render efficient service in the brilliant operations in the southwest, and to contribute to the victories of the national arms over the rebel forces in Georgia under command of Johnston and Hood. On all occasions and in every service to which they were assigned their duty as patriotic volunteers was performed with alacrity and courage, for which they are entitled to, and are hereby tendered the national thanks.—*Executive order, Oct. 1, 1864.* X, 237.

Civil War, Indiana troops thanked—The thanks of the nation will follow you, and may God's blessing rest upon you now and forever.—*Response to 12th Indiana regiment, reported by the New York* Evening Post, *May 15, 1862.* VII, 165.

Civil War, issue in hands of dissatisfied citizens—In your hands, my dissatisfied fellow-countrymen, and not in mine, is the momentous issue of civil war. The government will not assail you. You can have no conflict without yourselves being aggressors. You have no oath registered in Heaven to destroy the government, while I shall have the most solemn one to "preserve, protect and defend" it.—*First inaugural, March 4, 1861.* Basler, 588.

2.—You can forbear the assault upon it [the government]; I cannot shrink from the defense of it. With you, not with me, is the solemn question of "Shall it be peace or a sword?"—*Original draft of first inaugural, changed at Seward's suggestion.* R.T.L.

Civil War, man power unimpaired by—The election [of 1864] has exhibited another fact, not less valuable to be known—the fact that we do not approach exhaustion in the most important branch of the national resources—that of living men. While it is melancholy to reflect that the war has filled so many graves, and carried mourning to so many hearts, it is some relief to know that, compared with the surviving, the fallen have been so few. While corps, and divisions, and brigades, and regiments, have been formed and fought, and dwindled and gone out of existence, a great majority of the men who composed them are still living. The same is true of the naval service. The election returns prove this. So many voters could not else be found.—*Fourth annual message, Dec. 6, 1864.* X, 305.

2.—The important fact remains demonstrated that we have more men now than we had when the war began; that we are not exhausted, nor in process of exhaustion; that we are gaining strength, and may, if need be, maintain the contest indefinitely.—*Fourth annual message, Dec. 6, 1864.* X, 307.

Civil War, "most terrible"—War, at the best, is terrible, and this war of ours, in its magnitude and its duration, is one of the most terrible. It has deranged business, totally in many localities, and partially in all localities. It has destroyed property and ruined homes; it has produced a national debt and taxation unprecedented, at least in this country; it has carried mourning to almost every home, until it can almost be said that the "Heavens are hung in black."—*Speech, Philadelphia, June 16, 1864.* X, 127.

Civil War, moves country won't allow—The country will not allow us to send our whole western force down the Mississippi while the enemy sacks Louisville and Cincinnati. Probably it would be better if the country would allow this, but it will not. I confidently believed last September that we could end the war by allowing the enemy to go to Harrisburg and Philadelphia, only that we could not keep down mutiny, and utter demoralization among the Pennsylvanians. And this, though unhandy sometimes, is not at all strange. I presume if an army was starting today for New Orleans, and you confidently believed that St. Louis would be sacked in consequence, you would be in favor of stopping such army.—*To Judge S. Treat, St. Louis, Nov. 19, 1862.* Angle, 309.

Civil War, national progress in spite of—Needful diversions of wealth and of strength from the fields of peaceful industry to the national defense have not arrested the plow, the shuttle or the ship; the ax has enlarged the borders of our settlements, and the mines, as well of iron and coal as of the precious metals, have yielded even more abundantly than heretofore. Population has steadily increased notwithstanding the waste that has been made in the camp, the siege and battlefield, and the country, rejoicing in the consciousness of augmented strength and vigor,

is permitted to expect continuance of years with large increase of freedom.—*Thanksgiving Proclamation, Oct. 3, 1863.* IX, 152.

2.—It is easy to see that under the sharp discipline of civil war the nation is beginning a new life.—*Third annual message, Dec. 8, 1863.* IX, 231.

3.—Voluntary contributions . . . [for soldiers give] proof that the national resources are not all exhausted, and that the national spirit of patriotism is even firmer and stronger than at the commencement of the war.—*Speech, Philadelphia, June 16, 1864.* X, 128.

4.—It is of noteworthy interest that the steady expansion of population, improvement, and government institutions over the new and unoccupied portions of our country have scarcely been checked, much less impeded or destroyed, by our great civil war, which at first glance would seem to have absorbed almost the entire energies of the nation.—*Fourth annual message, Dec. 6, 1864.* X, 298.

5.—The national resources, then, are unexhausted, and, as we believe, inexhaustible.—*Fourth annual message, Dec. 6, 1864.* X, 307.

Civil War, no armistice acceptable—An armistice—a cessation of hostilities—is the end of the struggle, and the insurgents would be in peaceable possession of all that has been struggled for.—*Unfinished letter to Isaac M. Schermerhorn, Sept. 12, 1864.* X, 222.

Civil War, Ohio National Guard thanked—The term of one hundred days for which the National Guard of Ohio volunteered having expired, the President directs an official acknowledgment to be made of their patriotic and valuable services during the recent campaigns. . . . In the Valley of the Shenandoah, on the Peninsula, in the operations on the James river, around Petersburg and Richmond, in the battle of Monocacy and in the entrenchments at Washington and in other important services, the National Guard of Ohio performed with alacrity the duty of patriotic volunteers, for which they are entitled to and are hereby tendered through the governor of their state, the national thanks.—*Executive order, Sept. 10, 1864* X, 219.

Civil War, Ohio troops thanked—I thank you for your promptness in responding to the call for troops. Your services were never more needed than now.—*Remarks to Ohio regiment, June 11, 1864.* X, 124.

2.—I am greatly obliged to you, and to all who have come forward at the call of their country.—*Speech to 164th Ohio regiment, Aug. 18, 1864.* X, 199.

3.—For the services you have done in this great struggle in which we are all engaged, I present you sincere thanks for myself and the country.—*Speech to 166th Ohio regiment, Aug. 22, 1864.* X, 202.

4.—Permit me in the name of the people to thank you for the part you have taken in this struggle for the life of the nation.—*Speech to 148th Ohio regiment, Aug. 31, 1864.* X, 208.

See CIVIL WAR, Ohio National Guard thanked.

Civil War, people not aware of the seriousness of— See CIVIL WAR, strategy overemphasized.

Civil War, "people's contest"—See PEOPLE, Civil War their contest.

Civil War, President blamed if it fails—I certainly know that if the war fails, the administration fails, and that I will be blamed for it, whether I deserve it or not. And I ought to be blamed if I could do better. You think I could do better; therefore, you blame me already. I think I could not do better; therefore, I blame you for blaming me.—*To Gen. Schurz, Nov. 24, 1862.* VIII, 85.

Civil War, progress of—Maryland, Kentucky and Missouri, neither of which would promise a single soldier at first, have now an aggregate of not less than 40,000 in the field for the Union, while of their citizens certainly not more than a third of that number, and they of doubtful whereabouts and doubtful existence, are in arms against it.—*First annual message, Dec. 3, 1861.* VII, 53.

2.—Missouri is comparatively quiet, and, I believe, cannot again be overrun by the insurrectionists.—*First annual message, Dec. 3, 1861.* VII, 53.

3.—The cause of the Union is advancing steadily and certainly southward.—*First annual message, Dec. 3, 1861.* VII, 54.

4.—An insurgent force of about 1500 for months dominating the narrow peninsular region . . . and known as the eastern shore of Virginia, together with some contiguous parts of Maryland, have laid down their arms, and the people there have renewed their allegiance to and accepted the protection of the old flag. This leaves no armed insurrectionist north of the Potomac or east of the Chesapeake.—*First annual message, Dec. 3, 1861.* VII, 54.

5.—The signs look better. The Father of Waters again goes unvexed to the sea.—*To J. C. Conkling, Aug. 26, 1863.* IX, 100.

6.—Peace does not appear so distant as it did. I hope it will come soon; and so come as to be worth the keeping in all future time.—*To J. C. Conkling, Aug. 26, 1863.* IX, 101.

7.—The rebel borders are pressed still further back, and by the complete opening of the Mississippi the country dominated by the rebellion is divided into distinct parts, with no practical communications between them.—*Third annual message, Dec. 8, 1863.* IX, 246.

8.—Tennessee and Arkansas have been substantially cleared of insurgent control.—*Third annual message, Dec. 8, 1863.* IX, 246.

9.—The war continues. Since the last annual message all important lines and positions then occupied by our forces have been maintained and our arms have steadily advanced, thus liberating the regions left in the rear.—*Fourth annual message, Dec. 6, 1864.* X, 302.

10.—The progress of our arms, upon which all else chiefly depends, is as well known to the public as to myself, and it is, I trust, reasonably satisfactory and encouraging to all. With high hopes for the future, no prediction in regard to it is ventured.—*Second inaugural, March 4, 1865.* XI, 44.

Civil War, "prolonged indefinitely"—See GETTYSBURG, full advantage of victory sacrificed, 2.

Civil War, reluctant to accept—The world knows how reluctantly I accepted this issue of battle forced upon me on my advent to this place by the internal enemies of our country.—*Reply to Evangelical Lutherans, May 6, 1862.* VII, 154.

Civil War, results of, involve future—The struggle of today is not altogether for today; it is for the vast future also.—*First annual message, Dec. 3, 1861.* VII, 60.

2.—[This] important crisis . . . involves, in my judgment, not only the civil and religious liberties of our own dear land, but in a large degree the civil and religious liberties of mankind in many countries and through many ages.—*Response to Evangelical Lutherans, May 6, 1862.* VII, 154.

3.—It became necessary for me to choose whether . . . I should let the government fall at once into ruin, or whether . . . I would make an effort to save it with all its blessings for the present age and for posterity.—*Message to Congress, May 26, 1862.* VII, 196.

4.—May our children and our children's children for a thousand generations continue to enjoy the benefits conferred upon us by a united country; and have cause yet to rejoice under those glorious institutions bequeathed us by Washington and his compeers!—*Speech, Frederick, Md., Oct. 4, 1862.* XI, 125.

5.—Whatever shall tend to turn our thoughts from the unreasoning and uncharitable passions, prejudices, and jealousies incident to a great national trouble such as ours, and to fix them upon the vast and long-enduring consequences, for weal or woe, which are to result from the struggle . . . cannot but be well for all of us.—*To Rev. Alexander Reed, Feb. 22, 1863.* VIII, 217.

6.—Thanks to all [for recent victories]; for the great Republic—for the principle it lives by and keeps alive—for man's vast future.—*To J. C. Conkling, Aug. 26, 1863.* IX, 101.

7.—It is not merely for today, but for all time to come, that we should perpetuate for our children's children that great and free government which we have enjoyed all our lives. . . . It is in order that each one of you may have, through this free government which we have enjoyed, an open field and a fair chance for your industry, enterprise, and intelligence; that you may all have equal privileges in the race of life, with all its desirable human aspirations. It is for this the struggle should be maintained, that we may not lose our birthright. . . . The nation is worth fighting for, to secure such an inestimable jewel.—*Speech to 166th Ohio regiment, Aug. 22, 1864.* X, 202.

Civil War, situation at start of—Immediately afterward [fall of Fort Sumter] all the roads and avenues to this city were obstructed, and the capital was put into the condition of a siege. The mails in every direction were stopped and the lines of telegraph cut off by the insurgents, and military and naval forces which had been called out by the government for the defense of Washington were prevented from reaching the city by organized and combined treasonable resistance in the state of Maryland. There was no adequate and effective organization for the public defense.—*Message to Congress, May 26, 1862.* VII, 189.

2.—The several departments of government at that time contained so large a number of disloyal persons that it would have been impossible to provide safely through official agents only for the performance of the duties thus confided to citizens favorably known for their ability, loyalty and patriotism. The several orders issued upon these occurrences were transmitted by private messengers, who pursued a circuitous way to the seaboard cities, inland across the states of Pennsylvania and Ohio and the northern lakes. I believe that by these and similar measures taken in that crisis, some of which were without any authority of law, the government was saved from overthrow. I am not aware that a dollar of the public funds thus confided to unofficial persons was either lost or wasted, although apprehensions of such misdirection occurred to me as objections to those proceedings, and were necessarily overruled.—*Message to Congress, May 26, 1862.* VII, 192.

3.—Their [insurgents'] sympathizers pervaded all departments of the government and nearly all communities of the people. From this material under cover of "liberty of speech," "liberty of the press" and "*habeas corpus*" they hoped to keep on foot amongst us a most efficient corps of spies, informers, suppliers, and aiders and abettors of their cause in a thousand ways. They knew that in such times as they were inaugurating, by the Constitution itself the *habeas corpus* might be suspended; but they also knew they had friends who would make a question as to who was to suspend it; meanwhile their spies and others might remain at large to help their cause.—*To Erastus Corning, June 12, 1863.* VIII, 301.

See WAR POWERS, use of, defended.

Civil War, slavery, cause of—Without the institution of slavery, and the colored race as a basis, the [civil] war could not have an existence.—*Speech to free colored men, Aug. 14, 1862.* VIII, 3.

2.—Slavery is the root of the rebellion, or at least its *sine qua non.* The ambition of politicians may have instigated them to act, but they would have been impotent without slavery as their instrument.—*Reply to committee from Chicago churches, Sept. 13, 1862.* VIII, 32.

3.—Without slavery the rebellion could never have existed; without slavery it could not continue.—*Second annual message, Dec. 1, 1862.* VIII, 117.

4.—One eighth of the whole population [on the eve of war] were colored slaves, not distributed generally over the Union, but localized in the southern part of it. These slaves constituted a peculiar and powerful interest. All knew that this interest was somehow the cause of the war. To strengthen, perpetuate and extend this interest was the object for which the insurgents would rend the Union even by war, while the government claimed no right to do more than to restrict the territorial enlargement of it.—*Second inaugural, March 4, 1865.* XI, 45.

See SLAVERY, sole threat to Union.

Civil War, some dazzled by—Some of our Northerners seem bewildered and dazzled by the excitement of the hour. Doolittle seems inclined to think that this war is to result in the entire abolition of slavery. Old Col. Hamilton, a venerable and most respectable gentleman, impresses upon me most earnestly the propriety of enlisting the slaves in our army.—*To John Hay, May 7, 1861.* War Years I, 291.

Civil War, strategy overemphasized—The fact is the people have not yet made up their minds that we are at war with the South. They have not buckled down to the determination to fight this war through; for they have got the idea into their heads that we are going to get out of this fix somehow by strategy! That's the word—strategy! Gen. McClellan thinks he is going to whip the rebels by strategy; and the army has got the same notion. They have no idea that the war is to be carried on and put through by hard, tough fighting that will hurt somebody, and no headway is going to be made while this delusion lasts. . . . Gen. McClellan is responsible for the delusion that is untoning the whole army—that the South can be conquered by strategy.—*To Mary A. Livermore and friend, Sept., 1862. War Years I, 553.*

Civil War, suggested strategy for—I state my general idea of this war to be that we have the greater numbers, and the enemy has the greater facility of concentrating forces upon points of collision; that we must fail unless we can find some way of making our advantage an overmatch for his; and that this can only be done by menacing him with superior forces at different points at the same time, so that we can safely attack one or both if he makes no change; and if he weakens one to strengthen the other, forbear to attack the strengthened one, gaining so much.—*To Gen. Buell, Jan. 13, 1862. VII, 83.*
2.—If [the enemy] makes a stand at Winchester, moving neither north nor south, I would fight him there, on the idea that if we cannot beat him when he bears the wastage of coming to us, we can never bear the wastage of going to him. This proposition is a simple truth and is too important to be lost sight of for a moment. In coming to us he tenders us an advantage which we should not waive.—*To Gen. McClellan, Oct. 13, 1862. VIII, 59.*
3.—The two armies are face to face, with a narrow river between them. Our communications are shorter and safer than those of the enemy. For this reason we can, with equal powers, fret him more than he can us. . . . While he remains intact I do not think we should take the disadvantage of attacking him in his entrenchments; but we should continually harass and menace him, so that he shall have no leisure nor safety in sending away detachments. If he weakens himself, then pitch into him.—*Indorsement on Hooker's plan against Richmond, April 11, 1863. VIII, 243.*

Civil War, thanks to civilians—Honor also to the citizen who cares for his brother in the field, and serves, as he best can, the same cause—honor to him only less than to him who braves, for the common good, the storms of Heaven and the storms of battle.—*To George Opdyke and others, Dec. 2, 1863. IX, 216.*

Civil War, to make "short and decisive"—It is now recommended that you give the legal means for making this contest a short and decisive one; that you place at the control of the government for the work at least 400,000 men and $400,000,000.—*Message to Congress, July 4, 1861. VI, 311.*

Civil War, western victories—You propose also to celebrate our western victories. Freed from the apprehension of wounding the just sensibilities of brave soldiers fighting elsewhere, it would be exceedingly agreeable to me to join in a suitable acknowledgment to those of the great West with whom I was born and have passed my life.—*To George Opdyke and others, Dec. 2, 1863. IX, 215.*

Civil War, when will it end?—If I had 50,000 additional troops here now, I believe I could substantially close the war in two weeks.—*To governors, July 3, 1862. VII, 254.*
2.—Still, let us not be over sanguine of a speedy, final triumph. Let us be quite sober.—*To J. C. Conkling, Aug. 26, 1863. IX, 102.*
3.—If we can hold Chattanooga and East Tennessee, I think the rebellion must dwindle and die.—*To Gen. Rosecrans, Sept. 4, 1863. IX, 154.*
4.—It is a pertinent question, often asked in the mind privately, when is the war to end? . . . I do not wish to name a day, a month or year, when it will end. . . . We accepted this war for an object, a worthy object, and the war will end when that object is attained. Under God, I hope it will never end until that time. Speaking of the present campaign, Gen. Grant is reported to have said, "I am going through on this line if it takes all summer." The war has taken three years; it was begun or accepted upon the line of restoring the national authority over the whole national domain, and for the American people, as far as my knowledge enables me to speak, I say we are going through on this line if it takes three years more.—*Speech, Philadelphia, June 16, 1864. X, 129.*
5.—The war will cease on the part of the government whenever it shall have ceased on the part of those who began it.—*Fourth annual message, Dec. 6, 1864. X, 310.*

See CIVIL WAR, determination to continue, 1.

Civil War, why South wins battles—You ask, "Why is it the North with her great armies so often is found with inferiority of numbers face to face with the armies of the South?" . . . I suppose the cause of its continuance lies mainly [in the fact that] the enemy holds the interior and we the exterior lines; and that we operate where people convey information to the enemy, while he operates where they convey none to us.—*To Count A. de Gasparin, Aug. 4, 1862.* VII, 302.

Civil War, will end slavery if continued—The incidents of war cannot be avoided. If the war continues long, as it must if the object [preservation of the Union] be not sooner attained, the institution [slavery] in your states will be extinguished by mere friction and abrasion—by the mere incidents of war. It will be gone, and you will have nothing valuable in lieu of it. Much of its value is gone already.— *To border-state congressmen, July 12, 1862.* VII, 271.

Civil War, working people have most at stake in— *See* WORKING PEOPLE, have most at stake in war.

Civilization, Commerce and—*See* COMMERCE, resumption of, foreseen.

Civilization, high function of—To correct evils, great and small, which spring from want of sympathy, and from positive enmity among strangers, as nations or as individuals, is one of the highest functions of civilization.—*Speech, Milwaukee, Sept. 30, 1859.* V, 236.

Civilization, new country most favorable to—*See* EMANCIPATION (THOUGHT), new country favors.

Civilization, on continent depends on Union victory —*See* HONORARY DEGREE, thanks for.

"Claws Burnt Off to Gristle"—*See* PIERCE, FRANKLIN, cat's-paw.

See BUCHANAN, JAMES, "claws burnt off."

Clay, Henry, America's debt to—Our country is prosperous and powerful; but could it have been quite all it has been, and is, and is to be, without Henry Clay? Such a man the times have demanded, and such in the providence of God, was given us.—*Speech, Springfield, July 16, 1852.* II, 177.

Clay, Henry, death-bed scene—*See* WHIG PARTY, apple-sized tears from.

Clay, Henry, devotion of, to liberty—Mr. Clay's efforts in behalf of South Americans, and afterward in behalf of the Greeks, in the times of their respective struggles for civil liberty, are among the finest on record, upon the noblest of all themes, and bear ample corroboration of what I have said was his ruling passion—a love of liberty and right, unselfishly for their own sakes.—*Speech, Springfield, July 16, 1852.* II, 171.

Clay, Henry, devotion of, to Union—*See* UNION, Clay's devotion to.

Clay, Henry, disciple of—Finally the judge [Douglas] invokes against me the memory of Clay and Webster. They were great men, and men of great deeds. But where have I assailed them? For what is it that their life-long enemy shall now make profit by assuming to defend them against their life-long friend?—*Speech, Peoria, Oct. 16, 1854.* II, 261.

See CLAY, HENRY, slavery decried by, 4.

Clay, Henry, education of—Mr. Clay's education to the end of his life was comparatively limited. I say "to the end of his life," because I have understood that from time to time he added something to his education during the greater part of his whole life.— *Speech, Springfield, July 16, 1852.* II, 160.

See EDUCATION, opportunities for, in America.

Clay, Henry, eloquence of—Mr. Clay's eloquence did not consist, as many fine specimens of eloquence do, of types and figures, of antitheses and elegant arrangement of words and sentences, but rather of that deeply earnest and impassioned tone and manner which can proceed only from great sincerity, and a thorough conviction in the speaker of the justice and importance of his cause. This it is that truly touches the chords of sympathy; and those who heard Mr. Clay never failed to be moved by it, or ever after forgot the impression. All his efforts were made for practical effect. He never spoke merely to be heard.— *Speech, Springfield, July 16, 1852.* II, 163.
2.—Brightly, and captivatingly as it had previously shown, it was now perceived that his great eloquence was a mere embellishment, or at most a helping hand, to his inventive genius, and his devotion to his country in the day of her extreme peril.—*Speech, Springfield, July 16, 1852.* II, 171.

Clay, Henry, "lost" speech of—Several of his [Henry Clay's] speeches on these occasions [discussions of whether to declare war in 1812] were reported and are still extant, but the best of them all never was. During its delivery the reporters forgot their vocations, dropped their pens and sat enchanted from near the beginning to quite the close. The speech now lives only in the memory of a few old men, and the enthusiasm with which they cherish their recollection of it is absolutely astonishing.—*Speech, Springfield, July 16, 1852.* II, 166.
2.—The precise language of this ["lost"] speech we shall never know; but we do know—we cannot help knowing—that with deep pathos it pleaded the cause of the injured sailor, that it invoked the genius of the Revolution, that it apostrophized the names of Otis, of Henry, and of Washington, that it appealed to the

interest, the pride, the honor, and the glory of the nation, that it shamed and taunted the timidity of friends, that it scorned and scouted and withered the temerity of domestic foes, that it bearded and defied the British lion, and, rising and maddening in its course, it sounded the onset, till the charge, the shock, the steady struggle, the glorious victory, all passed in vivid review before the entranced hearers.—*Speech, Springfield, July 16, 1852.* II, 167.

Clay, Henry, Missouri Compromise and—*See* MISSOURI COMPROMISE, Clay engineered.

Clay, Henry, no chance for—Mr. Clay's chance for an election [to the Presidency] is just no chance at all. He might get New York, and that would have elected him in 1844, but it will not now, because he must now, at the least, lose Tennessee, which he had then, and in addition the fifteen new votes of Florida, Texas, Iowa and Wisconsin.—*To Archibald Williams, April 30, 1848.* II, 17.

Clay, Henry, Presidency escapes—In 1824 he [Clay] was first a candidate for the Presidency, and was defeated; and, although he was successively defeated for the same office in 1832 and 1844, there has never been a moment since 1824, till after 1848, when a very large proportion of the American people did not cling to him with an enthusiastic hope and purpose of still electing him to the Presidency. With other men, to be defeated was to be forgotten; but with him defeat was but a trifling incident, neither changing him nor the world's estimate of him. Even those of both political parties who have been preferred to him for the highest office have run far briefer courses than he, and left him still shining high in the heavens of the political world.—*Speech, Springfield, July 16, 1852.* II, 162.

Clay, Henry, responsible for compromise acts—*See* COMPROMISE OF 1850, Clay led in.

Clay, Henry, sectional attitude avoided—As a politician or statesman, no one was so habitually careful [as Clay] to avoid all sectional grounds. Whatever he did he did for the whole country. In the construction of his measures, he carefully surveyed every part of the field, and duly weighed every conflicting interest. —*Speech, Springfield, July 16, 1852.* II, 164.

Clay, Henry, slavery decried by—He [Henry Clay] was on principle and in feeling opposed to slavery. The very earliest, and one of the latest, public efforts of his life, separated by a period of more than 50 years, were both made in favor of gradual emancipation. He did not perceive that on a question of human right the negroes were to be excepted from the

human race. And yet Mr. Clay was the owner of slaves. Cast into life where slavery was already widely spread and deeply seated, he did not perceive, as I think no wise man has perceived, how it could be at once eradicated, without producing a greater evil even to the cause of human liberty itself. His feeling and his judgment, therefore, ever led him to oppose both extremes of opinion on the subject.—*Speech, Springfield, July 16, 1852.* II, 172.

2.—Not that he [Clay] hated slavery less, but that he loved the whole Union more.—*Speech, Bloomington, May 29, 1856.* Lapsley II, 267.

3.—They ["the hosts of slavery"] have slaughtered one of his [Clay's] most cherished measures [Missouri Compromise], and his ghost would arise to rebuke them.—*Speech, Bloomington, May 29, 1856.* Lapsley II, 268.

4.—Henry Clay, my beau ideal of a statesman, the man for whom I fought all my humble life—Henry Clay once said of a class of men who would repress all tendencies to liberty and ultimate emancipation, that they must, if they would do this, go back to the era of our independence, and muzzle the cannon which thunders its annual joyous return; they must blow out the moral lights around us; they must penetrate the human soul, and eradicate there the love of liberty; and then, and not till then, could they perpetuate slavery in this country.—*Debate, Ottawa, Aug. 21, 1858.* III, 255.

5.—When Henry Clay says that in laying the foundations of societies in our territories where it does not exist, he would be opposed to the introduction of slavery as an element, I insist that we have his warrant—his license—for insisting upon the exclusion of that element which he declared in such strong and emphatic language was most hateful to him.—*Debate, Alton, Oct. 15, 1858.* V, 44.

Clay, Henry, tribute to—Within the first year of that [the nation's] declared independence, and while its maintenance was yet problematical—while the bloody struggle between those resolute rebels and their haughty would-be masters was still waging . . . Henry Clay was born. The infant nation and the infant child began the race of life together. For three-quarters of a century they have traveled hand in hand. They have been companions ever. The nation has passed its perils, and it is free, prosperous and powerful. The child has reached his manhood, his middle age, his old age, and is dead. In all that has concerned the nation the man ever sympathized; and now the nation mourns the man.—*Speech, Springfield, July 16, 1852.* II, 155.

2.—Throughout that long period [half a century] he

[Henry Clay] has constantly been the most beloved and most implicitly followed by friends, and most dreaded by opponents, of all living American politicians. In all the great questions which have agitated the country, and particularly in those fearful crises, the Missouri question, the nullification question, and the late slavery question, as connected with the newly acquired territory, involving and endangering the stability of the Union, his has been the leading and most conspicuous part.—*Speech, Springfield, July 16, 1852. II, 162.*

3.—The spell—the long-enduring spell—with which the souls of men were bound to him [Clay] is a miracle. Who can compass it? It is probably true he owed his prominence to no one quality, but to a fortunate combination of several. He was surpassingly eloquent; but many eloquent men fail utterly, and they are not, as a class, generally successful. His judgment was excellent; but many men of good judgment live and die unnoticed. His will was indomitable; but this quality often secures to its owner nothing better than a character for useless obstinacy. These, then, were Mr. Clay's leading qualities. No one of them is very uncommon; but all together are rarely combined in a single individual, and in this is probably the reason why such men as Henry Clay are so rare in the world.—*Speech, Springfield, July 16, 1852. II, 163.*

See CLAY, JOHN M., son of honored father.

Clay, Henry, War of 1812 and—*See* WAR OF 1812, Clay's influence for.

Clay, John M., son of honored father—The snuff-box you sent . . . was received yesterday. Thanks for this memento of your great and patriotic father [Henry Clay]. Thanks also for your assurance that, in these days of dereliction, you remain true to his principles. In the concurring sentiment of your venerable mother, so long the partner of his bosom and his honors, and lingering now where he was but for the call to rejoin him where he is, I recognize his voice, speaking, as it ever spoke, for the Union, the Constitution and the freedom of mankind.—*To Mr. Clay, Aug. 9, 1862. VII, 307.*

Clay, Lucretia Hart (wife of Henry), tribute to—*See* CLAY, JOHN M., son of honored father.

Clemency, refused—I cannot postpone the execution of a convicted spy on a mere telegraphic dispatch signed with a name I never heard before.—*To Christiana A. Sack, May 21, 1864. X, 106.*

Climate, no bar to slavery—It is argued that slavery will not go to Kansas and Nebraska, in any event. This is a palliation, a lullaby. I have some hope that

it will not; but let us not be too confident. As to climate, a glance at the map shows that there are five slave states . . . and also the District of Columbia, all north of the Missouri Compromise line. . . . It is not climate, then, that will keep slavery out of those territories. . . . Climate will not, no peculiarity of the country will, nothing in nature will. Will the disposition of the people prevent it? Those nearest the scene are all in favor of the extension. The Yankees who are opposed to it may be most numerous; but, in military phrase, the battlefield is too far from their base of operations.—*Speech, Peoria, Oct. 16, 1854. II, 219.*

Repeated at Urbana, Oct. 24, 1854. Hertz II, 640.

2.—In the early days of the Constitution slavery was recognized, by South and North alike, as an evil, and the division of sentiment about it was not controlled by geographical lines or considerations of climate, but by moral and philanthropic views.—*Speech, Bloomington, May 29, 1856. Lapsley II, 256.*

3.—He [Douglas] will tell you, men of Ohio, that if you choose here to have laws against slavery, it is in conformity to the idea that your climate is not suited to it; that your climate is not suited to slave labor. . . . Let us attend to that argument for a little while, and see if it be sound. You do not raise sugar-cane . . . because you can't raise it profitably, because the climate don't suit it. . . . Is there, then, anything in the constitution or laws of Ohio against raising sugar-cane? . . . No man desires to raise sugar-cane in Ohio; but if any man did desire to do so, you would say it was a tyrannical law that forbids his doing so; and whenever you shall agree with Douglas, whenever your minds are brought to adopt his argument, as surely you will have reached the conclusion that although slavery is not profitable in Ohio, if any man wants it, it is a wrong to him not to let him have it.—*Speech, Cincinnati, Sept. 17, 1859. V, 201.*

Cliquism, eschew—*See* RECONSTRUCTION, must not repudiate emancipation, 2.

Clothing, origin of—His [man's] first discovery was the fact that he was naked; and his first invention was the fig-leaf apron. This simple article, the apron made of leaves, seems to have been the origin of clothing—the one thing for which nearly half of the toil and care of the human race has ever since been expended.—*Lecture, Springfield, Feb. 22, 1859. Hertz II, 796.*

"Cock-and-Bull Story"—*See* ABOLITIONIZE, plot to, parties denied, 3.

Code of Conduct, rules for personal guidance—I may be wrong in regard to any or all of them [opinions expressed] but, holding it a sound maxim that it is better only sometimes to be right than at all times to be wrong, so soon as I discover my opinions to be erroneous, I shall be ready to renounce them.—*Address to Sangamon County, March 9, 1832.* I, 8.

2.—I made a point of honor and conscience in all things to stick to my word, especially if others had been induced to act upon it.—*To Mrs. O. H. Browning, April 1, 1838.* I, 89.

3.—I . . . feel myself bound not to hinder him [Hardin] in any way from getting the [congressional] nomination. I should despise myself to attempt it.—*To M. M. Morris, March 26, 1843.* I, 264.

4.—Now, if I have sought the nomination in an improper manner, you have the right, to that extent, to be dissatisfied. But I deny all impropriety on my part, in the matter.—*To John J. Hardin, Feb. 7, 1846.* Angle, 22.

5.—You are compelled to speak; and your only alternative is to tell the truth or a lie.—*To W. H. Herndon, Feb. 1, 1848.* I, 352.

6.—I wish at all times in no way to practice any fraud upon the House or the committee, and I also desire to do nothing which may be very disagreeable to any of the members.—*Speech in Congress, June 20, 1848.* II, 28.

7.—I wish to do justice to all.—*Speech, Congress, July 27, 1848.* II, 85.

8.—In relation to these pledges [relative to recommendations for office] I must not only be chaste but above suspicion.—*To W. B. Warren and others, April 7, 1849.* II, 111.

9.—I do not propose to question the patriotism or to assail the motives of any man or class of men. . . . I also wish to be no less than national in all the positions I may take.—*Speech, Peoria, Oct. 16, 1854.* II, 192.

10.—If it is decreed that I should go down because of this speech, then let me go down linked to the truth—let me die in the advocacy of what is just and right.—*To friends trying to dissuade Lincoln from delivering "house divided" speech, June 15, 1858.* Herndon, 400.

11.—I planted myself upon the truth and the truth only, so far as I knew it, or could be brought to know it.—*Speech, Springfield, July 17, 1858.* III, 170.

12.—If I have brought forward anything not a fact, if he [Douglas] will point it out, it will not even ruffle me to take it back.—*Debate, Ottawa, Aug. 21, 1858.* III, 242.

13.—I have never tried to conceal my opinions, nor tried to deceive anyone in reference to them.—*Debate, Freeport, Aug. 27, 1858.* III, 336.

14.—If I should never be elected to any office, I trust I may go down with no stain of falsehood upon my reputation, notwithstanding the hard opinions Judge Douglas chooses to entertain of me.—*Debate, Freeport, Aug. 27, 1858.* III, 339.

15.—It used to be a fashion amongst men that when a charge was made, some sort of proof was brought forward to establish it, and if no proof was found to exist, the charge was dropped.—*Debate, Jonesboro, Sept. 15, 1858.* IV, 35.

16.—I do not state a thing and say I know it when I do not. . . . I mean to put a case no stronger than the truth will allow.—*Debate, Jonesboro, Sept. 15, 1858.* IV, 51.

17.—I have always wanted to deal with everyone I meet candidly and honestly. If I have made any assertion not warranted by facts, and it is pointed out to me, I will withdraw it cheerfully.—*Debate, Charleston, Sept. 18, 1858.* IV, 113.

18.—I don't want to be unjustly accused of dealing illiberally or unfairly with an adversary, either in court, or in a political canvass, or elsewhere. I would despise myself if I supposed myself ready to deal less liberally with an adversary than I was willing to be treated myself.—*Debate, Charleston, Sept. 18, 1858.* IV, 190.

19.—I am altogether unconscious of having attempted any double-dealing anywhere. . . . Upon one occasion I may say one thing and leave other things unsaid, and *vice versa;* but that I have said anything on one occasion that is inconsistent with what I have said elsewhere, I deny—at least, I deny it so far as the intention is concerned.—*Debate, Quincy, Oct. 13, 1858.* IV, 319.

20.—It really hurts me very much to suppose that I have wronged anybody on earth.—*Debate, Quincy, Oct. 13, 1858.* IV, 327.

21.—I am glad of all the support I can get anywhere, if I can get it without practicing any deception to obtain it.—*Debate, Quincy, Oct. 13, 1858.* IV, 376.

22.—His [Douglas's] proposition [is] that they [Lincoln's speeches] show rascality or double-dealing. I deny that they do.—*Debate, Quincy, Oct. 13, 1858.* IV, 383.

23.—I confess, when I propose a certain measure of policy, it is not enough for me that I do not intend anything evil in the result, but it is incumbent on me to show that it has not a tendency to that result.—*Debate, Alton, Oct. 15, 1858.* V, 51.

24.—What is done [regarding slavery should] be comely and not altogether outrageous.—*To W. H. Seward, Feb. 1, 1861.* IV, 104.

25.—In the position I have assumed [the Presidency] I wish to do more than I have ever given reason to believe I would do.—*Reply to Pennsylvania delegation, March 5, 1861.* XI, 117.

26.—As the President in the administration of the government, I hope to be man enough not to know one citizen of the United States from another, nor one section from another.—*Reply to Massachusetts delegation, March 5, 1861.* XI, 118.

27.—I wish to avoid violations of law and bad faith. —*To Gen. Halleck, Oct. 3, 1862.* VIII, 53.

28.—Most certainly I intend no injustice to any, and if I have done any I deeply regret it.—*To Gen. McClellan, Oct. 27, 1862.* VIII, 69.

29.—I will not perform the ungrateful task of comparing cases of failure.—*To Gen. Schurz, Nov. 24, 1862.* VIII, 86.

30.—I must bear this load which the country has entrusted to me as well as I can, and do my best.—*To Wendell Phillips and others, Jan. 24, 1863.* Kelley, 87.

31.—If both factions, or neither, shall abuse you, you will probably be about right. Beware of being assailed by one and praised by the other.—*To Gen. Schofield, May 27, 1863.* VIII, 283.

See LINCOLN, ABRAHAM, personal traits and reactions.

Coercion, none intended—*See* SOUTH, no cause for fear by, 10.

Coercion, what is it?—*See* INVASION AND COERCION, words used loosely.

Colfax, Schuyler, why not invited to cabinet—When I said to you the other day that I wished to write you a letter, I had reference, of course, to my not having offered you a cabinet appointment. I meant to say, and now do say, you were most honorably and amply recommended, and tender of the appointment was not withheld, in any part, because of anything happening in 1858. Indeed, I should have decided as I did easier than I did, had that matter never existed. I had partly made up my mind in favor of Mr. Smith —not conclusively, of course—before your name was mentioned in that connection. When you were brought forward I said, "Colfax is a young man, is already in position, is running a brilliant career, and is sure of a bright future in any event; with Smith it is now or never."—*To Mr. Colfax, March 8, 1861.* VI, 187.

Coles, Edward, governor of Illinois—*See* ILLINOIS, saved to freedom.

Collamer, Jacob—God help me. It is said I have offended you. I hope you will tell me how.—*To Senator Collamer, March 12, 1861.* XI, 119.

Colleges, devotion of, to Union—*See* HONORARY DEGREE, thanks for.

Colombia, United States of, cordial relation with— It would be doing an injustice to an important South American state not to acknowledge the directness, frankness and cordiality with which the United States of Colombia have entered into intimate relations with this government.—*Fourth annual message, Dec. 6, 1864.* X, 284.

Colonization, appeal for, to free colored men—Why . . . should the people of your race be colonized? . . . You and we are different races. We have between us a broader difference than exists between any other two races. Whether it is right or wrong I need not discuss; but this physical difference is a great disadvantage to both of us, as I think. Your race suffers very greatly, many of them, by living among us, while ours suffers from your presence. In a word we suffer on each side. If this is admitted, it affords a reason, at least, why we should be separated. . . . I suppose one of the principal difficulties in the way of colonization is that the free colored man cannot see that his comfort would be advanced by it. You may believe that you can live in Washington, or elsewhere in the United States, the remainder of your life as easily, perhaps more so, than you can in any foreign country; and hence you may come to the conclusion that you have nothing to do with the idea of going to a foreign country. This is—I speak in no unkind sense —an extremely selfish view of the case. You ought to do something to help those who are not so fortunate as yourselves. . . . If we deal with those who are not free at the beginning, and whose intellects are clouded by slavery, we have very poor material to start with. . . . It is exceedingly important that we have men at the beginning capable of thinking as white men, and not those who have been systematically oppressed. . . . For the sake of your race you should sacrifice something of your present comfort for the purpose of being as grand in that respect as the white people. . . . If you will engage in the enterprise [colonization] I will spend some of the money entrusted to me [by Congress]. I am not sure you will succeed. The government may lose the money but we cannot succeed unless we try; and we think, with care, we can succeed. . . . The practical thing I want to ascertain is whether I can get a number of able-bodied men, with their wives and children, who are willing to go when I present evidence of encouragement and protection. . . . If I could find [even] twenty five able-bodied men, with a mixture of women and children—good things in the family relation, I think—I could make a successful commencement. —*Speech to free colored men, Aug. 14, 1862.* VIII, 2.

Colonization, applications for—Applications have been made to me by many free Americans of African descent to favor their emigration, with a view to such colonization as was contemplated in recent acts of Congress. Other parties, at home and abroad—some from interested motives, others upon patriotic considerations, and still others influenced by philanthropic sentiments—have suggested similar measures; while, on the other hand, several of the Spanish-American republics have protested against the sending of colonies to their respective territories. Under these circumstances I have declined to move any such colony to any state without first obtaining the consent of its government, with an agreement on its part to receive and protect such immigrants in all the rights of free men; and I have at the same time offered to the several states situated within the tropics, or having colonies there, to negotiate with them, subject to the advice and consent of the Senate, to favor the voluntary emigration of persons of that class to their respective territories, upon conditions which shall be equal, just and humane. Liberia and Hayti are as yet the only countries to which colonists of African descent from here could go with certainty of being received and adopted as citizens; and I regret to say such persons contemplating colonization do not seem so willing to migrate to those countries as to some others. I believe, however, opinion among them in this respect is improving and that ere long there will be an augmented and considerable migration to both these countries from the United States.—*Second annual message, Dec. 1, 1862.* VIII, 97.

Colonization, argument for—On this whole proposition [of colonization], including the appropriation of money with the acquisition of territory, does not the expediency amount to absolute necessity—that without which the government itself cannot be perpetuated?—*First annual message, Dec. 3, 1861.* VII, 51.

Colonization, Central America as site for—The place I am thinking about for a colony [of American negroes] is in Central America. . . . The particular place I have in view is to be on a great highway from the Atlantic or Caribbean Sea to the Pacific ocean. . . . On both sides are harbors—among the finest in the world. Again there is evidence of very rich coal mines. . . . Coal land is the best thing I know with which to commence an enterprise.—*Speech to free colored men, Aug. 14, 1862.* VIII, 6.
2.—The political affairs in Central America are not in quite as satisfactory a condition as I wish. There are contending factions in that quarter; but, it is true, all the factions are agreed alike on the subject of colonization, and want it, and are more generous

than we are here.—*Speech to free colored men, Aug. 14, 1862.* VIII, 8.

Colonization, Clay hoped for—If to such a consummation [colonization of negroes in Africa] the efforts of Mr. Clay shall have contributed, it will be what he most ardently wished, and none of his labors will have been more valuable to his country and his kind. —*Speech, Springfield, July 16, 1852.* II, 177.

Colonization, difficulties in way of—See COLONIZATION, appeal for, to free colored men.

Colonization, effect on labor—See LABOR, supply and demand.

Colonization, forfeited persons recommended for— Under and by virtue of the act of Congress entitled "An act to confiscate property used for insurrectionary purposes," approved Aug. 6, 1861, the legal claims of certain persons to the labor and services of certain other persons have become forfeited and numbers of the latter thus liberated are already dependent on the United States and must be provided for in some way. Besides this, it is not impossible that some of the states will pass similar enactments for their own benefit respectively and by operation of which persons of the same class will be thrown upon them for disposal. In such case I recommend that Congress provide for accepting such persons from such states according to some mode of valuation, in lieu, *pro tanto,* of direct taxes or upon some other plan to be agreed on with such states respectively; that such persons on such acceptance by the general government be at once deemed free, and that in any event steps be taken for colonizing both classes—or the one first mentioned if the other shall not be brought into existence—at some place or places in a climate congenial to them. It might be well to consider, too, whether the free colored people already in the United States could not, so far as individuals may desire, be included in such colonization.—*First annual message, Dec. 3, 1861.* VII, 49.

Colonization, "glorious consummation"—If, as the friends of colonization hope, the present and coming generations of our countrymen shall by any means succeed in freeing our land from the dangerous presence of slavery, and at the same time in restoring a captive people to their long lost fatherland with bright prospects for the future, and this too so gradually that neither races nor individuals shall have suffered by the change, it will indeed be a glorious consummation.—*Speech, Springfield, July 16, 1852.* II, 176.

Colonization, homes for white men—If it be said that the only legitimate object in acquiring territory is to furnish homes for white men, this [colonization] measure effects that object, for the emigration of colored men leaves additional room for white men remaining or coming here.—*First annual message, Dec. 3, 1861.* VII, 50.

Colonization, indorsement iterated—I . . . proclaim and declare . . . that the effort to colonize persons of African descent with their consent upon this continent or elsewhere, with the previously obtained consent of the governments existing there, will be continued.—*Proclamation, Sept. 22, 1862.* VIII, 37.
2.—I cannot make it better known than it already is that I strongly favor colonization.—*Second annual message, Dec. 1, 1862.* VIII, 126.

Colonization, only way to separate races—Separation [of the races] if ever effected at all, must be effected by colonization; and no political party, as such, is now doing anything directly for colonization. Party operations at present only favor or retard colonization incidentally. The enterprise is a difficult one; but "where there is a will there is a way," and what colonization needs most is a hearty will. . . . Let us be brought to believe it is morally right, and at the same time favorable to, or at least not against, our interest to transfer the African to his native clime, and we shall find a way to do it; however great the task may be.—*Speech, Springfield, June 27, 1857.* II, 337.

Colonization, redemption of Africa by—This suggestion [of Clay's] of the possible ultimate redemption of the African race and African continent was made 25 years ago. Every succeeding year has added strength to the hope of its realization. May it indeed be realized!—*Speech, Springfield, July 16, 1852.* II, 176.

Colonization, some colonists wish to return—You are directed to have a transport . . . sent to the colored colony established by the United States at the island of Vache, on the coast of San Domingo, to bring back to this country such of the colonists there as desire to return. . . . The colonists will be brought to Washington, unless otherwise hereafter directed, and be employed and provided for at the camps for colored persons around that city.—*To Sec. Stanton, Feb. 1, 1864.* IX, 301.

Colonization, South America as site for—Room in South America for colonization can be obtained cheaply and in abundance, and when numbers shall be large enough to be company and encouragement for one another, the freed people will not be so reluctant to go.—*To border-state congressmen, July 12, 1862.* VII, 272.

Colonization, why Liberia not favored for—*See* LIBERIA, difficulties in colonizing.

Colorado, resources invite immigrants—The abundant natural resources of these territories [Colorado, Dakota, Nevada], with the security and protection afforded by organized government, will doubtless invite to them a large immigration when peace shall restore the business of the country to its accustomed channels.—*First annual message, Dec. 3, 1861.* VII, 48.

Colorado, territory of, organized—The territories of Colorado, Dakota and Nevada, created by the last Congress, have been organized, and civil administration has been inaugurated there under auspices especially gratifying when it is considered that the leaven of treason was found existing in some of these new countries when the federal officers arrived. . . . I submit the resolutions of the legislature of Colorado, which evidence the patriotic spirit of the people of the territory.—*First annual message, Dec. 3, 1861.* VII, 48.

Color Blindness, recommended—*See* NEGRO TROOPS, importance of, 12.

Comet, Pope's bull against—*See* EMANCIPATION, against immediate proclamation, 2.

Commerce, liberal policy urged—The United States, I think, ought not to be exceptionally illiberal to international trade and commerce.—*Third annual message, Dec. 8, 1863.* IX, 233.

Commerce, mutual advantage in—If we here raise a barrel of flour more than we need, and Louisianians raise a barrel of sugar more than they want, it is mutual advantage to exchange. That produces commerce, brings us together, and makes us better friends. We like one another the more for it. . . . These mutual accommodations are the cements which bind together the different parts of this Union.—*Debate, Alton, Oct. 15, 1858.* V, 53.

Commerce, resumption of, foreseen—It is hoped that with the return of domestic peace the country will be able to resume with energy and advantage its former high career of commerce and civilization.—*Fourth annual message, Dec. 6, 1864.* X, 286.

Commerce, war's effect on—*See* CIVIL WAR, foreign nations' attitude toward, 3.

Commerce, would discontinue in part—If I be asked whether I would destroy all commerce, I answer, Certainly not; I would continue it where it is necessary, and discontinue it where it is not. An instance: I would continue commerce so far as it is employed in bringing us coffee, and I would discontinue it so far as it is employed in bringing us cotton goods.—*Tariff memorandum, Dec. 1, 1847.* I, 310.

Compassion, shown litigant—I could have got a judgment against Turley, if I had pressed to the utmost; but I am really sorry for him—poor and crippled as he is. He begged time to try to find evidence. . . . I do not suppose he will get any such evidence, but I allowed him until next court to try.—*To L. M. Hays, Oct. 27, 1852.* Angle, 110.

Compensation, world of—*See* FREEDOM, none who denies deserves, 2.

Compensatory Assessments, resort to, "only sparingly" —*See* WAR VICTIMS, assessments to compensate.

Compliment, acceptable—*See* CONGRESS, seeks nomination for, 3.

Compromise, Douglas's attitude toward—*See* DOUGLAS, STEPHEN A., attitude toward compromises.

Compromise, no, on slavery—*See* SLAVERY, no compromise on.

Compromise, of principle—Compromises of principle break down of their own weight.—*To John J. Crittenden, Dec. 22, 1859.* Tracy, 121.

Compromise, spirit of, fruitful—The spirit of compromise . . . of mutual concession . . . first gave us the Constitution . . . and has thrice saved the Union. —*Speech, Peoria, Oct. 16, 1854.* II, 240.
2.—Not that compromises are not often proper.— *Message to Congress, July 4, 1861.* VI, 324.

See MISSOURI COMPROMISE, restoration of, urged, 2.

Compromise of 1850, Clay led in—In the days of nullification and more recently in the reappearance of the slavery question connected with our territory newly acquired of Mexico, the task of devising a mode of adjustment seems to have been cast upon Mr. Clay by common consent—and his performance of the task in each case was little else than a literal fulfillment of the public expectation.—*Speech, Springfield, July 16, 1852.* II, 171.
2.—I had thought that the pen of history had written, acknowledged and recorded as facts, that Henry Clay, more than any other man, or perhaps than any other ten men, was the originator of that system of measures [Compromise of 1850]; and he, together with Webster and Pearce of Maryland—not Gen.

Pierce—were its most efficient supports in its progress. —*Speech, Chicago, Aug. 14, 1852.* Angle, 87.

Compromise of 1850, Douglas's defense of—*See* DOUGLAS, STEPHEN A., characterized, 3.

Compromise of 1850, extension of, not intended— The intention to extend the law is not only not mentioned in the law, but is not mentioned in any contemporary history. Both the law itself, and the history of the times, are a blank as to any principle of extension; and by neither the known rules of construing statutes and contracts, nor by common sense can such principle be inferred.—*Speech, Peoria, Oct. 16, 1854.* II, 210.

Compromise of 1850, Nebraskaism and—The North consented to this provision [allowing Utah and New Mexico local option on slavery] not because they considered it right in itself, but because they were compensated—paid for it. They at the same time got California into the Union as a free state. . . . They also got the area of slavery somewhat narrowed in the settlement of the boundary of Texas. Also they got the slave-trade abolished in the District of Columbia. —*Speech, Peoria, Oct. 16, 1854.* II, 213.
2.—The North could afford to yield something [in Compromise of 1850]; and they did yield to the South the Utah and New Mexico provision.—*Speech, Peoria, Oct. 16, 1854.* II, 214.
3.—I have always maintained so far as I was able that there was nothing of the principle of the Nebraska bill in the Compromise of 1850—nothing whatever.—*Debate, Galesburg, Oct. 7, 1858.* IV, 270.
4.—Where can you find the principle of the Nebraska bill in that compromise [of 1850]? The two pieces of the compromise organizing the territories of Utah and New Mexico . . . expressly provided . . . that when they came to be admitted into the Union, they should be admitted with or without slavery, as they should choose, by their own constitutions. Nothing was said in either of those acts as to what was to be done in relation to slavery during the territorial existence of those territories, while Henry Clay constantly made the declaration—Judge Douglas recognizing him as leader—that in his opinion, the old Mexican law would control that question during the territorial existence, and that those old Mexican laws excluded slavery. How can that be used as a principle for declaring that during the territorial existence, as well as at the time of framing the constitution, the people, if you please, might have slaves if they wanted them? . . . The acts [comprising the compromise] . . . were a part of the general system of compromises. They did not lay down what was proposed as a regu-

lar policy for the territories.—*Debate, Galesburg, Oct. 7, 1858.* IV, 271.

5.—They [Utah and New Mexico] were allowed to come in [to the Union] in that shape, because in another way it was paid for—considering that as part of that system of measures called the Compromise of 1850, which finally included half a dozen acts. It included the admission of California as a free state, which was kept out of the Union for half a year because it had framed a free constitution. It included the settlement of the boundary of Texas. . . . It included the abolition of the slave trade in the District of Columbia. It included the passage of a new fugitive slave law. . . . The New Mexico and Utah bills . . . could not be taken as models . . . for the future territories.—*Debate, Galesburg, Oct. 7, 1858.* IV, 272.

6.—My own opinion is that a thorough investigation will show most plainly that the New Mexico and Utah bills were part of a system of compromises, and not designed as patterns for future territorial legislation, and that this Nebraska bill did not follow them as a pattern at all.—*Debate, Galesburg, Oct. 7, 1858.* IV, 273.

Compromise of 1850, not partisan—I had understood and now understand, as the indelibly written history of the country, that the compromise measures were not party measures—that for praise or blame, they belong to neither party to the exclusion of the other; but that the chief leaders in their origin and adoption were Whigs, not Democrats.—*Speech, Springfield, Aug. 14, 1852.* Angle, 87.

Compromise of 1850, origin of—There were other points of dispute connected with the general question of slavery. . . . These points needed adjustment, and they were held up, perhaps wisely, to make them help adjust one another. The Union now, as in 1820, was thought to be in danger, and devotion to the Union rightfully inclined men to yield somewhat in points, where nothing else could have so inclined them. A compromise was finally effected. . . . This is the Compromise of 1850.—*Speech, Peoria, Oct. 16, 1854.* II, 202.

Compromise of 1850, promise of, broken—Preceding the presidential election of 1852, each of the great political parties, Democrats and Whigs, met in convention and adopted resolutions indorsing the Compromise of 1850, as a "finality," a final settlement, so far as those parties could make it so, of all slavery agitation.—*Speech, Peoria, Oct. 16, 1854.* II, 203.

2.—The compromises of 1850 were declared to be a full and final settlement of the [slavery] question. The two great parties, each in national convention, adopted resolutions declaring the settlement made by the Compromise of 1850 was a finality—that it would last forever. Yet how long before it was unsettled again? It broke out again in 1854, and blazed higher and raged more furiously than ever before, and the agitation has not rested since.—*Speech, New Haven, Conn., March 6, 1860.* V, 342.

Repeated at Norwich, Conn., March 9, 1860. VI, 2.

Conceit, decried—

> Conceited whelp! We laugh at thee—
>   Now, mind, that not a few
> Of pompous, two-legged dogs there be,
>   Conceited, quite as you—
>   *Verses, about 1846.* Angle, 31.

Conciliation, efforts for—The consolidation [of cavalry units] throws out one set of officers, and whichever it may be, it offends either the governor or a U.S. senator. We cannot afford to offend either, while we can avoid it.—*To Sec. Stanton, April 4, 1864.* Angle, 345.

Condolence, letter of, to grieving daughter—It is with deep regret that I learn of the death of your kind and brave father, and especially that it is affecting your young heart beyond what is common in such cases. In this sad world of ours sorrow comes to all, and to the young it comes with bitterer agony because it takes them unawares. . . . Perfect relief is not possible, except with time. You cannot now realize that you will ever feel better. Is not this so? And yet it is a mistake. You are sure to be happy again. To know this, which is certainly true, will make you somewhat less miserable now. I have had experience enough to know what I say, and you need only believe it to feel better at once. The memory of your dear father, instead of an agony, will yet be a sad, sweet feeling in your heart, of a purer and holier sort than you have known before.—*To Fanny McCullough, Dec. 23, 1862.* VIII, 152.

Condolence, letter of, to mother of heroes—*See* BIXBY LETTER.

Condolence, letter of, to parents of lost son—In the untimely loss of your noble son [Col. E. E. Ellsworth], our affliction is scarcely less than your own. So much of promised usefulness to one's country, and of bright hopes for one's self and friends, have rarely been so suddenly dashed as in his fall. . . . He was singularly modest and deferential in social intercourse. . . . To me he appeared to have no indulgences or pastimes; and I never heard him utter a profane or intemperate word. May God give you that consolation which is beyond all earthly power.—*To parents of Col. Ellsworth, May 25, 1861.* VI, 287.

Confederacy of Free States—*See* SECTIONALISM, Washington's warning against.

Confederate Constitution, questions concerning—Our adversaries have adopted some declarations of independence, in which, unlike the good old one penned by Jefferson, they omit the words "all men are created equal." Why? They have adopted a temporary national constitution, in the preamble of which, unlike our good old one signed by Washington, they omit "We, the people," and substitute "We, the deputies of the sovereign and independent states." Why? Why this deliberate pressing out of view the rights of men and the authority of the people?—*Message to Congress, July 4, 1861.* Basler, 607.

Confederate Constitution, secession and—The seceders insist that our Constitution admits secession. They have assumed to make a national constitution of their own, in which of necessity they have either discarded or retained the right of secession, as they insist it exists in ours. If they have discarded it, they merely admit that on principle it ought not to be in ours. If they have retained it, by their own construction of ours they show that to be consistent they must secede from one another whenever they shall find it the easiest way of settling their debts or effecting any other selfish or unjust object.—*Message to Congress, July 4, 1861.* VI, 318.

Confederate Declarations of Independence—*See* CONFEDERATE CONSTITUTION, questions concerning.

Confederate Generals, might have been arrested—Of how little value the constitutional provision [touching suspension of habeas corpus] . . . will be rendered if arrest shall never be made until defined crimes shall have been committed, may be illustrated by a few notable examples: Gen. John C. Breckinridge, Gen. Robert E. Lee, Gen. Joseph E. Johnston, Gen. John B. Magruder, Gen. William B. Preston, Gen. Simon B. Buckner and Commodore Franklin Buchanan, now occupying the very highest places in the rebel service, were all within the power of the government since the rebellion began, and were nearly as well known to be traitors then as now. Unquestionably if we had seized and held them, the insurgent cause would be much weaker. But no one of them had then committed any crime defined by law. Every one of them, if arrested, would have been discharged on *habeas corpus* were the writs allowed to operate.—*To Erastus Corning and others, June 12, 1863.* VIII, 305.

Confederate scrip, plan for use of, vetoed—You tell me you have in your hands some $270,000 "Confederate scrip," which was forced upon Union men of Kentucky, in exchange for supplies, by the rebels during their late raid into that state; and you wish government authority for you to take this scrip into the cotton states, exchange it for cotton if found practicable, and to bring the cotton out. . . . I feel constrained to decline it. It would come to something, or it would come to nothing—that is, you would get cotton for the scrip, or you would not. If you should get any, to precisely that extent this government would have aided in giving currency to this scrip—that is, men, seeing that the scrip would bring cotton, would gladly produce for the scrip; and hence a scramble for it, as for gold, would ensue. . . . This would run till at length I should have to abandon all restraint, or put a stop to what is now much easier not to begin.—*To W. L. Vance, Nov. 22, 1862.* VIII, 83.

Confederate States, army dominates—The strength of the rebellion is in its military, its army. That army dominates all the country and all the people within its range.—*To J. C. Conkling, Aug. 26, 1863.* IX, 96.

Confederate States, assumption of independence rejected—Whatever may be military will be readily received if offered through the well-understood military channel. Of course nothing else will be received by the President when offered, as in this case, in terms assuming the independence of the so-called Confederate States; and anything will be received, and carefully considered by him, when offered by any influential person or persons in terms not assuming the independence of the so-called Confederate States.—*Draft of telegram (not sent) to Rear Admiral S. P. Lee, July 4, 1863.* IX, 16.
2.—As to the Alexander H. Stephens matter, so much pressed by you, I can only say that he sought to come to Washington in the name of the "Confederate States," in a vessel of the "Confederate States navy," and with no pretence even that he would bear any proposal for peace; but with language showing that his mission would be military and not civil or diplomatic. Nor has he at any time since pretended that he had terms of peace, so far as I know or believe. On the contrary, Jefferson Davis has, in the most formal manner, declared that Stephens had no terms of peace. I thought we could not afford to give this quasi-acknowledgment of the independence of the Confederacy, in a case where there was not even an intimation of anything for our good.—*To Horace Greeley, Aug. 9, 1864.* X, 185.

See PEACE, conditions essential to.

Confederate States, should be barred from family of nations—Whereas, while heretofore, states and nations have tolerated slavery, recently, for the first time in the world, an attempt has been made to construct a new nation, upon the basis of, and with, the primary and fundamental object to maintain, enlarge, and perpetuate human slavery; therefore, Resolved, That no such embryo state should ever be recognized by, or admitted into, the family of Christian and civilized nations; and that all Christian and civilized men everywhere should, by all lawful means, resist to the utmost, such recognition or admission.—*To John Bright, April 17, 1863.* Hertz II, 893.

Confiscation, curb put on—Allow no one to assume the functions of confiscating property under the law of Congress, or otherwise, except upon orders from here.—*To Gen. Schofield, Oct. 1, 1863.* IX, 149.

Confiscation, discrimination difficult—The principle of seizing and appropriating the property of the persons [in rebellion] . . . is certainly not very objectionable; but a justly discriminating application of it would be very difficult, and to a great extent impossible.—*Message to House, July 17, 1862.* VII, 283.

Confiscation, Mrs. Stephen A. Douglas reassured—[Mrs. Douglas fears property of her children in the South will be confiscated] I expect the United States will overcome the attempt to confiscate property because of loyalty to the government; but if not, I still do not expect the property of absent minor children will be confiscated. . . . But it is especially dangerous for my name to be connected with the matter; for nothing would more certainly excite the secessionists to do the worst they can against the children.—*To Mrs. Douglas, Nov. 27, 1861.* R.T.L.

Confiscation, property taken by, must bear cost of further war—This remission of confiscation [of rebel property] being within the executive power, if the war be now further persisted in by those opposing the government, the making of confiscated property at the least to bear the additional cost will be insisted on, but confiscations—except in case of third party intervening interests—will be remitted to the people of any state which shall now promptly and in good faith withdraw its troops from further resistance to the government. What is now said as to the remission of confiscation has no reference to supposed property in slaves.—*Unsigned memorandum given J. A. Campbell, April 5, 1865.* XI, 72.
Repeated in memorandum, April 13, 1865. Hertz II, 967.
2.—Judge Campbell . . . called on me [in Richmond] and made such representations as induced me to put

in his hands an informal paper, repeating the propositions in my letter of instructions to Mr. Seward, which you remember, and adding that if the war be now further persisted in by the rebels, confiscated property shall at the least bear the additional cost, and that confiscation shall be remitted to the people of any state which will now promptly and in good faith withdraw its troops and other support from resistance to the government.—*To Gen. Grant, April 6, 1865.* XI, 73.

Confiscation, remission of—Would it not be wise to place a power of remission somewhere, so that those persons [losing property by confiscation] may know they have something to lose by persisting [in rebellion] and something to save by desisting?—*Message to House, July 17, 1862.* VII, 283.
2.—I promised . . . a remission to the people of the state [Virginia], except in certain cases, of the confiscation of their property. I meant this, and no more.—*To Gen. Weitzel, April 12, 1865.* XI, 93.

See CONFISCATION, property taken by, must bear cost of further war.

Confiscation, when justified—The traitor against the general government forfeits his slave at least as justly as he does any other property; and he forfeits both to the government against which he offends.—*Message to House, July 17, 1862.* VII, 282.
2.—Without any special act of Congress, I think our military commanders, when, in military phrase, "they are within the enemy's country," should, in an orderly manner, seize and use whatever of real or personal property may be necessary or convenient for their commands; at the same time preserving in some way the evidence of what they do.—*Message to House, July 17, 1862.* VII, 283.
3.—The true rule for the military is to seize such property as is needed for military uses and reasons, and let the rest alone.—*To Gen. J. J. Reynolds, Jan. 20, 1864.* IX, 288.

See WAR, enemy property in.

Congress, legislation should rest with—Were I President, I should desire the legislation of the country to rest with Congress, uninfluenced by the Executive in its origin or progress, and undisturbed by the veto unless in very special and clear cases.—*Memorandum, July 1, 1848.* II, 56.
2.—In a certain sense, and to a certain extent, he [the President] is the representative of the people. He is elected by the people, as well as Congress is, but can he, in the nature of things, know the wants of the people as well as 300 other men, coming from

all the various localities of the nation? If so, where is the propriety of having a Congress?—*Speech in Congress, July 27, 1848.* II, 64.

3.—That the Constitution gives the President a negative in legislation, all know; but that this negative should be so combined with platforms and other appliances as to enable him, and in fact almost compel him, to take the whole legislation into his own hands, is what we [Whigs] object to; is what Gen. Taylor objects to, and is what constitutes the broad distinction between you [Democrats] and us.—*Speech in Congress, July 27, 1848.* II, 64.

4.—To thus transfer legislation [from Congress to President, by abuse of the veto power] is clearly to take it from those who understand with minuteness the interests of the people and give it to one who does not and cannot so well understand it.—*Speech in Congress, July 27, 1848.* II, 65.

5.—We [Whigs] and our candidate [Gen. Taylor] are in favor of making presidential elections, and the legislation of the country distinct matters; so that the people can elect whom they please, and afterward legislate just as they please, without any hindrance, save only so much as may guard against infractions of the Constitution, undue haste, and want of consideration. . . . That we are right we cannot doubt. —*Speech in Congress, July 27, 1848.* II, 69.

6.—By the Constitution, the Executive may recommend measures which he thinks proper, and he may veto those he thinks improper, and it is supposed that he may add to these certain indirect influences to affect the action of Congress. My political education strongly inclines me against a very free use of any of these means by the Executive to control the legislation of the country. As a rule, I think it better that Congress should originate as well as perfect its measures without external bias.—*Speech, Pittsburgh, Feb. 15, 1861.* VI, 128.

Congress, not much pleased in—Being elected to Congress, though I am very grateful to our friends for having done it, has not pleased me as much as I expected.—*To Joshua F. Speed, Oct. 22, 1846.* Lapsley II, 17.

Congress, power of, relative to slavery—*See* EMANCIPATION, District of Columbia, 1, 7.

Congress, President and—In full view of his responsibilities, he [the President] has, so far, done what he has deemed his duty. You will now, according to your own judgment, perform yours.—*Message to Congress, July 4, 1861.* VI, 324.

See CONGRESS, legislation should rest with.

Congress, Reelection to, discussed—It is very pleasant to learn from you that there are some who desire that I should be re-elected [to Congress]. I most heartily thank them for their kind partiality; and can say, as Mr. Clay said of the annexation of Texas, that "personally I would not object" to a re-election, although I thought at the time, and still think, it would be quite as well for me to return to the law at the end of a single term. I made the declaration that I would not be a candidate again, more from a wish to deal fairly with others, to keep peace among our friends, and to keep the district from going to the enemy, than for any cause personal to myself; so that, if it should so happen that no one else wishes to be elected, I could not refuse the people the right of sending me again. But to enter myself as a competitor of others, or to authorize anyone so to enter me, is what my word and honor forbid.—*To W. H. Herndon, Jan. 8, 1848.* I, 325.

2.—I am not a candidate for renomination or election.—*To Richard S. Thomas, March 1, 1848.* Tracy, 28.

Congress, refuses candidacy for—An article in the Tazewell *Mirror* in which my name is prominently used, makes me fear that my position, with reference to the next congressional election in this district, is misunderstood, and that such misunderstanding may work injury to the cause of our friends. I therefore take occasion to say that I neither seek, expect, or desire, a nomination for a seat in the next Congress; that I prefer my name should not be brought forward in that connection; and that I would peremptorily forbid the use of it, could I feel entirely at liberty to do so.—*To editors of Illinois Journal, June 5, 1850.* Angle, 66.

2.—Let me assure you that I decline to be a candidate for Congress, on my clear conviction that my running would hurt and not help the cause. I am willing to make any personal sacrifice, but I am not willing to do what, in my own judgment, is a sacrifice of the cause itself.—*To Julian M. Sturtevant, Sept. 27, 1856.* Angle, 164.

Congress, representation in, unequal—The United States House of Representatives is constituted on the principle that each member is sent by the same number of people that each other one is sent by; and yet, in practice, no two of the whole number, much less the whole number, are ever sent by precisely the same number of constituents. The districts cannot be made precisely equal in population at first, and if they could, they would become unequal in a single day, and much more so in the ten years which the districts, once made, are to continue. They cannot

be remodeled every day; nor, without too much expense and labor, even every year.—*Opinion on draft
law, Aug. 15, 1863.* IX, 82.

See SLAVE STATES, have advantage in Congress.

Congress, seeks nomination to—Now if you should
hear any one say that Lincoln don't want to go to
Congress, I wish you as a personal friend of mine
would tell him you have reason to believe he is mistaken. The truth is, I would like to go very much.
Still, circumstances may happen which may prevent
my being a candidate. If there are any who be my
friends in such an enterprise, what I want now is
that they shall not throw me away just yet.—*To
Richard S. Thomas, Feb. 14, 1843.* Tracy, 9.
2.—Your county and ours are almost sure to be
placed in the same congressional district. I would like
to be its representative, still circumstances may happen to prevent my even being a candidate. If, however, there are any Whigs in Tazewell who would as
soon I should represent them as any other person,
I would be glad if they not cast me aside until they
see and hear farther what turn things take. Do not
suppose, Esqr., that in addressing this letter to you,
I assume that you will be for me against all other
Whigs; I only mean, that I know you to be my personal friend, a good Whig, and an honorable man,
to whom I may, without fear, communicate a fact
which I wish my particular friends—if I have any—
to know.—*To Alden Hull, Feb. 14, 1843.* Angle, 16.
3.—You say you shall instruct your delegates for me
[for Congress] unless I object. I certainly shall not
object. That would be too pleasant a compliment for
me to tread in the dust. . . . If in those instructions
I were named as first choice, it would gratify me
very much.—*To M. M. Morris, March 26, 1843.* I,
264.
4.—I wish you would let nothing appear in your
paper which may operate against me.—*To B. F.
James, Nov. 17, 1845.* I, 278.
5.—I now wish to say to you that if it be consistent
with your feelings, you would set a few stakes for me.
I do not certainly know, but I strongly suspect, that
Gen. Hardin wishes to run again.—*To Harry E.
Dummer, Nov. 18, 1845.* Tracy, 15.
6.—If Hardin and I stood precisely equal, if neither
of us had been in Congress, or, if we both had—it
would not only accord with what I have always done,
for the sake of peace, to give way to him; and I
expect I should do it. . . . But to yield to Hardin
under present circumstances, seems to me as nothing
else than yielding to one who would sacrifice me
altogether. This I would rather not submit to.—*To
Dr. Robert Boal, Jan. 7, 1846.* I, 280.

7.—[Your statement] is a direct imputation that I
procured, or worked out, or in some way directly or
indirectly, had a hand in, the nominating of you for
governor; and the imputation is to the utmost hair-
breadth of it, unjust.—*To John J. Hardin, Feb. 7,
1846.* Angle, 24.
8.—If I am not—in service done the party and in
capacity to serve in future—near enough your equal,
when added to the fact of your having had a turn
[as congressman], to entitle me to the nomination, I
scorn it on any and all other grounds.—*To John J.
Hardin, Feb. 7, 1846.* Angle, 26.
9.—If I am not, in what I have done, and am able
to do, for the party, near enough the equal of Gen.
Hardin to entitle me to the nomination, now that
he has one, I scorn it on any and all other grounds.
—*To B. F. James, Feb. 9, 1846.* Tracy, 19.

See HARDIN, JOHN J., characterized.

See HARDIN, JOHN J., tribute to.

Congress, slave states have advantage in—*See* SLAVE
STATES, have advantage in Congress.

Congress, war-making power of, explained—The provision of the Constitution giving the war-making
power to Congress was dictated, as I understand it,
by the following reasons: Kings had always been involving and impoverishing their people in wars,
pretending generally, if not always, that the good of
the people was the object. This our convention
understood to be the most oppressive of all kingly
oppressions, and they resolved to so frame the Constitution that no man should hold the power of
bringing this oppression upon us.—*To W. H. Herndon, Feb. 15, 1848.* II, 2.

See MEXICAN WAR, acts of aggression, 4.

Congress, war supporters only—As you ask my opinion, I give it, that the supporters of the war should
send no man to Congress who will not pledge himself
to go into caucus with the unconditional supporters
of the war, and to abide the action of such caucus
and vote for the person therein nominated for
speaker.—*To Henry Winter Davis, March 18, 1863.*
VIII, 229.

Conkling, J. C., commended—He has ample business
qualifications, is entirely trustworthy; and withal is
my personal friend of long standing.—*To quarter-
master general, Jan. 31, 1863.* Angle, 314.

Conkling, Roscoe, "good enough"—I am for the regular nominee in all cases. . . . No one could be more
satisfactory to me as the nominee in that district
than Mr. [Roscoe] Conkling. I do not mean to say

there [are] not others as good as he in the district; but I think I know him to be at least good enough.—*To Ward Hunter, Aug. 16, 1864.* X, 193.

Connecticut, loyal and patriotic—Be assured, my dear sir, that I am deeply gratified by this new proof [resolutions adopted by the legislature] of the loyalty and patriotic devotion of the people of your state [Connecticut], and that I most gratefully appreciate their expressions toward myself, which are at once so generous and so kind.—*To Gov. Buckingham, Jan. 12, 1863.* VIII, 185.

Conscience, clear before his own—At least I should have done my duty, and have stood clear before my own conscience.—*Memorandum, Aug. 23, 1864.* X, 204.

Consciences, differ—Consciences differ in different individuals.—*Notes, Oct. 1, 1858.* IV, 213.

Conscription—*See* MILITARY DRAFT.

Conscription, Southern policy characterized—*See* MILITARY DRAFT, can't wait, 2.

Consent of the Governed—*See* SELF-GOVERNMENT, defined.

Conservatism, defined—*See* REPUBLICAN PARTY, conservative, 4.

Considerateness, Lincoln trait—I should be with Judge Douglas at your town on the 4th had he not intimated in his published letter, that my presence would be an intrusion.—*To J. F. Alexander, Aug. 2, 1858.* Angle, 181.
2.—I should be at your town today with Judge Douglas, had he not strongly intimated in his letter, which you have seen in the newspapers, that my presence, on the days or evenings of his meetings would be considered an intrusion.—*To J. T. Eccles, Aug. 2, 1858.* Angle, 182.
3.—I trust that in the freedom with which I have canvassed your views I have not in any respect injured your feelings.—*Reply to Chicago church committee, Sept. 13, 1862.* VIII, 33.

Constitution, amendment of, opposed—I wish now to submit a few remarks on the general proposition of amending the Constitution. As a general rule, I think we would much better let it alone. No slight occasion should tempt us to touch it. Better not take the first step, which may lead to a habit of altering it. Better, rather, habituate ourselves to think of it as unalterable. It can scarcely be made better than it is. New provisions would introduce new difficulties, and thus create an increased appetite for further change.

No, sir; let it stand as it is. New hands have never touched it. The men who made it have done their work, and have passed away. Who shall improve on what they did?—*Speech in Congress, June 20, 1848.* II, 44.
2.—I do not . . . propose to destroy, or alter or disregard the Constitution. I stand to it, fairly, fully and firmly.—*Speech, Peoria, Oct. 16, 1854.* II, 235.
3.—Don't interfere with anything in the Constitution. That must be maintained, for it is the only safeguard of our liberties.—*Speech, Kalamazoo, Mich., Aug. 27, 1856.* Stern, 407.
4.—I do not desire any amendment of the Constitution. Recognizing, however, that questions of such amendment rightfully belong to the American people, I should not feel justified nor inclined to withhold from them, if I could, a fair opportunity of expressing their will thereon through either of the modes prescribed in the instrument.—*To Duff Green, Dec. 28, 1860.* VI, 88.
5.—The people of Illinois do not desire any change in our federal constitution.—*Resolution, Illinois Legislature, Feb. 1, 1861.* Hertz II, 809.

Constitution, amendment of, urged—*See* THIRTEENTH AMENDMENT, favorable action on, urged.

See EMANCIPATION, constitutional amendment urged.

Constitution, as each "understands it"—*See* JACKSON, ANDREW, Supreme Court and bank decision, 1, 3.

See POLITICAL PLATFORMS, proposals for 1860 rejected, 3.

Constitution, Electoral College and—*See* ELECTORAL COLLEGE, argument for retaining.

Constitution, Fugitive Slave Act and—*See* FUGITIVE SLAVE ACT, attitude toward, 2.

Constitution, higher law and—*See* HIGHER LAW, conditionally condemned.

Constitution, in war and peace—*See* WAR POWER, use of, defended.

Constitution, "measures otherwise unconstitutional" —*See* WAR POWER, use of, defended, 15.

Constitution, men who pervert—*See* PEOPLE, masters in America, 6.

Constitution, methods of amendment—To me the convention mode [of amending the Constitution] seems preferable, in that it allows amendments to originate with the people, instead of permitting them to take or reject propositions originated by others, not especially chosen for the purpose, and which might not be precisely such as they would wish to accept or reject.—*First inaugural, March 4, 1861.* VI, 182.

Constitution, minorities protected by—*See* SECESSION, no excuse for, 3.

Constitution, negro citizenship and—*See* NEGRO CITIZENSHIP, opposed to.

Constitution, noninterference amendment indorsed —*See* SLAVERY, no interference with, in slave states, 34

Constitution, North and South devoted to—I believe the devotion to the Constitution is equally great on both sides of the [Ohio] river. It is only a difference of understanding of that instrument that causes difficulty. The only dispute on both sides is, "What are their rights?"—*Speech, Steubenville, Ohio, Feb. 14, 1861.* V, 123.

Constitution, oath to defend—In the choice of evils, war may not always be the worst. Still, I would do all in my power to avoid it, except to neglect a constitutional duty.—*Reply to committee from peace congress, Feb. 24, 1861.* Table Talk, 92.
2.—I take the oath today with no mental reservations, and with no purpose to construe the Constitution or laws by any hypercritical rules.—*First inaugural, March 4, 1861.* VI, 172.
3.—It was in the oath I took that I would, to the best of my ability, preserve, protect and defend the Constitution of the United States. . . . Nor was it my view that I ought to take an oath to get power, and break the oath in using the power.—*To A. G. Hodges, April 4, 1864.* X, 65.
4.—My oath to preserve the Constitution to the best of my ability imposed upon me the duty of preserving, by every indispensable means, that government— that nation, of which the Constitution was the organic law. Was it possible to lose the nation and yet preserve the Constitution? . . . I could not feel that to the best of my ability I had even tried to preserve the Constitution, if, to save slavery, or any minor matter, I should permit the wreck of government, country and Constitution, altogether.—*To A. G. Hodges, April 4, 1864.* X, 66.

See CIVIL WAR, issue in hands of dissatisfied citizens.

Constitution, obedience to—Let us continue to obey the Constitution and the laws.—*Speech, Bloomington, May 29, 1856.* Lapsley II, 273.

Constitution, preservation of, first duty—*See* UNION, preservation of, first duty.

Constitution, questions not answered by—*See* SLAVERY, questions Constitution does not answer.

Constitution, safeguard of liberties—*See* CONSTITUTION, amendment of, opposed, 5.

Constitution, secession for and against—*See* WEST VIRGINIA, argument for admission of, 6.

Constitution, slavery not mentioned in—At the framing and adoption of the Constitution they forebore to so much as mention the word "slave" or "slavery" in the whole instrument. In the provision for the recovery of fugitives, the slave was spoken of as a "person held to service or labor." In that prohibiting the abolition of the African slave trade for twenty years, that trade is spoken of as the "migration or importation of such persons as any of the states now existing shall think proper to admit," etc. These are the only provisions alluding to slavery.—*Speech, Peoria, Oct. 16, 1854.* II, 244.

2.—The framers of the Constitution were particular to keep out of that instrument the word "slave," the reason being that slavery would ultimately come to an end, and they did not wish to have any reminder that in this free country human beings were ever prostituted to slavery.—*Speech, Bloomington, May 29, 1856.* Lapsley II, 254.
3.—We must make good in essence as well as in form Madison's avowal that "the word 'slave' ought not to appear in the Constitution"; and we must even go further, and decree that only local law, and not that time-honored instrument, shall shelter a slave-holder. —*Speech, Bloomington, May 29, 1856.* Lapsley II, 274.
4.—There is no allusion to slavery in the Constitution—and Madison says it was omitted that future generations might not know such a thing ever existed —and that the Constitution might yet be a "national charter of freedom."—*Speech, Carlinville, Aug. 31, 1858.* Angle, 189.
5.—The institution of slavery is only mentioned in the Constitution of the United States two or three times, and in neither of these cases does the word "slavery" or "negro race" occur; but covert language is used each time, and for a purpose full of significance . . . and that purpose was that in our Constitution, which it was hoped, and is still hoped, will endure forever—when it should be read by intelligent and patriotic men, after the institution of slavery had passed from among us—there should be nothing on the face of the great charter of liberty suggesting that such a thing as negro slavery had existed among us.—*Debate, Alton, Oct. 15, 1858.* V, 48.
6.—Neither the word "slave" nor "slavery" is to be found in the Constitution, nor the word "property"

even, in any connection with language alluding to the things slave, or slavery. . . . Wherever in that instrument the slave is alluded to, he is called a person; and whenever his master's legal right in relation to him is alluded to, it is spoken of as "service or labor which may be due"—as a debt payable in service or labor. Also it would be open to show, by contemporaneous history, that this mode of alluding to slaves and slavery, instead of speaking of them, was employed on purpose to exclude from the Constitution the idea that there could be property in man.—*Cooper Institute address, New York, Feb. 27, 1860.* V, 321.

7.—When men are framing a supreme law and chart of government to secure blessings and prosperity to untold generations yet to come, they use language as short and direct and plain as can be found to express their meaning. In all matters but this of slavery the framers of the Constitution used the very clearest, shortest, and most direct language. But the Constitution alludes to slavery three times without mentioning it once! The language becomes ambiguous, roundabout, and mystical. . . . We cannot doubt that it was done on purpose. Only one reason is possible, and that is supplied us by one of the framers of the Constitution—and it is not for men to conceive of any other. They expected and desired that the system would come to an end, and meant that when it did the Constitution should not show that there ever had been a slave in this good free country. —*Speech, New Haven, Conn., March 6, 1860.* V, 356.

Constitution, South insists on interpreting—*See* UNION, South proposes rule or ruin of.

Constitution, spirit of—It is said the devil takes care of his own. Much more should a good spirit—the spirit of the Constitution and the Union—take care of its own. I think it cannot do less and live.— *Opinion on admission of West Virginia, Dec. 31, 1862.* VIII, 158.

Constitution, stand on, to stab—The object of the charge [of Judge Carmichael to a grand jury], I understand, was to procure prosecution and punishment of some men for arresting and doing violence to some secessionists—that is, the judge was trying to help a little by giving the protection of the law to those who were endeavoring to overthrow the supreme law—trying if he could find a safe place for certain men to stand on the Constitution, whilst they should stab it in another place.—*To John W. Crisfield, June 26, 1862.* VII, 237.

Constitution, support of, defined—*See* FREEPORT DOCTRINE, fallacy of, 5, 17.

Constitution, thirteenth amendment of, urged—*See* THIRTEENTH AMENDMENT, favorable action on, urged.

Constitution, war-making power—*See* CONGRESS, war-making power of, explained.

Constitution, wholly satisfactory to none—It has been said, and I believe truly, that the Constitution itself is not altogether such as any one of its framers would have preferred. It was the joint work of all, and certainly the better that it was so.—*Opinion on draft law (never published), Aug. 15, 1863.* IX, 78.

Constitution, who shall suspend guarantees?—*See* HABEAS CORPUS, Who shall suspend?

Constitutions, must free-state, go?—I am also aware that they [men of the South] have not as yet in terms demanded the overthrow of our free-state constitutions. Yet these constitutions declare the wrong of slavery with more solemn emphasis than do all the other sayings against it; and when all these other sayings shall have been silenced, the overthrow of these constitutions will be demanded, and nothing left to resist the demand.—*Speech, New Haven, Conn., March 6, 1860.* V, 369.

Consuls, tax exemption urged for foreign—The proper officers of the treasury have deemed themselves required by law . . . to demand a tax upon the incomes of foreign consuls in this country. While such a demand may not in strictness be in derogation of public law, or perhaps of any existing treaty . . . the expediency of so far modifying the act as to exempt from tax the income of such consuls as are not citizens of the United States, derived from emoluments of their office or from property not situated in the United States, is submitted to your serious consideration. I make this suggestion upon the ground that a comity which ought to be reciprocated exempts our consuls in all other countries from taxation to the extent thus indicated.—*Third annual message, Dec. 8, 1863.* IX, 232.

Consultation, desirable—I am really glad you have come, and wish that more of you southern gentlemen would call and see me, as these are times when there should be a full, fair and frank interchange of sentiment among all who have the good of the country at heart.—*To Congressman Boteler, March 3, 1861.* War Years I, 116.

Controversies, too many family—I have too many family controversies, so to speak, already on my hands to voluntarily, or so long as I can avoid it, take up another. You are doing well—well for the country, and well for yourself—much better than you could possibly do if engaged in open war with Gen. Halleck.—*To Gen. McClernand, Jan. 22, 1863.* VIII, 201.

Convention of 1860, time and place of—I find some of our friends here attach more consequence to getting the national convention into our state than I do. . . . As to the time, it must certainly be after the Charleston fandango; and I think, within bounds of reason, the later the better.—*To N. B. Judd, Dec. 14, 1859.* V, 283.

Convention of 1864, satisfied with—. . . with which, of course, I am very well satisfied.—*Reply to Ohio delegation, June 9, 1864.* X, 121.

Convention System, recommended—It is to induce our friends to act upon this important and universally acknowledged truth [that "union is strength"] that we urge the adoption of the convention system. . . . If two friends aspire to the same office it is certain that both cannot succeed. Would it not, then, be much less painful to have the question decided by mutual friends some time before, than to snarl and quarrel until the day of election, and then both be beaten by the common enemy?—*Whig circular, March 1, 1843.* I, 255.

Convictions, stand up to, and clouds will pass—You, as a portion of the great American people, need only to maintain your composure, stand up to your sober convictions of right, to your obligations to the Constitution, and act in accordance with these convictions, and the clouds now on the horizon will be dispelled, and we shall have a bright and glorious future; and when this generation has passed away, tens of thousands will inhabit this country where only thousands inhabit it now.—*Speech, Buffalo, Feb. 16, 1861.* VI, 134.

Cooper Institute Address, no objection to improving—So far as it is intended merely to improve in grammar and elegance of composition, I am quite agreed [to having the address revised for publication]; but I do not wish the sense changed, or modified, to a hair's breadth. And you, not having studied the particular points so closely as I have, cannot be quite sure that you do not change the sense when you do not intend it.—*To Charles C. Nott, May 31, 1860.* Tracy, 149.

Copperheads, would scoff—The Copperheads would be sure to say [if the Jaquess enterprise were sanctioned] I had shown the white feather, and resorted to back-door diplomacy to get out of a bad scrape.

This, whether true or not, would discourage loyal people. You see, I don't want to be like the dog that crossed the brook with a piece of meat in his mouth, and dropped it to catch its enlarged shadow in the water.—*To James R. Gilmore, late May, 1863.* Gilmore, 157.

Corkran, F. S., "disobliges" Lincoln—*See* PATRONAGE, "disobliged."

Corporations, "enthroned"—*See* CIVIL WAR, aftermath feared.

Corruption, "in high places" foreseen—*See* CIVIL WAR, aftermath feared.

Corruption, volcano of political—I know that the volcano at Washington, aroused and directed by the evil spirit that reigns there, is belching forth the lava of political corruption in a current broad and deep, which is sweeping with frightful velocity over the whole length and breadth of the land, bidding fair to leave unscathed no green spot of living thing; while on its bosom are riding, like demons on the waves of hell, the imps of that evil spirit, and fiendishly taunting all those who dare resist its destroying course with the hopelessness of their effort.—*Speech, Springfield, Dec. 20, 1839.* I, 137.

Cost of Living, dangerous steps toward higher—I think it my duty to express my sincere regret that it has been found necessary to authorize so large an additional issue of United States notes, when this circulation and that of the suspended banks together have become so redundant as to increase prices beyond real values, thereby augmenting the cost of living, to the injury of labor, and the cost of supplies, to the injury of the whole country.—*Message to Congress, Jan. 17, 1863.* VIII, 192.

Cotton, blockade and—*See* BLOCKADE, cotton and.

Cotton, exports of, affect currency—*See* GOLD, affected by cotton escaping through blockade.

Cotton, need for, as policy motive abroad—*See* CIVIL WAR, foreign nations' attitude toward, 3.

Cotton, shippers of, hampered—*See* BLACKMAIL AND SPOILS.

Cotton, speculation in, criticized—*See* SPECULATION, diverts army from fighting.

Cotton, tariff and—*See* TARIFF, useless labor as a factor, 2.

Cotton Gin, slavery policy affected by—*See* SLAVERY, perpetuation of, 6, 8, 9.

"Counterfeit Logic"—See RACIAL AMALGAMATION, opposed to, 1, 4.

Country (America)—See AMERICA.

Court of Claims, needs more authority—It was intended by the organization of the court of claims mainly to remove this branch of business [investigation and adjudication of claims against the government] from the halls of Congress; but while the court has proved to be an effective and valuable means of investigation it in great degree fails to effect the object of its creation for want of power to make its judgments final. . . . I commend to your careful consideration whether this power of making judgments final may not properly be given to the court, reserving the right of appeal on questions of law to the Supreme Court.—First annual message, Dec. 3, 1861. VII, 43.

"Court of Negroes"—See DRED SCOTT DECISION, challenged, 11.

Courts, uneasy about—I am not easy about the courts. I am satisfied with them as they are, but shall not care much if the judges are made elective by the people, and their term of office limited. I fear, however, something more, and, as I think, much worse than all this, to wit "a puppy court," that is, a judge in each county with civil jurisdiction in all cases up to a thousand dollars, and criminal in all cases not capital. A "migratory supreme court" and salaries so low as to exclude all respectable talent. From these—may God preserve us.—To O. H. Browning, June 24, 1847. Tracy, 22.

Cousin Lizzie, "no indelicacy"—See GRIMSLEY, ELIZABETH TODD, suggested appointment of, "troubles me."

Cowardly legs, Caesar and—A witty Irish soldier, who was always boasting of his bravery when no danger was near, but invariably retreated without orders at the first charge of an engagement, being asked by his captain why he did so, replied: "Captain, I have as brave a heart as Julius Caesar ever had, but somehow or other, whenever danger approaches, my cowardly legs will run away with it.—Speech, Springfield, Dec. 20, 1839. I, 136.

Cowardly Legs, how can he help?—If the Lord gives a man a pair of cowardly legs, how can he help their running away with him?—To Gen. Meade, Sept. 11, 1863. IX, 117.

Cowards, argument for—Address that argument to cowards and knaves; with the free and the brave it will effect nothing.—Speech, Springfield, Dec. 20, 1839. I, 137.

Crisis, artificial—There is no crisis, excepting such a one as may be gotten up at any time by turbulent men aided by designing politicians.—Speech, Pittsburgh, Feb. 15, 1861. VI, 125.
2.—I think there is no occasion for any excitement. I think the crisis, as it is called, is altogether an artificial one. . . . What they do who seek to destroy the Union is altogether artificial. . . . It [the crisis] has no foundation in fact. It can't be argued up, and it can't be argued down. Let it alone, and it will go down of itself.—Speech, Cleveland, Feb. 15, 1861. VI, 130.
3.—It is true . . . that there is great anxiety amongst the citizens of the United States at this time. I deem it a happy circumstance that this dissatisfied portion of our fellow-citizens does not point us to anything in which they are being injured or about to be injured; which reason I have felt all the while justified in concluding that the crisis, the panic, the anxiety of the country, at this time, is artificial—Speech, reply to mayor of Philadelphia, Feb. 21, 1861. VI, 154.
4.—Oh, well! I guess we'll manage to keep house.—To W. T. Sherman, March, 1861. Reveille, 49.

Critical Days, confront North—We are living in a trying time.—Speech, Bloomington, May 29, 1856. Lapsley II, 248.
2.—We have more serious business than to dally with temporary measures.—Speech, Bloomington, May 29, 1856. Lapsley II, 249.
3.—Chase says we can't raise any more money; Pope is licked and McClellan has the diarrhoea. What shall I do? The bottom is out of the tub; the bottom is out of the tub.—To Gen. Meigs, Sept. 1, 1862. War Years I, 533.
4.—I have no word of encouragement to give! The military situation is far from bright; and the country knows it as well as I do.—To Mary A. Livermore and friend, Sept., 1862. War Years I, 533.
5.—We are on the brink of destruction. It appears to me that the Almighty is against us, and I can hardly see any ray of hope.—To O. H. Browning, Dec. 18, 1862. Stephenson, 329.

See DEITY, dependence on, 3.

Crittenden, John J., "always loved"—Still, to heighten the wonder, a senator [Crittenden] from Kentucky, whom I have always loved with an affection as tender and endearing as I have ever loved any man, was writing letters into Illinois to secure the re-election of Douglas.—Speech, Cincinnati, Sept. 17, 1859. V, 216.

Crittenden, John J., nothing dishonorable from—The emotions of defeat at the close of a struggle in which I felt more than a selfish interest, and to which defeat the use of your name contributed largely, are fresh upon me; but even in this mood I cannot for a moment suspect you of anything dishonorable.—*To Sen. Crittenden, Nov. 4, 1858.* V, 91.

Crittenden-Montgomery Bill—*See* REPUBLICAN PARTY, warned against Douglas, 17.

See RULE OF THREE.

Crocodile, negro and—*See* NEGRO, tendency to dehumanize, 7, 9, 10, 11.

Cuba, inhumanity against, charged—Their [filibusters'] butchery [in Cuba] was, as it seemed to me, most unnecessary and inhumane.—*Speech, Springfield, Aug. 26, 1852.* Angle, 105.

Cuba, South might demand—*See* SLAVERY, no compromise on, 6.

Cuba, unfit for civil liberty—*See* LIBERTY, CIVIL, Cubans unfit for.

Currency—*See* BANKING AND CURRENCY.

Curtin, Andrew C., appointment offered to—If, after the expiration of your present term as governor of Pennsylvania, I shall continue in office here, and you shall desire to go abroad, you can do so with one of the first-class missions.—*To Gov. Curtin, April 13, 1863.* VIII, 246.

Curtis, Samuel R., no censure of—I did not relieve Gen. Curtis because of any full conviction that he had done wrong by commission or omission.—*To Gen. Schofield, May 27, 1863.* VIII, 282.
2.—I did not mean to base any censure upon you, nor to indorse any of the charges made against you by others. With me the presumption is still in your favor; that you are honest, capable, faithful and patriotic.—*To Gen. Curtis, June 8, 1863.* VIII, 295.
3.—I have received such evidence and explanations, in regard to the supposed cotton transactions of Gen. Curtis as fully restore in my mind the fair presumption of his innocence; and as he is my friend, and what is more, as I think, the country's friend, I would be glad to relieve him from the impression that I think him dishonest by giving him a command. —*To Sec. Stanton, Dec. 18, 1863.* IX, 265.

Cushing, William B., Congress asked to thank—I most cordially recommend that Lieut. William B. Cushing, United States navy, receive a vote of thanks from Congress for his important, gallant and perilous achievement in destroying the rebel steamer *Albemarle,* on the night of the 27th of October, 1864, at Plymouth, N. C. The destruction of so formidable a vessel, which had resisted the continued attacks of a number of our vessels on former occasions, is an important event touching our future naval and military operations, and would reflect honor on any officer, and redounds to the credit of this young officer and the few brave comrades who assisted in that successful and daring undertaking.—*Message to Congress, Dec. 5, 1864.* X, 281.

"Cut Its Own Fodder"—*See* POST OFFICE, "cut its own fodder."

Cuttlefish, Douglas plays—*See* DOUGLAS, STEPHEN A., characterized, 28.

Cutts, James M.—*See* "QUARREL NOT AT ALL," advice to army captain.

Dahlgren, John A., Congress asked to thank—I recommend that the thanks of Congress be given . . . Commander John A. Dahlgren [U.S.N.] for distinguished services in the line of his profession, improvements in ordnance, and zealous and efficient labors in the ordnance branch of the service.—*Message to Congress, July 11, 1862.* VII, 267.

Dakota, Territory of, organized—*See* COLORADO, Territory of, organized.

See COLORADO, resources invite immigrants.

Dana, N. J. T., asked to explain—The attached document, purporting to be an order issued by your authority, is sent you with the request that you will inform me whether such an order has been issued by you, and if it has, please inform me by what authority it is that you undertake to impose terms in the premises not imposed by the government, and which in effect entirely thwart and defeat the object of the government.—*To Gen. Dana, Jan. 6, 1865.* X, 331.

Dark Ages, printing ended—*See* PRINTING, "better half" of writing, 2.

Davis, Charles Henry, Congress asked to thank—I recommend that the thanks of Congress be given . . . Capt. Charles Henry Davis [U.S.N.] for distinguished services in conflict with the enemy at Fort Pillow, at Memphis, and for successful operations at other points in the waters of the Mississippi River.—*Message to Congress, July 11, 1862.* VII, 267.

Davis, Jefferson, army his only hope—Davis is right. His army is his only hope, not only against us, but against his own people. If that were crushed the people would be ready to swing back to their old bearings.—*To John Hay, Aug. 9, 1863.* Hay, 77.

Davis, Jefferson, Douglas and Mason—*See* SLAVERY, nationalization of, 10.

Davis, Jefferson, "let him try me"—If Jefferson Davis wishes for himself, or for the benefit of his friends at the North, to know what I would do if he were to offer peace reunion, saying nothing about slavery, let him try me.—*Unfinished letter to Charles D. Robinson, Aug. 17, 1864.* X, 197.

Davis, Jefferson, would pardon—I will pardon Jeff Davis, if he asks for it.—*To W. C. Bibb, April 12, 1865.* DuBose, 458.

Davis, John W., way to free self from prison—*See* PRISON, release from, by taking oath of allegiance.

Dayton, William L., difficulty in placing—It is not necessary to speak to me in praise of Mr. Dayton; I have known him since we served in the different houses of Congress at the same time, and there is no public man for whose character I have a higher admiration. When the telegraph wires brought to Springfield the news of my election, my first thought was that I would have him associated with me in council, and would make him secretary of state. But New York is a great state, and Mr. Seward has many friends, and I was compelled by the pressure upon me to give up the thought. I then desired to arrange for him some other cabinet position, commensurate with his abilities; but Pennsylvania—another great state, you know—was bound to have a place for Mr. Cameron, and I again reluctantly yielded. I then said to myself, Mr. Dayton deserves the best place abroad, and I will send him to the Court of St. James. But New England pressed her claims for notice, and united upon Mr. Adams, and I was driven from that purpose. I then thought of the French mission, and wondered if that would not suit him. I have put my foot down now, and will not be moved. I shall offer that place to Mr. Dayton, and hope it will prove satisfactory to him and his friends.—*Reply to delegation of New Jersey citizens, Feb. or March, 1861.* Hertz II, 810.

Dayton, William L., tribute to—When you meet Judge Dayton, present my respects, and tell him I think him a far better man than I for the position he is in [candidate for Vice President], and that I shall support both him and Col. Frémont most cordially.—*To John Van Dyke, June 27, 1856.* II, 289.

Deadheads—*See* UNION, do-nothing friends of, 3.

Dead-Letter Laws—*See* TAXATION, ideal plan impracticable, 1.

Death, great men's most impressive—The death of the late President [Taylor] may not be without its use, in reminding us that we, too, must die. Death, abstractly considered, is the same with the high as with the low; but practically, we are not so much aroused to the contemplation of our own mortal natures, by the fall of many undistinguished, as that of one great, and well known name.—*Speech, Chicago, July 25, 1850.* Angle, 75.

Debater, vocation of—If I have reasoned to a false conclusion, it is the vocation of an able debater to show by argument that I have wandered to an erroneous conclusion.—*Debate, Ottawa, Aug. 21, 1858.* III, 242.

Declaration of Independence, appeals for—Let us readopt the Declaration of Independence, and with it the practices and policy which harmonize with it.—*Speech, Peoria, Oct. 16, 1854.* II, 248.

2.—Let us revere the Declaration of Independence.—*Speech, Bloomington, May 29, 1856.* Lapsley II, 273.

3.—My countrymen, if you have been taught doctrines conflicting with the great landmarks of the Declaration of Independence; if you have listened to suggestions which would take away from its grandeur and mutilate the fair symmetry of its proportions; if you have been inclined to believe that all men are not created equal in those inalienable rights enumerated in our charter of liberty, let me entreat you to come back! Return to the fountain whose waters spring close by the blood of the Revolution. You may do anything with me you choose, if you will but heed these sacred principles. I charge you to drop every paltry and insignificant thought of any man's success. It is nothing; I am nothing; Judge Douglas is nothing. But do not destroy that immortal emblem of humanity—the Declaration of Independence.—*Speech, Beardstown, Aug. 12, 1858.* Hertz II, 713.

4.—Think nothing of me—take no thought for the political fate of any man whomsoever—but come back to the truths of the Declaration of Independence. You may do anything with me you choose, if you will but heed these sacred principles. You may not only defeat me for the Senate, but you may take me and put me to death . . . but do not destroy that immortal emblem of humanity.—*Speech, Lewiston, Aug. 17, 1858.* Richards, 194.

5.—We had slaves among us; we could not get our Constitution unless we permitted them to remain in slavery; we could not secure the good we did secure, if we grasped for more; but having by necessity submitted to that much, it does not destroy the principle that is the charter of our liberties. Let that charter stand as our standard.—*Speech, Chicago, July 10, 1858.* III, 50.

Declaration of Independence, can principles of, save the country?—*See* SELF-GOVERNMENT, can it survive?

Declaration of Independence, "Charter of Liberties" —*See* DECLARATION OF INDEPENDENCE, appeals for, 5.

Declaration of Independence, Clay supports Lincoln —In the sentiments I have occasionally advanced upon the Declaration of Independence, I am entirely borne out by the sentiments advanced by our old Whig leader, Henry Clay.—*Debate, Quincy, Oct. 13, 1858.* IV, 319.

Declaration of Independence, "emblem of humanity" —*See* DECLARATION OF INDEPENDENCE, appeals for, 3, 4.

Declaration of Independence, "glittering generalities" —*See* DECLARATION OF INDEPENDENCE, hostility toward, **5.**

Declaration of Independence, "Hawked at and torn" —*See* DECLARATION OF INDEPENDENCE, hostility toward, **6.**

Declaration of Independence, hostility toward—So far as I have learned, the first American of any note to do or attempt this [ridicule the Declaration] was John C. Calhoun; and if I mistake not, it soon after found its way into some of the messages of the governor of South Carolina.—*Speech, Springfield, July 16, 1852.* II, 173.

2.—When [Senator] Pettit, in connection with his support of the Nebraska bill, called the Declaration of Independence "a self-evident lie," he only did what consistency and candor require all other Nebraska men to do.—*Speech, Peoria, Oct. 16, 1854.* II, 247.

3.—Of the forty-odd Nebraska senators who were present and heard him [Pettit], no one rebuked him. Nor am I apprised that any Nebraska newspaper, or any Nebraska orator, in the whole nation has ever rebuked him. If this had been said among Marion's men, southerners though they were, what would have become of the man who said it? If it had been said to the men who captured André, the man who said it would have been hung sooner than André was. If it had been said in old Independence Hall 78 years ago, the very doorkeeper would have throttled the man and thrust him into the street.—*Speech, Peoria, Oct. 16, 1854.* II, 247.

4.—When we were the political slaves of King George, and wanted to be free, we called the maxim that "all men are created equal" a self-evident truth, but now when we have grown fat, and have lost all

dread of being slaves ourselves, we have become so greedy to be masters that we call the same maxim "a self-evident lie."—*To George Robertson, Aug. 15, 1855.* II, 279.

5.—Meanwhile the helpless negro is the fruitful subject of reprisals in other quarters. John Pettit, whom Tom Benton paid his respects to, you will recollect, calls the immortal Declaration "a self-evident lie"; while at the birthplace of freedom—in the shadow of Bunker Hill and of the "cradle of Liberty," at the home of the Adamses, and Warren and Otis— Choate, from our side of the House, dares to fritter away the birthday promise of liberty by proclaiming the Declaration to be "a string of glittering generalities"; and the southern Whigs, working hand and hand with pro-slavery Democrats, are making Choate's theories practical.—*Speech, Bloomington, May 29, 1856.* Lapsley II, 253.

6.—In those days [of the Revolution] our Declaration of Independence was held sacred by all; and thought to include all; but now, to aid in making the bondage of the negro universal and eternal, it is assailed and sneered at and construed, and hawked at and torn, till, if its framers could rise from their graves, they could not at all recognize it.—*Speech, Springfield, June 26, 1857.* II, 327.

7.—Why, that object [the justification of the revolting colonies in the eyes of the world, as argued by Douglas] having been effected some eighty years ago, the Declaration is of no practical use now—mere rubbish, old wadding left to rot on the battlefield after the victory is won.—*Speech, Springfield, June 26, 1857.* Basler, 362.

8.—We can no longer express our admiration for the Declaration of Independence without their [proslavery men's] petty sneers. And it is thus they are fast bringing that sacred instrument into contempt.— *Speech, Carlinville, Aug. 31, 1858.* Angle, 192.

9.—In support of the Nebraska bill, on its first discussion in the Senate, Senator Pettit of Indiana declared the equality of men, as asserted in the Declaration of Independence to be "a self-evident lie."— *Notes, Oct. 1, 1858.* IV, 200.

10.—[Friends of slavery] are laboring at a common object, and . . . that common object is to subvert, in the public mind, and in practical administration, our old and only standard of free government, that "all men are created equal" and to substitute for it some different standard. What that substitute is to be is not difficult to perceive. It is to deny the equality of men, and to assert the natural, moral, and religious right of one class to enslave another.—*Notes, Oct. 1, 1858.* IV, 201.

11.—There were men, who, finding this assertion

[that "all men are created equal"] constantly in the way of their schemes to bring about the ascendancy and perpetuation of slavery, denied the truth of it. I know that Mr. Calhoun and the politicians of his school denied the truth of it. I know that it ran along in the mouths of some southern men for a period of years, ending at last in that shameful though rather forceful declaration of Pettit of Indiana upon the floor of the United States Senate, that the Declaration was in that respect a "self-evident lie."—*Debate, Alton, Oct. 15, 1858.*   V, 37.

12.—I say, with a perfect knowledge of all this hawking at the Declaration without directly attacking it, that three years ago there had never lived a man who ventured to assail it in the sneaking way of pretending to believe it and then asserting it did not include the negro.—*Debate, Alton, Oct. 15, 1858.* V, 37.

See SLAVERY, "sacred right of," 3.

See KNOW-NOTHING PARTY, principles of, challenged, 2.

Declaration of Independence, most distinguished signers of—See ADAMS, JOHN, death of.

Declaration of Independence, origin of popular sovereignty—See POPULAR SOVEREIGNTY, origin of.

Declaration of Independence, "self-evident lie."—See DECLARATION OF INDEPENDENCE, hostility toward, 2, 4, 9, 11.

Declaration of Independence, slave-trade denunciation omitted from—On the second day of July 1776, the draft of a Declaration of Independence was reported to Congress by the committee, and in it the slave-trade was characterized as "an execrable commerce," as "a piratical warfare," and as the "opprobrium of infidel powers," and as "a cruel war against human nature." All agreed on this except South Carolina and Georgia, and in order to preserve harmony, and from the necessities of the case, these expressions were omitted.—*Speech, Bloomington, May 29, 1856.* Lapsley II, 257.

Declaration of Independence, source of political creed—I adhere to the Declaration of Independence.—*Speech, Springfield, June 26, 1857.* Stern, 455.

2.—I have never had a feeling, politically, that did not spring from the sentiments embodied in the Declaration of Independence. I have often pondered over the dangers which were incurred by the men who assembled here and framed and adopted that Declaration. I have pondered over the toils that were endured by the officers and soldiers of the army who achieved that independence. I have often inquired of myself what great principle or idea it was that kept

this confederacy so long together. It was not the mere matter of separation of the colonies from the motherland, but that sentiment in the Declaration of Independence which gave liberty not alone to the people of this country, but hope to all the world, for all future time. It was that which gave promise that in due time the weights would be lifted from the shoulders of all men, and that all should have an equal chance. This is the sentiment embodied in the Declaration of Independence.—*Speech, Independence Hall, Philadelphia, Feb. 22, 1861.* VI, 157.

Declaration of Independence, stumbling block to tyrants—Its [the Declaration's] authors meant it to be—as, thank God, it is now proving itself—a stumbling block to all those who in after times might seek to turn a free people back into the hateful paths of despotism. They knew the proneness of prosperity to breed tyrants, and they meant when such should reappear in this fair land and commence their vocation, they should find left for them at least one hard nut to crack.—*Speech, Springfield, June 27, 1857.* II, 331.

2.—Wise statesmen as they [authors of the Declaration of Independence] were, they knew the tendency of prosperity to breed tyrants, so they established those great self-evident truths, that when in the distant future some man, some faction, some interest, should set up a doctrine that none but rich men, none but white men, or none but Anglo-Saxon white men, were entitled to life, liberty and the pursuit of happiness, their posterity might look up again to the Declaration of Independence and take courage to renew the battle which their fathers began.—*Speech, Beardstown, Aug. 12, 1858.* Hertz II, 714.

3.—It [the Declaration] has proved a stumbling block to tyrants, and always will, unless brought into contempt by its pretended friends.—*Speech, Carlinville, Aug. 31, 1858.* Angle, 191.

Declaration of Independence, who will destroy?—If that Declaration is not the truth, let us get the statute-book in which we find it, and tear it out! Who is so bold as to do it? If it is not true, let us tear it out! [Cries of "No! No!"] Let us stick to it then; let us stand firmly by it then.—*Speech, Chicago, July 10, 1858.* III, 50.

Deeds, Not Words—Tell him [Gen. J. H. Lane] when he starts, to put it through—not to be writing or telegraphing back here, but put it through.—*To Sec. Cameron, June 20, 1861.* VI, 294.

Defeat, Lincoln in—We have had a convention for nominating candidates in this county. . . . I was much, very much, wounded myself at not being nominated.—*To John T. Stuart, March 26, 1840.* I, 151.

2.—I regret my defeat [for United States senator] moderately; but I am not nervous about it. . . . On the whole, it is perhaps as well for our general cause that Trumbull is elected.—*To E. B. Washburne, Feb. 9, 1855.* II, 277.

3.—The election is over, the session is ended, and I am not senator. I have to content myself with the honor of having been the first choice of a large majority of the 51 members who finally made the election. My larger number of friends had to surrender to Trumbull's smaller number, in order to prevent the election of Matteson, which would have been a Douglas victory. I started with 44 votes and T. with 5. It is rather hard for the 44 to have to surrender to the 5 and a less good-humored man than I, perhaps, would not have consented to it,—and it would not have been done without my consent. I could not, however, let the whole political result go to smash, on a point merely personal to myself.—*To W. H. Henderson, Feb. 21, 1855.* Hertz II, 658.

4.—Well, the election is over; and in the main point, we are beaten. Still my view is that the fight must go on. Let no one falter. The question is not half settled. New splits and divisions will soon be upon our adversaries, and we shall fuse again.—*To Eleazar A. Paine, Nov. 19, 1858.* Tracy, 95.

5.—You doubtless have seen ere this the result of the election here. Of course I wished, but did not much expect, a better result. . . . I am glad I made the late race [for senator against Douglas]. It gave me a hearing on the great and durable question of the age, which I could have had in no other way; and though I now sink out of view, and shall be forgotten, I believe I have made some marks which will tell for the cause of civil liberty long after I am gone.—*To A. G. Henry, Nov. 19, 1858.* V, 95.

6.—I expect the result of the election went hard with you. So it did with me, too, perhaps not quite so hard as you may have supposed. I have an abiding faith that we shall best them in the long run. Step by step the objects of the leaders will become too plain for the people to stand them. . . . I write merely to let you know that I am neither dead nor dying.—*To Alexander Sympson, Dec. 13, 1858.* V, 97.

7.—While I desired the result of the late canvass [for United States senator] to have been different, I still regard it as an exceeding small matter. I think we have fairly entered upon a durable struggle as to whether this nation is ultimately to become all slave or all free, and though I fall early in the contest, it is nothing if I shall have contributed, in the least degree, to the final restful result.—*To H. D. Sharpe, Dec. 18, 1858.* V, 96.

8.—Of course I would have preferred success; but failing in that, I have no regrets for having rejected all advice to the contrary, and resolutely made the struggle.—*To Salmon P. Chase, April 30, 1859.* Tracy, 109.

9.—Returning from the campaign [Black Hawk War], and encouraged by his great popularity among his immediate neighbors, he the same year [1832] ran for the legislature, and was beaten—his own precinct, however, casting its votes 277 for and 7 against him. . . . This was the only time Abraham was ever beaten on a direct vote of the people.—*Autobiography, June 1, 1860.* VI, 31.

De Gasparin, Count A., book by—Allow me to return my cordial thanks for your kindness in sending me a copy of your translation of the Count De Gasparin's *America Before Europe.* I shall read it with pleasure and with gratitude.—*To Mary L. Booth, Aug. 1, 1862.* Angle, 299.

De Gasparin, Count A., "much admired"—You are much admired in America for the ability of your writtings, and much loved for your generosity to us and your devotion to liberal principles generally.—*To Count de Gasparin, Aug. 4, 1862.* VII, 302.

"Dallying with Douglas"—*See* REPUBLICAN PARTY, warned against Douglas, 7, 9, 10.

Deity, "Almighty Architect"—*See* AMERICA, devotion to, 2.

Deity, American flag and—*See* AMERICAN FLAG, each star brings happiness.

Deity, American people and—I turn, then, and look to the great American people, and to that God who has never forsaken them.—*Speech to Ohio legislature, Feb. 13, 1861.* VI, 121.

See DEITY, trust in, 3, 4, 5.

See WASHINGTON, GEORGE, task greater than that of.

Deity, argument for existence of—The universal sense of mankind on any subject is an argument, or at least an influence, not easily overcome. The success of the argument in favor of the existence of an overruling Providence mainly depends upon that sense.—*Speech, Springfield, Feb. 22, 1842.* I, 200.

2.—Surely God would not have created such a being as man, with an ability to grasp the infinite, to exist only for a day! No, no, man was made for immortality.—*To Chicago group, Sept., 1857.* Layman's Faith, 28.

Deity, attitude toward good and evil—*See* GOOD AND EVIL, God's prohibition.

Deity, "author of man"—*See* SLAVERY, wrong of, 18.

Deity, blessing of—*See* AMERICAN FLAG, each star brings happiness.

Deity, blessing of, asked—*See* UNION, "we know how to save."
For "all good Union men"—*See* "READ SLOWLY."
For Andrew Johnson—*See* RECONSTRUCTION, Tennessee, 5.
For Gen. Grant—*See* GRANT, U. S., appreciation of, 7, 9, 10, 15.
For Gen. McClellan—*See* MC CLELLAN, GEORGE B., appreciation of, 4.
For Gen. Rosecrans—*See* ROSECRANS, W. S., appreciation of, 1.
For Gen. Sheridan—*See* SHERIDAN, PHILIP H., appreciation of, 1.
For Indiana soldiers—*See* CIVIL WAR, Indiana troops thanked.
For Italy—*See* ITALY, never faltered.
For Japan—*See* JAPAN, good wishes for.
For Kentucky's sons—*See* KENTUCKY, attitude of, toward Union, 3.
For Methodists and all churches—*See* METHODIST CHURCH, thanked, 2.
For rulers of San Marino—*See* SAN MARINO, complimented.
For soldiers and seamen—*See* UNION TROOPS, tributes to, 16.
For women of America—*See* WOMEN, tribute to, 1.

Deity, both sides invoke—The rebel soldiers are praying with a great deal more earnestness, I fear, than our own troops, and expecting God to favor their side.—*Reply to committee from Chicago churches, Sept. 13, 1862.* VIII, 29.
2.—Doctor, if it had been left to you and me, there would have been no war. If it had been left to you and me, there would have been no cause for this war. God has allowed men to make slaves of their fellows. He permits this war. He has before Him a strange spectacle. We on our side are praying Him to give us victory, because we believe we are right; but those on the other side pray Him, too, for victory, believing they are right. What must He think of us? And what is coming from the struggle? What will be the effect of it all on the whites and negroes?—*To Rev. Byron Sunderland, Dec. 28, 1862.* War Years II, 12.

See DEITY, purpose of, toward slavery.

Deity, braving the arm of—*See* SLAVERY, Jefferson versus Douglas on, 3.

Deity, chastises Americans for sins—*See* DEITY, dependence on, 13.

See DEITY, mercy of, 1, 3.

See DEITY, purpose of, in war, 2.

Deity, consolation of—*See* CONDOLENCE, letter of, to parents of lost son.

Deity, creator—*See* FATHER, advised to trust God.

Deity, dependence on—Yet, under all circumstances, trusting to our Maker, and through His wisdom and beneficence, to the great body of our people, we will not despair nor despond.—*Speech, Chicago, July 25, 1850.* Angle, 75.
2.—Let us strive to deserve, as far as mortals may, the continued care of Divine Providence, trusting that in future national emergencies He will not fail to provide us the instruments of safety and security.—*Speech, Springfield, July 16, 1852.* II, 177.
3.—The Union is undergoing a fearful strain; but it is a stout old ship, and has weathered many a hard blow, and "the stars in their courses," aye, an invisible Power greater than the puny efforts of men, will fight for us.—*Speech, Bloomington, May 29, 1856.* Lapsley II, 273.
4.—All we want is time, patience and a reliance on that God who has never forsaken this people.—*Speech, Columbus, Ohio, Feb. 13, 1861.* VI, 122.
5.—If we have patience, if we restrain ourselves, if we allow ourselves not to run off in a passion, I still have confidence that the Almighty, the Maker of the Universe, will, through the instrumentality of this great and intelligent people, bring us through this as He has through all the other difficulties of our country.—*Speech, New York Legislature, Feb. 18, 1861.* VI, 141.
6.—With my own ability I cannot succeed, without the sustenance of Divine Providence, and of this great free, happy and intelligent people. Without these I cannot hope to succeed; with them, I cannot fail.—*Speech, Newark, N.J., Feb. 21, 1861.* Hertz II, 807.
7.—Intelligence, patriotism, Christianity, and a firm reliance on Him who has never yet forsaken this favored land, are still competent to adjust in the best way all our present difficulties.—*First inaugural, March 4, 1861.* VI, 184.
8.—With a reliance on Providence all the more firm and earnest, let us proceed in the great task which events have devolved upon us.—*First annual message, Dec. 3, 1861.* VII, 60.
9.—It is most cheering and encouraging for me to know that in the efforts which I have made and am making for the restoration of a righteous peace to our country, I am upheld and sustained by the good wishes and prayers of God's people. No one is more deeply than myself aware that without His favor our

highest wisdom is but as foolishness and that our most strenuous efforts would avail nothing in the shadow of His displeasure. . . . It seems to me that if there be one subject upon which all good men may unitedly agree, it is imploring the gracious favor of the God of Nations upon the struggles our people are making for the preservation of their precious birthright of civil and religious liberty.—*To Iowa Quakers, Jan. 5, 1862.* Hertz II, 847.
Repeated to Caleb Russell and Sallie A. Fenton, *Jan. 5, 1863.* VIII, 174.

10.—You all may recollect that in taking up the sword . . . forced into our hands, the government appealed to the prayers of the pious and the good, and declared that it placed its whole dependence upon the favor of God. I now, humbly and reverently, in your presence, reiterate the acknowledgment of that dependence, not doubting that, if it shall please the Divine Being who determines the destinies of nations, that this shall remain a united people, and that they will, humbly seeking Divine guidance, make their prolonged national existence a source of new benefits to themselves and their successors, and to all classes and conditions of mankind.—*Response to Evangelical Lutherans, May 6, 1862.* VII, 154.

11.—I can only say that I have acted upon my best convictions, without selfishness or malice, and that by the help of God I shall continue to do so.—*To Count A. de Gasparin, Aug. 4, 1862.* VII, 303.

12.—Whatever shall be sincerely, and in God's name, devised for the good of the soldiers and seamen in their hard spheres of duty, can scarcely fail to be blest.—*To Rev. Alexander Reed, Feb. 22, 1863.* VIII, 217.

13.—It is the duty of nations as well as of men to own their dependence upon the overruling power of God, and to confess their sins and transgressions in humble sorrow, yet with assured hope that genuine repentence will lead to mercy and pardon, and to recognize the sublime truth, announced in Holy Scripture, and proven by all history, that those nations only are blessed whose God is the Lord. And, insomuch as we know that by His divine law nations, like individuals, are subjected to punishments and chastisements in this world, may we not justly fear that the awful calamity of civil war which now desolates the land may be but a punishment inflicted upon us for our presumptuous sins, to the needful end of our national reformation as a whole people? We have been the recipients of the choicest bounties of Heaven; we have been preserved these many years in peace and prosperity; we have grown in numbers, wealth and power as no other nation has ever grown. But we have forgotten God. We have forgotten the

gracious hand which has preserved us in peace and multiplied and enriched and strengthened us, and we have vainly imagined, in the deceitfulness of our hearts, that all these blessings were produced by some superior wisdom and virtue of our own. Intoxicated with unbroken success, we have become too self-sufficient to feel the necessity of redeeming and preserving grace, too proud to pray to the God that made us. It behooves us, then, to humble ourselves before the offended power, to confess our national sins and to pray for clemency and forgiveness.—*Fast Day Proclamation, March 30, 1863.* VIII, 235.

14.—From the beginning I saw that the issue of our great struggle depended on the divine interposition and favor. If we had that, all would be well. . . . Relying, as I do, upon the Almighty power . . . with the support which I receive from Christian men I shall not hesitate to use all the means at my control to secure the termination of this rebellion, and will hope for success.—*Reply to Presbyterian General Assembly, May 30, 1863.* VIII, 287.

15.—Let us diligently apply the means, never doubting that a just God, in His own good time, will give us the rightful result.—*To J. C. Conkling, Aug. 26, 1863.* IX, 102.

See METHODIST CHURCH, thanked, 1.

See PEOPLE, relied on to save Union, 17.

See WASHINGTON, GEORGE, task greater than that of.

Deity, faith in—With a firm reliance on the strength of our free government, and the ultimate loyalty of the people to the just principles upon which it is founded, and above all, an unshaken faith in the Supreme Ruler of nations, I accept this trust.—*To notification committee, Feb. 26, 1861.* Angle, 262.

See ELECTION OF 1860, result accepted.

See ELECTION OF 1864, gratitude without taint, 3.

Deity, "Father of Mercies"—*See* DEITY, gratitude to, 12.

Deity, fulfills promise to—*See* EMANCIPATION PROCLAMATION (PRELIMINARY), timed to circumstances, 1.

Deity, glory to—*See* OHIO, "saves" nation.

Deity, governing world—*See* INAUGURAL, SECOND, should "wear well."

Deity, gratitude to—In the midst of unprecedented political troubles we have cause of great gratitude to God for unusual good health and abundant harvests.—*First annual message, Dec. 3, 1861.* VII, 28.

2.—It is . . . recommended to the people of the United States . . . that they especially acknowledge and render thanks to our Heavenly Father for those inestimable blessings ["signal victories" in the war]; that they . . . implore spiritual consolation in behalf of all who have been brought into affliction by the casualties and calamities of sedition and civil war and that they reverently invoke the divine guidance for our national counsels to the end that they may speedily result in the restoration of peace, harmony and unity throughout our borders, and hasten the establishment of fraternal relations among all the countries of the earth.—*Proclamation, April 10, 1862. VII, 144.*

3.—For this [Gettysburg victory] he [the President] especially desires that on this day He whose will, not ours, should ever be done, be everywhere remembered and revered with profoundest gratitude.—*Executive announcement, July 4, 1863. IX, 17.*

4.—I do most sincerely thank Almighty God for the occasion on which you have called.—*Response to serenade, July 7, 1863. IX, 20.*

5.—It has pleased Almighty God to hearken to the supplications and prayers of an afflicted people and to vouchsafe to the army and navy of the United States victories on land and on the sea so signal and so effective as to furnish reasonable grounds for augmented confidence that the Union of these states will be maintained, their constitution preserved and their peace and prosperity permanently restored. . . . I invite the people of the United States [on Aug. 6] to . . . render the homage due to the Divine Majesty for the wonderful things He has done in the nation's behalf and to invoke the influence of His Holy Spirit to subdue the anger which has produced and so long sustained a needless and cruel rebellion, to change the hearts of the insurgents.—*Thanksgiving Proclamation, July 15, 1863. IX, 32.*

6.—It has seemed to me fit and proper that they [gifts of God] should be solemnly, reverently, and gratefully acknowledged as with one heart and one voice by the whole American people. I do, therefore, invite my fellow-citizens in every part of the United States, and also those who are at sea and those who are sojourning in foreign lands, to set apart and observe the last Thursday of November next as a day of thanksgiving and praise to our beneficent Father who dwelleth in the heavens.—*Thanksgiving Proclamation, Oct. 3, 1863. IX, 152.*

7.—Reliable information being received that the insurgent force is retreating from East Tennessee under circumstances rendering it probable that the Union forces cannot hereafter be dislodged from that important position, and esteeming this to be of high na-

tional consequence, I recommend that all loyal people, on receipt of this information, assemble at their places of worship and render special homage and gratitude to Almighty God for this great advancement of the national cause.—*Proclamation, Dec. 7, 1863. IX, 217.*

8.—Another year of health, and of sufficiently abundant harvests, has passed. For these, and especially for the improved condition of our national affairs, our renewed and profoundest gratitude to God is due.—*Third annual message, Dec. 8, 1863. IX, 224.*

9.—Enough is known of the army operations within the last five days to claim our especial gratitude to God, while what remains undone demands our most sincere prayers to and reliance upon Him, without whom all human efforts are vain. I recommend that all patriots, at their homes, in their places of public worship and wherever they may be unite in common thanksgiving and prayer to Almighty God.—*Executive order, May 9, 1864. X, 94.*

10.—While we are grateful to all the brave men and officers for the events of the past few days, we should, above all, be very grateful to Almighty God, who gives us the victory.—*Response to serenade, May 9, 1864. X, 95.*

11.—I am indeed very grateful to the brave men who have been struggling with the enemy in the field, to their noble commanders who have directed them, and especially to our Maker.—*Response to serenade, May 13, 1864. Hertz II, 929.*

12.—The signal success that Divine Providence has recently vouchsafed to the operations of the United States fleet and army in the harbor of Mobile and the reduction of Fort Powell, Fort Gaines and Fort Morgan, and the glorious achievements of the army of Maj. Gen. Sherman in the state of Georgia, resulting in the capture of the city of Atlanta, call for devout acknowledgment to the Supreme Being, in whose hands are the destinies of nations. It is, therefore, requested that on next Sunday, in all places of public worship in the United States, thanksgiving be offered to Him for His mercy in preserving our national existence against the insurgent rebels who so long have been waging a cruel war against the government of the United States for its overthrow; and also that prayer be made for the divine protection to our brave soldiers and their leaders in the field, who have so often and so gallantly periled their lives in battling with the enemy, and for blessing and comfort from the Father of Mercies to the sick, wounded and prisoners, and to the orphans and widows of those who have fallen in the service of their country; and that He will continue to uphold the government of the United States against all efforts of public enemies and secret foes.—*Executive order, Sept. 3, 1864.* X, 211.

13.—It has pleased Almighty God to prolong our national life another year, defending us with His guardian care against unfriendly designs from abroad and vouchsafing to us in His mercy many and signal victories over the enemy, who is of our own household. It has also pleased our Heavenly Father to favor as well our citizens in their homes as our soldiers in their camps and our sailors on the rivers and seas with unusual health. He has largely augmented our free population by emancipation and immigration, while He has opened to us new sources of wealth and has crowned the labor of our workingmen in every department of industry with abundant rewards. Moreover, He has been pleased to animate and inspire our minds and hearts with fortitude, courage and resolution sufficient for the great trial of civil war into which we have been brought by our adherence as a nation to the cause of freedom and humanity, and to afford to us reasonable hopes of an ultimate and happy deliverance from all our dangers and afflictions. . . . I . . . recommend to my fellow-citizens that . . . they do reverently humble themselves in the dust and from thence offer up penitent and fervent prayers and supplications to the Great Disposer of Events for a return of the inestimable blessings of peace, union and harmony throughout the land which it has pleased Him to assign as a dwelling place for ourselves and our posterity throughout all generations.—*Thanksgiving Proclamation, Oct. 20, 1864.* X, 245.

14.—Again the blessings of health and abundant harvests claim our profoundest gratitude to Almighty God.—*Fourth annual message, Dec. 6, 1864.* X, 283.

15.—In the midst of this [celebration of the war's end], however, He from whom all blessings flow must not be forgotten.—*Last public speech, April 11, 1865.* XI, 84.

See ELECTION OF 1864, gratitude without taint, 1, 2.

Deity, "Great Disposer of events"—*See* DEITY, gratitude to, 13.

Deity, "instrument in the hands of"—I believe God made me one of the instruments of bringing your Fanny and you together, which union I have no doubt He had foreordained.—*To Joshua F. Speed, July 4, 1842.* I, 218.

2.—I shall be most happy indeed if I shall be a humble instrument in the hands of the Almighty and of this, his almost chosen people, for perpetuating the object of that great struggle [Revolutionary War].—*Speech, New Jersey Senate, Feb. 21, 1861.* VI, 151.

3.—In the very responsible position in which I happen to be placed, being a humble instrument in the hands of our Heavenly Father, as I am, and as we all are, to work out His just purposes, I have desired that all my works and acts may be according to His will, and that it might be so, I have sought His aid; but if, after endeavoring to do my best in the light which He affords me, I find my efforts fail, I must believe that for some purpose unknown to me, He wills it otherwise. If I had had my way, this war would never have been commenced. If I had been allowed my way, this war would have ended before this; but we find it still continues, and we must believe that He permits it for some wise purpose of His own, mysterious and unknown to us; and though with our limited understandings we may not be able to comprehend it, yet we cannot but believe that He who made the world still governs it.—*To Mrs. Eliza Gurney, Sept. 28, 1862.* VIII, 50.

4.—God selects his own instruments, and sometimes they are queer ones; for instance, He chose me to steer the ship through a great crisis.—*To James R. Gilmore, late May, 1863.* Gilmore, 158.

5.—Don't kneel to me—that is not right. You must kneel to God only, and thank Him for the liberty you will hereafter enjoy. I am but God's humble instrument; but you may rest assured that as long as I live no one shall put a shackle on your limbs, and you shall have all the rights which God has given to any other free citizen of this republic.—*To negroes in Richmond, April 4, 1865.* Hertz II, 964.

See TRENTON, BATTLE OF, inspiration of.

Deity, justice and goodness of—At the end of three years' struggle, the nation's condition is not what either party, or any man, devised or expected. God alone can claim it. Whither it is tending seems plain. If God now wills the removal of a great wrong [slavery], and wills also that we of the North as well as you of the South, shall pay fairly for our complicity in that wrong, impartial history will find therein new cause to attest and revere the justice and goodness of God.—*To A. G. Hodges, April 4, 1864.* X, 68.

See FREEDOM, none who denies deserves, 1.

Deity, "kindred to"—It is difficult to make a man miserable while he feels he is worthy of himself and claims kindred to the great God who made him.—*Address to free colored men, Aug. 14, 1862.* VIII, 5.

Deity, liberty and—*See* LIBERTY, bulwark of.

Deity, line across continent—*See* SLAVERY, line across continent, 1, 3.

Deity, men not "flattered"—Men are not flattered by being shown that there has been a difference of purpose between the Almighty and them.—*To Thurlow Weed, March 15, 1865.* XI, 54.

Deity, mercy of—Whereas our beloved country, once, by the blessings of God, united, prosperous and happy, is now afflicted with faction and civil war, it is peculiarly fit for us to recognize the hand of God in this terrible visitation, and in sorrowful remembrance of our own faults and crimes as a nation and as individuals, to humble ourselves before Him and to pray for His mercy—to pray that we may be spared further punishment, though most justly deserved; that our arms may be blessed and made effectual for the re-establishment of law, order, and peace throughout the wide extent of our country; and that the inestimable boon of civil and religious liberty, earned under His guidance and blessing by the labors and sufferings of our fathers, may be restored in all its original excellence.—*Fast Day Proclamation, Aug. 12, 1861.* VI, 342.

2.—In granting this respite it becomes my painful duty to admonish the prisoner [Nathaniel Gordon, condemned slave trader] that, relinquishing all expectation of pardon by human authority, he refer himself alone to the mercy of the common God and Father of all men.—*Executive order, Feb. 4, 1862.* VII, 96.

3.—No human counsel hath devised nor hath any mortal hand worked out these great things. They are the gracious gifts of the Most High God, who, while dealing with us in anger for our sins, hath nevertheless remembered mercy.—*Thanksgiving Proclamation, Oct. 3, 1863.* Basler, 728.

See FATHER, advised to trust God.

Deity, never deserted by—The Lord has never yet deserted me, and I did not believe He would this time.—*To Sec. Seward, July, 1864.* War Years, III, 117.

2.—When I finally struck the name of Fessenden as Gov. Chase's successor, I felt as if the Lord hadn't forsaken me yet.—*To Noah Brooks, July, 1864.* War Years, III, 118.

Deity, "One mouth and two hands"—*See* SLAVERY, wrong of, 18, 20.

Deity, perfection of—*See* DEITY, purpose of, in war, 3.

See EQUALITY, doctrine of Declaration explained, 4.

Deity, providence of—The year that is drawing to its close, has been filled with the blessings of fruitful fields and healthful skies. To these bounties, which are so constantly enjoyed that we are prone to forget the source from which they come, others have been added, which are of so extraordinary a nature, that they cannot fail to penetrate and soften even the heart which is habitually insensible to the ever-watchful providence of Almighty God.—*Thanksgiving Proclamation, Oct. 3, 1863.* Basler, 727.

Deity, purpose of, in war—In great contests each party claims to act in accordance with the will of God. Both may be, and one must be, wrong. God cannot be for and against the same thing at the same time. In the present civil war it is quite possible that God's purpose is something different from the purpose of either party; and yet the human instrumentalities, working just as they do, are the best adaption to effect His purpose. I am almost ready to say that this is probably true; that God wills this contest, and wills that it shall not end yet. By His mere great power on the minds of the now contestants, He could either have saved or destroyed the Union without a human contest. Yet the contest began. And, having begun, He could give the final victory to either side any day. Yet the contest proceeds.—*Meditation, Sept. 30, 1862.* VIII, 52.

2.—I fear the war must go on till North or South have both drunk of the cup to the very dregs—till both have worked out in pain and grief, and bitter humiliation, the sin of 200 years. It has seemed to me that God so wills it.—*To James R. Gilmore, late May, 1863.* Gilmore, 160.

3.—The purposes of the Almighty are perfect, and must prevail, though we erring mortals may fail to accurately perceive them in advance. We hoped for a happy termination of this terrible war long before this; but God knows best, and has ruled otherwise. We shall yet acknowledge His wisdom, and our own error therein. Meanwhile we must work earnestly in the best lights He gives us, trusting that so working still conduces to the great ends He ordains. Surely, He intends some great good to follow this mighty convulsion, which no mortal could make, and no mortal could stay.—*To Mrs. Eliza Gurney, Sept. 4, 1864.* X, 215.

Deity, purpose of, toward slavery—Both [North and South] read the same Bible and pray to the same God, and each invokes His aid against the other. . . . The prayers of both could not be answered. That of neither has been fully answered. The Almighty has His own purposes. "Woe unto the world because of offences; for it must needs be that offences come, but woe to that man by whom the offences cometh." If we shall suppose that American slavery is one of these offences which, in the providence of God, must needs come, but which, having continued through His appointed time, He now wills to remove, and that He gives to both North and South this terrible war as the woe due to those by whom the offence came, shall we discern therein any departure from those divine attributes which believers in a living God always ascribe to Him?—*Second inaugural, March 4, 1865.* XI, 45.

See DEITY, purpose of, in war.

See SLAVERY, theology of.

See SLAVERY, line across the continent, 1, 3.

Deity, ready to follow—I am conscious of no desire for my country's welfare that is not in consonance with His will, and no plan upon which we may not ask His blessing.—*To Iowa Quakers, Jan. 5, 1862.* Hertz II, 847.

2.—Unless I am more deceived in myself than I often am, it is my earnest desire to know the will of Providence in this matter. And if I can learn what it is, I will do it.—*Reply to Chicago church committee, Sept. 13, 1862.* Stern, 720.

3.—Whatever shall appear to be God's will I will do. —*Reply to Chicago church committee, Sept. 13, 1862.* Stern, 723.

See REVELATION, no direct, expected.

Deity, responsibility to—In full view of my great responsibility to my God and my country, I earnestly beg the attention of Congress to the subject [compensated emancipation].—*Message to Congress, March 6, 1862.* VII, 115.

Deity, revelations of—*See* REVELATION, no direct, expected.

Deity, reversing rule of—*See* REPUBLICAN PARTY, advice to, 19.

Deity, right and—If we do right God will be with us, and if God is with us we cannot fail.—*Proclamation, July 7, 1864.* X, 149.

Deity, ruler of nations—*See* INAUGURAL, SECOND, should "wear well."

See PEOPLE, justice of, 1.

Deity, speech "direct gift of"—*See* SPEECH, "direct gift of Creator."

Deity, submission to—It is fit and becoming in all people at all times to acknowledge and revere the supreme government of God, and to bow in humble submission to His chastisements, to confess and deplore their sins and transgressions in the full conviction that the fear of the Lord is the beginning of wis-

dom, and to pray with all fervency and contrition for the pardon of their offences and for a blessing upon their present and prospective action.—*Fast Day Proclamation, Aug. 12, 1861.* VI, 341.

2.—Fondly do we hope, fervently do we pray, that this mighty scourge of war may speedily pass away. Yet, if God wills that it continue until all the wealth piled up by the bondsman's 250 years of unrequited toil shall be sunk, and until every drop of blood drawn with the lash shall be paid by another drawn with the sword, as was said 3,000 years ago, so still must it be said, "the judgments of the Lord are true and righteous altogether."—*Second inaugural, March 4, 1865.* XI, 46.

Deity, supplication to—The problem [slavery] is too mighty for me—may God, in his mercy, superintend the solution.—*To George Robertson, Oct. 15, 1855.* II, 280.

2.—May the God of the right give you the victory now, as He surely will in the end.—*To C. D. Gilfillan, May 9, 1857.* Hertz II, 703.

3.—May the Almighty grant that the cause of truth, justice and humanity shall in no wise suffer at my hands.—*To J. R. Giddings, May 21, 1860.* VI, 14.

4.—I invite the people of the United States [on Aug. 6] . . . to invoke the influence of His Holy Spirit . . . to guide the counsels of the government with wisdom adequate to so great a national emergency, and to visit with tender care and consolation throughout the length and breadth of our land all those who, through the vicissitudes of marches, voyages, battles, and sieges have been brought to suffer in mind, body, or estate, and finally to lead the whole nation through the paths of repentence and submission to the Divine will back to the perfect enjoyment of union and fraternal peace.—*Thanksgiving Proclamation, July 15, 1863.* IX, 32.

5.—I recommend to them [the American people] that while offering up ascriptions justly due to Him for such singular deliverances and blessings, they also, with humble penitence for our national perverseness and disobedience, commend to His tender care all those who have become widows, orphans, mourners, or sufferers in the lamentable civil strife in which we are unavoidably engaged, and fervently implore the interposition of the Almighty hand to heal the wounds of the nation and to restore it to the full enjoyment of peace, harmony, tranquility and union.— *Proclamation, Oct. 3, 1863.* IX, 153.

6.—I do hereby . . . invite and request the heads of the executive departments of this government, together with all legislators, all judges and magistrates, and all other persons exercising authority in the land, whether civil, military or naval, and all soldiers, sea-men, and marines in the national service and all the other loyal and law-abiding people of the United States to assemble in their preferred places of public worship on that day [first Thursday of August] and there and then render to the Almighty and merciful Ruler of the Universe such homages and such confessions and to offer to Him such supplications as the Congress . . . have . . . so solemnly, so earnestly and so reverently recommended.—*Fast Day Proclamation, July 7, 1864.* X, 151.

See BIXBY LETTER.

See EMANCIPATION PROCLAMATION, text of.

See FAREWELL TO SPRINGFIELD.

See GETTYSBURG, Lincoln's prayer for.

See "HOUSE DIVIDED AGAINST ITSELF," cannot stand, 1.

See NOMINATION OF 1860, accepted.

Deity, trust in—Whatever He designs He will do for me yet. "Stand still, and see the salvation of the Lord" is my text just now.—*To Joshua F. Speed, July 4, 1842.* I, 219.

2.—Let us strive to deserve, as far as mortals may, the continued care of Divine Providence, trusting that in future national emergencies He will not fail to provide us the instruments of safety and security.—*Speech, Springfield, July 16, 1852.* II, 177.

3.—[I trust] through the good sense of the American people, on all sides of all rivers in America, under the providence of God, who has never deserted us, that we shall again be brethren, forgetting all parties, ignoring all parties.—*Speech, Cincinnati, Feb. 12, 1861.* VI, 119.

4.—Your worthy mayor has thought fit to express the hope that I may be able to relieve this country from the present, or, I should say, the threatened, difficulties. I am sure I bring a heart true to the work. For the ability to perform it, I must trust in that Supreme Being which has never forsaken this favored land, through the instrumentality of this great and intelligent people. Without that assistance I shall surely fail; with it, I cannot fail.—*Speech, Buffalo, Feb. 16, 1861.* VI, 133.

5.—I still have confidence that the Almighty, Maker of the universe, will, through the instrumentality of this great and intelligent people, bring us through this as He has through all other difficulties of our country.—*Speech, New York Legislature, Feb. 18, 1861.* VI, 141.

6.—Having thus chosen our course, without guile and with pure purpose, let us renew our trust in God and go forward without fear and with manly hearts.—*Message to Congress, July 4, 1861.* VI, 325.

7.—Since your last annual assembling another year of health and bountiful harvests has passed; and while it has not pleased the Almighty to bless us with a return of peace, we can but press on, guided by the best light He gives us, trusting that in His good time and wise way all will yet be well.—*Second annual message, Dec. 1, 1862.* VIII, 93.

See EMANCIPATION PROCLAMATION (PRELIMINARY), deliberate policy.

See FAREWELL TO SPRINGFIELD, 3.

See SLAVERY, Taylor's death impedes settlement of.

Deity, will not be evaded—*See* POLK, JAMES K., "Where Washington sat."

Delaware, characterized—South of the [Mason and Dixon] line noble little Delaware led off [for the Union] right from the first.—*First annual message, Dec. 3, 1861.* VII, 52.

Delaware, cost of freeing slaves in—*See* EMANCIPATION, financial aspects of compensated, 3.

Deliberation, urged—We must be calm and moderate. . . . We must not be led by excitement and passion to do that which our sober judgment would not approve in our cooler moments.—*Speech, Bloomington, May 29, 1856.* Lapsley II, 249.

Democracy—*See* SELF-GOVERNMENT.

Democracy, "sacred name" of—And was the sacred name of Democracy ever before made to indorse such an enormity [collection of revenue in specie under the subtreasury plan] against the rights of the people?—*Speech, Springfield, Dec. 20, 1839.* I, 105.

Democracy, true—True democracy makes no inquiry about the color of the skin, or place of nativity, or any other similar circumstance or condition.—*Speech, Cincinnati, May 6, 1842.* Hertz II, 531.

Democratic Party, alleged bargain to sell out—*See* ABOLITIONIZE, plot to, parties denied.

Democratic Party, antislavery men of—*See* SLAVERY, Democrats appealed to.

Democratic Party, attitude of, toward slavery—*See* SLAVERY, Democratic policy toward.

Democratic Party, attitude of, toward war effort—I cannot overlook the fact that the [Albany] meeting speaks as "Democrats." . . . In this time of national peril I would have preferred to meet you upon a level one step higher than any party platform, because I am sure that from such more elevated position we could do better battle for the country we all love than we possibly can from those lower ones where, from the force of habit, the prejudices of the past and selfish hopes of the future, we are sure to expend much of our ingenuity and strength in finding fault with and aiming blows at each other. But since you have denied me this, I will yet be thankful for the country's sake that not all Democrats have done so. He on whose discretionary judgment Mr. Vallandigham was arrested and tried is a Democrat, having no old party affinity with me, and the judge who rejected the constitutional view expressed in these [Albany] resolutions, by refusing to discharge Mr. Vallandigham on habeas corpus, is a Democrat of better days than these, having received his judicial mantle at the hands of President Jackson. And still more, of all those Democrats who are nobly exposing their lives and shedding their blood on the battle-field, I have learned that many approve the course taken with Mr. Vallandigham, while I have not heard of a single one condemning it.—*To Erastus Corning and Others, June 12, 1863.* VIII, 310.

2.—The slightest knowledge of arithmetic will prove to any man that the rebel armies cannot be destroyed by Democratic strategy. It would sacrifice all the white men of the north to do it. There are now in the service of the United States nearly 150,000 able-bodied colored men, most of them under arms, defending and acquiring Union territory. The Democratic strategy demands that these forces be disbanded, and that the masters be conciliated by restoring them to slavery. The black men who now assist Union prisoners to escape are to be converted into our enemies, in the vain hope of gaining the good-will of their masters. We shall have to fight two nations instead of one. You cannot conciliate the South if you guarantee to them ultimate success; and the experience of the present war proves their success is inevitable if you fling the compulsory labor of millions of black men into their side of the scale.—*Interview, Gov. Randall, Aug. 15, 1864.* X, 189.

3.—We have to hold the territory in inclement and sickly places; where are the Democrats to do this? It was a free fight, and the field was open to the war Democrats to put down this rebellion by fighting both master and slave, long before the present policy was inaugurated.—*Interview, Gov. Randall, Aug. 15, 1864.* X, 190.

See UNION, fate of, to be decided by 1864 election.

Democratic Party, classes negroes as brutes—*See* NEGRO, tendency to dehumanize.

Democratic Party, deserts Jeffersonian principles—*See* JEFFERSON, THOMAS, supporters and opponents of, trade creeds.

Democratic Party, outraged by Kansas-Nebraska bill—When this Nebraska bill was first introduced into Congress the sense of the Democratic party was outraged. That party has ever prided itself that it was a friend of individual, universal freedom. It was that principle upon which they carried their measures. When the Kansas scheme was conceived, it was natural that this respect and sense should have been outraged. Now I make this appeal to the Democratic citizens here. Don't you find yourselves making arguments in support of these measures which you never would have made before? Did you ever do it before this Nebraska bill compelled you to do it? If you answer this in the affirmative, see how a whole party have been turned away from their love of liberty.—*Speech, Kalamazoo, Mich., Aug. 27, 1856.* Stern, 407.

Democratic Party, party of negation—*See* CAMPAIGN OF 1852, Democrats' do-nothing platform.

Democratic Party, program of, would destroy Union—*See* UNION, fate of, to be decided by 1864 election.

Demonstration, two methods of—There are two ways of establishing a proposition. One is by trying to demonstrate it upon reason, and the other is to show that great men in former times have thought so and so, and thus to pass it by the weight of pure authority.—*Speech, Columbus, Ohio, Sept. 16, 1859.* V, 172.

Depression, not to be checked by "fawning"—I am not insensible to any commercial or financial depression that may exist, but nothing is to be gained by fawning around the "respectable scoundrels" who got it up. Let them go to work and repair the mistake of their own making, and then perhaps they will be less greedy to do the like again.—*To Truman Smith, Nov. 10, 1860.* VI, 69.

Designing Men, beware of—*See* UNION, appeals for support of, 8.

Despotism, Declaration of Independence "hard nut" for—*See* DECLARATION OF INDEPENDENCE, stumbling block to tyrants, 1.

Despotism, seeds of—Destroy this spirit [of liberty] and you have planted the seeds of despotism at your doors. Accustomed to trample on the rights of others, you have lost the genius of your own independence and become fit subjects of the first cunning tyrant who rises among you.—*Speech, Edwardsville, Sept. 13, 1858.* XI, 110.

2.—In my present position I could scarcely be justified were I to omit raising a warning voice against this approach of returning despotism [as seen in insurgent documents].—*First annual message, Dec. 3, 1861.* VII, 5.

Despotism, those who deny Jefferson are vanguards of—These expressions [denying Jeffersonian principles] differing in form, are identical in object and effect—the supplanting the principles of free government, and restoring those of classification, cast and legitimacy. . . . They are the vanguard, the miners and sappers, of returning despotism. We must repulse them or they will subjugate us.—*To H. L. Pierce and others, April 6, 1859.* V, 126.

Despotism, without hypocrisy in Russia—See KNOW-NOTHING PARTY, principles of, challenged, 2.

Determination Comes First—Determine that the thing can and shall be done, and then we shall find a way.—*Speech in Congress, June 20, 1848.* II, 46.

Devil, outdone by "holy men of the South"—See CHURCH, insulted by "professedly holy men of the South."

Devil, "takes care of his own"—See CONSTITUTION, spirit of.

"Dews of Heaven"—See EMANCIPATION, states appealed to for compensated, 2.

Dictatorship, Frémont proclamation smacks of—See FRÉMONT, JOHN C., proclamation of, disapproved, 3.

Dictatorship, "I will risk"—See HOOKER, JOSEPH, talk of dictatorship challenged.

Diddling, no—Please look into this, and write me. I can and will pay it if it is right; but I do not wish to be diddled.—*To Cincinnati hotel proprietors, June 5, 1860.* Angle, 248.

Diligence, "leading rule"—See LAW, advice to lawyers.

Disappointment, familiar with—But if the good people in their wisdom shall see fit to keep me in the background, I have been too familiar with disappointments to be very much chagrined.—*Address to Sangamon County, March 9, 1832.* I, 9.

Discovery, man's first—See CLOTHING, origin of.

Discretion, exercised for peace—The cause here indicated will be followed unless current events and experience shall show a modification or change to be proper, and in every case and exigency my best discretion will be exercised according to circumstances actually existing, and with a view and a hope of a peaceful solution of the national troubles and the restoration of fraternal sympathies and affections.—*First inaugural, March 4, 1861.* VI, 176.

Discretion, left to commander in field—Knowing how hazardous it is to bind down a distant commander in the field to specific lines and operations, as so much always depends on a knowledge of localities and passing events, it is intended, therefore, to leave a considerable margin for the exercise of your judgment and discretion.—*To commander, Department of the West, Oct. 24, 1861.* VII, 11.

Disobedience, boys guilty of, not needed—See BOYS, disobedient, not needed.

Dissension, dangers of—See REPUBLICAN PARTY, threats to unity of.

Distance, lulls the mind—Great distance in either time or space has wonderful power to lull and render quiescent the human mind.—*Speech, Springfield, Feb. 22, 1842.* I, 202.

Distinction, agrees to acquire—As you are all so anxious for me to distinguish myself [in Congress], I have concluded to do so before long.—*To W. H. Herndon, Dec. 13, 1847.* I, 317.

District of Columbia, Republican attitude toward slavery in—See SLAVERY, Republican policy toward, 5.

District of Columbia, restoration of original boundaries urged—The present insurrection shows, I think, that the extension of this District across the Potomac River at the time of establishing the capital here was eminently wise and consequently that the relinquishment of that portion of it which lies within the State of Virginia was unwise and dangerous. I submit for your consideration the expediency of regaining that part of the District and the restoration of the original boundaries thereof through negotiations with the State of Virginia.—*First annual message, Dec. 3, 1861.* VII, 44.

District of Columbia, slavery in—The North clamored for the abolition of a peculiar species of slave trade in the District of Columbia, in connection with which, in view from the windows of the capitol, a sort of negro livery stable, where droves of negroes were collected, temporarily kept, and finally taken to southern markets, precisely like droves of horses, had been openly maintained for fifty years.—*Speech, Peoria, Oct. 16, 1854.* II, 202.
Repeated at Urbana, Oct. 24, 1854. Hertz, II, 631.
2.—In the measures of 1850 Congress had the subject

of slavery in the District expressly in hand. If they were then establishing the principle of allowing the people to do as they please [as argued by Douglas] why did they not apply the principle to that people? —*Speech, Peoria, Oct. 16, 1854.* II, 215.

See EMANCIPATION, District of Columbia.

District of Columbia, war causes suffering in—I recommend to the favorable consideration of Congress the interests of the District of Columbia. The insurrection has been the cause of much suffering and sacrifice to its inhabitants and as they have no representative in Congress that body should not overlook their just claims upon the government.—*First annual message, Dec. 3, 1861.* VII, 48.

Dix, John A., "zealous and able"—Upon the subject of your letter, I have to say that it is beyond my province to interfere with New York City politics; that I am very grateful to Gen. Dix for the zealous and able military and quasi-civil support he has given the government during the war, and that if the people of New York should tender him the mayoralty, and he accept it, nothing on that subject could be more satisfactory to me. . . . To state it in another way, if Gen. Dix's present relation to the general government lays any restraint upon him in this matter, I wish to remove that restraint.—*To J. J. Astor, Jr., R. B. Roosevelt and N. Sands, Nov. 9, 1863.* IX, 202.

"Dixie," song captured—I have always thought "Dixie" one of the best tunes I ever heard. I have heard that our adversaries over the way have attempted to appropriate it as a national air. I insisted yesterday that we had fairly captured it. I presented the question to the attorney general, and he gives his opinion that it is our lawful prize. I ask the band to give us a good turn upon it.—*Response to serenade, April 10, 1865.* Hertz II, 965.

Doctrine, testing truth of—*See* SECTIONALISM, what constitutes? 7, 8.

"Doctrine of necessity"—*See* RELIGION, attitude toward.

Do-Nothing, policy decried—Do nothing at all [those who resist internal improvements argue], lest you do something wrong.—*Speech in Congress, June 20, 1848.* II, 31.
2.—We must reject them [arguments against internal improvements] as insufficient, or lie down and do nothing by any authority.—*Speech in Congress, June 20, 1848.* II, 31.
3.—If this argument of "irregularity" is sufficient anywhere, it is sufficient everywhere, and puts an end to

[internal] improvements altogether.—*Speech in Congress, June 20, 1848.* II, 36.

Dog, "Better give the path to"—*See* QUARREL NOT AT ALL.

Dog That Crossed the Brook, does not want to be like—*See* COPPERHEADS, would scoff.

"Dog to a Bladder of Beans"—*See* CASS, LEWIS D., military figure of, 1.

Dogmas of the Past, inadequate for the present—The dogmas of the quiet past are inadequate to the stormy present. The occasion is piled high with difficulty and we must rise with the occasion. As our case is new, so we must think anew and act anew. We must disenthral ourselves, and then we shall save our country.—*Second annual message, Dec. 1, 1862.* VIII, 131.

Douglas, Adele Cutts—*See* CONFISCATION, Mrs. Stephen A. Douglas reassured.

Douglas, Stephen A., "Abolitionist"—*See* ABOLITION, strongest argument for, 3.

Douglas, Stephen A., apotheosis of—Does he [Douglas] expect to stand up in majestic dignity, and go through his apotheosis and become a god, in the maintaining of a principle which neither man nor mouse in all God's creation is opposing?—*Speech, Springfield, July 17, 1858.* III, 164.

Douglas, Stephen A., "aptest way to kill"—Douglas has gone south, making characteristic speeches, and seeking to reinstate himself in that section. The majority of the Democratic politicians of the nation mean to kill him; but I doubt whether they will adopt the aptest way to do it. Their true way is to present him with no new test, let him into the Charleston convention, and then out-vote him, and nominate another. On the other hand, if they push a slave code upon him as a test, he will bolt at once, turn upon us, as in the case of Lecompton, and claim that all northern men shall make common cause in electing him President as the best means of breaking down this slave power.—*To Lyman Trumbull, Dec. 11, 1858.* Tracy, 97.

Douglas, Stephen A., at Clay's death-bed—*See* WHIG PARTY, apple-sized tears from.

Douglas, Stephen A., attitude of, toward compromises—You [Kentuckians] ought to remember how long, by precedent, Judge Douglas holds himself obliged to stick by compromises. You ought to remember that by the time you yourselves think you are ready to inaugurate measures for the revival of the African slave trade, sufficient time will have arrived, by precedent, for Judge Douglas to break through that compromise. He says now nothing more strong than he said in 1849 when he declared in favor of the Missouri Compromise—that precisely four years and a half after he declared that compromise to be a sacred thing, which "no ruthless hand would ever dare to touch" he, himself, brought forward the measure ruthlessly to destroy it. By a mere calculation of time it will only be four years more until he is ready to take back his profession about the sacredness of the compromise [allegedly in the Constitution] abolishing the slave trade.—*Speech, Cincinnati, Sept. 17, 1859.* V, 210.

Douglas, Stephen A., attitude toward court decisions —See JUDICIAL DECISIONS, Douglas's attitude toward.

See DRED SCOTT DECISION, Douglas's devotion to.

Douglas, Stephen A., attitude toward Lincoln—Those who heard Mr. Douglas recollect that he indulged himself in a contemptuous expression of pity for me. "Now he's got me," thought I. But when he went on to say that $5,000,000 of the expenditure of 1838 were payments of the French indemnities, which I knew to be untrue; that $5,000,000 had been spent for the post office, which I knew to be untrue; that $10,000,000 had been for the Maine boundary war, which I not only knew to be untrue, but supremely ridiculous; and when I saw he was stupid enough to hope that I would permit such groundless and audacious assertions to go unexposed,—I readily consented that, on the score both of veracity and sagacity, the audience should judge whether he or I were the more deserving of the world's contempt.—*Speech, Springfield, Dec. 20, 1839.* I, 135.

2.—[Reading an extract from a Douglas speech] Well now, Gentlemen, is not that very alarming? Just to think of it! Right at the outset of his [Douglas's] canvass, I, a poor, amiable, intelligent gentleman—I am to be slain in this way.—*Speech, Chicago, July 10, 1858.* III, 20.

3.—It is fortunate for me that I can keep as good-humored as I do, when the judge [Douglas] acknowledges that he has been trying to make a question of veracity with me. I know the judge is a great man, while I am only a small one.—*Debate, Ottawa, Aug. 21, 1858.* III, 240.

4.—He [Douglas] is very much in the habit, when he argues me up into a position I never thought of occupying, of very cozily saying he has no doubt Lincoln is "conscientious" in saying so.—*Debate, Freeport, Aug. 27, 1858.* III, 284.

5.—The judge [Douglas] has set about seriously trying to make the impression that when we meet at different places I am literally in his clutches—that I am a poor, helpless, decrepit mouse, and that I can do nothing at all. . . . I don't want to quarrel with him—to call him a liar—but when I come square up to him, I don't know what else to call him, if I must tell the truth out.—*Debate, Jonesboro, Sept. 15, 1858.* IV, 69.

6.—When he [Douglas] has burlesqued me into a position which I never thought of assuming myself, he will, in the most benevolent and patronizing manner imaginable, compliment me by saying "he has no doubt I am perfectly conscientious about it." I thank him for that word "conscientious." It turns my attention to the wonderful evidences of conscience he manifests. When he assumes to be the first discoverer and sole advocate of the right of a people to govern themselves, he is conscientious. When he affects to understand that a man, putting a hundred slaves through under the lash, is simply governing himself, he is more conscientious. When he affects not to know that the Dred Scott decision forbids a territorial legislature to exclude slavery, he is most conscientious. When . . . he declares that I say, unless I shall play my batteries successfully, so as to abolish slavery in every one of the states, the Union shall be dissolved, he is absolutely bursting with conscience. It is nothing that I never said any such thing. —*Notes, Oct. 1, 1858.* IV, 212.

7.—At Bloomington . . . he [Douglas] . . . said that I had used language ingeniously contrived to conceal my intentions, or words to that effect. Now I understand this is an imputation upon my veracity and candor. . . . Judge Douglas may not understand that he implicated my truthfulness and my honor when he said I was doing one thing and pretending another. . . . At Galesburg, when he [Douglas] brings forward a speech made at Chicago, and an extract from a speech made at Charleston, to prove that I was trying to play a double part—that I was trying to cheat the public and get votes upon one set of principles at one place and upon another set of principles at another place—I do not understand but what he impeaches my honor, my veracity, and my candor; and because he does this, I do not understand that I am bound, if I see a truthful ground for it, to keep my hands off of him.—*Debate, Quincy, Oct. 13, 1858.* IV, 325.

8.—He [Douglas] did not make a mistake, in one of his early speeches, when he called me an "amiable" man, though perhaps he did when he called me an "intelligent" man.—*Debate, Quincy, Oct. 13, 1858.* IV, 327.

9.—He [Douglas] asks me, or he asks the audience, if I wish to push this matter to the point of personal difficulty. I tell him, No. . . . I very much prefer, when this canvass shall be over, however it may result, that we at least part without any bitter recollections of personal difficulties.—*Debate, Quincy, Oct. 13, 1858.* IV, 327.

10.—Judge Douglas . . . has strongly impressed me with the belief of a predetermination on his part to misrepresent me.—*Debate, Alton, Oct. 15, 1858.* V, 31.

See DOUGLAS, STEPHEN A., characterized.

Douglas, Stephen A., best way to combat—My recent experience shows that speaking at the same place the next day after D[ouglas] is the very thing—is, in fact, a concluding speech on him.—*To William Fithian, Sept. 3, 1858.* III, 348.

Douglas, Stephen A., care-not policy of, toward slavery—*See* SLAVERY, Douglas's care-not policy.

Douglas, Stephen A., characterized—A report is in circulation that he [Douglas] has abandoned the idea of going to Washington, though the report does not come in a very authentic form, so far as I can learn—though, by the way, speaking of authenticity, you know that if we heard Douglas say that he had abandoned the contest, it would not be very authentic.—*To John T. Stuart, Nov. 14, 1839.* I, 198.

2.—The Richmond speech [by Douglas], though marked with the same species of "shirks and quirks" as the old ones, was not marked with any greater ability.—*Speech, Springfield, Aug. 14, 1852.* Angle, 85.

3.—I considered it [Douglas's Chicago speech defending Compromise of 1850] a very able production—by far superior to anything I had ever seen from Judge Douglas, and compared favorably with anything from any source, which I had seen, on that general subject.—*Speech, Springfield, Aug. 14, 1852.* Angle, 88.

4.—His [Douglas's] old friends have deserted him in such numbers as to leave him too few to live by. He came to his own, and his own received him not; and lo! he turns unto the Gentiles.—*Speech, Peoria, Oct. 16, 1854.* II, 261.

5.—There is certainly a double game being played somehow. Possibly—even probably—Douglas is temporarily deceiving the president. . . . Unless he plays his double game more successfully than we have often seen done, he cannot carry many Republicans North, without at the same time losing a larger number of his old friends South.—*To E. B. Washburne, May 27, 1858.* II, 362.

6.—This man Douglas, who misrepresents his constituents and who has exercised his highest talents in that direction.—*Speech, Bloomington, May 29, 1856.* Lapsley II, 264.

7.—Douglas is a great man—at keeping from answering questions he doesn't want to answer.—*Speech, Kalamazoo, Mich., Aug. 27, 1856.* Stern, 401.

8.—Douglas clings to that hope [of nailing the charge on his adversaries that they favor indiscriminate race amalgamation] as a drowning man to the last plank.—*Speech, Springfield, June 26, 1857.* II, 329.

9.—Don't you know how apt he [Douglas] is—how exceedingly anxious he is at all times—to seize upon anything and everything to persuade you that something he has done you did yourself? Why, he tried to persuade you last night that our Illinois legislature instructed him to introduce the Nebraska bill. There was nobody in that legislature ever thought of such a thing.—*Speech, Chicago, July 10, 1858.* III, 42.

10.—I have just returned from Chicago. Douglas took nothing by his motion there—in fact, by his rampant indorsement of the Dred Scott decision he drove back a few Republicans who were favorably inclined toward him. His tactics just now, in part, is to make it appear that he is having a triumphal entry into, and march through the country; but it is all as bombastic and hollow as Napoleon's bulletins sent back from his campaign in Russia.—*To Gustave Koerner, July 15, 1858.* Tracy, 89.

11.—Senator Douglas is of world-wide renown. All the anxious politicians of his party, or who have been of his party for years past have been looking upon him as certainly, at no distant day, to be President of the United States. They have seen in his round jolly, fruitful face, postoffices, land offices, marshalships and cabinet appointments, chargeships and foreign missions, bursting and sprouting out in wonderful exuberance, ready to be laid hold of by their greedy hands. . . . On the contrary, nobody has ever expected me to be President. On my poor lean, lank face nobody has ever seen that any cabbages were sprouting out.—*Speech, Springfield, July 17, 1858.* III, 157.

12.—He [Douglas] then quotes, or attempts to quote, from my speech. I will not say that he wilfully misquotes, but he does fail to quote accurately.—*Speech, Springfield, July 17, 1858.* III, 171.

13.—It would be amusing, if it were not disgusting, to see how quick these compromise-breakers [like Douglas] administer on the political effects of their adversaries, trumping up claims never before heard of, and dividing the assets among themselves.—*Speech, Springfield, July 17, 1858.* III, 184.

14.—He [Douglas] cares nothing for the South; he

knows he is already dead there. He only leans southward more to keep the Buchanan party from growing in Illinois. . . . At all events he means to hold on to his chances in Illinois.—*To Henry Asbury, July 31, 1858.* III, 198.

15.—Seeing that Douglas had had the process served on him, that he had taken notice of such service, that he had come into court and pleaded to a part of the complaint, but had ignored the main issue, I took a default on him. I held that he had no plea to make to the general charge [that his course on Nebraska bill was friendly to slavery].—*Speech, Beardstown, Aug. 12, 1858.* Angle, 186.

16.—I repeat, and renew, and shall continue to repeat and renew, this "charge" until he [Douglas] denies the evidence, and then I shall so fasten it upon him that it will cling to him as long as he lives.—*Speech, Beardstown, Aug. 12, 1858.* Angle, 187.

17.—[Douglas goes] vociferating about the country that possibly he may hint that somebody is a liar.—*Speech, Beardstown, Aug. 12, 1858.* Angle, 187.

18.—Judge Douglas is a man of vast influence, so great that it is enough for many men to profess to believe anything when they once find out that Judge Douglas professes to believe it.—*Debate, Ottawa, Aug. 21, 1858.* III, 252.

19.—When we consider who Judge Douglas is—that he is a distinguished senator of the United States; that he has served nearly twelve years as such; that his character is not at all limited as an ordinary senator of the United States, but that his name has become of world-wide renown,—it is most extraordinary that he should so far forget all the suggestions of justice to an adversary or of prudence to himself, as to venture upon the assertion of that which the slightest investigation would have shown him to be wholly false. I can only account for his having done so upon the supposition that that evil genius which has attended him through his life, giving to him an apparent astonishing prosperity, such as to lead very many good men to doubt there being any advantage in virtue over vice—I say I can only account for it on the supposition that that evil genius has at last made up its mind to forsake him.—*Debate, Freeport, Aug. 27, 1858.* III, 282.

20.—Another extraordinary feature of the judge's conduct in this canvass . . . is, that he is in the habit, in almost all his speeches, of charging falsehood upon his adversaries, myself and others. I now ask whether he is able to find in anything that Judge Trumbull, for instance, has said, or in anything I have said, a justification at all compared with what we have, in this instance, for that sort of vulgarity.—*Debate, Freeport, Aug. 27, 1858.* III, 282.

21.—Douglas will tell a lie to 10,000 people one day, even though he knows he may have to deny it to 5,000 the next.—*Speech, Clinton, Sept. 8, 1858.* Stephenson, 159.

22.—Judge Douglas, why didn't you tell the truth? I would like to know why you didn't tell the truth about it.—*Debate, Jonesboro, Sept. 15, 1858.* IV, 67.

23.—[Douglas's statement, at Joliet, that Lincoln "had to be carried from the platform at Ottawa"] furnishes a subject for philosophical contemplation. I have been treating it in that way, and I have really come to the conclusion that I can explain it in no other way than by believing the judge is crazy. If he was in his right mind, I cannot conceive how he would have risked disgusting the four or five thousand of his own friends who stood there and knew, as to my having been carried from the platform—that there was not a word of truth in it. [Douglas: "Didn't they carry you off?"] There; that question illustrates the character of this man Douglas exactly. He smiles now and says, "Didn't they carry you off?" But he said then, "He had to be carried off"; and he said it to convince the country that he had so completely broken me down by his speech that I had to be carried away. . . . Yes, they did [carry him away]. But, Judge Douglas, why didn't you tell the truth?—*Debate, Jonesboro, Sept. 15, 1858.* IV, 67.

24.—Judge Douglas, when he made that statement, must have been crazy, and wholly out of his sober senses.—*Debate, Jonesboro, Sept. 15, 1858.* IV, 68.

25.—He [Douglas] is merely making an issue upon the meaning of words.—*Debate, Charleston, Sept. 18, 1858.* IV, 97.

26.—It is said that a bear is sometimes hard enough pressed to drop a cub, and so I presume it was in this case. I presume the truth is that Douglas put it [a provision of the Kansas-Nebraska bill] in and afterward took it out.—*Debate, Charleston, Sept. 18, 1858.* IV, 104.

27.—Judge Douglas [at Ottawa] attacked me in regard to a matter ten years old [Lincoln's Mexican War record]. Isn't he a pretty man to be whining about people making charges against him only two years old!—*Debate, Charleston, Sept. 18, 1858.* IV, 193.

28.—Judge Douglas is playing cuttlefish, a small species of fish that has no mode of defending itself except by throwing out a black fluid, which makes the water so dark the enemy cannot see it and thus it escapes. Is not Judge Douglas playing the cuttlefish?—*Debate, Charleston, Sept. 18, 1858.* IV, 195.

29.—When Judge Douglas is drawn up to a distinct point, there is significance in all he says, and in all he omits to say.—*Notes, Oct. 1, 1858.* IV, 208.

30.—Does not Judge Douglas equivocate when he pretends not to know that the Supreme Court has decided that the people of a territory cannot exclude slavery prior to forming a state constitution?—*Notes, Oct 1, 1858.* IV, 208.

31.—In the main I shall trust an intelligent community to learn my objects and aims from what I say and do myself, rather than from what Judge Douglas may say of me.—*Notes, Oct. 1, 1858.* IV, 212.

32.—Judge Douglas speaks with greater conscience than most men. It corresponds with his other points of greatness.—*Notes, Oct. 1, 1858.* IV, 213

33.—He [Douglas] speaks . . . with increased confidence and recklessness of assertion.—*Notes, Oct. 1, 1858.* IV, 215.

34.—Judge Douglas is a man of large influence. His bare opinion goes far to fix the opinions of others. Besides this, thousands hang their hopes upon forcing their opinions to agree with his. It is a party necessity with them to say they agree with him, and there is danger they will repeat the saying till they really come to believe it. Others dread, and shrink from, his denunciations, his sarcasms and his ingenious misrepresentations. The susceptible young hear lessons from him, such as their fathers never heard when they were young.—*Notes, Oct. 1, 1858.* IV, 223.

35.—He [Douglas] says when he discovered there was a mistake in that case [*See* FORGERY, alleged] he came forward magnanimously, without my calling his attention to it, and explained it. I will tell you how he became so magnanimous. When the newspapers of our side had discovered and published it, and put it beyond his power to deny it, then he came forward and made a virtue of necessity by acknowledging it. . . . He has taken credit for great magnanimity in coming forward and acknowledging what is proved on him beyond even the capacity of Judge Douglas to deny, and he has more capacity in that way than any other living man.—*Debate, Quincy, Oct. 13, 1858.* IV, 386.

36.—In his quotations from that speech [by Lincoln at Springfield] as he has made them upon former occasions, the extracts were taken in such a way as, I suppose, brings them within the definition of what is called garbling—taking portions of a speech which, when taken by themselves, do not present the entire sense of the speaker as expressed at the time.—*Debate, Alton, Oct. 15, 1858.* V, 33.

37.—He [Douglas] is so put up by nature that a lash upon his back would hurt him, but a lash on anybody else's back does not hurt him.—*Speech, Columbus, Ohio, Sept. 16, 1859.* V, 159.

38.—Is it not a most extraordinary spectacle, that a man should stand up and ask for any confidence in his statements, who sets out as he does [in his *Harper's* essay] with portions of history, calling upon people to believe that it is a true and fair representation, when the leading part and controlling feature of the whole history is carefully suppressed?—*Speech, Columbus, Ohio, Sept. 16, 1859.* V, 170.

39.—The wonderful capacity of the man; the power he has of doing what would seem to be impossible.—*Speech, Cincinnati, Sept. 17, 1859.* V, 216.

See GAG, can't fashion, for Douglas.

See "HOUSE DIVIDED AGAINST ITSELF," cannot stand, 3.

Douglas, Stephen A., challenges "good man"—*See* "HOUSE DIVIDED AGAINST ITSELF," does Douglas say it can stand? 2.

Douglas, Stephen A., claims too much credit for Lecompton defeat—*See* LECOMPTON CONSTITUTION, who defeated?

Douglas, Stephen A., "conscientious"—*See* DOUGLAS, STEPHEN A., attitude toward Lincoln, 6.

Douglas, Stephen A., contrast between, and Lincoln—*See* DOUGLAS, STEPHEN A., characterized, 11.

Douglas, Stephen A., cotton gin and slavery—*See* SLAVERY, perpetuation of, 6, 9.

Douglas, Stephen A., Democrats stick to, reluctantly—The impulse of almost every Democrat is to stick to Douglas; but it horrifies them to have to follow him out of the Democratic party. A good many are annoyed that he did not go for the English contrivance, and thus heal the breach. They begin to think there is a "negro in the fence"—that Douglas really wants to have a fuss with the President—that sticks in their throats.—*To J. M. Lucas, May 10, 1858.* II, 358.

Douglas, Stephen A., expected to turn Republican—His [Douglas's] hope rested on the idea of enlisting the great "Black Republican" party, and making it the tail of his own kite. He knows he was then expecting from day to day to turn Republican and place himself at the head of our organization. He has found that these despised "Black Republicans" estimate him by a standard which he has taught them only too well. Hence he is crawling back into his old camp, and you will find him eventually installed in full fellowship with those whom he has been battling, and with whom he now pretends to be at such fearful variance.—*Debate, Freeport, Aug. 27, 1858.* III, 347.

Douglas, Stephen A., "explanations explanatory"—*See* POPULAR SOVEREIGNTY, Douglas troubled by, 1.

Douglas, Stephen A., how, became judge—*See* JUDI-CIAL DECISIONS, Douglas's attitude toward, 4, 5, 10.

Douglas, Stephen A., "hydrophobia and spasms of rage"—*See* "IRREPRESSIBLE CONFLICT," difference in who says it, 4.

Douglas, Stephen A., ingenuity of—*See* CAMPAIGN OF 1858, in review, 2.

Douglas, Stephen A., interpreter of English—What wonderful acumen the judge [Douglas] displays on the construction of language! According to this criticism of his, the word "with" is equivalent to the word "notwithstanding," and also to the phrases, "although I defy" and "although I spit upon." Verily, these are wonderful substitutes for the word "with."—*Speech, Springfield, Aug. 14, 1852.* Angle, 91.

See EQUALITY, Douglas's interpretation of the Declaration.

Douglas, Stephen A., interprets Popular Sovereignty—*See* POPULAR SOVEREIGNTY, Douglas's interpretation of.

Douglas, Stephen A., Jefferson and, on slavery—*See* SLAVERY, Jefferson versus Douglas.

Douglas, Stephen A., Jefferson and Jackson—I might as well preach Christianity to a grizzly bear as to preach Jefferson and Jackson to him [Douglas].—*Notes, Oct. 1, 1858.* IV, 221.

Douglas, Stephen A., lion or bear?—"A living dog is better than a dead lion." Judge Douglas, if not a dead lion for this work [overthrowing the "political dynasty" at Washington] is at least a caged and toothless one. How can he oppose the advances of slavery?—*Speech, Springfield, June 16, 1858.* III, 13.
2.—My friend, the judge [Douglas] is not only, as it turns out, not a dead lion, nor even a living one—he is a rugged Russian bear.—*Speech, Chicago, July 10, 1858.* III, 21.

Douglas, Stephen A., "most dangerous enemy of liberty"—*See* REPUBLICAN PARTY, warned against Douglas, 12.

Douglas, Stephen A., Ohio warned against—It is useless for me to say to you—and yet I cannot refrain from saying it—that you must not let your approaching election in Ohio so result as to give encouragement to Douglasism. That is all which now stands in the way of an early and complete success of Republicanism.—*To Salmon P. Chase, Sept. 21, 1859.* Hertz II, 758.

Douglas, Stephen A., opposes equality doctrine—*See* EQUALITY, Douglas's interpretation of the Declaration, 8.

Douglas, Stephen A., part of proslavery conspiracy—*See* SLAVERY, conspiracy to promote.

Douglas, Stephen A., profitable thievery by—I will venture to suggest that if he [Douglas] had stolen none of the ideas of Henry Clay and Daniel Webster, and other Whigs, which he had been listening to for the last preceding six or eight months, he might not have been able to get up quite so creditable a speech at Chicago as he did.—*Speech, Springfield, Aug. 14, 1852.* Angle, 88.

Douglas, Stephen A., prophet—*See* PROPHECY, false, touching slavery, 2, 3, 5, 6, 8.

Douglas, Stephen A., second to say Declaration does not include negro—*See* EQUALITY, Douglas's interpretation of the Declaration, 11.

Douglas, Stephen A., sees peril in Scott's nomination—*See* SCOTT, WINFIELD, peril to Union?

Douglas, Stephen A., some Republicans favor—*See* CAMPAIGN OF 1858, some Republicans favor Douglas.

Douglas, Stephen A., South should magnify—Will you [men of the South] give Douglas no credit for impressing that sentiment [that the negro should be treated as a beast] on the northern mind for your benefit? Why, you should magnify him to the utmost, in order that he may impress it more deeply, broadly, and surely.—*Speeches in Kansas, Dec. 1-5, 1859.* V, 273.

Douglas, Stephen A., strategy of, in 1860—*See* CAMPAIGN OF 1860, Douglas's strategy.

Douglas, Stephen A., suggested for legislature—*See* RACIAL AMALGAMATION, opposed to, 8.

Douglas, Stephen A., suggested for President—I . . . propose to try to show you [Kentuckians] that you ought to nominate for the next Presidency, at Charleston, my distinguished friend, Judge Douglas. . . . He is as sincerely for you [on the slavery issue], and more wisely for you, than you are for yourselves. . . . What do you want more than anything else to make successful your views of slavery?—to advance the outspread of it and to secure and perpetuate the nationality of it? . . . What is needed absolutely? . . . Why, if I may be allowed to answer the question, it is to retain a hold upon the North—it is to retain support and strength from the free states. If you can get this support and strength from the free states, you can succeed. . . . If that proposition be admitted,—and it is undeniable—, then the next thing I say to you is, that Douglas of all the men in this nation is the only man that affords you any hold upon the free states.—*Speech, Cincinnati, Sept. 17, 1859.* V, 195.

2.—It is my opinion that it is for you [Kentucky proslavery men] to take him [Douglas, as presidential candidate] or be defeated; and that if you do take him you may be beaten. You will surely be beaten if you do not take him. We, the Republicans and others forming the opposition of the country, intend to "stand by our guns," to be patient and firm, and in the long run to beat you whether you take him or not.—*Speech, Cincinnati, Sept. 17, 1859.* V, 217.

Douglas, Stephen A., thought Lincoln joking—The judge insists that, in the first speech I made, in which I very distinctly made that charge [of conspiracy to promote slavery] he thought for a good while I was in fun—that I was playful.—*Debate, Freeport, Aug. 27, 1858.* III, 283.

Douglas, Stephen A., Trumbull charges against—*See* TRUMBULL, LYMAN, charges of, against Douglas.

Douglas, Stephen A., "turns unto the Gentiles"—*See* DOUGLAS, STEPHEN A., characterized, 4.

Douglas, Stephen A., two against giant—I dislike the appearance of unfairness of two attacking one. After all, however, as the judge is a giant, and Edwards and I are but common mortals, it may not be very unfair. —*Speech, Springfield, Aug. 26, 1852.* Angle, 95.

Douglas, Stephen A., unable to check extension of slavery—There are those who denounce us [Republicans] openly to their own friends, and yet whisper us softly that Senator Douglas is the aptest instrument there is with which to effect that object [overthrow of the proslavery Democratic "dynasty"]. They wish us to infer all from the fact that he now has a little quarrel with the present head of the dynasty; and that he has regularly voted with us on a single point upon which he and we have never differed. They remind us that he is a great man and the largest of us are very small ones. But . . . how can he oppose the advances of slavery? He don't care anything about it. His avowed mission is impressing the "public heart" to care nothing about it.—*Speech, Springfield, June 16, 1858.* III, 13.

Douglas-Buchanan Feud, Republicans welcome—I know of no effort to unite the Reps. and Buc. men, and believe there is none. Of course the Republicans do not try to keep the common enemy from dividing; but, as far as I know, or believe, they will not unite with either branch of the division. Indeed it is difficult for me to see on what grounds they could unite. —*To Samuel Wilkinson, June 10, 1858.* Hertz II, 709.

2.—In relation to the charge of an alliance between the Republicans and the Buchanan men in this state, if being rather pleased to see a division in the ranks of the Democracy, and not do anything to prevent it, be such an alliance, then there is such an alliance,— at least that is true of me. But if it is intended to charge that there is any alliance by which there is to be any concession of principle on either side, or furnishing of the sinews, or partition of offices, or swapping of votes, to any extent; or the doing of anything, great or small, on the one side, for a consideration, express or implied, on the other, no such thing is true, so far as I know or believe.—*To Lyman Trumbull, June 23, 1858.* Tracy, 87.

3.—Whether there be such an alliance [of Republicans and Buchanan Democrats, as charged by Douglas] depends, so far as I know, upon what may be the right definition of the term "alliance." If for the Republican party to see the other great party to which they are opposed divided among themselves and not try to stop the division, and rather be glad of it, if that is an alliance, I confess I am in it; but if it is meant to be said that the Republicans had formed an alliance going beyond that, by which there is contribution of money or sacrifice of principle on the one side or the other, so far as the Republican party is concerned, if there be any such thing, I protest that I neither know anything of it nor do I believe it.—*Speech, Chicago, July 10, 1858.* III, 21.

4.—I have said upon a former occasion, and I do not propose to suppress it now, that I have no objection to the division in the judge's party. He got it up himself. . . . I can give all fair friends of Judge Douglas here to understand exactly the view that Republicans take in regard to that division. Don't you remember how two years ago the opponents of the Democratic party divided between Frémont and Fillmore? I guess you do. Any Democrat who remembers that division will remember also that he was at the time very glad of it, and then he will be able to see all there is between the National Democrats and the Republicans. What we now think of the two divisions of Democrats, you then thought of the Frémont and Fillmore divisions. That is all there is to it.—*Debate, Galesburg, Oct. 7, 1858.* IV, 276.

5.—Judge Douglas has again for, I believe, the fifth time, if not the seventh, in my presence, reiterated his charge of a conspiracy or combination between the National Democrats and Republicans. What evidence Douglas has upon this subject I know not, inasmuch as he never favors us with any. . . . I am very free to confess to Judge Douglas that I have no objection to the division [among the Democrats]; but I defy the judge to show any evidence that I have in any way promoted that division.—*Debate, Galesburg, Oct. 7, 1858.* IV, 276.

6.—If the judge [Douglas] continues to put forward the declaration that there is an unholy, unnatural alliance between the Republicans and the National Democrats I want now to enter my protest against receiving him as an entirely competent witness upon that subject.—*Debate, Galesburg, Oct. 7, 1858.* IV, 277.

7.—All I can say now is to re-commend to them [Democratic factions] what I then commended—to prosecute the war against one another in the most vigorous manner. I say to them again, "Go it, husband; go it, bear!"—*Debate, Alton, Oct. 15, 1858.* V, 29.

8.—At Quincy . . . I told [Douglas] to "give it to them with all the power he had," and as some of them were present, I told them I would be very much obliged if they would give it to him in about the same way.—*Debate, Alton, Oct. 15, 1858.* V, 29.

Douglass, Frederick, Lincoln to—*See* LINCOLN, ABRAHAM, personal traits and reactions, 17.

Drama, unprofessional criticism—For one of my age I have seen very little of the drama. . . . Some of Shakespeare's plays I have never read; while others I have gone over perhaps as frequently as any unprofessional reader. . . . I think nothing equals "Macbeth." It is wonderful. Unlike you gentlemen of the profession, I think the soliloquy in "Hamlet" commencing "Oh, my offense is rank" surpasses that commencing "To be or not to be."—*To James H. Hackett, Aug. 17, 1863.* IX, 84.

Dram-Sellers, defense of—*See* TEMPERANCE, early reformers erred, 2.

Dram-Sellers, excoriated — *See* SALOON SMASHERS, women, defended.

Dreams, subject to—I now have no doubt that it is the peculiar misfortune of both you and me to dream dreams of Elysium far exceeding all that anything earthly can realize.—*To Joshua F. Speed, Feb. 25, 1842.* I, 212.

2.—Colonel, did you ever dream of a lost friend, and feel that you were holding sweet communion with that friend, and yet have a sad consciousness that it was not a reality? Just so I dream of my boy, Willie. —*To Col. Cannon, no date.* Hertz II, 852.

3.—Think you had better put "Tad's" pistol away. I had an ugly dream about him.—*To Mrs. Lincoln, June 9, 1863.* VIII, 296.

4.—I had this strange dream again last night, and we shall, judging from the past, have great news very soon. I think it must be from Sherman. My thoughts are in that direction, as are most of yours.—*To members of cabinet, April 14, 1865.* Welles II, 283.

Dred Scott Decision, analyzed—That decision declares two propositions—first, that a negro cannot sue in the United States courts; and secondly, that Congress cannot prohibit slavery in the territories.—*Speech, Springfield, June 26, 1857.* II, 320.

2.—He [Douglas] and everyone knows that the [Dred Sott] decision of the Supreme Court, which he approves and makes special ground of attack upon me for disapproving forbids the people of a territory to exclude slavery.—*Speech, Springfield, July 17, 1858.* III, 162.

3.—This change in our national policy [effected by the Kansas-Nebraska Act] is decided to be constitutional, although the court would not decide the only question before them—whether Dred Scott was a slave or not—and did decide, too, that a territorial legislature cannot exclude slavery in behalf of the people, and if their premises be correct a state cannot exclude it, for they tell us that the negro is property anywhere in the light that horses are property.—*Speech, Carlinville, Aug. 31, 1858.* Angle, 189.

4.—They [members of the court] reach the conclusion that as the Constitution of the United States expressly recognizes property in slaves, and prohibits any person from being deprived of property without due process of law, to pass an act of Congress by which a man who owned a slave on one side of a line would be deprived of him if he took him on the other side, is depriving him of that property without due process of law . . . and the difficulty is, how is it possible to exclude slavery from the territory unless in violation of that decision? That is the difficulty.—*Debate, Jonesboro, Sept. 15, 1858.* IV, 57.

5.—After having argued that Congress had no power to pass a law excluding slavery from a United States territory, they [members of the Supreme Court] then used language to this effect: That inasmuch as Congress itself could not exercise such a power, it followed as a matter of course that it could not authorize a territorial government to exercise it, for the territorial legislature can do no more than Congress could do. Thus it expressed its opinion emphatically against the power of a territorial legislature to exclude slavery.—*Debate, Jonesboro, Sept. 15, 1858.* IV, 66.

6.—After stating that Congress cannot prohibit slavery in the territories, the court adds: "And if Congress cannot do this, if it be beyond the powers conferred by the federal Constitution, it will be admitted, we presume, that it could not authorize a territorial government to exercise them; it could confer no power on any local government, established by its authority, to violate the provisions of the Constitution." Can any mortal man misunderstand this language?—*Notes, Oct. 1, 1858.* IV, 208.

7.—The Dred Scott decision . . . may be reduced to three points. The first is that a negro cannot be a citizen. . . . The second point is that the United States Constitution protects slavery, as property, in all the United States territories, and that neither Congress, nor the people of the territories, nor any other power, can prohibit it at any time prior to the formation of state constitutions. . . . The third point decided is that the voluntary bringing of Dred Scott into Illinois by his master, and holding him here a long time as a slave, did not operate to his emancipation—did not make him free.—*Notes, Oct. 1, 1858.* IV, 233.

8.—The essence of the Dred Scott decision is compressed into the sentence which I will now read: "Now, as we have already said in an earlier part of this opinion, upon a different point, the right of property in a slave is distinctly and expressly affirmed in the Constitution."—*Debate, Galesburg, Oct. 7, 1858.* IV, 283.

9.—I never have complained especially of the Dred Scott decision because it held that a negro could not be a citizen, and the judge is always wrong when he says I ever did so complain of it.—*Debate, Alton, Oct. 15, 1858.* V, 31.

10.—It [Dred Scott decision] is a long opinion, but it is all embodied in this short statement: "The Constitution of the United States forbids Congress to deprive a man of his property without due process of law; the right of property in slaves is distinctly and expressly affirmed in that Constitution; therefore, if Congress shall undertake to say that a man's slave is no longer his slave when he crosses a certain line into a territory, that is depriving him of his property without due process of law, and is unconstitutional." There is the whole of the Dred Scot decision.—*Speech, Columbus, Ohio, Sept. 16, 1859.* V, 177.

11.—I know the opinion of the judges [in the Dred Scott case] states that there is a total absence of power [to do anything about slavery in the territories]; but that is, unfortunately, not all it states; for the judges add that the right of property in a slave is distinctly and expressly affirmed in the Con-

stitution. . . . Its language is equivalent to saying that it is embodied and so woven into that instrument that it cannot be detached without breaking the Constitution itself—in a word, it is part of the Constitution.—*Speech, Columbus, Ohio, Sept. 16, 1859.* V, 180.

12.—This Dred Scott decision says that the right of property in a slave is affirmed in that Constitution which is the supreme law of the land, any state constitution or law notwithstanding.—*Speech, Columbus, Ohio, Sept. 16, 1859.* V, 181.

13.—As the [territorial] legislature has not the power to drive slaves out, they have no power by indirection, by tax, or by imposing burdens in any way on the property, to effect the same end, and . . . any attempt to do so would be held by the Dred Scott court unconstitutional.—*Speech, Cincinnati, Sept. 17, 1859.* V, 212.

Dred Scott Decision; argument for abolition—*See* ABOLITION, strongest argument for, 1.

Dred Scott Decision, challenged—We think the Dred Scott decision is erroneous. We know the court that made it has often overruled its own decisions, and we shall do what we can to have it overrule this. We offer no resistance to it. . . . If this important decision had been made by the unanimous concurrence of the judges, and without any apparent partisan bias, and in accordance with legal public expectation and with the steady practice of the departments throughout our history, and had been in no part based on assumed historical facts which are not really true; or, if wanting in some of these, it had been before the court more than once, and had there been affirmed and re-affirmed through a course of years, it then might be, perhaps would be, factious, nay, even revolutionary, not to acquiesce in it as precedent. But when, as is true, we find it wanting in all these claims to the public confidence, it is not resistance, it is not factious, it is not even disrespectful, to treat it as not having yet quite established a settled doctrine for the country.—*Speech, Springfield, June 26, 1857.* II, 321.

2.—It may well puzzle older heads than yours to understand how, as the Dred Scott decision holds, Congress can authorize a territorial legislature to do everything else, and cannot authorize them to prohibit slavery. That is one of the things the court can decide, but can never give an intelligible reason for. —*To J. W. Somers, June 25, 1858.* III, 16.

3.—Another of the issues he [Douglas] says that is to be made with me, is upon his devotion to the Dred Scott decision, and my opposition to it. . . . I should be allowed to state the nature of that opposition. . . .

All that I am doing is refusing to obey it as a political rule.—*Speech, Chicago, July 10, 1858.* III, 38.

4.—If I were in Congress, and a vote should come up on the question whether slavery should be prohibited in a new territory, in spite of the Dred Scott decision, I would vote that it should.—*Speech, Chicago, July 10, 1858.* III, 38.

5.—We will try to reverse that decision. . . . Somebody has to reverse that decision, since it is made; and we mean to reverse it, and we mean to reverse it peaceably.—*Speech, Chicago, July 10, 1858.* III, 39.

6.—It is based upon falsehood in the main as to the facts—allegation of facts upon which it stands are not facts at all in many instances—and no decision made on any question—the first instance of a decision made under so many unfavorable circumstances—thus placed, has ever been held by the profession as law, and it has needed confirmation before the lawyers regarded it as settled law.—*Speech, Chicago, July 10, 1858.* III, 40.

7.—Decisions apparently contrary to that [Dred Scott] decision, or that good lawyers thought were contrary to that decision, have been made by that very [Supreme] court before. It is the first of its kind; it is an astonisher in legal history. It is a new wonder of the world.—*Speech, Chicago, July 10, 1858.* III, 40.

8.—I am opposed to that [Dred Scott] decision in a certain sense, but not in the sense which he [Douglas] puts it. I say that in so far as it decided in favor of Dred Scott's master, and against Dred Scott and his family, I do not propose to disturb or resist the decision. I never have proposed to do any such thing. I think that in respect for judicial authority, my humble history would not suffer in comparison with that of Judge Douglas. . . . By resisting it as a political rule, I disturb no right of property, create no disorder, excite no mobs.—*Speech, Springfield, July 17, 1858.* III, 177.

9.—The power claimed for the Supreme Court by Judge Douglas [in relation to the Dred Scott decision], Mr. [Thomas] Jefferson holds, would reduce us to the despotism of an oligarchy.—*Speech, Springfield, July 17, 1858.* III, 179.

10.—[The decision] helps to nationalize slavery.—*Speech, Springfield, July 17, 1858.* III, 181.

11.—Will you [Douglas] not graciously allow us to do with the Dred Scott decision precisely as you did with the [national] bank decision? You succeeded in breaking down the moral effect of that decision; did you find it necessary to amend the Constitution?—or to set up a court of negroes in order to do it?—*Speech, Springfield, July 17, 1858.* III, 183.

12.—Suppose, now, a provision in a state constitution should negative all the above propositions [contained in the Fifth Amendment], declaring directly or substantially that "any person may be deprived of life, liberty or property without due process of law," a direct contradiction—collision—would be pronounced between the United States Constitution and such state constitution. And can there be any doubt but that which is declared to be the supreme law would prevail over the other to the extent of the collision? Such state constitution would be unconstitutional. There is no escape from this conclusion but in one way, and that is to deny that the Supreme Court, in the Dred Scott case, properly applied this constitutional guaranty of property.—*Notes, Oct. 1, 1858.* IV, 211.

13.—That burlesque upon judicial decisions [in the Dred Scott case] and slander and profanation upon the honored names and sacred history of republican America, must be overruled and expunged from the books of authority.—*Notes, Oct. 1, 1858.* IV, 235.

14.—I believe that [contrary to the Dred Scott decision] the right of property in a slave is not distinctly and expressly affirmed in the Constitution. . . . I say, therefore, that I think one of the premises [on which the decision was based] is not true in fact.—*Debate, Galesburg, Oct. 7, 1858.* IV, 284.

15.—We [Republicans] oppose the Dred Scott decision in a certain way. . . . We do not propose that when Dred Scott has been decided to be a slave by the court, we, as a mob, will decide him to be free. We do not propose that, when any other one, or one thousand, shall be decided by that court to be slaves, we will in any violent way disturb the rights of property thus settled; but we nevertheless do oppose that decision as a political rule. . . . We think it lays the foundation not merely of enlarging and spreading out what we consider an evil, but it lays the foundation for spreading that evil into the states themselves.—*Debate, Quincy, Oct. 13, 1858.* IV, 329.

16.—We . . . oppose that decision as a political rule which shall be binding on the members of Congress or the President to favor no measure that does not actually concur with the principles of that decision. We do not propose to be bound by it as a political rule in that way. We propose so resisting it as to have it reversed, if we can, and a new judicial rule established upon this subject.—*Debate, Quincy, Oct. 13, 1858.* IV, 330.

17.—I do not believe it is a constitutional right to hold slaves in a territory of the United States. I believe the decision was improperly made, and I go for reversing it.—*Debate, Alton, Oct. 15, 1858.* V, 68.

18.—When I say the [Dred Scott] decision was made in a sort of way, I mean it was made in a divided court, by a bare majority of the judges, and they not quite agreeing with one another in the reasons for making it; that it is so made that its avowed supporters disagree with one another about its meaning; and that it was mainly based upon a mistaken statement of fact—the statement in the opinion that the "right of property in a slave is distinctly and expressly affirmed in the Constitution."—*Cooper Institute address, New York, Feb. 27, 1860. V, 321.*

Dred Scott Decision, determined by election—It is my opinion that the Dred Scott decision, as it is, would never have been made in its present form if the party that made it had not been sustained previously by the election. My own opinion is that the new Dred Scott decision, deciding against the right of the people of the states to exclude slavery, will never be made if that [Democratic] party is not sustained by the elections.—*Debate, Galesburg, Oct. 7, 1858. IV, 286.*

Dred Scott Decision, Douglas's devotion to—The sacredness that Judge Douglas throws around this decision is a degree of sacredness that has never before been thrown around any other decision. I never heard of such a thing. . . . Judge Douglas will have it that all hands must take this extraordinary decision made under these extraordinary circumstances, and give their votes in Congress in accordance with it, yield to it, and obey it in every possible sense. Circumstances alter cases.—*Speech, Chicago, July 10, 1858. III, 39.*

2.—He [Douglas] boldly takes ground in favor of that decision. This is one half the onslaught [against Lincoln] and one third of the entire plan of the campaign. . . . He would have the citizen conform his vote to that decision; the member of Congress, his; the President, his use of the veto power. He would make it a rule of political action for the people and all the departments of the government.—*Speech, Springfield, July 17, 1858. III, 177.*

3.—It is part of the plan of his [Douglas's] campaign, and he will cling to it with a desperate grip. Even turn it upon him—the sharp point against him, and gaff him through—he will still cling to it till he can invent some new dodge to take its place.—*Speech, Springfield, July 17, 1858. III, 178.*

4.—He [Douglas] says this Dred Scott decision is . . . but an abstraction. I submit that the . . . thing which determines whether a man is free or a slave is rather concrete than abstract.—*Speech, Springfield, July 17, 1858. III, 181.*

5.—This man [Douglas] sticks to a decision which forbids the people of a territory to exclude slavery, and he does this, not because he says it is right in itself—he does not give any opinion as to that—but because

it has been decided by the court.—*Debate, Ottawa, Aug. 21, 1858. III, 252.*

6.—He [Douglas] did not commit himself on account of the merit or demerit of the [Dred Scott] decision, but it is a "Thus saith the Lord." The next decision, as much as this, will be a "Thus saith the Lord."—*Debate, Ottawa, Aug. 21, 1858. III, 252.*

7.—There is nothing that can divert or turn him [Douglas] away from this [Dred Scott] decision.—*Debate, Ottawa, Aug. 21, 1858. III, 253.*

8.—I cannot shake Judge Douglas's teeth loose from the Dred Scott decision. Like some obstinate animal—I mean no disrespect—that will hang on when he has once got his teeth fixed,—you may cut off a leg, or you may tear away an arm, still he will not relax his hold. And so I may point out to the Judge, and say that he is bespattered all over, from the beginning of his political life to the present time, with attacks upon judicial decisions,—I may cut limb after limb of his public record, and strive to wrench from him a single dictum of the court, yet I cannot divert him from it. He hangs to the last to the Dred Scott decision.—*Debate, Ottawa, Aug. 21, 1858. III, 255.*

9.—Forthwith Judge Douglas espouses the decision, and denounces all opposition to it in no unmeasured terms. He adheres to it with extraordinary tenacity; and under rather extraordinary circumstances. He espouses it not on any opinion of his that it is right within itself. On this he forbears to commit himself. He espouses it exclusively on the ground of its binding authority on all citizens—a ground which commits him as fully to the next decision as to this.—*Notes, Oct. 1, 1858. IV, 220.*

10.—These things warrant me in saying that Judge Douglas adheres to the Dred Scott decision under rather extraordinary circumstances—circumstances suggesting the question, "Why does he adhere to it so pertinaciously? Why does he thus belie his whole past life? Why, with a record more marked for hostility to judicial decisions than almost any living man, does he cling to this with a devotion that nothing can baffle?—*Notes, Oct. 1, 1858. IV, 222.*

11.—Now in this very devoted adherence to this [Dred Scott] decision, in opposition to all the great political leaders whom he has recognized as leaders—in opposition to his former self and history—there is something very marked.—*Debate, Galesburg, Oct. 7, 1858. IV, 287.*

Dred Scott Decision, Douglas works for second—[Douglas's attitude toward the Dred Scott decision] commits him to the next [Dred Scott] decision, whenever it comes, as being as obligatory as this one, since he does not investigate it, and won't inquire whether this opinion is right or wrong. He teaches men this doctrine, and in so doing, prepares the public mind to take the next decision when it comes without any inquiry. In this I think I argue fairly—without questioning motives at all—that Judge Douglas is most ingeniously and powerfully preparing the public mind to take that decision when it comes.—*Debate, Galesburg, Oct. 7, 1858.* IV, 278.

Dred Scott Decision, effect of, in Kansas—*See* KANSAS, Dred Scott decision and.

Dred Scott Decision, how reverse?—*See* JUDICIAL DECISIONS, Douglas's attitude toward, 11.

Dred Scott Decision, Negro citizenship and—*See* NEGRO CITIZENSHIP, opposed to.

Dred Scott Decision, resistance to, denied—He [Douglas] denounces all who question the correctness of that decision, as offering violent resistance to it. But who resists it? Who has, in spite of the decision, declared Dred Scott free, and resisted the authority of his master over him?—*Speech, Springfield, June 26, 1857.* II, 320.

2.—What is fairly implied by the term . . . "resistance to the decision"? I do not resist. . . . All I am doing is refusing to obey it as a political rule.—*Speech, Chicago, July 10, 1858.* III, 38.

Dred Scott Decision, second, forecast—While the opinion of the [United States Supreme] court, by Chief Justice Taney, in the Dred Scott case, and the separate opinions of all the concurring judges, expressly declare that the Constitution of the United States neither permits Congress nor a territorial legislature to exclude slavery from any United States territory, they all omit to declare whether or not the same Constitution permits a state, or the people of a state, to exclude it.—*Speech, Springfield, June 16, 1858.* III, 11.

2.—We may, ere long see . . . another Supreme Court decision declaring that the Constitution of the United States does not permit a state to exclude slavery from its limits. . . . Such a decision is all that slavery now lacks of being alike lawful in all the states. Welcome or unwelcome, such a decision is probably coming, and will soon be upon us, unless the power of the present political dynasty shall be met and overthrown.—*Speech, Springfield, June 16, 1858.* III, 12.

3.—What is necessary to make the institution [slavery] national? Not war. There is no danger that the people of Kentucky will shoulder their muskets and, with a young nigger stuck on every bayonet, march into Illinois and force them upon us. There is no danger of our going over there to make war upon them. Then what is necessary for the nationalization of slavery? It is simply the next Dred Scott decision. It is merely for the Supreme Court to decide that no state under the Constitution can exclude it, just as they have already decided that under the Constitution neither Congress nor the territorial legislature can do it.—*Debate, Ottawa, Aug. 21, 1858.* Basler, 458.

4.—When . . . Judge Douglas shall succeed in bringing public sentiment to an exact accord with his own views—when these vast assemblages shall echo back all these sentiments—when they shall come to repeat his views and to avow his principles, and to say all that he says on these mighty questions—then it needs only the formality of the second Dred Scott decision, which he indorses in advance, to make slavery alike lawful in all the states—old as well as new, North as well as South.—*Debate, Ottawa, Aug. 21, 1858.* III, 256.

5.—I propose to show, in the teeth of Judge Douglas's ridicule, that such a decision [second Dred Scott decision, that states cannot exclude slavery] does logically and necessarily follow the [first] Dred Scott decision. In that case the court holds that Congress . . . cannot prohibit slavery in the territories, because to do so would infringe on the "right of property" guaranteed to the citizen by the fifth amendment to the Constitution. . . . I propose to show, beyond the power of quibble, that the guarantee applies with all the force, if not more, to states than it does to territories. . . . It is a case where the guarantee is expressly given to the individual citizen, in and by the organic law of the general government; and the duty of maintaining that guarantee is imposed upon that general government, over-riding all obstacles.—*Notes, Oct. 1, 1858.* IV, 209.

6.—In the [Kansas-Nebraska] bill the provision about the people of "states" is the odd half of something, the other half of which was not quite ready for exhibition. What is the other half to be? Another Supreme Court decision, declaring that the people of a state cannot exclude slavery, is exactly fitted to be that other half. As the power of the people of the territories and of the state is cozily set down in the Nebraska bill as being the same; so the constitutional limitations on that power will then be judicially held to be precisely the same in both territories and states —that is, that the Constitution permits neither a territory nor a state to exclude slavery.—*Notes, Oct. 1, 1858.* IV, 219.

7.—If our presidential election, by a mere plurality, and of doubtful significance, brought one Supreme

Court decision that no power can exclude slavery from a territory, how much more shall a public sentiment, in exact accordance with the sentiments of Judge Douglas, bring another that no power can exclude it from a state?—*Notes, Oct. 1, 1858.* IV, 224.

8.—I believe, further, that it [second Dred Scott decision] is just as sure to be made as tomorrow is to come, if that [Democratic] party should be sustained [by the elections].—*Debate, Galesburg, Oct. 7, 1858.* IV, 286.

9.—I have examined that [Dred Scott] decision with a good deal of care, as a lawyer examines a decision, and so far as I have been able to do so, the court has nowhere in its opinions said that the states have the power to exclude slavery, nor have they used other language substantially that. I also say, so far as I can find, not one of the concurring judges has said that the states can exclude slavery, nor said anything that was substantially that.—*Debate, Quincy, Oct. 13, 1858.* IV, 321.

10.—If public sentiment has not been debauched already to this point [of conceding the negro is not included in the Declaration of Independence] a new turn of the screw in that direction is all that is wanting; and this is constantly being done by the teachers of this insidious popular sovereignty. You need but one or two turns further until your minds, now ripening under these teachings, will be ready for all these things, and you will receive and support, or submit to, the slave-trade revived with all its horrors, a slave-code enforced in our territories, and a new Dred Scott decision to bring slavery up into the very heart of the free North.—*Speech, Columbus, Ohio, Sept. 16, 1859.* V, 188.

Dred Scott Decision, threat to states—If the Constitution gives the master a right of property in negroes above the jurisdiction of territorial laws, enacted in the sovereignty of the people, it only requires another favorable decision from the same court to make the rights of property alike in states as well as territories and that by virtue of the Constitution and in disregard of local laws to the contrary. Buchanan takes this position now.—*Speech, Carlinville, Aug. 31, 1858.* Angle, 189.

2.—He [Douglas] has an object in these denunciations, and is it not to prepare our minds for acquiescence in the next decision regarding slavery to exist in the states?—*Speech, Carlinville, Aug. 31, 1858.* Angle, 192.

3.—By the Dred Scott decision, pushed to its legitimate consequences, slavery would be established in all the states as well as in the territories.—*Debate, Quincy, Oct. 13, 1858.* IV, 320.

4.—We think it lays the foundation not merely for enlarging and spreading out what we consider an evil, but it lays the foundation for spreading that evil into the states themselves.—*Debate, Quincy, Oct. 13, 1858.* IV, 330.

5.—That [Dred Scott] decision lays down the principles, which, if pushed to their logical conclusion—I say pushed to their logical conclusion—would decide that the constitutions of the free states, forbidding slavery, are themselves unconstitutional.—*Speech, Columbus, Ohio, Sept. 16, 1859.* V, 147.

See DRED SCOTT DECISION, second, forecast.

See STATES, freedom of, endangered.

Dred Scott Decision, will judges reconsider?—When this obvious mistake of the judges [in saying the Constitution affirms the right of property in slaves] shall be brought to their attention, is it not reasonable to expect that they will withdraw the mistaken statement, and reconsider the conclusion based upon it?—*Cooper Institute address, New York, Feb. 27, 1860.* V, 322.

Drugs, use of, in peace and war—*See* WAR POWER, use of, defended, 8, 9.

Drunkards, defended—*See* TEMPERANCE, defense of drunkards.

"Due Process of Law," slavery and—The Constitution itself impliedly admits that a person may be deprived of property by "due process of law," and the Republicans hold that if there be a law of Congress or territorial legislature telling the slaveholder in advance that he should not bring his slave into the territory upon pain of forfeiture, and he still will bring him in, he will be deprived of his property in such slave by "due process of law." And the same would be true in the case of taking a slave into a state against a state constitution or laws prohibiting slavery.—*Notes, Oct. 1, 1858.* IV, 211.

See DRED SCOTT DECISION, challenged, 12.

DuPont, Samuel F., Congress asked to thank—I cordially recommend that Capt. Samuel F. DuPont receive a vote of thanks of Congress for his services and gallantry displayed in the capture of Forts Walker and Beauregard, commanding the entrance of Port Royal harbor, on the 7th of November, 1861.—*Message to Congress, Feb. 4, 1862.* VII, 98.

2.—I cordially recommend that Capt. Samuel F. DuPont receive a vote of thanks of Congress for his services and gallantry displayed in the capture, since the 21st of December, 1861, of various points on the coast of Georgia, and Florida, particularly Brunswick,

Cumberland Island and Sound, Amelia Island, the towns of St. Mary's, St. Augustine, Jacksonville and Fernandina.—*Message to Congress, March 20, 1862.* VII, 137.

"Durable Curse of the Race"—*See* LABOR, free and slave, compared.

Duty, understands own, best—Without claiming to be your superior, which I do not, my position enables me to understand my duty in all these matters better than you possibly can, and I hope you do not yet doubt my integrity.—*To I. N. Arnold, May 26, 1863.* Stephenson, 352.

Dynasty, Democratic, to advance slavery—*See* DOUGLAS, STEPHEN A., unable to check extension of slavery.

Eagle, reading through—*See* SLAVERY, profit motive in, 6.

"Economy of the Universe"—*See* EQUALITY, Fathers' interpretation of the Declaration.

Editorials, Lincoln writes newspaper—*See* KANSAS-NEBRASKA ACT, opens territories to slavery, 1.

See CABINET, Southern men for? 1.

See KANSAS-NEBRASKA ACT, parable of starving cattle.

Education, better teaching sought—That the committee on education be instructed to inquire into the expediency of providing by law for the examination as to the qualifications of persons offering themselves as school teachers, that no teacher shall receive any part of the public school fund who shall not have successfully passed such examination.—*Resolution, in Illinois Legislature, Dec. 2, 1840.* Tarbell I, 168.

Education, importance of—That every man may receive at least a moderate education, and thereby be enabled to read the histories of his own and other countries, by which he may duly appreciate the value of our free institutions, appears to be an object of vital importance, even on this account alone, to say nothing of the advantages and satisfaction to be derived from all being able to read the Scriptures, and other works both of a religious and moral nature for themselves. For my part I desire to see the time when education—and by its means, morality, sobriety, enterprise and industry—shall become much more general than at present, and should be gratified to have it in my power to contribute something to the advancement of any measure which might have a tendency to accelerate that happy period.—*Address to Sangamon County, March 9, 1832.* I, 7.

Education, labor and—*See* LABOR, education and.

Education, Lincoln's—Education, defective.—*Autobiography, June 15, 1858.* II, 368.

2.—I am not a master of language; I have not a fine education; I am not capable of entering into a disquisition upon dialectics, as I believe you call it; but I do not believe the language I employed [in a speech at Springfield] bears any such construction as Judge Douglas puts upon it.—*Speech, Chicago, July 10, 1858.* III, 32.

3.—There were some schools so-called [in Spencer County, Indiana, which became Lincoln's home in his eighth year], but no qualification was ever required of a teacher beyond "readin', writin' and cipherin' " to the rule of three. . . . There was absolutely nothing to excite ambition for education. Of course, when I came of age I did not know much. Still, somehow, I could read, write and cipher to the rule of three, but that was all. I have not been to school since. The little advance I now have upon this store of education, I have picked up from time to time under the pressure of necessity. I was raised to work, which I continued till I was twenty-two.—*To J. W. Fell, Dec. 20, 1859.* V, 287.

4.—Well, as to education, the newspapers are correct; I never went to school more than six months in my life. But, as you say, this ["the unusual power of 'putting things' "] must be a product of culture in some form. I have been putting the question you ask me to myself, while you have been talking. I can say this, that among my earliest recollections I remember how, when a mere child, I used to get irritated when anybody talked to me in a way I could not understand. I don't think I ever got angry at anything else in my life. But that always disturbed my temper, and has ever since. I can remember going to my little bedroom, after hearing the neighbors talk of an evening with my father, and spending no small part of the night walking up and down, and trying to make out what was the exact meaning of some of their, to me, dark sayings. I could not sleep, though I often tried to, when I got on such a hunt after an idea, until I had caught it; and when I thought I had got it, I was not satisfied until I had repeated it over and over, until I put it in language plain enough, as I thought, for any boy I knew to comprehend. This was a kind of passion with me, and it has stuck by me; for I am never easy now, when I am handling a thought, till I have bounded it north, and bounded it south, and bounded it east and bounded it west. Perhaps that accounts for the characteristic you observe in my speeches, though I never put the two things together before.—*To J. P. Gulliver, March 10, 1860.* Carpenter, 312.

5.—While here [in Indiana] Abraham [the future

President] went to A.B.C. schools by littles. . . . Abraham now thinks that the aggregate of all his schooling did not amount to one year. He was never in a college or academy as a student, and never inside a college or academy building till since he had a law license. What he has in the way of education he has picked up. After he was 23 and had separated from his father, he studied English grammar—imperfectly, of course, but so as to speak and write as well as he does now. He studied and nearly mastered the six books of Euclid since he was a member of Congress. He regrets his want of education, and does what he can to supply the want.—*Autobiography, June 1, 1860.* VI, 27.

See AUTOBIOGRAPHY, Lincoln's.

Education, opportunities for, in America—Mr. [Henry] Clay's lack of a more perfect early education, however it may be regretted generally, teaches at least one profitable lesson; it teaches that in this country one can scarcely be so poor but that, if he will, he can acquire sufficient education to get through the world respectably.—*Speech, Springfield, July 16, 1852.* II, 160.

Education, universal, demanded by free labor—See LABOR, education and, 3.

Egg and Fowl—Concede that the new government of Louisiana is only what it should be as the egg is to the fowl, we shall sooner have the fowl by hatching the egg than by smashing it.—*Last public speech, April 11, 1865.* XI, 91.

Egypt, punished for slavery—See SLAVERY, Egypt's experience with.

Egypt, thanks to viceroy of—I have received from Mr. Thayer, consul-general of the United States at Alexandria, a full account of the liberal, enlightened and energetic proceedings which, on his complaint, you have adopted in bringing to speedy and condign punishment of the parties, subjects of your Highness in Upper Egypt, who were concerned in an act of criminal persecution against Faris, an agent of certain Christian missionaries in Upper Egypt. I pray Your Highness to be assured that these proceedings, at once so prompt and so just, will be regarded as a new and unmistakable proof equally of Your Highness's friendship for the United States and of the firmness, integrity, and wisdom with which the government of Your Highness is conducted.—*To Mohammed Said Pasha, viceroy of Egypt, Oct. 11, 1862.* VII, 7.

Egypt (Southern Illinois), almost at home in—[Douglas declared at Joliet] that he was going to

"trot me down to Egypt." Thereby he would have you infer that I would not come to Egypt unless he forced me—that I could not be got here, unless he giant-like, had hauled me down here. That statement he makes, too, in the teeth of the knowledge that I made the stipulation to come down here, and that he himself had been very reluctant to enter into the stipulation. More than all this, Judge Douglas, when he made that statement, must have been crazy, and wholly out of his sober senses, or else he would have known that, when he got me down here, that promise—that windy promise—of his powers to annihilate me wouldn't amount to anything. . . . Did the Judge talk of trotting me down to Egypt to scare me to death? Why, I know this people better than he does. I was raised just a little east of here. I am a part of this people.—*Debate, Jonesboro, Sept. 15, 1858.* IV, 68.

"Egypt of the West"—*See* UNION, commercial argument for, 3.

Elder-Stalk Squirts—*See* CIVIL WAR, determination to continue, 4.

Election of 1840, no victory by fraud—In 1840 we [Whigs] carried the nation by more than 140,000 majority. Our opponents charged that we did it by fraudulent voting; but, whatever they may have believed, we know the charge to be untrue.—*Whig circular, March 1, 1843.* I, 256.

Election of 1844, Whigs should win—In the great contest of 1840 some more than 2,100,000 votes were cast, and so surely as there shall be that many, with the ordinary increase added, cast in 1844, that surely will a Whig be elected President of the United States. —*Whig circular, March 1, 1843.* I, 259.

Election of 1844, why lost?—If the Whig abolitionists of New York had voted with us [Whigs] last fall, Mr. Clay would now be President, Whig principles in the ascendent, and Texas not annexed; whereas, by the division, all that either [groups, Whigs or Liberty men] had at stake in the contest was lost.—*To Williamson Durley, Oct. 3, 1845.* I, 275.

Election of 1856, Conflicting interpretations of—The President [Pierce] thinks the great body of us Frémonters, being ardently attached to liberty, in the abstract, were duped by a few wicked and designing men. There is a slight difference of opinion in this. We think he, being ardently attached to the hope of a second term, in the concrete, was duped by men who had liberty every way.—*Speech, Chicago, Dec. 10, 1856.* II, 309.

Election of 1859, "glorious"—The general result in the state [Ohio]—and in other states—is, indeed, glorious.—*To W. M. Dickson, Oct. 17, 1859.* Angle, 226.

Election of 1860, possible danger foreseen—Our adversaries have us now clearly at disadvantage on the second Wednesday of February, when the votes should be officially counted. If the two houses refuse to meet at all, or meet without a quorum of each, where shall we be? I do not think that this counting is constitutionally essential to the election, but how are we to proceed in the absence of it?—*To William H. Seward, Jan. 3, 1861.* Lapsley V, 201.

Election of 1860, result accepted—With deep gratitude to my countrymen for this mark of their confidence, with a distrust of my own ability to perform the required duty under the most favorable circumstances, now rendered doubly difficult by existing national perils, yet with a firm reliance on the strength of our free government and the ultimate loyalty of the people to the just principles upon which it is founded, and above all, an unbroken faith in the Supreme Ruler of nations, I accept this trust.—*To Senate inauguration committee, Jan. 26, 1861.* Hertz II, 811.

Election of 1860, "wisest thing" not done—I do not say that in the recent election the people did the wisest thing that they could have done; indeed, I do not think they did; but I do say that in accepting the great trust committed to me, which I do with a determination to endeavor to prove worthy of it, I must rely upon you, upon the people of the whole country, for support.—*Speech, Poughkeepsie, N. Y., Feb. 19, 1861.* VI, 143.

Election of 1862, explained—We have lost the elections; and it is natural that each of us will believe, and say, it has been because his peculiar views were not made sufficiently prominent. I think I know what it was, but I may be mistaken. Three main causes told the whole story. 1. The Democrats were left in a majority by our friends going to war. 2. The Democrats observed this and determined to reinstate themselves in power, and 3. Our newspapers, by vilifying and disparaging the administration, furnished them all the weapons to do it with. Certainly, the ill-success of the war had much to do with this.—*To Gen. Schurz, Nov. 10, 1862.* Tracy, 213.
2.—The popular elections then just held indicated uneasiness among ourselves.—*Third annual message, Dec. 8, 1863.* IX, 245.

Election of 1863, "very glad"—I am very glad the elections this autumn have gone favorably, and that

I have not, by native depravity or under evil influences, done anything bad enough to prevent the good result.—*To Zachariah Chandler, Nov. 20, 1863.* IX, 213.

Election of 1864, gratitude without taint—I am thankful to God for this approval of the people; but, while deeply grateful for this mark of their confidence in me, if I know my heart, my gratitude is free from any taint of personal triumph. I do not impugn the motives of any one opposed to me. It is no pleasure to me to triumph over any one, but I give thanks to the Almighty for this evidence of the people's resolution to stand by free government and the rights of humanity.—*Response to serenade, Nov. 9, 1864.* X, 262.
2.—While I am duly sensible of the high compliment of a re-election, and duly grateful, as I trust to Almighty God, for having directed my countrymen to a right conclusion, as I think, for their good, it adds nothing to my satisfaction that any other man may be disappointed by the result.—*Response to serenade, Nov. 10, 1864.* X, 264.
3.—With deep gratitude to my countrymen for this mark of their confidence; with a distrust of my own ability to perform the duty required under the most favorable circumstances, and now rendered doubly difficult by existing national perils; yet with a firm reliance on the strength of our free government, and the eventual loyalty of the people to the just principles upon which it is founded, and above all with an unshaken faith in the Supreme Ruler of nations, I accept this trust.—*Reply to committee reporting electoral count, Feb. 9, 1865.* XI, 10.

Election of 1864, no bitterness after—May I ask those who have not differed from me to join with me in this same spirit toward those who have?—*Response to serenade, Nov. 9, 1864.* X, 265.

Election of 1864, of lasting advantage—I cannot at this hour say what has been the result of the election. But, whatever it may be, I have no desire to modify this opinion; that all who have labored today in behalf of the Union have wrought for the best interests of the country and the world; not only for the present, but for all future ages.—*Response to serenade, Nov. 9, 1864.* X, 262.
2.—The election, along with its incidental and undesirable strife, has done good too. It has demonstrated that a people's government can sustain a national election in the midst of a great civil war. Until now, it has not been known to the world that this was a possibility. It shows also how sound and strong we are. It shows that, even among candidates of the same

party, he who is most devoted to the Union and most opposed to treason can receive most of the people's votes.—*Response to serenade, Nov. 10, 1864.* X, 264.

Election of 1864, "people's business"—Well, I cannot run the political machine; I have enough on my hands without that. It is the people's business—the election is in their hands. If they turn their backs to the fire and get scorched in the rear, they'll find they have got to sit on the blisters.—*To a cabinet secretary, Aug. 1864.* Hertz II, 941.

Election of 1864, shows agreement on value of Union —*See* UNION, maintenance of, insisted on in election.

See UNION, friends of, get most votes.

Election of 1864, "voice of the people"—*See* THIRTEENTH AMENDMENT, favorable action on, urged, 3.

Election of 1864, will decide Union's fate—*See* UNION, fate of, to be decided by 1864 election.

Elections, indicate public purpose—The most reliable indication of public purpose in this country is derived through our popular elections.—*Fourth annual message, Dec. 6, 1864.* X, 304.

Elections, minority, not impressive—*See* BUCHANAN, JAMES, minority choice.

Elections, must be free—I wish all qualified voters in Maryland and elsewhere to have the undisturbed privilege of voting at elections; and neither my authority nor my name can be properly used to the contrary.—*To Thomas Swan, Oct. 27, 1863.* IX, 185.

Elections, necessary to free government—We cannot have free government without elections; and if the rebellion could force us to forego or postpone a national election, it might fairly claim to have already conquered and ruined us. The strife of the election is but human nature practically applied to the facts in the case. What has occurred in this case [1864 election] must ever recur in similar cases. . . . In any great national trial, compared with the men of this, we shall have as wise, as bad and as good. Let us, therefore, study the incidents of this as philosophy to learn wisdom from, and none of them as wrongs to be avenged.—*Response to serenade, Nov. 10, 1864.* X, 263.

Elections, no interference in presidential—By the Constitution and laws, the President is charged with no duty in the conduct of a presidential election in any state.—*To W. B. Campbell and others, Oct. 22, 1864.* X, 250.

2.—Except it be to give protection against violence, I decline to interfere in any way with any presiden-

tial election.—*To W. B. Campbell and others, Oct. 22, 1864.* X, 251.

Elections, not always accurate guide—I understand your idea that if a presidential candidate avow his opinion upon a given question, or rather upon all questions, and the people, with full knowledge of this, elect him, they thereby distinctly approve all these opinions. By means of it, measures are adopted or rejected contrary to the wishes of the whole of one party, and often nearly half of the other. Three, four, or half a dozen questions are prominent at a given time; the party selects its candidate, and he takes his position on each of these questions. On all but one his positions have already been indorsed at former elections, and his party fully committed to them; but that one is new, and a large portion of them are against it. But what are they to do? The whole was strung together; and they must take all or reject all. They cannot take what they like, and leave the rest. What they are already committed to being the majority, they shut their eyes and gulp the whole.— *Speech in Congress, July 27, 1848.* II, 65.

Elections, people united after—When an election is past, it is altogether fitting a free people, as I suppose, that, until the next election, they should be one people.—*Speech, reply to New York governor, Albany, Feb. 18, 1861.* VI, 139.

Elective Franchise, dishonestly exercised—*See* ALIENS, status of, in war, 4.

Elective Franchise, loyalty test for—The remaining point of your letter is a protest against any person offering to vote being put to any test not found in the laws of Maryland. This brings us to a difference between Missouri and Maryland. With the same reason in both states, Missouri has, by law, provided a test for the voter with reference to the present rebellion, while Maryland has not.—*To Gov. A. W. Bradford, Nov. 2, 1863.* IX, 197.

Electoral College, argument for retaining—I was once of your opinion . . . that presidential electors should be dispensed with, but a more thorough knowledge of the causes that first introduced them has made me doubt. The convention that framed the Constitution had this difficulty: the small states wished to so form the new government as that they might be equal to the large ones, regardless of the inequality in population; the large ones insisted on equality of population. They compromised it by basing the House of Representatives on population, and the Senate on states regardless of population, and the execution of both principles by the electors in each state, equal in number to her senators and representatives. Now throw away the machinery of electors and the compromise is broken up and the whole yielded to the principle of the larger states. There is one thing more. In the slave states you have representatives, and consequently electors, partly upon the basis of your slave population, which would be swept away by the change you seem to think desirable.—*To Josephus Hewett, Feb. 13, 1848. I, 355.*

Electoral College, veto power and—*See* EXECUTIVE POWER, electoral votes and.

"Electric Cord," of the Declaration of Independence —*See* EQUALITY, Declaration's message to foreign-born.

Elephants, Siam's offer declined—I appreciate most highly your Majesty's tender of good offices in forwarding to this government a stock from which a supply of elephants, might be raised on our soil. This government would not hesitate to avail itself of so generous an offer if the object were one which could be made practically useful in the present condition of the United States. Our political jurisdiction, however, does not reach a latitude so low as to favor the multiplication of the elephant, and steam on land as well as on water has been our best and most efficient agent of transportation in internal commerce.—*To King of Siam, Feb. 3, 1862. Tracy, 202.*

Ellsworth, E. E., tribute to—Ever since the beginning of our acquaintance, I have valued you highly as a personal friend, and at the same time—without much capacity of judging—have had a very high estimate of your military talent, accordingly, I have been, and still am, anxious for you to have the best position in the military which can be given you, consistently with justice and proper courtesy toward the older officers of the army.—*To Col. Ellsworth, April 15, 1861. Hertz II, 828.*

See CONDOLENCE, letter of, to parents of lost son.

Elysium—*See* DREAMS, subject to, 1.

Emancipation, against immediate proclamation—I think Sumner and the rest of you would upset our applecart altogether, if you had your way. We'll fetch 'em; just give us a little time. We didn't go into the war to put down slavery, but to put the flag back; and to act differently at this moment would, I have no doubt, not only weaken our cause, but smack of bad faith; for I never should have had votes enough to send me here, if the people had supposed I should try to use my power to upset slavery. Why, the first thing you would see would be a mutiny in the army.

No! We must wait until every other means have been exhausted. This thunderbolt will keep.—*To friends of Senator Sumner, Sept., 1861. War Years I, 356.*
2.—What good would a proclamation of emancipation from me do, especially as we are now situated? I do not wish to issue a document that the whole world will see must necessarily be inoperative, like the Pope's bull against the comet. Would my word free the slaves, when I cannot even enforce the Constitution in the rebel states? Is there a single court, or magistrate, or individual that would be influenced by it there? And what reason is there to think it would have any greater effect upon the slaves than the late law of Congress, which I approved, and which offers protection and freedom to the slaves of rebel masters who come within our lines? Yet I cannot learn that that law has caused a single slave to come over to us. . . . Do not misunderstand me because I have mentioned these objections. . . . I have not decided against a proclamation of liberty to the slaves, but hold the matter under advisement; and I can assure you that the subject is on my mind, day and night, more than any other.—*Reply to Chicago church committee, Sept. 13, 1862. VIII, 30.*

See BORDER STATES, attitude of, toward Union, 2.

Emancipation, argument for compensated—The emancipation [as proposed by Lincoln in suggested constitutional amendment] will be unsatisfactory to the advocates of perpetual slavery; but the length of time [37 years] should mitigate their dissatisfaction. The time spares both races from the evils of sudden derangement—in fact, from the necessity of any derangement; while most of those whose habitual course of thought will be disturbed by the measure will have passed away before its consummation. They will never see it. Another class will hail the prospect of emancipation, but will deprecate the length of time. They will feel that it gives too little to the now living slaves. But it really gives them much. It saves them from the vagrant destitution which must largely attend immediate emancipation in localities where their numbers are very great; and it gives the inspiring assurance that their posterity shall be free forever. The plan leaves to each state choosing to act under it to abolish slavery now, or at the end of the century, or at any intermediate time, or by degrees extending over the whole or any part of the period; and it obliges no two states to proceed alike. It also provides for compensation, and generally the mode of making it. This, it would seem, must further mitigate the dissatisfaction of those who favor perpetual slavery, and especially of those who are to receive the compensation. Doubtless some of those who are to pay, and not receive, will object. Yet the measure is both just and economical.—*Second annual message, Dec. 1, 1862.* VIII, 118.

2.—Is it doubted that it [proposed amendment] would restore the national authority and national prosperity, and perpetuate both indefinitely?—*Second annual message, Dec. 1, 1862.* VIII, 119.

3.—The plan is recommended as a means, not in exclusion of, but additional to, all others for restoring and preserving the national authority throughout the Union. . . . The plan would, I am confident, secure peace more speedily and maintain it more permanently than can be done by force alone, while all it would cost, considering amounts and manner of payment and times of payment, would be easier paid than will the additional cost of the war if we rely solely upon force. It is much, very much, that it would cost no blood at all.—*Second annual message, Dec. 1, 1862.* VIII, 129.

4.—Does the mere fact that the North has come suddenly to a contrary opinion [that slaves are property] give us the right to take the slaves from their owners without compensation? . . . If we have to fight this war till the South is subjugated, then I think we shall be justified in freeing the slaves without compensation. But in any settlement arrived at before they force things to that extremity, is it not right and fair that we should make payment for the slaves?—*To James R. Gilmore, late May, 1863.* Gilmore, 159.

5.—I should be disposed to make compensation for the slaves; but I doubt if my cabinet or the country would favor that.—*To James R. Gilmore, late May, 1863.* Gilmore, 158.

See EMANCIPATION, financial aspects of compensated.

Emancipation, bill for compensated, recommended—Herewith is the draft of a bill to compensate any state which may abolish slavery within its limits, the passage of which substantially as presented I respectfully and earnestly recommend.—*Message to Congress, July 14, 1862.* VII, 276.

Emancipation, Clay favored gradual—*See* CLAY, HENRY, slavery decried by, 1.

Emancipation, compensated, might soon end war—I intend no reproach or complaint when I assure you [border-state congressmen] that, in my opinion, if you all had voted for the resolution in the gradual [compensated] emancipation message of last March, the war would now be substantially ended. And the plan therein proposed is yet one of the most potent and swift means of ending it. Let the states which are in rebellion see definitely and certainly that in no

event will the states you represent ever join their proposed confederacy, and they cannot much longer maintain the contest. But you cannot divest them of their hope to ultimately have you with them so long as you show a determination to perpetuate the institution within your own states. . . . You and I know what the lever of their power is. Break that lever before their faces, and they can shake you no more.—*To border-state congressmen, July 12, 1862.* VII, 270.

Emancipation, compensated, would avoid bloodshed —*See* BLOODSHED, emancipation avoids.

Emancipation, constitutional—The proposition [compensated emancipation] now submitted does not encounter any constitutional difficulty.—*Interview with border-state congressmen, March 10, 1862.* VII, 125.

Emancipation, constitutional amendment urged—I recommend the adoption of the following resolution amendatory to the Constitution of the United States: "Every state wherein slavery now exists which shall abolish the same therein at any time before the first of January, 1900, shall receive compensation from the United States. . . . The President of the United States shall deliver to every such state bonds of the United States . . . said bonds to be delivered to such state by instalments, or in one parcel at the completion of the abolishment, accordingly as the same shall have been gradual or at one time within such state. . . . Any state having received bonds as aforesaid, and afterward reintroducing or tolerating slavery therein, shall refund to the United States the bonds so received, or the value thereof, and all interest paid thereon. All slaves which shall have enjoyed actual freedom by the chances of the war at any time before the end of the rebellion shall be forever free; but all owners of such who shall not have been disloyal shall be compensated for them at the same rates as are provided for the states adopting abolishment of slavery, but in such way that no slave shall be twice accounted for.—*Second annual message, Dec. 1, 1862.* Basler, 679.

Emancipation, desired in Maryland—I am very anxious for emancipation to be effected in Maryland in some substantial form. . . . My wish is that all who are for emancipation in any form shall co-operate, all treating all respectfully, and all adopting and acting upon the major opinion when fairly ascertained. What I have dreaded is the danger that by jealousies, rivalries, and consequent ill-blood—driving one another out of meetings and conventions—perchance from the polls—the friends of emancipation themselves may divide, and lose the measure altogether.—*To John A. J. Creswell, March 7, 1864.* X, 30.

2.—It needs not be a secret that I wish success to emancipation in Maryland. It would aid much to end the rebellion.—*To John A. J. Creswell, March 17, 1864.* X, 43.

3.—I presume the only feature of the instrument [proposed Maryland constitution] about which there is serious controversy is that which provides for the extinction of slavery. It needs not to be a secret, and I presume is not a secret, that I wish success to this provision. I wish all men to be free. I wish the material prosperity of the already free, which I feel sure the extinction of slavery would bring. I wish to see in process of disappearing the only thing which ever could bring this nation to civil war. . . . I only add that I shall be gratified exceedingly if the good people of the state shall, by their votes, ratify the new constitution.—*To H. W. Hoffman, Oct. 10, 1864.* X, 239.

Emancipation, destruction of property by—In a certain sense the liberation of slaves is the destruction of property—property acquired by descent or by purchase, the same as any other property. . . . If, then, for a common object this property is to be sacrificed, is it not just that it be done at a common charge?—*Second annual message, Dec. 1, 1862.* VIII, 119.

Emancipation, District of Columbia—They [Sangamon County representatives in Illinois legislature] believe that the Congress of the United States has the power, under the Constitution, to abolish slavery in the District of Columbia, but that the power ought not to be exercised, unless at the request of the people of the District.—*Protest in Illinois Legislature, March 3, 1837.* I, 52.

2.—Be it enacted . . . that no person not now within the District of Columbia, nor now owned by any person or persons now resident within it, shall ever be held in slavery within said District. . . . That no person now within said District, or now owned by any person or persons now resident within the same, or hereafter born within it, shall ever be held in slavery without the limits of said District. . . . That all children born of slave mothers within said District, on or after the first day of January, in the year of our Lord, 1850, shall be free. . . . That all persons now within the District, lawfully held as slaves, or now owned by any person or persons now resident within said District, shall remain such at the will of their respective owners, their heirs, and legal representatives; Provided that such owner [and so forth] may at any time receive from the treasury of the United States the full value of his or her slave . . .

upon which [sale] such slave shall be forthwith and forever free. . . . That [a special election be held and] if a majority of them [votes] be found for this act, [the President will] forthwith issue his proclamation giving notice of the fact; and this act shall only be in full force and effect on and after the day of such proclamation.—*Bill offered in House, Jan. 16, 1849.* II, 97.

3.—[In Washington six years ago] I heard no one express a doubt that a system of gradual emancipation, with compensation to owners, would meet the approbation of a large majority of the white people of the district. But without the action of Congress they could say nothing; and Congress said "no"—*Speech, Peoria, Oct. 16, 1854.* II, 215.

4.—I do not stand pledged to the abolition of slavery in the District of Columbia. . . . [Yet] I should be exceedingly glad to see slavery abolished in the District of Columbia. I believe that Congress possesses the constitutional power to abolish it. Yet as a member of Congress, I should not with my present views be in favor of endeavoring to abolish slavery in the District of Columbia unless it would be upon these conditions: First, that the abolition should be gradual; second, that it should be on a vote of a majority of the qualified voters in the District; and, third, that compensation should be made to unwilling owners. With these three conditions, I confess, I would be exceedingly glad to see Congress abolish slavery in the District of Columbia, and in the language of Henry Clay, "sweep from our capital that foul blot upon our nation."—*Debate, Freeport, Aug. 27, 1858.* III, 273.

5.—I have not thought of recommending the abolition of slavery in the District of Columbia, nor the slave trade among the slave states . . . and if I were to make such recommendation, it is quite clear Congress would not follow it.—*To John A. Gilmer, Dec. 15, 1860.* VI, 80.

6.—I am a little uneasy about the abolishment of slavery in the District, not but I would be glad to see it abolished, but as to the time and manner of doing it. If some one or more of the border states would move first, I should greatly prefer it, but if this cannot be, in a reasonable time, I would like the bill to have these main features—gradual compensation—and vote of the people.—*To Horace Greeley, March 24, 1862.* Hertz II, 854.

7.—The act entitled "An act for the release of certain persons held to service or labor in the District of Columbia" has this day been approved and signed. I have never doubted the constitutional authority of congress to abolish slavery in this district, and I have ever desired to see the national capital freed from the institution in some satisfactory way. Hence there has never been in my mind any question upon the subject except the one of expediency, arising in view of all the circumstances. . . . I am gratified that the two principles of compensation and colonization are both recognized and practically applied in the act.—*Message to Congress, April 16, 1862.* VII, 146.

See DISTRICT OF COLUMBIA, slavery in, 1.

See SLAVERY, Republican policy on, 5.

Emancipation, early examples of gradual—While all this was passing in the general government [adoption of measures to stop the slave trade], five or six of the original slave states had adopted systems of gradual emancipation, by which the institution was rapidly becoming extinct within their limits.—*Speech, Peoria, Oct. 16, 1854.* II, 246.

2.—Several of the old states, in the last quarter of the last century, did adopt systems of gradual emancipation by which the institution has finally become extinct within their limits.—*Speech, Peoria, Oct. 16, 1854.* II, 252.

Emancipation, financial aspect of compensated—In the mere financial or pecuniary view any member of Congress with the census tables and treasury reports before him can readily see for himself how very soon the current expenditures of this war would purchase, at fair valuation, all the slaves in any named state.—*Message to Congress, March 6, 1862.* VII, 113.

2.—I am grateful to the New York journals, and not less so to the *Times* than to the others, for their kind notices of the late special message to Congress. Your paper, however, intimates that the proposition [for compensated emancipation], though well-intentioned, must fail on the score of expense. I do hope you will reconsider this. Have you noticed the facts that less than one-half day's cost of this war would pay for all the slaves in Delaware—that 87 days' cost of this war would pay for all in Delaware, Maryland, District of Columbia, Kentucky, and Missouri at the same price? Were these states to take the step, do you doubt that it would shorten the war more than 87 days, and thus be an actual saving of expense? Please look at these things and consider whether there should not be another article in the *Times*.—*To Henry J. Raymond, editor of Times, March 9, 1862.* VII, 119.

3.—Less than one-half day's cost of this war would pay for all the slaves in Delaware at $400 a head. . . . Again, less than 87 days' cost of this war would, at the same price, pay for all in Delaware, Maryland, District of Columbia, Kentucky and Missouri. . . . Do you doubt that taking the initiatory steps on the part of those states and the District would shorten

the war more than 87 days, and thus be an actual saving of expense?—*To James A. McDougall, March 14, 1862.* VII, 132.

4.—A word as to the time and manner of incurring the expense [of compensated emancipation]. Suppose, for instance, a state devises and adopts a system by which the institution [slavery] absolutely ceases therein by a named day—say Jan. 1, 1882. Then let the sum to be paid to such state by the United States be ascertained by taking from the census of 1860 the number of slaves within the state, and multiplying that number by four hundred—the United States to pay such sum to the state in 20 equal annual installments, in 6 per cent bonds of the United States. The sum thus given, as to time and manner, I think, would not be half as onerous as would be an equal sum raised now for the indefinite prosecution of the war.—*To James A. McDougall, March 14, 1862.* VII, 133.

5.—How much better to thus save the money which else we sink forever in the war! How much better to do it while we can, lest the war ere long render us pecuniarily unable to do it!—*To border-state congressmen, July 12, 1862.* VII, 271.

6.—The war requires large sums, and requires them at once. The aggregate sum necessary for compensated emancipation would of course be large. But it would require no ready cash, nor the bonds even, any faster than the emancipation progresses. . . . This might not, and probably would not, close before the end of the 37 years. At that time we shall probably have 100,000,000 people to share the burden, instead of the 31,000,000 as now. . . . The proposed emancipation would shorten the war, perpetuate peace, insure this increase of population, and proportionately the wealth of the country. With these, we should pay all the emancipation would cost, together with our other debt, easier than we should pay our other debt without it. . . . Is it doubted, then, that the plan I propose, if adopted, would shorten the war, and thus lessen the expenditure of money and blood?—*Second annual message, Dec. 1, 1862.* VIII, 118.

7.—If, with less money, or money more easily paid, we can preserve the benefits of the Union by this means, than we can by war alone, is it not also economical to do it? Let us consider it then. Let us ascertain the sum we have expended in the war since compensated emancipation was proposed last March, and consider whether, if that measure had been promptly accepted by even some of the slave states, the same sum would not have done more to close the war than has been done otherwise. If so, the measure would save money, and in that view would be a prudent and economical measure. Certainly it is not so easy to pay something as it is to pay nothing, but it is easier to pay a large sum than it is to pay a larger one. And it is easier to pay any sum when we are able than to pay it before we are able.—*Second annual message, Dec. 1, 1862.* Basler, 681.

8.—This fact [that time helps pay the national debt] would be no excuse for delaying payment of what is justly due; but it shows the great importance of time in this connection—the great advantage of a policy by which we should not have to pay, until we number 100,000,000, what by a different policy we would have to pay now when we number but 31,000,000. In a word, it shows that a dollar will be much harder to pay for the war than will a dollar for emancipation on the proposed plan.—*Second annual message, Dec. 1, 1862.* VIII, 125.

9.—The subject is presented exclusively in its economical aspects. The plan would, I am confident, secure peace more speedily, and maintain it more permanently, than can be done by force alone; while all it would cost, considering amounts and manner of payment, would be easier paid than will the additional cost of the war if we rely solely on force.—*Second annual message, Dec. 1, 1862.* VIII, 129.

10.—I suggested compensated emancipation, to which you replied that you wished not to be taxed to buy negroes. But I had not asked you to be taxed to buy negroes, except in such a way as to save you from greater taxation to save the Union exclusively by other means.—*To J. C. Conkling, Aug. 26, 1863.* IX, 97.

Emancipation, for forfeited slaves—The government, so far as there can be ownership, thus owns the forfeited slaves, and the question for Congress in regard to them is, "Shall they be made free or sold to new masters?" I perceive no objection to Congress deciding in advance that they shall be free. . . . Indeed I do not believe it possible for the general government to return persons so circumstanced to actual slavery. I believe there would be physical resistance to it which could neither be turned aside by argument nor driven away by force.—*Message to House, July 17, 1862.* VII, 282.

Emancipation, free hand for states—I have very earnestly urged the slave states to adopt emancipation; and it ought to be, and is, an object with me not to overthrow or thwart what any of them may in good faith do to that end.—*To Gen. Schofield, June 22, 1863.* VIII, 330.

Emancipation, freedom to slave and free.—*See* UNION, "we know how to save."

Emancipation, gains favor in states formerly hostile —In each [of the states of Arkansas and Tennessee] owners of slaves and advocates of slavery at the beginning of the rebellion, now declare openly for emancipation in their respective states.—*Third annual message, Dec. 8, 1863.* IX, 246.

2.—Of the states not included in the Emancipation Proclamation, Maryland and Missouri, neither of which three years ago would tolerate any restraint upon the extension of slavery into new territories, only dispute now as to the best mode of removing it within their own limits.—*Third annual message, Dec. 8, 1863.* IX, 246.

3.—The movements by state action for emancipation in several of the states not included in the Emancipation Proclamation are matters of profound gratulation.—*Third annual message, Dec. 8, 1863.* IX, 251.

Emancipation, Georgians urged to accept—If I resided in Georgia, with my present sentiments, I'll tell you what I would do if I were in your place. I would go home and get the governor of the state to call the legislature together, and get them to recall all the state troops from the war; elect senators and members to Congress, and ratify this constitutional amendment prospectively, so as to take effect—say in five years. . . . I have looked into the subject, and think such a prospective ratification would be valid. Whatever may have been the views of your people before the war, they must be convinced now that slavery is doomed. It cannot last long in any event, and the best course, it seems to me, for your public men to pursue would be to adopt such a policy as will avoid, as far as possible, the evils of immediate emancipation. This would be my course, if I were in your place.—*To Confederate peace commissioners, Hampton Roads, Feb. 3, 1865.* Tarbell, IV, 7.

Emancipation, gradual, "might be adopted"—It does seem to me that systems of gradual emancipation might be adopted, but for their tardiness in this I will not undertake to judge our brethren of the South.—*Speech, Peoria, Oct. 16, 1854.* II, 207.

Emancipation, gradual, preferred—In my judgment gradual and not sudden emancipation is better for all. —*Message to Congress, March 6, 1862.* VII, 112.

2.—I do not speak of emancipation at once, but of a decision at once to emancipate gradually.—*To border-state congressmen, July 12, 1862.* VII, 272.

3.—I believe some plan substantially being gradual emancipation would be better for both white and black.—*To Gen. Hurlbut, July 31, 1863.* IX, 52.

4.—I think it probable that my expressions of a preference for gradual over immediate emancipation, are misunderstood. I had thought the gradual would pro-duce less confusion and destitution, and therefore would be more satisfactory; but if those who are better acquainted with the subject, and more deeply interested in it, prefer the immediate, most certainly I have no objection to their judgment prevailing.—*To John A. J. Creswell, March 7, 1864.* X, 30.

Emancipation, imaginary perils of—There is an ob-jection urged against free colored persons remaining in the country which is largely imaginary, if not sometimes malicious. It is insisted that their presence would injure and displace white laborers. . . . Is it true, then, that colored people can displace any more white labor by being free than by remaining slaves? If they stay in their old places they jostle no white laborers; if they leave their old places, they leave them open to white laborers. Logically, then, there is neither more nor less of it. Emancipation, even with-out deportation, would probably enhance the wages of white labor, and very surely would not reduce them. Thus the customary amount of labor would still have to be performed—the freed people would surely not do more than their old proportion of it, and very probably for a time would do less, leaving an increased part to white laborers, bringing their labor into greater demand and consequently enhanc-ing the wages of it. With deportation—colonization—even to a limited extent, enhanced wages to white labor is mathematically certain.—*Second annual mes-sage, Dec. 1, 1862.* VIII, 126.
2.—It is dreaded that the freed people will swarm forth and cover the whole land. Are they not already in the land? Will liberation make them any more numerous? Equally distributed among the whites of the whole country, there would be but one colored to seven whites. Could the one in any way greatly dis-turb the seven? There are many communities now having more than one free colored person to seven whites, and this without any apparent consciousness of evil from it. . . . The District [of Columbia] has more than one free colored person to six whites and yet in its frequent petitions to Congress I believe it has never presented the presence of free colored per-sons as one of its grievances. But why will emancipa-tion south send the free people north? People of any color seldom run unless there be something to run from. Heretofore colored people to some extent have fled north from bondage, and now perhaps from both bondage and destitution. But if gradual emancipation and deportation be adopted, they will have neither to flee from. Their old masters will give them wages at least until new laborers can be procured, and the freedmen in turn will gladly give their labor for the

wages till new homes can be found for them in con-genial climes and with people of their own blood and race. . . . In any event, cannot the North decide for itself whether to receive them? Again, as practice proves more than theory in any case, has there been any irruption of colored people northward because of the abolition of slavery in this District last spring? —*Second annual message, Dec. 1, 1862.* VIII, 127.
3.—No servile insurrection or tendency to violence or cruelty has marked the measures of emancipation and arming the blacks. . . . The annual elections follow-ing are highly encouraging to those whose official duty it is to bear the country through this great trial. Thus we have the new reckoning.—*Third annual message, Dec. 8, 1863.* IX, 247.
4.—The proposed acquiescence of the national execu-tive in any reasonable temporary state arrangement for the freed people is made with the view of possibly modifying the confusion and destitution which must at best attend all classes by the total revolution of labor throughout the whole states. It is hoped that the already deeply afflicted people in those states may be somewhat more ready to give up the cause of their affliction if to this extent this vital matter be left to themselves.—*Third annual message, Dec. 8, 1863.* IX, 250.

Emancipation, joint resolution for compensated, urged—I recommend the adoption of a joint resolu-tion, which shall be substantially as follows: "That the United States ought to co-operate with any state which may adopt gradual abolishment of slavery, giv-ing to such state pecuniary aid, to be used by such state, in its discretion, to compensate for the incon-veniences, public and private, produced by such change of system." If the proposition . . . does not meet the approval of Congress and the country, there is the end; but if it does command such approval I deem it of importance that the states and the people immediately interested should be at once distinctly notified of the fact, so that they may begin to consider whether to accept or reject it. The federal govern-ment will find its highest interest in such a measure, as one of the most efficient means of self-preservation. The leaders of the existing insurrection entertain the hope that this government will ultimately be forced to acknowledge the independence of some part of the disaffected region, and that all the slave states north of such part will then say, "The Union for which we struggled being already gone, we now choose to go with the southern section." To deprive them of this hope substantially ends the rebellion, and the initia-tion of emancipation completely deprives them of it as to all the states initiating it. The point is that not all the states tolerating slavery would very soon, if at all, initiate emancipation; but that . . . the more northern shall by such initiation make it certain to the more southern that in no event will the former ever join the latter in their proposed confederacy. . . . Such a proposition on the part of the general government sets up no claim of a right by federal authority to interfere with slavery, within state limits, referring, as it does, the absolute control of the subject in each case to the state and its people immediately interested.—*Message to Congress, March 6, 1862.* VII, 112.

2.—I respectfully recommend that a joint resolution, substantially as follows, be adopted so soon as practicable by your honorable bodies [House and Senate]: —"That the President . . . is hereby empowered, in his discretion, to pay $400,000,000 to the states of Alabama, Arkansas, Delaware, Florida, Georgia, Kentucky, Louisiana, Maryland, Mississippi, Missouri, North Carolina, South Carolina, Tennessee, Texas, Virginia and West Virginia, in the manner and on the conditions following, to wit: The payment to be made in 6 per cent government bonds, and to be distributed among said states *pro rata* on their respective slave populations as shown by the census of 1860, and no part of said sum to be paid unless all resistance to the national authority shall be abandoned and cease, on or before the first day of April next; and upon such abandonment and ceasing of resistance one-half of said sum to be paid in manner aforesaid, and the remaining half to be paid only upon the amendment of the National Constitution recently proposed by Congress [Thirteenth Amendment] becoming valid law, on or before the first day of July next, by the action thereon of the requisite number of states."—*To Congress, Feb. 5, 1865.* [Disapproved by cabinet; not signed or sent.] XI, 1.

Emancipation, justified only when indispensable— *See* EMANCIPATION, war measure, 3.

Emancipation, Missouri proposal for, discussed— Your dispatch, asking in substance whether, in case Missouri shall adopt gradual emancipation, the general government will protect slave holders in that species of property during the short time it shall be permitted by the state to exist within it, has been received. Desirous as I am that emancipation shall be adopted by Missouri, and believing as I do that gradual can be made better than immediate for both black and white, except when military necessity changes the case, my impulse is to say that such protection would be given. I cannot know exactly what shape an act of emancipation may take. If the period from the initiation to the final end should be com-

paratively short, and the act should prevent persons being sold during that period into more lasting slavery, the whole would be easier. I do not wish to pledge the general government to the affirmative support of even temporary slavery, beyond what can be fairly claimed under the Constitution.—*To Gen. Schofield, June 22, 1863.* VIII, 329.

2.—The Missouri plan [for gradual emancipation] recently adopted, I do not object to on account of the time for ending the institution; but I am sorry the beginning should have been postponed for seven years, leaving all that time to agitate for the repeal of the whole thing. It should begin at once, giving at least the new-born a vested interest in freedom which could not be taken away.—*To Gen. Hurlbut, July 31, 1863.* IX, 52.

Emancipation, motives for desiring—As an anti-slavery man I have a motive to desire emancipation which pro-slavery men do not have; but even they have strong enough reason to thus place themselves again under the shield of the Union; and to thus perpetually hedge against the recurrence of the scenes through which we are now passing.—*To Gen. Banks, Aug. 5, 1863.* IX, 57.

Emancipation, no hope for voluntary—So far as peaceful voluntary emancipation is concerned, the condition of the negro slave in America, scarcely less terrible to the contemplation of a free mind, is now as fixed and hopeless of change for the better, as that of the lost souls of the finally impenitent.—*To George Robertson, Aug. 15, 1855.* II, 280.

Emancipation, plan for compensated, merely initiatory—While it is true that the adoption of the proposed resolution would be merely initiatory and not within itself a practical measure, it is recommended in the hope that it would soon lead to important practical results.—*Message to Congress, March 6, 1862.* VII, 115.

Emancipation, plan for Louisiana—*See* RECONSTRUCTION, Louisiana, 8.

Emancipation, policy of, necessary to success—No human power can subdue the rebellion without the use of the emancipation policy, and every other policy calculated to weaken the moral and physical forces of the rebellion.—*Interview, Gov. Randall, Aug. 15, 1864.* X, 191.

Emancipation, President's purpose declared—I hereby make known that it is my purpose, upon the next meeting of Congress, to again recommend the adoption of a practical measure for tendering pecuniary aid to the free choice or rejection of any and all states which may then be recognizing and practically sustaining the authority of the United States and which may then have voluntarily adopted, or thereafter may voluntarily adopt, gradual abolishment of slavery within such state or states; that the object is to practically restore, thenceforward to be maintained, the constitutional relation between the general government and each and all the states, wherein that relation is now suspended or disturbed; and that for this object the war, as it has been, will be prosecuted.—*First draft of preliminary proclamation, July 22, 1862.* VII, 289.

2.—I . . . proclaim and declare . . . that it is my purpose, upon the next meeting of Congress, to again recommend the adoption of a practical measure tendering pecuniary aid to the free acceptance or rejection of all slave states, so-called, the people whereof may not then be in rebellion against the United States, and which states may then have voluntarily adopted, or thereafter may voluntarily adopt, immediate or gradual abolishment of slavery within their respective limits.—*Proclamation, Sept. 22, 1862.* VIII, 36.

Emancipation, "pressed with a difficulty" over Hunter proclamation—I am pressed with a difficulty . . . which threatens division among those who, united, are none too strong. Gen. Hunter . . . proclaimed all men free within certain states, and I repudiated the proclamation. He expected more good and less harm from the measure than I could believe would follow. Yet, in repudiating it, I gave dissatisfaction, if not offense, to many whose support the country cannot afford to lose. And this is not the end of it. The pressure in this direction is still upon me, and is increasing.—*To border-state congressmen, July 12, 1862.* VII, 272.

Emancipation, principle of Revolution inspired—But [says Douglas] the principle of the Nebraska bill abolished slavery in several of the old states. . . . Is there not some reason to suspect that it was the principle of the Revolution, and not the principle of the Nebraska bill, that led to emancipation in those old states?—*Speech, Peoria, Oct. 16, 1854.* II, 251.

Emancipation, probable effect on labor—*See* EMANCIPATION, imaginary perils of, 1, 2.

Emancipation, progress toward compensated—The movements by state action, for emancipation in several of the states not included in the Emancipation Proclamation, are matters of profound gratulation. And while I do not repeat in detail what I have heretofore so earnestly urged upon the subject, my general views and feelings remain unchanged; and I

trust that Congress will omit no fair opportunity of aiding these important steps to a great consummation.—*Third annual message, Dec. 8, 1863.* IX, 251.

Emancipation, rejected in Missouri—*See* SLAVERY, Democratic policy toward, 5.

Emancipation, repudiated—*See* HUNTER, DAVID, proclamation of, voided.

See EMANCIPATION, "pressed with a difficulty" over Hunter proclamation.

See FRÉMONT, JOHN C., proclamation of, disapproved.

Emancipation, reserved for executive decision—I . . . make known that whether it be competent for me, as commander-in-chief of the army and navy, to declare the slaves of any state or states free, and whether at any time, in any case, it shall have become a necessity indispensable to the maintenance of the government to exercise such supposed power are questions which, under my responsibility, I reserve to myself.—*Proclamation, May 19, 1862.* VII, 171.

Emancipation, slave states "need not be hurt" by—Even the people of the states included [in the proclamation] need not be hurt by it. Let them adopt systems of apprenticeship for the colored people, conforming substantially to the most approved plans of gradual emancipation; and with the aid they can have from the general government they may be nearly as well off, in this respect, as if the present trouble had not occurred, and much better off than they can possibly be if the contest continues persistently.—*To Gen. McClernand, Jan. 8, 1863.* VIII, 182.

Emancipation, states appealed to for compensated—The proposition now made, though an offer only, I hope it may be esteemed no offense to ask whether the pecuniary consideration tendered would not be of more value to the states and private persons concerned than are the institution and property in it, in the present aspect of affairs.—*Message to Congress, March 6, 1862.* VII, 114.

2.—To the people of those states [which may be ready to accept the assistance offered by a congressional resolution just passed] I now earnestly appeal. I do not argue—I beseech you to make the argument yourselves; you cannot, if you would, be blind to the signs of the times. I beg of you a calm and enlarged consideration of them, ranging, if it may be, far above personal and partisan politics. This proposal makes common cause for a common object, casting no reproaches upon any. It acts not the Pharisee. The change it contemplates would come gently as the dews of Heaven, not rending or wrecking anything.

Will you embrace it? So much good has not been done by one effort in all past time as, in the Providence of God, it is now your high privilege to do. May the vast future not have to lament that you have neglected it.—*Proclamation, May 19, 1862.* VII, 172.

3.—Can you, for your states, do better than to take the course I urge? Discarding punctilio and maxims adapted to more manageable times, and looking only to the unprecedentedly stern facts of our case, can you do better in any possible event?—*To border-state congressmen, July 12, 1862.* VII, 271.

4.—How much better for you and for your people to take the step which at once shortens the war and secures substantial compensation for that which is sure to be wholly lost in any event! How much better for you as seller, and the nation as buyer, to sell out and buy out that without which the war could never have been, than to sink both the things to be sold and the price of it in cutting one another's throats!—*To border-state congressmen, July 12, 1862.* VII, 272.

5.—You are patriots and statesmen, and as such I pray you consider this proposition, and at least commend it to the consideration of your states and people.—*To border-state congressmen, July 12, 1862.* VII, 273.

6.—I have very earnestly urged the slave states to adopt emancipation; and it ought to be, and is, an object with me not to overthrow or thwart what any of them may in good faith do to that end.—*To Gen. Schofield, June 22, 1863.* VIII, 330.

Emancipation, war measure—But you must bear in mind that I have no right to emancipate slaves, except for the preservation of the Union.—*To James R. Gilmore, April 13, 1861.* Gilmore, 19.

2.—I view this matter as a practical war measure, to be decided on according to the advantages or disadvantages it may offer to the suppression of the rebellion.—*Reply to Chicago church committee, Sept. 13, 1862.* VIII, 32.

3.—When, early in the war, Gen. Frémont attempted military emancipation, I forbade it, because I did not then think it an indispensable necessity. When, a little later, Gen. Cameron, then secretary of war, suggested arming the blacks, I objected because I did not yet think it an indispensable necessity. When, still later, Gen. Hunter attempted military emancipation, I again forbade it, because I did not yet think the indispensable necessity had come.—*To A. G. Hodges, April 4, 1864.* X, 66.

4.—When in March and May and July, 1862, I made earnest and successive appeals to the border states to favor compensated emancipation, I believed the indispensable necessity for military emancipation and arming the blacks would come unless averted by that measure. They declined the proposition, and I was, in my best judgment, driven to the alternative of surrendering the Union and with it the Constitution, or of laying strong hands upon the colored element.—*To A. G. Hodges, April 4, 1864.* X, 67.

Emancipation, weakens enemy—You say you will not fight to free negroes. . . . I thought that in your struggle for the Union, to whatever extent the negroes should cease helping the enemy, to that extent it weakened the enemy in his resistance to you. Do you think differently?—*To J. C. Conkling, Aug. 26, 1863.* IX, 100.

2.—Freedom has given us 150,000 men; raised on southern soil. . . . Just so much it has subtracted from the enemy, and, instead of alienating the South, there is now evidence of a fraternal feeling growing up between our men and the rank and file of the rebel soldiers.—*Interview with Gov. Randall, Aug. 15, 1864.* X, 191.

Emancipation, would help in some places—Emancipation would help us in Europe, and convince them that we are incited by something more than ambition, I grant, further, that it would help somewhat in the North, though not so much, I fear, as you and those you represent imagine.—*Reply to committee from Chicago churches, Sept. 13, 1862.* VIII, 32.

Emancipation (Mind)—See FREEDOM OF THOUGHT, printing helped achieve.

Emancipation (Thought), new country favors—It is . . . a curious fact that a new country is most favorable—almost necessary—to the emancipation of thought, and the consequent advancement of civilization and the arts.—*Lecture, Springfield, Feb. 22, 1859.* V, 112.

Emancipation Proclamation, argument against extension of—Knowing your great anxiety that the Emancipation Proclamation shall now be applied to certain parts of Virginia and Louisiana which were exempted from it last January, I state briefly what appears to me to be the difficulties in the way of such a step. The original proclamation has no constitutional or legal justification, except as a military measure. The exemptions were made because the military necessity did not apply to the exempted localities. Nor does that necessity apply to them now any more than it did then. If I take the step, must I not do so without the arguments of military necessity, and so without any argument except the one that I think the measure politically expedient and morally right? Would it not thus give up all footing upon the Constitution or law? Would I not thus be in the boundless field of absolutism? Could it fail to be perceived that without any further stretch I might do the same in Delaware, Maryland, Kentucky, Tennessee and Missouri, and even change any law in any state? Would not many of our own friends shrink away appalled? Would it not lose us the elections and with them the very cause we seek to advance?—*Draft of letter to Secretary Chase, Sept. 2, 1863.*   IX, 108.

Emancipation Proclamation, "driven to it"—I have studied this matter [issuance of proclamation] well; my mind is made up. It must be done. I am driven to it. There is no other way out of our troubles. But although my duty is plain, it is in some respects painful, and I trust the people will understand that I act not in anger, but in expectation of a greater good.—*To John Covada, late Dec., 1862.*   War Years II, 14.

Emancipation Proclamation, gains due to—In [adopting the policy of the proclamation] . . . I hoped for greater gain than loss; but of this, I was not entirely confident. More than a year of trial now shows no loss by it in our foreign relations, none in our home popular sentiment, none in our white military force— no loss by it anyhow anywhere. On the contrary, it shows a gain of quite 130,000 soldiers, seamen and laborers. These are palpable facts, about which, as facts, there can be no caviling. We have the men; and we could not have had them without the measure.—*To A. G. Hodges, April 4, 1864.*   X, 67.

Emancipation Proclamation, military measure—I made the peremptory proclamation on what appeared to be military necessity. And being made, it must stand.—*To Gen. McClernand, Jan. 8, 1863.*   VIII, 182.

See EMANCIPATION PROCLAMATION, argument against extension of.

Emancipation Proclamation, must not be sacrificed— *See* RECONSTRUCTION, must not repudiate emancipation.

Emancipation Proclamation, no retraction of—To use a coarse but expressive figure, "broken eggs cannot be mended." I have issued the Emancipation Proclamation, and I cannot retract it. After commencement of hostilities, I struggled for nearly a year and a half to get along without "touching" the institution [of slavery]; and when finally I conditionally determined to touch it, I gave a hundred days' fair notice of my purpose to all states and people, within which time they could have turned it wholly aside by simply again becoming good citizens of the United States. They chose to disregard it.—*To Gen. McClernand, Jan. 8, 1863.*   VIII, 182.

2.—Those who shall have tasted actual freedom [by reason of emancipation] I believe can never be slaves or quasi-slaves again.—*To Gen. Hurlbut, July 31, 1863.*   IX, 52.

3.—For my own part, I think I shall not, in any event, retract the Emancipation Proclamation; nor, as Executive, ever return to slavery any person who is free by the terms of that proclamation, or by any of the acts of Congress.—*To Gen. Banks, Aug. 5, 1863.*   IX, 57.

4.—I am sure you will not, on due reflection, say that the promise [of the proclamation] being made must be broken at the first opportunity. I am sure you would not desire me to say, or leave an inference, that I am ready, whenever convenient, to join in reenslaving those who shall have served us in consideration of our promise. As matter of morals, could such treachery by any possibility escape the curses of Heaven, or of any good man? As matter of policy, to announce such a policy would ruin the Union cause itself. All recruiting of colored men would instantly cease and all colored men now in our service would instantly desert us. And rightly, too. Why should they give their lives for us, with full notice of our purpose to betray them?—*Unfinished draft of letter to Charles D. Robinson, Aug. 17, 1864.*   X, 195.

5.—The [Emancipation] Proclamation, as law, either is valid or is not valid. If it is not valid it needs no retraction; if it is valid it cannot be retracted any more than the dead can be brought to life.—*To J. C. Conkling, Aug. 26, 1863.*   IX, 98.

6.—Negroes, like other people, act upon motives. Why should they do anything for us if we will do nothing for them? If they stake their lives for us they must be prompted by the strongest motive, even the promise of freedom. And the promise, being made, must be kept.—*To J. C. Conkling, Aug. 26, 1863.*   IX, 100.

7.—While I remain in my present position I shall not attempt to retract or modify the Emancipation Proclamation, nor shall I return to slavery any person who is free by the terms of that proclamation or by any of the acts of Congress.—*Third annual message, Dec. 8, 1863.*   IX, 249.

8.—To abandon them [laws and proclamations against slavery] would be not only to relinquish a lever of power, but would also be a cruel and astounding breach of faith.—*Third annual message, Dec. 8, 1863.*   IX, 249.

9.—There have been men base enough to propose to me to return to slavery the black warriors of Port Hudson and Olustee, and thus win the respect of the masters they fought. Should I do so, I should deserve to be damned in time and eternity. Come what will, I will keep my faith with friends and foe.—*Interview, Gov. Randall, Aug. 15, 1864.* X, 191.

10.—Nor is it possible for any administration to retain the services of these [colored] people with the express or implied understanding that, upon the first convenient occasion, they are to be re-enslaved.— *Unfinished draft of letter to Isaac M. Schermerhorn, Sept. 12, 1864.* X, 222.

11.—I retract nothing heretofore said as to slavery. I repeat the declaration made a year ago, that "while I remain in my present position I shall not attempt to retract or modify the Emancipation Proclamation, nor shall I return to slavery any person who is free by the terms of that proclamation or by any of the acts of Congress." If the people should, by whatever mode or means, make it an executive duty to re-enslave such persons, another, and not I, must be their instrument to perform it.—*Fourth annual message, Dec. 6, 1864.* X, 310.

Emancipation Proclamation, not unconstitutional— I think it [the proclamation] is valid in law, and will be so held by the courts. I think I shall not retract or repudiate it.—*To Gen. Hurlbut, July 31, 1863.* IX, 52.

2.—You say it [the proclamation] is unconstitutional. I think differently.—*To J. C. Conkling, Aug. 26, 1863.* IX, 98.

Emancipation Proclamation, original draft of, given for soldiers' benefit—According to the request made in your behalf, the original draft of the Emancipation Proclamation is herewith inclosed. . . . I have some desire to retain the paper; but if it shall contribute to the relief or comfort of the soldiers that will be better.—*To women of Chicago Sanitary Commission, Oct. 26, 1863.* R.T.L.

Emancipation Proclamation, place of, in history— If my name ever gets into history, it will be for this act [signing the proclamation], and my whole soul is in it.—*To Sec. Seward, Jan. 1, 1863.* Arnold, 265.

2.—As affairs have turned, it [signing of the proclamation] is the central act of my administration, and the great event of the nineteenth century.—*To F. B. Carpenter, Feb., 1865.* Carpenter, 90.

Emancipation Proclamation, precipitates crisis—It was all the while deemed possible that the necessity for it [emancipation] might come, and that if it should, the crisis of the contest would then be presented. It came, as was anticipated, and was followed by dark and doubtful days. Eleven months having passed, we are now permitted to take another review.

The crisis which threatened to divide the friends of the Union is past.—*Third annual message, Dec. 8, 1863.* IX, 246.

Emancipation Proclamation, refusal to indorse, no proof of disloyalty—Disloyalty, without any statement of the evidence supposed to have proved it, is assigned as the cause of dismissal [of Capt. Schaadt]; and he represents at home—as I am told—that the sole evidence was his refusal to sanction a resolution —indorsing the Emancipation Proclamation, I believe—; and our friends assure me that this statement is doing the Union cause great harm in his neighborhood and county. . . . It is hoped . . . that if there is no evidence but his refusal to sanction the resolution, you will restore him.—*To Gen. Hunter, April 30, 1863.* VIII, 260.

Emancipation Proclamation, text of—By virtue of the power and for the purpose aforesaid [in the preliminary proclamation of Sept. 22, 1862] I do order and declare that all persons held as slaves [in states and parts of states in rebellion] are and henceforward shall be free, and that the executive government of the United States, including the military and naval authorities thereof, will recognize and maintain the freedom of said persons. And I hereby enjoin upon the people so declared to be free to abstain from all violence, unless in necessary self-defense; and I recommend to them that in all cases when allowed they labor faithfully for reasonable wages. . . . Upon this act, sincerely believed to be an act of justice, warranted by the Constitution upon military necessity, I invoke the considerate judgment of mankind, and the gracious favor of Almighty God.—*Emancipation Proclamation, Jan. 1, 1863.* VIII, 163.

Emancipation Proclamation (Preliminary), deliberate policy—What I did [issue the proclamation] I did after full deliberation, and under a heavy and solemn sense of responsibility. I can only trust in God I have made no mistake. . . . It is now for the country and the world to pass judgment, and, maybe, take action upon it.—*Reply to serenade, Sept. 24, 1862.* VIII, 44.

Emancipation Proclamation (Preliminary), doubtfully received—While I hope something from the proclamation, my expectations are not as sanguine as are those of some friends. The time for its effect southward has not come; but northward the effect should be instantaneous. . . . While commendation in newspapers and by distinguished individuals is all that a vain man could wish, the stocks have declined and troops come forward more slowly than ever. . . .

The North responds to the proclamation sufficiently in breath, but breath alone kills no rebels.—*To Vice President Hamlin, Sept. 28, 1862.* VIII, 49.

Emancipation Proclamation (Preliminary), text of— I . . . proclaim and declare . . . that on the 1st day of January, A.D. 1863, all persons held as slaves within any state or designated part of a state the people whereof shall then be in rebellion against the United States shall be then, thenceforward and forever free; and the executive government of the United States, including the military and naval authority thereof, will recognize and maintain the freedom of such persons, and will do no act or acts to repress such persons, or any of them, in any efforts they may make for their actual freedom.—*Proclamation, Sept. 22, 1862.* VIII, 37.

Emancipation Proclamation (Preliminary), text of first draft—As a fit and necessary military measure for effecting this object [bringing insurgent states back into the Union], I, as commander-in-chief of the army and navy of the United States, do order and declare that on the first day of January, in the year of our Lord one thousand eight hundred and sixty-three, all persons held as slaves within any state or states wherein the constitutional authority shall not then be practically recognized, submitted to, and maintained, shall then, thenceforward, and forever be free.—*Proclamation (not issued), July 22, 1862.* VII, 289.

Emancipation Proclamation (Preliminary), timed to circumstances—I determined, as soon as it [rebel army] should be driven out of Maryland, to issue a proclamation of emancipation, such as I thought most likely to be useful. I said nothing to anyone, but I made the promise to myself and (hesitating a little) to my Maker. The rebel army is now driven out, and I am going to fulfill that promise. I have got you together to hear what I have written down. I do not wish your advice about the main matter, for that I have determined for myself. This I say without intending anything but respect for any one of you. But I already know the views of each of you upon this question. They have been heretofore expressed, and I have considered them as thoroughly and carefully as I can. What I have written is that which my reflections have determined me to say.—*To cabinet, Sept. 22, 1862.* Hertz II, 882.

2.—It had got to be midsummer, 1862. Things had gone from bad to worse, until I felt that we had reached the end of our rope on the plan of operations we had been pursuing; that we had about played our last card, and must change our tactics, or lose the game. I now determined upon the adoption of the emancipation policy; and without consultation with, or the knowledge of, the cabinet, I prepared the original draft of the proclamation, and, after much anxious thought, called a cabinet meeting upon the subject. . . . Nothing was offered that I had not fully anticipated and settled in my own mind, until Secretary Seward spoke. He said in substance, "Mr. President, I approve of the proclamation, but I question the expediency of its issue at this juncture. The depression of the public mind consequent upon our repeated reverses, is so great that I fear the effect of so important a step. It may be viewed as the last measure of an exhausted government, a cry for help; the government stretching forth its hands to Ethiopia, instead of Ethiopia stretching forth her hands to the government. . . . I suggest, sir, that you postpone its issue until you can give it to the country supported by military success, instead of issuing it, as would be the case now, upon the greatest disasters of the war." The wisdom of the view . . . struck me with very great force. . . . The result was that I put the draft of the proclamation aside. . . . From time to time I added or changed a line, touching it up here and there, anxiously watching the progress of events. Well, the next news we had was of Pope's disaster at Bull Run. Things looked darker than ever. Finally came the week of the battle of Antietam. I determined to wait no longer. The news came, I think, on Wednesday, that the advantage was on our side. . . . I finished writing the second draft . . . called the cabinet together to hear it, and it was published on the following Monday.—*Related to F. B. Carpenter, Feb. 6, 1864.* X, 1.

3.—The moment came when I felt that slavery must die that the nation might live. . . . Many of my strongest supporters urged emancipation before I thought it indispensable, and, I may say, before I thought the country was ready for it. It is my conviction that, had the proclamation been issued even six months earlier than it was, public sentiment would not have sustained it.—*To deputation of anti-slavery men, April 7, 1864.* Carpenter, 76.

Embarrassment, cure for—I have found that when one is embarrassed, usually the shortest way to get through with it is to quit talking and thinking about it, and go at something else.—*Speech, Cincinnati, Sept. 17, 1859.* V, 190.

Employment, how to make, secure—*See* TARIFF, prices and employment.

Ends and Means—When an end is lawful and obligatory, the indispensable means to it are also lawful and obligatory.—*Message to Congress, July 4, 1861.* VI, 323.

See UNION, inviolability of, 12.

Enemies, not, but friends—I am loath to close. We are not enemies, but friends. We must not be enemies. Though passion may have strained, it must not break our bonds of affection. The magic chords of memory, stretching from every battlefield and patriot grave to every living heart and hearthstone all over this broad land, will yet swell the chorus of the Union when again touched, as surely they will be, by the better angels of our nature.—*First inaugural, March 4, 1861.* VI, 185.

2.—Americans, all, we are not enemies but friends. We have sacred ties of affection which, though strained by passion, let us hope can never be broken. —*Indorsement on letter of O. H. Browning, Feb. 17, 1861.* R.T.L.

Enemies, to thwart—Our adversaries think they can gain a point if they force me to openly deny the charge [that he had attended a Know-Nothing Lodge], by which some degree of offense would be given to the Americans. For this reason it must not publicly appear that I am paying any attention to the charge.—*To A. Jonas, July 21, 1860.* VI, 47.

"Entangling Details"—Mr. Miller's system doubtless is well intended, but from what I hear I fear that, if persisted in, it would fall down dead within its own entangling details.—*To Gen. Thomas, Feb. 28, 1864.* X, 24.

Equality, appeal for old faith—Let us discard all this quibbling about this man and the other man, this race and that race and the other race, being inferior and therefore they must be placed in an inferior position. Let us discard all these things, and unite as one people throughout this land, until we shall once more stand up declaring that all men are created equal.—*Speech, Chicago, July 10, 1858.* III, 51.

Equality, basic American principle—Nearly 80 years ago we began by declaring that all men were created equal; but now from that beginning we have run down to the other declaration that for some men to enslave others is a "sacred right of self-government." —*Speech, Urbana, Oct. 24, 1854.* Hertz II, 654.

2.—I believe the declaration that "all men are created equal" is the great fundamental principle upon which our free institutions rest. That negro slavery is violative of that principle.—*Notes, Sept. 16, 1858.* IV, 88.

3.—How long is it?—eighty-odd years since on the Fourth of July, for the first time in the history of the

world, a nation, by its representatives assembled, declared, as a self-evident truth, that "all men were created equal."—*Response to serenade, July 7, 1863.* IX, 20.

4.—Four score and seven years ago our fathers brought forth on this continent a new nation, conceived in liberty, and dedicated to the proposition that all men are created equal.—*Gettysburg Address, Nov. 19, 1863.* IX, 209.

See GOVERNMENT (AMERICAN), based on equal rights.

Equality, beats inequality—Equality in society beats inequality, whether the latter be of the British aristocratic sort or the domestic slavery sort.—*Fragment, July 1, 1854.* II, 184.

Equality, "central idea at beginning"—Public opinion, on any subject, always has a "central idea," from which all its minor thoughts radiate. The "central idea" in our public opinion at the beginning was, and until recently has continued to be, "the equality of men." And although it has always submitted patiently to whatever of inequality there seemed to be as a matter of actual necessity, its constant working has been a steady progress toward the practical equality of all men. The late presidential election was a struggle by one party to discard that "central idea" and to substitute for it the opposite idea that slavery is right in the abstract, the working of which as a "central idea" may be the perpetuity of human slavery and its extension to all countries and colors.— *Speech, Chicago, Dec. 10, 1856.* II, 310.

Equality, Declaration's message to foreign-born—Perhaps half our people . . . are not descendants at all of these men [founders of the government]; they are men who have come from Europe . . . themselves or whose ancestors have come hither and settled here, finding themselves our equal in all things. If they look back through this history to trace their connection with those days of blood, they find they have none; they cannot carry themselves back into that glorious epoch and make themselves feel that they are a part of us, but when they look through that old Declaration of Independence, they find that those old men say that "we hold these truths to be self-evident, that all men are created equal," and then they feel that the moral sentiment in that day evidences their relation to those men, that it is the father of all moral principle in them, and they have a right to claim it as if they were blood of the blood, and flesh of the flesh, of the men who wrote that Declaration, and so they are. That is the electric cord in the Declaration that links the hearts of patriotic and liberty-loving men together, that will link those patriotic hearts as long as the love of freedom exists in the minds of men throughout the world.—*Speech, Chicago, July 10, 1858.* III, 47.

Equality, doctrine of Declaration explained—I think the authors of that notable instrument intended to include all men, but they did not intend to declare all men equal in all respects. They did not mean to say all men were equal in color, size, intellect, moral development or social capacity. They defined with tolerable distinction in what respects they did consider all men created equal—equal with "certain inalienable rights, among which are life, liberty and the pursuit of happiness." This they did say, and this they meant. They did not mean to assert the obvious untruth that all were then actually enjoying that equality, nor yet that they were about to confer it immediately upon them. In fact, they had no power to confer such a boon. They meant simply to declare the right; so that enforcement of it might follow as fast as circumstances should permit.—*Speech, Springfield, June 27, 1857.* II, 330.
Repeated at Alton, Oct. 15, 1858. V, 35.
2.—They [authors of the Declaration] meant to set up a standard maxim for free society, which should be familiar to all, and revered by all; constantly labored for, and even though never perfectly attained, constantly approximated, and thereby constantly spreading and deepening its influence and augmenting the happiness and value of life to all people of all colors everywhere.—*Speech, Springfield, June 27, 1857.* II, 331.
3.—In some respects she [colored woman] certainly is not my equal; but in her natural right to eat the bread she earns with her own hands, without asking leave of anyone else, she is my equal, and the equal of all others.—*Speech, Springfield, Dec. 10, 1857.* II, 329.
4.—It is said in one of the admonitions of our Lord, "As your Father in Heaven is perfect, be ye also perfect." The Savior, I suppose, did not expect that any human creature could be perfect as the Father in Heaven; but He . . . set that up as a standard, and he who did most toward reaching that standard attained the highest degree of moral perfection. So I say in relation to the principle that all men are created equal, let it be as nearly reached as we can.—*Speech, Chicago, July 10, 1858.* Basler, 403.
5.—In relation to the principle that all men are created equal, let it be as nearly reached as we can. If we cannot give freedom to every creature, let us do nothing that will impose slavery upon any other creature. Let us, then, turn this government back into the channel in which the framers of the Constitution

originally placed it.—*Speech, Chicago, July 10, 1858.* III, 51.
6.—I do not understand the Declaration [of Independence] to mean that all men are created equal in all respects. They [negroes] are not our equal in color; but I suppose that it does mean to declare that all men are equal in some respects; they are equal in their right to "life, liberty, and the pursuit of happiness." Certainly, the negro is not our equal in color—perhaps not in many other respects; still, in the right to put into his mouth the bread that his own hands have earned, he is the equal of every other man. In pointing out that more has been given you, you cannot be justified in taking away the little which has been given him. All I ask for the negro is that if you do not like him, let him alone. If God gave him but little, that little let him enjoy.—*Speech, Springfield, July 17, 1858.* III, 186.
7.—I agree with Judge Douglas that he [the negro] is not my equal in many respects—certainly not in color, perhaps not in moral or intellectual endowment. But in the right to eat the bread, without the leave of anybody else, which his own hand earns, he is my equal and the equal of Judge Douglas, and the equal of every living man.—*Debate, Ottawa, Aug. 21, 1858.* III, 229.
8.—Negroes have natural rights, however, as other men have, although they cannot enjoy them here. . . . But though it [Declaration] does not declare that all men are equal in their attainments or social position, yet no sane man will attempt to deny that the African upon his own soil has all the natural rights that instrument vouchsafes to all mankind.—*Speech, Carlinville, Aug. 31, 1858.* Angle, 191.
9.—Mr. [Henry] Clay says it is true as an abstract principle that all men are created equal, but that we cannot practically apply it in all cases.—*Debate, Alton, Oct 15, 1858.* V, 41.

Equality, Douglas's interpretation of the Declaration—The founder of the Democratic party declared that all men were created equal. His successor in the leadership [Douglas] has written the word "white" before men, making it read, "all white men are created equal." Pray, will or may not the Know-Nothings, if they should get into power, add the word "Protestant," making it read, "all Protestant white men"?—*Speech, Bloomington, May 29, 1856.* Lapsley II, 253.
2.—"They [authors of the Declaration, according to Douglas] were speaking of British subjects on this continent being equal to British subjects born and residing in Great Britain." Why, according to this, not only negroes but white people outside of Great Britain and America were not spoken of in that in-

strument. . . . The French, Germans and other white people of the world are all gone to pot along with the judge's inferior races. I had thought the Declaration promised something better than the condition of British subjects; but no, it only meant that we should be equal to them in their oppressed and unequal condition. According to that, it gave no promise that, having kicked off the king and lords of Great Britain, we should not at once be saddled with a king and lords of our own. I had thought the Declaration contemplated the progressive improvement in the condition of all men everywhere; but no, it merely "was adopted for the purpose of justifying the colonists in the eyes of the civilized world in withdrawing their allegiance from the British crown, and dissolving their connection with the mother country."—And now I appeal to all—to Democrats as well as others —are you really willing that the Declaration shall thus be frittered away?—thus left no more, at most, than an interesting memorial of the dead past?—thus shorn of its vitality and practical value, and left without the germ or even the suggestion of the individual rights of man in it?—*Speech, Springfield, June 27, 1857.* II, 332.

3.—But I suppose you will celebrate [the Fourth], and will even go as far as to read the Declaration. Suppose, after you read it once in the old-fashioned way, you read it once more with Judge Douglas's version. It will then run thus: "We hold these truths to be self-evident, that all British subjects who were on this continent 81 years ago were created equal to all British subjects born and then residing in Great Britain."—*Speech, Springfield, Dec. 10, 1857.* II, 334.

4.—For the purpose of squaring things with this [Douglas's] idea of "don't care if slavery is voted up or voted down," for sustaining the Dred Scott decision, for holding that the Declaration of Independence did not mean anything at all, we have Judge Douglas giving his exposition of what the Declaration of Independence means, and we have him saying that the people of America are equal to the people of England. According to his construction, you Germans are not connected with it.—*Speech, Chicago, July 10, 1858.* III, 48.

5.—In his construction of the Declaration [of Independence] last year, he [Douglas] said it only meant that Americans in America were equal to Englishmen in England. Then, when I pointed out to him that by that rule he excludes Germans, the Irish, the Portuguese, and all the other people who have come amongst us since the Revolution, he reconstructs his construction. In his last speech he tells us it meant Europeans. I press him a little further, and ask if it meant to include Russians in Asia? . . . I expect ere

long he will introduce another amendment to his definition. He is not at all particular. He is satisfied with anything which does not endanger the nationalization of negro slavery.—*Speech, Springfield, July 17, 1858.* III, 185.

6.—If Judge Douglas and his friends are not willing to stand by it [Declaration], let them come up and amend it. Let them make it read that all men are created equal, except negroes. Let us have it decided whether the Declaration of Independence, in this blessed year of 1858, shall be thus amended.—*Speech, Springfield, July 17, 1858.* III, 185.

7.—Douglas says no man can defend it except on the hypothesis that it referred to British white subjects, and that no other white men are included; that it does not speak alike to the down-trodden of all nations—German, French, Spanish, etc., but simply meant that the English were born equal and endowed by their Creator with certain natural or equal rights, among which were life, liberty, and the pursuit of happiness, and that it means nobody else.—*Speech, Carlinville, Aug. 31, 1858.* Angle, 191.

8.—Senator Douglas regularly argues against the doctrine of the equality of men; and while he does not draw the conclusion that the superiors ought to enslave the inferiors, he evidently wishes his hearers to draw that conclusion. He shirks the responsibility of pulling the house down, but he digs under it that it may fall of its own weight.—*Notes, Oct. 1, 1858.* IV, 200.

9.—The judge has . . . insisted . . . that it is a slander upon the framers of that instrument [Declaration] to suppose that negroes were meant therein; and he asks you: Is it possible to believe that Mr. Jefferson, who penned the immortal paper, could have supposed himself applying the language of that instrument to the negro race, and yet hold a portion of that race in slavery?—*Debate, Galesburg, Oct. 7, 1858.* IV, 262.

10.—I believe the entire records of the world from the date of the Declaration of Independence up to within three years ago, may be searched in vain for one single affirmation, from one single man, that the negro was not included in the Declaration of Independence; I think I may defy Judge Douglas that he ever said so; that any President ever said so; that any member of Congress ever said so; or that any living man upon the whole earth ever said so, until the necessities of the present policy of the Democratic party in regard to slavery, had to invent that affirmation.—*Debate, Galesburg, Oct. 7, 1858.* IV, 263.

11.—I believe the first man who ever said it [that the Declaration does not include the negro] was Chief Justice Taney in the Dred Scott case, and the next to him was our friend, Stephen A. Douglas. And now it has become the catchword of the entire party.—*Debate, Alton, Oct. 15, 1858.* V, 37.

12.—I would like to call upon his [Douglas's] friends everywhere, to consider how they come in so short a time to view this matter in a way so entirely different from their former belief; to ask whether they are not being borne along by an irresistible current, whither, they know not.—*Debate, Alton, Oct. 15, 1858.* V, 38.

13.—Five years ago no living man had expressed the opinion that the negro had no share in the Declaration of Independence. . . . Within the space of five years Senator Douglas, in the argument of this question, has got his entire party, so far as I know, without exception, to join in saying that the negro has no share in the Declaration of Independence. . . . This is a vast change in the northern public sentiment upon that question. . . . The tendency of that change is to bring the public mind to the conclusion that when men are spoken of, the negro is not meant; that when negroes are spoken of, brutes alone are contemplated.—*Speech, Cincinnati, Sept. 17, 1859.* V, 201.

14.—Five years ago no living man had placed on record, nor, as I believe, verbally expressed, a denial that negroes have a share in the Declaration of Independence. Two or three years since, Douglas began to deny it; and now every Douglas man in the nation denies it.—*Speeches in Kansas, Dec. 1-5, 1859.* V, 270.

15.—Is there a Democrat, especially one of the Douglas wing, but will declare that the Declaration of Independence has no application to the negro? It would be safe to offer a moderate premium for such a man. . . . Not one of them said it five years ago. I never heard it till I heard it from the lips of Judge Douglas. . . . Not a man of them said it till then—they all say it now. This is a long stride toward establishing the policy of indifference—one more stride, I think, would do it.—*Speech, Hartford, Conn., March 5, 1860.* V, 131.

16.—Do you know any Democrat . . . who declares that he believes that the Declaration of Independence has any application to the negro? Judge Taney declares that it has not, and Judge Douglas even villifies me personally and scolds me roundly for saying the Declaration applies to all men, and that negroes are men.—*Speech, New Haven, Conn., March 6, 1860.* V, 350.

Equality, efforts to overthrow principle—Now on this last Fourth of July, when we have a gigantic rebellion, at the bottom of which is an effort to overthrow the principle that all men are created equal, we have the surrender of a most powerful position and an army on that very day. And not only so, but in a succession of battles in Pennsylvania, near to us, through three days, so rapidly fought that they might be called one great battle, on the first, second and third of the month of July; and on the fourth the cohorts of those opposed to the declaration that all men are created equal "turned tail" and ran.—*Response to serenade, July 7, 1863.* IX, 21.

Equality, essential to liberty—In what I have done I cannot claim to have acted from any peculiar consideration of the colored people as a separate and distinct class in the community, but from the simple conviction that all the individuals of that class are members of the same community, and, in virtue of their manhood, entitled to every original right enjoyed by any other member. We feel, therefore, that all legal distinction between individuals of the same community founded in any such circumstances as color, origin, and the like, are hostile to the genius of our institutions, and incompatible with the true history of American liberty. Slavery and oppression must cease, or American liberty must perish.—*Speech, Cincinnati, May 6, 1842.* Hertz II, 531.

Equality, Fathers' interpretation of the Declaration—This was their majestic interpretation of the economy of the universe. This was their lofty, and wise, and noble, understanding of the justice of the Creator to His creatures—yes, gentlemen, to all His creatures, to the whole great family of men. In their enlightened belief, nothing stamped with the divine image and likeness was sent into the world to be trodden on and degraded and imbruited by its fellows. They grasped not only the whole race of men then living, but they reached forward and seized upon the farthermost posterity.—*Speech, Beardstown, Aug. 12, 1858.* Hertz II, 713.

Equality, Free-state principle—The free states carry on their government on the principle of the equality of men.—*Speech, Hartford, Conn., March 5, 1860.* V, 330.

Equality, Jeffersonian Democrats challenged on—Are Jeffersonian Democrats willing to have that gem [equality] taken from the magna carta of human liberty in this shameful way? Or will they maintain that its declaration of equality of natural rights among all men is correct?—*Speech, Carlinville, Aug. 31, 1858.* Angle, 191.

Equality, largest degree of, under American government—*See* LIBERTY, largest degree of, in America.

Equality, negroes and the Declaration—There is no reason in the world why the negro is not entitled to all the natural rights enumerated in the Declaration of Independence—the right to life, liberty and the pursuit of happiness. I hold that he is as much entitled to these as the white man.—*Debate, Ottawa, Aug. 21, 1858.* III, 229.

Repeated at Quincy, Oct. 13, 1858. IV, 318.

Repeated at Columbus, Ohio, Sept. 16, 1859. V, 143.

2.—Clay and other great men were ever ready to express their abhorrence of slavery; but we of the North dare not use his noble language when he said, to force its [slavery's] perpetuation and extension you must muzzle the cannon that annually proclaims liberty, and repress all tendencies in the human heart to justice and mercy. We can no longer express our admiration for the Declaration of Independence without their petty sneers. And it is true they are fast bringing that sacred instrument into contempt.—*Speech, Carlinville, Aug. 31, 1858.* Angle, 191.

3.—I have said that in their right to "life, liberty and the pursuit of happiness," as proclaimed in that old Declaration, the inferior races are our equals.—*Debate, Galesburg, Oct. 7, 1858.* IV, 266.

4.—I think the negro is included in the word "men" used in the Declaration of Independence.—*To J. N. Brown, Oct. 18, 1858.* V, 87.

5.—Did you ever, five years ago, hear of anybody in the world saying that the negro had no share in the Declaration of Independence; that it did not mean negroes at all, and when "all men" were spoken of negroes were not included? . . . If you think that now, and did not think it then, the next thing that strikes me to remark is that there has been a change wrought in you, and a very significant change it is, being no less than changing the negro, in your estimation, from the rank of a man to that of a brute.—*Speech, Columbus, Ohio, Sept. 16, 1859.* V, 86.

6.—We think, most of us, that this charter of freedom applies to the slave as well as to ourselves; that the class of arguments put forward to batter down that idea [that it does not apply to slaves] is also calculated to break down the very idea of free government, even for white men, and to undermine the very foundations of free society.—*Speech, New Haven, Conn., March 6, 1860.* V, 344.

7.—Is there a Democrat here who does not deny that the Declaration applies to a negro? Do any of you know of one? . . . I venture to defy the whole party to produce one man that ever uttered the belief that the Declaration did not apply to negroes before the repeal of the Missouri Compromise.—*Speech, New Haven, Conn., March 6, 1860.* V, 351.

8.—To us [men of the North] it appears natural to think of slaves as human beings; that some of the things, at least, stated in the Declaration of Independence apply to them as well as to us.—*Speech, Norwich, Conn., March 9, 1860.* VI, 3.

See EQUALITY, doctrine of the Declaration explained, 3, 6, 7, 8.

See SLAVERY, wrong of.

Equality, recent interpretation of Declaration—*See* EQUALITY, Douglas's interpretation of the Declaration, 9, 10, 11, 12, 13.

Equality, sentiment will live again—The human heart is with us; God is with us. We shall again be able not to declare that "all states as states are equal," nor yet that "all citizens as citizens are equal," but to renew the broader, better declaration, including both these and much more, that "all men are created equal."—*Speech, Chicago, Dec. 10, 1856.* II, 311.

Equality, steady progress toward—*See* EQUALITY, "central idea at beginning."

Equality, who shall judge?—Who shall say, "I am the superior, and you are the inferior?—*Speech, Springfield, July 17, 1858.* III, 186.

Errors, confessed—I claim not to be more free from errors than others—perhaps scarcely so much.—*Speech, Springfield, July 17, 1858.* III, 169.

2.—I cannot claim that I am entirely free from all error in the opinions I advance.—*Debate, Galesburg, Oct. 7, 1858.* IV, 267.

3.—You must not lay too much stress on the blunder about Mr. Adams; for I made a more mischievous one in the first printed speech of mine on the slavery question—October, 1854. I stated that the prohibition of slavery in the Northwest Territory was made a condition in the Virginia deed of cession, while, in fact, it was not.—*To James O. Putnam, Sept. 13, 1860.* Angle, 254.

4.—I frequently make mistakes myself in the many things I am compelled to do hastily.—*To Gen. Rosecrans, May 20, 1863.* VIII, 279.

5.—In my administration I may have committed some errors. It would indeed be remarkable if I had not.—*Reply to Presbyterian General Assembly, May 30, 1863.* VIII, 287.

Escort, not wanted—On reflection I think it will not do, as a rule, for the adjutant-general to attend me wherever I go; not that I have any objection to his presence, but that it would be an uncompensating encumbrance both to him and me. When it shall occur to me to go anywhere, I wish to be free to go at once, and not to have to notify the adjutant-general and wait till he can get ready.—*To Sec. Stanton, Jan. 22, 1862.* VII, 87.

2.—I believe I need no escort, and unless the secretary of war directs, none will attend me.—*Indorsement on letter, July 4, 1864.* Tracy, 242.

Ethiopia—*See* EMANCIPATION PROCLAMATION (PRELIMINARY), timed to circumstances, 2.

Euclid, "disproving" a theorem—If you have ever studied geometry, you remember that by a course of reasoning Euclid proves that all the angles in a triangle are equal to two right angles. Euclid has shown you how to work it out. Now, if you undertake to disprove that proposition, and to show that it is erroneous, would you prove it to be false by calling Euclid a liar?—*Debate, Charleston, Sept. 18, 1858.* IV, 199.

Euclid, essential to proof—One would state with great confidence that he could convince any sane child that the simpler propositions of Euclid are true; but nevertheless he would fail, utterly, with one who should deny the definitions and axioms.—*Speech, Springfield, March 1, 1858.* V, 126.

Euclid, example for Douglas—If Judge Douglas will demonstrate somehow that this is popular sovereignty —the right of one man to make a slave of another, without any right in that other, or anyone else, to object,—demonstrate it as Euclid demonstrated propositions—there is no objection.—*Speech, Columbus, Ohio, Sept. 16, 1859.* V, 172.

Evangelical Lutheran Church, response to—*See* DEITY, dependence on, 10.

See CIVIL WAR, reluctant to accept.

Eve—*See* ADAM, joins Eve in first invention.

Events, "have controlled me"—I claim not to have controlled events, but confess plainly that events have controlled me.—*To A. G. Hodges, April 4, 1864.* X, 68.

Everett, Edward, tribute to—No gentleman is better able to correct misunderstandings in the minds of foreigners in regard to American affairs.—*Letter "to whom it may concern," Sept. 24, 1862.* VIII, 43.

2.—His [Edward Everett's] life was a truly great one, and I think the greatest part of it was that which crowned its closing years.—*Reply to committee, Jan. 24, 1865.* X, 346.

Evil Genius, Douglas's attendant—*See* DOUGLAS, STEPHEN A., characterized, 19.

Ewing, Thomas, opinion of—Ewing [ex-senator from Ohio] won't do anything. He is not worth a damn.— *To John T. Stuart, Feb. 14, 1839.* XI, 98.

2.—By the way, I have a better opinion of Mr. Ewing [Secretary of Interior] than you, perhaps, suppose I have.—*To J. M. Lucas, Nov. 17, 1849.* Angle, 60.

3.—As to Mr. Ewing [Secretary of Interior], his position has been one of great difficulty. I believe him, too, to be an able and faithful officer.—*To editor of Chicago Journal, Nov. 21, 1849.* II, 131.

Executive and Legislative, interference decried—*See* CONGRESS, legislation should rest with.

Executive Power, electoral votes and—The joint resolution . . . "declaring certain states not entitled to representation in the Electoral College," has been signed by the Executive, in deference to the view of Congress implied in its passage and presentation to him. In his own view, however, the two houses of Congress, convened under the twelfth article of the Constitution, has complete power to exclude from counting all electoral votes deemed by them to be illegal; and it is not competent for the Executive to defeat or obstruct that power by a veto, as would be the case if his action were at all essential in the matter. He disclaims all right of the Executive to interfere in any way in the matter of canvassing or counting electoral votes; and he also disclaims that, by signing said resolution, he has expressed any opinion on the recitals of the preamble, or any judgment of his own upon the subject of the resolution. —*Message to Congress, Feb. 8, 1865.* XI, 8.

Executive Power, in relation to peace—The executive power itself would be greatly diminished by the cessation of actual war. Pardons and remissions of forfeitures, however, would still be within executive control. In what spirit and temper this control would be exercised can be fairly judged by the past.—*Fourth annual message, Dec. 6, 1864.* X, 309.

Expediency, constitutionality and—No one who is satisfied of the expediency of making [internal] improvements needs be much uneasy in his conscience about its constitutionality.—*Speech in Congress, June 20, 1848.* II, 44.

2.—No one who has sworn to support the Constitution can conscientiously vote for what he understands to be an unconstitutional measure, however expedient he may think it; but one may and ought to vote against a measure which he deems constitutional if he deems it inexpedient.—*Cooper Institute address, New York, Feb. 27, 1860.* V, 302.

3.—It is clear that a constitutional law may not be

expedient or proper.—*Opinion on draft law never issued, Aug. 15, 1863.* IX, 77.

Expediency, rules emancipation issue in District of Columbia—There has never been in my mind any question upon the subject [of abolition in the District of Columbia] except the one of expediency, arising in view of all the circumstances.—*Message to Congress, April 16, 1862.* VIII, 146.

See EMANCIPATION, District of Columbia, 7.

Experience, teacher—We know nothing of what will happen in future, but by the analogy of past experience.—*Speech, Springfield, Dec. 20, 1839.* I, 113.
2.—We dare not disregard the lessons of experience. —*To Sec. of State John M. Clayton, July 28, 1849.* Tracy, 39.
3.—We all feel that we know that a blast of wind would extinguish the flame of the candle that stands by me. How do we know it? We have never seen this flame thus extinguished. We know it because we have seen through all our lives that a blast of wind extinguishes the flame of a candle whenever it is thrown fully upon it. Again, we all feel we know that we have to die. How? We have never died yet. We know it because we know, at least we think that of all the beings, just like ourselves, who have been coming into the world for 6,000 years, not one is now living who was here 200 years ago.—*Speech, Springfield, Dec. 20 1839.* I, 112.

Extra-Legal Acts—*See* WAR POWER, use of defended.

Eye, wonderful power of—Notice the wonderful power of the eye in conveying ideas to the mind from writing. Take the . . . example of the numbers from one to one hundred written down, and you can run your eye over the list, and be assured that every number is in it, and in about half the time it would require to pronounce the words with the voice; and not only so, but you can in the same short time determine whether every word is spelled correctly, by which it is evident that every separate letter, amounting to 864, has been recognized and reported to the mind within the incredibly short space of twenty seconds, or one third of a minute.—*Lecture, Springfield, Feb. 22, 1859.* V, 109.

Factions, beware of—*See* CODE OF CONDUCT, rules for personal guidance, 31.

Faith, appeal to—Let us have faith that right makes might, and in that faith let us to the end dare to do our duty as we understand it.—*Cooper Institute address, New York, Feb. 27, 1860.* V, 328.
Repeated at New Haven, Conn., March 6, 1860. V, 371.

Faith, government should keep—It is bad faith in the government to force new terms upon such as have kept faith with it—at least, so it seems to me.—*To Sec. Stanton, Aug. 21, 1863.* IX, 90.

Falsehood, in proslavery reasoning—*See* NEGRO, no necessary conflict between, and white man, 3.

See SLAVERY, policy of the fathers, 27, 33.

Falsehood, maxim in morals—I believe it is an established maxim in morals that he who makes an assertion without knowing whether it is true or false is guilty of falsehood, and the accidental truth of the assertion does not justify or excuse him.—*To editor of Illinois* Gazette, *Aug. 11, 1846.* Quarterly, March, 1942, p. 3.

Fame, fixed by "cloud of witnesses"—My belief is that the permanent estimate of what a general does in the field is fixed by the "cloud of witnesses" who have been with him in the field; and that, relying on these, he who has been right needs not to fear.—*To Gen. McClellan, Aug. 12, 1863.* IX, 73.

Farewell to Springfield—I assure you Springfield and its citizens are very dear to me. It will only be a matter of time—if I live—and return again with the dispensation of Divine Providence.—*To I. R. Diller, Feb. 10, 1861.* Hertz II, 804.
2.—If I live, I am coming back some time, and then we'll go right on practicing law, as if nothing had happened.—*To W. H. Herndon, Feb. 10, 1861.* Tarbell II, 203.
3.—No one, not in my position, can appreciate my feeling of sadness at this parting. To this place, and the kindness of these people, I owe everything. Here I have lived a quarter of a century, and have passed from a young man to an old man. Here my children have been born, and one is buried. I now leave, not knowing when or whether ever I may return, with a task before me greater than that which rested upon Washington. Without the assistance of that Divine Being who ever attended him I cannot succeed. With the assistance, I cannot fail. Trusting in Him who can go with me, and remain with you, and be everywhere for good, let us confidently hope that all will yet be well. To His care commending you, as I hope in your prayers you will commend me, I bid you an affectionate farewell.—*Farewell Speech, Springfield, Feb. 11, 1861.* VI, 110.
4.—I love the people here, Billy, and owe them all that I am. If God spares my life to the end, I shall come back among you and spend the remnant of my days.—*To W. H. Herndon, Feb., 1861.* Townsend, 10.

Farragut, David G., Congress asked to thank—I cordially recommend that Capt. D. G. Farragut receive a vote of thanks of Congress for his services and gallantry displayed in the capture, since the 21st of December, 1861, of Forts Jackson and St. Philip, city of New Orleans, and the destruction of various rebel gunboats, rams, etc.—*Message to Congress, May 14, 1862.* VII, 160.

Farragut, David G., thanked for victories—The national thanks are tendered by the president to Admiral Farragut and Maj. Gen. Canby for the skill and harmony with which the recent operations in Mobile harbor and against Fort Powell, Fort Gaines and Fort Morgan were planned and carried into execution; also to Admiral Farragut and Maj. Gen. Granger under whose immediate command they were conducted, and to the gallant commanders on sea and land, and to the sailors and soldiers engaged in the operations, for their energy and courage, which, under the blessing of Providence, have been crowned with brilliant success and have won for them the applause and thanks of the nation.—*Executive order, Sept. 3, 1864.* X, 212.

Fashion, influence of—It is said by some that men will think and act for themselves; that none will disuse spirits or anything else because his neighbors do; and that moral influence is not that powerful engine contended for. Let us examine this. Let me ask the man who could maintain this position most stiffly, what compensation he will accept to go to church some Sunday and sit during the sermon with his wife's bonnet upon his head? Not a trifle, I'll venture. And why not? There would be nothing irreligious in it, nothing immoral, nothing uncomfortable—then why not? Is it not because there would be something egregiously unfashionable in it? Then it is the influence of fashion; and what is the influence of fashion but the influence that other people's actions have on our actions—the strong inclination each of us feels to do as we see all our neighbors do?—*Speech, Springfield, Feb. 22, 1842.* I, 205.

Fasting, days of, proclaimed—I . . . do appoint the last Thursday in September next as a day of humiliation, prayer, and fasting for all the people of the nation. And I do earnestly recommend to all the people, and especially to all ministers and teachers of religion, of all denominations, and to all heads of families, to observe and keep that day, according to their several creeds and modes of worship, in all humility and with all religious solemnity, to the end that the united prayer of the nation may ascend to the Throne of Grace, and bring down plentiful bless-

ings upon our country.—*Fast Day Proclamation, Aug. 12, 1861.* VI, 342.

2.—I do by this proclamation designate and set apart Thursday, the 30th day of April, 1863, as a day of national humiliation, fasting and prayer. And I do hereby request all the people to abstain from their ordinary secular pursuits, and to unite at their several places of public worship and their respective homes in keeping the day holy to the Lord, and devoted to the humble discharge of the religious duties proper to that solemn occasion. All this being done in sincerity and truth, let us then rest humbly in the hope authorized by the divine teachings, that the united cry of the nation will be heard on high, and answered with blessings no less than the pardoning of our national sins, and the restoration of our now divided and suffering country to its former happy condition of unity and peace.—*Fast Day Proclamation, March 30, 1863.* VIII, 237.

"Fatal Heresy"—*See* "IRREPRESSIBLE CONFLICT," difference in who says it, 3.

Father, advised to trust God—I sincerely hope father may recover his health, but in all events, tell him to remember to call upon and confide in our great and good and merciful Maker, who will not turn away from him in any extremity. He notes the fall of a sparrow, and numbers the hairs of our heads, and He will not forget the dying man who puts his trust in Him. Say to him that . . . if it be his lot to go now, he will soon have a joyous meeting with many loved ones, gone before, and where the rest of us, through the help of God, hope ere long to join them.—*To John D. Johnston, Jan. 12, 1851.* II, 148.

"Father of Waters Again Goes Unvexed to the Sea"—*See* CIVIL WAR, progress of, 5.

Fathers of the Republic, characterized—That people were few in numbers and without resources, save only their wise heads and stout hearts.—*Speech, Springfield, July 16, 1852.* II, 155.

2.—We find a race of men living in that day whom we claim as our fathers and grandfathers; they were iron men.—*Speech, Chicago, July 10, 1858.* III, 46.

3.—Those noble fathers, Washington, Jefferson, and Madison.—*Speech, Cincinnati, Sept. 17, 1859.* V, 218.

Fathers of the Republic, fame of, depended on success—Their all was staked upon it [success of the new Republic]; their destiny was inseparably linked with it. Their ambition aspired to display before an admiring world a practical demonstration of the truth of a proposition which had hitherto been considered at best no better than problematical—namely the capability of a people to govern themselves. If they succeeded they were to be immortalized; their names were to be transferred to counties, and cities, and rivers, and mountains; and to be revered and sung, and toasted through all time. If they failed, they were to be called knaves, and fools, and fanatics for a fleeting hour; then to sink and be forgotten. They succeeded. The experiment is successful, and thousands have won their deathless names in making it so.—*Speech, Springfield, Jan. 27, 1837*. I, 45.

Fathers of the Republic, obligation to—They [blessings enjoyed by Americans] are a legacy bequeathed us by a once hardy, brave, and patriotic, but now lamented and departed, race of ancestors. Theirs was the task—and nobly they performed it—to possess themselves, and through themselves us, of this goodly land, and to uprear upon its hills and valleys a political edifice of liberty, and equal rights; 'tis ours only to transmit these—the former unprofaned by the foot of an invader, the latter undecayed by the lapse of time and untorn up usurpation—to the latest generation that fate shall permit the world to know.—*Speech, Springfield, Jan. 27, 1837*. I, 35.
2.—This task of gratitude to our fathers, justice to ourselves, duty to posterity, and love for our species in general, all imperatively require us to faithfully perform.—*Speech, Springfield, Jan. 27, 1837*. I, 36.
3.—I love the sentiments of those old-time men, and shall be most happy to abide by their opinions.—*Speech, Peoria, Oct. 16, 1854*. II, 229.
4.—By what they then did it has followed that the degree of prosperity which we now enjoy has come to us.—*Speech, Chicago, July 10, 1858*. III, 46.

Fathers of the Republic, slavery control views of—Of our 39 fathers who framed the original Constitution, 21—a clear majority of the whole—certainly understood that no proper division of local from federal authority, nor any part of the Constitution, forbade the federal government to control slavery in the federal territories; while all the rest had probably the same understanding.—*Cooper Institute address, New York, Feb. 27, 1860*. V, 304.

See SLAVERY, policy of the fathers.

Fathers of the Republic, when to differ with—I do not mean to say we are to follow implicitly in whatever our fathers did. To do so would be to discard all the lights of current experience—to reject all progress, all improvement. What I do say is that if we would supplant the opinions and policy of our fathers in any case, we should do so upon evidence so conclusive, and argument so clear, that even their great authority, fairly considered, and weighed, cannot stand.—*Cooper Institute address, New York, Feb. 27, 1860*. V, 308.

"Favor," rejected—I am told that . . . you stated publicly that you were in possession of a fact or facts which, if known to the public, would entirely destroy the prospects of N. W. Edwards and myself at the ensuing election; but that, through favor to us, you should forbear to divulge them. No one has needed favors more than I, and, generally speaking, few have been less unwilling to accept them; but in this case favor to me would be injustice to the public, and therefore I must beg your pardon for declining it. That I once had the confidence of the people of Sangamon, is sufficiently evident; and if I have since done anything, either by design or misadventure, which if known would subject me to a forfeiture of that confidence, he that knows of that thing, and conceals it, is a traitor to his country's interest.—*To Col. Robert Allen, June 21, 1836*. I, 15.

Fear, discernible in writer—If a man is scared when he writes, I can detect it, when I see what he writes.—*To William Schouler, Aug. 28, 1848*. Tracy, 35.

Federal Forts, must be retaken—The most we can do now is to watch events, and be as well prepared as possible for any turn things may take. If the forts fall, my judgment is that they are to be retaken.—*To Gen. Hunter, Dec. 22, 1860*. VI, 86.

Federal Offices, may be left vacant—Where hostility to the United States in any interior locality shall be so great and universal as to prevent competent resident citizens from holding the federal offices, there will be no attempt to force obnoxious strangers among the people for that object. While the strict legal right may exist in the government to enforce the exercise of these offices, the attempt to do so would be so irritating and so nearly impracticable withal that I deem it better to forego for the time the uses of such offices.—*First inaugural, March 4, 1861*. VI, 176.

Fence, over at a leap—*See* POPULAR SOVEREIGNTY, Douglas's essay in *Harper's*.

Ferguson, Benjamin, tribute to—In his intercourse with his fellow men he possessed that uprightness of character which was evidenced by his having no disputes or bickerings of his own, while he was ever the chosen arbiter to settle those of his neighbors.—*Speech, Springfield, Feb. 8, 1842*. Hertz II, 530.

Fessenden, William P., qualifications of—It is very singular, considering that this appointment of Fessenden [as Chase's successor in the cabinet] is so popular when made, that no one ever mentioned his name to me for that place. Thinking over the matter two or three points occurred to me. First, he knows the ropes thoroughly; as chairman of the Senate committee on finance he knows as much of this special subject as Mr. Chase. Second, he is a man possessing a national reputation and the confidence of the country. Third, he is a radical—without the petulant and vicious fretfulness of many radicals.—*To John Hay, July 1, 1864.* Hay, 202.

"Few Things Wholly Evil"—*See* GOOD AND EVIL, balance of.

Fiddler, paying the—It is an old maxim and a very sound one that he that dances should always pay the fiddler. Now, sir, if any gentlemen, whose money is a burden to them, choose to lead off a dance, I am decidedly opposed to the people's money being used to pay the fiddler.—*Speech in Illinois Legislature, Jan. 11, 1837.* Basler, 66.

"Fifty-four, Forty or Fight," Polk's subterfuge.—*See* MEXICAN WAR, acts of aggression, 4.

Fight, Lincoln sees historical parallel in—I remember being once much amused at seeing two partially intoxicated men engaged in a fight with their great coats on, which fight after a long and rather harmless contest, ended in each having fought himself out of his own coat and into that of the other. If the two leading parties of this day are really identical with the two in the days of Jefferson and Adams, they have performed the same feat as the two drunken men.—*To H. L. Pierce and others, April 6, 1859.* V, 125.

Fight, refuses to—I am informed that my distinguished friend [Douglas] yesterday became a little excited—nervous, perhaps—and he said something about fighting, as though referring to a pugilistic encounter between him and myself. . . . I am informed further, that somebody in his audience, rather more excited or nervous than himself, took off his coat and offered to take the job off Douglas's hands, and fight Lincoln himself. . . . Well, I merely desire to say that I shall fight neither Judge Douglas nor his second. I shall not do this for two reasons. . . . In the first place a fight would prove nothing which is an issue in this contest. It might establish that Judge Douglas is a more muscular man than I, or it might demonstrate that I am more muscular than Judge Douglas. But this question is not referred to in the Cincinnati platform, nor in either of the Springfield platforms. Neither result would prove him right or me wrong. And so of the gentleman who volunteered

to do his fighting for him. If my fighting Judge Douglas would not prove anything, it would certainly prove nothing for me to fight his bottleholder. My second reason for not having a personal encounter with the judge is that I don't believe he wants it himself. He and I are about the best friends in the world, and when we get together he would no more think of fighting me than of fighting his wife. Therefore, ladies and gentlemen, when the judge talked about fighting, he was not giving vent to any ill-feeling of his own, but merely trying to excite—well, enthusiasm against me on the part of his audience. And as I find he was tolerably successful, we will call it quits.—*Speech, Havana, Aug. 13, 1858.* Hertz II, 714.

Fig-Leaf Apron—*See* ADAM, joins Eve in first invention.

See CLOTHING, origin of.

Figures of Speech—The point—the power to hurt—of all figures [of speech] consist in the truthfulness of their application.—*Speech in Congress, July 27, 1848.* II, 74.

Filibuster, invitation to—*See* TERRITORY, grab for new, feared, 2, 3.

Fillmore, Millard, attitude toward slavery—Fillmore tickles a few of his friends with the notion that he is not the cause of the door [opened to slavery by the Kansas-Nebraska Act] being open. Well, it brings him into this position: he tries to get both sides, one by denouncing those who opened the door, and the other by hinting that he doesn't care a fig for its being open.—*Speech, Kalamazoo, Mich., Aug. 27, 1856.* Stern, 402.

Fillmore, Millard, endangers Frémont—*See* CAMPAIGN OF 1856, Fillmore endangers Frémont.

See DOUGLAS-BUCHANAN FEUD, Republicans welcome, 4.

Fillmore, Millard, "most national"—Fillmore, however, will go out of this contest the most national man we have. He has no prospect of having a single vote on either side of Mason and Dixon's line, to trouble his poor soul about.—*Speech, Kalamazoo, Mich., Aug. 27, 1856.* Stern, 404.

Fillmore, Millard, responsibilities of—The Whigs hold no department of the government but the executive, and that is in the hands of Mr. Fillmore. What can they be responsible for which he is not?—*Speech, Springfield, Aug. 26, 1852.* Angle, 104.

Finance, "will rule"—Finance will rule the country for the next 50 years.—*To William Pitt Kellogg, April 12, 1865.* Quarterly, Sept., 1945, p. 334.

Fire, smoke best proof of—We better know there is a fire whence we see much smoke rising than we could know it by one or two witnesses swearing to it. The witnesses may commit perjury, but the smoke cannot. —*Unfinished draft of letter to J. R. Underwood and H. Grider, Oct. 26, 1864.* X, 254.

"Fizzlegigs and Fireworks"—Auxiliary to these main points [as urged by Douglas] . . . are their thunderings or cannon, their marching and music, their fizzlegigs and fireworks; but I will not waste time with them. They are but the little trappings of the campaign.—*Speech, Springfield, July 17, 1858.* III, 160.

Florida, would shirk part of national debt—*See* SECESSION, national debt and, 1.

Florida War, money thrown away—The large sums foolishly, not to say corruptly, thrown away in that war constitute one of the just causes of complaint against the administration.—*Speech, Springfield, Dec. 20, 1839.* I, 130.

"Fondly Do We Hope, Fervently Do We Pray"—*See* DEITY, submission to, 2.

"Fools Rush In"—Some poet has said: "Fools rush in where angels fear to tread." At the hazard of being thought one of the fools of this quotation, I meet that argument—I rush in—I take that bull by the horns. —*Speech, Peoria, Oct. 16, 1854.* II, 226.

"Foot Down Firmly"—*See* PEACE, devotion to, 1.

Foote, Andrew H., Congress asked to thank—I most cordially recommend that Capt. Andrew H. Foote, of the United States Navy, receive a vote of thanks of Congress for his eminent services in organizing the flotilla on the western waters, and for his gallantry at Fort Henry, Fort Donelson, Island Number Ten, and at various other places, whilst in command of the naval forces, embracing a period of nearly ten months. —*Message to Congress, July 1, 1862.* VII, 253.

Force, to repel, by—*See* VIRGINIA, policy toward.

See WAR POWER, use of, defended.

Foreign-Born Citizens, message of Declaration of Independence to—*See* EQUALITY, Declaration's message to foreign-born.

Foreign-Born Citizens, no discrimination against— Your note asking me, in behalf of yourself and other German citizens, whether I am for or against the constitutional provision in regard to naturalized citizens, lately adopted by Massachusetts . . . is received. Massachusetts is a sovereign and independent state; and it is no privilege of mine to scold her for what

she does. Still, if from what she has done an inference is sought to be drawn as to what I would do, I may without impropriety speak out. I say, then, that, as I understand the Massachusetts provision, I am against its adoption in Illinois, or in any other place where I have a right to oppose it. Understanding the spirit of our institutions to aim at the elevation of men, I am opposed to whatever tends to degrade them. I have some little notoriety for commiserating the oppressed negro; and I should be strangely inconsistent if I would favor any project for curtailing the existing rights of white men, even though born in different lands, and speaking different languages from myself.—*To Theodore Canisius, May 17, 1859.* V, 129.

Foreign-Born Citizens, some abuse privileges—There is also reason to believe that foreigners frequently become citizens of the United States for the sole purpose of evading duties imposed by the laws of their native countries, to which on becoming naturalized here they at once repair, and though never returning to the United States they still claim the interposition of this government as citizens. Many altercations and great prejudices have heretofore arisen out of this abuse. It might be advisable to fix a limit beyond which no citizen of the United States residing abroad may claim interposition of his government.—*Third annual message, Dec. 8, 1863.* IX, 228.

Foreign Nations, attitude toward American war struggle—*See* CIVIL WAR, foreign nations' attitude toward.

Foreigners—*See* ALIENS.

Forgery, alleged—In order to fix extreme Abolitionism upon me, Judge Douglas read [at Ottawa] a set of resolutions which he declared had been passed by a Republican state convention . . . and he declared I had taken part in that convention. . . . So apparent had it become that the resolutions which he read had not been passed . . . by any state convention in which I had taken part, that seven days afterward, at Freeport, Judge Douglas declared that he had been misled by Charles H. Lanphier, editor of the *State Register,* and Thomas L. Harris, member of Congress in that district. . . . A fraud, an absolute forgery, was committed, and the perpetration of it was traced to the three—Lanphier, Harris and Douglas.—*Debate, Galesburg, Oct. 7, 1858.* IV, 277.

2.—The publication in the [Illinois State] *Register* was a forgery then, and the question is still behind, which of the three [Lanphier, Harris and Douglas], if not all of them, committed that forgery. The idea that it was done by mistake is absurd. The article in the Illinois *State Register* contains part of the real proceedings of the Springfield convention, showing that the writer of the article had the real proceedings before him, and purposely threw out the genuine resolutions passed by the convention, and fraudulently substituted the others.—*Debate, Galesburg, Oct. 7, 1858.* IV, 278.

3.—Lanphier then [when the fraudulent resolutions were published], as now, was the editor of the *Register,* so that there seems to be little room for his escape [from responsibility]. But then it is to be borne in mind that Lanphier had less interest in the object of that forgery than either of the other two. The main object of that forgery at that time was to beat Yates and elect Harris to Congress, and that object was known to be exceedingly dear to Judge Douglas at that time.—*Debate, Galesburg, Oct. 7, 1858.* IV, 279.

4.—The fraud having been apparently successful upon that occasion, both Harris and Douglas have more than once since then been attempting to put it to new uses. . . . On the 9th of July, 1856, Douglas attempted a repetition of it upon Trumbull on the floor of the Senate of the United States. . . . On the 9th of August Harris attempted it again upon Norton in the House of Representatives. . . . On the 21st of August last, all three— Lanphier, Douglas and Harris —reattempted it upon me at Ottawa. It has been clung to and played out again and again as an exceedingly high trump by this blessed trio.—*Debate, Galesburg, Oct. 7, 1858.* IV, 279.

5.—He [Douglas], Lanphier and Harris are just as cozy now, and just as active in the concoction of new schemes as they ever were before the general discovery of this fraud. Now all this is very natural if they are all alike guilty in that fraud, and it is very unnatural if any one of them is innocent.—*Debate, Galesburg, Oct. 7, 1858.* IV, 280.

6.—After all, the question still recurs upon us, how did that fraud originally get into the *State Register?* Lanphier, then as now, was the editor of that paper. Lanphier knows. Lanphier cannot be ignorant of how and by whom it was originally concocted. Can he be induced to tell, or if he has told, can Judge Douglas be induced to tell, how it was originally concocted?—*Debate, Galesburg, Oct. 7, 1858.* IV, 281.

7.—I do dare to say forgery when it's true; and don't dare to say forgery when it's false. . . . I have not dared to say he [Douglas] committed a forgery, and I never shall until I know it; but I did dare to say— just to suggest to the judge—that a forgery had been committed, which by his own showing had been traced to him and two of his friends.—*Debate, Quincy, Oct. 13, 1858.* IV, 324.

8.—I will tell Judge Douglas again the facts upon which I "dared" to say they proved a forgery. I pointed out at Galesburg that the publication of those resolutions in the Illinois *State Register* could not have been the result of accident, as the proceedings of that meeting bore unmistakable evidence of being done by a man who knew it was a forgery; that it was a publication partly taken from the real proceedings of a convention at another place; which showed that he had the real proceedings before him, and, taking one part of the resolutions, he threw out another part, and substituted false and fraudulent ones in their stead. I pointed that out to him, and also that his friend Lanphier, who was editor of the *Register* at that time and now is, must have known how it was done. Now whether he did it, or got some friend to do it for him, I could not tell, but he certainly knew all about it. I pointed out to Judge Douglas that in his Freeport speech he had promised to investigate the matter. . . . I call upon him to tell here today why he did not keep that promise. That fraud has been traced up so that it lies between him, Harris and Lanphier.—*Debate, Quincy, Oct. 13, 1858.* IV, 383.

9.—He [Douglas] says my oath would not be taken against the bare word of Charles H. Lanphier or Thomas L. Harris. Well, that is altogether a matter of opinion. It is certainly not for me to vaunt my word against the oaths of these gentlemen.—*Debate, Quincy, Oct. 13, 1858.* IV, 383.

10.—As he [Douglas] has said that he would investigate it [alleged forgery], and implied that he would tell us the result of his investigation, I demand of him to tell why he did not investigate, if he did not; and if he did, why he won't tell the result.—*Debate, Quincy, Oct. 13, 1858.* IV, 384.

Forgery, defined—What is forgery? It is the bringing forward something in writing or in print purporting to be of certain effect when it is altogether untrue.— *Debate, Charleston, Sept. 18, 1858.* IV, 112.

Forgery, seems not to suspect—The Illinois *State Register,* edited by Lanphier, then, as now, the central organ of both [Congressmen Thomas L.] Harris and Douglas, continues to din the public ear with these assertions without seeming to suspect that they are all lacking in title to belief.—*Debate, Galesburg, Oct. 7, 1858.* IV, 281.

Forgiveness, principle of, rejected—See OATH, form of, disliked.

Forquer, George—See LIGHTNING ROD, sign of guilty conscience.

Fort Donelson, importance of—*See* HALLECK, HENRY W., appeals to, 1.

Fort Gaines, reduction of—*See* DEITY, gratitude to, 12.

See FARRAGUT, DAVID G., thanked for victories.

Fort Kearny, desertion report a humbug?—I have another letter, from a writer unknown to me, saying the officers of the army at Fort Kearny have determined, in case of Republican success at the approaching presidential election, to take themselves and the arms at that point, South, for the purpose of resistance to the government. While I think there are many chances to one that this is a humbug, it occurs to me that any real movement of this sort in the army would leak out and become known to you. In such case, if it would not be unprofessional or dishonorable—of which you are to be the judge—I shall be much obliged if you will apprise me of it.—*To Maj. David Hunter, Oct. 26, 1860.* VI, 65.

Fort Morgan, reduction of—*See* DEITY, gratitude to, 12.

See FARRAGUT, DAVID G., thanked for victories.

Fort Pickens—*See* FORT SUMTER, decision not to abandon.

Fort Pillow, advice sought—It is now quite certain that a large number of colored soldiers, with their white officers, were by the rebel force massacred after they had surrendered, at the recent capture of Fort Pillow. . . . I will thank you to prepare, and give me in writing, your opinion as to what course the government should take in the case.—*To members of cabinet, May 3, 1864.* X, 92.

Fort Pillow, retribution will follow—A painful rumor—true, I fear—has reached us of the massacre by the rebel forces at Fort Pillow . . . of some three hundred colored soldiers, and white officers, who had just been overpowered by their assailants. There seems to be some anxiety in the public mind whether the government is doing its duty to the colored soldier, and to the service, at this point. . . . It is a mistake to suppose that the government is indifferent to this matter, or is not doing the best it can in regard to it. . . . We are having the Fort Pillow affair thoroughly investigated. . . . If there has been the massacre of three hundred there, or even the tenth part of three hundred, it will be conclusively proved; and being so proved, the retribution shall as surely come. —*Speech, Baltimore, April 18, 1864.* X, 78.

See RETALIATION, haste in, to be avoided.

Fort Powell, reduction of—*See* DEITY, gratitude to, 12.

See FARRAGUT, DAVID G., thanked for victories

Fort Sumter, decision not to abandon—It was believed . . . that to . . . abandon that position [Fort Sumter] under the circumstances would be utterly ruinous; that the necessity under which it was to be done would not be fully understood; that by many it would be construed as a part of a voluntary policy; that at home it would discourage the friends of the Union, embolden its adversaries, and go far to insure to the latter a recognition abroad; that, in fact, it would be our national destruction consummated. This could not be allowed. Starvation was not yet upon the garrison, and ere it would be reached Fort Pickens might be reenforced. This last would be a clear indication of policy, and would better enable the country to accept the evacuation of Fort Sumter as a military necessity.—*Message to Congress, July 4, 1861.* VI, 301.

Fort Sumter, ends hope of peace—The last ray of hope for preserving the Union peaceably expired at the assault upon Fort Sumter.—*First annual message, Dec. 3, 1861.* VII, 52.
2.—On the 12th day of April, 1861, the insurgents committed the flagrant act of civil war by the bombardment and capture of Fort Sumter, which cut off the hope of immediate conciliation.—*Message to Congress, May 26, 1862.* VII, 189.

Fort Sumter, surrender of, foreseen—Dispatches have come here two days in succession, that the forts in South Carolina will be surrendered by the order, or consent at least, of the President. I can scarcely believe this; but if it prove true, I will, if our friends at Washington concur, announce publicly at once that they are to be retaken after the inauguration. This will give the Union men a rallying cry, and preparation will proceed somewhat on their side, as well as on the other.—*To Lyman Trumbull, Dec. 24, 1860.* Tracy, 173.

Fort Sumter, unprovoked assault on—The assault upon and reduction of Fort Sumter was in no sense a matter of self-defense on the part of the assailants. They well knew that the garrison in the fort could by no possibility commit aggression upon them. They knew—they were expressly notified—that the giving of bread to the few brave and hungry men of the garrison was all which would on that occasion be attempted, unless themselves, by resisting so much, should provide more. They knew that this government desired to keep the garrison in the fort, not to assail them, but merely to maintain visible possession, and thus to preserve the Union from actual and immediate dissolution. . . . They assailed and reduced the fort for precisely the reverse object—to drive out the visible authority of the Federal Union, and thus force it to immediate dissolution. . . . Then and thereby the assailants of the government began the conflict of arms, without a gun in sight or in expectancy to return their fire, save only the few in the fort, sent to that harbor years before for their own protection and still ready to give that protection in whatever way was lawful. In this act, discarding all else, they have forced upon the country the distinct issue, "immediate dissolution or blood."—*Message to Congress, July 4, 1861.* VI, 303.

Fourth of July, day for firecrackers—The Fourth of July has not quite dwindled away; it is still a great day—for burning firecrackers!!!—*To George Robertson, Aug. 15, 1855.* II, 280.

Fourth of July, significance of—We hold this annual celebration to remind ourselves of all the good done in this process of time, of how it was done and who did it; and we go from these meetings in better humor with ourselves—we feel more attached the one to the other, and more firmly bound to the country we inhabit. In every way we are better men, in the age, and race and country in which we live, for these celebrations.—*Speech, Chicago, July 10, 1858.* III, 46.

Fox, Gustavus V., appreciation of—I sincerely regret that the failure of the late attempt to provision Fort Sumter should be the source of any annoyance to you. The practicability of your plan was not, in fact, brought to a test. . . . I most cheerfully and truly declare that the failure of the undertaking has not lowered you a particle, while the qualities you developed in the effort have greatly heightened, you in my estimation.—*To Mr. Fox, May 1, 1861.* VI, 261.
2.—He [Fox] is a live man, whose services we cannot dispense with.—*To Sec. Welles, 1861.* War Years I, 486.

France, vindicates neutrality—*See* CIVIL WAR, foreign nations' attitude toward, 12.

Francis, Simeon, recommended as secretary of Oregon —*See* OREGON, offices in, declined.

Fredericksburg, battle of—*See* ARMY OF THE POTOMAC, praised for Fredericksburg.

Free Government—*See* SELF-GOVERNMENT.

Free Government, "end to, on earth"—*See* SELF-GOVERNMENT, can it survive? 5.

Free Government, gives chance to all—It is in order that each one of you, through this free government which we have enjoyed, have an open field and a fair chance for your industry, enterprise and intelligence. . . . It is for this the struggle should be maintained.—*To 166th Ohio regiment, Aug. 22, 1864.* X, 302.

Free Institutions, encourage popular demonstrations —I could not look upon this vast assemblage without being made aware that all parties were united in this reception. This is as it should be. . . . I think what has occurred here could not have occurred in any other country on the face of the globe, without the influence of the free institutions which we have unceasingly enjoyed for three-quarters of a century. There is no country where the people can turn out and enjoy this day precisely as they please, save under the benign influence of the free institutions of our land.—*Speech, Cincinnati, Feb. 12, 1861.* VI, 115.

Free Institutions, "enduring support of"—As these sentiments [expressed in New Year's address by workingmen of London] are manifestly the enduring support of the free institutions of England, so I am sure also they constitute the only reliable basis for free institutions throughout the world.—*Reply to workers of London, Feb. 2, 1863.* VIII, 211.

Free Institutions, fundamental principle of—*See* EQUALITY, basic American principle, 2.

Free Institutions, interest in maintaining—I think we have an ever growing interest in maintaining the free institutions of our country.—*Speech, Kalamazoo, Mich., Aug. 27, 1856.* Stern, 405.

Free Institutions, raise condition of whole people— It may be affirmed without extravagance that the free institutions we enjoy have developed the powers and improved the condition of our whole people beyond any example in the world. Of this we now have a striking and impressive illustration. So large an army as the government has now on foot was never before known without a soldier in it but who had taken his place there of his own free choice. But more than this, there are many single regiments whose members, one and another, possess full practical knowledge of all the arts, sciences, professions, and whatever else, whether useful or elegant, is known in the world; and there is scarcely one from which there could not be selected a President, a cabinet, a Congress and perhaps a court, abundantly competent to administer the government itself. Nor do I say this is not true in the army of our late friends, now adversaries in this contest; but if it is, so much better the reason why the government which has conferred such benefits on both them and us should not be broken up.—*Message to Congress, July 4, 1861.* VI, 319.

Free Love, Southern view of the Union arrangement —*See* UNION, free-love arrangement.

Free Society—The principles of Jefferson are the definitions and maxims of free society.—*Speech, Chicago, March 1, 1859.* V, 126.

Free Soil Party, slavery extension sole concern of— If their [Free-Soilers'] platform contains any other principle [than opposition to slavery extension] it is in such a general way that it is like the pair of pantaloons the Yankee peddler offered for sale; "large enough for any man, small enough for any boy."— *Speech, Worcester, Mass., Sept. 12, 1848.* II, 92.

Free Speech—*See* FREEDOM OF SPEECH.

Freedmen, work for, praised—Your statement to Maj. Gen. Hurlbut of the condition of the freedmen in your department, and of your success in the work of their moral and physical elevation, has reached me and given me much pleasure. . . . The blessing of God and the efforts of good and faithful men will bring us an earlier and happier consummation than the most sanguine friends of the freedmen could reasonably expect.—*To Thomas W. Conway, April 1, 1864.* Lapsley VII, 327.

See RECONSTRUCTION, freedmen in.

Freedom, army of—We must all lay aside our prejudices and march, shoulder to shoulder, in the great army of freedom.—*Speech, Bloomington, May 29, 1856.* Lapsley II, 259.

Freedom, basis of battle for—The battle of freedom is to be fought out on principle.—*Speech, Bloomington, May 29, 1856.* Lapsley II, 267.

Freedom, "disenthralled"—*See* UNION TROOPS, tributes to, 11.

Freedom, Douglas would disestablish—There is this vital difference between all those states [of the North originally having slavery] and the judge's [Douglas's] Kansas experiment; that they sought to disestablish slavery which had been already established, while the judge seeks, so far as he can, to disestablish freedom, which had been established there by the Missouri Compromise.—*Speech, Bloomington, May 29, 1856.* Lapsley II, 273.

Freedom, fathers clung to—Through their whole course, from first to last, they clung to freedom.— *Speech, Columbus, Ohio, Sept. 16, 1859.* V, 171.

Freedom, for all men—The thing which determines whether a man is free or a slave is rather concrete than abstract.—*Speech, Springfield, July 17, 1858.* III, 181.
2.—I certainly wish that all men could be free.—*To James C. Conkling, Aug. 26, 1863.* IX, 96.
3.—I intend no modification of my often personally expressed wish that all men everywhere could be free. —*To Gen. Grant, July 10, 1864.* Hertz II, 936.
4.—It has always been a sentiment with me that all mankind should be free.—*Reply to committee, Sept. 7, 1864.* X, 217.
5.—I wish all men to be free.—*To H. W. Hoffman, Oct. 10, 1864.* X, 239.
6.—I have always thought that all men should be free.—*Speech to Indiana regiment, March 17, 1865.* XI, 56.

See EQUALITY.

Freedom, home of—*See* UNION TROOPS, tributes to, 11.

Freedom, individual, defined—I believe each individual is naturally entitled to do as he pleases with himself and the fruits of his labor, so far as it in no wise interferes with any other man's rights.—*Speech, Chicago, July 10, 1858.* III, 35.

Freedom, negroes fight for promise of—*See* NEGRO, fights for promise of freedom.

Freedom, new birth of—*See* CIVIL WAR, dedication to task of winning.

Freedom, none who denies, deserves—Those who deny freedom to others deserve it not for themselves; and, under the rule of a just God, cannot long retain it.—*To H. L. Pierce and others, April 6, 1859.* V, 126.
Repeated at Bloomington, May 29, 1856. Lapsley II, 274.
2.—This is a world of compensation; and he who would be no slave must consent to have no slave.— *To H. L. Pierce and others, April 6, 1859.* V, 126.

Freedom, universality of—*See* SLAVERY, perpetuation of, 5.

Freedom of Choice, due at ballot box—The correct principle, I think, is that all our friends should have absolute freedom of choice among our friends. My wish, therefore, is that you will do as you think fit with your own suffrage in the case, and not constrain any of your subordinates to do other than as he thinks fit with his.—*Memorandum of interview with Philadelphia postmaster, June 20, 1864.* X, 132.
Repeated to John P. Scripps, July 4, 1864. X, 142.

Freedom of Opinion—If we ever have a government on the principles we profess, we should remember, while we exercise our opinion, that others have also rights to the exercise of their opinions, and that we should endeavor to allow those rights, and act in such a manner as to create no bad feeling.—*Response to Pennsylvania delegation, March 5, 1861.* XI, 117.

2.—Under your recent order, which I have approved, you will only arrest individuals and suppress assemblies or newspapers when they may be working palpable injury to the military in your charge, and in no other case will you interfere with the expression of opinion in any form or allow it to be interfered with violently by others.—*To Gen. Schofield, Oct. 1, 1863.* IX, 148.

3.—Men will speak their minds freely in this country. —*To Sec. Stanton, July 14, 1864.* War Years III, 148.

Freedom of Press—*See* PRESS, freedom of.

Freedom of Speech, part of guarantee—Free speech and discussion and immunity from whip and tar and feathers, seem implied by the guarantee to each state of a republican form of government.—*To John J. Crittenden, Dec. 22, 1859.* Tracy, 121.

Freedom of Thought, printing helped achieve—To emancipate the mind from this under-estimate of itself [the belief that only the superior are capable of education] is the great task which printing came into the world to perform. It is difficult for us now and here to conceive how strong this slavery of the mind was, and how long it did of necessity take to break its shackles and to get the habit of freedom of thought established.—*Lecture, Springfield, Feb. 22, 1859.* V, 112.

Freeport Doctrine, defined—The second interrogatory that I propounded to him [Douglas, at Freeport] was this: "Can the people of a United States territory, in any lawful way, against the wishes of any citizen of the United States, exclude slavery from its limits prior to the formation of a state constitution?" To this Judge Douglas answered that they can lawfully exclude slavery from the territory prior to the formation of a state constitution. He goes on to tell us how it can be done. As I understand him, he holds that it can be done by the territorial legislature refusing to make any enactments for the protection of slavery in the territory, and especially by adopting legislation unfriendly to it. For the sake of clearness, I state it again: that they can exclude slavery from the territory—first, by withholding what he assumes to be an indispensable assistance to it in the way of legislation; and, second, by unfriendly legislation.— *Debate, Jonesboro, Sept. 15, 1858.* IV, 56.

Freeport Doctrine, Douglas shifts ground—In 1856, on the floor of the Senate, Judge Trumbull asked Judge Douglas the direct question: "Can the people of a territory exclude slavery prior to the forming of a state constitution?"—and Judge Douglas answered, "That is a question for the Supreme Court". . . . But now, when the Supreme Court has decided that the people of a territory cannot so exclude slavery, Judge Douglas shifts his ground, saying the people can exclude it, and thus virtually saying it is not a question for the Supreme Court.—*Notes, Oct. 1, 1858.* IV, 207.

2.—There was something about that answer [given by Douglas to Lincoln at Freeport] that has probably been a trouble to the judge ever since. . . . The judge does not any longer say that the people [of a territory] can exclude slavery. . . . He does not say the people can drive it out, but they can control it as other property. . . . What do the men who are in favor of slavery want more than this?—*Speech, Columbus, Ohio, Sept. 16, 1859.* V, 174.

3.—He [Douglas] escapes, to some extent, the absurd position I have stated by changing his language entirely. . . . The language is different; we should consider whether the sense is different. . . . What do they [proslavery men] really want, other than that slavery, being in the territories, shall be controlled as other property?—*Speech, Columbus, Ohio, Sept. 16, 1859.* V, 174.

4.—You remember . . . that he, last year, said the people of the territories can, in spite of the Dred Scott decision, exclude your [Kentuckians'] slaves from the territories. . . . You ought, however, to bear in mind that he has never said it since. . . . He has always since then declared the "Constitution does not carry slavery into the territories of the United States beyond the power of the people legally to control it, as other property.". . . I should think the controlling it as other property would be just about what you in Kentucky should want. I understand the controlling of property means the controlling of it for the benefit of the owner of it.—*Speech, Cincinnati, Sept. 17, 1859.* V, 211.

5.—Douglas is not willing to stand by his first proposition that they [the people of a territory] can exclude it [slavery], because we have seen that that proposition amounts to nothing more nor less than the naked absurdity that you may lawfully drive out that which has a lawful right to remain. . . . He is not willing to stand in the face of that direct, naked, and impudent absurdity; he has, therefore, modified his language into that of being "controlled as other property."—*Speech, Cincinnati, Sept. 17, 1859*. V, 212.

See FREEPORT DOCTRINE, fallacy of.

Freeport Doctrine, Dred Scott decision and, inconsistent—This position [taken by Douglas in the Freeport Doctrine] and the Dred Scott decision are absolutely inconsistent. The judge furiously indorses the Dred Scott decision; and that decision holds that the United States Constitution guarantees to the citizens of the United States the right to hold slaves in the territories, and that neither Congress nor a territorial legislature can destroy or abridge that right. In the teeth of this, where can the judge find room for his unfriendly legislation against their right?—*Notes, Oct. 1, 1858*. IV, 204.

Freeport Doctrine, fallacy of—The Supreme Court of the United States has decided that any congressional prohibition of slavery in the territories is unconstitutional. . . . How is it possible for any power to exclude slavery from the territory unless in violation of that decision?—*Debate, Jonesboro, Sept. 15, 1858*. IV, 56.

2.—I hold that the proposition that slavery cannot enter a new country without police regulations is historically false. It is not true at all. I hold that the history of this country shows that the institution of slavery was originally planted upon this continent without those "police regulations" which the judge [Douglas] now thinks necessary for the actual establishment of it.—*Debate, Jonesboro, Sept. 15, 1858*. IV, 59.

3.—There is vigor enough in slavery to plant itself in a new country even against unfriendly legislation. It takes not only law but the enforcement of law to keep it out.—*Debate, Jonesboro, Sept. 15, 1858*. IV, 59.

4.—It being understood that the Constitution of the United States guarantees property in slaves in the territories, if there is any infringement of the rights of that property, would not the United States courts, organized for the government of the territory, apply such remedy as might be necessary in that case?—*Debate, Jonesboro, Sept. 15, 1858*. IV, 60.

5.—What do you understand by supporting the constitution of a state or of the United States? Is it not to give such constitutional helps to the rights established by that constitution as may be practically needed? Can you, if you swear to support the Constitution and believe that the Constitution establishes a right, clear your oath without giving it support? Do you support the Constitution if, knowing or believ-

ing there is a right established under it which needs specific legislation, you withhold that legislation? Do you not violate and disregard your oath? I can conceive of nothing plainer in the world.—*Debate, Jonesboro, Sept. 15, 1858*. IV, 60.

6.—And what I say here will hold with still more force against the judge's [Douglas's] doctrine of "unfriendly legislation."—*Debate, Jonesboro, Sept. 15, 1858*. IV, 60.

7.—Is not Congress under obligation to give legislative support to any right that is established under the United States Constitution? . . . A member of Congress swears to support the Constitution of the United States, and if he sees a right established by that Constitution which needs specific legislative protection, can he clear his oath without giving that protection? —*Debate, Jonesboro, Sept. 15, 1858*. IV, 61.

8.—If I acknowledge, with Judge Douglas, that this [Dred Scott] decision properly construes the Constitution, I cannot conceive that I would be less than a perjured man if I should in Congress refuse to give such protection to that property [in slaves] as in its nature it needed.—*Debate, Jonesboro, Sept. 15, 1858*. IV, 63.

9.—The members of a territorial legislature are sworn to support the Constitution of the United States. How dare they legislate unfriendly to a right guaranteed by that Constitution? And if they should, how quickly would the courts hold their work to be unconstitutional and void! But doubtless the judge's chief reliance to sustain his proposition that the people can exclude slavery, is based on non-action—upon withholding friendly legislation. But can members of a territorial legislature, having sworn to support the Constitution of the United States, conscientiously withhold necessary legislative protection to a right guaranteed by that Constitution? Again, will not the courts, without territorial legislation, find a remedy for the evasion of a right guaranteed by the Constitution of the United States?—*Notes, Oct. 1, 1858*. IV, 204.

10.—As a matter of fact, non-action, both legislative and judicial, will not exclude slavery from any place. . . . Slavery, having actually gone into a territory to some extent [as in the Dred Scott case], without local legislation in its favor, and against congressional prohibition, how much more will it go there now that by a judicial decision that congressional prohibition has been swept away, and the constitutional guaranty of property declared to apply to slavery in the territories.—*Notes, Oct. 1, 1858*. IV, 205.

11.—Judge Douglas says: "The sovereignty of a territory remains in abeyance, suspended in the United States, in trust for the people, until they shall be admitted into the Union as a state." If so—if they have no active living sovereignty—how can they readily enact the judge's unfriendly legislation to slavery?—*Notes, Oct. 1, 1858.* IV, 206.

12.—Slavery was originally planted on this continent without the aid of friendly legislation. History proves this. After it was actually in existence to a sufficient extent to become, in some sort, a public interest, it began to receive legislative attention, but not before. How futile, then, is the proposition that the people of a territory can exclude slavery by simply not legislating in its favor.—*Notes, Oct. 1, 1858.* IV, 206.

13.—We will say you are a member of the territorial legislature, and, like Judge Douglas, you believe that the right to take and hold slaves there is a constitutional right. The first thing you do is to swear you will support the Constitution and all rights guaranteed therein; that you will, whenever your neighbor needs your legislation to support his constitutional rights, not withhold that legislation. If you withheld that necessary legislation for the support of the Constitution and constitutional rights, do you not commit perjury? I ask every sensible man if that is not so. That is undoubtedly just so, say what you please. Now, that is precisely what Judge Douglas says—that this is a constitutional right. Does the judge mean to say that the territorial legislature may, by withholding necessary laws or by passing unfriendly laws, nullify that constitutional right? Does he mean that?—*Debate, Quincy, Oct. 13, 1858.* IV, 378.

14.—Does he [Douglas] mean to ignore the proposition so long and well established in law, that what you cannot do directly you cannot do indirectly?—*Debate, Quincy, Oct. 13, 1858.* IV, 379.

15.—Judge Douglas constantly said, before the [Dred Scott] decision, that whether they [people of the territories] could or could not [exclude slavery] was a question for the Supreme Court. But after the court has made the decision, he virtually says it is not a question for the Supreme Court, but for the people. And how is it he tells us they can exclude it? He says it needs "police regulations," and that admits of "unfriendly legislation." Although it is a right established by the Constitution of the United States to take a slave into a territory of the United States and hold him as property, yet unless the territorial legislature will give friendly legislation, and, more especially if they adopt unfriendly legislation, they can practically exclude him. . . . Why, this is a monstrous sort of talk about the Constitution of the United States! There has never been as outlandish or lawless a doctrine from the mouth of any respectable man on earth.—*Debate, Alton, Oct. 15, 1858.* V, 67.

16.—Judge Douglas is furious against those who go for reversing a [Supreme Court] decision. But he is for legislating it out of all force while the law itself stands. I repeat that there has never been so monstrous a doctrine uttered from the mouth of a respectable man.—*Debate, Alton, Oct. 15, 1858.* V, 68.

17.—Let us take the gentleman who looks me in the face before me, and let us suppose that he is a member of the territorial legislature. The first thing he will do will be to swear to support the Constitution of the United States. His neighbor by his side in the territory has slaves and needs territorial legislation to enable him to enjoy that constitutional right. Can he withhold the legislation which his neighbor needs for the enjoyment of a right which is fixed in his favor in the Constitution of the United States which he has sworn to support?—*Debate, Alton, Oct. 15, 1858.* V, 68.

18.—No man can deny his obligation to give the necessary legislation to support slavery in a territory, who believes it is a constitutional right to have it there.—*Debate, Alton, Oct. 15, 1858.* V, 69.

19.—The process will probably be about this: Some territorial legislature will adopt unfriendly legislation [toward slavery]; the Supreme Court will decide that legislation to be unconstitutional, and the advocates of the present compound absurdity will acquiesce in the decision.—*Speeches in Kansas, Dec. 1–5, 1858.* V. 270.

20.—When all the trash, the words, the collateral matter, was cleared away from it,—all the chaff was fanned out of it [Douglas's argument at Freeport]—it was a bare absurdity; no less than that a thing may be lawfully driven away from where it has a lawful right to be. Clear it of all the verbiage, and that is the naked truth of his proposition—that a thing may be lawfully driven from a place where it has a lawful right to stay.—*Speech, Columbus, Ohio, Sept. 16, 1859.* V, 174.

21.—I undertake to give the opinion, at least, that if the territories attempt by any direct legislation to drive the man with his slave out of the territory, or to decide that his slave is free because of his being taken in there, or to tax him to such an extent that he cannot keep him there, the Supreme Court will unhesitatingly decide all such legislation unconstitutional, as long as that Supreme Court is constructed as the Dred Scott Supreme Court is.—*Speech, Columbus, Ohio, Sept. 16, 1859.* V, 177.

22.—As to this indirect mode by "unfriendly legislation" [for keeping slavery out of the territories], all lawyers here will readily understand that such a proposition cannot be tolerated for a moment, because a legislature cannot indirectly do that which it cannot accomplish directly.—*Speech, Columbus, Ohio, Sept. 16, 1859.* V, 178.

23.—I have no doubt . . . that as the legislature has not the power to drive slaves out, they have no power by indirection, by tax, or by imposing burdens in any way on that property, to effect the same end, and that any attempt to do so would be held by the Dred Scott Supreme Court unconstitutional.—*Speech, Cincinnati, Sept. 17, 1859.* V, 212.

24.—When one of these acts of unfriendly legislation [as suggested by Douglas] shall impose such heavy burdens as to, in effect, destroy property in slaves in a territory, and show plainly enough that there can be no mistake in the purpose of the legislation to make them so burdensome, this same Supreme Court [as made the Dred Scott decision] will decide that law to be unconstitutional.—*Speech, Cincinnati, Sept. 17, 1859.* V, 213.

25.—While I have no doubt the Supreme Court of the United States would say "God speed" to any of the territorial legislatures that should thus control slave property ["as other property"] they would sing quite a different tune if by the pretense of controlling it, they were to undertake to pass laws which virtually excluded it.—*Speech, Cincinnati, Sept. 17, 1859.* V, 212.

26.—If it be said that it [slavery] cannot be planted, in fact, without protective law, that assertion is already falsified by history, for it was originally planted in this continent without protective law.—*Speeches in Kansas, Dec. 1–5, 1859.* V, 266.

27.—. . . the absurdity which asserts that a thing may be lawfully driven from a place, at which place it has a lawful right to remain.—*Speeches in Kansas, Dec. 1–5, 1859.* V, 270.

28.—If your first settlers [in Kansas] had so far decided in favor of slavery as to have got 5,000 slaves planted on your soil, you could by no moral possibility have adopted a free-state constitution. Their owners would be influential voters among you, as good men as the rest of you, and, by their great wealth, and consequently greater capacity to assist the more needy, perhaps the most influential among you. You could not wish to destroy, or injuriously interfere with, their property. You would not know what to do with the slaves after you had made them free. You would not wish to keep them as underlings; nor yet to elevate them to social and political equality. You could not send them away. The slave states would not let you send them there; and the free states would not let you send them there. All the rest of your property would not make a free state if the first half of your own numbers had got 5,000 slaves fixed upon the soil. . . . There they would have stuck, in spite

of you, to plague you and your children and your children's children.—*Speech, Leavenworth, Dec. 3, 1859.* Angle, 232.

See ABOLITION, strongest argument for, 3.

Freeport Doctrine, forecast—You shall have hard work to get him [Douglas] directly to the point whether a territorial legislature has or has not the power to exclude slavery. But if you succeed in bringing him to it—though he will be compelled to say it possesses no such power—he will instantly take ground that slavery cannot actually exist in the territories unless the people desire it, and so give it protection by territorial legislation. If this offends the South, he will let it offend them, as at all events he means to hold on to his chances in Illinois.—*To Henry Asbury, July 31, 1858.* Stern, 461.

Freeport Doctrine, fugitive slaves and—*See* ABOLITION, strongest argument for.

Frémont, Jessie Benton, avoids quarrel with—I sent him [Montgomery Blair, to Missouri] as Frémont's friend. He passed on the way Mrs. Frémont coming to see me. She sought an audience with me at midnight and taxed me so violently with many things that I had to exercise all the awkward tact I have to avoid quarreling with her. She surprised me by asking why their enemy, Montgomery Blair, had been sent to Missouri. She more than once intimated that if Gen. Frémont should try conclusions with me he could set up for himself.—*To White House group, Dec. 9, 1863.* Hay, 133.

Frémont, John C., balancing accounts with—I am ready to come to a fair settlement of accounts with you on the fulfilment of understanding. . . . I beg you to believe that as surely as you have done your best, so have I.—*To Gen. Frémont, June 16, 1862.* Lapsley VI, 47.

Frémont, John C., characterized—Why, just now, he [Douglas] and Frémont would make the closest race imaginable in the southern states.—*Notes, Oct. 1, 1858.* IV, 229.

2.—Gen. Frémont needs assistance which it is difficult to give him. He is losing the confidence of men near him, whose support any man in his position must have to be successful. His cardinal mistake is that he isolates himself and allows no one to see him, and by which he does not know what is going on in the very matter he is dealing with. He needs to have by his side a man of large experience. Will you not, for me, take that place? Your rank is one grade too high to be ordered to it, but will you not serve the country and oblige me by taking it voluntarily?—*To Gen. Hunter, Sept. 9, 1861.* VI, 352.

3.—No impression has been made on my mind against the honor or integrity of Gen. Frémont, and I now enter my protest against being understood as acting in any hostility toward him.—*To Mrs. Frémont, Sept. 12, 1861.* VI, 354.

4.—Do not misunderstand me. I do not say you have not done all you could. I presume you met unexpected difficulties; and I beg you to believe that as surely as you have done your best, so have I.—*To Gen. Frémont, June 16, 1862.* VII, 225.

5.—I thought well of Frémont. Even now I think well of his impulses. I only think he is the prey of wicked and designing men, and I think he has absolutely no military capacity.—*To White House group, Dec. 9, 1863.* Hay, 133.

6.—[Frémont] is like Jim Jett's brother. Jim used to say that his brother was the damnedest scoundrel that ever lived, but in the infinite mercy of Providence he was also the damnedest fool.—*To John Hay, May 22, 1864.* Hay, 183.

Frémont, John C., election of, endangered by Fillmore—*See* CAMPAIGN OF 1856, Fillmore endangers Frémont.

Frémont, John C., explanation from, demanded—I see that you are at Moorefield, You were expressly ordered to march to Harrisonburg. What does this mean?—*To Gen. Frémont, May 27, 1862.* VII, 195.

Frémont, John C., for Vice President at most—*See* WHIG PARTY, members of, and Buchanan's nomination.

Frémont, John C., insurrection followed defeat of—When the Democrats of Tennessee continually asserted in their canvass of '56 that Frémont's election would free the negroes, though they did not believe it themselves, their slaves did; and as soon as the news of Frémont's defeat came to the plantations the disappointment of the slaves flashed into insurrection.—*To John Hay, Nov. 24, 1863.* Hay, 126.

Frémont, John C., proclamation of, disapproved—Two points in your proclamation of Aug. 30 give me some anxiety: First. Should you shoot a man, according to the proclamation, the Confederates would very certainly shoot our best men in their hands in retaliation; and so, man for man, indefinitely. It is, therefore, my order that you allow no man to be shot under the proclamation without first having my approbation or consent. Second. I think there is great danger that the closing paragraph, in relation to the confiscation of property, and the liberating of slaves

of traitorous owners, will alarm our southern Union friends and turn them against us; perhaps ruin our rather fair prospects for Kentucky. Allow me, therefore, to ask that you will, as of your own motion, modify that paragraph so as to conform to the first and fourth sections of the Act of Congress entitled, "An act to confiscate property used for insurrectionary purposes". . . . This letter is written in a spirit of caution, and not of censure.—*To Gen. Frémont, Sept. 2, 1861.* VI, 350.

2.—Your answer, just received, expresses the preference on your part that I should make an open order for the modification [of Frémont's emancipation proclamation], which I very cheerfully do. It is therefore ordered that the said clause of the said proclamation be so modified, held and construed as to conform to, and not to transcend, the provisions of the Act of Congress entitled, "An act to confiscate property used for insurrectionary purposes."—*To Gen. Frémont, Sept. 11, 1863.* VI, 353.

3.—Gen. Frémont's proclamation as to confiscation of property and the liberation of slaves is purely political and not within the range of military law or necessity. If a commanding general finds a necessity to seize the farm of a private owner for a pasture, an encampment, or a fortification, he has the right to do so, and to hold it as long as the necessity lasts; and this is within military law, because within military necessity. But to say the farm shall no longer belong to the owner, or his heirs forever, and this as well when the farm is not needed for military purposes as when it is, is purely political, without the savor of military law about it. And the same is true of slaves. If the general needs them, he can seize them and use them; but when the need is past, it is not for him to fix their permanent future condition. That must be settled according to laws made by law-makers, and not by military proclamations. The [Frémont] proclamation in the point in question is simply "dictatorship." It assumes that the general may do anything he pleases—confiscate the lands and free the slaves of loyal people, as well as disloyal ones.—*To O. H. Browning, Sept. 22, 1861.* VI, 358.

4.—You speak of it [Frémont's proclamation freeing slaves] as being the only means of saving the government. On the contrary, it is itself the surrender of the government. Can it be pretended that it is any longer the government of the United States—any government of constitution and laws—wherein a general or a President may make permanent rules of property by proclamation? I do not say that Congress might not with propriety pass a law on the point, just such as Gen. Frémont proclaimed. I do not say I might not, as a member of Congress, vote for it.

What I object to is, that I, as President, shall expressly or impliedly seize and exercise the permanent legislative functions of the government.—*To O. H. Browning, Sept. 22, 1861.* VI, 359.

Frémont, John C., proclamation of, arouses Kentuckians—*See* KENTUCKY, attitude of, toward Union, 1.

Frémont, John C., support for, urged—*See* CAMPAIGN OF 1856.

Frémont, John C., supporters of, Abolitionists?—*See* ABOLITION, How define?

Frémont, John C., thanked—Many thanks for yourself, officers and men, for the gallant battle of last Sunday.—*To Gen. Frémont, June 12, 1862.* VII, 219.

Frémont-Fillmore Division, like Douglas-Buchanan feud—*See* DOUGLAS-BUCHANAN FEUD, Republicans welcome, 4.

"Fret Him and Fret Him"—*See* HOOKER, JOSEPH, suggestions to, 2.

Friends, how to make—"A drop of honey catches more flies than a gallon of gall." So with men. If you would win a man to your cause, first convince him that you are his sincere friend.—*Speech, Springfield, Feb. 22, 1842.* I, 197.

Friends, importance of—The better part of one's life consists of his friendships.—*To Joseph Gillespie, July 13, 1849.* II, 125.
2.—The loss of enemies does not compensate for the loss of friends.—*To Sec. Seward, June 30, 1862.* VII, 245.

Friends, no distinction among—You distinguish between yourself and my original friends—a distinction which, by your leave, I propose to forget.—*To Schuyler Colfax, May 26, 1860.* Hertz II, 774.

Friends, old, preferred—We much prefer standing with old friends, to being driven to form new ones.—*To Joseph Gillespie, Feb. 11, 1854.* Angle, 122.

Friends, responsive to—I have always been in the habit of acceding to almost any proposal that a friend would make.—*To John J. Hardin, Jan. 19, 1845,* I, 274.

Friends, Society of, given pledge of peace—A domestic affliction, of which doubtless you are informed, has delayed me so long in making acknowledgement of the very kind and appropriate letter . . . of the Society of Friends for New England. . . . Engaged as I am in a great war, I fear it will be difficult for the world to understand how fully I appreciate the prin-

ciples of peace inculcated in this letter and everywhere by the Society of Friends. Grateful to the good people you represent for the prayers in behalf of our common country, I look forward hopefully to an early end of the war and return to peace.—*To Dr. Samuel Boyd Tobey, March 19, 1862.* VII, 135.

See PEACE, devotion to, 2.

Friends, Society of, "hard dilemma" of—Your people, the Friends, have had, and are having a very great trial. On principle and faith opposed to both war and oppression, they can only practically oppose oppression by war. In this hard dilemma some have chosen one horn and some the other. For those appealing to me on conscientious grounds I have done, and shall do, the best I could and can, in my conscience, under my oath to the law. That you believe this I doubt not; and, believing it, I shall still receive for our country and myself your earnest prayers to our Father in Heaven.—*To Mrs. Eliza P. Gurney, Sept. 4, 1864.* Basler, 758.

Friends, some of their advice distrusted—You are ready to say that I apply to friends what is due only to enemies. I distrust the wisdom if not the sincerity of friends who would hold my hands while my enemies stab me. This appeal of professed friends has paralyzed me more in this struggle than any other one thing.—*To Reverdy Johnson, July 26, 1862.* VII, 293.

Friends, things "miserably arranged"—How miserably things seem to be arranged in this world! If we have no friends, we have no pleasure; and if we have them, we are sure to lose them, and be doubly pained by the loss.—*To Joshua F. Speed, Feb. 25, 1842.* I, 210.

Frye, Speed S., appreciation of—I have a very strong impression . . . that Gen. Frye is a worthy gentleman and a meritorious officer.—*Indorsement, Feb. 9, 1863.* Angle, 315.

Fugitive-Slave Act, attitude toward—I would give them ["our brethren of the South"] any legislation for the reclaiming of their fugitive slaves which should not in its stringency be more likely to carry a free man into slavery than our ordinary criminal laws are to hang an innocent one.—*Speech, Peoria, Oct. 16, 1854.* II, 207.
Repeated at Ottawa, Aug. 21, 1858. III, 228.
Repeated at Carlinville, Aug. 31, 1858. Angle, 190.
2.—I avow, without any mental reservation, my full indorsement of the fugitive-slave law. It was formulated in obedience to a plain constitutional requirement, as one of the compromises of the Constitution,

without which that instrument would not probably have come into being, and it should be as fully and honestly respected and obeyed as any other provision in that instrument, and any law to carry it into effect should be enforced like any other laws.—*Speech, Urbana, Oct. 24, 1854.* Hertz II, 634.

3.—We grant a fugitive-slave law because it is so "nominated in the bond"; because our fathers so stipulated—had to—and we are bound to carry out this agreement.—*Speech, Bloomington, May 29, 1856.* Lapsley II, 261.

4.—I do not now, nor ever did, stand in favor of the unconditional repeal of the fugitive-slave law. . . . I have never hesitated to say, and I do not now hesitate to say, that I think under the Constitution of the United States, the people of the southern states are entitled to a congressional fugitive-slave law. Having said that, I have nothing to say in regard to the existing fugitive-slave law, further than that I think it should have been framed so as to be free from some of the objections that pertain to it, without lessening its efficiency. And inasmuch as we are now in an agitation in regard to an alteration or modification of that law, I would not be the man to introduce it as a new subject of agitation upon the general question of slavery.—*Debate, Freeport, Aug. 27, 1858.* III, 273.

5.—On what ground would a member of Congress who is opposed to slavery in the abstract vote for a fugitive-slave law, as I would deem it my duty to do? Because there is a constitutional right which needs legislation to enforce it.—*Debate, Jonesboro, Sept. 15, 1858.* IV, 62.

6.—Let me ask you why many of us who are opposed to slavery upon principle give our acquiescence to a fugitive-slave law. Why do we hold ourselves under obligations to pass such a law and abide by it when it is passed? Because the Constitution makes provision that the owners of slaves shall have the right to reclaim them. It gives the right to reclaim slaves, and that right is, as Judge Douglas says, a barren right, unless there is legislation that will enforce it.—*Debate, Jonesboro, Sept. 15, 1858.* IV, 62.

7.—We must not withhold an efficient fugitive-slave law, because the Constitution requires us, as I understand it, not to withhold such a law.—*Speech, Cincinnati, Sept. 17, 1859.* V, 232.

8.—I suppose most of us—I know it of myself—believe that the people of the southern states are entitled to a congressional fugitive-slave law; that it is a right fixed in the Constitution. But it cannot be made available to them without congressional legislation. . . . And, as the right is constitutional, I agree that the legislation shall be granted to it. Not that

we like the institution of slavery; we profess to have no taste for running and catching negroes—at least I profess no taste for that job at all. Why then do I yield to a fugitive-slave law? Because I do not understand that the Constitution, which guarantees that right, can be supported without it.—*Debate, Alton, Oct. 15, 1858.* V, 69.

9.—The legal right of the southern people to reclaim their fugitives I have constantly admitted.—*Speech, Springfield, Oct. 30, 1858.* Angle, 197.

10.—My view has been, and is, simply this: the U.S. Constitution says the fugitive slave "shall be delivered up," but it does not expressly say who shall deliver him up. Whatever the Constitution says "shall be done" and has omitted saying who shall do it, the government established by that Constitution, *ex vi termini,* is vested with the power of doing; and Congress is, by the Constitution, expressly empowered to make all laws which shall be necessary and proper for carrying into execution all powers vested by the Constitution in the government of the United States.—*To Salmon P. Chase, June 20, 1859.* Hertz II, 755.

11.—In any law upon this subject [return of fugitive slaves] ought not all the safeguards of liberty known in civilized and humane jurisprudence to be introduced, so that a free man be not in any case surrendered as a slave? And might it not be well at the same time to provide by law for the enforcement of that clause of the Constitution which guarantees that "the citizens of each state shall be entitled to all the privileges and immunities of citizens in the several states"?—*First inaugural, March 4, 1861.* VI, 172.

Fugitive-Slave Act, early proposals—A fugitive-slave law was passed in 1793, with no dissenting voice in the Senate, and but seven dissenting votes in the House. It was, however, a wise law, moderate, and, under the Constitution, a just one. Twenty-five years later, a more stringent law was proposed and defeated; and 35 years after that, the present law, drafted by Mason of Virginia, was passed by northern votes. . . . The proposed law of 1817 was far less offensive than the present one.—*Speech, Bloomington, May 29, 1856.* Lapsley II, 256.

Fugitive-Slave Act, New Hampshire Republicans criticized for "tilting against"—See REPUBLICAN PARTY, threats to unity, 3.

Fugitive-Slave Act, Ohio Republican action regretted—It appears by the papers that the late Republican state convention of Ohio adopted a platform, of which the following is one plank, "A repeal of the atrocious fugitive-slave law." This is already damaging us here. I have no doubt that if that plank be ever introduced into the next Republican national convention, it will explode it. . . . I assure you the cause of Republicanism is hopeless in Illinois, if it be in any way made responsible for that plank. I hope you can, and will, contribute something to relieve us from it.—*To Salmon P. Chase, June 9, 1859.* Hertz II, 754.

2.—Two things done by the Ohio Republican convention—the repudiation of Judge Swan, and the "plank" for a repeal of the fugitive-slave law—I very much regretted. These two things are of a piece; and they are viewed by many good men, sincerely opposed to slavery, as a struggle against, and in disregard of, the Constitution itself. And it is the very thing that will greatly endanger our cause, if it be not kept out of our national convention.—*To Samuel Galloway, July 28, 1859.* V, 136.

See REPUBLICAN PARTY, threats to unity of, 3.

Fugitive-Slave Clause, secession would surrender— The fugitive-slave clause of the Constitution and the law for the suppression of the foreign slave trade are each as well enforced, perhaps, as any law can ever be in a community where the moral sense of the people imperfectly supports the law itself. . . . It would be worse in both cases after the separation of the sections than before. The foreign slave trade, now imperfectly suppressed, would be ultimately revived without restriction in one section, while fugitive slaves, now only partially surrendered, would not be surrendered at all by the other.—*First inaugural, March 4, 1861.* VI, 180.
Repeated in second annual message, Dec. 1, 1862. VIII, 111.

2.—The fact of separation [of the Union], if it comes, gives up on the part of the seceding section the fugitive-slave clause, along with all the other constitutional obligations upon the section seceded from.—*Second annual message, Dec. 1, 1862.* VIII, 113.

Fugitive-Slave Clause, should be enforced—You know I think the fugitive-slave clause of the Constitution ought to be enforced—to put it in its mildest form, ought not to be resisted.—*To William Kellogg, Dec. 11, 1860.* VI, 78.

2.—All opposition, real and apparent, to the fugitive-slave clause of the Constitution ought to be withdrawn.—*To Thurlow Weed, Dec. 17, 1860.* VI, 82.

3.—It is but repetition for me to say I am for an honest enforcement of the Constitution—fugitive-slave clause included.—*To Lyman Trumbull, Dec. 17, 1860.* Tracy, 171.

4.—The fugitive-slave clause of the Constitution ought to be enforced by a law of Congress, with effi-

cient provisions for that object, not obliging private persons to assist in its execution, and with the usual safeguards to liberty, securing free men from being surrendered as slaves. . . . All state laws, if there be such, really or apparently in conflict with such law of Congress, ought to be repealed; and no opposition to the execution of such law of Congress ought to be made.—*Memorandum, Dec. 22, 1860.* XI, 115.

See FUGITIVE-SLAVE ACT, attitude toward.

Fugitive-Slave Clause, sworn to support—It is scarcely questioned that this provision [Art. IV, Sect. 3, United States Constitution] was intended by those who made it for the reclaiming of what we call fugitive slaves; and the intention of the lawgiver is the law. All members of Congress swear their support of the whole Constitution—to this provision as much as to any other. To the proposition, then, that slaves whose cases come within the terms of this clause "shall be delivered up" their oaths are unanimous—*First inaugural, March 4, 1861.* VI, 171.

Fugitive-Slave Clause, who enforces?—There is some difference of opinion whether this [fugitive-slave] clause [of the Constitution] should be enforced by national or by state authority, but surely that difference is not a material one. If the slave is to be surrendered, it can be of but little consequence to him or to others by which authority it is done. And should anyone in any case be content that his oath shall go unkept on a merely unsubstantial controversy as to how it shall be kept?—*First inaugural, March 4, 1861.* VI, 172.

Fugitive Slaves, "dirty disagreeable job"—There are constitutional relations between the slave and free states which are degrading to the latter. We are under legal obligations to catch and return their runaway slaves to them; a sort of dirty, disagreeable job, which, I believe, as a general rule, the slave-holders will not perform for one another.—*Speech, Peoria, Oct. 16, 1854.* II, 233.

Fugitive Slaves, "may as well surrender the contest" —Do you know that I may as well surrender the contest as to make any order the obvious purpose of which would be to return fugitive slaves [who have taken refuge behind the Union lines]?—*Letter (not sent) to George Robertson, Nov. 20, 1862.* VIII, 78.

Fugitive Slaves, military not to return—Allow no part of the military under your command to be engaged in either returning fugitive slaves or enticing slaves from their homes, and, so far as practicable, enforce the same forbearance upon the people.—*To Gen. Schofield, Oct. 1, 1863.* IX, 148.

Fusion, political, for 1860—*See* CAMPAIGN OF 1860, North-South fusion suggested.

Future, Civil War fought for—*See* CIVIL WAR, results of, involve future.

Future, consequences of war important to—*See* DEITY, dependence on, 10.

Future, self-government a promise for—*See* SELF-GOVERNMENT, makes America great.

Future, who labor for Union labor for the—*See* ELECTION OF 1864, of lasting advantage, 1.

Gag, can't fashion, for Douglas—If a man will stand up and assert, and repeat and reassert, that two and two do not make four, I know nothing in the power of argument that can stop him. I think I can answer the judge, so long as he sticks to the premises; but when he flies from them, I cannot work an argument into the consistency of a maternal gag, and actually close his mouth with it.—*Speech, Peoria, Oct. 16, 1854.* Basler, 323.
2.—I don't know how to meet this kind of argument. I don't want to have a fight with Judge Douglas, and I have no way of making an argument up into the consistency of a corncob and stopping his mouth with it.—*Debate, Jonesboro, Sept. 15, 1858.* IV, 35.

Gallows of Haman, no mourning—If, like Haman, they [proslavery men in Kansas] should hang upon the gallows of their own building, I shall not be among the mourners of their fate.—*To Joshua F. Speed, Aug. 24, 1855.* II, 284.

See CAMPAIGN OF 1848, victory forecast.

Gamble, H. R., characterized—An honest and true man.—*To Gen. Curtis, Jan. 5, 1863.* VIII, 171.

Gamble, H. R., won't read letter from—My private secretary has just brought me a letter; says it is a very "cross" one from you. . . . As I am trying to preserve my own temper by avoiding irritants so far as possible, I decline to read the cross letter.—*To Gov. Gamble, July 23, 1863.* IX, 40.

Gamblers, "worse than useless"—Abstractly considered, the hanging of the gamblers at Vicksburg was of little consequence. They constitute a portion of the population that is worse than useless in any community; and their death, if no pernicious example be set by it, is never a matter of reasonable regret with any one. If they were annually swept from the stage of existence by the plague or smallpox, honest men would perhaps be much profited by the operation.—*Speech, Springfield, Jan. 27, 1837.* I, 39.

Garbled Speeches—*See* DOUGLAS, STEPHEN A., characterized, 36.

"Gates of Hell," shall not prevail—Upon these [reverence for the Constitution and laws] let the proud fabric rest, as the rock of its basis, and as truly as has been said of the only greater institution, "the gates of hell shall not prevail against it."—*Speech, Springfield, Jan. 27, 1837.* I, 50.
2.—The people when they rise in mass in behalf of the Union and the liberties of their country, truly may it be said, "The gates of hell cannot prevail against them ".—*Speech, Indianapolis, Feb. 11, 1861.* VI, 111.

See REPUBLICAN PARTY, advice to, 1.

General Land Office, Butterfield not entitled to—Like you, I fear the land office is not going as it should; but I know nothing I can do. . . . As to Butterfield, he is my personal friend, and is qualified to do the duties of the office; but of the quite one hundred Illinoisans equally well qualified, I do not know one with less claims to it. In the first place, what you say about Lisle Smith is the first intimation I have had of anyone in Illinois desiring Butterfield to have an office. Now, I think if anything be given the state, it should be so given as to gratify our friends and to stimulate them to future exertions. As to Mr. Clay having recommended him, that is *quid pro quo.* He fought for Clay against Gen. Taylor to the bitter end, as I understand; and I do not believe I misunderstand. Lisle Smith, too, was a Clay delegate at Philadelphia, and against my most earnest entreaties took the lead in filling two vacancies from my own district with Clay men. It will now mortify me deeply if Gen. Taylor's administration shall trample all my wishes in the dust merely to gratify these men.—*To J. M. Lucas, April 25, 1849.* II, 114.
2.—It is a delicate matter to oppose the wishes of a friend; and consequently I address you on the subject I now do, with no little hesitation. Last night I received letters assuring me it was not improbable that Justin Butterfield of Chicago, Ill., would be appointed commissioner of the general land office. . . . Mr. Butterfield is my friend, is well qualified and, I suppose, would be faithful to the office. So far, good. But now for the objections. In 1840 we fought a fierce and laborious battle in Illinois, many of us spending almost the entire year in the contest. The general victory came, and with it, the appointment of a set of drones, including this same Butterfield, who never spent a dollar or lifted a finger in the fight. The place he got was that of district attorney. . . . Again, winter and spring before the last, when

you and I were almost sweating blood to have **Gen. Taylor** nominated, the same man was ridiculing the idea, and going for Mr. Clay; and when Gen. T. was nominated, if he went out of the city of Chicago to aid in his election, it is more than I ever heard, or believe. Yet, when the election is secured, by other men's labor, and even against his effort, why, he is the first man on hand for the best office that our state lays any claim to. Shall this thing be? Our Whigs will throw down their arms and fight no more, if the fruit of their labor is thus disposed of. . . . What influence operates for him I cannot conceive. . . . Be assured nothing can more endanger it [success of the Taylor administration] than making appointments through old-hawker foreign influences.—*To W. B. Preston, May 16, 1849.* Hertz, II, 597.

3.—Butterfield will be commissioner of the general land office, unless prevented by strong and speedy efforts. Ewing is for him, and he is only not appointed yet because Old Zach. hangs fire. I have reliable information of this. Now, if you agree with me that this appointment would dissatisfy rather than gratify the Whigs of this state, that it would slacken their energies in future contests, that his appointment in '41 is an old sore with them which they will not patiently have reopened—in a word that his appointment now would be a fatal blunder to the administration and our political men here in Illinois, write Crittenden to that effect. He can control the matter.—*To Joseph Gillespie, May 19, 1849.* Lapsley, II, 135.

See GENERAL LAND OFFICE, candidate for.

General Land Office, candidate for—If the office could be secured to Illinois by my consent to accept it, and not otherwise, I give that consent. . . . With this understanding you are at liberty to procure me the offer of the appointment if you can; and I shall feel complimented by your effort, and still more by its success.—*To W. B. Warren and others, April 7, 1849.* II, 110.

2.—If you can conscientiously do so, I wish you to write Gen. Taylor at once, saying that either I or the man I recommend should, in your opinion, be appointed to that [general land] office, if anyone from Illinois shall be.—*To E. Embree, May 25, 1849.* Lapsley II, 136.

3.—The appointment of Mr. Butterfield will be an egregious political blunder. I believe it will gratify no single Whig in the state, except it be Mr. B. himself. Now the favor I ask of you is, that you will see Gen. Taylor at once, saying that in your opinion, either I, or the man I recommend, should be appointed to that office, if anyone from Illinois shall be.—*To Col. R. W. Thompson, May 25, 1849.* Hertz II, 598.

4.—It is now certain that either Mr. Butterfield or I will be commissioner of the general land office. If you are willing to give me the preference, please write me to that effect. . . . There is not a moment to be lost.—*To J. B. Herrick, June 3, 1849.* Angle, 55.

5.—I understand the President has determined to give the general land office to Illinois; and if you quite as soon I should have it as any other Illinoisan, I shall be grateful if you will write me to that effect. . . . A private dispatch . . . tells me the appointment has been postponed three weeks from the first Inst. for my benefit. No time to lose.—*To Willie P. Mangum, June 4, 1849.* Angle, 56.

6.—I do not know that it would, but I can well enough conceive it might, embarrass you to now give a letter recommending me for the general land office. Could you not, however, without embarrassment or any impropriety, so far vindicate the truth of history as to briefly state to me, in a letter, what you did say to me last spring on my arrival here from Washington, in relation to my becoming an applicant for that office? Having at last concluded to be an applicant, I have thought it perhaps due me to be enabled to show the influences which brought me to the conclusion, and of which influences the wishes and opinions you expressed were not the least.—*To N. Pope, June 8, 1849.* II, 124.

7.—Nothing in my papers questions Mr. B's competency or honesty, and, I presume, nothing in his questions mine. Being equal so far, if it does not appear that I am preferred by the Whigs of Illinois, I lay no claim to the office. But if it does appear I am preferred, it will be argued that the whole Northwest, and not Illinois alone, should be heard. I answer I am strongly recommended by Ohio and Indiana, as well as Illinois and further, that when the many appointments were made for Ohio, as for the Northwest Illinois was not consulted. . . . In each of them, the state whose citizen was appointed was allowed to control, I think rightly. I only ask that Illinois be not cut off with less deference.—*To President Taylor, June 19, 1849.* Angle, 56.

8.—I would not now accept the land office, if it were offered me.—*To John Addison, Aug. 9, 1850.* Hertz II, 604.

See GENERAL LAND OFFICE, Butterfield not entitled to.

General Welfare—*See* SLAVERY, general welfare impaired by.

See AFRICAN SLAVE TRADE, revival of, resisted.

Generals, good and bad—*See* RESPONSIBILITY, must center somewhere, 1.

Generals, quarreling—We had the enemy in the hollow of our hands on Friday; if our generals, who were vexed with Pope, had done their duty; all of our present difficulties and reverses have been brought upon us by these quarrels of the generals.—*To Sec. Welles, Sept. 8, 1862.* Welles I, 116.

Genius, ambition and, dangerous combination—*See* AMBITION, driving power of, 3.

Genius of Discord—*See* MISSOURI COMPROMISE, sacrificed by Genius of Discord.

Georgia, "right of, to buy slaves in Africa"—*See* AFRICAN SLAVE TRADE, slavery extension akin to, 9, 14.

Georgia, urged to accept emancipation—*See* EMANCIPATION, Georgians urged to accept.

Georgia, "well-known costume" of—If that's the plan, they should begin at the foundation, and adopt the well-known Georgia costume of a shirt and a pair of spurs.—*Speech, Hartford, Conn., March 5, 1860.* V, 337.

German Revolution, sympathy for—*See* REVOLUTION, American sympathy for.

Germans, attitude of, toward Fillmore—*See* CAMPAIGN OF 1856, plan to save Illinois.

Germans, Douglas and the Declaration—*See* EQUALITY, Douglas's interpretation of the Declaration, 2, 5, 7.

Germans, "true and patriotic"—The Germans are true and patriotic, and so far as they get cross in Missouri it is upon mistake and misunderstanding.—*To Gen. Halleck, Jan. 15, 1862.* VII, 85.

Germans, "what about?"—What about Carl Schurz [for a diplomatic appointment], or, in other words, what about our German friends?—*To Sec. Seward, March 18, 1861.* VI, 224.

Gettysburg, Army of the Potomac thanked for—*See* ARMY OF POTOMAC, praised for Gettysburg.

Gettysburg, full advantage of victory sacrificed—I left the telegraph office a good deal dissatisfied. You know I did not like the phrase—in Orders, No. 68, I believe—"Drive the invaders from our soil." [This and other facts] all appear to me to be connected with a purpose to cover Baltimore and Washington, and to get the enemy across the river without further collision, and they do not appear connected with a purpose to prevent his crossing and to destroy him.—*To Gen. Halleck, July 6, 1863.* IX, 18.

2.—I have been oppressed nearly ever since the battle of Gettysburg by what appeared to be evidences that

yourself, Gen. Couch and Gen. Smith were not seeking a collision with the enemy but were trying to get him across the river without another battle. . . . You fought and beat the enemy at Gettysburg and, of course, to say the least, his loss was as great as yours. He retreated, and you did not, as it seemed to me, pressingly pursue him; but a flood in the river detained him till, by slow degrees, you were again upon him. . . . You stood and let the flood run down, bridges be built, and the enemy move away at his leisure without attacking him. . . . I do not believe you appreciate the magnitude of the misfortune involved in Lee's escape. He was within your easy grasp, and to have closed upon him would, in connection with our other late successes, have ended the war. As it is, the war will be prolonged indefinitely.—*To Gen. Meade, July 14, 1863 (not signed or sent).* IX, 28.

3.—We had them [Lee's army] within our grasp. We had only to stretch forth our hands and they were ours. And nothing I could say or do could make the [Union] army move.—*To John Hay, July 14, 1863.* Hay, 67.

4.—And that, my God, is the last of this Army of the Potomac! There is bad faith somewhere. Meade has been pressed and urged, but only one of his generals was for an immediate attack, was ready to pounce on Lee; the rest held back. What does it mean, Mr. Welles? Great God, what does it mean?—*To Sec. Welles, July 14, 1863.* Welles, I, 370.

5.—Your golden opportunity is gone, and I am distressed immeasurably because of it.—*To Gen. Meade, July 14, 1863 (not sent).* IX, 30.

6.—I would give much to be relieved of the impression that Meade, Couch, Smith, and all since the battle of Gettysburg, have striven only to get Lee over the river without another fight.—*To Simon Cameron, July 15, 1863.* IX, 31.

7.—He [Meade] has committed a terrible mistake, but we will try him further.—*To Sec. Welles, July 17, 1863.* Welles I, 374.

8.—Our army held the war in the hollow of their hand and they would not close it. We had gone through all the labor of tilling and planting an enormous crop and when it was ripe we did not harvest it.—*To John Hay, July 19, 1863.* Hay, 69.

9.—I was deeply mortified by the escape of Lee across the Potomac, because the substantial destruction of his army would have ended the war, and because I believed such destruction was perfectly easy—believed that Gen. Meade and his noble army had expended all the skill, and toil, and blood, up to the ripe harvest, and then let the crop go to waste.—*To Gen. Howard, July 21, 1863.* IX, 39.

10.—Well, to be candid, I have no faith that Meade

will attack Lee; nothing looks like it to me. I believe he can never have another as good opportunity as that which he trifled away. Everything since has dragged with him. No, I don't believe he is going to fight.—*To Sec. Welles, July 26, 1863.* Welles I, 383.
11.—True, I desired Meade to pursue Lee across the Potomac, hoping, as has proved true, that he would thereby clear the Baltimore & Ohio Railroad, and get some advantage by harassing him on his retreat.— *To Gen. Halleck, July 29, 1863.* IX, 47.

Gettysburg, Lincoln's prayer for—Well, I will tell you how it was. In the pinch of the campaign up there [at Gettysburg] when everybody seemed panic-stricken and nobody could tell what was going to happen, oppressed by the gravity of our affairs, I went to my room one day and locked the door and got down on my knees before Almighty God and prayed to Him mightily for victory at Gettysburg. I told Him that this war was His war, and our cause His cause, but we could not stand another Fredericksburg or Chancellorsville. . . . And after that, I don't know how it was, and I cannot explain it, but soon a sweet comfort crept into my soul. The feeling came that God had taken the whole business into His own hands and that things would go right at Gettysburg and that is why I had no fears about you.—*To Gen. Daniel E. Sickles, July 5, 1863.* Hill, 339.

Gettysburg, Meade's opportunity—We have certain information that Vicksburg surrendered to Gen. Grant on the fourth of July. Now if Gen. Meade can complete his work, so gloriously prosecuted this far, by the literal or substantial destruction of Lee's army, the rebellion will be over.—*To Gen. Halleck, July 7, 1863.* IX, 22.
2.—I am more than satisfied with what has happened north of the Potomac so far, and am anxious and hopeful for what is to come.—*To J. K. Dubois, July 11, 1863.* IX, 25.

See GETTYSBURG, full advantage of victory sacrificed.

Gettysburg Address, manuscript of, given for soldiers' benefit—I send herewith the manuscript of my remarks at Gettysburg, which, with my note to you of Nov. 20th, you are at liberty to use for the benefit of our soldiers, as you have requested.—*To Edward Everett, Feb. 4, 1864.* R.T.L.

Gettysburg Address, "not entirely a failure"—In our respective parts yesterday [at the Gettysburg dedication], you could not have been excused to make a short address, nor I a long one. I am pleased to know that, in your judgment, the little I did say was not

entirely a failure.—*To Edward Everett, Nov. 20, 1863.* IX, 210.

Gettysburg Battlefield, dedication of—We have come to dedicate a portion of that field [of Gettysburg] as a final resting place for those who here gave their lives that that nation might live. It is altogether fitting and proper that we should do this. But in a larger sense, we cannot dedicate—we cannot consecrate—we cannot hallow—this ground. The brave men, living and dead, who struggled here have consecrated it far above our poor power to add or detract. The world will little note nor long remember what we say here, but it can never forget what they did here.—*Gettysburg Address, Nov. 19, 1863.* IX, 209.

Giddings, Joshua R.—*See* OHIO, famous for cheese.

Ginger Bread, Hoosier and—*See* LINCOLN, ABRAHAM, personal traits and reactions, 8.

Glory, field of, harvested—This field of glory [establishment of the Republic] has been harvested, and the crop is already appropriated. But new reapers will arise, and they will seek a field.—*Speech, Springfield, Jan. 27, 1837.* I, 46.

Goats, Tad Lincoln's—Tell Dear Tad poor "Nanny Goat" is lost, and Mrs. Cuthbert and I are in distress about it. The day you left, Nanny was found resting herself and chewing her little cud on the middle of Tad's bed; but now she's gone.—*To Mrs. Lincoln, Aug. 8, 1863.* IX, 61.
2.—Tell Tad the goats and father are very well, especially the goats.—*To Mrs. Lincoln, April 28, 1864.* XI, 89.
3.—All well, including Tad's pony and the goats.— *To Mrs. Lincoln, Sept. 8, 1864.* X, 219.

Gold, affected by cotton escaping through blockade— We cannot give up the blockade, and hence it becomes immensely important to us to get the cotton away from him [the enemy]. Better give him guns for it than let him, as now, get both guns and ammunition for it. But even this only presents part of the public interest to get out cotton. Our finances are greatly involved in the matter. The way cotton goes now [through the blockade] carries so much gold out of the country as to leave us paper currency only, and that so far depreciated as that for every hard dollar's worth of supplies we obtain, we contract to pay two and a half hard dollars hereafter. This is much to be regretted; and, while I believe we can live through it, at all events it demands an earnest effort on the part of all to correct it.—*To Gen. Canby, Dec. 12, 1864.* X, 313.

Gold, men better than—Gold is good in its place, but living, brave, patriotic men are better than gold.—*Response to serenade, Nov. 10, 1864.* X, 264.

Goldsborough, Louis M., appreciation of—I avail myself of the occasion to thank you for your courtesy and all your conduct, so far as known to me, during my brief visit here [at Fort Monroe, Va.]—*To Flag Officer Goldsborough, May 10, 1862.* VII, 158.

Goldsborough, Louis M., Congress asked to thank—I cordially recommend that Louis M. Goldsborough receive a vote of thanks of Congress for his services and gallantry displayed in the combined attack of the forces commanded by him and Brig. Gen. Burnside in the capture of Roanoke Island and the destruction of rebel gunboats on the 7th, 8th and 10th of February, 1862.—*Message to Congress, Feb. 15, 1862.* VII, 105.

Good, greatest, to greatest number—I hold that while man exists it is his duty to improve not only his own condition, but to assist in ameliorating mankind. . . . I am for those means which will give the greatest good to the greatest number.—*Speech to Germans, Cincinnati, Feb. 12, 1861.* VI, 120.

Good and Evil, balance of—The true rule, in determining to embrace or reject anything, is not whether it have any evil in it, but whether it have more of evil than of good. There are few things wholly evil or wholly good. Almost everything, especially of government policy, is an inseparable compound of the two; so that our best judgment of the preponderance between them is continually demanded. . . . Why, as to [internal] improvements, magnify the evil and stoutly refuse to see any good in them?—*Speech in Congress, July 20, 1848.* II, 37.

See TEXAS, Abolitionist reasoning relative to.

Good and Evil, God's prohibition—God did not place good and evil before man, telling him to make his choice [as declared by Douglas]. On the contrary, He did tell him there was one tree of the fruit of which he should not eat, upon pain of certain death. I should scarcely wish so strong a prohibition against slavery in Nebraska.—*Speech, Peoria, Oct. 16, 1854.* II, 253.

Good Neighborhood Policy, outlined—The United States have no enmities, animosities, or rivalries, and no interests which conflict with the welfare, safety, and rights or interests of any other nation. Their own prosperity, happiness, and aggrandizement are sought most safely and advantageously through the preservation not only of peace on their own part, but peace among all other nations. But while the United States

are thus friends to all other nations, they do not seek to conceal the fact that they cherish especial sentiments of friendship for, and sympathies with, those who, like themselves have founded their institutions on the principles of the equal rights of men; and such nations being more prominently neighbors of the United States, the latter are co-operating with them in establishing civilization and culture on the American continent.—*To Peruvian minister, March 4, 1862.* Lapsley V, 438.

See LATIN-AMERICA, Salvador and the good-neighborhood policy.

Government, bulwark of—. . . the strongest bulwark of any government, and particularly of those constituted like ours . . . I mean the attachment of the people.—*Speech, Springfield, Jan. 27, 1837.* I, 41.

Government, first purpose of—*See* SELF-GOVERNMENT, can it survive? 4.

Government, if men were just—If all men were just, there still would be some, though not so much, need of government.—*Fragment, July 1, 1854.* R.T.L.

See GOVERNMENT, Why have?

Government, no interference by—In all that the people can individually do as well for themselves, government ought not to interfere.—*Fragment, July 1, 1854.* II, 187.

Government, purposes of—*See* GOVERNMENT, Why have?

Government, responsibility in face of wrongs—*See* WRONGS, government responsibility in regard to.

Government, sometimes oppressive—The best framed and best administered governments are necessarily expensive; while by errors in frame and maladministration most of them are more onerous than they need be, and some of them very oppressive.—*Fragment, July 1, 1854.* II, 182.

Government, why have?—Why . . . should we have government? Why not each individual take to himself the whole fruit of his labor, without having any of it taxed away, in services, corn or money? Why not take just so much land as he can cultivate with his own hands, without buying it of anyone? The legitimate object of government is "to do for the people what needs to be done, but which they cannot, by individual effort, do at all, or do so well, for themselves." There are many such things—some of them exist independently of the injustice in the world. Making and maintaining roads, bridges and the like; providing for the helpless young and afflicted; common schools; and disposing of deceased men's property, are instances. But a far larger class of objects springs from the injustice of men. If one people will make war upon another, it is a necessity with that other to unite and cooperate for defence. Hence the military department. If some men will kill, or beat, or constrain others, or despoil them of property, by force, fraud, or noncompliance with contracts, it is a common object with peaceful and just men to prevent it. Hence the criminal and civil departments.—*Fragment, July 1, 1854.* II, 182.

2.—The desirable things which the individuals of a people cannot do, or cannot well do, for themselves [thus requiring government] fall into two classes: Those which have relation to wrongs, and those which have not. . . . The first—that in relation to wrongs —embraces all crimes, misdemeanors, and non-performance of contracts. The other embraces all which, in its nature, and without wrong, requires combined action, as public roads and highways, public schools, charities, pauperism, orphanage, estates of the deceased, and the machinery of government itself.—*Fragment, July 1, 1854.* II, 187.

Government (American), administration and—Let the friends of the government first save the government, and then administer it to their liking.—*To Henry Winter Davis, March 18, 1863.* VIII, 229.

2.—The government is to be supported though the administration may not in every case wisely act.—*Reply to Presbyterian General Assembly, May 30, 1863.* VIII, 288.

3.—The constitutional administration of our government must be sustained, and I beg of you not to allow your minds or your hearts to be diverted from the support of all necessary measures for that purpose, by any miserable picayune arguments addressed to your pockets, or inflammatory appeals made to passions and prejudices.—*Speech to 148th Ohio regiment, Aug. 31, 1864.* X, 208.

4.—It is vain and foolish to arraign this man or that for the part he has taken or has not taken, and to hold the government responsible for his acts. In no administration can there be perfect equality of action and uniform satisfaction rendered by all.—*Speech to 148th Ohio regiment, Aug. 31, 1864.* X, 209.

5.—I had inferred that you were of that portion of my countrymen who think that the best interests of the nation are to be subserved by the support of the present administration. I do not pretend to say that you, who think so, embrace all the patriotism and loyalty of the country, but I do believe, and I trust without personal interest, that the welfare of the

country does require that such support and indorsement should be given.—*Response to serenade, Nov. 9, 1864.* X, 261.

Government (American), alienation of affections from—*See* LAW, respect for, 2.

Government (American), based on equal rights—Most governments have been based, practically, on the denial of the equal rights of men . . . ours began by affirming those rights. They said, some men are too ignorant and vicious to share in government. Possibly so, said we; and, by your system, you would always keep them ignorant and vicious. We proposed to give all a chance; and we expected the weak to grow stronger, the ignorant wiser and all better and happier together. We made the experiment, and the fruit is before us. . . . Look at it in its aggregate grandeur.—*Fragment, July 1, 1854.* II, 184.

2.—Judge Douglas remarked [in speech at Springfield] that he had always considered this government was made for the white people and not for the negroes. Why, in point of mere fact, I think so too.—*Speech, Peoria, Oct. 16, 1854.* II, 259.

3.—He [Douglas] avows that the Union was made by white men and for white men and their descendants. As matter of fact, the first branch of the proposition is historically true; the government was made by white men, and they were and are the superior race. This I admit. But the cornerstone of the government, so to speak, was the declaration that "all men are created equal," and are entitled to "life, liberty, and the pursuit of happiness."—*Speech, Bloomington, May 29, 1856.* Lapsley II, 254.

Government (American), best—It is said that we have the best government the world ever knew, and I am glad to meet you, the supporters of that government. —*Speech to 189th New York regiment, Oct. 24, 1864.* X, 252.

Government (American), change of form threatened —*See* LIBERTY, danger to, 3.

Government (American), contrasted with others—*See* GOVERNMENT (AMERICAN), based on equal rights, 1.

Government (American), dictatorship for, suggested —*See* HOOKER, JOSEPH, talk of dictatorship challenged.

Government (American), division of interest between general, and state—*See* STATES, national power and.

Government (American), great principle of—*See* LABOR, no permanent class, 4.

Government (American), no "seizure" of—*See* GOVERNMENT (AMERICAN), preservation of, first duty, 7.

Government (American), not surprising it survived— That our government should have been maintained in its original form, from its establishment until now, is not much to be wondered at. It had many props to support it through that period, which are now decayed and crumbled away. Through that period it was felt by all to be an undecided experiment, now it is understood to be a successful one. Then all that sought celebrity and fame and distinction expected to find them in the success of that experiment. Their all was staked upon it; their destiny was inseparably linked with it. Their ambition aspired to display before an admiring world a practical demonstration of the truth which had hitherto been considered at best no better than problematical—namely, the capability of a people to govern themselves.—*Speech, Springfield, Jan. 27, 1837.* I, 45.

Government (American), people will save—*See* PEOPLE, relied on to save Union.

Government (American), permeated with disloyalty —*See* CIVIL WAR, situation at start of, 2, 3.

Government (American), preservation of, first duty— Now and ever I shall do all in my power for peace consistently with the maintenance of the government. —*To Gov. Hicks and Mayor Brown, April 20, 1861.* V, 251.

2.—He [the Executive] desires to preserve this government that it may be administered for all, as it was administered by the men who made it.—*Message to Congress, July 4, 1861.* VI, 323.

3.—I am a patient man—always willing to forgive on the Christian terms of repentence, and also to give ample time for repentence. Still, I must save this government, if possible. . . . It may as well be understood, once for all, that I shall not surrender this game, leaving any available cards unplayed.—*To Reverdy Johnson, July 26, 1862.* VII, 293.

4.—I am in no boastful mood. I shall not do more than I can, but I shall do all I can to save the government, which is my sworn duty as well as my personal inclination.—*To Cuthbert Bullitt, July 28, 1862.* VII, 298.

5.—In every case and at all hazards the government must be perpetuated.—*Reply to Presbyterian General Assembly, May 30, 1863.* VIII, 288.

6.—This government must be preserved in spite of the acts of any man or set of men. It is worthy of your every effort. Nowhere in the world is presented a government of so much liberty and equality. To the humblest and poorest amongst us are held out the highest privileges and positions.—*Speech to 148th Ohio regiment, Aug. 31, 1864.* X, 209.

7.—Something said by the secretary of state, in his recent speech at Auburn, has been construed by some into a threat that if I shall be beaten at the election, I will, between then and the end of my constitutional term, do what I may be able to ruin the government. Others regard the fact that the Chicago convention [which nominated McClellan] adjourned not *sine die,* but to meet again if called to do so by a particular individual, as the intimation of a purpose that if their nominee shall be elected he will at once seize control of the government. I hope the good people will permit themselves to suffer no uneasiness on either point. I am struggling to maintain the government, not to overthrow it. I therefore say that if I shall live I shall remain President until the 4th of next March; and that whoever shall be constitutionally elected therefor, in November, shall be duly installed as President on the 4th of March; and that, in the interval, I shall do my utmost that whoever is to hold the helm for the next voyage shall start with the best possible chance to save the ship. This is due to the people both in principle and under the Constitution. —*Response to serenade, Oct. 19, 1864.* X, 243.

See UNION, preservation of, first duty.

Government (American), should have best—I am for the government having the best articles in spite of patent controversies.—*Memorandum, March 10, 1864.* X, 35.

Government (American), successful experiment—*See* GOVERNMENT (AMERICAN), not surprising it survived.

Government (American), two points settled and one remains—*See* SELF-GOVERNMENT, Can it survive? 6.

Governors, importance of—The governors of the northern states are the North. What they decide must be carried out.—*To N. F. Dixon, June 28, 1862.* Hertz II, 870.

Granada, "must be friends"—Your country contains one of the principal highways of commerce and intercourse between the Atlantic and Pacific states of this Union. The people of the two countries cannot, therefore, be strangers to each other; they must be friends, and in some measure allies. It shall be no fault of mine, if they ever cease to be such.—*To Granadan minister, June 4, 1861.* Hertz II, 836.

"Grandson of Milliken's Bend"—The writer of the accompanying letter is one of Mrs. Lincoln's numerous cousins. He is a grandson of Milliken's Bend, near Vicksburg—that is, a grandson of the man who gave name to Milliken's Bend—*To Sec. Chase, Oct. 26, 1863.* IX, 183.

Granger, Gordon—*See* FARRAGUT, David G., thanked for victories.

Grant, U. S., advice to—Hold on with a bull-dog grip and chew and choke as much as possible.—*To Gen. Grant, Aug. 17, 1864. X, 193.*

Grant, U. S., appreciation of—I congratulate you and all concerned in your recent battles and victories. How does it all sum up?—*To Gen. Grant. Oct. 8, 1862. VIII, 55.*

2.—I can't spare this man—he fights!—*To A. K. McClure, 1862. War Years, I, 478.*

3.—Whether Gen. Grant shall or shall not consummate the capture of Vicksburg, his campaign from the beginning of the month up to the 22nd day of it is one of the most brilliant in the world.—*To Isaac N. Arnold, May 26, 1863. Tracy, 225.*

4.—I do not remember that you and I have ever met personally. I write this now as a grateful acknowledgment for the most inestimable service you have done the country.—*To Gen. Grant, July 13, 1863. IX, 26.*

5.—Gen. Grant is a copious worker and fighter, but a very meager writer or telegrapher.—*To Gen. Burnside, July 27, 1863. IX, 45.*

6.—Well done! Many thanks to all.—*To Gen. Grant, Nov. 25, 1863. IX, 214.*

7.—I wish to tender you, and all under your command, my more than thanks, my profoundest gratitude, for the skill, courage and perseverance with which you and they, over so great difficulties, have effected that important object [occupation of Chattanooga and Knoxville]. God bless you all!—*To Gen. Grant. Dec. 8, 1863. IX, 253.*

8.—True, these troops are, in strict law, only to be removed by my order; but Gen. Grant's judgment would be the highest incentive to me to make such an order.—*To Gov. Bramlette, Jan. 6, 1864. IX, 278.*

9.—The nation's appreciation of what you have done, and its reliance upon you for what remains to do, in the existing great struggle, are now presented with this commission constituting you lieutenant-general of the Army of the United States. With this high honor devolves upon you also a corresponding responsibility. As the country herein trusts you, so, under God, it will sustain you. I scarcely need add, that with what I here speak for the nation goes my own hearty personal concurrence.—*To Gen. Grant, March 9, 1864. X, 33.*

10.—You are vigilant and self-reliant; and, pleased with this, I wish not to obtrude any constraints upon you. . . . And now, with a brave army and a just cause, may God sustain you.—*To Gen. Grant, April 30, 1864. X, 90.*

11.—I believe, I know—and am specially grateful to know—that Gen. Grant has not been jostled in his purposes, that he has made all his points, and today he is on his line as he purposed before he moved his armies. I will volunteer to say that I am very glad at what has happened, but there is a great deal still to be done.—*Response to serenade, May 9, 1864. X, 95.*

12.—I commend you to keep yourselves in the same tranquil mood that is characteristic of that brave and loyal man [Grant].—*Response to serenade, May 9, 1864. X, 96.*

13.—It is the dogged pertinacity of Grant that wins. —*To John Hay, May 9, 1864. Hay, 180.*

14.—My previous high estimate of Gen. Grant has been maintained and heightened by what has occurred in the remarkable campaign he is now conducting, while the magnitude and difficulty of the task before him do not prove less than I expected. He and his brave soldiers are in the midst of their great trial.—*To F. A. Conkling, June 3, 1864. X, 112.*

15.—I begin to see it; you will succeed. God bless you all.—*To Gen. Grant, June 15, 1864. X, 126.*

16.—If Grant could be more useful in putting down the rebellion as President, I would be content. He is pledged to our policy of emancipation, and the employment of negro soldiers; and if this policy is carried out, it won't make much difference who is President.—*To friend, 1864. History and Overthrow, 501.*

17.—I wish you to be judge and master on these points.—*To Gen. Grant, Feb. 7, 1865. XI, 5.*

18.—Please accept for yourself and all under your command the renewed expression of my gratitude for your and their arduous and well-performed public service.—*To Gen. Grant, March 7, 1865. XI, 48.*

19.—Allow me to tender to you and all with you the nation's grateful thanks for this additional and magnificent success.—*To Gen. Grant, April 2, 1865. Lapsley II, 351.*

20.—To Gen. Grant, his skillful officers and brave men, all belongs.—*Last public address, April 11, 1865. XI, 84.*

Grant, U. S., explanation to—I send this as an explanation to you, and to do justice to the secretary of war. I was induced, upon pressing application, to authorize the agents of one of the districts of Pennsylvania to recruit in one of the prison depots in Illinois; and the thing went so far before it came to the knowledge of the secretary that, in my judgment, it could not be abandoned without greater evil than would follow its going through. I did not know at that time that you had protested against that class of thing being done; and I now say that while this particular job must be completed, no other of the sort will be authorized, without an understanding with you, if at all. The secretary of war is wholly free from any part of this blunder.—*To Gen. Grant, Sept. 22, 1864.* X, 228.

Grant, U. S., no interference with—Let nothing which is transpiring change, hinder or delay your military movements or plans.—*To Gen. Grant, Feb. 1, 1865.* X, 354.

2.—I do not wish to modify anything I have heretofore said as to your having entire control whether anything in the way of trade shall pass either way through your lines.—*To Gen. Grant, March 13, 1865.* Angle, 372.

3.—Nothing that I have done, or probably shall do, is to delay, hinder, or interfere with your work.—*To Gen. Grant, April 6, 1865.* XI, 74.

Grant, U. S., vigilance urged on—It will never be done nor attempted, unless you watch it every day and hour, and force it.—*To Gen. Grant, Aug. 3, 1864.* X, 180.

2.—Gen. Sheridan says "if the thing is pressed, I think that Lee will surrender." Let the thing be pressed.—*To Gen. Grant, April 7, 1865.* XI, 77.

Grass, every blade a study—Every blade of grass is a study; and to produce two where there was but one is both a profit and a pleasure.—*Speech, Milwaukee, Sept. 30, 1859.* V, 253.

Grass, no, in streets—[William E. Dodge said to the President: "It is for you, sir, to say whether the whole nation shall be plunged into bankruptcy, whether the grass shall grow in the streets of our commercial cities."] If it depends upon me, the grass will not grow anywhere except in the fields and meadows.—*To Mr. Dodge, Feb. 27, 1861.* Foner, 273.

Gratitude, country's, to men who serve—But he [Zachary Taylor] is gone. The conqueror at last is conquered. The fruits of his labors, his name, his memory and example, are all that is left us—his example, verifying the great truth that "he that humbleth himself shall be exalted"; teaching us that to serve one's country with a singleness of purpose, gives assurance of that country's gratitude, secures its best honors, and makes "a dying bed soft as downy pillows are."—*Speech, Chicago, July 25, 1850.* Angle, 75.

Gratitude, testimony to—I have just heard of your deep affliction, and the arrest of your son for murder. I can hardly believe he can be capable of the crime alleged against him. It does not seem possible. I am anxious that he should be given a fair trial at any rate; and gratitude for your long-continued kindness

to me in adverse circumstances prompts me to offer my humble services gratuitously in his behalf. It will afford me an opportunity to requite, in a small degree, the favors I received at your hand, and that of your lamented husband, when your roof afforded me a grateful shelter, without money and without price.—*To Mrs. Hannah Armstrong, Sept. 1857.* Tracy, 79.

Great Britain, blamed for slavery—They [the fathers] found the institution existing among us, which they could not help, and they cast blame on the British king for having permitted its introduction.—*Speech, Peoria, Oct. 16, 1854.* II, 244.

2.—Our forefathers . . . declared, as we have done in later years, the blame [for the existence of slavery in America] rested on the mother government of Great Britain. We constantly condemn Great Britain for not preventing slavery from coming amongst us. She would not interfere to prevent it, and so individuals were enabled to introduce the institution without opposition. I have alluded to this, to ask if this is not exactly the policy of Buchanan and his friends, to place this government in the attitude then occupied by the government of Great Britain—placing the nation in position to authorize the territories to reproach it, for refusing to allow them to hold slaves.—*Speech, Kalamazoo, Mich., Aug. 27, 1856.* Stern, 401.

See SLAVERY, American colonies and.

Great Britain, enemy of freedom—That there is nothing in the past history of the British government, or in its present expressed policy, to encourage the belief that she will aid, in any manner, in the delivery of continental Europe from the rope of despotism; and that her treatment of Ireland, of O'Brien, Mitchell, and other worthy patriots, forces the conclusion that she will join her efforts to the despots of Europe in suppressing every effort of the people to establish free governments based upon the principles of true religious and civil liberty.—*Resolutions on behalf of Hungarian freedom, Jan. 9, 1852.* Angle, 82.

Great Britain, friendship of, for America—The people of the United States are kindred of the people of Great Britain. With all our distant national interests, objects and aspirations, we are conscious that our moral strength is largely derived from that relationship, and we think we do not deceive ourselves when we suppose that by constantly cherishing cordial friendship and sympathy with the other branches of the family to which we belong, we impart to them not less strength than we receive from the same connection. Accidents, however, incidental to all states, and passions, common to all nations, often tend to disturb the harmony so necessary and proper, and to convert them into enemies. It was reserved for Your Majesty in sending your son, the heir apparent of the British throne, on a visit among us, to inaugurate a policy destined to counteract these injurious tendencies, as it has been Your Majesty's manifest endeavor through a reign already of considerable length and of distinguished success, to cultivate the friendship on our part so earnestly desired. It is for this reason you are honored on this side of the Atlantic as a friend of the American people.—*To Queen Victoria, Feb. 1, 1862.* Hertz II, 849.

2.—I hail this interchange of sentiment [between workers of Manchester, and the American President] as an augury that whatever else may happen, whatever misfortune may befall your country or my own, the peace and friendship which now exist between the two nations will be, as it shall be my desire to make them, perpetual.—*To workers of Manchester, Jan. 19, 1863.* VIII, 195.

3.—Great Britain and the United States, by the extended and varied forms of commerce between them, the contiguity of positions of their possessions, and the similarity of their language and laws, are drawn into constant and intimate intercourse. At the same time they are from the same causes exposed to frequent occasions of misunderstanding, only to be averted by mutual forbearance. So eagerly are the people of the two countries engaged throughout almost the whole world in the pursuit of similar commercial enterprises, accompanied by natural rivalries and jealousies, that at first sight it would almost seem that the two governments must be enemies or at best, cold calculating friends. So devoted are the two nations throughout all their domain, and even in their remote territorial and colonial possessions, to the principles of civil rights and constitutional liberty, that, on the other hand, the superficial observer might erroneously count upon a continued concert of action and sympathy, amounting to an alliance between them. Each is charged with the development of the progress and liberty of a considerable portion of the human race. Each in its sphere is subject to difficulties and trials, not participated in by the other. The interest of civilization and of humanity require that the two should be friends. I have always known and accepted as a fact, honorable to both countries, that the queen of England is a sincere and honest well-wisher to the United States. I have been equally frank and explicit in the opinion that the friendship of the United States toward Great Britain is enjoined by all the considerations of interest and senti-

ment affecting the character of both.*—To Sir Frederick Bruce, British representative at Washington, April 14, 1865.* Hertz II, 969.

"Great Cry and Little Wool"—It was his Satanic majesty, clipping the hog, that founded the old proverb, "Great cry and little wool"; but the war demand should make your sheep farmers very happy and patriotic.—*To J. B. Grinnell (no date).* War Years II, 51.

Great Lakes, fortification of, suggested—I . . . ask the attention of Congress to our great lakes and rivers. I believe that some fortifications and depots of arms and munitions, with harbor navigation improvements, all at well-selected points upon these, would be of great importance to the national defense and preservation.—*First annual message, Dec. 3, 1861.* VII, 30.

2.—In view of the insecurity of life and property in the region adjacent to the Canadian border, by recent assaults and depredations committed by inimical and desperate persons who are harbored there, it has been thought proper to give notice that after the expiration of six months, the period conditionally stipulated in the existing arrangement with Great Britain, the United States must hold themselves at liberty to increase their naval armament upon the lakes if they shall find that proceeding necessary. The condition of the border will necessarily come into consideration in connection with the question of continuing or modifying the rights of transit from Canada through the United States, as well as the regulation of imports, which were temporarily established by the reciprocity treaty of the 5th of June, 1854. I desire, however, to be understood while making this statement that the colonial authorities of Canada are not deemed to be intentionally unjust or unfriendly toward the United States, but, on the contrary, there is every reason to expect that, with the approval of the Imperial Government, they will take the necessary measures to prevent new excursions across the border.—*Fourth annual message, Dec. 6, 1864.* X, 289.

"Great Sores, Small Plasters"—*See* SLAVERY, why issue is not settled, 3.

Greatest Good to the Greatest Number—I hold that while man exists it is his duty to improve not only his own condition, but to assist in ameliorating mankind; and, therefore, without entering upon the details of the question, I will simply say that I am for those means which will give the greatest good to the great-

---

* Written a few hours before the assassination and read some days later by a secretary.

est number.—*Speech to Germans, Cincinnati, Feb. 12, 1861.* VI, 120.

Greece, Clay's efforts for—*See* CLAY, HENRY, devotion of, to liberty.

Greeley, Horace, appreciation of—I do not know how you estimate [Horace] Greeley, but I consider him incapable of corruption or falsehood. He denies that he directly is taking part in favor of Douglas, and I believe him. Still his feeling constantly manifests itself in his paper, which, being so extensively read in Illinois, is, and will continue to be, a drag upon us.—*To Charles L. Wilson, June 1, 1858.* II, 363.
2.—I do not charge that G[reeley] was corrupt in this [talking with Douglas and then urging his re-election to the Senate]. I do not think he was, or is.—*To William Kellogg, Dec. 11, 1859.* Angle, 237.
3.—I need not tell you that I have the highest confidence in Mr. [Horace] Greeley. He is a great power. Having him firmly behind me will be as helpful to me as an army of one hundred thousand men. That he has ever kicked the traces has been owing to his not being fully informed. . . . If he ever objects to my policy, I shall be glad to have him state to me his views frankly and fully. I shall adopt his if I can. If I cannot, I will at least tell him why. He and I should stand together, and let no minor differences come between us; for we both seek one end, which is the saving of our country.—*To Gov. Walker, Nov. 21, 1861.* XI, 121.
4.—This is a longer letter than I have written in a month—longer than I would have written for any other man than Horace Greeley.—*To Gov. Walker, Nov. 21, 1861.* XI, 122.

Greeley, Horace, correspondence censored—The parts of your letters I wish suppressed are only those which, as I think, give too gloomy an aspect to our cause, and those which present the carrying of elections as a motive of action. I have, as you see, drawn a red pencil over the parts I wish suppressed.—*To Horace Greeley, Aug. 9, 1864.* X, 184.
2.—I have proposed to Mr. Greeley that the Niagara correspondence be published, suppressing only the parts of his letters over which the red pencil is drawn in the copy which I herewith send. He declines giving his consent to the publication of his letters unless these parts be published with the rest. I have concluded it is better for me to submit for the time to the consequence of the false position in which I consider he has placed me than to subject the country to the consequences of publishing their discouraging and injurious parts.—*To Henry J. Raymond, Aug. 15, 1864.* X, 191.

Greeley, Horace, favors Douglas over Lincoln for Senate—*See* CAMPAIGN OF 1858, some Republicans favor, 2.

Greeley, Horace, critic—*See* NEGRO, cannot prevent auction of, back to slavery.

Greeley, Horace, interview with Douglas—I have been a good deal relieved this morning by a sight of [Horace] Greeley's letter to you published in the *Tribune.* Before seeing it, I much feared you had, in charging interviews between Douglas & Greeley, stated what you believed, but did not certainly know, to be true; and that it might be untrue, and our enemies would get an advantage of you. However, as G. admits the interviews, I think it will not hurt you that he denies conversing with D. about his re-election to the Senate. G., I think, will not tell a falsehood; and I think he will scarcely deny that he had the interview with D. in order to assure himself from D.'s own lips, better than he could from his public acts and declarations, whether to try to bring the Republican party to his support generally, including his re-election to the Senate. What else could the interviews be for? Why immediately followed in the *Tribune* the advice that all anti-Lecompton Democrats should be re-elected? The world will not consider it anything that D's re-election to the Senate was not specifically talked of by him and G. Now, Wash, I do not charge that G. was corrupt in this. I do not think he was, or is. It was his judgment that the course he took was the best way of serving the Republican cause.—*To William Kellogg, Dec. 11, 1859.* Angle, 237.

Greeley, Horace, letter to, on Lincoln's "paramount object"—*See* UNION, policy in saving, 5.

Greeley, Horace, "old shoe"—[The President said that Greeley is an old shoe—good for nothing now, whatever he had been.] In early life, and with few mechanics and but little means in the west, we used to make our shoes last a great while with much mending, and sometimes when far gone, we found the leather so rotten the stitches would not hold. Greeley is so rotten that nothing can be done with him. He is not truthful; the stitches all tear out.—*To members of cabinet, Aug. 19, 1864.* Welles II, 111.

Greeley, Horace, proposed as mouthpiece—I have thought over the interview which Mr. Gilmore has had with Mr. Greeley, and the proposal that Greeley has made to Gilmore, namely that he—Gilmore—shall communicate to him—Greeley—all that he learns from you of the inner workings of the administration, in return for which his—Greeley's—giving such aid as he can to the new administration, and allowing you

—Walker—from time to time the use of his—Greeley's—columns when it is desirable to feel of, or forestall, public opinion on important subjects. The arrangement meets my unqualified approval. . . . But all this must be on the express and implicit understanding that the fact of these communications coming from me shall be absolutely confidential—not to be disclosed by Greeley to his nearest friend, or any of his subordinates. He will be, in effect, my mouthpiece, but I shall not be known to be the speaker.—*To Gov. Walker, Nov. 21, 1861.* XI, 120.

Greeley, Horace, "unprecedented agreement"—*See* WEED, THURLOW, unprecedented agreement.

Greeley, Horace, will not help, to Senate—A certain gentleman in your state [is] claiming . . . to be authorized to use my name to advance the chances of Mr. Greeley for an election to the United States Senate. It is very strange that such things should be said by anyone. The gentleman . . . did speak to me of Mr. Greeley in connection with the senatorial election, and I replied in terms of kindness toward Mr. Greeley, which I really feel, but always with an expressed protest that my name must not be used in the senatorial election in favor of, or against, anyone. Any other representation of me is a misrepresentation.—*To Thurlow Weed, Feb. 4, 1861.* VI, 104.

Greenbacks, origin of—*See* BANKING AND CURRENCY, greenbacks' origin.

Grimsley, Elizabeth Todd, suggested appointment of, "troubles me"—Cousin Lizzie shows me your letter of the 27th. The question of giving her the Springfied post office troubles me. You see I have already appointed William Jayne a territorial governor and Judge Trumbull's brother to a land office. Will it do for me to go on and justify the declaration that Trumbull and I have divided all the offices among our relatives? . . . I see by the papers, a vote is to be taken as to the post office. Could you not set up Lizzie and beat them all? She, being here [in Washington], need know nothing of it, so therefore there would be no indelicacy on her part.—*To John T. Stuart, March 30, 1861.* VI, 231.

Grizzly Bear, preaching Christianity to—*See* DOUGLAS, STEPHEN A., Jefferson and Jackson.

Guinea, seeing through—*See* SLAVERY, profit motive in, 9.

Gulf States, would suffer if slavery is retained—*See* SLAVERY, Gulf States would suffer.

Habeas Corpus, "cover for insurgents"—Or if, as has happened, the executive should suspend the writ

without ruinous waste of time, instances of arresting innocent persons might occur, as are always likely to occur in such cases; and then a clamor could be raised in regard to this, which might be at least some service to the insurgent cause. It needed no very keen perception to discover this part of the enemy's program; so soon as by open hostilities their machinery was fairly put in motion.—*To Erastus Corning and others, June 12, 1863.* VIII, 302.

Habeas Corpus, little value in, if curtailed—*See* CONFEDERATE GENERALS, might have been arrested.

Habeas Corpus, not jeopardized by military arrests—*See* WAR POWER, use of, defended, 8.

Habeas Corpus, suspended—Be it ordered that the writ of *habeas corpus* is suspended in respect to all persons arrested, or who are now, or hereafter during the rebellion shall be, imprisoned in any fort, camp, arsenal, military prison or other place of confinement by any military authority or by the sentence of any court-martial or military commission.—*Proclamation, Sept. 24, 1862.* VIII, 42.

2.—I . . . proclaim and make known to all whom it may concern that the privilege of the writ of *habeas corpus* is suspended throughout the United States in the several cases before mentioned [persons held under the command or in custody of military, naval or civil officers of the United States, "either as prisoners of war, spies, or aiders or abettors of the enemy, or officers or soldiers or seamen enrolled or drafted or mustered or enlisted in or belonging to the land or naval forces of the United States, or as deserters therefrom, or otherwise amenable to military law or the rules or regulations prescribed for the military or naval services . . . or for resisting a draft or for any other offense against the military or naval service"] and that this suspension will continue throughout the duration of the said rebellion or until it shall be modified or revoked.—*Proclamation, Sept. 15, 1863.* IX, 122.

3.—I . . . hereby require of the military officers in the said state [Kentucky] that the privilege of the writ of *habeas corpus* be effectually suspended within the said state according to the aforesaid proclamation [of Sept. 15, 1863], and that martial law be established therein to take effect from the date of this proclamation, the said suspension and establishment of martial law to continue until this proclamation shall be revoked or modified, but not beyond the period when the said rebellion shall have been suppressed or come to an end.—*Proclamation, July 5, 1864.* X, 147.

Habeas Corpus, suspension of, conditionally ordered If at any point on or in the vicinity of any military line which is now or which shall be used between the city of Philadelphia and the city of Washington you find resistance which renders it necessary to suspend the writ of *habeas corpus* for the public safety, you personally, or through the officer in command at the point at which resistance occurs, are authorized to suspend that writ.—*To Gen. Winfield Scott, April 27, 1861*. VI, 258.

2.—I . . . direct the commander of the forces of the United States on the Florida coast . . . if he shall find it necessary, to suspend there the writ of *habeas corpus*.—*Proclamation, May 10, 1861*. VI, 271.

3.—You are engaged in suppressing an insurrection against the laws of the United States. If at any point on or in the vicinity of any military line which is now or which shall be used between the city of New York and the city of Washington you find resistance which renders it necessary to suspend the writ of *habeas corpus* for the public safety, you . . . are authorized to suspend that writ.—*To Gen. Winfield Scott, July 2, 1861*. VI, 295.

4.—The military line of the United States for the suppression of the insurrection may be extended so far as Bangor, Me. You and any officer acting under your authority are hereby authorized to suspend the writ of *habeas corpus* in any place between that place and the city of Washington.—*To Gen. Winfield Scott, Oct. 14, 1861*. VII, 8.

5.—As an insurrection exists in the United States, and is in arms in the state of Missouri, you are hereby authorized and empowered to suspend the writ of *habeas corpus* within the limits of the military division under your command, and to exercise martial law as you find it necessary in your discretion to secure the public safety and the authority of the United States.—*To Gen. Halleck, Dec. 2, 1861*. VII, 26.

6.—You or any officer you may designate will in your discretion suspend the writ of *habeas corpus* so far as may relate to Major Chase . . . now alleged to be guilty of treasonable practices against this government.—*To Gen. McClellan, Jan. 20, 1862*. VII, 87.

See MARYLAND, legislature of, under surveillance.

Habeas Corpus, suspension of, defended—Soon after the first call for militia it was considered a duty to authorize the commanding general in proper cases, according to his discretion, to suspend the privilege of the writ of *habeas corpus*. . . . This authority has purposely been exercised but very sparingly. Nevertheless, the legality and propriety of what has been done under it are questioned, and the attention of the country has been called to the proposition that one who is sworn to "take care that the laws be faith-

fully executed" should not himself violate them. Of course some consideration was given to the questions of power and propriety before this matter was acted upon. The whole of the laws which were required to be faithfully executed were being resisted and failing of execution in nearly one-third of the states. Must they be allowed to finally fail of execution, even had it been perfectly clear that by the use of the means necessary to their execution some single law, made in such extreme tenderness of the citizen's liberty that practically it relieves more of the guilty than of the innocent, should to a very limited extent be violated?—*Message to Congress, July 4, 1861*. VI, 308.

2.—The provision of the Constitution that "the privilege of the writ of *habeas corpus* shall not be suspended unless when, in cases of rebellion or invasion, the public safety may require it" is equivalent to a provision—is a provision—that such privilege may be suspended when, in cases of rebellion or invasion, the public safety does require it. It was decided that we have a case of rebellion and that the public safety does require the qualified suspension of the privilege of the writ which was authorized to be made.—*Message to Congress, July 4, 1861*. VI, 308.

3.—Are all the laws but one to go unexecuted, and the government itself to go to pieces, lest that one be violated? Even in such a case, would not the official oath be broken, if the government should be overthrown, when it was believed that disregarding that single law would tend to preserve it? But it was not believed that this question was presented. It was not believed that any law was violated.—*Message to Congress, July 4, 1861*. VI, 309.

4.—Ours is a case of rebellion . . . in fact, a clear, flagrant, and gigantic case of rebellion; and the provision of the Constitution that "the privilege of the writ of *habeas corpus* shall not be suspended unless when, in cases of rebellion or invasion, the public may require it," is a provision which specially applies to our present case. This provision plainly attests the understanding of those who made the Constitution that ordinary courts of justice are inadequate to "cases of rebellion"—attests the purpose that, in such cases, men may be held in custody whom the courts, acting on ordinary rules, would discharge.—*To Erastus Corning and others, June 12, 1863*. Basler, 702.

5.—The provision of the Constitution that "the privilege of the writ of *habeas corpus* shall not be suspended unless when, in cases of rebellion or evasion, the public safety may require it," is the provision which specifically applies to our present case. . . . This is precisely our present case—a case of rebellion, wherein the public safety does require the suspension. . . . I think the time not unlikely to come when

I shall be blamed for having made too few arrests rather than too many.—*To Erastus Corning and others, June 12, 1863.* VIII, 304.

6.—The benefit of the writ of *habeas corpus* is the great means through which the guarantees of personal liberty are conserved and made available in the last resort. . . . But by the Constitution the benefit of the writ of *habeas corpus* itself may be suspended when in the case of rebellion or invasion, the public safety may require it.—*To M. Birchard and others, presenting resolution of Ohio Democratic state convention, June 29, 1863.* IX, 3.

7.—You [representing Ohio Democratic state convention] claim that men may, if they choose, embarrass those whose duty it is to combat a giant rebellion, and then be dealt with in turn, only as if there were no rebellion. The Constitution itself rejects this view.—*To M. Birchard and others, June 29, 1863.* IX, 4.

See CONFEDERATE GENERALS, might have been arrested.

See WAR POWER, use of, defended.

Habeas Corpus, who shall suspend?—Now it is insisted that Congress, and not the Executive, is vested with this power [to suspend the writ] but the Constitution itself is silent as to which or who is to exercise the power, and as the provision was plainly made for a dangerous emergency, it cannot be believed that the framers of the instrument intended that in every case the danger should run its course until Congress could be called together, the very assembling of which might be prevented, as was intended in this case, by the rebellion.—*Message to Congress, July 4, 1861.* VI, 310.

2.—The Constitution contemplates the question [of suspending habeas corpus] as likely to occur for decision, but it does not expressly declare who is to decide it. By necessary implication, when rebellion or invasion comes, the decision is to be made from time to time; and I think the man whom, for the time, the people have, under the Constitution, made commander-in-chief of their army and navy, is the man who holds the power and bears the responsibility of making it.—*To M. Birchard and others, June 29, 1863.* IX, 4.

Habeas Corpus, would have saved men known to be traitors—*See* CONFEDERATE GENERALS, might have been arrested.

Hahn, Michael, congratulated—*See* NEGRO SUFFRAGE, favored, 3.

"Hair's breath—*See* CAMPAIGN OF 1860, North-South fusion suggested, 3.

See CONGRESS, seeks nomination to, 7.

See MEADE, GEORGE G., appreciation of, 4.

Haiti, recognition of, urged—*See* LIBERIA, recognition of, urged.

"Half-Insane Mumblings of a Fever Dream"—*See* MEXICAN WAR, Polk's attempt to justify, 3.

"Half Slave and Half Free"—*See* "HOUSE DIVIDED AGAINST ITSELF," cannot stand.

Halleck, Henry W., appeals to—Our success or failure at Fort Donelson is vastly important, and I beg you to put your soul in the effort.—*To Gen. Halleck, Feb. 16, 1862.* VII, 106.

2.—If in such a difficulty as this you do not help, you fail me precisely in the point for which I sought your assistance. . . . Your military skill is useless to me if you do not do this.—*To Gen. Halleck, Jan. 1, 1863.* VIII, 165.

Halleck, Henry W., attack of, on postmaster general rebuffed—*See* CABINET, dismissals from, up to President alone, 1.

Halleck, Henry W., confidence in—My dear general, I feel justified to rely very much on you. I believe you, and the brave officers and men with you, can and will get the victory at Corinth.—*To Gen. Halleck, May 24, 1862.* VII, 180.

Halleck, Henry W., deference to—If you are satisfied . . . I am content. If you are not so satisfied, please look to it.—*To Gen. Halleck, July 6, 1863.* IX, 18.

2.—Halleck knows better than I what to do. He is a military man, has had military education. I brought him here to give me military advice. His views and mine are widely different. It is better that I, who am not a military man, should defer to him, rather than he to me.—*To Sec. Welles, July 14, 1863.* Welles I, 371.

Halleck, Henry W., "first-rate clerk"—I who am not a specially brave man have had to sustain the sinking courage of these professional fighters in critical times. When it was proposed to station Halleck here in general command, he insisted, to use his own language, on the appointment of a general-in-chief who should be held responsible for results. We appointed him and all went well enough until after Pope's defeat, when he broke down—nerve and pluck all gone—and has ever since evaded all possible responsibility—little more since then than a first-rate clerk.—*To John Hay, April 28, 1864.* Hay, 176.

Halleck, Henry W., tribute to—Halleck is wholly for the service. He does not care who succeeds or who fails, so the service is benefited.—*To John Hay, Aug. 30, 1862.* Hay, 45.

Halleck, Henry W., vigilance urged on—You have Fort Donelson safe, unless Grant shall be overcome from without; to prevent which latter will, I think, require all the vigilance, energy, and skill of yourself and Buell, acting in full co-operation.—*To Gen. Halleck, Feb. 16, 1862.* VII, 105.

Hamilton, Andrew Jackson, tribute to—I really believe him [Gen. Hamilton] to be a man of worth and ability; and one who, by his acquaintance there [in Texas], can scarcely fail to be efficient in reinaugurating the national authority. He has suffered so long and painful an exile, from his home and family, that I feel a deep sympathy for him.—*To Gen. Banks, Sept. 19, 1863.* Tracy, 233.

Hamlin, Hannibal, letter to, relative to preliminary proclamation—*See* EMANCIPATION PROCLAMATION (PRELIMINARY), doubtfully received.

Hamlin, Hannibal, remembered—I remember distinctly while I was in Congress to have heard you make a speech in the Senate. I was very much struck with that speech, Senator, particularly struck with it, and for the reason that it was filled chock up with the very best kind of anti-slavery doctrine.—*To Mr. Hamlin, Nov. 1860.* War Years I, 154.

Handwriting, irked by—I have already been bored more than enough by it; not the least of which annoyance is his [Louis H. Chandler's] cursed, unreadable and ungodly handwriting.—*To W. H. Herndon, Jan. 19, 1848.* I, 351.

Harbor Improvements—*See* GREAT LAKES, fortification of, suggested, 1.

Hardin, John J., characterized—Hardin is a man of desperate energy and perseverance, and one that never backs out; and, I fear, to think otherwise is to be deceived in the character of our adversary.—*To B. F. James, Jan. 14, 1846.* I, 283.

Hardin, John J., tribute to—We do it because we like you personally.—*To Mr. Hardin, May 11, 1843.* I, 266.
2.—Let nothing be said against Hardin. . . . Nothing deserves to be said against him.—*To B. F. James, Dec. 6, 1845.* Tracy, 16.
3.—I have constantly spoken of you in the most kind and commendatory terms, as to your talents, your services, and your goodness of heart. If I falsify in

this, you can convict me. The witnesses live and can tell.—*To Mr. Hardin, Feb. 7, 1846.* Angle, 25.
4.—You have — and deservedly — many devoted friends; and they have been gratified by seeing you in Congress, and taking a stand that did high credit to you and to them.—*To Mr. Hardin, Feb. 7, 1846.* Angle, 27.

See "TURN ABOUT IS FAIR PLAY"; rule in politics.

Hardy, C. M.—A highly intelligent, worthy, and honorable gentleman.—*To diplomatic agents, Feb. 22, 1861.* Angle, 261.

Harper's Ferry.—*See* BROWN, JOHN.

Harper's Ferry, attack on, wrong—The attack of John Brown is wrong for two reasons: It is a violation of law and it is, as all such attacks must be, futile as to any effect it may have on the extinction of a great evil.—*Speech, Elwood, Kan., Dec. 3, 1859.* Hertz II, 759.

Harper's Ferry, Democrats rejoice in raid on—You [Democrats] never dealt with us [Republicans] fairly in relation to that affair [Brown's raid]—and I will say frankly that I know of nothing in your character that should lead us to suppose that you would. . . . You rejoiced at the occasion and were only troubled that there were not three times as many killed in the affair. You were in evident glee; there was no sorrow for the killed nor for the peace of Virginia disturbed; you were rejoicing that by charging Republicans with this thing you might get an advantage of us in New York and other states. You pulled that string as tightly as you could, but your very generous and worthy expectations were not quite fulfilled.—*Speech, New Haven, Conn., March 6, 1860.* V, 359.

Harper's Ferry, raid not influenced by Republican doctrines—Some of you [men of the South] admit that no Republican designedly aided or encouraged the Harper's Ferry affair, but still insist that our doctrines and declarations necessarily lead to such results. We do not believe it. We know we hold to no doctrine and make no declaration, which were not held to and made by our fathers who framed the government under which we live. You never dealt with us fairly in relation to this affair.—*Cooper Institute address, New York, Feb. 27, 1860.* V, 315.
Repeated at New Haven, Conn., March 6, 1860. V, 359.

Harper's Magazine, Douglas's essay in—*See* POPULAR SOVEREIGNTY, Douglas troubled by, 1.

See POPULAR SOVEREIGNTY, Douglas's essay in **Harper's.**

See TERRITORIES, "all the South wants," 1, 3.

See TERRITORIES, large and small issues in, 1.

Harris, Thomas L.—See FORGERY, alleged, 1, 4, 5, 9.

Harrison, William Henry., death balked Whig program—It is true, the [Whig] victory of 1840 did not produce the happy results anticipated, but it is equally true, as we believe, that the unfortunate death of Gen. Harrison was the cause of the failure. It was not the election of Gen. Harrison that was expected to produce happy effect, but the measures to be adopted by his administration. By means of his death, and the unexpected course of his successor, these measures were never adopted. How could the fruits follow?—*Whig circular, March 4, 1843.* I, 257.

Hassaurek, F.—One of our best German Republican workers in America, residing at Cincinnati.—*To W. H. Seward, March 14, 1861.* VI, 191.

Hat, Lincoln's useful—My hat, where I carry all my packages.—*To C. R. Welles, Feb. 20, 1849.* Tracy, 37.
2.—I am ashamed of not sooner answering your letter. . . . When I received the letter I put it in my old hat, and buying a new one the next day, the old one was set aside, and so the letter was lost sight of for a time.—*To Richard S. Thomas, June 27, 1850.* Tracy, 42.

"Hath No Relish of Salvation"—See KANSAS-NEBRASKA ACT, not Union-saving.

Hawaiian Islands, importance of—In every light in which the state of the Hawaiian Islands can be contemplated, it is an object of profound interest for the United States. Virtually it was once a colony. It is a haven of shelter and refreshment for our merchants, fishermen, seaman and other citizens, when on their lawful occasions they are navigating the eastern seas and oceans. Its people are free, and its laws, language and religion are largely the fruit of our own teaching and example.—*To Hawaiian envoy, June 11, 1864.* XI, 132.

Head and Heart—I promise you that I bring to the work a sincere heart. Whether I will bring a head equal to that heart will be for future times to determine.—*Speech, reply to Philadelphia mayor, Feb. 21, 1861.* VI, 155.
2.—As I have often had occasion to say, I repeat to you—I am quite sure I do not deceive myself when I tell you that I bring to the work an honest heart; I dare not tell you that I bring a head sufficient for it.—*Speech, reply to Gov. Curtin, Harrisburg, Feb. 22, 1861.* VI, 161.

"Heal the Wounds of the Nation"—See DEITY, supplication to, 5.

Heart High Road to Reason—[A man's] heart . . . say what he will, is the great high road to his reason. —*Speech, Springfield, Feb. 22, 1842.* I, 197.

Hearts, who shall judge?—I understand you now to be willing to accept the help of men who are not Republicans, provided they have "heart in it." Agreed. I want no other. But who is to be the judge of hearts, or of "heart in it"?—*To Gen. Schurz, Nov. 24, 1862.* VIII, 85.

Heaven, not the way to reach—See RELIGION, "not the sort."

Heaven, place in, held cheap—You say you would almost give your place in Heaven for seventy or eighty dollars. Then you value your place in Heaven very cheap, for I am sure you can, with the offer I make, get the seventy or eighty dollars for four or five months' work.—*To John D. Johnston, Jan. 2, 1851.* II, 145.

"Heavens Hung in Black"—See CIVIL WAR, "most terrible."

Hell, feeling like—I believe, according to a letter of yours to Hatch, you are "feeling like Hell yet." Quit it. You will soon feel better. Another "blow-up" is coming; and we shall have fun again.—*To Dr. C. H. Ray, Nov. 20, 1858.* XI, 111.

Helm, Emily T.—Last December Mrs. Emily T. Helm, half-sister of Mrs. Lincoln, and widow of the rebel general, Ben Hardin Helm, stopped here on her way from Georgia to Kentucky, and I gave her a paper, as I remember, to protect her against the mere fact of her being Gen. Helm's widow. I hear a rumor today that you recently sought to arrest her, but were prevented by her presenting the paper from me. I do not intend to protect her against the consequences of disloyal words or acts, spoken or done by her since her return to Kentucky, and if the paper given her by me can be construed to give her protection for such words or acts, it is hereby revoked *pro tanto.* Deal with her for current conduct just as you would with any other.—*To Gen. Burbridge, Aug. 8, 1864.* X, 184.
2.—I hear you have arrested my relative, Mrs. Helm, and released her on her showing you a letter from me. If it contains anything that allows her to talk or act treason, disregard it and treat her as you would other rebels.—*To Gen. Burbridge, Dec., 1864.* Hertz II, 953.

Henry, Anson G., recommended—I believe, nay, I know, he [Henry] has done more disinterested labor in the Whig cause, than any other one, two, or three men in the state.—*To Sec. Ewing, March 22, 1850.* Angle, 65.

Henry, John, "astounded and mortified"—[Congressman] Henry was my personal and political friend; and, as I thought, a very good man; and when I first heard of that vote [Henry's against Mexican War supplies], I well remember how astounded and mortified I was.—*To J. Medill, June 25, 1858.* Angle, 180.

"Hermitage Lion," "hungry ticks" on tail of—Like a horde of hungry ticks you [Democrats] have stuck to the tail of the Hermitage lion to the end of his life; and you are still sticking to it, and drawing a loathesome substance from it after he is dead.—*Speech in Congress, July 27, 1848.* II, 73.

Herndon, William H., estimate of—Now, in what I have said, I am sure you will suspect nothing but sincere friendship. I would save you from a fatal error. You have been a laborious, studious young man. You are far better informed on almost all subjects than I have been. You cannot fail in any laudable object, unless you allow your mind to be improperly directed.—*To Mr. Herndon, July 10, 1848.* II, 57.

Hickman, John, has "genuine ring"—Now while I am speaking of Hickman, let me say I know little about him. I have never seen him, and know scarcely anything about the man; but I will say this much: of all the anti-Lecompton Democracy that has been brought to my notice, he alone has the true, genuine ring of the metal.—*Speech, Columbus, Ohio, Sept. 16, 1859.* V, 155.

See "IRREPRESSIBLE CONFLICT," difference in who says it, 2.

Hickory, useful party emblem—Your campaign papers have constantly been "Old Hickories"; with rude likenesses of the old general upon them; hickory poles and hickory brooms your never-ending emblems; Mr. Polk himself was "Young Hickory," or something so; and even now your campaign paper here is proclaiming Cass and Butler are of the true "hickory stripe."—*Speech in Congress, July 27, 1848.* II, 72.

"Higher Law," conditionally condemned—I never read the speech in which that proclamation [by Senator Seward] is said to have been made; so that I cannot by its connection judge its import and purpose; and I therefore have only to say of it now, that in so far as it may attempt to foment disobedience to

the Constitution, or to the constitutional laws of the country, it has my unqualified condemnation.—*Speech, Springfield, Aug. 26, 1852.* Angle, 108.

Highwayman, threat of South like that of—*See* SOUTH, will not accept Republican President, 3.

History, cannot be escaped—Fellow citizens, we cannot escape history. We of this Congress and this administration will be remembered in spite of ourselves. No personal significance or insignificance can spare one or another of us. The fiery trial through which we pass will light us down in honor or dishonor to the latest generation.—*Second annual message, Dec. 1, 1862.* VIII, 131.

History, Douglas denies—This [argument of Douglas's] is no more than a bold denial of the history of the country. If we do not know that the compromises of 1850 were dependent on each other; if we do not know that Illinois came into the Union as a free state —we do not know anything. If we do not know these things we do not know we ever had a Revolutionary War or such a chief as Washington. To deny these things is to deny our national axioms,—or dogmas, at least,—and it puts an end to all argument.—*Speech, Peoria, Oct. 16, 1854.* II, 261.

History, living—At the close of that struggle [Revolutionary War], nearly every adult male had been a participator in some of its scenes. The consequence was that of those scenes in the form of a husband, a father, a son, or a brother, a living history was to be found in every family—a history bearing the indubitable testimonies of its own authenticity, in the limbs mangled, in the scars of wounds received, in the midst of the very scenes related—a history, too, that could be read and understood alike by all, the wise and the ignorant, the learned and the unlearned. But those histories are gone. They can be read no more forever.—*Lyceum speech, Springfield, Jan., 1837.* I, 49.

History, repeats—What has once happened will invariably happen again when the same circumstances which combined to produce it shall again combine in the same way.—*Speech, Springfield, Dec. 20, 1839.* I, 112.
2.—And so history repeats itself; and even as slavery has kept its course by craft, intimidation, and violence in the past, so it will persist, in my judgment, until met and dominated by the will of a people bent on its restriction.—*Speech, Bloomington, May 29, 1856.* Lapsley II, 265.
3.—Like causes produce like effects.—*Debate, Jonesboro, Sept. 15, 1858.* IV, 40.

4.—Do you think that the . . . same causes that produced agitation at one time will not have the same effect at another?—*Debate, Jonesboro, Sept. 15, 1858.* IV, 41.

History, truth in—History is not history unless it is the truth.—*To W. H. Herndon, 1856.* Herndon II,. 147.

"Hive the Enemy"—If you can hold your present position, we shall hive the enemy yet.—*To Gen. McClellan, July 5, 1862.* VII, 261.

Hogs, adding weight of—This is as plain as adding up the weight of three small hogs.—*To Harrison Maltby, Sept. 8, 1856.* II, 297.
Repeated to Ed. Lawrence and Luther Hale, same date. Hertz II, 687 and 688.

Hogs, "equally divided"—I have heard some things from New York, and if they are true, one might well say of your party there, as a drunken fellow once said when he heard the reading of an indictment for hog-stealing. The clerk read on till he got to and through the words, "did steal, take and carry away ten boars, ten sows, ten shoats and ten pigs," at which he exclaimed, "Well, by golly, that is the most equally divided gang of hogs I ever did hear of!" If there is any other gang of hogs more equally divided than the Democrats of New York are about this time, I have not heard of it.—*Speech in Congress, July 27, 1848.* II, 88.

Holt, Joseph—Faithful and vigilant secretary of war.—*To Gen. Winfield Scott, March 9, 1861.* VI, 188.

"Holy Men of the South"—*See* CHURCH, insulted by "professedly holy men of the South."

Home Front, honor to those who serve—Honor to the soldier and sailor everywhere who bravely bears his country's cause. Honor also to the citizen who cares for his brother in the field, and serves, as he best can, the same cause—honor to him, only less than to him who braves, for the common good, the storms of heaven and the storms of battle.—*To George Opdyke and others, Dec. 2, 1863.* IX, 216.

"Homeopathic Soup"—*See* POPULAR SOVEREIGNTY, killed by Supreme Court, 4.

Homes, difficulty of procuring—*See* PUBLIC LANDS, sale of, if money volume is reduced.

Homestead Law, amendment of, suggested—This policy [of encouraging settlement] has received its most signal and beneficient illustration in the recent enactment granting homesteads to actual settlers. I cordially concur in the recommendation of the secretary of the interior, suggesting a modification of the act in favor of those engaged in the military and naval service of the United States.—*Third annual message, Dec. 8, 1863.* IX, 242.

Homestead Law, principle of, favored—In regard to the homestead law, I have to say that in so far as the government lands can be disposed of, I am in favor of cutting up the wild lands into parcels, so that every poor man may have a home.—*Speech to Germans, Cincinnati, Feb. 12, 1861.* VI, 120.

"Homicides on Punctilio"—It seems we could send white men to recruit better than to send negroes and thus inaugurate homicides on *punctilio.—To Gen. Schenck, Oct. 22, 1863.* IX, 179.

Honest Man—In very truth he [Benjamin Ferguson] was the noblest work of God—an honest man.—*Speech, Springfield, Feb. 8, 1842.* Hertz II, 530.

Honesty, inference establishes—In the absence of a more adequate motive than the evidence discloses, I am wholly unable to believe in the existence of criminal or fraudulent intent on the part of the men of such well-established good character. If the evidence went so far as to establish a guilty profit of one or two hundred thousand dollars, as it does of one or two hundred dollars, the case would, on the question of guilt, bear a far different aspect. That on this contract, involving some twelve hundred thousand dollars, the contractors would plan, and attempt to execute, a fraud, which, at the most, could profit them only one or two hundred dollars, is to my mind beyond the power of rational belief. That they did not, in such a case, make far greater gains, proves that they did not, with guilty or fraudulent intent, make any at all.—*Executive order, March 18, 1865.* XI, 58.

Honesty, lawyers should cherish—*See* LAW, advice to lawyers.

Honesty, no common assurance of—With however much care selections may be made, there will be some unfaithfulness and dishonesty in both classes [public officers and bankers]. The experience of the whole world, in all bygone times, proves this true. The Saviour of the world chose twelve disciples, and even one of that small number, selected by superhuman wisdom, turned out a traitor and a devil.—*Speech, Springfield, Dec. 20, 1839.* I, 114.

Honey and Gall—Don't you go and forget the old maxim that "one drop of honey catches more flies than a half-gallon of gall. Load your musket with this maxim, and smoke it in your pipe.—*To George E. Pickett, Feb. 22, 1842.* I, 192.

See FRIENDS, how to make.

See PERSUASION, rule for successful.

Honorary Degree, thanks for—I have the honor to acknowledge the reception of your note . . . conveying the announcement that the trustees of the College of New Jersey had conferred on me the degree of Doctor of Laws. The assurance conveyed by this high compliment, that the course of the government which I represent has received the approval of a body of gentlemen of such high character and intelligence, in this time of public trial is most grateful to me. Thoughtful men must feel that the fate of civilization upon this continent is involved in the issue of the contest. Among the most gratifying proofs of this conviction is the hearty devotion everywhere exhibited by our schools and colleges. I am most thankful if my labors have seemed to conduce to the preservation of these institutions under which alone we can expect good government—and in its train sound learning and the progress of the liberal arts.—*To John Maclean, Dec. 27, 1864.* X, 326.

Hooker, Joseph, "can't help but win"—We cannot help beating them [the enemy], if we have the man. How much depends in military matters on one master mind! Hooker may commit the same fault as McClelland and lose his chance. We shall soon see, but it appears to me he can't help but win.—*To Sec. Welles, June 26, 1863.* Welles I, 344.

Hooker, Joseph, cautioned—And now beware of rashness. Beware of rashness, but with energy and sleepless vigilance go forward and give us victories.—*To Gen. Hooker, Jan. 26, 1863.* VIII, 207.

Hooker, Joseph, characterized—I think as much as you or any other man of Hooker, but—I fear he gets excited.—*To Sec. Welles, Jan. 22, 1863.* Welles II, 229.
2.—Hooker talks badly; but the trouble is, he is stronger with the country today than any other man. —*To Henry J. Raymond, Feb. 24, 1863.* Stephenson, 343.

Hooker, Joseph, criticized and promoted—I have placed you at the head of the Army of the Potomac. Of course I have done this upon what appears to me to be sufficient reasons, and yet I think it best for you to know that there are some things in regard to which I am not quite satisfied with you. I believe you to be a brave and skillful soldier, which of course I like. I also believe you do not mix politics with your profession, in which you are right. You have confidence in yourself, which is a valuable if not indispensable quality. You are ambitious, which, within rea-

sonable bounds, does good rather than harm; but I think that during Gen. Burnside's command of the army you have taken counsel of your ambition and thwarted him as much as you could, in which you did a great wrong to the country and to a most meritorious and honorable brother officer. . . . I much fear that the spirit which you aided to infuse into the army, of criticizing their commander and withholding confidence from him, will now turn upon you.—*To Gen. Hooker, Jan. 26, 1863.* VIII, 206.

Hooker, Joseph, deference to—While I am anxious, please do not suppose that I am impatient, or waste a moment's thought on me, to your own hindrance or discomfort.—*To Gen. Hooker, April 28, 1863.* Angle, 323.

Hooker, Joseph, "painful intimations"—I must tell you that I have some painful intimations that some of your corps and division commanders are not giving you their entire confidence. This would be ruinous if true, and you should therefore, first of all, ascertain the real facts beyond all possibility of doubt.—*To Gen. Hooker, May 14, 1863.* VIII, 275.

Hooker, Joseph, relations with Gen. Slocum—Unfortunately the relations between Gens. Hooker and Slocum are not such as promise good, if their present relative positions remain. Therefore, let me beg—almost enjoin upon you—that on their reaching you, you will make a transposition by which Gen. Slocum with his corps may pass from under the command of Gen. Hooker, and Gen. Hooker, in turn, receive some other equal force.—*To Gen. Rosecrans, Sept. 28, 1863.* IX, 142.

Hooker, Joseph, relations with Halleck—When you say I have long been aware that you do not enjoy the confidence of the major-general commanding, you state the case much too strongly. You do not lack his confidence in any degree to do you any harm. . . . I believe Halleck is dissatisfied with you to this extent only, that he knows that you write or telegraph —"report," as he calls it—to me. I think he is wrong to find fault with this; but I do not think he withholds any support from you on account of it.—*To Gen. Hooker, June 16, 1863.* VIII, 320.
2.—If you and he [Halleck] would use the same frankness to one another, and to me, that I use to both of you, there would be no difficulty.—*To Gen. Hooker, June 16, 1863.* VIII, 321.
3.—To remove all misunderstanding, I now place you in the strict military relation to Gen. Halleck of a commander of one of the armies to the general-in-chief of all the armies. I have not intended differently, but as it seems to be differently understood I

shall direct him to give you orders, and you to obey them.—*To Gen. Hooker, June 16, 1863.* VIII, 323.

Hooker, Joseph, suggestions to—I would not take any risk of being entangled upon the [Rappahannock] river, like an ox jumped half over a fence, and liable to be torn by dogs front and rear without a fair chance to gore one way or kick the other.—*To Gen. Hooker, June 5, 1863.* VIII, 291.

2.—If he [the enemy] goes toward the Upper Potomac follow on his flank and on his inside track, shortening your lines while he lengthens his. Fight him, too, when opportunity offers. If he stays where he is, fret him and fret him.—*To Gen. Hooker, June 10, 1863.* VIII, 297.

3.—If the head of Lee's army is at Martinsburg and the tail of it on the plank road between Fredericksburg and Chancellorsville, the animal must be very slim somewhere. Could you not break him?—*To Gen. Hooker, June 14, 1863.* VIII, 315.

Hooker, Joseph, talk of dictatorship challenged—I have heard, in such a way as to believe it, of your recently saying that both the army and the government needed a dictator. . . . Only those generals who gain successes can set up dictators. What I now ask of you is military success, and I will risk the dictatorship.—*To Gen. Hooker, Jan. 26, 1863.* VIII, 207.

Hope, power of—The power of hope upon human exertion and happiness is wonderful.—*Fragment, July 1, 1854.* II, 185.

See LABOR, free and slave compared, 2.

Horse, "patting and petting"—[Preparation for the second Dred Scott decision] looks like the cautious patting and petting of a spirited horse, preparatory to mounting him, when it is dreaded that he may give the rider a fall.—*Speech, Springfield, June 16, 1858.* III, 9.

Horsechestnut and Chestnut Horse—He [Douglas] runs on step by step, in the horsechestnut style of argument.—*Speech, Springfield, July 17, 1858.* III, 239.

2.—When Douglas ascribes such to me, he does so, not by argument, but by mere burlesque on the art and name of argument—by such fantastic arrangements of words as prove "horsechestnuts" to be "chestnut horses."—*Notes, Oct. 1, 1858.* IV, 212.

See RACIAL EQUALITY, neither desired nor intended, 5.

Horses, "sore-tongued and fatigued"—*See* MC CLELLAN, GEORGE B., criticized, 12.

Horses, would not swap, midstream—I do not allow myself to suppose that either the [Republican national] convention or the [National Union] League have concluded to decide that I am either the greatest or best man in America, but rather they have concluded that it is not best to swap horses while crossing the river, and have further concluded that I am not so poor a horse that they might not make a botch of it in trying to swap.—*Reply to delegation from National Union League, June 9, 1864.* X, 123.

House-Burning, "mutual discontinuance" urged—The secretary of war and I concur that you had better confer with Gen. Lee, and stipulate for a mutual discontinuance of house-burning and other destruction of private property.—*To Gen. Grant, Aug. 14, 1864.* X, 187.

"House Divided Against Itself," Author of—*See* UNION, strength in.

"House Divided Against Itself," cannot stand—Our political problem now is, Can we as a nation continue together permanently—forever—half slave and half free? The problem is too mighty for me—may God, in His mercy, superintend the solution.—*To George Robertson, Aug. 15, 1855.* II, 280.

2.—"A house divided against itself cannot stand." I believe this government cannot endure permanently half slave and half free. I do not expect the Union to be dissolved—I do not expect the house to fall—but I do expect it will cease to be divided. It will become all one thing or all the other. Either the opponents of slavery will arrest the further spread of it, and place it where the public mind shall rest in the belief that it is in the course of ultimate extinction; or its advocates will push it forward till it shall become alike lawful in all the states, old as well as new, North as well as South.—*Speech, Springfield, June 16, 1858.* III, 2.

Repeated at Chicago, July 10, 1858. III, 30.
Repeated at Springfield, July 17, 1858. III, 173.
Repeated at Clinton, Sept. 8, 1858. III, 351.
Repeated at Alton, Oct. 15, 1858. V, 44.

3.—I repeat that I do not believe this government can endure permanently half slave and half free, yet I do not admit, nor does it at all follow, that the admission of a single slave state will permanently fix the character and establish this as a universal slave nation. The judge [Douglas] is very happy indeed at working up these quibbles.—*Debate, Freeport, Aug. 27, 1858.* III, 340.

4.—I believe the government cannot endure permanently half slave and half free. I expressed this belief a year ago; and subsequent developments have but confirmed me.—*Notes, Oct. 1, 1858.* IV, 233.

5.—I think we have fairly entered upon a durable struggle as to whether this nation is to ultimately become all slave or all free.—*To H. D. Sharpe, Dec. 8, 1858.* V, 96.

See UNION, strength in.

"House Divided Against Itself," does Douglas say it can stand?—He [Douglas] has read from my speech in Springfield in which I say that "a house divided against itself cannot stand." Does the judge say it can stand? I don't know whether he does or not. . . . If he does, then there is a question of veracity, not between him and me, but between the judge and an authority of a somewhat higher character.—*Debate, Ottawa, Aug. 21, 1858.* III, 231.

2.—But he [Douglas] is not quite so vain as to say that the Good Man uttered a falsehood when He said, "A house divided against itself cannot stand." Does he believe this thing [slavery] will always stand as it is now—neither expand nor diminish?—*Speech, Carlinville, Aug. 31, 1858.* Angle, 189.

"House Divided Against Itself," importance of speech —If I had to draw a pen across my record, and erase my whole life from sight, and I had one poor gift or choice left as to what I save from the wreck, I should choose that speech and leave it to the world unerased. —*Statement, June 16, 1858.* Tarbell, II, 100.

"House Divided Against Itself," slavery divides it—*See* SLAVERY, disturbing element.

"House Divided Against Itself," use of expression defended—That expression is a truth of all human experience; a house divided against itself cannot stand. . . . The proposition is indisputably true, and has been true for more than 6,000 years. . . . I want to use some universally known figure, expressed in language as universally known, that it may strike home to the minds of men in order to rouse them to the peril of the times. I would rather be defeated with this expression in the speech and it held up and discussed before the people than to be victorious without it.—*To W. H. Herndon, June 16, 1858.* Quarterly, Dec., 1844, p. 184.

Houseless, admonished—Let not him who is houseless pull down the house of another, but let him work diligently and build one for himself, thus by example assuring that his own shall be safe from violence when built.—*Reply to committee of Workingmen's Association of New York, March 21, 1864.* X, 54.

Huckleberries, Harrison and Cass pick—*See* CASS, LEWIS D., military figure of, 1, 2.

"Hug Tighter"—*See* BARGAIN, "hug tighter" if bad.

Human Bondage, chains of—Familiarize yourselves with the chains of bondage, and you prepare your own limbs to wear them.—*Speech, Edwardsville, Sept. 13, 1858.* XI, 110.

Human Bondage, challenged as basis of government— *See* SELF-GOVERNMENT, Can it survive? 9.

Human Eel Trap—The fisherman's wife whose drowned husband was brought home with his body full of eels, said when she was asked what was to be done with him, "Take the eels out and set him again." —*Debate, Galesburg, Oct. 7, 1858.* IV, 279.

Human Freedom, challenged—*See* SELF-GOVERNMENT, Can it survive? 9.

Human Nature, does not change—Human nature . . . is God's decree and can never be reversed.—*Speech, Springfield, Feb. 22, 1842.* I, 197.

2.—Repeal the Missouri Compromise, repeal all compromises, repeal the Declaration of Independence, repeal all past history, you still cannot repeal human nature.—*Speech, Peoria, Oct. 16, 1854.* II, 238.

3.—Human action can be modified to some extent, but human nature cannot be changed.—*Cooper Institute address, New York, Feb. 27, 1860.* V, 319.

4.—Human nature is the same—people at the South are the same as those at the North, barring the difference in circumstances.—*Speech, Hartford, Conn., March 5, 1860.* V, 330.

Human Nature, entitled to progress—*See* LABOR, no permanent class, 4.

Human Nature, shown in elections—The strife of the election is but human nature practically applied to the facts of the case. What has occurred in this case [election of 1864] must ever recur in similar cases. In any future great national trial, compared with the men of this, we shall have as weak and as strong, as silly and as wise, as bad and as good. Let us, therefore, study the incidents of this as philosophy to learn wisdom from, and none of them as wrongs to revenge.—*Response to serenade, Nov. 10, 1864.* X, 263.

Human race, curse of—As labor is the common burden of our race, so the effort of some to shift their share of the burden onto the shoulders of others is the great durable curse of the race.—*Fragment, July 1, 1854.* II, 185.

Human Right, endangered—*See* SELF-GOVERNMENT, Can it survive? 11.

Humility, Lincoln trait—I am humble Abraham Lincoln.—*Speech, Pappville, March, 1832.* XI, 97.

2.—Considering the great probability that the framers of those laws [under discussion] were wiser than myself, I should prefer not meddling with them, unless they were first attacked by others; in which case I should feel it both a privilege and a duty to take that stand which, in my view, might tend most to the advancement of justice.—*Address to Sangamon County, March 9, 1832.* I, 8.

3.—Considering the great degree of modesty which should always attend youth, it is probable I have already been more presuming than becomes one.—*Address to Sangamon County, March 9, 1832.* I, 8.

4.—So soon as I discover my opinions to be erroneous I shall be ready to renounce them.—*Address to Sangamon County, March 9, 1832.* I, 8.

5.—I am, indeed, apprehensive, that the few who have attended [the present meeting] have done so more to spare me mortification than in the hope of being interested in anything I may be able to say. This circumstance casts a damp upon my spirits, which I am sure I shall be unable to overcome during the evening.—*Speech, Springfield, Dec. 20, 1859.* I, 101.

6.—In this view, humble as I am, I wish to review, and contest as well as I may, the general positions of this veto message [on internal improvements]—*Speech in Congress, June 20, 1848.* II, 30.

7.—Being the man I am, and speaking where I do, I feel that in any attempt at an original constitutional argument, I should not be, and ought not to be, listened to patiently.—*Speech in Congress, June 20, 1848.* II, 38.

8.—. . . not being learned myself.—*Speech in Congress, July 27, 1848.* II, 70.

9.—Your note, requesting my "signature with a sentiment," was received. . . . I am not a very sentimental man; and the best sentiment I can think of is, that if you collect the signatures of all persons who are no less distinguished than I, you will have a very undistinguishing mass of names.—*To C. U. Schlater, Jan. 5, 1849.* Basler, 254.

10.—There is nothing about me to authorize me to think of a first-class office, and a second-class one would not compensate my being sneered at by others who want it for themselves.—*To Joshua F. Speed, Feb. 20, 1849.* II, 105.

11.—I am not an accomplished lawyer. I find quite as much material for a lecture in those points wherein I have failed, as in those wherein I have been moderately successful.—*Notes, July 1, 1850.* II, 140.

12.—He says he intends to keep me down—put me down, I should not say, for I have never been up.—*Speech, Chicago, July 10, 1858.* III, 24.

13.—I am, in a certain sense, made the standard-bearer in behalf of the Republicans. I was made so merely because there had to be some one so placed, I being in no wise preferable to any other one of the 25, perhaps 100, we have in the Republican ranks.—*Speech, Springfield, July 17, 1858.* III, 158.

14.—If I should be found dead tomorrow morning, nothing but my insignificance could prevent a speech being made on my authority, before the end of next week.—*Speech, Springfield, July 17, 1858.* III, 184.

15.—. . . so far as my humble ability was capable of showing.—*Speech, Springfield, July 17, 1858.* III, 236.

16.—I know the judge is a great man, while I am only a small man, but [on this point] I feel that I have got him.—*Speech, Springfield, July 17, 1858.* III, 239.

17.—. . . an insignificant individual like Lincoln.—*Debate, Freeport, Aug. 27, 1858.* III, 290.

18.—. . . trying to help poor me to be elected.—*Debate, Jonesboro, Sept. 15, 1858.* IV, 47.

19.—This is but an opinion, and the opinion of one very humble man.—*Debate, Galesburg, Oct. 7, 1858.* IV, 286.

20.—. . . so humble an individual as myself.—*Debate, Alton, Oct. 15, 1858.* V, 36.

21.—I must in candor say I do not think myself fit for the Presidency. I certainly am flattered and gratified that some partial friends think of me in that connection.—*To T. J. Pickett, April 16, 1859.* V, 127.

22.—I fear you have formed an estimate of me which can scarcely be sustained on a personal acquaintance. . . . I must say I do not think myself fit for the Presidency.—*To Samuel Galoway, July 28, 1859.* V, 138.

23.—I feel that it will be well for you, as for me, that you should not raise your expectations [as to this speech] to that standard to which you would have been justified in raising them had one of these distinguished men [Ohioans: Corwin, Chase, Wade] appeared before you. You would perhaps be only preparing a disappointment for yourselves, and, as a consequence of your disappointment, mortification for me.—*Speech, Columbus, Ohio, Sept. 16, 1859.* V, 140.

24.—Now, Gentlemen, if it were not for my excessive modesty I would say that I told that very thing [that the Dred Scott decision looked toward slavery in unwilling states] to Judge Douglas quite a year ago.—*Speech, Columbus, Ohio, Sept. 16, 1859.* V, 179.

25.—And in such suggestions by me, quite likely very little will be new to you, and a large part of the rest will be possibly already known to be erroneous.—*Speech, Milwaukee, Sept. 30, 1859.* V, 239.

26.—Remembering that when not a very great man begins to be mentioned for a very great office, his head is very likely to be a little turned.—*To R. M. Corwine, April 6, 1860.* Tracy, 138.

27.—I am not a professional lecturer. Have never got

up but one lecture, and that I think rather a poor one. —*To John M. Carson, April 7, 1860.* Tracy, 141.

28.—My friend, I do not see much in my life yet to write about.—*To friend at Springfield, May 18, 1860.* Stephenson, 201.

29.—Holding myself the humblest of all whose names were before the convention, I feel in special need of the assistance of all.—*To Salmon P. Chase, May 26, 1860.* VI, 20.

30.—I confess with gratitude, be it understood, that I did not suppose my appearance among you would create the tumult which I now witness. I am gratified because it is a tribute which can be paid to no man as a man.—*Speech, Springfield, Aug. 14, 1860.* VI, 49.

31.—I thank you for the good opinion you express of me, fearing, at the same time, I may not be able to maintain it through life.—*To Mrs. M. J. Green, Sept. 22, 1860.* Tracy, 164.

32.—I give the leave, begging only that the inscription may be in modest terms, not representing me as a man of great learning, or a very extraordinary one in any respect.—*To W. D. Kelly, Oct. 13, 1860.* Lang, 86.

33.—It is a great piece of folly to attempt to make anything out of me or my early life. It can all be condensed into a single sentence, and that sentence you will find in Gray's "Elegy": "The short and simple annals of the poor." That's my life, and that's all you or anyone else can make out of it.—*To J. L. Scripps, 1860.* Herndon, 2.

34.—I remember that people used to say, without disturbing my self-respect, that I was not lawyer enough to hurt me.—*Interview, Thurlow Weed, Dec. 1860.* Weed, 611.

35.—I fear that the great confidence placed in my ability is unfounded. Indeed I am sure it is.—*Speech, Steubenville, Ohio, Feb. 14, 1861.* VI, 122.

36.—I am not vain enough to believe that you are here from any wish to see me as an individual, but because I am for the time being the representative of the American people.—*Speech, Rochester, N. Y., Feb. 18, 1861.* VI, 135.

37.—It is much more gratifying to me that this reception has been given to me as the elected representative of a free people, than it could possibly be if tendered merely as an evidence of devotion to me, or to any one man personally.—*Speech, New York Legislature, Feb. 18, 1861.* VI, 140.

38.—It is true that, while I hold myself, without mock modesty, the humblest of all individuals that have ever been elevated to the Presidency, I have a more difficult task to perform than any of them.—*Speech, New York Legislature, Feb. 18, 1861.* VI, 140.

39.—As to my wisdom in conducting affairs so as to tend to the preservation of the Union, I fear too great

confidence may have been placed in me.—*Speech, reply to New York mayor, Feb. 20, 1861.* VI, 149.

40.—I appropriate to myself very little of the demonstrations of respect with which I have been greeted. I think little should be given to any man, but that it should be a manifestation of adherence to the Union and the Constitution.—*Speech, New Jersey Assembly, Feb. 21, 1861.* VI, 152.

41.—I don't know anything about diplomacy. I will be very apt to make blunders.—*To R. M. Schleiden, March 2, 1861.* War Years I, 98.

42.—I do not wish you to believe that I assume to be better than others who have gone before me [in the Presidency]. — *Reply to Pennsylvania delegation, March 5, 1861.* XI, 117.

43.—I know very well that others might, in this matter [issuance of preliminary Emancipation Proclamation] as in others, do better than I can; and if I was satisfied that the public confidence was more fully possessed by any one of them than by me, and knew any constitutional way in which he could be put in my place, he should have it.—*To cabinet, Sept. 22, 1862.* Hertz II, 882.

44.—While I commend him [Edward Everett] to the consideration of those whom he may meet [in Europe], I am quite conscious that he could better introduce me than I him.—*Letter "to whom it may concern," Sept. 24, 1862.* VIII, 43.

45.—I do not . . . forget that some of you are my seniors, nor that many of you have more experience than I in the conduct of public affairs. Yet I trust that in view of the great responsibility resting upon me you will perceive no want of respect to yourselves in any undue earnestness I may seem to display.—*Second annual message, Dec. 1, 1862.* VIII, 130.

46.—Have you already in your mind a plan wholly or partially formed? If you have, prosecute it without interference from me. If you have not, please inform me, so that I, incompetent as I may be, can try and assist in the formation of some plan for the army.—*To Gen. Hooker, May 7, 1863.* VIII, 265.

47.—All I ask is that you will be in such mood that we can get into our actions the best cordial judgment of yourself and Gen. Halleck, with my poor mite added, if indeed he and you shall think it entitled to any consideration at all.—*To Gen. Hooker, June 16, 1863.* VIII, 321.

48.—I am not without anxiety lest I appear to be importunate in thus recalling your attention to a subject upon which you have so recently acted, and nothing but a deep conviction that the public interest demands it could induce me to incur the hazard of being misunderstood on this point.—*Message to Senate, Jan. 5, 1864.* IX, 276.

See AMERICAN FLAG, its raising an omen.

See HORSES, would not swap, midstream.

See PEACE, devotion to, 2.

See WASHINGTON, GEORGE, task greater than that of.

Hundred-Day Volunteers, thanked—*See* CIVIL WAR, hundred-day volunteers thanked.

Hundred Days' Notice—*See* EMANCIPATION PROCLAMATION, no retraction of, 1.

Hung Jury, sometimes preferred—A jury too often has at least one member more ready to hang the panel than to hang the traitor.—*To Erastus Corning and others, June 12, 1863.* VIII, 303.

Hungarian Revolution, American recognition urged —That, in their present glorious struggle for liberty, the Hungarians command our highest admiration and have our warmest sympathy; that they have our prayers for their speedy triumph and final success; that the government of the United States should acknowledge the independence of Hungary as a nation of free men at the very earliest moment consistent with our amicable relations with the government against which they are contending; that, in the opinion of this meeting, the immediate acknowledgment of the independence of Hungary by our government is due from American free men to their struggling brethren, to the general cause of republican liberty, and not violative of the just rights of any nation or people.—*Resolutions, Sept. 12, 1849.* Lapsley II, 141.

Hungarian Revolution, Russia acted illegally in— That the late interference of Russia in the Hungarian struggle was, in our opinion, such illegal and unwarrantable interference. That to have resisted Russia in that case, or to resist any power in like case, would be no violation of our own cherished principles of non-intervention, but, on the contrary, would be ever meritorious, in us, or any independent nation.— *Resolutions, Jan. 9, 1852.* Angle, 81.

Hunkerism—*See* MISSOURI, factions worry President, 1.

Hunt, Sallie Ward, willing to accommodate—*See* WOMEN AND MARRIAGE, attitude toward, 11.

Hunter, David, asked to help Fremont—*See* FRÉMONT, JOHN C., characterized, 2.

Hunter, David, complaint answered—Yours of the 23d is received, and I am constrained to say it is difficult to answer so ugly a letter in good temper. I am, as you intimate, losing much of the great confidence I placed in you, not from any act or omission of yours

touching the public service, up to the time you were sent to Leavenworth, but from the flood of grumbling dispatches and letters I have seen from you since. . . . With as tender a regard for your honor and your sensibilities as I had for my own, it never occurred to me that you were being "humiliated, insulted, and disgraced," nor have I, up to this day, heard an intimation that you have been wronged, coming from anyone but yourself. . . . You constantly speak of being placed in command of only 3,000. Now tell me, is this not mere impatience? Have you not known all the while that you are to command four or five times that many? I have been, and am sincerely your friend; and if, as such, I dare to make a suggestion, I would say you are adopting the best possible way to ruin yourself.—*To Gen. Hunter, Dec. 31, 1861.* VII, 68.

Hunter, David, appreciation of—Gen. Hunter is an honest man. He was, and I hope still is, my friend. I value him none the less for agreeing with me in the general wish that all men everywhere could be free.— *To border-state congressmen, July 12, 1862.* VII, 272. 2.—I assure you, and you may feel authorized in stating, that the recent change of commanders in the Department of the South was made for no reasons which convey any imputation upon your known energy, efficiency, and patriotism.—*To Gen. Hunter, June 30, 1863.* IX, 14. 3.—The order you complain of was only nominally mine, and was framed by those who really made it with no thought of making you a scapegoat. . . . Gen. Grant wishes you to remain in command of the department, and I do not wish to order otherwise.—*To Gen. Hunter, July 17, 1864.* X, 161.

Hunter, David, proclamation of, voided—I . . . proclaim and declare that . . . neither Gen. Hunter nor any other commander or person has been authorized by the government of the United States to make proclamations declaring the slaves of any state free, and that the supposed proclamation now in question, whether genuine or false, is altogether void so far as respects such declaration.—*Proclamation, May 19, 1862.* VII, 171.

See EMANCIPATION, "pressed with a difficulty" over Hunter proclamation.

Hunter, David, vigilance urged on—The utmost caution and vigilance is necessary on our part.—*To Gen. Hunter, April 1, 1863.* VIII, 239.

Hurlbut, Stephen A., advice to—As your friend, which you know I am, I would advise you not to come to Washington, if you could safely come without leave. You now stand well with the Sec. of War, and with

Gen. Halleck, and it would lessen you with both to make your appearance here. I advise you by all means to dismiss the thought of coming here.—*To Gen. Hurlbut, Jan. 22, 1863.* Angle, 312.

2.—From one standpoint a court of inquiry is most just, but if your case were mine, I would not allow Gens. Grant and Sherman [to] be diverted by it just now.—*To Gen. Hurlbut, May 2, 1864.* X, 91.

Hurlbut, Stephen A., confidence in—The secretary of war and Gen. Halleck are very partial to you, as you know I am. We all wish you to reconsider the question of resigning.—*To Gen. Hurlbut, July 31, 1683.* IX, 51.

2.—My friendship and confidence for you remain unabated.—*To Gen. Hurlbut, May 2, 1864.* X, 91.

Hypochondria, victim of—You recollect that I mentioned at the outset of this letter that I had been unwell. That is the fact, though I believe I am about well now; but that, with other things I cannot account for, have conspired, and have gotten my spirits so low that I feel I would rather be any place in the world than here.—*To Mary Owens, Dec. 13, 1836.* I, 18.

2.—Tell your sister I don't want to hear any more about selling out and moving. That gives me the "hypo" whenever I think of it.—*To Mary Owens, May 7, 1837.* I, 54.

3.—What I wish now is to speak of our post office. You know I desired Dr. Henry to have that place when you left; I now desire it more than ever. I have within the last few days been making a most discreditable exhibition of myself in the way of hypochondriasm and thereby got an impression that Dr. Henry is necessary to my existence. Unless he gets that place he leaves Springfield. You therefore see how much I am interested in the matter. . . . My heart is very much set upon it. Pardon me for not writing more; I have not sufficient composure to write a long letter.—*To John T. Stuart, Jan. 20, 1841.* Angle, 8.

4.—Yours of the 3d instant is received, and I proceed to answer it as well as I can, though from the deplorable state of my mind at this time I fear I shall give you but little satisfaction.—*To John T. Stuart, Jan. 23, 1841.* I, 157.

5.—I am now the most miserable man living. If what I feel were equally distributed to the whole human family, there would not be one cheerful face on the earth. Whether I shall ever be better, I cannot tell; I awfully forbode I shall not. To remain as I am is impossible; I must die or be better, it appears to me.—*To John T. Stuart, Jan. 23, 1841.* I, 159.

6.—I have been quite clear of "hypo" since you left; even better than I was along in the fall.—*To Joshua F. Speed, Jan. 3, 1842.* I, 187.

7.—I must gain my confidence in my own ability to keep my resolves when they are made. In that ability you know I once prided myself. . . . I have not yet regained it; and until I do, I cannot trust myself in any matter of much importance.—*To Joshua F. Speed, July 4, 1842.* I, 218.

Idaho, partially organized—Idaho and Montana, by reason of their great distance and the interruption of communication with them by Indian hostilities, have been only partially organized; but it is understood that these difficulties are about to disappear, which will permit their governments, like those of the others, to go into speedy and full operation.—*Fourth annual message, Dec. 6, 1864.* X, 298.

Idleness, to be avoided—I think if I were you, in case my mind were not exactly right, I would avoid being idle. I would immediately engage in some business, or go to making preparations for it, which would be the same thing.—*To Joshua F. Speed, Feb. 3, 1842.* I, 188.

2.—Universal idleness would speedily result in universal ruin.—*Tariff memorandum, Dec. 1, 1847.* I, 314.

3.—No country can sustain in idleness more than a small percentage of its numbers. The great majority must labor at something productive.—*Speech, Milwaukee, Sept. 30, 1859.* V, 251.

See WORK, desire to, rare.

"If I Blab Too Much"—*See* STANTON, EDWIN M., censor.

Illinois, antislavery men of, not united—*See* SLAVERY, perpetuation of, 3.

Illinois, "home pride" in—In my present position I must care for the whole nation; but I hope it will be no injustice to any other state for me to indulge a little home pride that Illinois does not disappoint us. —*To Gen. McClernand, Nov. 10, 1861.* VII, 19.

Illinois, honored by Mexican War soldiers—Many of them, Whigs and Democrats, are my constituents and personal friends; and I thank them—more than thank them—one and all, for the high imperishable honor they have conferred on our common state.—*Speech in Congress, July 27, 1848.* II, 85.

Illinois, many in, wanted slavery—[In 1821] five thousand citizens of Illinois, out of a voting mass of less than twelve thousand, deliberately, after a long and heated contest, voted to introduce slavery in Illinois; and today a large party in the free state of Illinois are willing to vote to fasten the shackles of slavery on the fair domain of Kansas, notwithstanding it received the dowry of freedom long before its birth as a political community.—*Speech, Bloomington, May 29, 1856.* Lapsley II, 258.

2.—Even after the Ordinance of 1787, the settlers of Indiana and Illinois—it was all one government then—tried to get Congress to allow slavery temporarily, and petitions to that end were sent from Kaskaskia, and Gen. Harrison, the governor, urged it from Vincennes, the capital. If that had succeeded, goodbye to liberty here. But John Randolph of Virginia made a vigorous report against it; and although they persevered so well as to get three favorable reports for it, yet the United States Senate, with the aid of some slave states, finally squelched it for good. And that is why this hall is today a temple for free men, instead of a negro livery stable.—*Speech, Bloomington, May 29, 1856.* Lapsley II, 270.

Illinois, never a slave state—But he [Douglas] says Illinois came into the Union as a slave state. Silence, perhaps, would be the best answer to this flat contradiction of the known history of the country.—*Speech, Peoria, Oct. 16, 1854.* II, 250.

2.—Allow me but a little while to state to you what facts there are to justify him [Douglas] in saying that Illinois came into the Union as a slave state. I have mentioned to you that there were a few old French slaves there. . . . Besides that, there had been a territorial law for indenturing black persons. Under that law, in violation of the Ordinance of '87 . . . there had been a small number of slaves introduced as indentured persons. Owing to this, the clause for the prohibition of slavery was slightly modified. Instead of running like yours [in Ohio] . . . they said that neither slavery nor involuntary servitude should thereafter be introduced, and that the children of indentured servants should be born free. . . . How far the facts sustain the conclusion that he [Douglas] draws, it is for intelligent and impartial men to decide.—*Speech, Cincinnati, Sept. 17, 1859.* V, 226.

Illinois, obligation of, to help others to freedom—Now, can we [men of Illinois], mindful of the blessings of liberty which the early men of Illinois left to us, refuse a like privilege to the free men who seek to plant Freedom's banner on our western outposts? Should we not stand by our neighbors who seek to better their conditions in Kansas and Nebraska?—*Speech, Bloomington, May 29, 1856.* Lapsley II, 270.

Illinois, saved to freedom—It was by that policy [of using ballots rather than bullets] that here in Illinois the early fathers fought the good fight and gained the victory. In 1824 the free men of our state, led by Gov. [Edward] Coles—who was a native of Maryland and President Madison's private secretary—determined that these beautiful groves should never re-echo the dirge of one who has no title to himself. By their resolute determination, the winds that sweep across our broad prairies shall never cool the parched brow, nor shall the unfettered streams that bring joy and gladness to our free soil water the tired feet, of a slave; but so long as these heavenly breezes and sparkling streams bless the land, or the groves and their fragrance remain, the humanity to which they minister shall be forever free.—*Speech, Bloomington, May 29, 1856.* Lapsley II, 269.

Illinois, troops innocent—They [members of an Illinois regiment] did not misbehave, and I am satisfied; so that they should receive no treatment, nor have anything withheld from them, by way of punishment.—*To Sec. Stanton, Dec. 26, 1862.* Angle, 310.

Illinois, troops lag—I certainly cannot conceive what it was I said which can be construed as injustice to Illinois. I knew by your dispatch that Ills. had raised an unexpectedly large number of troops, and my impatience was that none of them could be got forward.—*To Gov. Yates, Aug. 25, 1862.* Brown, 22.

Illinois, volunteers thanked for services—*See* CIVIL WAR, hundred-day volunteers thanked.

Illinois and Michigan Canal, importance of—Nothing is so local as not to be of some general benefit. Take, for instance, the Illinois and Michigan canal. Considered apart from its effects, it is perfectly local. Every inch of it is within the state of Illinois. That canal was first opened for business last April. In a very few days we were all gratified to learn, among other things, that sugar had been carried from New Orleans through this canal to Buffalo, in New York. . . . Supposing benefit of the reduction in the cost of carriage to be shared between seller and buyer, the result is that the New Orleans merchant sold his sugar a little dearer, and the people of Buffalo sweetened their coffee a little cheaper than before—a benefit resulting from the canal, not to Illinois, where the canal is, but to Louisiana and New York, where it is not.—*Speech in Congress, June 20, 1848.* II, 35.

2.—This suggests . . . the favorable action of Congress upon the projects now pending . . . for enlarging the capacities of the great canals in New York and Illinois, as being of vital and rapidly increasing importance to the whole nation, and especially to the vast interior region. . . . The military and commercial importance of enlarging the Illinois and Michigan canal and improving the Illinois river . . . I respectfully ask attention to.—*Second annual message, Dec. 1, 1862.* VIII, 108.

3.—The military and commercial importance of enlarging the Illinois and Michigan canal and improving the Illinois river is presented in the report of Col. Webster to the secretary of war, and now transmitted to Congress. I respectfully ask attention to it. —*Second annual message, Dec. 1, 1862.* VIII, 109.

4.—The attention of Congress during the last session was engaged to some extent with a proposition for enlarging the water communication between the Mississippi river and the northeastern seaboard. . . . Since then, upon a call of the greatest respectability, a convention has been held at Chicago upon the same subject. . . . That this interest is one which ere long will force its own way I do not entertain a doubt, while it is submitted entirely to your wisdom as to what can be done now. Augmented interest is given this subject by the actual commencement of work upon the Pacific Railroad, under auspices so favorable to rapid progress and completion. The enlarged navigation becomes a palpable need to the great road.—*Third annual message, Dec. 8, 1863.* IX, 244.

Illinois State Register, continues to assert—*See* FORGERY, seems not to suspect.

See PRESS, Whig, ignores speeches.

Illinois Supreme Court—*See* JUDICIAL DECISIONS, Douglas's attitude toward, 4, 5, 6, 7, 10, 11.

Ills, flying to and flying from—*See* UNION, appeals for support of, 2.

Immigration, encouragement for—In regard to Germans and foreigners, I esteem them not better than other people, nor any worse. It is not my nature when I see a people borne down by the weight of their shackles—the oppression of tyranny—to make their life more bitter by heaping upon them greater burdens; but rather would I do all in my power to raise the yoke than to add anything that would tend to crush them. Inasmuch as our country is extensive and new, and the countries of Europe are densely populated, if there are any abroad who desire to make this the land of their adoption, it is not in my heart to throw aught in their way to prevent them from coming to the United States.—*Speech to Germans, Cincinnati, Feb. 12, 1861.* VI, 120.

2.—I again submit to your consideration the expediency of establishing a system for the encouragement of immigration. Although this source of national wealth and strength is again flowing with greater freedom than for several years before the insurrection occurred, there is still a great deficiency of laborers in many fields of industry, especially in agricul-

ture and in our mines, as well of iron and coal as of the precious metals. While the demand for labor is much increased here, tens of thousands of persons destitute of remunerative employment, are thronging our foreign consulates and offering to emigrate to the United States if essential, but very cheap, assistance can be afforded them.—*Third annual message, Dec. 8, 1863.* IX, 230.

3.—The act passed at the last session for the encouragement of immigration has so far as possible been put into operation. It seems to need amendment which will enable officers of the government to prevent the practice of frauds against the immigrants while on their way and on their arrival in the ports, so as to secure them here a free choice of avocations and places of settlement. A liberal disposition toward this great national policy is manifested by most of the European states, and ought to be reciprocated on our part by giving the immigrants effective national protection. I regard our immigrants as one of the principal replenishing streams which are appointed by Providence to repair the ravages of internal war and its wastes of national strength and health.—*Fourth annual message, Dec. 6, 1864.* X, 290.

Immigration, immigrants need not fear military service—*See* MILITARY DRAFT, immigrants need not fear.

Immigration, right to bar applicants—For myself I have no doubt of the power and duty of the executive, under the law of nations, to exclude enemies of the human race from an asylum in the United States. —*Fourth annual message, Dec. 6, 1864.* X, 288.

Immortality—*See* DEITY, argument for existence of, 2.

Inaugural, first, "great delicacy" felt—I am thankful for . . . your sanction of what I have enunciated in my inaugural address. This is very grateful to my feelings. The object was one of great delicacy, in presenting views at the opening of an administration under the peculiar circumstances attending my entrance upon the official duties connected with the government. I studied all the points with great anxiety, and presented them with whatever of ability and sense of justice I could bring to bear.—*Response to Massachusetts delegation, March 5, 1861.* XI, 118.

Inaugural, first, principles to control—I hope, then, [in the inaugural] not to be false to anything that you have to expect of me.—*Speech to Germans, Cincinnati, Feb. 12, 1861.* VI, 119.

2.—I hope I may say nothing in opposition to the spirit of the Constitution, contrary to the integrity of the Union, or which will prove inimical to the liberties of the people, or to the peace of the whole country. And, furthermore, when the time arrives for me to speak on this great subject [the crisis before the country], I hope I may say nothing to disappoint the people generally throughout the country, especially if the expectation has been based on anything which I may have heretofore said.—*Speech, Pittsburgh, Feb. 15, 1861.* VI, 125.

3.—When I shall speak authoritatively, I hope to say nothing inconsistent with the Constitution, the Union, the rights of all the states, of each state, and of each section of the country, and not to disappoint the reasonable expectations of those who have confided to me their votes.—*Speech, Buffalo, Feb. 16, 1861.* VI, 134.

4.—When the time comes, I shall speak, as well as I am able, for the good of the present and future of this country—for the good both of the North and the South—for the good of the one and the other, and of all sections of the country.—*Speech, New York Legislature, Feb. 18, 1861.* VI, 141.

5.—I have said several times upon this journey, and I now repeat it to you, that when the time does come [for Lincoln to speak] I shall then take the ground that I think is right—right for the North, for the South, for the East, for the West; for the whole country. And in doing so, I hope to feel no necessity pressing upon me to say anything in conflict with the Constitution; in conflict with the continued union of these states, in conflict with the perpetuation of the liberties of this people, or anything in conflict with anything whatever that I have ever given you reason to expect from me.—*Speech, New York, Feb. 19, 1861.* VI, 147.

6.—I shall endeavor to take the ground that I deem most just to the North, the East, the West, the South, and the whole country. . . . I shall do what may be in my power to promote a peaceful settlement of all our difficulties.—*Speech to New Jersey Assembly, Feb. 21, 1861.* VI, 153.

7.—If I do speak then [next Monday week], it is useless for me to do so now. When I do speak, I shall take such ground as I deem best calculated to restore peace, harmony, and prosperity to the country, and tend to the perpetuity of the nation and the liberty of these states and these people.—*Speech, reply to mayor of Philadelphia, Feb. 21, 1861.* VI, 155.

See SILENCE, post-election explained.

Inaugural, second, should "wear well"—Everyone likes a compliment. Thank you for yours on my little ratification speech and on the recent inaugural address. I expect the latter to wear as well as—perhaps better than—anything I have produced; but I believe it is not immediately popular. Men are not flat-

tered by being shown that there has been a difference of purpose between the Almighty and them. To deny it, however, in this case, is to deny that there is a God governing the world. It is a truth which I thought needed to be told, and, as whatever of humiliation there is in it falls most directly upon myself, I thought others might afford for me to tell it.—*To Thurlow Weed, March 15, 1865.* XI, 54.

Income tax, exemption urged for foreign consuls—*See* CONSULS, tax exemption urged for foreign.

Independence, national, conserved by republican system—*See* SELF-GOVERNMENT, Can it survive? 4.

Independence Hall, source of inspiration—Your worthy mayor has expressed the wish, in which I join him, that it were convenient for me to remain in your city long enough to consult your merchants and manufacturers; or, as it were, to listen to those breathings rising within the consecrated walls wherein the Constitution of the United States, and, I will add, the Declaration of Independence, were originally framed and adopted. I assure you and your mayor that I had hoped on this occasion, and upon all occasions during my life, that I shall do nothing inconsistent with the teaching of these holy and most sacred walls. I have never asked anything that does not breathe from these walls. All my political warfare has been in favor of the teachings that came forth from these sacred walls. May my right hand forget its cunning and my tongue cleave to the roof of my mouth if ever I prove false to those teachings.—*Speech, reply to mayor of Philadelphia, Feb. 21, 1861.* VI, 156.

2.—I am filled with deep emotion at finding myself standing in this place, where were collected together the wisdom, the patriotism, the devotion to principle, from which sprang the institutions under which we live. . . . All the political sentiments I entertain have been drawn, so far as I have been able to draw them, from the sentiments which originated in and were given to the world from this [Independence] hall.—*Speech, Independence Hall, Philadelphia, Feb. 22, 1861.* V, 156.

Indian Tribes, disturbed by war—The relations of the government with the Indian tribes have been greatly disturbed by the insurrection, especially in the southern superintendency, and in New Mexico. . . . It has been stated in the public press that a portion of those Indians have been organized as a military force, and are attached to the army of the insurgents. . . . It is believed that upon the repossession of the country by the federal forces the Indians will readily cease all hostile demonstrations and resume their former relations to the government.—*First annual message, Dec. 3, 1861.* VII, 46.

Indian Tribes, friendlier relations with, foreseen— It is hoped that the effect of these treaties [agreements with various tribes for "extinguishing the possessory rights of the Indians to large and valuable tracts of land"] will result in the establishment of permanent friendly relations with such of these tribes as have been brought into frequent and bloody collision with our outlying settlements and emigrants. Sound policy and our imperative duty to these wards of the government demand our anxious and constant attention to their material well-being, to their progress in the arts of civilization, and above all, to that moral training which under the blessing of Divine Providence will confer upon them the elevated and sanctifying influences, the hopes and consolations of the Christian faith.—*Third annual message, Dec. 8, 1863.* IX, 243.

Indian Tribes, paroled prisoners to curb—I know it is your purpose to send the paroled prisoners to the seat of the Indian difficulties; and I write this only to urge that this be done with all possible dispatch. Gen. Wool telegraphs that, including those from Harper's Ferry, there are now twenty thousand at Annapolis, requiring four good unparoled regiments to guard them. This should not be endured beyond the earliest moment possible to change it. Arm them and send them away just as fast as the railroads will carry them.—*To Sec. Stanton, Sept. 20, 1862.* Angle, 306.

Indian Tribes, system needs revision—I submit for your special consideration whether our Indian system shall not be remodeled. Many wise and good men have impressed me with the belief that this can be profitably done.—*Second annual message, Dec. 1, 1862.* VIII, 108.
2.—I suggested in my last annual message the propriety of remodeling our Indian system. Subsequent events have satisfied me of its necessity.—*Third annual message, Dec. 8, 1863.* IX, 243.
3.—It was recommended in my last annual message that our Indian system be remodeled. Congress at its last session, acting upon the recommendation, did provide for reorganizing the system in California, and it is believed that under the present organization the management of the Indians there will be attended with reasonable success. Much yet remains to be done to provide for the proper government of the Indians in other parts of the country, to render it secure for the advancing settler, and to provide for the welfare of the Indian.—*Fourth annual message, Dec. 6, 1864.* X, 300.

Indiana, soldier vote urged—The state election of Indiana occurs on the 11th of October, and the loss of it, to the friends of the government, would go far toward losing the whole Union cause. . . . Indiana is the only important state, voting in October, whose soldiers cannot vote in the field. Anything you can safely do to let her soldiers, or any part of them, go home and vote at the state election will be greatly to the point.—*To Gen. Sherman, Sept. 19, 1864.* X, 225.

Indiana, sought privilege of having slaves—I believe Indiana once or twice, if not Ohio, petitioned the general government for the privilege of suspending that provision [of the Ordinance of 1787, prohibiting slavery in the Northwest Territory] and allowing them to have slaves. . . . The action was to refuse them the privilege of violating the Ordinance of '87. —*Speech, Columbus, Ohio, Sept. 16, 1859.* V, 170.
2.—In her [Indiana's] territorial condition she more than once petitioned Congress to abrogate the ordinance [of 1787] entirely, or at least so far as to suspend its operation for a time, in order that they should exercise the "popular sovereignty" of having slaves, if they wanted them. The men then controlling the general government, imitating the men of the Revolution, refused Indiana that privilege. And so we have the evidence that Indiana supposed she could have slaves, if it were not for that ordinance.— *Speech, Cincinnati, Sept. 17, 1859.* V, 223.

Indiana Troops, thanked—*See* CIVIL WAR, Indiana troops thanked.

See PEOPLE, relied on to save Union, 22.

Individual Right—I believe each individual is naturally entitled to do as he pleases with himself and the fruit of his labor, so far as it in no wise interferes with any other men's rights.—*Speech, Chicago, July 10, 1858.* III, 35.

Inference, fact and—Does not this fact cut up your inference by the roots?—*To Rev. J. M. Peck, May 21, 1848.* II, 23.

Injunction, defined—The word "injunction" in common language imports a command that some person or thing shall not move or be removed; in law it has the same meaning.—*To editor of Sangamo Journal, Oct. 28, 1837.* I, 81.

Inland Waterways, contrasted with railroads—*See* RAILROADS, contrasted with waterways.

Inland waterways—*See* INTERNAL IMPROVEMENTS.

See ILLINOIS AND MICHIGAN CANAL.

Insurgents—*See* CIVIL WAR.

Insurrection—*See* CIVIL WAR.

Intemperance—*See* TEMPERANCE.

Internal Improvements, "arrayed against themselves"—I suppose all, or nearly all, Democrats will vote for him [Cass for President]. Many of them will do so, not because they like his position on this question, [of improvements] but because they prefer him, being wrong on this, to another whom they consider farther wrong on other questions. In this way the internal-improvement Democrats are to be, by a sort of forced consent, carried over and arrayed against themselves on this measure of policy.—*Speech in Congress, June 20, 1848.* II, 30.

Internal Improvements, budget plan suggested for—I would not borrow money. I am against an overwhelming, crushing system. Suppose that, at each session, Congress shall first determine how much money can, for that year, be spared for [internal] improvements; then apportion that sum to the most important objects. . . . Adopt and adhere to this course, and, it seems to me, the difficulty is cleared.—*Speech in Congress, June 20, 1848.* II, 47.

Internal Improvements, Chancellor Kent thought Congress had power—Many great and good men have been against the power; but it is insisted that quite as many, as great and as good, have been for it; and it is shown that, on a full survey of the whole, Chancellor Kent was of the opinion that the arguments of the latter were vastly superior. This is but the opinion of a man; but who was that man? He was one of the ablest and most learned lawyers of his age, or of any age. It is no disparagement of Mr. Polk, nor indeed of anyone who devotes much time to politics, to be placed far behind Chancellor Kent as a lawyer.—*Speech in Congress, June 20, 1848.* II, 40.

Internal Improvements, conflicting interests—All can recur to instances of this difficulty [urged by President Polk in opposing federal financing of internal improvements] in the case of county roads, bridges, and the like. One man is offended because a road passes over his land, and another is offended because it does not pass over his; one is dissatisfied because the bridge for which he is taxed crosses the river on a different road from that which leads from his house to town; another cannot bear that the county should be got in debt for those same roads and bridges; while not a few struggle hard to have roads located

over their lands, and then stoutly refuse to let them be opened until they are first paid the damages. Even between the different wards and streets of towns and cities we find this same wrangling and difficulty.—*Speech in Congress, June 20, 1848.* II, 45.

Internal Improvements, Congress can control expenditures—The President . . . tells us that at a certain point in our history more than two hundred millions of dollars had been applied for to make improvements; and this he does to prove that the treasury would be overwhelmed by such a system. Why did he not tell us how much was granted? . . . These [the four years of the J. Q. Adams administration], if any, must have been the days of the two hundred millions. And how much do you suppose was really expended for improvements during that four years? Two hundred millions? One hundred? Fifty? Ten? Five? No, sir, less than two millions. . . . This fact shows that when the power to make improvements "was fully asserted and exercised" [the President's expression], the Congress did keep within reasonable limits; and what has been done, it seems to me, can be done again.—*Speech in Congress, June 20, 1848.* II, 32.

Internal Improvements, crisis in—The question of [internal] improvements is verging to a final crisis; and the friends of this policy must now battle manfully, or surrender all.—*Speech in Congress, June 20, 1848.* II, 30.

Internal Improvements, do-nothing policy of Polk—*See* DO-NOTHING, policy decried.

Internal Improvements, favored—I am in favor of the internal improvement system.—*Reputed first public speech, March, 1832.* XI, 97.
2.—Time and experience have verified to a demonstration the public utility of internal improvements.—*Address to Sangamon County, March 9, 1832.* I, 1.

Internal Improvements, folly of, if uncompleted—That the poorest and most thinly populated countries would be greatly benefited by the opening of good roads, the clearing of navigable streams within their limits, is what no person will deny. Yet it is folly to undertake works of this or any other kind without first knowing that we are able to finish them—as half-finished work generally proves to be labor lost.—*Address to Sangamon County, March 9, 1832.* I, 1.

Internal Improvements, "inequality" argument answered—The burdens of [internal] improvements [says the President] would be general, while their benefits would be local and partial, involving an obnoxious inequality. . . . No commercial object of government patronage can be so exclusively general as not to be of some peculiar local advantage. The navy, as I understand it, was established, and is maintained, at a great annual expense, partly to be ready for war when war shall come, and partly also, and perhaps chiefly, for the protection of our commerce on the high seas. The latter object is, for all I can see, in principle the same as internal improvements. The driving a pirate from the track of commerce on the broad ocean, and removing a snag from its more narrow part in the Mississippi river, cannot, I think, be distinguished in principle.—*Speech in Congress, June 20, 1848.* II, 33.

2.—The next most general object I can think of would be improvements on the Mississippi river and its tributaries. They touch thirteen of our states. . . . Now I suppose it will not be denied that these thirteen states are a little more interested in improvements on that great river than are the remaining seventeen. . . . There is something of local advantage in the most general objects. But the converse is also true. Nothing is so local as not to be of some general benefit.—*Speech in Congress, June 20, 1848.* II, 35.

3.—If the nation refuse to make improvements of the more general kind because their benefits may be somewhat local, a state may for the same reason refuse to make an improvement because its benefits may be somewhat general. . . . Thus it is seen that if this argument of "inequality" is sufficient anywhere, it is sufficient everywhere, and puts an end to improvements altogether.—*Speech in Congress, June 20, 1848.* II, 35.

4.—Inequality is certainly never to be embraced for its own sake; but is every good thing to be discarded which may be inseparably connected with some degree of it? If so, we must discard all government.—*Speech in Congress, June 20, 1848.* II, 36.

5.—No work—no object—can be so general as to dispense its benefits with precise equality; and this inequality is chief among the "portentous consequences" for which he [Polk] declares that government should be arrested.—*Speech in Congress, June 20, 1848.* II, 44.

Internal Improvements, nation and states should cooperate—I hope and believe that if both the nation and the states would, in good faith, in their respective spheres, do what they could in the way of improvements, what of inequality might be produced in one place might be compensated in another and the sum of the whole might not be very unequal.—*Speech in Congress, June 20, 1848.* II, 36.

2.—From these [statistics] it would readily appear where a given amount of expenditure [for internal improvements] would do the most good. . . . In this way, and by these means, let the nation take hold of the larger works, and the states the smaller ones; and thus, working in a meeting direction, discreetly, but steadily and firmly, what is made unequal in one place may be equalized in another, extravagance avoided, and the whole country put on that career of prosperity which shall correspond with its extent of territory, its natural resources, and the intelligence and enterprise of its people.—*Speech in Congress, June 20, 1848.* II, 48.

Internal Improvements, only objections to—There cannot justly be any objection to having railroads and canals, any more than to any other good things, provided they cost nothing. The only objection is to paying for them; and the objection arises from want of ability to pay.—*Address to Sangamon County, March 9, 1848.* I, 2.

2.—Particularity—expending the money of the whole people for an object which will benefit only a portion of them—is the greatest objection to [internal] improvements.—*Speech in Congress, July 27, 1848.* II, 68.

Internal Improvements, Polk dodges own conclusions—When the President intimates that something in the way of improvements may properly be done by the general government, he is shrinking from the conclusions to which his own arguments would force him.—*Speech in Congress, June 20, 1848.* II, 44.

Internal Improvements, public-lands revenue urged for—I go for distributing the proceeds of the sales of public lands to the several states, to enable our state, in common with others, to dig canals and construct railroads without borrowing money and paying interest on it.—*To editor of Sangamon Journal, June 13, 1832.* I, 15.

2.—The distribution of the proceeds of the sale of public lands, upon the principles of Mr. Clay's bill, accords with the best interests of the nation, and particularly with those of the state of Illinois.—*Whig circular, March 1, 1843.* I, 241.

3.—In every light in which we can view this question, it amounts simply to this: Shall we accept our share of the proceeds under Mr. Clay's bill, or shall we rather reject that and get nothing?—*Whig circular, March 1, 1843.* I, 251.

Internal Improvements, tendency to "undue expansion"—The first position [of President Polk] is that a system of internal improvements would overwhelm the treasury. That in such a system [spending federal funds for internal improvements] there is a tendency to undue expansion, is not to be denied. Such ten-

dency is founded in the nature of the subject. A member of Congress will prefer voting for a bill which contains an appropriation for his district, to voting for one which does not; and when a bill shall be expanded till every district shall be provided for, that it will be too greatly expanded is obvious. But is this any more true in Congress than in a state legislature [where the President suggests the problem be handled]?—*Speech in Congress, June 20, 1848.* II, 31.
2.—The tendency to undue expansion is unquestionably the chief difficulty. How to do something, and still not do too much, is the desideratum.—*Speech in Congress, June 20, 1848.* II, 46.

International Law—*See* REVOLUTION, American policy of nonintervention.

See CIVIL WAR, Foreign nations' attitude toward, 10.

Interoceanic Transit Route, difficulties adjusted—It is a source of much satisfaction that the difficulties which for the moment excited some political apprehensions and caused a closing of the interoceanic transit route have been amicably adjusted, and that there is a good prospect that the route will soon be reopened with an increase of capacity and adaptation. We could not exaggerate either the commercial or political importance of that great improvement.—*Fourth annual message, Dec. 6, 1864.* X, 284.

Intrigue, danger of, foreseen—I understand a bill is before Congress, by your instigation, for taking your office from the control of the Department of the Interior, and considerably enlarging the powers and patronage of your office. . . . If the change is made, I do not think I can allow you to retain the office, because that would be encouraging officers to be constantly intriguing, to the detriment of the public interest, in order to profit themselves.—*To B. B. French, March 25, 1864.* X, 56.

Invasion, dangerous authority to concede—Allow the President to invade a neighboring nation whenever he shall deem it necessary to repel an invasion, and you allow him to do so whenever he may choose to say he deems it necessary for such purpose, and you allow him to make war at pleasure. . . . If today he should choose to say he thinks it necessary to invade Canada to prevent the British from invading us, how could you stop him? You may say to him, "I see no probability of the British invading us"; but he will say to you, "Be silent; I see it, if you don't."—*To W. H. Herndon, Feb. 15, 1848.* II, 2.

Invasion, of America "impossible"—Shall we expect some transatlantic military giant to step the ocean and crush us at a blow? Never! All the armies of Eu-

rope, Asia and Africa combined, with all the treasures of the earth—our own excepted—in their military chest, with a Bonaparte for a commander, could not by force take a drink from the Ohio or make a track on the Blue Ridge in a trial of a thousand years.—*Speech, Springfield, Jan. 27, 1837.* I, 36.

Invasion, policy toward—I denounce the lawless invasion by armed force of the soil of any state or territory, no matter under what pretext, as the greatest of crimes.—*To Duff Green, Dec. 28, 1860.* VI, 88.
2.—The power confided in me will be used to hold, occupy, and possess the property and places belonging to the government, and to collect the duties and imposts; but beyond what may be necessary for these objects, there will be no invasion, no using of force against or among the people anywhere.—*First inaugural, March 4, 1861.* VI, 175.

See VIRGINIA, policy toward.

Invasion, safe from lawless—*See* PEOPLE, "influenced by reason."

"Invasion and Coercion," words used loosely—The words "coercion" and "invasion" are much used in these days, and often with some temper and hot blood. . . . What, then, is "coercion"? What is "invasion"? Would the marching of an army into South Carolina without consent of her people, and with hostile intent toward them, be "invasion"? I certainly think it would; and it would be "coercion" also if the South Carolinians were forced to submit. But if the United States should merely hold and retake its own forts and other property, and collect the duties on foreign importations, or even withhold the mails from places where they were habitually violated, would any or all of these things be "invasion" or "coercion"? Do our professed lovers of the Union, who spitefully resolve that they will resist invasion and coercion, understand that such things as these on the part of the United States would be coercion or invasion of a state? If so, their idea of means to preserve the object of their great affection would seem to be exceedingly thin and airy. If sick, the little pills of the homeopathist would be much too large for them to swallow. —*Speech, Indiana Legislature, Feb. 12, 1861.* VI, 113.

"Invasions and Insurrections"—*See* SOUTH, what will satisfy? 2.

Invention, first—*See* ADAM, joins Eve in first invention.

Invention, indispensable to—To be fruitful in invention, it is indispensable to have a habit of observation and reflection.—*Lecture, Springfield, Feb. 22, 1859.* V, 103.

2.—If he [Adam] should do anything in the way of inventions, he had first to invent the art of invention, the instance, if not the habit, of observation and re-flection.—*Lecture, Springfield, Feb. 22, 1859.* V, 104.

Iowa, all honor to—All thanks and all honor to Iowa! But Iowa is out of all danger, and it is no time for us, when the battle [for Frémont] still rages, to pay holy-day visits to Iowa.—*To Henry O'Conner, Sept. 14, 1856.* II, 299.

Iowa, volunteers from, thanked—*See* CIVIL WAR, hundred-day volunteers thanked.

Ipse Dixit, use of, denied—I must be allowed to say that Judge Douglas recurs again, as he did upon one or two other occasions, to the enormity of Lincoln . . . upon his ipse dixit charging a conspiracy upon a large number of members of Congress, the Supreme Court, and two Presidents, to nationalize slavery. I want to say that, in the first place, I have made no charge of this sort upon my ipse dixit. I have only arrayed the evidence tending to prove it, and presented it to the understanding of others, saying what I think it proves, but giving you the means of judging whether it proves it or not. . . . I have not placed it upon my ipse dixit at all.—*Debate, Freeport, Aug. 27, 1858.* III, 290.

Irishmen, characterized—He [Edward Hannegan] was the son of an Irishman, with a bit of the brogue still lingering on his tongue; and with a large share of that sprightliness and generous feeling which generally characterize Irishmen who have anything of a fair chance in the world.—*Speech, Springfield, Aug. 14, 1852.* Angle, 97.

Irish Revolution, sympathy for—*See* GREAT BRITAIN, enemy of freedom.

See REVOLUTION, American sympathy for.

Iron, early importance of—The discovery of the property of iron, and the making of iron tools, must have been among the earliest of important discoveries and inventions. We can scarcely conceive the possibility of making much of anything else, without the use of iron tools. Indeed an iron hammer must have been very much needed to make the first iron hammer with.—*Lecture, Springfield, no date.* Hertz II, 797.

"Irrepressible Conflict," difference in who says it—He [Douglas] . . . has complained of Seward for declaring that there is an "irrepressible conflict" between the principles of free and slave labor. . . . But neither I nor Seward . . . is entitled to the enviable

or unenviable distinction of having first expressed that idea. That same idea was expressed by the Richmond *Enquirer* in Virginia, in 1856, quite two years before it was expressed by the first of us. And while Douglas was pluming himself that in his conflict with my humble self, last year, he had "squelched out" that fatal heresy, as he delighted to call it, and had suggested that if he only had had a chance to be in New York and meet Seward he would have "squelched" it there also, it never occurred to him to breathe a word against [Roger A.] Pryor [editor of the *Enquirer*]. . . . Pryor was brought to Washington City and made the editor of the *par excellence* Douglas paper after making use of that expression, which, in us, is so unpatriotic and heretical. From all this my Kentucky friends may all see that this opinion is heretical in his view only when it is expressed by men suspected of a desire that the country shall become free, and not when expressed by those fairly known to entertain the desire that the whole country shall become slave.—*Speech, Cincinnati, Sept. 17, 1859.* V, 214.

2.—Since that time [John] Hickman of Pennsylvania expressed the same sentiment ["irrepressible conflict," and so forth]. He [Douglas] has never denounced Hickman. Why? There is a little chance, notwithstanding that opinion in the mouth of Hickman, that he may yet be a Douglas man. That is the difference. It is not unpatriotic to hold that opinion, if a man is a Douglas man.—*Speech, Cincinnati, Sept. 17, 1859.* V, 214.

3.—Last year Gov. Seward and myself expressed the belief that this government cannot endure half slave and half free. This gave great offense to Douglas, and after the fall election in Illinois, he became quite rampant upon it. . . . He denounced it as a "fatal heresy." With great pride he claimed that he had crushed it in Illinois, and modestly regretted that he could not have been in New York to crush it there too. How the heresy is fatal to anything, or what the thing is to which it is fatal, he never paused to tell us. At all events, it is a fatal heresy in his view when expressed by a northern man. Not so when expressed by men of the South. In 1856 Roger A. Pryor, editor of the Richmond *Enquirer*, expressed the same belief in that paper, quite two years before it was expressed by either Seward or me. But Douglas perceived no "heresy" in him—talked not of going to Virginia to crush it out; nay, more, he now has that same Mr. Pryor at Washington, editing the *States* newspaper, as his special organ.—*Speeches in Kansas, Dec. 1-5, 1859.* V, 271.

4.—There is the "irrepressible conflict." How they rail at Seward for saying that! . . . Almost every good man since the formation of our government has uttered the same sentiment, from Gen. Washington, who "trusted that we should yet have a confederacy of free states," with Jefferson, Jay, Monroe, down to the latest days. . . . Even Roger A. Pryor, editor of the Richmond *Enquirer,* uttered the same sentiment in almost the same language, and yet so little offense did it give the Democrats that he was sent for to Washington to edit the *States*—the Douglas organ there, while Douglas goes into hydrophobia and spasms of rage because Seward dared to repeat it.— *Speech, New Haven, Conn., March 6, 1860.* V. 358.

"Irrepressible Conflict," how produced—These two ideas—the property idea that slavery is right and the idea that it is wrong—come into collision, and do actually produce that irrepressible conflict which Mr. Seward has been so roundly abused for mentioning. The two ideas conflict, and must forever conflict.— *Speech, New Haven, Conn., March 6, 1860.* V, 345. Repeated at Norwich, Conn., March 9, 1860. VI, 3.

Italy, never faltered—I am free to confess that the United States have in the course of the last three years encountered vicissitudes and been involved in controversies which have tried the friendship and even the forbearance of other nations, but at no stage in this unhappy fraternal war in which we are only endeavoring to save and strengthen the foundations of our national unity has the king or the people of Italy faltered in addressing to us the language of respect, confidence, and friendship. . . . I pray God to have your country in His holy keeping, and to vouchsafe to crown with success her noble aspirations to renew, under the auspices of her present enlightened government, her ancient career, so wonderfully illustrated in the achievements of art, science, and freedom.—*Reply to Italian Envoy Bertinatti, July 23, 1864.* X, 169.

Jackson, Andrew, fruitful popularity of—You [Democrats] not only twice made a President of him [Jackson] out of it [Jackson's popularity], but you have had enough of the stuff left to make Presidents of several comparatively small men since; and it is your chief reliance now to make still another.—*Speech in Congress, July 27, 1848.* II, 73.

Jackson, Andrew, "military coat-tails" of—*See* "MILITARY COAT-TAILS," 1.

Jackson, Andrew, "Samson's locks"—*See* MAN OF STRAW, President must avoid being.

Jackson, Andrew, Supreme Court and bank decision Judge Douglas will have it that all hands must take this extraordinary [Dred Scott] decision . . . and . . .

yield to it and obey it in every possible sense. Circumstances alter cases. Do not gentlemen here remember that case of that same Supreme Court, some 25 or 30 years ago, deciding that a national bank was constitutional? . . . The bank charter ran out, and a recharter was granted by Congress. That recharter was laid before Gen. Jackson. It was urged upon him, when he denied the constitutionality of the bank, that the Supreme Court had decided that it was constitutional; and Gen. Jackson then said the Supreme Court had no right to lay down a rule to govern a co-ordinate branch of the government, the members of which had sworn to support the Constitution— that each member had sworn to support the Constitution as he understood it. . . . I have heard Judge Douglas say that he approved of Gen. Jackson for that act.—*Speech, Chicago, July 10, 1858.* III, 40.
2.—The case [against the National Bank] went to the Supreme Court, and therein it was decided that the bank was constitutional. The whole Democratic party revolted against that decision. Gen. Jackson himself asserted that he, as President, would not be bound to hold a national bank to be constitutional, even though the court had decided it to be so. . . . The declaration that Congress does not possess this constitutional power to charter a bank has gone into the Democratic platform. . . . They have contended for that declaration in the very teeth of the Supreme Court for more than a quarter of a century.—*Speech, Springfield, July 17, 1858.* III, 180.
3.—Gen. Jackson once said that each man was bound to support the Constitution, "as he understood it." Now, Judge Douglas understands the Constitution according to the Dred Scott decision, and he is bound to support it as he understands it. I understand it another way, and therefore I am bound to support it in the way in which I understand it.—*Debate, Quincy, Oct. 13, 1858.* IV, 378.

See JUDICIAL DECISIONS, Douglas's attitude toward, 8.

See NATIONAL BANK, constitutionality of, affirmed, 1.

Jackson, "Stonewall," "game" suspected—I think Jackson's game—his assigned work—now is to magnify the accounts of his numbers and reports of his movements, and thus by constant alarms keep three or four times as many of our troops away from Richmond as his own force amounts to. Thus he helps his friends at Richmond three or four times as much as if he were there.—*To Gen. Frémont, June 15, 1862.* VII, 222.

Japan, Funayma Solace incident—A war steamer called the *Funayma Solace,* having been built in this country for the Japanese government and at the instance of that government, it is deemed to comport with the public interest, in view of the unsettled condition of the relations of the United States with that empire, that the steamer should not be allowed to proceed to Japan. If, however, the secretary of the navy should ascertain that the steamer is adapted to our service he is authorized to purchase her.—*Executive order, Dec. 3, 1864.* XI, 133.

Japan, Fusigama incident—The Japanese government having caused the construction at New York of a vessel of war called the *Fusigama,* and application having been made for clearance of the same, in order that it may proceed to Japan, it is ordered that, in view of the state of affairs in that country and of its relation with the United States, that a compliance with the application be for the present suspended.— *Executive order, Oct. 12, 1864.* Messages, VIII, 3443.

Japan, good wishes for—Wishing abundant prosperity and length of years to the great state over which you preside, I pray God to have your Majesty always in his safe and holy keeping.—*Reply to tycoon of Japan, Aug. 1, 1861.* VI, 337.

Japan, "inconstant and capricious"—Owing to the peculiar situation of Japan and the anomalous form of its government, the action of that empire in performing treaty stipulations is inconstant and capricious. . . . Our own pecuniary claims have been allowed or put in course of settlement, and the inland sea has been reopened to commerce. There is reason also to believe that these proceedings have increased rather than diminishd the friendship of Japan toward the United States.—*Fourth annual message, Dec. 6, 1864.* X, 287.

Japan, relations with, in "serious jeopardy"—In common with other western powers, our relations with Japan have been brought into serious jeopardy through the perverse opposition by the heriditary aristocracy of the empire to the enlightened and liberal policy of the tycoon, designed to bring the country into the society of nations. It is hoped, although not with entire confidence, that these difficulties may be peacefully overcome.—*Third annual message, Dec. 8, 1863.* IX, 229.

Jaquess, James F., tribute to—Here is a man, cool, deliberate, God-fearing, of exceptional sagacity, and worldly wisdom, who undertakes a project that strikes you and me as chimerical; he attempt to bring about single-handed, and on his own hook, a peace between two great sections. . . . He is very far from being a fanatic. He is remarkably level-headed; I never saw a man more so.—*To James R. Gilmore, late May, 1863.* Gilmore, 160.

Jaquess, James F.—*See* COPPERHEADS, would scoff.

Jefferson, Thomas, death of—*See* ADAMS, JOHN, death of.

Jefferson, Thomas, Democrats forget—There was once in this country a man by the name of Thomas Jefferson, supposed to be a Democrat—a man whose principles and policies are not very prevalent among Democrats today.—*Speech, Columbus, Ohio, Sept. 16, 1859.* V, 159.

Jefferson, Thomas, denial of principles of, looks toward despotism—*See* DESPOTISM, those who deny Jefferson are vanguards of.

Jefferson, Thomas, "most distinguished politician"— Mr. [Thomas] Jefferson . . . was, is, and perhaps will continue to be, the most distinguished politician of our history.—*Speech, Peoria, Oct. 16, 1854.* II, 193. Repeated at Urbana, Oct. 24, 1854. Hertz II, 628.

Jefferson, Thomas, favored abolition—*See* ABOLITION, Virginians advocated, 2, 3.

Jefferson, Thomas, nothing derogatory of—I never said anything derogatory of Mr. Jefferson in McDonough County or elsewhere.—*To J. H. Reed, Sept. 1, 1860.* VI, 60.

Jefferson, Thomas, principles of, threatened—It is now no child's play to save the principles of Jefferson from total overthrow in this nation. . . . The principles of Jefferson are the definitions and axioms of free society. And yet they are denied and evaded, with no small show of success. One dashingly calls them "glittering generalities." Another bluntly calls them "self-evident lies." And others insidiously argue that they apply to "superior races."—*To H. L. Pierce and others, April 6, 1859.* V, 126.

Jefferson, Thomas, quoted on judicial decisions—*See* JUDICIAL DICTATORSHIP, way to, 2.

Jefferson, Thomas, slavery and Northwest Territory —*See* ORDINANCE OF 1787, fruits of, 2.

Jefferson, Thomas, slavery decried by—While Mr. Jefferson was the owner of slaves, as undoubtedly he was, in speaking upon this very subject, he used the strong language that "he trembled for his country when he remembered that God was just."—*Debate, Galesburg, Oct. 7, 1858.* IV, 263.
2.—In contemplation of this thing [slavery], we all know he [Jefferson] was led to exclaim, "I tremble for

my country when I remember that God is just."—*Speech, Columbus, Ohio, Sept. 16, 1859.* V, 159.

See SLAVERY, Jefferson versus Douglas on, 1.

Jefferson, Thomas, supporters and opponents of, trade creeds—Remembering . . . that the Jefferson party was formed upon its supposed superior devotion to the personal rights of men, holding the rights of property to be secondary only, and greatly inferior, and assuming that the so-called Democracy of today are the Jeffersonian, and their opponents the anti-Jeffersonian, party, it will be . . . interesting to note how completely the two have changed hands as to the principle upon which they were originally supposed to be divided. The Democracy of today hold the liberty of one man to be absolutely nothing, when in conflict with another man's right of property; Republicans, on the contrary, are for both the man and the dollar, but in case of conflict the man before the dollar.—*To H. L. Pierce and others, April 6, 1859.* V, 125.

Jefferson, Thomas, tribute to—All honor to Jefferson—to the man, who, in the concrete pressure of a struggle for national independence by a single people, had the coolness, forecast and capacity to introduce into a merely revolutionary document an abstract truth, applicable to all men and all times, and so to embalm it there that today and in all coming days it shall be a rebuke and a stumbling block to the very harbingers of reappearing tyranny and oppression.—*To H. L. Pierce and others, April 6, 1859.* V, 126.

See FREE SOCIETY.

Jefferson, Thomas, veto power and—*See* VETO, Taylor agrees with Jefferson.

Jefferson, Thomas, yields scruples—*See* LOUISIANA PURCHASE.

Jett, Jim, brother of—*See* FRÉMONT, JOHN C., characterized, 6.

Johnson, Andrew, asked to raise negro troops—*See* NEGRO TROOPS, importance of, 1.

Johnson, Andrew, proclamation of, approved—I have seen and examined Gov. Johnson's proclamation [ordering an election in Tennessee], and am entirely satisfied with his plan, which is to restore the state government and place it under the control of citizens truly loyal to the government of the United States.—*To E. H. East, Feb. 27, 1864.* X, 21.

Johnson, Andrew, proposal of, rejected—Do you not, my good friend, perceive that what you ask is simply to put you in command in the West? I do not suppose you desire this. You only wish to control in your own localities, but this you must know may disarrange all other parts.—*To Gov. Johnson, July 11, 1862.* Hertz II, 872.

Johnson, Andrew, "true and valuable"—Gov. Johnson . . . is a true and valuable man—indispensable to us in Tennessee.—*To Gen. Halleck, July 11, 1862.* VII, 269.

Johnson, Reverdy, answered—*See* RECONSTRUCTION, Louisiana, 1.

See FRIENDS, some of their advice distrusted.

Johnston, Joseph E., might have been arrested—*See* CONFEDERATE GENERALS, might have been arrested.

Judas—*See* TREASON, Judas an example.

Judd, N. B., confidence in—The vague charge that you played me false last year I believe to be false and outrageous; but it seems I can make no impression by expressing that belief.—*To Mr. Judd, Dec. 9, 1859.* V, 281.
2.—I have never believed, and do not now believe, that on that occasion [senatorial campaign, 1858] there was any unfairness in the conduct of Mr. Judd toward me, or anything blamable on his part. I have always believed, and now believe, that during that canvass he did his whole duty toward me and the Republican party. . . . I neither know nor suspect anything unfair in his conduct toward myself in any way. There is not one of them [avowed friends in 1858] in whose honor and integrity I have more confidence than in that of Mr. Judd.—*To George W. Dole and others, Dec. 14, 1858.* V, 284.

Judgment, must follow own—If I must discard my own judgment and take yours, I must also take that of others; and by the time I should reject all I should be advised to reject, I should have none left, Republicans or others, not even yourself.—*To Gen. Schurz, Nov. 24, 1862.* VIII, 85.
2.—I have acted according to my best judgment in every case.—*Reply to Presbyterian General Assembly. —May 30, 1863.* VIII, 287.

Judgment Deferred—There is something so ludicrous in promises of good or threats of evil a great way off as to render the whole subject with which they are connected turned into ridicule. "Better lay down that spade you are stealing, Paddy; if you don't, you'll pay for it at the day of Judgment." "By the powers, if ye'll credit me so long, I'll take another jist."—*Speech, Springfield, Feb. 22, 1842.* I, 202.

Judicial Decisions, Douglas's attitude toward—That [National Bank] decision, I repeat, is repudiated in the Cincinnati [Democratic] platform; and still, as if to show that effrontery can go no further, Judge Douglas vaunts, in the very speech in which he denounces me for opposing the Dred Scott decision, that he stands on the Cincinnati platform.—*Speech, Springfield, July 17, 1858.* III, 180.

2.—The plain truth is simply this—Judge Douglas is for Supreme Court decisions when he likes, and against them when he does not like them. He is for the Dred Scott decision because it tends to nationalize slavery—because it is part of the original combination for that object.—*Speech, Springfield, July 17, 1858.* III, 181.

3.—I will tell him, though, that he now claims to stand on the Cincinnati platform, which affirms that Congress cannot charter a national bank, in the teeth of that old standing decision [of the Supreme Court] that Congress can charter a bank.—*Debate, Ottawa, Aug. 21, 1858.* III, 253.

4.—I remind him [Douglas] of another piece of history on the question of respect for judicial decisions; and it is a piece of Illinois history, belonging to a time when a large party to which Judge Douglas belongs were displeased with a decision of the supreme court of Illinois, because they had decided that a governor could not remove a secretary of state. . . . Judge Douglas will not deny that he was then in favor of overslaughing that decision by the mode of adding five new judges, so as to vote down the four old ones. Not only so, but it ended in the judge's sitting down on the very bench as one of the five new judges. . . . It was in this way precisely that he got his title of judge.—*Debate, Ottawa, Aug. 21, 1858.* III, 254.

5.—Douglas demands that we shall bow to all decisions. If the courts are to decide on political subjects, how long will it be till Jefferson's fears of a political despotism are realized? He denounces all opposed to the Dred Scott opinions, in disregard of his former opposition to real decisions and the fact that he got his title of judge by breaking down a decision of our supreme court.—*Speech, Carlinville, Aug. 31, 1858.* Angle, 192.

6.—He [Douglas] was once a leading man in Illinois to break down a court because it had made a decision he did not like. But he now . . . denounces all men that do not swear by the courts as unpatriotic, as bad citizens.—*Speech, Cincinnati, Sept. 17, 1859.* V, 213.

7.—I remind him [Douglas] of a piece of Illinois history about Supreme Court decisions—of a time when the Supreme Court of Illinois, consisting of four judges, because of one decision made, and one ex-

pected to be made, were overwhelmed by the adding of five new judges to their number; that he, Judge Douglas, took a leading part in that onslaught. . . . Why with a longer record more marked for hostility to judicial decisions than almost any living man, does he cling to this [Dred Scott decision] with a devotion that nothing can baffle? *Notes, Oct. 1, 1858.* IV, 221.

8.—I point out to him [Douglas] that Mr. Jefferson and Gen. Jackson were both against him on the binding political authority of Supreme Court decisions. No response. . . . I tell him I have often heard him denounce the Supreme Court decision in favor of a national bank.—*Notes, Oct. 1, 1858.* IV, 221.

9.—I remind him [Douglas] that he, even now, indorses the Cincinnati platform, which declares that Congress has no constitutional power to charter a bank; and that in the teeth of a Supreme Court decision that Congress has such power. This he cannot deny; and so he remembers to forget it.—*Notes, Oct. 1, 1858.* IV, 221.

10.—I have asked his [Douglas's] attention to the fact that he himself was one of the most active instruments at one time in breaking down the Supreme Court of Illinois, because it had made a decision distasteful to him—a struggle ending in the remarkable circumstance of his sitting down as one of the new judges who were to overslaugh that decision, getting his title as judge in that very way.—*Debate, Galesburg, Oct. 7, 1858.* IV, 287.

11.—He [Douglas] is desirous of knowing how we are going to reverse the Dred Scott decision. Judge Douglas ought to know how. Did not he and his political friends find a way to reverse the decision of that same court in favor of the constitutionality of the national bank? Didn't they find a way to do it so effectually that they have reversed it as completely as any decision was ever reversed, so far as its practical operation is concerned? And, let me ask you, didn't Judge Douglas find a way to reverse the decision of our [Illinois] Supreme Court, when it decided that Carlin's father—old Gov. Carlin—had not the constitutional power to remove a secretary of state? Did he not appeal to the "mobs," as he calls them? Did he not make speeches in the lobby to show how villainous that decision was, and how it ought to be overthrown? Did he not succeed, too, in getting an act passed by the legislature to have it overthrown? . . . If there is villainy in using disrespect or making opposition to Supreme Court decisions, I commend it to Judge Douglas's earnest consideration. I know of no man in the state of Illinois who ought to know so well about how much villainy it takes to oppose a decision of the Supreme Court as our honorable friend, Stephen A. Douglas.—*Debate, Quincy, Oct. 13, 1858.* IV, 377.

See DRED SCOTT DECISION, Douglas's devotion to, 6.

See JACKSON, ANDREW, Supreme Court and bank decision, 1, 3.

Judicial Decisions, obedience to and respect for—We believe as much as Judge Douglas—perhaps more—in obedience to, and respect for, the judicial department of government. We think its decisions on constitutional questions, when fully settled, should control not only the particular cases decided, but the general policy of the country, subject to be disturbed only by amendments to the Constitution as provided in that instrument itself. More than this would be revolution.—*Speech, Springfield, Dec. 10, 1857.* II, 320.

2.—I wish to stand erect before the country, as well as Judge Douglas, on this question of judicial authority.—*Speech, Springfield, July 17, 1858.* III, 178.

3.—It so happens, singularly enough, that I never stood opposed to a decision of the Supreme Court till this [Dred Scott]. On the contrary, I have no recollection that he [Douglas] was ever particularly in favor of one till this.—*Speech, Springfield, July 17, 1858.* III, 181.

4.—Such decisions [of the Supreme Court] must be binding in any case, upon the parties to the suit, while they are also entitled to very high respect and consideration in all parallel cases by all other departments of the government. And while it is obviously possible that such decisions may be erroneous in any given case, still the evil effects following it, being limited to that particular case, with the chance that it may be overruled and never become a precedent for other cases, can better be borne than could the evils of a different practice.—*First inaugural, March 4, 1861.* VI, 179.

See DRED SCOTT DECISION, challenged.

Judicial Decisions, two uses of—Judicial decisions have two uses—first, to absolutely determine the case decided; and, secondly, to indicate to the public how other similar cases will be decided when they arise. For the latter use they are called "precedents" and "authorities."—*Speech, Springfield, June 27, 1857.* II, 320.

2.—What are the uses of decisions of courts? They have two uses. As rules of property they have two uses. First—they decide upon the question before the court. They decide in this case that Dred Scott is a slave. Nobody resists that. Not only that, but they say to everybody else that persons standing just as Dred

Scott stands are as he is. That is, they say that when a question comes up upon another person, it will be so decided again, unless the court decides in another way, unless the court overrules its decision.—*Speech, Chicago, July 10, 1858.* III, 39.

Judicial Dictatorship, way to—If the courts are to decide upon political subjects, how long will it be till Jefferson's fears of a political despotism are realized? —*Speech, Carlinville, Aug. 31, 1858.* Angle, 192.

2.—Jefferson said that "judges are as honest as other men and not more so." And he said, substantially, that whenever a free people should give up in absolute submission to any department of government, retaining for themselves no appeal from it, their liberties were gone.—*Debate, Galesburg, Oct. 7, 1858.* IV, 286.

3.—The candid citizen must confess that if the policy of government upon vital questions affecting the whole people is to be irrevocably fixed by decisions of the Supreme Court, the instant they are made in ordinary litigation between parties in personal actions, the people will have ceased to be their own rulers, having to that extent practically resigned their government into the hands of that eminent tribunal. Nor is there in this view any assault upon the court or the judges. . . . It is no fault of theirs if others seek to turn their decisions to political purposes.— *First inaugural, March 4, 1861.* VI, 180.

Judicial Integrity, Douglas "ought to know"—When the judge tells me that men appointed conditionally to sit as members of a court will have to be catechised beforehand upon some subject, I say, "You know, Judge; you have tried it." When he says a court of this kind will lose the confidence of all men, will be prostituted and disgraced by such a proceeding, I say, "You know best, Judge; you have been through the mill."—*Debate, Ottawa, Aug. 21, 1858.* III, 254.

Judiciary, elective, approved—*See* COURTS, uneasy about.

Judiciary, independence of, endangered—Respect for public opinion, and regard for the rights and liberties of the people, have hitherto restrained the spirit of party from attacks upon the independence and integrity of the judiciary. . . . Men professing respect for public opinion . . . were unwilling to see the temples of justice and the seats of independent judges occupied by the tools of faction. . . . [Now, we believe] that the independence of the judiciary has been destroyed, and hereafter our courts will be independent of the people, and entirely dependent upon the legislature; that our rights of property and liberty of conscience can no longer be regarded as safe from the encroachments of unconstitutional legislation.—*Whig committee circular, Feb. 9, 1841.* I, 161.

2.—[We, Whig members of legislature] cannot assent to the passage of the [pending] bill . . . [for] the reorganization of the judiciary, because—1. It violates the great principle of free government by subjecting the judiciary to the legislature. 2. It is a fatal blow at the independence of the judges.—*Protest, Illinois Legislature, Feb. 26, 1841.* I, 166.

Judiciary, politics and—By the way, if we should nominate him [John McLean for President] how would we save ourselves the chance of filling his vacancy in the [U.S. Supreme] court? Have him hold on up to the moment of his inauguration? Would that course be no drawback upon us in the canvass?—*To Lyman Trumbull, April 29, 1860.* Tracy, 143.

Juggernaut—*See* POLITICAL PARTIES, power of the lash, 4.

Justice, certain to prevail—*See* PEOPLE, justice of.

Justice, for and against government—It is as much the duty of government to render prompt justice against itself, in favor of citizens, as it is to administer the same between private individuals.—*First annual message, Dec. 3, 1861.* VII, 42.

Justice, not best if too severe—The severest justice may not always be the best policy. The principle of seizing and appropriating the property of persons [engaged in rebellion] is certainly not objectionable, but a justly discriminating application of it would be very difficult, and to a great extent impossible.—*Message to House, July 17, 1862.* VII, 283.

Justice, "only political wisdom"—*See* SLAVERY, wrong of, 15.

Justice, sacrificed to party—The immutable principles of justice are to make way for party interests, and the bonds of social order are to be rent in twain, in order that a desperate faction may be sustained at the expense of the people.—*Whig circular, Feb. 8, 1841.* I, 164.

Justice, walls of—Your hisses will not blow down the walls of justice.—*Speech, Cincinnati, Sept. 17, 1859.* Hertz II, 731.

"Justice and Fairness to All"—*See* CAMPAIGN OF 1860; silence is candidate's best policy, 1, 3.

"Justice to All," rule in patronage—*See* PATRONAGE, "Justice to all."

See CODE OF CONDUCT, rules for personal guidance, 7.

Kansas, advice to Republicans—If I might advise my Republican friends here, I would say to them: Leave your Missouri neighbors alone. Have nothing whatever to do with their slaves. Have nothing whatever to do with the white people except in a friendly way. Drop past differences, and so conduct yourselves that, if you cannot be at peace with them, the fault shall be wholly theirs.—*Speech, Leavenworth, Kan., Dec. 3, 1859.* Angle, 234.

Kansas, Douglas would disestablish freedom in—*See* FREEDOM, Douglas would disestablish.

Kansas, Dred Scott decision and—Kansas was settled, for example, in 1854. It was a territory yet, without having formed a constitution, in a very regular way, for three years. All this time negro slavery could be taken in by any few individuals, and by that decision of the Supreme Court which the judge [Douglas] approves, all the rest of the people cannot keep it out; but when they come to make a constitution they may say they will not have slavery. But it is there; they are obliged to tolerate it some way, and all experience shows it will be so—for they will not take the negro slaves and absolutely deprive the owners of them. . . . All that space of time that runs from the beginning of the settlement of the territory until there is sufficiency of people to make a state constitution—all that portion of time popular sovereignty is given up. The seal is absolutely put down upon it by the court decision, and Judge Douglas puts his own upon top of that; yet he is appealing to the people to give him vast credit for his devotion to popular sovereignty.—*Speech, Chicago, July 10, 1858.* III, 25.

Kansas, election in, a "farce"—The returns [from the Kansas election] are as yet very incomplete; but so far as they go, they indicate that only about one-sixth of the registered voters have really voted; and this, too, when not more, perhaps, than one-half of the rightful voters have been registered, thus showing the thing to have been altogether the most exquisite farce ever enacted.—*Speech, Springfield, June 26, 1857.* II, 319.

Kansas, eve of statehood—You are, as yet, people of a territory; but you probably soon will be the people of a state of the Union. Then you will be in possession of new privileges, and new duties will be upon you. You will have to bear a part in all that pertains to the administration of the national government.—*Speech, Leavenworth, Kan., Dec. 3, 1859.* Angle, 230.

Kansas, evidence of bad faith in—I do not admit that good faith in taking a negro to Kansas to be held in slavery is a probability with any.—*To Joshua F. Speed, Aug. 24, 1855.* II, 286.

Kansas, freedom denied in—By every principle of law ever held by any court north or south, every negro taken to Kansas is free; yet, in utter disregard of this, in the spirit of violence merely—, that beautiful legislature gravely passes a law to hang any man who shall venture to inform a negro of his legal rights.—*To Joshua F. Speed, Aug. 24, 1855.* II, 284.
2.—You say that if Kansas fairly votes herself a free state, as a Christian you will rejoice at it. All decent slave-holders talk that way, and I do not doubt their candor. But they never vote that way.—*To Joshua F. Speed, Aug. 24, 1855.* II, 286.
3.—It is a felony, by the local law of Kansas, to deny that slavery exists there even now. By every principle of law a negro in Kansas is free; yet the bogus legislature makes it an infamous crime to tell him that he is free.—*Speech, Bloomington, May 29, 1856.* Lapsley II, 251.
4.—As you see by the Kansas slave code, which, as you know, is the Missouri slave code, merely ferried across the river, it is a felony to even express an opinion hostile to that foul blot in the land of Washington and the Declaration of Independence.—*Speech, Bloomington, May 29, 1856.* Lapsley II, 259.

Kansas, if force is necessary—While, in all probability, no resort to force will be needed [to save Kansas from slavery], our moderation and forbearance will stand in good stead when, if ever, we must make an appeal to battle and to the God of hosts.—*Speech, Bloomington, May 29, 1856.* Lapsley II, 275.

Kansas, if slaves had come to—*See* FREEPORT DOCTRINE, fallacy of, 28.

Kansas, Missouri and, in relation to slavery—*See* MISSOURI COMPROMISE, rescind!

Kansas, must be free—*See* MISSOURI COMPROMISE, restoration of, urged, 9.

See REPUBLICAN PARTY, advice to, 3.

Kansas, no peace in—*See* PROPHECY, false, touching slavery, 4, 7.

Kansas, Northern sympathy for—All true men North should sympathize with them [Kansans], and ought to be willing to do any possible and needful thing to right their wrongs.—*Speech, Bloomington, May 29, 1856.* Lapsley II, 249.

Kansas, Northwest Territory and—You, the people of Kansas, furnish the example of the first application of this new policy [that slavery is not wrong]. At the end of about five years, after having almost continual struggles, fire and bloodshed, over this very question, and after having framed several state constitutions,

you have, at last, secured a free-state constitution under which you will probably be admitted to the Union. You have at last, at the end of all this difficulty, attained what we, in the old Northwestern Territory, attained without any difficulty at all. Compare, or rather contrast, the actual working of this new policy with that of the old, and say whether, after all, the old way—the way adopted by Washington and his compeers—was not the better way.—*Speech, Leavenworth, Kan., Dec. 3, 1859.* Angle, 231.

Kansas, no free-state Democrat in—Allow me to barely whisper my suspicion that there were no such things in Kansas as "free-state Democrats" [mentioned by Douglas]—that they were altogether mythical, good only to figure in newspapers and speeches in the free states. If there should prove to be one real living free-state Democrat in Kansas, I suggest that it might be well to catch him, and stuff and preserve his skin as an interesting specimen of that soon-to-be-extinct variety of the genus Democrat.—*Speech, Springfield, June 27, 1857.* II, 319.

Kansas, partiality for—If I went west, I think I would go to Kansas—to Leavenworth or Atchison. Both of them are, and will continue to be, fine growing places.—*To J. W. Somers, March 17, 1860.* VI, 6.

Kansas, people of, "just as good"—The merits of the Kansas people need not be argued to me. They are just as good as any other loyal and patriotic people, and as such, to the best of my ability, I have always treated them.—*To Gov. Carney, May 14, 1864.* X, 100.

Kansas, slavery's test case—If we lose Kansas to freedom, an example will be set which will prove fatal to freedom in the end. We, therefore, in the language of the Bible, must "lay the ax to the root of the tree." Temporizing will not do longer; now is the time for decision—for firm, persistent, resolute action.—*Speech, Bloomington, May 29, 1856.* Lapsley II, 250.
2.—Kansas—the battle-ground of slavery.—*Speech, Bloomington, May 29, 1856.* Lapsley II, 265.

Kansas, Texas and, in relation to slavery—*See* TEXAS, by what right a slave state?

Kansas-Nebraska Act—*See* MISSOURI COMPROMISE.

Kansas-Nebraska Act, African slave trade and—*See* AFRICAN SLAVE TRADE, slavery extension akin to.

Kansas-Nebraska Act, amendment of, repeals Missouri Compromise—*See* MISSOURI COMPROMISE, repealed by Douglas amendment, 1.

Kansas-Nebraska Act, bloodshed invited by—Is it not probable that the contest [in Nebraska] will come to blows and bloodshed? Could there be a more apt invention to bring about collision and violence, on the slavery question, than this Nebraska project is? I do not charge, or believe, that such was intended by Congress; but if they had literally formed a ring, and placed champions within it to fight out the controversy, the fight could be no more likely to come off than it is.—*Speech, Peoria, Oct. 16, 1854.* II, 239.

2.—Unless popular opinion makes itself strongly felt and a change is made in our present course, blood will flow on account of Nebraska, and brother's hands will be raised against brother.—*Speech, Bloomington, May 29, 1856.* Lapsley II, 248.

Kansas-Nebraska Act, Cass invented issue—Nebraskaism did not originate as a piece of statesmanship. Gen. Cass, in 1848, invented it as a political maneuver, to secure himself the Democratic nomination for the Presidency. It served its purpose then, and sank out of sight. Six years later Judge Douglas fished it up, and glozed it over with what he called, and still persists in calling, "sacred right of self-government." —*Notes, Oct. 1, 1858.* IV, 231.

Kansas-Nebraska Act, Chase amendment to—*See* SLAVERY, conspiracy to promote.

Kansas-Nebraska Act, Dred Scottism and—The combined charge of Nebraskaism and Dred Scottism must be repulsed and rolled back.—*Notes, Oct. 1, 1858.* IV, 235.

Kansas-Nebraska Act, ended period of peace—The very allaying plaster of Judge Douglas stirred it [slavery agitation] up again.—*Debate, Alton, Oct. 15, 1858.* V, 45.

Kansas-Nebraska Act, fruits of—In your assumption that there may be a fair decision of the slavery question in Kansas, I plainly see you and I would differ about the Nebraska law.—*To Joshua F. Speed, Aug. 24, 1855.* II, 283.

2.—You may say men ought to be hung for the way they are executing the law; I say the way it is being executed is quite as good as any of its antecedents. It is being executed in the precise way which was intended from the first, else why does no Nebraska man express astonishment or condemnation?—*To Joshua F. Speed, Aug. 24, 1855.* II, 283.

3.—Freedom's share [of the fruits of the Missouri Compromise] is about to be taken by violence—by the force of misrepresentative votes, not called for by the popular will. What name can I, in common decency, give to this wicked transaction?—*Speech, Bloomington, May 29, 1856.* Lapsley II, 263.

4.—We have, this very afternoon, heard bitter denunciations of Brooks [and others] in Washington. . . . I certainly am not going to advocate or shield them; but they and their acts are but the necessary outcome of the Nebraska law. We should reserve our highest censure for the authors of the mischief, and not for the cat's-paws which they use. . . . In my opinion, this man Douglas and the northern men in Congress who advocate "Nebraska" are more guilty than a thousand Jones and Stringfellows, with all their murderous practices.—*Speech, Bloomington, May 29, 1856.* Lapsley II, 265.

5.—All the fruits of this Nebraska bill are like the poisoned source from which they come.—*Speech, Bloomington, May 29, 1856.* Lapsley II, 269.

Kansas-Nebraska Act, future use of—The authors of Nebraska are not at all satisfied with the destruction of the compromise—an indorsement of this principle they proclaim to be their object. With them Nebraska alone is a small matter—to establish a principle for future use is what they particularly desire. That future use is to be the planting of slavery wherever in the wide world local and unorganized opposition cannot prevent it.—*Speech, Peoria, Oct. 16, 1854.* II, 242.
Repeated at Urbana, Oct, 24, 1854. Hertz II, 652.

Kansas-Nebraska Act, Illinois Democrats and—*See* POLITICAL PARTIES, power of the lash, 3.

Kansas-Nebraska Act, issue defined—*See* SLAVERY, Douglas's care-not policy, 10, 11.

Kansas-Nebraska Act, new policy—No, sir; the Nebraska bill finds no model in the [compromise] acts of '50 or the Washington [territorial] act. It finds no model in any law from Adam till today.—*Speech, Peoria, Oct. 16, 1854.* II, 253.

2.—But lately, I think—and in this I charge nothing in the judge's motives—lately, I think, that he, and those acting with him, have placed that institution [slavery] on a new basis, which looks to the perpetuity and nationalization of slavery.—*Debate, Ottawa, Aug. 21, 1858.* III, 233.

3.—On the fourth day of January, 1854, Judge Douglas introduced the Kansas-Nebraska bill. He initiated a new policy, and that policy, as he says, was to put an end to the agitation of the slavery question. Whether that was his object or not, I will not stop to discuss, but at all events some kind of a policy was initiated; and what has been the result? Instead of the quiet times and good feeling which was promised us by the self-styled author of Popular Sovereignty, we have had nothing but ill-feeling and agitation.— *Speech, Clinton, Sept. 8, 1858.* III, 352.

4.—Judge Douglas and his friends have broken that policy [of the fathers] and placed it [slavery] upon a new basis, by which it is to become national and perpetual.—*Debate, Jonesboro, Sept. 15, 1858.* IV, 32.

5.—Anyone who will read his [Douglas's] speech of the 22d of last March will see that he then makes an open confession, showing that he set about fixing the institution [slavery] upon an altogether different set of principles. . . . He has himself changed the whole policy of the government in that regard.—*Debate, Jonesboro, Sept. 15, 1858.* IV, 34.

6.—I turn and ask him [Douglas] why he was driven to the necessity of introducing a new policy in regard to it [slavery]? He has himself said he introduced a new policy. . . . I ask him why he could not let it remain where our fathers placed it.—*Debate, Alton, Oct. 15, 1858.* V, 51.
Repeated at Rushville, Oct. 20, 1859. Hertz II, 730.

7.—In the beginning of the year 1854, a new policy was inaugurated with the avowed purpose and confident promise that it would entirely and forever put an end to the slavery agitation. It was again and again declared that under this policy, when once successfully established, the country would be forever rid of this whole question. Yet under the operations of that policy this agitation has not only not ceased, but it has been constantly augmented.—*Speech, New Haven, Conn., March 6, 1860.* V, 340.

Kansas-Nebraska Act, not Union-saving—Nebraska [Kansas-Nebraska Act] is urged as a great Union-saving measure. Well, I go for saving the Union. . . . But when I go to Union-saving, I must believe, at least, that the means I employ have some adaptation to the end. To my mind, Nebraska has no such adaptation. "It hath no relish of salvation in it."—*Speech, Peoria, Oct. 16, 1854.* II, 236.

Kansas-Nebraska Act, objections to—I particularly object to the new position which the avowed principle of this Nebraska law gives to slavery in the body politic. I object to it because it assumes that there can be moral right in the enslaving of one man by another. I object to it as a dangerous dalliance for a free people—a sad evidence that, feeling prosperity, we forget right—that liberty, as a principle, we have ceased to revere. I object to it because the fathers of the republic eschewed and rejected it.—*Speech, Peoria, Oct. 16, 1854.* II, 244.
Repeated at Urbana, Oct. 24, 1854. Hertz II, 653.

2.—As Phillips says of Napoleon, the Nebraska Act is grand, gloomy and peculiar, wrapped in the solitude of its own originality, without a model and without a shadow upon the earth.—*Speech, Peoria, Oct. 16, 1854.* II, 259.

3.—He [Douglas] has seen himself superseded in a presidential nomination by one indorsing the general doctrine of his measure [Kansas-Nebraska Act] but at the same time standing clear of the odium of its untimely agitation and its gross breach of public faith. —*Speech, Springfield, June 26, 1857.* Stern, 421.

4.—I am fighting it upon these "original principles" —fighting it in the Jeffersonian, Washingtonian, Madisonian fashion.—*Debate, Ottawa, Aug. 21, 1858.* III, 236.

5.—That Nebraska policy . . . has been nothing but a living, creeping lie from the time of its introduction till today.—*Debate, Alton, Oct. 15, 1858.* V, 46.

Kansas-Nebraska Act, opens territories to slavery— The state of the case in a few words is this: The Missouri Compromise excluded slavery from the Kansas-Nebraska territory. The repeal opened the territories to slavery. If there is any meaning to the declaration in the 14th section [of the Act] that it does not mean to legislate slavery into the territories, [it] is this: that it does not require slaves to be sent there. The Kansas and Nebraska territories are now as open to slavery as Mississippi or Arkansas were when they were territories.—*Editorial, Illinois Journal, Sept. 11, 1854.* Angle, 132.

2.—To get slaves into the territory simultaneously with the whites in the incipient stages of settlement is the precise stake played for and won in this Nebraska measure.—*Speech, Peoria, Oct. 16, 1854.* II, 221.

3.—It could not but be expected by its [the Kansas-Nebraska bill's] author that it would be looked upon as a measure for the extension of slavery, aggravated by a gross breach of faith. Argue as you will, and long as you will, this is the naked front and aspect of the measure.—*Speech, Peoria, Oct. 16, 1854.* II, 237.
Repeated at Urbana, Oct. 24, 1854. Hertz II, 649.

4.—He [Douglas] denied [at Springfield] that this [extension of slavery] was intended [in the passage of the Kansas-Nebraska bill] or that this effect would follow. . . . That such was the intention the world believed at the start, and will continue to believe. This was the countenance of the thing, and both friends and enemies instantly recognized it as such. That countenance cannot now be changed by argument. You can as easily argue the color out of the negro's skin. Like the "bloody hand," you may wash it and wash it, the red witness of guilt sticks and stares horribly at you.—*Speech, Peoria, Oct. 16, 1854.* II, 249.

5.—The Nebraska bill, or rather Nebraska law, is not one of wholesome legislation, but was and is an act of legislative usurpation, whose result, if not indeed intention, is to make slavery national; and unless headed off in some effective way, we are in a fair way to see this land of boasted freedom converted into a land of slavery in fact. Just open your two eyes, and see if this is not so.—*Speech, Bloomington, May 29, 1856.* Lapsley II, 251.

6.—I understand that, by the Nebraska bill, a door has been opened for the spread of slavery in the territories. Examine, if you please, and see if they [Buchanan and Fillmore] have ever done any such thing as try to shut the door.—*Speech, Kalamazoo, Mich., Aug. 27, 1856.* Stern, 402.

7.—This [Act] opened all the national territory to slavery.—*Speech, Springfield, June 16, 1858.* III, 3.

See KANSAS-NEBRASKA ACT, parable of starving cattle.

Kansas-Nebraska Act, parable of starving cattle—To illustrate the case—Abraham Lincoln has a fine meadow, containing beautiful springs of water, well fenced, which John Calhoun had agreed with Abraham—originally owning the land in common—should be his, and the agreement had been consummated in a most solemn manner, regarded by both as sacred. John Calhoun, however, in the course of time, had become owner of an extensive herd of cattle. The prairie grass had become dried up, and there was no convenient water to be had. John Calhoun then looks with a longing eye on Lincoln's meadow, and goes to it and throws down the fences, and exposes it to the ravages of his starving and famishing cattle. "You rascal," says Lincoln, "what have you done? What do you do this for?" "Oh," replies Calhoun, "everything is right. I have taken down your fence, but nothing more. It is my true intent and meaning not to drive my cattle into your meadow, nor to exclude them therefrom, but to leave them perfectly free to form their own notions of the feed, and to direct their movements in their own way." Now would not the man who committed this outrage be deemed both a knave and a fool,—a knave in removing the restrictive fence, which he had solemnly pledged himself to sustain; and a fool in supposing that there could be one man found in the country to believe that he had not pulled down the fence for the purpose of opening the meadow for his cattle?—*Editorial, Illinois Journal, Sept. 11, 1854.* Angle, 133.

Kansas-Nebraska Act, "perfect liberty" under—Some men who drew their first breath—and every other breath of their lives—under this very restriction [imposed against slavery in the Northwest Territory], now live in dread of absolute suffocation if they should be restricted in the "sacred right" of taking slaves to Nebraska. That perfect liberty they sigh for —the liberty of making slaves of other people—

Jefferson never thought of, their own fathers never thought of, they never thought of themselves, a year ago. How fortunate for them they did not sooner become sensible of their great misery! Oh, how difficult it is to treat with respect such assaults upon all we ever really held sacred.—*Speech, Peoria, Oct. 16, 1854.* II, 195.

Kansas-Nebraska Act, principle of, gave slavery to Illinois—The principle of the Nebraska bill, he [Douglas] says, expelled slavery from Illinois. The principle of that bill first planted it here—that is, it first came because there was no law to prevent it, first came before we owned the country.—*Speech, Peoria, Oct. 16, 1854.* II, 251.

Kansas-Nebraska Act, safety amendment rejected— *See* SLAVERY, conspiracy to promote.

Kansas-Nebraska Act, speeches against, needed—You know how anxious I am that this Nebraska measure shall be rebuked and condemned everywhere. . . . You are and always have been honestly and sincerely a Democrat; and I know how painful it must be to an honest, sincere man to be urged by his party to the support of a measure which in his conscience he believes to be wrong. You have had a severe struggle with yourself, and you have determined not to swallow the wrong. Is it not just to yourself that you should, in a few public speeches, state your reasons, and thus justify yourself? I wish you would; and yet I say "don't do it if you think it would injure you."— *To J. M. Palmer, Sept. 7, 1854.* II, 187.

2.—Harris will be with you, head up and tail up for Nebraska. You must have some one to make an anti-Nebraska speech.—*To A. B. Moreau, March 23, 1855.* XI, 100.

Kansas-Nebraska Act, spirit of—The spirit of '76 and the spirit of Nebraska are utter antagonisms; and the former is being rapidly replaced by the latter.— *Speech, Peoria, Oct. 16, 1854.* II, 247.

2.—The spirit of the Revolution and the spirit of Nebraska are antipodes.—*Speech, Urbana, Oct. 24, 1854.* Hertz II, 655.

Kansas-Nebraska Act, structure of, peculiar—The structure, too, of the Nebraska bill is very peculiar. The people are to decide the question of slavery for themselves; but when are they to decide, or how are they to decide, or whether, when the question is once decided, it is to remain so or is to be subject to an indefinite succession of new trials, the law does not say. Is it to be decided by the first dozen settlers who arrive there, or is it to await the arrival of a hundred? Is it to be decided by a vote of the people or by a vote of the legislature, or, indeed, by a vote of any sort? To these questions the law gives no answer.—*Speech, Peoria, Oct. 16, 1854.* II, 238.

Kansas-Nebraska Act, variety of weapons used against —Our senator [Douglas] also objects that those who oppose him in this matter [Kansas-Nebraska Act] do not entirely agree with one another. . . . He should remember that he took us by surprise—astounded us by this measure. We were thunderstruck and stunned, and we reeled and fell in utter confusion. But we rose, each fighting, grasping whatever he could first reach—a scythe, a pitchfork, a chopping-ax, or a butcher's cleaver. We struck in the direction of the sound, and we were rapidly closing in upon him. He must not think to divert us from our purpose by showing us that our drill, our dress, and our weapons are not entirely perfect and uniform.—*Speech, Peoria, Oct. 16, 1854.* II, 260.

Kansas-Nebraska Act, violence marks—I look upon that enactment [Kansas-Nebraska Act] not as a law, but as a violence from the beginning. It was considered in violence, is maintained in violence, and is being executed in violence. I say it was conceived in violence, because the destruction of the Missouri Compromise, under the circumstances, was nothing less than violence. It was passed in violence because it could not have been passed at all but for the votes of many members in violence of the known will of their constituents. It was maintained in violence, because the elections since already clearly demand its repeal; and the demand is openly disregarded.—*To Joshua F. Speed, Aug. 24, 1855.* II, 283.

2.—Any man who has sense enough to be controller of his own property has too much sense to misunderstand the outrageous character of the whole Nebraska business.—*To Joshua F. Speed, Aug. 24, 1855.* II, 285.

3.—The repeal of the Missouri Compromise was by violence. It was a violation of both law and the sacred obligations of honor, to overthrow and trample under foot a solemn compromise, obtained by the fearful loss of freedom to one of the fairest of our western domains. Congress violated the will and confidence of its constituents in voting for the [Kansas-Nebraska] bill; and while public sentiment, as shown by the elections of 1854, demanded the restoration of this compromise, Congress violated its trust by refusing simply because it had the force of numbers to hold on to it. And murderous violence is being used now, in order to force slavery on to Kansas; for it cannot be done in any other way.—*Speech, Bloomington, May 29, 1856.* Lapsley II, 255.

4.—The necessary result [of the Kansas-Nebraska

policy] was to establish the rule of violence—force, instead of the rule of law and reason; to perpetuate and spread slavery, and in time to make it general. We see it at both ends of the line. In Washington, on the very spot where the outrage started, the fearless Sumner is beaten to insensibility, and is now slowly dying; while senators who claim to be gentlemen and Christians stood by, countenancing the act, and then applauding it afterward in their places in the Senate. Even Douglas, our man, saw it all and was within helping distance, yet let the murderous blow fall unopposed. Then, at the other end of the line, at the very time Sumner was being murdered, Lawrence was being destroyed for the crime of freedom. It was the most prominent stronghold of liberty in Kansas, and must give way to the all-dominating power of slavery.—*Speech, Bloomington, May 29, 1856.* Lapsley II, 255.

5.—The repeal of the sacred Missouri Compromise has installed the weapons of violence; the bludgeon, the incendiary torch, the death-dealing rifle, the bristling cannon—the weapons of kingcraft, of the inquisition, of ignorance, of barbarism, of oppression. We see its fruits in the dying bed of the heroic Sumner; in the ruins of the "Free State" hotel; in the smoking embers of the *Herald of Freedom;* in the free-state governor of Kansas chained to a stake on freedom's soil like a horse thief, for the crime of freedom. We see it in Christian statesmen, and Christian newspapers, and Christian pulpits applauding the cowardly act of a low bully who crawled upon his victim behind his back and dealt the deadly blow.—*Speech, Bloomington, May 29, 1856.* Lapsley II, 268.

Kansas-Nebraska Bill, Democratic party outraged by —*See* DEMOCRATIC PARTY, outraged by Kansas-Nebraska bill.

Keep Cool, safest course—I appreciate your desire to keep down excitement; and I promise you to "keep cool" under all circumstances.—*To John J. Hardin, Jan. 19, 1845.* I, 272.

2.—Be careful to give no offence, and keep cool under all circumstances.—*To M. W. Delahay, May 12, 1860.* Angle, 243.

3.—My advice . . . is to keep cool. If the great American people only keep their temper on both sides of the line, the troubles will come to an end, and the question which now distracts the country will be settled, just as surely as all other difficulties of a like character which have originated in this government have been adjusted. Let the people on both sides keep their self-possession, and just as other clouds have cleared away in due time, so will this great nation continue to prosper as heretofore.—*Speech, Pittsburgh, Feb., 15, 1861*. VI, 125.

4.—Let us be vigilant, but keep cool. I hope neither Baltimore nor Washington will be sacked.—*To T. Swan and others, July 10, 1864*. X, 155.

Kellogg, William, friendship for—I believe you will not doubt the sincerity of my friendship for you.— *To Mr. Kellogg, Dec. 11, 1859*. Angle, 238.

See LETTER, refuses to read.

Kent, James, estimate of—His attitude was most favorable to correct conclusions. He wrote coolly, and in retirement. He was struggling to rear a durable monument of fame; and he well knew that truth and thoroughly sound reasoning were the only foundations.—*Speech in Congress, June 20, 1848*. II, 41.

See INTERNAL IMPROVEMENTS, Chancellor Kent thought Congress had power.

Kentucky, attitude of, toward Union—The Kentucky legislature would not budge till the [Frémont] proclamation was modified; and Gen. Anderson telegraphed me that on the news of Gen. Frémont having actually issued deeds of manumission, a whole company of our volunteers threw down their arms and disbanded. I was so assured as to think it probable that the very arms we had furnished Kentucky would be turned against us.—*To O. H. Browning, Sept. 22, 1861*. VI, 359.

2.—Kentucky, too, for some time in doubt, is now decidedly and I think unchangeably ranged on the side of the Union.—*First annual message, Dec. 3, 1861*. VII, 53.

3.—I am very anxious to have the special force in Kentucky raised and armed. But the changed conduct toward me of some of her members of Congress and the ominous outgivings as to what the governor and legislature of Kentucky intend doing, admonish me to consider whether any additional arms I may send there are not to be turned against the government. I hope this may clear up on the right side. So far as I can see, Kentucky's sons in the field are acting loyally and bravely. God bless them! I cannot help thinking the mass of the people feel the same way.—*To Green Adams, Jan. 7, 1863*. VIII, 175.

Kentucky, governor of, lukewarm toward Union—It is with regret I search [for], and cannot find, in your not very short letter any declaration or intimation that you entertain any desire for the preservation of the Federal Union.—*To Gov. Beriah Magoffin, Aug. 24, 1861*. Basler, 612.

Kentucky, importance of, to Union—I think to lose Kentucky is nearly the same as to lose the whole game. Kentucky gone, we cannot hold Missouri, nor, I think, Maryland. These all against us, and the job on our hands is too large for us. We would as well consent to separation at once, including the surrender of this capital.—*To O. H. Browning, Sept. 22, 1861*. VI, 360.

See LOUISVILLE, defense of.

Kentucky, Lincoln chooses not to visit—You suggest that a visit to the place of my nativity might be pleasant to me. Indeed it would. But would it be safe? Would not the people lynch me?—*To Samuel Haycraft, June 4, 1860*. VI, 39.

2.—A correspondent of the New York *Herald*, who was here [in Springfield] a week ago, writing to that paper, represents me as saying I had been invited to visit Kentucky, but that I suspected it was a trap to inveigle me into Kentucky in order to do violence to me. I said no such thing.—*To Samuel Haycraft, Aug. 16, 1860*. VI, 51.

3.—I am annoyed some by the printed paragraph below, in relation to myself, taken from the N. Y. *Herald's* correspondence from this place [Springfield] of August 8th:

He had, he said, on one occasion been invited to go into Kentucky and revisit some of the scenes with whose history his father in his lifetime had been identified. On asking by letter whether Judge Lynch would be present, he received no response; and he therefore came to the conclusion that the invitation was a trap laid by some designing person to inveigle him into a slave state for the purpose of doing violence to his person.

This is decidedly wrong. I did not say it. I do not impugn the correspondent. I suppose he misconceived the statement from the following incident. Soon after the Chicago nomination I was written to by a highly respectable gentleman of Hardin County, Ky., . . . and, among other things (he—did not invite me—but simply inquired if it would not be agreeable to me to revisit the scenes of my childhood). I replied, among other things, "It would, indeed, but would you not lynch me?" He did not write again. I have playfully— and never otherwise—related this incident several times; and I suppose I did so to the *Herald* correspondent, though I do not remember it. . . . Now, I dislike exceedingly, for Kentuckians to understand that I am charging them with a purpose to inveigle me, and then do violence to me. Yet I cannot go into the newspapers. Would not the editor of the *Herald* upon being shown this letter, insert the short correction which you find upon the inclosed scrap?—*To George G. Fogg, Aug. 16, 1860*. Tracy, 157.

Kentucky, no armed force into—So far I have not sent an armed force into Kentucky, nor have I any present purpose to do so. I sincerely desire that no necessity for it be presented.—*Memorandum to Gen. Buckner, July 10, 1861.* VI, 325.

Kentucky, pacification and harmony for—The secretary of war and myself are trying to devise means of pacification and harmony for Kentucky, which we hope to effect soon, now that the passion-exciting subject of the election is past.—*To Gov. Bramlette, Nov. 22, 1864.* X, 276.

Kentucky, peace of, disturbed by insurgents—Many citizens of the state of Kentucky have joined the forces of the insurgents, and such insurgents have on several occasions entered the said state of Kentucky in large force, and, not without aid and comfort furnished by disaffected and disloyal citizens of the United States residing therein, have not only greatly disturbed the public peace, but have overborne the civil authorities and made flagrant civil war, destroying property and life in various parts of that state.—*Proclamation, July 5, 1864.* X, 146.

Kentucky, praised for freeing slaves—To the high honor of Kentucky, as I am informed, she has been the owner of some slaves by escheat and has sold none, but liberated all. I hope the same is true of some other states.—*Message to the House, July 17, 1862.* VII, 282.

Kentucky, proslavery men advised to name Douglas for President—*See* DOUGLAS, STEPHEN A., suggested for President.

Kentucky, rejects emancipation—In Kentucky—my state—in 1849, on a test vote, the mighty influence of Henry Clay and many other good men could not get a symptom of expression in favor of gradual emancipation on a plain issue of marching toward the light of civilization with Ohio and Illinois; but the state of Boone and Hardin and Clay, with a nigger under each arm, took the black trail toward the deadly swamps of barbarism.—*Speech, Bloomington, May 29, 1856.* Lapsley II, 259.

Kentucky, son of—It is understood among us Kentuckians.—*Speech, Bloomington, May 29, 1856.* Lapsley II, 270.

See KENTUCKY, rejects emancipation.

Kerr, Orpheus, appreciation of—Why, have you not read those papers [by Kerr]? They are in two volumes; anyone who has not read them must be a heathen.—*To Gen. Meigs, June 17, 1863.* Welles I, 333.

2.—I read it [book by Kerr] when my brain is weary, and I must be unbent. When a boy, the owner of a bow and arrow, I found I must let up on the bow if the arrow is to have force. Read Kerr and then pity me chained here in the Mecca of office seekers.—*To J. B. Grinnell, no date.* War Years II, 50.

Key, John J., dismissal of, explained—In regard to my dismissal of yourself from the military service, it seems to me you misunderstand me. I did not charge, or intend to charge, you with disloyalty. I had been brought to fear that there was a class of officers in the army, not very inconsiderable in numbers, who were playing a game not to beat the enemy when they could, on some peculiar notion as to the proper way of saving the Union; and when you were proved to me, in your presence, to have avowed yourself in favor of that "game," and did not attempt to controvert the proof, I dismissed you as an example and warning to that supposed class. I bear you no ill will, and I regret that I could not have the example without wounding you personally. But can I now, in view of the public interest, restore you to the service, by which the army would understand that I indorse and approve that game myself?—I am really sorry for the pain the case gives you; but I do not see how, consistently with duty, I can change it.—*To Maj. Key, Nov. 24, 1862.* VIII, 48.

Kingcraft, argument for—*See* SLAVERY, wrong of, 11.

Kingly Oppressions, most oppressive of—*See* CONGRESS, war-making power of, explained.

Kings, "divine right" of—*See* SLAVERY, "divine right of kings" and.

Kings, tyrannical principle of—*See* SLAVERY, wrong of, 14.

Kirkland, Charles P., thanked—I have just received and hastily read your published letter to Hon. Benjamin R. Curtis. Under the circumstances I may not be the most competent judge, but it appears to me to be a paper of great ability, and for the country's sake, more than my own, I thank you for it.—*To Mr. Kirkland, Dec. 7, 1862.* VIII, 136.

Kissing, not averse to—*See* WOMEN AND MARRIAGE, attitude toward, 6, 9.

Knave, reports by, false—Reports are often false, and always false when made by a knave to cloak his knavery.—*Speech, Springfield, Dec. 20, 1838.* I, 118.

Know-Nothing Party, "hoped it would die"—Not even you are more anxious to prevent the extension of slavery than I. And yet the political atmosphere is such, just now, that I fear to do anything, lest I do wrong. Know-Nothingism has not yet entirely tumbled to pieces. . . . Until we can get the elements of this organization there is not sufficient material to successfully combat the Nebraska democracy with. We cannot get them so long as they cling to a hope of success under their own organization; and I fear an open push by us now may offend them and tend to prevent our ever getting them. About us here, they are mostly my old personal and political friends and I have hoped this organization would die out without the painful necessity of my taking an open stand against them.—*To Owen Lovejoy, Aug. 11, 1855.* Tracy, 59.

Know-Nothing Party, not a member of—You inquire where I now stand. . . . I am not a Know Nothing; that is certain.—*To Joshua F. Speed, Aug. 24, 1855.* II, 286.

2.—I am not, nor ever have been, connected with the party called the Know-Nothing party, or the party calling themselves the American party.—*To Edward Lusk, Oct. 30, 1858.* V, 90.

3.—I never belonged to the American party organization; nor ever to a party called a Union party, though I hope I neither am, nor ever have been, less devoted to the Union than yourself or any other patriotic man.—*To Samuel Haycraft, June 4, 1860.* VI, 39.

4.—That I was never in a Know-Nothing lodge in Quincy, I should expect could be easily proved by respectable men who were always in the lodges and never saw me there.—*To A. G. Henry, July 4, 1860.* VI, 46.

5.—I suppose as good or even better men than I may have been in American or Know-Nothing lodges; but, in point of fact, I was never in one at Quincy or elsewhere.—*To A. Jonas, July 21, 1860.* VI, 45.

Know-Nothing Party, principles of, challenged—Of their [Know-Nothing party followers'] principles I think little better than I do those of the slavery extensionists. Indeed I do not perceive how anyone professing to be sensitive to the wrongs of the negroes, can join in a league to degrade a class of white men. I have no objection to "fuse" with anybody provided I can fuse on ground which I think right. And I believe the opponents of slavery extension could now do this if it were not for the K.N.ism.—*To Owen Lovejoy, Aug. 11, 1855.* Tracy, 59.

2.—As a nation we began by declaring that "all men are created equal." We now practically read it, "all men are created equal except negroes." When the Know-Nothings get control, it will read, "all men

are created equal, except negroes and foreigners and Catholics." When it comes to this, I shall prefer emigrating to some country where they make no pretence of loving liberty—to Russia, for instance, where despotism can be taken pure, and without the base alloy of hypocrisy.—*To Joshua F. Speed, Aug. 24, 1855.* II, 286.

3.—How can anyone who abhors the oppression of negroes be in favor of degrading classes of white people.—*To Joshua F. Speed, Aug. 24, 1855.* II, 287.

Koerner, Gustave, appraised—He [Gov. Koerner] is an educated and talented German, as true a man as lives.—*To Gen. Halleck, Jan. 15, 1862.* VII, 85.

Kossuth, Louis, tribute to—That we recognize in Gov. Kossuth of Hungary the most worthy and distinguished representative of the cause of civil and religious liberty on the continent of Europe. A cause for which he and his nation struggled until they were overwhelmed by the armed intervention of a foreign despot, in violation of the more sacred principles of the laws of nature and nations—principles held dear by the friends of freedom everywhere, and more especially by the people of these United States.—*Resolutions on Hungarian freedom, Jan. 9, 1852.* Angle, 82.

See REVOLUTION, American sympathy for.

Labor, argument of free—*See* SLAVERY, wrong of, 18.

Labor, education and—Henceforth educated people must labor. Otherwise, education itself would become a positive and intolerable evil.—*Speech, Milwaukee, Sept. 30, 1859.* V, 250.

2.—By the "mud-sill" theory it is assumed that labor and education are incompatible, and any practicable combination of them impossible.—*Speech, Milwaukee, Sept. 30, 1859.* V, 251.

3.—In a word, free labor insists on universal education.—*Speech, Milwaukee, Sept. 30, 1859.* V, 252.

4.—I suppose, however, I shall not be mistaken in assuming as a fact that the people of Wisconsin prefer free labor, with its natural companion, education.—*Speech, Milwaukee, Sept. 30, 1859.* V, 252.

5.—Education—cultivated thought—can best be combined with agricultural labor, or any labor, on the principle of thorough work.—*Speech, Milwaukee, Sept. 30, 1859.* V, 254.

Labor, emancipation and—*See* EMANCIPATION, imaginary perils of.

Labor, free and slave, compared—As labor is the common burden of our race, so the effort of some to shift their share of the burden onto the shoulders of others is the great durable curse of the race. Originally a curse for transgression upon the whole race, when, as by slavery, it is concentrated on a part only, it becomes the double-refined curse of God upon his creatures.—*Fragment, July 1, 1854*. II, 184.

2.—Free labor has the inspiration of hope; pure slavery has no hope. The slave whom you cannot drive with the lash to break seventy-five pounds of hemp in a day, if you task him to break a hundred, and promise to pay him for all he does over, will break you one hundred and fifty. You have substituted hope for the lash. And yet it does not perhaps occur to you that to the extent of your gain in the case, you have given up the slave system and adopted the free system of labor.—*Fragment, July 1, 1854*. II, 185.

3.—They [men of the South] insist that their slaves are better off than northern free men. What a mistaken view do these men have of northern laborers.—*Speech, Kalamazoo, Mich., Aug. 27, 1856*. Stern 404.

Labor, freedom to strike welcomed—I am glad to see that a system of labor prevails in New England under which laborers can strike when they want to. . . . I like the system which lets a man quit when he wants to, and wish it might prevail everywhere.—*Speech, New Haven, Conn., March 6, 1860*. V, 360.

Labor, if all should cease—If at any time all labor should cease, and all existing provisions be equally divided among the people, at the end of a single year there could scarcely be one human being left alive; all would have perished by want of subsistence.—*Tariff memorandum, Dec. 1, 1847*. I, 314.

Labor, international organization suggested—*See* WORKING PEOPLE, have most at stake in war, 2.

See WEALTH, defense of, 2.

Labor, "mud-sill" theory—By some it is assumed . . . that whoever is once a hired laborer, is fatally fixed in that condition for life; and thence again, that his condition is as bad as, or even worse than, that of a slave. This is the "mud-sill" theory.—*Speech, Milwaukee, Sept. 30, 1859*. V, 248.

2.—According to that [the "mud-sill"] theory, a blind horse upon a tread-mill is a perfect illustration of what a laborer should be—all the better for being blind, that he could not kick understandingly. According to that theory, the education of laborers is not only useless, but pernicious and dangerous. In fact, it is, in some sort, deemed a misfortune that laborers should have heads at all. Those same heads are regarded as explosive materials, only to be safely kept in damp places, as far as possible from that peculiar sort of fire which ignites them. A Yankee

who could invent a strong-handed man without a head would receive the everlasting gratitude of the "mud-sill" advocates.—*Speech, Milwaukee, Sept. 30, 1859*. V, 251.

See LABOR, education and, 2.

Labor, no good achieved without—In the early days of our race the Almighty said to the first of our race, "In the sweat of thy face shalt thou eat bread"; and since then, if we except the light and the air of heaven, no good thing has been or can be enjoyed by us without having first cost labor. And inasmuch as most good things are produced by labor, it follows that all such things of right belong to those whose labor has produced them. But it has so happened, in all ages of the world, that some have labored, and others have without labor enjoyed a large proportion of the fruits. This is wrong, and should not continue. To secure to each laborer the whole product of his labor, or as nearly as possible, is a worthy object of any good government.—*Tariff memorandum, Dec. 1, 1847*. I, 306.

Labor, no permanent class—There is no permanent class of hired laborers amongst us. Twenty-five years ago I was a hired laborer. The hired laborer of yesterday labors on his own account today, and will hire others to labor for him tomorrow.—*Fragment, July 1, 1854*. II, 184.

2.—They [men of the South] think that men are always to remain as laborers here—but there is no such class. The man who labored for another last year, this year labors for himself, and next year will hire others to labor for him.—*Speech, Kalamazoo, Mich., Aug. 27, 1856*. Stern, 405.

3.—The assumption that the slave is in a better condition than the hired laborer includes the further assumption that he who is once a hired laborer always remains a hired laborer; that there is a certain class of men who remain through life in a dependent condition. Then they endeavor to point out that when they get old they have no kind masters to take care of them, and that they fall dead in the traces, with the harness of actual labor upon their feeble backs. In point of fact that is a false assumption. There is no such thing as a man who is a hired laborer, of a necessity, always remaining in his early condition. The general rule is otherwise.—*Speech, Cincinnati, Sept. 17, 1859*. Follett, 146.

4.—When at an early age I was myself a hired laborer, at $12 a month; and therefore I do know that there is not always the necessity for actual labor because once there was propriety in being so. My understanding of the hired laborer is this: A young man himself of an age to be dismissed from parental control, has for his capital nothing, save two strong hands that God has given him, a heart willing to labor, and a freedom to choose the mode of his work and the manner of his employment; has got no soil, nor shop, and he avails himself of the opportunity of hiring himself to some man who has capital to pay him a fair day's wages for a fair day's work. He is benefited by availing himself of that privilege. He works industriously, he behaves soberly, and the result of a year or two's labor is a surplus of capital. Now he buys land on his own hook; he settles, he marries, begets sons and daughters, and in course of time he too has enough capital to hire some new beginner. In this same way every member of the whole community benefits and improves his condition. . . . There is no such case [of a man "chained throughout life" to labor for another] unless he be of that confiding and leaning disposition that makes it preferable for him to choose that course, or unless he be a vicious man, who, by reason of his vice, is, in some way prevented from improving his condition, or else he be a singularly unfortunate man. There is no such thing as a man being bound down in a free country through his life as a laborer. The progress by which the poor, honest, industrious and resolute man raises himself, that he may work on his own account, and hire somebody else, is that progress that human nature is entitled to, is that improvement in condition that is intended to be secured by those institutions under which we live, is the great principle for which this government was really formed.—*Speech, Cincinnati, Sept. 17, 1859.* Follett, 147.

5.—If any continue through life in the condition of the hired laborer, it is not the fault of the [economic] system, but because of either a dependent nature, or improvidence, or a singular misfortune.—*Speech, Milwaukee, Sept. 30, 1859.* V, 250.

6.—The prudent, penniless beginner in the world labors for wages awhile, saves a surplus with which to buy tools or land for himself, and then labors on his own account another while, and at length hires another new beginner to help him. This, says its advocate, is free labor—the just and generous and prosperous system, which opens the way for all, gives hope to all, and energy, and progress, and improvement of condition to all.—*Speech, Milwaukee, Sept. 30, 1859.* V, 250.

7.—When one starts poor, as most do in the race of life, free society is such that he knows he can better his condition; he knows that there is no fixed condition of labor for his whole life. . . . I want every man to have a chance—and I believe a black man is entitled to it—in which he can better his condition;

when he may look forward and hope to be a hired laborer this year and the next, work for himself afterward, and finally to hire men to work for him. This is the true system.—*Speech, New Haven, Conn., March 6, 1860.* V, 361.

8.—There is not of necessity any such thing as the free hired laborer being fixed to that condition for life. Many independent men everywhere in these states a few years back in their lives were hired laborers.—*First annual message, Dec. 5, 1861.* VII, 57.

Repeated to workingmen of New York, March 21, 1864. X, 52.

Labor, only man improves—Man is not the only animal who labors; but he is the only one who improves his workmanship.—*Speech, Springfield, no date.* Hertz II, 796.

Labor, product of, belongs to—*See* LABOR, no good achieved without.

Labor, property is fruit of—*See* WEALTH, defense of, 2.

Labor, relationship of, and capital—Some men assume that there is a necessary connection between capital and labor, and that connection draws within it the whole of the labor of the community. They assume that nobody works unless capital excites them to work. They begin next to consider what is the best way [to induce men to labor]. They say there are but two ways—one is to hire men and to allure them to labor by their consent; the other is to buy the men and drive them to it, and that is slavery. Having assumed that, they proceed to discuss the question of whether the laborers themselves are better off in the condition of slaves or of hired laborers, and they usually decide that they are better off in the condition of slaves. . . . I say the whole thing is a mistake. That there is a certain relation between capital and labor, I admit. . . . That men who are industrious and sober and honest in the pursuit of their own interests should after a while accumulate capital, and after that should be allowed to enjoy it in peace, and also if they should choose, when they have accumulated it, to use it to save themselves from actual labor, and hire other people to labor for them, is right. . . . Thus a few men that own capital hire a few others, and these establish the relation of capital and labor rightfully—a relation of which I make no complaint. But I insist that the relation, after all, does not embrace more than one-eighth of the labor of the country.—*Speech, Cincinnati, Sept. 17, 1859.* V, 229.

2.—Take the state of Ohio. Out of eight bushels of

wheat, seven are raised by those men who labor for themselves, aided by their boys growing to manhood, neither being hired nor hiring, but literally laboring upon their own hook, asking no favor of capital, of hired laborer or of the slave. This is the true condition of the larger portion of all the labor done in this community, or that should be the condition of labor in well-regulated communities of agriculturists. —*Speech, Cincinnati, Sept. 17, 1859.* Follett, 146.

3.—It is assumed that labor is available only in connection with capital; that nobody labors unless somebody else, owning capital, somehow by use of it, induces him to labor. This assumed, it is next considered whether it is best that capital shall hire laborers and thus induce them to work by their own consent, or buy them and drive them to it without their consent. Having proceeded so far, it is naturally concluded that all laborers are either hired laborers or what we call slaves. And further it is assumed that whoever is once a hired laborer is fixed in that condition for life. Now there is no such relationship between capital and labor as assumed, nor is there any such thing as a free man being fixed for life in the condition of a hired laborer. Both these assumptions are false, and all inferences from them are groundless. —*First annual message, Dec. 3, 1861.* Basler, 633.

4.—Labor is prior to and independent of capital. Capital is only the fruit of labor; and could not have existed if labor had not first existed. Labor is the superior of capital and deserves much the higher consideration. Capital has its rights, which are as worthy of protection as any other rights. . . . A few men own capital and that few avoid labor themselves, and with their capital hire or buy another few to labor for them. A large majority belong to neither class—neither work for others nor have others work for them. In most of the southern states a majority of the whole people, of all colors are neither slaves nor masters, while in the northern a large majority are neither hirers nor hired. Men with their families —wives, sons and daughters—work for themselves on their farms, in their houses or in their shops, taking the whole product to themselves and asking no favors of capital on the one hand nor of hired laborers or slaves on the other. It is not forgotten that a considerable number of persons mingle their own labor with capital; that is, they labor with their own hand and also buy or hire others to labor for them, but this is only a mixed and not a distinct class. No principle stated is disturbed by the existence of this mixed class.—*First annual message, Dec. 3, 1861.* VII, 57.

5.—There is, and probably always will be, a relationship between capital and labor producing mutual benefits. The error is in assuming that the whole labor of a community exists within that relationship. —*To Workingmen's Association of New York, March 21, 1864.* X, 52.

Labor, source of comforts—Labor is the great source from which nearly all, if not all, human comforts and necessities are drawn.—*Speech, Cincinnati, Sept. 17, 1859.* V, 229.

2.—The world is agreed that labor is the source from which human wants are mainly supplied. There is no dispute upon this point.—*Speech, Milwaukee, Sept. 30, 1859.* V, 247.

Labor, supply and demand—Labor is like any other commodity in the market—increase the demand for it and you increase the price of it. Reduce the supply of black labor by colonizing the black laborer out of the country and precisely so much you increase the demand for, and wages of, white labor.—*Second annual message, Dec. 1, 1862.* VIII, 127.

Labor, three classes—Upon this subject the habits of our whole species fall into three great classes—useful labor, useless labor, and idleness. Of these the first only is meritorious, and to it all the products of labor rightfully belong; but the two latter, while they exist, are heavy pensioners upon the first, robbing it of a large portion of its rights. The only remedy for this is to, so far as possible, drive useless labor and idleness out.—*Tariff Memorandum, Dec. 1, 1847.* I, 307.

Labor, useless, condemned—*See* TARIFF, useless labor as a factor.

See LABOR, three classes.

Labor, two methods of procuring—*See* LABOR, relationship of, and capital, 1.

Labor, wages for women—I know not how much is within the legal power of the government in this case; but it is certainly true in equality that the laboring women in our [government's] employment should be paid at least as much as they were at the beginning of the war.—*To Sec. Stanton, July 27, 1864.* Hertz II, 938.

Labor, white, would benefit by emancipation—*See* EMANCIPATION, imaginary perils of, 1.

Labor and Capital—*See* LABOR, relationship of, and capital.

Land, rising cost of—The cost of land is a great item, even in new countries, and it constantly grows greater and greater, in comparison with other items, as the country grows older.—*Speech, Milwaukee, Sept. 20, 1859.* V, 241.

"Land of the Free, Home of the Brave," is America? —Every Fourth of July our young orators all proclaim this to be "the land of the free and the home of the brave." Well, now, when you orators get that off next year, and maybe, this very year, how would you like some old, grizzled farmer to get up in the grove and deny it?—*Speech, Bloomington, May, 29, 1856.* Lapsley II, 259.
2.—Suppose Kansas comes in as a slave state, and all the "border ruffians" have barbecues about it, and free-state men come trailing back to the dishonored North, like whipped dogs with their tails between their legs, it is—ain't it?—evident that this is no more the "land of the free," and if we let it go so, we won't dare to say "home of the brave" out loud.— *Speech, Bloomington, May 29, 1856.* Lapsley II, 259.

Land to bury in—Part with the land you have, and, my life upon it, you will never after own a spot big enough to bury you in.—*To John D. Johnston, Nov. 4, 1851.* II, 150.

Lane, S. H., relations with Carney—*See* CARNEY, THOMAS, relations with Lane.

"Lane Expedition"—I have not intended, and do not now intend, that it ["Lane expedition"] shall be a great, exhausting affair, but a snug, sober column of 10,000 or 15,000.—*To Sec. Stanton, Jan. 31, 1862.* VII, 90.

Language, construction of—I will not stand upon the construction of language.—*Unfinished letter to Charles D. Robinson, Aug. 15, 1864.* X, 194.

Lanphier, Charles H.—*See* FORGERY, alleged.

Lardner, John L., Congress asked to thank—I recommend that the thanks of Congress be given . . . Capt. John L. Lardner (U.S.N.) for meritorious conduct at the battle of Port Royal, and distinguished services on the coast of the United States against the enemy.— *Message to Congress, July 11, 1862.* VII, 267.

Lash, hurts only Douglas's back—*See* DOUGLAS, STEPHEN A., characterized, 37.

"Last Best Hope of Earth"—*See* UNION, we know how to save.

Latin America, Salvador and the "good neighborhood" policy—Several of the republics of this hemisphere, among which is Salvador, are alarmed at a supposed sentiment tending to reactionary movements against republican institutions on this continent. It seems, therefore, to be proper that we should show to any of them who may apply for that purpose, that compatibly with our cardinal policy and with an enlightened view of our own interests, we are willing to encourage them by strengthening our ties of good will and good neighborhood with them.—*Message to Senate, May 30, 1862.* Messages, VIII, 3281.

Law, advice to lawyers—The leading rule for the lawyer, as for the man of every other calling, is diligence. Leave nothing for tomorrow which can be done today. . . . Whatever piece of business you have in hand, before stopping, do all the labor pertaining to it which can then be done. . . . Extemporaneous speaking should be practiced and cultivated. It is the lawyer's avenue to the public. However able and faithful he may be in other respects, people are slow to bring him business if he cannot make a speech. And there is not a more fatal error to young lawyers than relying too much on speech-making. If anyone, upon his rare powers of speaking, shall claim an exemption from the drudgery of the law, his case is a failure in advance. . . . Discourage litigation. Persuade your neighbors to compromise whenever you can. . . . Never stir up litigation. . . . Who can be more nearly a fiend than he who habitually overhauls the register of deeds in search of defects in titles, whereon to stir up strife, and put money in his pocket. A moral tone ought to be infused into the profession which should drive such men out of it. . . . There is a vague popular belief that lawyers are necessarily dishonest. . . . Let no young man choosing the law for a calling for a moment yield to the popular belief—resolve to be honest at all events; and if in your judgment you cannot be an honest lawyer, resolve to be honest without being a lawyer.—*Notes, July 1, 1850.* II, 140.

See LEGAL FEES, discussed, 2.

Law, advice to students of—I am from home too much of my time, for a young man to read law with me advantageously. If you are resolutely determined to make a lawyer of yourself, the thing is more than half done already. It is but a small matter whether you read with anybody or not. I did not read with anyone. Get the books, and read and study them till you understand them in their principal features; and that is the main thing.—*To Isham Reaves, Nov. 5, 1855.* Tracy, 61.
2.—If you wish to be a lawyer, attach no consequence to the place you are in, or the person you are with; but get books, sit down anywhere, and go to reading for yourself. That will make a lawyer of you quicker

than any other way.—*To William H. Grigsby, Aug. 3, 1858.* Angle, 183.

3.—I am absent altogether too much to be a suitable instructor for a law student. When a man has reached the age Mr. [John H.] Widner has, and has already been doing for himself, my judgment is, that he read the books for himself without an instructor. That is precisely the way I came to the law. Let Mr. Widner read Blackstone's Commentaries, Chitty's Pleadings, Greenleaf's Evidence, Story's Equity, and Story's Equity Pleadings, get a license, and go to the practice, and still keep reading.—*To James T. Thornton, Dec. 2, 1858.* XI, 114.

4.—[You ask] "the best mode of obtaining a thorough knowledge of the law." . . . The mode is very simple, though laborious and tedious. It is only to get the books and read and study them carefully. . . . Work, work, work, is the main thing.—*To J. W. Brockman, Sept. 26, 1860.* VI, 59.

Law, construction of—[Am I] not right when I say that where a law has been passed in terms so general as to require a construction to be put upon it—and this is the case with most laws—and constructions of its provisions are accordingly given, and a second law is afterward passed referring to the first, this second law is held to recognize and to confirm the constructions put upon that first passed?—*Speech, in Congress, Jan. 5, 1848.* Hertz II, 558.

Law, cure for bad—Let me not be misunderstood as saying there are no bad laws, or that grievances may not arise for the redress of which no legal provisions have been made. I mean to say no such thing. But I do mean to say that although bad laws, if they exist, should be repealed as soon as possible, still, while they continue in force, for the sake of example, they should be religiously observed.—*Speech, Springfield, Jan. 27, 1837.* I, 44.

Law, caution as to implied—Nothing should ever be implied as law which leads to unjust or absurd consequences.—*Message to Congress, July 4, 1861.* VI, 317.

Law, codification of statute, urged—I respectfully recommend to the consideration of Congress the present condition of the statute laws, with the hope that Congress will be able to find an easy remedy for many of the inconveniences and evils which constantly embarrass those engaged in the practical administration of them. Since the organization of the government Congress has enacted some 5,000 acts and joint resolutions which fill more than 6,000 closely printed pages and are scattered through many vol-

umes. Many of these acts have been drawn in haste and without sufficient caution, so that their provisions are often obscure in themselves or in conflict with each other, or at least so doubtful as to render it very difficult for even the best-informed persons to ascertain precisely what the statute really is. It seems to me very important that the statute laws should be made as plain and intelligible as possible and be reduced to as small a compass as may consist with the fullness and precision of the will of the legislature and perspicuity of its language.—*First annual message, Dec. 3, 1861.* VII, 39.

Law, dangerous implication—Are men now to be entrapped by a legal implication, extracted from covert language, introduced perhaps for the very purpose of entrapping them?—*Speech, Peoria, Oct. 16, 1854.* II, 257.

Law, enforcement of, depends on public sentiment—No law is stronger than is the public sentiment where it is to be enforced.—*To John J. Crittenden, Dec. 22, 1859.* Tracy, 121.

See FUGITIVE-SLAVE CLAUSE, secession would surrender, 1.

Law, good lawyers sometimes befog—*See* MEXICAN WAR, Polk's attempt to justify, 1.

Law, how Lincoln studied—During the canvass [for Lincoln's first election to the legislature, 1834] in a private conversation he [John T. Stuart] encouraged Abraham to study law. After the election he borrowed books of Stuart, took them home with him, and went at it in good earnest. He studied with nobody. He still mixed in surveying to pay board and clothing bills. When the legislature met, the law books were dropped, but were taken up again at the end of the session. . . . In the autumn of 1836 he obtained a law license.—*Autobiography, June 1, 1860.* VI, 32.

Law, intention determines—It [Missouri Compromise Act] could have no principle beyond the intention of those who made it.—*Speech, Peoria, Oct. 16, 1854.* II, 210.

2.—Did they [Congress] then—could they—establish a principle contrary to their own intention?—*Speech, Peoria, Oct. 16, 1854.* II, 215.

3.—The intention of the lawgiver is the law.—*First inaugural, March 4, 1861.* VI, 171.

Law, lawyers as temperance advocates—*See* TEMPERANCE, early reformers erred, 1.

Law, maxim of—I understand that it is a maxim of law that a poor plea may be a good plea to a bad declaration.—*Debate, Jonesboro, Sept. 15, 1858.* IV, 44.

Law, no, is free—The negative principle that no law is free law is not much known except among lawyers. —*Speech, Peoria, Oct. 16, 1858.* II, 222.

2.—No law is free law; such is the understanding of all Christendom.—*Speech, Bloomington, May 29, 1856.* Lapsley II, 260.

Law, policy in pleading—In law it is good policy to never plead what you need not, lest you oblige yourself to prove what you cannot.—*To U. F. Linder, Feb. 20, 1848.* II, 3.

Law, positive and general—*See* TERRITORIES, positive law needed to keep slavery out.

Law, private enforcement of, dangerous—So far as practicable, you will, by means of your military force, expel guerrillas, marauders, and murderers, and all who are known to harbor, aid or abet them. But in like manner you will repress assumptions of unauthorized individuals to perform the same service because, under pretense of doing this, they become marauders and murderers themselves.—*To Gen. Schofield, Oct. 1, 1863.* IX, 149.

Law, respect for—I hope I am over wary; but if I am not, there is even now something of ill omen amongst us. I mean the increasing disregard for law which pervades the country—the growing disposition to substitute the wild and furious passions in lieu of the sober judgment of courts, and the worse than savage mobs for the executive ministers of justice. . . . Accounts of outrages committed by mobs form the everyday news of the times.—*Speech, Springfield, Jan. 27, 1837.* I, 37.

2.—I know the American people are much attached to their government. I know they would suffer much for its sake; I know they would endure evils long and patiently before they would ever think of exchanging it for another—yet, notwithstanding all this, if the laws be continually despised and disregarded, if their rights to be secure in their persons and property are held by no better tenure than the caprice of a mob, the alienation of their affections from the government is a natural consequence; and to that, sooner or later, it must come.—*Speech, Springfield, Jan. 27, 1837.* I, 42.

3.—As the patriots of '76 did to the support of the Declaration of Independence, so to the support of the Constitution and laws let every American pledge his life, his property and his sacred honor. Let every man remember that to violate the law is to trample on the blood of his fathers, and to tear the charter

of his own and his children's liberty.—*Speech, Springfield, Jan. 27, 1837.* I, 43.

4.—Let us continue to obey the Constitution and the laws.—*Speech, Bloomington, May 29, 1856.* Lapsley II, 273.

5.—I . . . suggest that it will be much safer for all, both in official and private station, to conform to and abide by all those acts [of Congress] which stand unrepealed than to violate any of them, trusting to find immunity in having them held unconstitutional.— *First inaugural, March 4, 1861.* VI, 173.

6.—Being a law, it must be treated as such by all of us.—*To Gen. Sherman, July 18, 1864.* X, 167.

See LAW, reverence for.

See MOB LAW.

See MOBOCRATIC SPIRIT, warning against.

Law, reverence for—Let every American, every lover of liberty, every well-wisher to his posterity, swear by the blood of the Revolution never to violate in the least particular the laws of the country, and never to tolerate their violence by others. . . . Let reverence for the laws be breathed by every American mother to the lisping babe that prattles on her lap; let it be taught in schools, seminaries, and in colleges; let it be written in primers, spelling books, and in almanacs; let it be preached from the pulpit, proclaimed in legislative halls, and enforced in courts of justice. And, in short, let it become the political religion of the nation.—*Speech, Springfield, Jan. 27, 1837.* I, 42.

2.—Let it [reverence for law] become the political religion of the nation; and let the old and young, the rich and the poor, the grave and the gay of all sexes and tongues and colors and conditions, sacrifice unceasingly upon its altars.—*Speech, Springfield, Jan. 27, 1837.* I, 43.

See LAW, respect for.

Law, sometimes unjustly administered—A law may be both constitutional and expedient, and yet may be administered in an unjust and unfair way.—*Opinion on draft law, Aug. 15, 1863.* IX, 81.

Law, when not a—An unconstitutional act is not a law.—*Speech, Galena, Aug. 1, 1856.* II, 294.

Law of War—*See* WAR POWER.

"Lawfully Driven from Place Where It Has Lawful Right to Remain"—*See* FREEPORT DOCTRINE, fallacy of, 27.

Laws and Treaties, compared—*See* SECESSION, after, what? 4.

Lawyer, too lazy for anything but—*See* LINCOLN, ABRAHAM, personal traits and reactions, 22.

Lawyer or Liar—If he [James Adams] is not a lawyer, he is a liar, for he proclaimed himself a lawyer, and got a man hanged by depending on him—*To editor Sangamo* Journal, *Oct. 28, 1837.* I, 78.

"Leaven of Treason"—*See* COLORADO, Territory of, organized.

Lecompton Constitution, Democrats "hobbling along"—Nearly all the Democrats here stick to Douglas [on the Lecompton issue]; but they are hobbling along with the idea that there is no conflict between him and Buchanan.—*To Lyman Trumbull, Dec. 18, 1857.* Tracy, 83.

Lecompton Constitution, issue defined—This dispute was upon the question of fact, whether the Lecompton constitution had been fairly formed by the people or not. Mr. Buchanan and his friends have not contended for the contrary principle [that the people have not the right to make their own state constitutions] any more than the Douglas men or the Republicans. . . . The question was, was it a fair emanation of the people? It was a question of fact and not of principle. As to the principle, all men were agreed. . . . He [Douglas] and they [Republicans] by their voices and votes, denied that it was a fair emanation of the people. The administration affirmed that it was.—*Speech, Springfield, July 17, 1858.* III, 163.

Lecompton Constitution, Republicans should "stand clear"—*See* REPUBLICAN PARTY, advice to, 9.

Lecompton Constitution, should be throttled—The Lecompton constitution . . . should be throttled and killed as hastily and heartily as a rabid dog.—*Notes, Oct. 1, 1858.* IV, 229.

Lecompton Constitution, who defeated?—In voting together in opposition to a constitution being forced upon the people of Kansas, neither Judge Douglas nor the Republicans have conceded anything which was ever in dispute between them.—*To J. F. Alexander, May 15, 1858.* Angle, 176.

2.—I agree that in opposing the Lecompton constitution, so far as I can perceive, he [Douglas] was right. . . . All the Republicans in the nation opposed it; and they would have opposed it just as much without Judge Douglas's aid as with it. They had all taken ground against it long before he did. . . . The argument that he makes why that constitution should not be adopted, that the people were not fairly represented nor allowed to vote, I pointed out in a speech a year ago.—*Speech, Chicago, July 10, 1858.* III, 27.

3.—The Lecompton constitution, as the judge tells us, was defeated. . . . Who defeated it? [Voice: "Judge Douglas."] Yes, he furnished himself, and if you suppose he controlled the other Democrats that went with him, he furnished three votes, while the Republicans furnished twenty. That is what he did to defeat it.—*Speech, Chicago, July 10, 1858.* III, 28.

4.—The Republicans could not have done it without Judge Douglas. Could he have done it without them? Which could have come the nearest to doing it without the other? . . . Ground was taken against it by the Republicans long before Judge Douglas did it. The proportion of opposition to that measure is about five to one.—*Speech, Chicago, July 10, 1858.* III, 29.

5.—I wish to know what there is in the opposition of Judge Douglas to the Lecompton constitution which entitles him to be considered the only opponent of it—as being *par excellence* the very quintessence of that opposition. . . . He in the Senate, and his class of men there, formed the number of three and no more. In the House of Representatives his class of men—the anti-Lecompton Democrats—formed a number of about twenty. It took 120 to defeat the measure against 112. Of the votes of that 120, Judge Douglas's friends furnished twenty, to add to which there were six Americans and 94 Republicans. . . . Why is it that twenty shall be entitled to all the credit of doing that work and the hundred none of it?—*Speech, Springfield, July 17, 1858.* III, 165.

6.—He [Douglas] declares the dividend of credit for defeating Lecompton upon a basis which seems unprecedented and incomprehensible.—*Speech, Springfield, July 17, 1858.* III, 166.

7.—It is said by the judge that the defeat was a good and proper thing. If it was a good thing, why is he entitled to more credit than others for the performance of that good act, unless there was something in the antecedents of the Republicans that might induce everyone to expect them to join in that good work, and at the same time something leading them to doubt that he would? Does he place his superior claim to credit on the ground that he performed a good act which was never expected of him?—*Speech, Springfield, July 17, 1858.* III, 166.

8.—He [Douglas] reminds us that he opposed Lecompton before the vote was taken declaring whether the state was to be free or slave. But he forgets to say that our Republican senator, Trumbull, made a speech against Lecompton even before he did.—*Speech, Springfield, July 17, 1858.* III, 167.

See LOST SHEEP, parable of.

Lee, Robert E., might have been arrested—*See* CONFEDERATE GENERALS, might have been arrested.

Legal Fee, part of, returned—I have just received yours of the 16th, with check on Flagg & Savage for $25. You must think I am a high-priced man. You are too liberal with your money. Fifteen dollars is enough for the job. I send you a receipt for fifteen dollars, and return to you a ten dollar bill.—*To George P. Floyd, Feb. 21, 1856.* Tracy, 66.

Legal Fees, discussed—Whatever fees we [Judge Logan and I] earn at a distance, if not paid before, we have noticed, we never hear of after the work is done. We, therefore, are growing a little sensitive on that point.—*To James S. Irwin, Nov. 2, 1842.* XI, 99.
2.—The matter of fees is important, far beyond the mere question of bread and butter involved. Properly attended to, fuller justice is done to both lawyer and client. An exorbitant fee should never be claimed. As a general rule, never take your whole fee in advance, nor any more than a small retainer. When fully paid beforehand you are more than a common mortal if you can feel the same interest in the case as if something was still in prospect for you, as well as for your client. And when you lack interest in the case the job will very likely lack skill and diligence in the performance. Settle the amount of fee and take a note in advance. Then you will feel that you are working for something, and you are sure to do your work faithfully and well.—*Fragment, July 1, 1850.* II, 142.
3.—I have heard news from Ottawa that we win our Gallatin and Saline county cases. As the Dutch justice said when he married folks, "Now vere ish my hundred tollars?"—*To Andrew McCallen, July 4, 1851.* Tracy, 45.

Legislation, adjudication and, depend on social progress—Legislation and adjudication must follow and conform to the progress of society.—*Notes for law case, June 15, 1858.* II, 366.
Repeated in notes, Dec., 1858. XI, 112.

Legislation, executive interference in—*See* CONGRESS, legislation should rest with.

Legislation, special and general—Special legislation always trenches upon the judicial department, and in so far violates section two of the Constitution. Just reasoning—policy—is in favor of general legislation, else the legislature will be loaded down with the investigation of smaller cases—a work which the courts ought to perform, and can perform much more perfectly.—*Notes, June 15, 1858.* II, 366.
2.—Let him [a purchaser], say we, have general law in advance . . . so that when he acquires a legal right he will have no occasion to wait for additional legislation.—*Notes, June 15, 1858.* II, 367.

Legislature, power of, limited—A legislature cannot indirectly do that which it cannot accomplish directly.—*Speech, Columbus, Ohio, Sept. 16, 1859.* V, 178.
2.—What a legislature cannot directly do, it cannot do by indirection.—*Speech, Cincinnati, Sept. 17, 1859.* V, 212.

Legs, "question of"—*See* ACTION, pleas for, 13.

Leniency, limit on—I cannot postpone the execution of a convicted spy on a mere telegraphic dispatch signed with a name I never heard before.—*To Christiana A. Sack, May 21, 1864.* X, 106.

"Let Bygones Be Bygones"—*See* REPUBLICAN PARTY, advice to, 8.

"Let Me Stay and Rot Here,"—Let the judge [Douglas] go on, and after he is done with his half hour, I want you all, if I can't go home myself, to let me stay and rot here; and if anything happens to the judge, if I cannot carry him to the hotel, and put him to bed, let me stay here and rot.*—*Debate, Jonesboro, Sept. 15, 1858.* IV, 69.

"Let the Past As Nothing Be"—*To W. H. Herndon, July 11, 1848.* Angle, 46.
Same to N. B. Judd, Nov. 15, 1858. V, 92.

"Let the Thing Be Pressed"—*See* GRANT, U. S., vigilance urged on, 2.

Letter, refuses to read—I understand my friend [William] Kellogg is ill-natured, therefore, I do not read his letter.—*Indorsement on letter from Mr. Kellogg, April, 1863.* R.T.L.

See GAMBLE, H. R., won't read letter from.

Liberal Arts, dependent on free institutions—*See* HONORARY DEGREE, thanks for.

Liberals, world's, warn Americans against slavery extension—*See* SLAVERY, extension of, opposed, 12.

Liberator, Garrison's newspaper—*See* CHARLESTON MERCURY, "salivated by."

Liberia, difficulties in colonizing—My first impulse [had I "all earthly power"] would be to free all the slaves and send them to Liberia, to their own native land. But a moment's reflection would convince me that whatever of high hope—as I think there is—may be in this in the long run, its sudden execution is impossible. If they were all landed there in a day,

* Douglas had said at Joliet six days before: "The very notice that I was going to take him [Lincoln] down to Egypt made him tremble in the knees so that he had to be carried from the platform."

they would all perish in the next ten days; and there is not surplus shipping and surplus money to carry them there in many times ten days.—*Speech, Peoria, Oct. 16, 1854.* II, 206.

Repeated at Ottawa, Aug. 21, 1858. III, 227.

2.—The colony of Liberia has been in existence a long time. In a certain sense it is a success. . . . Something less than 12,000 have been sent thither from this country. . . . The question is, if the colored people are persuaded to go anywhere, why not there? One reason for unwillingness to do so is that some of you would rather remain within reach of the country of your nativity.—*Speech to deputation of free colored men, Aug. 14, 1862.* VIII, 5.

Liberia, gunboat suggested for—I solicit your authority to furnish to the republic [Liberia] a gunboat at moderate cost, to be reimbursed to the United States by installments. Such a vessel is needed for the safety of that state against the native African races, and in Liberian hands it would be more effective in arresting the African slave trade than a squadron in our own hands.—*Fourth annual message, Dec. 6, 1864.* X, 285.

Liberia, progress in—Official correspondence has been freely opened with Liberia, and it gives us a pleasing view of the social and political progress in that republic. It may be expected to derive new vigor from American influence, improved by the rapid disappearance of slavery in the United States.—*Fourth annual message Dec. 6, 1864.* X, 285.

Liberia, recognition of, urged—If any good reason exists why we should persevere longer in withholding our recognition of the independence and sovereignty of Hayti and Liberia, I am unable to discern it. . . . I submit for your consideration the expediency of an appropriation for maintaining a *chargé d'affaire* near each of these new states.—*First annual message, Dec. 3, 1861.* VII, 33.

Liberty, America may lose—*See* AMERICA, dedication to, 1.

Liberty, American inheritance—Theirs [our American ancestors'] was the task—and nobly they performed it—to possess themselves, and through themselves us, of this goodly land, and to uprear upon its hills and its valleys a political edifice of liberty and equal rights; 'tis ours only to transmit these—the former unprofaned by the foot of an invader, the latter undecayed by the lapse of time and untorn by usurpation—to the latest generation that fate shall permit the world to know.—*Speech, Springfield, Jan. 27, 1837.* I, 36.

Liberty, bulwark of—What constitutes the bulwark of our own liberty and independence? It is not our frowning battlements, or bristling seacoasts, our army and navy. These are not our reliance against tyranny. All of those may be turned against us without making us weaker for the struggle. Our reliance is in the love of liberty which God has planted in us. Our defense is in the spirit which prized liberty as the heritage of all men, in all lands everywhere. Destroy this spirit and you have planted the seeds of despotism at your own doors.—*Speech, Edwardsville, Sept. 13, 1858.* XI, 110.

Liberty, civil, boon of—*See* CLAY, HENRY, devotion of, to liberty.

See GREAT BRITAIN, enemy of freedom.

See SLAVERY, extension of, opposed, 2.

See WASHINGTON, GEORGE, tributes to, 1.

Liberty, Civil—Cubans unfit for—Their [filibusters'] fault was that the real people of Cuba had not asked for their assistance; were neither desirous of, nor fit for, civil liberty.—*Speech, Springfield, Aug. 26, 1852.* Angle, 105.

Liberty, civil, fight for, must go on—The fight must go on. The cause of civil liberty must not be surrendered at the end of one or even one hundred defeats.—*To Henry Asbury, Nov. 19, 1858.* V, 94.

Liberty, civil and religious, American system conduces to—We find ourselves under the government of a system of political institutions conducing more essentially to the ends of civil and religious liberty than any of which the history of former times tells us.—*Speech, Springfield, Jan. 27, 1837.* I, 35.

Liberty, civil and religious, "noblest of causes"—*See* REVOLUTIONARY WAR, influence of, 2.

See AMERICA, inheritance.

See CIVIL WAR, results of, involve future, 2.

See DEITY, dependence on, 9.

See DEITY, mercy of, 1.

See WORLD SIGNIFICANCE OF AMERICAN AFFAIRS, 2.

Liberty, civil and religious, thanks for support of—You have generously tendered me the support—the united support—of the great Empire State. For this, in behalf of the nation—in behalf of the present and future of the nation—in behalf of civil and religious liberty for all time to come, most gratefully do I thank you.—*Speech, New York Legislature, Feb. 18, 1861.* VI, 141.

Liberty, Clay's "predominant sentiment"—Mr. Clay's predominant sentiment, from first to last, was a deep devotion to the cause of human liberty—a strong sympathy with the oppressed everywhere, and an ardent wish for their elevation. With him this was a primary and all-controlling passion. . . . He loved his country partly because it was his own country, and mostly because it was a free country; and he burned with zeal for its advancement, prosperity and glory, because he saw in such the advancement, prosperity and glory of human liberty, human right and human nature.—*Speech, Springfield, July 16, 1852.* II, 164.

Liberty, constitution and Union—I return most sincerely my thanks, not for myself, but for liberty, the Constitution, and Union.—*Speech, Cleveland, Feb. 15, 1861.* VI, 132.

Liberty, danger to—Slavery and oppression must cease, or American liberty must perish.—*Speech, Cincinnati, May 31, 1842.* Hertz II, 531.
2.—Is there no danger to liberty itself in discarding the earlier practice and first precept of our ancient faith?—*Speech, Peoria, Oct. 16, 1854.* II, 248.
3.—Now I ask you, in all soberness, if all these things [urged by Douglas], if indulged in, if ratified, if confirmed and indorsed, if taught to our children, and repeated to them, do not tend to rub out the sentiment of liberty in the country, and to transform this government into a government of some other form. —*Speech, Chicago, July 10, 1858.* III, 48.

Liberty, definitions of, differ—The world has never had a good definition of the word "liberty," and the American people, just now, are much in need of one. We all declare for liberty; but in using the same word we do not all mean the same thing. With some the word "liberty" may mean for each man to do as he pleases with himself, and the product of his labor; while with others the same word may mean for some men to do as they please with other men, and the product of other men's labor. Here are two, not only different, but incompatible things, called by the same name, "liberty." And it follows that each of the things is, by the respective parties, called by two different and incompatible names—"liberty" and "tyranny."—*Speech, Baltimore, April 18, 1864.* X, 77.
2.—The shepherd drives the wolf from the sheep's throat, for which the sheep thanks the shepherd as a liberator; while the wolf denounces him, for the same

act, as the destroyer of liberty, especially as the sheep was a black one. Plainly, the sheep and the wolf are not agreed upon the word "liberty"; and precisely the same difference prevails today among us human creatures, even in the north, and all professing to love liberty. . . . Recently, as it seems, the people of Maryland have been doing something to define liberty and, thanks to them, the wolf's dictionary has been repudiated.—*Speech, Baltimore, April 18, 1864.* X, 77.

Liberty, jewel of—They [negroes in Louisiana] would probably help, in some trying time to come, to keep the jewel of liberty within the family of freedom.— *To Gov. Hahn, March 13, 1864.* X, 39.

Liberty, lamp of—I leave you, hoping that the lamp of liberty will burn in your bosoms until there shall no longer be a doubt that all men are created free and equal.—*Speech, Chicago, July 10, 1858.* III, 52.

Liberty, largest degree of, in America—This government must be preserved in spite of the acts of any man or set of men. . . . Nowhere in the world is presented a government of so much liberty and equality. To the humblest and poorest amongst us are held out the highest privileges and positions. The present moment finds me at the White House, yet there is as good a chance for your children as there was for my father's.—*Speech to 148th Ohio Regiment, Aug. 31, 1864.* X, 209.

Liberty, motive to preserve—Surely each man has as strong a motive now to preserve our liberties as each had then [in the Revolution] to establish them.— *Message to Congress, July 4, 1861.* VI, 312.

Liberty, no abstraction—I submit that the proposition that the thing which determines whether a man is free or a slave is rather concrete than abstract. I think you would conclude that it was if your liberty depended on it, and so would Judge Douglas if his liberty depended on it.—*Speech, Springfield, July 17, 1858.* III, 181.

Liberty, pillars of temple of—*See* REVOLUTIONRY WAR, tribute to soldiers of, 2.

Liberty, preservation of, a duty—If there is anything which it is the duty of the whole people to never intrust to any hands but their own, that thing is the preservation and perpetuity of their own liberties and institutions.—*Speech, Peoria, Oct. 16, 1854.* II, 235.
Repeated at Urbana, Oct. 24, 1854. Hertz II, 648.
2.—We must make this a land of liberty in fact, as it

is in name.—*Speech, Bloomington, May 29, 1856.* Lapsley II, 274.

Liberty, prosperity and, threatened by slavery—What is that we hold most dear amongst us? Our own liberty and prosperity. What has ever threatened our liberty and prosperity save and except this institution of slavery? If this is true, how do you propose to improve the condition of things by enlarging slavery—by spreading it out and making it bigger? You may have a wen or a cancer upon your person, and not be able to cut it out lest you bleed to death; but surely it is no way to cure it, to engraft it and spread it over your whole body.—*Debate, Alton, Oct. 15, 1858.* V, 61.

Liberty, race distinctions incompatible with—In what I have done I cannot claim to have acted from any peculiar consideration of the colored people as a separate and distinct class in the community, but from the simple conviction that all the individuals of that class are members of the community, and, in virtue of their manhood, entitled to every original right enjoyed by any other member. We feel, therefore, that all legal distinction between individuals of the same community, founded in any such circumstances as color, origin, and the like, are hostile to the genius of our institutions, and incompatible with the true history of American liberty.—*Speech, Cincinnati, May 31, 1842.* Hertz II, 531.

Liberty, temperance and—*See* TEMPERANCE, revolution compared with Revolutionary War.

"Liberty and Union"—In the joint names of liberty and Union let us labor to give it [emancipation] legal form and practical effect.—*To notification committee, June 7, 1864.* X, 117.

Life and Limb—By general law, life and limb must be protected, yet often a limb must be amputated to save a life; but a life is never wisely given to save a limb.—*To A. G. Hodges, April 4, 1864.* X, 66.

Lightning Rod, does church need?—What you suggest reminds me of a man out west, who was not over pious, but rich, and built a church for the poor people of his neighborhood. When the church was finished, the people took it into their heads that it needed a lightning rod, and they went to the rich man, and asked for money to help pay for it. "Money for a lightning rod!" he said. "Not a red cent! If the Lord wants to thunder down His own house, let Him thunder it down, and be damned!"—*To James R. Gilmore, late May, 1863.* Gilmore, 161.

Lightning Rod, sign of guilty conscience—I desire to live, and I desire place and distinction; but I would rather die now than, like the gentleman [George Forquer], live to see the day that I would change my politics for an office worth $3,000 a year, and then feel compelled to erect a lightning rod to protect a guilty conscience from an offended God.—*Speech, Springfield, 1836.* Herndon, 163.

"Like Whipped Dogs"—*See* "LAND OF THE FREE, HOME OF THE BRAVE," is America?

Lincoln, Abraham, affectionate husband and father—I did not get rid of the impression of that foolish dream about dear Bobby till I got your letter written the same day. What did he and Eddy think of the little letters father sent them? Don't let the blessed fellows forget father.—*To Mrs. Lincoln, April 16, 1848.* Angle, 42.

2.—In this troublesome world we are never quite satisfied. When you were here, I thought you hindered me some in attending to business, but now, having nothing but business—no vanity—it has grown exceedingly tasteless to me. I hate to sit down and direct accounts, and I hate to stay in the old room by myself. . . . Are you entirely free from headache? That is good—considering it is the first spring you have been free from it since we were acquainted—I am afraid you will get so well and fat and young as to be wanting to marry again.—*To Mrs. Lincoln, April 16, 1848.* Hertz II, 568.

3.—Come on just as soon as you can—I want to see you, and our dear, dear boys very much. Everybody here wants to see our dear Bobby.—*To Mrs. Lincoln, June 12, 1848.* Stern, 315.

4.—The leading matter in your letter is your wish to return to this side of the mountains—Will you be a good girl in all things, if I consent? Then come along, and that as soon as possible. Having got the idea in my head, I shall be impatient till I see you.—*To Mrs. Lincoln, June 12, 1848.* Hertz II, 574.

5.—By the way, do you intend to do without a girl, because the one you had has left you? Get another as soon as you can to take care of the dear codgers. . . . Kiss and hug the dear rascals.—*To Mrs. Lincoln, July 2, 1848.* Angle, 46.

6.—My poor boy, he was too good for this earth. God has called him home. I know that he is much better off in Heaven, but then we loved him so. It is hard, hard to have him die.—*To Elizabeth Keckley, Feb. 20, 1862.* Keckley, 103.

7.—Allow me to thank you in behalf of my little son for your present of white rabbits. He is very much pleased with them.—*To Michael Crock, April 2, 1862.* Angle, 291.

8.—Ted wants some flags. Can he be accommodated? *To Sec. Stanton, April 10, 1865.* Angle, 373.

9.—I am engaged to go to the theater with Mrs. Lincoln. . . . It is the kind of engagement I never break. —*To Sen. W. M. Stewart, April 14, 1865.* Hertz II, 968.

See LINCOLN, ROBERT T.

Lincoln, Abraham, aspires to Congress—*See* CONGRESS, seeks nomination to.

Lincoln, Abraham, aspires to Senate—*See* UNITED STATES SENATE, aspires to.

See CAMPAIGN OF 1858.

Lincoln, Abraham, aspirant for land office—*See* GENERAL LAND OFFICE, candidate for.

Lincoln, Abraham, autobiography of—*See* AUTOBIOGRAPHY, Lincoln's.

Lincoln, Abraham, chooses not to visit Kentucky—*See* KENTUCKY, Lincoln chooses not to visit.

Lincoln, Abraham, churches' attitude toward—*See* CHURCH, opposed to Lincoln.

Lincoln, Abraham, citizen of San Marino—*See* SAN MARINO, complimented.

Lincoln, Abraham, could have married southern girl —*See* SOUTH, no cause for fear by, 2.

Lincoln, Abraham, financial—I keep some money loaned at 10 per cent.—*To Maria L. Bullock, Jan. 3, 1859.* Angle, 203.

2.—I never keep anybody's money, which I collect, an hour longer than I can find a chance to turn it over to him.—*To Mrs. Deziah Vance, June 9, 1860.* Hertz II, 777.

See POVERTY, confessed.

Lincoln, Abraham, holds no secret purposes—*See* REPUBLICAN PARTY, platforms of, binding, 2.

Lincoln, Abraham, humility of—*See* HUMILITY, Lincoln trait.

Lincoln, Abraham, in politics, did not wait—*See* POLITICS, young men, in, 1.

Lincoln, Abraham, "I should deserve to be damned" —*See* EMANCIPATION PROCLAMATION, no retraction of, 9.

Lincoln, Abraham, "military hero"—By the way, Mr. Speaker, did you know that I am a military hero? Yes, sir; in the days of the Black Hawk War I fought, bled and came away. Speaking of Gen. Cass's career

reminds me of my own. I was not at Stillman's defeat, but I was about as near it as Cass was to Hull's surrender; and, like him, I saw the place very soon afterward.—*Speech in Congress, July 27, 1848.* II, 75.

See CASS, LEWIS D., military figure of.

Lincoln, Abraham, "my final reckoning"—*See* SLAVERY, wrong of, 29.

Lincoln, Abraham, no expectation of Presidency— *See* DOUGLAS, STEPHEN A., characterized, 11.

Lincoln, Abraham, no longer young—Reading from speeches is a very tedious business, particularly for an old man who has to put on spectacles, and more so if the man be so tall that he has to bend over to the light.—*Speech, Chicago, July 10, 1858.* III, 28.

2.—[Voice: "Put on your specs."] Yes, sir, I am obliged to do so. I am no longer a young man.—*Debate, Ottawa, Aug. 21, 1858.* III, 225.

Lincoln, Abraham, no pleasure in another's defeat— *See* ELECTION OF 1864, gratitude without taint.

Lincoln, Abraham, "old stump speaker"—*See* PRESIDENCY, puts curb on speech, 9.

Lincoln, Abraham, opposition to re-election of, no offense—I can scarcely believe that Gen. John B. Houston has been arrested "for no other offense than opposition to my re-election". . . . If, however, Gen. Houston has been arrested for no other cause than opposition to my re-election, Gen. Burbridge will discharge him at once.—*To Gov. T. E. Bramlette, Nov. 10, 1864.* X, 265.

Lincoln, Abraham, personal description of—Perhaps you have forgotten me. Don't you remember a long black fellow who rode on horseback with you from Tremont to Springfield nearly ten years ago, swimming our horses over the Mackinaw on the trip? Well, I am the same old fellow yet.—*To Josephus Hewett, Feb. 13, 1848.* I, 355.

2.—If any personal description of me is thought desirable, it may be said that I am, in height, six feet four inches, nearly; lean in flesh, weighing an average one hundred and eighty pounds; dark complexion, with coarse black hair, and dark eyes. No other marks or brands recollected.—*To F. W. Fell, Dec. 20, 1859.* V, 288.

Lincoln, Abraham, personal traits and reactions—At your request I send you a receipt for the postage on your paper. I am somewhat surprised at your request. . . . The law requires newspaper postage to be paid in advance, and now that I have waited a full year you choose to wound my feelings by insinuating that unless you get a receipt I will probably make you pay it again.—*To George Spear, 1833 or 1834.* I, 11.

2.—You see I have a congenital aversion to failure.—*To George F. Pickett, Feb. 22, 1842.* I, 191.

3.—Although you know I am not a petulant man, I declare I was almost out of patience with Mr. Everett's importunity.—*To Joshua F. Speed, March 27, 1842.* I, 216.

4.—I did the labor of writing one [Whig party] address this year; and got thunder for my reward.—*To John J. Hardin, May 11, 1843.* I, 267.

5.—Suppose you do not prefix the "Hon." to the address on your letters to me any more. I like your letters very much but would rather they should not have that upon them.—*To Mrs. Lincoln, April 16, 1848.* Angle, 42.

6.—The other day one of the gentlemen from Georgia . . . came down upon us [Whigs] astonishingly. He spoke in what the Baltimore *American* calls the "scathing and withering style." At the end of his second severe flash I was struck blind, and found myself feeling with my fingers for an assurance of my continued existence. A little of the bone was left, and I gradually recovered.—*Speech in Congress, July 27, 1848.* II, 70.

7.—It pains me to have to say that I forgot to attend to your business when I was in Clinton at court in May last. Your best way would be to address me a letter at Clinton, about the time I go there to court in the fall—Oct. 16th, I think—and then it will be fresh & I will not forget or neglect it.—*To M. K. Alexander, June 13, 1854.* Angle, 130.

8.—I was not very much accustomed to flattery, and it came the sweeter to me. I was rather like the Hoosier with the ginger bread, when he said he reckoned he loved it better than any other man, and got less of it.—*Debate, Ottawa, Aug. 21, 1858.* III, 238.

9.—For once in my life I will play Gen. Jackson, and to the just extent I take the responsibility.—*Debate, Charleston, Sept. 18, 1858.* IV, 93.

10.—I was not entirely sure that I should be able to hold my own with him [Douglas, in the debates], but at least I had the purpose made to do as well as I could upon him; and now I say that I will not be the first to cry "Hold!"—*Debate, Quincy, Oct. 13, 1858.* IV, 326.

11.—Let me talk to some gentleman down there among you who looks me in the face.—*Debate, Quincy, Oct. 31, 1858.* IV, 378.

12.—If, after all, the indictment shall be quashed it will indicate that my forte is as a statesman rather than a prosecutor.—*To Ward H. Lamon, April 28, 1860.* Tracy, 138.

13.—Doubtless you begin to understand how disagreeable it is for me to do a thing arbitrarily when it is unsatisfactory to others associated with me.—*To Gen. Scott, June 5, 1861.* VI, 290.

14.—Gen. Schurz thinks I was a little cross in my last note to you. If I was, I ask pardon. If I do get up a little temper I have no sufficient time to keep it up.—*To Franz Sigel, Feb. 5, 1863.* Tracy, 221.

15.—I shall have to cut this knot!—*To Charles Sumner, April 29, 1863.* Welles I, 289.

16.—For once in my life I gave my temper the rein and I talked to those men [D. D. Field and George Opdyke] pretty damned plainly. Opdyke may be right in being cool to me. I may have given him reason this morning.—*To John Hay, Oct. 30, 1863.* Hay, 112.

17.—Mr. Douglass, I have been charged with being tardy, and the like. I am charged with vacillating; but, Mr. Douglass, I do not think that charge can be sustained; I think it cannot be shown that when I have once taken a position, I have ever retreated from it.—*To Frederick Douglass. Reported by Douglass to American Anti-Slavery Society, Philadelphia, Dec. 4, 1863.*

18.—I did this [ordered a commutation of sentence], not on any merit in the case, but because I am trying to evade the butchering business lately.—*Indorsement Jan. 7, 1864.* IX, 279.

19.—I wish you and Lane would make a sincere effort to get out of the mood you are in. It does neither of you any good. It gives you the means of tormenting my life out of me, and nothing else.—*To S. C. Pomeroy, May 12, 1864.* X, 98.

20.—As to your demand that I will accept or reject your proposition to furnish troops made to me yesterday, I have to say I took the proposition under advisement in good faith, as I believe you know; that you can withdraw it if you wish; but while it remains before me, I shall neither accept nor reject it until, with reference to the public interest, I shall feel that I am ready.—*To Gov. Carney, May 14, 1864.* X, 101.

21.—For such an awkward fellow I am pretty sure-footed. It used to take a pretty dexterous man to throw me.—*To White House group, Nov. 7, 1864.* Hay, 234.

22.—How many times I have laughed at your telling me plainly that I was too lazy to be anything but a lawyer.—*To Col. E. D. Taylor, Dec. 1864.* Hertz II, 957.

23.—Last night at 10:16 P.M., when it was dark as a rainy night without a moon could be, a furious cannonade, soon joined in by a heavy musketry fire, opened near Petersburg and lasted about two hours.

The sound was very distinct here as also were the flashes of the guns upon the clouds. It seemed to me a great battle, but the older hands here scarcely noticed it, and sure enough this morning it was found that very little had been done.—*To Sec. Stanton, from City Point, Va., March 30, 1865.* XI, 64.

24.—[In a dream Lincoln was recognized as President by someone who exclaimed: "He's a very common-looking man."] Friend, the Lord prefers common-looking people. That is the reason he makes so many of them.—*Morgan, 149* (no date).

See CODE OF CONDUCT, rules for personal guidance.

Lincoln, Abraham, "politician"—I am . . . in some sort a politician and in no sort a farmer.—*Speech, Milwaukee, Sept. 30, 1859.* V, 238.

See POLITICIANS, characterized.

Lincoln, Abraham, portrait criticized—Your picture presented by Mr. Lutz is, in the main, very good. From a line across immediately above the eyebrows, downward, it appears to me perfect. Above such line I think it is not so good—that is, while it gives perhaps a better forehead, it is not quite true to the original.—*To E. C. Middleton, Dec. 30, 1864.* Angle, 366.

Lincoln, Abraham, reporting lost case—Our case is decided against us. . . . Very sorry, but there is no help. . . . I do not think I could ever have argued the case better than I did. I did nothing else, but prepare to argue and argue this case, from Friday morning till Monday evening. Very sorry for the result; but I do not think it could have been prevented.—*To Charles Hoyt, Jan. 11, 1852.* II, 146.

Lincoln, Mary Todd, affectionate husband to—See LINCOLN, ABRAHAM, affectionate husband and father.

Lincoln, Mary Todd, "mistake" explained—Your note about the little paragraph in the *Republican* was received yesterday, since which time I have been too unwell to notice it. I had not supposed you wrote or approved it. The whole originated in a mistake. You know by the conversation with me that I thought the establishment of the paper was unfortunate, but I always expected to throw no obstacle in its way, and to patronize it to the extent of taking and paying for one copy. When the paper was brought to my house, my wife said to me, "Now are you going to take another worthless little paper?" I said to her evasively "I have not directed the paper to be left." From this, in my absence, she sent the message to the carrier.—*To John E. Rosette, Feb. 20, 1857.* II, 313.

Lincoln, Robert T., appraisal of—Bob is "short and low," and I expect always will be. He talks very plainly—almost as plainly as anybody. He is quite smart. I sometime fear that he is one of the little rare-ripe sort that are smarter at about five than ever after. He has a great deal of that sort of mischief that is the offspring of such animal spirits. Since I began this letter a messenger came to tell me Bob was lost; but by the time I reached the house his mother had found him and had whipped him, and by now, very likely he is run away again.—*To Joshua F. Speed, Oct. 22, 1846.* I, 298.

2.—Our oldest boy, Bob, has been away from us nearly a year at school, and will enter Harvard University next month. He promises very well, considering we never controlled him much.—*To A. G. Henry, July 4, 1860.* VI, 43.

Lincoln, Robert T., place sought for—Please read and answer this letter as though I was not President, but only a friend. My son, now in his twenty-second year, having graduated at Harvard, wishes to see something of the war before it ends. I do not wish to put him in the ranks, nor yet to give him a commission, to which those who have already served long are better entitled and better qualified to hold. Could he, without embarrassment to you or detriment to the service, go into your military family with some nominal rank, I, and not the public, furnishing his necessary means? If no, say so without the least hesitation, because I am as anxious and as deeply interested that you shall not be encumbered as you can be yourself. —*To Gen. Grant, Jan. 19, 1865.* X, 343.

Lincoln, Sarah Bush, son's care for—*See* MOTHER, care of.

Lincoln, Thomas, "without education"—Owing to my father being left an orphan at the age of six, in poverty, and in a new country, he became a wholly uneducated man.—*To Solomon Lincoln, March 6, 1848.* Hertz II, 565.

2.—Thomas [Lincoln, father of the President] . . . by the early death of his father and very narrow circumstances of his mother, even in childhood was a wandering laboring boy, and grew up literally without education. He never did more in the way of writing than to bunglingly write his own name.—*Autobiography, June 1, 1860.* VI, 25.

Lincoln-Douglas Debates, "in the face of the world" —I was aware, when it was first agreed that Judge Douglas and I were to have these seven joint discussions, that they were the seven successive acts of a drama—perhaps I should say, to be enacted not merely in the face of audiences like this, but in the face of the nation, and to some extent, by my relation to him, and not from anything in myself, in the face of the world; and I am anxious that they should be conducted with dignity and in the good temper which would be befitting the vast audience before which it was conducted.—*Debate, Quincy, Oct. 13, 1858.* IV, 324.

See CAMPAIGN OF 1858.

Lion or Bear, which is Douglas?—*See* DOUGLAS, STEPHEN A., lion or bear?

Liquor, appetite for, a disease—The victims of it [formerly] were to be pitied and compassionated, just as are the heirs of consumption and other hereditary diseases. Their failing was treated as a misfortune, and not as a crime, or even a disgrace.—*Speech, Springfield, Feb. 22, 1842.* I, 200.

Liquor, consumption of, "old as the world"—To all of us who now inhabit the world, the practice of drinking them [intoxicating liquors] is just as old as the world itself—that is, we have seen the one just as long as we have seen the other. When all such of us as have now reached the years of maturity first opened our eyes upon the stage of existence, we found intoxicating liquor recognized by everybody, used by everybody, repudiated by nobody. It commonly entered into the first draught of the infant and the last draught of the dying man. From the sideboard of the parson down to the ragged pocket of the houseless loafer, it was constantly found. Physicians prescribed it in this, that and the other disease; government provided it for soldiers and sailors; and to have a rolling or raising, a husking or "hoedown," anywhere about without it was positively insufferable.—*Speech, Springfield, Feb. 22, 1842.* I, 199.

Liquor, mankind favors its banishment—Whether or not the world would be vastly benefited by a total and final banishment from it of all intoxicating drinks seems to me not now an open question. Three-fourths of mankind confess the affirmative with their tongues, and, I believe, all the rest acknowledge it in their hearts. Ought any, then, to refuse their aid in doing what the good of all demands.—*Speech, Springfield, Feb. 22, 1842.* I, 204.

Liquor, manufacture was "honorable and respectable"—It [intoxicating liquor] was everywhere a respectable article of manufacture and merchandise. The making of it was regarded as an honorable livelihood, and he who could make most was the most enterprising and respectable. Large and small manufactories of it were everywhere erected, in which all the earthly goods of their owners were invested. . . . Merchants bought and sold it . . . with precisely the same feelings on the part of the seller, the buyer, and bystander as are felt at the selling and buying of plows, beef, bacon, or any other of the real necessaries of life. Universal public opinion not only tolerated but recognized and adopted its use.—*Speech, Springfield, Feb. 22, 1842.* I, 199.

Liquor, use and abuse of—It is true that even then it was known and acknowledged that many were greatly injured by it; but none seemed to think the injury arose from the use of a bad thing, but from the abuse of a very good thing.—*Speech, Springfield, Feb. 22, 1842.* I, 200.

"Loaves and Fishes," policy of, decried—*See* REPUBLICAN PARTY, advice to, 15.

Locke, David Ross—*See* NASBY, PETROLEUM V.

"Locos on the Blind Side"—*See* CAMPAIGN OF 1848, victory forecast, 1.

London, workers of—*See* FREE INSTITUTIONS, "enduring support of."

London Times, power of—The London *Times* is one of the greatest powers in the world—in fact, I don't know anything which has much more power—except, perhaps, the Mississippi.—*Interview, William Howard Russell, March 27, 1861.* Russell, I, 57.

Lost Sheep, parable of—He [Douglas] says I have a proneness for quoting Scripture. If I should do so now, it occurs that perhaps he places himself somewhat upon the ground of the parable of the lost sheep which went astray upon the mountains, and when the owner of the hundred sheep found the one that was lost, and threw it upon his shoulders, and came home rejoicing, it was said that there was more rejoicing over the one sheep that was lost and had been found, than over the ninety and nine in the fold. . . . And now, if the judge claims the benefit of this parable, let him repent.—*Speech, Springfield, July 17, 1658.* III, 166.

See SOUTH, "lost sheep."

Lost Speech, Henry Clay's—*See* CLAY, HENRY, "lost" speech of.

Lot, quickest way out—*See* POPULAR SOVEREIGNTY, Douglas's essay in *Harper's.*

Louisiana, free constitution for, defended—*See* RECONSTRUCTION, Louisiana, 12.

Louisiana, provisional court for—The insurrection which has for some time prevailed in several of the states of the Union, including Louisiana, has temporarily subverted and swept away the civil institutions of that state, including the judiciary and the judicial authorities of the Union, so that it has become necessary to hold the state in military occupation, and it being indispensably necessary that there shall be some judicial tribunal existing there capable of administering justice, I have therefore thought it proper to appoint, and I do hereby constitute, a provisional court, which shall be a court of record for the state of Louisiana.—*Executive order, Oct. 20, 1862.* VIII, 64.

Louisiana, slavery restrictions in Territory of—*See* TERRITORIES, slavery in, once controlled by Congress, 3.

Louisiana, submissive majority—*See* MAJORITY RULE, essential to safety, 3.

Louisiana Purchase—The power [of the government to acquire territory] was questioned at first by Mr. Jefferson, who, however, in the purchase of Louisiana yielded his scruples on the plea of great expediency. . . . Mr. Jefferson placed the importance of procuring Louisiana more on political and commercial grounds than on providing room for population.—*First annual message, Dec. 3, 1861.* VII, 50.

Louisville, defense of—As to Kentucky, you do not estimate that state as more important than I do, but I am compelled to watch all points. While I write this I am, if not in range, at least in hearing, of cannon shot from an army of enemies more than 100,000 strong. I do not expect them to capture the city; but I know they would if I were to send the men and arms from here to defend Louisville, of which there is not a single hostile armed soldier within forty miles, nor any force known to be moving upon it from any distance.—*To Gov. O. P. Morton, Sept. 29, 1861.* VII, 2.

Louisville Journal, Letter to editor of—*See* CAMPAIGN OF 1860, silence is candidate's best policy, 7, 8.

Lovejoy, Elijah P., biblical comparison—Both your father and Lovejoy were pioneer leaders in the cause of freedom, and it has always been difficult for me to see why your father . . . never aroused nor encountered any of that mob violence which . . . pursued Lovejoy and finally doomed him to a felon's death and a martyr's crown. Perhaps the two cases are a little parallel with those of John and Peter. John was bold and fearless at the scene of the Crucifixion, standing near the cross, receiving the Savior's request to care for his mother, but was not annoyed; while Peter, whose disposition [was] to shrink from public view, seemed to catch the attention of members of the mob on every hand, until finally to throw public attention off, he denied his Master with an oath; though later the grand old apostle redeemed himself grandly, and like Lovejoy, died a martyr to his faith. Of course, there was no similarity between Peter's treachery at the Temple and Lovejoy's splendid courage when the pitiless mob were closing around him. —*To Rev. James Lemen, March 2, 1857.* Tracy, 72.

2.—The madness and pitiless determination with which the mob steadily pursued Lovejoy to his doom, marks it as one of the most unreasoning and unreasonable in all time, except that which doomed the Savior to the cross.—*To Rev. James Lemen, March 2, 1857.* Stern, 415.

Lovejoy, Owen, advice to—Your danger [as candidate for Congress] has been that the democracy would wheedle some Republican to run against you without a nomination, relying mainly on Democratic votes. I have seen the strong men who could make the most trouble in that way, and find that they view the thing in the proper light, and will not consent to be so used. But they have been urgently tempted by the enemy; and I think it is still the point for you to guard most vigilantly.—*To Mr. Lovejoy, March 8, 1858.* Angle, 175.

Lovejoy, Owen, tribute to—Many of you have known Mr. [Owen] Lovejoy longer than I have, and are better able than I to do his memory complete justice. My personal acquaintance with him commenced only about ten years ago, since when it has become quite intimate, and every step in it has been one of increasing respect and esteem, ending, with his life, in no less than affection on my part. It can truly be said of him that while he was personally ambitious he bravely endured the obscurity which the unpopularity of his principles imposed, and never accepted official honors until those honors were ready to admit his principles with him. Throughout very heavy and perplexing duties here to the day of his death, it would scarcely wrong any other to say he was my most generous friend. Let him have the marble monument along with the well-assured and more enduring one in the hearts of those who love liberty unselfishly for all men.—*To John H. Bryant, May 30, 1864.* X, 111.

Lovejoy, Owen, "turned me blind"—It turned me blind when I first heard Swett was beaten and Lovejoy nominated; but after much reflection I really believe it is best to let it stand.—*To W. C. Whitney, July 9, 1856.* Lapsley II, 276.

Loyalty, cannot be assumed—In this struggle for the nation's life I cannot so confidently rely on those whose election [to office] may have depended on disloyal votes. Such men, when elected, may prove true; but such votes are given them in the expectation that they will prove false.—*To Gov. Bradford, Nov. 2, 1863.* IX, 197.

Lullaby Arguments—Another lullaby argument is that taking slaves to new countries does not increase their number, does not make anyone a slave who would otherwise be free.—*Speech, Peoria, Oct. 16, 1854.* II, 222.

Lynch, Judge, assisted by general—*See* BLUNT, JAMES, G., accused of helping Judge Lynch.

McClellan, George B., admonished—Stand well on your guard, hold all your ground, or yield only inch by inch and in good order.—*To Gen. McClellan, June 1 1862.* VII, 208.

McClellan, George B., appreciation of—With the retirement of Gen. Scott came the executive duty of appointing in his stead a general-in-chief of the army. It is a fortunate circumstance that neither in council nor country was there, so far as I know, any difference of opinion as to the proper person to be selected. The retiring chief repeatedly expressed his judgment in favor of Gen. McClellan for the position, and in this the nation seemed to give unanimous concurrence. The designation of Gen. McClellan is therefore in considerable degree the selection of the country as well as that of the executive, and hence there is better reason to hope there will be given him the confidence and cordial support thus by fair implication promised, and without which he cannot with so full efficiency serve the country.—*First annual message, Dec. 3, 1861.* VII, 55.

2.—I am satisfied that yourself, officers, and men have done the best you could. All accounts say better fighting was never done. Ten thousand thanks for it!—*To Gen. McClellan, July 3, 1862.* VII, 257.

3.—Be assured the heroism and skill of yourself, officers, and men is, and forever will be, appreciated.—*To Gen. McClellan, July 6, 1862.* VII, 261.

4.—God bless you, and all with you. Destroy the rebel army, if possible.—*To Gen. McClellan, Sept. 13, 1862.* VIII, 34.

5.—Unquestionably he [McClellan] has acted badly toward Pope! He wanted him to fail. That is unpardonable, but he is too useful just now to sacrifice.—*To John Hay, Sept. 5, 1862.* Hay, 47.

McClellan, George B., criticized—Your dispatches, complaining that you are not properly sustained,

while they do not offend me, do pain me very much. . . . After you left [here] I ascertained that less than 20,000 unorganized men, without a single field battery, were all you designed to be left for the defense of Washington and Manassas Junction. . . . This presented—or would present when McDowell and Sumner should be gone—a great temptation to the enemy to turn back from the Rappahannock and sack Washington. . . . I suppose the whole force which has gone forward to you is with you by this time; and if so, I think it is the precise time for you to strike a blow.—*To Gen. McClellan, April 9, 1862.* VII, 141.

2.—I now think it indispensable for you to know how your struggle against it [army corps organization] is received in quarters which we cannot entirely disregard. It is looked upon as merely an effort to pamper one or two pets and to persecute and degrade their supposed rivals.—*To Gen. McClellan, May 9, 1862.* VII, 156.

3.—Let me say, not as applicable to you personally, that senators and representatives speak of me in their places as they please without question, and that officers of the army must cease addressing insulting letters to them for taking no greater liberty with them.—*To Gen. McClellan, May 9, 1862.* VII, 157.

4.—I give you all I can, and act on the presumption that you will do the best you can with what you have, while you continue, ungenerously, I think, to assume that I could give more if I would.—*To Gen. McClellan, June 26, 1862.* VII, 235.

5.—I have not said you were ungenerous for saying you needed reinforcements. I thought you were ungenerous in assuming that I did not send them as fast as I could. I feel any misfortune to your army as keenly as you feel it yourself.—*To Gen. McClellan, June 28, 1862.* VII, 240.

6.—I can never feel confident that he [McClellan] will do anything effectual.—*To Sec. Welles, Sept. 8, 1862.* Welles I, 116.

7.—I put McClellan in command here to defend the city, for he has great powers of organization and discipline; he comprehends and can arrange military combinations better than any of our generals, and there his usefulness ends. He can't go ahead—he can't strike a blow.—*To White House group, Sept. 12, 1862.* Welles I, 124.

8.—You remember my speaking to you of what I called your over-cautiousness. Are you not overcautious when you assume you cannot do what the enemy is constantly doing? Should you not claim to be at least his equal in prowess, and act upon the claim?—*To Gen. McClellan, Oct. 13, 1862.* VIII, 57.

9.—One of the standard maxims of war, as you know, is to "operate upon the enemy's communications as much as possible without exposing your own." You seem to act as if this applies against you, but cannot apply in your favor.—*To Gen. McClellan, Oct. 13, 1862.* VIII, 58.

10.—Change positions with the enemy, and think you not he would break your communications with Richmond within the next 24 hours?—*To Gen. McClellan, Oct. 13, 1862.* VIII, 58.

11.—It is all easy if our troops march as well as the enemy, and it is unmanly to say they cannot do it.—*To Gen. McClellan, Oct. 13, 1862.* VIII, 61.

12.—I have just read your dispatch about soretongued and fatigued horses. Will you pardon me for asking what the horses of your army have done since the battle of Antietam that fatigues anything?—*To Gen. McClellan, Oct. 24, 1862.* VIII, 67.

13.—To be told, after more than five weeks' total inaction of the army, and during which period we sent to the army every fresh horse we possibly could, amounting to 7,918, that the cavalry horses were too much fatigued to move, presents a very cheerless, almost hopeless, prospect for the future, and it may have forced something of impatience in my dispatch. If not recruited and rested then, when could they ever be?—*To Gen. McClellan, Oct. 27, 1862.* VIII, 69.

McClellan, George B., demotion of, explained—After the battle of Antietam I went up to the field to try to get him [McClellan] to move, and came back thinking he would move at once. But when I got home he began to argue why he ought not to move. I peremptorily ordered him to advance. It was 19 days before he put a man across the river. It was 9 days longer before he got his army across, and then he stopped again delaying on little pretexts of wanting this or that. I began to fear he was playing false —that he did not want to hurt the enemy. I saw how he could intercept the enemy on the way to Richmond. I determined to make that the test. If he let them get away I would remove him. He did, so I relieved him.—*To John Hay, Sept. 24, 1864.* Hay, 218.

McClellan, George B., difficulties of replacing, in command—I beg you to be assured that no one out of my position can know so well as if he were in it the difficulties and involvements of replacing Gen. McClellan in command, and this aside from any imputations upon him.—*To Gov. Parker, June 30, 1863.* IX, 13.

McClellan, George B., had he beaten Lincoln in 1864—I would say, "General, the election has demonstrated that you are stronger, have more influence with the American people, than I. Now let us get together, you with your influence, and I with the executive power of the government, and try to save the country. You raise as many troops as you possibly can for this final trial, and I will devote all my energy to assisting and pushing the war.—*To cabinet, Nov. 11, 1864.* Stephenson, 436.

McClellan, George B., no rebuke—I wish to do this, and yet I do not wish to be understood as rebuking you.—*To Gen. McClellan, May 21, 1862.* Lapsley VI, 13.

McClellan, George B., opposition of, to corps organization—*See* ARMY CORPS ORGANIZATION, favored by all except McClellan.

See MC CLELLAN, GEORGE B., criticized, 2.

McClellan, George B., overemphasizes strategy—*See* CIVIL WAR, strategy overemphasized.

McClellan, George B., plea to, for reasonableness— The success of your army and the cause of the country are the same, and, of course, I only desire the good of the cause.—*To Gen. McClellan, May 9, 1862.* VII, 157.

2.—Please understand this, and do the best you can with the force you have.—*To Gen. McClellan, May 25, 1862.* VII, 188.

3.—The idea of sending you 50,000 or any other considerable force, promptly, is simply absurd. If, in your frequent mention of responsibility, you have the impression that I blame you for not doing more than you can, please be relieved of such impression. I only beg that in like manner you will not ask impossibilities of me.—*To Gen. McClellan, July 2, 1862.* VII, 254.

McClellan, George B., "quarrel" with Stanton—*See* STANTON, EDWIN M., appreciation of, 3.

McClellan, George B., "Save your army"—Save your army at all events. Will send reinforcements as fast as we can.—*To Gen. McClellan, June 28, 1862.* VII, 239.

2.—Maintain your ground if you can, but save the army at all events, even if you fall back to Fort Monroe. We still have strength enough in the country, and will bring it out.—*To Gen. McClellan, July 2, 1862.* VII, 253.

3.—Save the army, material and personal, and I will strengthen it for the offensive as fast as I can.—*To Gen. McClellan, July 2, 1862.* VII, 254.

4.—Save the army—first, where you are, if you can; secondly, by removal, if you must. You, on the ground, must be the judge as to which you will attempt, and of the means of effecting it.—*To Gen. McClellan, July 4, 1862.* VII, 259.

McClellan, George B., successors of, and Buell disappoint—I certainly have been dissatisfied with the slowness of Buell and McClellan; but before I relieved them I had great fears I should not find successors to them who would do better; and I am sorry to add that I have seen little to relieve those fears.—*To Gen. Schurz, Nov. 24, 1862.* VIII, 85.

McClellan, George B., support of—Draw on me for all the sense I have, and all the information.—*To Gen. McClellan, Nov. 1, 1861.* Hay, 33.
2.—Have done and shall do all I could and can to sustain you.—*To Gen. McClellan, May 15, 1862.* VII, 163.
3.—I have omitted and shall omit no opportunity to send you reinforcements whenever I possibly can.—*To Gen. McClellan, June 26, 1862.* VII, 235.

McClellan, George B., urged to action—*See* ACTION, pleas for, 6, 7, 8, 11.

McClellan, George B., works like beaver—McClellan is working like a beaver. He seems to be aroused to doing something by the sort of snubbing he got last week. The cabinet yesterday was unanimous against him.—*To John Hay, Sept. 5, 1862.* War Years I, 544.

"McClellan's Body-Guard"—*See* ARMY OF THE POTOMAC, McClellan's body-guard.

McClernand, John A., admonition and compliment—I have too many family controversies, so to speak, already on my hands to voluntarily so long as I can avoid it, take up another. You are doing well—well for the country and well for yourself—much better than you could possibly do if engaged in open war with Gen. Halleck. Allow me to beg that, for your sake, for my sake, and for the country's sake, you give your whole attention to the better work. Your success upon the Arkansas was both brilliant and valuable, and is fully appreciated by the country and government.—*To Gen. McClernand, Jan. 22, 1863.* VIII, 201.

McClernand, John A., painful to both—I doubt whether your present position [relieved of his command by Grant] is more painful to you than to myself. Grateful for the patriotic stand so early taken by you in this life-and-death struggle of the nation, I have done whatever has appeared practicable to advance you and the public interest together. . . . Gen. Grant and yourself have been conspicuous in our most important successes; and for me to interfere and thus magnify a breach between you could not but be of evil effect.—*To Gen. McClernand, Aug. 12, 1863.* IX, 72.

McClernand, John A., thanked—This is not an official, but a social letter. You have had a battle, and without being able to judge as to the precise measure of its value, I think it is safe to say that you and all with you have done honor to yourselves and the flag, and service to the country. Most gratefully do I thank you and them.—*To Gen. McClernand, Nov. 10, 1861.* VII, 18.

McCullough, Fanny, letter to—*See* CONDOLENCE, letter of, to grieving daughter.

McFingal's Kicking Gun—This opinion of Mr. Jefferson, in one branch at least, is, in the hands of Mr. Polk, like McFingal's gun—"bears wide and kicks the owner over."—*Speech in Congress, June 20, 1848.* II, 39.

McLean, John, too old for 1860 nomination—I can scarcely give an opinion as to what effect a nomination of Judge [John] McLean, by the Union convention, would have. I do not believe that he would accept it; and if he did, that fact alone, would shut him out of the Chicago convention. If he were ten years younger he would be our best candidate.—*To Lyman Trumbull, April 7, 1860.* Tracy, 140.

See CAMPAIGN OF 1860, preconvention candidates appraised.

McLean, John, tribute to—. . . long and brilliant judicial career.—*First annual message, Dec. 3, 1861.* VII, 38.

McLean, John, urged for President in 1856—*See* WHIG PARTY, members of, and Buchanan's nomination.

Madison, James, explains why Constitution does not mention slavery—*See* CONSTITUTION, slavery not mentioned in, 3, 4.

Madison, James, favored abolition—*See* ABOLITION, Virginians advocated, 2.

Magic, neither, nor miracles—*See* MIRACLES, neither magic nor.

"Magna Carta of Human Liberty"—*See* EQUALITY, Jeffersonian Democrats challenged on.

See REVOLUTION, constitutional substitute for.

Magnanimity, America's appreciated—They [American people] will rejoice with me in the new evidences which your proceedings furnish that the magnanimity they are exhibiting is justly estimated by the true friends of freedom and humanity in foreign countries. —*To workers of London, Feb. 2, 1863.* VIII, 212.

Magoffin, Beriah, lukewarm toward Union—*See* KENTUCKY, governor of, lukewarm toward Union.

Magruder, John B., might have been arrested—*See* CONFEDERATE GENERALS, might have been arrested.

Mail Subsidies, suggestions of, merit consideration—The views presented by the postmaster general on the subject of special grants by the government in aid of the establishment of new lines of ocean mail steamships, and the policy he recommends for the development of increased commercial intercourse with adjacent and neighboring countries should receive the careful consideration of Congress.—*Fourth annual message, Dec. 6, 1864.* X, 297.

Maine, strength of, in Congress compared with South Carolina's—*See* SLAVE STATES, have advantage in Congress, 4.

Maine, thanks to—On behalf of the Union, thanks to Maine.—*To J. G. Blaine, Sept. 13, 1864.* X, 224.

Majority Rule, essential to safety—If the majority should not rule, who would be the judge? Where is such a judge to be found? We should all be bound by the majority of the American people; if not, then the minority must control. Would that be right? Would it be generous? Assuredly, not! I reiterate that the majority should rule.—*Speech, Steubenville, Ohio, Feb. 14, 1861.* VI, 123.
2.—If the minority will not acquiesce, the majority must, or the government must cease. There is no other alternative; for continuing the government is acquiescence on the one side or the other.—*First inaugural, March 4, 1861.* VI, 178.
3.—The first part of the letter [Durant to Bullitt] is devoted to an effort to show that the secession ordinance of Louisiana was adopted against the will of a majority of the people. This is probably true, and in that fact may be found some instruction. Why did they allow the ordinance to go into effect? Why did they not assert themselves? Why stand passive and allow themselves to be trodden down by a minority?— *To Cuthbert Bullitt, July 28, 1862.* VII, 294.
4.—In a great national crisis like ours, unanimity of action among those seeking a common end is very desirable—almost indispensable. And yet no approach to such unanimity is attainable unless some deference shall be paid to the will of the majority, simply be-

cause it is the will of the majority.—*Fourth annual message, Dec. 6, 1864.* X, 304.

See SECESSION, means disintegration, 2.

Malice, party—*See* PRESS, some papers unfair.

Malice, without—I take it, I hope, in good temper, certainly with no malice toward any section.—*Speech, New Jersey Assembly, Feb. 21, 1861.* Basler, 576.
2.—I now have to beg that you will not do me the injustice to suppose for a moment that I remember anything against you in malice.—*To Schuyler Colfax, March 8, 1861.* XI, 188.
3.—I shall do nothing in malice. What I deal with is too vast for malicious dealing.—*To Cuthbert Bullitt, July 28, 1862.* VII, 298.
4.—When I wrote the letter to Gen. Schofield I was totally unconscious of any malice or disrespect toward you.—*To Gov. Gamble, July 23, 1863.* IX, 41.
5.—I can only say that I have acted upon my best convictions, without selfishness or malice, and that by the help of God I shall continue to do so.—*To Count A. de Gasparin, Aug. 4, 1862.* VII, 303.
6.—I say this without malice in my heart toward those who have done otherwise.—*Speech, Frederick, Md., Oct. 4, 1862.* XI, 125.
7.—With malice toward none, with charity for all, with firmness in the right as God gives us to see the right, let us strive on to finish the work we are in, to bind up the nation's wounds, to care for him who shall have borne the battle and for his widow and his orphan, to do all which may achieve and cherish a just and lasting peace among ourselves and with all nations.—*Second inaugural, March 4, 1865.* XI, 46.

Mammon—*See* SLAVERY, "sacred right" of, 3.

See NEGRO, condition of, grows worse, 2.

Man, acts correctly unless—I believe it is universally understood and acknowledged that all men will act correctly unless they have a motive to do otherwise.— *Speech in legislature, Jan., 1837.* I, 29.

Man, chance for every—*See* LABOR, no permanent class.

Man in the Moon—Forces now beyond Carlisle to be joined by regiments still at Harrisburg, and the united force again to join Pierce somewhere, and the whole to move down the Cumberland valley, will, in my unprofessional opinion, be quite as likely to capture the "man in the moon" as any part of Lee's army.—*To Gen. Lorenzo Thomas, July 8, 1863.* IX, 23.

Man, "neither living nor dead"—*See* REPUBLICAN PARTY, advice to, 19.

Man, objects to being driven—It is not much in the nature of man to be driven to anything; still less to be driven about that which is exclusively his own business; and least of all where such driving is to be submitted to at the expense of pecuniary interest or burning appetite.—*Speech, Springfield, Feb. 22, 1842.* I, 196.

2.—Assume to dictate to his [man's] judgment, or to command his action, or to mark him as one to be shunned and despised, and he will retreat within himself, close all the avenues to his head and his heart; and though your cause be naked truth itself, transferred to the heaviest lance, harder than steel, and sharper than steel can be made, and though you throw it with more than herculean force and precision, you shall be no more able to pierce him than to penetrate the hard shell of a tortoise with a rye straw. Such is man, and so must he be understood by those who would lead him, even to his own best interests.—*Speech, Springfield, Feb. 22, 1842.* I, 197.

"Man of Straw," Douglas fights—He [Douglas] is but fighting a man of straw when he assumes that I am contending against the rights of the states to do as they please about it [slavery].—*Debate, Alton, Oct. 15, 1858.* V, 57.

"Man of Straw," President must avoid being—It is understood that the President [Taylor] at first adopted, as a general rule, to throw the responsibility of the appointments upon the respective departments; and that such rule is adhered to and practiced upon. This course I at first thought proper, and, of course, I am not now complaining of it. Still I am disappointed with the effect of it on the public mind. It is fixing for the President the unjust and ruinous character of being a mere man of straw. This must be arrested, or it will damn us all inevitably. It is said Gen. Taylor and his officers held a council of war at Palo Alto—I believe—and that he then fought the battle against the unanimous opinion of those officers. This fact—whether rightfully or wrongfully—gives him more popularity than ten thousand submissions, however really wise and magnanimous those submissions may be. The appointments need be no better than they have been, but the public must be brought to understand that they were the President's appointments. He must occasionally say, or seem to say, "By the Eternal! I take the responsibility." These phrases were the "Samson's locks" of Gen. Jackson, and we dare not disregard the lessons of experience.—*To*

Sec. of State John M. Clayton, July 28, 1849. Tracy, 39.

Man Power, north's unimpaired by war—*See* CIVIL WAR, man power unimpaired by.

Man, whole or fraction of—*See* SLAVE STATES, have advantage in Congress, 1, 3.

Manchester, suffering of workers of, deplored—I know and deeply deplore the sufferings which the workingmen at Manchester and in all Europe, are called to endure in this crisis. . . . Under the circumstances, I cannot but regard your decisive utterance upon the question as an instance of sublime Christian heroism which has not been surpassed in any age or in any country. It is indeed an energetic and re-inspiring assurance of the inherent power of truth, and of the ultimate and universal triumph of justice, humanity, and freedom.—*To workers of Manchester, Jan. 19, 1863.* VIII, 196.

Manifest Destiny, Young America* invents—He [Young America] knows all that can possibly be known; inclines to believe in spiritual rappings, and is the unquestioned inventor of "Manifest Destiny." —*Speech, Springfield, Feb. 22, 1859.* V, 101.

Mankind, all should be free—*See* FREEDOM, for all men, 4.

Mankind, inherent right of—That they [men] are to go forth and improve their condition . . . is the inherent right given to mankind directly by the Maker. —*Speech, Cincinnati, Sept. 17, 1859.* Follett, 148.

Mankind, issues of war involve—*See* CIVIL WAR, results of, involve future.

Mankind, universal sense of—*See* DEITY, argument for existence of, 1.

Marriage, dreaded like halter—*See* WOMEN AND MARRIAGE, attitude toward, 3.

Martial Law—*See* HABEAS CORPUS.

See WAR POWER.

Maryland, adopts emancipation—I am notified that this is a compliment paid me by the loyal Marylanders resident in this District. I infer that the adoption of the new constitution for the state furnishes the occasion, and that in your view the extirpation of slavery constitutes the chief merit of the new constitution. Most heartily do I congratulate you, and Maryland, and the nation, and the world, upon this event. I regret that it did not occur two years sooner,

* See footnote, page 3.

which, I am sure, would have saved to the nation more money than would have met all the private loss incident to the measure, but it has come at last, and I sincerely hope its friends may fully realize all the anticipations of good from it, and that its opponents may by its effects be agreeably and profitably disappointed.—*Response to serenade, Oct. 19, 1864.* X, 243.

Maryland, calamities of—*See* BALTIMORE, calamities of, deplored.

Maryland, changed attitude of—Maryland was made to seem against the Union. Our soldiers were assaulted, bridges were burned and railroads torn up within her limits and we were many days at one time without the ability to bring a single regiment over her soil to the capital. Now her bridges and railroads are repaired and open to the government; she already gives seven regiments to the cause of the Union and none to the enemy; and her people at a regular election have sustained the Union by a large majority and a larger aggregate vote than they ever before gave to any candidate on any question.—*First annual message, Dec. 3, 1861.* VII, 53.

2.—Of those states not included in the Emancipation Proclamation, Maryland and Missouri, neither of which three years ago would tolerate any restraint upon the extension of slavery into new territories, only dispute now as to the best mode of removing it within their own limits.—*Third annual message, Dec. 8, 1863.* IX, 246.

3.—Maryland presents the example of complete success [in organizing to sustain the Union]. Maryland is secure to Liberty and Union for all the future. The genius of rebellion will no longer claim Maryland. Like another foul spirit being driven out, it may seek to tear her, but it will woo her no more.—*Fourth annual message, Dec. 6, 1864.* X, 303.

Maryland, cities of, might be bombarded—*See* MARYLAND, legislature under surveillance.

Maryland, defines liberty—*See* LIBERTY, definitions of, differ, 2.

Maryland, emancipation desired in—*See* EMANCIPATION, desired in Maryland.

Maryland, good state to leave—Maryland must, I think, be like New Hampshire, a good state to move from.—*Interview, Thurlow Weed, Dec., 1860.* Weed, 607.

Maryland, legislature under surveillance—I . . . conclude that it is only left to the commanding general [of the army] to watch and await their [the legisla-

tors'] action, which, if it shall be to arm their people against the United States, he is to adopt the most prompt and efficient means to counteract, even, if necessary, to the bombardment of their cities, and, in the extremest necessity, to suspension of *habeas corpus.*—*To Gen. Scott, April 25, 1861.* VI, 256.

Maryland, lost to Union if Kentucky goes—*See* KENTUCKY, importance of, to the Union.

Maryland, troops must cross—You, gentlemen, come here to me and ask for peace on any terms, and yet have no word of condemnation for those who are making war on us. You express great horror of bloodshed, and yet would not lay a straw in the way of those who are organizing in Virginia and elsewhere to capture this city. The rebels attack Fort Sumter, and your citizens attack troops sent to the defense of the government, and the lives and property in Washington, and yet you would have me break my oath and surrender the government without a blow. There is no Washington in that—no Jackson in that—no manhood nor honor in that. I have no desire to invade the South; but I must have troops to defend the capital. Geographically, it lies surrounded by the soil of Maryland; and mathematically the necessity exists that they should come over her territory. Our men are not moles, and they can't dig under the earth; they are not birds, and can't fly through the air. There is no way but to march across, and that they must do. But in doing this there need be no collision. Keep your rowdies in Baltimore, and there will be no blood shed. Go home and tell your people that if they will not attack us, we will not attack them; but if they do attack us, we will return it, and that severely.—*Reply to Baltimore committee, April 28, 1861.* Hertz II, 830.

Mason, George, abolition speech by—*See* ABOLITION, Virginians advocated, 4.

Mason, James M., Douglas and Davis—*See* SLAVERY, nationalization of, 10.

Mason and Dixon Line, no insurgent support north of—The insurgents confidently claimed a strong support from north of the Mason and Dixon's Line, and the friends of the Union were not free from apprehension on the point. This, however, was soon settled definitely and on the right side.—*First annual message, Dec. 3, 1861.* VII, 52.

Mason and Slidell—*See* NEUTRAL RIGHTS, Mason and Slidell case.

Masquerade Party, to, "with clean face"—*See* VALLANDIGHAM, C. L., return of.

Massachusetts, constitutional provision disapproved —See FOREIGN-BORN CITIZENS, no discrimination against.

Massachusetts, Republicans cautioned against dissension—See REPUBLICAN PARTY, threats to unity of, 3.

Massachusetts, Virginia and, asked for abolition—See ABOLITION, Virginians advocated, 1.

Massacre, Fort Pillow—See FORT PILLOW.

Masses—See PEOPLE.

Matheny, James H., "cock-and-bull story" by—See ABOLITIONIZE, plot to, parties denied, 3.

Matheny, James H., tribute to—That I have long esteemed Mr. Matheny as a man and a friend is known to you all. But that I should mete out to you the full measure of his worth I shall not now attempt to do.—*Speech to Springfield bar, Dec. 20, 1856.* Hertz II, 693.

Meade, George G., appreciation of—I have seen your dispatch to Gen. Halleck, asking to be relieved of your command because of a supposed censure of mine. I am very, very grateful to you for the magnificent success you gave the cause of the country at Gettysburg; and I am sorry now to be the author of the slightest pain to you.—*To Gen. Meade, July 14, 1863 (not sent).* IX, 28.
2.—I am very grateful to Meade for the great service he did at Gettysburg.—*To John Hay, July 19, 1863.* Hay, 77.
3.—I have always believed—making my belief a hobby, possibly—that the main rebel army going north of the Potomac could never return, if well attended to. . . . A few days having passed, I am now profoundly grateful for what was done [at Gettysburg] without criticism for what was not done. Gen. Meade has my confidence as a brave and skillful officer and a true man.—*To Gen. Howard, July 21, 1863.* IX, 39.
4.—Do not lean a hair's breadth against your own judgment of the public service on the idea of gratifying me.—*To Gen. Meade, July 27, 1863.* IX, 45.
5.—I regret that I cannot be present to witness the presentation of a sword by gallant Pennsylvania Reserve Corps to one so worthy to receive it as Gen. Meade.—*To Gen. Crawford, Aug. 28, 1863.* IX, 106.
6.—I have seen your dispatches about operations on the Rappahannock on Saturday, and I wish to say, "Well done!"—*To Gen. Meade, Nov. 9, 1863.* IX, 204.
7.—Your letter to Col. Townsend, inclosing a slip from the *Herald,* and asking a court of inquiry, has

been laid before me by the secretary of war. . . . It is quite natural that you should feel some sensibility on the subject, yet I am not impressed with the belief that your honor demands, or the public interest demands, such an inquiry. The country knows that in all events you have done good service; and I believe it agrees with me that it is much better for you to be engaged in trying to do more than to be diverted, as you necessarily would be, by a court of inquiry.—*To Gen. Meade, March 29, 1864.* X, 61.

Meade, George G., blamed for Lee's escape—See GETTYSBURG, full advantage of victory sacrificed.

"Mecca of Office Seekers"—See KERR, ORPHEUS, appreciation of, 2.

Meditation on Divine Will—See DEITY, purpose of, in war, 1.

Meigs, Montgomery C., tribute to—I have come to know Col. Meigs quite well for a short acquaintance, and, so far as I am capable of judging, I do not know one who combines the qualities of masculine intellect, learning, and experience of the right sort, and physical power of labor and endurance, so well as he.—*To Gen. Scott, June 5, 1861.* VI, 290.

Melancholy—A tendency to melancholy . . . let it be observed, is a misfortune, not a fault.—*To Mary Speed, Sept. 27, 1841.* I, 80.

Menard Index (newspaper), forged article in—See PRESS, forgery in, best ignored.

Mercer, Samuel, no criticism—You will, on receipt of this order, turn over the command of your vessel to Lieut. David D. Porter, who is to proceed in her on an important service. . . . I do not desire in the least to reflect upon your zeal or patriotism; on the contrary, I have the fullest confidence in your ability to perform the duty in question.—*To Capt, Mercer, April 1, 1861.* Hertz II, 827.
2.—The government does not in the least reflect upon your efficiency or patriotism; on the contrary, have fullest confidence in your ability to perform any duty required of you.—*To Capt. Mercer, April 2, 1861.* VI, 238.

Merchant Ships, arming of—By the act of the 5th of August last, Congress authorized the President to instruct the commanders of suitable vessels to defend themselves against and to capture pirates. . . . For the more effectual protection of our extensive and valuable commerce in the eastern seas especially it seems to me that it would also be advisable to authorize the commanders of sailing vessels to recapture any prizes which pirates may make of United States vessels and their cargoes.—*First annual message, Dec. 3, 1861.* VII, 33.

Message, safety in sending—I am unable to conceive how a message can be less safe by the express than by a staff officer. If you send a verbal message, the messenger is one additional person let into the secret. —*To Gen. Rosecrans, June 8, 1864.* X, 116.

Methodist Church, thanked—These kind words of approval, coming from so numerous a body of intelligent Christian people, and so far from all suspicion of sinister motives, are indeed encouraging to me. By the help of an all-wise Providence, I shall endeavor to do my duty, and I shall expect the continuance of your prayers for a right solution of our national difficulties and the restoration of our country to peace and prosperity.—*Reply to East Baltimore conference, May 15, 1862.* VII, 163.

2.—Nobly sustained as the government has been by all the churches, I would utter nothing which might in the least appear invidious against any. Yet without this it may fairly be said that the Methodist Episcopal Church, not less devoted than the rest, is by its greater numbers the most important of all. It is no fault in others that the Methodist Church sends more soldiers to the field, more nurses to the hospital, and more prayers to Heaven than any. God bless the Methodist Church. Bless all the churches, and blessed be God, who, in this our great trial, giveth us the churches.—*Reply to Methodist delegation, May 14, 1864.* X, 100.

Methodist Church, "they complain"—If his recommendations are satisfactory, and I recollect them to have been so, the fact that he is urged by the Methodists should be in his favor, as they complain of us some.—*To Sec. Chase, July 26, 1861.* Tracy, 190.

Mexican War, acquired territory and slavery—In a final treaty of peace [terminating the Mexican War] we shall probably be under a sort of necessity of taking some territory; but it is my desire that we shall not acquire any extending so far south as to enlarge and aggravate the distracting subject of slavery.— *Memorandum, July 1, 1848.* II, 56.

Mexican War, acts of aggression—I own that finding in the oration [by Peck] a labored justification of the administration on the origin of the Mexican War disappointed me, because it is the first effort of the kind I have known made by one appearing to me to be intelligent, right-minded and impartial.—*To Rev. J. M. Peck, May 21, 1848.* II, 23.

2.—[You say] "the conviction to my mind is irresist-ible that the government of the United States committed no aggression on Mexico." . . . If you admit that they [assertions made by Lincoln] are facts, then I shall be obliged for a reference to any law of language, law of states, law of nations, law of morals, law of religions, any law, human or divine, in which an authority can be found for saying those facts constitute "no aggression."—*To Rev. J. M. Peck, May 21, 1848.* II, 25.

3.—Possibly you consider those acts [committed by the United States against Mexico] too small for notice. Would you venture to so consider them had they been committed by any nation on earth against the humblest of our people? I know you would not. Then I ask, is the precept "Whatsoever ye would that men should do to you, do ye even so to them" obsolete? of no force? of no application?—*To Rev. J. M. Peck, May 21, 1848.* II, 26.

4.—Mr. Lincoln thought [as a member of Congress] that the act of sending an armed force among the Mexicans was unnecessary, inasmuch as Mexico was in no way molesting or menacing the United States or the people thereof; and that it was unconstitutional, because the power of levying war is vested in Congress, and not in the President. He thought the principal motive for the act was to divert public attention from the surrender of "Fifty-four, forty or fight" to Great Britain on the Oregon boundary question.—*Autobiography, June 1, 1860.* VI, 36.

See MEXICAN WAR, voting record explained.

Mexican War, Fort Brown relieved—And now the din of battle nears the fort and sweeps obliquely by; a gleam of hope flies through the half-imprisoned few; they fly to the wall; every eye is strained—it is— it is—the stars and stripes are still aloft! Anon the anxious brethren meet; and while hand strikes hand, the heavens are rent with a loud, long, glorious, gushing cry of "Victory! Victory!! Victory!!!"—*Speech, Chicago, July 25, 1850.* Angle, 70.

Mexican War, heroes of, praised—I think of all those brave men [who fought in the Mexican War] as Americans, in whose proud fame, as an American, I too have a share. Many of them, Whigs and Democrats, are my constituents and personal friends; and I thank them—more than thank them—one and all, for the high imperishable honor they have conferred on our common state.—*Speech, in Congress, July 27, 1848.* II, 85.

Mexican War, Polk's attempt to justify—My way of living leads me to be about the courts of justice; and there I have sometimes seen a good lawyer, struggling for his client's neck in a desperate case, employing every artifice to work around, befog, and cover up with many words some point arising in the case which he dared not admit and yet could not deny. Party bias may help to make it appear so, but with all the allowances I can make for such bias, it still does appear to me that just such, and from just such necessity, is the President's struggle in this case [that is, to justify the war].—*Speech in Congress, Jan. 12, 1848.* I, 337.

2.—If he [President Polk] cannot or will not do this [answer Lincoln's "interrogations" touching the war] —if, on any pretence or no pretence he shall refuse or omit it—then I shall be fully convinced of what I more than suspect already—that he is deeply conscious of being in the wrong; that he feels the blood of this war, like the blood of Abel, is crying to Heaven against him; that originally having some strong motive—what, I will not stop now to give my opinion concerning—to involve the two countries in a war, and trusting to escape scrutiny by fixing the public gaze upon the exceeding brightness of military glory—that attractive rainbow that arises in showers of blood—that serpent's eye that charms to destroy—he plunged into it, and has swept on and on till, disappointed in his calculations of the ease with which Mexico might be subdued, he now finds himself he knows not where.—*Speech in Congress, Jan. 12, 1848.* I, 340.

3.—How like the half-insane mumblings of a fever dream is the whole [Mexican] war part of his [President Polk's] late message.—*Speech in Congress, Jan. 12, 1848.* I, 341.

4.—The President [Polk] is in no wise satisfied with his own positions [relative to the Mexican War]. First he takes up one, and in attempting to argue us into it he argues himself out of it, then seizes another and goes through the same process, and, then, confused at being able to think of nothing new, he snatches up the old one again, which he has some time before cast off.—*Speech in Congress, Jan. 12, 1848.* I, 344.

5.—His [President Polk's] mind, taxed beyond its power, is running hither and thither like some tortured creature on a burning surface, finding no position on which it can settle down and be at ease.— *Speech in Congress, Jan. 12, 1848.* I, 344.

6.—He [President Polk] is a bewildered, confounded and miserably perplexed man. God grant he may be able to show there is not something about his conscience more painful than all his mental perplexity. —*Speech in Congress, Jan. 12, 1848.* I, 345.

Mexican War, Santa Anna and his "treaty"—I next consider the President's statement that Santa Anna in his treaty with Texas recognized the Rio Grande as the western boundary of Texas. . . . During the first ten years of the existence of that document it was never by anybody called a treaty. . . . It has none of the distinguishing features of a treaty. . . . It does not call itself a treaty. Santa Anna does not therein assume to bind Mexico. . . . He did not recognize the independence of Texas; he did not assume to put an end to the war. . . . He did not say one word about boundary.—*Speech in Congress, Jan. 12, 1848.* I, 334.

Mexican War, territorial indemnity—The President is resolved under all circumstances to have full territorial indemnity for the expenses of the war; but he forgets to tell us how we are to get the excess after those expenses shall have surpassed the value of the whole of the Mexican territory. . . . He insists that the separate national existence of Mexico shall be maintained; but he does not tell us how this can be done, after we shall have taken all her territory.— *Speech in Congress, Jan. 12, 1848.* I, 342.

2.—The war has gone on some twenty months; for the expense of which, together with an inconsiderable old score, the President now claims about one-half of the Mexican territory, and that by far the better half, so far as concerns our ability to make anything of it. It is comparatively uninhabited; so that we could establish land offices in it, and raise some money in that way.—*Speech in Congress, Jan. 12, 1848.* I, 342.

3.—If the prosecution of the war has in expenses already equalled the better half of the country [Mexico], how long its future prosecution will be in equalling the less valuable half is not a speculative, but a practical, question, pressing closely upon us.— *Speech in Congress, Jan. 12, 1848.* I, 343.

Mexican War, Texas boundary where?—*See* TEXAS, "true boundary of."

Mexican War, voting record explained—When the [Mexican] war began, it was my opinion that all those who because of knowing too little, or because of knowing too much, could not conscientiously approve the conduct of the President in the beginning of it should nevertheless, as good citizens and patriots, remain silent on that point, at least till the war should be ended. . . . I adhered to it [this view] and acted upon it, until since I took my seat here [in Congress]; and I think I should still adhere to it were it not that the President and his friends will not allow it to be so.—*Speech in Congress, Jan. 12, 1848.* I, 328.

2.—Because of my vote for Ashmun's amendment you fear that you and I disagree about the war. . . . That vote affirms that the [Mexican] war was unnecessarily and unconstitutionally commenced by the President; and I will stake my life that if you had been in my place you would have voted just as I did. Would you have voted what you felt and knew to be a lie? I know you would not. Would you have gone out of the House—skulked the vote? I expect not. If you had skulked one vote, you would have had to skulk many more before the end of the session. . . . No man can be silent if he would. You are compelled to speak; and your only alternative is to tell the truth or a lie. I cannot doubt which you would do.—*To W. H. Herndon, Feb. 1, 1848.* I, 351.

3.—This vote [declaring the beginning of the war unconstitutional] has nothing to do in determining my votes on the question of supplies. I have always intended, and still intend, to vote supplies, perhaps not in the precise form recommended by the President but in a better form for all purposes, except Locofoco party purposes.—*To W. H. Herndon, Feb. 1, 1848.* I, 352.

4.—If, when the [Mexican] war had begun, and had become the cause of the country, the giving of our [Whig] money and our blood, in common with yours [Democrats'] was support of the war . . . it is not true that we have always opposed the war. With few individual exceptions, you have constantly had our votes here for all the necessary supplies. And, more than this, you have had the services, the blood, and the lives of our political brethren in every trial and on every field.—*Speech in Congress, July 27, 1848.* II, 84.

5.—Give yourself no concern about my voting against the supplies, unless you are without faith that a lie can be successfully contradicted. There is not a word of truth in the charge.—*To Henry C. Whitney, June 24, 1858.* XI, 104.

6.—Your letter inclosing the attack of the [Chicago] *Times* upon me was received this morning. . . . There is not a word of truth in the charge, and I am just considering a little as to the best shape to put a contradiction in.—*To Henry C. Whitney, June 24, 1858.* XI, 104.

7.—You may safely deny that I ever gave any vote for withholding any supplies whatever from officers or soldiers of the Mexican War.—*To J. Medill, June 25, 1858.* Hertz II, 711.

8.—My friend, the judge [Douglas] is . . . at fault when he charges me at the time when I was in Congress of having opposed our soldiers who were fighting the Mexican War. . . . You remember I was an old Whig, and whenever the Democratic party tried to get me to vote that the war had been righteously begun by the President I would not do it. But when-

ever they asked for any money, or land-warrants, or anything to pay the soldiers there, during all that time, I gave the same vote that Judge Douglas did.—*Debate, Ottawa, Aug. 21, 1858.* III, 230.

9.—Whenever there was an attempt to procure a vote of mine which would indorse the origin and justice of the war, I refused to give such indorsement and voted against it; but I never voted against the supplies for the army. . . . You know they have charged that I voted against the supplies, by which I starved the soldiers who were out fighting the battles of their country. I say . . . it is false.—*Debate, Charleston, Sept. 18, 1858.* IV, 191.

10.—Much has been said of his [Lincoln's] course in Congress in regard to this [Mexican] war. A careful examination of the *Journal* and Congressional *Globe* shows that he voted for all the supply measures in any way favorable to the officers, soldiers, and their families, who conducted the war through; with the exception that some of these measures passed without yea's and nay's, leaving no record as to how particular men voted. The *Journal* and *Globe* also show him voting that the war was unnecessarily and unconstitutionally begun by the President of the United States.—*Autobiography, June 1, 1860.* VI, 35.

11.—Mr. Lincoln thought the act of sending an armed force among the Mexicans was unnecessary, inasmuch as Mexico was in no way molesting or menacing the United States or the people thereof; and that it was unconstitutional, because the power of levying war is vested in Congress, and not in the President,—*Autobiography, June 1, 1860.* VI, 36.

12.—I dislike to waste a word on a merely personal point, but I must respectfully assure you that you will find yourselves at fault should you ever seek for evidence to prove your assumption that I "opposed, in discussions before the people, the policy of the Mexican war."—*To M. Birchard and others, June 29, 1863.* IX, 2.

Mexican War, Whig attitude toward—The Locos are untiring in their efforts to make the impression that all who vote supplies or take part in the war do of necessity approve the President's conduct in the beginning of it; but the Whigs here [in Congress] from the beginning made and kept the distinction between the two. In the very first act nearly all the Whigs voted against the preamble declaring that war existed by the act of Mexico; and yet nearly all of them voted for the supplies.—*To W. H. Herndon, Feb. 1, 1848.* I, 352.

2.—As to the Whig men who have participated in the war, so far as they have spoken in my hearing, they do not hesitate to denounce as unjust the President's conduct at the beginning of the war.—*To W. H. Herndon, Feb. 1, 1848.* I, 352.

3.—The news reached Washington of the commencement of hostilities on the Rio Grande, and of the great peril of Gen. Taylor's army. Everybody, Whigs and Democrats, was for sending them aid, in men and money. It was necessary to pass a bill for this. The Locos had a majority in both houses, and they brought in a bill with a preamble, saying, Whereas, war exists by the act of Mexico, therefore we send Gen. Taylor money. The Whigs moved to strike out the preamble, so that they could vote to send the men and money, without saying anything about how the war commenced; but being in the minority, they were voted down, and the preamble was retained. Then, on passage of the bill, the question came upon them, Shall we vote for preamble and bill together, or against them both together? They did not want to vote against sending help to Gen. Taylor and therefore they voted for both together.—*To W. H. Herndon, June 22, 1848.* II, 52.

4.—You Democrats say we Whigs have always opposed the [Mexican] war. . . . The declaration . . . is true or false, according as one may understand the term "oppose the war." If to say "the war was unnecessarily and unconstitutionally commenced by the President" is opposing the war, then the Whigs have very generally opposed it. . . . The marching an army into the midst of a peaceful Mexican settlement, frightening the inhabitants away, leaving their growing crops and other property to destruction, to you may appear a perfectly amiable, peaceful, unprovoking procedure; but it does not appear so to us. So to call such an act, to us appears no other than a naked, impudent absurdity, and we speak of it accordingly. But if, when the war had begun, and had become the cause of the country, the giving of our money and our blood, in common with yours, was support of the war, then it is not true that we have always opposed the war. With few individual exceptions, you have constantly had our votes here for all the necessary supplies. And, more than this, you have had the services, the blood, and the lives of our political brethren in every trial and on every field.— *Speech in Congress, July 27, 1848.* II, 84.

5.—Through suffering and death, by disease and in battle, they [Whigs] have fought and fell with you. . . . Nor were the Whigs few in number, or laggard in the day of danger. In that fearful, bloody, breathless struggle at Buena Vista, where each man's hard task was to beat back five foes or die himself, of the five high officers who perished, four were Whigs.— *Speech in Congress, July 27, 1848.* II, 85.

6.—The distinction between the cause of the Presi-

dent in beginning the [Mexican] war, and the cause of the country after it was begun is a distinction which you [Democrats] cannot perceive. . . . We [Whigs] see the distinction, as we think, clearly enough; and our friends who have fought in the war have no difficulty in seeing it also.—*Speech in Congress, July 27, 1848.* II, 86.

Mexican War, Whigs not permitted silence—You ask . . . "Would it not have been just as easy to have elected Gen. Taylor without opposing the war as by opposing it?" I answer, I suppose it would, if we could do neither—could be silent on the question; but the Locofocos here will not let the Whigs be silent. Their very first act in Congress was to present a preamble declaring that war existed by the act of Mexico, and the Whigs were obliged to vote on it— and this policy is followed up by them, so that they are compelled to speak, and their only option is whether they will, when they do speak, tell the truth, or tell a foul, villainous, and bloody falsehood—But, while on this point, I protest against your calling the condemnation of Polk "opposing the war". . . . I think you fall into one of the artfully set traps of Locofocoism.—*To Usher F. Linder, March 22, 1848.* Basler, 221.

Mexican War, whose soil?—If . . . he [Polk] can show that the soil was ours where the first blood of the war was shed—that it was not within an inhabited country, or, if within such, that the inhabitants had submitted themselves to the civil authority of Texas or of the United States and that the same is true of the site of Fort Brown,—then I am with him for his justification. In that case I shall be most happy to reverse the vote I gave the other day.—*Speech in Congress, Jan. 12, 1848.* I, 340.

2.—Their [Polk's and his friends'] only positions [to justify the start of the war] are first, that the soil was ours when the hostilities commenced; and second, that whether it was rightfully ours or not, Congress had annexed it, and the President for that reason was bound to defend it; both of which are as clearly proved to be false in fact as you can prove that your house is mine. The soil was not ours, and Congress did not annex or attempt to annex it.—*To W. H. Herndon, Feb. 15, 1848.* II, 2.

3.—It is a fact that the United States Army in marching to the Rio Grande marched into a peaceful Mexican settlement, and frightened the inhabitants away from their homes and their growing crops. It is a fact that Fort Brown, opposite Matamoras, was built by that army within a Mexican cotton field, on which at the time the army reached it a young cotton crop was growing, and which crop was wholly destroyed and the field itself greatly and permanently injured. . . . It is a fact that when the Mexicans captured Capt. Thornton and his command, they found and captured them within another Mexican field.—*To Rev. J. M. Peck, May 21, 1848.* II, 25.

Mexico, "disorganized"—*See* SLAVERY, no compromise on, 9.

Mexico, good wishes toward—You have hitherto resided with us. . . . You know how sincerely and how profoundly during that residence the United States desired that Mexico might always enjoy the blessings of domestic and foreign peace with perfect security, prosperity, independence and freedom. . . . I have the pleasure of assuring you that in all things, as well affecting your country as yourself personally, these feelings remain unchanged.—*To Ambassador Romero, Oct. 29, 1863.* Hertz II, 915.

Mexico, nation of "mongrels"—I understand that there is not more than one person there [in Mexico] out of eight who is a pure white, and I suppose from the judge's [Douglas's] previous declaration that when we get Mexico, or any considerable portion of it, he will be in favor of these mongrels settling the question [of slavery], which would bring him somewhat into collision with his horror of an inferior race.—*Debate, Galesburg, Oct. 1, 1858.* IV, 292.

See TERRITORY, grab for new, feared, 1.

Mexico, slavery abolished by—*See* TEXAS, By what right a slave state?

Military Appointments, merit controls—I have scarcely appointed a Democrat to a [military] command, who was not urged by many Republicans and opposed by none. . . . But, after all, many Republicans were appointed; and I mean no disparagement to them when I say I do not see that their superiority of success has been so marked as to throw great suspicion on the good faith of those who are not Republicans.—*To Gen. Schurz, Nov. 10, 1862.* Stern, 734.

2.—I cannot even conjecture what junior of yours you suppose I contemplate promoting over you. True, seniority has not been my rule in this connection; but in considering military merit, the world has abundant evidence that I disregard politics.—*To Col. W. R. Morrison, Nov. 5, 1862.* VIII, 72.

3.—If a brigade was promised him [Charles Wiegand] by the War Department, I know nothing of it; and not knowing whether he is fit for any place, I could not with propriety recommend him for any.—*Memorandum, March 24, 1863.* VIII, 231.

4.—I beg you to believe we do not act in a spirit of disregarding merit.—*To Gen. Sherman, July 26, 1864.* X, 175.

Military Arm, hopes not to use—It is not with any pleasure that I contemplate the possibility that a necessity may arise in this country for the use of the military arm.—*Speech, Pennsylvania Legislature, Feb. 22, 1861.* VI, 164.

Military Arrests—*See* WAR POWER, use of, defended, 5, 7.

"Military Coat-Tails"—The gentleman from Georgia further says we [Whigs] have deserted all our principles, and taken shelter under Gen. Taylor's military coat-tails, and he seems to think this is exceedingly degrading. Well, as his faith is, so be it unto him. But can he remember no other military coat-tail under which a certain other party has been sheltering for more than a quarter of a century? Has he no acquaintance with the ample military coat-tail of Gen. Jackson? Does he not know that his own party have run the last five presidential races under that coat-tail? And that they are now running the sixth under the same cover? Yes, sir, that coat-tail was used not only for Gen. Jackson himself, but has been clung to, with the grip of death, by every Democratic candidate since. You have never ventured, and dare not now venture, from under it.—*Speech in Congress, July 27, 1848.* II, 72.

2.—Old horses and military coat-tails, or tails of any sort, are not figures of speech such as I would be the first to introduce into discussions here; but as the gentleman from Georgia has seen fit to introduce them, he and you are welcome to all you have made, or can make by them. If you have any more old horses, trot them out; any more tails, just cock them and come to us.—*Speech in Congress, July 27, 1848.* II, 73.

Military Courts (for collection of debts against insurgents), recommendation for, resisted—There are no courts nor officers to whom the citizens of other states may apply for the enforcement of their lawful claims against citizens of the insurgent states, and there is a vast amount of debt constituting such claims. Some have estimated it as high as $200,000,000, due in large part from insurgents in open rebellion to loyal citizens who are even now making great sacrifices in the discharge of the patriotic duty to support the government. . . . I have been urgently solicited to establish by military power courts to administer summary justice in such cases. I have thus far declined it, not because I had any doubt that the end proposed—the collection of the debts—was just and right in itself but because I have been unwilling to go beyond the pressure of necessity in the unusual exercise of power.—*First annual message, Dec. 3, 1861.* VII, 41.

Military Draft, "Are we degenerate?"—Shall we shrink from the necessary means to maintain our free government, which our grandfathers employed to establish it and our own fathers have already employed once to maintain it? Are we degenerate? Has the manhood of our race run out?—*Opinion (never published) on draft law, Aug. 15, 1863.* IX, 80.

Military Draft, authorized by Constitution—They tell us the [draft] law is unconstitutional. It is the first instance, I believe, in which the power of Congress to do a thing has ever been questioned in a case where the power is given by the Constitution in express terms. Whether a power can be implied when it is not expressed has often been the subject of controversy; but this is the first case in which the degree of effrontery has been ventured upon by denying a power which is plainly and distinctly written down in the Constitution. The Constitution declares that "the Congress shall have power . . . to raise and support armies." . . . The whole scope of the conscription is "to raise and support armies." There is nothing else in it. . . . The power is given fully, completely, unconditionally. It is not a power to raise armies if state authorities consent; nor if the men to compose the armies are entirely willing; but it is a power . . . given to Congress by the Constitution, without an "if."—*Opinion (never published) on draft law, Aug. 15, 1863.* IX, 75.
2.—This law was considered, discussed, modified, and amended by Congress at great length, and with much labor; and was finally passed with a near approach to unanimity.—*Opinion (never published) of draft law, Aug. 15, 1863.* IX, 78.

Military Draft, buying of substitutes defended—Much complaint is made of that provision of the conscription law which allows a drafted man to substitute $300 for himself; while, as I believe, none is made of that provision which allows him to substitute another man for himself. Nor is the $300 provision objected to for unconstitutionality; but for inequality, for favoring the rich against the poor. The substitution of men is the provision, if any, which favors the rich to the exclusion of the poor. But this, being a provision in accordance with an old and well-known practice in the raising of armies, is not objected to. There would have been great objection if that provision had been omitted. And yet, being in, the money provision really modifies the inequality which

the other introduces. It allows men to escape the service who are too poor to escape but for it. Without the money provision, competition among the more wealthy might, and probably would, raise the price of substitutes above $300, thus leaving the man who could raise only $300 no escape from personal service. True, by the law as it is, the man who cannot raise so much as $300, nor obtain a personal substitute for less, cannot escape; but he can come quite as near escaping as he could if the money provision were not in the law. To put it another way: is an unobjectionable law which allows only the man to escape who can pay $1,000 made objectionable by adding a provision that any one may escape who can pay the smaller sum of $300? This is the exact difference at this point between the present law and all former draft laws.—*Opinion (never published) on draft law, Aug. 15, 1863.* IX, 78.
2.—It is true that by this law a somewhat larger number will escape [military service] than could under a law allowing personal substitutes only; but each additional man thus escaping will be a poorer man than could have escaped by the law in the other form. The money provision enlarges the class of exempts from actual service simply by admitting poorer men into it. How, then, can the money provision be a wrong to the poor man? The inequality complained of pertains in greater degree to the substitution of men, and is really modified and lessened by the money provision.—*Opinion (never published) on draft law, Aug. 15, 1863.* IX, 80.

Military Draft, can't wait—It is a very delicate matter to postpone the draft in one state, because of the argument it furnishes others to have postponements also.—*To Gov. Joel Parker, July 20, 1863.* IX, 36.
2.—I do not object to abide a decision of the United States Supreme Court . . . on the constitutionality of the draft law . . . but I cannot consent to lose the time while it is being obtained. We are contending with an enemy, who, as I understand, drives every able-bodied man he can reach into his ranks, very much as a butcher drives bullocks into a slaughter-pen. No time is wasted, no argument used. This produces an army which will soon turn upon our now victorious soldiers, already in the field, if they shall not be sustained by recruits as they should be. It produces an army with a rapidity not to be matched on our side, if we waste time to re-experiment with the volunteer system already deemed by Congress, and palpably, in fact, so far exhausted as to be, inadequate, and then more time to obtain a court decision as to whether a law is constitutional which requires a part of those not now in the service to go

to the aid of those who are already in it, and still more time to determine with absolute certainty that we get those who are to go in the precisely legal proportion to those who are not to go.—*To Gov. Horatio Seymour, Aug. 7, 1863. IX, 60.*

3.—Looking to time, as heretofore, I am unwilling to give up a drafted man now even for the certainty, much less the mere chance, of getting a volunteer hereafter.—*To Horatio Seymour, Aug. 16, 1863. IX, 83.*

Military Draft, discretion given Congress—If the Constitution had prescribed a mode [for raising armies], Congress could and must follow that mode; but, as it is, the mode necessarily goes to Congress, with the power expressly given.—*Opinion (never published) on draft law, Aug. 15, 1863. IX, 77.*

Military Draft, distributes burdens—This law belongs to a class, which class is composed of those laws whose object is to distribute burdens or benefits on the principle of equality.—*Opinion (never published) on draft law, Aug. 15, 1863. IX, 81.*

Military Draft, feared effect on navy—It has been found . . . that the operation of the draft, with the high bounties paid for army recruits, is beginning to affect injuriously the naval service, and will, if not corrected, be likely to impair its efficiency by detaching seamen from their proper vocation and inducing them to enter the army.—*Third annual message, Dec. 8, 1863. IX, 238.*

Military Draft, immigrants need not fear—All that is necessary is to secure the flow of that stream [immigration] in its present fullness, and to that end the government must in every way make it manifest that it neither needs nor designs to impose involuntary military service upon those who come from other lands to cast their lot in our country.—*Fourth annual message, Dec. 6, 1864. X, 291.*

Military Draft, necessary—It matters not. We must have the men. If I go down I intend to go like the *Cumberland,* with my colors flying.—*To George W. Dole, Aug., 1864. War Years III, 187.*

Military Draft, principle guiding—The principle to which I purpose adhering, which is to proceed with the draft, at the same time applying infallible means to avoid any great wrongs.—*To Horatio Seymour, Aug. 11, 1863. IX, 69.*

2.—The government is bound to administer the law with such an approach to exactness as is usual in analogous cases, and as entire good faith and fidelity will reach.—*Opinion (never published) on draft law, Aug. 15, 1863. IX, 82.*

3.—I feel bound to tell you it is my purpose to see the draft law faithfully executed.—*Opinion (never published) on draft law, Aug. 15, 1863. IX, 83.*

Military Draft, principle of, not new—The principle of the draft, which simply is involuntary or enforced service, is not new. It has been practiced in all ages of the world. It was well known to the framers of our Constitution as one of the modes of raising armies. . . . It had been used just before in establishing our independence, and it was also used under the Constitution in 1812.—*Opinion (never published) on draft law, Aug. 15, 1863. IX, 80.*

Military Draft, reason for—At the beginning of the war, and ever since, a variety of motives, pressing, some in one direction and some in the other, would be presented to the mind of each man physically fit for a soldier, upon the combined effect of which motives, he would, or would not, voluntarily enter the service. Among these motives would be patriotism, political bias, ambition, personal courage, love of adventure, want of employment, and convenience, or the opposites of some of these. We already have, and have had in the service, as appears, substantially all that can be obtained upon this voluntary weighing of motives. And yet we must somehow obtain more, or relinquish the original object of the contest, together with all the blood and treasure already expended in the effort to secure it. To meet this necessity the law for the draft has been enacted.—*Opinion (never published) on draft law, Aug. 15, 1863. IX, 74.*

2.—The republican institutions and territorial integrity of our country cannot be maintained without the further raising and supporting of armies. There can be no army without men. Men can be had only voluntarily or involuntarily. We have ceased to obtain them voluntarily, and to obtain them involuntarily is the draft—the conscription. If you dispute this fact, and declare that men can still be had voluntarily in sufficient numbers, prove the assertion by yourselves volunteering in such numbers, and I shall gladly give up the draft.—*Opinion (never published) on draft law, Aug. 15, 1863. IX, 77.*

Military Draft, some dislike—You who do not wish to be soldiers do not like this law. This is natural; nor does it imply lack of patriotism. Nothing can be so just and necessary as to make us like it if it is disagreeable to us. We are prone, too, to find false argument with which to excuse ourselves for opposing such disagreeable things. In this case, those who desire the rebellion to succeed, and others who seek reward in a different way, are very active in accommodating us with this class of arguments.—*Opinion (never published) on draft law, Aug. 15, 1863.* IX, 75.

Military Draft, volunteers and drafted men compared—Be not alarmed if you shall learn that we have resorted to a draft. . . . It seems strange even to me, but it is true, that the government is now pressed to this course. Thousands who wish not to enter the service, are nevertheless anxious to pay and send substitutes, provided they can have assurance that unwilling persons, similarly situated, will be compelled to do likewise. Besides this, volunteers mostly choose to enter newly forming regiments, while drafted men can be sent to fill up the old ones, wherein man for man they are quite doubly as valuable.—*To Count A. de Gasparin, Aug. 4, 1862.* VII, 301.

Military Glory, "rainbow that arises in showers of blood"—*See* MEXICAN WAR, Polk's attempt to justify, 2.

Military Glory, "serpent's eye"—*See* MEXICAN WAR, Polk's attempt to justify, 2.

Military "Impedimenta," threatens ruin—*See* BANKS, NATHANIEL P., chided for "impedimenta."

Military Necessity, war power and—*See* WAR POWER, military necessity alone justifies use of.

Military Raids, recommended—In no other way does the enemy give us so much trouble at so little expense to himself as by the raids of rapidly moving small bodies of troops, largely if not wholly mounted, harassing and discouraging loyal residents, supplying themselves with provisions, clothing, horses and the like, surprising and capturing small detachments of our forces and breaking our communications. . . . I think we should organize proper forces and make counter-raids.—*To Gen. Rosecrans, Feb. 17, 1863.* VIII, 215.

Military Rank, not impressed by, on paper—I do not appreciate this matter of rank on paper as you officers do. The world will not forget that you fought the battle of Stone River, and it will never care a fig whether you rank Gen. Grant on paper, or he so ranks you.—*To Gen. Rosecrans, March 17, 1863.* VIII, 228.

Militia, remains in Missouri—*See* MISSOURI, militia will remain.

Militia, uniform basis for, urged—The recommendation of the secretary [of war] for an organization of the militia upon a uniform basis is a subject of vital importance to the future safety of the country.—*First annual message, Dec. 3, 1861.* VII, 36.

"Millionaire," calls himself one—I'm a millionaire myself. I got a minority of a million in the votes cast last November.—*To W. H. Aspinwall, Feb. 20, 1861.* War Years I, 64.

Milroy, R. H., appreciation of—I have never doubted your courage and devotion to the cause. But you have just lost a division, and, *prima facie,* the fault is upon you.—*To Gen. Milroy, June 29, 1863.* IX, 11. 2.—He [Milroy] is not a difficult man to satisfy—sincerity and courage being his strong traits. Believing in our cause, and wanting to fight for it, is the whole matter with him.—*To Gen. Grant, Dec. 19, 1863.* IX, 266.

Milroy, R. H., defeat of, justifies no serious blame—I cannot say that in this case any of the officers are deserving of serious blame.—*Opinion on loss of Milroy's division, Oct. 27, 1863.* IX, 185.

Milroy, R. H., cautioned—I have scarcely seen anything from you at any time that did not contain imputations against your superiors, and a chafing against acting the part they had assigned you. You have constantly urged the idea that you were being persecuted because you did not come from West Point. . . . This, my dear General, is, I fear, the rock on which you have split.—*To Gen. Milroy, June 29, 1863.* IX, 12.

Mind, single, must be master—*See* RESPONSIBILITY, must center somewhere.

"Miners and Sappers"—*See* AFRICAN SLAVE TRADE, slavery extension akin to, 13.

See DESPOTISM, those who deny Jefferson are vanguards of.

See NEGRO, "tendency to dehumanize," 6.

See REPUBLICAN PARTY, warned against Douglas, 13.

Mining, above ground—There are more mines above the earth's surface than below it. All nature—the whole world, material, moral and intellectual—is a mine. . . . It was the destined work of Adam's race to develop, by discoveries, inventions and improvements, the hidden treasures of this mine.—*Speech, Springfield, Feb. 22, 1859.* V, 103.

Mining, "every man a miner"—All creation is a mine, and every man a miner. The whole earth, and all within it, upon it, and round about it, including himself, in his physical, moral and intellectual nature, and his susceptibilities, are the infinitely various "leads," from which man, from the first, was to dig out his destiny. In the beginning the mine was unopened, and the miner stood naked and knowledgeless upon it.—*Speech, Springfield, Feb. 22, 1859.* Hertz II, 796.

Mining, wealth from—The immense mineral resources of some of these [American] territories ought to be developed as rapidly as possible. Every step in that direction would have a tendency to improve the revenues of the government, and diminish the burdens of the people. It is worthy of your serious consideration whether some extraordinary measures to promote that end cannot be adopted.—*Second annual message, Dec. 1, 1862.* VIII, 100.

2.—Numerous discoveries of gold, silver and cinnabar mines have been added to the many heretofore known, and the country occupied by the Sierra Nevada and Rocky Mountains and the subordinate ranges now teems with enterprising labor, which is richly remunerative. It is believed that the product of the mines of precious metals in that region has during the year reached, if not exceeded, one hundred millions in value.—*Fourth annual message, Dec. 6, 1864.* X, 300.

3.—I want you to take a message from me to the miners whom you visit. I have very large ideas of the mineral wealth of our nation. I believe it practically inexhaustible. It abounds all over the western country —from the Rocky Mountains to the Pacific, and its development has scarcely commenced. During the war, when we were adding a couple of millions of dollars every day to our national debt, I did not care about encouraging the increase in the volume of our precious metals. We had the country to save first. But now that the rebellion is overthrown, and we know pretty nearly the amount of our national debt, the more gold and silver we mine makes the payment of that debt so much the easier. Now I am going to encourage that in every possible way. We shall have hundreds of thousands of disabled soldiers, and many have feared that their return home in such great numbers might paralyze industry by furnishing suddenly a greater supply of labor than there will be a demand for. I am going to try to attract them to the hidden wealth of our mountain ranges, where there is room enough for all. . . . Tell the miners for me that I shall promote their interests to the utmost of my ability, because their prosperity is the prosperity of the nation; and we shall prove, in a very few years, that we are indeed the treasury of the world.—*To Schuyler Colfax, April 14, 1865.* Hertz II, 967.

Minorities, "rights" of—*See* SECESSION, *fanciful illustration.*

Miracles, neither magic nor—The way these measures [emancipation and use of colored soldiers] were to help the [Union] cause was not to be by magic or

miracles.—*To Charles D. Robinson, Aug. 17, 1864.* X, 194.

Miracles, not the days of—*See* REVELATION, *no direct, expected.*

Misrepresentation, not safe to ignore—*See* OHIO STATESMAN (newspaper), *mistaken.*

Misrepresentation, sometimes amusing—When a man hears himself somewhat misrepresented, it provokes him—at least I find it so myself; but when misrepresentation becomes very gross and palpable, it is more apt to amuse him.—*Debate, Ottawa, Aug. 21, 1858.* III, 223.

Mississippi, slavery restrictions in territory—*See* TERRITORIES, *slavery in, once controlled by Congress, 2.*

Mississippi River, God's law respecting—*See* VICKSBURG, *Lincoln's prayer for.*

Mississippi River, importance of opening—The job was a great national one, and let none be banned who bore an honorable part in it. And while those who have cleared the great river may well be proud, even that is not all.—*To J. C. Conkling, Aug. 26, 1863.* IX, 101.

Missouri, Blair's fight for emancipation—*See* SLAVERY, *Democratic policy on, 5, 11.*

Missouri, changed attitude toward slavery—*See* MARYLAND, *changed attitude of, 2.*

Missouri, disappointed in—Three months ago today I wrote you about Missouri affairs, stating, on the word of Gov. Shepley, as I understood him, that Mr. Durant was taking a registry of citizens preparatory to the election of a constitutional convention for that state. . . . Nothing has yet been done. This disappoints me bitterly.—*To Gen. Banks, Nov. 5, 1863.* IX, 200.

Missouri, factions worry President—I am having a good deal of trouble with Missouri matters. . . . One class of friends believe in greater severity and another in greater leniency in regard to arrests, banishments, and assessments. As usual in such cases, each questions the other's motives. On the one hand, it is insisted that Gov. Gamble's unionism, at most, is not better than a secondary spring of action; that hunkerism and a wish for political influence stand before unionism with him. On the other hand, it is urged that arrests, banishments, and assessments are made more for private malice, revenge and pecuniary interest than for the public good. . . . Now, my belief is that Gov. Gamble is an honest and true man, not less so than yourself; that you and he could confer together on this and other Missouri questions with great advantage to the public. . . . May I not hope that you and he will attempt this?—*To Gen. Curtis, Jan. 5, 1863.* VIII, 171.

2.—It is very painful to me that you in Missouri cannot or will not settle your factional quarrels among yourselves. I have been tormented with it beyond endurance for months by both sides. Neither side pays the least respect for my appeals to your reason. —*To H. T. Blow, C. D. Drake, and others, May 15, 1863.* VIII, 276.

3.—The Union men of Missouri, constituting, when united, a vast majority of the whole people, have entered into a pestilential factional quarrel among themselves—Gen. Curtis, perhaps not of choice, being the head of one faction and Gov. Gamble that of the other. After months of labor to reconcile the difficulty, it seemed to grow worse and worse; until I felt it my duty to break it up somehow; as I could not remove Gov. Gamble, I had to remove Gen. Curtis.— *To Gen. Schofield, May 27, 1863.* VIII, 282.

See MISSOURI, Radicals and Conservatives.

Missouri, Germans of—*See* GERMANS, "true and patriotic."

Missouri, lost to Union if Kentucky goes—*See* KENTUCKY, importance of, to Union.

Missouri, militia will remain—As to the enrolled militia, I shall endeavor to ascertain better than I now know what is its exact value. Let me say now, however, that your proposal to substitute national forces for the enrolled militia implies that in your judgment the latter is doing something which needs to be done; and if so, the proposition to throw that force away and to supply its place by bringing other forces from the field where they are urgently needed seems to me very extraordinary. . . . So far from finding cause to object, I confess to a sympathy for whatever relieves our general force in Missouri and allows it to serve elsewhere. I, therefore, as at present advised, cannot attempt the destruction of the enrolled militia of Missouri.—*To Charles D. Drake and others, Oct. 5, 1863.* IX, 162.

Missouri, national military needed—There is no organized military force in avowed opposition to the general government now in Missouri. . . . Still, the condition of things both here and elsewhere is such as to render it indispensable to maintain for a time the United States military establishment in that state. . . . Your immediate duty in regard to Missouri now is to advance the efficiency of that establishment, and

to use it as far as practicable to compel the excited people there to leave one another alone.—*To Gen. Schofield, Oct. 1, 1863.* IX, 147.

Missouri, plan for emancipation—*See* EMANCIPATION, Missouri proposal for, discussed.

Missouri, Radicals and Conservatives—I do not feel justified to enter upon the broad field you present in regard to the political differences between Radicals and Conservatives [in Missouri]. From time to time I have done and said what appeared to me proper to do and say. The public knows it all. It obliges nobody to follow me, and I trust it obliges me to follow nobody. The Radicals and Conservatives each agree with me on some things and disagree on others. I could wish both to agree with me in all things, for then they would agree with each other, and would be too strong for any foe from any quarter. They, however, choose to do otherwise; and I do not question their right. I too shall do what seems to be my duty. —*To C. D. Drake and others, Oct. 5, 1863.* IX, 163.

2.—I know these radical men [of Missouri] have in them the stuff which must save the state and on which we must mainly rely. They are absolutely uncorrosive by the virus of secession. . . . If one side must be crushed out and the other cherished there could be no doubt which side we would choose as fuller of hope for the future. We would have to side with the radicals. But just there is where their wrong begins. They insist that I shall hold and treat Gov. Gamble and his supporters—men appointed by loyal people of Missouri as representative of Missouri loyalty, and who have done their whole duty in the war faithfully and promptly—when they have disagreed with me have been silent and kept about the good work—that I shall treat these men as Copperheads and enemies to the government. This is simply monstrous.—*To White House group, Dec. 10, 1863.* Hay, 135.

See MISSOURI, factions worry President.

Missouri, repose promised to—I am very glad to believe that the late military operations in Missouri and Arkansas are at least promising of repose to southwest Missouri.—*To S. T. Glover, Jan. 20, 1863.* VIII, 197.

Missouri, soldiers must be allowed to vote—*See* SOLDIER VOTE, must be allowed.

Missouri, state or federal troops?—Few things perplex me more than this question between Gov. Gamble and the war department, as to whether the peculiar force organized by the former in Missouri are state troops or United States troops. Now, this is either immaterial or a mischievous question. First, if more is desired than to have it settled what name this force is to be called by, it is immaterial. Secondly, if it is desired for more than the fixing a name, it can only be to get a position from which to draw practical inferences; then it is mischievous. . . . I believe the force is not strictly either "state troops" or "United States troops." It is of mixed character.—*To Att. Gen. Bates, Nov. 29, 1862.* VIII, 90.

2.—Instead of settling one dispute by deciding the question [whether the military force are state troops or United States troops] I should merely furnish a nestful of eggs for hatching new disputes.—*To Att. Gen. Bates, Nov. 29, 1862.* VIII, 91.

3.—After a good deal of reflection, I concluded that it was better to make a rule for the practical matter in hand [the removal of officers and acceptance of resignations] than to decide a general question—to wit: Whether the forces are state troops, which while it might embrace the practical question mentioned, might also be the nest in which forty other troublesome questions would be hatched.—*To Gov. Gamble, Dec. 20, 1862.* VIII, 155.

Missouri, system invites dishonesty—To restrain contraband intelligence and trade, a system of searches, seizures, permits and passes, had been introduced, I think, by Gen. Frémont. When Gen. Halleck came, he found and continued the system, and added an order, applicable to some parts of the state, to levy and collect contributions from noted rebels, to compensate losses and relieve destitution caused by the rebellion. . . . That there was a necessity for something of the sort was clear, but that it could only be justified by stern necessity and that it was liable to great abuse in administration was equally clear. Agents to execute it, contrary to the great prayer, were led into temptation. Some might, while others would not, resist that temptation. It was not possible to hold any to a very strict accountability, and those yielding to the temptation would sell permits and passes to those who would pay most and most readily for them; and would seize property and collect levies in the aptest way to fill their own pockets. Money being the object, the man having money, whether loyal or disloyal, would be a victim.—*To Charles D. Drake and others, Oct. 5, 1863.* IX, 158.

2.—A controversy in regard to it [system of seizures and permits] rapidly grew into almost unmanageable proportions. One side ignored the necessity and magnified the evils of the system, while the other ignored the evils and magnified the necessity, and each bitterly assailed the motives of the other. . . . I exhausted my wits, and very nearly my patience, also.—*To Charles D. Drake and others, Oct. 5, 1863.* IX, 159.

Missouri, violence in, explained—*See* WAR, how men act in.

Missouri, way to peace in—It is represented to me that there is so much irregular violence in northern Missouri as to be driving away the people and almost depopulating it. Please gather information, and consider whether an appeal to the people there to go to their homes and let one another alone—recognizing as a full right of protection for each that he lets the other alone, and banning only him who refuses to let others alone—may not enable you to withdraw the troops, their presence itself [being] a cause of irritation and constant apprehension, and thus restore peace and quiet, and returning prosperity.—*To Gen. Dodge, Jan. 15, 1865.* X, 340.

2.—It seems there is now no organized military force of the enemy in Missouri, and yet that destruction of property and life is rampant everywhere. Is not the cure for this within easy reach of the people themselves? It cannot but be that every man not naturally a robber or cut-throat would gladly put an end to this state of things. A large majority in every locality must feel alike upon the subject; and if so, they only need to reach an understanding, one with another. Each leaving all others alone solves the problem, and surely each would do this but for his apprehension that others will not leave him alone. Cannot this mischievous distrust be removed? Let neighborhood meetings be everywhere called and held, of all entertaining a sincere purpose for mutual security in the future, whatever they may heretofore have thought, said, or done about the war, or about anything else. Let all such meet, and, waiving all else, pledge each to cease harassing others, and to make common cause against whoever persists in making, aiding, or encouraging further disturbance. The practical means they will best know how to adopt and apply. At such meetings old friendships will cross the memory, and honor and Christian charity will come in to help.—*To Gov. Fletcher, Feb. 20, 1865.* XI, 38.

Missouri, would make free state of—*See* MISSOURI COMPROMISE, Rescind!

Missouri Compromise—*See also* KANSAS-NEBRASKA ACT.

Missouri Compromise, Clay engineered—Important and exciting as was the war question of 1812, it never so alarmed the sagacious statesmen of the country for the safety of the Republic as afterward did the Missouri question. This sprang from that unfortunate source of discord—negro slavery. When our federal Constitution was adopted we owned no territory beyond the limits or ownership of the states, except the territory northwest of the River Ohio and east of the

Mississippi. . . . But in 1803 we purchased Louisiana of the French, and it included, with much more, what has since been formed into the state of Missouri. With regard to it, nothing had been done to forestall the question of slavery. When, therefore, in 1819 Missouri, having formed a state constitution without excluding slavery, and with slavery already actually existing within its limits, knocked at the door of the Union for admission, almost the entire representation of the non-slave-holding states objected. A fearful and angry struggle instantly followed. . . . Mr. Clay was in Congress, and, perceiving the danger [to the Union], he at once engaged his whole energies to avert it. . . . After several failures, and great labor on the part of Mr. Clay to so present the question that a majority could consent to the admission [of Missouri as a state], it was by a vote rejected, and, as all seemed to think, finally. A sullen gloom hung over the nation. All felt that the rejection of Missouri was equivalent to a dissolution of the Union. . . . Mr. Clay, though worn down and exhausted, was appealed to by members to renew his efforts at compromise. He did so, and by some judicious modifications of his plan, coupled with laborious efforts with individual members and his own over-mastering eloquence, upon that floor, he finally secured the admission of the state.—*Speech, Springfield, July 16, 1852.* II, 167.

2.—Mr. Clay was the leading spirit in making the Missouri Compromise; is it very credible that if now alive he would take the lead in the breaking of it?—*Speech, Peoria, Oct. 16, 1854.* II, 261.

3.—When the Missouri constitution came before the Congress for its approval, it forbade any free negro or mulatto from entering the state . . . and the controversy was thus revived. Then it was that Mr. Clay's talents shone out conspicuously, and the controversy that shook the Union to its foundation was finally settled to the satisfaction of the conservative parties on both sides of the line, though not the extremists on either.—*Speech, Bloomington, May 29, 1856.* Lapsley II, 263.

4.—Henry Clay perfected and forced through the compromise which secured to slavery a great state as well as a political advantage. Not that he hated slavery less, but that he loved the whole Union more. . . . They [proslavery men] have slaughtered one of his most cherished measures, and his ghost would arise to rebuke them.—*Speech, Bloomington, May 29, 1856.* Lapsley II, 267.

Missouri Compromise, fruits of repeal—See KANSAS-NEBRASKA ACT, violence marks.

See KANSAS-NEBRASKA ACT, fruits of, 3, 5.

Missouri Compromise, gave Missouri slaves—When the measure [compromise] came before President Monroe for his approval, he put to each member of his cabinet this question: "Has Congress the constitutional right to prohibit slavery in a territory?" And John C. Calhoun and William H. Crawford from the South, equally with John Quincy Adams, Benjamin Rush and Smith Thompson from the North, answered, Yes! without qualification or equivocation; and this measure, of so great consequence to the South, was passed, and Missouri was, by means of it, finally enabled to knock at the door of the Republic for an open passage to its brood of slaves. . . . In short, our Illinois "black laws" were hidden away in their constitution.—*Speech, Bloomington, May 29, 1856.* Lapsley II, 263.

Missouri Compromise, not repealed in 1850—My own opinion is that a careful investigation of all the arguments to sustain the position that that [Missouri] compromise was virtually repealed by the Compromise of 1850 would show that they are the merest fallacies.—*Debate, Jonesboro, Sept. 15, 1858.* IV, 38.

See MISSOURI COMPROMISE, rescind!

Missouri Compromise, origin of—In 1818 or '19 Missouri showed signs of a wish to come in [to the Union] with slavery. . . . The controversy lasted several months, and became very angry and exciting —the House of Representatives voting steadily for the prohibition of slavery in Missouri, and the Senate voting steadily for it. Threats of the breaking up of the Union were freely made, and the ablest of the public men of the day became seriously alarmed. At length a compromise was made, in which, as in all compromises, both sides yielded something. It was a law passed on the 6th of March, 1820, providing that Missouri might come into the Union with slavery, but that in all the remaining part of the territory purchased of France, which lies north of 36.30 north latitude, slavery should never be permitted. This provision of law is the "Missouri Compromise."—*Speech, Peoria, Oct. 16, 1854.* II, 196.

Missouri Compromise, parable of starving men—After an angry and dangerous controversy [between friends and foes of slavery extension] the parties made friends by dividing the bone of contention [by adopting the Missouri Compromise]. The one party first appropriates her own share beyond all power to be disturbed in the possession of it, and then seizes the share of the other party. It is as if two starving men had divided their only loaf; the one had hastily swallowed his half, and then grabbed the other's half just

as he was putting it to his mouth.—*Speech, Peoria, Oct. 16, 1854.* II, 219.
Repeated at Urbana, Oct. 24, 1854. Hertz II, 640.

Missouri Compromise, repeal of, aroused Lincoln to action—I was losing interest in politics when the repeal of the Missouri Compromise aroused me again. —*To J. W. Fell, Dec. 20, 1859.* V, 288.
2.—In 1854 his [Lincoln's] profession had almost superseded the thought of politics in his mind, when the repeal of the Missouri Compromise aroused him as he had never been before.—*Autobiography, June 1, 1860.* VI, 27.

See SLAVERY, extension of, opposed, 16.

Missouri Compromise, repeal of, condemned—I think, and I shall try to prove, that it [repeal of the Missouri Compromise] is wrong—wrong in its direct effect, letting slavery into Kansas and Nebraska; and wrong in its prospective principle, allowing it to spread to every other part of the wide world where men can be found inclined to take it.—*Speech, Peoria, Oct. 16, 1854.* II, 205.
Repeated at Urbana, Oct. 24, 1854. Hertz II, 633.
Repeated at Ottawa, Aug. 21, 1858. III, 226.
2.—We [opponents of slavery extension] have held the Missouri Compromise as a sacred thing, even when against ourselves as well as when for us.—*Speech, Peoria, Oct. 16, 1854.* II, 212.
3.—Take the particular case. A controversy had arisen between the advocates and opponents of slavery, in relation to its establishment within the country we had purchased of France. The southern, and then best, part of the purchase was already in as a slave state. The controversy was settled by also letting in Missouri in as a slave state; but with the agreement that within all the remaining part of the purchase, north of a certain line, there should never be slavery. As to what was to be done with the remaining part south of the line, nothing was said; but perhaps the fair implication was, it should come in with slavery if it should so choose. The southern part, except a portion heretofore mentioned, afterward did come in with slavery, as the state of Arkansas. All these many years, since 1820, the northern part had remained a wilderness. At length settlements began in it also. . . . Finally the sole remaining part north of the line—Kansas and Nebraska—was to be organized; and it is proposed, and carried, to blot out the old dividing line of 34 years' standing, and to open the whole of that country to slavery. Now, this to my mind, is manifestly unjust.—*Speech, Peoria, Oct. 16, 1854.* II, 218.
4.—This [opposition to slavery extension] is good

Whig ground. To desert such ground because of any company is to be less than a Whig—less than a man —less than an American.—*Speech, Peoria, Oct. 16, 1854.* II, 243.
5.—I now come to consider whether the repeal, with its avowed principles, is intrinsically right. I insist it is not.—*Speech, Peoria, Oct. 16, 1854.* II, 218.

Missouri Compromise, repeal of, embitters slavery issue—It [repeal] is an aggravation, rather, of the one thing which ever endangers the Union. When it came upon us, all was peace and quiet. The nation was looking to the forming of new bonds of union, and a long course of peace and prosperity seemed to lie before us. In the whole range of possibility, there scarcely appears to me anything out of which the slavery agitation could have been revived, except the very project of repealing the Missouri Compromise.— *Speech, Peoria, Oct. 16, 1854.* II, 237.
2.—What shall we have in lieu of it [the spirit of concession reflected in the Missouri Compromise]? The South flushed with triumph and tempted to excess; the North, betrayed as they believe, brooding on wrong and burning to revenge. One side will provoke, the other resent. The one will taunt, the other defy; one aggresses, the other retaliates. Already a few in the North defy all constitutional restraints, resist the execution of the fugitive-slave law, and even menace the institution of slavery in the states where it exists. Already a few in the South claim the constitutional right to take and to hold slaves in the free states—demand the revival of the slave trade—and demand a treaty with Great Britain by which fugitive slaves may be reclaimed from Canada. As yet they are but few on either side. It is a grave question for lovers of the Union, whether the final destruction of the Missouri Compromise will or will not embolden and embitter each of these, and fatally increase the number of both.—*Speech, Peoria, Oct. 16, 1854.* II, 240.

Missouri Compromise, repeal of, not demanded by public—I deny that the public ever demanded any such thing [as repeal of the Missouri Compromise]— ever repudiated the Missouri Compromise, ever commanded its repeal. I deny it, and call for the proof. —*Speech, Peoria, Oct. 16, 1854.* II, 209.
2.—The public never demanded the repeal of the Missouri Compromise.—*Speech, Peoria, Oct. 16, 1854.* II, 218.
3.—I ask why he [Douglas] could not have left that [Missouri] compromise alone? We were quiet from the agitation of the slavery question. We were making no fuss about it.—*Debate, Jonesboro, Sept. 15, 1858.* IV, 38.

Missouri Compromise, repealed by Douglas amendment—About a month after the introduction of the [Kansas-Nebraska] bill, on the judge's [Douglas's] own motion it is so amended as to declare the Missouri Compromised inoperative and void; and, substantially, that the people who go and settle there may establish slavery, or exclude it, as they may see fit. In this shape the bill passed both branches of Congress and became a law.—*Speech, Peoria, Oct. 16, 1854.* II, 204.

Repeated at Urbana, Oct. 24, 1854. Hertz II, 633.

2.—Judge Douglas now argues that the subsequent express repeal [of Missouri Compromise] is no substantial alteration of the [Kansas-Nebraska] bill. This argument seems wonderful to me. It is as if one should argue that white and black are not different. He admits, however, that there is a literal change in the bill, and that he made the change in deference to other senators who would not support the bill without. This proves that the other senators thought the change a substantial one, and that the judge thought their opinions worth deferring to.—*Speech, Peoria, Oct. 16, 1854.* II, 217.

Missouri Compromise, repealed by violence—See KANSAS-NEBRASKA ACT, violence marks.

Missouri Compromise, rescind!—It is, I believe, a principle in law that when one party to a contract violates it so grossly as to chiefly destroy the object for which it is made, the other party may rescind it. . . . Well, now if that be right, I go for rescinding the whole, entire Missouri Compromise, and thus turning Missouri into a free state; and I should like to know the difference—should like for anyone to point out the difference—between our making a free state of Missouri and their making a slave state of Kansas. There ain't a bit of difference, except that our way would be a great mercy to humanity.—*Speech, Bloomington, May 29, 1856.* Lapsley II, 261.

Missouri Compromise, restoration of, urged—The Missouri Compromise ought to be restored. For the sake of the Union, it ought to be restored. We ought to elect a House of Representatives which will vote its restoration. If by any means we omit to do this, what follows? . . . We shall have repudiated—discarded from the councils of the nation—the spirit of compromise; for who, after this, will ever trust in a national compromise? The spirit of mutual concession—that spirit which first gave us the Constitution and which has thrice saved the Union—we shall have strangled and cast from us forever.—*Speech, Peoria, Oct. 16, 1854.* II, 240.

Repeated at Urbana, Oct. 24, 1854. Hertz II, 651.

2.—But restore the Missouri Compromise, and what then? We thereby restore the national faith, the national confidence, the national feeling of brotherhood. We thereby reinstate the spirit of concession and compromise—that spirit which has never failed us in past perils, and which may be safely trusted for all the future. The South ought to join in doing this.—*Speech, Peoria, Oct. 16, 1854.* II, 241.

3.—[Restoration] would be worth to the nation a hundred years' purchase of peace and prosperity.—*Speech, Peoria, Oct. 16, 1854.* II, 241.

4.—Even if we fail technically to restore the compromise, it is still a great point to carry a popular vote in favor of the restoration. The moral weight of such a vote cannot be estimated too highly.—*Speech, Peoria, Oct. 16, 1854.* II, 242.

5.—Some men, mostly Whigs, who condemn the repeal of the Missouri Compromise, nevertheless hesitate to go for its restoration, lest they be thrown in company with the Abolitionists. Will they allow me, an old Whig, to tell them good-humoredly, that I think this is very silly? Stand with anybody that stands right. Stand with him while he is right, and part with him when he goes wrong. Stand with the Abolitionist in restoring the Missouri Compromise, and stand against him when he attempts to repeal the fugitive-slave law. In the latter case you stand with the southern disunionist. What of that? You are still right. In both cases you are right. In both cases you expose the dangerous extremes.—*Speech, Peoria, Oct. 16, 1854.* Basler, 312.

Repeated at Urbana, Oct. 24, 1854. Hertz II, 652.

6.—I shall address you upon the recent repeal . . . of the Missouri Compromise, so-called, and the expediency, if not, indeed, necessity, that that repeal be itself repealed.—*Speech, Urbana, Oct. 24, 1854.* Hertz II, 627.

7.—In my humble sphere, I shall advocate the restoration of the Missouri Compromise as long as Kansas remains a territory, and when, by all these foul means, it seeks to come into the Union as a slave state, I shall oppose it.—*To Joshua F. Speed, Aug. 24, 1855.* II, 284.

8.—We come [to the state convention] . . . to place the nation, so far as it may be possible now, as it was before the repeal of the Missouri Compromise; and the plain way to do this is to restore the Compromise, and to demand and determine that Kansas shall be free!—*Speech, Bloomington, May 29, 1856.* Lapsley II, 250.

9.—We must highly resolve that Kansas must be free! We must reinstate the birthday promise of the Republic; we must re-affirm the Declaration of Independence.—*Speech, Bloomington, May 29, 1856.* Lapsley II, 274.

10.—The conclusion of all is, that we must restore the Missouri Compromise.—*Speech, Bloomington, May 29, 1856.* Lapsley II, 274.

Missouri Compromise, sacrificed by Genius of Discord—The Genius of Discord himself could scarcely have invented a way of again setting us by the ears but by turning back and destroying the peace measures [relating to slavery] of the past. The counsels of that Genius seem to have prevailed. The Missouri Compromise was repealed; and here we are in the midst of a new slavery agitation, such, I think, as we have never seen before.—*Speech, Peoria, Oct. 16, 1854.* II, 237.

Repeated at Urbana, Oct. 24, 1854. Hertz II, 649.

Missouri Compromise, South should help restore—The South ought to join in doing this. The peace of the nation is as dear to them as to us. In memories of the past and hopes of the future, they share as largely as we. It would be on their part a great act—great in its spirit, and great in its effect. . . . And what sacrifice would they make? They only surrender what they gave up for a consideration long, long ago; what they have not now asked for, struggled or cared for; what has been thrust upon them, not less to their astonishment than to ours.—*Speech, Peoria, Oct. 16, 1854.* II, 241.

Missouri Compromise, Southern triumph—The scheme [compromise], as a whole, was, of course, a Southern triumph. It is idle to contend otherwise, as is now being done by the Nebraskaites; it was shown by the votes and quite as emphatically by the expressions of representative men.—*Speech, Bloomington, May 29, 1856.* Lapsley II, 262.

Missouri Compromise, why disturb?—I ask why he [Douglas] could not have left that compromise alone? We were quiet from the agitation of the slavery question. We were making no fuss about it. All had acquiesced in the compromise measures of 1850. We never had been seriously disturbed by an abolition agitation before that period.—*Debate, Jonesboro, Sept. 15, 1858.* IV, 38.

2.—When he [Douglas] came to form governments for the territories north of the line 36 degrees 30 minutes, why could he not have left that matter stand as it was standing? Was it necessary to the organization of a territory? Not at all.—*Debate, Jonesboro, Sept. 15, 1858.* IV, 38.

Missouri Compromise, Wilmot Proviso and—To argue that we thus [by supporting the Wilmot Pro-

viso] repudiated the Missouri Compromise is no less absurd than it would be to argue that because we have so far foreborne to acquire Cuba, we have thereby, in principle, repudiated our former acquisitions and determined to throw them out of the Union. No less absurd than it would be to say that because I may have refused to build an addition to my house, I thereby have decided to destroy the existing house.—*Speech, Peoria, Oct. 16, 1854.* II, 211.

"Mr. Whiskey"—*See* SALOON SMASHERS, women, defended.

Mob Law, danger of—When men take it in their heads to hang gamblers or burn murderers, they should recollect that in the confusion usually attending such transactions they will be as likely to hang or burn someone who is neither a gambler nor a murderer as one who is, and that, acting upon the example they set, the mob of tomorrow may, and probably will, hang or burn some of them by the very same mistake. And not only so; the innocent, those who have even set their faces against violations of law in every shape, alike with the guilty fall victims to the ravages of mob law; and thus it goes up, step by step, till all the walls erected for the defence of the person and property of individuals are trodden down and disregarded. But all this, even, is not the full extent of the evil. By such examples, by instances of the perpetrators of such acts going unpunished, the lawless in spirit are encouraged to become lawless in practice; and having been used to no restraint but the dread of punishment, they thus become absolutely unrestrained. Having ever regarded government as their deadliest bane, they make a jubilee of the suspension of its operations, and pray for nothing so much as its total annihilation. While, on the other hand, good men, men who love tranquillity, who desire to abide by the laws and enjoy their benefits, who would gladly spill their blood in defence of their country, seeing their property destroyed, their families insulted, and their lives endangered, their persons injured, and seeing nothing in prospect that forebodes a change for the better, become tired of and disgusted with a government that offers them no protection, and are not much averse to a change in which they imagine they have nothing to lose. Thus . . . the strongest bulwark of any government, and particularly of those constituted like ours, may effectually be broken down and destroyed—I mean the attachment of the people. Whenever this effect shall be produced among us; whenever the vicious portion of population shall be permitted to gather in bands of hundreds and thousands, and burn churches, ravage and rob provision stores, throw printing presses into rivers, shoot editors, and hang and burn obnoxious persons at pleasure and with impunity, depend on it, this government cannot last. . . . I know the American people are much attached to their government; I know they would suffer much for its sake; I know they would endure evils long and patiently before they would ever think of exchanging it for another—yet, notwithstanding all this, if the laws be continually despised and disregarded, if their rights to be secure in their persons and property are held by no better tenure than the caprice of a mob, the alienation of the affections from the government is the natural consequence; and to that, sooner or later, it must come.—*Speech, Springfield, Jan. 27, 1837.* I, 40.

Mob Law, dangerously familiar—Such are the effects of mob law, and such are the scenes becoming more and more frequent in this land so lately famed for love of law and order, and the stories of which have even now grown too familiar to attract anything more than idle remark. . . . Its direct consequences are, comparatively speaking, but a small evil, and much of its danger consists in the proneness of our minds to regard its direct as its only consequences.—*Speech, Springfield, Jan. 27, 1837.* I, 39.

Mob Law, never justified—There is no grievance that is a fit object of redress by mob law. In any case that may arise as, for instance, the promulgation of abolitionism, one of the two positions is necessarily true—that is, the thing is right within itself, and therefore deserves the protection of all law and all good citizens, or it is wrong, and therefore proper to be prohibited by legal enactments; and in neither case is the interposition of mob law either necessary, justifiable or excusable.—*Speech, Springfield, Jan. 27, 1837.* I, 44.

Mob Law, pervades country—They [mobs] have pervaded the country from New England to Louisiana; they are neither peculiar to the eternal snows of the former nor the burning suns of the latter; they are not the creature of climate, neither are they confined to the slave-holding or the non-slave-holding states. Alike they spring up among the pleasure-hunting masters of southern slaves, and the order-loving citizens of the land of steady habits. Whatever, then, their case may be, it is common to the whole country.—*Speech, Springfield, Jan. 27, 1837.* I, 37.

Mobile, capture of—*See* DEITY, gratitude to, 12.

See FARRAGUT, DAVID G., thanked for victories.

Mobile, expedition against, not favored—I see by a dispatch of yours that you incline quite strongly toward an expedition against Mobile. This would appear tempting to me also, were it not that, in view of recent events in Mexico, I am greatly impressed with the importance of re-establishing the national authority in western Texas as soon as possible.—*To Gen. Grant, Aug. 9, 1863.* IX, 64.

Mobocratic Spirit, warning against—I am opposed to encouraging that lawless and mobocratic spirit . . . which is already abroad in the land; and is spreading with rapid and fearful impetuosity to the ultimate overthrow of every institution, of even moral principle, in which persons and property have hitherto found security.—*Speech, Illinois Legislature, Jan. 27, 1837.* I, 33.

Moderation, best policy—In grave emergencies, moderation is generally safer than radicalism.—*Speech, Bloomington, May 29, 1856.* Lapsley II, 266.
2.—We will grow strong by calmness and moderation.—*Speech, Bloomington, May 29, 1856.* Lapsley II, 267.
3.—Now let us harmonize, my friends, and appeal to the moderation and patriotism of the people.—*Speech, Bloomington, May 29, 1856.* Lapsley II, 268.
4.—The utmost care will be observed, consistently with the objects aforesaid [repossession of lost federal property] to avoid any devastation, any destruction of or interference with property, or any disturbance of peaceful citizens in any part of the country.—*Proclamation, April 15, 1861.* VI, 247.
5.—I have an imploring appeal in behalf of citizens, who say your Order No. 8 will compel them to go north of Nashville. This is in no sense an order, nor is it even a request that you will do anything which in the least shall be a drawback upon your military operations, but anything you can do consistently with those operations for these suffering people I shall be glad of.—*To Gen. Sherman, May 4, 1864.* X, 93.

Moles, soldiers are not—*See* MARYLAND, troops must cross.

Monarchy, could be established by bribery—Standing as a unit among yourselves [proslavery men], you can, directly or indirectly, bribe enough of our men to carry the day [admitting Kansas as a slave state] as you could on the open proposition to establish a monarchy. Get hold of some man in the North whose position and ability is such that he can make the support of your measure, whatever it may be, a Democratic party necessity, and the thing is done.—*To Joshua F. Speed, Aug. 24, 1855.* II, 285.

Monarchy, "possible refuge"—Monarchy itself is sometimes hinted at [in Confederate documents] as a possible refuge from the power of the people.—*First annual message, Dec. 3, 1861*.   VII, 56.

Money, decrease in volume would bring disaster—When one hundred millions, or more, of the [money] circulation we now have shall be withdrawn [as threatened by the subtreasury plan] who can contemplate without terror the distress, ruin, bankruptcy, and beggary, that must follow. A man who has purchased any article—say a horse—on credit, at one hundred dollars, when there are two hundred millions circulating in the country, if the quantity be reduced to one hundred millions by the arrival of payday, will find the horse but sufficient to pay half the debt; and the other half must either be paid out of his other means, and thereby become a clear loss to him, or go unpaid, and thereby becomes a clear loss to his creditor. What I have here said of a single case of the purchase of a horse will hold good in every case of a debt existing at the time a reduction in the quantity of money occurs, by whomever, and for whatsoever, it may have been contracted.—*Speech, Springfield, Dec. 20, 1839*.   I, 106.
2.—The general distress thus created will, to be sure, be temporary, because whatever change may occur in the quantity of money in any community, time will adjust the derangement produced; but while that adjustment is progressing, all suffer more or less, and very many lose everything that renders life desirable. —*Speech, Springfield, Dec. 20, 1839*.   I, 107.

See PUBLIC LANDS, sale of, if money volume is reduced.

Money, in politics—*See* POLITICS, money in.

Money, public lands and decrease in volume of—*See* PUBLIC LANDS, sale of, if money volume is reduced.

Money, "rusting"—By the subtreasury . . . the money is performing no nobler office than that of rusting in iron boxes.—*Speech, Springfield, Dec. 20, 1839*.   I, 103.

Money, temptation in—There is powerful temptation in money.—*To Gen. Rosecrans, March 7, 1863*.   VIII, 227.

Money, when valuable—Any person who will reflect that money is only valuable while in circulation will readily perceive that any device which will keep government revenues in constant circulation, instead of being locked up in idleness, is of no inconsiderable advantage.—*Speech, Springfield, Dec. 20, 1839*.   I, 102.

"Money Kings"—*See* AGRICULTURE, fosters independence.

"Money Power," feared—*See* CIVIL WAR, aftermath feared.

Monitor, could be easily captured—I have just seen Lieut. Worden, who says the *Monitor* could be boarded and captured very easily; first, after boarding, by wedging the turret, so that it would not turn, and then by pouring water in her & drowning her machinery.—*To Sec. Welles, March 10, 1862*.   Hertz II, 853.

Monitor and Merrimac—*See* WORDEN, JOHN L., Congress asked to thank.

Montana, partially organized—*See* IDAHO, partially organized.

Moon, "territories of" the—[The provision of the compromises of 1850 relating to Utah and New Mexico] had no more direct reference to Nebraska than it had to the territories of the Moon.—*Speech, Peoria, Oct. 16, 1854*.   II, 213.
2.—I am just as much responsible for the resolutions at Kane county as those at Springfield, the amount of the responsibility being exactly nothing in either case —no more than there would be in regard to a set of resolutions passed in the Moon.—*Debate, Freeport, Aug. 27, 1858*.   III, 281.

See MAN IN THE MOON.

Moral Perfection, goal to strive for—It is said in one of the admonitions of our Lord, "Be ye [therefore] perfect even as your Father which is in heaven is perfect." The Savior, I suppose, did not expect that any human creature could be as perfect as the Father in heaven. . . . He set that up as a standard, and he who did most toward reaching that standard attained the highest degree of moral perfection.—*Speech, Chicago, July 10, 1858*.   III, 50.

Morris, George U., Congress asked to thank—I most cordially recommend that Lieut.-Commander George U. Morris, United States Navy, receive a vote of thanks of Congress for the determined valor and heroism displayed in his defense of the United States ship of war *Cumberland* temporarily under his command, in the naval engagement of Hampton Roads on the 8th of March, 1862, with the rebel iron-clad steam-frigate *Merrimac*.—*Message to Congress, Dec. 10, 1862*.   VIII, 138.

Morris, I. N., "never at variance" with—Without supposing that you and I are any nearer together, politically, than heretofore, allow me to tender you my sincere thanks for your Union resolution, expressive of views upon which we never were, and, I trust, never will be at variance.—*To Mr. Morris, Dec. 24, 1860.* VI, 87.

Morrison, William R., groundless suspicions—Your words of kindness are very grateful, but your suspicions that I intend you an injustice are very painful to me. I assure you such suspicions are groundless.—*To Col. Morrison, Nov. 5, 1862.* VIII, 72.

Morton, Oliver P., "Bravo!"—Bravo for Indiana and for yourself personally.—*To Gov. Morton, Oct. 13, 1864.* X, 242.

Morton, Oliver P., no purpose to stab—No appointments have been made or will be made by me for the purpose of stabbing you.—*To Gov. Morton, June 28, 1862.* VII, 243.

Mosquitoes, "bloody struggles with"—*See* CASS, LEWIS D., military figure of, 1.

Mother, care of—Your proposal about selling the east 40 acres of land is all that I want or could claim for myself; but I am not satisfied with it on mother's account. I want her to have her living, and I feel that it is my duty, to some extent, to see that she is not wronged. She . . . has the use of the whole of the east 40 as long as she lives; but you propose to sell it for $300, take the $100 away with you, and leave her $200 at 8 per cent, making her the enormous sum of $16 a year. Now, if you are satisfied with treating her in that way, I am not. It is true that you are to have that 40 for $200 at mother's death, but you are not to have it before. I am confident that land can be made to produce for mother at least $30 a year, and I cannot consent that she shall be put on an allowance of $16 a year.—*To John D. Johnston, Nov. 25, 1851.* II, 152.

Mother, tribute to—All that I am, or hope to be, I owe to my angel mother.—*To W. H. Herndon, date uncertain.* Townsend, 6.

"Mud-Sill" Theory, of labor—*See* LABOR, "mud-sill" theory.

Mulattoes, census comparison between Virginia and New Hampshire—*See* RACIAL AMALGAMATION, census of mulattoes, 3.

Music, Lincoln's youthful delight—I would beg to remind you that music is a very useful art. Many persons are now busy to ascertain what your next President delighted in during his younger days. I will tell you confidentially that my greatest pleasure when taking a rest after splitting rails, was to play a solo on the Jews harp. Now keep this to yourselves.—*To St.*

Marie Brass Band and St. Cecelia Society, Nov. 16, 1860. Hertz II, 791.

Namesake, "best wishes" for—I shall have to acknowledge very briefly your letter informing me of the prosperity of your little boy whom you so kindly named after me. You may rest assured that my little namesake has my very best wishes that he may grow to be a good man and a good citizen.—*To Mrs. Alice C. Smith, Oct. 12, 1863.* Angle, 333.

Napoleon, Douglas borrows from—*See* DOUGLAS, STEPHEN A., characterized, 10.

Nasby, Petroleum V.—For the genius to write these things [of Nasby's] I would gladly give up my office. —*To Sen. Sumner, March 18, 1865.* Stephenson, 455.

Nation, defined—A nation may be said to consist of its territory, its people and its laws. The territory is the only part which is of certain durability.—*Second annual message, Dec. 1, 1862.* VIII, 110.

Nation, test of its power to survive—*See* SELF-GOVERNMENT, Can it survive?

National Bank, compared with subtreasury—Of the subtreasury, then, as contrasted with a national bank . . . I lay down the following propositions, to wit: (1) It will injuriously affect the community by its operation on the circulating medium. (2) It will be a more expensive fiscal agent. (3) It will be a less secure depository of the public money.—*Speech, Springfield, Dec. 20, 1839.* I, 102.
2.—By the late national bank we had the public revenue received, safely kept, transferred, and disbursed, not only without expense, but we actually received of the bank $75,000 annually for its privileges while rendering us those services. By the subtreasury, according to the estimate of the secretary of the treasury, who is a warm advocate of the system—and which estimate is the lowest made by anyone—the same services are to cost $60,000. Mr. Rives, who, to say the least, is equally talented and honest, estimates that these services, under the subtreasury system, cannot cost less than $600,000. For the sake of liberality, let us suppose that the estimates of the secretary and Mr. Rives are the two extremes, and that their mean is about the true estimate, and we shall then find that when the sum is added to the $75,000 which the bank paid us, the difference between the two systems, in favor of the bank against the subtreasury, is $405,000 a year. This sum, though small when compared to the many millions annually expended by the general government, is, when viewed, by itself, very large; and much too large, when viewed in any light, to be

thrown away once a year for nothing.—*Speech, Springfield, Dec. 20, 1839.* I, 111.

3.—By the subtreasury scheme the public money is to be kept, between the times of its collection and disbursement, by treasurers of the mint, custom-house officers, land officers, and some new officers to be appointed in the same way that those first enumerated are. Has a year passed, since the organization of the government, that numerous defalcations have not occurred among this class of officers? . . . But turn to the history of the national banks of this country, and we shall see that those banks performed the fiscal operations of the government through a period of 40 years, received, safely kept, transferred, disbursed an aggregate of nearly $500,000,000; and that, in all this time, and with all that money, not one dollar, nor one cent, did the government lose by them.—*Speech, Springfield, Jan. 20, 1839.* I, 113.

4.—The interest of the subtreasurer is against his duty; while the interest of the bank is on the side of its duty.—*Speech, Springfield, Jan. 20, 1839.* I, 115.

5.—Our opponents say there is no express authority in the Constitution to establish a bank, and therefore, a bank is unconstitutional; but we with equal truth may say there is no express authority in the Constitution to establish a subtreasury, and, therefore, a subtreasury is unconstitutional. Who, then, has the advantage of this "express authority" argument? . . . Our position is that both are constitutional.—*Speech, Springfield, Dec. 20, 1839.* I, 123.

National Bank, constitutionality of, affirmed—As a sweeping objection to a national bank, and consequently an argument in favor of the subtreasury as a substitute for it, it has often been urged . . . that such a bank is unconstitutional. . . . A majority of the Revolutionary patriarchs, who ever acted officially upon the question, commencing with Gen. Washington, and embracing Gen. Jackson, the larger number of the signers of the Declaration of Independence and of the framers of the Constitution, who were in the Congress of 1791, have decided upon their oaths that such a bank is constitutional. . . . The votes of Congress have more often been in favor of than against its constitutionality. In addition to all this . . . the Supreme Court—that tribunal which the Constitution has itself established to decide constitutional questions—has solemnly decided that such a bank is constitutional.—*Speech, Springfield, Dec. 20, 1839.* I, 122.

2.—Upon the question of constitutionality [we] content ourselves with remarking the facts that the first national bank was established chiefly by the same men who formed the Constitution, at a time when that instrument was but two years old, and receiving the sanction, as President, of the immortal Washington; that the second received the sanction of Mr. Madison, to whom common consent has awarded the proud title of "Father of the Constitution"; and subsequently the sanction of the Supreme Court, the most enlightened judicial tribunal in the world.—*Whig circular, March 1, 1843.* I, 248.

National Bank, Dred Scott decision and—*See* JUDICIAL DECISIONS, Douglas's attitude toward, 11.

National Bank, expediency of—Upon the question of expediency we only ask you to examine the history of the times during the existence of the two banks, and compare those times with the miserable present. —*Whig circular, March 1, 1843.* I, 248.

National Bank, favored—I am in favor of a national bank.—*Reputed first public speech, March, 1832.* XI, 97.

2.—A national bank, properly restricted, is highly necessary and proper to the establishment and maintenance of a sound currency, and for the cheap and safe collection, keeping and disbursing of the public revenue.—*Resolution, Whig convention, Springfield, March 1, 1843.* I, 241.

See NATIONAL BANK, compared with subtreasury.

National Bank, government aid insures success of— We do not pretend that a national bank can establish and maintain a sound and uniform state of currency in the country, in spite of the national government; but we do say that it has established and maintained such a currency, and can do so again, by the aid of that government.—*Speech, Springfield, Dec. 20, 1839.* I, 110.

National Bank, help to public credit—*See* PUBLIC CREDIT, helped by banking law.

National Bank, incentive to honesty—Besides the government money deposited with it, it is doing business upon a large capital of its own. If it proves faithful to the government, it continues its business; if unfaithful, it forfeits its charter, breaks up its business, and thereby loses more than all it can make by seizing upon the government funds in its possession. Its interest, therefore, is on the side of its duty.—*Speech, Springfield, Jan. 20, 1839.* I, 115.

National Bank, paid for privilege—The late Bank of the United States paid the government $75,000 annually for the privilege of using the public money between the times of its collection and disbursement. Can any man suppose that the bank would have paid this sum annually for twenty years, and then offered to renew its obligation to do so, if in reality there was no time intervening between the collection and disbursement of the revenue, and consequently no privilege of using the money extended to it?—*Speech, Springfield, Dec. 20, 1839.* I, 109.

National Bank, system gains rapidly—Changes from the state [banking] systems to the national system are rapidly taking place, and it is hoped that very soon there will be in the United States no banks of issue not authorized by Congress and no bank-note circulation not secured by the government. That the government and the people will derive great benefit from this change in the banking systems of the country can hardly be questioned.—*Fourth annual message, Dec. 6, 1864.* X, 295.

National Bank, Tyler helped defeat—If they [Democrats] ask us [Whigs] for the sufficient and sound currency we promised [in 1840], let them be answered that we only promised it through the medium of a national bank, which they, aided by Mr. Tyler, prevented our establishing.—*Whig circular, March 1, 1843.* I, 258.

National Bank, would not reagitate question of—The question of a national bank is at rest. Were I President, I should not urge its reagitation upon Congress; but should Congress see fit to pass an act to establish such an institution, I should not arrest it by the veto, unless I should consider it subject to some constitutional objection from which I believe the two former banks to have been free.—*Fragment (July 1) 1848.* II, 55.

National Capitol, shall it be moved?—So far as they [internal improvements] involve "obnoxious inequality" [as Polk argues], this capitol is built at public expense, for the public benefit; but does anyone doubt that it is of some peculiar advantage to the property-holders and business people of Washington? Shall we remove it for this reason? And if so, where shall we set it down, and be free from the difficulty? To make sure of our object, shall we locate it nowhere? and let Congress hereafter to hold its sessions, as the loafer lodged, "in spots about"?—*Speech in Congress, June 20, 1848.* II, 36.

National Credit—*See* PUBLIC CREDIT.

National Debt, calls for tariff revision—*See* TARIFF, protective, favored, 5.

National Debt, not burdensome—*See* NATIONAL DEBT, time helps pay.

National Debt, owed to ourselves—Held as it [the national debt] is, for the most part, by our own peo-

ple, it has become a substantial branch of national, though private, property. For obvious reasons the more nearly this property can be distributed among the people the better. To favor such general distribution, greater inducements to become owners might, perhaps, with good effect and without injury be presented to persons of limited means. With this view I suggest whether it might not be both competent and expedient for Congress to provide that a limited amount of some future issue of public securities might be held by any *bona fide* purchaser exempt from taxation and from seizure for debt, under such restrictions and limitations as might be necessary to guard against abuse of so important a privilege. This would enable every prudent person to set aside a small annuity against a possible day of want. . . . The great advantage of citizens being creditors as well as debtors with relation to the public debt is obvious. Men readily perceive that they cannot be much oppressed by a debt which they owe themselves.—*Fourth annual message, Dec. 6, 1864.* X, 293.

National Debt, patriotic contributions—The patriotism of the people has placed at the disposal of the government the large means demanded by the public exigencies. Much of the national loan has been taken by citizens of the industrial classes, whose confidence in their country's faith and zeal for their country's deliverance from present peril have induced them to contribute to the support of the government the whole of their limited acquisitions.—*First annual message, Dec. 3, 1861.* VII, 34.
2.—It is gratifying to know that the expenditures made necessary by the rebellion are not beyond the resources of the loyal people, and to believe that the same patriotism which has thus far sustained the government will continue to sustain it till peace and union shall again bless the land.—*First annual message, Dec. 3, 1861.* VII, 35.

National Debt, rapid growth of, deprecated—For several years past the revenues of the government have been unequal to its expenditures, and consequently loan after loan, sometimes direct and sometimes indirect in form, has been resorted to. By this means a new national debt has been created, and is still growing on us with a rapidity fearful to contemplate—a rapidity only reasonably to be expected in time of war. This state of things has been produced by a prevailing unwillingness to increase the tariff or resort to direct taxation. . . . The present debt must be paid. . . . The system of loans is but temporary in its nature, and must soon explode. . . . As an individual who undertakes to live by borrowing soon finds his original means devoured by interest, and, next, no one left to borrow from, so must it be with a government.—*Whig circular, March 4, 1843.* I, 245.

National Debt, suggestion to Chase—Suppose you change your 5 per cent loan to 6, allowing the holders of the 5's already out to convert them into 6's, upon taking each an additional amount at 6. You will understand better than I the reasons *pro* and *con*, among which probably will be the rise of the rate of interest in Europe.—*To Sec. Chase, May 18, 1864.* X, 102.

National Debt, time helps pay—If we had allowed our old national debt to run at 6 per cent per annum, simple interest, from the end of our revolutionary struggle until today, without paying anything on either principal or interest, each man of us would owe less upon that debt now than each man owed upon it then; and this because our increase of men through the whole period has been greater than 6 per cent. Thus time alone relieves a debtor nation, so long as its population increases faster than unpaid interest accumulates on its debt.—*Second annual message, Dec. 1, 1862.* VIII, 124.
2.—A debt of $600,000,000 now is a less sum per head than was the debt of our Revolution when we came out of that struggle, and the money value in the country now bears even a greater proportion to what it was then than does the population.—*Message to Congress, July 4, 1861.* VI, 311.

National Debt, who pays, if all states secede?—*See* SECESSION, national debt and, 1.

National Democracy, name has new significance—In the contest of 1856 his [Douglas's] party delighted to call themselves together as the "National Democracy," but now, if there should be a notice put up anywhere for a meeting of the "National Democracy," Judge Douglas and his friends would not come. They would not suppose themselves invited. They would understand that it was a call for those hateful postmasters whom he talks about.—*Debate, Galesburg, Oct. 7, 1858.* IV, 264.

National Democracy, Republicans deny charge of conspiracy with—*See* DOUGLAS-BUCHANAN FEUD, Republicans welcome, 2, 3, 6.

National Union League—*See* NOMINATION OF 1864, only small part compliment.

Natural Resources, greater than those of any other country—Our country has advantages superior to any other nation in our resources of iron and timber, with inexhaustible quantities of fuel in the immediate

vicinity of both, and all available and in close proximity to navigable water. Without the advantage of public works, the resources of the nation have been developed, and its power displayed in the construction of a navy of such magnitude, which has at the very period of its creation rendered signal service to the Union.—*Third annual message, Dec. 6, 1863.* IX, 238.

Naturalization, abuses of, in war—*See* ALIENS, status of, in war, 3, 4.

Nature, "all, is a mine"—*See* MINING, above ground.

Naval Academy, work of, commended—I commend to your consideration the suggestions of the secretary of the navy in regard to the policy of fostering and training seamen, and also the education of officers and engineers for the naval service. The Naval Academy is rendering signal service in preparing midshipmen for the highly responsible duties which in after life they will be required to perform. The school is now more full and complete than at any former period, and in every respect entitled to the favorable consideration of Congress.—*Third annual message, Dec. 8, 1863.* IX, 239.

Naval Yards, steam calls for changes—The change that has taken place in naval vessels and naval warfare since the introduction of steam as a motive power for ships of war demands either a corresponding change in some of our existing navy yards or the establishment of new ones for the construction and necessary repair of modern naval vessels. No inconsiderable embarrassment, delay and public injury have been experienced from the want of such government establishments.—*Third annual message, Dec. 8, 1863.* IX, 237.

Navy, argument for internal improvements—*See* INTERNAL IMPROVEMENTS, "inequality" argument answered, 1.

Navy, complimented—Besides blockading our extensive coast, squadrons larger than ever before assembled under our flag have been put afloat and performed deeds which have increased our naval renown.—*First annual message, Dec. 3, 1861.* VII, 37.
2.—The duties devolving on the naval branch of the service during the year and throughout the whole of this unhappy contest have been discharged with fidelity and eminent success. . . . The events of the war give an increased interest and importance to the navy which will probably extend beyond the war itself.—*Third annual message, Dec. 8, 1863.* IX, 236.
3.—Satisfactory and important as have been the performances of the heroic men of the navy at this in-

teresting period, they are scarcely more wonderful than the success of our mechanics and artisans in the production of war vessels, which has created a new form of naval power.—*Third annual message, Dec. 8, 1863.* IX, 238.

4.—Allow me to wish you a great success. With the old fame of the navy made brighter in the present war, you cannot fail. . . . To all, from rear-admiral to honest Jack, I tender the nation's admiration and gratitude.—*Telegram to Sailor's Fair, Boston, Nov. 8, 1864.* X, 260.

5.—It is a subject of congratulation and laudable pride to our countrymen that a navy of such vast proportions has been organized in so brief a period and conducted with so much efficiency and success.—*Fourth annual message, Dec. 6, 1864.* X, 296.

6.—The gallant navy stood ready [as the war ended], but was not in reach to take active part.—*Last public address, April 11, 1865.* XI, 84.

See NATURAL RESOURCES, greater than those of any other country.

See UNION TROOPS, tributes to, 3, 11, 15.

Navy, draft may impair—*See* MILITARY DRAFT, feared effect on navy.

Navy, growth of—Such have been the additions by construction and purchase that it may almost be said a navy has been created and brought into service since our difficulties commenced.—*First annual message, Dec. 3, 1861.* VII, 37.

Navy, natural resources help—*See* NATURAL RESOURCES, greater than those of any other country.

Navy, requires real secretary—"Wooden midshipmen" answer very well in novels, but we must have a live secretary of the navy.—*Interview, Thurlow Weed, Dec., 1860.* Weed, 611.

Nebraska, character of, supposedly fixed—As to Nebraska, I regarded its character as being fixed by the Missouri Compromise for 30 years—as unalterably fixed as that of my own home in Illinois.—*Speech, Peoria, Oct. 16, 1854.* II, 216.

Nebraska, Missouri Compromise and—The restriction of slavery by the Missouri Compromise directly applies to it [Nebraska]—in fact was first made, and has since been maintained, for it.—*Speech, Peoria, Oct. 16, 1854.* II, 203.

Nebraska, no need for compromise repeal—If that country [Nebraska] was in need of a territorial organization, could it not have had it as well without as with repeal?—*Speech, Peoria, Oct. 16, 1854.* II, 208.

Nebraskaism—*See* KANSAS-NEBRASKA ACT.

See SLAVERY, Douglas's care-not policy, 10.

Necessity—To the extent that a necessity is imposed upon a man, he must submit to it.—*Speech, Chicago, July 10, 1858.* III, 50.
Repeated at Alton, Oct. 15, 1858. V, 34.

Negative, cannot be proved—*See* PROOF REQUIRED.

Negro, apprenticeship for—*See* EMANCIPATION, slave states "need not be hurt by."

Negro, arming, would be dangerous—If we were to arm them, I fear that in a few weeks the arms would be in the hands of the rebels.—*Reply to Chicago church committee, Sept. 13, 1862.* VIII, 32.

Negro, attitude of, toward white race—I do not know how much attachment you may have toward our race. It does not strike me that you have the greatest reason to love them. But still you are attached to them, at all events.—*Speech, to free colored men, Aug. 14, 1862.* VIII, 6.

Negro, cannot prevent auction of, back to slavery—I am told that whenever the rebels take any black prisoners, free or slave, they immediately auction them off. They did so with those they took from a boat that was aground in the Tennessee river. And then I am ungenerously attacked for it! For instance, when, after the late battles at and near Bull Run, an expedition went out from Washington under a flag of truce to bury the dead and bring in the wounded, and the rebels seized the blacks who went along to help, and sent them into slavery, Horace Greeley said in his paper that the government would probably do nothing about it. What could I do?—*Reply to committee from Chicago churches, Sept. 13, 1862.* VIII, 31.

Negro, citizenship for—*See* NEGRO CITIZENSHIP.

Negro, condition of, grows worse—So far as peaceful voluntary emancipation is concerned, the condition of the negro slave in America . . . is now as fixed and hopeless of change for the better, as that of the lost souls of the finally impenitent. The autocrat of all the Russias will resign his crown and proclaim his subjects free republicans sooner than will our American masters voluntarily give up their slaves.—*To George Robertson, Aug. 15, 1855.* II, 280.
2.—The chief justice [Taney in the Dred Scott decision] does not directly assert, but plainly assumes, as a fact, that the public estimate of the black man is more favorable now than it was in the days of the Revolution. This assumption is a mistake. In some

trifling particulars the condition of that race has been ameliorated; but as a whole, in this country, the change between then and now is decidedly the other way; and their ultimate destiny has never appeared so hopeless as in the last three or four years. In two of the five states—New Jersey and North Carolina—that then gave the free negro the right of voting, the right has since been taken away, and in a third—New York—it has been greatly abridged; while it has not been extended, so far as I know, in a single state, though the number of states has more than doubled. In those days, as I understand, masters could, at their own pleasure, emancipate their slaves; but since then such legal restraints have been made upon emancipation as to amount almost to prohibition. In those days legislatures held the unquestioned power to abolish slavery in their respective states, but now it is becoming quite fashionable for state constitutions to withhold that power from legislatures. In those days, by common consent, the spread of the black man's bondage to new countries was prohibited, but now Congress decides that it will not continue the prohibition and the Supreme Court decides that it could not if it would. . . . All the powers of earth seem rapidly combining against him. Mammon is after him, ambition follows, philosophy follows, and the theology of the day is fast joining the cry. They have him in his prison-house; they have searched his person and left no prying instrument with him. One after another they have closed the heavy iron doors upon him; and now they have him, as it were, bolted in with a lock of a hundred keys, which can never be unlocked without the concurrence of every key—the keys in the hands of a hundred different men, and they scattered to a hundred different and distant places; and they stand musing as to what invention, in all the dominions of mind and matter, can be produced to make the impossibility of his escape more complete than it is.—*Speech, Springfield, June 27, 1857.* II, 326.

Negro, Declaration of Independence construed to harm—*See* DECLARATION OF INDEPENDENCE, hostility toward, 6.

Negro, education for young—*See* RECONSTRUCTION, Louisiana, 8.

Negro, employment of, as army laborer—I think it is proper for our military commanders to employ as laborers as many persons of African descent as can be used to advantage.—*Message to Congress, July 17, 1862.* VII, 284.

Negro, fights for promise of freedom—You say you will not fight to free negroes. Some of them seem willing to fight for you. . . . Negroes, like other people, act upon motives. Why should they do anything for us if we will do nothing for them? If they stake their lives for us they must be prompted by the strongest motive, even the promise of freedom. And the promise, being made, must be kept.—*To J. C. Conkling, Aug. 26, 1863.* IX, 100.

Negro, homes for, welcomed—If . . . Massachusetts wishes to afford a permanent home within her borders for all or even a large number of colored persons who will come to her, I shall be only too glad to know it. It would give relief in a very difficult point.—*To Gov. Andrews, Feb. 18, 1864.* X, 13.

Negro, "invention of"—It is but justice to the fruitfulness of that period to mention . . . the invention of negroes, or of the present mode of using them, in 1434.—*Speech, Feb. 22, 1859.* V, 110.

Negro, justice to—Let the negro possess the little he has in independence; if he has but one talent, he should be permitted to keep the little he has.—*Speech, Bloomington, May 29, 1856.* Lapsley II, 254.
2.—All I ask for the negro is that if you do not like him, let him alone. If God gave him but little, that little let him enjoy.—*Speech, Springfield, July 17, 1858.* III, 186.
3.—I do not perceive that because the white man is to have the superior position the negro should be denied everything.—*Debate, Charleston, Sept. 18, 1858.* IV, 89.
4.—Suppose it is true that the negro is inferior to the white in the gifts of nature; is it not the exact reverse of justice that the white should for that reason take from the negro any part of the little which he has had given him. "Give to him that is needy" is the Christian rule of charity; but "take from him that is needy" is the rule of slavery.—*Notes, Oct. 1, 1858.* IV, 201.

Negro, man or property?—*See* SELF-GOVERNMENT, defined, 3.

See EQUALITY, Douglas's interpretation of the Declaration, 13.

See NEGRO, tendency to dehumanize, 5.

See SLAVERY, slaves as property.

Negro, no necessary conflict between, and white man —The first inference seems to be that if you do not enslave the negro, you are wronging the white man in some way or other; and that whoever is opposed to the negro being enslaved is in some way or other against the white man. Is not that a falsehood? If there was a necessary conflict between the white man and the negro, I should be for the white man as much as Judge Douglas; but I say there is no such necessary conflict. I say there is room enough for us all to be free.—*Speech, Cincinnati, Sept. 17, 1859.* V, 204.

2.—The proposition that there is a struggle between the white man and the negro contains a falsehood. There is no struggle. . . . I never had to struggle to keep a negro from enslaving me, nor did a negro ever have to fight to keep me from enslaving him.— *Speech, Hartford, Conn., March 5, 1860.* V, 332.

3.—"In the struggle between the white man and the negro" [phrase of proslavery men], assumes that there is a struggle in which either the white man must enslave the negro or the negro must enslave the white. There is no such struggle. It is merely an ingenious falsehood to degrade and brutalize the negro. Let each let the other alone, and there is no struggle about it.—*Speech, New Haven, Conn., March 6, 1860.* V, 351.

4.—This good earth is plenty broad enough for the white man and negro both, and there is no need of either pushing the other off.—*Speech, New Haven, Conn., March 6, 1860.* V, 352.

Negro, some will remember—There will be some black men who [after the war] can remember that with silent tongue, and clenched teeth, and steady eye, and well-poised bayonet, they have helped mankind on to this great consummation, while I fear there will be some white ones unable to forget that with malignant heart and deceitful speech they strove to hinder it.—*To James C. Conklin, Aug. 26, 1863.* IX, 102.

Negro, "tendency to dehumanize"—Equal justice to the South, it is said, requires us to consent to the extension of slavery to new countries. That is to say, inasmuch as you do not object to my taking my hog to Nebraska, therefore I must not object to your taking your slave. Now, I admit that this is perfectly logical, if there is no difference between hogs and negroes.—*Speech, Peoria, Oct. 16, 1854.* II, 223. Repeated at Urbana, Oct. 24, 1858. Hertz II, 642.

2.—Why will you ask us to deny the humanity of the slave, and estimate him as only the equal of the hog? —*Speech, Peoria, Oct. 16, 1854.* II, 226.

3.—The judge [Douglas] has no very vivid impression that the negro is human, and consequently has no idea that there can be any moral question in legislating about him.—*Speech, Peoria, Oct. 16, 1854.* II, 259.

4.—As I read once, in a blackletter law book, "a slave is a human being who is legally not a person but a

thing."—*Speech, Bloomington, May 29, 1856.* Lapsley II, 253.

5.—When this new principle [that the Declaration of Independence does not include the negro]—this new proposition that no human being ever thought of three years ago—is brought forward, I combat it as having an evil tendency, if not an evil design. I combat it as having a tendency to dehumanize the negro —to take away from him the right of ever striving to be a man. I combat it as being one of the thousand things constantly done in these days to prepare the public mind to make property, and nothing but property, of the negro in all the states of this Union. —*Debate, Alton, Oct. 15, 1858.* V, 42.

6.—If this principle is established, that there is no wrong in slavery; that . . . between us and the negro there is no sort of question, but that at the South the question is between the negro and the crocodile . . . —when this is done, where this doctrine prevails, the miners and sappers will have formed public opinion for the slave trade.—*Speech, Columbus, Ohio, Sept. 16, 1859.* V, 185.

7.—If you think that now [that the Declaration of Independence does not include the negro], and did not think it then [five years ago] . . . there has been a change wrought in you, and a very significant change it is, being no less than changing the negro, in your estimation, from the rank of a man to that of a brute. They are taking him down, and placing him, when spoken of, among reptiles and crocodiles, as Judge Douglas himself expresses it.—*Speech, Columbus, Ohio, Sept. 16, 1859.* V, 187.

8.—That change in public sentiment has already degraded the black man in the estimation of Douglas and his followers from the condition of a man of some sort, and assigned him to the condition of a brute.—*Speech, Cincinnati, Sept. 17, 1859.* V. 202.

9.—In the struggle between the negro and the crocodile he [Douglas] is for the negro. Well, I don't know that there is any struggle between the negro and the crocodile. . . . But . . . what is this proposition? I believe it is a sort of proposition in proportion, which may be stated thus: "As the negro is to the white man, so is the crocodile to the negro; and as the negro may rightfully treat the crocodile as a beast or reptile, so the white man may rightfully treat the negro as a beast or reptile." That is really the point of all that argument of his.—*Speech, Cincinnati, Sept. 17, 1859.* V, 204.

10.—Douglas [declares he is] for the negro against the crocodile, but for the white man against the negro. . . . As the negro ought to treat the crocodile as a beast, so the white man ought to treat the negro as a beast.—*Speeches in Kansas, Dec. 1–5, 1859.* V, 272.

11.—[Douglas has the idea] that down where the crocodile inhabits, a white man can't labor; it must be nothing else but crocodile or negro; if the negro does not, the crocodile must possess the earth; in that case he declares for the negro. . . . This . . . has a tendency to still further brutalize the negro, and to bring public opinion to the point of utter indifference whether men so brutalized are enslaved or not.— *Speech, New Haven, Conn., March 6, 1860.* V, 352.

See SLAVERY, Democratic policy toward, 9, 10.

Negro, Why so many free?—*See* SLAVERY, Why so many free negroes?

Negro Breeding, Virginia "changed its tune"—Yet within less than 50 years Virginia changed its tune, and made negro breeding for the cotton and sugar states one of its leading industries.—*Speech, Bloomington, May 29, 1856.* Lapsley II, 258.

Negro Citizenship, opposed to—I am not in favor of negro citizenship. . . . My opinion is that the different states have the power to make a negro a citizen under the Constitution of the United States, if they choose. The Dred Scott decision decides that they have not that power. If the state of Illinois had that power, I should be opposed to the exercise of it.— *Debate, Charleston, Sept. 18, 1858.* IV, 184.

"Negro Livery Stable"—*See* DISTRICT OF COLUMBIA, slavery in, 1.

See ILLINOIS, many in, wanted slavery, 2.

Negro Suffrage, favored—I embrace, with pleasure, this opportunity of declaring my disapprobation of that clause of the Constitution which denies to a portion of the colored people the right of suffrage. . . . I regard, therefore, the exclusion of the colored people as a body from the elective franchise as incompatible with true democratic principles.—*Speech, Cincinnati, May 6, 1842.* Hertz II, 531.

2.—You desire to know, in the event of our complete success in the field, the same being followed by a loyal and cheerful submission on the part of the South, if universal amnesty should not be accompanied with universal suffrage. . . . I cannot see, if universal amnesty is granted, how, under the circumstances, I can avoid asking in return universal suffrage or at least suffrage on the basis of intelligence and military service. . . . I think I am clear and decided as to what course I shall pursue in the premises, regarding it as a religious duty, as the nation's guardian of these people who have so heroically vindicated their man-

hood on the battle-field, where, in assisting to save the life of the Republic, they have demonstrated in blood their right to the ballot, which is but the human protection of the flag they have so fearlessly defended. *To Gen. James Wadsworth, Jan. or Feb., 1864.* XI, 130.

3.—I congratulate you [Michael Hahn] on having fixed your name in history as the first free-state governor of Louisiana. Now you are about to have a convention which, among other things, will probably define the elective franchise. I barely suggest for your private consideration, whether some of the colored people may not be let in—as, for instance, the very intelligent, and especially those who have fought gallantly in our ranks. They would probably help, in some trying time to come, to keep the jewel of liberty within the family of freedom.—*To Gov. Hahn, March 13, 1864.* X, 38.

4.—It is also unsatisfactory to some that the elective franchise is not given to the colored man [by the Lousiana constitution]. I would myself prefer that it were now conferred on the very intelligent, and on those who serve our cause as soldiers.—*Last public address, April 11, 1865.* XI, 89.

Negro Suffrage, opposed to—[Quoting from a previous speech, in answer to the Columbus newspaper Ohio *Statesman:*] In it [this speech] you not only perceive, as a probability, that in that contest [with Douglas in 1858] I did not at any time say I was in favor of negro suffrage; but the absolute proof that twice—once substantially and once expressly—I declared against it.—*Speech, Columbus, Ohio, Sept. 16, 1859.* V, 145.

See RACIAL EQUALITY, neither intended nor desired, 8.

Negro Troops, importance of—I am told you have at least thought of raising a negro military force. In my opinion the country now needs no specific thing so much as some man of your ability and position to go to this work. When I speak of your position I mean that of an eminent citizen of a slave state and himself a slaveholder. . . . The bare sight of 50,000 armed and drilled black soldiers upon the banks of the Mississippi would end the rebellion at once; and who doubts that we can present that sight if we but take hold in earnest.—*To Gov. Andrew Johnson, March 26, 1863.* VIII, 233.

2.—The colored population is the great available and yet unavailed force for restoring the Union.—*To Gov. Johnson, March 26, 1863.* VIII, 233.

3.—Hon. Daniel Ullman [and others propose to raise] . . . a colored brigade. To now avail ourselves of this element of force is very important, if not indispensable.—*To Gen. Banks, March 29, 1863.* VIII, 234.

4.—I am glad to see the accounts of your colored force at Jacksonville, Fla. I see the enemy are driving at them fiercely, as is to be expected. It is important to the enemy that such a force shall not take shape and grow and thrive in the South, and in precisely the same proportion it is important to us that it shall. . . . The enemy will make extra efforts to destroy them, and we should do the same to preserve and increase them.—*To Gen. Hunter, April 1, 1863.* VIII, 239.

5.—I desire that a renewed and vigorous effort be made to raise colored forces along the shores of the Mississippi.—*To Sec. Stanton, July 21, 1863.* IX, 37.

6.—Gen. Thomas has gone again to the Mississippi valley, with the view of raising colored troops. . . . I believe it is a resource which if vigorously applied now will soon close the contest. It works doubly, weakening the enemy and strengthening us. We were not fully ripe for it, until the river was opened. Now, I think at least 100,000 can and ought to be rapidly organized along its shores, relieving all white troops to serve elsewhere.—*To Gen. Grant, Aug. 9, 1863.* IX, 65.

7.—I know as fully as one can know the opinions of others that some of the commanders of our armies in the field, who have given us our most important successes, believe the emancipation policy and the use of colored troops constitute the heaviest blow yet dealt to the rebellion, and that at least one of these important successes could not have been achieved when it was but for the aid of black soldiers.—*To J. C. Conkling, Aug. 26, 1863.* IX, 99.

8.—I thought that whatever negroes can be got to do as soldiers, leaves just so much less for white soldiers to do in saving the Union. Does it appear otherwise to you?—*To J. C. Conkling, Aug. 27, 1863.* IX, 100.

9.—Of those who were slaves at the beginning of the rebellion full 100,000 are now in the United States military service, about one-half of which number actually bear arms in the ranks, thus giving the double advantage of taking so much labor from the insurgent cause and supplying the places which otherwise must be filled by so many white men. So far as tested, it is difficult to say they are not as good soldiers as any.—*Third annual message, Dec. 8, 1863.* IX, 246.

10.—Let any Union man who complains of the [emancipation] measure test himself by writing down in one line that he is for subduing the rebellion by force of arms; and in the next, that he is for taking these 130,000 men [brought to the Union side by emancipation] from the Union side, and placing them where they would be but for the measure he con-

demns. If he cannot face his case so stated, it is only because he cannot face the truth.—*To A. G. Hodges, April 4, 1864.* X, 67.

11.—There is a witness in every white man's bosom that he would rather go to the war having the negro to help him than to help the enemy against him.—*To Charles D. Robinson, April 17, 1864.* X, 196.

12.—I was opposed on nearly every side when I first favored the raising of colored regiments; but they have proved their efficiency, and I am glad they have kept pace with the white troops in the recent assaults. When we wanted every able-bodied man who could be spared to go to the front, and my opposers kept objecting to the negroes, I used to tell them that at such times it was just as well to be a little color-blind.—*To Gen. Grant, June, 1864.* Hertz II, 934.

13.—Our colored forces . . . unlike white recruits, help us where they come from, as well as where they go.—*To Gen. Sherman, July 18, 1864.* X, 167.

14.—Abandon all the posts now garrisoned by black men, take 150,000 men from our side and put them in the battle-field or corn-field against us, and we would be compelled to abandon the war in three weeks.—*Interview, Gov. Randall, Aug. 15, 1864.* X, 190.

15.—Drive back to the support of the rebellion the physical force which the colored people now give and promise us, and neither the present, nor any coming administration can save the Union. Take from us and give to the enemy the hundred and thirty, forty, or fifty thousand colored persons now serving us as soldiers, seamen, and laborers, and we cannot longer maintain the contest. . . . It is not a question of sentiment or taste, but one of physical force, which can be measured and estimated as horsepower and steampower are measured and estimated. And, by measurement, it is more than we can lose and live.—*Unfinished letter to Charles D. Robinson, Aug. 17, 1864.* X, 195.

16.—Any different policy [than that adopted] in regard to the colored men deprives us of his help, and this is more than we can bear. We cannot spare the hundred and forty or fifty thousand now serving us as soldiers, seamen and laborers. . . . Keep it [this physical force], and you can save the Union. Throw it away and the Union goes with it. It is not possible for any administration to retain the service of these people with the express or implied understanding that, upon the first convenient occasion, they are to be re-enslaved. It cannot be, and it ought not to be.—*Unfinished letter to Isaac M. Schermerhorn, Sept. 12, 1864.* X, 222.

17.—Just so, as to the subsequent action in reference to enlisting blacks in the border states. The step, taken sooner, could not have been carried out. A man watches his pear tree day after day, impatient for the ripening of the fruit. Let him attempt to force the process, and he may spoil both fruit and tree. But let him patiently wait, and the ripe pear at length falls into his lap. We have seen this great revolution in public sentiment slowly but surely progressing, so that, when final action came, the opposition was not strong enough to defeat the purpose. I can now solemnly assert that I have a clear conscience in regard to my action on this momentous question. I have done what no man could have helped doing, standing in my place.—*To deputation of antislavery men, Feb. 3, 1865.* Carpenter, 77.

Negro Troops, Massachusetts wants Virginians—You are engaged in trying to raise colored troops for the United States, and wish to take recruits from Virginia through Washington to Massachusetts for that object, and the loyal governor of Virginia is also trying to raise troops for us, objects to your taking his material away, while we, having to care for all and being responsible alike to all, have to do as much for him as we would have to do for you if he was by our authority taking men from Massachusetts to fill up Virginia regiments.—*To Gov. Andrews, Feb., 1864.* X, 12.

2.—I understand . . . that there are a hundred colored men in Alexandria who desire to go to Massachusetts and enlist in the United States service. Let them go.—*Indorsement, Aug., 1864.* War Years III, 181.

Negro Troops, protection of—It is the duty of every government to give protection to its citizens of whatever class, color or condition, and especially to those who are duly organized as soldiers in the public service. . . . The government of the United States will give the same protection to all its soldiers.—*Executive order, July 30, 1863.* IX, 48.

2.—For every soldier of the United States killed in violation of the laws of war, a rebel soldier shall be executed, and for every one enslaved by the enemy or sold into slavery, a rebel soldier shall be placed at hard labor on the public works and continued at such labor until the other shall be released and receive the treatment due a prisoner of war.—*Executive order, July 30, 1863.* IX, 48.

3.—At the beginning of the war, and for some time, the use of colored troops was not contemplated. . . . Upon a clear conviction of duty I resolved to turn that element of strength to account; and I am responsible for it to the American people, to the Christian world, to history, and in my final account to God. Having determined to use the negro as a soldier,

there is no way but to give him all the protection given to any other soldier.—*Speech, Baltimore, April 18, 1864.* X, 78.

4.—Complaint is made to me that in the vicinity of Henderson [Ky.] our militia are seizing negroes and carrying them off without their own consent, and according to no rules whatever, except those of absolute violence. . . . See that the making soldiers of negroes is done according to the rules you are acting upon, so that unnecessary provocation and irritation be avoided.—*To Gen. Thomas, June 13, 1864.* X, 125.

5.—Complaint is made to me that you are forcing negroes into the artillery service, and even torturing them—riding them on rails and the like—to extort their consent. I hope this may be a mistake. The like must not be done by you, or anyone under you. You must not force negroes any more than white men. Answer me on this.—*To Lieut. Col. Glenn, Feb. 7, 1865.* XI, 5.

Neighbors, influence of—*See* FASHION, influence of.

Nest, for hatching troubles—*See* MISSOURI, state or federal troops? 2, 3.

Neutral Rights, conventions urged to consider—A civil war occurring in a country where foreigners reside and carry on trade under treaty stipulation is necessarily fruitful of complaints of the violation of neutral rights. All such collisions tend to excite misapprehensions, and possibly produce mutual recriminations between nations which have a common interest in preserving peace and friendship. In clear cases of these kinds I have so far as possible heard and redressed complaints which have been presented by friendly powers. There is still, however, a large and augmenting number of doubtful cases upon which the government is unable to agree with the government whose protection is demanded by the claimants. There are, moreover, many cases in which the United States or their citizens suffer wrongs from the naval or military authorities of foreign nations which the governments of those states are not at once prepared to redress. I have proposed to some of the foreign states thus interested mutual conventions to examine and adjust such complaints.—*Second annual message, Dec. 1, 1862.* VIII, 95.

Neutral Rights, instructions to Secretary of Navy—First: You will avoid the reality, and as far as possible the appearance, of using any neutral port to watch neutral vessels, and then to dart out and seize them on their departure. Second: You will not in any case detain the crew of a captured neutral vessel or any other subject of a neutral power on board such vessel, as prisoners of war or otherwise, except the small number necessary as witnesses in the prize court.—*To Sec. Welles, July 25, 1863.* XI, 127.

Neutral Rights, Mason and Slidell case—We must stick to American principles concerning the rights of neutrals. We fought Great Britain for insisting by theory and practice on the right to do exactly what Capt. Wilkes has done [captured Mason and Slidell]. If Great Britain shall now protest against the act and demand their release, we must give them up, apologize for the act as a violation of our doctrine, and thus forever bind her over to keep the peace in relation to neutrals, and so acknowledge that she has been wrong for sixty years.—*To Benson J. Lossing, Nov. 15, 1861.* Hertz II, 844.

Nevada, admitted as state—The organization and admission of the state of Nevada has been completed in conformity with law, and thus our excellent system is firmly established in the mountains, which once seemed a barren and uninhabitable waste between the Atlantic states and those which have grown up on the coast of the Pacific ocean.—*Fourth annual message, Dec. 6, 1864.* X, 298.

Nevada, Territory of, organized—*See* COLORADO, Territory of, organized.

See COLORADO, resources invite immigrants.

"New Birth of Freedom"—*See* CIVIL WAR, dedication to task of winning.

New England, labor system of, praised—*See* LABOR, freedom to strike welcomed.

New England, poor in soil but rich in men—Up here in New England you have a soil that scarcely sprouts black-eyed beans, and yet where will you find wealthy men so wealthy, and poverty so rarely in extremity. There is not another such place on earth.—*Speech, New Haven, Conn., March 6, 1860.* V, 361.

New Hampshire, comparison with Virginia in number of mulattoes—*See* RACIAL AMALGAMATION, census of mulattoes, 3.

New Hampshire, good state to leave—*See* MARYLAND, good state to leave.

New Hampshire, Republicans cautioned against dissension—*See* REPUBLICAN PARTY, threats to unity of, 3.

New Mexico, gets local option on slavery—*See* COMPROMISE OF 1850, Nebraskaism and.

New York, canals of—*See* ILLINOIS AND MICHIGAN CANAL, importance of, 2.

New York Day-Book—A Buchanan paper in the North.—*Notes, Oct. 1, 1858.* IV, 200.

New York Evening Post—Questions asked editor of—May I ask whether the *Evening Post* has not assailed me for supposed too lenient dealing with persons charged with fraud and crime? And that in cases of which the *Post* could know but little of the facts?—*To William Cullen Bryant, June 27, 1864.* X, 136

New York Herald, correspondent of, corrected—*See* KENTUCKY, Lincoln chooses not to visit, 2, 3.

New York Herald, correspondent of, reinstated—Whereas it appears to my satisfaction that Thomas W. Knox, a correspondent of the New York *Herald,* has been by the sentence of a court-martial excluded from the military department under command of Maj. Gen. Grant, and also that Gen. Thayer and Maj. Gen. McClernand, in command of a corps of that department, and many other respectable persons, are of opinion that Mr. Knox's offense was technical rather than wilfully wrong, and that the sentence should be revoked; now, therefore, said sentence is hereby so far revoked as to allow Mr. Knox to return to Gen. Grant's headquarters, and to remain if Gen. Grant shall give his express assent, and to again leave the department if Gen. Grant shall refuse such assent.—*Executive order, March 20, 1863.* VIII, 230.

New York Herald, no discrimination against—The administration will not discriminate against the *Herald,* especially while it sustains us so generously, and the cause of the country as ably as it has been doing.—*To James Gordon Bennett, Sept. 22, 1861.* Hertz II, 842.

New York Herald, thanked—Thanking you again for the able support given by you, through the *Herald,* to what I think the true cause of the country, and also for your expressions toward me personally.—*To James Gordon Bennett, May 21, 1862.* Hertz II, 867.

New York Journal of Commerce, suppressed—*See* NEW YORK WORLD, suppressed.

New York Times, asked to reconsider—*See* EMANCIPATION, financial aspects of, compensated, 2.

New York Times, correspondent of, "very mad"—What a very mad man your correspondent, Smedley, is. Mr. Lincoln is not pledged to the ultimate extinction of slavery; does not hold the black man to be the equal of the white, unqualifiedly as Mr. S. states it; and never did stigmatize their white people as immoral or unchristian; and Mr. S. cannot prove one of his assertions true. Mr. S. seems sensitive on the questions of morals and Christianity. What does he think of a man who makes charges against another which he does not know to be true, and could easily learn to be false? As to the pitcher story, it is a forgery out and out. I was never in a meeting of negroes in my life; and never saw a pitcher presented by anybody to anybody.—*To Henry J. Raymond, Dec. 18, 1860.* VI, 83.

New York Times, "true to Union"—The *Times*, I believe, is always true to .the Union, and therefore should be treated at least as well as any.—*To E. A. Paul, May 24, 1864.* X, 107.

New York Tribune, forged article in—*See* PRESS, forgery best ignored.

New York World, suppressed—Whereas there has been wickedly and traitorously printed and published this morning in the New York *World* and New York *Journal of Commerce* . . . a false and spurious proclamation purporting to be signed by the President and to be countersigned by the secretary of state, which publication is of a treasonable nature, designed to give aid and comfort to the enemies of the United States and to the rebels now at war against the government and their aiders and abettors, you are therefore hereby commanded forthwith to arrest and imprison . . . the editors, proprietors and publishers of the aforesaid newspapers, and all such persons as, after public notice has been given of the falsehood of such publication, print and publish the same with intent to give aid and comfort to the enemy; and you will hold the persons so arrested in close custody until they can be brought to trial before a military commission for their offense. You will also take possession by military force of the printing establishments of the New York *World* and *Journal of Commerce* . . . and prohibit any further publication therefrom.—*To Gen. Dix, May 18, 1864.* X, 103.

Newell, M. W., appreciation of—He . . . enjoyed the reputation of a most competent and faithful man. . . . I never heard anything against him personally or professionally.—*Indorsement, Aug. 21, 1862.* Angle, 302.

Newell, W. A., recommended—He is a .true friend of the Union, and every way a reliable gentleman.—*To Simeon Draper, Sept. 8, 1864.* Angle, 356.

Newspapers—*See* PRESS (also individual names of papers).

Niagara Falls, reflections on—Niagara Falls . . . calls up the indefinite past. When Columbus first sought this continent—when Christ suffered on the cross—when Moses led Israel through the Red Sea—nay, even when Adam first came from the hand of his Maker, then, as now, Niagara was roaring here. The eyes of that species of extinct giants whose bones fill the mounds of America have gazed on Niagara, as ours do now. Contemporary with the first race of men, and older than the first man, Niagara is strong and fresh today as ten thousand years ago. The mammoth and mastodon, so long dead that fragments of their monstrous bones alone testify that they ever lived, gazed on Niagara—in that long, long time never still for a moment, never froze, never slept, never rested. —*Notes, July 1, 1850.* II, 138.

2.—There is no mystery about the thing itself. Every effect is just as any intelligent man, knowing the causes, would anticipate without seeing it. . . . Its power to excite reflection and emotion is its great charm.—*Notes, July 1, 1850.* II, 138.

Nicaragua, good wishes toward—On behalf of the United States I fully reciprocate toward your government [Nicaragua] and people the kind wishes and friendly purposes you so generously express toward ours. Please communicate to His Excellency, the President of Nicaragua, my high esteem and consideration, and my earnest wish for his health, happiness, and long life.—*To Nicaraguan minister, March 17, 1861.* VI, 222.

Nineteenth Century, "great event of"—*See* EMANCIPATION PROCLAMATION, place of, in history, 2.

"No More Argument"—I know you are dissatisfied, which pains me very much, but I wish not to be argued with further.—*To Gen. Banks, Dec. 2, 1864.* X, 278.

"Nobly Save or Meanly Lose"—*See* UNION, we know how to save.

Nomination of 1860, accepted—I accept the nomination tendered me by the convention. . . . The declaration of principles and sentiments which accompanies your letter meets my approval; and it shall be my care not to violate or disregard it in any part. Imploring the assistance of Divine Providence, and with due regard to the views and feelings of all who were represented in the convention—to the rights of all the states and territories and people of the nation; to the inviolability of the Constitution; and the perpetual Union, harmony, and prosperity of all—I am most happy to cooperate for the practical success of the principles declared by the convention.—*To George Ashmun and convention, May 23, 1860.* VI, 14.

Nomination of 1860, attitude toward—As to myself, let me pledge you my word that neither I, nor any friend so far as I know, has been setting stake against Gov. Seward. No combination has been made with me, or proposed to me, in relation to the next presidential candidate.—*To Charles L. Wilson, June 1, 1858.* II, 363.

2.—I am not directly or indirectly committed to anyone, nor has anyone made any advance to me upon the subject.—*To Charles L. Wilson, June 1, 1858.* II, 363.

3.—As I would not like the public to know, so I would not like myself to know, I had entered a combination with any man to the prejudice of all others whose friends respectively may consider them preferable [for the 1860 nomination].—*To W. E. Frazer, Nov. 1, 1859.* V, 258.

4.—I am not in a position where it would hurt much for me not to be nominated on the national ticket; but I am where it would hurt some for me not to get the Illinois delegates. What I expected when I wrote the letter to Messrs. Dole and others [*See* JUDD, N. B., confidence in] is now happening. Your discomfited assailants are most bitter against me; and they will, for revenge upon me, lay to the Bates egg in the South, and to the Seward egg in the North, and go far toward squeezing me out in the middle with nothing. Can you not help me a little in your end of the vineyard?—*To N. B. Judd, Feb. 9, 1860.* V, 291.

5.—As to the presidential nomination, claiming no greater exemption from selfishness than is common, I still feel that my whole aspiration should be, and therefore must be, to be placed anywhere, or nowhere, as may appear most likely to advance our cause.—*To James F. Babcock, April 14, 1860.* Hertz II, 771.

6.—As your request, I will be entirely frank. The taste is in my mouth a little. . . . You may confidently rely, however, that by no advice or consent of mine, shall my pretensions be pressed to the point of endangering our common cause.—*To Lyman Trumbull, April 29, 1860.* Tracy, 142.

7.—I have not asked the nomination and I will not buy it with pledges.—*To friends on eve of convention.* Tribune I, 124.

8.—Remembering that Peter denied his Lord with an oath, after most solemnly protesting that he never would, I will not swear I will make no committals, but I do not think I will.—*To Lyman Trumbull, June 5, 1860.* Tracy, 154.

9.—If I fail, it will be lack of ability, and not of purpose.—*To Joshua R. Giddings, June 26, 1860.* Tracy, 155.

10.—If my record would hurt any, there is no hope that it will be overlooked; so that if friends can help any with it, they may as well do so.—*To R. W. Thompson, July 10, 1860.* Hertz II, 779.

See POLITICS, money in.

Nomination of 1860, chances for, appraised—If I have any chance, it consists mainly in the fact that the whole opposition would vote for me if nominated—I don't mean to include the pro-slavery opposition of the South, of course—My name is new in the field, and I suppose I am not the first choice of a very great many. Our policy, then, is to give no offense to others—leave them in a mood to come to us if they shall be compelled to give up their first love.—*To Samuel Galloway, March 24, 1860.* VI, 7.

2.—After what you have said, it is perhaps proper I should post you, so far as I am able, as to the "lay of the land." First I think the Illinois delegation will be unanimous for me at the start; and no other delegation will. A few individuals in other delegations would like to go for me at the start, but may be restrained by their colleagues. It is represented to me by men who ought to know, that the whole of Indiana might not be difficult to get. You know how it is in Ohio. I am certainly not the first choice there; and yet I have not heard that anyone makes any positive objection to me. It is just so everywhere so far as I can perceive. Everywhere, except here in Illinois and possibly Indiana, one or another is preferred to me, but there is no positive objection. This is the ground as it now appears.—*To R. M. Corwine, May 2, 1860.* Tracy, 146.

Nomination of 1860, "Deeply and even painfully sensible"—Deeply and even painfully sensible of the great responsibility which is inseparable from this high honor—a responsibility which I could almost wish had fallen upon some one of the far more eminent men and experienced statesmen whose distinguished names were before the convention—I shall, by your leave, consider more fully the resolutions of the convention, denominated the platform, and without any unnecessary or unreasonable delay respond to you, Mr. Chairman, in writing, not doubting that the platform will be found satisfactory, and the nomination gratefully accepted.—*To notification committee, May 19, 1860.* VI, 13.

Nomination of 1860, no bargains—I authorize no bargains and will be bound by none.—*Fragment, May 17, 1860.* Hertz II, 773.

2.—Make no contracts that will bind me.—*To W. H. Herndon, no date.* Hertz II, 773.

3.—I am not wanting in the purpose, though I may fail in the strength, to maintain my freedom from bad influences. . . . May the Almighty grant that the cause of truth, justice, and humanity shall in no wise suffer at my hands.—*To J. R. Giddings, May 21, 1860.* V, 13.

4.—It is indeed most grateful to my feelings that the responsible position assigned to me comes without conditions, save only such honorable ones as are fairly implied.—*To J. R. Giddings, May 21, 1860. VI, 14.*

Nomination of 1864, accepted—The nomination is gratefully accepted, as the resolutions of the convention, called the platform are heartily approved. While the resolution in regard to the supplanting of republican government upon the western continent is fully concurred in, there might be misunderstanding were I not to say that the position of the government in relation to the action of France in Mexico, as assumed through the state department, and approved and indorsed by the convention among the measures and acts of the executive, will be faithfully maintained so long as the state of facts shall leave the position pertinent and applicable.—*To William Dennison and others, June 27, 1864. X, 136.*

Nomination of 1864, gratified by—I will neither conceal my gratification nor restrain the expression of my gratitude that the Union people, through their convention, in their continued effort to save and advance the nation, have deemed me not unworthy to remain in my present position.—*Reply to committtee notifying President of renomination, June 9, 1864. X, 116.*

Nomination of 1864, only small part compliment—I am not insensible at all to the personal compliment there is in this [nomination], and yet I do not allow myself to believe that any but a small portion of it is to be appropriated as a personal compliment. That really the convention and the Union League assembled with a higher view—that of taking care of the interests of the country for the present and the great future—and that the part I am entitled to appropriate as a compliment is only that part which I may lay hold of as being the opinion of the convention and of the league that I am not entirely unworthy to be entrusted with the place which I have occupied for the last three years.—*Reply to delegation from National Union League, June 9, 1864. X, 122.*

See HORSES, would not swap, midstream.

Nonsense, hurts no one—If I were as I have been for most of my life, I might, perhaps talk nonsense to you for half an hour, and it wouldn't hurt anybody. —*Speech, Fredericksburg, Oct. 4, 1862. XI, 125.*

Norfolk, Va., no vote needed—*See* WAR POWER, military necessity alone justified.

North, too numerous for South to whip—*See* SECESSION, after, what? 2.

North American Review, thanked for article—The number for this month and year of the *North American Review* was duly received, and for which please accept my thanks. I am not the most impartial judge; yet, with due allowance for this, I venture to hope that the article entitled "The President's Policy" will be of value to the country. I fear I am not quite worthy of all which is therein kindly said of me personally.—*To Crosby and Nichols, Jan. 16, 1864. IX, 284.*

Northwest Territory, Jefferson and—*See* ORDINANCE OF 1787, fruits of, 2.

Northwest Territory, slavery barred from—*See* ORDINANCE OF 1787, fruits of.

Norwegian Bark, indemnification for, urged—*See* ADMIRAL P. TORDENSKIOLD.

"Not Enemies but Friends"—*See* ENEMIES, not, but friends.

"Not Much of Me"—*See* AUTOBIOGRAPHY, Lincoln's, 6.

"Not Worth a Damn"—*See* EWING, THOMAS, opinion of, 1.

"Nothing That Really Hurts"—*See* SECESSION, no excuse for, 1.

"Now or Never," secessionists' idea—*See* UNION, destruction of, openly sought, 1.

Oath, form of, disliked—On principle I dislike an oath which requires a man to swear he has never done wrong. It rejects the Christian principle of forgiveness on terms of repentance. I think it is enough if the man does no wrong hereafter.—*Indorsement to Sec. Stanton, Feb. 5, 1864. IX, 303.*

Oath "Registered in Heaven"—*See* CIVIL WAR, issue in hands of dissatisfied citizens.

Oath of Allegiance, offers freedom from prison—*See* PRISON, release from, by taking oath.

"Of the People, by the People, for the People"—*See* CIVIL WAR, dedication to task of winning.

Office Holding, vocations and—Nor is it perceived how being a physician or farmer should qualify a man for office. Whatever of sound views of government are acquired by the physician and farmer are acquired not in their regular occupations, but by reading and reflection in the hours of relaxation from their regular occupations. It is probable that the leisure time for such reading and reflection would, in times of peace, be quite as abundant with an officer of the army as with a physician or farmer.—*Speech, Springfield, Aug. 26, 1852.* Angle, 98.

Office Seekers, troubles with—Mr. [F. B.] Marshall [of Massachusetts] appears to be a very intelligent gentleman, and well acquainted with the affairs of the Sandwich Islands. The California delegation also expects the place for some one of their citizens. In self-defense, I am disposed to say, "Make a selection and send it to me."—*To Sec. Seward, March 7, 1862.* VII, 115.

2.—If our American society and the United States government are demoralized and overthrown, it will come from the voracious desire for office, this wriggle to live without toil, work and labor from which I am not free myself.—*To W. H. Herndon, no date.* R. T. L.

See KERR, ORPHEUS, appreciation of, 2.

See PATRONAGE.

"Oh! Why Should the Spirit of Mortal Be Proud?"—I would give all I am worth, and go in debt, to be able to write so fine a piece as I think that is [William Knox's poem].—*To William Johnston, April 18, 1846.* I, 289.

Ohio, famous for cheese—Connecticut, I think, owned the little remaining part of Ohio [the Northwest Territory took the rest], being the same where they now send [Joshua R.] Giddings to Congress, and beat all creation in making cheese.—*Speech, Peoria, Oct. 16, 1854.* II, 193.
Repeated at Urbana, Oct. 24, 1854. Hertz II, 628.

Ohio, grateful to—I am grateful to the state of Ohio for many things, especially for the brave soldiers and officers she has given in the present national trial to the armies of the Union.—*To M. Birchard and others, June 29, 1863.* IX, 5.

Ohio, had slaves been present—You did so [formed a free-state constitution]unembarrassed by the actual presence of the institution [slavery] among you—if they [slaves] had been among you, embarrassing difficulties most probably, would have induced you to tolerate a slave constitution instead of a free one.—*Speech, Cincinnati, Sept. 17, 1859.* V, 221.

Ohio, must not falter—You must not let your approaching election in Ohio so result as to give encouragement to Douglasism. That ism is all that now stands in the way of an early and complete success of Republicanism; and nothing would help it or hurt us so much as for Ohio to go over or falter just now. You must, one and all, put your souls into the effort. —*To Salmon P. Chase, Sept. 21, 1859.* Hertz II, 758.

Ohio, no insult to—I am unable to perceive an insult to Ohio in the case of Mr. Vallandigham. Quite surely nothing of the sort was or is intended.—*To M. Birchard and others, June 29, 1863.* IX, 5.

Ohio, "saves nation"—Glory to God in the highest! Ohio has saved the nation.—*To John Brough, Oct. 13, 1863.* Hertz II, 914.

Ohio Democrats, attitude of, toward the war—The convention you represent have nominated Mr. Vallandigham for governor of Ohio, and both they and you have declared the purpose to sustain the national Union by all constitutional means. But of course they and you in common reserve to yourselves to decide what are constitutional means; and . . . you omit to state or intimate that in your opinion an army is a constitutional means of saving the Union against a rebellion, or even to intimate that you are conscious of an existing rebellion being in progress with the avowed object of destroying that very Union.—*To M. Birchard and others, June 29, 1863.* IX, 7.

2.—Your nominee for governor [Vallandigham], in whose behalf you appeal, is known to you and to the world to declare against the use of an army to suppress the rebellion. Your own attitude, therefore, encourages desertions, resistance to the draft, and the like because it teaches those who incline to desert and to escape the draft to believe it is your purpose to protect them, and to hope that you will become strong enough to do so.—*To M. Birchard and others, June 29, 1863.* IX, 8.

Ohio National Guard, thanked—*See* CIVIL WAR, Ohio national guard thanked.

Ohio Statesman (newspaper), editor of, given opportunity—I presume the editor of that paper [*Statesman*] is an honest and truth-loving man, and that he will be greatly obliged to me for furnishing him thus early an opportunity to correct the misrepresentation he has made, before it has run so far that malicious people can call him a liar.—*Speech, Columbus, Ohio, Sept. 16, 1859.* V, 145.

Ohio Statesman (newspaper) mistaken—In this paper [*Statesman*] I have read an article in which, among other statements, I find the following: "In debating with Senator Douglas during the memorable contest last fall, Mr. Lincoln declared in favor of negro suffrage, and attempted to defend that vile conception against the Little Giant." I mention this now . . . for the purpose of making three comments upon it. The first . . . —it furnishes me an introductory topic; the second is to show that the gentleman is mistaken; thirdly, to give him an opportunity to correct it. . . .

I have found that it is not entirely safe, when one is misrepresented under his very nose, to allow the misrepresentation to go uncontradicted.—*Speech, Columbus, Ohio, Sept. 16, 1859.* V, 141.

Old Fogy—*See* YOUNG AMERICA, compared with Old Fogy.

See YOUNG AMERICA, horror for Old Fogy.

"Old Serpent's Tail"—*See* SLAVERY, "reptile," 3.

Oligarchy, threatened by court decision—*See* DRED SCOTT DECISION, challenged, 9.

"On the Blind Side"—*See* CAMPAIGN OF 1848, victory forecast, 1.

"On This Line"—*See* CIVIL WAR, when will it end?

"One Common Country," Davis understood—Today Mr. [F. P.] Blair tells me . . . that at the time of delivering it [Lincoln's letter to Blair] Mr. [Jefferson] Davis read it over twice in Blair's presence, at the close of which he, Blair, remarked that the part about "our one common country" related to the part of Mr. Davis's letter about "the two countries," to which Mr. Davis replied that he so understood it.—*Indorsement, Jan. 28, 1865.* X, 347.

One Leak for Another—Do we gain anything by opening one leak to stop another? Do we gain anything by quieting one clamor merely to open another, and probably a larger one?—*To Col. A. K. McClure, June 30, 1863.* IX, 14.

"One Mouth and Two Hands"—*See* SLAVERY, wrong of, 15, 18, 20.

One Worth Two—One man there [Southerner in Union regiment] is worth two here in this, that it adds one to us, and takes one from the enemy.—*To Sec. Stanton, Oct. 10, 1862.* Hertz II, 884.

Only Voters Who Vote Count—It is not the qualified voters, but the qualified voters who choose to vote, that constitute the political power of the state.—*Opinion on admission of West Virginia, Dec. 31, 1862.* VIII, 157.

"Open Field and Fair Chance"—*See* CIVIL WAR, results involve future, 7.

Ordinance of 1787—*See also* SLAVERY, policy of the Fathers, 1, 19.

Ordinance of 1787, Congress dissents from—Now Congress declares this [prohibition of slavery] ought never to have been, and the like of it must never be again.—*Speech, Peoria, Oct. 16, 1854.* II, 195.

Ordinance of 1787, fruits of—With the author of the Declaration of Independence, the policy of prohibiting slavery in the new territory originated. Thus way back to the Constitution, in the pure, fresh, free breath of the Revolution, the state of Virginia and the national Congress put that policy into practice. Thus, through more than 60 of the best years of the Republic, did that policy work to its great and beneficent end.—*Speech, Peoria, Oct. 16, 1854.* II, 194.

Repeated at Urbana, Oct. 24, 1854. Hertz II, 628.

2.—It [Northwest Territory] is now what Jefferson foresaw and intended—the happy home of teeming millions of free, white, prosperous people, and no slave among them.—*Speech, Peoria, Oct. 16, 1854.* II, 194.

3.—Thus, in those five states [comprising the former Northwest Territory] and in five millions of free, enterprising peoples, we have before us the rich fruits of [Jefferson's] policy [of prohibiting slavery in new territory].—*Speech, Peoria, Oct. 16, 1854.* II, 195.

4.—If the Ordinance of '87 did not keep slavery out of the Northwest Territory [as Douglas insists], how happens it that the northwest shore of the Ohio river is entirely free of it, while the southeast shore, less than a mile distant, along nearly the whole length of the river, is entirely covered with it?—*Speech, Peoria, Oct. 16, 1854.* II, 250.

5.—Here is this fine city of Cincinnati, and over there is the little town of Covington. Covington has just as good a location as Cincinnati, and a fine country back of it. It was settled before Cincinnati. Why is it not a bigger city? Just because of slavery, and nothing else. My people used to live over there, and I know.—*To Ralph Emerson, Sept. 1855.* Starr, 157.

6.—Begin with the men of the Revolution, and go down for 60 entire years and until the last scrap of that territory comes into the Union in the form of the state of Wisconsin, everything was made to conform to that Ordinance of '87, excluding slavery from that vast extent of country.—*Speech, Columbus, Ohio, Sept. 16, 1859.* V, 169.

7.—There was nothing said in the Constitution in regard to the spread of slavery into the territories . . . but there was something said about it by the same generation of men in the adoption of the old Ordinance of 1787, through the influence of which you here in Ohio, our neighbors in Indiana, we in Illinois, our neighbors in Michigan and Wisconsin, are happy, prosperous, teeming millions of free men.—*Speech, Cincinnati, Sept. 17, 1859.* V, 209.

8.—Tell me not, then, that the Ordinance of '87 had nothing to do with making Indiana a free state [as argued by Douglas], when we find some men chafing against, and only restrained by that barrier.—*Speech, Cincinnati, Sept. 17, 1859.* V, 223.

9.—I think all these facts abundantly prove that my friend Judge Douglas's proposition that the Ordinance of '87 or the national restricting of slavery, never had a tendency to make a free state, is a fallacy—a proposition without the shadow of substance of truth about it.—*Speech, Cincinnati, Sept. 17, 1859.* V, 225.

See INDIANA, sought privilege of having slaves.

See JEFFERSON, THOMAS, slavery decried by.

See SLAVERY, Illinois and Missouri in contrast.

See SLAVERY, Ohio and Kentucky in contrast.

Oregon, offices in, declined—I cannot but be grateful to you and to all other friends who have interested themselves in having the governorship of Oregon offered me; but on as much reflection as I have had time to give the subject, I cannot consent to accept it. As to the secretaryship—of Oregon—I have already recommended our friend Simeon Francis of the *Journal.*—*To John Addison, Sept. 27, 1849.* II, 129.

2.—Your letter of the 17th inst., saying you had received no answer to yours informing me of my appointment as secretary of Oregon, is received, and surprises me very much. I received that letter, accompanied by the commission, in due course of mail, and answered it two days after, declining the office and warmly recommending Simeon Francis for it.—*To Sec. of State Clayton, Sept. 27, 1849.* II, 130.

Orme, W. M., appreciation of—. . . whom I also know to be one of the most active, competent and best men in the world.—*To Gen. Halleck, Aug. 2, 1862.* Angle, 300.

"Out at Elbows and Out at Toes"—*See* SHIELDS, JAMES, division of, "out of shape."

Overcoat, gift of, acknowledged—Your note of the 1st, together with the very substantial and handsome overcoat which accompanied it by express, were duly received by me. . . . Permit me now to thank you sincerely for your elegant and valuable New Year's gift.—*To Isaac Fenno, Jan. 22, 1861.* Angle, 260.

Owen, Robert Dale, characterized— . . . an intelligent, disinterested and patriotic gentleman.—*To Gen. Ripley, Jan. 22, 1861.* XI, 116.

Ox-Bows, wood for—Like wood for ox-bows, they [advocates of Douglas's "absurdity" concerning Dred Scott and slavery in the territories] are being merely soaked in it [the "absurdity"] preparatory to the

bending [that is, acquiesence in the expected court decision to nationalize slavery].—*Fragment, speeches in Kansas, Dec. 1-5, 1859.* V, 271.

Ox on Fence—*See* HOOKER, JOSEPH, suggestions to, 1.

Pacific Railroad—*See* ILLINOIS AND MICHIGAN CANAL, importance of, 4.

Pacific Telegraph, promising—Satisfactory arrangements have been made with the emperor of Russia, which, it is believed, will result in effecting a continuous line of telegraph through that empire from our Pacific coast.—*Third annual message, Dec. 8, 1863.* IX, 229.

2.—The proposed overland telegraph between America and Europe, by way of Behring's Straits and Asiatic Russia, which was sanctioned by Congress at the last session, has been undertaken under very favorable circumstances, by an association of American citizens, with the cordial good will and support of Great Britain and Russia. Assurances have been received from most of the South American states of their high appreciation of the enterprise and their readiness to cooperate in constructing lines tributary to that world-encircling communication.—*Fourth annual message, Dec. 6, 1864.* X, 286.

See ATLANTIC TELEGRAPH, favored.

Painting, gift of, acknowledged—When I received the spirited and admirable painting, "Waiting for the Hour," I directed my secretary not to acknowledge its arrival at once, preferring to make my personal acknowledgments of the thoughtful kindness of the donors; and waiting for some leisure hour, I have committed the discourtesy of not replying at all. I hope you will believe that my thanks, though late, are most cordial, and request that you will convey them to those associated with you in this flattering and generous gift.—*To William Lloyd Garrison, Jan. 24, 1865.* X, 345.

Palmer, John M., characterized—He is a good and true man.—*To J. A. Pickrell, Nov. 3, 1859.* Angle, 227.

2.—I do not want him to resign, unless there be some reason not yet known to me.—*To Sec. Stanton, Dec. 12, 1863.* Angle, 336.

Panic, "artificial"—*See* CRISIS, artificial, 3.

Panic, feared if more troops are called—*See* CIVIL WAR, determination to continue, 3.

Paroles, Confederate parole plan rejected—Gen. Stuart, of the rebel army, has sent in a few of our prisoners under a flag of truce, paroled with terms to prevent their fighting the Indians, and evidently seeking to commit us to their right to parole our prisoners in that way. My inclination is to send the prisoners back with a distinct notice .that we will recognize no paroles given to our prisoners by rebels as extending beyond the prohibition against fighting them; yet I wish your opinion upon it.—*To Gen. Halleck, Oct. 3, 1862. VIII, 53.*

Parts and the Whole—I would then like to know how it comes about that when each piece of a story is true, the whole story turns out false? . . . Then I ask the original question, if each of the pieces of testimony is true, how is it possible that the whole is a falsehood?—*Debate, Charleston, Sept. 18, 1858. IV, 195.*
2.—Nebraska, while a territory . . . is part of ourselves. If you say we shall not control it, because it is only part, the same is true of every other part; and when all the parts are gone, what has become of the whole? What is there left of us? What use for the general government, when there is nothing left for it to govern?—*Speech, Peoria, Oct. 16, 1854. II, 231.*

"Party Measures"—*See* PRESIDENCY, Northern aspirants for, bid for Southern help.

Party Responsibility—*See* POLITICAL PARTIES, not answerable for individual members.

Passion, future enemy—Passion has helped us [to establish the Republic], but can do no more. It will in future be our enemy.—*Speech, Springfield, Jan. 27, 1837. I, 50.*

Patent System, achievement of—The patent system . . . secured to the inventor for a limited time exclusive use of his invention, and thereby added the fuel of interest to the fire of genius in the discovery and production of new and useful things.—*Lecture, Springfield, Feb. 22, 1859. V, 113.*

Patent System, agricultural fairs and—In this these [agricultural] fairs are kindred to the patent clause of the Constitution of the United States, and to the department and practical system based upon that clause.—*Speech, Milwaukee, Sept. 30, 1859. V, 238.*

Patience, Republican purpose to exercise—We [Republicans] don't intend to be very impatient about it [defeating the slave power]. We mean to be as deliberate and calm about it as it is possible to be, but as firm and resolved as it is possible for men to be.—*Speech, Cincinnati, Sept. 17, 1859. V, 218.*

Patriotism, no corner on—I do not pretend to say that you, who think so [that the administration merits support], embrace all the patriotism and loyalty of the country, but I do believe, and I trust without

personal interest, that the welfare of the country does require that such support and indorsement should be given.—*Response to serenade, Nov. 9, 1864. X, 261.*

Patronage, both men good but one better—There are several aspirants for the office of United States marshal for the district of Illinois, among the most prominent of whom is Benjamin Bond, Esq., of Carlyle, and ——— Thomas, Esq., of Galena. Mr. Bond I know to be personally in every way worthy of the office; and he is very numerously and most respectably recommended. . . . I solicit for his claims a full and fair consideration. Having said this much, I add that in my individual judgment the appointment of Mr. Thomas would be the better.—*To Sec. of State Clayton, March 10, 1849. II, 106.*

Patronage, "demoralizing"—In my opinion, there is not a more foolish or demoralizing way of conducting political rivalry than these fierce and bitter struggles for patronage.—*To Gov. Carney, May 14, 1864. X, 101.*
2.—If ever this free people, if ever this government itself, shall become utterly demoralized, it will come from this human wriggle and struggle for office; a way to live without work—from which complaint I am not free myself.—*To Henry Wilson, no date. War Years II, 33.*

Patronage "disobliged"—I am quite sure you are not aware how much I am disobliged by the refusal to give Mr. F. S. Evans a place in the Customs House. I had no thought that the men to whom I had given the higher offices would be so ready to disoblige me. —*To F. S. Corkran, May 6, 1861. Hertz II, 832.*
2.—I have been greatly—I might say grievously—disappointed and disobliged by Mr. Corkran's refusal to make Mr. Evans deputy naval officer, as I requested him to do.—*To Sec. Chase, May 6, 1861. Angle, 272.*

Patronage, friends get most—The administration came into power, very largely in a minority of the popular vote. Notwithstanding this, it distributed to its party friends as nearly all the civil patronage as any administration ever did.—*To Gen. Schurz, Nov. 10, 1862. Tracy, 215.*

Patronage, government official cautioned—*See* INTRIGUE, danger of, foreseen.

Patronage, imperative case—You must make a job for the bearer of this—make a job of it with the collector, and have it done. You can do this for me, and you must.—*To James Pollock, Aug. 15, 1861. VI, 344.*

Patronage, "justice to all"—In regard to the patronage sought with so much earnestness and jealousy, I have prescribed for myself the maxim, "Justice to all"; and I earnestly beseech your co-operation in keeping the maxim good.—*To W. H. Seward, Dec. 8, 1860.* VI, 77.

2.—As to the matter of dispensing patronage, it perhaps will surprise you to learn that I have information that you claim to have my authority to arrange that matter in New York. I do not believe that you have so claimed; but still so some men say. On that subject you know all I have said is, "Justice to all," and I have said nothing more particular to anyone.—*To Thurlow Weed, Feb. 4, 1861.* VI, 104.

Patronage, localities "accommodated"—As to the use of patronage in the slave states, where there are few or no Republicans, I do not expect to inquire for the politics of the appointee, or whether he does or does not own slaves. I intend in that matter to accommodate the people in the sevaral localities, if they themselves will allow me to accommodate them.—*To John R. Gilmer, Dec. 15, 1860.* VI, 80.

Patronage, Minnesota men object—I was nearly as sorry as you at not being able to give Mr. Luce the appointment you desired for him. Of course, I could have done it; but it would have been against the united, earnest, and, I add, angry protest of the Republican delegation of Minnesota, in which state the office is located. So far as I understand, it is unprecedented [to] send an officer into a state against the wishes of the members of Congress of that state, and of the same party.—*To J. K. Dubois, March 30, 1861.* Angle, 264.

Patronage, no commitments—I have not promised an office to any man, nor have I, but in a single instance, mentally committed myself to an appointment.—*Interview, Thurlow Weed, Dec., 1860.* Weed, 612.

Patronage, preference due soldiers—Two cases . . . occurring on the same day brought me to reflect more attentively than I had before done, as to what is fairly due from us here in the dispersing of patronage toward the men who, by fighting our battles, bear the chief burden of saving our country. My conclusion is that, other claims and qualifications being equal, they have the better right; and this is especially applicable to the disabled soldier and the deceased soldier's family.—*To Postmaster General Blair, July 24, 1863.* IX, 42.

2.—I shall at all times be ready to recognize the paramount claims of the soldiers of the nation in the disposition of public trusts.—*To Gen. Scott and others, March 1, 1865.* XI, 42.

See UNION TROOPS, consideration due to.

Patronage, qualifications for—I did tell him [Walter Davis] that, if the distribution of the offices should fall into my hands, he should have something. . . . I said this to him, because, as I understand, he is of good character, is one of the young men, is of the mechanics, and always faithful, and never troublesome Whig, and is poor, with the support of a widow mother thrown almost exclusively on him by the death of his brother—If these are wrong reasons, then I have been wrong.—*To W. H. Herndon, Jan. 5, 1849.* Hertz II, 590.

Patronage, resistance to—I am, as you know, opposed to removals to make places for our friends.—*To John T. Stuart, Dec. 17, 1840.* I, 156.

2.—Mr. Holman will not be jostled from his place with my knowledge and consent.—*To Mrs. J. F. Speed, Sept. 16, 1863.* Hertz II, 908.

3.—I dislike to make changes in office as long as they can be avoided. It multiplies my embarrassments immensely.—*To W. Jayne, Feb. 26, 1864.* X, 20.

Patronage, Taylor warned—I suppose Gen. Taylor, because both of his declarations and his inclinations, will not go the doctrine of removals very strongly; and hence the greater reason, when an office or a job is already in Democratic hands, that it should be given to a Whig. Even at this, full half the government patronage will still be in the hands of our opponents at the end of four years; and if still less than this is done for our friends, I think they will have just cause to complain, and I verily believe the administration cannot be sustained.—*To W. B. Preston, April 20, 1849.* Hertz II, 595.

See ADVERTISING, Democrats get too much.

See GENERAL LAND OFFICE, Butterfield not entitled to, 2, 3.

Patronage, troubled by post-office jobs—I have troubles enough; when I last saw you I was having little troubles; they filled my mind full; since then I have big troubles and they can do no more—what do you think has annoyed me more than any one thing? . . . I don't mean affairs forced by events, and which a single man can't do much about, but I mean matters wholly mine to arrange. Now, I will tell you; the fight over two postoffices—one at our Bloomington and the other in Pennsylvania.—*To Henry C. Whitney, July 26, 1861.* War Years I, 310.

Patronage, would welcome vacancy—If it be true, as I have been informed, that the office is of no pecuniary consequence to you, it would be quite a relief to me to have it at my disposal.—*To John Z. Goodrich, March 13, 1865.* XI, 54.

Paymasters, warned—Please say to these gentlemen [army paymasters] that if they do not work quickly, I will make quick work with them.—*To Gov. Andrews, Aug. 12, 1862.* Hertz II, 876.

Payments, easy and otherwise—*See* EMANCIPATION, financial aspects of compensated, 7.

Peace, by negotiation impossible—On careful consideration of all the evidence accessible it seems to me that no attempt at negotiation with the insurgent leader could result in any good. He would accept nothing short of severance of the Union, precisely what we will not and cannot give. His declarations to that effect are explicit and oft-repeated. He does not attempt to deceive us. He affords us no excuse to deceive ourselves. He cannot voluntarily reaccept the Union; we cannot voluntarily yield it. Between him and us the issue is distinct, simple and inflexible.—*Fourth annual message, Dec. 6, 1864.* X, 307.

2.—It is an issue which can only be tried by war, and decided by victory. If we yield, we are beaten; if the southern people fail him [the enemy] he is beaten.—*Fourth annual message, Dec. 6, 1864.* X, 308.

Peace, conditions essential to—[You write:] "On the 25th of November last I was advised . . . that the southern states would send representatives to the next Congress, provided that a full and general amnesty should permit them to do so. . . ." I strongly suspect your information will prove to be groundless; nevertheless, I thank you for communicating it to me. Understanding that the phrase . . . "the southern states would send representatives to the next Congress"—to be substantially the same as that "the people of the southern states would cease resistance, and would reinaugurate, submit to, and maintain the national authority within the limits of such states under the Constitution of the United States," I say that in such case the war would cease on the part of the United States; and that if within a reasonable time "a full and general amnesty" were necessary to such an end, it would not be withheld.—*To Fernando Wood, Dec. 12, 1862.* VIII, 142.

2.—We can make no overtures to the rebels. If they want peace, all they have to do is to lay down their arms.—*To James R. Gilmore, late May, 1863.* Gilmore, 150.

3.—Let Rosecrans tell him [Jaquess] that we shall be liberal on collateral points; that the country will do everything for safety, nothing for revenge.—*To James R. Gilmore, late May, 1863.* Gilmore, 158.

4.—My views are, peace on any terms consistent with the abolition of slavery and the restoration of the Union.—*To James R. Gilmore, late May, 1863.* Gilmore, 158.

5.—There are but three conceivable ways [to attain peace]; first, to suppress the rebellion by force of arms. This I am trying to do. Are you for it? If you are, so far we are agreed. If you are not for it, a second way is to give up the Union. I am against this. Are you for it? If you are, you should say so plainly. If you are not for force, nor yet for dissolution, there only remains some imaginable compromise. I do not believe any compromise embracing the maintenance of the Union is now possible.—*To James C. Conkling, Aug. 26, 1863.* IX, 96.

6.—Any offer of terms made by any man or men within that range [of the Confederate Army's control], in opposition to that army, is simply nothing for the present, because such man or men have no power whatever to enforce their side of a compromise, if one were made with them.—*To J. C. Conkling, Aug. 26, 1863.* IX, 96.

7.—A compromise [for peace], to be effective, must be made either with those who control the rebel army, or with the people first liberated from the domination of that army by the success of our own army.—*To J. C. Conkling, Aug. 26, 1863.* IX, 97.

8.—If you can find any person, anywhere, professing to have any proposition of Jefferson Davis in writing, for peace, embracing the restoration of the Union and abandonment of slavery, whatever else it embraces, say to him he may come to me with you; and that if he really brings such proposition, he shall at the least have safe conduct with the paper—and without publicity, if he chooses—to the point where you shall have met him. The same, if there be two or more persons.—*To Horace Greeley, July 9, 1864.* X, 154.

9.—Any proposition which embraces the restoration of peace, the integrity of the whole Union and the abandonment of slavery, which comes by and with an authority that can control the armies now at war against the United States, will be received and considered by the executive government of the United States, and will be met by liberal terms on other substantial and collateral points.—*Executive announcement, July 18, 1864.* X, 161.

10.—To me it seems plain that saying reunion and abandonment of slavery would be considered, if offered, is not saying that nothing else or less would be considered, if offered.—*Unfinished letter to Charles D. Robinson, Aug. 17, 1864.* X, 194.

11.—No one, having control of the rebel armies, or, in fact, having any influence whatever in the rebellion, has offered, or intimated, a willingness to a restoration of the Union, in any event, or on any condition whatever.—*Unfinished letter to Charles D. Robinson, Aug. 17, 1864.* X, 196.

12.—Shall we be weak enough to allow the enemy to distract us with an abstract question which he himself refuses to present as a practical one?—*Unfinished letter to Charles D. Robinson, Aug. 17, 1864.* X, 197.

13.—You will proceed forthwith and obtain, if possible, a conference for peace with Hon. Jefferson Davis, or any person by him authorized for that purpose. You will address him in entirely respectful terms, at all events, and in any that may be indispensable to secure the conference. At said conference you will propose, on behalf of this government, that upon the restoration of the Union and the national authority, the war shall cease at once, all remaining questions to be left for adjustment by peaceful modes. If this be accepted, hostilities to cease at once. If it be not accepted, you will then request to be informed what terms, if any, embracing restoration of the Union would be accepted. If any such be presented to you in answer, you will forthwith report the same to this government, and await further instructions. If the presentation of any terms embracing the restoration of the Union be declined, you will then request to be informed what terms of peace would be accepted; and, on receiving any answer, report the same to this government, and await further instructions.—*Draft of letter (never sent) to Henry J. Raymond, Aug. 24, 1864.* X, 204.

14.—I am as yet unprepared to give up the Union for a peace which, so achieved, could not be of much duration.—*Unfinished letter to Isaac M. Schermerhorn, Sept. 12, 1864.* X, 220.

15.—What is true . . . of him who heads the insurgent cause is not necessarily true of those who follow. Although he cannot reaccept the Union, they can. Some of them, we know, already desire peace and reunion. The number of such may increase. They can at any moment have peace simply by laying down their arms and submitting to the national authority under the Constitution. After so much the government could not, if it would, maintain war against them. The loyal people would not sustain or allow it. If questions should remain, we would adjust them by the peaceful means of legislation, conference, courts and votes, operating only in constitutional and lawful channels.—*Fourth annual message, Dec. 6, 1864.* X, 308.

16.—Stating a single condition of peace, I mean simply to say that the war will cease on the part of the government whenever it shall have ceased on the part of those who began it.—*Fourth annual message, Dec. 6, 1864.* X, 310.

17.—You may say to him [Jefferson Davis] that I have constantly been, am now, and shall continue, ready to receive any agent whom he or any other influential person now resisting the national authority may informally send to me with the view of securing peace to the people of our common country.—*To F. P. Blair, Jan. 18, 1865.* X, 342.

18.—Three things are indispensable [to peace], to wit: 1, The restoration of the national authority throughout all the states; 2, No receding by the Executive of the United States on the slavery question from the position assumed thereon in the late annual message to Congress and in preceding documents; 3, No cessation of hostilities short of an end of the war and the disbanding of all forces hostile to the government.—*To Sec. Seward, Jan. 31, 1865.* X, 351.

Identical terms repeated in unsigned memorandum given to J. A. Campbell, April 5, 1865. XI, 72.

Again repeated in memorandum, April 13, 1865. Hertz II, 967.

19.—If there be any who are ready for these indispensable terms . . . on any conditions whatever, let them say so, and state their conditions, so that the conditions can be known and considered.—*Unsigned memorandum given J. A. Campbell, April 5, 1865.* XI, 72.

Peace, devotion to—The man does not live who is more devoted to peace than I am, none who would do more to preserve it, but it may be necessary to put the foot down firmly.—*Speech, New Jersey Assembly, Feb. 21, 1861.* VI, 154.

2.—I hope no one of the [Society of] Friends who originally settled here, or who lived here since that time, or who live here now, have been or is a more devoted lover of peace, harmony and concord than my humble self.—*Speech, reply to Gov. Curtin, Harrisburg, Pa., Feb. 22, 1861.* VI, 161.

3.—I am extremely anxious to see these sectional troubles settled peaceably and satisfactorily to all concerned. To accomplish that, I am willing to make almost any sacrifice, and do anything in reason consistent with my sense of duty.—*To Congressman Boteler, March 3, 1861.* War Years I, 118.

4.—Now and ever I shall do all in my power for peace, consistently with the maintenance of the government.—*Reply to Gov. Hicks and Mayor Brown, April 20, 1861.* VI, 251.

5.—Engaged as I am in a great war, I fear it will be difficult for the world to understand how fully I appreciate the principles of peace inculcated in this letter and everywhere by the Society of Friends. —*To Dr. Samuel Boyd Tobey, March 19, 1862.* VII. 136.

6.—I want peace; I want to stop this terrible waste of

life and property.—*To James R. Gilmore, late May, 1863.* Gilmore, 157.

7.—I not only intend a serious effort for peace, but I intend that you shall be a personal witness that it is made.—*To Horace Greeley, July 15, 1864.* X, 159.

8.—No man desires peace more ardently than I.—*Unfinished letter to Isaac M. Schermerhorn, Sept. 12, 1864.* X, 220.

See FRIENDS, Society of, given pledge of peace.

Peace, great lesson of—*See* WAR, folly of beginning.

Peace, South cherishes—The peace of the nation is as dear to them [people of the South] as to us. In memories of the past and hopes of the future, they share as largely as we.—*Speech, Peoria, Oct. 16, 1854.* II, 241.

Pear Tree, watching—*See* NEGRO TROOPS, importance of, 17.

Pearce, James A.—*See* COMPROMISE OF 1850, Clay led in, 2.

Peculation, only way to expose—Long experience has shown that nothing short of an actual demand of the money will expose an adroit peculator. Ask him for reports, and he will give them to your heart's content; send agents to examine and count the money in his hands, and he will borrow of a friend, merely to be counted and then returned, a sufficient sum to make the sum square. Try what you will, it will all wait till you demand the money; then and not till then, the truth will come.—*Speech, Springfield, Dec. 20, 1839.* I, 118.

Peddler's Pantaloons—*See* FREE SOIL PARTY, slavery extension sole concern of.

Penitence, sole requirement for pardon—*See* AMNESTY, penitence alone essential.

Pennsylvania, best security for—The best possible security for Pennsylvania is putting the strongest force possible into the enemy's rear.—*To Gov. Curtin, Sept. 12, 1862.* VIII, 26.

Pennsylvania, no invasion foreseen—I hope I am not less anxious to do my duty to Pennsylvania than yourself, but I really do not yet see the justification for incurring the trouble and expense of calling out the militia. Our forces are exactly between the enemy and Pennsylvania.—*To Gov. Curtin, May 2, 1863.* VIII, 261.

2.—As bearing on the question of your coming home, I do not think the raid in Pennsylvania amounts to anything at all.—*To Mrs. Lincoln, June 16, 1863.* VIII, 322.

3.—I think there is not much danger of a raid into Pennsylvania.—*To Gov. Curtin, Oct. 17, 1864.* X, 243.

Pennsylvania, thanked—I thank your great commonwealth for the overwhelming support it recently gave, not me personally, but the cause which I think a just one, in the late election.—*Speech to Pennsylvania Legislature, Feb. 22, 1861.* VI, 162.

Pensions, "diligently administered"—The liberal provisions made by Congress for paying pensions to invalid soldiers and sailors of the Republic and to the widows, orphans and dependent mothers of those who have fallen in battle or died of disease contracted or of wounds received in the service of their country have been diligently administered.—*Fourth annual message, Dec. 6, 1864.* X, 301.

Pensions, purge recommended—There is reason to believe that many who are now upon the pension rolls and are in receipt of the bounty of the government are in the ranks of the insurgent army or giving them aid and comfort. . . . I recommend that Congress authorize that office [secretary of the interior] to cause the names of such persons to be stricken from the pension rolls.—*First annual message, Dec. 3, 1861.* VII, 45.

Pensions, Revolutionary War—[The estimated economy of a national bank over a subtreasury system] is sufficient to pay the pensions of more than 4,000 Revolutionary soldiers, or to purchase a 40-acre tract of government land for each of more than 8,000 poor families.—*Speech, Springfield, Dec. 20, 1839.* I, 111.

People, alone can reverse their decisions—The people themselves, and not their servants, can safely reverse their own deliberate decisions.—*Message to Congress, July 4, 1861.* VI, 324.

People, attached to government—*See* LAW, respect for, 2.

People, Civil War their contest—This is essentially a people's contest. . . . I am most happy to believe that the plain people understand and appreciate this. . . . They understand without an argument that the destroying the government which was made by Washington means no good to them.—*Message to Congress, July 4, 1861.* VI, 321.

People, devoted to Union—Had the [presidential] election fallen to any other of the distinguished candidates instead of me, under the peculiar circumstances, to say the least, it would have been proper for all citizens to have greeted him as you now greet me. It is an evidence of the devotion of the whole people to the Constitution, the Union, and the perpetuity of the liberties of this country.—*Speech, Buffalo, Feb. 16, 1861.* VI, 133.

2.—. . . in testimony of the universal, unanimous devotion of the whole people to the Constitution, the Union, and to the perpetual liberties of the succeeding generations in this country.—*Speech, reply to governor, Albany, Feb. 18, 1861.* VI, 139.

3.—For the great principles of our government the people are nearly or quite unanimous.—*Speech, reply to mayor, New York, Feb. 20, 1861.* VI, 149.

4.—. . . gentlemen . . . united by the single purpose to perpetuate the Constitution, the Union, and the liberties of the people.—*Speech, New Jersey Senate, Feb. 21, 1861.* VI, 152.

5.—The public purpose to re-establish and maintain the national authority is unchanged, and, as we believe, unchangeable.—*Fourth annual message, Dec. 6, 1864.* X, 307.

See PEOPLE, relied on to save Union.

People, "do well if done well by"—I think very much of the people as an old friend said he thought of women. He said when he lost his first wife, who had been a great help to him in business, he thought he was ruined, that he could never find another to fill her place. At length, however, he married another, who he found did quite as well as the first, and his opinion now was that any woman would do well who was well done by. So I think of the whole people of this nation; they will ever do well if well done by. We will try to do well by them in all parts of the country, North and South, with entire confidence that all will be well with all of us.—*Speech, Bloomington, Nov. 21, 1860.* Hertz II, 793.

People, Douglas's attitude toward—Judge Douglas, alluding to the death of Gen. Taylor, says it was the hand of Providence which saved us from our first and only military administration. This reminds me of Douglas's so much wanted confidence in the people. The people had elected Gen. Taylor; and, as is appointed to all men once to do, he dies. Douglas chooses to consider this a special interference of Providence, against the people, and in favor of Locofocoism. After all, his confidence in the people seems to go no farther than this, that they may be safely trusted with their own affairs, provided Providence retains and exercises a sort of veto upon their act, whenever they fall into the "marvelous hallucination," as the judge calls it, of electing some one to office contrary to the dictation of a Democratic convention.—*Speech, Springfield, Aug. 26, 1852.* Angle, 102.

People, fooling—You can fool all the people some of the time and some of the people all of the time, but you can't fool all of the people all of the time.—*Speech, Clinton, Sept. 8, 1858.* III, 349.

People, government of, by, for—*See* SELF-GOVERNMENT, resolution to perpetuate.

People, "influenced by reason"—Our people are easily influenced by reason. They have determined to prosecute this matter with energy but with the most temperate spirit. You are entirely safe from lawless invasion.—*To visitors from Baltimore, April 19, 1861.* Hay, 4.

People, issue of compromise in their hands—This thing [the issue of compromise] will hereafter be, as it now is, in the hands of the people; if they desire to call a convention to remove any grievance complained of [by the South] or to give guarantees of permanence of vested rights, it is not mine to oppose. —*To editors Chicago Tribune, Jan., 1861.* Tribune, I, 171.

People, justice of—Why should there not be a patient confidence in the ultimate justice of the people; Is there any better or equal hope in the world? In our present differences, is either party without faith of being in the right? If the Almighty Ruler of nations, with His eternal truth and justice, be on your side of the North, or on yours of the South, that truth and that justice will surely prevail by the judgment of this great tribunal of the American people.—*First inaugural, March 4, 1861.* VI, 183.

People, know their rights—The people know their rights, and they are never slow to assert and maintain them, when they are invaded.—*Speech, Springfield, Jan., 1837.* I, 26.

People, masters in America—To us [Whigs] it appears like principle, and the best sort of principle at that,—the principle of allowing the people to do as they please with their own business.—*Speech in Congress, July 27, 1848.* II, 64.

2.—In leaving the people's business in their own hands, we cannot be wrong.—*Speech in Congress, July 27, 1848.* II, 69.

3.—Wisdom and patriotism, in a public office, under institutions like ours, are wholly inefficient and worthless, unless they are sustained by the confidence and devotion of the people.—*Speech, Chicago, July 25, 1850.* Angle, 74.

4.—If the people remain right your public men can never betray you. . . . Cultivate and protect that sentiment [that the principles of liberty are eternal], and your ambitious leaders will be reduced to the position of servants instead of masters.—*Speech, Lawrenceburg, Ind., Feb. 11, 1861.* Hertz II, 806.

5.—This country, with its institutions, belongs to the people who inhabit it. Whenever they shall grow weary of the existing government, they can exercise their constitutional right of amending it or their revolutionary right to dismember or overthrow it.—*First inaugural, March 4, 1861.* VI, 182.

6.—The people of these United States are the rightful masters of both congresses and courts, not to overthrow the Constitution, but to overthrow the men who pervert the Constitution.—*Speech, Cincinnati, Sept. 17, 1859.* V, 232.

7.—Their [the people's] will, constitutionally expressed, is the ultimate law for all. If they should deliberately resolve to have immediate peace, even at the loss of their country and their liberty, I know not the power or the right to resist them. It is their own business, and they must do as they please with their own. I believe, however, they are still resolved to preserve their country and their liberty; and in this, in office or out of it, I am resolved to stand by them.—*Response to serenade, Oct. 19, 1864.* X, 244.

See UNION, inviolability of, 6.

People, much alike—Our down East friends did, indeed, treat me with great kindness, demonstrating what I before believed, that all good, intelligent people are very much alike.—*To William Gooding, April 6, 1860.* Hertz II, 771.

People, opposed to violence—The opposition politicians are so blinded with rage seeing themselves unable to control the politics of the government that they may be able to manage the Chicago [Democratic national] convention for some violent end, but they cannot transfer the people, the honest though misguided masses, to the same course.—*To John Hay, June 17, 1864.* Hay, 193.

People, patriotic instinct of—*See* UNION TROOPS, tributes to, 2.

People, President and—If I, in my brief connection with public affairs, shall be wicked or foolish, and if you remain true and honest, you cannot be betrayed. My power is temporary; yours as eternal as the principles of liberty.—*Speech, Lawrenceburg, Ind., Feb. 11, 1861.* Hertz, II, 806.

2.—If I adopt a wrong policy, the opportunity for condemnation will occur in four years' time. Then I can be turned out, and a better man with better views put in my place.—*Speech, Steubenville, Ohio, Feb. 14, 1861.* VI, 123.

3.—The chief magistrate derives all his authority from the people, and they have conferred none upon him to fix terms for the separation of the states. The people themselves can do this also if they choose; but the Executive, as such, has nothing to do with it.—*First inaugural, March 4, 1861.* VI, 183.

4.—By the frame of the government under which we live this same people have wisely given their public servants but little power for mischief, and have with equal wisdom provided for a return of that little to their own hands at very short intervals. While the people retain their virtue and vigilance no administration by any extreme of wickedness or folly can very seriously injure the government in the short space of four years.—*First inaugural, March 4, 1861.* VI, 183.

5.—I am, you know, only the servant of the people. —*To James R. Gilmore, April 13, 1861.* Gilmore, 19.

6.—In justice to myself you must remember that Abraham Lincoln is President of the United States. Anything that the President of the United States does, right or wrong, will be the act of Abraham Lincoln, and Abraham Lincoln will, by the people, be held responsible for the President's action.—*To N. F. Dixon, June 28, 1862.* Hertz II, 870.

7.—I know very well that many others might in this matter [issuance of the preliminary Emancipation Proclamation], as in others, do better than I can; and if I was satisfied that the public confidence was more fully possessed by any one of them than by me, and knew any constitutional way in which he could be put in my place, he should have it. I would gladly yield to him. But, though I believe that I have not so much of the confidence of the people as I had some time since, I do not know that, all things considered, any other person has more; and however this may be, there is no way in which I can have any other man put where I am. I am here; I must do the best I can, and bear the responsibility of taking the course which I feel I ought to take.—*To cabinet, Sept. 22, 1862.* Hertz II, 882.

8.—I freely acknowledge myself the servant of the people according to the bond of service—the United States Constitution—and that, as such, I am responsible to them.—*To James C. Conkling, Aug. 26, 1863.* IX, 97.

9.—If he [the President] uses the power [to suspend habeas corpus] the same people will probably justify him; if he abuses it, he is in their hands to be dealt with by all the modes they have reserved to themselves in the Constitution.—*To M. Birchard and others, June 29, 1863.* IX, 4.

See UNION, inviolability of, 6.

People, relied on to save Union—I am pleased to have the assurance that in the event of trouble or danger, you and others are ready to give both your lives and your fortunes for the defense and maintenance of the government and the Union.—*To Peter Page, Jan. 21, 1861.* Hertz II, 802.

2.—I wish you to remember, now and forever, that it is your business, and not mine; that if the union of these states and the liberties of this people shall be lost, it is but little to any one man of 52 years of age, but a great deal to the thirty millions of people who inhabit these United States, and to their posterity in all coming time. It is your business to rise up and preserve the Union and liberty for yourselves, and not for me.—*Speech, Indianapolis, Feb. 11, 1861.* VI, 111.

3.—In all trying positions in which I shall be placed —and doubtless I shall be placed in many such, my reliance will be placed upon you and the people of the United States.—*Speech, Indianapolis, Feb. 11, 1861.* VI, 111.

4.—I appeal to you to constantly bear in mind that not with Presidents, not with office-seekers, but with you is the question Shall the Union, shall the liberties of this country, be preserved to the latest generations.—*Speech, Indianapolis, Feb. 11, 1861.* VI, 112.

5.—We are bound together in Christianity, civilization, and patriotism and our attachment to our country and our whole country. While some of us may differ in political opinions, still we are all united in one feeling for the Union. We all believe in the maintenance of the Union, of every star and stripe of the glorious flag.—*Speech, Lafayette, Ind., Feb. 11, 1861.* Hertz II, 805.

6.—Encompassed by vast difficulties as I am, nothing shall be wanting on my part, if sustained by God and the American people.—*Speech, Steubenville, Ohio, Feb. 14, 1861.* VI, 123.

7.—It is, fellow-citizens, for the whole American people, and not for one single man alone, to advance the great cause of the Union and the Constitution. And in a country like this, where every man bears on his face the marks of intelligence, where every man's clothing, if I may so speak, shows signs of comfort, and every dwelling signs of happiness and contentment, where schools and churches abound on every side, the Union can never be in danger.—*Speech, Cleveland, Feb. 15, 1861.* VI, 130.

8.—It [this reception] is an evidence of the devotion of the whole people to the Constitution, the Union, and the perpetuity of the liberties of this country.—*Speech, Buffalo, Feb. 16, 1861.* VI, 133.

9.—Allow me to say that you, as a portion of the great American people, need only to maintain your composure, stand up to your sober convictions, and act in accordance with those convictions, and the clouds now on the horizon will be dispelled.—*Speech, Buffalo, Feb. 16, 1861.* VI, 134.

10.—This reception . . . indicates an earnest desire on the part of the whole people, without regard to political differences, to save—not the country, because the country will save itself—but to save the institutions under which, in the last three-quarters of a century, we have grown to be a great, an intelligent, and a happy people—the greatest, the most intelligent, and the happiest people in the world.—*Speech, Poughkeepsie, N.Y., Feb. 19, 1861.* VI, 143.

11.—If, as it ever must be, some have been successful in the recent election, and some have been beaten, if some are satisfied and some are dissatisfied, the defeated party are not in favor of sinking the ship, but are desirous of running it through the tempest in safety.—*Speech, Poughkeepsie, N.Y., Feb. 19, 1861.* VI, 143.

12.—With their sustaining aid, even I, humble as I am, cannot fail to carry the Ship of State through the storm.—*Speech, Poughkeepsie, N.Y., Feb. 19, 1861.* VI, 144.

13.—I do say that in accepting the great trust entrusted to me, which I do with a determination to endeavor to prove worthy of it, I must rely upon you, upon the people of the whole country, for support. —*Speech, Poughkeepsie, N.Y., Feb. 19, 1861.* VI, 144.

14.—I trust that in the course I shall pursue I shall be sustained not only by the party that elected me, but by the patriotic people of the whole country.— *Speech, Peekskill, N.Y., Feb. 19, 1861.* VI, 145.

15.—I will say in a single sentence, in regard to the difficulties that lie before me and our beloved country, that if I can only be as generously and unanimously sustained as the demonstrations I have witnessed indicate I shall be, I shall not fail; but without your sustaining hands I am sure that neither I nor any other man can hope to surmount those difficulties.—*Speech, Peekskill, N.Y., Feb. 19, 1861.* VI, 145.

16.—For the great principles of our government the people are pretty nearly or quite unanimous.— *Speech, New York, Feb. 20, 1861.* VI, 149.

17.—I feel that, under God, in the strength of the arms and wisdom of the heads of these masses, after all, must be my support.—*Speech, reply to Gov. Curtin, Harrisburg, Feb. 22, 1861.* VI, 160.

18.—If my own strength should fail, I shall at least fall back on these masses, who, I think, under any circumstances will not fail.—*Speech, reply to Gov. Curtin, Harrisburg, Feb. 22, 1861.* VI, 161.

19.—In the whole transaction [of flag raising] I was in the hands of the people who had arranged it, and if I can have the same generous cooperation of the people of this nation, I think the flag of our country may yet be kept floating gloriously.—*Speech to Pennsylvania Legislature, Feb. 22, 1861.* VI, 162.

20.—The people will save their government if the government itself will do its part only indifferently well.—*Message to Congress, July 4, 1861.* VI, 312.

21.—The integrity of our country and the stability of our government mainly depend . . . on the loyalty, virtue, patriotism, and intelligence of the American people.—*First annual message, Dec. 3, 1861.* VII, 30.

22.—Your colonel has thought fit, on his own account and in your name, to say that you are satisfied with the manner in which I have performed my part in the difficulties which have surrounded the nation. . . . I assure you that the nation is more indebted to you, and such as you, than to me. It is upon the brave hearts and strong arms of the people of the country that our reliance has been placed in support of free government and free institutions.—*Speech to 12th Indiana regiment, reported in New York* Evening Post, *May 15, 1862.* VII, 164.

23.—I cannot but congratulate you and the country . . . upon the spectacle of devoted unanimity presented by the people at home, the citizens that form our marching columns, and the citizens that fill our squadrons on the sea, all animated by the same determination to complete the work our fathers began and transmitted. The work of the Plymouth emigrants was the glory of their age. While we reverence their memory, let us not forget how vastly greater is our opportunity.—*To Joseph H. Choate, Dec. 19, 1864.* X, 319.

See CONVICTIONS, stand up to, and clouds will pass.

See "KEEP COOL," safest course, 3.

See PEOPLE, devoted to Union.

See WASHINGTON, GEORGE, task greater than that of.

People, responsibility to—We should do neither more nor less than we gave the people reason to believe we would when they gave us their votes.—*Speech, Pittsburgh, Feb. 15, 1861.* VI, 126.

People set the pace—*See* UNION, policy in saving, 4.

People should rule on District emancipation—*See* EMANCIPATION, District of Columbia, 1, 4.

People, voice of—*See* THIRTEENTH AMENDMENT, favorable action on, urged, 3.

Perjury—*See* FREEPORT DOCTRINE, fallacy of, 8.

"Pernicious Abstraction"—*See* RECONSTRUCTION, policy in, 5.

Persuasion, rule for successful—When the conduct of men is designed to be influenced, persuasion, kind, unassuming persuasion, should ever be adopted. It is an old and true maxim "that a drop of honey catches more flies than a gallon of gall." So with men. If you would win a man to your cause, first convince him that you are his sincere friend. Therein is a drop of honey that catches his heart, which, say what he will, is the great high-road to his reason, and which, when once gained, you will find but little trouble in convincing his judgment of the justice of your cause, if indeed that cause really is a good one.—*Speech, Springfield, Feb. 22, 1842.* I, 197.

Perthshire, British ship—I invite your attention to the correspondence between Her Britannic Majesty's minister accredited to this government and the secretary of state relative to the detention of the British ship *Perthshire* in June last by the United States Steamer *Massachusetts* for a supposed breach of the blockade. As this detention was occasioned by an obvious misapprehension of the facts, and as justice requires that we should commit no belligerent act not founded in strict right as sanctioned by public law, I recommend that an appropriation be made to satisfy the reasonable demand of the owners of the vessel for her detention.—*First annual message, Dec. 3, 1861.* VII, 32.

Peru, friendship with—You may be assured, sir, that in all things this government will deal justly, frankly, and, if it be possible, even liberally with Peru.—*To Peruvian minister, March 4, 1862.* Lapsley V, 439.

2.—An earnest and cordial friendship continues to exist between the two countries [United States and Peru] and such efforts as were in my power have been used to remove misunderstanding and avert a threatened war between Peru and Spain.—*Fourth annual message, Dec. 6, 1864.* X, 284.

Peter, Simon—*See* NOMINATION OF 1860, attitude toward, 8.

Petersburg, Va., evacuation of—*See* RICHMOND, evacuation of.

Pettit, John, critic of Declaration—*See* DECLARATION OF INDEPENDENCE, hostility toward, 2, 3, 5, 9, 11.

Pharisees, avoid being like—We must remember that the people of all the states are entitled to all the privileges and immunities of the citizens of the several states. We should bear this in mind, and act in such a way as to say nothing insulting or irritating. I would inculcate this idea, so that we may not, like Pharisees, set ourselves up to be better than other people.—*Reply to Pennsylvania delegation, March 5, 1861.* XII, 117.

Phelps, John S., tribute to—Mr. Phelps is too zealous and efficient and understands his ground too well for us to lose his services.—*To Sec. Cameron, Aug. 7, 1861.* VI, 340.

Philosophy, election incidents as—See HUMAN NATURE, shown in elections.

Philosophy, false—See SLAVERY, silence will not check, 2.

Phonetic Writing, difficult of conception and execution—[That] the invention of phonetic writing, as distinguished from the clumsy picture-writing of some of the nations . . . was difficult of conception and execution is apparent . . . by the . . . fact that so many tribes of men have come down from Adam's time to our own without ever having possessed it. Its utility may be conceived by the reflection that to it we owe everything which distinguishes us from savages. Take it from us, and the Bible, all history, all science, all government, all commerce, and nearly all social intercourse go with it.—*Speech, Springfield, Feb. 22, 1859.* V, 108.

Pickett, George E., advice to—See TRUTH, prudence and.

Pierce, Franklin—*See also* SLAVERY, conspiracy to promote, 5,9.

Pierce, Franklin, adopts "state equality"—See "STATE EQUALITY," not yet approved.

Pierce, Franklin, "arguments" for—It soon came to light that the first thing ever urged in his favor as a candidate was his having given a strange boy a cent to buy candy with. . . . Forthwith also appears a biographical sketch of him, in which he is represented at the age of seventeen, to have spelled "but" for his father, who was unable to spell it for himself.—By the way, I do wish Frank had not been present on that trying occasion. I have a great curiosity to know how "old dad" would have spelled that difficult word, if he had been left entirely to himself.—*Speech, Springfield, Aug. 26, 1852.* Angle 99.

Pierce, Franklin, cat's paw—The President [Pierce] thinks the great body of us Frémonters, being ardently attached to liberty, in the abstract, were duped by a few wicked and designing men. . . . We think he, being ardently attached to the hope of a second term, in the concrete, was duped by men who had

liberty every way. He is the cat's-paw. By much dragging of chestnuts from the fire for others to eat, his claws are burnt off to the gristle, and he is thrown aside as unfit for further use.—*Speech, Chicago, Dec. 10, 1856.* II, 309.

Pierce, Franklin, falsehood charged against—So far as the President [Pierce] charges us [antislavery] men "with a desire to change the domestic institutions of existing states," and of "doing everything in our power to deprive the Constitution and the laws of normal authority," for the whole [Republican] party on belief, and for myself on knowledge, I pronounce the charge an unmixed and unmitigated falsehood.—*Speech, Chicago, Dec. 10, 1856.* II, 309.

Pierce, Franklin, fugitive-slave law and—The indispensable necessity with the Democrats of getting these New York Free Soil votes, to my mind, explains why they nominated a man [for President] who "loathes the fugitive-slave law." In December or January last, Gen. Pierce made a speech in which, according to two newspaper reports, published at the time in his vicinity and never questioned by him or anyone else till after the nomination, he publicly declared his loathing of the slave law. Now we shall allow ourselves to be very green, if we conclude the Democratic convention did not know of this when they nominated him. On the contrary, his supposed efficacy to win Free Soil votes was the very thing that secured his nomination. His southern allies will continue to bluster and pretend to disbelieve the report, but they would not, for any consideration, have him to contradict it. And he will not contradict it—mark me, he will not contradict it.—*Speech, Springfield, Aug. 26, 1852.* Angle, 109.

Pierce, Franklin, "ludicrous" attempt to boost—Gen. Pierce's history being as it is, the attempt to set him up as a great general is simply ludicrous and laughable.—*Speech, Springfield, Aug. 14, 1852.* Angle, 86.

Pierce, Franklin, only chance of, for Presidency—Why, Pierce's only chance for the Presidency is to be born into it, as a cross between New York and hunkerism, the latter predominating in the offspring.—*Speech, Springfield, Aug. 26, 1852.* Angle, 110.

Pierce, Franklin, plodding partisan—Gen. Pierce has been in the state legislature and in Congress; and I misread his history if it does not show him to have had just sufficient capacity, and no more, of setting his foot down in the track, as his partisan leader lifted his out of it, and so trudging along in the party train without a single original thought or independent action.—*Speech, Springfield, Aug. 26, 1852.* Angle, 98.

Pierce, Franklin, "shelled peascod"—As the fool said to King Lear, when his daughters had turned him out of doors, "He's a shelled peascod."—*Speech, Chicago, Dec. 10, 1856.* II, 309.

Pierce, Franklin, Winfield Scott and—Scott, on the contrary [in contrast with Pierce], has on many occasions been placed in the lead, when originality of thought and independence of action, both of the highest order, have been indispensable to success; and yet he failed in none. What he has performed in these stations bears much stronger resemblance to the duties he would have to perform as President than anything Gen. Pierce has ever done. Indeed, they were literally, in every instance, executive duties—functions delegated to Gen. Scott by the President, because the President could not perform them in person.—*Speech, Springfield, Aug. 26 1852.* Angle, 98.
2.—Let it be alike forgotten that Gen. Pierce ever fainted, or that Gen. Scott ever made a "fuss" or wore a "feather." Let them be placed in the scales solely on what they have done alone, giving evidence of capacity for civil administration; and let him kick the beam who is found lightest.—*Speech, Springfield, Aug. 26, 1852.* Angle, 99.

See CAMPAIGN OF 1852, Democrats' do-nothing platform.

Pierpoint, Frank, appreciation of—Gov. Pierpoint is a good man.—*To Gen. J. G. Foster, Aug. 8, 1863.* IX, 63.
2.—I must tell you I have no less confidence in those [loyalty and patriotism] of Gov. Pierpoint and the attorney-general. The former at first as the loyal governor of Virginia, including that which is now West Virginia, in organizing and furnishing troops, and in all other proper matters—was as earnest, honest, and efficient to the extent of his means as any other loyal governor.—*To Gen. Butler, Aug. 9, 1864 (but not sent until Dec. 21).* X, 321.

Pilgrims, our opportunities greater—*See* PEOPLE, relied on to save Union, 23.

"Pill of Sectionalism"—*See* SECTIONALISM, Douglas guilty of, 3.

Pinched Toes—Ready are we all to cry out and ascribe motives when our own toes are pinched.—*To Gen. Rosecrans, March 17, 1863.* VIII, 228.

Piracy, defense against—*See* MERCHANT SHIPS, arming of.

Pitcher, story of, denied—*See* NEW YORK TIMES, correspondent of, "very mad."

Plank, drowning man on—*See* RACIAL AMALGAMATION, opposed to, 3.

Plank, two men on a—If two men are adrift at sea on a plank which will bear up but one, the law justifies either in pushing the other off.—*Speech, Hartford, Conn., March 5, 1860.* V, 332.
2.—If it was like two wrecked seamen on a narrow plank, where each must push the other off or drown himself, I would push the negro off—or a white man either; but it is not: the plank is large enough for both.—*Speech, New Haven, Conn., March 6, 1860.* V, 352.

Platform, declined—I see you have erected a very fine and handsome platform here for me, and I presume you expect me to speak from it. If I should go upon it, you would imagine that I was about to deliver you a much longer speech than I am. . . . I wish you to understand that, though I am unwilling to go upon this platform, you are not at liberty to draw any inferences concerning any other platform with which my name has been or is connected.—*Speech, Syracuse, N.Y., Feb. 18, 1861.* VI, 135.
2.—You have provided a platform, but I shall have to decline standing upon it. The superintendent tells me I have not time during our brief stay to leave the train. I had to decline standing on some very handsome platforms prepared for me yesterday. But I say to you, as I said to them, you must not on this account draw the inference that I have any intention to desert any platform I have a legitimate right to stand on.—*Speech, Hudson, N.Y., Feb. 19, 1861.* VI, 144.

Plato, cited—*See* YOUNG AMERICA, longs for territory.

"Plymouth Emigrants"—*See* PEOPLE, relied on to save Union, 23.

Political Consistency—No party can command respect which sustains this year what it opposed last.—*To Samuel Galloway, July 28, 1859.* V, 136.

Political Freedom, temperance as an ally of—*See* TEMPERANCE, revolution compared with Revolutionary War, 1.

Political Parties, candidates' struggles harmful—It is certain that struggles between candidates do not strengthen a party; but who are most responsible for these struggles, those who are willing to live and let live, or those who are resolved, at all hazards, to take care of "No. 1"?—*To John J. Hardin, Feb. 7, 1846.* Angle, 27.

Political Parties, importance of—A free people in times of peace and quiet—when pressed by no common danger—naturally divide into parties. At such times the man who is of neither party is not, cannot be, of any consequence.—*Speech, Springfield, July 16, 1852.* II, 165.

2.—In this country, and in any country where freedom of thought is tolerated, citizens attach themselves to political parties. It is but an ordinary degree of charity to attribute this act to the supposition that in thus attaching themselves to the various parties, each man in his own judgment supposes he thereby best advances the interests of the whole country.—*Reply to governor, Albany, Feb. 18, 1861.* VI, 138.

Political Parties, not answerable for individual members—No party can be justly held responsible for what individual members of it may say or do.—*To Gov. Gamble, Oct. 19, 1863.* IX, 178.

Political Parties, not strong enough to disturb general peace—There never was a party in the history of this country, and there probably never will be, of sufficient strength to disturb the general peace of the country. Parties themselves may be divided and quarrel on minor questions, yet it extends not beyond the parties themselves.—*Debate, Alton, Oct. 15, 1858.* V, 55.

Political Parties, outsiders no help—I have scarcely known a party preceding an election to call in help from the neighboring states, but they lost the state. . . . Generally, it seems to stir up more enemies than friends.—*To William Grimes, July 12, 1856.* II, 291.

2.—I think too much reliance is placed in noisy demonstrations, importing speakers from a distance and the like. They excite prejudice and close the avenues to sober reason. The "home production" principle in my judgment is the best.—*To Andrew McCollen, June 19, 1858.* Tracy, 85.

Political Parties, power of the lash—The merits of men and measures, therefore, became the subject of discussion in caucus, instead of the halls of legislation, and decisions there made by a minority of the legislature have been executed and carried into effect by the force of party discipline, without any regard whatever to the rights of the people or the interests of the state.—*Whig circular, Feb. 8, 1841.* I, 161.

2.—The party lash and the fear of ridicule will overawe justice and liberty; for it is a singular fact, and well known by the most common experience, that men will do things under the terror of the party lash that they would not on any account or for any consideration do otherwise.—*Speech, Bloomington, May 29, 1856.* Lapsley II, 252.

3.—Judge Douglas introduced his Nebraska bill in January; and we had an extra session of our legislature in the succeeding February, in which were 75 Democrats; and at a party caucus, fully attended, there were just three votes, out of the whole 75, for the measure. But in a few days orders came from Washington, commanding them to approve the measure; the party lash was applied, and it was brought up again in caucus, and passed by a large majority.—*Speech, Bloomington, May 29, 1856.* Lapsley II, 252.

4.—The masses were against it [Kansas-Nebraska bill] but party necessity carried it; and it was passed through the lower house of Congress against the will of the people, for the same reason. Here is where the greatest danger lies—that while we profess to be a government of law and reason, law will give way to violence on demand of this awful crushing power. Like the great Juggernaut—I think that is the name—the great idol, it crushes everything that comes in its way.—*Speech, Bloomington, May 29, 1856.* Lapsley II, 252.

Political Parties, when to forget—When an election is past, it is altogether befitting a free people, as I suppose, that, until the next election, they should be one people.—*Speech, New York, Feb. 18, 1861.* VI, 138.

Political Platforms, candidates and—I am in, and shall go for anyone nominated [for President] unless he be "platformed" expressly, or impliedly, on some ground which I may think wrong.—*To Lyman Trumbull, June 7, 1856.* Lore, June 16, 1941.

2.—I do not deny that there are as good men in the South as the North. . . . For my single self I would be willing to risk some Southern man without a platform; but I am satisfied that is not the case with the Republican party generally.—*To Nathan Sargent, June 23, 1859.* Lore, June 16, 1941.

3.—In the absence of formal written platforms, the antecedents of candidates become their platforms. On just such platforms all our earlier and better Presidents were elected.—*Speeches in Kansas, Dec. 1-5, 1859.* V, 276.

4.—The St. Louis *Intelligencer* is out in favor of a good man for President, to be run without a platform. Well, I am not wedded to the formal written platform system; but a thousand to one the editor is not himself in favor of his plan, except with the qualification that he and his sort are to select and name the "good man." To bring him to a test, is he willing to take Seward without a platform?—*Speeches in Kansas, Dec. 1-5, 1859.* V, 276.

Political Platforms, higher level preferred—See DEMOCRATIC PARTY, attitude of, toward war effort. 1.

Political Platforms, proposals for 1860 rejected—I am not in favor of a party of Union, Constitution and laws to suit Mr. Bell or Mr. Everett, and [to] be construed variously in as many sections as there are states.—*To Alexander H. Stephens, Jan, 19, 1859.* Tracy, 129.

2.—Of course I would be pleased to see all the elements of the opposition [to slavery extension] united for the approaching contest of 1860; but I confess I have not much hope of seeing it. You state a platform for such union in these words: "Opposition to the opening of the slave trade; and eternal hostility to the rotten Democracy". . . . Well, I say such a platform, unanimously adopted by a national convention, with two of the best men living placed upon it as candidates, would probably carry Maryland, and would certainly not carry a single other state. It would gain nothing in the South, and lose everything in the North. Mr. Goggin has just been beaten in Virginia on just such a platform. Last year the Republicans of Illinois cast 125,000 votes; on such a platform as yours they cannot cast as many as 50,000. You could not help perceiving this, if you would but reflect that the Republican party is utterly powerless everywhere, if it will, by any means, drive from it all those who came to it from the Democracy for the sole object of preventing the spread and nationalization of slavery. Whenever this object is waived by the organization, they will drop the organization; and the organization itself will dissolve into thin air. Your platform proposes to allow the spread and nationalization of slavery to proceed without let or hindrance, save only that it shall not receive supplies directly from Africa. . . . If the rotten Democracy shall be beaten in 1860, it has to be done by the North; no human invention can deprive them of the South. I do not deny there are as good men in the South as in the North; and I guess we will elect one of them if he will allow us to do so on Republican ground. I think there can be no other ground of union.—*To Nathan Sargent, June 23, 1859.* Tracy, 111.

3.—I should not care to be a candidate of a party having as its only platform "The Constitution, the Union and the enforcement of the laws." "The Constitution as we understand it" has been the shibboleth of every party or malcontent from the Hartford convention that wanted to secede from slave territory and the "Blue Light" burners who were in British sympathy in 1812, to John C. Calhoun and South Carolina nullification. . . . Its [the Union's] Constitution and laws made in pursuance thereof must and shall remain the "supreme law of the land." The enforcement of what laws? If they are those which give the use of jails and domestic police for

masters seeking "fugitives from labor," that means war in the North.—*To John J. Crittenden, Dec. 22, 1859.* Tracy, 120.

See CAMPAIGN OF 1860, North-South fusion suggested.

Political Speeches, no charge for—It is not true that I ever charged anything for a political speech in my life; but this much is true; last October I was requested by letter to deliver some sort of speech in Mr. Beecher's church in Brooklyn—two hundred dollars being offered in the first letter. I wrote that I could do it in February, provided they would take a political speech if I could find time to get up no other. They agreed; and subsequently I informed them the speech would have to be a political one. When I reached New York, I for the first time learned that the place was changed to Cooper Institute. I made the speech, and left for New Hampshire, where I have a son at school, neither asking for pay, nor having any offered me. Three days after a check for two hundred dollars was sent to me at New Hampshire; and I took it, and did not know it was wrong. My understanding now is—though I knew nothing of it at the time—that they did charge for admittance to the Cooper Institute, and that they took in more than twice two hundred dollars. I have made this explanation to you as a friend; but I wish no explanation made to our enemies. What they want is a squabble and a fuss, and they can have it if we explain; and they cannot have it if we don't. . . . My judgment is, and therefore my request is, that you give no denial and no explanations.—*To C. F. McNeil, April 6, 1860.* VI, 8.

Politicians—*See also* POLITICS.

Politicians, characterized—This work is exclusively the work of politicians; a set of men who have interests aside from the interests of the people, and who, to say the most of them, are, taken as a mass, at least one long step removed from honest men. I say this with the greater freedom because, being a politician myself, none can regard it as personal.—*Speech, Springfield, Jan., 1837.* I, 27.

Politicians, "designing"—*See* CRISIS, artificial, 1.

Politicians, not responsible for slavery agitation—Judge Douglas has intimated . . . that all this difficulty in regard to the institution of slavery is the mere agitation of office seekers and ambitious northern politicians. . . . But is it true that all the difficulty and agitation we have in regard to this institution of slavery springs from office seeking . . . from the mere ambition of politicians? . . . Does not this question make a disturbance outside of political circles? . . . Is it not this same mighty, deep-seated power that somehow operates on the minds of men, exciting and stirring them up in every avenue of society—in politics, in religion, in literature, in morals, and all the manifold relations of life? Is this the work of politicians?—*Debate, Alton, Oct. 15, 1858.* V, 54.

Politicians, sound false alarm—It is the politician who is the first to sound the alarm [against the state bank]—which, by the way, is a false one. It is he who, by these unholy means, is endeavoring to blow up a storm that he may ride upon and direct.—*Speech, Springfield, Jan. 11, 1837.* Basler, 67.

Politics—*See also* POLITICIANS.

Politics, "doing what I can"—As to politics, I am doing what I can for the cause.—*To Albert Parker, Aug. 10, 1858.* Angle, 184.

Politics, money in—I cannot enter the ring [for the 1860 nomination] on the money basis—first, because in the main it is wrong; and secondly, I have not and cannot get the money. I say, in the main, the use of money is wrong; but for certain objects in a political contest, the use of some is both right and indispensable. . . . I now distinctly say this—if you shall be appointed a delegate to Chicago, I will furnish one hundred dollars to bear the expenses of the trip.—*To unnamed correspondent, March 16, 1860.* VI, 5.

Politics, young men in—Now, as to the young men. You must not wait to be brought forward by the older men. For instance, do you suppose that I should have ever got into notice if I had waited to be hunted up and pushed forward by older men? You young men get together and form a "Rough and Ready Club" and have regular meetings and speeches. . . . Let everyone play the part he can play best,—some speak, some sing, and all "holler."—*To W. H. Herndon, June 22, 1848.* II, 49.
2.—A young man before the enemy has learned to watch him, can do more good [in politics] than any other. Pitch in and try.—*To P. Quinn Harrison, Nov. 3, 1859.* Tracy, 119.

Polk, James K., compared to Chancellor Kent—*See* INTERNAL IMPROVEMENTS, Chancellor Kent thought Congress had power.

Polk, James K., "miserably perplexed"—*See* MEXICAN WAR, Polk's attempt to justify, 6.

Polk, James K., war attitude criticized—*See* MEXICAN WAR, Polk's attempt to justify.

See MEXICAN WAR, voting record explained, 1.

Polk, James K., "where Washington sat"—Let him remember he sits where Washington sat and, so remembering, let him answer [Lincoln's inquiries relative to the Mexican War] as Washington would answer. As a nation should not, and the Almighty will not, be evaded, so let him attempt no evasion—no equivocation.—*Speech in Congress, Jan. 12, 1848.* I, 340.

Polygamy—*See* UTAH, polygamy and statehood.

Pomeroy, Samuel C., "tormenting my life out of me"—I wish you and Lane would make a sincere effort to get out of the mood you are in. It does neither of you any good. It gives you the means of tormenting my life out of me.—*To Sen. Pomeroy, May 12, 1864.* X, 98.

Pomeroy Circular, not disturbed by—I have not yet read it [Pomeroy circular, boosting Chase for President in 1864] and I think I shall not. . . . I have known just as little of these things as my friends have allowed me to know. They bring the documents to me, but I do not read them; they tell me what they think fit to tell me, but I do not inquire for more.—*To Sec. Chase, Feb. 29, 1864.* X, 25.

Pope, John, criticized—He [Pope] has retired to Centreville where he says he will be able to hold his men. I don't like the expression. I don't like to hear him admit that his men need "holding."—*To John Hay, Aug. 31, 1862.* Hay, 46.

Pope, John, tributes to—. . . reposing special trust and confidence in the patriotism, valor, fidelity and abilities of John Pope.—*Executive order, March 22, 1862.* Hertz II, 853.
2.—I fully appreciate Gen. Pope's splendid achievements, with their invaluable results.—*To R. Yates and William Butler, April 10, 1862.* VII, 145.

Popular Government—*See* SELF-GOVERNMENT.

Popular Sovereignty, African slave trade and—*See* AFRICAN SLAVE TRADE, slavery extension akin to.

Popular Sovereignty, attitude of the fathers toward—He [Douglas] asks the community to believe that the men of the Revolution were in favor of his great principle [popular sovereignty], when we have the naked history that they themselves dealt with this very subject-matter of his principle, and utterly repudiated his principle, acting upon a precisely contrary ground. It is as impudent and absurd as if a prosecuting attorney should stand up before a jury, and ask them to convict A as the murderer of B, while B was walking alive before them.—*Speech, Columbus, Ohio, Sept. 16, 1859.* V, 171.

Popular Sovereignty, Clay versus Douglas—It so happens that in that "popular sovereignty" with which Mr. [Henry] Clay was identified, the Missouri Compromise was expressly reserved; and it was a little singular if Mr. Clay cast his mantle upon Judge Douglas on purpose to have that compromise repealed.—*Speech, Springfield, July 17, 1858.* III, 184.
2.—In a pre-eminent degree these popular sovereigns [disciples of Douglas] are at this work: blowing out the moral lights around us [Clay's expression]; teaching that the negro is no longer a man, but a brute; that the Declaration of Independence has nothing to do with him! that he ranks with the crocodile and the reptile; that man, with body and soul, is a matter of dollars and cents.—*Speech, Columbus, Ohio, Sept. 16, 1859.* V, 189.

Popular Sovereignty, Clay's death-bed scene—*See* WHIG PARTY, apple-sized tears from.

Popular Sovereignty, "deceitful pretense"—*See* UTAH, Rebellion and sovereignty.

Popular Sovereignty, defined—The essence of squatter or popular sovereignty—I don't care how you call it—is that if one man chooses to make a slave of another, no third man shall be allowed to object.—*Speech, Bloomington, May 29, 1856.* Lapsley II, 271.
2.—I suppose about everyone knows that, in this controversy, whatever has been said has had reference to the question of negro slavery. We have not been in a controversy about the right of the people to govern themselves in the ordinary matters of domestic concern in the states and territories. . . . Hence, when hereafter I speak of popular sovereignty, I wish to be understood as applying what I say to the question of slavery only.—*Speech, Springfield, July 17, 1858.* III, 161.
3.—I will state—and I have an able man to watch me—my understanding is that popular sovereignty, as now applied to the question of slavery, does allow the people of a territory to have slavery if they want to, but does not allow them not to have it if they do not want it.—*Debate, Ottawa, Aug. 21, 1858.* III, 234.

Popular Sovereignty, denounced—"Popular sovereignty" [argument used by Douglas against Lincoln] . . . is to be labeled upon the cars in which he travels; put upon the hacks he rides in; is to be flaunted upon the arches he passes under, and the banners which wave over him. It is to be dished up in as many varieties as a French cook can produce soup from potatoes. . . . The whole thing is the most arrant quixotism that was ever enacted before a com-

munity.—*Speech, Springfield, July 17, 1858.* III, 160.
2.—I pass from this . . . question of popular sovereignty [as defined by Douglas] as the most arrant humbug that has ever been attempted on an intelligent community.—*Speech, Springfield, July 17, 1858.* III, 164.

Popular Sovereignty, does Douglas mean to deceive?—Does Judge Douglas, when he says that several of the past years of his life have been devoted to the question of "popular sovereignty," and that all the remainder of his life shall be devoted to it, mean to say that he has been devoting his life to securing to the people of the territories the right to exclude slavery from the territories? If he means to say so, he means to deceive; because he and everyone knows that the decision of the Supreme Court, which he approves and makes special ground of attack upon me for disapproving, forbids the people of the territory to exclude slavery. This covers the whole ground, from the settlement of a territory till it reaches the degree of maturity entitling it to vote for a state constitution. So far as all that group is concerned, the judge is not sustaining popular sovereignty, but absolutely opposing it.—*Speech, Springfield, July 17, 1858.* III, 161.

Popular Sovereignty, Douglas's essay in Harper's—I do not propose . . . to enter into a detailed examination of the historical statements he [Douglas] has made [in his *Harper's* essay]. . . . I avoid doing so upon this principle—that if it were important to me to pass out of this lot in the least period of time possible, and I came to that fence and saw by a calculation of my strength and agility that I could clear it at a bound, it would be folly for me to stop and consider whether I could or could not crawl through a crack. So I say of the whole history contained in his essay, where he endeavored to link the men of the Revolution to popular sovereignty. It only required an effort to leap out of it—a single bound to be entirely successful.—*Speech, Columbus, Ohio, Sept. 16, 1859.* V, 164.

Popular Sovereignty, Douglas's interpretation of—He [Douglas] discovered that the right to breed and flog negroes in Nebraska was popular sovereignty.—*Speech, Paris, Sept. 8, 1858.* XI, 106.
2.—After fighting through more than three hours, if you will undertake to read it [Douglas's essay in *Harper's*] he at last places the whole matter [of popular sovereignty] under the control of that power [Congress] which he had been contending against, and arrives at a result directly contrary to what he had been laboring to do. He at last leaves the whole

matter to the control of Congress.—*Speech, Columbus, Ohio, Sept. 16, 1859.* V, 164.

3.—Douglas's popular sovereignty, as a principle, is simply this: If a man chooses to make a slave of another, neither that man nor anybody else has a right to object. Apply it to government, as he seeks to apply it, and it is this: If, in a new territory, into which a few people are beginning to enter for the purpose of making their homes, they choose either to exclude slavery from their limits, or to establish it there, however one or the other may affect the persons to be enslaved or the infinitely greater number of persons who are afterward to inhabit the territory, or the other members of the family of communities of which they are but an incipient member, or the general head of the family of states as parent of all—however their action may affect one or the other of these, there is no power or right to interfere. That is Douglas's popular sovereignty applied.—*Speech, Columbus, Ohio, Sept. 16, 1859.* V, 149.
Repeated at Cincinnati, Sept. 17, 1859. V, 227.

4.—There is a broad distinction between real popular sovereignty and Douglas popular sovereignty. . . . Douglas popular sovereignty, as a matter of principle [is] simply this: If one man would enslave another, neither that other nor any third man has a right to object. Douglas popular sovereignty as he practically applies it, is: If any organized political community, however new and small, would enslave men or forbid their being enslaved within its own territorial limits; however the doing the one or the other may affect the men sought to be enslaved, or the vastly superior number of men who are afterward to come within those limits, or the family of communities of which it is but a member, or the head of that family, as the present and common guardian of the whole—however any or all of those are to be affected, neither any nor all may interfere.—*Speeches in Kansas, Dec. 1-5, 1859.* V, 261.

5.—It is a concealed assumption of Douglas's popular sovereignty that slavery is a little, harmless, indifferent thing, having no wrong in it and no power for mischief about it.—*Speeches in Kansas, Dec. 1-5, 1859.* V, 264.

6.—. . . some for the "gur-reat pur-rinciple" that "if one man would enslave another, no third man should object," fantastically called "popular sovereignty."—*Cooper Institute address, New York, Feb. 27, 1860.* V, 313.

See POPULAR SOVEREIGNTY, does Douglas mean to deceive?

See POPULAR SOVEREIGNTY, Douglas troubled by.

See POPULAR SOVEREIGNTY, killed by Supreme Court.

See POPULAR SOVEREIGNTY, what did Douglas invent?

Popular Sovereignty, Douglas troubled by—He [Douglas] has a good deal of trouble with popular sovereignty. His explanations explanatory of explanations explained are interminable. The most lengthy and, as I suppose, the most maturely considered of his long series of explanations is his great essay in *Harper's Magazine.*—*Speech, Columbus, Ohio, Sept. 16, 1859.* V, 150.

2.—[Douglas's "do-nothing" sovereignty] is precisely no other than the putting of that most unphilosophical proposition that two bodies can occupy the same space at the same time.—*Debate, Quincy, Oct. 13, 1858.* IV, 380.

Popular Sovereignty, genuine, defined—What does that [popular sovereignty] mean? It means the sovereignty of the people over their own affairs—in other words, the right of the people to govern themselves.—*Speech, Paris, Sept. 8, 1858.* XI, 105.

2.—Here [in the Declaration of Independence] we are told that governments are instituted among men, deriving their just powers from the consent of the governed. If this is not popular sovereignty, then I have no conception of the meaning of words.—*Speech, Paris, Sept. 8, 1858.* XI, 105.

3.—I believe there is a genuine popular sovereignty. I think a definition of genuine popular sovereignty, in the abstract, would be about this: That each man shall do precisely as he pleases with himself, and with all those things which exclusively concern him. Applied to government, this principle would be, that a general government shall do all those things which pertain to it, and all the local governments shall do precisely as they please in respect to those matters which exclusively concern them. I understand that this government of the United States, under which we live, is based upon this principle, and I am misunderstood if it is supposed that I have any war to make upon that principle.—*Speech, Columbus, Ohio, Sept. 16, 1859.* V, 149.

4.—That the nation shall control what concerns it; that a state or any minor political community shall control what exclusively concerns it; and that an individual shall control what exclusively concerns him—is the real popular sovereignty, which no Republican opposes.—*Speeches in Kansas, Dec. 1-5, 1859.* V, 261.

See REPUBLICAN PARTY, warned against Douglas, 13.

Popular Sovereignty, killed by Supreme Court—Under the Dred Scott decision "squatter sovereignty" squatted out of existence, tumbled down like temporary scaffolding—like the mold at the foundry, served through one blast and fell back into loose sand—helped to carry an election, and then kicked to the winds.—*Speech, Springfield, June 16, 1858.* Basler, 375.

2.—Popular sovereignty! Everlasting popular sovereignty! Let us for a moment inquire into this vast matter of popular sovereignty. What is popular sovereignty? We recollect that at an earlier period in the history of this struggle, there was another name for the same thing—squatter sovereignty. . . . Vast credit is taken by our friend, the judge [Douglas] in regard to his support of it, when he declares the last years of his life have been, and all the future years of life shall be, devoted to this matter of popular sovereignty. . . . Now I wish you to mark what has become of that squatter sovereignty. . . . Can you get anyone to tell you now that the people of a territory have any authority to govern themselves, in regard to this mooted question of slavery, before they form a state constitution? . . . No more than a year ago it was decided by the Supreme Court of the United States, and is insisted on today, that the people of a territory have no right to exclude slavery from a territory; that if any one man chooses to take slaves into a territory, all the rest of the people have no right to keep them out. . . . When that is so, how much is left of the vast matter of squatter sovereignty, I should like to know—*Speech, Chicago, July 10, 1858.* III, 23.

3.—All that space of time that runs from the beginning of the settlement of the territory until there is a sufficiency of people to make a state constitution—all that portion of time popular sovereignty is given up. The seal is absolutely put down upon it by the [Dred Scott] court decision.—*Speech, Chicago, July 10, 1858.* III, 25.

4.—Judge Douglas has sung peans to his "popular sovereignty" doctrine until his Supreme Court, co-operating with him, has squatted his squatter sovereignty out. But he will keep up this species of humbuggery about squatter sovereignty. He has at last invented this sort of do-nothing sovereignty—that the people may exclude slavery by a sort of "sovereignty" that is exercised by doing nothing at all. Is not that running his popular sovereignty down awfully? Has it not got down as thin as the homeopathic soup that was made by boiling the shadow of a pigeon that had starved to death? But at last, when it is brought to the test of close reasoning, there is not even that thin concoction of it left. It is a presumption impossible in the domain of thought. It is precisely no other than the putting of that most unphilosophical propo-

sition, that two bodies can occupy the same space at the same time. The Dred Scott decision covers the whole ground, and while it occupies it, there is no room even for the shadow of starved pigeon to occupy the same ground.—*Debate, Quincy, Oct. 13, 1858.* IV, 379.

Popular Sovereignty, origin of—I suppose that Judge Douglas will claim in a little while that he is the inventor of the idea that the people should govern themselves; that nobody ever thought of such a thing until he brought it forward. We remember that in that old Declaration of Independence it is said that "We hold these truths to be self-evident, that all men are created equal; that they are endowed by their Creator with inalienable rights; that among these are life, liberty and the pursuit of happiness; that to secure these rights, governments are instituted among men, deriving their just powers from the consent of the governed." There is the origin of popular sovereignty.—*Speech, Chicago, July 10, 1858.* III, 27.

2.—The idea of popular sovereignty was floating about several ages before the author of the Nebraska bill was born—indeed, before Columbus set foot on this continent. In the year 1776 it took form in the noble words which you are familiar with: "We hold these truths to be self-evident, that all men are created equal," etc. Was not this the origin of popular sovereignty as applied to the American people?—*Speech, Paris, Sept. 8, 1858.* XI, 105.

See POPULAR SOVEREIGNTY, what did Douglas invent?

Popular Sovereignty, Republicans not opposed to—Whoever will undertake to examine the platform and the speeches of responsible men of the party, and of irresponsible men, too, if you please, will be unable to find one word from anybody in the Republican ranks opposed to that popular sovereignty which Judge Douglas thinks he has invented.—*Speech, Chicago, July 10, 1858.* III, 26.

Popular Sovereignty, slavery and—The new year of 1854 found slavery excluded from more than half the states by state constitutions, and from most of the national territory by congressional prohibition. Four days later commenced the struggle which ended in repealing that congressional prohibition. This opened all the national territory to slavery, and was the first point gained. But so far, Congress only had acted; and an indorsement by the people, real or apparent, was indispensable to save the point already gained and give chance for more. This necessity had not been overlooked, but had been provided for, as well might be, in the notable argument of "squatter sovereignty," otherwise called "sacred right of self-government," which latter phrase, though expressive of the most rightful basis of any government, was so perverted in this attempted use of it as to amount to just this; that if any one man chooses to enslave another, no third man shall be allowed to object.—*Speech, Springfield, June 16, 1858.* III, 3.

2.—I am sorry any Republican inclines to dally with Pop. Sov. of any sort. It acknowledges that slavery has equal rights with liberty, and surrenders all we have contended for.—*To J. D. DeFrees, Dec. 18, 1860.* Hertz II, 795.

Popular Sovereignty, "sugar-coated name"—*See* SLAVERY, Douglas's care-not policy, 20.

Popular Sovereignty, trespassers under—Popular sovereignty by his [Douglas's] own words, does not pertain to the few persons who wander upon the public domain in violation of law. . . . When it does pertain to them is when they are sufficient to be formed into an organized political community, and he fixes the minimum for that at 10,000. . . . Now I would like to know what is to be done with the 9,000? Are they all to be treated, until they are large enough to be organized into a political community, as wanderers upon the public land in violation of law? And if so treated and driven out, at what point of time would there ever be 10,000?—*Speech, Columbus, Ohio, Sept. 16, 1859.* V, 162.

2.—If they [Douglas's trespassers] were not driven out, but remained there as trespassers upon the public land in violation of the law, can they establish slavery there? No; the judge says popular sovereignty don't pertain to them. Can they exclude it, then? No; popular sovereignty don't pertain to them, then. I would like to know, in the case covered by the essay [Douglas's in *Harper's*] what condition the people of the territory are in before they reach the number of 10,000?—*Speech, Columbus, Ohio, Sept. 16, 1859.* V, 163.

3.—Is it his [Douglas's] plan that at any time before they [people of a territory] reach the required number [for statehood] those who are on hand shall be driven out as trespassers? If so, it will probably be a good while before a sufficient number to organize will get in.—*Speeches in Kansas, Dec. 1–5, 1859.* V, 265.

Popular Sovereignty, what did Douglas invent?—Let us inquire what Judge Douglas really invented when he introduced the Nebraska bill. . . . Was it the right of emigrants to Kansas and Nebraska to govern themselves, and a lot of "niggers," too, if they wanted? Clearly, this was no invention of his, because Gen. Cass put forth the same doctrine in 1848 in his so-called Nicholson letter, six years before Judge Doug-

las thought of such a thing. Then what was it that the "Little Giant" invented? It never occurred to Gen. Cass to call his discovery by the odd name of popular sovereignty. He had not the face to say that the right of the people to govern "niggers" was the right of the people to govern themselves. His notions of the fitness of things were not moulded to the brazenness of calling the right to put a hundred "niggers" through under the lash in Nebraska a "sacred right" of self-government—*Speech, Paris, Sept. 8, 1858.* XI, 105.

Population, prophecy—There are already among us those who, if the Union be preserved, will live to see it contain 250,000,000.—*First annual message, Dec. 3, 1861.* VII, 59.

2.—The great interior region . . . already has above 10,000,000 people, and will have 50,000,000 within 50 years if not prevented by any political folly or mistake. It contains more than one third of the country owned by the United States—certainly more than 1,000,000 square miles.—*Second annual message, Dec. 1, 1862.* VIII, 113.

3.—At that time [1900] we shall probably have 100,-000,000 of people to share the burden [of compensated emancipation], instead of 31,000,000 as now. And not only so, but the increase in our population may be expected to continue for a long time after that period as rapidly as before, because our territory will not have become full.—*Second annual message, Dec. 1, 1862.* VIII, 121.

See AMERICAN FLAG, each star brings happiness.

See POPULATION, secession would curtail.

Population, scarcely checked by war—*See* CIVIL WAR, national progress in spite of, 1, 4.

Population, secession would curtail—At the same ratio of increase which we have maintained, on an average, from our first national census in 1790 until that of 1860, we should in 1900 have a population of 103,208,415. . . . Figures show that our country may be as populous as Europe now is at some point between 1920 and 1930—say about 1925—our country at 73⅓ persons to the square mile—the European figure—being of capacity to contain 217,186,000. And we will reach this, too, if we do not ourselves relinquish the chance by the follies and evils of disunion or by long and exhausting war springing from the only great element of national discord among us. While it cannot be foreseen exactly how much one huge example of secession, breeding lesser ones indefinitely, would retard population, civilization and prosperity, no one can doubt that the extent of it would be very great and injurious.—*Second annual message, Dec. 1, 1862.* VIII, 121.

Port Privileges, policy of retaliation—Whereas, for some time past, vessels of war of the United States have been refused, in certain foreign ports, privileges and immunities to which they are entitled by treaty, public law, or the comity of nations . . . therefore, I . . . do hereby make known, that if, after a reasonable time shall have elapsed for intelligence of this proclamation to reach any foreign country in whose ports the said privileges and immunities shall have been refused, as aforesaid, they shall continue to be so refused; then and thenceforth the same privileges and immunities shall be refused to the vessels of war of that country in the ports of the United States.—*Proclamation, April 11, 1865.* XI, 83.

Porter, David D., Congress asked to thank—I recommend that the thanks of Congress be given . . . Commander David D. Porter, U.S.N., for distinguished services in the conception and preparation of the means used for the capture of the forts below New Orleans, and for the highly meritorious conduct in the management of the mortar flotilla during the bombardment of Forts Jackson and St. Phillip.—*Message to Congress, July 11, 1862.* VII, 268.
2.—I most cordially recommend that Commander David D. Porter, U.S.N., acting rear-admiral commanding the Mississippi squadron, receive a vote of thanks of Congress for the bravery and skill displayed in the attack on the post of Arkansas, which surrendered to the combined military and naval forces on the 10th instant.—*Message to Congress, Jan. 28, 1863.* VIII, 207.

Porter, Fitz-John, confidence in—. . . reposing special trust and confidence in the patriotism, valor, fidelity, and abilities of Fitz-John Porter.—*Executive order, July 16, 1862.* Pen and Voice, 175.

Porter, Fitz-John, court-martial of, approved—And it is ordered that the said Fitz-John Porter be, and he hereby is, cashiered and dismissed from the service of the United States as a major-general of volunteers, and as colonel and brevet brigadier-general in the regular service of the United States, and forever disqualified from holding any office of trust or profit under the government of the United States.—*Indorsement, Jan. 21, 1863.* VIII, 199.

Post Office, "cut its own fodder"—That department of the government has become a charge upon the treasury, whereas under Mr. [J. Q.] Adams and the Presidents before him it not only, to use a homely phrase, cut its own fodder, but actually threw a surplus into

the treasury.—*Speech, Springfield, Dec. 20, 1839.* I, 131.

Post Office, may become self-sustaining—It is manifest, therefore, that the Post Office Department may become self-sustaining in a few years.—*Third annual message, Dec. 8, 1863.* IX, 240.

Post Offices, appointments to, most annoying—*See* PATRONAGE, troubled by.

Posterity, few care to labor for—Few can be induced to labor exclusively for posterity; and none will do it enthusiastically. Posterity has done nothing for us; and, theorize on it as we may, practically we should do very little for it, unless we are made to think we are at the same time doing something for ourselves.—*Speech, Springfield, Feb. 22, 1842.* I, 201.
2.—What an ignorance of human nature it exhibits, to ask or expect a whole community to rise up and labor for the temporal happiness of others, after themselves shall be consigned to the dust, a majority of which community takes no pains whatever to secure their own eternal welfare at no more distant day? . . . Pleasures to be enjoyed, or pains to be endured, after we shall be dead and gone, are but little regarded even in our own cases, and much less in the case of others.—*Speech, Springfield, Feb. 22, 1842.* I, 202.

Poverty, confessed—I am so poor and make so little headway in the world, that I drop back in a month of idleness as much as I gain in a year's sowing.—*To Joshua F. Speed, July 4, 1842.* I, 219.
2.—I lost nearly all the working-part of last year, giving my time to the canvass; and I am altogether too poor to lose two years together.—*To William Grimes, Aug., 1857.* II, 339.
3.—I have been on expenses so long without earning anything that I am absolutely without money now for even household purposes. Still, if you can put in $250 for me toward discharging the debt of the committee, I will allow it when you and I settle the private matter between us. This, with what I have already paid, and with an outstanding note of mine, will exceed my subscription of $500. This, too, is exclusive of my ordinary expenses during the campaign, all of which being added to my loss of time and business bears pretty heavily upon one no better off in this world's goods than I.—*To N. B. Judd, Nov. 16, 1858.* V, 93.
4.—It is bad to be poor. I shall go to the wall for bread and meat, if I neglect my business this year as well as last.—*To Hawkins Taylor, Sept. 6, 1859.* V, 138.
5.—As to the pecuniary matter . . . I again appealed

to our friend Turner by letter, but he never answered. I can but repeat to you that I am so pressed myself, as to be unable to assist you, unless I could get it from him.—*To Mark W. Delahay, Oct. 17, 1859.* Tracy, 117.

6.—I could not raise $10,000, if it would save me from the fate of John Brown. Nor have my friends, so far as I know, yet reached the point of staking any money on my chances of success.—*To E. Stafford, March 17, 1860.* VI, 7.

See LINCOLN, ABRAHAM, financial.

Poverty, encourages trust—No men living are more worthy to be trusted than those who toil up from poverty.—*First annual message, Dec. 3, 1861.*

Practice Better Than Theory—Practice proves more than theory, in any case.—*Second annual message, Dec. 1, 1862.* VIII, 128.

Prayer, Lincoln's for Gettysburg—*See* GETTYSBURG, Lincoln's prayer for.

Prayer, Lincoln's for Vicksburg—*See* VICKSBURG, Lincoln's prayer for.

Prayer, rebels engage in—The rebel soldiers are praying with a great deal more earnestness, I fear, than our own troops, and expecting God to favor their side.—*Reply to deputation of Chicago churchmen, Sept. 13, 1862.* VIII, 29.

Preachers, as temperance advocates—*See* TEMPERANCE, early reformers erred.

Preble, George H.—Dismiss him. If that is your opinion, it is mine. I will do it.—*To Sec. Welles, Sept. 20, 1862.* Welles I, 141.

Precedent, no, to guide—As our cause is new, so must we think anew and act anew.—*Second annual message, Dec. 1, 1862.* VIII, 131.

2.—We must disenthrall ourselves, and then we shall save our country.—*Second annual message, Dec. 1, 1862.* VIII, 131.

Precedent, war and peace—A measure made expedient by a war is no precedent for times of peace.—*Opinion on admission of West Virginia, Dec. 31, 1862.* VIII, 160.

Prentice, George D., attitude of, toward Lincoln—*See* CAMPAIGN OF 1860, silence is candidate's best policy, 7.

Preparedness—I think the necessity of being ready increases. Look to it.—*To Gov. Curtin, April 8, 1861.* Angle, 266.

Presidency, example of inequality—I make no allusion to the present President when I say there are few stronger cases in the world of "burden to the many and benefit to the few," of "inequality," than the Presidency itself is by some thought to be.—*Speech in Congress, June 20, 1848.* II, 37.

Presidency, "greatly distinguished citizens" in—It is 72 years since the first inauguration of a President under our national Constitution. During that period fifteen different and greatly distinguished citizens have, in succession, administered the executive branch of the government. They have conducted it through many perils, and generally with great success.—*First Inaugural, March 4, 1861.* VI, 173.

Presidency, "no bed of roses"—The Presidency, even to the most experienced politicians, is no bed of roses; and Gen. Taylor like others, found thorns within it.—*Speech, Chicago, July 25, 1850.* Angle, 74.

2.—In my position I am environed with difficulties.—*Reply to serenade, Sept. 24, 1862.* VIII, 44.

Presidency, no thought of Lincoln in connection with—*See* DOUGLAS, STEPHEN A., characterized, 11.

Presidency, Northern aspirants for, bid for Southern help—The total withdrawal of Southern aspirants for the Presidency multiplies the number of Northern ones. These last, in competing with each other, commit themselves to the utmost verge that, through their own greediness, they have the least hope their Northern supporters will bear. Having got committed in a race of competition, necessity drives them into union to sustain themselves. Each at first secures all he can on personal attachments to him and through hopes resting on him personally. Next they unite with one another and with the perfectly banded South, to make the offensive position they have got into "a party measure."—*Fragment, Oct. 1, 1856.* II, 305.

Presidency, puts curb on speech—In my present position it is hardly proper for me to make speeches. Every word is so closely noted that it will not do to make foolish ones, and I cannot be expected to be prepared to make sensible ones. If I were as I have been most of my life, I might, perhaps, talk nonsense to you for half an hour, and it wouldn't hurt anybody.—*Speech, Frederick, Md., Oct. 4, 1862.* XI, 124.

2.—In my position it is somewhat important that I should not say any foolish thing. [Voice: "If you can help it."] It very often happens that the only way to help it is to say nothing at all.—*Speech, Gettysburg, Nov. 19, 1863.* Hertz II, 919.

3.—I have appeared before you to apologize for not speaking rather than to speak. . . . Everything I say, necessarily, in consequence of my position, goes into print. If it is foolish, it does not do me or the nation any good. If I make any mistakes it may do myself and the nation harm. It is difficult to always say sensible things. I therefore hope you will accept my sincere thanks for this charitable enterprise in which you are engaged.—*Speech, Washington, Feb. 22, 1864.* Quarterly, Sept., 1945, p. 341.

4.—It is not very becoming for one in my position to make speeches at great length.—*Speech, Baltimore, April 18, 1864.* X, 78.

5.—In the excitement of the moment I am sure to say something which I am sorry for when I see it in print. So I have it here in black and white, and there are no mistakes made. People attach too much importance to what I say anyhow.—*To Noah Brooks, Nov. 9, 1864.* War Years IV, 116.

6.—Everything I say, you know, goes into print. If I make a mistake it doesn't merely affect me, or you, but the country. I, therefore, ought at least try not to make mistakes.—*Response to serenade, April 10, 1865.* Hertz II, 965.

7.—If there should be such a demonstration I, of course, shall have to respond to it, and I shall have nothing to say if I dribble it out before.—*Response to serenade, April 10, 1865.* Hertz II, 965.

8.—As a general rule, I abstain from reading the reports of attacks upon myself, wishing not to be provoked by that to which I cannot properly offer an answer.—*Last public speech, April 11, 1865.* XI, 85.

9.—I know what you are thinking about. You think it mighty queer that an old stump-speaker like myself should not be able to address a crowd like this outside without a written speech. But you must remember I am, in a certain way, talking to the country, and I have to be mighty careful.—*To White House group, April 12, 1865.* Hertz II, 966.

Presidency, second term in—A second term would be a great honor and a great labor, which, together, perhaps I would not decline if tendered.—*To E. B. Washburne, Oct. 26, 1863.* IX, 183.

Presidency, South doesn't want—If a southern man aspires to be President, they choke him down instantly, in order that the glittering prize of the Presidency may be held up on southern terms to the greedy eyes of northern ambition. With this they tempt us and break in upon us.—*Fragment, Oct. 1, 1856.* II, 304.

2.—"Actions speak louder than words" is the old maxim, and if true the South now distinctly says to the North, "Give us the measures and you take the man."—*Fragment, Oct. 1, 1856.* II, 304.

3.—The Democratic party in 1844 elected a southern President. Since then they have neither had a southern candidate for election or nomination. Their conventions of 1848, 1852 and 1856 have been struggles exclusively among northern men, each vying to outbid the others for the southern vote; the South standing calmly by to finally cry, "Going, going, gone!" to the highest bidder, and at the same time to make its power more distinctly seen, and thereby to secure a still higher bid at the next succeeding struggle.—*Fragment, Oct. 1, 1856.* II, 304.

Presidency, uncertainty as to successor in—It is something on the question of time to remember that it cannot be known who is next to occupy the position I now hold, nor what he will do.—*To Gov. Andrew Johnson, Sept. 11, 1863.* IX, 117.

President, "law of war" and—*See* WAR POWER, use of, defended, 13.

President, wages of, and laborer—*See* WAGES, inequality in.

Press, forgery in, best ignored—Yours of the 8th inclosing the forged article from the New York *Tribune* published in the *Menard Index* was received yesterday. Although the getting up of the thing was intended to deceive, and was very malicious and wicked, I do not think much could be made by exposing it. When you shall have exposed it, they will then say they meant it as a "take off" and never intended to be understood as genuine.—*To R. M. Ewing, Nov. 12, 1856.* Tracy, 70.

Press, freedom of, to be protected—*See* FREEDOM OF SPEECH, part of guarantee.

See CHICAGO TIMES, embarrassed by suspension of.

See FREEDOM OF OPINION.

See REPUBLICAN INSTITUTIONS, inquiry and discussion best sustains.

Press, garbles—Please pardon me for suggesting that if papers like yours which heretofore have persistently garbled and misrepresented what I have said, will now fully and fairly place it before their readers, there can be no further misunderstanding. I beg you to believe me sincere when I declare I do not say this in a spirit of complaint or resentment; but that I urge it as the true cure for any real uneasiness in the country that my course may be other than conservative.—*To N. P. Paschall, Nov. 16, 1860.* VI, 70.

Press, grateful to New York newspapers—*See* EMANCIPATION, financial aspect of compensated, 2.

Press, papers "vilify and disparage"—See ELECTION OF 1862, explained, 1.

Press, reporters characterized—. . . those villainous reporters Douglas has with him.—*To M. P. Sweet, Sept. 16, 1858.* Angle, 194.

Press, some papers unfair—On the 20th instant Senator Trumbull made a short speech, which I suppose you have seen and approved. Has a single newspaper, heretofore against us, urged that speech upon its readers with a purpose to quiet the public anxiety? Not one, so far as I know. On the contrary, the Boston *Courier* and its class hold me responsible for that speech, and endeavor to inflame the North with the belief that it foreshadows an abandonment of Republican ground by the incoming administration; while the Washington *Constitution* and its class hold the same speech up to the South as an open declaration of war against them. This is just what I expected, and just what would happen with any declaration I could make. These political fiends are not sick enough yet. Party malice, and not public good, possesses them entirely.—*To Henry J. Raymond, Nov. 28, 1860.* VI, 74.

Press, sustains republican institutions—See REPUBLICAN INSTITUTIONS, inquiry and discussion best sustain.

Press, Washington papers complain—I am appealed to by the proprietors of papers here, because they have to get telegraphed back to them from New York matter which goes from the War Department. Might not this be avoided without harm or inconvenience to any?—*To Sec. Stanton, Sept. 9, 1864.* Tracy, 244.

Press, Whig, ignores speeches—Thinking it would be most natural that the newspapers would feel interested to give at least some of the speeches to their readers, I at the beginning of the session made arrangements to have one copy of the [Congressional] *Globe* and "Appendix" regularly sent to each Whig paper of the district. And yet, with the exception of my own little speech, which was published in two only of the then five, now four, Whig papers, I do not remember having seen a single speech, or even extract from one, in any single one of the papers. With equal and full means on both sides, I venture that the *State Register* has thrown before its readers more of Locofoco speeches in a month than all the Whig papers of the district have done of Whig speeches during the session.—*To W. H. Herndon, June 22, 1848.* II, 51.

Preston, William B., might have been arrested—See CONFEDERATE GENERALS, might have been arrested.

Presumption, "impossible"—[Douglas's "do-nothing sovereignty"] is a presumption impossible in the domain of thought.—*Debate, Quincy, Oct. 13, 1858.* IV, 380.

Principles, must be inflexible—Important principles may and must be inflexible.—*Last public address, April 11, 1865.* XI, 92.

Printing, "better half . . . of writing"—Printing . . . is but the other half, and in reality the better half, of writing; and . . . both together are but the assistants of speech in the communication of thoughts between man and man.—*Lecture, Springfield, Feb. 22, 1859.* V, 110.
2.—For 3,000 years during which printing remained undiscovered after writing was in use, it was only a small portion of the people who could write, or even read writing, and consequently the field of invention, though much extended, still continued very limited. At length printing came. It gave ten thousand copies of any written matter quite as cheaply as ten were given before; and consequently a thousand minds were brought into the field where was but one before. This was a great gain—and history shows a great change corresponding to it—in point of time. I will venture to consider it the true termination of that period called the "dark ages." Discoveries, inventions, and improvements, followed rapidly and have been increasing their rapidity ever since.—*Lecture, Springfield, Feb. 22, 1859.* V, 111.

Printing, encouraged freedom of thought—See FREEDOM OF THOUGHT, printing helped achieve.

Prison, release from, by taking oath—Mr. [John W.] Davis [a Baltimore police commissioner] could at the time of his arrest, could at any time since, and can now, be released [from prison] by taking a full oath of allegiance to the government of the United States. . . . If Mr. Davis is still so hostile to the government, and so determined to aid its enemies in destroying it, he makes his own choice.—*Indorsement on letter of Mr. Davis's, Sept. 15, 1861.* VI, 355.

Prisoners of war, civilized treatment of—See WAR, no barbarities in civilized, 1.

Prisoners of War, object to exchange—I am so pressed in regard to prisoners of war in our custody, whose homes were within our lines, and who wish not to be exchanged, but to take the oath and be discharged, that I hope you will pardon me for again calling up the subject. My impression is that we will not ever force the exchange of any of this class; that, taking the oath and being discharged, none of them will again go to the rebellion; but the rebillion again coming to them, a considerable percentage of them, probably not a majority, would rejoin it; that, by a cautious discrimination, the number so discharged would not be large enough to do any considerable mischief in any event, will relieve distress in at least some meritorious cases, and would give me some relief from intolerable pressure. I shall be glad, therefore, to have your cheerful assent to the discharge of those whose names I may send, which I will only do with circumspection.—*To Sec. Stanton, March 18, 1864.* X, 44.

Prize Courts, commended—It is especially gratifying that our prize courts, by the impartiality of their adjudications, have commanded the respect and confidence of maritime powers.—*Third annual message. Dec. 8, 1863.* IX, 225.

Procrustean Bed, no—*See* RECONSTRUCTION, Louisiana, 10.

Promises, bad—Bad promises are better broken than kept.—*Last public speech, April 11, 1865.* XI, 87.

Promises, caution as to—We must not promise what we ought not, lest we be called on to perform what we cannot.—*Speech, Bloomington, May 29, 1856.* Lapsley II, 249.

Promise, reasonable construction of, necessary—I have just received your telegram saying that the "secretary of war telegraphed after the battle of Stone River: 'Anything you and your command want you can have,'" and then specifying several things you have requested and have not received. . . . The promise of the secretary, as you state it, is certainly pretty broad. . . . Still, the promise must have a reasonable construction.—*To Gen. Rosecrans, March 17, 1863.* VIII, 226.

Proof Required—A man cannot prove a negative, but he has a right to claim that when one makes an affirmative charge he must offer some proof to show the truth of what he says.—*Debate, Ottawa, Aug. 21, 1858.* III, 225.

Property, effect on public opinion—*See* PUBLIC OPINION, property basis of.

Property, love of, and sense of wrong—The love of property and consciousness of right or wrong have conflicting places in organization, which often make a man's course seem crooked, his conduct a riddle.— *Speech, Hartford, Conn., March 5, 1860.* V, 331.

Property, "posititve good"—*See* WEALTH, defense of, 2.

Prophecy, false, touching slavery—We are now far into the fifth year since a policy was initiated with the avowed object and confident promise of putting an end to slavery agitation. Under the operation of that policy, that agitation has not only not ceased, but has constantly augmented.—*Speech, Springfield, June 16, 1858.* III, 1.

2.—Did the angry debates which took place at Washington during the last session of Congress lead you to suppose that the slavery agitation was settled? . . . But Judge Douglas says the slavery question is settled. He says the bill which he introduced into the Senate of the United States on the fourth day of January, 1854, settled the slavery question forever.—*Speech, Clinton, Sept. 8, 1858.* III, 353.

3.—Instead of the quiet times and good feeling which was promised us by the self-styled author of Popular Sovereignty, we have had nothing but ill feeling and agitation. According to Judge Douglas, the passage of the Nebraska bill would tranquilize the whole country—there would be no more slavery agitation in or out of Congress, and the vexed question would be left entirely to the people of the territories. Such was the opinion of Judge Douglas, and such were the opinions of the leading men of the Democratic party. —*Speech, Clinton, Sept. 8, 1858.* III, 352.

4.—Even as late as the spring of 1856 Mr. Buchanan said, a short time subsequent to his nomination by the Cincinnati convention, that the Territory of Kansas would be tranquil in less than six weeks. Perhaps he thought so, but Kansas has not been and is not tranquil, and it may be a long time before she will be.—*Speech, Clinton, Sept. 8, 1858.* III, 353.

5.—He [Douglas] introduced the Nebraska bill in 1854 to put another end to the slavery agitation. He promised that it would finish it all up immediately. . . . Now, at this day in the history of the world we can no more tell when the end of this slavery agitation will be than we can see the end of the world itself.—*Debate, Charleston, Sept. 18, 1858.* IV, 186.

6.—Judge Douglas amuses himself by saying I wish to go into the Senate on my qualifications as a prophet. He says he has known some other prophets, and does not think very well of them. Well, others of us have also known some prophets. We know who nearly five years ago prophesied that the "Nebraska bill" would put an end to slavery agitation in next to no time—one who renewed that prophecy at least as often as quarter-yearly ever since; and still the prophecy has not been fulfilled. That one might very well go out of the Senate on his qualifications as a false prophet.—*Notes, Oct. 1, 1858.* IV, 213.

7.—When Mr. Buchanan accepted the presidential nomination, he felicitated himself with the belief that the whole thing [agitation over the Kansas-Nebraska bill] would be quieted and forgotten in about six weeks. In his inaugural, and in his Silliman letter, at their respective dates, he was just not quite in reach of the same happy consummation.—*Notes, Oct. 1, 1858.* IV, 232.

8.—In every speech you heard Judge Douglas make, until he got into this "imbroglio," as they call it, with the administration about the Lecompton Constitution —every speech on that Nebraska bill was full of his felicitations that we were just at the end of the slavery agitation. . . . But has it proved so?—*Debate, Alton, Oct. 15, 1858.* V, 46.

See COMPROMISE OF 1850, promise of, broken.

Prosperity, primary cause of—Without the Constitution and the Union we could have attained the result, but even these are not the primary cause of our great prosperity. There is something back of these, entwining itself more and more closely about the human heart. That something is the principle of "liberty to all"—the principle that clears the path for all—gives hope to all—and, by consequence, enterprise and industry to all. The expression of that principle in our Declaration of Independence was most happy and fortunate. Without this, as well as with it, we could have declared our independence of Great Britain; but without it we could not, I think, have secured our free government and consequent prosperity. No oppressed people will fight and endure, as our fathers did without the promise of something better than a mere change of masters.—*Fragment, date uncertain.* Angle, 240.

Prosperity, promise of—*See* INTERNAL IMPROVEMENTS, nation and states should cooperate, 2.

Prosperity, slavery and—*See* LIBERTY, prosperity and, threatened by slavery.

Providence, practical definition of—I agree with you in providence, but I believe in the providence of the most men,—the longest purse and the largest cannon.—*Fragment, 1856.* Hertz II, 690.

Pryor, Roger A., pass for—Allow the bearer, Roger A. Pryor [Confederate brigadier general] to pass to Gen. Grant, and report to him for exchange [as a prisoner of war].—*Feb. 25, 1865.* Angle, 370.

Pryor, Roger A., perplexed by—I am in a little perplexity. I was induced to authorize a gentleman to bring Roger A. Pryor here with a view of effecting an exchange of him; but since then I have seen a dispatch of yours showing that you specially object to his exchange. Meantime he has reached here and re-ported to me. It is an ungracious thing for me to send him back to prison, and yet inadmissible for him to remain here long. Cannot you help me out with it.—*To Gen. Grant, Feb. 24, 1865.* XI, 39.

Pryor, Roger A., rewarded for what Douglas condemns others for saying—*See* "IRREPRESSIBLE CONFLICT," difference in who says it, 1, 3.

Public Confidence, who has more?—Though I believe I have not so much of the confidence of the people as I had some time since, I do not know that, all things considered, any other person has more.—*To cabinet, Sept. 22, 1862.* Hertz II, 883.

See HUMILITY, Lincoln trait.

Public Credit, helped by banking law—The public credit, moreover, would be greatly improved and the negotiations of new loans greatly facilitated by the steady market demand for government bonds which the adoption of the proposed [banking] system would create.—*Second annual message, Dec. 1, 1862.* VIII, 102.

2.—The enactment . . . of a national banking law has proved a valuable support of the public credit, and the general legislation in relation to loans has fully answered the expectations of its favorers.—*Third annual message, Dec. 8, 1863.* IX, 233.

3.—The national [banking] system will create a reliable and permanent influence in support of the national credit, and protect the people against losses in the use of paper money.—*Fourth annual message, Dec. 6, 1864.* X, 295.

Public Credit, maintained in spite of war—The vast expenditures incident to the military and naval operations required for the suppression of the rebellion have hitherto been met with a promptitude and certainty unusual in similar circumstances, and the public credit has been fully maintained. The continuance of the war, however, and the increased disbursements made necessary by the augmented forces now in the field demand your best reflections as to the best modes of providing the necessary revenue without injury to business and with the least possible burdens upon labor.—*Second annual message, Dec. 1, 1862.* VIII, 100.

Public Credit, uniform currency needed to sustain— In order to raise money by loans most easily and cheaply, it is clearly necessary to give every possible support to the public credit. To that end a uniform currency, in which taxes, subscriptions to loans and all other ordinary public dues, as well as all private dues, may be paid, is almost, if not quite, indispensable.—*Message to Congress, Jan. 17, 1863.* VIII, 193.

Public Defense, recommended—I recommend that adequate and ample measures be adopted for maintaining the public defense on every side.—*First annual message, Dec. 3, 1861.* VII, 30.

Public-Land Bill, Clay's, and Illinois farmer—Many silly reasons are given [against Clay's land bill]. . . . One is that by giving us [the states] the proceeds of the lands, we impoverish the national treasury, and thereby render necessary an increase of the tariff. This may be true; but if so, the amount of it only is that those whose pride, whose abundance of means, prompt them to spurn the manufactures of our country, and to strut in British cloaks and coats and pantaloons, may have to pay a few cents more on the yard for the cloth that makes them. A terrible evil, truly, to the Illinois farmer, who never wore, nor ever expects to wear, a single yard of British goods in his whole life.—*Whig circular, March 4, 1843.* I, 249.

Public Lands, majority of states want prices of, up—The states in which none, or few, of the public lands lie, and those consequently interested against parting with them except for the best price, are the majority; and a moment's reflection will show that they must ever continue the majority, because by the time one of the original new states—Ohio, for example—becomes populous and gets weight in Congress, the public lands in her limits are so nearly sold out that in every point material to this question she becomes an old state. She does not wish the price reduced, because there is none left for her citizens to buy; she does not wish them ceded to the states in which they lie, because they no longer lie in her limits, and she will get nothing by the cession. In the nature of things, the states interested in the reduction of price . . . never can be the majority.—*Whig circular, March 1, 1843.* I, 250.

Public Lands, proceeds for states—*See* INTERNAL IMPROVEMENTS, public-lands revenue urged for.

See PUBLIC-LAND BILL, Clay's, and Illinois farmer.

Public Lands, revenue from, secondary consideration—It has long been a cherished opinion of some of our wisest statesmen that the people of the United States had a higher and more enduring interest in the early settlement and substantial cultivation of the public lands than in the amount of direct revenue to be derived from the sale of them. This opinion has had a controlling influence in shaping legislation upon the subject of our national domain. . . . This policy has received its most signal and beneficent illustration in the recent enactment granting homesteads to actual settlers.—*Third annual message, Dec. 8, 1863.* IX, 241.

Public Lands, sale of, if money volume is reduced—When the quantity of money shall be reduced [as threatened by the subtreasury plan], and consequently everything under individual control brought down in proportion, the price of those [public] lands, being fixed by law, will remain as now. Of necessity, it will follow that the produce or labor that now raises money sufficient to purchase 80 acres will then but be sufficient to purchase 40, or perhaps not that much; and this difficulty and hardship will last as long, in some degree, as any portion of these lands remain undisposed of. Knowing, as I well do, the difficulty that poor people now encounter in procuring homes, I hesitate not to say that when the price of the public lands shall be doubled or trebled, or, which is the same thing, produce and labor cut down to one-half or one-third of their present prices, it will be little less than impossible for them to procure those homes at all.—*Speech, Springfield, Dec. 20, 1839.* I, 108.

Public Office, Virginians' hunger for—Were it believed that vacant places could be had at the North Pole, the road there would be lined with dead Virginians.—*To Donn Piatt, Feb. 11, 1861.* Diplomat, 16.

Public Opinion, Douglas tries to mold—If . . . he [Douglas] shall succeed in molding public sentiment to a perfect accordance with his own; in bringing all men to indorse all court decisions, without caring to know whether they are right or wrong; in bringing all tongues to as perfect a silence as his own, as to there being any wrong in slavery; in bringing all to declare, with him, that they care not whether slavery be voted up or voted down; that if any people want slaves they have a right to have them; that negroes are not men, have no part in the Declaration of Independence; that there is no moral question about slavery; that liberty and slavery are perfectly consistent—indeed necessary accompaniments; that for a strong man to declare himself the superior of a weak one, and thereupon enslave the weak one, is the very essence of liberty, the most sacred right of self-government . . . in the name of Heaven, what barrier will be left against slavery being made lawful everywhere?—*Notes, Oct. 1, 1858.* IV, 223.

2.—I call upon your mind to inquire, if you were going to get the best instrument you could, and then set it to work in the most ingenious way, to prepare the public mind for this movement [to make slavery national], operating in the free states, where there is now an abhorrence of the institution of slavery, could you find an instrument so capable of doing it as Judge

Douglas, or one employed in so apt a way to do it?—*Debate, Galesburg, Oct. 7, 1858. IV, 289.*

3.—I lay down the proposition that . . . in every possible way he [Douglas] can, he molds the public opinion of the North to your [Kentuckians'] ends.—*Speech, Cincinnati, Sept. 17, 1859. V, 197.*

4.—Douglas is molding the public opinion of the North, first to say that the thing [slavery] is right in your state [Kentucky] over the Ohio river, and hence to say that that which is right there is not wrong here, and that all laws and constitutions here, recognizing it as being wrong, are themselves wrong and ought to be repealed and abrogated.—*Speech, Cincinnati, Sept. 17, 1859. V, 200.*

Public Opinion, government rests in—Our government rests in public opinion. Whoever can change public opinion can change the government practically just so much.—*Speech, Chicago, Dec. 10, 1856. II, 310.*

2.—We know that in a government like this, a government of the people, where the voice of all the men of the country, substantially, enters into the administration of the government, what lies at the bottom of all of it is public opinion.—*Speech, Cincinnati, Sept. 17, 1859. V, 197.*

Public Opinion, importance of—A universal feeling, whether well or ill-founded, cannot safely be disregarded.—*Speech, Peoria, Oct. 16, 1854. II, 207.* Repeated at Urbana, Oct. 24, 1854. Hertz II, 634. Repeated at Carlinville, Aug. 31, 1858. Angle, 190.

2.—There is both a power and a magic in popular opinion.—*Speech, Bloomington, May 29, 1856.* Lapsley II, 275.

3.—In this and like communities, public sentiment is everything. With public sentiment nothing can fail; without it, nothing can succeed. Consequently he who molds public sentiment goes deeper than he who enacts statutes or pronounces decisions. He makes statutes and decisions possible or impossible to be executed.—*Debate, Ottawa, Aug. 21, 1858. III, 252.*

4.—Public opinion in this country is everything.—*Speech, Columbus, Ohio, Sept. 16, 1859. V, 188.*

5.—Public opinion settles everything here [in the North]. Any policy to be permanent must have public opinion at the bottom—something in accordance with the human mind as it is.—*Speech, Hartford, Conn., March 5, 1860. V, 331.*

6.—No policy that does not rest upon philosophical public opinion can be permanently maintained.—*Speech, New Haven, Conn., March 6, 1860. V, 346.*

7.—. . . the great loyal public sentiment of the country, which is, indeed, the foundation of all else that

is valuable in this great national trial.—*To Sec. Stanton, March 28, 1864. Hertz II, 924.*

Public Opinion, law and—*See* LAW, enforcement of, depends on public sentiment.

Public Opinion, property basis of—Public opinion is founded, to a great extent, on a property basis.—*Speech, Hartford, Conn., March 5, 1860. V, 330.*

Public Opinion, slavery and—*See* SLAVERY, Douglas's care-not policy, 4, 11, 17, 21.

Public Opinion, "steady process of debauching"—I suggest to this portion of the Ohio Republicans, or Democrats if there be any present, that there is now going on among you a steady process of debauching public opinion on this subject [slavery.]—*Speech, Columbus, Ohio, Sept. 16, 1859. II, 189.*

Public Sentiment—*See* PUBLIC OPINION.

Public Speaking—*See* SPEAKING.

Punctilio—Please do not ruin us on punctilio.—*To Gov. Yates, Aug. 23, 1862. Hertz II, 876.*

See EMANCIPATION, states appealed to for, compensated, 3.

See "HOMICIDES ON PUNCTILIO."

Punctuation, "Matter of feeling"—With educated people, I suppose, punctuation is a matter of rule; with me it is a matter of feeling. But I must say I have a great respect for the semicolon; it's a useful little chap.—*To Noah Brooks, Dec. 3, 1864. Scribner's, February, 1878.*

Punishment, form of, disapproved—A poor widow by the name of Baird has a son in the army, that for some offense has been sentenced to serve a long time without pay, or at most with very little pay. I do not like this punishment of withholding pay—it falls so very hard on poor families.—*To Sec. Stanton, March 1, 1864. X, 27.*

Punishment, no cure—Will the punishment of the thief bring back the stolen money? No more so than the hanging of a murderer restores his victim to life.—*Speech, Springfield, Jan. 20, 1839. I, 120.*

"Puppy Court"—*See* COURTS, uneasy about.

Purpose and Expectation—Cannot the judge [Douglas] perceive a distinction between a purpose and an expectation? I have often expressed an expectation to die, but I have never expressed a wish to die.—*Speech, Springfield, July 17, 1858. III, 173.*

Putting Foot Down Firmly—The man does not live who is more devoted to peace than I am, but it may be necessary to put the foot down firmly.—*Speech, New Jersey Assembly, Feb. 21, 1861.* VI, 154.

"Quarrel Not at All," advice to army captain—The advice of a father to his son, "Beware of entrance to a quarrel, but being in, so bear it that the opposed may beware of thee," is good, and yet not the best. Quarrel not at all. No man resolved to make the most of himself, can spare time for personal contention. Still less can he afford to take all the consequences, including the vitiating of his temper, and the loss of self-control. Yield larger things to which you can show no more than equal right, and yield lesser ones, though clearly your own. Better give your path to a dog, than be bitten by him in contesting the right. Killing the dog would not cure the bite. In the mood indicated deal henceforth with your fellow men, and especially with your brother officers; and even the unpleasant events you are passing from will not have been profitless to you.—*To Capt. James M. Cutts, Oct. 26, 1863.* R. T. L.

Quarrels, waste time—A man has not time to spend half his life in quarrels. If a man ceases to attack me, I never remember the past against him.—*To group in Stanton's office, Nov. 8, 1864.* Hay, 234.

2.—In the difficulty between us, of which you speak, you say you think I was the aggressor. I do not think I was. You say "my words imported insult." I meant them as a fair set-off to your own statements, and not otherwise; and in that light alone I wish you to understand them. You ask for my present "feeling on the subject." I entertain no unkind feelings to you, and none of any sort upon the subject, except a sincere regret that I permitted myself to get into such an altercation.—*To W. G. Anderson, Oct. 31, 1840.* I, 151.

"Question of Legs"—*See* ACTION, pleas for, 13.

Quibbling, Douglas enjoys—The judge is very happy indeed at working up these quibbles.—*Debate, Freeport, Aug. 27, 1858.* III, 340.

2.—It would take all my time to meet all the quibbling arguments of Judge Douglas.—*Debate, Jonesboro, Sept. 15, 1858.* IV, 38.

3.—Why does he [Douglas] stand playing upon the meaning of words, and quibbling around the edges of the evidence?—*Debate, Charleston, Sept. 18, 1858.* IV, 198.

Races, separation of—*See* RACIAL AMALGAMATION, separation of races best preventive of.

Racial Amalgamation, census of mulattoes—In 1850 there were in the United States 405,751 mulattoes. Very few of these are the offspring of whites and free blacks; nearly all have sprung from black slaves and white masters. . . . A few free colored persons may get into the free states, in any event; but their number is too insignificant to amount to much in the way of mixing blood. In 1850 there were in the free states 56,649 mulattoes; but for the most part they were not born there—they came from the slave states ready made up. In the same year the slave states had 348,-874 mulattoes, all of home production.—*Speech, Springfield, June 26, 1857.* II, 335.

2.—You know that Virginia has more mulattoes than all the northern states.—*Speech, Carlinville, Aug. 31, 1858.* Angle, 191.

3.—Judge Douglas . . . pretends to fear that the success of our [Republican] party will result in the amalgamation of blacks and whites. I think I can show plainly . . . that Judge Douglas's fears are groundless. The census of 1850 tells us that in that year there were over 400,000 mulattoes in the United States. Now let us take what is called an abolition state—the Republican slavery-hating state of New Hampshire—and see how many mulattoes we can find in her borders. The number amounts to just 184. In the Old Dominion—in the Democratic and aristocratic state of Virginia—there were a few more mulattoes than the census takers found in New Hampshire. How many do you suppose there were? Seventy-nine thousand, seven hundred and seventy—23,000 more than there were in all the free states! In the slave states there were in 1850, 348,000 mulattoes—all of home production; and in the free states there were less than 60,000 mulattoes—and a large number of them were imported from the South.—*Speech, Clinton, Sept. 8, 1858.* III, 355.

Racial Amalgamation, opposed to—There is a natural disgust in the minds of nearly all white people at the idea of an indiscriminate amalgamation of the white and black races. . . . He [Douglas] finds the Republicans insisting that the Declaration of Independence includes all men, black as well as white, and forthwith he boldly denies that it includes negroes at all, and proceeds to argue gravely that all who contend that it does do so only because they want to vote, and eat, and sleep, and marry with negroes. . . . Now I protest against the counterfeit logic which concludes that, because I do not want a black woman for a slave, I must necessarily want her for a wife. I need not have her for either. I can just leave her alone.—*Speech, Springfield, June 27, 1857.* II, 329.

2.—Judge Douglas is especially horrified at the

thought of the mixing of blood by the white and black races. Agreed for once—a thousand times agreed. There are white men enough to marry all the white women, and black men enough to marry all the black women; and so let them be married. . . . When he shall show that his policy [slavery extension] is better adapted to prevent amalgamation than ours, we shall drop ours and adopt his.—*Speech, Springfield, June 27, 1857.* II, 334.

3.—If he [Douglas] can, by much drumming and repeating, fasten the odium of that idea upon his adversaries, he thinks he can struggle through the storm. He therefore clings to this hope, as a drowning man to the last plank.—*Speech, Springfield, June 27, 1857.* II, 329.

4.—I protest, now and forever, against that counterfeit logic which presumes that because I do not want a negro woman for a slave, I do necessarily want her for a wife. My understanding is that I need not have her for either; but, as God has made us separate, we can leave one another alone, and do one another much good thereby.—*Speech, Chicago, July 10, 1858.* III, 45.

5.—He [Douglas] thinks—he says, at least—that the Republican party is in favor of allowing whites and blacks to intermarry, and that a man can't be a good Republican unless he is willing to elevate black men to office, and to associate with them on terms of perfect equality. He knows that we advocate no such doctrines as those.—*Speech, Clinton, Sept. 8, 1858.* III, 354.

6.—I have never had the least apprehension that I or my friends would marry negroes if there was no law to keep them from it; but as Judge Douglas and his friends seem to be in great apprehension that they might, if there was no law to keep them from it, I give him the most solemn pledge that I will to the very last stand by the law of this state which forbids the marrying of white people with negroes.—*Debate, Charleston, Sept. 18, 1858.* IV, 90.

7.—I do not understand that because I do not want a negro woman for a slave I must necessarily want her for a wife. My understanding is that I can just let her alone. I am now in my 50th year, and I certainly never had a black woman for either a slave or a wife. —*Debate, Charleston, Sept. 18, 1858.* IV, 90. Repeated at Columbus, Ohio, Sept. 16, 1859. V, 144.

8.—I do not understand that there is any place where an alteration of the social and political relations of the negro and the white race can be made except in the state legislature—not in the Congress of the United States—and as Judge Douglas seems to be in constant horror that some such danger is rapidly approaching, I propose, as the best means to prevent it, that the judge be kept at home and placed in the state legislature to fight the measure.—*Debate, Charleston, Sept. 17, 1858.* IV, 91.

9.—The judge [Douglas] will have it that if we [Republicans] do not confess that there is a sort of inequality between the white and black races which justifies us in making them slaves, we must, then, insist that there is a degree of equality that requires us to make them our wives. . . . I have all the while maintained that in so far as it should be insisted that there was an equality between the white and black races that should produce social and political equality, it was an impossibility.—*Debate, Galesburg, Oct. 7, 1858.* IV, 265.

10.—I have lived until my 50th year, and have never had a negro woman either for a slave or a wife, and I think I can live 50 centuries, for that matter, without having one for either.—*Debate, Quincy, Oct. 13, 1858.* IV, 382.

11.—I shall never marry a negress, but I have no objection to anyone else doing so. If a white man wants to marry a negro woman, let him if the negro can stand it.—*To David R. Locke, Sept. 16, 1859.* Locke, 446.

See RACIAL EQUALITY, neither intended nor desired.

Racial Amalgamation, separation of races best preventive of,—Could we [Republicans] have had our way [in the Dred Scott case] the chance of these black girls [daughters of Dred Scott] ever mixing their blood with that of white people would have been diminished at least to the extent that it could not have been without their consent. But Judge Douglas is delighted to have them decided to be slaves . . . and thus left subject to the forced concubinage of their masters, and liable to become mothers of mulattoes in spite of themselves; the very state of case that produces nine-tenths of all the mulattoes—all the mixing of blood in the nation.—*Speech, Springfield, June 27, 1857.* II, 336.

2.—A separation of the races is the only perfect preventive of amalgamation; but as an immediate separation is impossible, the next best thing is to keep them apart where they are not already together. If white and black people never get together in Kansas, they will never mix blood in Kansas.—*Speech, Springfield, June 27, 1857.* II, 335.

3.—The judge [Douglas] regales us with the terrible enormities that take place by the mixture of races; that the inferior race bears the superior down. Why, Judge, if we do not let them get together in the territories, they won't mix there. I should say at least that is a self-evident truth.—*Speech, Chicago, July 10, 1858.* III, 45.

4.—What I would most desire would be the separation of the white and black races.—*Speech, Springfield, July 17, 1858.* III, 187.

5.—Douglas pretends to be horrified at amalgamation, yet had he not opened the war for slavery in Kansas, could there have been any amalgamation there? If you keep the two races separate, is there any danger of amalgamation? . . . Douglas says he does not care whether they vote slavery up or down in Kansas; then I submit to this audience which is the more favorable to amalgamation, he who would not raise a finger to keep it out, or I who would give my vote and use my lawful means to prevent its extension.—*Speech, Carlinville, Aug. 31, 1858.* Angle, 191.

6.—It is better for both of us [white men and negroes] . . . to be separated.—*Speech to free colored men, Aug. 14, 1862.* VIII, 3.

See COLONIZATION, only way to separate races.

See RACIAL AMALGAMATION, slavery source of.

Racial Amalgamation, slavery source of—Statistics show that slavery is the greatest source of amalgamation; and, next to it, not the elevation, but the degradation, of free blacks. Yet Judge Douglas dreads the slightest restraints on the spread of slavery, and the slightest human recognition of the negro, as tending horribly to amalgamation.—*Speech, Springfield, June 27, 1857.* II, 336.

Racial Equality, difficult to attain—Even when you cease to be slaves, you are yet far removed from being placed on an equality with the white race. You are cut off from many of the advantages which the other race enjoys. The aspiration of men is to enjoy equality with the best when free, but on this broad continent not a single man of your race is made the equal of a single man of ours. Go where you are treated the best, and the ban is still upon you.—*Speech to deputation of free colored men, Aug. 14, 1862.* VIII, 2.

Racial Equality, necessary to reconstruction—See RECONSTRUCTION, racial equality essential to.

Racial Equality, neither intended nor desired—What next? Free them, and make them politically and socially our equals? My own feelings will not admit of this, and if mine would, we well know that those of the great mass of whites will not. . . . We cannot, then, make them equals.—*Speech, Peoria, Oct. 16, 1854.* II, 206.
Repeated at Urbana, Oct. 24, 1854. Hertz II, 634.
Repeated at Ottawa, Aug. 21, 1858. III, 227.
Repeated at Carlinville, Aug. 31, 1858. Angle, 190.

2.—What then? Free them all and keep them among us as underlings? Is it quite certain that this betters their condition?—*Speech, Peoria, Oct. 16, 1854.* II, 207.

3.—Let it not be said that I am contending for the establishment of political or social equality between the whites and blacks. I have already said the contrary.—*Speech, Peoria, Oct. 16, 1854.* II, 229.
Repeated at Urbana, Oct. 24, 1854. Hertz II, 645.

4.—Last night Judge Douglas tormented himself with horrors about my disposition to make negroes perfectly equal with white men in social and political relations. He did not stop to show that I have ever said any such thing, or that it legitimately follows anything I have said, but he rushes on with his assertion.—*Speech, Springfield, July 17, 1858.* III, 184.

5.—Anything that argues me into his [Douglas's] idea of perfect social and political equality with the negro is but a specious and fantastic arrangement of words, by which a man can prove a horsechestnut to be a chestnut horse.—*Debate, Ottawa, Aug. 21, 1858.* III, 229.
Repeated at Quincy, Oct. 13, 1858. IV, 317.

6.—I have no purpose to introduce political and social equality between the white and black races. There is a physical difference between the two which, in my judgment, will probably forever forbid their living together upon the footing of perfect equality; and inasmuch as it becomes a necessity that there must be a difference, I, as well as Judge Douglas, am in favor of the race to which I belong having the superior position.—*Debate, Ottawa, Aug. 21, 1858.* III, 229.
Repeated at Quincy, Oct. 13, 1858. IV, 318.
Repeated at Columbus, O. Sept. 16, 1859, V, 142.

7.—Douglas tries to make capital by charges of negro equality against me. My speeches have been printed and before the country for some time on this question, and Douglas knows the utter falsity of such a charge.—*Speech, Carlinville, Aug. 31, 1858.* Angle, 190.

8.—I will say, then, that I am not, nor ever have been, in favor of bringing about, in any way, the social and political equality of the white and black races; that I am not, nor ever have been, in favor of making voters or jurors of negroes, nor of qualifying them to hold office, or intermarry with white people.—*Debate, Charleston, Sept. 18, 1858.* IV, 89.
Repeated at Quincy, Oct. 13, 1858. IV, 315.
Repeated at Columbus, O., Sept. 16, 1859. V, 143.

9.—I have never seen, to my knowledge, a man, woman, or child who was in favor of producing a perfect equality, social and political, between negroes and white men.—*Debate, Charleston, Sept. 18, 1858.* IV, 90.

10.—I have all the while maintained that in so far as it should be insisted there was an equality between the white and black races that should produce a perfect social and political equality, it was an impossibility.—*Debate, Galesburg, Oct. 7, 1858.* IV, 266.

11.—It does not follow that social and political equality between white and black must be incorporated, because slavery must not.—*To J. N. Brown, Oct. 18, 1858.* V, 89.

12.—At Ottawa I read an extract from an old speech of mine, made nearly four years ago . . . in which I expressly declared that my own feelings would not admit of a social and political equality between the white and black races, and that even if my own feelings would admit it, I still knew that the public sentiment of the country would not, and that such a thing was an utter impossibility, or substantially that. —*Debate, Quincy, Oct. 13, 1858.* IV, 317.

13.—When I first saw by the dispatches that Douglas had run from the Senate while you were speaking I did not quite understand it; but seeing by the report that you were cramming down his throat that infernal stereotyped lie of his about "negro equality," the thing became plain.—*To Lyman Trumbull, March 16, 1860.* Tracy, 136.

See LIBERTY, race distinctions incompatible with.

See RACIAL AMALGAMATION, opposed to.

See WHITE RACE, superior position for, preferred.

Racial Relations, "contact" important—*See* RECONSTRUCTION, Louisiana, 8.

Racial Relations, to promote better—*See* RECONSTRUCTION, Louisiana, 8.

Raffle—The President has no authority as to whether you may raffle for the benevolent object you mention. If there is no objection in the Iowa laws, there is none here.—*To Mother Mary Gonyeag, Dec. 15, 1863.* IX, 259.

"Ragmen"—*See* SUBTREASURY, specie provision argues against proposal.

Rail Splitter—I cannot say whether I made those rails or not, but I am quite sure I have made a great many just as good.—*Statement at Decatur, May 8, 1860.* Tarbell II, 134.

See AUTOBIOGRAPHY, Lincoln's, 9, 11.

Railroad, Atlantic to Pacific—The great enterprise of connecting the Atlantic with the Pacific states by railways and telegraph lines has been entered upon with a vigor that gives assurance of success; notwithstanding the embarrassments arising from the prevailing high prices of materials and labor.—*Fourth annual message, Dec. 6, 1864.* X, 299.

Railroad, contrasted with waterways—It [the railroad] is a never failing source of communication between places of business remotely situated from each other. Upon the railroad the regular progress of commercial intercourse is not interrupted by either high or low water, or freezing weather, which are the principal difficulties that render our future hopes of water communication precarious and uncertain.— *Address to Sangamon County, March 9, 1832.* I, 2.

Railroad, home folk must show faith in—An effort is being made to build a railroad from Springfield to Alton. A charter has been granted by the legislature, and books are now open for subscriptions to the stock. The chief reliance for taking the stock must be on the eastern capitalists; yet, as an inducement to them, we, here, must do something. We must stake something of our own in the enterprise, to convince them that we believe it will succeed, and to place ourselves between them and subsequent unfavorable legislation, which, it is supposed, they very much dread.—*Address to Sangamon County, June 30, 1847.* Angle, 33.

Railroad, line in Kentucky urged—I deem it of importance that the loyal regions of East Tennessee and western North Carolina should be connected with Kentucky and other faithful parts of the Union by railroad. I therefore recommend as a military measure that Congress provide for the construction of such a road as speedily as possible. Kentucky will no doubt co-operate and through her legislature make the most judicious selection of a line. . . . Kentucky and the general government co-operating, the work can be completed in a very short time and when done it will be not only of vast present usefulness, but also a valuable permanent improvement, worth its cost in all the future.—*First annual message, Dec. 3, 1861.* VII, 31.

Railroad, Mississippi will see—At no distant day, a railroad connecting the eastern cities with some point on the Mississippi will surely be built.—*Address to Sangamon County, June 30, 1847.* Angle, 36.

Railroad, Sangamon plan too costly—No other improvement that reason will justify us in hoping for can equal in utility the railroad. . . . Yet, however desirable an object the construction of a railroad through our country may be; however high our imaginations may be heated at thoughts of it—there is always a heart-appalling shock accompanying the amount of its cost, which forces us to shrink from our pleasing anticipations. The probable cost of this contemplated railroad is estimated at $290,000; the bare statement of which, in my opinion, is sufficient to justify the belief that the improvement of the Sangamon river is an object much better suited to our infant resources.—*Address to Sangamon County, March 9, 1832.* I, 2.

Railroad Pass, request for renewal of,—Says Tom to John: "Here's your old rotten wheelbarrow. I've broke it, usin' on it. I wish you would mend it, case I shall want to borrow it this afternoon." Acting on this as a precedent, I say: "Here's your old 'chalked hat.' I wish you would take it, and send me a new one; case I shall want to use it the first of March.—*To R. P. Morgan, Feb. 13, 1856.* II, 289.

Rancor, marks Lincoln's contests—It is a little singular that I, who am not a vindictive man, should have always been before the people for election in canvasses marked for their bitterness: always but once; when I came to Congress it was a quiet time. But always besides that the contests in which I have been prominent have been marked with great rancor.—*To John Hay, Nov. 8, 1864.* Hay, 233.

Rashness, cautioned against—[I do not] wish anything done in desperation or rashness.—*To Gen. Hooker, May 7, 1863.* VIII, 265.
2.—I would not push you to any rashness, but I am very anxious that you do your utmost, short of rashness, to keep Bragg from getting off to help Johnston against Grant.—*To Gen. Rosecrans, May 28, 1863.* VIII, 284.

Rashness, repented—Although I was fixed "firm as the surge-repelling rock" in my resolution, I found I was continually repenting the rashness which had led me to make it.—*To Mrs. O. H. Browning, April 1, 1837.* I, 90.

Raymond, Henry J., letters to—See PRESS, some papers unfair.

See EMANCIPATION, financial aspects of compensated, 2.

"Read Slowly"—I cannot leave here now. Herewith is a letter instead. You are one of the best public readers. I have but one suggestion—read it very slowly. And now God bless you, and all good Union men.—*To James C. Conkling, Aug. 26, 1863.* IX, 102.

Reading—A capacity and taste for reading gives access to whatever has been discovered by others. It is the key, or one of the keys, to the already solved prob-

lems. And not only so; it gives a relish and facility for successfully pursuing the unsolved ones.—*Speech, Milwaukee, Sept. 30, 1859.* V, 253.

Reading Through an Eagle—*See* SLAVERY, profit motive, 6.

Reason, reign of, hailed—Happy day when—all appetites controlled, all poisons subdued, all matter subjected—mind, all-conquering mind, shall live and move, the monarch of the world. Glorious consummation! Hail, fall of fury! Reign of reason, all hail.—*Speech, Springfield, Feb. 22, 1842.* I, 209.

Reason, source of national security—Reason, cold, calculating, unimpassioned reason—must furnish all the materials for our future [national] support and defence. Let those materials be molded into general intelligence, sound morality, and, in particular, a reverence for the Constitution, and laws.—*Speech, Springfield, Jan. 1, 1837.* I, 50.

"Rebellion," why term "secession" is preferred—*See* SECESSION, sophism of.

"Rebellion Sugar-Coated"—*See* SECESSION, sophism of.

Recommendation, refused—Not knowing whether he [Charles Wiegand] is fit for any place, I could not with propriety recommend him for any.—*Memorandum, March 24, 1863.* VIII, 231.

Reconstruction, Arkansas—I understand that Senator [William K.] Sebastian of Arkansas thinks of offering to resume his place in the Senate. Of course, the Senate, and not I, would decide whether to admit or reject him. Still I shall feel great interest in the question. It may be so presented as to be one of the very greatest national importance.—*To Gen. Hurlbut, July 31, 1863.* IX, 51.
2.—If Senator Sebastian would come with something of this sort [a properly conceived emancipation measure] from Arkansas, I, at least, should take great interest in his case; and I believe a single individual will have scarcely done the world so great a service.—*To Gen. Hurlbut, July 31, 1863.* IX, 51.
3.—I wish to afford the people of Arkansas an opportunity of taking the oath prescribed in the proclamation of Dec. 8, 1863, preparatory to reorganizing a state government there. Accordingly, I send you by Gen. Kimball some blank books and other blanks, the manner of using which will in the main, be suggested by an inspection of them; and Gen. Kimball will add some verbal explanations.—*To Gen. Steele, Jan. 5, 1864.* IX, 277.
4.—Be sure to retain [in the proposed constitution] the free-state constitutional provision in some unques-

tionable form, and you and he [Mr. Gantt] can fix the rest.—*To Gen. Steele, Jan. 27, 1864. IX, 296.*

5.—Whatever of conflict there is between the [Arkansas] convention and me is accidental, not designed, I having acted in ignorance that the convention would act. I yield to the convention, and have so notified Gen. Steele who is master, and is to cut any knots which cannot be untied.—*To Gen. Thayer, Feb. 15, 1864. X, 8.*

6.—I should have fixed no day for an election [in Arkansas], presented no plan for reconstruction, had I known the convention was doing the same thing.—*To Gen. Steele, Feb. 17, 1864. X, 11.*

7.—When I fixed a plan for an election in Arkansas I did it in ignorance that your convention was doing the same work. Since I learned the latter fact I have been constantly trying to yield my plan to them.—*To W. M. Fishback, Feb. 17, 1864. X, 11.*

8.—Do your best to get out the largest vote possible, and of course as much of it as possible on the right side.—*To Gov. Murphy, March 12, 1864. X, 37.*

9.—Will do my best to protect people and new state government, but can act with no better intentions than have always done.—*To Gov. Murphy, March 18, 1864. X, 49.*

10.—I understand that Congress declines to admit to seats the persons sent as senators and representatives from Arkansas. These persons apprehend that, in consequence, you may not support the new state government there as you otherwise would. My wish is that you give that government and the people there the same support and protection that you would if the members had been admitted, because in no event, nor in any view of the case, can this do any harm, while it will be the best you can do toward suppressing the rebellion.—*To Gen. Steele, June 29, 1864. X, 139.*

Reconstruction, cabinet approved plan—This [general reconstruction] plan was in advance submitted to the then cabinet, and distinctly approved by every member of it.—*Last public speech, April 11, 1865. XI, 87.*

Reconstruction, cliques to be avoided—Of all things, avoid, if possible, a dividing into cliques among the friends of the common object. Be firm and resolute against such as you can perceive would make confusion and division.—*To Gen. Steele, Jan. 30, 1864. IX, 299.*

Reconstruction, Florida—I understand an effort is being made by some worthy gentlemen to reconstruct a loyal state government in Florida. . . . It is desirable for all to co-operate, but if differences of opinion shall arise, you are master. I wish the thing done in the most speedy way possible, so that when done, it lie within the range of the late proclamation on the subject.—*To Gen. Gillmore, Jan. 13, 1864. IX, 283.*

Reconstruction, "fraught with difficulty"—Reconstruction . . . is fraught with great difficulty. Unlike a case of war between independent nations, there is no authorized organization for us to treat with—no one man has authority to give up the rebellion for any other man. We simply must begin with and mold from disorganized and discordant elements. Nor is it a small additional embarrassment that we, the loyal people, differ among ourselves as to the mode, manner, and measure of reconstruction.—*Last public address, April 11, 1865. XI, 85.*

Reconstruction, freedmen in—I have said, and say again, that if a new state government, acting in harmony with this government, and consistently with general freedom, shall think best to adopt a reasonable temporary arrangement in relation to the landless and homeless freed people, I do not object; but my word is out to be for and not against them on the question of their permanent freedom.—*To Gen. Banks, Nov. 5, 1863. IX, 201.*

2.—I do further proclaim, declare, and make known, that any provision which may be adopted by said government in relation to the freed people of such state, which shall recognize and declare their permanent freedom, provide for their education, and which may yet be consistent, as a temporary arrangement, with their present condition as a laboring, landless and homeless class, will not be objected to by the national executive.—*Proclamation, Dec. 8, 1863. IX, 222.*

3.—You have enquired how the government would regard and treat cases wherein the owners of plantations, in Arkansas, for instance, might fully recognize the freedom of those formerly slaves, and by fair contracts of hire with them, recommence the cultivation of their plantations. I answer, I should regard such cases with great favor, and should as a principle treat them precisely as I would treat the same number of white people in the same relation and condition. Whether white or black, reasonable effort should be made to give government protection.—*To Alpheus Lewis, Jan. 23, 1864. IX, 292.*

4.—[Mr. Lewis] hopes to be useful, without charge to the government, in facilitating the introduction of the free labor system on the Mississippi plantations. . . . He will show you two letters of mine on this subject. . . . I desire that all I promise in these letters, so far as practicable, may be in good faith carried out.—*To Gen. Thomas, March 1, 1864. X, 27.*

Reconstruction, Louisiana—The people of Louisiana —all intelligent people everywhere—know full well that I never had a wish to touch the foundations of their society or any right of theirs. With perfect knowledge of this, they forced a necessity upon me to send armies among them, and it is their own fault, not mine, that they are annoyed by the presence of Gen. Phelps. They know the remedy—how to be cured of Gen. Phelps. Remove the necessity for this presence. . . . If they can conceive of anything worse than Gen. Phelps within my power, would they not better be looking out for it? They very well know the way to avert all this is simply to take their place in the Union upon the old terms. If they will not do this, should they not receive harder blows rather than lighter ones?—*To Reverdy Johnson, July 26, 1862.* VII, 292.

2.—The people of Louisiana who wish protection to person and property have but to reach forth their hands and take it. Let them in good faith reinaugurate the national authority, and set up a state government conforming thereto under the Constitution. They know how to do it, and can have the protection of the army while doing it. The army will be withdrawn so soon as such state government can dispense with its presence; and the people of the state can then, upon the old constitutional terms, govern themselves to their own liking. This is very simple and easy.—*To Cuthbert Bullitt, July 28, 1862.* VII, 297.

3.—Broken eggs cannot be mended; but Louisiana has nothing to do now but to take her place in the Union as it was, barring the already broken eggs. The sooner she does so, the smaller will be the amount of that which will be past mending.—*To August Belmont, July 31, 1862.* VII, 299.

4.—In all available ways give the people a chance to express their wishes at those elections [in Louisiana]. Follow forms of law as far as convenient, but at all events get the largest number of people possible. . . . Of course the men elected [to office] should be gentlemen of character, willing to swear support to the Constitution, as of old, and known to be above reasonable suspicion of duplicity.—*To Gen. Butler and others, Oct. 14, 1862.* VIII, 62.

5.—In my mind there could be no possible object in such an election [of men not citizens of Louisiana as Congressmen from that state]. . . . What we do want is conclusive evidence that respectable citizens of Louisiana are willing to be members of Congress and to swear support of the Constitution, and that other respectable citizens there are willing to vote for them and send them. To send a parcel of northern men here as representatives, elected, as would be understood—and perhaps really so—at the point of the bayonet, would be disgusting and outrageous; and were I a member of Congress here, I would vote against admitting any such man to a seat.—*To Gov. G. F. Shepley, Nov. 21, 1862.* VIII, 79.

6.—I wish elections for congressmen to take place in Louisiana; but I wish it to be a movement of the people of the districts, and not a movement of our military and quasi-military authorities there. I merely wish our authorities to give the people a chance—to protect them against secession interference. . . . Knots must be cut, the main object being to get an expression of the people. If they would fix a day and a way for themselves, all the better; but if they stand idle, not seeming to know what to do, do you fix these things for them by proclamation. And do not waste a day about it.—*To Gov. G. F. Shepley, Nov. 21, 1862.* VIII, 80.

7.—The people of Louisiana shall not lack an opportunity for a fair election for both federal and state officers by want of anything within my power to give them.—*To E. E. Malhiot, B. Johnson, and T. Cottman, June 19, 1863.* VIII, 328.

8.—While I very well know what I would be glad for Louisiana to do, it is quite a different thing for me to assume direction of the matter. I would be glad for her to make a new constitution, recognizing the Emancipation Proclamation, and adopting emancipation in those parts of the state to which the proclamation does not apply. And while she is at it, I think it would not be objectionable for her to adopt some practical system by which the two races could gradually live themselves out of their old relation to each other, and both come out better prepared for the new. Education for young blacks should be included in the plan. After all, the power or element of "contact" may be sufficient for this probationary period, and by its simplicity and flexibility may be the better. . . . Gov. Shepley has informed me that Mr. Durant is now taking a registry, with a view to the election of a constitutional convention in Louisiana. This, to me, appears proper. If such convention were to ask my views, I could present little else than what I now say to you.—*To Gen. Banks, Aug. 5, 1863.* IX, 56.

9.—Gov. Shepley has special instructions from the War Department. I wish him . . . without waiting for more territory, to go to work and give me a tangible nucleus which the remainder of the state may rally around as fast as it can, and which I can at once recognize and sustain as the true state government. And in that work I wish you and all under your command to give them a hearty sympathy and support.— *To Gen. Banks, Nov. 5, 1863.* IX, 201.

10.—You were so kind as to say this morning that

you desire to return to Louisiana, and to be guided by my wishes, to some extent, in the part you may take in bringing that state to resume her rightful relation to the general government. My wishes were in a general way expressed, as well as I can express them, in the proclamation issued on the 8th of the present month, and in that part of the annual message which relates to that proclamation. . . . I have not put forth the plan . . . as a Procrustean bed, to which exact conformity is indispensable; and, in Louisiana particularly, I wish that labor already done, which varies from that plan in no important particular, may not be thrown away.—*To Dr. Thomas Cottman, Dec. 15, 1863. IX, 256.*

11.—I have all the while intended you to be master, as well in regard to reorganizing a state government for Louisiana, as in regard to military matters of the department. . . . I now tell you that in every dispute with whomsoever, you are master. . . . You are master of all. . . . I wish you to take the case as you find it, and give us a free state reorganization in Louisiana in the shortest possible time.—*To Gen. Banks, Dec. 24, 1863. IX, 273.*

12.—I have just seen the new constitution adopted by the convention in Louisiana; and I am anxious that it shall be ratified by the people. I will thank you to let the civil officers in Louisiana, holding under me, know that this is my wish, and let me know at once who of them openly declare for the constitution, and who of them, if any, decline to so declare.—*To Gen. Banks, Aug. 9, 1864. X, 186.*

13.—Few things since I have been here have impressed me more painfully than what, for four or five months past, has appeared a bitter military opposition to the new state government of Louisiana. . . . A very fair proportion of the people of Louisiana have inaugurated a new state government, making an excellent constitution. . . . During the formation of the new government and constitution they were supported by nearly every loyal person and opposed by every secessionist. . . . Every advocate of slavery naturally desires to see blasted and crushed the liberty promised the black man by the new constitution. But why Gen. Canby and Gen. Hurlbut should join on the same side is to me incomprehensible.—*To Gen. Hurlbut, Nov. 14, 1864. X, 266.*

14.—To make assurance against misunderstanding, I repeat that in the existing condition of things in Louisiana, the military must not be thwarted by the civil authority; and I add that on points of difference the commanding general must be judge and master. But I also add that in the exercise of this judgment and control, a purpose, obvious and scarcely unavowed, to transcend all military necessity, in order to crush out the civil government, will not be overlooked.—*To Gen. Hurlbut, Nov. 14, 1864. X, 268.*

15.—It is a worthy object to again get Louisiana into proper practical relations with the nation, and we can never finish this if we never begin it. Much good work is already done, and surely nothing can be gained by throwing it away.—*To Gen. Canby, Dec. 12, 1864. X, 313.*

16.—Even before Gen. Banks went to Louisiana I was anxious for the loyal people there to move for reorganization and restoration of proper practical relations with the Union; and when he at last expressed his decided conviction that the thing was practicable, I directed him to give his official co-operation to effect it.—*To Lyman Trumbull, Jan. 9, 1865. X, 333.*

17.—From about July, 1862, I had corresponded with different persons supposed to be interested in the reconstruction of a state government in Louisiana. When the message of 1863, with the plan before mentioned, reached New Orleans, Gen. Banks wrote me that he was confident the people, with his military co-operation, would reconstruct substantially on that plan. I wrote him and some of them to try it. They tried it and the result is known. Such has been my only agency in getting up this Louisiana government.—*Last public speech, April 11, 1865. XI, 87.*

18.—The question is not whether the Louisiana government, as it stands, is quite all that is desirable. The question is, will it be wiser to take it as it is and help to improve it, or to reject and disperse it? . . . Some 12,000 voters in the heretofore slave state . . . have sworn allegiance to the Union, assumed to be the rightful political power of the state, held elections, organized a state government, adopted a free-state constitution, giving the benefit of public schools equally to black and white, and empowering the legislature to confer the elective franchise upon the colored man. Their legislature has already voted to ratify the constitutional amendment recently passed by Congress, abolishing slavery throughout the nation. These 12,000 persons are thus fully committed to the Union and to perpetual freedom in the state—committed to the very things, and nearly all of the things, the nation wants—and they ask the nation's recognition and its assistance to make good their committal. Now, if we reject and spurn them, we do our utmost to disorganize and disperse them. We, in effect, say to the white man: You are worthless or worse; we will neither help you nor be helped by you. To the blacks we say: This cup of liberty which these, your old masters, hold to your lips we will dash from you, and leave you to the chances of gathering the spilled and scattered contents in some vague and indefinite when, where and how. If this course, discouraging and paralyzing both white and black, has any tendency to bring Louisiana into proper practical relations with the Union, I have so far been unable to perceive it. If, on the contrary, we recognize and sustain the new government of Louisiana, the converse of all this is made true.—*Last public speech, April 11, 1865.* XI, 89.

19.—[If the federal government sustains the new Missouri constitution] we encourage the hearts and nerve the arms of 12,000 [who established it] to adhere to their work, and argue for it, and proselyte for it, and fight for it, and feed it, and grow it, and ripen it to a complete success. The colored man, too, in seeing all united for him, is inspired with vigilance, and energy, and daring, to the same end. Grant that he desires the elective franchise, will he not attain it sooner by saving the already advanced steps toward it than by running backward over them?—*Last public speech, April 11, 1865.* XI, 90.

20.—I am trying to blaze a way through the swamp [in Louisiana].—*To William Pitt Kellogg, April 12, 1865.* Quarterly, Sept., 1945. p. 333.

Reconstruction, must not repudiate emancipation—If a few professedly loyal men [in Louisiana] shall draw the disloyal about them, and colorably set up a state government, repudiating the Emancipation Proclamation, and re-establishing slavery, I cannot recognize or sustain their work. I shall fall powerless in the attempt. This government in such an attitude would be a house divided against itself.—*To Gen. Banks, Nov. 5, 1863.* IX, 201.

2.—I deem the sustaining of the Emancipation Proclamation, where it applies, as indispensable [in a state seeking re-admission to the Union]. . . . The strongest wish I have . . . is that . . . all sincere Union men would stoutly eschew cliquism, and, each yielding something in minor matters, all work together. Nothing is likely to be so baleful in the great work before us as stepping aside from the main object to consider who will get the offices if a small matter shall go thus, and who else will get them if it shall go otherwise. It is a time now for real patriots to rise above all this.—*To Dr. Thomas Cottman, Dec. 15, 1863.* IX, 257.

Reconstruction, national help in—The constitutional obligation of the United States to guarantee to every state in the Union a republican form of government and to protect the state in the cases stated [against invasion and domestic violence] is explicit and full. But why tender the benefits of this provision only to a state government set up in this particular way? This section of the Constitution contemplates a case wherein the element within a state favorable to republican government in the Union may be too feeble for an opposite and hostile element external to, or even within, the state; and such are precisely the cases with which we are now dealing. An attempt to guarantee and protect a revived state government constructed in whole or in preponderating part from the very element against whose hostility and violence it is to be protected is simply absurd. There must be a test by which to separate the opposing elements, so as to build only from the sound; and that test is sufficiently one which accepts as sound whoever will make a sworn recantation of his former unsoundness. —*Third annual message, Dec. 8, 1863.* IX, 248.

Reconstruction, no inflexible plan for—While the mode presented is the best the Executive can suggest, with his present impressions, it must not be understood that no other possible mode would be acceptable.—*Proclamation, Dec. 8, 1863.* IX, 223.

2.—Saying that reconstruction will be accepted if presented in a specified way, it is not said it will never be accepted in any other way.—*Third annual message, Dec. 8, 1863.* IX, 251.

3.—I . . . am unprepared . . . to be inflexibly committed to any single plan of restoration, and while I am also unprepared to declare that the free state constitutions and governments already adopted and installed in Arkansas and Louisiana shall be set aside and held for naught, thereby repelling and discouraging the loyal citizens which have set up the same as to further effort, or to declare a constitutional competency in Congress to abolish slavery in states, but I am at the same time sincerely hoping and expecting that a constitutional amendment abolishing slavery throughout the nation may be adopted; nevertheless, I am fully satisfied with the system for restoration contained in the bill as one very proper plan for the loyal people of any state choosing to adopt it, and I am and at all times shall be prepared to give the executive aid and assistance to any such people as soon as the military resistance to the United States shall have been suppressed in any such state and the people thereof shall have sufficiently returned to their obedience to the Constitution and the laws of the United States, in which cases military governors will be appointed with directions to proceed according to the bill.—*Proclamation, July 8, 1864.* X, 152.

4.—So great peculiarities pertain to each state, and such important and sudden changes occur in the same state, and withal so new and unprecedented is the whole case that no exclusive and inflexible plan can safely be prescribed as to details and collaterals. Such exclusive and inflexible plan would surely become a new entanglement.—*Last public speech, April 11, 1865.* XI, 91.

See RECONSTRUCTION, Louisiana, 10.

Reconstruction, none but trusted men admissible in —*See* RECONSTRUCTION, Tennessee, 3.

Reconstruction, policy in—The proposed acquiescence of the national executive in any reasonable temporary state arrangement for the freed people is made with the view of possibly modifying the confusion and destitution which must at best attend all classes by a total revolution of labor throughout whole states. It is hoped that the already deeply afflicted people in those states may be somewhat more ready to give up the cause of their affliction, if, to this extent, this vital matter is left to themselves.— *Third annual message, Dec. 8, 1863.* IX, 250.

2.—It was to obviate this question [whether rebel states were in or out of the Union] that I earnestly favored the movement for an amendment to the Constitution abolishing slavery. . . . I thought it much better, if it were possible, to restore the Union without the necessity of a quarrel among its friends as to whether certain states have been in or out of the Union during the war; a mere metaphysical question and one unnecessary to be forced into the discussion. —*To group at Capitol, July 4, 1864.* Hay, 205.

3.—I must have some consciousness of being somewhere near right. I must keep some standard or principle fixed within myself.—*To John Hay, July 4, 1864.* Hay, 206.

4.—It is my wish for you to relieve the people from all burdens, harassments, and oppressions, so far as it is possible consistently with your military necessities; that the object of the war being to restore and maintain the blessings of peace and good government, I desire you to help and not hinder every advance in that direction.—*To commanders in western Tennessee, Feb. 13, 1865.* XI, 34.

5.—I have been shown a letter . . . in which the writer expresses regret that my mind has not seemed definitely fixed on the question whether the seceded states, so called, are in the Union or out of it. . . . As appears to me, that question has not been, nor yet is, a practically material one, and that any discussion of it, while it remains thus practically immaterial, could have no effect other than the mischievous one of dividing our friends. And yet, whatever it may hereafter become, that question is bad as the basis of a controversy, and good for nothing at all— a merely pernicious abstraction.—*Last public speech, April 11, 1865.* XI, 87.

6.—We all agree that the seceded states, so called, are out of their proper practical relation with the Union, and that the sole object of the government, civil and military, in regard to these states, is to again get them into that proper practical relation. I believe it is not only possible, but in fact easier, to do this without deciding or even considering whether these states have ever been out of the Union, than with it. Finding themselves safely at home, it would be utterly immaterial whether they had ever been abroad. Let us all join in doing the acts necessary to restoring the practical relations between these states and the Union, and each forever after innocently indulge his own opinion whether in doing the acts he brought the states from without into the Union, or only gave them proper assistance, they never having been out of it.—*Last public speech, April 11, 1865.* XI, 88.

7.—I hope there will be no persecution, no bloody work after the war is over. . . . Enough lives have been sacrificed. We must extinguish our resentment, if we expect harmony and reunion. There is too much desire on the part of our very good friends to be masters, to interfere with and dictate to those states, to treat the people not as fellow citizens; there is too little respect for the right. I don't sympathize with those feelings.—*To cabinet, April 14, 1865.* Stephenson, 467.

See SOUTH, no cause for fear by.

Reconstruction, progress in—Important movements have . . . occurred during the year to the effect of molding society for the durability of the Union. Although short of complete success, it is much in the right direction that 12,000 citizens in each of the states of Arkansas and Louisiana have organized loyal state governments, with free constitutions, and are earnestly struggling to administer them. The movements in the same direction, more extensive though less definite, in Missouri, Kentucky and Tennessee should not be overlooked. But Maryland presents the example of complete success.—*Fourth annual message, Dec. 6, 1864.* X, 303.

Reconstruction, proposed proclamation—I . . . do proclaim, declare and make known, that on the conditions therein stated [*See* EMANCIPATION, joint resolution for compensated, urged] the power conferred on the executive in and by said joint resolution will be fully exercised; that war will cease and armies reduced to a basis of peace; that all political offenses will be pardoned; that all property, except slaves, liable to confiscation or forfeiture, will be released therefrom, except in cases of intervening interests of third parties; and that liberality will be recommended to Congress upon all points not lying within executive control.—*To Congress, Feb. 5, 1865 (disapproved by cabinet; not signed or sent).* XI, 2.

Reconstruction, racial equality essential to—The restoration of the rebel states to the Union must rest upon the principle of civil and political equality of both races; and it must be sealed by general amnesty. —*To Gen. Wadsworth, Jan., or Feb., 1864.* XI, 131.

Reconstruction, state identities to remain—It is suggested as not improper that, in constructing a loyal state government in any state, the name of the state, the boundary, the subdivisions, the constitution, and the general code of laws, as before the rebellion, be maintained, subject only to the modifications made necessary by the conditions hereinbefore stated, and such others, if any, not contravening said conditions, and which may be deemed expedient by those framing the new state government.—*Proclamation, Dec. 8, 1863.* IX, 222.

2.—The suggestion in the proclamation [of Dec. 8] as to maintaining the political framework of the states in what is called reconstruction is made in the hope that it may do good without danger of harm. It will save labor, and avoid great confusion.—*Third annual message, Dec. 8, 1863.* IX, 250.

Reconstruction, Tennessee—If we could, somehow, get a vote of the people of Tennessee and have it result properly, it would be worth more to us than a battle gained. How long before we can get such a vote?—*To Gov. Johnson, July 11, 1862.* Hertz II, 871.

2.—The bearer of this, Thomas R. Smith, a citizen of Tennessee, goes to that state seeking to have such of the people thereof as desire to avoid the unsatisfactory prospect before them and to have peace again upon the old terms under the Constitution of the United States, to manifest such desire by elections of members to the Congress of the United States particularly, and perhaps a legislature, state officers, and a U.S. senator friendly to their object. I shall be glad for you and each of you to aid him, and all others acting for this object, as much as possible. In all available ways give the people a show to express their wishes at these elections.—*To Gen. Grant and others, Oct. 21, 1862.* Hertz II, 885.

3.—The reinauguration must not be such as to give control of the state and its representation in Congress to the enemies of the Union, driving its friends there into political exile. . . . Let the reconstruction be the work of such men only as can be trusted for the Union. Exclude all others, and trust that your government so organized will be recognized here as being the one of republican form to be guaranteed to the

state, and to be protected against invasion and domestic violence.—*To Gov. Johnson, Sept. 11, 1863.* IX, 116.

4.—All Tennessee is now clear of armed insurrectionists. You need not be reminded that it is the nick of time for reinaugurating a loyal state government. Not a moment should be lost.—*To Gov. Johnson, Sept. 11, 1863.* IX, 116.

5.—I see that you have declared for emancipation in Tennessee, for which may God bless you. Get emancipation into your new state government—constitution —and there will be no such word as fail for your case. —*To Gov. Johnson, Sept. 11, 1863.* IX, 117.

6.—You are hereby authorized to exercise such powers as may be necessary and proper to enable the loyal people of Tennessee to present such a republican form of state government as will entitle the state to the guaranty of the United States therefor, and to be protected under such state government against invasion and domestic violence.—*To Gov. Johnson, Sept. 19, 1863.* IX, 127.

7.—In the county and state elections of Tennessee, the oath prescribed in the proclamation of Gov. Johnson on the 26th of January, 1864 . . . is entirely satisfactory to me as a test of loyalty of all persons proposing or offering to vote in said elections; and coming from him would better be observed and followed. There is no conflict between the oath of amnesty in my proclamation of the 8th of December, 1863, and that prescribed by Gov. Johnson.—*To E. H. East, Feb. 27, 1864.* X, 21.

8.—If any election shall be held, and any votes shall be cast in the state of Tennessee for President and Vice President of the United States, it will belong, not to the military agents, nor yet to the executive department, but exclusively to another department of the government, to determine whether they are entitled to be counted in conformity with the Constitution and laws of the United States.—*To W. B. Campbell and others, Oct. 22, 1864.* X, 250.

Reconstruction, terms for, declared—And I do further proclaim, declare, and make known that whenever, in any of the [seceding] states . . . a number of persons, not less than one tenth in number of the votes cast in such state at the presidential election of the year of our Lord one thousand eight hundred and sixty, each having taken the oath [of allegiance] aforesaid and not having since violated it, and being qualified voters by the election laws of the state existing immediately before the so-called act of secession, and excluding all others, shall re-establish a state government which shall be republican, and in no wise contravening said oath, such shall be recognized as the true government of the state.—*Proclamation, Dec. 8, 1863.* IX, 221.

Reconstruction, war power and—*See* WAR POWER, main reliance.

Reconstruction, why a proclamation?—But why a proclamation now upon this subject? The question· is beset with conflicting views that the step might be delayed too long or be taken too soon. In some states the element for resumption seems ready for action, but remains inactive apparently for want of a rallying point. . . . By the proclamation a plan is presented which may be accepted by them as a rallying point, and which they are assured in advance will not be rejected here. This may bring them to act sooner than they otherwise would.—*Third annual message, Dec. 8, 1863.* IX, 250.

Recreation, man needs—Constituted as man is, he has positive need of occasional recreation, and whatever can give him this associated with virtue and advantage, and free from vice and disadvantage, is a positive good.—*Speech, Milwaukee, Sept. 30, 1859.* V, 237.

"Red Cotton Handkerchief," cost of a slave—*See* AFRICAN SLAVE TRADE, slavery extension akin to, 2.

Rejected Lover—In getting Baker the nomination I shall be fixed a good deal like a fellow who is made groomsman to a man who has cut him out and is marrying his own dear "gal."—*To Joshua F. Speed, March 24, 1843.* I, 261.
2.—Like a rejected lover, making merry at the wedding of his rival, the President [Pierce] felicitates himself hugely over the late presidential election.—*Speech, Chicago, Dec. 10, 1856.* II, 308.

Religion, attitude toward—That I am not a member of any Christian church is true; but I have never denied the truth of the Scriptures; and I have never spoken with intentional disrespect of religion in general, or of any denomination of Christians in particular. It is true that in early life I was inclined to believe in what I understand is called the "Doctrine of Necessity"—that is, that the human mind is impelled to action, or held in rest, by some power, over which the mind itself has no control; and I have sometimes, with one, two or three, but never publicly, tried to maintain this opinion in argument. The habit of arguing thus, however, I have entirely left off for more than five years. And, I add here, I have always understood this same opinion to be held by several of the Christian denominations. . . . I do not think I could myself be brought to support a man for office whom I knew to be an open enemy of, or

scoffer at, religion. Leaving the higher matter of eternal consequences between himself and his Maker, I still do not think any man has the right thus to insult the feelings, and injure the morals, of the community in which he may live.—*Address to voters, July 31, 1846.* Quarterly, March, 1942, p. 4.
2.—I am not a Christian. God knows I would be one.—*To Newton Bateman, before the 1860 election.* Brooks, 208.
3.—I know there is a God, and that He hates injustice and slavery. I see the storm coming, and I know His hand is in it. If He has a place and work for me, and I think He has, I believe I am ready. I am nothing, but truth is everything. I know I am right, for Christ teaches it, and Christ is God. I have told that a house divided against itself cannot stand, and Christ and reason say the same thing; and they will find it so. Douglas doesn't care whether slavery is voted up or voted down, but God cares, and humanity cares, and I care; and with God's help I shall not fail. I may not see the end, but it will come and I shall be vindicated; and these men [majority of Springfield men opposed Lincoln for President] will find that they have not read their Bibles aright.—*To Newton Bateman, before the 1860 election.* Brooks, 209.
4.—When any church will inscribe over its altar, as its sole qualification for membership, the Savior's condensed statement of the substance of both law and Gospel, "Thou shalt love the Lord thy God with all thy heart, and with all thy soul and thy neighbor as thyself," that church will I join with all my heart and all my soul.—*To Henry Champion Deming, no date.* Eulogy, 42.

Religion, "not the sort"—You say your husband is a religious man; tell him when you meet him that I say I am not much of a judge of religion, but that, in my opinion, the religion that sets men to rebel and fight against their government because, as they think, that government does not sufficiently help some men to eat their bread in the sweat of other men's faces, is not the sort of religion upon which people can get to Heaven.—*Memorandum, Dec. 3, 1864.* X, 280.

Religious Duty—*See* NEGRO SUFFRAGE, favored, 2.

Religious Liberty—*See* LIBERTY, CIVIL AND RELIGIOUS.

Repentance, calling righteous to—*See* REPUBLICAN PARTY, advice to, 19.

Repentance, forgiveness on terms of—*See* OATH, form of, disliked.

See AMNESTY, penitence alone essential.

Repentance, required of Douglas—Repentance before forgiveness is a provision of the Christian system, and on that condition alone will the Republicans grant, him [Douglas] forgiveness.—*Speech, Springfield, July 17, 1858.* III, 167.

Repentance, willing to accept—*See* GOVERNMENT (American), preservation of, first duty, 3.

Representative, creed for a—While acting as their [peoples'] representative, I shall be governed by their will on all subjects upon which I have the means of knowing what their will is; and upon all others, I shall do what my own judgment teaches me will best advance their interests.—*To editor, Sangamo Journal, June 13, 1836.* I, 15.
2.—You [Democrats] violated the primary, the one great living principle of all democratic representative government—the principle that the representative is bound to carry out the known will of his constituents. —*Speech in Congress, July 27, 1848.* I, 71.
3.—For a senator to be the impartial representative of his whole state is so plain a duty that I pledge myself to the observance of it without hesitation.—*To E. B. Washburne, Dec. 19, 1854.* II, 269.

Republic, "central ideas" of—Let us reinaugurate the good old "central ideas" of the Republic. We can do it.—*Speech, Chicago, Dec. 10, 1856.* II, 311.

Republican Form of Government—*See* SELF-GOVERNMENT.

Republican Institutions, inquiry and discussion best sustain—Compliance with this general wish [that postmasters be authorized to receive newspaper subscriptions] is deemed to be in accordance with our republican institutions, which can be best sustained by the diffusion of knowledge and the due encouragement of a universal, national spirit of inquiry and discussion of public events through the medium of the public press.—*Committee report to Congress, March 9, 1848.* II, 4.

Republican Party, adopts Jefferson's principles—*See* JEFFERSON, THOMAS, supporters and opponents of, trade creeds.

Republican Party, advice to—Let us, in building our new party, plant ourselves on the rock of the Declaration of Independence and the gates of hell shall not be able to prevail against us.—*Speech, Bloomington, May 29, 1856.* History and Overthrow, 93.
2.—We know that great political and moral wrongs are done, and outrages committed, and we denounce these wrongs and outrages, although we cannot, at present, do much more. But we desire to reach out beyond those personal outrages and establish a rule that will apply to all, and so prevent any further outrages.—*Speech, Bloomington, May 29, 1856.* Lapsley II, 249.
3.—I counsel you earnestly to bury all resentment, to sink all personal feeling, make all things work to a common purpose in which we are all united and agreed about, and which all present will agree is absolutely necessary—which must be done by any rightful mode if there be such; Slavery must be kept out of Kansas! The test—the pinch—is right there.— *Speech, Bloomington, May 29, 1856.* Lapsley II, 250.
4.—As this struggle [against slavery extension] is likely to be long and earnest, we must not by our action, repel any who are in sympathy with us in the main, but rather win all that we can to our standard. We must not belittle or overlook the facts of our condition—that we are new and comparatively weak, while our enemies are entrenched and relatively strong. They have the administration and the political power, and, right or wrong, at present they have the numbers. Our friends who urge an appeal to arms with so much force and eloquence should recollect that the government is arrayed against us, and that the numbers are arrayed against us as well; or, to state it nearer to the truth, they are not yet expressly and affirmatively for us; and we should repel friends rather than gain them by anything savoring of revolutionary methods. As it now stands, we must appeal to the sober sense and patriotism of the people.— *Speech, Bloomington, May 29, 1856.* Lapsley II, 266.
5.—Now, let us harmonize, my friends, and appeal to the moderation and patriotism of the people; to the sober second thought; to the awakened public conscience.—*Speech, Bloomington, May 29, 1856.* Lapsley II, 268.
6.—Whatever duty urges us to do or to omit must be done or omitted; and the recklessness with which our adversaries break the laws, or counsel their violation, should afford no example for us.—*Speech, Bloomington, May 29, 1856.* Lapsley II, 273.
7.—But let us, meanwhile, appeal to the sense and patriotism of the people, and not to their prejudice; let us spread the floods of enthusiasm here aroused all over these vast prairies so suggestive of freedom.— *Speech, Bloomington, May 29, 1856.* Lapsley II, 275.
8.—Let everyone who really believes, and is resolved, that free society is not and shall not be a failure, and who can conscientiously declare that in the past contest he has done only what he thought best—let every such one have charity to believe that every other one can say as much. Thus let bygones be bygones; let past differences as nothing be.—*Speech, Chicago, Dec. 10, 1856.* II, 311.

9.—What think you of the probable "rumpus" among the Democracy over the Kansas constitution? I think the Republicans should stand clear of it. In their view both the President and Douglas are wrong; and they should not espouse the cause of either, because they may consider the other a little the farther wrong of the two.—*To Lyman Trumbull, Nov. 30, 1857.* Tracy, 82.

10.—I believe we need nothing so much as to get rid of unjust suspicions of one another.—*To Charles L. Wilson, June 1, 1858.* II, 364.

11.—Two years ago the Republicans of the nation mustered over thirteen hundred thousand strong. We did this under the single impulse of resistance to a common danger, with every external circumstance against us. Of strange, discordant, and even hostile, elements we gathered from the four winds, and formed and fought the battle through, under the constant hot fire of a disciplined, proud and pampered enemy. Did we brave all to falter now?—now when that same enemy is wavering, dissevered and belligerent?—*Speech, Springfield, June 16, 1858.* III, 15.

12.—All you have to do is to keep the faith, to remain steadfast in the right, to stand by your banner. Nothing should lead you to leave your guns. Stand together, match in hand. Allow nothing to turn you to the right or the left.—*Speech, Chicago, March 1, 1859.* V, 123.

13.—I think the only temptation [in adopting party resolutions] will be to lower the Republican standard in order to gather recruits. In my judgment such a step would be a serious mistake, and open a gap through which would pass out more than pass in. And this would be the same whether the letting down should be in deference to Douglasism or to the southern opposition element; either would surrender the object of the Republican organization—the preventing of the spread and nationalization of slavery. This object surrendered, and the organization would go to pieces.—*To M. W. Delahay, May 14, 1859.* V, 128.

14.—In every locality we [Republicans] should look beyond our noses; and at least say nothing on points where it is probable we shall disagree.—*To Schuyler Colfax, July 6, 1859.* V, 132.

15.—If we [Republicans] shall adopt a platform that fails to recognize or express our purpose, or elect a man that declares himself inimical to our purpose, we not only take nothing by our success, but we tacitly admit that we act upon no other principle than a desire to have "the loaves and fishes," by which, in the end, our apparent success is really an injury to us.—*Speech, Cincinnati, Sept. 17, 1859.* V, 232.

16.—Now, let our friends bear, and forbear, and not quarrel over the spoils.—*To W. M. Dickson, Oct. 17, 1859.* Angle, 226.

17.—As to men for leaders, we must remember that "he who is not for us is against us; and he that gathereth not with us, scattereth."—*Speeches in Kansas, Dec. 1–5, 1859.* V, 280.

18.—It is exceedingly desirable that all parts of this confederacy shall be at peace, and in harmony one with another. Let us Republicans do our part to have it so. Even though much provoked, let us do nothing through passion and ill temper. Even though the southern people will not as much as listen to us, let us calmly consider their demands, and yield to them, if in our deliberate view of our duty, we possibly can.—*Cooper Institute address, New York, Feb. 27, 1860.* V, 323.
Repeated at New Haven, Conn., March 6, 1860. V, 367.

19.—Let us stand by our duty fearlessly and effectively. Let us be diverted by none of those sophistical contrivances wherewith we are so industriously plied and belabored—contrivances such as groping for some middle ground between the right and the wrong; vain as the search for a man who should be neither a living man nor a dead man . . . such as Union appeals beseeching true Union men to yield to disunionists, reversing the divine rule, and calling, not the sinners, but the righteous, to repentance.—*Cooper Institute address, New York, Feb. 27, 1860.* V, 327.
Repeated at New Haven, Conn., March 6, 1860. V, 371.

20.—Let us [not] be slandered from our duty by false accusations against us, nor frightened from it by menaces of destruction to the government, nor of dungeons to ourselves.—*Cooper Institute address, New York, Feb. 27, 1860.* V, 327.
Repeated at New Haven, Conn., March 6, 1860. V, 371.

21.—I rejoice with you in the success which has thus far attended that [the Republican] cause. Yet in all our rejoicings, let us neither express nor cherish any feelings toward any citizen who by his vote has differed with us.—*Speech, Springfield, Nov. 20, 1860.* VI, 72.

See REPUBLICAN PARTY, threats to unity of.

Republican Party, conservative—The chief and real purpose of the Republican party is conservative. It proposes nothing save and except to restore this government to its original tone in regard to this element of slavery.—*Speech, Columbus, Ohio, Sept. 16, 1859.* V, 147.

2.—You [Democrats] claim that you are conservative, and we are not. We deny it. What is conservatism? Preserving the old against the new. And yet you [you say] are conservative in struggling for the new and we are destructive in trying to maintain the old. Possibly you mean you are conservative in trying to maintain the existing institution of slavery. Very well, we are not trying to destroy it. The peace of society and structure of our government both require that we should let it alone, and we insist on letting it alone.—*Speech, Leavenworth, Kan., Dec. 3, 1859.* Angle, 234.

3.—You will find that our [Republican] policy is exactly the policy of the men who made the Union. Nothing more and nothing less. Do you [men of the South] really think you are justified to break up the government rather than have it administered by Washington, and other good and great men who made it? If you do you are very unreasonable; and more reasonable men cannot and will not submit to you.—*Speech, Leavenworth, Dec. 3, 1859.* Angle, 235.

4.—You [Democrats] say you are conservative—eminently conservative—while we [Republicans] are revolutionary, destructive or something of that sort. What is conservatism? Is it not adherence to the old and tried against the new and untried? We stick to, contend for, the identical old policy on the point in controversy [extension of slavery] which was adopted by "our fathers who framed the government under which we live" [words of Douglas]; while you with one accord reject, and scout, and spit upon that old policy, and insist on substituting something new.—*Cooper Institute Address, New York, Feb. 27, 1860.* V, 313.
Repeated at New Haven, Conn., March 6, 1860. V, 366.

5.—We [Republicans] know we hold no doctrine, and make no declaration, which was not held to and made by "our fathers who framed the government under which we live."—*Cooper Institute address, New York, Feb. 27, 1860.* V, 315.

6.—The Republicans desire to place this great question of slavery on the very basis on which our fathers placed it, and no other.—*Speech, New Haven, Conn., March 6, 1860.* V, 355.

7.—We [Republicans] know we hold to no doctrines and make no declarations which were not held to and made by "our fathers who framed the government under which we live," and we cannot see how declarations that were patriotic when they made them are villainous when we make them.—*Speech, New Haven, Conn., March 6, 1860.* V, 359.

Republican Party, devotion of, to principles—For the sake of their principles, in forming their party, they [Republicans] broke, and sacrificed the strongest mere party ties and advantages which can exist.—*Speeches in Kansas, Dec. 1–5, 1859.* V, 274.
2.—I [do not] believe we can ever advance our principles by supporting men who oppose our principles.—*Speeches in Kansas, Dec. 1–5, 1859.* V, 277.

Republican Party, difference between, and Douglas—As I understand, there remains all the difference there was between Judge Douglas and the Republicans—they insisting that Congress shall, and he insisting that Congress shall not, keep slavery out of the territories before and up to the time they form state constitutions. No Republican has ever contended that, when a constitution is to be formed, any but the people of the territory shall form it. Republicans have never contended that Congress should dictate a constitution to any state or territory; but they have contended that the people should be perfectly free to form their constitutions in their own way—as perfectly free from the presence of slavery amongst them as from every other improper influence.—*To J. F. Alexander, May 15, 1858.* Angle, 176.
2.—Now, as ever, I wish not to misrepresent Judge Douglas's position, question his motives, or do aught that can be personally offensive to him. Whenever, if ever, he and we can come together on principle so that our great cause may have assistance from his great ability, I hope to have interposed no adventitious obstacle. But clearly, he is not with us—he does not pretend to be—he does not promise ever to be.—*Speech, Springfield, June 16, 1858.* III, 14.
3.—All, or nearly all, of Judge Douglas's arguments are logical, if you admit that slavery is as good and as right as freedom, and not one of them is worth a rush if you deny it. This is the difference, as I understand it, between the Republican and Democratic parties.—*Speech, Edwardsville, Sept. 13, 1858.* XI, 109.
4.—Upon this radical difference of opinion with Judge Douglas, the Republican party was organized. There is all the difference between him and them now that there was then. He will not say that he has changed; have you?—*Notes, Oct. 1, 1858.* IV, 227.
5.—I suppose the real difference between Judge Douglas and friends and the Republicans . . . is that the judge is not in favor of making any difference between slavery and liberty—that he is in favor of eradicating, of pressing out of view, the question of preference in this country for free or slave institutions; and consequently every sentiment he utters

discards the idea that there is any wrong in slavery.—*Debate, Galesburg, Oct. 7, 1858.* IV, 273.

6.—Does the proper division of local from federal authority, or anything in the Constitution, forbid our federal government to control as to slavery in our federal territories? Upon this, Senator Douglas holds the affirmative, and we Republicans the negative.—*Cooper Institute address, New York, Feb. 27, 1860.* V, 295.

See REPUBLICAN PARTY, warned against Douglas.

See SLAVERY, party attitudes compared.

Republican Party, disunionist charges against, repelled—You further charge us with being disunionists. If you mean that it is our aim to dissolve the Union, I for myself answer that it is untrue; for those who act with me I answer that it is untrue. Have you heard us assert that as our aim? Do you really believe that such is our aim? Do you find it in our platform, our speeches, our conventions, or anywhere? If not, withdraw the charge. But you may say that, though it is not our aim [to dissolve the Union] it will be the result if we succeed, and that therefore we are disunionists in fact. This is a grave charge you make against us, and we certainly have a right to demand that you specify in what way we are to dissolve the Union. How can we effect this?—*Speech, Galena, Aug. 1, 1856.* II, 292.

2.—The Supreme Court of the United States is the tribunal to decide such a question [as to whether restoration of the restriction of 1820, making United States territory free territory, would dissolve the Union] and we will submit to its decisions; and if you do also, there will be an end of the matter. Will you? If not, who are the disunionists, you or we?—*Speech, Galena, Aug. 1, 1856.* II, 294.

3.—We [Republicans] claim we are the only true Union men.—*Speech, New Haven, Conn., March 6, 1860.* V, 346.

Republican Party, enlisted for success of—For my single self, I have enlisted for the permanent success of the Republican cause; and for this object I shall labor faithfully in the ranks unless, as I think not probable, the judgment of the party shall assign me a different position.—*To W. E. Frazer, Nov. 1, 1859.* V, 257.

Republican Party, handicaps of, in 1858—*See* CAMPAIGN OF 1858, Republican handicaps in.

Republican Party, how slaves hear of—For anything we [Republicans] say or do, the slaves would scarcely know there is a Republican party. I believe they would not, in fact, generally know it but for your [slavery advocates'] misrepresentations of us in their hearing.—*Cooper Institute address, New York, Feb. 27, 1860.* V, 316.

Republican Party, leaders of, Douglas would exterminate—He [Douglas] wants it understood that the mass of the Republican party are really his friends. It is only the leaders that are doing something, that are intolerant, and require extermination at his hands.—*Speech, Chicago, July 10, 1858.* III, 41.

Republican Party, no alliance with Democrats—*See* DOUGLAS-BUCHANAN FEUD, Republicans welcome.

Republican Party, no distinctions among states—I am altogether unaware that the Republicans are in favor of making any odious distinctions between the free and the slave states.—*Debates, Galesburg, Oct. 7, 1858.* IV, 273.

Republican Party, platforms of, binding—I have supposed myself since the organization of the Republican party at Bloomington, in May, 1856, bound as a party man by the platforms of the party then and since. If in any interrogations which I shall answer I go beyond the scope of what is within these platforms it will be perceived that no one is responsible but myself.—*Debate, Freeport, Aug. 27, 1858.* III, 272.

2.—If anyone expects of me, in case of my election [to the United States Senate] that I will do anything not signified by our Republican platform, and my answers here today, I tell you very frankly that person will be deceived. I do not ask for the vote of anyone who supposes that I have secret purposes or pledges that I dare not speak out.—*Debate, Freeport, Aug. 27, 1858.* III, 337.

3.—I have supposed that, in entering upon this canvass, I stood generally upon those [Republican] platforms.—*Debate, Quincy, Oct. 13, 1858.* IV, 312.

Republican Party, . . . principles of, will endure—I think the Republican party is made up of those who, as far as they can peaceably, will oppose the extension of slavery, and who will hope for its ultimate extinction. If they believe it is wrong in grasping up the new lands of the continent, and keeping them from the settlement of free white laborers, who want the land to bring up their families upon; if they are in earnest, although they make a mistake, they will grow restless, and the time will come when they will come back again and reorganize, if not by the same name, at least upon the same principles as their party now has. It is better, then, to save the work while it is begun. You have done the labor; maintain it, keep it. If men choose to serve you, go with them; but as you have made up your organization upon principle, stand by it; for, as surely as God reigns over you, and has inspired your mind, and given you a sense of propriety, and continues to give you hope, so surely will you cling to these ideas, and you will at last come back after your wanderings, merely to do your work over again.—*Speech, Chicago, July 10, 1858.* III, 44.

2.—I believe that the principles around which we have rallied and organized that [Republican] party will live; they will live under all circumstances, while we die. They would reproduce another party in the future. But in the meantime all the labor that has been done to build up the present Republican party would be entirely lost.—*Speech, Springfield, March 1, 1859.* V, 116.

3.—Our [Republican] principles would still live [even if the party had been wrecked by support of Douglas in Illinois], and ere long would produce a party; but we should have lost all our past labor and twenty years of time by the folly.—*Speeches in Kansas, Dec. 1-5, 1859.* V, 277.

4.—That our [Republican] principle, however baffled or delayed, will finally triumph, I do not permit myself to doubt. Men will pass away—die politically and naturally; but the principle will live, and live forever. Organizations rallied around that principle may, by their own dereliction, go to pieces, thereby losing all their time and labor; but the principle will remain, and will reproduce another, and another, till the triumph will come.—*Speeches in Kansas, Dec. 1-5, 1859.* V, 280.

5.—How much would it avail you [men of the South], if you could . . . break up the Republican organization? There is a judgment and a feeling against slavery in this nation, which cast at least a million and a half votes. You cannot destroy that judgment and feeling—that sentiment—by breaking up the political organization which rallies around it. You can scarcely scatter and disperse an army which has been formed into order in the face of your heaviest fire; but if you could, how much would you gain by forcing the sentiment which created it out of the peaceful channel of the ballot-box into some other channel? What would that other channel probably be? Would the number of John Browns be lessened or enlarged by the operation.—*Cooper Institute address, New York, Feb. 27, 1860.* V, 319.

Republican Party, purposes of, toward South—When we [Republicans] do as we say, beat you [proslavery men of the South] you perhaps want to know what we will do with you. I will tell you, so far as I am authorized to speak for the opposition. . . . We mean to treat you, as near as we possibly can, as Washington, Jefferson, and Madison treated you. We mean to leave you alone, and in no way to interfere with your institution; to abide by all and every compromise of the Constitution. . . . We mean to remember that you are as good as we are; that there is no difference between us other than the difference of circumstances. We mean to recognize and bear in mind always that you have as good hearts in your bosoms as other people, or as we claim to have, and treat you accordingly.—*Speech at Cincinnati, Sept. 17, 1859.* V, 218.
Repeated at Cincinnati, Feb. 12, 1861. VI, 117.

Republican Party, sectionalism charge against—*See* SECTIONALISM, what constitutes?

Republican Party, South's attitude toward—When you [men of the South] speak of us [Republicans] you do so only to denounce us as reptiles, or at best, no better than outlaws. You will grant a hearing to pirates or murderers, but nothing like it to "Black Republicans." In all your contentions with one another, each of you deems an unconditional condemnation of "Black Republicanism" as the first thing to be attended to. Indeed, such condemnation of us seems an indispensable prerequisite—license, so to speak—among you to be admitted or permitted to speak at all. Now can you or not be prevailed upon to pause and consider whether this is quite just to us, or even to yourselves. Bring forward your charges and specifications, and then be patient long enough to hear us deny or justify.—*Cooper Institute address, New York, Feb. 27, 1860.* V, 310.

Republican Party, temper of—I have said that in our present moral tone and temper we are strong enough for our open enemies, and so we are. But the chief effect of Douglasism is to change that tone and temper.—*Speeches in Kansas, Dec. 1-5, 1859.* V, 268.

Republican Party, threats to unity of—I am afraid of the result upon organized action where great results are in view, if any of us allow ourselves to seek out minor or separate points, on which there may be difference of views as to policy and right, and let them keep us from uniting in action upon a great principle in a cause on which we all agree; or are deluded into the belief that all can be brought to consider alike and agree upon every minor point before we unite and press forward in organization, asking the co-operation of all good men in that resistance to the extension of slavery upon which we all agree. I am afraid that such methods would result in keeping the friends of liberty waiting longer than we ought to. I say this for the purpose of suggesting that we consider whether it would not be better and wiser, so long as we all agree that this matter of slavery is a moral, political and social wrong, and ought to be treated as a wrong, not to let anything minor or subsidiary to that main principle and purpose make us fail to cooperate.—*Speech, Chicago, March 1, 1859.* V, 115.

2.—My main object . . . would be to hedge against divisions in the Republican ranks generally, and particularly for the contest of 1860. The point of danger is the temptation in different localities to "platform" for something which will be popular just there, but which, nevertheless, will be a firebrand elsewhere, and especially in a national convention. As instances, the movement against foreigners in Massachusetts; in New Hampshire, to make obedience to the fugitive-slave law punishable as a crime; in Ohio, to repeal the fugitive-slave law; and squatter sovereignty, in Kansas. In these things there is explosive enough to blow up half a dozen national conventions, if it gets into them. . . . What is desirable, if possible, is that in every local convocation of Republicans a point should be made to avoid everything which will disturb Republicans elsewhere. Massachusetts Republicans should have looked beyond their noses, and they could not have failed to see that tilting against foreigners would ruin us in the whole Northwest. New Hampshire and Ohio should forbear tilting against the fugitive-slave law in such a way as to utterly overwhelm us in Illinois with the charge of enmity to the Constitution itself. Kansas, in her confidence that she can be saved to freedom on "squatter sovereignty," ought not to forget that to prevent the spread and nationalization of slavery is a national concern, and must be attended to by the nation.— *To Schuyler Colfax, July 6, 1859.* V, 131.

3.—There can be no letting down about this [insistence that slavery is wrong]. Simultaneously with such letting down the Republican organization would go to pieces, and half its elements would go in a different direction, leaving an easy victory to the common enemy.—*Speeches in Kansas, Dec. 1-5, 1859.* V, 274.

See FUGITIVE SLAVE ACT, Ohio Republican action regretted.

See REPUBLICAN PARTY, advice to.

Republican Party, undesired members of—If it be true that on the ground which I occupy—ground which I occupy as frankly and boldly as Judge Douglas does his—my views, though partly coinciding with yours, are not as perfectly in accordance with your feelings as are his, I do say to you in all candor, go for him and not for me.—*Debate, Freeport, Aug. 27, 1858.* III, 338.

2.—If there be any man [in the Republican party] who does not believe that slavery is wrong in the three aspects I have mentioned, or in any one of them, that man is misplaced and ought to leave us. While, on the other hand, if there be any man in the Republican party who is impatient over the necessity springing from its actual presence, and is impatient of the constitutional guarantees thrown about it, and would act in disregard of these, he too is misplaced, standing with us. He will find his place somewhere else.—*Debate, Quincy, Oct. 13, 1858.* IV, 330.

3.—If there be a man amongst us [Republicans] who is so impatient of it [slavery] as a wrong as to disregard its actual presence among us and the difficulty of getting rid of it suddenly in a satisfactory way, and to disregard the constitutional obligations thrown about it, that man is misplaced if he is on our platform. We disclaim sympathy with him in practical action.—*Debate, Alton, Oct. 15, 1858.* V, 60.

Republican Party, victory ahead for—Unless truth be a mockery and justice a hollow lie, we will be in a majority after a while, and then the revolution which we will accomplish will be none the less radical from being the result of pacific measures.—*Speech, Bloomington, May 29, 1856.* Lapsley II, 267.

2.—The result is not doubtful. We shall not fail—if we stand firm, we shall not fail. Wise counsels may accelerate, or mistakes delay it, but, sooner or later, the victory is sure to come.—*Speech, Springfield, June 16, 1858.* III, 15.

3.—If we do not allow ourselves to be allured from the strict path of our duty by such a device as shifting our ground and throwing us into the rear of a leader which denies our first principle . . . then the future of the Republican cause is safe, and victory is assured.—*Speech, Chicago, March 1, 1859.* V, 123.

4.—Stand by your principles, stand by your guns, and victory, complete and permanent, is sure at the last.— *Speech, Chicago, March 1, 1859.* V, 123.

5.—We, the Republicans and others forming the opposition of the country, intend to "stand by our guns," to be patient and firm, and in the long run to beat you [Kentuckians] whether you take him [Douglas, for President] or not. We know that before we fairly beat you, we have to beat you both together. We know that "you are all of one feather," and that we have to beat you all together, and we expect to do it.—*Speech, Cincinnati, Sept. 17, 1859.* V, 218.

6.—I see the signs of the approaching triumph of the Republicans in the bearing of their political adversaries.—*Speech, New Haven, Conn., March 6, 1860.* V, 357.

See DEITY, supplication to, 2.

See REPUBLICAN PARTY, advice to.

Republican Party, warned against Douglas—If you indorse him [Douglas] you tell him you do not care whether slavery be voted up or voted down.—*Speech, Chicago, July 10, 1858.* III, 43.

2.—Now I could ask the Republican party, after all the hard names Judge Douglas has called them by, all his repeated charges of their inclination to marry with and hug negroes, all his declarations of Black Republicanism . . . if he be indorsed by Republican votes, where do you stand? Plainly, you stand ready saddled, bridled and harnessed, and waiting to be driven over to the slavery-extension camp of the nation—just ready to be driven over, tied together in a lot—to be driven over, every man with a rope around his neck, that halter being held by Judge Douglas.—*Speech, Chicago, July 10, 1858.* Basler, 399.

3.—Let us stand firmly by each other. If we do not do so we are tending in the contrary direction that our friend Judge Douglas proposes—not intentionally —working in the traces that tend to make this one universal slave nation. He is one that runs in that direction, and as such I resist him.—*Speech, Chicago, July 10, 1858.* III, 51.

4.—Like boys who have set a trap, they [Democratic followers of Douglas on the Lecompton issue] are watching to see if the [Republican] birds are picking at the bait and likely to go under.—*Notes, Oct. 1, 1858.* IV, 225.

5.—By so falling in [Republicans with Douglas] will we not be committed to, or at least compromised with, the Nebraska policy?—*Notes, Oct. 1, 1858.* IV, 226.

6.—[If Democrats give Douglas no cause to bolt the 1860 nomination] the Democratic party will go into a minority inevitably; and the struggle in the whole North will be, as it was in Illinois last summer and fall, whether the Republican party can maintain its identity, or be broken up to form the tail of Douglas's new kite. Some of our great Republican doctors will then have a splendid chance to swallow the pills they so eagerly prescribed for us last spring. . . . The truth is the Republican principle can in no wise live with Douglas; and it is arrant folly now, as it was last spring, to waste time, and scatter labor already performed, in dallying with him.—*To Lyman Trumbull, Dec. 11, 1858.* Tracy, 98.

7.—All dallying with Douglas by Republicans, who are such at heart, is, at the very least, time and labor lost; and all such, who dally with him, will yet bite their lips in vexation for their folly.—*To W. H. Wells, Jan. 8, 1859.* Hertz II, 739.

8.—I have believed that in the Republican situation in Illinois, if we, the Republicans of the state, had made Judge Douglas our candidate for the Senate of the United States last year, and had elected him, there would today be no Republican party in this Union.—*Speech, Chicago, March 1, 1859.* V, 116.

9.—Let the Republican party of Illinois dally with Judge Douglas; let them fall in behind him and make him their candidate, and they do not absorb him— he absorbs them.—*Speech, Chicago, March 1, 1859.* V, 118.

10.—The Republican party should not dally with Judge Douglas when it knows where his proposition and his leadership would take us, nor be disposed to listen to it because it was best somewhere else to support somebody occupying his ground.—*Speech, Chicago, March 1, 1859.* V, 122.

11.—Had we thrown ourselves into the arms of Douglas [in the 1858 campaign], as re-electing him by our votes would have done, the Republican cause would have been annihilated in Illinois, and, as I think, demoralized and prostrated everywhere for years, if not forever. As it is, in the language of Benton, "we are clean," and the Republican star gradually rises everywhere.—*To Salmon P. Chase, April 30, 1859.* Tracy, 109.

12.—There is another thing our [Republican] friends are doing which gives me some uneasiness. It is their leaning toward "popular sovereignty." There are three substantial objections to this. First, no party can command respect which sustains this year what it opposed last. Secondly, Douglas—who is the most dangerous enemy of liberty, because the most insidious one—would have little support in the North, and by consequence, no capital to trade on in the South, if it were not for his friends, thus magnifying him and his humbug. But lastly, and chiefly, Douglas's popular sovereignty, accepted by the public as a just principle, nationalizes slavery, and revives the African slave-trade inevitably.—*To Samuel Galloway, July 28, 1859.* V, 137.

13.—The most imminent danger that now threatens that purpose [of the Republican party] is that insidious Douglas popular sovereignty. This is the miner and sapper. I say this Douglas popular sovereignty—for there is a broad distinction as I now understand it, between that article and a genuine popular sovereignty.—*Speech, Columbus, Ohio, Sept. 16, 1859.* V, 148.

14.—This insidious Douglas popular sovereignty is

the measure that now threatens the purpose of the Republican party to prevent slavery from being nationalized in the United States.—*Speech, Columbus, Ohio, Sept. 16, 1859.* V, 181.

15.—It is only the insidious position of Douglas that endangers our [Republican] cause. That position is simply an ambuscade. By entering into contest with our open enemies, we are to be lured into his train; and then, having lost our organization and arms, we are to be turned over to those same open enemies.—*Speeches in Kansas, Dec. 1–5, 1859.* V, 268.

16.—Had we followed the advice [to support Douglas for senator] there would now be no Republican party in Illinois, and none to speak of anywhere else. The whole thing would now be floundering along after Douglas upon the Dred Scott and crocodile theory. It would have been the greatest "haul" for slavery ever yet made.—*Speeches in Kansas, Dec. 1–5, 1859.* V, 277.

17.—About a year ago all the Republicans in Congress voted for what was called the Crittenden-Montgomery bill; and forthwith Douglas claimed, and still claims, that they were all committed to his "gur-reat pur-rinciple." And Republicans have been so far embarrassed by the claim that they have ever since been protesting that they were not so committed, and trying to explain why.—*Speeches in Kansas, Dec. 1–5, 1859.* V, 277.

See REPUBLICAN PARTY, difference between, and Douglas.

See SLAVERY, Republican policy toward.

Republican Party, wars on slavery—*See* SLAVERY, Republican policy toward.

Republican Party, would not attend convention to organize—There was a call for a convention [in 1854] to form a Republican party at Springfield, and I think that my friend Mr. Lovejoy, who is here upon this stand, had a hand in it. I think this is true, and I think if he will remember accurately he will be able to recollect that he tried to get me into it, but I would not go. . . . It is true they did place my name, though without my authority, upon the committee, and afterward wrote me to attend the meeting of the committee, but I refused to do so, and I never had anything to do with that organization.—*Debate, Ottawa, Aug. 21, 1858.* III, 224.

Republican Platform, 1864, no interference in—*See* VICE PRESIDENCY, no interference in.

Republicanism, principles of—In accordance with an established custom and the principles of true republicanism, it becomes my duty to make known to you,

the people whom I propose to represent, my sentiments with regard to local affairs.—*Address to Sangamon County, March 9, 1832.* I, 1.

2.—We hold the true republican position. In leaving the people's business in their hands, we cannot be wrong.—*Speech in Congress, July 27, 1848.* II, 69.

Republicanism, "robe is soiled"—Our republican robe is soiled and trailed in the dust. Let us repurify it. Let us turn and wash it white in the spirit, if not the blood, of the Revolution.—*Speech, Peoria, Oct. 16, 1854.* II, 248.

Republicanism, "sheet anchor of"—*See* SELF-GOVERNMENT, defined, 6.

Resignation, Lincoln suggests his own—Gentlemen, I can't do it [emancipate and arm the slaves]. You may be right, and I may be wrong; but I'll tell you what I can do; I can resign in favor of Mr. Hamlin. Perhaps Mr. Hamlin could do it.—*To group of senators, early summer, 1862.* Tarbell in *McClure's,* Dec., 1898.

2.—They [critics in Congress] wish to get rid of me and I am sometimes half disposed to gratify them.—*To O. H. Browning, Dec. 18, 1862.* Stephenson, 329.

See CHASE, SALMON P., relations with Lincoln, 7.

"Respectable Scoundrels," responsible for depression—*See* DEPRESSION, not to be checked by "fawning."

Responsibility, must center somewhere—It has been said that one bad general is better than two good ones, and the saying is true if taken to mean no more than that an army is better directed by a single mind, though inferior, than by two superior ones at variance and cross purposes with each other. And the same is true in all joint operations wherein those engaged can have none but a common end in view and can differ only as to the choice of means. In a storm at sea no one on board can wish the ship to sink, and yet not infrequently all go down together because too many will direct and no single mind can be allowed to control.—*First annual message, Dec. 3, 1861.* VII, 55.

2.—Some single mind must be master, else there will be no agreement on anything.—*To W. H. Fishback, Feb. 17, 1864.* X, 12.

Responsibility, no evasion of—We have made the statements we have, because we know them to be true and we choose to live or die by them.—*To editor, Sangamo Journal, Oct. 28, 1837.* I, 84.

2.—But we ourselves must not decline the burden of responsibility, nor take counsel of unworthy passions.

—Speech, Bloomington, May 29, 1856. Lapsley II, 273.

3.—It strikes me there is some difference between holding a man responsible for an act which he has not done, and holding him responsible for an act that he has done.—*Debate, Quincy, Oct. 13, 1858.* IV, 285.

4.—I have said nothing but what I am willing to live by, and, if it be the pleasure of God, to die by.—*Speech, Independence Hall, Feb. 22, 1861.* VI, 158.

5.—In times like the present, men should utter nothing for which they would not willingly be responsible for through time and eternity.—*Second annual message, Dec. 1, 1862.* VIII, 126.

Retaliation—*See also* PORT PRIVILEGES, policy of retaliation.

Retaliation, haste in, to be avoided—We do not know today that a colored soldier, or white officer commanding colored soldiers, has been massacred [as reported at Fort Pillow]. We fear it—believe it, I may say—but we do not know it. To take the life of one of their prisoners on the assumption that they murder ours, when it is short of certainty that they do murder ours, might be too serious, too cruel a mistake.—*Speech, Baltimore, April 18, 1864.* X, 79.

Retaliation, to protect negro troops—*See* NEGRO TROOPS, protection of, 2.

Retreat, "last shriek on"—His [Seward's] idea was that it [preliminary Emancipation Proclamation] would be considered our last shriek on the retreat.—*To F. B. Carpenter, Feb. 6, 1864.* X, 2.

Revelation, no direct, expected—I hope it will not be irreverent for me to say that if it is probable that God would reveal His will to others on a point so connected with my duty [as in the issuance of a possible Emancipation Proclamation], it might be supposed he would reveal it directly to me; for, unless I am more deceived in myself than I often am, it is my earnest desire to know the will of Providence in this matter. And if I learn what it is, I will do it. These are not, however, the days of miracles, and I suppose it will be granted that I am not to expect a direct revelation. —*Reply to Chicago church committee, Sept. 13, 1862.* VIII, 29.

Revelations, Book of—*See* YOUNG AMERICA, longs for territory.

Revenge, to be avoided—In using the strong hand, as now compelled to do, the government has a difficult duty to perform. At the very best it will by turns do both too little and too much. It can properly have no motive of revenge, no purpose to punish merely for punishment's sake. While we must by all available means prevent the overthrow of the government, we should avoid planting and cultivating too many thorns in the bosom of society.—*To Sec. Stanton, April 18, 1864.* Stern, 803.

2.—I wish you to do nothing merely for revenge, but that what you may do shall be solely done with reference to the security of the future.—*To Gen. Rosecrans, Nov. 19, 1864.* X, 274.

Revolution, American policy of nonintervention— That it is the duty of our government to neither foment nor assist, such revolutions [as that in Hungary] in other governments. That, as we may not legally or warrantably interfere abroad to aid, so no other government may interfere abroad to suppress such revolutions; and that we should at once announce to the world our determination to insist upon this mutuality of non-intervention, as a sacred principle of the international law.—*Resolutions for Hungarian freedom, Jan. 9, 1852.* Angle, 81.

Revolution, American sympathy for—That the sympathies of this country, and the benefits of its position, should be exerted in favor of the people of every nation struggling to be free; and whilst we meet to do honor to Kossuth and Hungary, we should not fail to pour out the tribute of our praise and approbation to the patriotic efforts of the Irish, the Germans and the French, who have unsuccessfully fought to establish in their several governments the supremacy of the people.—*Resolutions for Hungarian freedom, Jan. 9, 1852.* Angle, 82.

Revolution, constitutional substitute for—The right of peaceable assembly and of petition, and by Article Fifth of the Constitution, the right of amendment, is the constitutional substitute for revolution. Here is our Magna Carta, not wrested by barons from King John, but the free gift of states to the nation they create.—*To Alexander H. Stephens, Jan. 19, 1859.* Tracy, 127.

Revolution, nature of—It is a quality of revolution not to go by old lines or old laws; but to break up both, and make new ones.—*Speech in Congress, Jan. 12, 1848.* I, 339.

2.—Be not deceived. Revolutions do not go backward.—*Speech, Bloomington, May 29, 1856.* Lapsley II, 253.

Revolution, right of—Any people anywhere, being inclined and having the power, have the right to rise up and shake off the existing government, and form a new one that suits them better. This is a most valuable, a most sacred right—a right which we hope and believe is to liberate the world. . . . More than this, a majority of any portion of such people may revolutionize, putting down a minority, intermingled with or near about them, who may oppose this movement. Such minority was precisely the case of the Tories in our own Revolution.—*Speech in Congress, Jan. 12, 1848.* I, 338.

2.—It is the right of any people, sufficiently numerous for national independence, to throw off, to revolutionize, their existing form of government, and to establish such other in its stead as they may choose.—*Resolutions for Hungarian freedom, Jan. 9, 1852.* Foner, 33.

3.—If by the mere force of numbers a majority should deprive a minority of any clearly written constitutional right, it might in a moral point of view justify revolution; certainly would if such right were a vital one.—*First inaugural, March 4, 1861.* VI, 177.

See PEOPLE, masters in America, 5.

Revolutionary war, compared with temperance revolution—*See* TEMPERANCE, revolution compared with Revolutionary War.

Revolutionary War, influence of—Another reason which once was but which, to the same extent, is now no more, has done much in maintaining our institutions thus far. I mean the powerful influence which the interesting scenes of the Revolution had upon the passions of the people as distinguished from their judgment. By this influence, the jealousy, envy, and avarice incident to our nature, and so common to a state of peace, prosperity and conscious strength, were for the time in a great measure smothered and rendered inactive.—*Speech, Springfield, Jan. 27, 1837.* I, 47.

2.—The deep-rooted principles of hate, and the forceful motive of revenge, instead of being turned against each other, were directed exclusively against the British nation. And thus from the force of circumstances, the basest principles of our nature were either made to lie dormant, or become the active agents in the advancement of the noblest of causes—that of establishing and maintaining civil and religious liberty.—*Speech, Springfield, Jan. 27, 1837.* I, 48.

Revolutionary War, sacrifices made in—*See* WASHINGTON, GEORGE, hardships endured by.

Revolutionary War, tribute to soldiers of—They were a fortress of strength; but what invading foeman could never do, the silent artillery of time has done —the leveling of its walls. They are gone. They were a forest of giant oaks; but the all-resistless hurri-

cane has swept over them, and left only here and there a lonely trunk, despoiled of its verdure, shorn of its foliage, unshading and unshaded, to murmur in a few more gentle breezes, and to combat with its mutilated limbs a few more rude storms, then to sink and be no more.—*Speech, Springfield, Jan. 27, 1837.* I, 49.

2.—They were pillars of the temple of liberty; and now that they have crumbled away, that temple must fall unless we, their descendants, supply their places with other pillars, hewn from the solid quarry of sober reason.—*Speech, Springfield, Jan. 27, 1837.* I, 49.

Richmond, evacuation of—The evacuation of Petersburg and Richmond, in Virginia, and the surrender of the principal insurgent army, give hope of a righteous and speedy peace, whose joyous expression cannot be restrained. In the midst of this, however, He from whom all blessings flow must not be forgotten.—*Last public address, April 11, 1865.* XI, 84.

Richmond, must be taken—Richmond . . . we must take with the least possible delay.—*To Governors of several states, June 30, 1862.* VII, 246.

Richmond, not the immediate goal—Our prime object is the enemy's army in front of us, and is not with or about Richmond at all, unless it be incidental to the main object.—*Indorsement on Hooker's plan against Richmond, April 11, 1863.* VIII, 243.

2.—Since then [McClellan's failure] I have constantly desired the Army of the Potomac to make Lee's army, and not Richmond, its objective point.—*To Gen. Halleck, Sept. 21, 1863.* Basler, 727.

Richmond Enquirer—*See also* "IRREPRESSIBLE CONFLICT," difference in who says it, 1, 3, 4.

Richmond Enquirer, Characterized—. . . a Buchanan paper in the South.—*Notes, Oct. 1, 1858.* IV, 200.

Richmond Enquirer, invented "state equality"—*See* "STATE EQUALITY," not yet approved.

Ridicule, used to—Through life . . . I have endured a great deal of ridicule without much malice; and have received a great deal of kindness not quite free from ridicule.—*To James H. Hackett, Nov. 2, 1863.* IX, 199.

Right, stand by—We are here to stand firmly for a principle—to stand firmly for a right.—*Speech, Bloomington, May 29, 1856.* Lapsley II, 249.

See MISSOURI COMPROMISE, restoration of, urged, 5.

Right and Wrong, contending principles—Do they really think that by right surrendering to wrong the hopes of our Constitution, our Union, and our liberties can possibly be bettered?—*Fragment, Oct. 1, 1856. II, 307.*

2.—You cannot institute any equality between right and wrong.—*Debate, Galesburg, Oct. 1, 1858. IV, 275.*

3.—[Slavery represents] the eternal struggle between these two principles—right and wrong—throughout the world. They are the two principles that have stood face to face from the beginning of time; and will ever continue to struggle.—*Debate, Alton, Oct. 15, 1858. V, 65.*

4.—The one [principle] is the common right of humanity and the other the divine right of kings. It is the same principle in whatever shape it develops itself. It is the spirit that says, "You work and toil and earn bread and I'll eat it." No matter in what shape it comes, whether from the mouth of a king who seeks to bestride the people of his own nation and live by the fruit of their labor, or from one race of men as an apology for enslaving another race, it is the same tyrannical principle.—*Debate, Alton, Oct. 15, 1858. V, 66.*

5.—Opposition to the right is wrong.—*Speech, New Haven, Conn., March 6, 1860. V, 346.*

See SLAVERY, wrong of.

"Right Makes Might"—*See* FAITH, appeal to.

"Right to Do Wrong"—*See* SLAVERY, Wrong of, 12.

See SLAVERY, Douglas's care-not policy, 14, 16.

Ringgold, Samuel, tribute to—. . . the gallant and accomplished, and noble Ringgold fell.—*Speech, Chicago, ¹uly 25, 1850. Angle, 70.*

Risk and Reward—My understanding is that, when a common job is done, if I put in five dollars to your one, I have a right to take out five dollars to your one.—*Speech, Springfield, July 17, 1858. III, 166.*

Rogers, John, Congress asked to thank—I most cordially recommend that Capt. John Rogers, United States Navy, receive a vote of thanks from Congress for the eminent skill and gallantry exhibited by him in the engagement with the rebel iron-clad steamer *Fingal*, alias *Atlanta*, whilst in command of the United States iron-clad steamer *Weehawken*, which led to her capture on the 17th of June, 1863; also for the zeal and general conduct shown by this officer on many occasions.—*Message to Congress, Dec. 8, 1863. IX, 252.*

Rosecrans, William S., appreciation of—Your dispatch announcing retreat of enemy just received here.

God bless you and all with you! Please tender to all, and accept for yourself, the nation's gratitude for your and their skill, endurance and dauntless courage.—*To Gen. Rosecrans, Jan. 5, 1863. VIII, 173.*

2.—I know not a single enemy of yours here. . . . And now be assured you wrong both yourself and us when you even suspect there is not the best disposition on the part of us all to oblige you.—*To Gen. Rosecrans, March 17, 1863. VIII, 226.*

3.—I cannot really say that I have ever heard any complaint of you.—*To Gen. Rosecrans, April 23, 1863. VIII, 255.*

4.—In no case have I intended to censure you or to question your ability.—*To Gen. Rosecrans, May 20, 1863. VIII, 279.*

5.—I have not abated in my kind feeling for and confidence in you. . . . Be assured once more that I think of you in all kindness and confidence and that I am not watching you with an evil eye.—*To Gen. Rosecrans, Aug. 10, 1863. IX, 66.*

6.—Be of good cheer. We have unabated confidence in you, and in your soldiers and officers.—*To Gen. Rosecrans, Sept. 21, 1863. IX, 132.*

7.—I repeat that my appreciation of you has not abated. I can never forget whilst I remember anything that about the end of last year and the beginning of this, you gave us a hard-earned victory, which, had there been a defeat instead, the nation could scarcely have lived over. Neither can I forget the check you so opportunely gave to a dangerous sentiment which was spreading in the North.—*To Gen. Rosecrans, Dec. 18, 1863. IX, 264.*

8.—I find it scarcely less than indispensable for me to do something for Gen. Rosecrans.—*To Sec. Stanton, Dec. 18, 1863. IX, 264.*

9.—So far you have got along in the Department of Missouri rather better than I dared hope, and I congratulate you and myself upon it.—*To Gen. Rosecrans, April 4, 1864. X, 64.*

Rosecrans, William S., opportunity of—If he [Rosecrans] can only maintain this position [in East Tennessee], without more, this rebellion can only eke out a short and feeble existence, as an animal sometimes may with a thorn in its vitals.—*To Gen. Halleck, Sept. 21, 1863. IX, 132.*

2.—You and Burnside now have him [the enemy] by the throat; and he must break your hold or perish.—*To Gen. Rosecrans, Oct. 12, 1863. IX, 167.*

Rosecrans, William S., order of, criticized—*See* AMNESTY, discretion urged.

"Rotten Wheelbarrow"—*See* RAILROAD PASS, request for renewal of.

Rowan, Stephen C., Congress asked to thank—I recommend that the thanks of Congress be given . . . Commander Stephen C. Rowan, U.S.N., for distinguished services in the waters of North Carolina, and particularly in the capture of Newbern, being in chief command of the naval forces.—*Message to Congress, July 11, 1862.* VII, 267.

Rule of Three—Let us state a question in the rule of three. If voting for the Crittenden-Montgomery bill entangle the Republicans with Douglas's dogmas for one year, how long would voting for Douglas himself entangle them?—*Speeches in Kansas, Dec. 1-5, 1859.* V, 278.

See EDUCATION, Lincoln's, 3.

Rule or Ruin, South insists on—*See* UNION, South proposes rule or ruin of.

"Run Over Like Sheep"—*See* AFRICAN SLAVE TRADE, slavery extension akin to, 12.

"Running Itch"—*See* VULNERABLE HEELS, Democratic affliction.

Russia, calls for American aid—*See* AMERICA, leads in improvements.

Russia, criticized for act against Hungarian Revolution—*See* HUNGARIAN REVOLUTION, Russia acted illegally in.

Russia, Czar of—*See* CAMERON, SIMON, confidence and esteem, 1.

Russia, where despotism is "pure"—*See* KNOW-NOTHING PARTY, principles of, challenged, 2.

Sabbath, observance of, urged—The President . . . desires and enjoins the orderly observance of the Sabbath by the officers and men in the military and naval service. The importance for man and beast of the prescribed weekly rest, the sacred rights of Christian soldiers and sailors, a becoming deference to the best sentiment of a Christian people, and a due regard for the divine will demand that Sunday labor in the army and navy be reduced to the measure of strict necessity. The discipline and character of the national forces should not suffer nor the cause they defend be imperilled by the profanation of the day or name of the Most High.—*Executive order, Nov. 15, 1862.* VIII, 76.

See WASHINGTON, GEORGE, order of, indicative.

Sacrifice, endurable when cheered by future—*See* WASHINGTON, GEORGE, hardships endured by.

St. Louis Democrat, factious—At the beginning of the administration I appointed one whom I understood to be an editor of the *Democrat* to be postmaster at St. Louis—the best office in my gift within Missouri. Soon after this our friends at St. Louis must needs break into factions, the *Democrat* being in my opinion justly chargeable with a full share of the blame for it. I have stoutly tried to keep out of the quarrel, and so mean to do.—*Indorsement on letter of T. Woodruff, April 16, 1863.* VIII, 249.

St. Louis Intelligencer—*See* POLITICAL PLATFORMS, candidates and, 4.

Salmon Trout, gift of, acknowledged—I have received at your hands a very fine specimen of the Mackinaw salmon trout, and I beg that you will convey to Mr. Williams my cordial thanks for his kind thoughtfulness.—*To J. F. Driggs, Feb. 3, 1865.* X, 355.

Saloon Smashers, women, defended—May it please the court, I will say a few words in behalf of the women who are arraigned before your Honor and the jury [for saloon smashing]. I would suggest, first, that there be a change in the indictment, so as to have it read, "The State against Mr. Whiskey," instead of "The State against the women." It would be more appropriate. Touching this question, there are three laws: First, the law of self-protection; second, the law of the statute; third, the law of God. The law of self-protection is the law of necessity, as shown when our fathers threw the tea into the Boston harbor; and in asserting their right to life, liberty, and the pursuit of happiness. This is the defense of these women. The man who has persisted in selling whiskey has had no regard for their well-being or the welfare of their husbands and sons. He has had no fear of God or regard for men; neither has he had any regard for the law of the statute. No jury can fix any damages or punishment for any violation of the moral law. The course pursued by this liquor dealer has been for the demoralization of society. His groggery has been a nuisance. These women, finding all moral suasion of no avail, with this fellow, oblivious to all tender appeal, alike regardless of their prayers and tears, in order to protect their households and promote the welfare of the community, united to suppress the nuisance. The good of society demands its suppression. They accomplished what otherwise could not have been done.—*Speech to jury, Clinton, 1839.* Hertz II, 523.

Salvation "Relish of"—*See* KANSAS-NEBRASKA ACT, not union-saving.

Sambo and Dr. Ross, slave's opinion not asked—*See* SLAVERY, theology of.

San Marino, complimented—I thank the council of San Marino for the honor of citizenship it has conferred upon me. Although your dominion is small, your state is, nevertheless, one of the most honored in all history. It has, by its experience demonstrated the truth, so full of encouragement to the friends of humanity, that government founded on republican principles is capable of being so administered as to be secure and enduring. . . . Wishing that your interesting state may endure and flourish forever, and that you may live long and enjoy the confidence and secure the gratitude of your fellow citizens, I pray God to have you in His holy keeping.—*To regent captains of San Marino, May 7, 1861.* Hertz II, 833.

Sanitary Commission, commended—The Sanitary Commission is doing a work of great humanity, and of direct practical value to the nation, in this time of trial. It is entitled to the gratitude and the confidence of the people, and I trust it will be generously supported.—*To Gen. Scott, Sept. 30, 1861.* VII, 3.
2.—The Sanitary Commission, with all its benevolent labors.—*Speech, Philadelphia, June 16, 1864.* X, 127.

Sanitary Fairs, services performed by—In this extraordinary war, extraordinary developments have manifested themselves, such as have not been seen in former wars; and amongst these manifestations nothing has been more remarkable than these fairs for the relief of suffering soldiers and their families.—*Speech, Washington, March 18, 1864.* X, 48.
2.—In what is contributed to his [the soldier's] comfort [by such organizations as the sanitary fairs] when he passes to and fro, and in what is contributed to him when he is sick and wounded, in whatever shape it comes, whether from the fair and tender hand of woman, or from any other source, it is much, very much. But I think that there is still that which is of as much value to him in the continual reminders he sees in the newspapers that while he is absent he is yet remembered by the loved ones at home. Another view of these various institutions, if I may so call them, is worthy of consideration, I think. They are voluntary contributions given zealously and earnestly, on top of all the disturbances of business, of all the disorders, of all the taxation, and of all the burdens that the war has imposed upon us, giving proof that the national resources are not at all exhausted, and that the national spirit of patriotism is even firmer and stronger than at the commencement of the war.—*Speech, Philadelphia, June 16, 1864.* X, 128.

Satan, Douglas wars like—He [Douglas] has warred upon them [Lincoln's antislavery sentiments] as Satan wars upon the Bible.—*Debate, Alton, Oct. 15, 1858.* V, 45.

Satan, rage of—The opposition men . . . will smile complacently at the angry snarl of the contending Van Buren candidates and their respective friends as the Christian does at Satan's rage.—*To Mary Owens, Dec. 13, 1836.* I, 18.

Savannah, thanks for—*See* SHERMAN'S MARCH TO THE SEA, thanks for Christmas gift.

Saying and Knowing—Did he know what he said, or did he say it without knowing it?—*To Anson Stager, May 24, 1862.* VIII, 281.

Schenck, Robert C., characterized—We're having a devil of a time just now. Schenck, can you fight? ["I don't know, sir, but I can try."] And I am sure you will succeed. You have it in your blood, and I am going to give you a chance. You shall be made a brigadier-general.—*To Gen. Schenck, May or June, 1861.* War Years I, 289.
2.—Schenck is wider across the head in the region of the ears, and loves fight for its own sake, better than I do.—*To John Hay, Oct. 22, 1863.* Hay, 105.

Schenck, Robert C., no intentional discourtesy—I beg you will not believe I have treated you with intentional discourtesy.—*To Gen. Schenck, July 23, 1863.* IX, 41.

Schofield, John M., advice to—I wish you . . . to exercise your own judgment, and do right for the public interest. Let your military measures be strong enough to repel the invader and keep the peace, and not so strong as to unnecessarily harass and persecute the people. It is a difficult role, and so much greater will be the honor if you perform it well.—*To Gen. Schofield, May 27, 1863.* VIII, 283.

Schofield, John M., appreciation of—Without disparaging any, I affirm with confidence that no commander of that department [Missouri] has, in proportion to his means, done better than Gen. Schofield.—*To Charles D. Drake and others, Oct. 5, 1863.* IX, 157.
2.—The charges that Gen. Schofield has purposely withheld protection from loyal people and purposely facilitated the objects of the disloyal are altogether beyond my power of belief.—*To Charles D. Drake and others, Oct. 5, 1863.* IX, 161.

Schofield, John M., criticized—I regret to learn of the arrest of the "Democrat" editor. I fear this loses you the middle position I desired you to occupy.—*To Gen. Schofield, July 13, 1863.* IX, 27.

Schofield, John M., removal of, eased—I believe Gen. Schofield must be relieved from command of the Department of Missouri; otherwise, a question of veracity, in relation to his declarations as to his interfering, or not, with the Missouri legislature, will be made with him, which will create an additional amount of trouble, not to be overcome by even a correct decision of the question. The question itself must be avoided. Now for the mode. Senator Henderson, his friend, thinks he can be induced to ask to be relieved, if he shall understand he will be generously treated; and, on this latter point, Gratz Brown will help his nomination as a major-general through the Senate. In no other way can he be confirmed; and upon his rejection alone it would be difficult for me to sustain him as commander of the department.—*To Sec. Stanton, Dec. 18, 1863.* IX, 264.

Schurz, Carl, advised not to leave military for politics Allow me to suggest that if you wish to remain in the military service, it is very dangerous for you to get temporarily out of it; because with a major-general once out, it is next to impossible for even the President to get him in again. . . . I would be very glad to have your service for the country in the approaching political canvass; but I fear we cannot properly have it without separating you from the military.—*To Gen. Schurz, March 13, 1864.* X, 39.
2.—I perceive no objection to your making a political speech when you are where one is to be made; but quite surely speaking in the North and fighting in the South at the same time are not possible; nor would I be justified to detail any officer to the political campaign during its continuance and then return him to the army.—*To Gen. Schurz, March 23, 1864.* X, 55.

Schurz, Carl, appreciation of—To the extent of our limited acquaintance no man stands nearer my heart than yourself.—*To Mr. Schurz, June 18, 1860.* Hertz II, 779.
2.—. . . his fidelity, probity and good conduct.—*To Queen of Spain, March 29, 1861.* Hertz II, 825.
3.—With my appreciation of your ability and correct principle.—*To Gen. Schurz, March 13, 1864.* X, 39.

Schurz, Carl, blamed for blaming President—*See* CIVIL WAR, President blamed if it fails.

Schurz, Carl, difficult to place—I appreciate him [Gen Schurz] as highly as you do; but you can never know until you have the trial, how difficult it is to find a place for an officer of so high rank when there

is no place seeking him.—*To Andrew Johnson, July 27, 1864.* X, 176.

"Scold Before They Think"—I am constantly pressed by those who scold before they think, or without thinking at all.—*To Gen. John A. McClernand, Aug. 12, 1863.* IX, 72.

Scott, Winfield, Douglas's eulogy of—As to the judge's [Douglas's] eulogy on Gen. Scott's military character, in which he says, "I will not depreciate his merits as a soldier because truth and honor forbid," I have but to remark that whoever will read the speech [Douglas's at Richmond] through and carefully note the imputations implying ignorance and stupidity, and duplicity and knavery, against Gen. Scott in almost every paragraph will, I think, conclude that the eulogy on his military character was dictated quite as much by the judge's view of the party impolicy of assailing that character as by a love of truth and honor.—*Speech, Springfield, Aug. 14, 1852.* Angle, 87.

Scott, Winfield, fitness of, for President—*See* PIERCE, FRANKLIN, Winfield Scott and.

Scott, Winfield, maligned by enemies—Nothing is too absurd for the malice of his fault-finding enemies.—*Speech, Springfield, Aug. 14, 1852.* Angle, 93.

Scott, Winfield, peril to Union?—The gist of all the judge's [Douglas's] views is that Scott's nomination, made as it was, is more perilous to the safety of the Union than all the scenes through which we have recently passed in connection with the slavery question. Well, we ought to be startled at the view of "peril to the Union," but it may be a little difficult for some short-sighted mortals to perceive such peril in the nomination of Scott. Mark you, it is the nomination, and not the election, which produces the peril. The judge does not say the election, and he cannot mean the election, because he constantly assures us there is no prospect of Scott's election. He could not be so alarmed at what he is so sure will never happen.—*Speech, Springfield, Aug. 14, 1852.* Angle, 90.

Scott, Winfield, tributes to—He has held a military commission a long time—over forty years. If you assert that this has bred in him a thirst for war, and a distaste for peace, "the known incidents of a long public life," abundantly prove the contrary. Among them are his successful efforts for peace and against war in the South Carolina nullification question, on the burning of the *Caroline,* and on the Maine boundary question.—*Speech, Springfield, Aug. 26, 1852.* Angle, 98.

2.—. . . most distinguished character as a military captain.—*To Gen. Scott, Nov. 9, 1860.* VI, 68.

3.—Permit me to renew to you the assurance of my high appreciation of the many past services you have rendered the Union, and my deep gratification of this evidence of your present active exertions to maintain the integrity and honor of the nation.—*To Gen. Scott, Jan. 11, 1861.* VI, 92.

4.—. . . great skill and experience.—*To Gen. Scott, March 9, 1861.* VI, 189.

5.—The American people will learn with sadness and deep emotion that Gen. Scott has withdrawn from the active control of the army, while the President and a unanimous cabinet express their own and the nation's sympathy in his personal affliction, and their profound sense of the important public services rendered by him to his country during his long and brilliant career, among which will ever be gratefully distinguished his faithful devotion to the Constitution, the Union and the flag when assailed by parricidal rebellion.—*Executive order, Nov. 1, 1861.* VII, 14.

6.—Since your last adjournment Lieut.-Gen. Scott has retired from the head of the army. During his long life the nation has not been unmindful of his merit; yet in calling to mind how faithfully, ably and brilliantly he has served the country, from a time far back in our history when few of the now living had been born, and thenceforward continually, I can not but think we are still his debtors.—*First annual message, Dec. 3, 1861.* VII, 54.

Scott, Winfield, urged to be ready—Please present my respects to the general [Winfield Scott], and tell him, confidentially, I shall be obliged to him to be as well prepared as he can to either hold or retake the forts, as the case may require, at and after the inauguration.—*To E. B. Washburne, Dec. 21, 1860.* VI, 84.

Secession, after, what?—I want to know what you [men of the South] are going to do with your half of it [the Union]? Are you going to split the Ohio down through, and push your half off a piece? Or are you going to keep it right alongside of us outrageous fellows? Or are you going to build up a wall some way between your country and ours, by which that movable property of yours can't come over here any more, to the danger of your losing it? Do you think you can better yourselves on that subject [slavery] by having us [of the North] bear no obligation whatever to return those specimens of your movable property that come hither?—*Speech, Cincinnati, Sept. 17, 1859.* V, 219.

2.—Will you [after the Union is dissolved] make war upon us [Northerners] and kill us all? Why, gentle-men, I think you are as gallant and as brave men as live; that you can fight as bravely in a good cause, man for man, as any other people living; that you have shown yourselves capable of this upon various occasions; but man for man you are not better than we are, and there are not so many of you as there are of us. You will never make much of a hand at whipping us. If we were fewer in numbers than you, I think you could whip us; if we were equal it would likely be a drawn battle; but inferior in numbers, you will make nothing by attempting to master us.—*Speech, Cincinnati, Sept. 17, 1859.* V, 219.

3.—You [will] have divided the Union because we would not do right with you, as you think, upon that subject [slavery]; when we cease to be under obligations to do anything for you, how much better off do you think you will be?—*Speech, Cincinnati, Sept. 17, 1859.* V, 221.

4.—Is it possible, then, to make that intercourse [between the sections] more advantageous or more satisfactory after separation than before? Can aliens make treaties easier than friends can make laws? Can treaties be more faithfully enforced between aliens than laws can among friends?—Suppose you go to war, you cannot fight always; and when, after much loss on both sides, and no gain on either, you cease fighting, the identical old terms of intercourse, are again upon you.—*First inaugural, March 4, 1861.* VI, 181.

5.—Whoever in any section proposes to abandon such a government [as that of the United States] would do well to consider in deference to what principle it is that he does it—what better is he likely to get in its stead—whether the substitute will give, or be intended to give, so much of good to the people?—*Message to Congress, July 4, 1861.* VI, 320.

Secession, disunionists in hurry—*See* UNION, destruction of, openly sought, 1.

Secession, fanciful illustration—If all the states save one should assert the power to drive that one out of the Union, it is presumed the whole class of seceder politicians would at once deny the power and denounce the act as the greatest outrage upon state rights. But suppose that precisely the same act, instead of being called "driving the one out," should be called "the seceding of the others from that one," it would be exactly what the seceders claim to do, unless, indeed, they make the point that the one, because it is a minority, may rightfully do what the others, because they are a majority, may not rightfully do. These politicians are subtle and profound on the rights of minorities.—*Message to Congress, July 4, 1861.* VI, 318.

Secession, for and against Constitution—*See* WEST VIRGINIA, argument for admission of, 6.

Secession, means disintegration—If a minority . . . will secede rather than acquiesce [in the rule of the majority] they make a precedent which in turn will divide and ruin them, for a minority of their own will secede from them whenever a majority refuses to be controlled by such minority. For instance, why may not any portion of a new confederacy a year or two hence arbitrarily secede again, precisely as portions of the present Union now claim to secede? All who cherish disunion sentiments are now being educated to the exact temper of doing this. Is there such perfect identity of interests among the states to compose a new union as to produce harmony only and prevent renewed secession?—*First inaugural, March 4, 1861.* VI, 178.

2.—Plainly the central idea of secession is the essence of anarchy. A majority held in restraint by constitutional checks and limitations, and always changing easily with deliberate changes of popular opinions and sentiments, is the only true sovereign of a free people. Whoever rejects it does of necessity fly to anarchy or to despotism. Unanimity is impossible. The rule of a minority, as a permanent arrangement, is wholly inadmissible; so that, rejecting the majority principle, anarchy or despotism in some form is all that is left.—*First inaugural, March 4, 1861.* VI, 179.

3.—The principle [of secession] itself is one of disintegration, and upon which no government can possibly endure.—*Message to Congress, July 4, 1861.* VI, 318.

See CONFEDERATE CONSTITUTION, secession and.

See MAJORITY RULE, essential to safety.

Secession, national debt and—The nation purchased with money the countries out of which several of these [seceding] states were formed. Is it just that they shall go off without leave and without refunding? The nation paid very large sums—in the aggregate, I believe, nearly a hundred millions—to relieve Florida of the aboriginal tribes. Is it just that she shall now be off without consent or without making any return? The nation is now in debt for money applied to the benefit of these so-called seceding states in common with the rest. Is it just either that creditors shall go unpaid or the remaining states pay the whole? . . . If one state may secede, so may another; and when all shall have seceded none is left to pay the debts. Is this quite just to creditors? Did we notify them of this sage view of ours when we borrowed their money?—*Message to Congress, July 4, 1861.* VI, 317.

2.—A part of the present national debt was contracted to pay the old debts of Texas. Is it just that she shall leave [the Union] and pay no part of this herself?—*Message to Congress, July 4, 1861.* VI, 317.

Secession, no compromise with—No compromise by public servants could, in this case, be a cure.—*Message to Congress, July 4, 1861.* VI, 324.

Secession, no excuse for—There is nothing going wrong. It is a consoling circumstance that when we look about there is nothing that really hurts anybody. We entertain different views upon political questions, but nobody is suffering anything.—*Speech to Ohio Legislature, Feb. 13, 1861.* VI, 122.

2.—What is happening to hurt them [men who seek to destroy the Union]? have they not all their rights now as they ever have had? Do not they have their fugitive slaves returned now as ever? Have they not the same Constitution that they have lived under for seventy-odd years? Have they not a position as citizens of this common country, and have we any power to change that position? What then is the matter with them? Why all this excitement? Why all these complaints?—*Speech, Cleveland, Feb. 15, 1861.* VI, 130.

3.—All the vital rights of minorities and of individuals are so plainly assured to them [men of the South] by affirmations and negations, guarantees and prohibitions, in the Constitution, that controversies never arise concerning them.—*First inaugural, March 4, 1861.* VI, 177.

4.—You all know, the world knows, the forces and resources the public agents have brought into employment to sustain a government against which there has been brought not one complaint of real injury committed against society at home or abroad.—*Reply to Evangelical Lutherans, May 6, 1862.* VII, 154.

See CRISIS, "artificial."

Secession, sophism of—It might seem at first thought to be of little difference whether the present movement at the South be called "secession" or "rebellion." The movers, however, well understand the difference. At the beginning they knew they could never raise their treason to any respectable magnitude by any name which implies violation of law. . . . Accordingly, they commenced by an insidious debauching of the public mind. They invented an ingenious sophism, which, if conceded, was followed by perfectly logical steps through all the incidents to the complete destruction of the Union. The sophism itself is that any state of the Union may, consistently with the national Constitution, and therefore lawfully and peacefully, withdraw from the Union without the consent of the Union or of any other state. The little disguise that the supposed right is to be exercised only for just cause, themselves to be the sole judge of its justice, is too thin to merit any notice. With rebellion thus sugar-coated they have been drugging the public mind of their section for more than 30 years, and until at length they have brought many good men to a willingness to take up arms against the government the day after some assemblage of men have enacted the farcical pretense of taking their state out of the Union who could have been brought to no such thing the day before.—*Message to Congress, July 4, 1861.* VI, 312.

Secession, wars on popular government—*See* SELF-GOVERNMENT, insurrection wars on.

Secessionists, face same fate as John Brown—*See* BROWN, JOHN, secessionists face same fate as.

Sectionalism, Democrats must avoid appearance of—The signs now are that Douglas and Breckinridge will each have a ticket in every state. They are driven to this to keep up their bombastic claims of nationality, and to avoid the charge of sectionalism which they have so much lavished upon us.—*To A. G. Henry, July 4, 1860.* VI, 43.

Sectionalism, Douglas guilty of—I understand that at one time the people of Chicago would not let Judge Douglas preach a certain favorite doctrine of his. I commend to his consideration the question, whether he takes that as a test of the unsoundness of what he wanted to preach.—*Debate, Galesburg, Oct. 7, 1858.* IV, 268.

2.—I ask his [Douglas's] attention also to the fact that by the rule of nationality, he is himself fast becoming sectional. I ask his attention to the fact that his speeches would not go current south of the Ohio River as they have formerly gone there.—*Debate, Galesburg, Oct. 7, 1858.* IV, 269.

3.—Whatever may be the result of this ephemeral contest between Judge Douglas and myself, I see the day rapidly approaching when his pill of sectionalism, which he has been thrusting down the throats of Republicans for years past, will be crowded down his own throat.—*Debate, Galesburg, Oct. 7, 1858.* IV, 270.

4.—It is an amusing fact, after all Douglas has said about nationality and sectionalism, that I had more votes from the southern section at Chicago than he had at Baltimore. In fact, there was more of the southern section represented at Chicago than in the

Douglas rump concern at Baltimore!—*To A. G. Henry, July 4, 1860.* VI, 43.

Sectionalism, how cure?—Who can help it [the evil of sectionalism]? Either side can help it, but how? Simply by yielding to the other side; there is no other way; in the whole range of possibility there is no other way.—*Fragment, Oct. 1, 1856.* II, 306.

Sectionalism, Washington's warning against—Some of you [men of the South] delight to flaunt in our [Republicans'] faces the warning against sectional parties given by Washington in his Farewell Address. Less than eight years before Washington gave that warning, he had, as President of the United States, approved and signed an act of Congress enforcing the prohibition of slavery in the Northwestern Territory, which act embodied the policy of the government upon that subject up to and at the very moment he penned that warning; and about one year after he penned it, he wrote Lafayette that he considered that prohibition a wise measure, expressing in the same connection his hope that we should at some time have a confederacy of free states. Bearing this in mind, and seeing that sectionalism has since arisen upon this same subject, is that warning a weapon in your hands against us, or in our hands against you? Could Washington himself speak, would he cast the blame of that sectionalism upon us, who sustain his policy, or upon you who repudiate it?—*Cooper Institute address, New York, Feb. 27, 1860.* V, 312.
Repeated at New Haven, Conn., March 6, 1860. V, 365.

Sectionalism, what constitutes?—It is said that our [Republican] party is a sectional party. . . . It is said we expect to elect Frémont by northern votes. Certainly we do not think the South will elect him. But let us ask the question differently. Does not Buchanan expect to be elected by southern votes?—*Speech, Kalamazoo, Mich., Aug. 27, 1856.* Stern, 405.

2.—It is constantly objected to Frémont and Dayton, that they are supported by a sectional party, who by their sectionalism endanger the national Union. . . . What is the question between the parties? . . . Simply this, "Shall slavery be allowed to extend into United States territories now legally free? . . . That is the naked issue, and the whole of it. . . . I beg to know how one side of that question is more sectional than the other.—*Fragment, Oct. 1, 1856.* II, 299.

3.—Frémont and Dayton are both residents of the free states, and this fact has been vaunted in high places as excessive sectionalism. While interested individuals become indignant and excited against this manifestation of sectionalism, I am very happy to know that the Constitution remains calm—keeps cool —upon the subject. It does say that the President and Vice President shall be residents of different states, but it does not say that one must live in a slave state and the other in a free state.—*Fragment, Oct. 1, 1856.* II, 301.

4.—With the friends of Frémont it is an expected necessity, but not an "avowed purpose," to elect him, if at all, principally by free-state votes; but it is with equal intensity true that Buchanan's friends expect to elect him, if at all, chiefly by slave-state votes. Here, again, the sectionalism is just as much on one side as on the other.—*Fragment, Oct. 1, 1856.* II, 302.

5.—And when by such means they [proslavery men] have got a large portion of northern people into a position [on slavery extension] contrary to their own honest impulses and sense of right, they have the impudence to turn upon those who do stand firm, and call them sectional. Were it not too serious a matter, this cool impudence would be laughable to say the least.—*Fragment, Oct. 1, 1856.* II, 306.

6.—Shall slavery be allowed to extend into United States territories now legally free? This is a sectional question—that is to say, it is a question in its nature calculated to divide the American people geographically. Who is to blame for that? Who can help it?— *Fragment, Oct. 1, 1865.* II, 306.

7.—He [Douglas] assumes that our party is altogether sectional—that the party to which he adheres is national; and the argument is that no party can be a rightful party—can be based on rightful principles— unless it can announce its principles everywhere. I presume that Judge Douglas could not go into Russia and announce the doctrine of our national Democracy; ... and it may be true of this country, that in some places we may not be able to proclaim a doctrine as clearly true as the truth of democracy, because there is a section so directly opposed to it that they will not tolerate us in doing so. Is it the true test of the soundness of a doctrine, that in some places people won't let you proclaim it?—*Debate, Galesburg, Oct. 7, 1858.* IV, 267.

8.—What has always been the evidence brought forward to prove that the Republican party is a sectional party? The main one was that in the southern portion of the Union the people did not let the Republicans proclaim their doctrines among them. ... The South have not taken hold of our principles as we announce them; nor does Judge Douglas grapple with these principles. ... If he had great confidence that our principles were wrong, he would take hold of them and demonstrate them to be wrong. ... The only evidence he has of their being wrong is the fact that there are people who won't allow us to preach them. I ask again is that the way to test the soundness of a doctrine?—*Debate, Galesburg, Oct. 7, 1858.* IV, 268.

9.—If the mere fact that we [Republicans] get no votes in the slave states make us sectional, whenever we shall get votes in those states we shall cease to be sectional; and we are sure to get votes, and a good many of them, too, in those states next year.—*Speech, Leavenworth, Kan., Dec. 3, 1859.* Angle, 234.

10.—Why [Democrats say], they [Republicans] have no existence, get no votes, in the South. But that depends on the South, and not on us. It is their volition, not ours; and if there be fault in it, it is primarily theirs, and remains so, unless they show that we repel them by some wrong principle. If they attempt this, they will find us holding no principle other than those held and acted upon by the men who gave us the government under which we live. They will find that the charge of sectionalism will not stop at us, but will extend to the very men who gave us the liberty we enjoy.—*Speech, Leavenworth, Kan., Dec. 3, 1859.* Angle, 234.

11.—You [men of the South] say we [Republicans] are sectional. We deny it. That makes an issue; and the burden of proof is upon you. You produce your proof; and what is it? Why, that our party has no existence in your section—gets no votes in your section. The fact is substantially true; but does it prove the issue? ... The fact that we get no votes in your section is a fact of your making, and not ours. And if there be fault in that fact, that fault is primarily yours, and remains so until you show that we repel you by some wrong principle or practice.—*Cooper Institute address, New York, Feb. 27, 1860.* V, 310. Repeated at New Haven, Conn., March 6, 1860. V, 363.

12.—If our [Republican] principles, put in practice, would wrong your section [South] for the benefit of ours, or for any other object, then our principle, and we with it, are sectional, and are justly opposed and denounced as such. Meet us, then, on the question of whether our principle, put in practice, would wrong your section; and so meet us as if it were possible that something may be said on our side.— *Cooper Institute address, New York, Feb. 27, 1860.* V, 311.

Repeated at New Haven, Conn., March 6, 1860. V, 364.

See SECTIONALISM, Washington's warning against.

Sedition Law, Douglas's new—[To satisfy the South] Senator Douglas's new sedition law must be enacted and enforced, suppressing any declarations that

slavery is wrong, whether made in politics, in presses, in pulpits, or in private.—*Cooper Institute address, New York, Feb. 27, 1860.* V, 325.
Repeated at New Haven, Conn., March 6, 1860. V, 368.

See SOUTH, what will satisfy? 1.

Self-Government, basic belief—I have said very many times . . . that no man believed more than I in the principle of self-government; that it lies at the bottom of all my ideas of just government from beginning to end. . . . I deny that any man has ever gone ahead of me in his devotion to the principle, whatever he may have done in efficiency in advocating it.—*Speech, Chicago, July 10, 1858.* III, 35.

Self-Government, be worthy of—Rise up to the height of a generation of men worthy of a free government. —*Speech to 164th Ohio regiment, Aug. 18, 1864.* X, 200.

Self-Government, can it survive?—Can this country be saved on that basis [of the Declaration of Independence]? If it can, I will consider myself one of the happiest men in the world if I can help save it. If it cannot be saved upon that principle, it will be truly awful. But if this country cannot be saved without giving up that principle, I was about to say I would rather be assassinated on this spot than surrender it. —*Speech, Independence Hall, Philadelphia, Feb. 22, 1861.* VI, 158.

2.—You have kindly adverted to the trial through which this republic is now passing. It is one of deep import. It involves the question whether a representative republic, extended and aggrandised so much as to be safe against foreign enemies, can save itself from the dangers of domestic faction. I have faith in a good result.—*To regent captains of San Marino, May 7, 1861.* Hertz II, 833.

3.—I consider the central idea pervading this struggle is the necessity that is upon us of proving that popular government is not an absurdity. We must settle this question now, whether in a free government the minority have the right to break up the government whenever they choose. If we fail it will go far to prove the incapability of the people to govern themselves. There may be one consideration used in stay of such final judgment, but that is not for us to use in advance. That is, that there exists in our case, an instance of so vast and far-reaching a disturbing element, which the history of no other nation will probably ever present. Taking the government as we found it, we will see if the majority can preserve it.—*To John Hay, May 7, 1861.* Hay, 19.

4.—The republican system of government, which has been adopted so generally on this continent, has proved its adaptation to what is the first purpose of government everywhere—the maintenance of national independence. It is my confident hope and belief that this system will be found, after sufficient trials, to be better adapted everywhere than any other to the other great interests of human society—namely, the preservation of peace, order, and national prosperity.—*To minister from Granada, June 4, 1861.* Hertz II, 836.

5.—This issue [of civil war] embraces more than the fate of these United States. It presents to the whole family of man the question whether a constitutional republic or democracy—government of the people by the same people—can or cannot maintain its territorial integrity against its own domestic foes. It presents the question whether discontented individuals too few in numbers to control administrations according to organic law in any case, can always, upon the pretenses made in this case, or on any other pretenses, or arbitrarily without any pretense, break up their government, and then practically put an end to free government upon the earth. It forces us to ask, Is there in all republics this inherent and fatal weakness? Must a government of necessity be too strong for the liberties of its own people, or too weak to maintain its own existence?—*Message to Congress, July 4, 1861.* VI, 304.

6.—Our popular government has often been called an experiment. Two points in it our people have already settled—the successful establishing and the successful administering of it. One still remains—its successful maintenance against a formidable internal attempt to overthrow it.—*Message to Congress, July 4, 1861.* VI, 322.

7.—No popular government can long survive a marked precedent that those who carry an election can only save the government from immediate destruction by giving up the main point upon which the people gave the election.—*Message to Congress, July 4, 1861.* VI, 324.

8.—Can this government stand, if it indulges constitutional constructions by which men in open rebellion against it are to be accounted, man for man, the equals of those who maintain their loyalty to it?— *Opinion on admission of West Virginia, Dec. 31, 1862.* VIII, 158.

9.—It seems to have devolved upon them [American people] to test whether a government established on the principles of human freedom can be maintained against an effort to build one upon the exclusive foundation of human bondage.—*To workers of London, Feb. 2, 1863.* VIII, 212.

10.—Now we are engaged in a great civil war, testing

whether that nation or any nation so conceived and so dedicated can long endure.—*Gettysburg address, Nov. 19, 1863. IX, 209.*

11.—We have, as all will agree, a free government, where every man has a right to be equal with every other man. In this great struggle [Civil War], this form of government and every form of human right is endangered if our enemies succeed. There is more involved in this contest than is realized by every one. There is involved in this struggle the question whether your children and my children shall enjoy the privileges we have enjoyed. . . . No small matter should divert us from our great purpose.—*Speech to 164th Ohio regiment, Aug. 18, 1864. X, 199.*

12.—It has long been a grave question whether any government, not too strong for the liberties of its people, can be strong enough to maintain its existence in great emergencies. On this point the present rebellion brought our Republic to a severe test, and a presidential election occurring in regular course during the rebellion added not a little to the strain.—*Response to serenade, Nov. 10, 1864. X, 264.*

Self-Government, Civil War fought to perpetuate— See CIVIL WAR, results of, involve future.

Self-Government, "deceitful cloak of"—See SLAVERY, "sacred right" of, 5.

Self-Government, defined—I admit that the emigrant to Kansas and Nebraska is competent to govern himself, but I deny his right to govern any other person without that person's consent.—*Memorandum, Oct. 4, 1854. Hertz II, 627.*

2.—My distinguished friend [Douglas] says it is an insult to the emigrants to Kansas and Nebraska to suppose they are not able to govern themselves. We must not slur over argument of this kind because it happens to tickle the ear. It must be met and answered. I admit that the emigrant to Kansas and Nebraska is competent to govern himself, but I deny his right to govern any other person without that person's consent.—*Speech, Springfield, Oct. 4, 1854. Bartlett, 65.*

3.—The doctrine of self-government has no just application as here attempted [by Douglas in his defense of the Missouri Compromise repeal]. Or perhaps I should rather say that whether it has such application depends upon whether a negro is not or is a man. If he is not a man, in that case he who is a man may as a matter of self-government do just what he pleases with him. But if the negro is a man, is it not to that extent a total destruction of self-government to say that he, too, shall not govern himself?—*Speech, Peoria, Oct. 16, 1854. II, 227.*

4.—I trust I understand and truly estimate the right of self-government. My faith in the proposition that each man should do precisely as he pleases with all that which is exclusively his own lies at the foundation of the sense of justice there is in me. I extend the principle to communities of men as well as to individuals. I so extend it because it is politically wise, as well as naturally just; politically wise in saving us from broils about matters which do not concern us.—*Speech, Peoria, Oct. 16, 1854. II, 227.*

5.—When the white man governs himself, that is self-government; but when he governs himself and also another man, that is more than self-government—that is despotism.—*Speech, Peoria, Oct. 16, 1845. II, 227.* Repeated at Urbana, Oct. 24, 1854. Hertz II, 644.

6.—No man is good enough to govern another man without that other man's consent. I say this is the leading principle, the sheet anchor, of American republicanism.—*Speech, Peoria, Oct. 16, 1854. II, 228.* Repeated at Urbana, Oct. 24, 1854. Hertz II, 228.

7.—The master not only governs the slave without his consent, but he governs him by a set of rules altogether different from those he prescribes for himself. —*Speech, Peoria, Oct. 16, 1854. II, 228.* Repeated at Urbana, Oct. 24, 1854. Hertz II, 645.

8.—According to our ancient faith, the just powers of government are derived from the consent of the governed. Now the relation of master and slave is *pro tanto* a total violation of this principle.—*Speech, Peoria, Oct. 16, 1854. II, 228.* Repeated at Urbana, Oct. 24, 1854. Hertz II, 645.

9.—Allow all the governed an equal voice in the government, and that, and that only, is self-government. —*Speech, Peoria, Oct. 16, 1854. II, 229.* Repeated at Urbana, Oct 24, 1854. Hertz II, 645.

10.—As I would not be a slave, so I would not be a master. This expresses my idea of democracy. Whatever differs from this, to the extent of the difference, is no democracy.—*Autograph, no date. Lang, 60.*

11.—I, too, believe in self-government as I understand it; but I do not understand that the privilege one man takes of making a slave of another, or holding him as such, is any part of self-government. To call it so is, to my mind, simply absurd and ridiculous. I am for the people of the whole nation doing just as they please in all matters which concern the whole nation; for those of each part doing just as they choose in all matters which concern no other part; and for each individual doing just as he chooses in all matters which concern nobody else. This is the principle.—*Notes, Oct. 1, 1858. IV, 231.*

12.—Our government was not established that one man might do with himself as he pleases, and with another man too.—*Speech, Cincinnati, Sept. 17, 1859. Follett, 148.*

Self-Government, Douglas and polygamy—*See* UTAH, polygamy and statehood.

Self-Government, election brings test of—*See* SELF-GOVERNMENT, can it survive? 12.

Self-Government, first principle of—*See* SELF-GOVERNMENT, insurrection wars on, 1.

Self-Government, importance of—Our common country is in great peril, demanding the loftiest views and boldest action to bring it speedy relief. Once relieved, its form of government is saved to the world, its beloved history and cherished memories are vindicated, and its happy future fully assured and rendered inconceivably grand.—*To border-state congressmen, July 12, 1862.* VII, 273.
2.—As you would perpetuate popular government for the best people in the world, I beseech you that you do in no wise omit this [compensated emancipation].—*To border-state congressmen, July 12, 1862.* VII, 273.
3.—No service can be more praiseworthy and honorable than that which is rendered for the maintenance of the Constitution and the Union and consequent preservation of free government.—*Proclamation, May 8, 1863.* VIII, 267.

Self-Government, insurrection wars on—It continues to develop that the insurrection is largely, if not exclusively, a war upon the first principle of popular government—the rights of the people.—*First annual message, Dec. 3, 1861.* VII, 56.
2.—Conclusive evidence of this [purpose to war on popular government] is found in the most grave and maturely considered documents as well as in the general tone of the insurgents. In these documents we find the abridgment of the existing right of suffrage and the denial to the people of all right to participate in the selection of public officers except the legislative, boldly advocated, with labored arguments to prove that large control of the people in government is the source of all political evil.—*First annual message, Dec. 3, 1861.* VII, 56.

Self-Government, Jefferson and—*See* DESPOTISM, those who deny Jefferson are vanguards of.

Self-Government, makes America great—From the first taking of our national census to the last are 70 years; and we find our population at the end of the period eight times as great as it was at the beginning. The increase of those other things which men deem desirable has been even greater. We thus have, at one view, what the popular principle, applied to government, through the machinery of the states and the Union, has produced in a given time; and also what, if firmly maintained, it promises for the future.—*First annual message, Dec. 3, 1861.* VII, 59.

Self-Government, requires elections—*See* ELECTIONS, necessary to free government.

Self-Government, resolution to perpetuate—We here highly resolve that these dead shall not have died in vain; that this nation, under God, shall have a new birth of freedom; and that government of the people, by the people and for the people shall not perish from the earth.—*Gettysburg address, Nov. 19, 1863.* IX, 210.

Self-Government, right—The doctrine of self-government is right—absolutely and eternally right.—*Speech, Peoria, Oct. 16, 1854.* II, 227.

Self-Government, sacred—I have done with this mighty argument of self-government. Go, sacred thing! Go in peace.—*Speech, Peoria, Oct. 16, 1854.* II, 236.

Self-Government, "sacred right" of—*See* EQUALITY, basic American principle, 1.

See AFRICAN SLAVE TRADE, slavery extension akin to, 3.

See SLAVERY, "sacred right" of, 1.

See SLAVE STATES, have advantage in Congress, 3.

Self-Government, strength of—*See* ELECTION OF 1864, gratitude without taint, 3.

Self-Government, success of, foreshadowed at Fredericksburg—*See* ARMY OF THE POTOMAC, praised for Fredericksburg.

Self-Interest—We have been mistaken all our lives if we do now know that whites, as well as blacks, look to their self-interest. Unless among those deficient in intellect, everybody you trade with makes something.—*Speech to delegation of free colored men, Aug. 14, 1862.* VIII, 7.

Self-Preservation, duty of—I have understood well that the duty of self-preservation rests solely with the American people.—*To workers of Manchester, Jan. 19, 1863.* VIII, 195.

Selfishness, foundation of slavery—*See* SLAVERY, wrong of, 5.

Selfishness, in politics—It pains me a little that you have deemed it necessary to point out to me how I may be compensated for throwing myself in the breach now [by running for Congress]. This assumes that I am merely calculating the chances of personal advancement.—*To J. M. Sturtevant, Sept. 27, 1856.* Angle, 163.

2.—I do not claim, gentlemen, to be unselfish; I do not pretend that I would not like to go to the United States Senate; I make no such hypocritical pretense.—*Speech, Chicago, July 1, 1858.* III, 42.

3.—I do not claim that I am any less so [selfish] than the average of men, but I do claim that I am not more selfish than Judge Douglas.—*Debate, Alton, Oct. 15, 1858.* V 54.

4.—The Bible says somewhere that we are desperately selfish. I think we would have discovered that fact without the Bible.—*Debate, Alton, Oct. 15, 1858.* V, 54.

Serenade, difficult to answer—The hardest of all speeches I have to answer is a serenade. I never know what to say on these occasions.—*Reply to delegation, June 9, 1864.* X, 121.

Serpent, slavery characterized as—*See* SLAVERY, "reptile."

Severity, not always best—*See* JUSTICE, not best if too severe.

Seward, William H., appraised as presidential candidate—*See* CAMPAIGN OF 1860, preconvention candidates appraised.

Seward, William H., "cannot afford"—I cannot afford to let Seward take the first trick.—*To John Hay, March 4, 1861.* War Years I, 141.

Seward, William H., caused delay in proclamation—*See* EMANCIPATION PROCLAMATION (Preliminary), timed to circumstances, 2.

Seward, William H., deference to—Gov. Seward, there is one part of my work that I shall have to leave largely to you. I shall have to depend upon you for taking care of these matters of foreign affairs of which I know so little, and with which I reckon you are familiar.—*To Mr. Seward, Feb. 24, 1861.* War Years I, 91.

Seward, William H., enemies of—I guess the southern people would hang Seward if they should catch him.—*To James R. Gilmore, April 13, 1861.* Gilmore, 21.

Seward, William H., no combination against—*See* NOMINATION OF 1860, attitude toward, 1.

Seward, William H., on "irrepressible conflict"—*See* IRREPRESSIBLE CONFLICT, difference in who says it, 1, 3, 4.

Seward, William H., proffer of office to—Rumors have got into the newspapers to the effect that the [state] department . . . would be tendered you as a compliment, with the expectation that you would decline it. I beg you to be assured that I have said nothing to justify these rumors. On the contrary, it has been my purpose, from the day of the nomination at Chicago, to assign you, by your leave, this place in the administration. . . . I now offer you the place in the hope that you will accept it, and with the belief that your position in the public eye, your integrity, ability, learning and great experience, will combine to render it an appointment eminently fit to be made.—*To Mr. Seward, Dec. 8, 1860.* VI, 76.

"Seward Egg in the North"—*See* NOMINATION OF 1860, attitude toward, 4.

Sewing Societies, mother of—That proceeding [Adam and Eve making the fig-leaf apron] may be reckoned as the mother of all "sewing societies," and the first and most perfect "World's Fair," all inventions and all inventors then in the world being on the spot.—*Lecture, Springfield, Feb. 22, 1859.* V, 106.

Seymour, Horatio, better acquaintance with, sought—You and I are substantially strangers, and I write this chiefly that we may become better acquainted. . . . In the performance of my duty the co-operation of your state, as that of others, is needed—in fact, is indispensable. This alone is sufficient reason why I should be at a good understanding with you.—*To Gov. Seymour, March 23, 1863.* VIII, 230.

Seymour, Horatio, Union sympathy of, assumed—As to maintaining the nation's life and integrity, I assume and believe there cannot be a difference of purpose between you and me. If we should differ as to the means, it is important that such difference should be as small as possible; that it should not be enhanced by unjust suspicions on one side or the other.—*To Gov. Seymour, March 23, 1863.* VIII, 231.

"Shadow of a Starved Pigeon"—*See* POPULAR SOVEREIGNTY, killed by Supreme Court, 4.

Shakespeare—*See* DRAMA, unprofessional criticism.

Sharp, Granville, enemy of slavery—*See* AFRICAN SLAVE TRADE, fight against, was long in Britain.

"Sheet Anchor of American Republicanism"—*See* SELF-GOVERNMENT, defined, 6.

"Shelled Peascod"—*See* PIERCE, FRANKLIN, "shelled peascod."

Shepherd, defines liberty—*See* LIBERTY, definitions of, differ, 2.

Sheridan, Philip H., appreciation of—Have just heard of your great victory. God bless you all, officers and men.—*To Gen. Sheridan, Sept. 20, 1864.* X, 227.

2.—With greatest pleasure I tender you and your brave army the thanks of the nation, and my own personal admiration and gratitude, for the month's operations in the Shenandoah Valley, and especially for the splendid work of Oct. 19, 1864.—*To Gen. Sheridan, Oct. 22, 1864.* X, 251.

Sherman, William T., appreciation of—My profoundest thanks to you and your whole army for the present campaign so far.—*To Gen. Sherman, July 26, 1864.* X, 175.

2.—The national thanks are tendered by the President to Maj. Gen. William T. Sherman and the gallant officers and soldiers of his command before Atlanta for the distinguished ability, courage and perseverance displayed in the campaign in Georgia, which, under divine favor, has resulted in the capture of the city of Atlanta. The marches, battles, sieges and other military operations that have signalized this campaign must render it famous in the annals of war, and have entitled those who have participated therein to the applause and thanks of the nation.—*Executive order, Sept. 3, 1864.* X, 213.

3.—Please make my grateful acknowledgments to your whole army—officers and men.—*To Gen. Sherman, Dec. 26, 1864.* X, 326.

Sherman, William T., deference to—Don't cheer, Boys. I confess I rather like it myself, but Col. Sherman here says it is not military, and I guess we had better defer to his opinion.—*To men in camp, summer, 1861.* War Years I, 307.

Sherman's March to the Sea, remarkable maneuver—The most remarkable feature in the military operations of the year is Gen. Sherman's attempted march of 300 miles directly through the insurgent region. It tends to show a great increase of our relative strength that our general-in-chief should feel able to confront and hold in check a very active force of the enemy, and yet to detach a well-appointed large army to move on such an expedition. The result not being known, conjecture in regard to it is not here indulged.—*Fourth annual message, Dec. 6, 1864.* X, 302.

2.—We know where he [Sherman] went in, but can't tell where he will come out.—*Response to serenade, Dec. 6, 1864.* X, 311.

Sherman's March to the Sea, thanks for Christmas gift—Many, many thanks for your Christmas gift, the capture of Savannah. When you were about leaving Atlanta for the Atlantic coast I was anxious if not fearful; but feeling that you were the better judge and remembering that "nothing risked, nothing gained," I did not interfere. Now, the undertaking being a success, the honor is all yours; for I believe none of us went further than to acquiesce.—*To Gen. Sherman, Dec. 25, 1864.* X, 325.

Shields, James, division of, "out of shape"—[Gen.] Shields' division has got so terribly out of shape, out at elbows, and out at toes, that it will require a long time to get it in again.—*To Gen. McClellan, June 15, 1862.* VII, 221.

Ship of State—*See also* PEOPLE, relied on to save Union, 11, 12.

Ship of State, "best exertions" for—As a pilot I have used my best exertions to keep afloat the Ship of State, and shall be glad to resign my trust at the appointed time to another pilot more skilful and successful than I may prove.—*Reply to Presbyterian General Assembly, May 30, 1863.* VIII, 288.

Ship of State, no pilot needed if wrecked now—If we do not make common cause to save the good old ship of the Union on this voyage, nobody will have a chance to pilot her on another voyage.—*Speech, Cleveland, Feb. 15, 1861.* VI, 132.

2.—Received as I am by members of a legislature the majority of whom do not agree with me in political sentiments, I trust that I may have their assistance in piloting the Ship of State through this voyage, surrounded by perils as it is; for if it should suffer wreck now, there will be no pilot ever needed for another voyage.—*Speech, New Jersey Assembly, Feb. 21, 1861.* VI, 154.

Ship of State, slavery as a figurehead—Henceforth it [slavery, if the Kansas-Nebraska principle wins] is to be the chief jewel of the nation—the very figurehead of the Ship of State.—*Speech, Peoria, Oct. 16, 1854.* II, 246.

Repeated at Urbana, Oct. 24, 1854. Hertz II, 654.

"Shirks and Quirks"—*See* DOUGLAS, STEPHEN A., characterized, 2.

Shorn Lamb, wind tempered to—How true it is that "God tempers the wind to the shorn lamb," or, in other words, that He renders the worst of human conditions tolerable, while He permits the best to be nothing better than tolerable.—*To Mary Speed, Sept. 27, 1841.* I, 179.

Short, James—. . . as honorable a man as there is in the world.—*To M. M. Morris, March 26, 1843.* I, 262.

Siam, elephants from, declined—*See* ELEPHANTS, Siam's offer declined.

Siam, gifts of, acknowledged—I have received Your Majesty's two letters of the date of Feb. 14, 1861. I have also received in good condition the royal gifts which accompanied the letters. . . . Your Majesty's letters show an understanding that our laws forbid the President from receiving these rich presents as personal treasures. They are, therefore, accepted, in accordance with Your Majesty's desire, as tokens of your good will and friendship for the American people. . . . I shall have occasion at no distant day to transmit to Your Majesty some token or indication of the high sense which this government entertains of Your Majesty's friendship.—*To king of Siam, Feb. 3, 1862.* Hertz II, 850.

Silence, best for presidential candidate—*See* CAMPAIGN OF 1860; silence is candidate's best policy.

See BIOGRAPHY, not authorized.

See CAMPAIGN OF 1864, public letter refused.

Silence, postelection explained—It is with most profound appreciation of your motive, and highest respect for your judgment, too, that I feel constrained for the present at least, to make no declaration for the public. First, I could say nothing which I have not already said, and which is in print, and open for the inspection of all. To press repetition of this upon those who have listened, is useless; to press it upon those who have refused to listen, and still refuse, would be wanting in self-respect, and would have an appearance of sycophancy and timidity which would excite the contempt of good men and encourage bad ones to clamor the more loudly.—*To Truman Smith, Nov. 10, 1860.* VI, 69.

2.—Mr. Ridgely showed me a letter of yours, in which you manifest some anxiety that I should make some public declaration with a view to favorably affect the business of the country. . . . I could say nothing which I have not already said, and which is in print, and accessible to the public. . . . If I thought a repetition would do any good I would make it. But in my judgment it would do positive harm. The secessionists *per se*, believing they had alarmed me, would clamor the louder.—*To N. P. Paschall, Nov. 16, 1860.* VI, 70.

3.—I am not in the habit of making speeches now, and I would therefore ask to be excused from entering upon any discussion of the political topics of the day.—*Speech, Lincoln, Nov. 21, 1860.* Angle, 258.

4.—[Any further statement relative to slavery] would make me appear as if I repented for the crime of having been elected, and was anxious to apologize and beg forgiveness. To so represent me would be the principal use made of any letter I might now thrust upon the public. My old record cannot be so used; and that is precisely the reason that some new declaration is so much sought.—*To John A. Gilmer, Dec. 15, 1860.* VI, 79.

5.—Is it desired that I shall shift the ground upon which I have been elected? I cannot do it.—*To John A. Gilmer, Dec. 28, 1860.* VI, 99.

6.—I am greatly averse to writing anything for the public at this time.—*To Duff Green, Dec. 28, 1860.* VI, 88.

7.—I deem it my duty—a duty which I owe to my constituents—to you, gentlemen, that I should wait until the last moment for a development of the present national difficulties before I express myself decidedly as to what course I shall pursue.—*Speech to Germans, Cincinnati, Feb. 12, 1861.* VI, 119.

8.—I have received from some a degree of credit for having kept silence, and from others some deprecation. I still think I was right.—*Speech, Columbus, Ohio, Feb. 13, 1861.* VI, 121.

9.—In the varying and repeatedly shifting scenes of the present, and without a precedent which could enable me to judge by the past, it has seemed fitting that before speaking upon the difficulties of the country, I should have gained a view of the whole field, being at liberty to modify and change the course of policy as future events may make a change necessary. —*Speech, Columbus, Ohio, Feb. 13, 1861.* VI, 122.

10.—It is natural to expect that I should say something on this subject ["present distracted condition of the country"]; but to touch upon it would involve an elaborate discussion of a great many questions and circumstances; requiring more time than I can at present command, and would, perhaps, unnecessarily commit me upon matters which have not yet fully developed themselves.—*Speech, Pittsburgh, Feb. 15, 1861.* VI, 124.

11.—When it is considered that these difficulties are without precedent, and have never been acted upon by any individual situated as I am, it is most proper I should wait and see developments, and get all the light possible, so that when I do speak authoritatively, I may be as near right as possible.—*Speech, Buffalo, Feb. 16, 1861.* VI, 134.

12.—I deem it just to you, to myself, to all, that I should see everything, that I should hear everything, that I should have every light that can be brought within my reach, in order that, when I do so speak, I shall have enjoyed every opportunity to take correct and true grounds.—*Speech, New York Legislature, Feb. 18, 1861.* VI, 141.

13.—I have not kept silence since the presidential election from any party wantonness, or from any indifference to the anxiety that pervades the minds of men about the aspect of the political affairs of the country. I have kept silence for the reason that I supposed it was peculiarly proper that I should do so until the time came when, according to the custom of the country, I could speak officially.—*Speech, New York, Feb. 19, 1861.* VI, 147.

14.—I still suppose that, while the political drama being enacted in this country, at this time, is rapidly shifting its scenes—forbidding an anticipation with any degree of certainty today of what we shall see tomorrow—it is peculiarly fitting that I should see it all, up to the last minute, before I should take ground that I might be disposed—by the shifting of scenes afterward—also to shift.—*Speech, New York, Feb. 19, 1861.* VI, 147.

15.—You, Mr. Speaker, have well said that this is a time when the bravest and wisest look with doubt and awe upon the aspect presented by our national affairs. Under these circumstances you will readily see why I should not speak in detail of the course I shall deem it best to pursue. It is proper that I should avail myself of all the information and all the time at my command, in order that when the time arrives in which I must speak officially, I shall be able to take the ground which I deem best and safest, and from which I may have no occasion to swerve.—*Speech, New Jersey Assembly, Feb. 21, 1861.* VI, 153.

16.—It were useless for me to speak of details of plans now; I shall speak officially next Monday week, if ever. If I should not speak then, it were useless for me to do so now. If I do speak then, it is useless for me to do so now.—*Speech, reply to Philadelphia mayor, Feb. 21, 1861.* VI, 155.

17.—As Solomon says, there is a time for all things, and I think the present is a time for silence.—*Speech, Lancaster, Pa., Feb. 22, 1861.* Hertz II, 808.

Simple-minded Boy, "must I shoot?"—*See* VALLANDIGHAM, C. L., arrest of, explained, 1.

"Skewhorn Principle"—Doubtless a small force of the enemy is flourishing about the northern part of Virginia on the "skewhorn" principle, on purpose to divert us in another quarter. I believe it is nothing more.—*To Gov. Curtin, April 28, 1863.* VIII, 257.

Skin, walking to save—Does Joe Heiskell's "walking to meet us" mean any more than that "Joe" was scared and wanted to save his skin?—*To Gov. Johnson, Aug. 2, 1864.* X, 179.

Slander, futility of—If you think you can slander a woman into loving you, or a man into voting for you, try it till you are satisfied.—*Speech, New Haven, Conn., March 6, 1860.* V, 360.

Slander, truth best vindication against—*See* CABINET, dismissals from, up to President alone, 1.

Slander, when malicious—Persisting in a charge which one does not know to be true is simply malicious slander.—*Cooper Institute address, Feb. 27, 1860.* V, 315.

Repeated at New Haven, Conn., March 6, 1860. V, 359.

See PRESS, some papers unfair.

Slave breeders—*See* SLAVE DEALERS AND BREEDERS, despised, 2.

Slave Children, asked to liberate—The petition of persons under eighteen, praying that I would free all slave children, and the heading of which it appears you wrote, was handed me a few days ago by Senator Sumner. Please tell these little people I am very glad their young hearts are so full of just and generous sympathy; and that, while I have not the power to grant all they ask, I trust they will remember God has, and that, as it seems, He wills to do so.—*To Mrs. Horace Mann, April 5, 1864.* X, 68.

Slave Code, Kansas gets, by ferry—*See* KANSAS, freedom denied in, 4.

Slave Code, only chance for—The advocates of a slave code are not now strong enough to master us; and they never will, unless recruits enough to make them so are tolled in through the gap of Douglasism. —*Speeches·in Kansas, Dec. 1-5, 1859.* V, 271.

Slave Code, prevention of, urged—We must prevent . . . the enacting by Congress of a territorial slave code.—*Speech, Cincinnati, Sept. 17, 1859.* V, 232.

Slave Dealers and Breeders, despised—You [people of the South] have among you a sneaking individual of the class of native tyrants known as the "slave dealer." He watches your necessities, and crawls up to buy your slaves at a speculating price. If you cannot help it, you sell to him; but if you can help it, you drive him from your door. You despise him utterly. You do not recognize him as an honest man. Your children must not play with his; they may rollick freely with the little negroes, but not with a slave dealer's children. Now, why is this? You do not so treat the man who deals in corn, cotton or tobacco.—*Speech, Peoria, Oct. 16, 1854.* II, 224.

2.—The slave breeders and slave traders are a small, odious and detested class among you [of the slave states]; and yet in politics they dictate the course of all of you, and are the masters of your own negroes. —*To Joshua F. Speed, Aug. 24, 1855.* II, 286.

Slave Empire—*See* SLAVERY, no compromise on, 10.

Slave Insurrections, charge denied—You [men of the South] charge that we [Republicans] stir up insurrections among your slaves. We deny it; and what is your proof?—*Cooper Institute address, New York, Feb. 27, 1860.* V, 314.

Slave Insurrections, no general, likely to occur—Slave insurrections are no more common now than they were before the Republican party was organized. . . . In the present state of things in the United States, I do not think a general, or even a very extensive, slave insurrection is possible. The indispensable concert of action cannot be attained. . . . Much is said by southern people about the affection of slaves for their masters and mistresses; and a part of it, at least, is true. A plot for an uprising could scarcely be devised and communicated to twenty individuals before some one of them, to save the life of a favorite master or mistress, would divulge it. . . . Occasional poisonings from the kitchen, and open or stealthy assassinations in the field, and local revolts extending to a score or so, will continue to occur as the natural results of slavery, but no general insurrection of slaves, as I think, can happen in this country for a long time. Whoever much fears, or much hopes for, such an event, will be alike disappointed. —*Cooper Institute address, New York, Feb. 27, 1860.* V. 316.

Slave States, admission of, to Union—I meant not to resist the admission of Utah and New Mexico, even should they ask to come in as slave states.—*Speech, Peoria, Oct. 16, 1854.* II, 216.
2.—If Kansas fairly votes herself a slave state she must be admitted, or the Union must be dissolved. But how if she votes herself a slave state unfairly, that is, by the very means for which you say you would hang men? Must she still be admitted, or the Union dissolved?—*To Joshua F. Speed, Aug. 24, 1855.* II, 283.
3.—That Kansas will form a slave constitution, and with it ask to be admitted into the Union, I take to be already a settled question.—*To Joshua F. Speed, Aug. 24, 1855.* II, 284.
4.—I do not understand the Republican party to be committed to the proposition "no more slave states." I think they are not so committed. Most certainly they prefer there should be no more, but I know there are many of them who think we are under obligations to admit slave states from Texas, if such shall be presented for admission; but I think the party as such is not committed either way.—*To Henry E. Dummer, July 20, 1858.* Tracy, 92.

5.—I do not now, nor ever did, stand pledged against the admission of any more slave states into the Union. . . . I would be exceedingly sorry ever to be put in a position of having to pass upon that question [admission of another slave state to the Union]. I should be exceedingly glad to know that there would never be another slave state admitted to the Union; but I must add, that if slavery shall be kept out of the territories during the territorial existence of any one given territory, and then the people shall, having a fair chance and a clear field, when they come to adopt the constitution, do such an extraordinary thing as to adopt a slave constitution, uninfluenced by the actual presence of the institution among them, I see no alternative, if we own the country, but to admit them into the Union.—*Debate, Freeport, Aug. 27, 1858.* III, 273.

Slave States, have advantage in Congress—In the control of the government—the management of the partnership affairs—they [the slave states] have greatly the advantage of us. By the Constitution each state . . . has a number of presidential electors equal to the whole number of its senators and representatives together. But in ascertaining the number of people for this purpose, five slaves are counted as being equal to three whites. The slaves do not vote; they are only counted and so used as to swell the influence of the white people's vote. . . . Each white man in South Carolina is more than the double of any man in Maine. . . . The South Carolinian has precisely the same advantage over the white man in every other free state. . . . When I am told I must leave it altogether to other people to say whether new partners are to be bred up and brought into the firm, on the same degrading terms against me, I respectfully demur. I insist that whether I shall be a whole man, or only the half of one, in comparison with others, is a question in which I am somewhat concerned, and one which no other man can have a sacred right of deciding for me.—*Speech, Peoria, Oct. 16, 1854.* II, 233.
Repeated at Urbana, Oct. 24, 1854. Hertz II, 647.
2.—It is an absolute truth, without an exception, there is no voter in any slave state but has more legal power in the government than any voter in any free state.—*Speech, Peoria, Oct. 16, 1854.* II, 234.
Repeated at Urbana, Oct. 24, 1854. Hertz II, 647.
3.—If it really be a sacred right of self-government in the man who shall go to Nebraska to decide whether he will be the equal of me or the double of me [in votes], then, after he shall have exercised that right, and thereby shall have reduced me to a still smaller fraction of a man than I already am, I should like

for some gentleman, deeply skilled in the mysteries of sacred rights, to provide himself with a microscope, and peep about, and find out, if he can, what has become of my sacred rights. They will surely be too small for detection with the naked eye.—*Speech, Peoria, Oct. 16, 1854.* Basler, 308.

4.—By our Constitution we are represented in Congress in proportion to numbers, and in counting the numbers that give us our representatives, three slaves are counted as two people. The state of Maine has six representatives in the lower house of Congress. The strength of South Carolina is equal to her. But stop! Maine has twice as many white people, and 32,000 to boot! And is that fair? I don't complain of it. This regulation was put in force when the exigencies of the times demanded it, and could not have been avoided. Now, one man in South Carolina is the same as two men here. Maine should have twice as many men in Congress as South Carolina.—*Speech, Kalamazoo, Mich., Aug. 27, 1856.* Stern, 403.

5.—It is a fact that any man in South Carolina has more influence and power in Congress than any two now before me. The same thing is true of all slave states, though it may not be in the same proportion. It is a truth that cannot be denied, that in all the free states no white man is the equal of the white man of the slave states. But this is in the Constitution, and we must stand up to it. The question, then, is, Have we no interest as to whether the white man of the North shall be the equal of the white man of the South?—*Speech, Kalamazoo, Mich., Aug. 27, 1856.* Basler, 341.

Slave Trade, African—*See* AFRICAN SLAVE TRADE.

Slave Trade, not pledged to prohibition of, between states—I do not stand pledged to the prohibition of the slave trade between the different states. . . . It is a subject to which I have not given that mature consideration that would make me feel authorized to state a position so as to hold myself entirely bound by it. . . . I must say, however, that if I should be of opinion that Congress does possess the constitutional power to abolish the slave-trade among the different states, I should still not be in favor of the exercise of that power unless upon some conservative principle as I conceive it, akin to what I have said in relation to the abolition of slavery in the District of Columbia. —*Debate, Freeport, Aug. 27, 1858.* III, 274.

Slavery, abolition of—*See* ABOLITION.

Slavery, abolition of, by amendment—*See* THIRTEENTH AMENDMENT.

Slavery, alternative policies in relation to—This government is sought to be put on a new track. Slavery is to be made a ruling element in our government. The question can be avoided in but two ways. By the one, we must submit, and allow slavery to triumph, or, by the other, we must triumph over the black demon. We [Republicans] have chosen the latter manner. . . . We would all like to have the question done away with, but we cannot submit.—*Speech, Kalamazoo, Mich., Aug. 27, 1856.* Stern, 406.

2.—That [national] government, from the beginning, has had, has now, and must continue to have, a policy in relation to domestic slavery. It cannot, if it would, be without a policy upon that subject; and that policy must, of necessity, take one of two directions. It must deal with the institution as being wrong, or as not being wrong.—*Speech, Leavenworth, Kan., Dec. 3, 1859.* Angle, 230.

Slavery, amendment to abolish, urged—*See* THIRTEENTH AMENDMENT, favorable action on, urged, 1.

Slavery, American colonies and—It has now been decided [in the Dred Scott case] that slavery cannot be kept out of our new territories by any legal means. In what do our new territories now differ in this respect from the old colonies when slavery was first planted in them? It was planted, as Mr. Clay once declared, and as history proves true, by individual men in spite of the wishes of the people; the mother government refusing to prohibit it, and withholding from the people of the colonies the authority to prohibit it themselves. Mr. Clay says this was one of the great and just causes of complaint against Great Britain by the colonies, and the best apology we can now make for having the institution amongst us. In that precise condition our Nebraska politicians have at last succeeded in placing our new territories; the government will not prohibit slavery within them, nor allow the people to prohibit it.—*Speech, Springfield, July 17, 1858.* III, 182.

See GREAT BRITAIN, blamed for slavery.

Slavery, appeal for unity against—For my part, I do hope that all of us, entertaining a common sentiment in opposition to what appears to us a design to nationalize and perpetuate slavery, will waive minor differences on questions which either belong to the dead past or the distant future, and all pull together in this struggle.—*Debate, Freeport, Aug. 27, 1858.* III, 338.

Slavery, argumentative pitfalls—If A can prove, however conclusively, that he may of right enslave B, why may not B snatch the same argument and prove equally that he may enslave A? You say A is white and B is black. It is color, then; the lighter having the right to enslave the darker? Take care! By this rule you are to be slave to the first man you meet with a fairer skin than your own. You do not mean color exactly? You mean the whites are intellectually the superior of the blacks, and therefore have the right to enslave them? Take care again! By this rule you are to be slave to the first man you meet with an intellect superior to your own. But, say you, it is a question of interest, and if you make it your interest you have the right to enslave another. Very well; and if he can make it his interest he has the right to enslave you.—*Fragment, July 1, 1854.* II, 186.

Slavery, ballot box and—*See* BALLOT, better than bullets, 3, 5.

Slavery, barred from Northwest Territory—*See* ORDINANCE OF 1787; fruits of.

Slavery, bayonets ineffective—The idea of forcing slavery into a free state, or out of a slave state, at the point of a bayonet, is alike nonsensical.—*Notes, Oct. 1, 1858.* IV, 220.

Slavery, best argument for—*See* SLAVERY, slaves as Confederate soldiers, 1.

Slavery, better to sell slaves than lose them by war—*See* EMANCIPATION, financial aspects of compensated, 5.

Slavery, Bible quoted against—*See* BIBLE, slavery and.

Slavery, Christian duty and—Can we as Christian men, and strong and free ourselves, wield the sledge or hold the iron which is to manacle anew an already oppressed race? "Woe unto them," it is written, "that decree unrighteous decrees and that write grievousness which they have prescribed." Can we afford to sin any more deeply against human liberty?—*Speech, Bloomington, May 29, 1856.* Lapsley II, 270.

Slavery, churches wrangle and crack—Just now it [slavery] is perplexing the mighty ones as no other subject ever did before. This is not confined to politics alone. Presbyterian assemblies, Methodist conferences, Unitarian gatherings, and single churches to an indefinite extent, are wrangling and cracking, and going to pieces on the same question.—*Notes, Oct. 1, 1858.* IV, 232.
2.—Does it [slavery agitation] not enter into the churches and rend them asunder? What divided the great Methodist Church into two parts, North and South? What has raised this constant disturbance in every Presbyterian general assembly that meets? What disturbed the Unitarian church in this very city two years ago?—*Debate, Alton, Oct. 15, 1858.* V, 55.

Slavery, Clay and Douglas on—But now Douglas snatches the robes of Clay and dubs me an Abolitionist! How do the principles of the two men agree? Clay always opposed the rightfulness of slavery. Douglas always took the opposite, or kept mum.—*Speech, Carlinville, Aug. 31, 1858.* Angle, 189.
2.—Mr. [Henry] Clay . . . said that "those who would repress all tendencies to liberty and ultimate emancipation [of slaves] must . . . go back to the era of our liberty and independence, and muzzle the cannon that thunders its annual joyous return—they must blot out the moral lights around us—they must penetrate the human soul, and eradicate the light of reason and the love of liberty." And I do think . . . that Judge Douglas, and whoever, like him, teaches that the negro has no share, humble though it may be, in the Declaration of Independence, is going back to the era of our liberty and independence, and, so far as in him lies, muzzling the cannon that thunders its annual joyous return; that he is blowing out the moral lights around us, when he contends that whoever wants slaves has a right to hold them; that he is penetrating, so far as lies in his power, the human soul, and eradicating the light of reason and the love of liberty, when he is in every possible way preparing the public mind, by his vast influence, for making the institution of slavery perpetual and national.—*Debate, Galesburg, Oct. 7, 1858.* IV, 289.

Slavery, Clay and Lincoln on—I can express all my views on the slavery question by quotations from Henry Clay. Doesn't this look like we are akin?—*Speech, Carlinville, Aug. 31, 1858.* Angle, 190.
2.—If I attempt, as Mr. Clay said all good men ought to do, to keep it [the equality principle of the Declaration of Independence] in view; if, in this "organized society," I ask to have the public eye turned upon it . . . —forthwith, I am villified, as you hear me today. What have I done that I have not the license of Henry Clay's illustrious example here in doing?—*Debate, Alton, Oct. 15, 1858.* V, 42.
3.—Even here today you heard Judge Douglas quarrel with me because I uttered a wish that it [slavery] might some day come to an end. Although Henry Clay could say he wished every slave in the United States was in the country of his ancestors, I am denounced by those pretending to respect Henry Clay, for uttering a wish that it might some time, in some peaceful way, come to an end.—*Debate, Alton, Oct. 15, 1858.* V, 63.

Slavery, Clay on perpetuation of—*See* CLAY, HENRY, slavery decried by, 4.

Slavery, climate no bar to—*See* CLIMATE, no bar to slavery.

See SLAVERY, Illinois and Missouri in contrast.

See SLAVERY, Ohio and Kentucky in contrast.

Slavery, confiscation of slaves—*See* JUSTICE, not best if too severe.

Slavery, conspiracy to promote—Let anyone who doubts [that slavery advocates hope to make slavery national] carefully contemplate that now almost complete legal combination—piece of machinery, so to speak—compounded of the Nebraska doctrine and the Dred Scott decision. Let him consider not only what work the machinery is adapted to do, and how well adapted; but also let him study the history of the construction, and trace, if he can, or rather fail, if he can, to trace, the evidences of design and concert of action among its chief architects, from the beginning.—*Speech, Springfield, June 16, 1858.* III, 2.

2.—Then [on the introduction of the Kansas-Nebraska bill] opened the roar of loose declamation in favor of "squatter sovereignty" and the "sacred right of self-government." "But," said opposition members [of Congress], "let us amend the bill so as to expressly declare that the people of the territory may exclude slavery." "Not we," said the friends of the measure; and down they voted the amendment.—*Speech, Springfield, June 16, 1858.* III, 4.

3.—The several points of the Dred Scott decision, in connection with Senator Douglas's "care not" policy, constitute the piece of machinery in its present state of advancement.—*Speech, Springfield, June 16, 1858.* III, 7.

4.—Several things will now appear less dark and mysterious than they did when they were transpiring. The people were [by the Kansas-Nebraska bill] to be left "perfectly free," "subject only to the Constitution." What the Constitution had to do with it outsiders could not then see. Plainly enough now, it was an exactly fitted niche for the Dred Scott decision to afterwards come in, and declare the perfect freedom of the people to be just no freedom at all. Why was the amendment [to the bill] expressly declaring the right of the people voted down? Plainly enough now, the adoption of it would have spoiled the niche for the Dred Scott decision. Why was the court decision held up? Why even a senator's individual opinion withheld till after the presidential election? Plainly enough now, the speaking out then would have damaged the "perfectly free" argument upon which the election was to be carried. . . . Why the delay of reargument? Why the incoming President's advance

exhortation in favor of the decision?—*Speech, Springfield, June 16, 1858.* III, 8.

5.—We cannot absolutely know that all these exact adaptations [of the proslavery program] are the result of preconcert. But when we see a lot of framed timbers, different portions of which we know have been gotten out at different times and places, and by different workmen—Stephen [Douglas], Franklin [Pierce], Roger [Taney] and James [Buchanan], for instance—and we see these timbers joined together, and see they exactly make the frame of a house or a mill, all the tenons and mortises exactly fitting, and all the lengths and proportions of these different pieces exactly adapted to their respective places, and not a piece too many or too few, not omitting even scaffolding—or, if a single piece is lacking, we see the place in the frame exactly fitted and prepared yet to bring such piece in—in such case we find it impossible not to believe that Stephen, Franklin, Roger and James all understood one another from the beginning, and all worked upon a common plan or draft drawn up before the first blow was struck.—*Speech, Springfield, June 16, 1858.* III, 9. Repeated at Ottawa, Aug. 21, 1858. III, 237.

6.—Upon that event [repeal of the Missouri Compromise] I became convinced that either I had been resting in a delusion, or the institution [slavery] was being placed on a new basis—a basis for making it perpetual, national and universal. Subsequent events have greatly confirmed me in that belief. I believe that [Kansas-Nebraska] bill to be the beginning of a conspiracy for that purpose.—*Speech, Springfield, July 17, 1858.* III, 174.

7.—I expressed [in a previous speech] my belief in the existence of a conspiracy to perpetuate and nationalize slavery. I did not profess to know, nor do I now. I showed the part Judge Douglas had played in the string of facts, constituting to my mind the proof of that conspiracy. . . . Judge Douglas . . . has not, so far as I know, contradicted those charges. . . . On his own tacit admission, I renew that charge.—*Speech, Springfield, July 17, 1858.* III, 187.

8.—I charge him [Douglas] with having been a party to that conspiracy, and to that deception, for the sole purpose of nationalizing slavery.—*Speech, Springfield, July 17, 1858.* III, 188.

9.—I made a speech in June last, in which I pointed out, briefly and consecutively, a series of public measures leading directly to the nationalization of slavery. . . . I enumerated the repeal of the Missouri Compromise, which every candid man must acknowledge conferred upon emigrants to Kansas and Nebraska the right to carry slaves there and hold them in bondage, whereas, formerly they had no such right. I alluded to events which followed that repeal—events in which Judge Douglas's name figures quite prominently. I referred to the Dred Scott decision, and the extraordinary means taken to prepare the public mind for that decision—the efforts put forth by President Pierce to make the people believe they had indorsed, in the election of James Buchanan, the doctrine that slavery may exist in the free territories of the Union—the earnest exhortation put forth by President Buchanan to the people to stick to that decision whatever it might be—the close-fitting niche in the Nebraska bill wherein the right of the people to govern themselves is made "subject to the Constitution of the United States"—the extraordinary haste displayed by Mr. Douglas to give this decision an indorsement at the capitol of Illinois. . . . I said that though I could not open the bosoms of men and find out their secret motives, yet, when I found the framework for a barn or bridge, or any other structure, built by a number of carpenters—Stephen and Franklin and Roger and James—and so built that each tenon had its proper mortise, and the whole forming a symmetrical piece of workmanship, I should say that these carpenters all worked on an intelligent plan, and understood each other from the beginning.—*Speech, Beardstown, Aug. 12, 1858.* Angle, 185.

10.—While the Nebraska bill was pending, Judge Douglas helped to vote down a clause giving the people of the territories the right to exclude slavery if they chose.—*Speech, Beardstown, Aug. 12, 1858.* Angle, 186.

11.—What if Judge Douglas never did talk with Chief Justice Taney and the President before the Dred Scott decision was made; does it not follow that he could have had as perfect an understanding without talking as with it? I am not disposed to stand upon my legal advantage. I am disposed to take his denial as being like an answer in chancery, that he neither had any knowledge, information, nor belief in the existence of such a conspiracy. I am disposed to take his answer as being as broad as though he had put in those words. And now, I ask, even if he had done so, have I not a right to prove it on him, and to offer the evidence of more than two witnesses, by whom to prove it; and if the evidence proves the existence of the conspiracy, does his broad answer, denying all knowledge, information, or belief, disturb the facts? It can only show that he was used by conspirators, and was not a leader of them.—*Debate, Ottawa, Aug. 21, 1858.* III, 241.

12.—"But," said in substance, a senator from Ohio—Mr. Chase, I believe—"we more than suspect that you [Douglas and his friends] do not mean to allow the people [under the Kansas-Nebraska bill] to exclude slavery if they wish to; and if you mean it, accept an amendment which I propose expressly authorizing the people to exclude slavery." And now, I state it as a fact, to be taken back if there is any mistake about it, that Judge Douglas and those acting with him voted that amendment down. I now think that those men who voted it down had a real reason for doing so. They know what that reason was. It looks to us, since we have seen the Dred Scott decision pronounced, holding that "under the Constitution the people cannot exclude slavery"—I say it looks to outsiders, poor, simple, "amiable, intelligent gentlemen" [Douglas's characterization of Lincoln] as though a niche was left as a place to put that Dred Scott decision in, which would have been spoiled by adopting the amendment.—*Debate, Ottawa, Aug. 21, 1858.* III, 243.

13.—There is in . . . the Nebraska bill this clause: "It being the true intent and meaning of this bill not to legislate slavery into any territory or state." I have always been puzzled to know what business the word "state" had in that connection. . . . The law they were passing was not about states, and was not making provision for states. . . . After seeing the Dred Scott decision which holds that the people cannot exclude slavery from a territory, if another Dred Scott decision shall come, holding that they cannot exclude it from a state, we shall discover that when the word was originally put there, it was in view of something which was to come in due time; and we shall see that it was the other half of something.—*Debate, Ottawa, Aug. 21, 1858.* III, 244.

14.—I have been in the habit of charging as a matter of belief on my part that, in the introduction of the Nebraska bill into Congress, there was a conspiracy to make slavery perpetual and national. I have arranged from time to time the evidence which establishes and proves the truth of this charge.—*Debate, Freeport, Aug. 27, 1858.* III, 283.

15.—I can conceive it possible for men to conspire to do a good thing, and I really find nothing in Judge Douglas's course of arguments that is contrary to or inconsistent with his belief of a conspiracy to nationalize and spread slavery as being a good and blessed thing, and so I hope he will understand that I do not at all question but that in all this matter he is entirely "conscientious."—*Debate, Freeport, Aug. 27, 1858.* III, 284.

16.—When he [Douglas] and some others began arguing that [through the Kansas-Nebraska Act] they were giving an increased degree of liberty to the people in the territories over and above what they already had on the question of slavery, a question was raised whether the law was enacted to give such unconditional liberty to the people; and to test the sincerity of this mode of argument, Mr. Chase of Ohio introduced an amendment, in which he made the law—if the amendment were adopted—expressly declare that the people of the territory should have the power to exclude slavery if they saw fit. . . . Judge Douglas, and those who acted with him, voted the amendment down, notwithstanding it expressed exactly the thing they said was the true intent and meaning of the law. . . . In subsequent times a decision of the Supreme Court has . . . declared that a territorial legislature has no constitutional right to exclude slavery. And I have argued and said that for men who did intend that the people of the territory should have the right to exclude slavery absolutely and unconditionally, the voting down of the Chase amendment is wholly inexplicable. . . . But . . . with men who did look forward to such a decision [as in the Dred Scott case] . . . the voting down of that amendment would be perfectly rational and intelligible. It would keep Congress from coming in collision with the decision when it was made. . . . It would be very rational for men expecting such a decision to keep the niche in that law clear for it.—*Debate, Freeport, Aug. 27, 1858.* III, 286.

17.—One of these ways [to keep the Chase amendment out of the law]—one of these excuses—was to ask [Senator Salmon P.] Chase to add to his proposed amendment a provision that the people [of a territory] might introduce slavery if they wanted to. They very well know Chase would do no such thing—that Mr. Chase was one of the men differing from them on the broad principle of his insistence that freedom was better than slavery—a man who would not consent to enact a law penned by his own hand, by which he was made to recognize slavery on the one hand and liberty on the other as precisely equal; and when they insisted on his doing this, they well knew they insisted on that which he would not for a moment think of doing, and that they were only bluffing him. —*Debate, Freeport, Aug. 27, 1858.* III, 288.

18.—They [proslavery men] went into a quibble with Chase to get him to add what they knew he would not add, and because he would not, they stand upon that flimsy pretext for voting down what they had argued was the meaning and intent of their own bill. They left room thereby for this Dred Scott decision, which goes very far to make slavery national throughout the United States.—*Debate, Freeport, Aug. 27, 1858.* III, 290.

19.—In it [speech to Republican convention] I arranged a string of incontestible facts which, I think, prove the existence of a conspiracy to nationalize slavery. The evidence is circumstantial only; but nevertheless it seemed inconsistent with every hypothesis, save that of the existence of such a conspiracy.—*Notes, Oct. 1, 1858.* IV, 214.

20.—I clearly see, as I think, a powerful plot to make slavery universal, and perpetual in this nation. The effort to carry that plot through will be persistent and long continued, extending far beyond the senatorial term for which Judge Douglas and I are just now struggling. I enter upon the contest to contribute my humble and temporary mite in opposition to that effort.—*Notes, Oct. 1, 1858.* IV, 214.

21.—I believe the facts can be explained today on no other hypothesis [than that of a conspiracy]. . . . From warp to woof his [Douglas's] handiwork is everywhere woven in.—*Notes, Oct. 1, 1858.* IV, 214.

22.—He [Douglas] seems to have grown confident and jubilant in the belief that he has entirely diverted me from my purpose of fixing conspiracy upon him and his co-workers. . . . I renew the charge against him.—*Notes, Oct. 1, 1858.* IV, 215.

23.—Suppose we construe it [Douglas's denial] as an answer in chancery, to be a denial of all knowledge, information, or belief in such conspiracy. Still I have the right to prove the conspiracy, even against his answer; and there is much more than the evidence of two witnesses to prove it by. Grant that he has no knowledge, information, or belief of such a conspiracy, and what of it? That does not disturb the facts in evidence. It only makes him the dupe, instead of a principal, of conspirators.—*Notes, Oct. 1, 1858.* IV, 216.

24.—What if he [Douglas] did not pass a word with Chief Justice Taney? Could he not have as distinct an understanding, and play his part just as well, without directly passing a word with Taney as with it?—*Notes, Oct. 1, 1858.* IV, 216.

25.—I have not affirmed that a conspiracy does exist. I have only stated the evidence, and affirmed my belief in its existence.—*Notes, Oct. 1, 1858.* IV, 217.

26.—There was some real reason for so voting it [Chase amendment] down. . . . I believe that reason was to keep the way clear for a court decision, then expected to come, and which has since come, in the case of Dred Scott.—*Notes, Oct. 1, 1858.* IV, 218.

27.—Did Judge Douglas, even then [during pendency of Kansas-Nebraska bill], intend that the people of a territory should have power to exclude slavery? If he did, why did he vote against an amendment expressly declaring they might exclude it? With men who then knew and intended that a Supreme Court decision should soon follow, declaring that the people of a territory could not exclude slavery, voting down such an amendment was perfectly rational. But with men not expecting or desiring such a decision, and really wishing the people to have such power, voting down such an amendment, to my mind, is wholly inexplicable.—*Notes, Oct. 1, 1858.* IV, 218.

28.—With persons looking forward to such additional [second Dred Scott] decision, the inserting of a provision about states in the Nebraska bill was perfectly rational, but to persons not looking for such decision it was a puzzle. There was a real reason for inserting such provision.—*Notes, Oct. 1, 1858.* IV, 219.

29.—Judge Douglas's present course by no means lessens my belief in the existence of a purpose to make slavery alike lawful in all the states. This can be done by a Supreme Court decision holding that the United States Constitution forbids a state to exclude slavery; and probably it can be done in no other way. —*Notes, Oct. 1, 1858.* IV, 220.

30.—He [Douglas] wants to know why I won't withdraw the charge in regard to a conspiracy to make slavery national. . . . I will withdraw it whenever a reasonable man shall be brought to believe that the charge is not true.—*Debate, Quincy, Oct. 13, 1858.* IV, 386.

31.—There is evidence about the [Dred Scott] case tending to show that it was a made-up case for the purpose of getting that decision. I have said that that evidence was very strong in the fact that when Dred Scott was declared to be a slave, the owner of him made him free, showing that he had had the case tried, and the question settled, for such use as could be made of that decision; he cared nothing about the property declared to be his by that decision.—*Debate, Quincy, Oct. 13, 1858.* IV, 387.

32.—I spoke of the Dred Scott decision in my Springfield speech, and I was then endeavoring to prove that the Dred Scott decision was a portion of a system or scheme to make slavery national in this country. I pointed out what things had been decided by the court. . . . I mentioned all these things together, as evidence tending to prove a combination and conspiracy to make the institution of slavery national.— *Debate, Alton, Oct. 15, 1858.* V, 31.

See SLAVERY, nationalization of.

Slavery, constitutional amendment to abolish, should be hastened—*See* THIRTEENTH AMENDMENT, favorable action on, urged, 3.

Slavery, constitutional amendment to protect, not opposed—*See* SLAVERY, no interference with, in slave states, 34.

Slavery, cotton-gin basis of—Judge Douglas could not let it [slavery issue] rest upon the basis where our

fathers placed it, but removed it, and put it upon the cotton-gin basis.—*Debate, Quincy, Oct. 13, 1858.* IV, 374.

See SLAVERY, perpetuation of, 6, 8, 9.

See SLAVERY, policy of the fathers, 22.

Slavery, "crucify their feelings" in North—You ought rather to appreciate how much the great body of northern people do crucify their feelings [touching slavery], in order to maintain their loyalty to the Constitution and the Union.—*To Joshua F. Speed, Aug. 24, 1855.* II, 282.

Slavery, "curse of God"—*See* LABOR, free and slave, compared, 1.

Slavery, "debauches"—This thing of slavery is more powerful than its supporters—even than the high priests that minister at its altars. It debauches even our greatest men. It gathers strength, like a rolling snowball, by its own infamy. Monstrous crimes are committed in its name by persons collectively which they would not dare to commit as individuals. Its aggressions and encroachments almost surpass belief. In a despotism one might not wonder to see slavery advance steadily and remorselessly into new dominions; but is it not wonderful, is it not even alarming, to see its steady advance in a land dedicated to the proposition that "all men are created equal"? It yields nothing itself; it keeps all it has, and gets all it can besides.—*Speech, Bloomington, May 29, 1856.* Lapsley II, 264.

2.—The public mind must be so far debauched as to square with this policy of caring not at all.—*Speech, New Haven, Conn., March 6, 1860.* V, 350.

Slavery, Democratic fight called bushwhacking—*See* BUSHWHACKING, war on Republican antislavery stand characterized.

Slavery, Democratic policy toward—I will not affirm that the Democratic party consider slavery morally, socially and politically right, though their tendency to that view has, in my opinion, been constant and unmistakable for the past five years. I prefer to take, as the accepted maxim of the party, the idea put forth by Judge Douglas, that he "don't care whether slavery is voted down or voted up." I am willing to believe that many Democrats would prefer that slavery should always be voted down, and I know that some prefer that it be "voted up"; but I have a right to insist that their action, especially if it be their constant action, shall determine their ideas and preferences on the subject.—*Speech, Edwardsville, Sept. 13, 1858.* XI, 107.

2.—Every measure of the Democratic party of late, bearing directly or indirectly on the slavery question, has corresponded with this notion of utter indifference whether slavery or freedom shall outrun in the race of empire across to the Pacific—every measure, I say, up to the Dred Scott decision, where, it seems to me, the idea is boldly suggested that slavery is better than freedom.—*Speech, Edwardsville, Sept. 13, 1858.* XI, 108.

3.—If there be a man in the Democratic party who thinks it [slavery] is a wrong, and yet clings to that party, I suggest to him in the first place that his leader don't talk as he does, for he never says it is wrong. In the second place, I suggest to him that if he will examine the policy proposed [by Douglas] to be carried forward, he will find that he carefully excludes the idea that there is anything wrong in it.— *Debate, Quincy, Oct. 13, 1858.* IV, 331.

4.—There is a sentiment in the country . . . which holds that slavery is not wrong, and therefore goes for the policy that does not propose dealing with it as a wrong. That policy is the Democratic policy, and the sentiment is the Democratic sentiment.—*Debate, Quincy, Oct. 13, 1858.* IV, 331.

5.—Frank Blair and Gratz Brown tried to get up a system of gradual emancipation in Missouri, had an election in August, and got beat; and you, Mr. Democrat, threw up your hat and hallooed, "Hurrah for Democracy."—*Debate, Quincy, Oct. 13, 1858.* IV, 332.

6.—Turn it in any way you can, in all the arguments sustaining the Democratic policy, and in that policy itself, there is a careful, studied exclusion of the idea that there is anything wrong in slavery.—*Debate, Quincy, Oct. 13, 1858.* IV, 333.

7.—There is a sentiment which treats it as not being wrong. That is the Democratic sentiment of this day. I do not mean to say that every man who stands within that range positively asserts that it is right. That class will include all who positively assert that it is right, and all who, like Judge Douglas, treat it as indifferent, and do not say it is either right or wrong. These two classes of men fall within the general class of those who do not look upon it as a wrong.—*Debate, Alton, Oct. 15, 1858.* V, 61.

8.—If there be among you anybody who supposes that he, as a Democrat, can consider himself "as much opposed to slavery as anybody," I would like to reason with him. You never treat it as a wrong. What other thing that you consider as a wrong do you deal with as you deal with that? . . . Finally, you will screw yourself up to the belief that if the people of the slave states should adopt a system of gradual emancipation on the slavery question, you would be

in favor of it. . . . But you are deceiving yourself.— *Debate, Alton, Oct. 15, 1858.* V, 62.

9.—All shades of Democracy, popular sovereignty as well as the rest, are fully agreed that slaves are property, and only property.—*Speech, Leavenworth, Kan., Dec. 3, 1859.* Angle, 234.

10.—The whole Democratic party has deliberately taken negroes from the class of men and put them in the class of brutes.—*Speech, New Haven, Conn., March 6, 1860.* V, 351.

11.—You [Democrats] may say that you think slavery a wrong, but you renounce all attempts to restrain it. . . . You will not let us do a single thing as if it was wrong; there is no place where you will allow it to be even called wrong. . . . Perhaps you will plead that if the people of slave states should themselves set on foot an effort for emancipation, you would wish them success and bid them God speed. Let us test that! In 1858 the emancipation party in Missouri, with Frank Blair at their head, tried to get up a movement for that purpose; and, having started a party, contested the state. Blair was beaten, apparently if not truly, and when the news came to Connecticut, you, who knew that Frank Blair was taking hold of this thing by the right end, and doing the only thing you say can properly be done to remove this wrong—did you bow your head in sorrow because of that defeat? . . . On the contrary, every man threw up his hat, and hallooed at the top of his lungs, "Hooray for Democracy!"—*Speech, New Haven, Conn., March 6, 1860.* V, 354.

See SLAVERY, party attitudes compared.

Slavery, Democrats appealed to—Now I make this appeal to the Democratic citizens here. Don't you find yourselves making arguments in support of these [proslavery] measures, which you never would have made before? . . . If you answer this in the affirmative, see how a whole party has been turned away from their love of liberty! And now, my Democratic friends, come forward. Throw off these things; and come to the rescue of this great principle of equality. —*Speech, Kalamazoo, Mich., Aug. 27, 1856.* Stern, 407.

2.—[For] men who want to adhere to the Democratic party, who have always belonged to that party, and are looking about for some excuse to stick to it, but nevertheless hate slavery, . . . Douglas's popular sovereignty is as good a way as any to oppose slavery. . . . We can do so without being called negro worshippers. We can do that without being subjected to the gibes and sneers that are so readily thrown out in place of argument where no argument can be found. So let us stick to this popular sovereignty—this insidious popular sovereignty!—*Speech, Columbus, Ohio, Sept. 16, 1859.* V, 186.

Slavery, destruction of, necessary—Slavery and oppression must cease, or American liberty must perish. —*Speech, Cincinnati, May 6, 1842.* Hertz II, 531.
2.—The blacks must be free. Slavery is the bone we are fighting over. It must be got out of the way, to give us permanent peace.—*To James R. Gilmore, late May, 1863.* Gilmore, 159.
3.—Let my enemies prove to the country that the destruction of slavery is not necessary to the restoration of the Union. I will abide the issue.—*Interview, Gov. Randall, Aug. 15, 1864.* X, 191.

See EMANCIPATION PROCLAMATION (PRELIMINARY), timed to circumstances, 3.

Slavery, disturbing element—The great variety of local institutions in the states . . . are bonds of union. They do not make "a house divided against itself," but they make a house united. . . . I leave it to you to say whether, in the history of our government, this institution of slavery has not always failed to be a bond of union, and, on the contrary, been an apple of discord and an element of division in the house. I ask you to consider whether, so long as the moral constitution of men's minds shall continue to be the same, after this generation and assemblage shall sink into the grave, and another race shall arise with the same moral and intellectual development we have—whether if that institution is standing in the same irritating position in which it now is, it will not continue an element of division.— *Debate, Ottawa, Aug. 21, 1858.* III, 232.
2.—This [slavery] was the cause of agitation resulting in the Missouri Compromise; this produced the troubles at the annexation of Texas, in the acquisition of the territory acquired in the Mexican War. Again, this was the trouble which was quieted by the compromise of 1850, when it was settled "forever," as both the great political parties declared in their national conventions. That "forever" turned out to be just four years, when Judge Douglas himself reopened it.—*Debate, Charleston, Sept. 18, 1858.* IV, 186.
3.—We have in this nation the element of domestic slavery. It is a matter of absolute certainty that it is the disturbing element. It is the opinion of all the great men who have expressed an opinion upon it that it is the dangerous element.—*Debate Quincy, Oct. 13, 1858.* IV, 327.
4.—It [slavery question] stands in the way and prevents the adjustment and the giving of necessary attention to other questions of national housekeeping. The people of the whole nation agree that this ques-

tion ought to be settled, and yet it is not settled.— *Speech, Norwich, Conn., March 9, 1860.* VI, 1.

Slavery, "divine right of kings" and—But this argument [by Douglas] strikes me as not a little remarkable in . . . its strong resemblance to the old argument for the "divine right of kings." By the latter, the king is to do just as he pleases with his white subjects, being responsible to God alone. By the former, the white man is to do just as he pleases with his black slaves, being responsible to God alone. The two things are precisely alike, and it is but natural that they should find similar arguments to sustain them.—*Speech, Peoria, Oct. 16, 1854.* II, 253.

Slavery, Douglas's care-not policy—In his [Douglas's] view the question of whether a new country shall be slave or free, is a matter of as utter indifference as it is whether his neighbor shall plant his farm with tobacco or stock it with horned cattle.—*Speech, Peoria, Oct. 16, 1854.* II, 259.
2.—At length a squabble springs up between the President and the author of the Nebraska bill, on the mere question of fact, whether the Lecompton constitution was or was not, in any just sense, made by the people of Kansas; and in that quarrel the latter declares that all he wants is a fair vote for the people, and that he cares not whether slavery be voted down or voted up. I do not understand his declaration that he cares not whether slavery be voted down or voted up to be intended by him other than as an apt definition of the policy he would impress upon the public mind—the principle for which he declares he has suffered so much, and is ready to suffer to the end.—*Speech, Springfield, June 16, 1858.* III, 6.
3.—The Nebraska doctrine, or what is left of it, is to educate and mold public opinion, at least northern public opinion, not to care whether slavery is voted down or voted up.—*Speech, Springfield, June 16, 1858.* III, 8.
4.—How can he [Douglas] oppose the advances of slavery? He don't care anything about it. His avowed mission is impressing the "public heart" to care nothing about it.—*Speech, Springfield, June 16, 1858.* III, 13.
5.—He [Douglas] looks upon all this matter of slavery as an exceedingly little thing—this matter of keeping one sixth of the population of the whole nation in a state of oppression and tyranny unequaled in the world. He looks upon it as being an exceedingly little thing, only equal to the question of the cranberry laws of Indiana—as something having no moral question in it, as something on a par with the question whether a man shall pasture his land with cattle or

plant it with tobacco.—*Speech, Chicago, July 10, 1858.* III, 36.

6.—He [Douglas] tells you . . . substantially . . . that he cares not if slavery is voted up or voted down.—*Speech, Chicago, July 10, 1858.* III, 43.

7.—Judge Douglas is going back to the era of our Revolution [in the words of Clay], and to the extent of his ability muzzling the cannon which thunders its annual joyous return. When he invites any people, willing to have slavery, to establish it, he is blowing out the moral lights around us. When he says he "cares not whether slavery is voted down or voted up" —that it is a sacred right of self-government—he is, in my judgment penetrating the human soul and eradicating the light of reason and the love of liberty in this American people.—*Debate Ottawa, Aug. 21, 1858.* III, 256.

8.—Douglas says he does not care whether they vote slavery up or down in Kansas.—*Speech, Carlinville, Aug. 31, 1858.* Angle, 191.

9.—He [Douglas] tells us in this very speech [in the Senate], expected to be so palatable to Republicans, that he cares not whether slavery is voted down or voted up. His whole effort is devoted to clearing the ring, and giving slavery and freedom a fair fight. For one who considers slavery as good as freedom, this is perfectly natural and consistent.—*Notes, Oct. 1, 1858.* IV, 227.

10.—I am glad Judge Douglas has, at last, distinctly told us that he cares not whether slavery is voted down or voted up. . . . I am glad because it affords such a true and excellent definition of the Nebraska policy itself. That policy, honestly administered, is exactly that. It seeks to bring the people of the nation to not care anything about slavery. This is Nebraska-ism in its abstract purity—in its very best dress.— *Notes, Oct. 1, 1858.* IV, 230.

11.—The Nebraska doctrine is to educate and mold public opinion to "not care whether slavery is voted up or voted down." At least, northern opinion must cease to care anything about it. Southern opinion, may, without offense, continue to care as much as it pleases.—*Notes, Oct. 1, 1858.* IV, 234.

12.—Every sentiment he [Douglas] utters discards the idea that there is any wrong in slavery. Everything that emanates from him or his coadjutors in their course of policy carefully excludes the thought that there is anything wrong in slavery. . . . If you will take the judge's speeches, and select the short and pointed sentences expressed by him—as his declaration that he don't care whether slavery is voted up or voted down—you will see at once that this is per-fectly logical, if you do not admit that slavery is wrong. If you admit that it is wrong, Judge Douglas

cannot logically say he don't care whether a wrong is voted up or voted down.—*Debate, Galesburg, Oct. 7, 1858.* IV, 274.

13.—The leading man—I think I may do my friend Judge Douglas the honor of calling him such— advocating the present Democratic policy, never him-self says it [slavery] is wrong. He has the high dis-tinction, so far as I know, of never having said slavery is either right or wrong. Almost everybody says one or the other, but the judge never does.— *Debate, Quincy, Oct. 13, 1858.* IV, 331.

14.—When Judge Douglas says he "don't care whether slavery is voted up or voted down," whether he means that as an individual expression of senti-ment, or only as a sort of statement of his views on national policy, it is alike true to say that he can thus argue logically if he don't see anything wrong in it; but he cannot say so logically if he admits that slavery is wrong. . . . When Judge Douglas says that whoever or whatever community wants slaves, they have a right to have them, he is perfectly logical if there is nothing wrong in the institution; but if you admit that it is wrong, he cannot logically say that anybody has a right to do wrong.—*Debate, Quincy, Oct. 13, 1858.* IV, 333.

15.—Is it not a false statesmanship that undertakes to build up a system of policy upon the basis of caring nothing about the very thing that everybody does care the most about—a thing which all experience has shown we care a very great deal about?—*Debate, Alton, Oct. 15, 1858.* V, 56.

16.—He [Douglas] says he "don't care whether it [slavery] is voted up or voted down" in the territories. . . . Any man can say that who does not see any-thing wrong in slavery, but no man can logically say it who does see a wrong in it; because no man can logically say he don't care whether a wrong is voted up or voted down. . . . He [Douglas] contends that whatever community wants slaves has a right to have them. So they have if it is not a wrong. But if it is a wrong, he cannot say people have a right to do wrong.—*Debate, Alton, Oct. 15, 1858.* V, 64.

17.—The judge [Douglas] never says your institution of slavery is wrong; he never says it is right, to be sure, but he never says it is wrong. . . . He leaves himself at perfect liberty to do all in your favor which he would be hindered from doing if he were to de-clare the thing to be wrong. On the contrary, he takes all the chances that he has for inveigling the senti-ment of the North, opposed to slavery, into your sup-port, by never saying it is right.—*Speech, Cincinnati, Sept. 17, 1859.* V, 197.

18.—He [Douglas] said upon the floor of the United States Senate, and he has repeated it, as I understand, a great many times, that he does not care whether slavery is "voted up or voted down"; . . . a man may say when he sees nothing wrong in a thing, that he cares not whether it be voted up or voted down; but no man can logically say that he does not care whether a thing goes up or goes down which appears to him to be wrong.—*Speech, Cincinnati, Sept. 17, 1859.* V, 198.

19.—The reasoning and sentiment advanced by Douglas in support of his policy as to slavery all spring from the view that slavery is not wrong. . . . He says he does not care whether it shall be voted down or voted up.—*Speeches in Kansas, Dec. 1–5, 1859.* V, 268.

20.—An effort has been made for a policy that shall treat it [slavery] as neither right nor wrong. It is based upon utter indifference. Its leading advocate has said: "I don't care whether it be voted up or down. . . ." It holds that it makes no more difference to us whether the territories become free or slave states than whether my neighbor stocks his farm with horned cattle or puts it into tobacco. All recognize this policy, the sugar-coated name of which is "popular sovereignty."—*Speech, New Haven, Conn., March 6, 1860.* V, 348.
Repeated at Norwich, Conn., March 9, 1860. VI, 4.

21.—[This care-not policy] can be maintained only by public opinion that shall say, "We don't care." There must be a change in public opinion; the public mind must so far be debauched as to square with this policy of caring not at all. . . . It is for you to say whether that can be done.—*Speech, New Haven, Conn., March 6, 1860.* V, 350.

Slavery, Douglas molds public opinion for—*See* PUBLIC OPINION, Douglas tries to mold.

See SLAVERY, Douglas's care-not policy, 11.

Slavery, drunkenness and—The one victory we can ever call complete will be that one which proclaims that there is not one slave or drunkard on the face of God's green earth.—*To George E. Pickett, Feb. 22, 1842.* I, 192.

Slavery, durable for discord—[I believe] that this slavery element is a durable element of discord among us, and we shall probably not have perfect peace in this country with it until it either masters the free principle in our government, or is so far mastered by the free principle as for the public mind to rest in the belief that it is going to its end.—*Speech, Columbus, Ohio, Sept. 16, 1859.* V, 151.

2.—Now it would seem to me that it might have occurred to Judge Douglas, or anybody who had turned his attention to these facts, that there was something in the nature of that thing—slavery—somewhat durable for mischief and discord.—*Speech, Columbus, Ohio, Sept. 16, 1859.* V, 152.

3.—Last year Gov. Seward and myself, at different times and occasions, expressed the opinion that slavery is a durable element of discord, and that we should not have peace with it until it either masters or is mastered by the free principle. This gave great offense to Judge Douglas, and his denunciations of it, and absurd inferences from it, have never ceased.—*Speeches in Kansas, Dec. 1–5, 1859.* V, 262.

Slavery, Egypt's experience with—Pharaoh's country was cursed with plagues, and his hosts were lost in the Red Sea, for striving to retain a captive people who had already served them more than 400 years. May like disasters never befall us.—*Speech, Springfield, July 16, 1852.* II, 176.

2.—The children of Israel, to such numbers as to include 400,000 fighting men, went out of Egyptian bondage in a body.—*Speech, Springfield, June 26, 1857.* II, 329.

Slavery, extension of, opposed—I am a northern man, or rather a western free-state man, with a constituency I believe to be, and with personal feelings I know to be, against the extension of slavery.—*Speech in Congress, July 27, 1848.* II, 66.

2.—This declared indifference, but, as I must think, covert real zeal, for the spread of slavery [manifest by the Missouri Compromise repeal] I cannot but hate. I hate it because it deprives our republican example of its just influence in the world; enables the enemies of free institutions with plausibility to taunt us as hypocrites; causes the real friends of freedom to doubt our sincerity; and especially because it forces so many good men among ourselves into an open war with the very fundamental principles of civil liberty, criticising the Declaration of Independence, and insisting that there is no right principle of action but self-interest.—*Speech, Peoria, Oct. 16, 1854.* II, 205.
Repeated at Urbana, Oct. 24, 1854. Hertz II, 633.
Repeated at Ottawa, Aug. 21, 1858. III, 226.

3.—Keep it [slavery] out [of a territory] until a vote is taken; and a vote in favor of it cannot be got in any population of 40,000 on earth, who have been drawn together by the ordinary motives of emigration and settlement.—*Speech, Peoria, Oct. 16, 1854.* II, 221.

4.—The opening of new countries to the institution [slavery] increases the demand for and augments the price of slaves, and so does, in fact, make slaves of free men, by causing them to be brought from Africa and sold into bondage.—*Speech, Peoria, Oct. 16, 1854.* II, 223.

310

5.—We know the opening of new countries to slavery tends to the perpetuation of the institution, and so does keep men in slavery who would otherwise be free.—*Speech, Peoria, Oct. 16, 1854.* II, 223.

6.—I am combatting what is set up as moral argument for allowing them [slaves] to be taken where they have never been—arguing against the extension of a bad thing.—*Speech, Peoria, Oct. 16, 1854.* II, 229.

7.—What better moral right have 31 citizens of Nebraska to say that the 32nd shall not hold slaves than the people of 31 states have to say that slavery shall not go into the 32nd state at all.—*Speech, Peoria, Oct. 16, 1854.* II, 231.

8.—The first few may get slavery in [to a territory], and the subsequent many cannot easily get it out.—*Speech, Peoria, Oct. 16, 1854.* II, 232.

9.—If they [Americans] shall think, as I do, that the extension of slavery endangers them [American "liberties and institutions"] more than any or all other causes, how recreant to themselves if they submit the question, and with it the fate of their country, to a mere handful of men bent only on self-interest.—*Speech, Peoria, Oct. 16, 1854.* II, 235.

10.—It could not but be expected by its [Kansas-Nebraska Act's] author that it would be looked upon as a measure for the extension of slavery, aggravated by a gross breach of faith. Argue as you will and long as you will, this is the naked aspect of the measure.—*Speech, Peoria, Oct. 16, 1854.* II, 237.

11.—It still will be the abundance of man's heart that slavery extension is wrong, and out of the abundance of his heart his mouth will continue to speak.—*Speech, Peoria, Oct. 16, 1854.* Basler, 309.

12.—Fellow-countrymen, Americans, South as well as North, shall we make no effort to arrest this [extension of slavery]? Already the liberal party throughout the world express the apprehension, "that the one retrograde institution in America is undermining the principles of progress, and fatally violating the noblest political system the world ever saw." This is not the taunt of enemies, but the warning of friends. Is it quite safe to disregard it?—*Speech, Peoria, Oct. 16, 1854.* II, 247.

13.—I do oppose the extension of slavery because my judgment and feeling so prompt me, and I am under no obligations to the contrary.—*To Joshua F. Speed, Aug. 24, 1855.* II, 282.

14.—Almost the entire North, as well as a large following in the border states, is radically opposed to the planting of slavery in free territory. Probably in a popular vote throughout the nation nine tenths of the voters in the free states, and at least one half in the border states, if they could express their senti-ments freely, would vote No on such an issue; and it is safe to say that two thirds of the voters of the entire nation would be opposed to it. And yet, in spite of this overbalancing of sentiment in this free country, we are in a fair way to see Kansas present itself for admission as a slave state.—*Speech, Bloomington, May 29, 1856.* Lapsley II, 251.

15.—We boldly say, let all who really think slavery ought to spread into free territory, openly go over against us; there is where they rightfully belong. But why should any go who really think slavery ought not to spread? Do they really think the right ought to yield to the wrong? Are they afraid to stand by the right?—*Fragment, Oct. 1, 1856.* II, 307.

16.—Although I have ever been opposed to slavery, so far [until the introduction of the Kansas-Nebraska bill] I rested in the hope and belief that it was in the course of ultimate extinction. For that reason it had been a minor question with me. I might have been mistaken; but I had believed, and now believe, that the whole public mind, that is, the mind of the great majority, had rested in that belief up to the repeal of the Missouri Compromise. But upon that event, I became convinced that either I had been resting in a delusion, or the institution was being placed on a new basis—a basis for making it perpetual, national and universal. Subsequent events have greatly confirmed me in that belief. . . . So believing, I have since then considered that question a paramount one.—*Speech, Springfield, July 17, 1858.* III, 174.

17.—Now I believe if we could arrest the spread [of slavery] and place it where Washington and Jefferson and Madison placed it, it would be in the course of ultimate extinction, and the public mind would, as for 80 years past, believe that it was in the course of ultimate extinction. The crisis would be past, and the institution might be let alone for a hundred years—if it should live that long—in the states where it exists, yet it would be going out of existence in the way best for both the black and the white races.—*Debate, Ottawa, Aug. 21, 1858.* III, 233.

18.—I am impliedly, if not expressly, pledged to a belief in the right and the duty of Congress to prohibit slavery in all the United States territories.—*Debate, Freeport, Aug. 27, 1858.* III, 274.

19.—I . . . would give my vote and use my lawful means to prevent its extension.—*Speech, Carlinville, Aug. 31, 1858.* Angle, 191.

20.—They [Republicans] will use every constitutional method to prevent the evil from becoming larger and involving more negroes, more white men, more soil, and more states in its deplorable consequences.—*Speech, Edwardsville, Sept. 13, 1858.* XI, 108.

21.—I say when this government was first established, it was the policy of its founders to prohibit the spread of slavery into the new territories of the United States, where it had not existed.—*Debate, Jonesboro, Sept. 15, 1858.* IV, 32.

22.—All the trouble and convulsion have proceeded from efforts to spread it [slavery] over more territory.—*Debate, Jonesboro, Sept. 15, 1858.* IV, 40.

23.—Slavery can only become extinct by being restricted to its present limits and dwindling out. It can only become national by a Supreme Court decision. To such a decision when it comes, Judge Douglas is fully committed. Such a decision, acquiesced in by the people, effects the whole object.—*Notes, Oct. 1, 1858.* IV, 220.

24.—Congress cannot dictate a constitution to a new state. All it can do at that point is to secure the people a fair chance to form one for themselves, and then to accept or reject it when they ask for admission into the Union. As I understand, Republicans claim no more than this. But they do claim that Congress can and ought to keep slavery out of a territory, up to the time of the people forming a state constitution.—*Notes, Oct. 1, 1858.* IV, 230.

25.—I have never manifested any impatience with the necessities that spring from the actual presence of black people amongst us and the actual presence of slavery amongst us where it does already exist, but I have insisted that, in legislating for new countries where it does not exist, there is no just rule other than that of moral and abstract right. With reference to those new countries, those maxims as to the right of a people to "life, liberty and the pursuit of happiness" were the just rules to be constantly referred to. There is no misunderstanding this except by men interested to misunderstand them.—*Debate, Galesburg, Oct. 7, 1858.* IV, 266.

26.—I believe . . . our government was so framed [relative to slavery in the states] because of the necessity springing from the actual presence of slavery, when it was framed. That such necessity does not exist in the territories where slavery is not at present.—*To J. N. Brown, Oct. 8, 1858.* V, 87.

27.—We [Republicans] also oppose it [slavery] as an evil so far as it seeks to spread itself. We insist on the policy that shall restrict it to its present limits.—*Debate, Quincy, Oct. 13, 1858.* IV, 329.

28.—When Mr. [Henry] Clay says that in laying the foundations of societies in our territories where it does not exist, he would be opposed to the introduction of slavery as an element, I insist that we have his warrant—his license for insisting upon the exclusion of that element which he declared in such strong

and emphatic language was most hateful to him.—*Debate, Alton, Oct. 15, 1858.* V, 44.

29.—I have said, and I repeat, my wish is that the further spread of it [slavery] may be arrested, and that it may be placed where the public mind shall rest in the belief that it is in the course of ultimate extinction.—*Debate, Alton, Oct. 15, 1858.* V, 47.

30.—Our controversy with him [Douglas] is in regard to [slavery in] the new territories. We agree that when the states come in as states they have the right and the power to do as they please. . . . What I insist upon is, that the new territories shall be kept free from it while in the territorial condition.—*Debate, Alton, Oct. 15, 1858.* V, 57.

31.—You see this peaceful way of dealing with it [slavery] as a wrong—restricting the spread of it, and not allowing it to go into new countries, where it has not already existed. That is the peaceful way, the old-fashioned way, the way in which the fathers themselves set us the example.—*Debate, Alton, Oct. 15, 1858.* V, 61.

32.—In resisting the spread of slavery to new territories, and with that, what appears to me to be a tendency to subvert the first principle of free government itself, my whole effort has consisted.—*Speech, Springfield, Oct. 30, 1858.* Angle, 198.

33.—Never forget that we have before us this whole matter of the right or wrong of slavery in this Union, though the immediate question is as to its spreading out into the territories and states. . . . I suppose it [slavery] may long exist; and perhaps the best way for it to come to an end peaceably is for it to exist for a length of time. But I say that the spread and strengthening and perpetuation of it is an entirely different proposition. There we should in every way resist it as a wrong, treating it as a wrong, with the fixed idea that it must and will come to an end.—*Speech, Chicago, March 1, 1859.* V, 122.

34.—To prevent the spread and nationalization of slavery is a national concern, and must be attended to by the nation.—*To Schuyler Colfax, July 6, 1859.* V, 132.

35.—The American people, on the first day of January, 1854, found the African slave-trade prohibited by a law of Congress. In a majority of the states of the Union, they found African slavery, or any other sort of slavery, prohibited by state constitutions. They also found a law existing, supposed to be valid, by which slavery was excluded from almost all the territory the United States then owned.—*Speech, Columbus, Ohio, Sept. 16, 1859.* V, 146.

36.—You need but one or two turns further, until your minds, now ripening under these teachings [by proslavery men] will be ready for . . . a slave code enforced in our territories.—*Speech, Columbus, Ohio, Sept. 16, 1859.* V, 188.

37.—I desire that it should be no further spread in these United States, and I should not object if it should gradually terminate in the whole Union.— *Speech, Cincinnati, Sept. 17, 1859.* V, 195.

38.—The federal government, however, as we [Republicans] insist, has the power of restraining the extension of the institution.—*Cooper Institute address, New York, Feb. 27, 1860.* V, 318.

39.—You [men of the South] will break up the Union rather than submit to a denial of your constitutional rights. . . . When you make these declarations you have a specific and well-understood allusion to an assumed constitutional right of yours to take slaves into the federal territories, and to hold them there as property. . . . We, on the contrary, deny that such a right has any existence in the Constitution, even by implication.—*Cooper Institute address, New York, Feb. 27, 1860.* V, 320.

See AFRICAN SLAVE TRADE, slavery extension akin to.

See CAMPAIGN OF 1856, issue defined.

See TERRITORIES, best use of.

Slavery, faith in victory—I have an abiding faith that we shall beat them [defenders of slavery] in the long run. Step by step the objects of the leaders will become too plain for the people to stand them. I write merely to let you know that I am neither dead nor dying.—*To Alexander Sympson, Dec. 12, 1858.* V, 97.

Slavery, first agitation against—This [admission of Missouri as slave state] was resisted by northern members of Congress; and thus began the first great slavery agitation in the nation.—*Speech, Peoria, Oct. 16, 1854.* II, 196.

Slavery, general welfare impaired by—I do not mean to say that this general government is charged with the duty of redressing all the wrongs in the world; but I do think it is charged with preventing and redressing all wrongs which are wrongs to itself. The government is expressly charged with the duty of providing for the general welfare. We believe that the spreading out and perpetuity of the institution of slavery impairs the general welfare.—*Speech, Cincinnati, Sept. 17, 1859.* V, 231.

2.—It [the government] is expressly charged with the duty of providing for the general welfare. We think slavery impairs and endangers the general welfare. . . . We must, by a national policy, prevent the spread of slavery into new territories . . . because the general welfare does demand such prevention.—*Speeches in Kansas, Dec. 1-5, 1859.* V, 279.

Slavery, geography and—See CLIMATE, no bar to slavery, 2.

Slavery, Great Britain blamed for—*See* GREAT BRITAIN, blamed for slavery.

Slavery, Gulf States would suffer—[To allow the Gulf States to retain slavery, as suggested by the Baltimore *American*] creates in those states a vast preponderance of the population of a servile and oppressed class. It fearfully imperils the life and safety of the ruling class. Now, the slaves are quiet, choosing to wait for the deliverance they hope from us, rather than endanger their lives by a frantic struggle for freedom. The society of the Southern States is now constituted on a basis entirely military. It would be easier now than formerly to repress a rising of unarmed and uneducated slaves. But if they should succeed in secession the Gulf States would be more endangered than ever. The slaves—despairing of liberty through us, would take the matter into their own hands, and, no longer opposed by the government of the United States, they would succeed.—*To John Hay, Nov. 24, 1863.* Hay, 126.

Slavery, helped by enemies—One of our greatest difficulties is that men who know that slavery is a detestable crime and ruinous to the nation are compelled, by our peculiar conditions and other circumstances, to advocate it concretely, though damning it in the raw. Henry Clay was a brilliant example of this tendency; others of our purest statesmen are compelled to do so; and thus slavery secures actual support from those who detest it at heart.—*Speech, Bloomington, May 29, 1856.* Lapsley II, 267.

Slavery, history of, repeats—*See* HISTORY, repeats, 2.

Slavery, horse stealing and—On the same principle a gang of Missouri horse thieves could come into Illinois and declare horse stealing to be legal, and it would be just as legal as slavery in Kansas.—*Speech, Bloomington, May 29, 1856.* Lapsley II, 260.

2.—It is a very strange thing, and not solvable by any moral law that I know of, that if a man loses his horse, the whole country will turn out to help hang the thief; but if a man but a shade or two darker than I am is himself stolen, the same crowd will hang one who aids in restoring him to liberty. Such are the inconsistencies of slavery, where a horse is more sacred than a man.—*Speech, Bloomington, May 29, 1856.* Lapsley II, 271.

Slavery, if government were formed anew—*See* SLAVERY, policy of the fathers, 36, 37.

Slavery, if nation owned slaves—It is startling to say that Congress can free a slave within a state, and yet if it be said the ownership of the slave had first been transferred to the nation and that Congress had then liberated him the difficulty would at once vanish.— *Message to the House, July 17, 1862.* VII, 281.

Slavery, Illinois and Missouri in contrast—if that ordinance [of 1787] did not keep it [slavery] out of Illinois [as Douglas says], what was it made the difference between Illinois and Missouri. They lie side by side, the Mississippi River only dividing them, while their early settlements were within the same latitude. Between 1810 and 1820, the number of slaves in Missouri increased 7,211, while in Illinois in the same ten years they decreased 51. . . . During this time the ordinance forbade slavery to go into Illinois, and nothing forbade it to go into Missouri. It did go into Missouri, and did not go into Illinois. That is the fact. Can anyone doubt as to the reason of it?—*Speech, Peoria, Oct. 16, 1854.* II, 250.

2.—Two years ago, at Springfield, Judge Douglas avowed that Illinois came into the Union as a slave state, and that slavery was weeded out by the operation of his great, patent, everlasting principle of "popular sovereignty." Well now, that argument must be answered, for it has a little grain of truth in it. I do not mean that it is true in essence, as he would have us believe. It could not be essentially true, if the Ordinance of '87 was valid. But, in point of fact, there were some degraded beings called slaves at Kaskaskia and the other French settlements when our first state constitution was adopted; that is a fact, and I don't deny it. Slaves were brought here as early as 1720, and were kept here in spite of the Ordinance of 1787 against it. But slavery did not thrive here. On the contrary, under the influence of the Ordinance, the number decreased 51 from 1810 to 1820; while under the influence of squatter sovereignty, right across the river in Missouri, they increased 7,211 in the same time; and slavery finally faded out in Illinois, under the influence of the law of freedom, while it grew stronger and stronger in Missouri, under the law and practice of "popular sovereignty."— *Speech, Bloomington, May 29, 1856.* Lapsley II, 272.

3.—There were French settlements in what is now Illinois, and at the same time there were French settlements in what is now Missouri. . . . In those French settlements negro slavery had existed for many years. . . . There was about the same number in each place. . . . Illinois and Missouri came into the Union about the same time in 1820. They have been filling up with American people about the same period of time, their progress enabling them to come into the Union

about the same time. At the end of that ten years, in which they had been so preparing . . ., the number of slaves in Illinois had actually decreased; while in Missouri, beginning with very few, at the end of that ten years there were about 10,000. This being so, and it being remembered that Missouri and Illinois are, to a certain extent, in the same parallel of latitude . . . so that climate would have the same effect upon one as upon the other; and that in the soil there is no material difference so far as it bears upon the question of slavery being settled upon one or the other; there being none of those natural causes to produce a difference in filling them, and yet there being a broad difference in their filling up, we are led again to inquire what was the cause of that difference. It is most natural to say that in Missouri there was no law to keep that country from filling up with slaves, while in Illinois there was the Ordinance of '87. The ordinance being there, slavery decreased during that ten years—the ordinance not being in the other, it increased from a few to ten thousand.—*Speech, Cincinnati, Sept. 17, 1859.* V, 224.

Slavery, impediment to progress—It [slavery] stands in the way and prevents the adjustment and the giving of necessary attention to other questions of national housekeeping.—*Speech, Norwich, Conn., March 9, 1860.* VI, 1.

Slavery, "insidious and crafty"—Slavery is an insidious and crafty power, and gains equally by open violence of the brutal as well as by sly management of the peaceful.—*Speech, Bloomington, May 29, 1856.* Lapsley II, 270.

Slavery, introduced without law—Wherever slavery is, it has been first introduced without law. The oldest laws we find concerning it are not laws introducing it; but regulating it as an already existing thing.— *Speech, Peoria, Oct. 16, 1854.* II, 221.

Repeated at Urbana, Oct. 24, 1854. Hertz II, 641.

2.—Once let slavery get planted in a locality, in ever so small numbers, and it is like the Canada thistle or Bermuda grass—you can't root it out. You yourself may detest slavery; but your neighbor has five or six slaves; and he is an excellent neighbor, or your son has married his daughter, and they beg you to help save their property, and you vote against your interests and principle to accommodate a neighbor, hoping that your vote will be on the losing side. And others do the same; and in those ways slavery gets a sure foothold. And when it is done the whole mighty Union—the force of the nation—is committed to its support.—*Speech, Bloomington, May 29, 1856.* Lapsley II, 271.

3.—We will suppose that there are ten men who go into Kansas to settle. Nine of these are opposed to slavery. One has ten slaves. The slaveholder is a good man in other respects; he is a good neighbor, and being a wealthy man, he is enabled to do to the others many neighborly kindnesses. They like the man, though they don't like the system by which he holds his fellow men in bondage. . . . Those ten men . . . live together three or four years; they intermarry; their family ties are strengthened. And who wonders that in time the people learn to look upon slavery with complacency? That is the way in which slavery is planted, and gains so firm a foothold.—*Speech, Kalamazoo, Mich., Aug. 27, 1856.* Stern, 402.

4.—I defy any man to find any difference between the policy which originally planted slavery in these [American] colonies and that policy which now prevails in our new territories. If it does not go into them, it is only because no individual wishes it to go. —*Speech, Springfield, July 17, 1858.* III, 183.

5.—It requires positive law to be both made and executed to keep slavery out of any territory where any owner chooses to take it.—*Notes, Oct. 1, 1858.* IV, 205.

6.—If it be said that it cannot be planted, in fact, without protective law, that assertion is already falsified by history; for it was originally planted in this continent without protective law.—*Speeches in Kansas, Dec. 1-5, 1859.* V, 266.

See FREEPORT DOCTRINE, fallacy of, 3, 10, 15.

Slavery, Jefferson originated territorial policy.—*See* ORDINANCE OF 1787, fruits of, 1.

Slavery, Jefferson versus Douglas on—Thomas Jefferson, a slaveholder, mindful of the moral element in slavery, solemnly declared that he trembled for his country when he remembered that God is just; while Judge Douglas, with an insignificant wave of the hand, "don't care whether slavery is voted up or voted down."—*Speech, Bloomington, May 29, 1856.* Lapsley II, 253.

2.—I will offer the highest premium in my power to Judge Douglas if he will show that he, in all his life, ever uttered a sentiment [on slavery] at all akin to that of Jefferson.—*Debate, Galesburg, Oct. 7, 1858.* IV, 264.

3.—That man [Jefferson] did not take exactly this view of the insignificance of the element of slavery which our friend Judge Douglas does. . . . There was danger to this country [Jefferson thought] danger of the avenging justice of God, in that little, unimportant popular sovereignty question of Judge Douglas. He supposed there was a question of God's eternal

justice wrapped up in the enslaving of any race of men, of any man, and that those who did so braved the arm of Jehovah—that when a nation thus dared the Almighty, every friend of that nation had cause to dread his wrath.—*Speech, Columbus, Ohio, Sept. 16, 1859.* V, 159.

4.—Choose ye between Jefferson and Douglas as what is the true view of this element [slavery] among us.— *Speech, Columbus, Ohio, Sept. 16, 1859.* V, 160.

Slavery, joint responsibility for—When southern men tell us they are no more responsible for the origin of slavery than we, I acknowledge the fact.—*Speech, Peoria, Oct. 16, 1854.* II, 206.
Repeated at Urbana, Oct. 24, 1854. Hertz II, 634.
Repeated at Ottawa, Aug. 21, 1858. III, 227.

2.—It is not less true for having been often said, that the people of the South are not more responsible for the original introduction of this [slave] property than are the people of the North; and when it is remembered how unhesitatingly we all use cotton and sugar and share the profits on dealing in them, it may not be quite safe to say that the South has been more responsible than the North for its continuance.— *Second annual message, Dec. 1, 1862.* VIII, 120.

Slavery, liberty and prosperity threatened by—*See* LIBERTY, prosperity and, threatened by slavery.

Slavery, Lincoln offers to pay for slave—I now understand [that] Col. Utley . . . has five slaves in his camp; four of whom belong to rebels, and one belonging to you. If this be true, convey yours to Col. Utley, so that he can make him free, and I will pay any sum not exceeding $500.—*To George Robertson, Nov. 26, 1862.* VIII, 88.

Slavery, line across continent—Suppose it is true that the Almighty has drawn a line across the continent [as proslavery men declare]. . . . Once we come to acknowledge that . . . it is the law of the Eternal Being for slavery to exist on one side of that line, have we any sure ground to object to slaves being held on the other side?—*Speech, Chicago, March 1, 1859.* V, 120.

2.—Once admit the position that a man rightfully holds another man as property on one side of the line, and you must, when it suits his convenience to come to the other side, admit that he has the same right to hold his property there. Once admit Judge Douglas's proposition, and we must finally all give way.—*Speech, Chicago, March 1, 1859.* V, 121.

3.—In a speech at Memphis . . . he [Douglas] distinctly told the people that there was a "line drawn by the Almighty across this continent, on one side of which the soil must always be cultivated by slaves. . . ." Whenever you can get these northern audiences to adopt the opinion that slavery is right on the other side of the Ohio . . . they will very readily make the other argument, which is perfectly logical, that that which is right on that side of the Ohio cannot be wrong on this side, and that if you have property [slaves] on that side of the Ohio, under the seal and stamp of the Almighty, when by any means it escapes over here, it is wrong to have constitutions and laws to "devil" you about it.—*Speech, Cincinnati, Sept. 17, 1859.* V, 199.

See UNION, no line of cleavage.

Slavery, local law alone should shelter—. . . and we must decree that only local law, and not that time-honored instrument [Constitution], shall shelter a slaveholder.—*Speech, Bloomington, May 29, 1856.* Lapsley II, 274.

Slavery, Lord Mansfield's decision on—*See* SLAVERY, positive law required for, 1.

Slavery, many in free states desire—There are many individual men in all the free states who desire to have slaves; and if you admit that slavery is not wrong, it is also tyranny to deny them the privilege. —*Speeches in Kansas, Dec. 1-5, 1859.* V, 269.

Slavery, masters who dodge facts—So long as we call slavery wrong, whenever a slave runs away they [the owners] will overlook the obvious fact that he ran because he was oppressed, and declare that he was stolen off. Whenever a master cuts his slaves with a lash, and they cry out under it, he will overlook the obvious fact that they cry out because they are hurt, and insist that they were put up to it by some rascally Abolitionist.—*Speech, New Haven, Conn., March 6, 1860.* V, 369.

Slavery, misunderstanding causes controversy—Much of the ill feeling that has existed between the people in the section from which I came and the people here, is dependent upon a misunderstanding of one another.—*Speech, Reply to mayor of Washington, Feb. 27, 1861.* VI, 165.

2.—Very much of the ill feeling that has existed between you and the people of your surroundings, and the people from among whom I come, has depended, and now depends, upon a misunderstanding. I hope that, if things go along as prosperously as I believe we all desire they may, I may have it in my power to remove something of this misunderstanding.—*Reply to serenade, Feb. 28, 1861.* VI, 167.

Slavery, Moloch of—Slavery will endure no test of logic or reason; and yet its advocates, like Douglas,

use a sort of bastard logic, or noisy assumption, it might better be termed . . . in order to prepare the mind for the gradual, but none the less certain, encroachments of the Moloch of slavery upon the fair domain of freedom.—*Speech, Bloomington, May 29, 1856.* Lapsley II, 255.

Slavery, nationalization of—We cannot be free men if this is, by our own national choice, to be a land of slavery.—*Speech, Bloomington, May 29, 1856.* Lapsley II, 274.

2.—In view of its importance and aggressive nature, I think it must come to a crisis—that it will become national by court verdicts, or local by the popular voice.—*Speech, Carlinville, Aug. 31, 1858.* Angle, 188.

3.—It can only become national by a supreme Court decision.—*Notes, Oct. 1, 1858.* IV, 220.

4.—Welcome or unwelcome, agreeable or disagreeable, whether this shall be an entire slave nation is the issue before us. Every incident—every little shifting of scenes or of actors—only clears away the intervening trash, compacts and consolidates the opposing hosts, and brings them more and more distinctly face to face. The conflict will be a severe one; and it will be fought through by those who do care for the result, and not by those who do not care—by those who are for, and those who are against, a legalized national slavery.—*Notes, Oct. 1, 1858.* IV, 235.

5.—Then what is necessary for the nationalization of slavery? It is simply the next Dred Scott decision. —*Debate, Ottawa, Aug. 21, 1858.* III, 236.

6.—The Dred Scott decision . . . goes very far to make slavery national throughout the United States. —*Debate, Freeport, Aug. 27, 1858.* III, 290.

7.—For my part, I do hope that all of us, entertaining a common sentiment in opposition to what appears to us as a design to nationalize and perpetuate slavery, will waive minor differences on questions which either belong to the dead past or the distant future, and all pull together in the struggle.—*Debate, Freeport, Aug. 27, 1858.* III, 338.

8.—In these general maxims about liberty—in his [Douglas's] assertions that "he don't care whether slavery is voted up or voted down"; that "whoever wants slavery has a right to have it"; that "upon principles of equality it should be allowed to go anywhere"; that "there is no inconsistency between free and slave institutions"—in this he is also [besides paving the way for a second Dred Scott decision] preparing—whether purposely or not—the way for making the institution of slavery national.—*Debate, Galesburg, Oct. 7, 1858.* IV, 288.

9.—Step by step, south of the judge's moral climate

line in the states, in the territories everywhere, and then in all the states—it is thus that Judge Douglas would lead us inevitably to the nationalization of slavery.—*Speech, Chicago, March 1, 1859.* V, 121.

10.—Douglas's position leads to the nationalization of slavery as surely as does that of Jeff Davis and [James M.] Mason of Virginia. The two positions are but slightly different roads to the same end—with this difference, that the nationalization of slavery can be reached by Douglas's route, and never can by the other.—*Speeches in Kansas, Dec. 1–5, 1859.* V, 268.

11.—Whether by his [Douglas's] doctrine of squatter sovereignty, or by the ground taken by him in his recent speeches in Memphis and through the South, that wherever the climate makes it the interest of the inhabitants to encourage slave property they will pass a slave code—whether it is covertly nationalized by congressional legislation or by Dred Scott decision, or by the sophistical and misleading doctrine he has last advanced, the same goal is inevitably reached by the one or the other device. It is only traveling to the same place by different roads.—*Speech, Chicago, March 1, 1859.* V, 121.

12.—The "don't care" policy leads just as surely to nationalizing slavery as Jeff Davis himself, but the doctrine is more dangerous because more insidious.—*Speech, Hartford, Conn., March 5, 1860.* V, 333.

13.—Even if fairly carried out, that policy [of not caring about slavery] is just as certain to nationalize slavery as the doctrine of Jeff Davis himself. These are only two roads to the same goal, and "popular sovereignty" is just as sure, and almost as short, as the other.—*Speech, New Haven, Conn., March 6, 1860.* V, 353.

See AFRICAN SLAVE TRADE, slavery extension akin to, 7.

See DRED SCOTT DECISION, challenged, 10.

See JUDICIAL DECISIONS, Douglas's attitude toward, 2.

See SLAVERY, conspiracy to promote.

See SLAVERY, no compromise on, 1.

See SLAVERY, perpetuation of, 1, 2.

See SLAVERY, republican policy toward, 8, 12.

Slavery, neutrality impossible—No man, and Judge Douglas no more than any other, can maintain a negative or merely neutral position on this question [slavery].—*Speech, Bloomington, May 29, 1856.* Lapsley II, 254.

2.—Nearly everybody does care something about slavery—is either for it or against it; and the statesmanship of a measure which conforms to the senti-

ments of nobody might well be doubted in advance —*Notes, Oct. 1, 1858.* IV, 231.

3.—A "don't care" policy won't prevail, for everybody does care.—*Speech, Hartford, Conn., March 5, 1860.* V, 331.

4.—There is nobody that "don't care." All the people do care, one way or the other.—*Speech, New Haven, Conn., March 6, 1860.* V, 349.

5.—Such a policy [as Douglas's "don't care"] may have a temporary run; it may spring up as necessary to the political prospects of some gentlemen—but it is utterly baseless; the people are not indifferent, and it can therefore have no durability or permanence.— *Speech, New Haven, Conn., March 6, 1860.* V, 349.

See SLAVERY, Douglas's care-not policy.

Slavery, no compromise on—Whoever desires the prevention of the spread of slavery and the nationalization of that institution, yields all when he yields to any policy that either recognizes slavery as being right, or as being an indifferent thing.—*Speech, Cincinnati, Sept. 17, 1859.* V, 231.

2.—Let there be no compromise on the question of extending slavery. If there be, all our labor is lost, and, ere long, must be done again. The dangerous ground—that into which some of our friends have a hankering to run—is Pop. Sov. Have none of it. Stand firm. The tug has to come, & better now than any time hereafter.—*To Lyman Trumbull, Dec. 10, 1860.* Tracy, 171.

3.—Entertain no proposition for a compromise in regard to the extension of slavery. The instant you do they have us under again; all our labor is lost, and sooner or later must be done over. Douglas is sure to be again trying to bring in his "popular sovereignty." Have none of it. The tug has to come, and better now than later.—*To Congressman William Kellogg, Dec. 11, 1860.* VI, 77.

4.—Prevent, as far as possible, any of our friends from demoralizing themselves and our cause by entertaining propositions of any sort on "slavery extension." There is no possible compromise upon it but which puts us under again, and leaves all our work to do over again.—*To E. B. Washburne, Dec. 13, 1860.* VI, 78.

5.—Should the convocation of governors of which you speak seem desirous to know my views on the present aspect of things, tell them you judge from my speeches that I will be inflexible on the territorial question.—*To Thurlow Weed, Dec. 17, 1860.* VI, 82.

6.—We have just carried an election on principles fairly stated to the people. Now we are told in advance the government shall be broken up unless we surrender to those we have beaten, before we take the offices. In this they are either attempting to play upon us or they are in dead earnest. Either way, if we surrender, it is the end of us and of the government. They will repeat the experiment upon us, *ad libitum*. A year will not pass till we shall have to take Cuba as a condition upon which they will stay in the Union.—*To J. T. Hale, Jan. 11, 1861*. VI, 93.

7.—No man can be elected President without some opponents, as well as some supporters; and if when elected, he cannot be installed, till he first appeases his enemies, by breaking his pledges, and betraying his friends, this government, and all popular government, is already at an end. . . . I do not deny the possibility that the people may err in an election; but if they do, the true [cure] is in the next election, and not in the treachery of the person elected.—*Speech to Kentuckians, Jan. 1861*. R.T.L.

8.—There is, in my judgment, but one compromise which would really settle the slavery question, and that would be a prohibition against acquiring any more territory.—*To J. T. Hale, Jan. 11, 1861*. VI, 94.

9.—I will suffer death before I will consent, or advise my friends to consent, to any concession or compromise which looks like buying the privilege of taking possession of the government to which we have a constitutional right; because, whatever I might think of the merit of various proposals before Congress, I should regard any concession in the face of menace as destructive of the government itself, and as a consent on all hands that our system should be brought down to the level existing in the disorganized state of affairs in Mexico.—*To editors Chicago* Tribune, *Jan., 1861*. Tribune, I, 170.

10.—On the territorial question—that is, the question of extending slavery under national auspices—I am inflexible. I am for no compromise which assists or permits the extension of the institution on soil owned by the nation. And any trick by which the nation is to acquire territory, and then allow some local authority to spread slavery over it, is as obnoxious as any other. I take it that to effect some such result as this, and put us again on the highroad to a slave empire, is the object of all these proposed compromises. I am against it.—*To William H. Seward, Feb. 1, 1861*. VI, 103.

11.—There is one point. . . . I can never surrender—that which was the main issue of the presidential canvass and decided at the late election, concerning the extension of slavery in the territories.—*To Congressman Boteler, March 3, 1861*. War Years I, 118.

See PEACE, conditions essential to.

Slavery, no interference with, in slave states—[We, representatives from Sangamon County] believe that the Congress of the United States has no power under the Constitution to interfere with the institution of slavery in the different states.—*Protest, Illinois Legislature, March 3, 1837*. I, 52.

2.—I hold it to be a paramount duty of us in the free states, due to the Union of states, and perhaps to liberty itself—paradox though it may seem—to let the slavery of the other states alone; while on the other hand, I hold it to be equally clear that we should never knowingly lend ourselves, directly or indirectly, to prevent that slavery from dying a natural death—to find new places for it to live in, when it can no longer exist in the old.—*To Williamson Durley, Oct. 3, 1845*. I, 277.

3.—I wish to make and to keep the distinction between the existing institution, and the extension of it, so broad and clear that no honest man can misunderstand me, and no dishonest one successfully misrepresent me.—*Speech, Peoria, Oct. 16, 1854*. II, 192.

4.—I am . . . not arguing against . . . a bad thing, which, where it already exists, we must of necessity manage as best we can—*Speech, Peoria, Oct. 16, 1854*. II, 229.

5.—I also acknowledge your rights and my obligations under the Constitution in regard to your slaves. —*To Joshua F. Speed, Aug. 24, 1855*. II, 282.

6.—I have never said, and the Whig party has never said, and those who oppose the Nebraska bill do not as a body say, that they have any intention of interfering with slavery in the slave states. Our platform says just the contrary.—*Speech, Bloomington, May 29, 1856*. Lapsley II, 261.

7.—We allow slavery to exist in the slave states, not because slavery is right or good, but from the necessities of our Union.—*Speech, Bloomington, May 29, 1856*. Lapsley II, 261.

8.—I am much flattered by the estimate you place on my late speech; and yet I am much mortified that any part of it should be construed so differently from anything intended by me. The language, "place it where the public mind shall rest in the belief that it is in course of ultimate extinction," I used deliberately, not dreaming then, nor believing now, that it asserts or intimates any power or purpose, to interfere with slavery in the states where it exists. But to not cavil about language, I declare that whether the clause used by me will bear such construction or not, I never so intended it. I have declared a thousand times, and now repeat, that, in my opinion, neither the general government, nor any other power outside the slave states, can constitutionally or rightfully interfere with slaves or slavery where it already exists. —*To John L. Scripps, June 23, 1858.* Tracy, 86. Same to Joseph Medill, same date. Tribune, I, 78.

9.—I have said a hundred times, and I now have no inclination to take it back, that I believe there is no right and ought to be no inclination in the people of the free states to enter into the slave states and interfere with the question of slavery at all.—*Speech, Chicago, July 10, 1858.* III, 34.

10.—We agree that, by the Constitution we assented to, in the states where it [slavery] exists we have no right to interfere with it, because it is in the Constitution.—*Speech, Chicago, July 10, 1858.* III, 37.

11.—I have again and again said that I would not enter into any of the states to disturb the institution of slavery.—*Speech, Springfield, July 17, 1858.* III, 172.

12.—I have no purpose, either directly or indirectly, to interfere with the institution of slavery in the states where it exists. I believe I have no lawful right to do so and I have no inclination to do so.—*Debate, Ottawa, Aug. 21, 1858.* III, 229. Repeated at Quincy, Oct. 13, 1858. IV, 318. Repeated at Columbus, Ohio, Sept. 16, 1859. V, 142. Repeated in first inaugural, March 4, 1861. VI, 305.

13.—I am standing up to our bargain for its maintenance where it lawfully exists.—*Speech, Carlinville, Aug. 31, 1858.* Angle, 188.

14.—Regarding it [slavery] as an evil, they [Republicans] will not molest it in the states where it exists; they will not overlook the constitutional guards which our fathers placed around it; they will do nothing that can give proper offence to those who hold slaves by legal sanction.—*Speech, Edwardsville, Sept. 13, 1858.* XI, 108.

15.—In so far as he [Douglas] has insisted that all the states have the right to do exactly as they please about all their domestic relations, including that of slavery, I agree entirely with him. . . . I hold myself under constitutional obligation to allow the people in all the states, without interference, direct or indirect, to do exactly as they please, and I deny that I have any inclination to interfere with them, even if there were no such constitutional obligation.—*Debate, Jonesboro, Sept. 15, 1858.* IV, 31.

16.—I believe . . . that by our form of government the states which have slavery are to retain or disuse it, at their own pleasure; and that all others—individuals, free states, and national government,—are constitutionally bound to leave them alone about it. —*Notes, Sept. 16, 1858.* IV, 88.

17.—I have never manifested any impatience with the necessity that springs from the actual presence of black people amongst us, and the actual existence of slavery amongst us where it does already exist; but I have insisted that, in legislating for new countries where it does not exist, there is no just rule other than that of moral and abstract right. With reference to these new countries, those maxims as to the right of a people to "life, liberty and the pursuit of happiness" were the just rules to be constantly referred to.—*Debate, Galesburg, Oct. 7, 1858.* IV, 266.

18.—We [antislavery men] have a due regard to the actual presence of it [slavery] amongst us, and the difficulties of getting rid of it in any satisfactory way, and all the constitutional obligations thrown about it. I suppose that in reference both to its actual existence in the nation, and to our constitutional obligations, we have no right at all to disturb it in the states where it exists, and we profess to have no more inclination to disturb it than we have right to do so.— *Debate, Quincy, Oct. 13, 1858.* IV, 328.

19.—I expressly declared in my opening speech that I had neither the inclination to exercise, nor the belief in the existence of, the right to interfere with the states of Kentucky or Virginia in doing as they please with slavery or any other existing institution. —*Debate, Quincy, Oct. 13, 1858.* IV, 375.

20.—I have never sought to apply these principles to the old states for the purpose of abolishing slavery in those states. It is nothing but a miserable perversion of what I have said, to assume that I have declared Missouri or any other slave state shall emancipate their slaves. I have proposed no such thing.— *Debate, Alton, Oct. 15, 1858.* V, 43.

21.—Our controversy with him [Douglas] is in regard to the new territories. We agree that when the states come in as states they have the right and the power to do as they please. We have no power as citizens of the free states, or in our federal capacity as members of the federal Union through the general government, to disturb slavery in the states where it exists. —*Debate, Alton, Oct. 15, 1858.* V, 57.

22.—By our form of government, the states which have slavery are to retain it, or surrender it, at their own pleasure; . . . all others—individuals, free states and national government—are constitutionally bound to leave them alone about it.—*To J. W. Brown, Oct. 18, 1858.* Hertz II, 717.

23.—The legal right of Congress to interfere with their institution [slavery] in the states I have constantly denied.—*Speech, Springfield, Oct. 30, 1858.* Angle, 197.

24.—I believe we have no power, under the Constitution of the United States, or rather under the form of government under which we live, to interfere with the institution of slavery, or any other of the institu-

tions of our sister states, be they free or slave states.—
Speech, Cincinnati, Sept. 17, 1859. V, 193.

25.—I have as little inclination to interfere with the institution of slavery where it now exists, through the instrumentality of the general government, or any other instrumentality, as I believe we have no power to do so.—*Speech, Cincinnati, Sept. 17, 1859.* V, 193.

26.—I [neither] have, nor ever had, any purpose in any way of interfering with the institution of slavery where it exists.—*Speech, Cincinnati, Sept. 17, 1859.* V, 193.

27.— We must not interfere with the institution of slavery in the states where it exists, because the Constitution forbids it, and the general welfare does not require us to do so.—*Speech, Cincinnati, Sept. 17, 1859.* V, 232.

28.—We must not disturb slavery in the states where it exists, because the Constitution and the peace of the country both forbid it.—*Speeches in Kansas, Dec. 1–5, 1859.* V, 279.

29.—Republican doctrines and declarations are accompanied with continual protest against any interference whatever with your slaves, or with you about your slaves. Surely, this does not encourage them to revolt.—*Cooper Institute address, New York, Feb. 27, 1860.* V, 315.

30.—Mr. Jefferson did not mean to say, nor do I, that the power of emancipation is in the federal government.—*Cooper Institute address, Feb. 27, 1860.* V, 318.

31.—Wrong as we think slavery is, we can yet afford to let it alone where it is, because that much is due to the necessity arising from its actual presence in the nation.—*Cooper Institute address, Feb. 27, 1860.* V, 327.
Repeated at New Haven, Conn., March 6, 1860. V, 370.

32.—Do the people of the South really entertain fears that a Republican administration would, directly or indirectly, interfere with the slaves, or with them about the slaves? If they do, I wish to assure you, as once a friend, and still, I hope, not an enemy, that there is no cause for such fears. The South would be in no more danger in this respect than it was in the days of Washington.—*To Alexander H. Stephens, Dec. 22, 1860.* VI, 85.

33.—I declare that the maintenance inviolate of the rights of the states, and especially the right of each state to order and control its own domestic institutions according to its own judgment exclusively, is essential to that balance of powers on which the perfection and endurance of our political fabric depends.—*To Duff Green, Dec. 28, 1860.* VI, 88.

34.—I understand a proposed amendment to the Con-

stitution . . . has passed Congress, to the effect that the federal government shall never interfere with the domestic institutions of the states, including that of persons held to service. . . . Holding such a provision to be now implied constitutional law, I have no objection to its being made express and irrevocable.—*First inaugural, March 4, 1861.* VI, 182.

35.—I have neither adopted nor proposed any measure [relative to slavery] which is not consistent with your view, provided you are for the Union.—*To J. C. Conkling, Aug. 26, 1863.* IX, 97.

36.—I do not see how any of us can deny and contradict all we have always said, that Congress has no constitutional power over slavery in the states.—*To group at the capitol, July 4, 1864.* Hay, 205.

See PIERCE, FRANKLIN, falsehood charged against.

Slavery, no man wishes, for himself—Although volume upon volume is written to prove slavery a very good thing, we never hear of a man who wishes to take the good of it by being a slave himself.—*Fragment, July 1, 1854.* II, 184.

2.—I never knew a man who wished to be himself a slave. Consider if you know any good thing, that no man desires for himself.—*Inscription in autograph album, March 22, 1864.* Tracy, 239.

3.—I have always thought that all men should be free; but if any should be slaves, it should be first those who desire it for themselves, and, secondly, those who desire it for others. Whenever I hear anyone arguing for slavery, I feel a strong impulse to see it tried on him personally.—*Speech to Indiana regiment, March 17, 1865.* XI, 56.

Slavery, no place to denounce—You [Democrats opposed to slavery] say it is wrong; but don't you constantly object to anybody else saying so? Do you not constantly argue that this is not the right place to oppose it? You say it must not be opposed in the free states, because slavery is not there; it must not be opposed in the slave states, because it is there; it must not be opposed in politics, because that will make a fuss; it must not be opposed in the pulpit, because it is not religion. Then where is the place to oppose it? —*Debate, Quincy, Oct. 13, 1858.* IV, 332.

2.—Although you [antislavery Democrats] pretend to say so [that slavery is wrong] yourselves, you can find no fit place to deal with it as a wrong. You must not say anything about it in the free states, because it is not there. You must not say anything about it in the slave states, because it is there. You must not say anything about it in the pulpit, because that is religion, and has nothing to do with it. You must not say anything about it in politics, because it will disturb the security of "my place." There is no place to talk about it as being a wrong, although you say yourselves it is a wrong.—*Debate, Alton, Oct. 15, 1858.* V, 62.

3.—They [Democrats opposed to slavery] don't treat it as they do other wrongs—they won't oppose it in the free states, for it isn't there; nor in the slave states, for it is there; don't want it in politics, for it makes agitation; not in the pulpit, for it isn't religion; not in a tract society, for it makes a fuss—there is no place for its discussion. Are they quite consistent in this?—*Speech, Hartford, Conn., March 5, 1860.* V, 334.

4.—There is no place where you [proslavery men] will allow it even to be called wrong. We must not call it wrong in the free states, because it is not there, and we must not call it wrong in the slave states, because it is there; we must not call it wrong in politics, because it is bringing morality into politics, and we must not call it wrong in the pulpit, because that is bringing politics into religion; we must not bring it into the tract society, or any other societies, because those are unsuitable places, and there is no single place, according to you, where this wrong thing can properly be called wrong.—*Speech, New Haven, Conn., March 6, 1860.* V, 354.

Slavery, no return to—*See* EMANCIPATION PROCLAMATION, no retraction of.

Slavery, North and South much alike—*See* SOUTH, no prejudice against.

Slavery, North fights, for principle only—*See* SLAVERY, profit motive in, 3, 5.

Slavery, not imposed by negroes—That the going many thousand miles, seizing a set of savages, bringing them here, and making slaves of them is a necessity imposed on us by them involves a species of logic to which my mind will scarcely assent.—*To C. H. Fisher, Aug. 27, 1860.* VI, 53.

Slavery, not mentioned in Constitution—*See* CONSTITUTION, slavery not mentioned in.

Slavery, Ohio and Kentucky in contrast—A portion of Kentucky, by reason of the course of the Ohio, is further north than this portion of Ohio in which we now stand. Kentucky is entirely covered with slavery; Ohio is entirely free from it. What made that difference? Was it the climate? No! A portion of Kentucky was further north than this portion of Ohio. Was it soil? No! There is nothing in the soil of the one more favorable to slave labor than the other. It was not climate or soil that caused one side of the line to be entirely covered with slavery and the other side free

of it. What was it? Study it over. Tell us, if you can, in all the range of conjecture, if there be anything you can conceive of that made that difference other than that there was no law of any sort keeping it out of Kentucky, while the Ordinance of '87 kept it out of Ohio.—*Speech, Cincinnati, Sept. 17 1859.* V, 222.

Slavery, party attitudes compared—The Republicans inculcate, with whatever of ability they can, that the negro is a man, that his bondage is cruelly wrong, and that the field of his oppression ought not to be enlarged. The Democrats deny his manhood; deny, or dwarf to insignificance, the wrong of his bondage; so far as possible, crush all sympathy for him, and cultivate and excite hatred and disgust against him; compliment themselves as Union savers for doing so; and call the indefinite outspreading of his bondage "a sacred right of self-government."—*Speech, Springfield, June 26, 1857.* Lapsley II, 306.

2.—The difference between the Republican and Democratic parties on the leading issues of the [senatorial] contest, as I understand it, is that the former consider slavery a moral, social and political wrong, while the latter do not consider it either a moral, social or a political wrong; and the action of each, as respects the growth of the country and the expansion of our population is squared to meet these views.—*Speech, Edwardsville, Sept. 13, 1858.* XI, 108.

3.—They [Republicans] will oppose, in all its length and breadth, the modern Democratic idea, that slavery is as good as freedom, and ought to have room for expansion all over the continent, if people can be found to carry it.—*Speech, Edwardsville, Sept. 13, 1858.* XI, 109.

4.—From this difference of sentiment—the belief on the part of one that the institution [slavery] is wrong, and a policy springing from that belief which looks to the arrest of the enlargement of that wrong; and this other sentiment, that it is no wrong, and a policy sprung from that sentiment which will tolerate no idea of preventing that wrong from growing larger, and looks to there never being an end of it through all the existence of things—arises the real difference between Judge Douglas and his friends on the one hand, and the Republicans on the other.—*Debate, Galesburg, Oct. 7, 1858.* IV, 275.

5.—The Democracy of today hold the liberty of one man to be absolutely nothing, when in conflict with another man's right of property; Republicans, on the contrary, are for both the man and the dollar, but in case of conflict the man before the dollar.—*To H. L. Pierce and others, April 6, 1859.* V, 125.

6.—You [Democrats] say we [Republicans] have made the question [slavery] more prominent than heretofore. We deny it. It is more prominent, but we did not make it so. Despite of us, you would have a change of policy; we resist the change, and, in the struggle, the greater prominence is given to the question. Who is responsible for that, you or we? If you would have the question reduced to its old proportions, go back to the old policy. That will effect it.—*Speech, Leavenworth, Kan., Dec. 3, 1859.* Hertz II, 235.

See JEFFERSON, THOMAS, supporters and opponents of, trade creeds.

See REPUBLICAN PARTY, differences between, and Douglas.

See SLAVERY, Democratic policy toward.

See SLAVERY, Republican policy toward.

Slavery, payment for loss of slaves—The executive will in due time recommend that all citizens . . . who have remained loyal . . . throughout the rebellion . . . be compensated for all losses by acts of the United States, including the loss of slaves—*Proclamation, Sept. 22, 1862.* VIII, 40.

Slavery, peace when?—In my opinion, it [slavery] will not cease until a crisis has been reached and passed.—*Speech, Springfield, June 16, 1858.* III, 1.
Repeated at Chicago, July 10, 1858. III, 30.
Repeated at Springfield, July 17, 1858. III, 172.
Repeated at Clinton, Sept. 8, 1858. III, 351.
Repeated at Alton, Oct. 15, 1858. V, 44.
2.—When the public mind shall rest in that belief [that slavery is in course of ultimate extinction] we shall have peace on the slavery question.—*Speech, Springfield, July 17, 1858.* III, 173.
3.—I think the public mind will never rest till the power of Congress to restrict the spread of it [slavery] shall again be acknowledged and exercised on the one hand, or, on the other, all resistance be entirely crushed out.—*Speech, Springfield, July 17, 1858.* III, 174.
4.—I say, and I have said, that I believe we shall not have peace upon the question until the opponents of slavery arrest the further spread of it, and place it where the public mind shall rest in the belief that it is in the course of ultimate extinction; or, on the other hand, that its advocates will push it forward until it shall become alike lawful in all the states, old as well as new, North as well as South.—*Debate, Ottawa, Aug. 21, 1858.* III, 233.
5.—If [slavery were] placed in the former attitude we should have peace.—*Speech, Carlinville, Aug. 31, 1858.* Angle, 189.
6.—Whenever it [slavery] has been limited to its pres-

ent bounds, and there has been no effort to spread it, there has been peace. All the trouble and convulsion has proceeded from efforts to spread it over more territory.—*Debate, Jonesboro, Sept. 15, 1858.* IV, 40.
7.—I appeal to this audience—very few of whom are my political friends—as national men, whether we have reason to expect that the agitation in regard to this subject [slavery] will cease while the causes that tend to reproduce agitation are actively at work?—*Debate, Jonesboro, Sept. 15, 1858.* IV, 40.
8.—What right have we then to hope that the trouble will cease, that the agitation [over slavery] will come to an end; until it shall either be placed back where it originally stood, and where the fathers originally placed it, or, on the other hand, until it shall entirely master all opposition.—*Debate, Jonesboro, Sept. 15, 1858.* IV, 41.
9.—From the adoption of the Constitution down to 1820 is the precise period in our history when we had comparative peace upon this [slavery] question. . . . This was the precise period of time in which our fathers adopted, and during which they followed, a policy restricting the spread of slavery, and the whole Union was acquiescing in it. The whole country looked forward to the ultimate extinction of the institution. It was when a policy had been adopted and was prevailing, which led all just and right-minded men to suppose that slavery was gradually coming to an end, and that they might be quiet about it, watching it as it expired.—*Speech, Columbus, Ohio, Sept. 16, 1859.* V, 152.
10.—Have we ever had any peace on this slavery question? When are we to have peace upon it, if it is kept in the position it now occupies? How are we ever to have peace upon it? . . . To be sure, if we will stop and allow Judge Douglas and his friends to march on in their present career until they plant the institution all over the nation, here and wherever else our flag waves, and we acquiesce in it, there will be peace. But let me ask Judge Douglas how he is going to get the people to do that? They have been wrangling over this question for at least 40 years.—*Debate, Charleston, Sept. 18, 1858.* IV, 186.
11.—There is no way of putting an end to the slavery agitation amongst us but to put it back where our fathers placed it; no way but to keep it out of our new territories—to restrict it forever to the old states where it now exists. Then the public mind will rest in the belief that it is in the course of ultimate extinction. That is one way of putting a stop to the slavery agitation. The other way is for us to surrender and let Judge Douglas and his friends have their way and plant slavery over all the states—cease speaking of it as in any way wrong—regard slavery as one

of the common matters of property, and speak of negroes as we do of our horses and cattle.—*Debate, Charleston, Sept. 18, 1858.   IV, 188.*

12.—Whenever we can get the question distinctly stated,—can get all these men who believe that slavery is in some of these respects wrong to stand and act with us in treating it as a wrong,—then, and not till then, I think, will we in some way come to an end of this slavery agitation.—*Debate, Quincy, Oct. 13, 1858. IV, 334.*

13.—We have sometimes had peace, but when was it? It was when the institution of slavery remained quiet where it was. We have had difficulty and turmoil whenever it has made a struggle to spread itself where it was not. I ask, then, if experience does not speak in thunder tones, telling us that the policy which has given peace to the country heretofore, being returned to, gives the greatest promise of peace again.—*Debate, Alton, Oct. 15, 1858.   V, 54.*

14.—I have intimated that I thought the agitation [over slavery] would not cease until a crisis should have been reached and passed. I have stated in what way I thought it would be reached and passed. I have said it might go one way or the other. We might, by arresting the further spread of it, and placing it where the fathers originally placed it, put it where the public mind should rest in the belief that it was in the course of ultimate extinction. Thus the agitation may cease. It may be pushed forward until it shall become alike lawful in all the states, old as well as new, North as well as South.—*Debate, Alton, Oct. 15, 1858.   V, 47.*

15.—Have we had any peace upon this [slavery] springing from any other basis [than that slavery was thought on its way to extinction]? I maintain that we have not.—*Speech, Rushville, Oct. 20, 1859.   Hertz II, 730.*

16.—If you [men of the South] would have the peace of the old times, readopt the precepts and policies of the old times.—*Cooper Institute address, New York, Feb. 27, 1860.   V, 314.*

See SLAVERY, policy of the Fathers.

See SLAVERY, toward ultimate extinction.

Slavery, peaceful extinction of, not in sight—You spoke of the "peaceful extinction of slavery," and used other expressions indicating your belief that the thing was at some time to have an end. Since then [the time of Robertson's speech] we have had 36 years of experience; and this experience has demonstrated, I think, that there is no peaceful extinction of slavery in prospect for us. . . . That spirit which desired the peaceful extinction of slavery has itself become extinct with the occasion and the men of the Revolution.—*To George Robertson, Aug. 15, 1855. II, 279.*

2.—I do not mean to say that when it takes a turn toward ultimate extinction it will be in a day, nor a year, nor in two years. I do not suppose that in the most peaceful way ultimate extinction [of slavery] would occur in less than a hundred years at least; but that it will occur in the best way for both races, in God's good time, I have no doubt.—*Debate, Charleston, Oct. 18, 1858.   IV, 188.*

Slavery, perpetuation of—[I call attention to] additional evidence of the change of sentiment upon this question of slavery in the direction of making it perpetual and national. I argue now as I did before, that there is such a tendency, and I am backed not merely by the facts, but by the open confession of the slave states.—*Speech, Springfield, July 17, 1858.   III, 176.*

2.—My main object [in Springfield speech] was to show . . . to the people of this country, what I believed was the truth—that there was a tendency, if not a conspiracy, among those who have engineered this slavery question for the last four or five years, to make slavery perpetual and universal in this nation. —*Debate, Ottawa, Aug. 21, 1858.   III, 236.*

3.—At the introduction of the Nebraska policy, we [Republicans of Illinois] believed there was a new era being introduced in the history of the Republic, which tended to the spread and perpetuation of slavery. But in our opposition to that measure we did not agree with one another in everything. The people in the north end of the state were for stronger measures of opposition than we of the central and southern portions of the state, but we were all opposed to the Nebraska doctrine. We had that one feeling and that one sentiment in common.—*Debate, Freeport, Aug. 27, 1858.   III, 336.*

4.—These men desire that slavery shall be perpetual and that we should not foster all lawful moves toward emancipation, and to gain their end they will endeavor to impress upon the public mind that the negro is not human, and even upon his own soil he has no rights which white men are bound to respect. —*Speech, Carlinville, Aug. 31, 1858.   Angle, 192.*

5.—If Douglas can make you believe that slavery is a sacred right; if we are to swallow Dred Scottism that the right of property in negroes is not confined to those states where it is established by local law; if by special sophisms he can make you believe that no nation except the English are born equal and are entitled to life, liberty, and the pursuit of happiness, upon their own soil, or when they are not constitutionally divested of the God-given rights to enjoy the fruits of their own labor, then may we truly despair of the universality of freedom, or the efficacy of those sacred principles enunciated by our fathers—and give in our adhesion to the perpetuation and unlimited extension of slavery.—*Speech, Carlinville, Aug. 31, 1858.* Angle, 192.

6.—[Preston S.] Brooks, the man who assaulted Senator Sumner on the floor of the Senate, and who was complimented with dinners, and silver pitchers, and gold-headed canes, and a good many other things for that feat, in one of his speeches declared that . . . the framers of our government did not have the knowledge that experience has taught us—that experience and the invention of the cotton-gin have taught us that slavery is a necessity. He insisted, therefore, upon its being changed from the basis upon which the fathers of the government left it to the basis of its perpetuation and nationalization. I insist that this is the difference between Judge Douglas and myself—that Judge Douglas is helping along that change. I insist upon this government being placed where our fathers originally placed it.—*Debate, Jonesboro, Sept. 15, 1858.* IV, 33.

7.—I wish to return to Judge Douglas my profound thanks for his public annunciation here today to be put on record, that his system of policy in regard to the institution of slavery contemplates that it shall last forever.—*Debate, Quincy, Oct. 13, 1858.* IV, 373.

8.—Mr. [Preston S.] Brooks of South Carolina once said, and said truly, that when this government was established, no one expected the institution of slavery to last until this day; and that the men who formed this government were wiser and better than the men of these days; but the men of these days had experience which the fathers had not, and that experience had taught them the invention of the cotton-gin, and this had made the perpetuation of the institution of slavery a necessity in this country.—*Debate, Quincy, Oct. 13, 1858.* IV, 374.

9.—[Preston S.] Brooks of South Carolina once declared that when this Constitution was framed, its framers did not look to the institution [slavery] existing until this day. When he said this, I think he stated a fact that is fully borne out by the history of the times. But he also said that they were better and wiser men than the men of these days; yet the men of these days had experience which they did not, and by the invention of the cotton-gin it became a necessity in this country that slavery should be perpetual. I now say that, willingly or unwillingly, purposely or without purpose, Judge Douglas has been the most prominent instrument in changing the position of the institution of slavery—which the fathers of the government expected to come to an end ere this,—and putting it upon Brooks's cotton basis—placing it where he openly confesses he has no desire there shall ever be an end of it.—*Debate, Alton, Oct. 15, 1858.* V, 66.

10.—I suppose it [slavery] may long exist; and perhaps the best way for it to come to an end peaceably is for it to exist for a length of time. But I say the spread and strengthening and perpetuation of it is an entirely different proposition. There we should in every way resist it as a wrong, treating it as a wrong, with the fixed idea that it must and will come to an end.—*Speech, Chicago, March 1, 1859.* V, 122.

11.—Judge Douglas is preparing the public mind for you in Kentucky, to make perpetual that good thing [slavery] in your estimation, about which you and I differ.—*Speech, Cincinnati, Sept. 17, 1859.* V, 201.

See SLAVERY, nationalization of.

See SLAVERY, toward ultimate extinction, 13.

Slavery, perplexing question—*See* UNION, slavery and, perplexing question.

Slavery, personal reaction to—If I ever get a chance to hit that thing, I'll hit it hard!—*To group at New Orleans, May, 1831.* Herndon, 67.

2.—I have been thinking about what you said in your speech. I reckon you are right. We have got to deal with this slavery question, and got to give much more attention to it hereafter than we have been doing.—*To William H. Seward, Oct. 15, 1848.* Tarbell II, 18.

3.—I think I would not hold one in slavery at any rate, yet the point is not clear enough for me to denounce people on.—*Speech, Peoria, Oct. 16, 1854.* II, 207.
Repeated at Ottawa, Aug. 21, 1858. III, 227.

4.—I suppose my opposition to the principle of slavery is as strong as that of any member of the Republican party; but I have also supposed that the extent to which I feel authorized to carry that opposition, practically, was not at all satisfactory to that party.—*To I. Codding, Nov. 27, 1854.* II, 264.

5.—You know I dislike slavery and you fully admit the abstract wrong of it.—*To Joshua F. Speed, Aug. 24, 1855.* II, 281.

6.—I confess I hate to see the poor creatures [slaves] hunted down and caught and carried back to their stripes and unrequited toil; but I bite my lips and keep quiet.—*To Joshua F. Speed, Aug. 24, 1855.* II, 282.

7.—In 1841 you and I together had a tedious low-water trip on a steamboat from Louisville to St. Louis. You remember, as I well do, that from Louisville to the mouth of the Ohio there were on board ten or a dozen slaves shackled together with irons. That sight was a continued torment to me, and I see something like it every time I touch the Ohio or any other slave border. It is not fair for you to assume that I have no interest in a thing which has, and continually exercises, the power of making me miserable.—*To Joshua F. Speed, Aug. 24, 1855.* II, 282.

8.—I have always hated slavery, I think, as much as any Abolitionist—I have been an old-line Whig—I have always hated it, but I have always been quiet about it until this new era of the introduction of the Nebraska bill began.—*Speech, Chicago, July 10, 1858.* III, 33.

9.—Nonsense! Wolves devouring lambs, not because it is good for their greedy maws, but because it is good for the lambs!—*Fragment, Oct. 1, 1858.* Basler, 478.

10.—I have never understood that the Presidency conferred upon me an unrestricted right to act officially upon this judgment and feeling [that slavery is wrong]. . . . I understood, too, that in ordinary civil administration this oath even forbade me to practically indulge my primary abstract judgment on the moral question of slavery. I had publicly declared this many times, and in many ways. And I aver that, to this day, I have done no official act in mere deference to my abstract judgment and feeling on slavery. —*To A. G. Hodges, April 4, 1864.* X, 64.

11.—I am naturally anti-slavery.—*To A. G. Hodges, April 4, 1864.* X, 65.

Slavery, philosophy essential to settlement of—Whenever this question shall be settled, it must be settled on some philosophical basis. No policy that does not rest upon philosophical public opinion can be permanently maintained.—*Speech, New Haven, Conn., March 6, 1860.* V, 346.

Slavery, policy of the Fathers—Senator Douglas has sought to bring to his aid [in defending Kansas-Nebraska Act] the opinions and examples of our Revolutionary fathers. . . . He shows that when it was in contemplation for the colonies to . . . set up a new government for themselves, several of the states instructed their delegates to go for the measure, provided each state should be allowed to regulate its domestic concerns in its own way. . . . This was right; I see nothing objectionable in it. I also think it probable that it had some reference to the existence of slavery among them. . . . But had it any reference to the carrying of slavery into new countries? That is the question, and we will let the fathers themselves answer it. This same generation of men, and mostly the same individuals of the generation . . .

passed the Ordinance of '87, declaring that slavery should never go to the Northwest Territory. I have no doubt Judge Douglas thinks they were very inconsistent in this.—*Speech, Peoria, Oct. 16, 1854.* II, 229.

2.—The argument of "necessity" was the only argument they [Fathers of the Republic] ever admitted in favor of slavery; and so far, and so far only, as it carried them did they ever go. They found the institution existing among us, which they could not help, and they cast blame upon the British king for having permitted its introduction.—*Speech, Peoria, Oct. 16, 1854.* II, 244.

3.—Less than this our fathers could not do, and more they would not do. Necessity drove them so far, and further they would not go. But this is not all. The earliest Congress under the Constitution took the same view of slavery. They hedged and hemmed it in to the narrowest limits of necessity.—*Speech, Peoria, Oct. 16, 1854.* II, 245.

4.—The plain, unmistakable spirit of that age [of the Fathers] toward slavery was hostility to the principle and toleration only by necessity.—*Speech, Peoria, Oct. 16, 1854.* II, 246.

5.—Let us turn slavery from its claims of "moral right" back upon its existing legal rights, and its arguments of "necessity."—Let us return it to the position our fathers gave it; and there let it rest in peace. —*Speech, Peoria, Oct. 16, 1854.* Basler, 315.

6.—But they [the Fathers] did not agree to introduce slavery in regions where it did not previously exist. On the contrary, they said by their example and teachings that they did not deem it expedient—did not consider it right—to do so; and it is wise and right to do just as they did about it. And that is what we propose—not to interfere with slavery where it exists—we have never tried to do it—and to give them a reasonable and efficient fugitive-slave law. It was part of the bargain, and I'm for living up to it; but I go no further; I'm not bound to do more, and I won't agree any further.—*Speech, Bloomington, May 29, 1856.* Lapsley II, 261.

7.—Let us, then, turn this government back into the channels in which the framers of the Constitution placed it.—*Speech, Chicago, July 10, 1858.* III, 51.

8.—The institution of slavery ought to be placed in the very attitude where the framers of this government placed it and left it.—*Speech, Springfield, July 17, 1858.* III, 172.

9.—When our government was established, we had the institution of slavery among us. We were in a certain sense compelled to tolerate its existence. It was a sort of necessity.—*Speech, Springfield, July 17, 1858.* III, 186.

10.—The framers of the Constitution found the institution of slavery amongst their other institutions at the time. They found that by an effort to eradicate it, they might lose much of what they had already gained. They were obliged to bow to the necessity. They gave power to Congress to abolish the slave trade at the end of twenty years. They also prohibited slavery in the territories where it did not exist. They did what they could and yielded to necessity for the rest. I also yield to all which follows from that necessity.—*Speech, Springfield, July 17, 1858. III, 186.*

11.—I account for it [the fact that the nation has been part slave and part free for 82 years] by looking at the position in which our fathers originally placed it [slavery]. . . . The public mind did rest in the belief that it was in the course of ultimate extinction.—*Debate, Ottawa, Aug. 21, 1858.   III, 233.*

12.—I am fighting it [slavery] upon these "original principles" [those of the founders of the Republic]—fighting it in the Jeffersonian, Washingtonian and Madisonian fashion.—*Debate, Ottawa, Aug. 21, 1858. III, 236.*

13.—Our fathers restricted its spread and stopped the importation of negroes, with the hope that it would remain in a dormant condition till the people saw fit to emancipate the negroes.—*Speech, Carlinville, Aug. 31, 1858.   Angle, 189.*

14.—He [Douglas] says, "why can't this Union endure permanently half slave and half free? . . ." I say when this government was first established, it was the policy of its founders to prohibit the spread of slavery into the new territory of the United States, where it had not existed. But Judge Douglas and his friends have broken up that policy, and placed it upon a new basis by which it is to become national and perpetual.—*Debate, Jonesboro, Sept. 15, 1858. IV, 32.*

15.—All I have asked or desired anywhere is that it [slavery] shall be placed back again upon the basis that the fathers of our government originally placed it upon. I have no doubt that it would become extinct, for all time to come, if we but readopted the policy of the fathers of restricting it to the limits it has already covered—restricting it from new territories.—*Debate, Jonesboro, Sept. 15, 1858. IV, 32.*

16.—When he [Douglas] asks me why we cannot get along with it [slavery] in the attitude where our fathers placed it, he had better clear up the evidences that he has himself changed it from that basis; that he has himself been chiefly instrumental in changing the policy of the fathers.—*Debate, Jonesboro, Sept. 15, 1858.   IV, 34.*

17.—All I ask of you, Judge Douglas, is to stick to the proposition that the men of the Revolution understood this subject [slavery] better than we do now; and, with that better understanding, they acted better than you are trying to act now.—*Speech, Columbus, Ohio, Sept. 16, 1859.   V, 173.*

18.—There is no way of putting an end to the slavery agitation amongst us but to put it back upon the basis where our fathers placed it, no way but to keep it out of new territories—to restrict it forever to the old states where it now exists. Then the public mind will rest in the belief that it is in course of ultimate extinction. That is the one way of putting a stop to the slavery agitation.—*Debate, Charleston, Sept. 18, 1858.   IV, 188.*

19.—They [Republicans] will, if possible, restore the government to the policy of the fathers—the policy of preserving the new territories from the baneful influence of human bondage, as the northwestern territories were sought to be preserved by the Ordinance of 1787, and the compromise act of 1820.—*Speech, Edwardsville, Sept. 13, 1858.   XI, 109.*

20.—The susceptible young hear lessons from him [Douglas] such as their fathers never heard when they were young.—*Notes, Oct. 1, 1858.   IV, 223.*

21.—I insist that our fathers did not make this nation half slave and half free, or part slave and part free [as argued by Douglas]. I insist that they found the institution of slavery existing here. They did not make it so, but they left it so because they knew of no way to get rid of it at that time. . . . More than that; when the fathers of the government cut off the source of slavery by the abolition of the slave trade, and adopted a system of restricting it from the new territories where it had not existed, I maintain that they placed it where they understood, and all sensible men understood, it was in the course of ultimate extinction. . . . It is precisely all I ask of him [Douglas] in relation to the institution of slavery, that it shall be placed upon the basis that our fathers placed it upon.—*Debate, Quincy, Oct. 13, 1858.   IV, 373.*

22.—Judge Douglas could not let it [slavery] stand upon the basis where our fathers placed it, but removed it, and put it upon the cotton-gin basis.—*Debate, Quincy, Oct. 13, 1858.   IV, 374.*

23.—Another form of his [Douglas's] question is, "Why can't we let it [slavery] stand as our fathers placed it?" That is the exact difficulty between us. I say that Judge Douglas and his friends have changed it from the position in which our fathers originally placed it. I say, in the way our fathers originally left the slavery question, the institution was in the course of ultimate extinction.—*Debate, Jonesboro, Sept. 15, 1858.   IV, 32.*

24.—I insist upon this government being placed

where our fathers originally placed it.—*Debate, Jonesboro, Sept. 15, 1858.* IV, 34.

25.—I entertain the opinion, upon evidence sufficient to my mind, that the fathers of this government placed that institution [slavery] where the public mind did rest in the belief that it was in the course of ultimate extinction. Let me ask why they made provision that the source of slavery—the African slave trade—should be cut off at the end of twenty years? Why did they make provision that in all the new territory we owned at that time, slavery should be forever inhibited? Why stop its spread in one direction and cut off its source in another, if they did not look to its being placed in the course of ultimate extinction?—*Debate, Alton, Oct. 15, 1858.* V, 47.

26.—The fathers of the government expected and intended the institution of slavery to come to an end. They expected and intended that it should be in the course of ultimate extinction. And when I say that I desire to see the further spread of it arrested, I only say I desire to see that done which the fathers have first done. When I say I desire to see it placed where the public mind will rest in the belief that it is in the course of ultimate extinction, I only say I desire to see it where they placed it.—*Debate, Alton, Oct. 15, 1858.* V, 49.

27.—When Judge Douglas asks me why we cannot let it [the Union] remain part slave and part free, as the fathers of the government made it, he asks a question based on an assumption which is itself a falsehood; and I turn upon him and ask him the question, when the policy that the fathers of the government adopted in relation to this element among us was the best policy in the world, the only wise policy, the only policy that we can ever safely continue upon, that will ever give us peace unless this dangerous element masters us all and becomes a national institution, I turn upon him and ask him why he could not let it alone?—*Debate, Alton, Oct. 15, 1858.* V, 50.

Repeated at Rushville, Oct. 20, 1859. Hertz II, 730.

28.—It is not true that our fathers, as Judge Douglas assumes, made this government part slave and part free. Understand the sense in which he puts it. He assumes that slavery is a rightful thing within itself—was introduced by the framers of the Constitution. The exact truth is, that they found the institution existing among us, and they left it as they found it. But in making the government they left the institution with many clear marks of disapprobation upon it. They found slavery among them and they left it among them because of the difficulty—the absolute impossibility—of its immediate removal.—*Debate, Alton, Oct. 15, 1858.* V, 50.

Repeated at Rushville, Oct. 20, 1858. Hertz II, 730.

29.—I have proposed nothing more than a return to the policy of the fathers [touching slavery].—*Debate, Alton, Oct 15, 1858.* V, 51.

Repeated at Rushville, Oct. 20, 1858. Hertz II, 730.

30.—There was nothing said in the Constitution in regard to the spread of slavery into the territories. I grant that, but there was something very important said about it by the same generation of men in the adoption of the old Ordinance of 1787.—*Speech, Cincinnati, Sept. 17, 1859.* V, 209.

31.—When you attempt it [dissolution of the Union] you will find that our [Republican] policy is exactly the policy of the men who made the Union. Nothing more and nothing less.—*Speech, Leavenworth, Kan., Dec. 3, 1859.* Angle, 235.

32.—I defy any man to show that any one of them [framers of the Constitution] ever, in his whole life, declared that, in his understanding, any proper division of local from federal authority, or any part of the Constitution, forbade the federal government to control as to slavery in the federal territories.—*Cooper Institute address, New York, Feb. 27, 1860.* V, 307.

33.—If any man . . . sincerely believes that a proper division of local from federal authority, or any part of the Constitution, forbids the federal government to control as to slavery in the federal territories, he is right to say so, and to enforce his position by all truthful evidence and fair argument which he can. But he has no right to mislead others, who have less access to history, and less leisure to study it, into the false belief that our fathers . . . were of the same opinion—thus substituting falsehood and deception for truthful evidence and fair argument.—*Cooper Institute address, New York, Feb. 27, 1860.* V, 308.

34.—As those fathers marked it, so let it again be marked, as an evil not to be extended, but to be tolerated and protected only because of and so far as its actual presence among us makes that toleration and protection a necessity. Let all the guarantees those fathers gave it be not grudgingly, but fully and fairly, maintained. For this Republicans are content, and with this, so far as I know or believe, they will be content.—*Cooper Institute address, New York, Feb. 27, 1860.* V, 309.

35.—It was not we [Republicans] but you [Democrats] who discarded the old policy of the fathers. . . . Would you have that question reduced to its former proportions? Go back to that old policy.—*Cooper Institute address, New York, Feb. 27, 1860.* V, 314.

36.—If we were to form a government anew, in view of the actual presence of slavery, we should find it necessary to frame just such a government as our fathers did; giving to the slaveholder the entire control where the system was established, while we possessed the power to restrain it from going outside those limits.—*Speech, New Haven, Conn., March 6, 1860.* V, 347.

Repeated at Norwich, Conn., March 9, 1860. VI, 4.

37.—From the necessities of the case [if we were to form a government anew] we should be compelled to form just such a government as our blessed fathers gave us; and surely if they have so made it, that adds another reason why we should let slavery alone where it exists.—*Speech, New Haven, Conn., March 6, 1860.* V, 347.

38.—In forming the Constitution they [the fathers] found the slave-trade existing, capital invested in it, fields depending on it for labor, and the whole system resting upon the importation of slave labor. They therefore did not prohibit the slave trade at once, but gave the power to prohibit it after 20 years. . . . Would they have done this had they not thought slavery wrong?—*Speech, New Haven, Conn., March 6, 1860.* V, 355.

39.—It is easy to demonstrate that "our fathers who framed the government under which we live" [Douglas's phrase] looked on slavery as wrong, and so framed it and everything about it as to square with the idea that it was wrong, so far as the necessities arising from its existence permitted.—*Speech, New Haven, Conn., March 6, 1860.* V, 355.

40.—The same men, the framers of the Constitution, cut off the supply and prohibited the spread of slavery; and both acts show conclusively that they considered that the thing was wrong.—*Speech, New Haven, Conn., March 6, 1860.* V, 356.

See SLAVERY, South not united on substitute policy.

See SLAVERY, toward ultimate extinction.

Slavery, positive law required for—In the Somerset case, decided nearly a century ago, the great Lord Mansfield held that slavery was of such a nature that it must take its rise in positive—as distinguished from natural—law; and that in no country or age could it be traced back to any other source. Will some one please tell me where is the positive law that established slavery in Kansas?—*Speech, Bloomington, May 29, 1856.* Lapsley II, 260.

See TERRITORIES, positive law needed to keep slavery out.

Slavery, principle for new societies—In legislating for new countries where it [slavery] does not exist, there is no just rule other than that of moral and abstract right.—*Debate, Galesburg, Oct. 1, 1858.* IV, 267.

2.—The principle [relating to slavery] upon which I have insisted in this canvass is in relation to laying the foundations of new societies.—*Debate, Alton, Oct. 15, 1858.* V, 43.

3.—In our new free territories a state of nature does exist. In them Congress lays the foundations of society; and, in laying those foundations, I say, with Mr. Clay, it is desirable that the declaration of the equality of all men shall be kept in view, as a great fundamental principle; and that Congress, which lays the foundations of society, should, like Mr. Clay, be strongly opposed to the incorporation of slavery among its elements.—*To J. N. Brown, Oct. 18, 1858.* V, 88.

See SLAVERY, extension of, opposed, 31.

Slavery, profit motive in—And you must recollect that the slave property is worth a billion dollars; while free-state men must work [against slavery] for sentiment alone.—*Speech, Bloomington, May 29, 1856.* Lapsley II, 271.

2.—Slavery is looked upon by men in the light of dollars and cents. The estimated worth of the slaves of the South is $1,000,000,000, and in a very few years, if the institution shall be admitted into the territories, they will have increased 50 per-cent in value.—*Speech, Kalamazoo, Mich., Aug. 27, 1856.* Stern, 406.

3.—[Why can't slavery restrictionists get votes in the slave states?] It is not because one side of the question . . . is more sectional than the other, nor because of any difference in the mental or moral structure of the people North and South. It is because in that question the people of the South have an immediate, palpable and immensely great pecuniary interest, while with the people of the North it is merely an abstract question of moral right, with only slight and remote pecuniary interest added.—*Fragment, Oct. 1, 1856.* II, 303.

4.—The slaves of the South, at a moderate estimate, are worth $1,000,000,000. Let it be permanently settled that this property may extend to new territory without restraint, and it greatly enhances, perhaps quite doubles, its value at once. This immense, palpable pecuniary interest on the question of extending slavery unites the Southern people as one man. But it cannot be demonstrated that the North will gain a dollar by restricting it.—*Fragment, Oct. 1, 1856.* II, 303.

5.—Moral principle is all, or nearly all, that unites us of the North [against slavery extension]. Pity 'tis, it is so, but this is a looser bond than pecuniary interest. Right here is the plain cause of their perfect union and our want of it.—*Fragment, Oct. 1, 1856.* II, 304.

6.—The plainest print cannot be read through a gold

eagle; and it will ever be hard to find many men who will send a slave to Liberia, and pay his passage, while they can send him to a new country—Kansas, for instance—and sell him for $1500, and the rise.—*Speech, Springfield, June 27, 1857.* II, 338.

7.—One sixth, and a little more, of the population of the United States, are slaves, looked upon as property, and nothing but property. The cash value of these slaves, at a moderate estimate, is $2,000,000,000. This amount of property value has a vast influence on the minds of its owners, very naturally. The same amount of property would have an equal influence upon us if owned in the North. What lessens the value of property is opposed; what enhances its value is favored.—*Speech, Hartford, Conn., March 5, 1860.* V, 330.

8.—About one sixth of the whole population of the United States are slaves. The owners of those slaves consider them property. The effect upon the minds of the owners is that of property and nothing else; it induces them to insist upon all that will favorably affect its value, to demand laws and institutions and a public policy that shall increase and secure its value, and make it durable, lasting, and universal.—*Speech, New Haven, Conn., March 6, 1860.* V, 343. Repeated at Norwich, Conn., March 9, 1860. VI, 2.

9.—The dissenting minister who argued with one of the established church was always met by the reply, "I can't see it so." He opened the Bible and pointed him to a passage, but the orthodox minister replied, "I can't see it so." Then he showed him a single word —"Can you see that?" "Yes, I see it," was the reply. The dissenter laid a guinea over the word, and asked, "Do you see it now?" So here. Whether the owners of this species of property [slavery] do really see it as it is, it is not for me to say; but if they do, they see it as it is through two billions of dollars, and that is a pretty thick coating. Certain it is that they do not see it as we see it. Certain it is that this two thousand million of dollars invested in this species of property is all so concentrated that the mind can grasp it at once. This immense pecuniary interest has its influence upon their minds.—*Speech, New Haven, Conn., March 6, 1860.* V, 344.

Slavery, questions Constitution does not answer— Shall fugitives from labor be surrendered by national or by state authority? The Constitution does not expressly say. May Congress prohibit slavery in the territories? The Constitution does not expressly say. Must Congress protect slavery in the territories? The Constitution does not expressly say. From questions of this class spring all our constitutional controversies, and we divide upon them into majorities and minorities.—*First inaugural, March 4, 1861.* VI, 178.

Slavery, radical opponents of—*See* ABOLITION, radical advocates of, receive execration.

Slavery, "reptile"—Let us draw a cordon, so to speak, around the slave states, and the hateful institution, like a reptile poisoning itself, will perish by its own infamy.—*Speech, Bloomington, May 29, 1856.* Lapsley II, 273.

2.—Turn it whatever way you will—whether it come from the mouth of a king, an excuse for enslaving the people of his country, or from the mouths of men of one race as a reason for enslaving the men of another, it is all the same old serpent.—*Speech, Chicago, July 10, 1858.* III, 49.

3.—[Douglas said] we were just at the end of the slavery agitation. The last tip of the last joint of the old serpent's tail was just drawing out of view.— *Debate, Alton, Oct. 15, 1858.* V, 46.

4.—If I find a venomous snake lying on the open prairie, I seize the first stick and kill him at once; but if that snake is in bed with my children, I must be more cautious; I shall, in striking the snake, also strike the children, or arouse the reptile to bite the children. Slavery is the venomous snake in bed with the children. But if the question is whether to kill it on the prairie or put it in bed with the children, I am inclined to think we'd kill it.—*Speech, Hartford, Conn., March 5, 1860.* V, 333.

5.—If I saw a venomous snake crawling in the road, any man would say I might seize the nearest stick and kill it; but if I found that snake in bed with my children, that would be another question. I might hurt the children more than the snake, and it might bite them. Much more, if I found it in bed with my neighbor's children, and I had bound myself by a solemn compact not to meddle with his children under any circumstances, it would become me to let that particular mode of getting rid of the gentleman alone. But if there was a bed newly made up, to which the children were to be taken, and it was proposed to take a batch of young snakes and put them there with them, I take it no man would say there was any question how I ought to decide. That is just the case. The new territories are the newly made bed to which our children are to go, and it lies with the nation to say whether they shall have snakes mixed up with them or not. It does not seem as if there could be much hesitation what our policy should be.—*Speech, New Haven, Conn., March 6, 1860.* V, 347.

6.—I want you to have a clean bed and no snakes in it!—*Speech, New Haven, Conn., March 6, 1860.* V, 362.

Slavery, Republican policy toward—I think the Republican party is made up of those who, as far as they can peaceably, will oppose the extension of slavery, and who will hope for its ultimate extinction. —*Speech, Chicago, July 10, 1858.* III, 44.

2.—The Republican party . . . hold that this government was instituted to secure the blessings of freedom, and that slavery is an unqualified evil to the negro, to the white man, to the soil, and to the state.— *Speech, Edwardsville, Sept. 13, 1858.* XI, 108.

3.—Republicans . . . think slavery is wrong; and that, like every other wrong which some men will commit if left alone, it ought to be prohibited by law. They consider it not only morally wrong, but a "deadly poison" in a government like ours, professedly based on the equality of men.—*Notes, Oct. 1, 1858.* IV, 227.

4.—They [Republicans] believe Congress ought to prohibit slavery wherever it can be done without violation of the Constitution, or of good faith.— *Notes, Oct. 1, 1858.* IV, 229.

5.—The Republican party think it [slavery] wrong— we think it is a moral, a social, a political wrong. We think it is a wrong not confining itself merely to the persons or the states where it exists, but that it is a wrong which in its tendency, to say the least, affects the existence of the whole nation. Because we think it is wrong, we propose a course of policy which shall deal with it as a wrong. We deal with it as with any other wrong, in so far as we can prevent its growing any larger, and so deal with it that in the run of time there may be some promise of an end to it. We have a due regard to the actual presence of it amongst us, and the difficulties of getting rid of it in any satisfactory way, and all the constitutional obligations thrown about it. . . . We have no right at all to disturb it in the states where it exists, and we profess that we have no more inclination to disturb it than we have the right to do it. We go further than that; we don't propose to disturb it where, in one instance, we think the Constitution would permit us. We think the Constitution would permit us to disturb it in the District of Columbia. Still, we do not propose to do that, unless it should be in terms which I don't suppose the nation is very likely soon to agree to—the terms of making emancipation gradual and compensating the unwilling owners. . . . We insist on the policy that shall restrict it [slavery] to its present limits.—*Debate, Quincy, Oct. 13, 1858.* IV, 328.

6.—The sentiment that contemplates the institution of slavery in this country as wrong is the sentiment of the Republican party. It is the sentiment around which all their actions, all their arguments, circle;

from which all their propositions radiate. They look upon it as being a moral, social, and political wrong; and while they contemplate it as such, they nevertheless have due regard for its actual existence among us; and the difficulties of getting rid of it in any satisfactory way, and to all the constitutional obligations thrown about it. Yet having due regard for these, they desire a policy in regard to it that looks to its not creating any more danger. They insist that it, as far as may be, be treated as a wrong, and one of the methods of treating it as a wrong is to make provision that it shall grow no larger. They also desire a policy that looks to a peaceful end of slavery some time, as being a wrong.—*Debate, Alton, Oct. 15, 1858.* V, 59.

7.—The Republican principle, the profound central truth that slavery is wrong and ought to be dealt with as a wrong,—though we are always to remember the fact of its actual existence amongst us and faithfully observe all the constitutional guarantees,—the unalterable principle never for a moment to be lost sight of, that it is a wrong, and ought to be dealt with as such, cannot advance at all upon Judge Douglas's ground. . . . The proposition now in our minds that this thing is wrong being once driven out and surrendered, then the institution of slavery necessarily becomes national.—*Speech, Chicago, March 1, 1859.* V, 119.

8.—. . . the object of the Republican organization— the preventing of the spread and nationalization of slavery.—*To M. W. Delahay, May 14, 1859.* V, 128.

9.—The Republican party . . . believes that there is a great danger of the institution of slavery being spread out and extended, until it is ultimately made alike lawful in all the states of this Union; so believing, to prevent that incidental and ultimate consummation is the original and chief purpose of the Republican organization.—*Speech, Columbus, Ohio, Sept. 16, 1859.* V, 147.

10.—We [Republicans] want and must have a national policy in regard to the institution of slavery that acknowledges and deals with that institution as a wrong. . . . Nothing will make you successful but setting up a policy which shall treat the thing as being wrong.—*Speech, Cincinnati, Sept. 17, 1859.* V, 230.

11.—The Republican party believe there is danger that slavery will be further extended, and ultimately made national in the United States; and to prevent this incidental and final consummation, is the purpose of this [Republican] organization.—*Speeches in Kansas, Dec. 1–5, 1859.* V, 260.

12.—Let them [Republicans] then keep constantly in view that the chief object of their organization is to prevent the spread and nationalization of slavery.— *Speeches in Kansas, Dec. 1–5, 1859.* V, 267.

13.—Republicans believe that slavery is wrong; and they insist, and will continue to insist, upon a national policy which recognizes it and deals with it as a wrong. There can be no letting down about this.— *Speeches in Kansas, Dec. 1–5, 1859.* V, 274.

14.—As those fathers marked it [slavery], so let it again be marked, as an evil not to be extended, but to be tolerated and protected only because of, and so far as, its actual presence among us makes that toleration and protection necessary. Let all the guarantees those fathers gave it be not grudgingly, but fully and fairly, maintained. For this Republicans contend, and with this, so far as I know or believe, they will be content.—*Cooper Institute address, New York, Feb. 27, 1860.* V, 309.

15.—In the organization of the Republican party this question of slavery was more important than any other.—*Speech, New Haven, Conn., March 6, 1860.* V, 339.

16.—What we [Republicans] want, and all we want, is to have with us the men who think slavery wrong. —*Speech, New Haven, Conn., March 6, 1860.* V, 353.

See REPUBLICAN PARTY, difference between, and Douglas.

See SLAVERY, party attitudes compared.

See SLAVERY, policy of the fathers.

Slavery, responsibility for—See SLAVERY, joint responsibility for.

Slavery, "sacred right" of—The "sacred right" of self-government is [according to Douglas] grossly violated by it [prohibition of slavery in territories]. We even find some men, who drew their first breath and every other breath of their lives under this very restriction, now live in dread of absolute suffocation, if they should be restricted in this "sacred right" of taking slaves to Nebraska.—*Speech, Peoria, Oct. 16, 1854.* II, 195.

2.—That perfect liberty they sigh for—the liberty of making slaves of other people—Jefferson never thought of, their own fathers never thought of, they never thought of themselves a year ago. How fortunate for them they did not sooner become sensible of their great misery.—*Speech, Peoria, Oct. 16, 1854.* II, 195.

3.—Now it [slavery] is to be transformed into a "sacred right." Nebraska brings it forth, places it on the high road to extension and perpetuity; and with a pat on its back, says to it, "Go and God speed you. . . ." Little by little, but steadily as a man's march

to the grave, we have been giving up the old for the new faith. Near 80 years ago we began by declaring that "all men are created equal"; but now, from that beginning, we have run down to the other declaration, that for some men to enslave others is a "sacred right of self-government." Those principles cannot stand together. They are as opposite as God and Mammon; and whoever holds to the one must despise the other.—*Speech, Peoria, Oct. 16, 1854.* II, 246.

4.—The notable argument of "squatter sovereignty," otherwise called "sacred right of self-government," which latter phrase, though expressive of the only rightful basis of any government, was so perverted in this attempted use of it as to amount to just this: That if any man chooses to enslave another, no third man shall be allowed to object.—*Speech, Springfield, June 16, 1858.* III, 3.

5.—The deceitful cloak of "self-government," wherewith "the sum of all villainies" seeks to protect and adorn itself, must be torn from its hateful carcass.— *Notes for speeches, Oct. 1, 1858.* IV, 235.

See AFRICAN SLAVE TRADE, slavery extension akin to, 3, 14, 15.

See SLAVERY, party attitudes compared, 1.

See SLAVERY, perpetuation of, 5.

Slavery, "second Dred Scott decision"—See DRED SCOTT DECISION, second, forecast.

Slavery, sectional views on, contrasted—In intellectual and physical structure, our southern brethren do not differ from us. They are, like us, subject to passions, and it is only their odious institution of slavery that makes the breach between us.—*Speech, Kalamazoo, Mich., Aug. 27, 1856.* Stern, 402.

2.—We keep up a controversy in regard to it [slavery]. That controversy necessarily springs from difference of opinion, and if we can learn exactly—can reduce to the lowest elements—what that difference of opinion is, we perhaps shall be better prepared for discussing the different systems of policy that we would propose in regard to that disturbing element. I suggest that the difference of opinion, reduced to its lowest terms, is no other than the difference between the men who think slavery a wrong and those who do not think it wrong.—*Debate, Quincy, Oct. 13, 1858.* IV, 327.

3.—The real issue in this controversy—the one pressing upon every mind—is the sentiment on the part of one class that looks upon the institution of slavery as a wrong, and of another class that does not look upon it as a wrong.—*Debate, Alton, Oct. 15, 1858.* V, 59.

4.—The issue between you [Kentuckians] and me, understand, is that I think slavery is wrong, and ought not to be outspread, and you think it is right, and ought to be extended and perpetuated.—*Speech, Cincinnati, Sept. 17, 1859.* V, 196.

5.—Their thinking it [slavery] right and our thinking it wrong is the precise fact upon which depends the whole controversy. Thinking it right, as they [men of the South] do, they are not to blame for desiring its full recognition as being right; but thinking it wrong, as we do, can we yield to them? Can we cast our votes with their view, and against our own? In view of our moral, social and political responsibilities, can we do this?—*Cooper Institute address, New York, Feb. 27, 1860.* V, 326.

Repeated at New Haven, Conn., March 6, 1860. V, 370.

6.—I have spoken of a policy based upon the idea that slavery is wrong, and a policy based upon the idea that it is right. But an effort has been made for a policy that shall treat it as neither right nor wrong. Its central idea is indifference. . . . All recognize this policy, the plausible, sugar-coated name of which is "popular sovereignty."—*Speech, Norwich, Conn., March 9, 1860.* VI, 4.

7.—You think slavery is right and ought to be extended; and we think it is wrong and ought to be restricted. For this neither has any just cause to be angry with the other.—*To John A. Gilmer, Dec. 15, 1860.* VI, 79.

8.—You think slavery is right and ought to be extended, while we think it is wrong and ought to be restricted. That, I suppose, is the rub. It certainly is the only substantial difference between us.—*To Alexander H. Stephens, Dec. 22, 1860.* VI, 86.

9.—One section of our country believes slavery is right and ought to be extended, while the other believes it is wrong and ought not to be extended. This is the only substantial dispute.—*First inaugural, Dec. 3, 1861.* VI, 180.

Repeated in second annual message, Dec. 1, 1862. VIII, 111.

10.—The war has educated our people into abolition, and they deny that slaves can be property. But there are two sides to that question; one is ours, the other the southern side; and those people are just as honest and conscientious in their opinion as we are in ours. They think they have a moral and legal right to their slaves, and until very recently the North has been of the same opinion; for 200 years the whole country has admitted it, and regarded and treated the slaves as property.—*To James R. Gilmore, late May, 1863.* Gilmore, 159.

Slavery, shall government protect temporarily?—Your dispatch, asking in substance whether, in case Missouri shall adopt gradual emancipation, the general government will protect slave-owners in that species of property during the short time it shall be permitted by the state to exist within it, has been received. Desirous as I am that emancipation shall be adopted by Missouri, and believing as I do that gradual can be made better than immediate for both black and white, except when military necessity changes the case, my impulse is to say that such protection would be given. I cannot know exactly what shape an act of emancipation may take. If the period from the initiation to the final end should be comparatively short, and the act should prevent persons being sold during that period into more lasting slavery, the whole would be easier. I do not wish to pledge the general government to the affirmative support of even temporary slavery beyond what can be fairly claimed under the Constitution.—*To Gen. Schofield, June 22, 1863.* VIII, 329.

Slavery, silence will not check—Is that irresistible power [the "endeavor to spread" slavery], which for 50 years has shaken the government and agitated the people, to be stilled and subdued by pretending that it is an exceedingly simple thing, and we ought not to talk about it? If you will get everybody else to stop talking about it, I assure you I will quit before they have half done so.—*Debate, Alton, Oct. 15, 1858.* V, 56.

2.—Where is the philosophy or statesmanship which assumes that you can quiet that disturbing element in our society which has disturbed us for more than half a century? . . . I say, where is the philosophy or statesmanship based on the assumption that we are to quit talking about it, and that the public mind is all at once to cease being agitated by it? Yet this is the policy here in the North that Douglas is advocating— that we are to care nothing about it! I ask you if it is not a false philosophy?—*Debate, Alton, Oct. 15, 1858.* V, 56.

Slavery, slaveholder argues to himself—The slaveholder does not like to be considered a mean fellow for holding that species of property [slaves], and hence he has to struggle within himself, and sets about arguing himself into the belief that slavery is right.—*Speech, New Haven, Conn., March 6, 1860.* V, 343.

Slavery, slaveholders' "sense of justice"—See SLAVERY, why so many free negroes?

See SLAVERY, wrong of, 3.

Slavery, slaves as Confederate soldiers—There is one [aspect of the war on which I have not already expressed my views]—the recent effort of "our erring brethren," sometimes so-called, to employ the slaves in their armies. The great question with them has been, "Will the negro fight for them?" They ought to know better than we, and doubtless do know better than we. I may incidentally remark, that having in my life heard many arguments—or strings of words meant to pass for arguments—intended to show that the negro ought to be a slave—if he shall now really fight to keep himself a slave, it will be a far better argument why he should remain a slave than I have ever heard before. He, perhaps, ought to be a slave if he desires it ardently enough to fight for it. Or, if one out of four will, for his own freedom, fight to keep the other three in slavery, he ought to be a slave for his selfish meanness.—*Speech to Indiana regiment, March 17, 1865.* XI, 55.

2.—There is one thing about the negro's fighting for the rebels which we can know as well as they can, and that is that they cannot at the same time fight in their armies and stay at home and make bread for them. And this being known and remembered, we can have but little concern whether they become soldiers or not. I am rather in favor of the measure, and would at any time, if I could, have loaned them a vote to carry it. We have to reach the bottom of the insurgent resources; and that they employ, or seriously think of employing the slaves as soldiers, gives us glimpses of the bottom.—*Speech to Indiana regiment, March 17, 1865.* XI, 56.

Slavery, slaves as property—He [Douglas] has done all in his power to reduce the whole question of slavery to one of a mere right of property.—*Speech, Springfield, June 16, 1858.* III, 14.

2.—Quite recently in Virginia, a man—the owner of slaves—made a will providing that after his death certain of his slaves should have their freedom if they should so choose, and go to Liberia, rather than remain in slavery. They chose to be liberated. But the persons to whom they would descend as property claimed them as slaves. A suit was instituted, which finally came up to the supreme court of Virginia, and was therein decided against the slaves, upon the ground that a negro cannot make a choice—that they had no legal power to choose—could not perform the condition upon which their freedom depended.—*Speech, Springfield, July 17, 1858.* III, 175.

3.—When he [Douglas] says that slave property and horse and hog property are alike to be allowed to go into the territories, upon the principles of equality, he is reasoning truly if there is no difference be-

tween them as property; but if the one is property, held rightfully, and the other is wrong, there is no equality between the right and wrong.—*Debate, Quincy, Oct. 13, 1858.* IV, 333.

4.—He [Douglas] says that upon the score of equality, slaves should be allowed to go into a new territory like other property. This is strictly logical if there is no difference between it and other property. If it and other property are equal, his argument is strictly logical.—*Debate, Alton, Oct. 15, 1858.* V, 64.

5.—I know that the judge [Douglas] sometimes squints at the argument that in controlling it as other property by unfriendly legislation they may control it to death, as you might in the case of a horse, perhaps feed him so lightly or ride him so much that he would die. But when you come to legislative control, there is something more to be attended to.—*Speech, Columbus, Ohio, Sept. 16, 1859.* V, 176.

6.—I have no doubt, myself, that if the territories should undertake to control slave property as other property—that is, control it in such a way that it would be the most valuable as property, and make it bear its just burdens as property,—really deal with it as property,—the Supreme Court of the United States will say, "God speed you, and amen."—*Speech, Columbus, Ohio, Sept. 16, 1859.* V, 176.

7.—Public opinion at the South regards slaves as property, and insists on treating them like other property.—*Speech, Hartford, Conn., March 5, 1860.* V, 330.

See DRED SCOTT DECISION, analyzed.

See DRED SCOTT DECISION, challenged, 14, 15, 18.

See NEGRO, tendency to dehumanize.

See WAR, enemy property in.

Slavery, slaves forfeit to government—The traitor against the general government forfeits his slave at least as justly as he does any other property, and he forfeits both to the government against which he offends.—*Message to Congress, July 17, 1862.* VII, 282.

Slavery, "social blessing"—Holding as they [men of the South] do that slavery is morally right and socially elevating, they cannot cease to demand a full national recognition of it, as a legal right and social blessing.—*Cooper Institute address, New York, Feb. 27, 1860.* V, 136.
Repeated at New Haven, Conn., March 6, 1860. V, 370.

Slavery, sole threat to Union—This slavery question has been the only one that has ever endangered our republican institutions—the only one that has ever threatened or menaced a dissolution of the Union—that has ever disturbed us in such a way as to make us fear for the perpetuity of our liberty.—*Debate, Galesburg, Oct. 7, 1858.* IV, 294.

2.—. . . the only serious danger that has threatened our institutions.—*Debate, Alton, Oct. 15, 1858.* V, 56.

3.—We believe—nay, we know—that [slavery] is the only thing that ever has threatened the perpetuity of the Union itself. The only thing that has ever menaced the destruction of the government, under which we live, is this very thing.—*Speech, Cincinnati, Sept. 17, 1859.* V, 231.

4.—In its political aspects does anything in any way endanger the perpetuity of this Union but that single thing—slavery?—*Speech, New Haven, Conn., March 6, 1860.* V, 345.

5.—Can any man believe that the way to save the Union is to extend and increase the only thing [slavery] that threatens the Union, and to suffer it to grow bigger and bigger?—*Speech, New Haven, Conn., March 6, 1860.* V, 346.

See CIVIL WAR, slavery cause of.

Slavery, sought not to touch—*See* EMANCIPATION PROCLAMATION, no retraction of, 1.

Slavery, South not content with—How common is the remark now in the slave states, "If we were only clear of our slaves, how much better it would be for us."—*Speech, Peoria, Oct. 16, 1854.* II, 232.

Slavery, South not united on substitute policy—You [men of the South] with one accord reject, and scout, and spit upon, that old policy [of the Fathers], and insist on substituting something new. True, you disagree among yourselves as to what the substitute shall be; you have a considerable variety of new propositions and plans. . . . Some of you are for reviving the foreign slave trade; some for a congressional slave code for the territories; some for Congress forbidding the territories to prohibit slavery within their limits; some for maintaining slavery in the territories through the judiciary; some for the "great principle" that if one man would enslave another, no third man should object, fantastically called "popular sovereignty"; but never a man among you in favor of federal prohibition of slavery in federal territories.—*Cooper Institute address, New York, Feb. 27, 1860.* V, 313.
Repeated at New Haven, Conn., March 6, 1860. V, 366.

Slavery, states may get—*See* DRED SCOTT DECISION, second, forecast.

Slavery, Sugar cane and—*See* CLIMATE, no bar to slavery, 3.

Slavery, Taylor and extension of—*See* WILMOT PROVISO, safe with Taylor.

Slavery, Taylor's death impedes settlement of—I fear the one great question of the day is not now so likely to be partially acquiesced in by the different sections of the Union, as it would have been, could Gen. Taylor have been spared to us. Yet under all the circumstances, trusting to our Maker, and through His wisdom and beneficence, to the great body of our people, we will not despair nor despond.—*Speech, Chicago, July 25, 1850.* Angle, 75.

Slavery, Texas annexation—*See* TEXAS, abolitionist reasoning relative to.

Slavery, theology of—The sum of pro-slavery theology seems to be this: "Slavery is not universally right, nor yet universally wrong; it is better for some people to be slaves; and, in such cases, it is the will of God that they be such." Certainly there is no contending against the will of God; but there is some difficulty in ascertaining and applying it to particular cases. For instance, we will suppose the Rev. Dr. Ross has a slave named Sambo, and the question is, "Is it the will of God that Sambo shall remain a slave, or be set free?" The Almighty gives no audible answer to the question, and his revelation, the Bible, gives none —or at most none but such as admits of a squabble as to its meaning; no one thinks of asking Sambo's opinion on it. So at last it comes to this, that Dr. Ross is to decide the question, and while he considers it, he sits in the shade, with gloves on his hands, and subsists on the bread that Sambo is earning in the burning sun. If he decides that God wills Sambo to continue a slave, he thereby retains his own comfortable position; but if he decides that God wills Sambo to be free, he thereby has to walk out of the shade, throw off his gloves, and delve for his own bread. Will Dr. Ross be actuated by the perfect impartiality which has ever been considered most favorable to correct decisions?—*Notes, Oct. 1, 1858.* IV, 201.

Slavery, "tired of"—They [men of the South] say they are tired of slavery agitation. We think the slaves, and white laboring men, too, have more reason to be tired of slavery than masters have to be tired of agitation about it.—*Speeches in Kansas, Dec. 1–5, 1859.* V, 274.

Slavery, toward ultimate extinction—I believe that wherever efforts to spread slavery into new territory, by whatever means, and into free states themselves by

Supreme Court decisions, shall be fairly headed off, the institution will then be in the course of ultimate extinction.—*To Joseph Medill, June 23, 1858.* Tribune, I, 78.

2.—I did not even say [at Springfield] that I desired that slavery should be put in course of ultimate extinction. I do say so now, however, so there need be no longer any difficulty about that.—*Speech, Chicago, July 10, 1858.* III, 32.

3.—I know that it [the country] has endured 82 years half slave and half free [as declared by Douglas]. . . . I believe it has endured because during all that time, until the introduction of the Nebraska bill, the public mind did rest all the time in the belief that slavery was in course of ultimate extinction. That was what gave us the rest that we had through that period of 82 years; at least, so I believe.—*Speech, Chicago, July 10, 1858.* III, 32.

4.—I always believed that everybody was against it [slavery], and that it was in course of ultimate extinction. . . . The great mass of the nation have rested in the belief. . . . They had reason so to believe.—*Speech, Chicago, July 10, 1858.* III, 33.

5.—The adoption of the Constitution and its attendant history led the people to believe so [that slavery was in course of ultimate extinction] and that such was the belief of the framers of the Constitution itself. Why did those old men, about the time of the adoption of the Constitution, decree that slavery should not go into the new territory, where it had not already gone? Why declare that within twenty years the African slave-trade . . . might be cut off by Congress? . . . Why were all these acts? . . . What were they but a clear indication that the framers of the Constitution intended and expected the ultimate extinction of that institution?—*Speech, Chicago, July 10, 1858.* III, 33.

6.—When I say that I think that the opponents of slavery will resist the further spread of it, and place it where the public mind shall rest in the belief that it is in course of ultimate extinction, I only mean to say that they will place it where the founders of this government originally placed it.—*Speech, Chicago, July 10, 1858.* III, 34.

7.—I think the Republican party is made up of those who, as far as they can peaceably, will oppose the extension of slavery, and who will hope for its ultimate extinction.—*Speech, Chicago, July 10, 1858.* III, 44.

8.—I do wish to see the spread of slavery arrested, and to see it placed where the public mind shall rest in the belief that it is in course of ultimate extinction. —*Speech, Springfield, July 17, 1858.* III, 173.

9.—Mr. [Preston S.] Brooks, of South Carolina, in one of his speeches, when they were presenting him

canes, silver plate, gold pitchers and the like, for assaulting Senator Sumner, distinctly affirmed his opinion that when this Constitution was formed, it was the belief of no man that slavery would last to the present day. He said, what I think, that the framers of our Constitution placed the institution of slavery where the public mind rested in the hope that it was in course of ultimate extinction.—*Speech, Springfield, July 17, 1858.* III, 175.

10.—I believe if we could arrest the spread [of slavery], and place it where Washington, Jefferson and Madison placed it, it would be in the course of ultimate extinction, and the public mind would, as for eighty years past, believe that it was in the course of ultimate extinction. The crisis would be past.—*Debate, Ottawa, Aug. 21, 1858.* III, 234.

11.—They [Republicans] will, if possible, place it where the public mind shall rest in the belief that it is in course of ultimate peaceable extinction in God's good time.—*Speech, Edwardsville, Sept. 13, 1858.* XI, 108.

12.—I have believed—and now believe—the public mind did rest in that belief [that slavery was in course of ultimate extinction] up to the introduction of the Nebraska bill.—*Speech, Springfield, July 17, 1858.* III, 174.

13.—I was glad to express my gratitude at Quincy, and I express it here to Judge Douglas,—that he looks to no end of the institution of slavery. That will help the people to see where the struggle really is. It will hereafter place with us all men who really do wish the wrong may have an end. Whenever we can get rid of the fog which obscures the real question,—when we can get Judge Douglas and his friends to avow a policy looking to its [slavery's] perpetuation—we can get out from among them that class of men and bring them to the side of those who treat it as a wrong. Then there will soon be an end of it, and that end will be its ultimate extinction.—*Debate, Alton, Oct. 1, 1858.* V, 65.

14.—I have said, and I repeat, my wish is that the further spread of it [slavery] may be arrested, and that it may be placed where the public mind shall rest in the belief that it is in the course of ultimate extinction. I have expressed that as my wish. I entertain the opinion upon evidence sufficient to my mind that the fathers of this government placed that institution where the public mind did rest in the belief that it was in the course of ultimate extinction. Let me ask why they made provision that the source of slavery—the African slave trade—should be cut off at the end of twenty years? Why did they make provision that in all the new territory we owned at that time it should be forever prohibited? Why stop its spread in one direction and cut off its source in another, if they did not look to its being placed in the course of ultimate extinction?—*Speech, Rushville, Oct. 20, 1859.* Hertz II, 729.

15.—The only comparative peace we have had with slavery . . . was in the period from the Revolution to 1820, precisely the period through which we were closing out the African slave trade, abolishing slavery in several of the states, and restraining the spread of it into new ones by the Ordinance of '87, precisely the period in which the public mind had reason to rest, and did rest, in the belief that slavery was in course of ultimate extinction.—*Speeches in Kansas, Dec. 1–5, 1859.* V, 263.

See SLAVERY, peace when?

See SLAVERY, policy of the Fathers.

Slavery, ultimately for all of nation or none—*See* "HOUSE DIVIDED AGAINST ITSELF," cannot stand.

Slavery, unavoidable issue—We can no more avoid it [consideration of slavery] than a man can live without eating. It is upon us; it attaches to the body politic as much and as closely as the natural wants attach to our natural bodies.—*Speech, New Haven, Conn., March 6, 1860.* V, 342.

Slavery, violates Declaration of Independence—*See* EQUALITY, basic American principle, 2.

Slavery, violence alone maintains—However much you may argue upon it, and smother it in soft phrases, slavery can only be maintained by force—by violence. . . . Murderous violence is being used now, in order to force slavery into Kansas; for it cannot be done in any other way.—*Speech, Bloomington, May 29, 1856.* Lapsley II, 255.

2.—Can you doubt that, even in spite of the people's will, slavery will triumph through violence, unless that will be made manifest and enforced?—*Speech, Bloomington, May 29, 1856.* Lapsley II, 260.

3.—I believe that, as a result of this moral and physical violence, Kansas will soon apply for admission as a slave state.—*Speech, Bloomington, May 29, 1856.* Lapsley II, 260.

Slavery, violence unnecessary in settlement of—Whenever the issue [of slavery] can be distinctly made, and all extraneous matter thrown out, so that men can fairly see the real difference between the parties, this controversy will soon be settled, and it will be done peaceably, too. There will be no war, no violence. It will be placed again where the wisest

and best men of the world placed it.—*Debate, Alton, Oct. 15, 1858.* V, 66.

Slavery, Virginia court adjudicates a will—*See* SLAVERY, slaves as property, 2.

Slavery, war will end, if continued—*See* CIVIL WAR, will end slavery if continued.

Slavery, way to satisfy South—*See* SOUTH, what will satisfy?

Slavery, white race injured by—In our greedy chase to make profit of the negro, let us beware lest we "cancel and tear in pieces" even the white man's charter of freedom.—*Speech, Peoria, Oct. 16, 1854.* II, 248.
Repeated at Urbana, Oct. 24, 1854. Hertz II, 655.

2.—If the safeguards to liberty are broken down, as is now attempted, when they have made things of all free negroes [as attempted in Kansas], how long, think you, before they will begin to make things of poor white men?—*Speech, Bloomington, May 29, 1856.* Lapsley II, 253.

3.—I held that if that course of argumentation that is made [by Douglas and others] for the purpose of convincing the public mind that we should not care about this [slavery] should be granted, it does not stop with the negro. I should like to know—taking this old Declaration of Independence which declares that all men are equal upon principle, and making exceptions to it,—where will it stop? If one man says it does not mean a negro, why not another say it does not mean some other man?—*Speech, Chicago, July 10, 1858.* III, 49.

4.—Sustain these men who support the implications of the Dred Scott decision, and negro equality will be abundant, as every white laborer will have occasion to regret when he is elbowed from his plow or his anvil by slave niggers.—*Speech, Carlinville, Aug. 31, 1858.* Angle, 189.

5.—The compromises of the Constitution we must all stand by, but where is the justness of extending the institution to compete with white labor and thus to degrade it? Is is not rather our duty to make labor more respectable by preventing all black competition, especially in the territories?—*Speech, Carlinville, Aug. 31, 1858.* Angle, 190.

6.—When . . . you have succeeded in dehumanizing the negro; when you have put him down and made it impossible for him to be but as the beasts of the field; when you have extinguished his soul in this world and placed him where the ray of hope is blown out as in the darkness of the damned, are you quite sure that the demon you have aroused will not turn and rend you?—*Speech, Edwardsville, Sept. 13, 1858.* XI, 110.

7.—[If the negro is] doomed, and damned, and forgotten, to everlasting bondage, is the white man quite certain that the tyrant demon will not turn upon him, too?—*Notes, Oct. 1, 1858.* IV, 224.

8.—I say it positively wrongs the mass of white men that the negro should be enslaved; that the mass of white men are really injured by the effects of slave labor in the vicinity of the fields of their own labor.—*Speech, Cincinnati, Sept. 17, 1859.* V, 204.

9.—Slavery is wrong in its effects upon white people and free labor.—*Speech, Hartford, Conn., March 5, 1860.* V, 331.

10.—I need not recount to you the effects upon the white men, growing out of the institution of slavery. I believe in its general evil effects on the white race. See our present condition—the country engaged in war—our white men cutting one another's throat—none knowing how far it will extend—and then consider what we know to be the truth. . . . Without the institution of slavery and the colored race as its basis, the war could not have an existence. It is better for us both, therefore, to be separated.—*Speech to colored men, Aug. 24, 1862.* VIII, 3.

See TERRITORIES, best use of, 6, 7.

Slavery, why issue is not settled—Why, when all desire to have this [slavery] controversy settled, can we not settle it satisfactorily? One reason is, we want it settled in different ways. Each faction has a different plan; they pull different ways and neither has a decided majority.—*Speech, Hartford, Conn., March 5, 1860.* V, 329.

2.—The people of the whole nation agree that this question ought to be settled, and yet it is not settled; and the reason is that they are not yet agreed how it shall be settled. All wish it done, but some wish one way and some another, and some a third, or fourth, or fifth; different bodies are pulling in different directions, and, none of them having a decided majority, are able to accomplish the common object.—*Speech, New Haven, Conn., March 6, 1860.* V, 340.

3.—I think that one of the causes of these repeated failures [to bring peace] is that our best and greatest men have greatly underestimated the size of the question. They have constantly brought forward small cures for great sores—plasters too small to cover the wound.—*Speech, Norwich, Conn., March 9, 1860.* VI, 2.

See UNION, slavery and, perplexing question, 1.

Slavery, why so many free negroes?—There are in the United States and territories, including the District of Columbia, 433,643 free blacks. At $500 per head they are worth over $200,000,000. How comes this vast amount of property to be running about without owners? We do not see free horses or free cattle running at large. How is this? All these free blacks are the descendants of slaves, or have been slaves themselves; and they would be slaves now but for something which has operated on their white owners, inducing them at vast pecuniary sacrifice to liberate them. What is that something? Is there any mistaking it? . . . It is your [slave owners'] sense of justice and human sympathy continually telling you that the poor negro has some natural right to himself.—*Speech, Peoria, Oct. 16, 1854.* II, 225. Repeated at Urbana, Oct. 24, 1854. Hertz II, 643.

Slavery, why tolerated 82 years?—*See* SLAVERY, policy of the Fathers, 11.

Slavery, will slaves fight to keep themselves in?—*See* SLAVERY, slaves as Confederate soldiers, 1.

Slavery, without reason or logic—*See* SLAVERY, Moloch of.

Slavery, would not know how to end—When it is said that the institution [slavery] exists, and that it is very difficult to get rid of it in any satisfactory way, I can understand and appreciate the saying. I surely will not blame them [men of the South] for not doing what I should not know how to do myself. If all earthly power were given me, I should not know what to do as to the existing institution.—*Speech, Peoria, Oct. 16, 1854.* II, 206. Repeated at Ottawa, Aug. 21, 1858. III, 227.

Slavery, wrong of—[We, representatives of Sangamon County] believe that the institution of slavery is founded on both injustice and bad policy, but that the promulgation of abolition doctrines tends rather to increase than abate its evils.—*Protest, Illinois Legislature, March 3, 1837.* I, 51.

2.—The ant who has toiled and dragged a crumb to his nest will furiously defend the fruit of his labor against whatever robber assails him. So plain that the most dumb and stupid slave that ever toiled for a master does constantly know that he is wronged. So plain that no one, high or low, does ever mistake it, except in a plainly selfish way.—*Fragment, July 1, 1854.* II, 183.

3.—But while you thus require me to deny the humanity of the negro, I wish to ask whether you of the South, yourselves, have ever been willing to do as

much? . . . The great majority, South as well as North, have human sympathies, of which they can no more divest themselves than they can of their sensibility to physical pain. These sympathies in the bosoms of the southern people manifest, in many ways, their sense of the wrong of slavery, and their consciousness that, after all, there is humanity in the negro. If they deny this, let me address them a few plain questions: In 1820 you joined the North, almost unanimously, in declaring the African slave-trade piracy, and in annexing to it the punishment of death. Why did you do this? If you did not feel that it was wrong, why did you join in providing that men should be hung for it? The practice was no more than bringing wild negroes from Africa to such as would buy them. But you never thought of hanging men for catching and selling wild horses, wild buffaloes or wild bears.—*Speech, Peoria, Oct. 16, 1854.* II, 223.
Repeated at Urbana, Oct. 24, 1854. Hertz II, 643.
4.—If the negro is a man, why then my ancient faith teaches me that "all men are created equal," and that there can be no moral right in connection with one man's making a slave of another.—*Speech, Peoria, Oct. 16, 1854.* II, 227.
Repeated at Urbana, Oct. 24, 1854. Hertz II, 644.
5.—Slavery is founded in the selfishness of man's nature—opposition to it in his love of justice. These principles are in eternal antagonism, and when brought into collision so fiercely as slavery extension brings them, shocks and throes and convulsions must ceaselessly follow.—*Speech, Peoria, Oct. 16, 1854.* II, 238.
Repeated at Urbana, Oct. 24, 1854. Hertz II, 649.
6.—The great mass of mankind . . . consider slavery a great moral wrong, and their feeling against it is not evanescent, but eternal. It lies at the very foundation of their sense of justice, and it cannot be trifled with. It is a great and durable element of popular action and I think no statesman can safely disregard it.—*Speech, Peoria, Oct. 16, 1854.* II, 259.
7.—We come—we are here assembled together—to protest as well as we can against a great wrong, and to take measures, as well as we now can, to make that wrong right.—*Speech, Bloomington, May 29, 1856.* Lapsley II, 250.
8.—Now, if slavery is right, or even negative, he [Douglas] has a right to treat it in this trifling manner. But if it is a moral and political wrong, as all Christendom considers it to be, how can he answer to God for this attempt to spread and fortify it?—*Speech, Bloomington, May 29, 1856.* Lapsley II, 254.
9.—Slavery is a violation of the eternal right. . . . As sure as God reigns and school children read, that black, foul lie can never be consecrated into God's

hallowed truth.—*Speech, Bloomington, May 29, 1856.* Lapsley II, 267.
10.—A vast portion of the American people . . . look upon it [slavery] as a vast moral evil; they can prove it as such by the writings of those who gave us the blessings of liberty which we enjoy, and that they so looked upon it, and not as an evil merely confining itself to the states where it was situated.—*Speech, Chicago, July 10, 1858.* III, 37.
11.—Arguments . . . that the inferior race are to be treated with as much allowance as they are capable of enjoying; that as much is to be done for them as their condition will allow—what are these arguments? They are the arguments that kings have made for enslaving the people in all ages of the world. You will find that all the arguments in favor of kingcraft were of this class; they always bestrode the necks of the people—not that they wanted to do it, but because the people were better off for being ridden! That is their argument, and this argument of the judge [Douglas, interpreting the Declaration of Independence] is the same old serpent that says, "You work and I eat, you toil and I will enjoy the fruits of it." —*Speech, Chicago, July 10, 1858.* III, 49.
12.—Judge Douglas declares that if any community wants slavery they have a right to have it. He can say that logically, if he says that there is no wrong in slavery; but if you admit that there is wrong in it, he cannot logically say that anybody has a right to do wrong.—*Debate, Galesburg, Oct. 7, 1858.* IV, 274.
13.—I confess myself as belonging to that class in this country who contemplate slavery as a moral, social and political evil, having due regard for its actual existence amongst us, and the difficulties of getting rid of it in any satisfactory way, and to the constitutional obligations which have been thrown about it; but who, nevertheless, desire a policy that looks to the prevention of it as a wrong, and looks hopefully to the time when as a wrong it may come to an end.— *Debate, Galesburg, Oct. 7, 1858.* IV, 275.
14.—It is the same spirit [as that which tries to justify slavery] that says, "You toil and work and earn bread, and I'll eat it." No matter in what shape it comes, whether from the mouth of a king who seeks to bestride the people of his nation and live by the fruits of their labor, or from one race of men as an apology for enslaving another race, it is the same tyrannical principle.—*Debate, Alton, Oct. 15, 1858.* V, 65.
15.—I find that every man comes into the world with a mouth to be fed and a back to be clothed; that each has also two hands, and I infer that those hands were meant to feed that mouth and to clothe that back. And I warn you, Kentuckians, that whatever institu-

tion would fetter those hands from so doing violates that justice which is the only political wisdom, and is sure to tumble around those who seek to uphold it. —*Speech, Cincinnati, Sept. 17, 1859.* Hertz II, 731.

16.—Slavery is wrong; the denial of that truth has brought on the angry conflict of brother with brother; it has kindled the fire of civil war in houses; it has raised the portents that overhang the future of our nation.—*Speech, Cincinnati, Sept. 17, 1859.* Hertz II, 731.

17.—And be you sure that no compromise, no political arrangement with slavery, will ever last which does not deal with it as a great wrong.—*Speech, Cincinnati, Sept. 17, 1859.* Hertz II, 731.

18.—Free labor argues that as the Author of man makes every individual with one head and one pair of hands, it was probably intended that heads and hands should co-operate as friends, and that that particular head should direct and control that pair of hands. As each man has one mouth to be fed, and one pair of hands to furnish food, it was probably intended that that particular pair of hands should feed that particular mouth—that each head is the natural guardian, director and protector of the hands and mouth inseparably connected with it; and that being so, every head should be cultivated and improved by whatever will add to its capacity for performing its charge.—*Speech, Milwaukee, Sept. 30, 1859.* V, 251.

19.—All those who believe slavery wrong should unite in a policy dealing with it as a wrong. They should be deluded into no deceitful contrivances, pretending indifference, but really working for that to which they are opposed.—*Speech, Leavenworth, Kan., Dec. 3, 1859.* Angle, 234.

20.—Our government was not established that one man might do with himself as he pleases, and with another man too. I hold that if there is any one thing that can be proved to be the will of Heaven by external nature around us, without reference to revelation, it is the proposition that whatever any one man earns with his hands by the sweat of his brow, he shall enjoy in peace. I say that, whereas God Almighty has given every man one mouth to be fed, and one pair of hands adapted to furnish food for that mouth, if anything can be proved to be the will of Heaven, it is proved by the fact that that mouth is to be fed by those hands, without being interfered with by any other man, who has also his mouth to feed and his hands to labor with. I hold, if the Almighty had ever made a set of men that should do all the eating and none of the work, He would have made them with mouths only and no hands; and if He had ever made another class that He intended should do all the work, and none of the eating, He

would have made them without mouths and with all hands. But inasmuch as He has not chosen to make men that way, if anything is proved it is that those hands and mouths are to be co-operative through life and not to be interfered with.—*Speech, Cincinnati, Sept. 17, 1859.* Follett, 148.

21.—There are many individual men in all the free states who desire to have slaves; and if you admit that slavery is not wrong, it is also tyranny to deny them the privilege.—*Speeches in Kansas, Dec. 1-5, 1859.* V, 269.

22.—There is no justification for prohibiting slavery anywhere, save only in the assumption that slavery is wrong; and whenever the sentiment that slavery is wrong shall give way in the North, all legal prohibitions of it will also give way.—*Speeches in Kansas, Dec. 1-5, 1859.* V, 270.

23.—If slavery is right, all words, acts, laws, and constitutions against it are themselves wrong, and should be silenced and swept away. If it is right, we cannot justly object to its nationality—its universality; if it is wrong, they [men of the South] cannot justly insist upon its extension—its enlargement. All they ask we could readily grant, if we thought slavery right; all we ask they could as readily grant, if they thought it wrong.—*Cooper Institute address, New York, Feb. 27, 1860.* V, 326.

Repeated at New Haven, Conn., March 6, 1860. V, 370.

24.—[That] slavery is morally wrong . . . is clearly proved, I think, by natural theology, apart from revelation. Every man, white, black or yellow, has a mouth to be fed, and two hands with which to feed it—and bread should be allowed to go to that mouth without controversy.—*Speech, Hartford, Conn., March 5, 1860.* V, 330.

25.—We think slavery a great moral wrong, and while we do not claim the right to touch it where it exists, we wish to treat it as a wrong in the territories, where our votes will reach it. We think that a respect for ourselves, a regard for future generations and for the God that made us, require that we put down this wrong where our votes will properly reach it. We think that species of labor an injury to free white men—in short, we think slavery a great moral, social and political evil, tolerable only because, and so far as, its actual existence makes it necessary to tolerate it, and that beyond that it ought to be treated as a wrong.—*Speech, New Haven, Conn., March 6, 1860.* V, 345.

26.—Your race is suffering, in my judgment, the greatest wrong inflicted on any people.—*Speech to free colored men, Aug. 14, 1862.* VIII, 2.

27.—If slavery is not wrong, nothing is wrong. I cannot remember when I did not so think and feel.—*To A. G. Hodges, April 4, 1864.* X, 65.

28.—To read in the Bible, as the word of God himself, that "in the sweat of thy face shall thou eat bread," and to preach therefrom that "in the sweat of other men's faces shall thou eat bread," to my mind, can scarcely be reconciled with honest sincerity.—*To Dr. Ide and others, May 30, 1864.* X, 109.

29.—When brought to my final reckoning, may I have to answer for robbing no man of his goods; yet more tolerable even this, than for robbing one of himself and all that was his.—*To Dr. Ide and others, May 30, 1864.* X, 110.

30.—It may seem strange that any men should dare to ask a just God's assistance in wringing bread from the sweat of other men's faces, but let us judge not, that we be not judged.—*Second inaugural, March 4, 1865.* XI, 45.

See REPUBLICAN PARTY, difference between, and Douglas.

See SLAVERY, Republican policy toward.

Slaves, Fugitive—*See* FUGITIVE SLAVES.

Slocum, Henry W., relations with Gen. Hooker—*See* HOOKER, JOSEPH, relations with Gen. Slocum.

Smith, W. C. S., commended—I am satisfied that he [W. C. S. Smith] is competent, and of good character. —*To Sec. McCulloch, April 13, 1865.* Angle, 373.

Smoke the Best Witness—We better know there is fire whence we see much smoke rising than we could know it by one or two witnesses swearing to it. The witnesses may commit perjury, but the smoke cannot.—*To J. R. Underwood and H. Grider, Oct. 26, 1864.* X, 254.

2.—Experience has already taught us in this war that holding these smoky localities responsible for the conflagrations within them has a very salutary effect.— *To J. R. Underwood and H. Grider, Oct. 26, 1864.* X, 254.

Snake, "scotched"—I have scotched the snake [proposal for a government-encouraged slave uprising], not actually killed it. When it is dead it will be time enough to preach its funeral sermon.—*To James R. Gilmore, late May, 1863.* Gilmore, 152.

Snakes in Bed—*See* SLAVERY, "reptile," 4, 5, 6.

Snuffbox, gift of, acknowledged—*See* CLAY, JOHN M., son of honored father.

Soap, not a competent judge of—Some specimens of your soap have been used at our house and Mrs. L. declares it is a superior article. She at the same time

protests that I have never given sufficient attention to the "soap question" to be a competent judge.—*To Prof. Gardner, Sept. 28, 1860.* VI, 60.

Society, thorns in bosom of—*See* REVENGE, to be avoided, 1.

Socks, gift of, acknowledged—I take great pleasure in acknowledging the receipt of your letter of Nov. 26; and in thanking you for the present by which it was accompanied. A pair of socks so fine, and soft, and warm, could hardly have been manufactured in any other way than the old Kentucky fashion.—*To Susannah Weathers, Dec. 4, 1861.* Hertz II, 846.

Soldier Vote, must be allowed—I have a report that you incline to deny the soldiers the right of attending the election in Missouri, on the assumed ground that they will get drunk and make a disturbance. . . . Wherever the law allows soldiers to vote, their officers must allow it.—*To Gen. Rosecrans, Sept. 26, 1864.* X, 234.

See INDIANA, soldier vote urged.

Solomon, quoted—*See* SILENCE, postelection, explained, 17.

"Some Speak, Some Sing and All Holler"—*See* POLITICS, young men in, 1.

"Sometimes Right"—It is better only sometimes to be right, than at all times to be wrong.—*Address to Sangamon County, March 9, 1832.* I, 8.

Sophism, ingenious invention—*See* SECESSION, sophism of.

See STATES, national power and, 6.

Soup from Potatoes—*See* POPULAR SOVEREIGNTY, denounced, 1.

South, attitude of, toward Republicans—*See* REPUBLICAN PARTY, South's attitude toward.

South, cherishes peace of nation—*See* PEACE, South cherishes.

South, has men suitable for President—*See* CAMPAIGN OF 1860, North-South fusion suggested.

South, human sympathies of—*See* SLAVERY, wrong of, 3.

See SLAVERY, why so many free negroes?

South, "lost sheep"—As to the disaffected portions of our fellow-citizens, I will say, as every good man throughout the country must feel, that there will be more rejoicing over one sheep that is lost, and is found, than over the ninety and nine which have not gone astray.—*Reply to serenade, March 4, 1861.* Hertz II, 820.

South, no cause for fear by—As I have not felt, so I have not expressed, any harsh sentiments toward our southern brethren. I have constantly declared, as I really believe, the only difference between them and us, is a difference of circumstances.—*Speech, Springfield, Oct. 30, 1858.* Angle, 198.

2.—When we do as we say, beat you [proslavery advocates], you perhaps want to know what we will do with you. . . . We mean to treat you, as near as we possibly can, as Washington, Jefferson and Madison treated you. We mean to leave you alone, and in no way to interfere with your institution [slavery]; to abide by all and every compromise of the Constitution. . . . We mean to remember that you are as good as we; that there is no difference between us other than the difference of circumstances. We mean to recognize and bear in mind always that you have as good hearts in your bosoms as other people, or as we claim to have, and to treat you accordingly. We marry your girls when we have a chance—the white ones, I mean, and I have the honor to inform you that I once did have a chance in that way.—*Speech, Cincinnati, Sept. 17, 1859.* V, 218.

3.—You ask, "In the event of your election to the Presidency, and of the election of a majority of Republicans to the next Congress, would you favor radicalism, to embitter still more the feelings of our southern brethren?" I certainly am in no temper, and have no purpose, to embitter the feelings of the South; but whether I am inclined to such a course as would in fact embitter their feelings, you can better judge by my published speeches than by anything I would say in a short letter, if I were inclined now, as I am not, to define my position anew.—*To L. Montgomery Bond, Oct. 15, 1860.* Tracy, 165.

4.—Rest fully assured that the good people of the South who will put themselves in the same temper and mood toward me which you do, will find no cause to complain of me.—*To Samuel Haycraft, Nov. 13, 1860.* VI, 69.

5.—In one word, I never have been, and am not now, and probably never shall be, in a mood of harassing the people either North or South.—*To John A. Gilmer, Dec. 15, 1860.* VI, 81.

6.—I have not now, and never have had, any other than as kindly feelings toward you [men of the South] as to the people of my own section. I have not now, and never have had, any disposition to treat you in any respect otherwise than as my own neighbors. I have not now any purpose to withhold from you any

of the benefits of the Constitution, under any circumstances, that I would not feel constrained to withhold from my own neighbors.—*Speech to mayor of Washington, Feb. 27, 1861.* VI, 166.

7.—We are in no wise disposed, if it were in our power, to oppress you [men of the South], to deprive you of any of your rights under the Constitution of the United States, or even narrowly to split hairs with you in regard to those rights, but are determined to give you as far as lies in our hands, all your rights under the Constitution—not grudgingly, but fully and fairly.—*Reply to serenade, Washington, Feb. 28, 1861.* VI, 167.

8.—Apprehension seems to exist among the people of the southern states that by the accession of a Republican administration their property and their peace and personal security are to be endangered. There has never been any reasonable cause for such apprehension. Indeed, the most ample evidence to the contrary has all the while existed and been open to their inspection. It is found in nearly all the published speeches of him who now addresses you. . . . I now reiterate these sentiments, and in doing so I only press upon the public attention the most conclusive evidence of which the case is susceptible that the property, peace and security of no section are to be in any wise endangered by the now incoming administration.—*First inaugural, March 4, 1861.* VI, 169.

9.—In every event the utmost care will be observed, consistently with the objects aforesaid [repossession of federal forts and property], to avoid any devastation, and destruction of or interference with property, or any disturbance of peaceful citizens in any part of the country.—*Proclamation, April 15, 1861.* VI, 247.

10.—Lest there be some uneasiness in the minds of candid men as to the course of the government toward the southern states after the rebellion shall have been suppressed, the Executive deems it proper to say it will be his purpose then, as ever, to be guided by the Constitution and the laws; and that he probably will have no different understanding of the powers and duties of the federal government relative to the rights of the states and the people, under the Constitution, than that expressed in the inaugural address. He desires to preserve the government, that it may be administered for all as it was administered by the men who made it. Loyal citizens everywhere have the right to claim this of their government, and the government has no right to withhold or neglect it. It is not perceived that in giving it there is any coercion, any conquest, or any subjugation, in any just sense of those terms.—*Message to Congress, July 4, 1861.* VI, 322.

11.—It is my duty, as I conceive it, to suppress an insurrection within the United States. I wish to do this with the least possible disturbance or annoyance to well-disposed people anywhere.—*To Gen. Buckner, July 10, 1861*. VI, 325.

12.—As to any dread of my having "a purpose to enslave or exterminate the whites of the South," I can scarcely believe that such dread exists. It is too absurd. I believe you can be my personal witness that no man is less to be dreaded for undue severity in any case.—*To Gen. McClernand, Jan. 8, 1863*. VIII, 183.

13.—The feeling [of the North] is against slavery, not against the South.—*To James R. Gilmore, late May, 1863*. Gilmore, 159.

See EMANCIPATION, slave states "need not be hurt by."

See SLAVERY, no interference with, in slave states.

South, No prejudice against—I think I have no prejudice against the southern people. They are just what we would be in their situation. If slavery did not now exist among them, they would not introduce it. If it did now exist among us, we should not instantly give it up. . . . We know that some southern men do free their slaves, go north and become tip-top abolitionists, while some northern ones go south and become most cruel slave-masters.—*Speech, Peoria, Oct. 16, 1854*. II, 205.
Repeated at Urbana, Oct. 24, 1854. Hertz II, 633.
Repeated at Ottawa, Aug. 21, 1858. III, 226.

South, too few in numbers to whip North—*See* SECESSION, after, what? 2.

South, welcomes military preparation of—I am rather glad of this military preparation in the South. It will enable the people the more easily to suppress any uprisings there, which their misrepresentation of purposes may have encouraged.—*Note to Lyman Trumbull, for inclusion in speech, Springfield, Nov. 20, 1860*. Hertz II, 793.

South, what will satisfy?—What will satisfy them [men of the South]. . . . This and only this; Cease to call slavery wrong, and join them in calling it right. And this must be done thoroughly—done in acts as well as in words. Silence will not be tolerated—we must place ourselves avowedly with them. Senator Douglas's new sedition law must be enacted, suppressing all declarations that slavery is wrong, whether made in politics, in presses, in pulpits, or in private. We must arrest and return their fugitive slaves with greedy pleasure. We must pull down our free-state constitutions. The whole atmosphere must be disinfected from all taint of opposition to slavery.—

Cooper Institute address, New York, Feb. 27, 1860. V, 324.
Repeated at New Haven, Conn., March 6, 1860. V, 368.

2.—Invasions and insurrections are the rage now [in the South's denunciation of the North]. Will it satisfy them if, in the future, we have nothing to do with invasions and insurrections? We know it will not. We so know, because we know we never had anything to do with invasions and insurrections; and yet this total abstaining does not exempt us from the charge and the denunciation.—*Cooper Institute address, New York, Feb. 27, 1860*. V, 324.
Repeated at New Haven, Conn., March 6, 1860. V, 367.

3.—We must not only let them alone, but we must somehow convince them that we do let them alone. This, we know by experience, is no easy task.—*Cooper Institute address, New York, Feb. 27, 1860*. V, 324.
Repeated at New Haven, Conn., March 6, 1860. V, 368.

4.—Will they be satisfied if the territories be unconditionally surrendered to them? We know they will not. In all their present complaints against us, the territories are scarcely mentioned.—*Cooper Institute address, New York, Feb. 27, 1860*. V, 324.
Repeated at New Haven, Conn., March 6, 1860. V, 367.

5.—The whole atmosphere must be disinfected from all taint of opposition to slavery, before they will cease to believe that all their troubles proceed from us.—*Cooper Institute address, New York, Feb. 27, 1860*. V, 325.

6.—Nothing will satisfy them but disinfecting the atmosphere entirely of all opposition to slavery.—*Speech, Hartford, Conn., March 5, 1860*. V, 337.

7.—Most of them [Southerners] would probably say to us [Northerners]: "Let us alone; do nothing to us, and say what you please about slavery. . . ." But we do let them alone; have never disturbed them,—so that, after all, it is what we say that dissatisfies them. They will continue to accuse us of doing, until we cease saying.—*Speech, New Haven, Conn., March 6, 1860*. V, 369.

See SEDITION LAW, Douglas's new.

See STRIKE, how to end.

South, will not accept Republican President—It has been said in high quarters that if Frémont and Dayton were elected the Union would be dissolved. The South do not think so. I believe it! I believe it! It is a shameful thing that the subject is talked of so much. Did we not have a southern President and

Vice President at one time? And yet the Union has not been dissolved.—*Speech, Kalamazoo, Mich., Aug. 27, 1856.* Basler, 343.

2.—But you [men of the South] are for the Union; and you greatly fear the success of the Republicans would destroy the Union. Why? Do the Republicans declare against the Union? Nothing like it. Your own statement of it is, that if the Black Republicans elect a President, you won't stand it. You will break up the Union. That will be your act, not ours. To justify it, you must show that our policy gives you just cause for such desperate action. Can you do that?—*Speech, Leavenworth, Dec. 3, 1859.* Angle, 235.

3.—You [men of the South] will not abide the election of a Republican President! In that supposed event, you say, you will destroy the Union; and then, you say, the great crime of having destroyed it will be upon us! That is cool. A highwayman holds a pistol to my ear, and mutters through his teeth, "Stand and deliver, or I shall kill you, and then you will be a murderer." To be sure, what the robber demanded of me—my money—was my own and I had a clear right to keep it; but it was no more my own than my vote is my own; and the threat of death to me, to extort my money, and the threat of destruction to the Union, to extort my vote, can scarcely be distinguished in principle.—*Cooper Institute address, New York, Feb. 27, 1860.* V, 323.

See BROWN, JOHN, secessionists face same fate as.

South America, Clay's efforts for—*See* CLAY, HENRY, devotion of, to liberty.

South Carolina, "eccentricities and heresies" in—We . . . look for and are not much shocked by political eccentricities and heresies in South Carolina.—*Speech, Springfield, July 16, 1852.* II, 173.

South Carolina, disunion sentiment in—*See* UNION, doubtful if more than one state majority against.

South Carolina, strength of, in Congress compared with Maine's—*See* SLAVE STATES, have advantage in Congress, 4.

Sovereignty, defined—What is "sovereignty" in the political sense of the term? Would it be far wrong to define it as "a political community without a political superior"? Tested by this, no one of our states except Texas ever was a sovereignty.—*Message to Congress, July 4, 1861.* VI, 315.

Sovereignty, do-nothing—*See* POPULAR SOVEREIGNTY, killed by Supreme Court, 4.

Spade, parable of stolen—*See* JUDGMENT DEFERRED.

Spain, characterized—. . . one of the worst governments in the world.—*Speech, Springfield, Aug. 26, 1852.* Angle, 105.

Spanish Moss, mob victims hang like—Thus went on this process of hanging [in Mississippi] from gamblers to negroes, from negroes to white citizens, and from these to strangers, till men were seen literally dangling from the boughs of trees upon every road side, and in numbers almost sufficient to rival the native Spanish moss of the country as a drapery of the forest.—*Speech, Springfield, Jan. 27, 1837.* I, 38.

Speaking, congressional, not different—I find speaking here [in Congress] and elsewhere about the same thing. I was about as badly scared, and no worse, as I am when I speak in court.—*To W. H. Herndon, Jan. 8, 1848.* Lapsley II, 26.

Speaking, difficulty encountered—The speech at New York, being within my calculation before I started [from home] went off passably well and gave me no trouble whatever. The difficulty was to make nine others, before reading audiences who had already seen all my ideas in print.—*To Mrs. Lincoln, March 4, 1860.* Hertz II, 770.

Speaking, extemporaneous, for lawyers—*See* LAW, advice to lawyers.

Speaking, no reading in—Allow me to say that I do not intend to indulge in that inconvenient mode sometimes adopted in public speaking, of reading from documents.—*Speech, Chicago, July 10, 1858.* III, 19.

2.—Gentlemen, reading from speeches is a very tedious business, particularly for an old man who has to put on spectacles, and more so if the man be so tall that he has to bend over to the light.—*Speech, Chicago, July 10, 1858.* III, 28.

Speaking, offensive, better than defensive—Your suggestions as to placing oneself on the offensive rather than the defensive are certainly correct. That is a point which I shall not disregard.—*To John Mathers, July 20, 1858.* III, 188.

Speaking, only for good purpose—I am very little inclined on any occasion to say anything unless I hope to produce some good by it.—*Speech, Washington, Aug. 6, 1862.* VII, 304.

Speaking, preparation essential for—Gentlemen, this is a glorious theme, and the occasion for a speech, but I am not prepared to make one worthy of the occasion.—*Response to serenade, July 7, 1863.* IX, 21.

2.—I believe I shall never be old enough to speak

without embarrassment when I have nothing to talk about.—*Response to serenade, Dec. 6, 1864.* X, 310.

See PRESIDENCY, puts curb on speech.

Specie, collection of revenue in, and subtreasury plan—*See* SUBTREASURY, specie provision argues against proposal.

Specie Payments, early return to, urged—The suspension of specie payments by the banks . . . made large issues of United States notes unavoidable. . . . The judicious legislation of Congress, securing the receivability of these notes for loans and internal duties and making them legal tender for other debts, has made them an universal currency, and has satisfied, partially at least, and for the time, the long-felt want of an uniform circulating medium, saving thereby to the people immense sums in discounts and exchanges. A return to specie payments, however, at the earliest period compatible with due regard to all interests concerned should ever be kept in mind.—*Second annual message, Dec. 1, 1862.* VIII, 100.

Speculation, diverts army from fighting—Few things are so troublesome to the government as the fierceness with which the profits in trading are sought. The temptation is so great that nearly everybody wishes to be in it; and, when in, the question of profit controls all, regardless of whether the cotton-seller is loyal or rebel, or whether he is paid in cornmeal or gunpowder. The officers of the army, in numerous instances, are believed to connive and share the profits, and thus the army itself is diverted from fighting the rebels to speculate in cotton, and steamboats and wagons in the pay of the government are set to gathering and carrying cotton, and the soldiers to loading cotton-trains and guarding them.—*To William Kellogg, June 29, 1863.* IX, 10.

Speech, "direct gift of Creator"—The inclination to exchange thoughts with one another is probably an original impulse of our nature. . . . To carry on such communications, some instrumentality is indispensable. Accordingly, speech—articulate sounds rattled off the tongue—was used by our first parents, and even by Adam before the creation of Eve. . . . From this it would appear that speech was not an invention of man, but rather the direct gift of his Creator.—*Lecture, Springfield, Feb. 22, 1859.* V, 104.

Speech, of small value alone—But speech alone, valuable as it ever has been and is, has not advanced the condition of the world much. This is abundantly evident when we look at the degraded condition of all those tribes of human creatures who have no consid-

erable additional means of communicating thoughts.—*Lecture, Springfield, Feb. 22, 1859.* V, 106.

Speech, Presidency curbs—*See* PRESIDENCY, puts curb on speech.

Speed, Joshua F., counseled as bridegroom—*See* BRIDEGROOM, counsel for.

Speed, Joshua F., friendly inquiry of—Are you possessing houses and lands, and oxen and asses, and men-servants and maid-servants, and begetting sons and daughters?—*To Mr. Speed, May 18, 1843.* I, 268.

Speed, Joshua F., friendship must not die—You, no doubt, assign the suspension of our correspondence to the true philosophic cause; though it must be confessed by both of us that this is rather a cold reason for allowing a friendship such as ours to die by degrees. I propose now that, upon receipt of this, you shall be considered in my debt, and under obligations to pay soon, and that neither shall remain long in arrears thereafter. Are you agreed?—*To Mr. Speed, Oct. 22, 1846.* Lapsley II, 17.

Spies—*See* CIVIL WAR, situation at start of, 3.

Spirit of '76—*See* KANSAS-NEBRASKA ACT, spirit of, 1.

Spoils—Now, let our friends bear and forbear, and not quarrel over spoils.—*To W. M. Dickson, Nov. 17, 1859.* Hertz II, 758.

Squatter Sovereignty—*See also* POPULAR SOVEREIGNTY.

Squatter Sovereignty, defined—What was squatter sovereignty? I suppose if it had any signification at all, it was the right of the people to govern themselves, to be sovereign in their own affairs, while they squatted down in a country not their own,—while they squatted in a territory that did not belong to them, in the sense that a state belongs to the people who inhabit it,—when it belonged to the nation; such right to govern themselves was called squatter sovereignty.—*Speech, Chicago, July 10, 1858.* III, 23.

Squatter Sovereignty, "squatted out"—*See* POPULAR SOVEREIGNTY, killed by Supreme Court, 1.

Stanley, Edward, commended—Your conduct as governor of North Carolina, as reported to me by Gen. Burnside, and as I have heard it personally from yourself, has my entire approbation.—*To Gov. Stanley, Sept. 29, 1862.* VIII, 51.

Stanton, Edwin M., appreciation of—I wish to correct an erroneous impression of yours in regard to the secretary of war. He mixes no politics whatever with his duties; he knew nothing of Gen. Hunter's proclamation; and he and I alone got up the counter-proclamation.—*To James Gordon Bennett, May 21, 1862.* Angle, 293.

2.—This note, as Col. [George Montagu] Hicks did verbally yesterday, attempts to excite me against the secretary of war and therein is offensive to me.—*Indorsement on letter of Hicks, May 22, 1862.* R. T. L.

3.—There has been a very wide-spread attempt to have a quarrel between Gen. McClellan and the secretary of war. Now, I occupy a position that enables me to observe that these two gentlemen are not nearly so deep in the quarrel as some pretending to be their friends. Gen. McClellan's attitude is such that, in the very selfishness of his nature, he cannot but wish to be successful, and I hope he will; and the secretary of war is in precisely the same situation. If the military commanders in the field cannot be successful, not only the secretary of war, but myself—for the time being master of them both—cannot but be failures. . . . Gen. McClellan has sometimes asked for things the secretary of war did not give him. Gen. McClellan is not to blame for asking for what he wanted and needed, and the secretary of war is not to blame for not giving when he had none to give. And I say here, as far as I know, the secretary has withheld no one thing at any time in my power to give him. I have no accusation against him. I believe he is a brave and able man, and I stand here, as justice requires me to do, to take upon myself what has been charged on the secretary of war, as withholding from him.—*Speech, Washington, Aug. 6, 1862.* VII, 304.

4.—As to Stanton—you know that it is hard to teach old dogs new tricks. He is terribly in earnest; and he does not always use the most conciliatory language. He very sensibly feels the need we have of victories, and he would take almost any means to get them. And the fact is, unless we have them soon the war is likely to be prolonged indefinitely.—*To James R. Gilmore, late May, 1863.* Gilmore, 155.

Stanton, Edwin M., censor—The secretary of war, you know, holds a pretty tight rein on the press, so that they shall not tell more than they ought to; and I am afraid that if I blab too much, he might draw a tight rein on me.—*Speech, Jersey City, June 24, 1862.* Lapsley VI, 56.

Stanton, Edwin M., deference to—I understand you say it rests with me under the law. Perhaps it does; but I do not wish to decide it without your concurrence.—*To Sec. Stanton, July 23, 1862.* Angle, 298.

Stanton, Edwin M., "quarrel" with McClellan—*See* STANTON, EDWIN M., appreciation of, 3.

"State Equality," not yet approved—Less than a year ago the Richmond *Enquirer,* an avowed advocate of slavery, regardless of color, invented the phrase "state equality," and now the President [Pierce] in his message, adopts the *Enquirer's* catch-phrase, telling us the people "have asserted the constitutional equality of each and all the states of the Union as states." The President flatters himself that the new central idea is completely inaugurated. . . . To us it is left to know that the majority of the people have not yet declared for it, and I hope that they never will.—*Speech, Chicago, Dec. 10, 1856.* II, 310.

States, freedom of, endangered—If the Constitution carries slavery into the territories beyond the powers of the people to control it as other property, then it also carries it into the states, because the Constitution is the supreme law of the land.—*Speech, Columbus, Ohio, Sept. 16, 1859.* V, 179.

2.—I think myself, and I repeat it here, that this [Dred Scott] decision does not merely carry slavery into the territories, but by its logical conclusion it carries it into the states in which we live.—*Speech, Columbus, Ohio, Sept. 16, 1859.* V, 180.

3.—To destroy a thing which is distinctly affirmed and supported by the supreme law of the land, even by a state constitution or law, is a violation of that supreme law, and there is no escape from it. In my judgment, there is no avoiding that result, save that the American people shall see that state constitutions are better construed than our Constitution is construed in that [Dred Scott] decision. They must take care that it is more faithfully and truly carried out than is there expounded.—*Speech, Columbus, Ohio, Sept. 16, 1859.* V, 181.

4.—I am quite aware . . . that they [men of the South] have not as yet in terms demanded the overthrow of our free-state constitutions. Yet these constitutions declare the wrong of slavery with more solemn emphasis than do all other sayings against it; and when all these other sayings shall have been silenced, the overthrow of these constitutions will be demanded, and nothing be left to resist the demand. . . . Demanding what they do, and for the reason they do, they can voluntarily stop nowhere short of this consummation.—*Cooper Institute address, New York, Feb. 27, 1860.* V, 325.

Repeated at New Haven, Conn., March 6, 1860. V, 369.

See DRED SCOTT DECISION, second, forecast.

See DRED SCOTT DECISION, threat to states.

States, guaranteed republican government—*See* UNION, inviolability of, 12.

States, help for—All the protection which, consistently with the Constitution and the laws, can be given, will be cheerfully given, to all the states when lawfully demanded, for whatever cause,—as cheerfully to one section as to another.—*First inaugural, March 4, 1861*. VI, 171.

States, national power and—I believe . . . that each community as a state, has a right to do exactly as it pleases with all the concerns within that state that interfere with the rights of no other state; and that the general government, upon principle, has no right to interfere with anything other than that general class of things that does concern the whole.—*Speech, Chicago, July 10, 1858*. III, 35.

2.—All the states' rights which they [states'-rights men] wished to retain are now and forever retained in the Union, including slavery; and so I have sworn loyalty to this constitutional Union, and for it let me live or let me die.—*To Alexander H. Stephens, Jan. 19, 1859*. Tracy, 128.

3.—I could hardly be justified, as a citizen of Illinois, or as President of the United States, to recommend the repeal of a statute of Vermont or South Carolina. —*To John A. Gilmer, Dec. 15, 1860*. VI, 79.

4.—The maintenance inviolate of the rights of the states, and especially the right of each state to order and control its own domestic institutions according to its own judgment exclusively, is essential to that balance of powers on which the perfection of our political fabric depends; and I denounce the lawless invasion by armed force of the soil of any state or territory, no matter under what pretext, as the gravest of crimes.—*To Duff Green, Dec. 28, 1860*. VI, 88.

5.—In what consists the special sacredness of a state? . . . I speak of that assumed primary right of a state to rule all which is less than itself, and to ruin all which is larger than itself. . . . On what rightful principle may a state, being not more than one fiftieth part of the nation in soil and population, break up the nation and then coerce a proportionately large subdivision of itself in the most arbitrary way? What mysterious right to play tyrant is conferred on a district of country with its people, by merely calling it a state?—*Speech, Indiana Legislature, Feb. 12, 1861*. VI, 114.

6.—This sophism [that a state is privileged to withdraw from the Union at will] derives much, perhaps the whole, of its currency from the assumption that there is some omnipotent and sacred supremacy pertaining to a state—to each state of our federal Union. Our states have neither more nor less power than that reserved to them in the Union by the Constitution, no one of them ever having been a state out of the Union. . . . Having never been states, either in substance or in name, outside of the Union, whence this magical omnipotence of "state rights," asserting a claim of power to lawfully destroy the Union itself? Much is said about the "sovereignty" of the states, but the word even is not in the national Constitution, nor, as is believed, in any of the state constitutions. . . . By conquest or purchase the Union gave each of them whatever of independence and liberty it has. The Union is older than any of the states, and, in fact, it created them as states. . . . Unquestionably, the states have the powers and rights reserved to them in and by the national Constitution; but among these surely are not included all conceivable powers, however mischievous or destructive, but at most only such as were known in the world at the time as governmental powers; and certainly a power to destroy the government itself had never been known as a governmental—as a merely administrative power.— *Message to Congress, July 4, 1861*. VI, 314.

7.—No one of our states, except Texas, was ever a sovereignty; and even Texas gave up the character on coming into the Union, by which act she acknowledged the Constitution of the United States and the laws and treaties of the United States made in pursuance of the Constitution to be for her the supreme law of the land.—*Message to Congress, July 4, 1861*. VI, 315.

8.—This relative matter of national power and state rights, as a principle, is no other than the principle of generality and locality. Whatever concerns the whole should be confided to the whole—to the general government—while whatever concerns only the state should be left exclusively to the state. This is all there is of original principle about it.—*Message to Congress, July 4, 1861*. VI, 316.

9.—The point made [by Everett at Gettysburg] against the theory of the general government being made only an agency whose principals are the states, was new to me, and, as I think, is one of the best arguments for the national supremacy.—*To Edward Everett, Nov. 20, 1863*. IX, 210.

See SLAVERY, no interference with, in slave states.

States, seceded, in or out of Union?—*See* RECONSTRUCTION, policy in, 2, 5, 6.

See UNION, inviolability of, 15.

States, "sovereignty" of—*See* STATES, national power and, 6, 7.

States, wholesome differences among—I do not believe in the right of Illinois to interfere with the cranberry laws of Indiana, the oyster laws of Virginia, or the liquor laws of Maine.—*Speech, Chicago, July 10, 1858.* III, 36.

2.—Now, so much for this nonsense—for I must call it so. The judge can have no issue with me on a question of establishing uniformity in the domestic regulations of the states.—*Speech, Chicago, July 10, 1858.* III, 38.

3.—As to the judge's [Douglas's] inference, that because I wish to see slavery placed in the course of ultimate extinction—placed where our fathers originally placed it—I wish to annihilate the state legislatures—to force cotton to grow upon the tops of the Green Mountains—to freeze ice in Florida—to cut lumber on the broad Illinois prairies. It seems to me it is a complete answer to all this to ask, if, when Congress did have the fashion of restricting slavery from free territories, when courts did have the fashion of deciding that taking a slave into a free country made him free—I say it is a sufficient answer to ask, if any of this ridiculous nonsense about consolidation and uniformity did actually follow?—*Speech, Springfield, July 17, 1858.* III, 176.

4.—When he [Douglas] undertakes to say that because I think this nation, so far as the question of slavery is concerned, will all become one thing or all the other, I am in favor of bringing about a dead uniformity in the various states in all their institutions, he argues erroneously. The great variety of the local institutions in the states, springing from differences in the soil, differences in the face of the country, and in the climate, are bonds of union. They do not make "a house divided against itself," but they make a house united.—*Debate, Ottawa, Aug. 21, 1858.* III, 232.

5.—Can it be true that placing this institution [slavery] upon the original basis—the basis upon which our fathers placed it—can have any tendency . . . to make the people of Vermont raise sugar-cane because they raise it in Louisiana, or that it can compel the people of Illinois to cut pine logs on the Grand Prairie, where they will not grow, because they cut pine logs in Maine where they do grow?—*Debate, Ottawa, Aug. 21, 1858.* III, 235.

6.—Douglas insists that I am in favor of perfect uniformity in the institutions of all the states. I believe in their right to do just as they please in this matter.—*Speech, Carlinville, Aug. 31, 1858.* Angle, 189.

7.—He [Douglas] tries to persuade us that there must be a variety in the different institutions of the states of the Union; that that variety necessarily proceeds from the variety of soil, climate, of the face of the country and the differences in the natural features of the states. I agree to all that. Have these matters ever produced any difficulty amongst us? Not at all. . . .

They don't make the house divided against itself. They are the props that hold up the house and sustain the Union.—*Debate, Jonesboro, Sept. 15, 1858.* IV, 39.

8.—Have we ever had any quarrel over the fact that they have laws in Louisiana designed to regulate the commerce that springs from the production of sugar? or because we have a different class relative to the production of flour in this state? Have they produced any differences? Not at all. They are the very cement of this Union.—*Debate, Jonesboro, Sept. 15, 1858.* IV, 59.

9.—He [Douglas] tries to show that variety in the domestic institutions of the different states is necessary and indispensable. I do not dispute it. . . . I shall very readily agree with him that it would be foolish for us to insist upon having a cranberry law here, in Illinois, where we have no cranberries, because they have a cranberry law in Indiana, where they have cranberries. I should insist that it would be exceedingly wrong in us to deny to Virginia the right to enact oyster laws, where they have oysters, because we want no such laws here. I understand, I hope, quite as well as Judge Douglas, or anybody else, that the variety in the soil and climate and face of the country, and consequent variety in the industrial pursuits and productions of a country, require systems of laws conforming to this variety in the natural features of the country. . . . But when I have admitted all this, I ask if there is any parallel between these things and this institution of slavery. I do not see that there is any parallel at all between them.—*Debate, Alton, Oct. 15, 1858.* V, 52.

10.—These mutual accommodations are the cements which bind together the different parts of this Union; that instead of being a thing to "divide the house"—figuratively expressing the Union,—they tend to sustain it; they are the props of the house tending always to hold it up. . . . When have we ever had any difficulty or quarrel among ourselves about the cranberry laws of Indiana, or the oyster laws of Virginia, or the pine-lumber laws of Maine, or the fact that Louisiana produces sugar, and Illinois flour? When have we had any quarrels over these things?—*Debate, Alton, Oct. 15, 1858.* V, 53.

See SLAVERY, disturbing element, 1.

States, (newspaper)—*See* "IRREPRESSIBLE CONFLICT," difference in who says it, 3.

States' Rights—*See* STATES, national power and.

Statesmanship, false—*See* SLAVERY, silence will not check, 2.

Statistical Bureau—*See* AGRICULTURE, bureau of, recommended.

Steam Power, delay in use of, surprising—The advantageous use of steam-power is, unquestionably, a modern discovery. And yet, as much as 2,000 years ago, the power of steam was not only observed, but an ingenious toy was actually made and put in motion by it, at Alexandria, in Egypt. What appears strange is that neither the inventor of the toy, nor anyone else, for so long a time afterward, should perceive that steam would move useful machinery, as well as a toy.—*Lecture, Springfield, no date.* Hertz II, 801.

Steam Power, in farming—*See* AGRICULTURE, steam power in.

Stepbrother, industry urged on—*See* WORK, urged on stepbrother.

Stephens, Alexander H., great speech of—I just take my pen to say that Mr. [Alexander H.] Stephens of Georgia, a little, slim, pale-faced, consumptive man, with a voice like Logan's, has just concluded·the very best speech of an hour's length I ever heard. My old withered dry eyes are full of tears yet.—*To W. H. Herndon, Feb. 2, 1848.* I, 354.

Stephens, Alexander H., unacceptable as peace envoy—You will not permit Mr. [Alexander H.] Stephens to proceed to Washington or to pass the blockade. He does not make known the subjects to which the communication in writing from Mr. [Jefferson] Davis relates, which he bears and seeks to deliver in person to the President, and upon which he desires to confer.—*To Rear-Admiral Lee, July 4, 1863 (not sent).* IX, 16.
2.—The request of A. H. Stephens is inadmissable. The customary agents and channels are adequate for all needful communications and conferences between the United States forces and the insurgents.—*To Rear Admiral Lee, July 4, 1863.* IX, 16.

See CONFEDERATE STATES, assumption of independence rejected, 2.

"Stick or Go Through"—We are in, and stick or go through, must be the word.—*To C. B. Smith, May 26, 1860.* VI, 21.

Stockings, octogenarian thanked for—Learning that you who have passed the 84th year of life, have given to the soldiers some 300 pairs of stockings, knitted by yourself, I wish to offer you my thanks.—*To Mrs. Esther Stockton, July 8, 1864.* Tracy, 243.

Story Telling, reasons for—I believe I have the popular reputation of being a story teller, but I do not de-serve the name in its general sense; for it is not the story itself but its purpose, or effect, that interests me. I often avoid a long and useless discussion by others or a laborious explanation on my own part by a short story that illustrates my point of view. So, too, the sharpness of a refusal or the edge of a rebuke may be blunted by an appropriate story, so as to save the wounded feeling and yet serve the purpose. No, I am not simply a story teller, but story telling as an emollient saves me much friction and distress.—*To Col. John D. Van Buren and others, June 26, 1863.* Burt.

"Strain a Point"—Please strain a point for him [William Kellogg] if you do not have to strain it too far.—*To Sec. Chase, June 25, 1863.* VIII, 333.

Strike, freedom to, commended—*See* LABOR, freedom to strike welcomed.

Strike, how to end—If, as the senator from Illinois asserts, this [shoe strike in New England] is caused by withdrawal of southern votes, consider briefly how you will meet the difficulty. You have done nothing, and have protested you have done nothing, to injure the South; and yet to get back the shoe trade, you must leave off doing something that you are doing. What is it? You must stop thinking slavery is wrong. Let your institutions be wholly changed; let your state constitutions be subverted; glorify slavery; and so you will get back the shoe trade.—*Speech, New Haven, Conn., March 6, 1860.* V, 362.

Stringham, Silas H., Congress asked to thank—I recommend that the thanks of Congress be given . . . Capt. Silas H. Stringham, now on the retired list, for distinguish-services in the capture of Forts Hatteras and Clark.—*Message to Congress, July 11, 1862.* VII, 268.

Subtreasury, arguments against—*See* NATIONAL BANK, compared with subtreasury.

Subtreasury, few versus many—In all candor let me ask, was such a system [as that of subtreasury] for benefitting the few at the expense of the many ever before devised?—*Speech, Springfield, Dec. 20, 1839.* I, 105.

Subtreasury, specie provision argues against proposal—By the [proposed] subtreasury [plan] the revenue is to be collected in specie. Now mark what the effect of this must be. By all estimates ever made there are but between sixty and eighty millions of specie in the United States. The expenditures of the government for the year 1838—the last for which we had the report—were forty millions. Thus it is seen that if the whole revenue be collected in specie, it will take more than half of all the specie in the nation to do it. By this means more than half of all the specie belonging to the fifteen millions of souls who compose the whole population of the country is thrown into the hands of the public-office holders, and other public creditors, composing in numbers perhaps not more than one quarter of a million, leaving the other fourteen millions and three-quarters to get along as best they can, with less than half the specie of the country, and whatever rags and shin plasters they may be able to put, and keep, in circulation. By this means, every office holder and other public creditor may, and most likely will, set up shaver; and a most glorious harvest will the specie men have of it—each specie man, upon a fair division, having to his share the fleecing of about fifty-nine ragmen. . . . Was the sacred name of democracy ever before made to indorse such an enormity against the rights of the people?—*Speech, Springfield, Dec. 20, 1839.* I, 105.

Success, most needed—I must say I need success more than I need sympathy, and that I have not seen so much greater evidence of getting success from my sympathizers than from those who are denounced as the contrary.—*To Gen. Schurz, Nov. 24, 1862.* VIII, 86.
2.—What we want still more than Baltimore conventions or presidential elections is success under Gen. Grant.—*Reply to delegation, June 9, 1864.* X, 122.

See HOOKER, JOSEPH, talk of dictatorship challenged.

Success, recipe for—Let none falter, who thinks he is right, and we may succeed.—*Speech, Springfield, Dec. 26, 1839.* Basler, 112.
2.—Always bear in mind that your own resolution to succeed is more important than any other one thing. —*To Isham Reaves, Nov. 5, 1855.* Stern, 396.
3.—The enterprise is a difficult one; but "where there is a will there is a way."—*Speech, Springfield, June 27, 1857.* II, 337.
4.—Having made the attempt [to enter Harvard] you must succeed in it. "Must" is the word. . . . Again I say let no feeling of discouragement prey upon you, and in the end you are sure to succeed.—*To George Latham, July 22, 1860.* Basler, 559.
5.—I say "try"; if we never try, we shall never succeed.—*To Gen. McClellan, Oct. 13, 1862.* VIII, 59.
6.—We can succeed only by concert. It is not "Can any of us imagine better?" but, "Can we all do better?"—*Second annual message, Dec. 1, 1862.* VIII, 130.

Suffrage, desired for loyal men—I wish all loyal qualified voters in Maryland and elsewhere to have the un-

disturbed privilege of voting at elections; and neither my authority nor my name can be properly used to the contrary.—*To Thomas Swann, Oct. 27, 1863.* IX, 185.

Sugar Cane, slavery and, in Ohio—*See* CLIMATE, no bar to slavery, 3.

"Sum of All Villainies"—*See* SLAVERY, "sacred right" of, 5.

Sumner, Charles, "my idea of a bishop"—He is a good piece of a man—Sumner, and a good man. I have never had much to do with bishops down where we live; but do you know, Sumner is just my idea of a bishop.—*To author, Diary of a Public Man, Feb. 28, 1861.* Diary, 55.

"Superiority," tribute to—It is not without a considerable degree of apprehension that I venture to cross the track of the gentleman from Coles [Mr. Linder]. Indeed, I do not believe I could muster a sufficiency of courage to come in contact with that gentleman, were it not for the fact that he, some days since, most graciously condescended to assure us that he would never be found wasting ammunition on small game. On the same fortunate occasion, he further gave us to understand that he regarded himself as being decidedly the superior of our common friend from Randolph; and feeling, as I really do, that I, to say the most of myself, am nothing more than the peer of our friend from Randolph, I shall regard the gentleman from Coles as decidedly my superior also. . . . In one faculty, at least, there can be no dispute on the gentleman's superiority over me, and most other men; and that is, the faculty of entangling a subject so far that neither himself nor any other man can find head or tail of it.—*Speech, Illinois Legislature, Jan., 1837.* I, 119.

Superstition, confessed—I was always superstitious. . . . Whatever He designs He will do for me yet. "Stand still and see the salvation of the Lord" is my text just now.—*To Joshua F. Speed, July 4, 1842.* I, 218.
2.—I am superstitious.—*To William Grimes, July 12, 1856.* II, 291.

Supreme Court, Characterized—*See* NATIONAL BANK, constitutionality of, affirmed, 2.

Supreme Court, duty of—It is a duty from which they [members of the court] may not shrink, to decide cases properly brought before them.—*First inaugural, March 4, 1861.* Basler, 586.

Supreme Court, Jackson's opinion of—*See* JACKSON, ANDREW, Supreme Court and bank decision, 1.

Supreme Court, "migratory," feared—*See* COURTS, uneasy about.

Supreme Court, modifications of, suggested—The accommodation of all parts of the country, with circuit courts, would create a [Supreme] court altogether too numerous for a judicial body of any sort. And the evil, if it be one, will increase as new states come into the Union. Circuit courts are useful, or they are not useful. If useful, no state should be denied them; if not useful, no state should have them. Let them be provided for all, or abolished as to all. These modifications occur to me; either of which I think, would be an improvement upon the present system. Let the Supreme Court be of convenient number in any event. Then, first, let the whole country be divided into circuits of convenient size, the supreme judges in a number of them corresponding to their own number, and independent circuit judges be provided for the rest. Or, secondly, let the supreme judges be relieved from circuit duties, and circuit judges provided for all the circuits. Or, thirdly, dispense with circuit courts altogether, leaving the judicial functions wholly to the district courts and an independent Supreme Court.—*First annual message, Dec. 3, 1861.* VII, 39.

Supreme Court, vacancies in, unfilled—There are three vacancies on the bench of the Supreme Court. . . . I have so far forborne making nominations to fill these vacancies for reasons I will now state. Two of the outgoing judges resided within the states now overrun by revolt, so that if successors were appointed in the same localities they could not now serve upon their circuits; and many of the most competent men there probably would not take the personal hazard of accepting to serve, even here, upon the supreme bench. I have been unwilling to throw all the appointments northward, thus disabling myself from doing justice to the South on the return of peace.—*First annual message, Dec. 3, 1861.* VII, 37.

Surplus Products, transportation and—*See* TRANSPORTATION, surplus products and.

Suspicion, get rid of—I believe we need nothing so much as to get rid of unjust suspicions of one another.—*To Charles L. Wilson, June 1, 1858.* II, 364.

Sweet, M. P., no offense to, intended—I write this to assure you that nothing can be farther from me than to feel, much less intentionally say, anything disrespectful to you.—*To Mr. Sweet, Sept. 16, 1858.* Angle, 194.

Taney, Roger Brooke, "conspiracy" by—*See* SLAVERY, conspiracy to promote, 5, 9.

Taney, Roger Brooke, first to say negro not included in Declaration—*See* EQUALITY, Douglas's interpretation of the Declaration, 11.

Tariff, direct taxation and—We are opposed to direct taxation for the support of the national government.—*Resolution, Whig convention, Springfield, March 1, 1843.* I, 241.
2.—Let us briefly compare the two systems [tariff and direct taxation]. The tariff is the cheaper system, because the duties, being collected in large parcels at a few commercial points, will require comparatively few officers in their collection; while by the direct-tax system the land must be literally covered with assessors and collectors, going forth like swarms of Egyptian locusts, devouring every blade of grass and other green thing. And, again, by the tariff system the whole revenue is paid by the consumers of foreign goods, and those chiefly the luxuries, and not the necessaries of life. By this system the man who contents himself to live upon the products of his own country pays nothing at all. And surely that country is extensive enough, and its products abundant and varied enough, to answer all the real wants of the people. In short, by this system the burthen of revenue falls almost entirely on the wealthy and luxurious few, while the substantial and laboring many who live at home, and upon the home products, go entirely free. By the direct tax system none can escape.—*Whig circular, March 4, 1843.* I, 246.
3.—A tariff sufficient for revenue, or a direct tax, must soon be resorted to. . . . Some of our opponents, in theory, admit the propriety of a tariff sufficient for revenue; but even they will not in practice vote for such a tariff; while others boldly advocate direct taxation. Inasmuch, therefore, as some of them boldly advocate direct taxation, and all the rest —or so nearly all as to make exceptions needless— refuse to adopt the tariff, we think it is doing them no injustice to class them all as advocates of direct taxation. Indeed, we believe they are only delaying an open avowal of the system until they can assure themselves that the people will tolerate it.—*Whig circular, March 4, 1843.* I, 246.
4.—However strictly the citizen may exclude from his premises all foreign luxuries—fine cloths, fine silks, rich wines, golden chains, and diamond rings—still for the possession of his house, his barn, and his homespun, he is [under a system of direct taxation] to be perpetually haunted and harassed by the tax-gatherer. . . . We leave it to be determined whether we or our opponents are the more truly democratic on the subject.—*Whig circular, March 4, 1843.* I, 247.

Tariff, Illinois farmer and—*See* PUBLIC LAND BILL, Clay's and the Illinois farmer.

Tariff, no matured judgment on—I have by no means a thoroughly matured judgment upon this subject [tariff], especially as to details; some general ideas are about all.—*Speech, Pittsburgh, Feb. 15, 1861.* VI, 127.

Tariff, "not to be agitated"—I now think the tariff question ought not to be agitated at the Chicago convention, but that all should be satisfied on that point with a presidential candidate whose antecedents give assurance that he would neither seek to force a tariff law by executive influence, nor yet to arrest a reasonable one by a veto or otherwise. Just such a candidate I desire to be put in nomination.—*To Dr. Edward Wallace, May 12, 1860.* VI, 11.

Tariff, perpetual question—The old question of tariff [is] a matter that will remain one of the chief affairs of national housekeeping to all time.—*Speech, New Haven, Conn., March 6, 1860.* V, 339.

2.—Assuming that direct taxation is not to be adopted, the tariff question must be as durable as the government itself. It is a question of national housekeeping. It is to the government what replenishing the meal-tub is to the family. Ever-varying circumstances will require frequent modifications as to the amount needed and the sources of supply. So far there is little difference of opinion among the people. It is as to whether, and how far, duties on imports shall be adjusted to favor home production in the home market, that controversy begins.—*Speech, Pittsburgh, Feb. 15, 1861.* VI, 126.

Tariff, prices and employment—It seems to be an opinion very generally entertained that the condition of a nation is best whenever it can buy cheapest; but this is not necessarily true, because if at the same time and by the same cause, it is compelled to sell correspondingly cheap, nothing is gained. Then it is said the best condition is when we can buy cheapest and sell dearest; but this again is not necessarily true, because with both these we might have scarcely anything to sell, or, which is the same thing, to buy with. . . . We must look not merely to buying cheap and selling dear, but also to having constant employment, so that we may have the largest possible amount of something to sell. This matter of employment can only be secured by an ample, steady and certain market to sell the products of labor in.—*Tariff memorandum, Dec. 1, 1847.* I, 304.

Tariff, protective, favored—I am in favor of . . . a high protective tariff.—*Reputed first political speech, March, 1832.* I, 98.

2.—A tariff of duties on imported goods, producing sufficient revenue for the payment of the necessary expenditures of the national government and so adjusted as to protect American industry, is indispensably necessary to the prosperity of the American people.—*Resolution, Whig convention, Springfield, March 1, 1843.* I, 240.

3.—I suppose the true effect of duties upon prices to be as follows: If a certain duty be levied upon an article which by nature cannot be produced in this country, as three cents a pound upon coffee, the effect will be that the consumer will pay one cent more per pound than before, the producer will take one cent less, and the merchant one cent less in profits; in other words, the burden of the duty will be distributed over consumption, production and commerce, and not confined to either. But if a duty amounting to full protection be levied upon an article which can be produced here with as little labor as elsewhere —as iron—that article will ultimately, and at no distant date, in consequence of such duty, be sold to our people cheaper than before, at least by the amount of the cost of carrying it from abroad.—*Tariff memorandum, Dec. 1, 1847.* I, 301.

4.—The abandonment of the protective policy by the American government must result in the increase of both useless labor and idleness, and so, in proportion, must produce want and ruin among our people.—*Tariff memorandum, Dec. 1, 1847.* I, 314.

5.—It appears to me that the national debt created by the war renders a modification of the existing tariff indispensable; and when it shall be modified I shall be pleased to see it adjusted with a due reference to the protection of our home industries. The particulars, it appears to me, must and should be left to the untrammeled discretion of Congress.—*Memorandum, July 1, 1848.* II, 55.

6.—I was an old Henry Clay-Tariff-Whig. . . . I have not since changed my views. I believe yet, if we could have a moderate, carefully adjusted protective tariff, so far acquiesced in as not to be a perpetual subject of political strife, squabbles, charges and uncertainties, it would be better for us. . . . I have not thought much on the subject recently but my general impression is that the necessity for a protective tariff will ere long force its old opponents to take it up; and then its old friends can join in and establish it on a more firm and durable basis.—*To Dr. Edward Wallace, Oct. 11, 1859.* V, 256.

7.—In 1844 I was on the Clay electoral ticket . . . and to the best of my ability, sustained, together, the tariff of 1842 and the tariff plank of the Clay platform. . . . I was one of a committee which reported, among others, a resolution in these words: "That we are in favor of an adequate revenue or duties from imports so levied as to afford ample protection to American industry." But, after all, was it really any more than the tariff plank of our present platform? And does not my acceptance pledge me to that?—*To J. E. Harvey, Oct. 2, 1860.* VI, 61.

8.—[I urge] such an adjustment of the tariff as shall produce a sufficient revenue, and in its other bearings, so far as possible, be just and equal to all sections of the country and classes of the people.—*Speech, Pittsburgh, Feb. 15, 1861.* VI, 129.

9.—Allusion has been made by one of your honored speakers to some remarks recently made by myself at Pittsburgh in regard to what is supposed to be the especial interest of this great commonwealth of Pennsylvania. I now wish only to say in regard to that matter, that the few remarks which I uttered on that occasion were rather carefully worded. I have seen no occasion since then to add to them or subtract from them. I leave them precisely as they stand, adding only now that I am pleased to have an expression from you, gentlemen of Pennsylvania, signifying that they are satisfactory to you.—*Speech, Pennsylvania Legislature, Feb. 22, 1861.* VI, 164.

See CAMPAIGN OF 1860, silence is candidate's best policy, 4.

Tariff, useless labor as a factor—All carrying, and incidents of carrying, of articles from the place of their production to a distant place for consumption, which articles could be produced of as good quality, in sufficient quantity and with as little labor, at the place of consumption as at the place carried from, is useless labor.—*Tariff memorandum, Dec. 1, 1847.* I, 301.

2.—The uselessness of the carrying labor [in the exchange of goods between nations] . . . is . . . glaringly obvious in relation to the cotton goods we purchase from abroad. The raw cotton from which they are made itself grows in our own country, is carried by land and by water to England, is there spun, wove, dyed, stamped, etc., and then carried back again and worn in the very country where it grew, and partly by the very persons who grew it. Why should it not be spun, wove, etc., in the very neighborhood where it both grows and is consumed, and the carrying thereby dispensed with?—*Tariff memorandum, Dec. 1, 1847.* I, 308.

3.—It appears to me that all labor done directly or indirectly in carrying articles to the place of consumption, which could have been produced in sufficient abundance, with as little labor, at the place of consumption as at the place they were carried from, is

useless labor.—*Tariff memorandum, Dec. 1, 1847.* I, 308.

4.—We may easily see that the cost of this useless labor is very heavy. It includes not only the cost of actual carriage, but also the insurances of every kind, and the profits of the merchants through whose hands it passes. All these create a heavy burden necessarily falling upon the useful labor connected with such articles, either depressing the price to the producer or advancing it to the consumer, or, what is more probable, doing both in part.—*Tariff memorandum, Dec. 1, 1847.* I, 309.

5.—Useless labor I would have discontinued, and those engaged in it added to the class of useful laborers.—*Tariff memorandum, Dec. 1, 1847.* I, 311.

6.—Universal idleness would speedily result in universal ruin; and . . . useless labor is, in this respect, the same as idleness.—*Tariff memorandum, Dec. 1, 1847.* I, 314.

7.—I have long thought it would be to our advantage to produce any necessary article at home which can be made of as good quality and with as little labor at home as abroad, at least by the difference of the carrying from abroad. In such case the carrying is demonstrably a dead loss of labor. . . . The condition of the treasury at this time would seem to render an early revision of the tariff indispensable.—*Speech, Pittsburgh, Feb. 15, 1861.* VI, 126.

See CAMPAIGN OF 1852, Democrats' do-nothing platform.

See LABOR, three classes.

Taxation, ideal plan impracticable—[No law] whose object is to distribute burdens or benefits on the principle of equality . . . can ever be practically administered with that exactness which can be conceived of in the mind. A tax law, the principle of which is that each owner shall pay in proportion to the value of his property, will be a dead letter if no one can be compelled to pay until he can be shown that every other one will pay in precisely the same proportion according to value; nay, even, it will be a dead letter if no one can be compelled to pay till it is certain that every other one will pay at all.—*Opinion on draft law, Aug. 15, 1863.* IX, 81.

2.—It is fair that each man shall pay taxes in exact proportion to the value of his property; but if we should wait before collecting a tax, to adjust the taxes upon each man in exact proportion with every other man, we should never collect any tax at all.—*Address to 164th Ohio regiment, Aug. 18, 1864.* X, 200.

Taylor, E. D., father of greenbacks—*See* BANKING AND CURRENCY, greenbacks' origin.

Taylor, Zachary, "administration's darkest hour"—I regret that the elections in the states have gone so badly; but I think there is some reason for hoping that this year has been the administration's darkest hour. The appointments were its most difficult task, and this year it has necessarily been viewed in connection with them alone. These are pretty much through with, and next we can get on grounds of measures—policy—where we can unite and rally again. It least, I hope so.—*To J. M. Lucas, Nov. 17, 1849.* Angle, 60.

Taylor, Zachary, agrees to anything people want—Now this is the whole matter. In substance, it is this: The people say to Gen. Taylor, "If you are elected President, shall we have a national bank?" He answers, "Your will, gentlemen, not mine." "What about the tariff"? "Say, yourselves." "Shall our rivers and harbors be improved?" "Just as you please. If you desire a bank, an alteration of the tariff, internal improvements, any or all, I will not hinder you. Send up your members of Congress from the various districts, with opinions according to your own, and if they are for these measures, or any of them, I shall have nothing to oppose."—*Speech in Congress, July 27, 1848.* II, 63.

2.—We [Whigs] prefer a candidate [for President] who, like Gen. Taylor, will allow the people to have their own way, regardless of his private opinions. . . . He would force nothing on them which they don't want.—*Speech in Congress, July 27, 1848.* II, 66.

Taylor, Zachary, Cass and slavery—Yet if I knew he would [veto the Wilmot Proviso], I still would vote for him. I should do this because, in my judgment, his election alone can defeat Gen. Cass; and because, should slavery thereby go into the territory we now have, just so much will certainly happen by the election of Cass, and, in addition a course of policy leading to new wars, new acquisitions of territory and still further extensions of slavery.—*Speech in Congress, July 27, 1848.* II, 67.

Taylor, Zachary, cited example of Jackson—*See* MAN OF STRAW, President must avoid being.

Taylor, Zachary, Col. Worth and—A short while before the [Mexican War] battles of the 8th and 9th of May, some question of precedence arose between [William J.] Worth—then a colonel—and some other officer, which question it seemed Gen. Taylor's duty to decide. He decided against Worth. Worth was greatly offended, left the army, came to the United States, and tendered his resignation. . . . He hesitated not to speak harshly and disparagingly of Gen. Taylor. . . . The government, both wisely and gen-

erously, I think, declined accepting his resignation: and he returned to Gen. Taylor. Then came Gen. Taylor's opportunity for revenge. The battle of Monterey was approaching, and even at hand. Taylor could, if he would, so place Worth in that battle that his name would scarcely be noticed in the report. But no. He felt it was due the service to assign the real post of honor to one of the best officers; he knew Worth was one of the best. . . . Accordingly, he assigned Col. Worth in that assault what was *par excellence* the post of honor; and the duties of which he executed so well, and so brilliantly, as to eclipse, in that battle, even Gen. Taylor himself.—*Speech, Chicago, July 25, 1850.* Angle, 72.

Taylor, Zachary, eulogy—Gen. Taylor is *par excellence* the hero of the Mexican War.—*Speech in Congress, July 27, 1848.* II, 84.

2.—Gen. Taylor himself, noblest Roman of them all. —*Speech in Congress, July 27, 1848.* II, 86.

3.—No one of the six battles he [Taylor] fought, excepting perhaps that of Monterey, presented a field which would have been selected by an ambitious captain upon which to gather laurels. So far as fame was concerned, the prospect—the promise in advance, was, "you may lose, but you cannot win." Yet Taylor, in his blunt, business-like view of things, seems never to have thought of this.—*Speech, Chicago, July 25, 1850.* Angle, 71.

4.—It did not happen to Gen. Taylor once in his life to fight a battle on equal terms, or on terms advantageous to himself—and yet he was never beaten, and never retreated. In all the odds were greatly against him; on each, defeat seemed inevitable; and yet in all he triumphed.—*Speech, Chicago, July 25, 1850.* Angle, 72.

5.—He was alike averse to sudden and to startling quarrels; and he pursued no man with revenge.—*Speech, Chicago, July 25, 1850.* Angle, 72.

6.—Gen. Taylor's battles were not distinguished for brilliant military maneuvers; but in all he seems rather to have conquered by the exercise of a sober and steady judgment, coupled with a dogged incapacity to understand that defeat was possible. His rarest military trait was a combination of negatives—absence of excitement and absence of fear. He could not be flurried, and he could not be scared.—*Speech, Chicago, July 25, 1850.* Angle, 72.

7.—No human being can fill that station [Presidency] and escape censure. Still I hope and believe when Gen. Taylor's official conduct shall come to be viewed in the calm light of history he will be found to have deserved as little as any who have succeeded him.—*Speech, Chicago, July 25, 1850.* Angle, 74.

8.—In Gen. Taylor's general public relations to his country, which will strongly impress a close observer, was his unostentatious, self-sacrificing devotion to duty. He indulged in no recreations, he visited no public places, seeking applause; but quietly, as the earth in its orbit, he was always at his post. Along our whole Indian frontier, thro' summer and winter, in sunshine and storm, like a sleepless sentinel, he watched, while we have slept for 40 years. How well might the dying hero say: "I have done my duty, I am ready to go."—*Speech, Chicago, July 25, 1850. Angle, 75.*

Taylor, Zachary, favored for President—I am decidedly in favor of Gen. Taylor as the Whig candidate for the next Presidency.—*To Whig committee, Feb. 9, 1848. Angle, 40.*

2.—I am in favor of Gen. Taylor as the Whig candidate for the Presidency because I am satisfied we can elect him, that he would give us a Whig administration, and that we cannot elect any other Whig—In Illinois his being our candidate would certainly give us one additional member of Congress, if not more; and probably would give us the electoral vote of the state.—*To T. S. Florney, Feb. 17, 1848. Hertz II, 564.*

3.—My prayer is that you let nothing discourage or baffle you, but that, in spite of every difficulty, you send us a good Taylor delegate from your circuit.—*To E. B. Washburne, April 30, 1848. II, 16.*

4.—In my judgment we can elect nobody but Gen. Taylor.—*To Archibald Williams, April 30, 1848. II, 17.*

Taylor, Zachary, no duelling for—Terrible as he was to his country's enemies, no man was so little disposed to have difficulty with his friends. During the period of his life, duelling was a practice not quite uncommon among gentlemen in the peaceful avocations of life, and still more common among the officers of the army and navy. Yet, so far as I can learn, a duel with Gen. Taylor has never been talked of.—*Speech, Chicago, July 25, 1850. Angle, 72.*

Taylor, Zachary, Presidency did not interest—Gen Taylor began to be named for the next Presidency, by letter writers, newspapers, public meetings and conventions in various parts of the country. . . . Up to this time I think it highly probable—nay, almost certain,—that Gen. Taylor had never thought of the Presidency in connection with himself. And there is reason for believing that the first intelligence of these nominations rather amused than seriously interested him. Yet I would be insincere, were I not to confess that, in my opinion, the repeated and steady mani-

festations in his favor did beget in his mind a laudable ambition to reach the high distinction of the presidential chair.—*Speech, Chicago, July 25, 1850. Angle, 73.*

Taylor, Zachary, relations with troops—As to Gen. Taylor's relations with his soldiers, details would be endless. It is perhaps enough to say—and it is far from the least of his honors that we can truly say—that of the many who served with him through the long course of 40 years, all testify to the uniform kindness, and his constant care for, and hearty sympathy with, their every want and every suffering; while none can be found to declare that he was ever a tyrant anywhere, in anything.—*Speech, Chicago, July 25, 1850. Angle, 73.*

Taylor, Zachary, veto power and—*See* VETO, Taylor agrees with Jefferson.

Taylor, Zachary, Wilmot Proviso and—*See* WILMOT PROVISO, safe with Taylor.

Telegraph, from Atlantic to Pacific—*See* RAILROAD, Atlantic to Pacific.

Temperance, ally of political freedom—*See* TEMPERANCE, revolution compared with Revolutionary War, 1.

Temperance, Christians won't object—"But," say some, "we are no drunkards, and we shall not acknowledge ourselves such by joining a reformed drunkards' society, whatever our influence might be." Surely, no Christian will adhere to this objection. If they believe, as they profess, that Omnipotence condescended to take on Himself the form of sinful man, and as such to die an ignominious death for their sakes, surely they will not refuse submission to the infinitely lesser condescension, for the temporal, and perhaps eternal salvation of a large, erring, and unfortunate class of their fellow creatures.—*Speech, Springfield, Feb. 22, 1842. I, 206.*

Temperance, defense of drunkards—In my judgment, such of us as have never fallen victims [of intemperance] have been spared more by the absence of appetite than from any mental or moral superiority over those who have. Indeed, I believe if we take habitual drunkards as a class, their heads and hearts will bear an advantageous comparison with those of any other class. There seems ever to have been a proneness in the brilliant and warm-blooded to fall into this vice—the demon of intemperance ever seems to have delighted in sucking the blood of genius and of generosity.—*Speech, Springfield, Feb. 22, 1842. I, 206.*

Temperance, early reformers erred—The warfare heretofore waged against the demon intemperance has somehow or other been erroneous. Either the champions engaged or the tactics they adopted have not been the most proper. These champions for the most part have been preachers, lawyers and hired agents. Between these and the mass of mankind there is a want of approachability, if the term be admissible, partially, at least, fatal to their success. They are supposed to have no sympathy of feeling or interest with those very persons whom it is their object to convince and persuade. . . . The preacher, it is said, advocates temperance because he is a fanatic, and desires a union of the church and state; and the lawyer from his pride and vanity of hearing himself speak; and the hired agent for his salary.—*Speech, Springfield, Feb. 22, 1842.* I, 194.

2.—Too much denunciation against dram-sellers and dram-drinkers was indulged in [in previous efforts to promote temperance]. This, I think, was both impolitic and unjust. . . . When the dram-seller and drinker were incessantly told—not in accents of entreaty and persuasion, diffidently addressed by erring man to erring brother, but in the thundering tones of anathema and denunciation with which the lordly judge often groups together all the crimes of the felon's life, and thrusts them in his face just as he passes sentence of death upon him—that they were the authors of all the vice and misery and crime in the land; that they were the manufacturers and material of all the thieves and robbers and murderers that infest the earth; that their houses were the workshops of the devil; and their persons should be shunned by all the good and virtuous, as moral pestilences—I say, when they were told all this, and in this way, it is not wonderful that they were slow, very slow, to acknowledge the truth of such denunciations, and to join the ranks of their denouncers in a hue and cry against themselves.—*Speech, Springfield, Feb. 22, 1842.* I, 196.

3.—Another error, it seems to me, into which the old reformers fell, was the position that all habitual drinkers were utterly incorrigible, and therefore must be turned adrift and damned without remedy in order that the grace of temperance might abound, to the temperate then, and to all mankind some hundreds of years thereafter. There is in this something so repugnant to humanity, so uncharitable, so cold-blooded and feelingless, that it never did nor ever can enlist the enthusiasm of a popular cause. . . . It looked so fiendishly selfish, so like throwing fathers and brothers overboard to lighten the boat for our security, that the noble-minded shrank from the mani-

fest meanness of the thing.—*Speech, Springfield, Feb. 22, 1842.* I, 201.

See TEMPERANCE, most effective advocates of, 3.

Temperance, evil of intemperance—Whether or not the world would be vastly benefited by a total and final banishment from it of all intoxicating drinks seems to me not now an open question. Three-fourths of mankind confess the affirmative with their tongues, and, I believe, all the rest acknowledge it in their hearts.—*Speech, Springfield, Feb. 22, 1842.* I, 204.

2.—He [demon of intemperance] ever seems to have gone forth like the Egyptian angel of death, commissioned to slay, if not the first, the fairest-born of every family. . . . Far around as human breath has ever blown he keeps our fathers, our brothers, our sons, and our friends prostrate in the chains of moral death.—*Speech, Springfield, Feb. 22, 1842.* I, 207.

3.—I think that the reasonable men of the world have long since agreed that intemperance is one of the greatest, if not the very greatest, of all evils among mankind. That is not a matter of dispute, I believe. That the disease exists, and that it is a very great one, is agreed upon by all. The mode of cure is one about which there may be differences of opinion.—*Reply to Sons of Temperance, Sept. 29, 1863.* IX, 145.

Temperance, "friend and sympathizer" of—Gentlemen, let us drink to our mutual good health in this wholesome drink which God has given us. It is the only drink I permit in my family and in all conscience let me not depart from this custom on this occasion. It is the purest Adam's ale, from the spring. —*To committee from Chicago convention, May 19, 1860.* Selby, 125.

2.—I can't permit to strangers what I do not do myself. No liquors, Billy! There's the tavern.—*To W. H. Herndon, May, 1860.* Townsend, 9.

3.—Having kept house sixteen years, and having never held the "cup" to the lips of my friends then, my judgment was that I should not, in my new position, change my habit in this respect. What actually occurred upon the occasion of the committee visiting me, I think it would be better for others to say.—*To J. Mason Haight, June 11, 1860.* Hertz II, 778.

4.—If I were better known than I am, you would not need to be told that in the advocacy of the cause of temperance you have a friend and sympathizer in me.—*Reply to Sons of Temperance, Sept. 29, 1863.* IX, 144.

5.—When I was a young man—long ago . . . I, in a humble way, made temperance speeches, and I think I may say that to this day I have never, by my example, belied what I then said.—*Reply to Sons of Temperance, Sept. 29, 1863.* IX, 144.

6.—No, I'm not a temperance man, but I am temperate in this, to wit: I don't drink.—*To Stephen A. Douglas, no date.* F. T. Hill, 36.

Temperance, in the army—To prevent intemperance in the army is even a part of the articles of war. It is part of the law of the land, and was so, I presume, long ago, to dismiss officers for drunkenness. I am not sure that, consistently with the public service, more can be done than has been done.—*Reply to Sons of Temperance, Sept. 29, 1863.* IX, 144.

2.—You have suggested that in an army—our army—drunkenness is a great evil, and one which, while it exists to a very great extent, we cannot expect to overcome so entirely as to have such successes in our arms as we might have without it. This undoubtedly is true, and while it is perhaps rather a bad source to derive comfort from, nevertheless in a hard struggle, I do not know but what it is some consolation to be aware that there is some intemperance on the other side, too; and, that they have no right to best us in physical combat on that ground.—*Reply to Sons of Temperance, Sept. 29, 1863.* IX, 145.

Temperance, most effective advocates of—When one who has long been known as a victim of intemperance bursts the fetters that have bound him, and appears before his neighbors "clothed and in his right mind," a redeemed specimen of long-lost humanity, and stands up, with tears of joy trembling in his eyes, to tell of the miseries once endured, now to be endured no more forever; of his once naked children, now clad and fed comfortably; of a wife long weighed down with woe, weeping, and a broken heart, now restored to health, happiness, and a renewed affection; and how easily it is all done, once it is resolved to be done; how simple is language!—there is logic and an eloquence in it that few with human feeling can resist. . . . In my judgment, it is to the battles of this new class of champions that our late success is greatly, perhaps chiefly, owing.—*Speech, Springfield, Feb. 22, 1842.* I, 195.

2.—Washingtonians [members of the Washington Temperance Society] greatly excel the temperance advocates of former times. Those whom they desire to convince and persuade are their old friends and companions. They know they are not demons, nor even the worst of men; they know that generally they are kind, generous, and charitable, even beyond the example of their more staid and sober neighbors. They are practical philanthropists; and they glow with a generous and brotherly zeal that mere theorizers are incapable of feeling. Benevolence and charity possess

their hearts entirely. . . . In this spirit they speak and act, and in the same they are heard and regarded. —*Speech, Springfield, Feb. 22, 1842.* I, 198.

3.—On every hand we behold those who but yesterday were the chief sinners, now the chief apostles of the cause. Drunken devils are cast out by ones, by sevens, by legions; and their unfortunate victims, like the poor possessed who were redeemed from their long and lonely wanderings in the tombs, are publishing to the ends of the earth how great things have been done for them. To these new champions and this new system of tactics our late success is mainly owing, and to them we must mainly look for the final consummation.—*Speech, Springfield, Feb. 22, 1842.* I, 203.

4.—They [new advocates of temperance] have been in that gulf from which they would teach others the means of escape. They have passed that prison wall, which others have long declared impassable; and who that has not shall dare to weigh opinions with them as to the mode of passing?—*Speech, Springfield, Feb. 22, 1842.* I, 203.

Temperance, new methods in promoting—By the Washingtonians [members of the Washington Temperance Society] this system of consigning the habitual drunkard to hopeless ruin is repudiated. They adopt a more enlarged philanthropy; they go for present as well as future good. They labor for all now living, as well as hereafter to live. They teach hope to all—despair to none. As applying to their cause, they deny the doctrine of unpardonable sin; as in Christianity it is taught, as in this they teach— "While the lamp holds out to burn, the vilest sinner may return."—*Speech, Springfield, Feb. 22, 1842.* I, 202.

Temperance, promising movement—The cause [temperance] seems suddenly transformed from a cold, abstract theory to a living, breathing, active and powerful chieftain, going forth "conquering and to conquer." The citadels of his great adversary are daily being stormed and dismantled; his temples and his altars, where the rites of his idolatrous worship have long been performed, and where human sacrifices have long been wont to be made, are daily desecrated and deserted. The triumph of the conqueror's fame is sounding from hill to hill, from sea to sea, and from land to land, and calling millions to his standard at a blast. For this new and splendid success we heartily rejoice.—*Speech, Springfield, Feb. 22, 1842.* I, 193.

2.—The ball is now rolling gloriously on, and none are so able as they [new champions of temperance] to increase its speed and its bulk, to add to its momentum and its magnitude.—*Speech, Springfield, Feb. 22, 1842.* I, 203.

Temperance, revolution compared with Revolutionary War—If the relative grandeur of revolutions shall be estimated by the great amount of human misery they alleviate, and the small amount they inflict, then indeed will this [temperance revolution] be the grandest the world shall ever have seen. Of our political revolution of '76 we are all justly proud. It has given us a degree of political freedom far exceeding that of any other nation of the earth. In it the world has found a solution of the long-mooted problem as to the capability of man to govern himself. In it was the germ which has vegetated, and still is to grow and expand into the universal liberty of mankind. But, with all these glorious results, past, present and to come, it had its evils too. It breathed forth famine, swam in blood, and rode in fire; and long, long after, the orphan's cry and the widow's wail continued to break the sad silence that ensued. These were the price, the inevitable price, paid for the blessings it bought. Turn now to the temperance revolution. In it we shall find a stronger bondage broken, a viler slavery manumitted, a greater tyrant deposed; in it, more of want supplied, more disease healed, and more sorrow assuaged. By it no orphans starving, no widows weeping. By it, none wounded in feeling, none injured in interest; even the drammaker and dram-seller will have glided into other occupations so gradually as never to have felt the change, and will stand ready to join all others in the universal song of gladness. And what a noble ally this is to the cause of political freedom; with such an aid its march cannot fail to be on and on, till every son of earth shall drink in rich fruition the sorrow-quenching draughts of perfect liberty.—*Speech, Springfield, Feb. 22, 1842.* I, 207.
2.—And when the victory shall be complete—when there shall be neither a slave nor a drunkard on the earth—how proud the title of that land which may truly claim to be the birthplace and the cradle of both these revolutions that shall have ended in that victory. How nobly distinguished that people which shall have planted and nurtured to maturity both the political and moral freedom of their species.—*Speech, Springfield, Feb. 22, 1842.* I, 209.

Temperance, why sign a pledge?—"But," says one, "what good can I do by signing the pledge? I never drink, even without signing." This question has already been asked and answered more than a million times. Let it be answered once more. For the man suddenly or in any other way to break off from the use of drams, who has indulged in them for a long

course of years, and until his appetite for them has grown ten or a hundred-fold stronger, and more craving than any natural appetite can be, requires most powerful moral effort. In such an undertaking he needs every moral support and influence that can possibly be brought to his aid and thrown around him.—*Speech, Springfield, Feb. 22, 1842.* I, 204.

Tennessee, believed loyal—The state of Tennessee, by a large majority of its citizens, is loyal to the federal Union.—*To governor of Tennessee (unsigned), May 1, 1861.* VI, 259.

Tennessee, East, difficult to rescue—I do as much for East Tennessee as I would or could if my own home and family were in Knoxville. The difficulties of getting a Union army into that region, and of keeping it there, are so apparent—so obvious—that none can fail to see them, unless it may be those who are driven mad and blind by their sufferings. Start by whatever route they may, their lines of supply are broken before they get halfway. A small force sufficient to beat the enemy now there would be of no value, because the enemy would reinforce to meet them, until we should have to give back or accumulate so large a force as to be very difficult to supply and as to ruin us entirely if a great disaster should befall it.—*To M. J. Fleming and R. Morrow, Aug. 9, 1863.* IX, 63.
2.—I am very anxious for East Tennessee; but I see and appreciate the difficulties you mention. The question occurs, Can the thing be done at all?—*To Gen. Rosecrans, Aug. 10, 1863.* IX, 67.

Tennessee, East, "driven to despair"—My distress is that our friends in East Tennessee are being hanged and driven to despair, and even now, I fear, are thinking of taking rebel arms for the sake of personal protection.—*To Gen. Buell, Jan. 1, 1862.* VII, 73.

Tennessee, East, important to hold—You do not estimate the holding of East Tennessee more highly than I do. There is no absolute purpose of withdrawing our forces from it, and only a contingent one to withdraw them temporarily for the purpose of not losing the position permanently.—*To John Williams and N. G. Taylor, Oct. 17, 1863.* XI, 129.

Tennessee, governor of, repulses call for troops—A legal call was recently made upon the said governor of Tennessee to furnish a quota of militia to suppress an insurrection against the United States, which call said governor responded to by a refusal couched in disrespectful and malicious language.—*To governor of Tennessee (unsigned), May 1, 1861.* VI, 259.

Territories, "all the South wants"—The question as to when they [people of a territory] shall have reached a sufficient number to be formed into a regular organized community is to be decided "by Congress." Judge Douglas says so [in his *Harper's* essay]. . . . That is what all those who are for slavery want. They do not want Congress to prohibit slavery from coming into the new territories, and they do not want popular sovereignty to hinder it; and, as Congress is to say when they are to be organized, all that the South has to do is to get Congress to hold off.—*Speech, Columbus, Ohio, Sept. 16, 1859.* V, 163.

2.—Let Congress hold off until they [people of a territory] are ready to be admitted as a state, and the South has all it wants in taking slavery into and planting it in all the territories.—*Speech, Columbus, Ohio, Sept. 16, 1859.* V, 165.

3.—Douglas tells us [in *Harper's*] that his popular sovereignty pertains to a people only after they are regularly organized into a political community; and that Congress in its discretion must decide when they are fit in point of numbers to be so organized. . . . Plainly enough, this . . . is a total surrender of his popular sovereignty.—*Speeches in Kansas, Dec. 1–5, 1859.* V, 265.

Territories, best use of—Whether slavery shall go into Nebraska, or other new territories, is not a matter of exclusive concern to the people who may go there. The whole nation is interested that the best use shall be made of these territories. We want them for homes of free white people.—*Speech, Peoria, Oct. 16, 1854.* II, 232.
Repeated at Urbana, Oct. 24, 1854. Hertz II, 646.

2.—Slave states are places for poor white people to remove from, not to remove to. New free states are the places for poor people to go to, and better their condition.—*Speech, Peoria, Oct. 16, 1854.* II, 232.
Repeated at Urbana, Oct. 24, 1854. Hertz II, 646.

3.—Have we no interest in the free territories of the United States—that they should be kept open for the homes of free white people? As our northern states are growing more and more in wealth and population, we are continually in want of an outlet, through which it may pass out to enrich our country. In this we have an interest—a deep and abiding interest.—*Speech, Kalamazoo, Mich., Aug. 27, 1856.* Stern, 404.

4.—Judge Douglas assumes that we have no interest in them—that we have no right whatever to interfere. I think we have some interest. I think that as white men we have. Do we wish for an outlet for our surplus population, if I may so express myself? Do we not feel an interest in getting to that outlet with such institutions as we would like to have prevail there?—*Debate, Alton, Oct. 15, 1858.* V, 57.

5.—I am in favor of this [keeping slavery out of the territories] not merely—I must say it here as I have elsewhere—for our own people who are born amongst us, but as an outlet for free white people everywhere, the world over—in which Hans, and Baptiste and Patrick, and all other men from all the world, may find new homes and better their condition in life.—*Debate, Alton, Oct. 15, 1858.* V, 58.

6.—I am still in favor of our new territories being in such a condition that white men may find a home—may find some spot where they can better their condition—where they can settle upon new soil, and better their condition in life.—*Debate, Alton, Oct. 15, 1858.* V, 58.

7.—In the exercise of this right [to "go forth and improve" your economic condition] you must have room. In the filling up of countries, it turns out after a while that we get so thick that we have not quite room enough for the exercise of that right, and we desire to go somewhere else. Where shall we go? Where shall you go to escape from over-population and competition? To those new territories which belong to us, which are God-given for that purpose.—*Speech, Cincinnati, Sept. 17, 1859.* Follett, 148.

8.—If, then, you will go to those territories that you may improve your condition, you have a right to keep them in the best condition for those going into them, and can they make that natural advance in their condition if they find the institution of slavery planted there?—*Speech, Cincinnati, Sept. 17, 1859.* Follett, 149.

9.—Let me ask you a question—you who have come from Virginia or Kentucky, to get rid of this thing of slavery; let me ask you what headway would you have made in getting rid of it, if by popular sovereignty you find slavery on that soil which you looked for to be free when you got there? You would not have made much headway if you had found slavery already here, if you had to sit down to your labor by the side of the unpaid workman.—*Speech, Cincinnati, Sept. 17, 1859.* Follett, 149.

10.—I say, then, that it is due to yourselves as voters, as owners of the new territories, that you shall keep those territories free, in the best condition for all such of your gallant sons as may choose to go there.—*Speech, Cincinnati, Sept. 17, 1859.* Follet, 149.

Territories, Congress controls—Congress, representing the whole people of the nation, have the power and responsibility under the Constitution of making all needful rules and regulation touching the territories.—*Speech, Urbana, Oct. 24, 1854.* Hertz II, 649.

Territories, "equality" one-sided—If you go to the territory opposed to slavery, and another man comes upon the same ground with his slave, upon the assumption that the things are equal, it turns out that he has the equal right all his way, and you have no part of it your way. If he goes in and makes it a slave territory, and by consequence a slave state, is it not time that those who desire to have a free state were on equal ground?—*Debate, Alton, Oct. 15, 1858. V, 57.*

Territories, large and small issues in—Judge Douglas . . . proceeds to assume [in his *Harper's Magazine* essay], without proving it, that slavery is one of those little, unimportant, trivial matters, which are of just about as much consequence as the question would be to me whether my neighbor should raise horned cattle or plant tobacco; that there is no moral question about it. . . . Judge Douglas ignores altogether the very well-known fact that we have never had a serious menace to our political existence, except it sprang from this thing, which he chooses to regard as only upon a par with onions and potatoes.—*Speech, Columbus, Ohio, Sept. 16, 1859. V, 156.*

2.—The question of who shall be governor of a territory for a year or two, and pass away, without his track being left upon the soil, or an act which he did for good or evil being left behind is [by Douglas's reasoning] a question of vast national magnitude—while this other matter of planting slavery upon a soil—a thing which once planted, cannot be eradicated . . . without infinite difficulty and a long struggle—he considers the power to prohibit it as one of those little, local, trivial things that the nation ought not to say a word about.—*Speech, Columbus, Ohio, Sept. 16, 1859. V, 157.*

3.—I ask any honest Democrat if the small, the trivial and temporary question is not, Who shall be governor?—while the durable, the important, and the mischievous one is, "Shall this soil be planted with slavery?"—*Speech, Columbus, Ohio, Sept. 16, 1859. V, 159.*

4.—They [territories] are fit, as he [Douglas] thinks, to decide upon the slavery question—the largest and most important with which they could possibly deal. . . . Oh, they are not fit to sit in Congress and decide upon rates of postage, or questions of *ad valorem* or specific duties on foreign goods, or live-oak timber contracts; they are not fit to decide these vastly important matters, which are national in their import, but they are fit, "from the jump," to decide the little negro question.—*Speech, Columbus, Ohio, Sept. 16, 1859. V, 160.*

5.—Douglas looks upon slavery as so insignificant that the people must decide that question for themselves; and yet they are not fit to decide who shall be their governor, judge or secretary, or who shall be any of their officers. These are vast national matters, in his estimation; but the little matter in his estimation is that of planting slavery there.—*Speech, Cincinnati, Sept. 17, 1859. V, 228.*

6.—Which is the greater, this [question of introducing slavery] or the [election of a] governor question? Which could the more safely be entrusted to the first few people who settle a territory? Is it that which, at most, can be but temporary and brief in its effects? or that which, being done by the first few, can scarcely ever be undone by the succeeding many?—*Speech, Leavenworth, Kan., Dec. 3, 1859. Angle, 232.*

Territories, loyal—So far the authority of the United States has been upheld in all the territories, as it is hoped it will be in the future.—*First annual message, Dec. 3, 1861. VII, 48.*

Territories, needed for expansion—*See* TERRITORIES, best use of.

Territories, positive law needed to keep slavery out—The question is asked us: "If slaves will go in [to a territory] notwithstanding the general principle of law liberates them, why would they not equally go in against positive statute law—go in, even if the Missouri restriction were maintained." I answer, because it takes a much bolder man to venture in, with his property, in the latter case than in the former; because the positive congressional enactment is known to, and respected by all, or nearly all.—*Speech, Peoria, Oct. 16, 1854. Basler, 300.*

See SLAVERY, positive law required for.

See SLAVERY, introduced without law, 5.

Territories, slavery in, once controlled by Congress—In 1794 they [Congress] prohibited an outgoing slave-trade—that is, the taking of slaves from the United States to sell. In 1798 they prohibited the bringing of slaves from Africa into the Mississippi Territory, this territory then comprising what are now the states of Mississippi and Alabama. . . . In 1800 they prohibited American citizens from trading in slaves between foreign countries. . . . In 1803 they passed a law in aid of one or two slave-state laws, in restraint of internal slave-trade. In 1807, in apparent hot haste, they passed the law nearly a year in advance—to take effect the first day of 1808, the very first day the Constitution would permit—prohibiting the African slave-trade by heavy pecuniary and corporal penalties. —*Speech, Peoria, Oct. 16, 1854. II, 245.*

2.—In 1798 Congress organized the Territory of Mississippi. In the act of organization they prohibited the bringing of slaves into the territory from any place without the United States, by fine, and giving freedom to the slaves thus brought.—*Cooper Institute address, New York, Feb. 27, 1860. V, 298.*

3.—Congress did not, in the [Louisiana] territorial act, prohibit slavery; but they did interfere with it— take control of it—in a more marked and extensive way than they did in the case of Mississippi. The substance of the provision therein made in relation to slaves was: That no slave should be imported into the territory from foreign parts; that no slave should be carried into it who had been imported into the United States since the first day of May, 1798; that no slave should be carried into it, except by the owner, and for his own use as a settler.—*Cooper Institute address, New York, Feb. 27, 1860. V, 299.*

See MISSOURI COMPROMISE, gave Missouri slaves.

Territories, undisturbed by war—The territories of the United States, with unimportant exceptions, have remained undisturbed by the civil war; and they are exhibiting such evidence of prosperity as justifies an expectation that some of them will soon be in a condition to be organized as states and be constitutionally admitted into the federal Union.—*Second annual message, Dec. 1, 1862. VIII, 99.*

Territories, what unfits?—What could they [territories] do by coming into the Union that they are not fit to do, according to his [Douglas's] mind, by staying out of it?—*Speech, Columbus, Ohio, Sept. 16, 1859. V, 160.*

2.—[Douglas assumes] that the states and territories differ only in the fact that the states are in the Union and the territories are not in it. But if this be the only difference, why not instantly bring the territories in? Why keep them out? Do you say they are unfitted for it? What unfits them? Especially what unfits them for any duty in the Union, after they are fit, if they choose, to plant the soil they sparsely inhabit with slavery, beyond the power of their millions of successors to eradicate it, and to the durable discord of the Union?—*Speeches in Kansas, Dec. 1–5, 1859. V, 263.*

Territory, acquisition of, and slavery—As to new acquisitions, I said, "Sufficient unto the day is the evil thereof." When we make new acquisitions, we will, as heretofore, try to manage them somehow.—*Speech, Peoria, Oct. 16, 1854. II, 17.*

2.—I am not generally opposed to honest acquisition of territory; and, in any given case, I would or would not oppose such acquisition, accordingly as I might

think such acquisition would or would not aggravate the slavery question among ourselves.—*Debate, Freeport, Aug. 27, 1858. III, 274.*

3.—It is, . . . I think, a very important question for the consideration of the American people, whether the policy of bringing in additional territory, without considering at all how it will operate upon the safety of the Union in reference to this one great disturbing element in our national politics [slavery] shall be adopted as the policy of the country.—*Debate, Galesburg, Oct. 7, 1858. IV, 293.*

4.—I think it is an exceedingly interesting and important question for this people to consider, whether we shall engage in the policy of acquiring additional territory, discarding altogether from our consideration, while obtaining new territory, the question how it may affect us in regard to this [slavery], the only endangering element to our liberties and national greatness.—*Debate, Galesburg, Oct. 7, 1858. IV, 295.*

See LOUISIANA PURCHASE.

See MEXICAN WAR, acquired territory and slavery.

Territory, acquisition of, no longer challenged—Having practiced the acquisition of territory for nearly 60 years, the question of constitutional power to do so is no longer an open one with us.—*First annual message, Dec. 3, 1861. VII, 50.*

Territory, grab for new, feared—If Judge Douglas's policy upon this question [slavery in the territories] succeeds . . . the next thing will be a grab for the territory of poor Mexico, an invasion of the rich lands of South America, then the adjoining islands will follow, each one of which promises additional slave-fields. And this question is to be left to the people of those countries for settlement. When we shall get to Mexico, I don't know whether the judge will be in favor of the Mexican people that we get with it settling that question for themselves and all others; because we know the judge has a great horror of mongrels, and I understand that the people are most decidedly a race of mongrels.—*Debate, Galesburg, Oct. 7, 1858. IV, 291.*

2.—We have no clear and certain way of determining or demonstrating how fast territory is needed by the necessities of the country. Whoever wants to go out filibustering, then, thinks that more territory is needed. Whoever wants wider slave fields feels sure that some additional territory is needed as slave territory. Then it is as easy to show the necessity of additional slave territory as it is to assert anything that is incapable of absolute demonstration. Whatever motive a man or set of men may have for making annexation of property or territory, it is very easy to assert, but much less easy to disprove, that it is necessary for the wants of the country.—*Debate, Galesburg, Oct. 7, 1858.* IV, 294.

3.—Once [popular sovereignty is] fastened on us as a settled policy, filibustering for all south of us, and making slave states of it, follows in spite of us.—*To J. D. Defrees, Dec. 18, 1860.* Hertz II, 795.

See SLAVERY, no compromise on, 6.

Territory, Young America longs for—*See* YOUNG AMERICA, longs for territory.

Texas, abolitionist reasoning relative to—As I always understood, the Liberty men [abolitionists] deprecated the annexation of Texas extremely; and this being so, why they should refuse to cast their votes so as to prevent it, even to me seemed wonderful. What was their process of reasoning, I can only judge from what a single one of them told me. It was this: "We are not to do evil that good may come." This general proposition is doubtless correct; but did it apply? If by your votes you could have prevented the extension, etc., of slavery, would it not have been good and not evil so to have used your votes, even though it involved the casting of them for a slaveholder? By the fruit the tree is to be known. An evil tree cannot bring forth good fruit. If the fruit of electing Mr. Clay would have been to prevent the extension of slavery could the act of electing him been evil?—*To Williamson Durley, Oct. 5, 1845.* I, 276.

Texas, boundary of, and slavery—The indefinite western boundary of Texas was to be settled [in the compromises of 1850]. She was a slave state, and consequently the farther west the slavery men could push the boundary, the more slave country they secured; and the farther east the slavery opponents could thrust the boundary back, the less slave ground was secured. . . . The North got the western boundary of Texas farther back eastward than the South desired; but, in turn, they gave Texas $10,000,000 with which to pay her old debts.—*Speech, Peoria, Oct. 16, 1854.* II, 202.

Texas, by what right a slave state?—Texas is a slave state, and four other slave states may be carved from its vast domain. And yet, in the year 1829, slavery was abolished throughout that vast region by a royal decree of the then sovereign of Mexico. Will you please tell me by what right slavery exists in Texas today? By the same right as, and no higher or greater than, slavery is seeking dominion in Kansas: by political force—peaceful if that will suffice; by the torch—as in Kansas—and the bludgeon—as in the Senate

chamber—if required.—*Speech, Bloomington, May 29, 1856.* Lapsley II, 265.

Texas, not much interested in—Individually, I never was much interested in the Texas question. I never could see much good to come of annexation, inasmuch as they were already a free republican people on our own model. On the other hand, I never could very clearly see how the annexation would augment the evil of slavery. It always seemed to me that slaves would be taken there in about equal numbers, with or without annexation. And if more were taken because of annexation, still there would be just so many the fewer left where they were taken from. It is possibly true, to some extent, that, with annexation, some slaves may be sent to Texas and continued in slavery that otherwise might have been liberated. To whatever extent this may be true, I think annexation an evil.—*To Williamson Durley, Oct. 3, 1845.* I, 276.

Texas, only state ever a sovereignty—*See* STATES, national power and, 7.

Texas, "true boundary" of—I propose to state my understanding of the true rule for ascertaining the boundary between Texas and Mexico. It is that wherever Texas was exercising jurisdiction was hers; and wherever Mexico was exercising jurisdiction was hers; and that whatever separated the actual exercise of jurisdiction of the one from the other was the true boundary between them.—*Speech in Congress, Jan. 12, 1848.* I, 338.

2.—Their [Whigs'] position, and in my opinion the true position, is that the boundary of Texas extended just so far as American settlements taking part in the revolution extended; and that as a matter of fact those settlements did extend, at one or two points, beyond the Nueces, but not anywhere near the Rio Grande at any point. The "stupendous desert" between the valleys of these two rivers, and not either river, has been insisted on by the Whigs as the true boundary.—*To Horace Greeley, June 27, 1848.* II, 53.

Texas, western, more important than attacking Mobile—*See* MOBILE, expedition against, not favored.

Texas, would shirk its part of national debt—*See* SECESSION, national debt and, 2.

Theology of Slavery—*See* SLAVERY, theology of.

Theory, practice better than—Practice proves more than theory, in any case.—*Second annual message, Dec. 1, 1862.* VIII, 128.

Thirteenth Amendment, favorable action on, urged—I approve the declaration [in the Republican national platform] in favor of so amending the Constitution as to prohibit slavery throughout the nation. When the people in revolt, with a hundred days of explicit notice that they could within those days resume their allegiance without the overthrow of their institution, and that they could not so resume it afterward, elected to stand out, such amendment of the Constitution as now proposed became a fitting and necessary conclusion to the final success of the Union cause. Such alone can meet and cover all cavils. Now the unconditional Union men, North and South, perceive its importance and embrace it.—*Response to committee notifying President of renomination, June 8, 1864.* X, 117.

2.—At the last session of Congress a proposed amendment of the Constitution abolishing slavery throughout the United States passed the Senate, but failed for lack of the requisite two-thirds vote in the House of Representatives. Although the present is the same Congress and nearly the same members, and without questioning the wisdom or patriotism of those who stood in opposition, I venture to recommend the reconsideration and passage of the measure at the present session. Of course, the abstract question is not changed; but an intervening election shows almost certainly that the next Congress will pass the measure if this does not. Hence there is only a question of time as to when the proposed amendment will go to the states for their action. And as it is so soon to go at all events, may we not agree that the sooner the better.—*Fourth annual message, Dec. 6, 1864.* X, 303.

3.—It is not claimed that the election has imposed a duty on members [of Congress] to change their views or their votes any further than, as an additional element to be considered, their judgment may be effected by it. It is the voice of the people now for the first time heard upon the question [of abolishing slavery by constitutional amendment]. In a great national crisis like ours, unanimity of action among those seeking a common end is very desirable—almost indispensable. And yet no approach to such unanimity is attainable unless some deference shall be paid to the will of the majority, simply because it is the will of the majority. In this case the common end is the maintenance of the Union, and among the means to secure that end such will, through the election, is most clearly declared in favor of such constitutional amendment.—*Fourth annual message, Dec. 6, 1864.* Basler, 785.

See "LIBERTY AND UNION."

Thirteenth Amendment, ratification of, should be unquestionable—It has been argued that no more than three-fourths of those states which have not attempted secession are necessary to validly ratify the [thirteenth] amendment. I do not commit myself against this further than to say that such a ratification would be questionable, and sure to be persistently questioned, while a ratification by three-fourths of all the states would be unquestioned and unquestionable.—*Last public speech, April 11, 1865.* XI, 91.

Thomas, George H., tribute to—It is doubtful whether his [Gen. Thomas's] heroism and skill exhibited last Sunday afternoon [at Chickamauga] has ever been surpassed in the world.—*To Robert A. Maxwell, Sept. 23, 1863.* Tracy, 234.
2.—Please accept for yourself, officers, and men, the nation's thanks for your good work of yesterday. You made a magnificent beginning; a grand consummation is within your easy reach. Do not let it slip.—*To Gen. Thomas, Dec. 16, 1864.* X, 315.

Thomas, Jesse B., tribute to—We, here in Illinois, should feel especially proud of the provision of the Missouri Compromise excluding slavery from what is now Kansas; for an Illinois man, Jesse B. Thomas, was its father. . . . Thomas was, beyond all controversy, the real author of the "slavery restriction" branch of the Compromise.—*Speech, Bloomington, May 29, 1856.* Lapsley II, 262.

"Thorn in Bosom"—So long as I have been here I have not willingly planted a thorn in any man's bosom.—*Response to serenade, Nov. 9, 1864.* X, 264.

See REVENGE, to be avoided, 1.

"Thorn in Its Vitals"—See ROSECRANS, WILLIAM S., opportunity of.

Thunder, rewards Lincoln—See LINCOLN, ABRAHAM, personal traits and reactions, 4.

"Thus Saith the Lord"—See DRED SCOTT DECISION, Douglas's devotion to, 6.

"Till the Britchen Broke"—I suspect that confidence [in Providence, as well as in people] is not more firmly fixed with the judge [Douglas] than it was with the old woman whose horse ran away with her in a buggy. She said she trusted Providence till the britchen broke; and then she didn't know what on earth to do.—*Speech, Springfield, Aug. 26, 1852.* Angle, 102.

Tod, David, regrets expressed to—See BROUGH, JOHN, nothing against.

Toes, pinched—Ready are we all to cry out and ascribe motives when our own toes are pinched.—*To Gen. Rosecrans, March 17, 1863.* VIII, 228.

Tongue, wonderful organ—Of the organs of speech the tongue is the principal; and if we shall test it, we shall find the capacities of the tongue, in the utterance of articulate sounds, absolutely wonderful.—*Lecture, Springfield, Feb. 22, 1859.* V, 105.

Tonnage Duties, inadequate to finance improvements—The President seems to think that enough may be done in the way of [internal] improvements, by means of tonnage duties under the state authority, with the consent of the general government. . . . I suppose it may be efficient, and perhaps sufficient, to make slight improvements and repairs in harbors already in use and not much out of repair. But if I have any correct general idea of it, it must be wholly inefficient for any general beneficent purposes of improvement.—*Speech in Congress, June 20, 1848.* II, 41.

2.—I know very little, or rather nothing at all, of the practical manner of levying and collecting tonnage duties; but I suppose one of its principles must be to lay a duty for the improvement of any particular harbor upon the tonnage coming into that harbor. . . . If I be right in this, how could we make any entirely new improvement by means of tonnage duties? How make a road, a canal, or clear a greatly obstructed river? . . . We shall never make a canal by tonnage duties until it shall already have been made a while, so the tonnage can get in.—*Speech in Congress, June 20, 1848.* II, 42.

See BOOTS, parable of new.

Tower of Babel, Douglas would have saved—When the builders of the Tower of Babel got into difficulty about languages, if they had just called on Judge Douglas he would at once have construed away the difficulty about languages, and enabled them to finish the structure, upon the truly Democratic platform on which they were building.—*Speech, Springfield, Aug. 14, 1852.* Angle, 91.

Trade, through Union lines—I do not wish to modify anything I have heretofore said as to your having entire control whether anything in the way of trade shall pass either way through your lines. I do say, however, that having known Judge [James] Hughes intimately during the whole of the rebellion, I do not believe he would knowingly betray any interest of the country and attempt to deceive you in the slightest degree. Please see him again.—*To Gen. Grant, March 13, 1865.* Angle, 372.

Transportation, surplus products and—Such products of the country as are to be consumed where they are produced need no roads or rivers, no means of trans-

portation, and have no very proper connection with this subject [internal improvements]. The surplus—that which is produced in one place to be consumed in another; the capacity of each locality for producing a greater surplus; the natural means of transportation, and their susceptibility of improvement; the hindrances, delays, and losses of life and property during transportation, and the causes of each, would be among the most valuable statistics in this connection.—*Speech in Congress, June 20, 1848.* II, 48.

Treason, Judas an example—The Savior of the world chose twelve disciples, and even one of that small number, selected by superhuman wisdom, turned out a traitor, and a devil.—*Speech, Springfield, Jan. 20, 1839.* I, 114.

"Treason," rebellion characterized—*See* SECESSION, sophism of.

Trenton, Battle of, inspiration of—May I be pardoned if, upon this occasion, I mention that away back in my childhood, the earliest days of my being able to read, I got hold of a small book . . . Weems's "Life of Washington." I remember all the accounts there given of battle-fields and struggles for the liberties of the country, and none fixed themselves upon my imagination so deeply as the struggle here at Trenton, N. J. . . . I recollect thinking then, boy even though I was, that there must have been something more than common that these men struggled for. I am exceedingly anxious that that thing—that something even more than national independence, that something that held out a great promise to all the people of the world to all time to come—I am exceedingly anxious that this Union, the Constitution, and the liberties of the people shall be perpetuated in accordance with the original idea for which that struggle was made, and I shall be most happy indeed if I shall be a humble instrument in the hands of the Almighty and of this, his almost chosen people, for perpetuating the object of that great struggle.—*Speech, New Jersey Senate, Feb. 21, 1861.* VI, 150.

Triumph, no pleasure in—*See* ELECTION OF 1864, gratitude without taint.

Troubles, one at a time—I would rather meet them ["troublesome questions"] as they come than before they come, trusting that some of them may not come at all.—*To Gov. Gamble, Dec. 30, 1862.* VIII, 155.

Trumbull, Lyman, charges of, against Douglas—When Judge Trumbull, our other senator in Congress, returned to Illinois in the month of August he made a speech at Chicago, in which he made what may be called a charge against Judge Douglas, which

I understand proved to be very offensive to him. . . . Upon a subsequent occasion Judge Trumbull spoke again before an audience at Alton, and upon that occasion not only repeated his charge against Douglas, but arrayed the evidence he relied on to substantiate it. . . . It had not originally been my purpose to discuss that matter at all. But inasmuch as it seems to be the wish of Judge Douglas to hold me responsible for it, then for once in my life I will play Gen. Jackson, and to the just extent I take the responsibility. . . . Trumbull's charge is in the following words: "That there was a plot entered into to have a constitution formed in Kansas, and put in force, without giving the people an opportunity to vote upon it, and that Mr. Douglas was in the plot. . . ." He [Douglas] says: "He [Trumbull] forges his evidence from beginning to end, and by falsifying the record he endeavors to bolster up his false charge. . . ." Upon my own authority I say that it is not true. . . . The point upon Judge Douglas is this: The [Kansas] bill that went into his hands had the provision in it for a submission of the constitution to the people; and I say its language amounts to an express provision for a submission, and that he took the provision out.—*Debate, Charleston, Sept. 18, 1858.* IV, 91.

Trumbull, Lyman, bargain with, denied—*See* ABOLITIONIZE, plot to, parties denied.

Trumbull, Lyman, no enmity toward—I am especially for Trumbull's re-election.—*To N. B. Judd, Oct. 15, 1858.* V, 92.
2.—Any effort to put enmity between you and me is as idle as the wind. . . . And I beg to assure you, beyond all possible cavil, that you can scarcely be more anxious to be sustained two years hence than I am that you shall be so sustained. I cannot conceive it possible for me to be a rival of yours, or to take sides against you in favor of any rival.—*To Senator Trumbull, Feb. 3, 1859.* Tracy, 100.
3.—I do not understand Trumbull and myself to be rivals. You know I am pledged to not enter a struggle with him for the seat in the Senate now occupied by him.—*To N. B. Judd, Dec. 9, 1859.* V, 282.
4.—To lose Trumbull's re-election next winter would be a great disaster.—*To William Fithian, Aug. 15, 1860.* Angle, 252.

Trumbull, Lyman, speech of, charged to Lincoln—*See* PRESS, some papers unfair.

Trumbull, Lyman, tributes to—You will find him a true and able man.—*To C. D. Gilfillan, May 9, 1857.* Angle, 166.
2.—[I said] that I believed him [Trumbull] to be a man of veracity—that I believed him to be a man of

capacity sufficient to know very well whether an assertion he was making, as a conclusion drawn from a set of facts, was true or false.—*Debate, Charleston, Sept. 18, 1858.* IV, 92.
3.—I do not choose to see Judge Trumbull calumniated, and the evidence he has brought forward [against Douglas] branded in general terms [as Douglas brands it] "a forgery from beginning to end."—*Debate, Charleston, Sept. 18, 1858.* IV, 113.
4.—When he [Douglas] asks me if I am ready to indorse Trumbull's veracity after he has broken a bargain with me, I reply that if Trumbull had broken a bargain with me, I would not be likely to indorse his veracity; but I am ready to indorse his veracity because neither in that thing, nor in any other, in all the years that I have known Lyman Trumbull, have I known him to fail of his word or tell a falsehood, large or small.—*Debate, Charleston, Sept. 18, 1858.* IV, 190.

Truth, best vindication against slander—*See* CABINET, dismissals from, up to President alone, 1.

Truth, inherent power of—*See* MANCHESTER, suffering of workers of, deplored.

Truth, loyalty to—*See* CODE OF CONDUCT, rules for personal guidance, 11.

Truth, "pole-star of"—Is it not a strong evidence that the general [Adams] is not traveling with the pole-star of truth in his front?—*To editor Sangamo Journal, Sept. 9, 1837.* I, 71.

Truth, prudence and—I never encourage deceit, and falsehood, especially if you have got a poor memory, is the worst enemy a fellow can have. The fact is truth is your truest friend, no matter what the circumstances are. Notwithstanding this copy-book preamble, my boy, I am inclined to suggest a little prudence on your part. You see, I have a congenital aversion to failure, and the sudden announcement to your Uncle Andrew of the success of your "lamp-rubbing" might possibly prevent your passing the severe physical examination to which you will be subjected in order to enter the Military Academy. You see, I should like to have a perfect soldier credited to dear old Illinois —no broken bones, scalp wounds, etc. So I think perhaps it might be wise to hand this letter from me in to your good uncle through his room window after he has had a comfortable dinner, and watch its effect from the top of the pigeon house.—*To George F. Pickett, Feb. 22, 1842.* I; 191.

"Tug Has to Come"—*See* SLAVERY, no compromise on, 2, 3.

"Turn About Is Fair Play," rule in politics—I know of no argument to give me a preference over him [Hardin] unless it be "Turn about is fair play."—*To Henry E. Dummer, Nov. 18, 1845.* Tracy, 15.

2.—Let the pith of the whole argument be "Turn about is fair play."—*To B. J. James, Dec. 6, 1845.* Tracy, 16.

3.—You know that my only argument is that "Turn about is fair play."—*To Dr. Robert Boal, Jan. 7, 1848.* I, 281.

4.—He [Hardin] has had a turn [in Congress] and my argument is "Turn about is fair play." I shall be pleased if this strikes you as a sufficient argument.—*To N. J. Rockwell, Jan. 21, 1846.* I, 286.

5.—I and my few friends say to the people that "Turn about is fair play." You and your friends do not meet this, and say "Turn about is not fair play"—but insist the argument itself ought not to be used. Fair or unfair, why not trust the people to decide it?—*To John J. Hardin, Feb. 7, 1846.* Angle, 23.

6.—I have said that "Turn about is fair play"; but this I have said just as I would, if that resolution [of Whig convention at Pekin] had never been thought of.—*To John J. Hardin, Feb. 7, 1846.* Angle, 26.

Tycoon of Japan—*See* JAPAN, good wishes for.

Tyler, John, unfair to Whigs—By the course of Mr. Tyler the policy of our opponents has continued in operation, still leaving them with the advantage of charging all its evils upon us as the results of a Whig administration.—*Whig circular, March 4, 1843.* I, 258.

See NATIONAL BANK, Tyler helped defeat.

Tyranny, invitation to—Accustomed to trample on the rights of others, you have lost the genius of your own independence and become the fit subjects for the first cunning tyrant who rises among you.—*Speech, Edwardsville, Sept. 13, 1858.* XI, 110.

Tyranny, prosperity breeds—*See* DECLARATION OF INDEPENDENCE, stumbling block to tyrants.

"Uncle Sam's Web Feet"—Nor must Uncle Sam's web feet be forgotten. At all watery margins they have been present. Not only on the deep sea, the broad bay, and the rapid river, also up the narrow, muddy bayou, and wherever the ground was a little damp, they have made their tracks.—*To J. C. Conkling, Aug. 26, 1863.* IX, 101.

"Unfriendly Legislation," Douglas challenged—*See* FREEPORT DOCTRINE, fallacy of, 6, 15.

Uniformity of Local Institutions, no thought of working for—*See* WAR BETWEEN THE STATES, no thought of precipitating, 1.

See STATES, wholesome difference among.

Union, appeals for support of—Let North and South—let all Americans—let all lovers of liberty everywhere join in the great and good work [of readopting policies harmonious with the Declaration of Independence]. If we do this, we shall not only have saved the Union, but we shall have so saved it as to make and keep it forever worthy of saving. We shall have so saved it that the succeeding millions of free, happy people, the world over, shall rise up and call us blessed to the latest generations.—*Speech, Peoria, Oct. 16, 1854.* II, 248.

Repeated at Urbana, Oct. 24, 1854. Hertz II, 655.

2.—Before entering upon so grave a matter as the destruction of our national fabric, with all its benefits, its memories and its hopes, would it not be wise to ascertain precisely why we do it? Will you hazard so desperate a step while there is any possibility that any portion of the ills you fly from have no real existence? Will you, while the certain ills you fly to are greater than all the real ones you fly from, risk the commission of so fearful a mistake? All profess to be content in the Union if all constitutional rights can be maintained. Is it true, then, that any right plainly written in the Constitution has been denied? I think not. Happily, the human mind is so constituted that no party can reach to the audacity of doing this. Think, if you can, of a single instance in which a plainly written provision of the Constitution has ever been denied.—*First inaugural, March 4, 1861.* VI, 177.

3.—Such of you as are now dissatisfied [and thinking of secession] still have the old Constitution unimpaired, and, on the sensitive point, the laws of your own framing under it; while the new administration will have no immediate power, if it would, to change either. If it were admitted that you who are dissatisfied hold the right side in the dispute, there still is no single good reason for precipitate action. Intelligence, patriotism, Christianity, and a firm reliance on Him who has never yet forsaken this favored land are still competent to adjust in the best way all our present difficulties.—*First inaugural, March 4, 1861.* VI, 184.

4.—My countrymen, one and all, think calmly and well upon this whole subject [of secession]. Nothing valuable can be lost by taking time. If there be an object to hurry any of you in hot haste to a step which you would never take deliberately, that object will be frustrated by taking time; but no good object can be frustrated by it.—*First inaugural, March 4, 1861.* VI, 184.

5.—I appeal to all loyal citizens to favor, facilitate,

and aid this effort [the raising of militia] to maintain the honor, the integrity, and the existence of our national Union, and the perpetuity of popular government; and to redress wrongs already too long endured.—*Proclamation, April 15, 1861.* R. T. L.

6.—I earnestly invoke the cooperation of all good citizens in the measures hereby adopted for the effectual suppression of unlawful violence, for the impartial enforcement of constitutional laws, and for the speediest possible restoration of peace and order, and, with these, of happiness and prosperity throughout the country.—*Proclamation, May 3, 1861.* VI, 264.

7.—The occasion is piled high with difficulty, and we must rise—with the occasion.—*Second annual message, Dec. 1, 1862.* Basler, 688.

8.—I admonish you not to be turned from your stern purpose of defending our beloved country and its free institutions by any arguments urged by ambitious and designing men, but to stand fast for the Union and the old flag.—*Speech to 148th Ohio regiment, Aug. 31, 1864.* X, 209.

9.—But the rebellion continues, and now that the election is over, may not all having a common interest unite in a common effort to save our common country?—*Response to serenade, Nov. 9, 1864.* X, 264.

Union, cannot be saved without negro help—*See* NEGRO TROOPS, importance of, 14, 15, 16.

Union, cements of—*See* STATES, wholesome differences among, 10.

See COMMERCE, mutual advantage in.

Union, "Chorus of"—*See* ENEMIES, not, but friends.

Union, Clay's devotion to—Feeling as he [Henry Clay] did, and as the truth surely is, that the world's best hope depended on the continued Union of these states, he was ever jealous of and watchful for whatever might have the slightest tendency to separate them.—*Speech, Springfield, July 16, 1852.* II, 164.

See ABOLITION, radical advocates of, receive execration.

Union, commercial argument for—The great interior region bounded east by the Alleghanies, north by the British dominions, west by the Rocky Mountains and south by the line along which the culture of corn and cotton meets, . . . once half as populous as Massachusetts already is, would have more than seventy-five millions of people ["if not prevented by any political folly or mistake"]. . . . In the production of provisions, grains, grasses and all which proceeds from

them this great interior region is naturally one of the most important in the world. . . . And yet this region has no seacoast—touches no ocean anywhere. As part of one nation, its people now find, and may forever find, their way to Europe by New York, to South America and Africa by New Orleans and to Asia by San Francisco; but separate our common country into two nations, as designed by the present rebellion, and every man of this great interior region is thereby cut off from some one or more of these outlets, not perhaps by a physical barrier but by embarrassing and onerous trade regulations.—*Second annual message, Dec. 1, 1862.* VIII, 113.

2.—And this is true wherever a dividing or boundary line may be fixed. Place it between the now free and slave country, or place it south of Kentucky or north of Ohio, and still the truth remains that none south of it can trade to any port or place north of it, and none north to any port or place south of it, except upon terms dictated by a government foreign to them. —*Second annual message, Dec. 1, 1862.* VIII, 114.

3.—Nor are the marginal regions [of the country] less interested in these communications to and through them to the great outside world. They, too, and each of them, must have access to this Egypt of the West without paying toll at the crossing of any national boundary.—*Second annual message, Dec. 1, 1862.* VIII, 115.

See UNION, no line of cleavage.

Union, destruction of, openly sought—Disunionists *per se* are now in hot haste to get out of the Union, precisely because they perceive they cannot, much longer, maintain an apprehension among the southern people that their homes, and firesides, and lives, are to be endangered by the action of the federal government. With such "now or never" is the maxim. —*Note to Lyman Trumbull for inclusion in speech, Springfield, Nov. 11, 1860.* Hertz II, 793.

2.—A disruption of the federal Union heretofore only menaced, is now formidably attempted.—*First inaugural, March 4, 1861.* VI, 173.

3.—The purpose to sever the federal Union was openly avowed.—*Message to Congress, July 4, 1861.* VI, 298.

4.—A disloyal portion of the American people have, during the whole year, been engaged in an attempt to divide and destroy the Union.—*First annual message, Dec. 3, 1861.* VII, 28.

5.—The insurrection . . . was clandestinely prepared during the winter of 1860 and 1861 and assumed an open organization in the form of a treasonable provisional government in Montgomery, in Alabama, on the 18th of February, 1861.—*Message to Congress, May 26, 1862.* VII, 189.

6.—On the occasion corresponding to this four years ago all thoughts were anxiously directed to an impending civil war. All dreaded it, all sought to avoid it. While the inaugural address was being delivered from this place, devoted altogether to saving the Union without war, insurgent agents were in the city seeking to destroy it without war—seeking to dissolve the Union and divide effects by negotiation. Both parties deprecated war, but one of them would make war rather than let the nation survive, and the other would accept war rather than let it perish, and the war came.—*Second inaugural, March 4, 1865.* XI, 44.

Union, destruction of, won't be permitted—We will say to the southern disunionists, We won't go out of the Union, and you shan't!—*Speech, Bloomington, May 29, 1856.* Lapsley II, 275.

2.—We will not secede, and you shall not.—*To Alexander H. Stephens, Jan. 19, 1859.* Tracy, 125.

3.—We, the majority, would not strive to dissolve the Union; and if any attempt is made, it must be by you, who so loudly stigmatize us as disunionists. But the Union, in any event, will not be dissolved. We don't want to dissolve it, and if you attempt it we won't let you. With the purse and the sword, the army and navy and treasury in our hands and at our command, you could not do it. This government would be very weak indeed if a majority with a disciplined army and navy and well-filled treasury could not preserve itself when attacked by an unarmed, undisciplined, unorganized minority.—*Speech, Galena, Aug. 1, 1856.* II, 294.

4.—All this talk about the dissolution of the Union is humbug, nothing but folly. We do not want to dissolve the Union; you shall not.—*Speech, Galena, Aug. 1, 1856.* II, 295.

5.—How is the dissolution of the Union to be consummated? They tell us that the Union is in danger. Who will divide it? A majority will never dissolve the Union. Can a minority do it?—*Speech, Kalamazoo, Mich., Aug. 27, 1856.* Stern, 407.

6.—While you elect the President, we submit, neither breaking nor attempting to break the Union. If we shall constitutionally elect a President, it will be our duty to see that you submit.—*Speech, Leavenworth, Kan., Dec. 3, 1859.* Angle, 235.

7.—The Union we intend to keep, and loyal states will not let disloyal ones break it.—*To John J. Crittenden, Dec. 22, 1859.* Tracy, 120.

Union, devotion to—To the best of my judgment I have labored [in the 1858 campaign] for, and not against, the Union.—*Speech, Springfield, Oct. 30, 1858.* Angle, 198.

2.—In my devotion to the Union I hope I am behind no man in the nation.—*Speech, reply to New York mayor, Feb. 20, 1861.* VI, 149.

Union, dissolution of, not expected—*See* "HOUSE DIVIDED AGAINST ITSELF," cannot stand, 2.

Union, do-nothing friends of—Yes, you Virginians are good Unionists, but always with an "if"! I don't like that sort of Unionism.—*To John B. Baldwin, April 4, 1861.* War Years I, 195.

2.—The paralysis—the dead palsy—of the government in this whole struggle is that this class of men will do nothing for the government, nothing for themselves, except demanding that the government shall not strike its open enemies, lest they be struck by accident.—*To Cuthbert Bullitt, July 28, 1862.* VII, 295.

3.—He [Thomas J. Durant] speaks [in his letter to Bullitt] of no duty—apparently thinks of none—resting upon Union men. He even thinks it injurious to the Union cause that they should be restrained in trade and passage without taking sides. They are to touch neither a sail nor a pump, but to be merely passengers—deadheads at that—to be carried snug and dry throughout the storm, and safely landed right side up. Nay, more; even a mutineer is to go untouched, lest these sacred passengers receive an accidental wound. Of course the rebellion will never be suppressed in Louisiana if the professed Union men there will neither help to do it nor permit the government to do it without their help.—*To Cuthbert Bullitt, July 28, 1862.* VII, 296.

4.—The man who stands by and says nothing when the peril of his government is discussed, cannot be misunderstood. If not hindered, he is sure to help the enemy; much more if he talks ambiguously—talks for his country with "buts," "ifs" and "ands."—*To Erastus Corning, June 12, 1863.* VIII, 305.

Union, doubtful if more than one state majority against—It may well be questioned whether there is today a majority of the legally qualified voters of any state, except, perhaps, South Carolina, in favor of disunion. There is much reason to believe that the Union men are the majority in many, if not in every other one, of the so-called seceding states. The contrary has not been demonstrated in any one of them.—*Message to Congress, July 4, 1861.* VI, 319.

Union, enemies of, must suffer—That those who make a causeless war should be compelled to pay the cost of it is too obviously just to be called in question. To give governmental protection to the property of persons who have abandoned it and gone on a crusade to overthrow that same government is absurd, if considered in the mere light of justice.—*Message to the House, July 17, 1862. VII, 283.*

2.—This government cannot much longer play a game in which it stakes all, and its enemies stake nothing. These enemies must understand that they cannot experiment for ten years trying to destroy the government, and if they fail still come back into the Union unhurt.—*To August Belmont, July 31, 1862. VII, 300.*

3.—You claim that men may, if they choose, embarrass those whose duty is to combat a great rebellion, and then be dealt with in turn, only as if there were no rebellion. The Constitution itself rejects this view.—*To M. Birchard and others, June 29, 1863. IX, 4.*

Union, fate of, to be decided by 1864 election—The men of the South recently—and perhaps still—at Niagara Falls tell us distinctly that they are in the confidential employment of the rebellion; and they tell us as distinctly that they are not empowered to offer terms of peace. Does anyone doubt that what they are empowered to do is to assist in selecting and arranging a candidate and a platform for the Chicago [Democratic national] convention. Who could have given them this confidential employment but he who, only a week since, declared to Jaquess and Gilmore, that he had no terms of peace but the independence of the South—the dissolution of the Union? Thus, the present presidential contest will almost certainly be no other than a contest between a Union and a disunion candidate, disunion certainly following the success of the latter. The issue is a mighty one, for all people, and all times; and whoever aids the right will be appreciated and remembered.—*To Abram Wakeman, July 25, 1864. X, 170.*

2.—Two or three weeks [at playing hermit in seclusion, as suggested by Gov. Randall] would do me no good. I cannot fly from my thoughts—my solicitude for this great country follows me wherever I go. I do not think it is personal vanity or ambition, though I am not free from these infirmities, but I cannot but feel that the weal or woe of this great nation will be decided [at the election] in November. There is no program offered by any wing of the Democratic party but that must result in the permanent destruction of the Union.—*Interview, Gov. Randall, Aug. 15, 1864. X, 189.*

Union "forever worthy of saving"—*See* UNION, appeals for support of, 1.

Union, "free-love arrangement"—In their [southerners'] view, the Union as a family relation would seem to be no regular marriage, but rather a sort of "free-love" arrangement, to be maintained on "passionate attractiveness."—*Speech, Indianapolis, Feb. 12, 1861. VI, 114.*

Union, friends of, get most votes—It [1864 election] shows that, even among candidates of the same party, he who is most devoted to the Union, and most opposed to treason, can receive most of the people's votes.—*Response to serenade, Nov. 10, 1864. X, 264.*

Union, if destroyed, would be restored—Our national strife springs not . . . from the land we inhabit; not from our national homestead. There is no possible severing of this but would multiply and not mitigate evils among us. In all its adaptations and aptitudes it demands union and abhors separation. In fact it would ere long force reunion, however much of blood and treasure the separation might have cost. Our strife pertains to ourselves—to the passing generation of men—and it can without convulsion be hushed forever with the passing of one generation.—*Second annual message, Dec. 1, 1862. VIII, 115.*

Union, importance of Kentucky to—*See* KENTUCKY, importance of, to Union.

Union, inviolability of—Let me say right here that only unanimous consent of all of the states can dissolve this Union.—*To Alexander H. Stephens, Jan. 19, 1859. Tracy, 125.*

2.—My opinion is, that no state can in any way get out of the Union without the consent of the others.—*To Thurlow Weed, Dec. 17, 1860. VI, 82.*

3.—I hold that in contemplation of universal law and of the Constitution the Union of these states is perpetual. Perpetuity is implied if not expressed, in the fundamental law of all national governments. It is safe to assert that no government proper ever had a provision in its organic law for its own termination. —*First inaugural, March 4, 1861. VI, 173.*

4.—If the United States be not a government proper but an association of states in the nature of a contract merely, can it, as a contract, be peaceably unmade by less than all the parties who made it? One party to a contract may violate it—break it, so to speak— but does it not require all to lawfully rescind it?— *First inaugural, March 4, 1861. VI, 174.*

5.—We find the proposition that in legal contemplation the Union is perpetual confirmed by the history of the Union itself. The Union is much older than the Constitution. It was formed, in fact, by the Articles of Association in 1774. It was matured and continued by the Declaration of Independence in 1776. It was further matured, and the faith of the then thirteen states expressly plighted and engaged that it should be perpetual, by the Articles of Confederation in 1778. And finally, in 1787, one of the declared objects for ordaining and establishing the Constitution was "to form a more perfect Union." But if destruction of the Union by one or by part only of the states be lawfully possible, the Union is less perfect than before the Constitution, having lost the vital element of perpetuity.—*First inaugural, March 4, 1861*. VI, 174.

6.—In view of the Constitution and the laws, the Union is unbroken, and to the extent of my ability I shall take care, as the Constitution expressly enjoins upon me, that the laws of the Union be faithfully executed in all the states. Doing this, I deem to be only a simple duty on my part, and I shall perform it so far as practicable unless my rightful masters, the American people, shall withhold the requisite means or in some authoritative manner direct the contrary. —*First inaugural, March 4, 1861*. VI, 175.

7.—No state upon its own mere motion can lawfully get out of the Union. . . . Resolves and ordinances to that effect are legally void, and . . . acts of violence within any state or states against the authority of the United States are insurrectionary or revolutionary, according to circumstances.—*First inaugural, March 4, 1861*. VI, 175.

8.—I consider the military posts and property situated within the states which claim to have seceded as yet belonging to the government of the United States as much as they did before the supposed secession.—*Reply to committee of Virginia convention, March 13, 1861*. VI, 245.

9.—By the Declaration of Independence . . . the "united colonies" were declared to be "free and independent states"; but even then the object plainly was not to declare their independence of one another or of the Union, but directly the contrary, as their mutual pledge and their mutual action before, at the time, and afterward, abundantly show. The express plighting of faith by each and all of the original thirteen in the Articles of Confederation, two years later, that the Union shall be perpetual, is most conclusive.—*Message to Congress, July 4, 1861*. VI, 314.

10.—The states have their status in the Union, and they have no other legal status. If they break from this, they can only do so against the law and by revolution. The Union, and not themselves separately procured their independence and their liberty.—*Message to Congress, July 4, 1861*. VI, 315.

11.—What is now combatted is the position that secession is consistent with the Constitution—is lawful and peaceful.—*Message to Congress, July 4, 1861*. VI, 316.

12.—The Constitution provides, and all the states have accepted the provision, that "the United States shall guarantee to every state in this Union a republican form of government." But if a state may lawfully go out of the Union, having done so it may discard the republican form of government; so that to prevent its going out is an indisputable means to the end of maintaining the guaranty mentioned.— *Message to Congress, July 4, 1861*. VI, 323.

13.—I have always thought the act of secession is legally nothing, and needs no repealing.—*To B. F. Flanders, Nov. 9, 1863*. IX, 203.

14.—I have never had a theory that secession could absolve states or people from their obligations. Precisely the contrary is asserted in the inaugural address; and it was because of my belief in the continuation of these obligations that I was puzzled for a time, as to denying the legal rights of those citizens who remained individually innocent of treason or rebellion.—*To Crosby and Nichols, Jan. 16, 1864*. IX, 285.

15.—This [reconstruction] bill and this position of these gentlemen seems to me to make the fatal admission [in asserting that rebel states are no longer in the Union] that states whenever they please may of their own motion dissolve their connection with the Union. Now we cannot survive that admission, I am convinced. If that be true, I am not President, these gentlemen are not Congress.—*To group at Capitol, July 4, 1864*. Hay, 205.

Union, knell of—Will not the first drop of blood so shed [over slavery in Nebraska] be the knell of the Union?—*Speech, Peoria, Oct. 16, 1854*. II, 240. Repeated at Urbana, Oct. 24, 1854. Hertz II, 651.

Union, maintenance of, insisted on in election—The most reliable indication of public purpose in this country is derived through our popular elections. Judging by the recent canvass and its results, the purpose of the people within the loyal states to maintain the integrity of the Union was never more firm nor more nearly unanimous than now. The extraordinary calmness and good order with which the millions of voters met and mingled at the polls give strong assurance of this. Not only those who supported the Union ticket, so-called, but a great majority of the opposing party also may be fairly claimed to entertain and to be actuated by the same purpose. It is an unanswerable argument to this effect that no candidate for any office whatever, high or low, has ventured to seek votes on the avowal that he was for giving up the Union. There have been much impugning of motives and much heated controversy as to the proper means and best mode of advancing the Union cause, but on the distinct issue of Union or no Union the politicians have shown their instinctive knowledge that there is no diversity among the people.—*Fourth annual message, Dec. 6, 1864. X, 304.*

Union, music of—Let us keep step to the music of the Union.—*Speech, Bloomington, May 29, 1856.* Lapsley II, 273.

Union, no compromise possible—I do not believe any compromise embracing the maintenance of the Union is now possible. All I learn leads to a directly opposite belief. The strength of the rebellion is its military, its army. That army dominates all the country and all the people within its range. Any offer of terms made by any man or men within that range, in opposition to that army, is simply nothing for the present, because such man or men have no power whatever to enforce their side of a compromise, if one were made with them. . . . In an effort at such a compromise we should waste time which the enemy would improve to our disadvantage; and that would be all.—*To J. C. Conkling, Aug. 26, 1863. IX, 96.*

Union, no effort probable to destroy—Many assurances I receive from the South, that in no probable event will there be any formidable effort to break up the Union. The people of the South have too much of good sense and good temper to attempt the ruin of the government rather than see it administered as it was administered by the men who made it. At least so I hope and believe.—*To John B. Fry, Aug. 15, 1860. VI, 50.*

Union, no line of cleavage—Physically speaking, we cannot separate. We cannot remove our respective sections from each other nor build an impassable wall between them. A husband and wife may be divorced and go out of the presence and beyond the reach of each other, but the different parts of our country cannot do this. They can but remain face to face, and intercourse, either amicable or hostile, must continue between them.—*First inaugural, March 4, 1861. VI, 181.*
Repeated in second annual message, Dec. 1, 1862. VIII, 112.
2.—That portion of the earth's surface which is owned and inhabited by the people of the United States is well adapted to be the home of one national family, and it is not well adapted for two or more. Its vast extent and its variety of climate and productions are of advantage in this age for one people, whatever they might have been in former ages. Steam, telegraphs and intelligence have brought these to be an advantageous combination for one united people. —*Second annual message, Dec. 1, 1862. VIII, 110.*

3.—There is no line, straight or crooked, suitable for a national boundary upon which to divide [the Union]. Trace through, from east to west, upon a line between the free and the slave country, and we shall find a little more than one third of its length are rivers, easy to be crossed, and populated, or soon to be populated, thickly upon both sides; while nearly all its remaining length are merely surveyors' lines, over which people may walk back and forth without any consciousness of their presence. No part of this line can be made any more difficult to pass by writing it down on paper or parchment as a national boundary.—*Second annual message, Dec. 1, 1862. VIII, 112.*
4.—True to themselves, they [people of the North] will not ask where a line of separation shall be, but will vow rather than there shall be no such line.— *Second annual message, Dec. 1, 1862. VIII, 115.*

See SLAVERY, line across continent.

See UNION, commercial argument for.

Union, no service more praiseworthy—No service can be more praiseworthy and honorable than that which is rendered for the maintenance of the Constitution and Union, and the consequent preservation of free government.—*Proclamation, May 8, 1863. VIII, 267.*

Union, people will save—*See* PEOPLE, relied on to save Union.

Union, policy in saving—Having at the beginning of my official term expressed my intended policy as plainly as I was able, it is with deep regret and some mortification I now learn that there is great and injurious uncertainty in the public mind as to what that policy is, and what course I intend to pursue. Not having as yet seen occasion to change, it is now my purpose to pursue the course marked out in the inaugural address.—*Reply to committee of Virginia convention, March 13, 1861. VI, 243.*
2.—In every event I shall, to the extent of my ability, repel force with force.—*Reply to committee from Virginia convention, April 13, 1861. VI, 244.*
3.—The policy chosen [by the administration] looked to the exhaustion of all peaceful measures before a resort to any stronger ones. It sought only to hold the public places and property not already wrested from the government and to collect the revenue, relying for the rest on time, discussion and the ballot box. It promised a continuance of the mails at government expense to the very people who were resisting the government, and it gave repeated pledges against any disturbance to any of the people or any of their rights. Of all that which a President might constitu-

tionally and justifiably do in such a case, everything was forborne, without which it was believed possible to keep the government on foot.—*Message to Congress, July 4, 1861.* Basler, 595.

4.—I shall go just so fast and only so fast as I think I am right and the people are ready for the step.—*To Sen. Horace Maynard, 1861.* Herndon, 508.

5.—I would save the Union. I would save it the shortest way under the Constitution. . . . If there be those who would not save the Union unless they could at the same time save slavery, I do not agree with them. If there be those who would not save the Union unless they could at the same time destroy slavery, I do not agree with them. My paramount object in this struggle is to save the Union, and is not either to save or to destroy slavery. If I could save the Union without freeing any slave, I would do it; and if I could save it by freeing all the slaves, I would do it; and if I could do it by freeing some and leaving the others alone, I would also do that. What I do about slavery and the colored race, I do because I believe it helps to save the Union; and what I forbear, I forbear because I do not believe it would help save the Union. I shall do less whenever I shall believe that what I am doing hurts the cause, and I shall do more whenever I shall believe doing more will help the cause. I shall try to correct errors when shown to be errors, and I shall adopt new views so fast as they shall appear to be true views.—*To Horace Greeley, Aug. 22, 1862.* VIII, 15.

6.—I can't afford to discourage our friends and encourage our enemies, and so, perhaps, make it more difficult to save the Union.—*To James R. Gilmore, late May, 1863.* Gilmore, 157.

7.—I must continue to do so much as may seem to be required by the public safety.—*To Erastus Corning and others, June 12, 1863.* VIII, 314.

8.—My purpose is to be in my action just and constitutional, and yet practical, in performing the important duty with which I am charged, of maintaining the unity and the free principles of our common country.—*To Horatio Seymour, Aug. 7, 1863.* IX, 61.

9.—I hope to "stand firm" enough not to go backward, and yet not go forward fast enough to wreck the country's cause.—*To Z. Chandler, Nov. 20, 1863.* IX, 213.

10.—Will you give our enemies such military advantages as insure success, and then depend on coaxing, flattery and concession to get them back into the Union?—*Interview, Gov. Randall, Aug. 15, 1864.* X, 190.

11.—The way these measures [emancipation and use of colored troops] were to help the cause was not by magic or miracles, but by inducing the colored people to come bodily over from the rebel side to ours.—*Unfinished letter to Charles D. Robinson, Aug. 17, 1864.* X, 194.

12.—When the rebellion broke out, my duty did not admit of a question. That was, first, by all strictly lawful means, to endeavor to maintain the integrity of the government. . . . The paramount idea of the Constitution is the preservation of the Union. It may not be specified in so many words, but that this was the idea of its founders is evident; for, without the Union, the Constitution would be worthless. It seems clear, then, that in the last extremity, if any local institution threatened the existence of the Union, the Executive could not hesitate to do his duty.—*To deputation of antislavery men, April 7, 1864.* Carpenter, 76.

13.—My present position in reference to the rebellion is the result of my best judgment, it is the only position upon which any Executive can or could save the Union. Any substantial departure from it insures the success of the rebellion.—*Unfinished letter to Isaac M. Schermerhorn, Sept. 12, 1864.* X, 221.

14.—In taking the various steps which have led to my present position in relation to the war, the public interest and my private interest have been perfectly parallel, because in no other way could I serve myself so well as by truly serving the Union.—*Unfinished letter to Isaac M. Schermerhorn, Sept. 12, 1864.* X, 221.

Union, preservation of, first duty—Much as I hate slavery, I would consent to the extension of it rather than see the Union dissolved, just as I would consent to any great evil to avoid a greater one.—*Speech, Peoria, Oct. 16, 1854.* II, 236.

Repeated at Urbana, Oct. 24, 1854. Hertz II, 648.

2.—I think you would do well to express [in the governor's inaugural] without passion, threat or appearance of boasting, but, nevertheless, with firmness, the purpose of yourself and your state to maintain the Union at all hazards.—*To Gov. A. G. Curtin, Dec. 21, 1860.* Angle, 260.

3.—The federal Union must be preserved.—*Memorandum, Dec. 22, 1860.* XI, 116.

4.—Until the people of these United States shall otherwise direct, the present federal Union must be preserved as it is, and the present Constitution and laws must be administered as they are.—*Resolution, Illinois Legislature, Feb. 1, 1861.* Hertz II, 809.

5.—There is nothing that could ever bring me to consent—willingly to consent—to the destruction of this Union . . . unless it would be that thing for which the Union itself was made. I understand that the ship is made for the carrying and preservation of the cargo; and so long as the ship is safe with the cargo, it shall not be abandoned. This Union shall never be abandoned, unless the possibility of its existence shall cease to exist without the necessity of throwing passengers and cargo overboard. So long, then, as it is possible that the prosperity and liberties of this people can be preserved within this Union, it shall be my purpose at all times to preserve it.—*Speech, New York, Feb. 20, 1861.* VI, 149.

6.—I have desired as sincerely as any man—I sometimes think more than any other man—that our present difficulties might be settled without the shedding of blood. I will not say that all hope is yet gone. But if the alternative is presented, whether the Union is to be broken in fragments, and the liberties of the people lost, or blood be shed, you will probably make the choice, with which I shall not be dissatisfied.—*To Frontier Guards, April 28, 1861.* Hertz II, 830.

7.—Finding this condition of things, and believing it to be an imperative duty upon the incoming Executive to prevent, if possible, the consummation of such an attempt to destroy the federal Union, a choice of means to that end became indispensable.—*Message to Congress, July 4, 1861.* VI, 299.

8.—In considering the policy to be adopted for suppressing the insurrection I have been anxious and careful that the inevitable conflict for this purpose shall not generate into a violent and remorseless revolutionary struggle. I have therefore in every case thought it proper to keep the integrity of the Union prominent as the primary object of the contest on our part, leaving all questions which are not of vital military importance to the more deliberate action of the Legislature.—*First annual message, Dec. 3, 1861.* VII, 51.

9.—The Union must be preserved; and hence all indispensable means must be employed. We should not be in haste to determine that radical and extreme measures, which may reach the loyal as well as the disloyal, are indispensable.—*First annual message, Dec. 3, 1861.* VII, 52.

10.—You prefer that the constitutional relation of the states to the nation shall be practically restored without disturbance of the institution [slavery]; and if this were done, my whole duty in this respect, under the Constitution and my oath of office, would be performed. But it is not done, and we are trying to accomplish it by war.—*To border-state congressmen, July 12, 1862.* VII, 271.

11.—I . . . proclaim and declare that hereafter, as heretofore, the war will be prosecuted for the object of practically restoring the constitutional relation between the United States and each of the states and the people thereof in which states that relation is or may be suspended or disturbed.—*Proclamation, Sept. 22, 1862.* VIII, 36.

12.—I never did ask more, nor ever was willing to accept less, than for all the states, and the people thereof, to take and hold their places and rights in the Union, under the Constitution of the United States. For this alone have I felt authorized to struggle and I seek neither more nor less now.—*To Gen. McClernand, Jan. 8, 1863.* VIII, 181.

13.—Whatever might have been the cause [of the Civil War], or whosesoever the fault, one duty paramount to all others, was before me [upon becoming President], namely, to maintain and preserve at once the Constitution and the integrity of the federal Republic. A conscientious purpose to perform this duty is the key to all the measures of administration which have been and to all which will hereafter be pursued.—*To workers of Manchester, Jan. 19, 1863.* VIII, 194.

14.—My purpose is to be in my action just and constitutional, and yet practical in performing the important duty with which I am charged, of maintaining the unity and the free principles of our common country.—*To Horatio Seymour, Aug. 7, 1863.* IX, 60.

15.—My enemies pretend that I am now carrying on the war for the sole purpose of abolition. So long as I am President it shall be carried on for the sole purpose of restoring the Union.—*Interview, Gov. Randall, Aug. 15, 1864.* X, 191.

16.—The administration accepted the war thus commenced for the sole avowed object of preserving the Union; and it is not true that it has since been, or will be, prosecuted by this administration for any other object. In declaring this I only declare what I can know and do know to be true, and what no other man can know to be false.—*Unfinished letter to Isaac M. Schermerhorn, Sept. 12, 1864.* X, 221.

17.—These rebels are violating the Constitution to destroy the Union; I will violate the Constitution, if necessary, to save the Union; and I suspect, Chase, that our Constitution is going to have a rough time of it before we get done with this war.—*To Sec. Chase, no date.* Hertz II, 897.

See GOVERNMENT (AMERICAN), preservation of, first duty.

Union, recipe for perpetuity of—Continue to execute all the express provisions of our national Constitution, and the Union will endure forever—it being impossible to destroy it except by some action not provided for in the instrument itself.—*First inaugural, March 4, 1861.* VI, 174.

Union, seceded states in or out of?—*See* RECONSTRUCTION, policy in, 2, 5, 6.

See UNION, inviolability of, 15.

Union, slavery and, perplexing question—Some [friends of the Union] would perpetuate slavery; some would abolish it suddenly and without compensation; some would abolish it gradually and with compensation; some would remove the freed people from among us, and some would retain them with us; and there are yet other minor diversities. Because of these diversities we waste much strength in struggles among ourselves. By concession we should harmonize and act together. This would be compromise, but it would be compromise among the friends and not with the enemies of the Union.—*Second annual message, Dec. 1, 1862.* VIII, 118.

2.—We are in a civil war. In such cases there always is a main question; but in this case that question is a perplexing compound—Union and slavery. It becomes a question, not of two sides merely; but of at least four sides, even among those who are for the Union, saying nothing of those who are against it. Thus, those who are for the Union with, but not without, slavery; those for it without, but not with; those for it with or without, but prefer it with; and those for it with or without, but prefer it without.—*To Charles D. Drake and others, Oct. 5, 1863.* IX, 156.

3.—Again there is a subdivision of those who are for gradual, but not for immediate, and those who are for immediate, but not for gradual extinction of slavery. It is easy to conceive that all these shades of opinion, and even more, may be sincerely entertained by honest and truthful men. Yet, all being for the Union, by reason of these differences each will prefer a different way of sustaining the Union.—*To Charles D. Drake and others, Oct. 5, 1863.* IX, 156.

Union, slavery sole threat to—*See* SLAVERY, sole threat to Union.

Union, South proposes rule or ruin of—You [men of the South] will break up the Union rather than submit to a denial of your constitutional rights. . . . When you make these declarations you have a specific and well-understood allusion to an assumed constitutional right of yours to take slaves into federal territories, and to hold them there as property. But no such right is specifically written in the Constitution. That instrument is literally silent about any such right. We, on the contrary, deny that such a right has any existence in the Constitution, even by implication. Your purpose, then, plainly stated, is that you will destroy the government, unless you be allowed to construe and force the Constitution as you please, on all points in dispute between you and us. You will rule or ruin in all events.—*Cooper Institute address, New York, Feb. 27, 1860.* V, 320.
See SOUTH, will not accept Republican President.

Union, strength in—That "union is strength" is a truth that has been known, illustrated, and declared in various ways and forms in all ages of the world. That great fabulist and philosopher, Aesop, illustrated it by his fable of the bundle of sticks; and He whose wisdom surpasses that of all philosophers has declared that "a house divided against itself cannot stand."—*Whig circular, March 1, 1843.* I, 255.

Union, "We know how to save"—We say we are for the Union. The world will not forget that we say this. We know how to save the Union. The world knows we do know how to save it. We, even we here, hold the power and bear the responsibility. In giving freedom to the slave we assure freedom to the free—honorable alike in what we give and what we preserve. We shall nobly save or meanly lose the last best hope of earth. Other means may succeed; this could not fail. The way is plain, peaceful, generous, just—a way which if followed the world will forever applaud and God must forever bless.—*Second annual message, Dec. 1, 1862.* VIII, 131.

Union, what preserved?—*See* DECLARATION OF INDEPENDENCE, source of political creed, 2.

Union, won't try to dissolve—In my opposition to the admission of Kansas [as a slave state] I shall have some company, but we may be beaten. If we are, I shall not on that account attempt to dissolve the Union.—*To Joshua F. Speed, Aug. 24, 1855.* II, 285.

Union League of Philadelphia, thanked for approval—I shall always bear with me the consciousness of having endeavored to do my duty in the trying times through which we are passing, and the generous approval of a portion of my fellow-citizens so intelligent and so patriotic as those composing your association assures me that I have not wholly failed.—*To George H. Boker, Oct. 26, 1863.* IX, 182.

"Union of hearts and hands"—I thank you for the assurance you give me that I shall be supported by conservative men like yourself, in the efforts I may make to restore the Union, so as to make it, to use your language, a Union of hearts and hands as well as of states.—*To Gen. Van Alen, April 14, 1865.* XI, 94.

"Union Party"—*See* KNOW-NOTHING PARTY, not a member of, 3.

Union Troops, consideration due to—Whatever shall be sincerely, and in God's name, devised for the good of the soldier and seaman in their hard spheres of duty, can scarcely fail to be blessed.—*To Rev. Alexander Reed, Feb. 22, 1863.* VIII, 217.

2.—We never should, and I am sure never will, be niggard of gratitude and benefaction to the soldiers who have endured toil, privations and wounds, that the nation may live.—*Statement, Aug. 10, 1863.* Hertz II, 905.

3.—I doubt not that Congress will cheerfully adopt such measures as will, without essentially changing the general features of the [public-lands] system, secure, to the greatest practicable extent, its benefits to those who have left their homes in defence of the country in this arduous crisis.—*Third annual message, Dec. 8, 1863.* IX, 242.

4.—Our soldiers are doing well, and must and will be done well by.—*To A. Mackay, May 20, 1864.* X, 105.

5.—I propose that you constantly bear in mind that the support you owe to brave officers and soldiers in the field is of the very first importance, and we should therefore bend all our energies to that point.—*Reply to Ohio delegation, June 9, 1864.* X, 122.

6.—Say what you will, after all, the most is due to the soldier who takes his life in his hands and goes to fight the battles of his country.—*Speech, Philadelphia, June 16, 1864.* X, 128.

7.—Nor must those whose harder part gives us the cause of rejoicing be overlooked. Their honors must not be parcelled out with others.—*Last public speech, April 11, 1865.* XI, 84.

See EMANCIPATION PROCLAMATION, original draft of, given for soldiers' benefit.

See GETTYSBURG ADDRESS, manuscript of, given for soldiers' benefit.

Union Troops, entitled to preference—*See* PATRONAGE, preference due soldiers.

See UNION TROOPS, consideration due to.

Union Troops, number tendered greater than ability to receive—One of the greatest perplexities of the government is to avoid receiving troops faster than it can provide for them.—*Message to Congress, July 4, 1861.* VI, 312.

2.—The plain matter of fact is, our good people have rushed to the rescue of the government faster than the government can find arms to put into their hands.—*To Gen. McClernand, Nov. 10, 1861.* VII, 19.

3.—It is gratifying to know that the patriotism of the people has proved equal to the occasion, and that the number of troops tendered greatly exceeds the force which Congress authorized me to call into the field.—*First annual message, Dec. 3, 1861.* VII, 35.

Union Troops, "only northern realities"—I don't believe there is any North. The seventh regiment [overdue at Washington] is a myth. Rhode Island is not known in our geography any longer. You are the only northern realities.—*To soldier group, April 24, 1861.* Hay, 11.

Union Troops, treated liberally—No considerable body of troops, it is believed, were ever more amply provided and more liberally and punctually paid [than are our northern soldiers] and it may be added that by no people were the burdens incident to a great war more cheerfully borne.—*Third annual message, Dec. 8, 1863.* IX, 233.

Union Troops, tributes to—I make no apology, gentlemen, for my weakness, but I knew poor [Col. E. E.] Ellsworth well and held him in high regard. . . . Poor fellow, it was doubtless an act of rashness, but it only shows the heroic spirit that animates our soldiers, from high to low, in this righteous cause of ours.—*To Sen. Wilson and others, May 3, 1861.* Hertz II, 822.

2.—Greatest honor is due to those officers who remained true, despite their treacherous associates; but the greatest honor, and most important fact of all, is the unanimous firmness of the common soldiers and common sailors. To the last man, so far as known, they have successfully resisted the traitorous efforts of those whose commands, but an hour before, they obeyed as absolute law. This is the patriotic instinct of the plain people.—*Message to Congress, July 4, 1861.* VI, 321.

3.—It is worthy of note that while in this government's hour of trial large numbers of those in the army and navy who have been favored with the offices have resigned and proved false to the hand which has pampered them, not one common soldier or sailor is known to have deserted his flag!—*Message to Congress, July 4, 1861.* VI, 321.

4.—I refer with pleasure to those portions of his [secretary of war's] report which makes allusion to the creditable degree of discipline already attained by our troops, and to the excellent sanitary condition of the entire army.—*First annual message, Dec. 3, 1861.* VII, 35.

5.—Be of good cheer; all is well. The country owes you an inextinguishable debt for your services. I am under immeasurable obligations to you. You have, like heroes, endured, and fought, and conquered. Yes, I say conquered; for though apparently checked, you conquered afterward and secured the position of your choice. You shall be strengthened and rewarded.—*Speech to troops, July, 1862.* War Years I, 496.

6.—With us every soldier is a man of character, and must be treated with more consideration than is customary in Europe.—*To Count A. De Gasparin, Aug. 4, 1862.* VII, 301.

7.—I am environed with difficulties. Yet they are scarcely so great as the difficulties of those who upon the battlefield are endeavoring to purchase with their blood and their lives the future happiness and prosperity of this country.—*Reply to serenade, Sept. 24, 1862.* VIII, 44.

8.—I return thanks to our gallant soldiers for the good service they have rendered, the energies they have shown, the hardships they have endured, the blood they have so nobly shed for this dear Union of ours.—*Speech, Frederick, Md., Oct. 4, 1862.* VIII, 125.

9.—I would like to speak in terms of praise due to the many brave officers and soldiers who have fought in the cause of the Union and liberties of their country from the beginning of the war.—*Response to serenade, July 7, 1863.* IX, 21.

10.—The brave men, living and dead, who struggled here, have consecrated it far above our poor power to add or detract. The world will little note nor long remember what we say here, but it can never forget what they did here.—*Gettysburg Address, Nov. 19, 1863.* IX, 210.

11.—Our chiefest care must still be directed to the army and navy, who have thus far borne their harder part so nobly and well; and it may be esteemed fortunate that in giving the greatest efficiency to these indispensable arms we do also honorably recognize the gallant men, from commander to sentinel, who compose them, and to whom more than to others the world must stand indebted for the home of freedom disenthralled, regenerated, enlarged and perpetuated.—*Third annual message, Dec. 8, 1863.* IX, 252.

12.—This extraordinary war . . . falls heavily upon all classes of people, but most heavily upon the soldier. For it has been said, all that a man hath he will give for his life; and while all contribute of their substance, the soldier puts his life at stake, and often yields it up in his country's cause. The highest merit, then, is due to the soldier.—*Speech, Washington, March 18, 1864.* X, 48.

13.—I am indeed very grateful to the brave men who have been struggling with the enemy in the field, and to their noble commanders who have directed them.—*Response to serenade, May 9, 1864.* X, 95.

14.—Say what you will, after all, the most is due the soldier who takes his life in his hands and goes to fight the battles of his country.—*Speech, Philadelphia, June 16, 1864.* X, 128.

15.—I am especially gratified that the soldier and seaman were not forgotten by the [Republican national] convention, as they forever must and will be remembered by the grateful country for whose salvation they devote their lives.—*To William Dennison and others, accepting nomination, June 27, 1864.* X, 137.

16.—In this purpose—to save the country and its liberties—no classes of people seem as nearly unanimous as the soldiers in the field and the sailors afloat. Do they not have the hardest of it? Who should quail when they do not? God bless the soldiers and seamen, with all their brave commanders.—*Response to serenade, Oct. 19, 1864.* X, 245.

17.—To you who render the hardest work in its [the government's] support should be given the greatest credit. Other who are connected with it, and who occupy higher positions, can be dispensed with, but we cannot get along without your aid. While others differ with the administration, and, perhaps, honestly, the soldiers have generally sustained it.—*Speech to 189th New York regiment, Oct. 24, 1864.* X, 252.

See FREE INSTITUTIONS, raise condition of whole people.

Union Troops, voted right—They have not only fought right, but, so far as can be judged from their actions, they have voted right, and I for one thank you for it.—*Speech to 189th New York regiment, Oct. 24, 1864.* X, 252.

Unit Rule, favored—The delegation of each county should go [to the convention] as a unit.—*To B. F. James, Jan. 27, 1846.* I, 287.

United States—*See* AMERICA.

United States Senate, Lincoln aspires to—You used to express a good deal of partiality for me and if you are still so, now is the time. Some friends here are really for me for the U.S. Senate, and I should be very grateful if you could make a mark for me among your members.—*To Charles Hoyt, Nov. 10, 1854.* II, 262.

2.—I have a suspicion that a Whig has been selected to the legislature from Edgar. If this is not so, why then *"nix cum arous,"* but if it is so then could you not make a mark with him for me for U.S. Senator? I really have some chance.—*To Jacob Harding, Nov. 11, 1854.* Tracy, 52.

3.—It has come round that a Whig may, by possibility, be elected to the United States Senate; and I want the chance of being the man. You are a member of the legislature, and have a vote to give. Think it over, and see whether you can do better than go for me.—*To T. J. Henderson, Nov. 27, 1854.* II, 263.

4.—I have really got it into my head to try to be United States senator. . . . But I know, and acknowledge, that you have as just claims to the place as I have; and therefore I cannot ask you to yield to me, if you are thinking of becoming a candidate yourself. If, however, you are not, then I should like to be remembered affectionately by you.—*To Joseph Gillespie, Dec. 1, 1854.* II, 265.

5.—Of course I prefer myself to all others [as candidate for senator]; yet it is neither in my heart nor my conscience to say that I am any better man than Mr. Williams. We shall have a desperate struggle with our adversaries. They are desperate and bent on desperate deeds.—*To T. J. Henderson, Dec. 15, 1854.* II, 268.

6.—Doubtless you have suspected for some time that I entertain a personal wish for a term in the United States Senate; and had the suspicion taken the shape of a direct charge, I think I could not have truthfully denied it.—*To N. B. Judd, Nov. 15, 1858.* V, 91.

7.—I would rather have a full term in the Senate than in the Presidency.—*To N. B. Judd, Dec. 9, 1859.* V, 282.

See CAMPAIGN OF 1858.

United States Supreme Court—*See* SUPREME COURT.

"Unprecedented Agreement"—*See* WEED, THURLOW, unprecedented agreement.

"Unvexed to the Sea"—*See* CIVIL WAR, progress of, 5.

See VICKSBURG, Lincoln's prayer for.

"Useless Labor," factor in tariff problem—*See* TARIFF, useless labor as a factor.

Usury, law proposed to limit—I would favor the passage of a law on this subject [usury] which might not be very easily evaded. Let it be such that the labor and difficulty of evading it could only be justified in cases of greatest necessity.—*Address to Sangamon County, March 9, 1832.* I, 2.

2.—It appears that the practice of loaning money at exorbitant rates of interest has already been opened as a field for discussion. . . . It seems as though we are never to have an end to this baneful and corroding system, acting almost as prejudicially to the general interests of the community as a direct tax of several thousand dollars annually laid on each county for the benefit of a few individuals only, unless there be a law made fixing the limits of usury.—*Address to Sangamon County, March 9, 1832.* I, 6.

Utah, gets local option on slavery—*See* COMPROMISE OF 1850, Nebraskaism and.

Utah, polygamy and statehood—If the people of Utah shall peacefully form a state constitution tolerating polygamy, will the Democracy admit them into the Union? There is nothing in the United States Constitution or law against polygamy; and why is it not a part of the judge's [Douglas's] "sacred right of self-government" for the people to have it, or rather to keep it, if they choose?—*Speech, Springfield, June 27, 1857.* II, 317.

Utah, rebellion and sovereignty—If it prove to be true, as is probable, that the people of Utah are in open rebellion against the United States, then Judge Douglas is in favor of repealing their territorial organization, and attaching them to the adjoining state for judicial purposes. I say so, too; if they are in rebellion, they ought to be somehow coerced to obedience, and I am not now prepared to admit or deny the judge's mode of coercing them is not as good as any. The Republicans can fall in with it, without taking back anything they ever said. To be sure, it would be a considerable backing down by Judge Douglas from his much-vaunted doctrine of self-government for the territories; but this is only additional proof of what was very plain from the beginning, that the doctrine was a mere deceitful pretense for the benefit of slavery.—*Speech, Springfield, June 27, 1857.* II, 315.

Vallandigham, C. L., arrest of, explained—It is asserted in substance [by the Albany meeting of May 16], that Mr. Vallandigham was, by a military commander, seized and tried "for no other reason than words addressed to a public meeting in criticism of the course of the administration, and in condemnation of the military orders of the general." Now . . . if this assertion is the truth and the whole truth, if there was no other reason for the arrest, then I concede that the arrest was wrong. But the arrest, as I understand, was made for a very different reason. . . . His [Vallandigham's] arrest was made because he was laboring, with some effect, to prevent the raising of troops, to encourage desertions from the army, and to leave the rebellion without an adequate military force to suppress it. He was not arrested because he was damaging the political prospects of the administration or the personal interests of the commanding general but because he was damaging the army, upon the existence and vigor of which the life of the nation depends. He was warring upon the military, and this gave the military constitutional jurisdiction to lay hands upon him. . . . Must I shoot a simple-minded boy who deserts, while I must not touch a hair of a wily agitator who induces him to desert? . . . I think that, in such a case, to silence the agitator and save the boy is not only constitutional, but withal a great mercy.—*To Erastus Corning and others, June 12, 1863.* VIII, 307.

2.—The military arrests and detentions which have been made, including those of Mr. Vallandigham, which are not different in principle from the others, have been for prevention, and not for punishment—as injunctions to stay injury, as proceedings to keep the peace; and hence, like proceedings in such cases and for like reasons, they have not been accompanied with indictments, or trials by jury, nor in a single case by any punishment whatever, beyond what is purely incidental to the prevention.—*To M. Birchard and others, June 29, 1863.* IX, 4.

3.—The original sentence of imprisonment in Mr. Vallandigham's case was to prevent injury to the military service only and the modification of it was made as a less disagreeable mode to him of securing the same prevention.—*To M. Birchard and others, June 29, 1863.* IX, 5.

4.—I certainly do not know that Mr. Vallandigham has specifically and by direct language advised against enlistments and in favor of desertions and resistance to drafting. We all know that combinations, armed in some instances, to resist the arrest of deserters began several months ago; that more recently the like has appeared in resistance to the enrollment preparatory to a draft; and that quite a number of assassinations have occurred from the same animus. . . . And now, under a sense of responsibility more weighty and enduring than any which is merely official, I solemnly declare my belief that this hindrance of the military, including maiming and murder, is due to the course in which Mr. Vallandigham has been engaged in a greater degree than to any other cause; and it is due to him personally in a greater degree than to any other one man. These things have been notorious, known to all, and of course known to Mr. Vallandigham. Perhaps I would not be wrong to say they originated with his special friends and adherents. With perfect knowledge of them, he has frequently if not constantly made speeches in Congress and before popular assemblies; and if it can be shown that, with these things staring him in the face, he has ever uttered a word of rebuke or counsel against them, it will be a fact greatly in his favor with me and one of which as yet I am totally ignorant. When it is known that the whole burden of his speeches has been to stir up men against the prosecution of the war, and that in the midst of resistance to it, he has not been known to counsel against such resistance, it is next to

impossible to repel the inference that he has counseled directly in favor of it.—*To M. Birchard and others, June 29, 1863.* IX, 6.

Vallandigham, C. L., arrested and tried by Democrats—See DEMOCRATIC PARTY, attitude of, toward war effort, 1.

Vallandigham, C. L., method suggested to effect release of—If it is a false hope [that Vallandigham's election as governor would mean immunity for deserters, and so forth] and one which you would willingly dispel, I will make the way exceedingly easy. I send you duplicates of this letter in order that you, or a majority of you, may, if you choose, indorse your names upon one of them and return it thus indorsed to me with the understanding that those signing are thereby committed to the following propositions, and to nothing else: 1. That there is now a rebellion in the United States, the object and tendency of which is to destroy the national Union; and that, in your opinion, the army and navy are constitutional means for suppressing that rebellion; 2. That no one of you will do anything which, in his own opinion, will tend to hinder the increase, or favor the decrease, or lessen the efficiency of the army or navy while engaged in the effort to suppress that rebellion; and 3. That each of you will, in his sphere, do all he can to have the officers, soldiers and seamen of the army and navy, while engaged in the effort to suppress the rebellion, paid, fed, clad, and otherwise well provided for and supported. And with the further understanding that upon receiving the letter and names thus indorsed, I will cause them to be published, which publication shall be, within itself, a revocation of the order in relation to Mr. Vallandigham. It will not escape observation that I consent to the release of Mr. Vallandigham upon terms not embracing any pledge from him or from others as to what he will or will not do. . . . I should expect that on his return he would not put himself practically in antagonism with the position of his friends. But I do it chiefly because I thereby prevail on other influential gentlemen of Ohio to so define their position as to be of immense value to the army.—*To M. Birchard and others, June 29, 1863.* IX, 8.

Vallandigham, C. L., regret that arrest was necessary—All the cabinet regretted the necessity of arresting . . . Vallandigham, some perhaps doubting there was a real necessity for it; but, being done, all were for seeing you through with it.—*To Gen. Burnside, May 29, 1863.* VIII, 286.

2.—I am specifically called upon [by the Albany resolutions] to discharge Mr. Vallandigham. . . . In response to such appeal I have to say, it gave me pain when I learned that Mr. Vallandigham had been arrested—that is, I was pained that there should have seemed to be a necessity for arresting him—and that it will afford me great pleasure to discharge him so soon as I can by any means believe the public safety will not suffer by it.—*To Erastus Corning and others, June 12, 1863*. VIII, 313.

3.—In my discretion I do not know whether I would have ordered the arrest of Mr. Vallandigham. While I cannot shift responsibility from myself, I hold that as a general rule, the commander in the field is the better judge of the necessity in any particular case.— *To Erastus Corning and others, June 12, 1863*. VIII, 313.

Vallandigham, C. L., return of—I don't believe that Vallandigham has returned; I never can believe it until he forces himself offensively upon the public attention. Then we shall have to deal with him. So long as he behaves himself decently, he is as effectually in disguise as the man who went to a masquerade party with a clean face.—*To Fernando Wood, June, 1864*. War Years III, 109.

Vallandigham, C. L., watch him—Consult freely together, watch Vallandigham and others close, and upon discovering any palpable injury or imminent danger to the military proceeding from him, them or any of them, arrest all implicated; otherwise, do not arrest without further order.—*To Gov. Brough and Gen. Heintzelman, June 20, 1864 (not sent)*. X, 134.

Van Buren, Martin, Cass and—*See* CASS, LEWIS D., Van Buren and.

Van Buren, Martin, death of—This event will occasion mourning in the nation, for the loss of a citizen and a public servant whose memory will be gratefully cherished. Although it has occurred at a time when his country is afflicted with division and civil war, the grief of his patriotic friends will be measurably assuaged by the consciousness that while suffering with disease and seeing his end approaching, his prayers were for the restoration of the authority of the government of which he had been the head, and for peace and good-will among his fellow-citizens.—*Executive order, July 25, 1862*. Messages, VII, 3319.

Van Buren, Martin, has no defense for—It is no business or inclination of mine to defend Martin Van Buren in the war of extermination now waging between him and his old admirers. I say, "Devil take the hindmost—and the foremost!"—*Speech in Congress, July 27, 1848*. II, 71.

Van Buren, Martin, "old horse"—Is not a certain Martin Van Buren an old horse which your own [Democratic] party have turned out to root? And is he not rooting a little to your own discomfort about now?—*Speech in Congress, July 27, 1848*. II, 70.

Vanderbilt, Cornelius, thanked—I have inadvertently omitted so long to inform you that in March last Mr. Cornelius Vanderbilt, of New York, gratuitously presented to the United States the ocean steamer *Vanderbilt*, by many esteemed the finest merchant ship in the world. . . . For the patriotic act of making this magnificent and valuable present to the country I recommend that some suitable acknowledgment be made.—*Message to Congress, July 17, 1862*. Lapsley VI, 93.

Venezuela—The government and people of the United States cannot but feel deep interest and earnest sympathy in the peace, the prosperity, and the progress of Venezuela.—*Reply to Venezuelan minister, Blas Bruzual, Sept. 5, 1864*. X, 217.

Veto, abuse of—*See* CONGRESS, legislation should rest with.

Veto, electoral votes and—*See* EXECUTIVE POWER, electoral votes and.

Veto, "Providence retains"—*See* PEOPLE, Douglas's attitude toward.

Veto, Taylor agrees with Jefferson—If we compare the opinions of Jefferson and [Zachary] Taylor [regarding the veto] . . . we find them more exactly alike than we can often find any two expressions having any literal difference. None but interested faultfinders, I think, can find any substantial variation.— *Speech in Congress, July 27, 1848*. II, 62.

Vice Admiral, new rank urged—I cordially concur in the recommendation of the secretary [of the navy] as to the propriety of creating the new rank of vice admiral in our navy service.—*Fourth annual message, Dec. 6, 1864*. X, 297.

Vice Presidency, no interference in—Wish not to interfere about Vice President. Cannot interfere about platform. Convention must judge for itself.— *Indorsement on letter, June 6, 1864*. X, 115.

Vicksburg, Lincoln's prayer for—The fact is—but don't say anything about this either just now—I have been praying to Almighty God for Vicksburg also. I have wrestled with Him, and told Him how much we need the Mississippi, and how it ought to flow unvexed to the sea, and how that great valley ought to be forever free, and I reckon He understands the whole business from "A to Izzard." I have done the very best I could to help Gen. Grant along, and all the rest of our generals, though some of them don't think so, and now it is kind of borne in upon me that somehow or other we are going to win at Vicksburg also. I can't tell how soon. But I believe we will. For this will save the Mississippi and cut the Confederacy in twain; and be in line with God's law besides.—*To Gen. Sickles, July 5, 1863.* Whitney, 274.

Victoria, Queen, respect and esteem for—It is now a pleasant duty to acknowledge the demonstration you have given of your desire that the spirit of amity and peace toward this country may prevail in the councils of your Queen, who is respected and esteemed in your country only more than she is by the kindred nation which has its home on this side of the Atlantic. —*To workers of Manchester, Jan. 19, 1863.* VIII, 195.

See GREAT BRITAIN, friendship of, for America, 1.

Victoria, Queen, sympathy for—I am informed of the overwhelming affliction which has fallen upon Your Majesty, by the untimely death of His Royal Highness, the late Prince Consort, Prince Albert of Saxe Coburg. The offer of condolence in such cases is a customary ceremony, which has its good uses, though it is conventional, and may sometimes be even insincere. But I would fain have Your Majesty apprehend on this occasion, that real sympathy can exist, as real truthfulness can be practiced, in the intercourse of nations. . . . The American people . . . deplore his death and sympathize in Your Majesty's irreparable bereavement with an unaffected sorrow. This condolence may not be altogether ineffectual, since we are sure it emanates from only virtuous motives and fraternal affection. I do not dwell upon it, however, because I know that the Divine hand that has wounded, is the only one that can heal: And so commending Your Majesty and the Prince Royal, the Heir Apparent, and all your afflicted family to the tender mercies of God.—*To Queen Victoria, Feb. 1, 1862.* Hertz II, 848.

Vigilance, urged on Union generals—*See* HALLECK, HENRY W., vigilance urged on.

See HUNTER, DAVID, vigilance urged on.

See GRANT, U. S., vigilance urged on.

Vindictiveness, no indulgence in—[Expressing the idea that no good comes of punishing political dereliction], I am in favor of short statutes of limitation in politics.—*To John Hay and others, Nov. 11, 1864.* Hay, 239.

Violence, marks Compromise repeal—*See* KANSAS-NEBRASKA ACT, violence marks.

Violence, safety from—*See* HOUSELESS, admonished.

Violet, stain is cherished—The sweet violet you inclosed came safely to hand, but it was so dry, and mashed so flat, that it crumbled to dust at the first attempt to handle it. The juice that mashed out of it stained a place in the letter, which I mean to preserve and cherish for the sake of her who procured it to be sent.—*To Joshua F. Speed, March 27, 1842.* I, 217.

Virginia, abolitionists of—*See* ABOLITION, Virginians advocated.

Virginia, changes tune—But within less than 50 years [after urging abolition] Virginia changed its tune, and made negro breeding for the cotton and sugar states one of its leading industries.—*Speech, Bloomington, May 29, 1856.* Lapsley II, 258.

Virginia, legislature refused recognition—It has been intimated to me that the gentlemen who have acted as the legislature of Virginia in support of the rebellion may now desire to assemble at Richmond and take measures to withdraw the Virginia troops and other support from resistance to the general government. If they attempt it, give them permission and protection, until, if at all, they attempt some action hostile to the United States, in which case you will notify them, give them reasonable time to leave, and at the end of which time arrest any who remain.—*To Gen. Weitzel, April 6, 1865.* XI, 75.
2.—I have just seen Judge Campbell's letter to you of the 7th. He assumes, it appears to me, that I have called the insurgent legislature of Virginia together, as the rightful legislature of the state, to settle all differences with the United States. I have done no such thing. I spoke of them, not as a legislature, but as "the gentlemen who have acted as the legislature of Virginia in support of the rebellion." I did this on purpose to exclude the assumption that I was recognizing them as a rightful body.—*To Gen. Weitzel, April 12, 1865.* XI, 92.
3.—Let my letter to you and the paper to Judge Campbell both be withdrawn, or countermanded, and he be notified of it. Do not allow them [members of the legislature] to assemble but if any have come, allow them safe return to their homes.—*To Gen. Weitzel, April 12, 1865.* XI, 93.

Virginia, "nest" of insurrection—The people of Virginia have thus allowed this giant insurrection to make its nest within its borders, and this government has no choice left but to deal with it where it finds it; and it has the less regret, as the loyal citizens have in due form claimed its protection. Those loyal citizens this government is bound to recognize and protect, as being Virginia.—*Message to Congress, July 4, 1861.* VI, 307.

Virginia, not much left of—The inauguration of West Virginia as a new state left to him [Gov. Pierpoint], as he assumed, the remainder of the old state; and the insignificance of the parts which are outside of the rebel lines, and consequently within his reach, certainly gives a somewhat farcical air to his dominion, and I suppose he, as well as I, has considered that it could be useful for little else than a nucleus to add to.—*To Gen. Butler, Aug. 9, 1864 (not sent until Dec. 21, 1864).* X, 321.

Virginia, objects to Massachusetts taking her negroes for soldiers—*See* NEGRO TROOPS, Massachusetts wants Virginians, 1.

Virginia, office-hungry citizens of—*See* PUBLIC OFFICE, Virginians' hunger for.

Virginia, policy toward—I have no objection to declare a thousand times that I have no purpose to invade Virginia or any other state, but I do not mean to let them invade us without striking back.—*To Reverdy Johnson, April 24, 1861.* Stern, 663.
2.—I have no purpose to invade Virginia . . . as I understand the word invasion. But, suppose Virginia sends her troops, or admits others through her borders, to assail this capital, am I not to repel them even to the crossing of the Potomac, if I can? Suppose Virginia erects, or permits to be erected, batteries on the opposite shore to bombard the city, are we to stand still and see it done? In a word, if Virginia strikes us, are we not to strike back, and as effectively as we can?—*To Reverdy Johnson, April 24, 1861.* VI, 254.

See INVASION, policy toward.

Virginia, popular will ignored in secession—The course taken in Virginia [to accomplish secession] was the most remarkable, perhaps the most important. A convention elected by the people of the state to consider this very question of disrupting the federal Union was in session at the capital of Virginia when Fort Sumter fell. To this body the people had chosen a large majority of professed Union men. Almost immediately after the fall of Fort Sumter many members of that majority went over to the original disunion minority, and with them adopted an ordinance for withdrawing the state from the Union. . . . Although they submitted the ordinance for ratification to a vote of the people, to be taken on a date then somewhat more than a month distant, the convention

and the legislature—which was also in session at the same time and place—with leading men of the state not members of either, immediately commenced acting as if the state were already out of the Union.—*Message to Congress, July 4, 1861.* VI, 305.

Virginia, slavery and the Northwest Territory—*See* ORDINANCE OF 1787, fruits of, 1.

Virginia, western, loyal—After a somewhat bloody struggle for months, winter closes on the Union people of western Virginia, leaving them masters of their own country.—*First annual message, Dec. 3, 1861.* VII, 53.

Vocation, relation of, to office holding—*See* OFFICE HOLDING, vocations and.

Volunteer Soldiers, drafted men and, compared—*See* MILITARY DRAFT, volunteers and drafted men compared.

Volunteer Soldiers, plea for—If . . . any one of you will volunteer, he for his single self will escape the horrors of the draft, and will thereby do only what each one of at least a million of his manly brethren have already done. Their toil and blood have been given as much for you as for themselves. Shall it all be lost rather than that you, too, will bear your part? —*Opinion on draft law, Aug. 15, 1863.* IX, 78.

Vote—*See* ELECTIVE FRANCHISE.

Voting Privilege—*See* SUFFRAGE, desired for loyal men.

See NEGRO SUFFRAGE.

Vulnerable Heels, Democratic affliction—[Mr. Lamborn says:] "The Democrats are vulnerable in the heels, but they are sound in the head and the heart." The first branch of the figure—that is, that the Democrats are vulnerable in the heels—I admit is not merely figurative, but literally true. Who that looks but a moment at their Swartouts, their Prices, their Harringtons, and their hundreds of others, scampering away with the public money to Texas, to Europe, and to every spot of the earth where a villain may hope to find refuge from justice, can at all doubt that they are most distressingly affected in their heels with a species of "running itch"? It seems that this malady of their heels operates on those sound-minded, and honest-hearted creatures very much like the cork leg in the comic song did on its owner; which, when he once got started on it, the more he tried to stop it, the more it would run away.—*Speech, Springfield, Dec. 20, 1839.* I, 136.

Wadsworth, James S., tribute to—No man has given himself up to the war with such self-sacrificing patriotism as Gen. Wadsworth. He went into the service not wishing or expecting great success or distinction in his military career and profoundly indifferent to popular applause, actuated only by a sense of duty which he neither evaded nor sought to evade.—*To John Hay, May 9, 1864.* Hay, 182.

Wages, inequality in—An honest laborer digs coal at about 70 cents a day, while the President [of the United States] digs abstractions at about $70 a day. The coal is clearly worth more than the abstractions, and yet what a monstrous inequality in the process.—*Speech in Congress, June 20, 1848.* II, 37.

Walker, Robert J., characterized—I know he's our American Solon. He is in favor of cutting straight across lots; but it's safer to go around by the road, and, sometimes, you get there just as soon.—*To James R. Gilmore, April 13, 1861.* Gilmore, 18.

Wall Street, gamblers of, condemned—Curtin, what do you think of those fellows in Wall Street who are gambling in gold at such a time as this? . . . For my part, I wish every one of them had his devilish head shot off.—*To Gov. Curtin, April 25, 1864.* Carpenter, 84.

War, enemy property in—The most that can be said against the [Emancipation] Proclamation—if so much —is that slaves are property. Is there—has there ever been—any question that by the law of war, property, both of enemies and friends, may be taken when needed? And is it not needed whenever taking it helps us, or hurts the enemy? Armies, the world over, destroy enemies' property when they cannot use it; and even destroy their own to keep it from the enemy.—*To J. C. Conkling, Aug. 26, 1863.* IX, 98.

See CONFISCATION, when justified.

War, folly of beginning—Such will be a great lesson of peace; teaching men that what they cannot take by an election, neither can they take by a war; teaching all the folly of being the beginners of a war.—*Message to Congress, July 4, 1861.* VI, 322.

War, how men act in—Actual war coming, blood grows hot, and blood is spilled. Thought is forced from old channels into confusion. Deception breeds and thrives. Confidence dies and universal suspicion reigns. Each man feels an impulse to kill his neighbor, lest he be first killed by him. Revenge and retaliation follow. . . . Every foul bird comes abroad and every dirty reptile rises up. These add crime to confusion. Strong measures deemed indispensable, but harsh at best, such men make worse by maladministration. Murders for old grudges, and murders for pelf, proceed under any cloak that will best cover for the occasion. These causes amply account for what has occurred in Missouri.—*To Charles D. Drake and others, Oct. 5, 1863.* IX, 156.

War, melioration of maritime—Although we have failed to induce some of the commercial powers to adopt a desirable melioration of the rigor of maritime war, we have removed all obstructions from the way of this humane reform, except such as are merely of temporary and accidental occurrence.—*First annual message, Dec. 3, 1861.* VII, 32.

War, no barbarities in civilized—The law of nations, and the usages and customs of war, as carried on by civilized powers, permit no distinction as to color in the treatment of prisoners of war as public enemies. To sell or enslave any captured person on account of his color, and for no offence against the laws of war, is a relapse into barbarism, and a crime against the civilization of the age.—*Executive order, July 30, 1863.* IX, 48.
2.—Civilized belligerents do all in their power to help themselves or hurt the enemy, except a few things regarded as barbarous or cruel. Among the exceptions are the massacre of vanquished foes and noncombatants, male and female.—*To J. C. Conkling, Aug. 26, 1863.* IX, 98.

See NEGRO TROOPS, protection of.

War, no holidays in—I sincerely wish war was an easier and pleasanter business than it is; but it does not admit of holidays.—*To T. H. Clay, Oct. 8, 1862.* VIII, 55.

War, no need of—*See* BLOODSHED, unnecessary.

War, those who cause should pay—*See* UNION, enemies of, must suffer.

War, trying to save Union without—*See* UNION, destruction of, openly sought, 6.

War Between the States, no thought of precipitating —I had no thought in the world [in speech at Springfield] that I was doing anything to bring about a war between the free and slave states [as Douglas charges]. I had no thought in the world that I was doing anything to bring about a political and social equality of the black and white races. It never occurred to me that I was doing anything or favoring anything to reduce to a dead uniformity all the local institutions of the various states. But I must say, in all fairness to him [Douglas], if he thinks I am doing something which leads to those bad results, it is none the better that I did not mean it. It is just as fatal to the country, if I have any influence in producing it, whether I intend it or not.—*Debate, Ottawa, Aug. 21, 1858.* III, 235.

2.—Can it be true, that placing this institution [slavery] upon the original basis—the basis upon which our fathers placed it—can have any tendency to set the northern and southern states at war with one another?—*Debate, Ottawa, Aug. 21, 1858.* III, 235.

3.—I ask you when he [Douglas] infers that I am in favor of setting the free and slave states at war, when the institution was placed in that attitude [looking toward ultimate extinction] by those who made the Constitution, did they make any war? If we had no war out of it when thus placed, wherein is the ground of belief that we shall have war out of it if we return to that policy?—*Debate, Alton, Oct. 15, 1858.* V, 51. Repeated at Rushville, Oct. 20, 1858. Hertz II, 730.

4.—I have not only made the declaration that I do not mean to produce a conflict between the states [over slavery] but I have tried to show by fair reasoning, and I think I have shown to the minds of all fair men, that I propose nothing but what has a most peaceful tendency.—*Debate, Alton, Oct. 15, 1858.* V, 52.

5.—On the point of my wanting to make war between the free and slave states, there has been no issue between us [Lincoln and Douglas].—*Debate, Alton, Oct. 15, 1858.* V, 59.

War-Making Power—*See* CONGRESS, war-making power of, explained.

War of 1812, Clay's influence for—Whether we should go to war with Great Britain [in 1812] being the question of the day, a minority opposed the declaration of war by Congress, while the majority, though apparently inclined to war, had for years wavered and hesitated to act decisively. Meanwhile, British aggressions multiplied, and grew more daring and aggravated. By Mr. Clay more than any other man the struggle was brought to a decision in Congress. The question, being now fully before Congress, came up in a variety of ways in rapid succession, on most of which occasions Mr. Clay spoke. Adding to all the logic of which the subject was susceptible, that noble inspiration which came to him as it came to no other, he aroused and nerved and inspired his friends, and confounded and bore down all opposition.—*Speech, Springfield, July 16, 1852.* II, 166.

See CLAY, HENRY, eloquence of.

War Power, main reliance—In the midst of other cares, however important, we must not lose sight of the fact that the war power is still our main reliance.

To that power alone can we look yet for a time, to give confidence to the people in the contested regions that the insurgent power will not again overrun them. Until that confidence shall be established, little can be done anywhere for what is called reconstruction.—*Third annual message, Dec. 8, 1863.* IX, 252.

War Power, military necessity alone justifies use of—Nothing justifies the suspension of the civil by the military authority, but military necessity; and of the existence of that necessity, the military commander . . . is to decide. And whatever is not within such necessity should be left undisturbed.—*To Gen. Butler, Aug. 9, 1864 (not sent until Dec. 21).* X, 322.

2.—If you, as department commander, find the cleansing of the city [Norfolk, Va.] necessary to prevent pestilence in your army; street lights and a fire department necessary to prevent assassinations and incendiarism among your men and stores; wharfage necessary to land and ship men and supplies, a large pauperism, badly conducted and at a needlessly large expense to the government; and find also that these things, or any of them, are not reasonably well attended to by the civil government, you rightfully may and must take them into your own hands. But you should do so upon your own avowed judgment of a military necessity, and not seem to admit that there is no such necessity by taking a vote of the people on the question.—*To Gen. Butler, Aug. 9, 1864 (not sent until Dec. 21).* X, 322.

War Power, need for using, decreases—As the war progresses, it appears to me, opinion and action, which were in great confusion at first, take shape and fall into more regular channels, so that the necessity for strong dealing with them gradually decreases. I have every reason to desire that it should cease altogether.—*To Erastus Corning and others, June 12, 1863.* VIII, 314.

2.—The executive power itself would be greatly diminished by the cessation of actual war.—*Fourth annual message, Dec. 6, 1864.* X, 309.

War Power, reluctant to use—It was with the deepest regret that the Executive found the duty of employing the war power in defense of the government forced upon him. He could but perform this duty or surrender the existence of the government.—*Message to Congress, July 4, 1861.* R.T.L.

2.—As a private citizen the Executive could not have consented that these institutions shall perish; much less could he in betrayal of so sacred a trust as these free people had confided in him. He felt that he had no moral right to shrink, nor even count the chances of his own life, in what might follow. In full view of his great responsibility he has so far done what he has deemed his duty.—*Message to Congress, July 4, 1861.* VI, 324.

3.—Thoroughly imbued with a reverence for the guaranteed rights of individuals, I was slow to adopt the strong measures which by degrees I have been forced to regard as being within the exceptions of the Constitution, and as indispensable to the public safety.—*To Erastus Corning and others, June 12, 1863.* VIII, 303.

War Power, use of, defended—So viewing the issue, no choice was left but to call out the war power of the government, and so to resist force employed for its destruction by force for its preservation.—*Message to Congress, July 4, 1861.* VI, 305.

2.—Measures, whether strictly legal or not, were ventured on [at outbreak of war] under what appeared to be a popular demand and a public necessity, trusting then, as now, that Congress would ratify them. It is believed that nothing had been done beyond the constitutional competency of Congress.—*Message to Congress, July 4, 1861.* VI, 308.

3.—It became necessary for me to choose whether, using only the existing means, agencies and processes which Congress had provided, I should let the government fall at once into ruins or whether, availing myself of the broader powers conferred by the Constitution in cases of insurrection, I would make an effort to save it, with all its blessings, for the present age and for posterity.—*Message to Congress, May 26, 1862.* VII, 190.

4.—I raise no objection to it on legal or constitutional grounds; for, as commander-in-chief of the army and navy, in time of war, I suppose I have a right to take any measure which may best subdue the enemy.—*Reply to Chicago church committee, Sept. 13, 1862.* VIII, 31.

5.—The [Albany] resolutions promise to support me in every constitutional and lawful measure to suppress the rebellion; and I have not knowingly employed, nor shall knowingly employ, any other. But the meeting, by their resolutions, assert and argue that certain military arrests and proceedings following them, for which I am ultimately responsible, are unconstitutional. I think they are not.—*To Erastus Corning and others, June 12, 1863.* VIII, 299.

6.—Civil courts are organized chiefly for trials of individuals, or, at most, a few individuals acting in concert—and this in quiet times, and on charges of crimes well defined in the law. Even in times of peace bands of horse thieves and robbers frequently grow too numerous and powerful for the ordinary courts. But what comparison, in numbers, have such bands

ever borne to the insurgent sympathizers even in many of the loyal states?—*To Erastus Corning and others, June 12, 1863.* VIII, 303.

7.—The meeting [at Albany] indicate their opinion that military arrests may be constitutional in localities where rebellion actually exists, but that such arrests are unconstitutional in localities where rebellion or insurrection does not actually exist. . . . Inasmuch, however, as the Constitution itself makes no such distinction, I am unable to believe that there is any such constitutional distinction. I consider that the class of arrests complained of can be constitutional only when, in cases of rebellion or invasion, the public safety may require them; and I insist that in such cases they are constitutional whenever the public safety does require them, as well in places to which they may prevent the rebellion extending, as in those where it may be already prevailing; as well where they may restrain mischievous interference with the raising and supplying of armies to suppress the rebellion, as where the rebellion may actually be; as well where they may restrain the enticing of men out of the army, as where they would prevent mutiny in the army; equally constitutional at all places where they will conduce to the public safety, as against the dangers of rebellion or invasion.—*To Erastus Corning and others, June 12, 1863.* VIII, 306.

8.—I am [not] able to appreciate the danger apprehended by the [Albany] meeting, that the American people will by means of military arrests during the rebellion lose the right of public discussion, the liberty of speech and the press, the law of evidence, trial by jury, and *habeas corpus* throughout the indefinite peaceful future which I trust lies before them, any more than I am able to believe that a man could contract so strong an appetite for emetics during temporary illness as to persist in feeding upon them during the remainder of his healthful life.—*To Erastus Corning and others, June 12, 1863.* VIII, 309.

9.—I can no more be persuaded that the government can constitutionally take no strong measure in time of rebellion, because it can be shown that the same could not be lawfully taken in time of peace, than I can be persuaded that a particular drug is not good medicine for a sick man because it can be shown to not be good food for a well one.—*To Erastus Corning and others, June 12, 1863.* Basler, 705.

10.—If I be wrong on this question of constitutional power, my error lies in believing that certain proceedings are constitutional when in case of rebellion or invasion the public safety requires them, which would not be constitutional when, in the absence of rebellion or invasion, the public safety does not require them; in other words that the Constitution is not, in its application, in all respects the same in cases of rebellion or invasion involving the public safety, as it is in times of profound peace and public security. The Constitution itself makes the distinction.—*To Erastus Corning and others, June 12, 1863.* VIII, 309.

11.—I [have] expressed the opinion that the Constitution is different in its application in cases of rebellion or invasion, involving the public safety, from what it is in times of profound peace and public security; and this opinion I adhere to, simply because, by the Constitution itself, things may be done in the one case which may not be done in the other. —*To M. Birchard and others, June 29, 1863.* IX, 2.

12.—In regard to Mr. Vallandigham and all others, I must hereafter, as heretofore, do so much as the public safety may seem to require.—*To M. Birchard and others, June 29, 1863.* IX, 10.

13.—I think the Constitution invests its commander-in-chief with the law of war in time of war.—*To J. C. Conkling, Aug. 26, 1863.* IX, 98.

14.—According to our political system, as a matter of civil administration, the general government had no lawful power to effect emancipation in any state, and for a long time it had been hoped that the rebellion could be suppressed without resorting to it as a military measure. It was all the while deemed possible that the necessity for it might come, and if it should, the crisis of the contest would then be presented.—*Third annual message, Dec. 8, 1863.* IX, 245.

15.—I felt that measures otherwise unconstitutional might become lawful by becoming indispensable to the preservation of the Constitution through the preservation of the nation.—*To A. G. Hodges, April 4, 1864.* X, 66.

16.—I conceive that I may in an emergency do things on military grounds which cannot be done constitutionally by Congress.—*To Sen. Chandler, July 4, 1864.* Hay, 204.

See CONGRESS, war-making power of, explained.

See HABEAS CORPUS, suspension of, defended.

See UNION, preservation of, first duty.

War Victims, assessments to compensate—It is represented to me that an officer has, by your authority, assessed and collected considerable sums of money from citizens of . . . Kentucky, to compensate Union men for depredations committed upon them in the vicinity by rebels; and I am petitioned to order the money refunded. . . . I write now to say that, in my opinion, in some extreme cases this class of proceeding becomes a necessity; but that it is liable to—

almost inseparable from—great abuses, and therefore should only be sparingly resorted to, and be conducted with great caution; that you, in your department, must be the judge of the proper localities and occasions for applying it; and that it will be as well for you to see that your subordinates be at all times ready to account for every dollar, as to why collected, of whom, and how applied. Without that, you will soon find some of them making assessments and collections merely to put money in their own pockets, and it will be impossible to correct errors in future and better times.—*To Gen. Burbridge, Oct. 27, 1864.* X, 255.

Ward, Artemus—I have a very funny book here, written by "Artemus Ward." Let me read you what he says about an outrage at Utica.—*To cabinet, Sept. 22, 1862.* Coffin, 342.

Washburne, E. B., appreciation of—. . . my grateful acknowledgments for the kind, active and continued interest you have taken for me.—*To Mr. Washburne, Feb. 9, 1855.* II, 277.

Washington, plight of—*See* CIVIL WAR, situation at start of, 1.

Washington, protection of, essential—No change in the base of operations of the Army of the Potomac shall be made without leaving in and about Washington such a force as in the opinion of the general in chief and the commanders of all the army corps shall leave the city entirely secure.—*General order, March 8, 1862.* VII, 117.

2.—My explicit order that Washington should, by the judgment of all the commanders of corps, be entirely secure, had been neglected.—*To Gen. McClellan, April 9, 1862.* VII, 142.

3.—A reasonable force should in every event be kept about Washington for its protection.—*To Sec. Seward, June 28, 1862.* VII, 241.

4.—But now, as heretofore, if you go to James river, a large part of the army must remain on or near the Fredericksburg line, to protect Washington. It is the old difficulty.—*To Gens. Franklin and Smith, Dec. 22, 1862.* VIII, 151.

See LOUISVILLE, defense of.

Washington, protection of, invites disaster—If you have had a drawn battle [at Richmond] or a repulse, it is the price we pay for the enemy not being in Washington. We protected Washington, and the enemy concentrated on you. Had we stripped Washington, he would have been upon us before the troops could have gotten to you.—*To Gen. McClellan, June 28, 1862.* VII, 240.

2.—The evacuation of Corinth and our delay by the flood of the Chickahominy have enabled the enemy to concentrate too much force in Richmond for McClellan to successfully attack. . . . But if we send all the force from here to McClellan, the enemy will, before we can know of it, send a force from Richmond and take Washington.—*To Sec. Seward, June 28, 1862.* VIII, 240.

Washington, George, favored abolition—*See* ABOLITION, Virginians advocated, 2.

Washington, George, hardships endured by—In the American Revolutionary War sacrifices were made by men engaged in it, but they were cheered by the future. Gen. Washington himself endured greater physical hardships than if he had remained a British subject, yet he was a happy man because he was engaged in benefitting his race, in doing something for the children of his neighbors, having none of his own.—*Speech, to free colored men, Aug. 14, 1862.* VIII, 5.

Washington, George, may children enjoy his bequests—May our children and our children's children for a thousand generations continue to enjoy the benefits conferred upon us by a united country, and have cause yet to rejoice under those glorious institutions bequeathed us by Washington and his compeers.—*Speech, Frederick, Md., Oct. 4, 1862.* XI, 125.

Washington, George, order of, indicative—The first general order issued by the Father of His Country after the Declaration of Independence indicates the spirit in which our institutions were founded and should ever be defended: "The general hopes and trusts that every officer and man will endeavor to live and act as becomes a Christian soldier, defending the dearest rights and liberties of his country."—*Executive order, Nov. 15, 1862.* VIII, 77.

Washington, George, task greater than that of—I cannot but know what you all know; that without a name, perhaps without reason why I should have a name, there has fallen upon me a task such as did not rest even upon the Father of His Country; and so feeling, I can turn and look for that support without which it will be impossible for me to perform that great task. I turn, then, and look to the American people, and to that God who has never forsaken them.—*Speech, Columbus, Ohio, Feb. 13, 1861.* VI, 121.

See FAREWELL TO SPRINGFIELD.

Washington, George, tributes to—[Washington's name], mightiest in the cause of civil liberty, still

mightiest in the cause of moral reformation, we mention in solemn awe, in naked, deathless splendor.—*To George E. Pickett, Feb. 22, 1842.* I, 192.

2.—Washington is the mightiest name of earth—long since mightiest in the cause of civil liberty, still mightiest in moral reformation. On that name no eulogy is expected. It cannot be. . . . To add brightness to the sun or glory to the name of Washington is alike impossible. Let none attempt it. In solemn awe pronounce the name, and in its naked, deathless splendor leave it shining.—*Speech, Springfield, Feb. 22, 1842.* I, 209.

Washington, George, Weems's life of—*See* TRENTON, BATTLE OF, inspiration of.

Washington Constitution (newspaper)—*See* PRESS, some papers unfair.

Washington Union (newspaper), not against editor alone—Judge Douglas says he made a charge upon the editor of the Washington *Union*, alone, of entertaining a purpose to rob the states of their power to exclude slavery from their limits. I undertake to say, and I make the direct issue, that he did not make his charge against the editor of the *Union* alone. I will undertake to prove by the record here that he made that charge against more and higher dignitaries than the editor of the Washington *Union*.—*Debate, Freeport, Aug. 27, 1858.* III, 341.

Washington Union (newspaper)—Thanks for support of—The judge [Douglas] has informed me, or informed this audience, that the Washington *Union* [an administration organ reputedly] is laboring for my election to the United States Senate. This is news to me—not very ungrateful news either. . . . I am glad of all the support I can get anywhere, if I can get it without practicing any deception to obtain it.—*Debate, Quincy, Oct. 13, 1858.* IV, 375.

Waterloo, incident at, cited—*See* BUSHWHACKING, war on Republican antislavery stand characterized.

"We Are Not Enemies, but Friends"—*See* ENEMIES, not, but friends.

Wealth, defense of—I take it that it is best for all to leave each man free to acquire property as fast as he can. Some will get wealthy. I don't believe in law to prevent a man from getting rich; it would do more harm than good. So while we do not propose any war upon capital, we do wish to allow the humblest man an equal chance to get rich with everybody else.—*Speech, New Haven, Conn., March 6, 1860.* V, 360.

2.—Nor should this [a union of "all working people,

of all nations, and tongues, and kindreds"] lead to a war upon property, or the owners of property. Property is the fruit of labor; property is desirable; it is a positive good in the world. That some should be rich shows that others may become rich, and hence is just encouragement to industry and enterprise.—*Reply to committee of Workingmen's Association of New York, March 21, 1864.* X, 54.

Wealth, "superfluity"—I cannot understand why men should be so eager after money. Wealth is simply a superfluity of what we don't need.—*To D. R. Locke, Oct. 12, 1864.* Coffin, 462.

Weather, affects nerves—Exposure to bad weather . . . my experience clearly proves to be very severe on defective nerves.—*To Joshua F. Speed, Jan. 3, 1842.* I, 183.

Weather, prophet repudiated—It seems to me Mr. Capen knows nothing about the weather in advance. He told me three days ago it would not rain again till the 30th of April or the 1st of May. It is raining now, and has been for ten hours. I cannot spare any more time to Mr. Capen.—*Indorsement on letter, April 28, 1863.* VIII, 256.

Webster, Daniel—*See* COMPROMISE OF 1850, Clay led in, 2.

See CLAY, HENRY, disciple of.

Weed, Thurlow, cautioned on patronage—*See* PATRONAGE, "Justice to all."

Weed, Thurlow, no enmity toward—You astonish me by saying Mr. Weed understands there is some alienation or enmity of feeling on my part toward him. Nothing like it. I shall be glad to see him any time, and have wondered at not having seen him already.—*To Sec. Seward, April 18, 1861.* Hertz II, 829.
2.—I have never entertained any unkind feeling or a disparaging thought toward you; and if I have said or done anything which has been construed into such unkindness or disparagement, it has been misconstrued. I am sure if we could meet we would not part with any unpleasant impressions on either side.—*To Mr. Weed, Oct. 14, 1863.* IX, 168.
3.—I have been both pained and surprised recently at learning that you are wounded because a suggestion of yours as to the mode of conducting our national difficulty has not been followed—pained because I very much wish you to have no unpleasant feeling proceeding from me; and surprised, because my impression is that I have seen you since the last message issued, apparently feeling cheerful and happy.—*To Mr. Weed, March 25, 1864.* X, 56.

Weed, Thurlow, no signs of intriguer—Weed was here, and saw me; but he showed no signs whatever of the intriguer. He asked for nothing.—*To Lyman Trumbull, June 5, 1860.* Tracy, 153.
2.—Some gentlemen, who have been quite nervous about the object of your visit here, would be surprised, if not incredulous, were I to tell that during the two days we have passed together you have made no application, suggestion or allusion to appointments.—*Interview, Thurlow Weed, Dec., 1860.* Weed, 613.
3.—You have the reputation of taking time by the forelock. I was warned to be on my guard against you; and the joke of the matter is that those who gave the warning are after the offices themselves, while you have avoided the subject.—*Interview, Mr. Weed, Dec., 1860.* Weed, 621.

Weed, Thurlow, unprecedented agreement—Mr. [Christopher] Adams is magnificently recommended; but the great point in his favor is that Thurlow Weed and Horace Greeley join in recommending him. I suppose the like never happened before.—*To Sec. Chase, May 8, 1861.* VI, 268.

Wen, slavery like—The thing [slavery] is hid away in the Constitution, just as an afflicted man hides away a wen or cancer which he dare not cut out at once, lest he bleed to death—with the promise, nevertheless, that the cutting may begin at a certain time.—*Speech, Peoria, Oct. 16, 1854.* II, 245.
2.—In front of us [on a car] sat an old gentleman with an enormous wen upon his neck. Everybody would say the wen was a great evil, and would cause the man's death after a while; but you couldn't cut it out for he'd bleed to death in a minute. But would you engraft the seeds of that wen on the necks of sound and healthy men? He must endure and be patient, hoping for possible relief. The wen represents slavery on the neck of this country. This only applies to those who think slavery is wrong. Those who think it right would consider . . . the wen an ornament.—*Speech, Hartford, Conn., March 5, 1860.* V, 333.

See LIBERTY, prosperity and, threatened by slavery.

West Point, advice to cadet—Your good mother tells me you are feeling very badly in your new situation. Allow me to assure you it is a perfect certainty that you will, very soon, feel better—quite happy—if you only stick to the resolution you have taken to procure a military education. I am older than you, have felt badly myself, and know what I tell you is true. Adhere to your purpose and you will soon feel as well as you ever did. On the contrary, if you falter, and give up, you will lose the power of keeping any resolution, and will regret it all your life. Take the advice of a friend, who, though he never saw you, deeply sympathizes with you, and stick to your purpose.—*To Quinton Campbell, June 28, 1862.* Hertz II, 870.

West Point, recommendation overruled—Herewith I return the papers in relation to the proposed reappointment of William Kellogg, Jr., to a cadetship. Upon Gen. Totten's statement of the case, I think it is natural that he should feel as he expresses himself. And yet the case comes upon me in the very strongest way to be painful to me. Hon. William Kellogg, the father, is not only a member of Congress from my state, but he is my personal friend of more than 20 years' standing, and of whom I had many personal kindnesses. This matter touches him very deeply—the feelings of a father for his child—as he thinks, all the future of his child. I cannot be the instrument to crush his heart. According to strict rule he has the right to make the renomination. Let the appointment be made. It needs not to become a precedent. Hereafter let no resignation be accepted under demerit amounting to cause for dismissal, unless upon express stipulation in writing that the cadet resigning shall not be renominated.—*To Sec. Stanton, June 5, 1862.* Angle, 294.

West Virginia, argument for admission of—The consent of the legislature of Virginia is constitutionally necessary to the bill for the admission of West Virginia becoming a law. A body claiming to be such legislature has given its consent. We cannot well deny that it is such, unless we do so upon the outside knowledge that the body was chosen at elections in which a majority of the qualified voters of Virginia did not participate.—*Opinion on admission of West Virginia, Dec. 31, 1862.* VIII, 157.
2.—It is a universal practice in the popular elections in all these states to give no legal consideration whatever to those who do not choose to vote, as against the effect of the votes of those who do choose to vote. Hence it is not the qualified voters, but the qualified voters who choose to vote, that constitute the political power of the state. Much less than to non-voters should any consideration be given those who did not vote in this case [the setting up of West Virginia as a state], because . . . they were not merely neglectful of their rights under and duty to this government, but were also engaged in open rebellion against it.—*Opinion on admission of West Virginia, Dec. 31, 1862.* VIII, 157.
3.—We cannot deny that the body which consents to the admission of West Virginia is the legislature of

Virginia.—*Opinion on admission of West Virginia as a state, Dec. 31, 1862.* VIII, 158.
4.—Her brave and good men regard her [West Virginia's] admission into the Union as a matter of life and death. They have been true to the Union under very severe trials. We have so acted as to justify their hopes, and we cannot fully retain their confidence and co-operation if we seem to break faith with them. —*Opinion on admission of West Virginia, Dec. 31, 1862.* VIII, 159.
5.—More than on anything else, it [the question of admission] depends on whether the admission or rejection of the new state would, under all the circumstances, tend the more strongly to the restoration of the national authority throughout the Union. That which helps most in this direction is the most expedient at this time. . . . We can scarcely dispense with the aid of West Virginia in this struggle; much less can we afford to have her against us, in Congress and in the field. . . . Again, the admission of the new state turns that much slave soil to free, and thus is a certain and irrevocable encroachment upon the cause of the rebellion.—*Opinion on admission of West Virginia, Dec. 31, 1862.* VIII, 159.
6.—It is said that the admission of West Virginia [to the Union] is secession, and tolerated only because it is our secession. Well, if we call it by that name, there is still difference enough between secession against the Constitution and secession in favor of the Constitution.—*Opinion on admission of West Virginia, Dec. 31, 1862.* VIII, 160.
7.—I believe the admission of West Virginia into the Union is expedient.—*Opinion on admission of West Virginia, Dec. 31, 1862.* VIII, 160.

West Virginia, leaves little to Virginia governor—*See* VIRGINIA, not much left of.

Where and Whither—If we could first know where we are, and whither we are tending, we could better judge what to do, and how to do it.—*Speech, Springfield, June 16, 1858.* III, 1.

Whig Party, advice to—To overthrow the trained bands that are opposed to us [the Whigs], whose salaried officers are ever on the watch, and whose misguided followers are ever ready to obey their smallest commands, every Whig must not only know his duty, but must firmly resolve, whatever of time and labor it may cost, boldly and faithfully to do it.—*Whig circular, Jan. 1, 1840.* I, 143.
2.—At every election, let every Whig act as though he knew the result to depend upon his action.—*Whig circular, March 4, 1843.* I, 259.

Whig Party, "always a majority"—When did the Whigs ever fail if they were fully aroused and united? —*Whig circular, March 4, 1843.* I, 258.
2.—We declare it to be our solemn conviction, that the Whigs are always a majority of this nation; and that to make them always successful needs but to get them all to the polls and to vote unitedly.—*Whig circular, March 4, 1843.* I, 259.

Whig Party, apple-sized tears from—Judge Douglas has a very affectionate leaning toward the Americans and Old Whigs. Last evening, in a sort of weeping tone, he described to us a death-bed scene. He had been called to the side of Mr. Clay, in his last moments, in order that the genius of "popular sovereignty" might duly descend from the dying man and settle upon him, the living and most worthy successor. He could do not less than promise that he would devote the remainder of his life to "popular sovereignty"; and then the great statesman departs in peace. By this part of the "plan of campaign," the judge has evidently promised himself that tears shall be drawn down the cheeks of all Old Whigs, as large as half-grown apples.—*Speech, Springfield, July 17, 1858.* III, 183.

Whig Party, beaten out on tariff—We, the Old Whigs, have been entirely beaten out of the tariff question, and we shall not be able to re-establish the policy until the absence of it shall have demonstrated the necessity for it in the minds of men heretofore opposed to it.—*To Dr. Edward Wallace, Oct. 11, 1859.* V, 257.

Whig Party, complimented—Honest Whigs—and nearly all of them are honest.—*To M. M. Morris, April 14, 1843.* I, 266.
2.—I am somewhat acquainted with the old-line Whigs. I was with the old-line Whigs from the origin to the end of that party; I became pretty well acquainted with them, and I know they always had some sense, whatever else you may ascribe to them.— *Debate, Alton, Oct. 15, 1858.* V, 38.

Whig Party "contented"—I suppose I cannot reasonably hope to convince you that we [Whigs] have any principles. The most I can expect is to assure you that we think we have, and are quite contented with them.—*Speech in Congress, July 27, 1848.* II, 70.
2.—Let our Democratic friend be comforted with the assurance that we [Whigs] are content with our position, content with our company, and content with our candidate; and that, although they in their generous sympathy think we ought to be miserable, we really are not.—*Speech in Congress, July 27, 1848.* II, 87.

Whig Party, despondency in—In about all the states we [Whigs] have fallen into the minority, and despondence seems to prevail universally among us. Is there just cause for this? . . . Every state which has fallen off from the Whig cause since 1840 has done so not by giving more Democratic votes than they did then, but by giving fewer Whig. . . . It is evident that tens of thousands in the late elections have not voted at all. . . . They can come forward and give us the victory again. That all, or nearly all, of them are Whigs is most apparent. . . . And why shall the Whigs not rally again? Are their principles less dear now than in 1840? Have any of their doctrines since then been discovered to be untrue?—*Whig circular, March 4, 1843.* I, 256.

Whig Party, Douglas calls, abolitionist—*See* WHIG PARTY, had to die to be called good.

Whig Party, had to die to be called good—I recollect in the presidential election which followed [the Compromise of 1850] . . . Judge Douglas was around berating us Whigs as Abolitionists, precisely as he does today—not a bit of difference. . . . We could do nothing when the old Whig party was alive that was not abolitionism, but it has got an extremely good name since it has passed away.—*Debate, Jonesboro, Sept. 15, 1858.* IV, 37.

Whig Party, members of, and Buchanan's nomination —The news of Buchanan's nomination came yesterday; and a good many Whigs, of conservative feelings, and slight pro-slavery proclivities, withal, are inclined to go for him; and will do so, unless the anti-Nebraska nomination shall be such as to divert them. The man to effect that object is Judge [John] McLean; and his nomination would save every Whig, except such as have already gone over hook and line. . . . J. T. Stuart, Anthony Thornton, James M. Davis —the old settler—and others like them, will heartily go for McLean, but every one will go for Buchanan, as against Chase, Banks, Seward, Blair or Frémont. I think they would stand Blair or Frémont for Vice President—but not more. Now there is a grave question to be considered. Nine tenths of the anti-Nebraska votes have to come from old Whigs. In setting stakes, is it safe to totally disregard them? So far they have been disregarded.—*To Lyman Trumbull, June 7, 1856.* Tracy, 66.

Whig Party, plan to abolitionize, denied—*See* ABOLITIONIZE, plot to, parties denied.

Whig Party, silk stockings oppose—Nearly all the old exclusive silk-stocking Whiggery is against us. I don't mean nearly all the old Whig Party, but merely all of the nice exclusive sort.—*To A. G. Henry, Nov. 19, 1858.* V, 95.

Whig Party, supports Mexican War—*See* MEXICAN WAR, Whig attitude toward.

Whiskers, "silly affectation"?—As to the whiskers, having never worn any, do you not think people would call it silly affectation, if I were to begin it now?—*To Grace Bedell, Oct. 19, 1860.* VI, 63.

White House, children of humblest may occupy—I happen, temporarily, to occupy the White House. I am a living witness that any one of your children may look to come here as my father's child has.—*Address to 166th Ohio regiment, Aug. 22, 1864.* X, 202.

See LIBERTY, largest degree of, in America.

White Race, degradation of—How can anyone who abhors the oppression of negroes be in favor of degrading classes of white people? Our progress in degeneracy appears to me to be pretty rapid.—*To Joshua F. Speed, Aug. 24, 1855.* II, 287.

White Race, injured by slavery—*See* SLAVERY, white race injured by.

White Race, some "unable to forget"—*See* NEGRO, some will remember.

White Race, superior position for, preferred—The government was made by white men, and they were and are the superior race.—*Speech, Bloomington, May 29, 1856.* Lapsley II, 254.
2.—There is a physical difference between the white and black races, which, I believe, will forever forbid the two races living together on terms of social and political equality. And inasmuch as they cannot so live, while they do remain together there must be the position of superior and inferior, and I, as much as any other man, am in favor of having the superior position assigned to the white race. . . . I do not perceive that because the white man is to have the superior position the negro should be denied everything.—*Debate, Charleston, Sept. 18, 1858.* IV, 89. Repeated at Columbus, Ohio, Sept. 16, 1859. V, 144.

See RACIAL EQUALITY, neither intended nor desired.

"Who Is Not for Us Is Against Us"—*See* BIBLE, maxims cited.

Widows and Orphans of the War—*See* DEITY, supplication to, 5.

Wife, neither, nor slave—*See* RACIAL AMALGAMATION, opposed to, 1, 4, 7, 10.

Wilberforce, William—*See* AFRICAN SLAVE TRADE, fight against, was long in Britain.

Wilcox, Nathaniel Green, tributes to—I consider him a gentleman of the highest honor.—*Recommendation, March 14, 1849.* Angle, 53.
2.—I have once seen his devotion to principle put to the severest test, and come out unshaken.—*To Sec. Ewing, June 19, 1849.* Angle, 57.

Will, origin of—Will springs from the two elements of moral sense and self-interest.—*Speech, Springfield, June 26, 1857.* II, 338.

Wilmot Proviso, Cass for and against—These extracts show that in 1846 Gen. Cass was for the proviso at once; that in March, 1847, he was still for it, but not just then; and that in December, 1847, he was against it altogether. This is a true index to the whole man.—*Speech in Congress, July 27, 1848.* II, 78.

Wilmot Proviso, origin of—Our war with Mexico broke out in 1846. When Congress was about adjourning that session President Polk asked them to place $2,000,000 under his control, to be used by him in the recess, if found practicable and expedient, in negotiating a treaty of peace with Mexico, and acquiring some part of her territory. A bill was duly gotten up for the purpose, and was progressing swimmingly in the House of Representatives, when a member by the name of David Wilmot, a Democrat from Pennsylvania, moved as an amendment, "Provided that in any territory thus acquired there shall never be slavery." This is the origin of the far-famed Wilmot Proviso.—*Speech, Peoria, Oct. 16, 1854.* II, 199.

Wilmot Proviso purpose of—When we voted for the Wilmot Proviso we were voting to keep slavery out of the whole Mexican acquisition, and little did we think we were thereby voting to let it into Nebraska, lying several hundred miles distant.—*Speech, Peoria, Oct. 16, 1854.* II, 211.

Wilmot Proviso, safe with Taylor—I am a northern man, or rather a western free-state man, with a constituency I believe to be, and with personal feelings I know to be, against the extension of slavery. As such, and with what information I have, I hope and believe Gen. Taylor, if elected, would not veto the [Wilmot] Proviso.—*Speech in Congress, July 27, 1848.* II, 66.

Wilmot Proviso, "stuck"—It [Wilmot Proviso] created a great flutter, but it stuck like wax.—*Speech, Peoria, Oct. 16, 1854.* II, 200.

Wilmot Proviso, support for, did not repudiate the Missouri Compromise—*See* MISSOURI COMPROMISE, Wilmot Proviso and.

Wilmot Proviso, voted for—I had the pleasure of voting for his [Wilmot's] Proviso, in one way or another, about 40 times. It was a Democratic measure then, I believe.—*Speech, Springfield, Oct. 4, 1854.* Bartlett, 64.

2.—I think I am a Whig; but others say there are no Whigs, and that I am an Abolitionist. When I was at Washington, I voted for the Wilmot Proviso as good as 40 times; and I never heard of anyone attempting to unwhig me for that.—*To Joshua F. Speed, Aug. 24, 1855.* II, 287.

Wind, as motive power—Of all the forces of nature, I should think the wind contains the largest amount of motive power—that is, power to move things. Take any given space of the earth's surface—for instance, Illinois; and all the power exerted by all the men, beasts, and running water, and steam, over and upon it; shall not equal the one-hundredth part of what is exerted by the blowing of the wind over and upon the same space.—*Speech, Springfield, no date.* Hertz II, 800.

Winslow, John A., Congress asked to thank—I most cordially recommend that Capt. John A. Winslow, United States Navy, receive a vote of thanks from Congress for the skill and gallantry exhibited by him in the brilliant action whilst in command of the United States steamer *Kearsarge,* which led to the total destruction of the piratical craft *Alabama,* on the 19th of June, 1864, a vessel superior in tonnage, superior in number of guns, and superior in number of crew.—*Message to Congress, Dec. 5, 1864.* X, 280.

Wisconsin, volunteers of, thanked for services—*See* CIVIL WAR, hundred-day volunteers thanked.

Wise, Henry A., characterized—. . . a man who believes in the divine right of slavery.—*Speech, Cincinnati, Sept. 17, 1859.* V, 216.

With Lash and Sword—*See* DEITY, submission to, 2.

"With Malice Toward None"—*See* MALICE, without, 7.

Wolf defines "liberty"—*See* LIBERTY, definitions of, differ, 2.

Woman Suffrage, limited measure for, endorsed—I go for all sharing the privileges of the government who assist in bearing its burdens. Consequently, I go for admitting all whites to the right of suffrage who pay taxes or bear arms—by no means excluding fe-

males.—*To Editor Sangamo* Journal, *June 13, 1836.* I, 14.

Women, tributes to—I am not accustomed to the use of the language of eulogy; I have never studied the art of paying compliments to women; but I must say, that if all that has been said by orators and poets since the creation of the world in praise of women were applied to the women of America, it would not do them justice for their conduct during this war. I will close by saying, God bless the women of America!—*Speech, Washington, March 18, 1864.* X, 48.

2.—In this extraordinary war extraordinary developments have manifested themselves such as have not been seen in former wars; and among these manifestations nothing has been more remarkable than these fairs for the relief of suffering soldiers and their families, and the chief agents in these fairs are the women of America.—*Speech, Washington, March 18, 1864.* X, 48.

3.—I am sure that you will join me in the hope for their [Union troops'] success; while yourselves, and other good mothers, wives, sisters, and daughters, do all you and they can to relieve and comfort the gallant soldiers who compose them [the armies].—*To Mrs. S. B. McConkey, May 9, 1864.* X, 96.

4.—I wish you to read, if you have not already done so, the eloquent and truthful words which he [Edward Everett] then [at Gettysburg dedication] spoke of the women of America. Truly, the services they have rendered to the defenders of our country in this perilous time, and are yet rendering, can never be estimated as they ought to be.—*Reply to committee, Jan. 24, 1865.* X, 346.

Women, wages for—*See* LABOR, wages for women.

Women and Marriage, attitude toward—Whatever woman may cast her lot with mine, should any ever do so, it is my intention to do all in my power to make her happy and contented; and there is nothing I can imagine that would make me more unhappy than to fail in the effort.—*To Mary Owens, May 7, 1837.* I, 53.

2.—I want in all cases to do right, and most particularly so in all cases with women.—*To Mary Owens, Aug. 16, 1837.* I, 57.

3.—I now spent my time planning how I might get along in life after my contemplated change in circumstances [marriage to Miss Owens] should have taken place, and how I might procrastinate the evil day for a time, which I really dreaded as much, perhaps more, than an Irishman does the halter.—*To Mrs. O. H. Browning, April 1, 1838.* I, 90.

4.—I have now come to the conclusion never again to

think of marrying, and for this reason—I can never be satisfied with anyone who would be blockhead enough to have me.—*To Mrs. O. H. Browning, April 1, 1838.* I, 92.

5.—Others have been made fools of by the girls, but this can never with truth be said of me. I most emphatically, in this instance made a fool of myself. —*To Mrs. O. H. Browning, April 1, 1838.* I, 92.

6.—Is little Siss Eliza Davis at your house yet? If she is, kiss her "o'er and o'er again" for me.—*To Mary Speed, Sept. 27, 1841.* Basler, 123.

7.—Since then [Jan. 1, 1841, when he did not appear for his marriage] it seems to me that I should have been entirely happy, but for the never-absent idea that there is one still unhappy whom I have contributed to make so. That still kills my soul. I cannot but reproach myself for even wishing to be happy while she is otherwise.—*To Joshua F. Speed, March 27, 1842.* I, 214.

8.—Nothing new here except my marriage which to me is matter of profound wonder.—*To Samuel D. Marshall, Nov. 11, 1842.* Tracy, 9.

9.—As to kissing a pretty girl, I know one very pretty one, but I guess she won't let me kiss her.—*To W. H. Herndon, July 11, 1848.* Angle, 47.

10.—The truth is I have never corresponded much with ladies; and hence I postpone writing letters to them, as a business which I do not understand.—*To Mrs. M. J. Green, Sept. 22, 1860.* Tracy, 164.

11.—I would not offer her [Sallie Ward Hunt, wife of a Confederate soldier] or any wife a temptation to a permanent separation from her husband, but if she shall avow that her mind is already independently and fully made up to such separation, I shall be glad for the property sought by her to be delivered to her, upon her taking the oath of Dec. 8, 1863.—*Statement, April 11, 1864.* Hertz II, 826.

Wool, John E., tribute to—Judgment and feeling go heartily with your sense of professional and official duty to the work. . . . I cannot be ignorant as to who Gen. Wool is, or what he has done. With my highest esteem and gratitude.—*To Gen. Wool, Jan. 14, 1861.* VI, 98.

Worden, John L., Congress asked to thank—I most cordially recommend that Commander John L. Worden, United States Navy, receive a vote of thanks of Congress for the eminent skill and gallantry exhibited by him in the late remarkable battle between the United States iron-clad steam *Monitor,* under his command, and the rebel iron-clad steamer *Merrimac,* in March last.—*Message to Congress, Dec. 8, 1862.* VIII, 136.

Work, desire to, rare—Wanting to work is so rare a want that it should be encouraged.—*To Maj. Ramsey, Oct. 17, 1861.* XI, 120.

2.—This man wants to work—so uncommon a want that I think it ought to be gratified.—*Memorandum, Jan. 23, 1862.* Angle, 287.

3.—I am always for the man who wishes to work.— *Indorsement, Aug. 15, 1864.* X, 192.

Work, recommended for sake of mind—See IDLENESS, to be avoided, 1.

Work, urged on stepbrother—You are not lazy, and still you are an idler. . . . You do not very much dislike to work, and still you do not work much, merely because it does not seem to you that you could get much for it. This habit of uselessly wasting time is the whole difficulty; it is vastly important to you, and still more so to your children, that you should break the habit. . . . You say if I will furnish you the money [$80] you will deed me the land, and, if you don't pay the money back, you will deliver possession. Nonsense! If you can't live with the land, how will you then live without it?—*To John D. Johnston, Jan. 2, 1851.* II, 144.

2.—You are anxious to sell the land and move to Missouri. . . . What can you do in Missouri better than here? Is the land any richer? Can you there, any more than here, raise corn and wheat and oats without work? Will anybody there, any more than here, do your work for you? . . . Half you will get for the land you will spend in moving to Missouri, and the other half you will eat, drink and wear out, and no foot of land will be bought. Now, I feel it my duty to have no hand in such a piece of foolery.—*To John D. Johnston, Nov. 4, 1851.* II, 150.

3.—Now do not misunderstand this letter. I do not write it in any unkindness. I write it in order, if possible, to get you to face the truth, which truth is, you are destitute because you have idled away all your time. Your thousand pretences for not getting along better are all nonsense; they deceive nobody but yourself. Go to work is the only cure for your case.—*To John D. Johnston, Nov. 4, 1851.* II, 151.

"Work, Work, Work Is the Main Thing"—SEE LAW, advice to students of, 4.

Workingmen—*See* WORKING PEOPLE.

Working People, basis of government—The workingmen are the basis of all government, for the plain reason that they are the most numerous.—*Speech, Cincinnati, Feb. 12, 1861.* VI, 119.

Working People, have most at stake in war—You comprehend, as your address shows, that the existing rebellion . . . is, in fact, a war upon the rights of all working people.—*Reply to committee of Workingmen's Association of New York, March 21, 1864.* X, 50.

2.—None are so deeply interested to resist rebellion as the working people. Let them beware of prejudices, working division and hostility among themselves. . . . The strongest bond of human sympathy, outside of the family relation, should be one uniting all working people, of all nations, and tongues, and kindred.—*Reply to committee of Workingmen's Association of New York, March 21, 1864.* X, 53.

Working People, international organization of, suggested—*See* WORKING PEOPLE, have most at stake in war, 2.

Working People, urged to retain political power— Let them [workingmen] beware of surrendering a political power which they already possess, and which, if surrendered, will surely be used to close the door of advancement against such as they, and fix new disabilities and burdens upon them, till all of liberty shall be lost.—*First annual message, Dec. 3, 1861.* VII, 59.

World, caters to Young America—*See* YOUNG AMERICA, world caters to.

World, moves—While all seems dead, the age itself is not. It liveth as sure as our Maker liveth. Under all this seeming want of life and motion, the world does move nevertheless.—*Speech, Springfield, June, 1856.* Herndon, 386.

World Significance of American Affairs—A right result at this time will be worth more to the world than ten times the men and ten times the money.—*Message to Congress, July 4, 1861.* VI, 312.

2.—. . . an important crisis which involves, in my judgment, not only the civil and religious liberties of our own dear land, but in a large degree the civil and religious liberties of mankind in many countries and through many ages.—*Reply to Evangelical Lutherans, May 6, 1862.* VII, 154.

3.—Once relieved [of slavery] its [America's] form of government is saved to the world, its beloved history and cherished memories are vindicated, and its happy future fully assured and rendered inconceivably grand.—*To border-state congressmen, July 12, 1862.* VII, 273.

See AMERICA, "beneficial toward mankind."

See CIVIL WAR, foreign nations' attitude toward, 8.

See CIVIL WAR, results of, involve future, 2.

See DECLARATION OF INDEPENDENCE, source of political creed, 2.

See ELECTION OF 1864, of lasting advantage, 1.

See JEFFERSON, THOMAS, tribute to.

See SELF-GOVERNMENT, can it survive? 4, 5.

See SELF-GOVERNMENT, importance of, 1.

See UNION, appeals for support of, 1.

See UNION TROOPS, tributes to, 10.

World's Fair, first and most perfect—*See* SEWING SOCIETIES, mother of.

Worth, William J., Taylor's generous treatment of— *See* TAYLOR, ZACHARY, Col. Worth and.

"Wriggle to Live"—*See* OFFICE SEEKERS, troubles with, 2.

Writing, "greatest invention"—Writing, the art of communicating thoughts to the mind through the eye, is the greatest invention of the world. Great is the astonishing range of analysis and combination which necessarily underlies the most crude and general conception of it—great, very great, in enabling us to converse with the dead, the absent, and the unborn, at all distances of time and space; and great, not only in its direct benefits, but greatest help to all other inventions.—*Lecture, Springfield, Feb. 22, 1859.* V, 107.

2.—Its utility may be conceived by the reflection that to it we owe everything which distinguishes us from savages. Take it from us, and the Bible, all history, all science, all government, all commerce, and nearly all social intercourse, go with it.—*Lecture Springfield, Feb. 22, 1859.* V, 109.

3.—When writing was invented, any important observation likely to lead to a discovery had at last a chance of being written down, and consequently a little chance of never being forgotten, and of being seen and reflected upon by a much greater number of persons; and thereby the chances of a valuable hint being caught proportionately augmented. By this means the observation of a single individual might lead to an important invention years, and even centuries, after he was dead. In one word, by means of writing, the seeds of invention were more permanently preserved and more widely sown.—*Lecture, Springfield, Feb. 22, 1859.* V, 110.

Writing, Old Fogies * invented—The precise period at which writing was invented is not known, but it certainly was as early as the time of Moses; from which

* See footnote, page 3.

we may safely infer that its inventors were Old Fogies.—*Lecture, Springfield, Feb. 22, 1859.* V, 107.

Wrongs, government responsibility in regard to—It is no just function of government to prohibit what is not wrong.—*Speeches in Kansas, Dec. 1–5, 1859.* V, 269.

2.—The United States government is not charged with the duty of redressing or preventing all the wrongs in the world. But the government rightfully may, and subject to the Constitution ought to, redress all wrongs which are wrongs to the nation itself.— *Speeches in Kansas, Dec. 1–5, 1859.* V, 279.

See SLAVERY, general welfare impaired by, 1.

Wrongs and Remedies—It is a maxim held by the courts, that there is no wrong without its remedy; and the courts have a remedy for whatever is acknowledged and treated as a wrong.—*Debate, Jonesboro, Sept. 15, 1858.* IV, 60.

Yellow Dog—A fellow once advertised that he had made a discovery by which he could make a new man out of an old one, and have enough of the stuff left to make a little yellow dog.—*Speech in Congress, June 27, 1848.* II, 73.

Young America,* compared with Old Fogy—The great difference between Young America and Old Fogy is the result of discoveries, inventions, and improvements. These, in turn, are the result of observation, reflection, and experiment.—*Lecture, Springfield, Feb. 22, 1859.* V, 102.

Young America,* horror for Old Fogy—His [Young America's] horror is for all that is old, particularly Old Fogy; and if there be anything old which he can endure, it is only old whiskey and old tobacco.—*Lecture, Springfield, Feb. 22, 1859.* V, 101.

Young America,* longs for territory—As Plato had for the immortality of the soul, so Young America has "a pleasing hope, a fond desire—a longing after" territory. He has a great passion—a perfect rage—for the "new"; particularly new men for office, and the new earth mentioned in the Revelations, in which, being no sea, there must be about three times as much land as in the present. He is a great friend of humanity; and his desire for land is not selfish, but merely an impulse to extend the area of freedom. He is very anxious to fight for the liberation of enslaved nations and colonies, provided, always, they have land, and have not any liking for his interference. As to those who have no land, and would be glad of help from any quarter, he considers they can afford

* See footnote, page 3.

to wait a few hundred years longer.—*Lecture, Springfield, Feb. 22, 1859.* V, 100.

Young America,* world caters to—We have all heard of Young America. . . . Some think him conceited and arrogant; but has he not reason to entertain a rather extensive opinion of himself? Is he not the inventor and owner of the present, and sole hope of the future? Men and things, everywhere, are ministering unto him. Look at his apparel, and you shall see cotton fabrics from Manchester and Lowell; flax linen from Ireland; wool cloth from Spain; silk from France; furs from the Arctic region; with a Buffalo robe from the Rocky Mountains, as a general outsider. At his table, besides plain bread and meat made at home, are sugar from Louisiana, coffee and fruits from the tropics, salt from Turk's Island, fish from Newfoundland, tea from China, and spices from the Indies. The whole of the Pacific furnishes his candle-light, he has a diamond ring from Brazil, a gold watch from California, and a Spanish cigar from Havana. He not only has a present supply of all these, and much more; but thousands of hands are engaged in producing fresh supplies, and other thousands in bringing them to him. The iron horse is panting and impatient to carry him everywhere in no time; and the lightning stands ready harnessed to take and bring his tidings in a trifle less than no time. He owns a large part of the world, by right of possessing it, and all the rest by right of wanting it, and intending to have it.—*Lecture, Springfield, Feb. 22, 1859.* V, 99.

Young Men, advice to—The way for a young man to rise is to improve himself every way he can, never suspecting that anybody wishes to hinder him. Allow me to assure you that suspicion and jealousy never did help any man in any situation. There may sometimes be ungenerous attempts to keep a young man down; and they will succeed, too, if he allows his mind to be diverted from its true channel to brood over the attempted injury.—*To W. H. Herndon, July 10, 1848.* II, 57.

Young Men, attitude toward—I cannot but think there is some mistake in your impression of the motives of the old men. I suppose I am now one of the old men; and I declare on my veracity, which I think is good with you, that nothing could afford me more satisfaction than to learn that you and others of my young friends at home were doing battle in the contest and endearing themselves to the people and taking a stand far above any I have been able to reach in their admiration. I cannot conceive that other men feel differently.—*To W. H. Herndon, July 10, 1848.* II, 56.

CHRONOLOGY

Born near Hodgenville, Ky.	Feb. 12, 1809
Moves with parents to Indiana	November, 1816
Mother dies	Oct. 5, 1818
Mary Todd born at Lexington, Ky.	Dec. 13, 1818
Father marries Sarah Bush Johnston	Dec. 2, 1819
Sister Sarah dies	Jan. 20, 1828
Moved with family to Illinois	March, 1830
Makes first political speech	March 9, 1831
Boat piloted by Lincoln sticks on dam	April 19, 1831
Announces candidacy for legislature	March 9, 1832
Elected captain of military company	April 21, 1832
Military company disbands	May 27, 1832
Mustered out of military service	July 16, 1832
Defeated for legislature	Aug. 6, 1832
Appointed postmaster at New Salem	May 7, 1833
Elected to legislature	Aug. 4, 1834
Ann Rutledge dies	Aug. 25, 1835
Reelected to legislature for second term	Aug. 1, 1836
Licensed to practice law	Sept. 9, 1836
Admitted to the bar in Illinois	March 1, 1837
Writes protest against legislative action on slavery	March 3, 1837
Moved from New Salem to Springfield	March 15, 1837
Forms law partnership with John T. Stuart	April 12, 1837
Delivers Lyceum address at Springfield	Jan. 27, 1838
Reelected to legislature for third term	Aug. 1, 1838
Speaks in legislative hall, on the subtreasury	Dec. 20, 1839
Sponsors Whig circular	Jan. 1, 1840
Reelected to legislature for fourth term	Aug. 1, 1840
Breaks engagement with Mary Todd	Jan. 1, 1841

Forms law partnership with Stephen T. Logan	May 14, 1841
Speaks to Washingtonian Temperance Society at Springfield	Feb. 22, 1842
Marries Mary Todd of Lexington, Ky.	Nov. 4, 1842
Sponsors Whig resolution	March 1, 1843
Robert Todd Lincoln, eldest child, born	Aug. 1, 1843
Buys home in Springfield	Jan. 7, 1844
Forms law partnership with William H. Herndon	Sept. 20, 1844
Edward Baker Lincoln, second child, born	March 10, 1846
Elected to Congress	Aug. 3, 1846
Leaves Springfield to serve congressional term	Oct. 25, 1847
Takes seat in Congress	Dec. 6, 1847
Introduces "spot resolutions" in Congress	Dec. 22, 1847
Speaks on "spot resolutions"	Jan. 12, 1848
Speaks in Congress on internal improvements	June 20, 1848
Speaks in Congress on Gen. Taylor's qualifications for President	July 27, 1848
Speaks at Worcester, Mass., advocating election of Taylor	Sept. 12, 1848
Speaks at Boston, advocating Taylor for President	Sept. 15 and Sept. 22, 1848
Introduces bill to free slaves in District of Columbia	Jan. 10, 1849
Member of arrangements committee for Taylor inaugural ball	March 4, 1849
Granted patent on boat-lifting device	May 30, 1849
Writes resolution of sympathy with Hungarian Revolution	Sept. 12, 1849
Edward Baker Lincoln, second child, dies	Feb. 1, 1850
William Wallace Lincoln, third child, born	Dec. 21, 1850
Father dies	Jan. 17, 1851
Delivers eulogy of Henry Clay at Springfield	July 16, 1852

Thomas ("Tad") Lincoln, fourth child, born	April 4, 1853
Speaks at Peoria on the repeal of the Missouri Compromise	Oct. 16, 1854
Defeated for United States senator by vote of legislature	Feb. 8, 1855
Delivers "lost speech" at Bloomington	May 29, 1856
Receives 110 convention votes for Vice President on the Frémont ticket	June 19, 1856
Speaks at Republican banquet at Chicago	Dec. 10, 1856
Speaks at Springfield on the Dred Scott decision	June 26, 1857
Argues Rock Island bridge case	Sept. 24, 1857
Defends Armstrong, who was charged with murder	May 7, 1858
Delivers "house divided" speech at Springfield	June 16, 1858
Speaks at Chicago on popular sovereignty and the Lecompton constitution	July 10, 1858
Speaks at Springfield, answering Douglas on the Dred Scott decision	July 17, 1858
First debate with Douglas at Ottawa	Aug. 21, 1858
Second debate, at Freeport	Aug. 27, 1858
Speaks at Paris on popular sovereignty and the Nebraska bill	Sept. 8, 1858
Speaks at Edwardsville on differences between the parties	Sept. 13, 1858
Third debate, at Jonesboro	Sept. 15, 1858
Fourth debate, at Charleston	Sept. 18, 1858
Fifth debate, at Galesburg	Oct. 7, 1858
Sixth debate, at Quincy	Oct. 13, 1858
Seventh and last debate, at Alton	Oct. 15, 1858
Defeated by Douglas for United States Senate	Nov. 2, 1858
First mentioned in press for Presidency	Nov. 5, 1858
Lectures at Springfield on inventions and discoveries	Feb. 22, 1859
Speaks at Chicago at Republican meeting celebrating city victory	March 1, 1859
Buys Chicago *Staats-Zeitung*	May 30, 1859
Speaks at Columbus, Ohio, on behalf of Republican state ticket	Sept. 16, 1859
Speaks at Cincinnati, continuing argument made at Columbus	Sept. 17, 1859
Speaks at Milwaukee on the importance of agriculture	Sept. 30, 1859
John Brown raid	Oct. 16, 1859
Letter to Alexander H. Stephens	Jan. 19, 1860
Cooper Institute address in New York	Feb. 27, 1860
Speaks at Hartford, Conn., on the slavery issue	March 5, 1860
Speaks at New Haven, Conn.	March 6, 1860
Nominated for the Presidency	May 18, 1860
Receives notification committee from the Chicago convention	May 19, 1860
Speaks at Springfield, acknowledging greetings of friends and neighbors	Aug. 14, 1860
Elected President	Nov. 6, 1860
Sells Chicago *Staats-Zeitung*	Dec. 6, 1860
Writes editorial for *Illinois State Journal*	Dec. 12, 1860
Writes memorandum on fugitive-slave clause of Constitution	Dec. 22, 1860
Delivers farewell to Springfield	Feb. 11, 1861
Delivers at Indianapolis first of speeches enroute to Washington	Feb. 11 and Feb. 12, 1861
Speaks to Ohio Legislature	Feb. 13, 1861
Speaks at Steubenville, Ohio	Feb. 14, 1861
Speaks at Pittsburgh	Feb. 15, 1861
Speaks at Cleveland	Feb. 15, 1861
Speaks at Buffalo	Feb. 16, 1861
Speaks at Rochester, N.Y.	Feb. 18, 1861
Speaks at Utica, N.Y.	Feb. 18, 1861
Speaks at Albany	Feb. 18, 1861
Speaks at Troy, N.Y.	Feb. 19, 1861
Speaks at Poughkeepsie, N.Y.	Feb. 19, 1861
Speaks at Hudson, N.Y.	Feb. 19, 1861
Speaks in New York City	Feb. 19 and Feb. 20, 1861
Speaks at Trenton, N.J.	Feb. 21, 1861
Speaks at Philadelphia	Feb. 21 and Feb. 22, 1861
Speaks to Pennsylvania Legislature	Feb. 22, 1861
Hoists flag at Independence Hall	Feb. 22, 1861
Arrives in Washington to assume Presidency	Feb. 23, 1861
Inaugurated as President	March 4, 1861
Orders relief of Fort Sumter	March 29, 1861
Answers Seward, relative to control of the administration	April 1, 1861
Replies to committee of Virginia convention	April 13, 1861
Fort Sumter falls	April 13, 1861
Calls for 75,000 volunteers	April 15, 1861
Proclaims blockade	April 19, 1861
Proclaims martial law	May 10, 1861
First message to Congress	July 4, 1861

Vested with war power by Congress — July 22, 1861

Proclaims Fast Day — Aug. 8, 1861

Appoints McClellan to command of Union armies — Nov. 1, 1861

First annual message to Congress — Dec. 3, 1861

Makes decision in Trent case — Dec. 26, 1861

Issues General War Order No. 1 — Jan. 27, 1862

William Wallace Lincoln, third child, dies — Feb. 20, 1862

Proclaims first Thanksgiving Day — April 10, 1862

Signs act freeing slaves in District of Columbia — April 16, 1862

Calls for 300,000 volunteers — July 1, 1862

Outlines plan for compensated emancipation — July 12, 1862

Speaks at Washington, touching on relations of Stanton and McClellan — Aug. 6, 1862

Replies to Horace Greeley editorial — Aug. 19, 1862

Issues preliminary Emancipation Proclamation — Sept. 22, 1862

Writes meditation on Divine Will — Sept. 30, 1862

Speaks at Frederick, Md. — Oct. 4, 1862

Relieves McClellan of command — Nov. 15, 1862

Second annual message — Dec. 1, 1862

Writes opinion on admission of West Virginia to Union — Dec. 31, 1862

Issues Emancipation Proclamation — Jan. 1, 1863

Letter to workingmen of Manchester — Jan. 19, 1863

Letter to workingmen of London — Feb. 2, 1863

Proclaims admission of West Virginia to Union — April 20, 1863

Orders Vallandigham beyond Union lines — May 19, 1863

Letter to Erastus Corning and others, concerning military arrests — June 12, 1863

Lee repulsed at Gettysburg — July 3, 1863

Vicksburg falls to Grant — July 4, 1863

Writes opinion on military draft — Aug. 15, 1863

Letter to J. C. Conkling and others, called Lincoln's "last stump speech," — Aug. 26, 1863

Delivers Gettysburg Address — Nov. 19, 1863

Proclaims amnesty and reconstruction — Dec. 8, 1863

Third annual message — Dec. 8, 1863

Appoints Grant to command Union armies — March 10, 1864

Replies to workingmen of New York — March 21, 1864

Frémont nominated for President by anti-Lincoln Republicans — May 31, 1864

Renominated for President — June 8, 1864

Proclaims Day of Prayer — July 7, 1864

Calls for 500,000 volunteers — July 18, 1864

Reelected President — Nov. 8, 1864

Writes letter of condolence to Mrs. Bixby — Nov. 21, 1864

Nominates Chase for chief justice — Dec. 6, 1864

Fourth annual message — Dec. 6, 1864

Meets Confederate envoys — Feb. 3, 1865

Reinaugurated as President — March 4, 1865

Issues proclamation, offering pardon to deserters — March 11, 1865

Visits Richmond — April 4, 1865

Notified of Lee's surrender — April 9, 1865

Delivers last public speech, in Washington — April 11, 1865

Shot by Booth — April 14, 1865

Dies at Washington — April 15, 1865